Financial ACCOUNTING

TWELFTH EDITION

C. William (Bill) Thomas
Baylor University

Wendy M. Tietz
Kent State University

Walter T. Harrison Jr.
Baylor University

Charles T. Horngren
Stanford University

Pearson

330 Hudson Street, NY, NY 10013

Vice President, Business, Economics, and UK Courseware: Donna Battista
Director of Portfolio Management: Adrienne D'Ambrosio
Specialist Portfolio Manager: Lacey Vitetta
Development Editor: Amy Ray
Editorial Assistant: Elisa Marks
Vice President, Product Marketing: Roxanne McCarley
Senior Product Marketer: Tricia Murphy
Product Marketing Assistant: Marianela Silvestri
Manager of Field Marketing, Business Publishing: Adam Goldstein
Field Marketing Manager: Nayke Popovich
Vice President, Production and Digital Studio, Arts and Business: Etain O'Dea
Director of Production, Business: Jeff Holcomb
Managing Producer, Business: Melissa Feimer
Content Producer: Emily Thorne
Operations Specialist: Carol Melville
Design Lead: Kathryn Foot
Manager, Learning Tools: Brian Surette
Content Developer, Learning Tools: Sarah Peterson
Managing Producer, Digital Studio and GLP, Media Production and Development: Ashley Santora
Managing Producer, Digital Studio and GLP: James Bateman
Managing Producer, Digital Studio: Diane Lombardo
Digital Studio Producer: Mary Kate Murray
Digital Studio Producer: Alana Coles
Digital Content Team Lead: Noel Lotz
Digital Content Project Lead: Martha LaChance
Project Manager: Kathy Smith, Cenveo® Publisher Services
Interior Design: Cenveo® Publisher Services
Cover Design: Cenveo® Publisher Services
Cover Art: Bloomicon/Shutterstock; Garagestock/Shutterstock
Printer/Binder: LSC Communications, Inc./Kendallville
Cover Printer: Phoenix Color/Hagerstown

Acknowledgments of third-party content appear on the appropriate page within the text.

Cataloging-in-Publication Data is available on file at the Library of Congress

2 18

Pearson

ISBN 10: 0-13-472598-0
ISBN 13: 978-0-13-472598-7

Question Help

MyLab Accounting homework and practice questions are correlated to the textbook, and many generate algorithmically to give students unlimited opportunity for mastery of concepts. If students get stuck, Learning Aids including Help Me Solve This, Demo Docs, videos and eText Pages walk them through the problem and identify helpful info in the text, giving them assistance when they need it most.

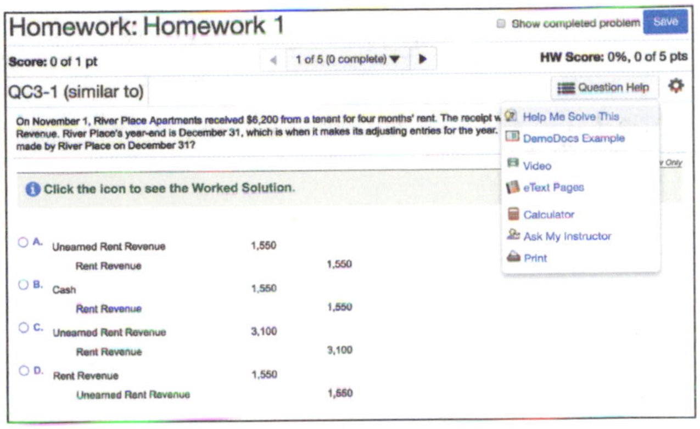

"Learning online can be a challenge. The Help Me Solve This option is incredibly helpful. It helped me see each step explained the way I needed it to be."

— Lauren Miller, Southern New Hampshire University

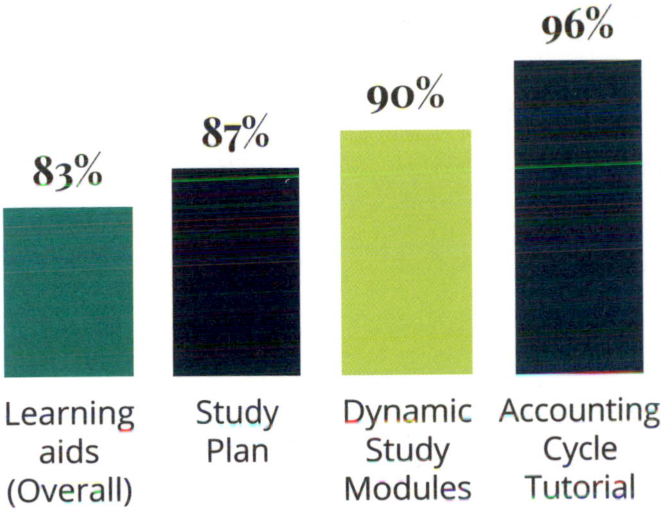

% of students who found learning tool helpful

Dynamic Study Modules help students study chapter topics effectively on their own by continuously assessing their **knowledge application** and performance in real time. These are available as graded assignments prior to class, and accessible on smartphones, tablets, and computers.

Pearson eText enhances student learning—both in and outside the classroom. Worked examples and videos bring learning to life, while algorithmic practice and self-assessment opportunities test students' understanding of the material. Accessible anytime, anywhere via MyLab or the app.

The **MyLab Gradebook** offers an easy way for students and instructors to view course performance. Item Analysis allows instructors to quickly see trends by analyzing details like the number of students who answered correctly/incorrectly, time on task, and median time spend on a question by question basis. And because it's correlated with the AACSB Standards, instructors can track students' progress toward outcomes that the organization has deemed important in preparing students to be **leaders.**

90%

of students would tell their instructor to keep using MyLab Accounting

For additional details visit: www.pearson.com/mylab/accounting

For my wife, Mary Ann.
C. William (Bill) Thomas

To my husband, Russ, who steadfastly supports me in every endeavor.
Wendy M. Tietz

About the Authors

C. William (Bill) Thomas is the J.E. Bush Professor of Accounting and a Master Teacher at Baylor University. A Baylor University alumnus, he received both his BBA and MBA there and went on to earn his PhD from The University of Texas at Austin.

With primary interests in the areas of financial accounting and auditing, Dr. Thomas has served as the J.E. Bush Professor of Accounting since 1995. He has been a member of the faculty of the Accounting and Business Law Department of the Hankamer School of Business since 1971 and served as chair of the department for 12 years. He has been recognized as an Outstanding Faculty Member of Baylor University as well as a Distinguished Professor for the Hankamer School of Business. Dr. Thomas has received many awards for outstanding teaching, including the Outstanding Professor in the Executive MBA Programs as well as the designation of Master Teacher.

Thomas is the author of textbooks in auditing and financial accounting, as well as many articles in auditing, financial accounting and reporting, taxation, ethics, and accounting education. His scholarly work focuses on the subject of fraud prevention and detection, as well as ethical issues among accountants in public practice. He presently serves as the accounting and auditing editor of *Today's CPA*, the journal of the Texas Society of Certified Public Accountants, with a circulation of approximately 28,000.

Thomas is a Certified Public Accountant in Texas. Prior to becoming a professor, Thomas was a practicing accountant with the firms of KPMG, LLP, and BDO Seidman, LLP. He is a member of the American Accounting Association, the American Institute of CPAs and Association of International Certified Professional Accountants, and the Texas Society of Certified Public Accountants.

Wendy M. Tietz is a professor in the Department of Accounting in the College of Business Administration at Kent State University. She teaches introductory financial and managerial accounting in a variety of formats, including large sections, small sections, and online sections.

Dr. Tietz is a Certified Public Accountant (Ohio), a Certified Management Accountant, and a Chartered Global Management Accountant. She is a member of the American Accounting Association, the Institute of Management Accountants, the American Institute of CPAs and Association of International Certified Professional Accountants, and the Sustainability Accounting Standards Board Alliance. She has published articles in such journals as *Issues in Accounting Education*, *Accounting Education: An International Journal*, *IMA Educational Case Journal*, and *Journal of Accounting & Public Policy*. Dr. Tietz is also the coauthor of a managerial accounting textbook, *Managerial Accounting*, with Dr. Karen Braun. She received the 2017 Bea Sanders/AICPA Innovation in Teaching Award for her web tool for financial accounting instructors, the Accounting Case Template. In 2016, Dr. Tietz was awarded the Jim Bulloch Award for Innovations in Management Accounting Education from the American Accounting Association/Institute of Management Accountants for her accounting educator blog, *Accounting in the Headlines*. She also received the 2014 Bea Sanders/AICPA Innovation in Teaching Award for her blog. She regularly presents at AAA regional and national meetings. She is intensely interested in the power of storytelling, interactivity, and social media as educational practices to promote engagement and understanding.

Dr. Tietz earned her PhD from Kent State University. She received both her MBA and BSA from the University of Akron. Prior to teaching, she worked in industry for several years, both as a controller for a financial institution and as the operations manager and controller for a recycled plastics manufacturer.

Walter T. Harrison Jr. is professor emeritus of accounting at the Hankamer School of Business, Baylor University. He received his BBA from Baylor University, his MS from Oklahoma State University, and his PhD from Michigan State University.

Professor Harrison, recipient of numerous teaching awards from student groups as well as from university administrators, has also taught at Cleveland State Community College, Michigan State University, the University of Texas, and Stanford University.

A member of the American Accounting Association and the American Institute of CPAs and Association of International Certified Professional Accountants, Professor Harrison has served as chairman of the Financial Accounting Standards Committee of the American Accounting Association, on the Teaching/Curriculum Development Award Committee, on the Program Advisory Committee for Accounting Education and Teaching, and on the Notable Contributions to Accounting Literature Committee.

Professor Harrison has lectured in several foreign countries and published articles in numerous journals, including *Journal of Accounting Research*, *Journal of Accountancy*, *Journal of Accounting and Public Policy*, *Economic Consequences of Financial Accounting Standards*, *Accounting Horizons*, *Issues in Accounting Education*, and *Journal of Law and Commerce*.

Professor Harrison has received scholarships, fellowships, and research grants or awards from PricewaterhouseCoopers, Deloitte & Touche, the Ernst & Young Foundation, and the KPMG Foundation.

Charles T. Horngren (1926–2011) was the Edmund W. Littlefield Professor of Accounting, emeritus, at Stanford University. A graduate of Marquette University, he received his MBA from Harvard University and his PhD from the University of Chicago. He was also the recipient of honorary doctorates from Marquette University and DePaul University.

A certified public accountant, Horngren served on the Accounting Principles Board for six years, the Financial Accounting Standards Board Advisory Council for five years, and the Council of the American Institute of Certified Public Accountants for three years. For six years he served as a trustee of the Financial Accounting Foundation, which oversees the Financial Accounting Standards Board and the Government Accounting Standards Board.

Horngren is a member of the Accounting Hall of Fame. As a member of the American Accounting Association, Horngren was its president and its director of research. He received its first annual Outstanding Accounting Educator Award. The California Certified Public Accountants Foundation gave Horngren its Faculty Excellence Award and its Distinguished Professor Award. He was the first person to have received both awards. The American Institute of Certified Public Accountants presented its first Outstanding Educator Award to Horngren. Horngren was named Accountant of the Year, in Education, by the national professional accounting fraternity, Beta Alpha Psi. Professor Horngren was also a member of the Institute of Management Accountants, from whom he received its Distinguished Service Award. He was a member of the institute's Board of Regents, which administers the Certified Management Accountant examinations.

Horngren is an author of these other accounting books published by Pearson: *Cost Accounting: A Managerial Emphasis*, Fifteenth Edition, 2015 (with Srikant M. Datar and Madhav V. Rajan); *Introduction to Financial Accounting*, Eleventh Edition, 2014 (with Gary L. Sundem, John A. Elliott, and Donna Philbrick); *Introduction to Management Accounting*, Sixteenth Edition, 2014 (with Gary L. Sundem, Jeff Schatzberg, and Dave Burgstahler); *Horngren's Financial & Managerial Accounting*, Fifth Edition, 2016 (with Tracie L. Miller-Nobles, Brenda L. Mattison, and Ella Mae Matsumura); and *Horngren's Accounting*, Eleventh Edition, 2016 (with Tracie L. Miller-Nobles, Brenda L. Mattison, and Ella Mae Matsumura). Horngren was the consulting editor for Pearson's Charles T. Horngren Series in Accounting.

Brief Contents

Contents

Preface

Financial Accounting gives readers a solid foundation in the fundamentals of accounting and the basics of financial statements, and then builds upon that foundation to offer more advanced and challenging concepts and problems. This scaffolded approach helps students to better understand the meaning and relevance of financial information and see its significance within a real-world context, as well as develop the skills needed to analyze financial information in both their courses and career.

Financial Accounting has a long-standing reputation in the marketplace for being readable and easy to understand. It drives home fundamental concepts using relevant examples from real-world companies in a reader-friendly way without adding unnecessary complexity. While maintaining hallmark features of accuracy, readability, and ease of understanding, the Twelfth Edition includes updated explanations, coverage, and ratio analysis with decision-making guidelines. These time-tested methodologies with the latest technology ensure that students learn basic concepts in accounting in a way that is relevant, stimulating, and fun, while exercises and examples from real-world companies help students gain a better grasp of the course material.

NEW TO THE TWELFTH EDITION

All Chapters

- New serial case on The Cheesecake Factory appears in every chapter in the end-of-chapter material.
- Throughout the book, an emphasis has been placed on making content flexible and modular to suit individual instructor preferences.
- Chapter content has been streamlined throughout the book to focus on the major concepts. References to material beyond the scope of an introductory financial accounting course have been eliminated to reduce "noise" in the learning process.

Chapter 1

- Updated and shortened the Disney case significantly, as well as the introduction, so students can more easily understand the major points.
- Shortened and eliminated many references to upcoming chapters and material (e.g., removed material on the board of directors and how corporate governance works since this is covered later in the text; "carrying value" and "high-quality earnings" were also removed since these concepts were too high level in the introductory chapter).
- Significantly shortened the discourse on GAAP versus IRFS.
- Updated Ethisphere's list of the World's Most Ethical Companies.

Chapter 2

- Combined learning objectives 1 and 2.
- Updated the Disney case.
- Streamlined the coverage of the different types of accounts.

- Deleted the "Account Formats" section.
- Deleted "Analyzing Transactions Using Only T-Accounts" section.

Chapter 3

- Significantly shortened the Global View box on the rules for recognizing revenue under U.S. GAAP versus IRFS.

Chapter 4

- Reversed Learning Objectives 3 and 4; "Evaluate Internal Controls" now comes before "Preparing a Bank Reconciliation."
- Eliminated Learning Objective 5, "Construct and Use a Cash Budget" and the associated materials in the chapter.
- Significantly shortened the Green Valley introductory case.
- Streamlined the coverage on the details of SOX.
- Streamlined the sections related to internal controls.
- Updated the section on computer controls to include malware, spyware, and ransomware.
- Streamlined the bank reconciliation and journal transactions sections.

Chapter 5

- This chapter underwent a major revision, so the Learning Objectives are significantly different.
- Short-term investments were moved from Chapter 5 to Appendix E.
- Updated the Apple introductory case.
- Sales Returns and Allowances and Sales Discounts are now separate learning objectives to allow for flexibility in coverage.
- Sales Returns and Allowances and Sales Discounts sections have been updated to reflect changes in revenue recognition standards.
- Sales Returns and Allowances section has been significantly pared down.
- New "Cooking the Books" on OCZ Technology Groups discusses misleading revenue recognition techniques.
- Several topics were eliminated, including internal controls over cash collections on account, credit card and debit card sales, and factoring.

Chapter 6

- Under Armour, Inc. case is updated and significantly streamlined.
- Discussion on consignment inventory has been pared down and focused.
- Updated and streamlined the section on periodic versus perpetual inventory systems.
- Section on keeping track of perpetual inventories under the LIFO and the weighted-average cost methods was eliminated.

- Streamlined the material on the disclosure principle.
- New "Cooking the Books" on LogiTech International's write down of inventory of parts related to its unsuccessful streaming device.

Chapter 7

- Updated the FedEx introductory case.
- Pared down the "Cooking the Books" feature on Waste Management.
- Significantly pared down the conditions and details related to asset impairment rules under U.S. GAAP versus IFRS.

Chapter 8

- Current and Contingent Liabilities, which were previously covered in Chapter 9, are now covered in this chapter.
- Long Term Investments is now covered in Appendix E.
- Time Value of Money is now covered in Appendix F.
- Updated the Amazon introductory case.
- New "Cooking the Engines" feature on the Volkswagen scandal as an example of disclosure principles for contingent liabilities.

Chapter 9

- Current and contingent liabilities are now in Chapter 8.
- Learning Objective 4, "Analyze and Differentiate Financing with Debt vs. Equity," has been moved to Chapter 10, which covers stockholders' equity.
- Shortened and updated Southwest Airlines introductory case.
- Clarified and streamlined the lease section to correspond with the FASB's revised standard.
- Added new Learning Objective on the impact of leverage on financial statements.

Chapter 10

- Learning Objective 5 has been changed from "Use Stock Values in Decision Making" to "Evaluate a Company's Performance Using New Ratios."
- Moved discussion of EPS calculations and PE ratio previously covered in Chapter 11 (Income Statement) to this chapter.
- Emphasized the coverage of EPS and removed coverage of the book value per share.
- Coverage of debt versus equity financing has been moved to this chapter (it was previously covered in Chapter 9, Liabilities).
- Updated and shortened the Home Depot introductory case.
- Tightened up the coverage of corporations and corporate governance.
- Eliminated several topics, including: redeemable preferred stock, redemption value, and liquidation value.

Chapter 11

- Some material previously found in Chapter 11 moved to Chapter 12, including earnings quality, footnotes, and differentiating between management and auditor responsibilities; revenue recognition moved to Chapter 5; earnings per share moved to Chapter 10.
- Coverage of Statement of Cash Flows moved from Chapter 12 in previous edition to Chapter 11.
- Updated and shortened the Google introductory case.
- Condensed the material on noncash activities.

Chapter 12

- Coverage of material previously found in Chapter 11 can now be found in this chapter, including: earnings quality, discussion on footnotes, and differentiating between management and auditor responsibilities.
- Under Armour's competitive position extensively updated.
- Several topics were eliminated, including: discussion of classes of stock (A, B, etc.), book value per share, Economic Value Added (EVA), and weighted average cost of capital.

Appendix E

- This new appendix combines and greatly condenses the coverage of all the investments in marketable securities, both short- and long-term (formerly in Chapters 5 and 8). All related problem materials were correspondingly shortened.

Appendix F

- This new appendix covers the time value of money, which was formerly located in Chapter 8. All related problem materials were correspondingly shortened.

SOLVING TEACHING AND LEARNING CHALLENGES

Dear Valued Colleagues,

Welcome to the Twelfth Edition of *Financial Accounting*. We are grateful for your support as an adopter of our text as we celebrate over 30 years of success in the market. The Twelfth Edition of *Financial Accounting* has been improved in many respects, as explained below.

Twelve chapters now rather than thirteen. We streamlined the content and the writing in this edition. We focused on students when working on this edition—we made the content more relevant to today's students with new stories and eliminated topics that are not relevant to introductory financial accounting. The first section of the book continues to be focused on the accounting cycle and basic financial statement preparation. The middle section of the book covers assets, liabilities, and stockholders' equity. The final two chapters cover the statement of cash flows and financial statement analysis. In this edition, the topics of investments and the time value of money are now appendices rather than a chapter. Chapter 9, Liabilities, from the 11th edition has been split into two chapters in this 12th edition: Chapter 8, Current Liabilities and Chapter 9, Long-Term Liabilities. We also integrated or eliminated the topics that were formerly in Chapter 11, Evaluating Performance: Earnings Quality, the Income Statement, and the Statement of Comprehensive Income, into other chapters. The book now has 12 chapters, making the content fit into a 15- or 16-week semester easily. We also focused on making the writing in the book more clear and understandable.

Author-created instructor resources. This book has a variety of instructor resources created by one of the authors, Wendy Tietz, to help instructors be both more efficient and more effective in their teaching. She has created 2–4 multiple-choice questions for each Accounting in the Headlines blog post. Those questions are in MyLab Accounting. She has also created a Learning Catalytics polling question for each blog post that is designed to start the conversation about that particular blog post. Dr. Tietz has created approximately 4–10 short videos about the major concepts in each chapter. In addition, she has created step-by-step videos for 3–6 of the homework exercises in each chapter. All of these videos are assignable through MyLab Accounting.

Try It in Excel®. As educators, we often have conversations with those who recruit our students. Based on these conversations, we found that students often complete their study of financial accounting without sufficient knowledge of how to use Excel® to perform accounting tasks. To respond to this concern, we have adapted most of the illustrations of key accounting tasks in the book to Excel® format and have added new sections in key chapters entitled "Try It in Excel®," which describe line-by-line how to retrieve and prepare accounting information (such as adjusted trial balance worksheets, ratio computations, depreciation schedules, bond discount and premium amortization schedules, and financial statement analysis) in Excel® format.

Student success. We feel we have the most advanced student learning materials in the market with MyLab Accounting. These include automatically graded homework, DemoDocs, and learning aid videos. We believe that the use of MyLab Accounting homework will greatly enhance student understanding of accounting with its instantaneous feedback. MyLab Accounting makes the study of financial accounting a more interactive and fun experience for students. In addition, we have adopted a scaffolding approach in the book and its resources. Chapter content and the end-of-chapter material build from the basic short exercise featuring a single concept to more advanced problems featuring multiple learning objectives. The student can practice at the basic level and then build upon that success to advance to more challenging problems.

Professor expectations. As professors, we know that you want a book that contains the most relevant and technically correct content available. We also know that you want excellent end-of-chapter material that is as up-to-date and error-free as possible. We reviewed and created the end-of-chapter questions, exercises, problems, and cases taking into account the types of assignments we ourselves use in class and assign as homework. Based on comments from adopters, we have thoroughly reviewed every end-of-chapter exercise and problem, with the goal of eliminating redundancy and adding relevance. The textbook and solutions manual have been put through a rigorous accuracy check to ensure that they are as complete and error-free as possible.

We welcome your comments and suggestions. Please don't hesitate to send feedback about this book to HorngrensAccounting@pearson.com. You are also welcome to reach out directly to author Bill Thomas at Bill_Thomas@baylor.edu or author Wendy Tietz at wtietz@kent.edu.

Bill Thomas
Wendy Tietz

REACH EVERY STUDENT WITH MYLAB ACCOUNTING.

MyLab is the teaching and learning platform that empowers you to reach every student. By combining trusted author content with digital tools and a flexible platform, MyLab personalizes the learning experience and improves results for each student. Learn more about MyLab Accounting.

EMPOWER EACH LEARNER

Each student learns at a different pace. Personalized learning pinpoints the precise areas where each student needs practice, giving all students the support they need—when and where they need it—to be successful.

IMPROVE STUDENT RESULTS

When you teach with MyLab, student performance improves. That's why instructors have chosen MyLab for over 20 years, touching the lives of over 50 million students.

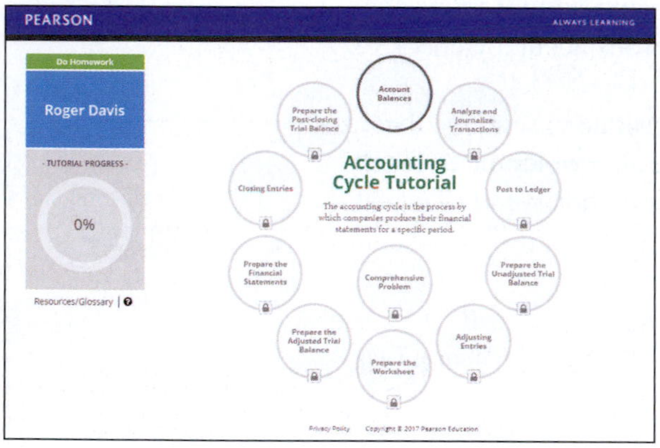

Accounting Cycle Tutorial (ACT) with Comprehensive Problem

MyLab Accounting's new interactive tutorial helps students master the accounting cycle for early and continued success in the Introduction to Accounting course. The tutorial, accessed by computer, Smartphone, or tablet, provides students with brief explanations of each concept of the accounting cycle through engaging videos and animations. Students are immediately assessed on their understanding, and their performance is recorded in the MyLab Accounting grade book. Whether the Accounting Cycle Tutorial is used as a remediation self-study tool or course assignment, students have yet-another resource within MyLab Accounting to help them be successful with the accounting cycle. This updated version includes a new comprehensive problem.

NEW—Time Value of Money Tutorial NEW!

The Time Value of Money Tutorial in MyLab ensures that students understand the basic theory and formulas of the TVM, while also helping test their ability to *apply* the TVM in the measurement of financial statement items. Students work through two sections. The first is to help them understand the theory—using whichever method the instructors choose (manually, through Excel®, with tables, or via a calculator), and the second is to give students the opportunity to apply the theory by giving them a number of scenarios regarding each financial statement.

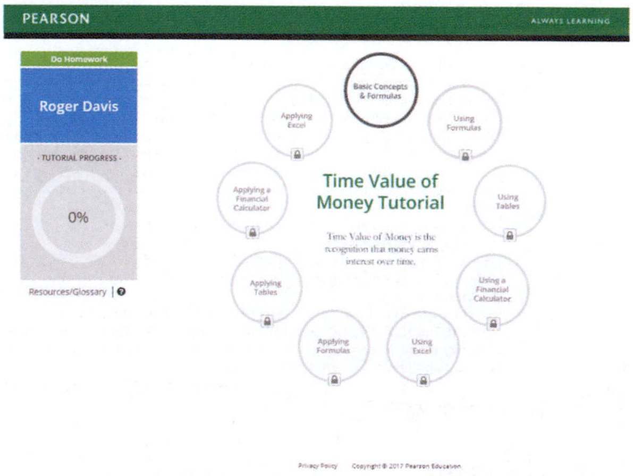

Deliver trusted content

You deserve teaching materials that meet your own high standards for your course. That's why we partner with highly respected authors to develop interactive content and course-specific resources that you can trust—and that keep your students engaged.

Try It

Found at various points in a chapter, this tool includes a question-and-answer snapshot asking students to apply what they just learned.

> **TRY IT**
>
> (Answers are given on p. 200.)
>
> **(1)** On March 15, a customer pays $3,133 for ten 4-day passes to Disney World for a vacation that will take place June 1–4. Did Disney earn the revenue on March 15?
>
> **(2)** On July 1, The Walt Disney Company prepays $60,000 in rent for a Disney Store building for the next six months. Did Disney incur the expense on July 1? If not, when will the company recognize rent expense?

> **Try It in Excel®**
>
> You can access the most current annual report of Southwest Airlines Company in Excel format at **www.sec.gov**. Using the "FILINGS" link on the toolbar at the top of the home page, select "Company Filings Search." This will take you to the "Edgar Company Filings" page. Type "Southwest Airlines" in the company name box, and select "Search." This will produce the "EDGAR Search Results" page showing the company name. Click on the "CIK" link beside the company name. Doing so will pull up a list of the reports the company has filed with the SEC. Under the "Filing Type" box, type "10-K" and click the search box. Form 10-K is the SEC form for the company's annual report. Find the year that you wish to view. Click on the "Interactive Data" box, which takes you to the "View Filing Data" page. Find and click on the "View Excel Document" link at the top of this page. You may choose to either open or download the Excel files containing the company's most recent financial statements.

Try It in Excel®

Describes line-by-line how to retrieve and prepare accounting information (such as adjusted trial balance work-sheets, ratio computations, depreciation schedules, bond discount and premium amortization schedules, and financial statement analysis) in Excel®.

Decision Guidelines

Illustrates how financial statements are used and how accounting information aids companies in decision making.

> **Decision Guidelines**
>
> **INVESTING IN STOCK**
>
> Suppose you've saved $5,000 to invest. You visit a nearby **Edward Jones** office, where the broker probes for your risk tolerance. Are you investing mainly for dividends or for growth in the stock price? These guidelines offer suggestions for what to consider when investing in stock.

Investor Decision	Guidelines
Which category of stock to buy for:	
• A safe investment?	Preferred stock is safer than common, but for even more safety, invest in high-grade corporate bonds or government securities.
• Steady dividends?	Cumulative preferred stock. However, the company is not obligated to declare preferred dividends, and the dividends are unlikely to increase.
• Increasing dividends?	Common stock, as long as the company's net income is increasing and the company has adequate cash flow to pay a dividend after meeting all obligations and other cash demands.
• Increasing stock price?	Common stock, but again only if the company's net income and cash flow are increasing.
• How to identify a good stock to buy?	There are many ways to pick stock investments. One strategy that works reasonably well is to invest in companies that consistently earn higher rates of return on assets and on equity than competing firms in the same industry. Another, called "value investing," is to invest in companies that have high earnings but relatively low price/earnings multiples compared to other companies in the same industry. Still another is to select companies with solid earnings in industries that are expected to grow.

> **Ethics Check**
>
> **EC3-1. Identify ethical principle violated**
>
> For each of the situations listed, identify which of three principles (integrity, objectivity and independence, or due care) from the AICPA Code of Professional Conduct is violated. Assume all persons listed in the situations are members of the AICPA. (Note: Refer to the AICPA Code of Professional Conduct contained on pages 25–27 in Chapter 1 for descriptions of the principles.)
>
> **a.** Drew purposely excludes a large amount of accrued salaries payable from this year's financial statements so his company's debt-to-equity ratio appears lower to investors.
>
> **b.** Abbey's company determines year-end bonuses based on revenue growth. Abbey records the sales of gift cards during this month as revenue rather than as unearned revenue. None of these gift cards have been used by customers as of the end of the current month. By recording the gift card sales as revenue in the current period, revenue will be higher and Abbey's bonus will, as a result, be higher as well.
>
> **c.** Debbie, a CPA, is an associate at a regional public accounting firm. Debbie's firm is auditing a local payroll company. Debbie does not disclose that her husband is a manager at the payroll company.
>
> **d.** A new revenue recognition standard has been issued by the Financial Accounting Standards Board (FASB) and the International Accounting Standards Board (IASB). John does not attend training on the new revenue recognition standard because he is busy dealing with the accounting impact of a merger.

Ethics Check

This new end-of-chapter feature presents students with several ethical business situations and asks them to identify which of the principles from the AICPA Code of Professional Conduct is violated.

Ethical Issue

This end-of-chapter feature presents students with ethical situations and has them work through the decision framework for making ethical judgments. Finally, they are asked to come to a decision and support it.

> **Ethical Issue**
>
> **C6-85.** During 2016, Coalmont, Inc., changed to the LIFO method. Suppose that during 2017, Coalmont changed back to the FIFO method. In 2018, the company switched back to LIFO again.
>
> **Requirements**
>
> 1. What would you think of a company's ethics if it changed accounting methods every year?
> 2. What accounting principle would changing methods every year violate?
> 3. Who can be harmed and how when a company changes its accounting methods too often?

Serial Case

C8-53. *(Learning Objective 5: Analyze contingent liabilities of a company in the restaurant industry)*

Note: This case is part of The Cheesecake Factory serial case contained in every chapter in this textbook.

Like many other large companies, **The Cheesecake Factory Incorporated** has several legal actions pending against it at any given time. It must accrue for and/or disclose certain contingent liabilities, such as pending or possible legal actions, in its financial statements and notes to its financial statements. The necessary reporting depends on the specific circumstances of the situations and the company's attorneys' assessment of the potential outcomes.

To follow are four *hypothetical* legal situations that might face The Cheesecake Factory.

Situation A: A former restaurant employee filed a class-action lawsuit alleging that The Cheesecake Factory violated the local law when it required employees to purchase their work uniforms. Legal counsel has indicated that the case will probably be settled for $2,500.
Situation B: A customer filed a lawsuit alleging that The Cheesecake Factory was negligent when she slipped and fell on a wet floor near the bar area in a Cheesecake Factory in Topeka, Kansas. Legal counsel has indicated that the company will most likely settle this case, but counsel is unable to estimate the dollar amount of the settlement.
Situation C: A customer filed a lawsuit alleging that The Cheesecake Factory caused her severe emotional distress when her favorite dessert was out of stock for her birthday dinner at the restaurant. Legal counsel has indicated that the chance of losing this lawsuit is remote.
Situation D: A former restaurant hourly employee filed a class-action lawsuit for $200,000 alleging that The Cheesecake Factory violated the local law by failing to pay overtime. Legal counsel has stated that it is reasonably possible, but not probable, that The Cheesecake Factory could lose the lawsuit.

NEW Cheesecake Factory Serial Case, consisting of several smaller cases—one per chapter, focuses on the same real-world company. This continuing case is meant to inspire critical thinking and to connect the content with real life by following one company through all of the chapters in financial accounting.

Teach your course your way

Your course is unique. So whether you'd like to build your own assignments, teach multiple sections, or set prerequisites, MyLab gives you the flexibility to easily create your course to fit your needs.

NEW Auto-Graded Excel® Projects NEW!

Using proven, field-tested technology, MyLab Accounting's new auto-graded Excel® Projects allow instructors to seamlessly integrate Excel® content into their course without having to manually grade spreadsheets. Students have the opportunity to practice important Accounting skills in Microsoft Excel®, helping them to master key concepts and gain proficiency with Excel®. Students simply download a spreadsheet, work live on an accounting problem in Excel®, and then upload that file back into MyLab Accounting, where they receive reports on their work that provide personalized, detailed feedback to pinpoint where they went wrong on any step of the problem.

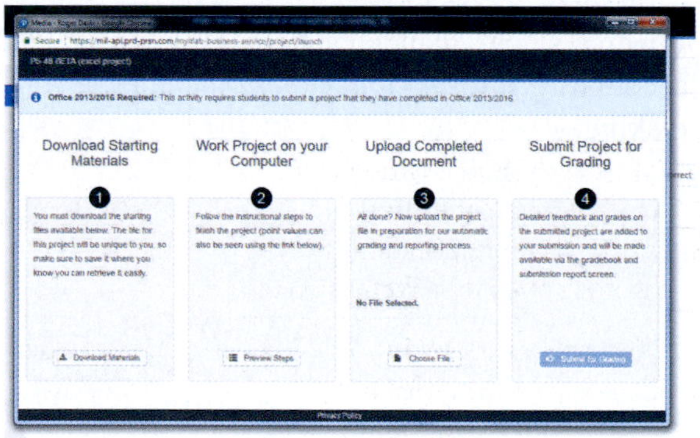

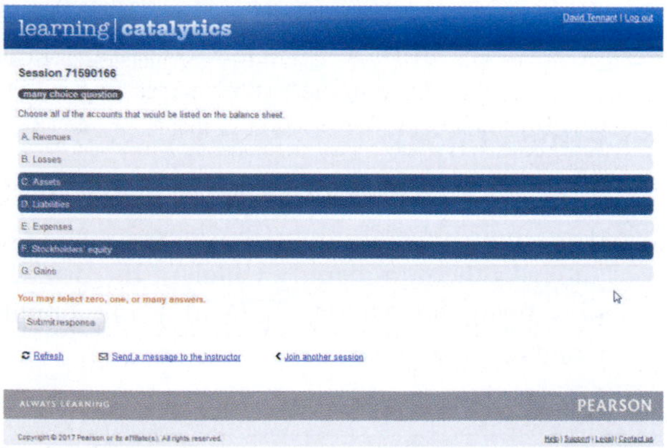

Learning Catalytics

Learning Catalytics, available through MyLab Accounting, is a "bring your own device" assessment and classroom activity system that expands the possibilities for student engagement. Using Learning Catalytics, you can deliver a wide range of automatically graded or open-ended questions that test content knowledge and build critical thinking skills. Eighteen different answer types provide great flexibility, including graphical, numerical, textual input, and more.

Pearson eText

Pearson eText enhances student learning. Worked examples, videos, and interactive tutorials bring learning to life, while algorithmic practice and self-assessment opportunities test students' understanding of the material.

INSTRUCTOR TEACHING RESOURCES

This program comes with the following teaching resources.

Supplements available to instructors at www.pearsonhighered.com/harrison	Features of the Supplement
Solutions Manual Created in collaboration with: Betsy Willis from Baylor University	Contains solutions to all end-of-chapter questions, including short exercises, exercises, problems and cases.
Instructor's Manual Created in collaboration with: Betsy Willis from Baylor University	Includes chapter outlines, suggested in-class activities, topics with which students struggle, as well as the following: • Assignment grid that outlines all end-of-chapter exercises, problems, and cases; the topic being covered in that particular exercise, problem, or case; estimated completion time; level of difficulty. • Ten-minute quizzes that quickly assess students' understanding of the chapter material.
Flipping Your Classroom Guide Created by author Wendy Tietz	Tips for each chapter on how to take your course from a traditional/in-class course to a hybrid, blended, or fully online format. Includes links to the discussion board prompts.
Discussion Board Prompts Created by author Wendy Tietz	Get the most out of online and in-class discussions and promote interaction and engagement with your financial accounting students. This supplement will aid instructors in facing the challenges of utilizing discussion prompts effectively in the online accounting classroom.
Multiple Choice Questions in MyLab Accounting for Accountingintheheadlines.com Created by author Wendy Tietz	These multiple choice questions are assignable in MyLab Accounting related to the chapter's blog post from accountingintheheadlines.com
Polling Questions in Learning Catalytics for Accountingintheheadlines.com Created by author Wendy Tietz	These Learning Catalytic polling questions related to blog posts at accountingintheheadlines.com can be used as a tool to get students actively engaged with the content during class.
Videos Created by author Wendy Tietz	• Concept videos reviewing chapter learning objectives • Step-by-step videos for selected homework problems
Directed Reading Created by author Wendy Tietz	Encourage students to actively read the textbook BEFORE coming to class and help direct them to what is important. Students should hand in these directed reading worksheets at the beginning of class before the chapter is covered in class.
Test Bank	Includes more than 2,000 questions. Both objective-based questions and computational problems are available. *Algorithmic test bank* is available in MyLab Accounting. Most computational questions are formulated with an algorithm so that the same question is available with unique values. This offers instructors a greater pool of questions to pull from and will help ensure each student has a different test. All questions include the following annotations: • Difficulty level (1 for straight recall, 2 for some analysis, 3 for complex analysis) • Type (Multiple-choice, true/false, short-answer, essay) • Learning objective • AACSB learning standard (Ethical Understanding and Reasoning; Analytical Thinking Skills; Information Technology; Diverse and Multicultural Work; Reflective Thinking; Application of Knowledge)

Continued

Computerized TestGen	TestGen allows instructors to: • Customize, save, and generate classroom tests • Edit, add, or delete questions from the Test Item Files • Analyze test results • Organize a database of tests and student results.
PowerPoint® Presentations	These presentations help facilitate classroom discussion. • Instructor PowerPoint® Presentations with lecture notes • Student PowerPoint® Presentations *Image Library* contains all image files from the text to assist instructors in modifying our supplied PowerPoint® presentations or in creating their own PowerPoint® presentations.
Working Papers	Available in both Excel® and PDF format, these documents can be used for completing end-of-chapter questions in preformatted templates

For Students

MyLab Accounting online Homework and Assessment Manager includes:

- Pearson eText
- Student PowerPoint® Presentations
- Accounting Cycle Tutorial
- Time Value of Money Tutorial
- Videos
- Demo Docs
- Flash Cards
- Dynamic Study Modules
- Excel® in Practice Data Files
- Working Papers
- Directed Reading

Student resource website: http://www.pearsonhighered.com/harrison
This website contains the following:

- The Excel® in Practice Data Files, related to select end-of-chapter problems
- Working Papers, for completing end-of-chapter questions in preformatted templates
- Directed Reading, to help direct students to what content in the chapter is important.
- Student PowerPoint® Presentations

ACKNOWLEDGMENTS

We sincerely thank the many friends and colleagues who have helped in the process of writing and revising this book. Betsy Willis deserves special mention for her dedication, feedback, and hard work throughout this project. We thank Carolyn Streuly for her amazing accuracy checking, Amy Ray for her clear, valuable feedback, and Kathy Smith for her incredible ability to manage multiple roles and people in this book revision process. We are also deeply grateful to Lacey Vitetta for her endless patience and support. Thank you to Donna Battista, Adrienne D'Ambrosio, Nayke Popovich, Tricia Murphy, Mary Kate Murray, Sarah Peterson, Martha LaChance, and Beth Geary for their continued help and support. Thanks also to Betsy Willis for preparing the *Instructor's Solutions Manual* and the *Instructor's Resource Manual*. Thank you also to the many professors and students who have used the book and provided feedback for improving it.

We would like to thank the following reviewers for the Twelfth Edition for their valuable input: Henri Akono, Maine Business School; John Babich, Kankakee Community College; Rodger Brannan, University of Minnesota Duluth; Esther Bunn, Stephen F. Austin State University; Andrew Dill, University of Southern Indiana; Caroline Falconetti, Nassau Community College; Ariana Gammel, Lake Forest College; Jane Garvin, Ivy Tech State College; Konrad Gunderson, Missouri Western State University; Frank Kane, Purdue University; Joung Yeon Kim, Indiana University Kokomo; William

Kresse, Governors State University; Jeff Paterson, Florida State University; Judy Peterson, Monmouth College; Sandra Roberson, Furman University; Chris Slinkard, Missouri State University; and Wendy Wilson, Southern Methodist University.

In revising previous editions of *Financial Accounting*, we had the help of instructors from across the country who have participated in online surveys, chapter reviews, and focus groups. Their comments and suggestions for both the text and the supplements have been a great help in planning and carrying out revisions, and we thank them for their contributions.

Past Reviewer Participants

Shawn Abbott, College of the Siskiyous
Linda Abernathy, Kirkwood Community College
Sol Ahiarah, SUNY College at Buffalo (Buffalo State)
M. J. Albin, University of Southern Mississippi
Gary Ames, Brigham Young University, Idaho
Elizabeth Ammann, Lindenwood University
Brenda Anderson, Brandeis University
Kim Anderson, Indiana University of Pennsylvania
Florence Atiase, University of Texas at Austin
Walter Austin, Mercer University, Macon
Brad Badertscher, University of Iowa
Sandra Bailey, Oregon Institute of Technology
Patrick Bauer, DeVry University, Kansas City
Barbara A. Beltrand, Metropolitan State University
Jerry Bennett, University of South Carolina–Spartanburg
Peg Beresewski, Robert Morris College
Lucille Berry, Webster University
John Bildersee, New York University, Stern School
Brenda Bindschatel, Green River Community College
Candace Blankenship, Belmont University
Charlie Bokemeier, Michigan State University
Patrick Bouker, North Seattle Community College
Amy Bourne, Oregon State University
Scott Boylan, Washington and Lee University
Robert Braun, Southeastern Louisiana University
Linda Bressler, University of Houston–Downtown
Michael Broihahn, Barry University
Rada Brooks, University of California, Berkeley
Carol Brown, Oregon State University
Elizabeth Brown, Keene State College
Helen Brubeck, San Jose State University
Scott Bryant, Baylor University
Marcus Butler, University of Rochester
Marci Butterfield, University of Utah
Mark Camma, Atlantic Cape Community College
Kay Carnes, Gonzaga University
Brian Carpenter, University of Scranton
Sandra Cereola, James Madison University
Kam Chan, Pace University
Hong Chen, Northeastern Illinois University
C. Catherine Chiang, Elon University
Freddy Choo, San Francisco State University
Charles Christy, Delaware Tech and Community College, Stanton Campus
Lawrence Chui, Opus College of Business, University of St. Thomas
Shifei Chung, Rowan University
Bryan Church, Georgia Tech at Atlanta
Carolyn Clark, Saint Joseph's University
Dr. Paul Clikeman, University of Richmond
Charles Coate, St. Bonaventure University
Dianne Conry, University of California State College Extension–Cupertino
Ellen D. Cook, University of Louisiana at Lafayette
John Coulter, Western New England College
Sue Counte, Saint Louis Community College–Meramec
Julia Creighton, American University
Sue Cullers, Buena Vista University
Donald Curfman, McHenry County College
Alan Czyzewski, Indiana State University
Laurie Dahlin, Worcester State College
Bonita Daly, University of Southern Maine
Kreag Danvers, Clarion University
Betty David, Francis Marion University
Patricia Derrick, Drexel University
Peter DiCarlo, Boston College
Charles Dick, Miami University
Barbara Doughty, New Hampshire Community Technical College
Allan Drebin, Northwestern University
Carolyn Dreher, Southern Methodist University
Emily Drogt, Grand Valley State University
Ada Duffey, University of Wisconsin-Waukesha
Carol Dutton, South Florida Community College
Reed Easton, Seton Hall University
James Emig, Villanova University
Ellen Engel, University of Chicago
Mary Ewanechko, Monroe Community College
Alan Falcon, Loyola Marymount University
Janet Farler, Pima Community College
Dr. Andrew Felo, Penn State Great Valley
Ken Ferris, Thunderbird College
Dr. Mary Fischer, The University of Texas at Tyler
Dr. Caroline Ford, Baylor University
Clayton Forester, University of Minnesota
Lou Fowler, Missouri Western State College
Timothy Gagnon, Northeastern University
Regan Garey, Lock Haven University
Terrie Gehman, Elizabethtown College
Lucille Genduso, Nova Southeastern University

Frank Gersich, Monmouth College
Bradley Gillespie, Saddleback College
Lisa Gillespie, Loyola University, Chicago
Marvin Gordon, University of Illinois at Chicago
Alesha Graves, Mount St. Joseph University
Brian Green, University of Michigan at Dearborn
Anthony Greig, Purdue University
Ronald Guidry, University of Louisiana at Monroe
Konrad Gunderson, Missouri Western State College
Dr. Geoffrey J. Gurka, Colorado Mesa University
William Hahn, Southeastern College
Jack Hall, Western Kentucky University
Gloria Halpern, Montgomery College
Penny Hanes, Mercyhurst College
Dr. Heidi Hansel, Kirkwood Community College
Kenneth Hart, Brigham Young University, Idaho
Al Hartgraves, Emory University
Michael Haselkorn, Bentley University
Thomas Hayes, University of North Texas
Larry Hegstad, Pacific Lutheran University
Candy Heino, Anoka-Ramsey Community College
Mary Hollars, Vincennes University
Anit Hope, Tarrant County College
Thomas Huse, Boston College
Fred R. Jex, Macomb Community College
Grace Johnson, Marietta College
Celina Jozsi, University of South Florida
John Karayan, Woodbury University
Beth Kern, Indiana University, South Bend
Irene Kim, The George Washington University
Hans E. Klein, Babson College
Robert Kollar, Duquesne University
Willem Koole, North Carolina State University
Emil Koren, Hillsborough Community College
Dennis Kovach, Community College of Allegheny County–North Campus
Maria U. Ku, Ohlone College & Diablo Valley College
Ellen Landgraf, Loyola University Chicago
Howard Lawrence, Christian Brothers University
Barry Leffkov, Regis College
Elliott Levy, Bentley University
Chao-Shin Liu, Notre Dame
Barbara Lougee, University of California, Irvine
Heidemarie Lundblad, California State University, Northridge
Joseph Lupino, Saint Mary's College of California
Anna Lusher, West Liberty State College
Shuai Ma, American University
Harriet Maccracken, Arizona State University
Susan Machuga, University of Hartford
Constance Malone Hylton, George Mason University
Carol Mannino, Milwaukee School of Engineering
Herb Martin, Hope College
Aziz Martinez, Harvard University, Harvard Business School
Anthony Masino, Queens University/NC Central
Lizbeth Matz, University of Pittsburgh, Bradford
Bruce Maule, College of San Mateo
Michelle McEacharn, University of Louisiana at Monroe
Molly McFadden-May, Tulsa Community College
Nick McGaughey, San Jose State University
Allison McLeod, University of North Texas
Cathleen Miller, University of Michigan–Flint
Cynthia J. Miller, Gatton College of Business & Economics, University of Kentucky
Mark Miller, University of San Francisco
Mary Miller, University of New Haven
Scott Miller, Gannon University
Frank Mioni, Madonna University
Dr. Birendra (Barry) K. Mishra, University of California, Riverside
Theodore D. Morrison III, Wingate University
Lisa Nash, Vincennes University
Rosemary Nurre, College of San Mateo
Bruce L. Oliver, Rochester Institute of Technology
Gary Olsen, Carroll University
Stephen Owen, Hamilton College
David Parker, Saint Xavier University
Charles Pedersen, Quinsigamond Community College
Richard J. Pettit, Mountain View College
George Plesko, Massachusetts Institute of Technology
David Plumlee, University of Utah
Brian Porter, Hope College
Gregory Prescott, University of South Alabama
Rama Ramamurthy, College of William and Mary
Craig Reeder, Florida A&M University
Barb Reeves, Cleary University
Bettye Rogers-Desselle, Prairie View A&M University
Darren Roulstone, University of Chicago
Brian Routh, University of Southern Indiana
Norlin Rueschhoff, Notre Dame
Anwar Salimi, California State Polytechnic University, Pomona
Philippe Sammour, Eastern Michigan University
Angela Sandberg, Jacksonville State University
George Sanders, Western Washington University
Betty Saunders, University of North Florida
Albert A. Schepanski, University of Iowa
William Schmul, Notre Dame
Arnie Schnieder, Georgia Tech at Atlanta
Randall Serrett, University of Houston—Downtown
Gim Seow, University of Connecticut
Itzhak Sharav, CUNY–Lehman Graduate School of Business
Allan Sheets, International Business College
Lily Sieux, California State University, East Bay
Alvin Gerald Smith, University of Northern Iowa
James Smith, Community College of Philadelphia
Virginia Smith, Saint Mary's College of California
Beverly Soriano, Framingham State College
Vic Stanton, Stanford University
Carolyn R. Stokes, Frances Marion University

J. B. Stroud, Nicholls State University
Gloria J. Stuart, Georgia Southern University
Al Taccone, Cuyamaca College
Diane Tanner, University of North Florida
Martin Taylor, University of Texas at Arlington
Dorothy Thompson, Ave Maria University
Howard Toole, San Diego State University
Vincent Turner, California State Polytechnic University, Pomona
Sue Van Boven, Paradise Valley Community College
Marcia Veit, University of Central Florida
Bruce Wampler, Louisiana State University, Shreveport
Suzanne Ward, University of Louisiana at Lafayette
Michelle Watts, Boise State University
Craig Weaver, University of California, Riverside
Frederick Weis, Claremont McKenna College
Frederick Weiss, Virginia Wesleyan College
Betsy Willis, Baylor University
Ronald Woan, Indiana University of Pennsylvania
Allen Wright, Hillsborough Community College
Dr. Jia Wu, University of Massachusetts, Dartmouth
Yanfeng Xue, George Washington University
Barbara Yahvah, University of Montana–Helena
Myung Yoon, Northeastern Illinois University
Lin Zeng, Northeastern Illinois University
Tony Zordan, University of St. Francis

1 The Financial Statements

LEARNING OBJECTIVES

1 **Explain** why accounting is critical to businesses

2 **Explain and apply** underlying accounting concepts, assumptions, and principles

3 **Apply** the accounting equation to business organizations

4 **Construct** financial statements and **analyze** the relationships among them

5 **Evaluate** business decisions ethically

Martin Beddall/Alamy Stock Photo

SPOTLIGHT

The Walt Disney Company

Where is the happiest place on earth? Walt Disney World or Disneyland, of course! The Disney theme parks in Orlando, Florida, and Anaheim, California, are famous for providing the ultimate family entertainment experience. However, these two parks are only a small part of **The Walt Disney Company**'s worldwide entertainment empire. The company owns vacation resorts, theme and water parks, hotels, motion-picture and recording studios, and cable TV networks throughout the world. Disney also sells billions of dollars of branded merchandise through retail, online, and wholesale distribution channels. How does Disney decide what to invest in and how to operate its businesses so as to maximize its profits? One way to find out is by studying its financial accounting information. ●

Most chapters of this book begin with an actual financial statement. **Financial statements** are the business documents companies use to report the results of their activities to people and groups that can include managers, investors, creditors, and regulatory agencies. These parties then use the reported information to make a variety of decisions, such as whether to invest in or loan money to the companies. The following four basic financial statements are used for these purposes:

- Income statement (sometimes known as the statement of operations)
- Statement of retained earnings (usually included in the statement of stockholders' equity)
- Balance sheet (sometimes known as the statement of financial position)
- Statement of cash flows

In Chapters 1–3, we will look at the contents of these statements using The Walt Disney Company as an example. For instance, the following financial statement is Disney's income statement for the year ended October 1, 2016.

Chapter 1 also explains generally accepted accounting principles, their underlying assumptions and concepts, and the bodies responsible for issuing accounting standards. Last, but not least, we examine the judgment process needed to make good accounting decisions.

	A	B	C	D	E
1	**The Walt Disney Company Consolidated Statements of Income**	**Fiscal 2016**	**Fiscal 2015**		
2		**12 Months Ended**			
3	**Adapted, in millions of $**	**Oct. 01, 2016**	**Oct. 03, 2015**		
4	Services revenue	$ 47,130	$ 43,894		
5	Products revenue	8,502	8,571		
6	Total revenues	55,632	52,465		
7	Cost of services	24,653	23,191		
8	Cost of products	5,340	5,173		
9	Selling, general, administrative and other	8,754	8,523		
10	Depreciation and amortization	2,527	2,354		
11	Total costs and expenses	41,274	39,241		
12	Income from operations	14,358	13,224		
13	Other items of income (expense), net	111	174		
14	Income before income taxes	14,469	13,398		
15	Income taxes	5,078	5,016		
16	Net income	$ 9,391	$ 8,382		
17					

Data from the U.S. Securities and Exchange Commission EDGAR Company Filings, www.sec.gov

Later chapters explain financial statements in more detail, as well as how the information contained in them is used to make business decisions.

Try It in Excel®

You can access the most current annual report of The Walt Disney Company in Excel® format at **www.sec.gov**. Using the "FILINGS" link on the toolbar at the top of the home page, select "Company Filings Search." This will take you to the "EDGAR Company Filings" page. Type "Walt Disney" in the company name box, and select "Search." This will produce the "EDGAR Search Results" page showing the company name. Click on the "CIK" link beside the company name. This will pull up a list of the reports the company has filed with the Securities and Exchange Commission (SEC). Under the "Filing Type" box, type "10-K," and click the "Search" box. Form 10-K is the SEC form for the company's annual report. Find the year you wish to view. Click on the "Interactive Data" box, which takes you to the "View Filing Data" page. Find and click on the "View Excel Document" link at the top of this page, and download the Excel file containing the selected 10-K report. Alternatively, you can click the listed section of the 10-K you would like to open.

The Walt Disney Company's managers make lots of decisions. What new films should be produced, and how should they be incorporated into new features in the company's theme parks? Should the company acquire another TV network? Which character dolls are the hottest sellers—Mickey, Donald, Elsa from *Frozen,* or Han Solo from *Star Wars*? Which theme parks are most and least profitable? Accounting information helps companies make these decisions.

Take a look at The Walt Disney Company's Consolidated Statements of Income. In accounting, the word *net* refers to an amount after a subtraction. Focus on Net income (line 16). Net income (profit) is the excess of revenues (net sales) over expenses. You can see that The Walt Disney Company earned $9,391 million of net income in the year ended October 1, 2016. That's good news because it means that the company had almost $9.4 billion more revenues than expenses for the year. Total revenues (line 6) increased by about 6% during the period compared to the previous year (from $52,465 million to $55,632 million). Net income increased by about 12% (from $8,382 million to $9,391 million).

Suppose you have $10,000 to invest. What information would you need before deciding to invest it in The Walt Disney Company? You can find some of that information in the company's financial statements, and to understand it, you must study accounting.

EXPLAIN WHY ACCOUNTING IS CRITICAL TO BUSINESSES

1 Explain why accounting is critical to businesses

Accounting is an information system that measures business activities, processes data into financial statements and reports, and communicates results to decision makers. Why study accounting? Accounting is the "language of business." You wouldn't think of moving to a foreign country without planning to learn the language(s) spoken there. Likewise, you shouldn't spend your career not knowing the language needed to measure and communicate business information. The better you understand the language of accounting, the better you can manage your own finances, as well as those of your business.

After you have completed this chapter, you'll begin to understand the nature of accounting, financial statements, and the relationships between them. By the end of Chapter 3, you'll understand the process by which a company's financial statements are prepared, called the **accounting cycle**.

Don't confuse bookkeeping and accounting. Bookkeeping is a mechanical part of accounting, just as arithmetic is a part of mathematics. Exhibit 1-1 below illustrates the flow of accounting information and its role in making business decisions.

Exhibit 1-1 | The Flow of Accounting Information

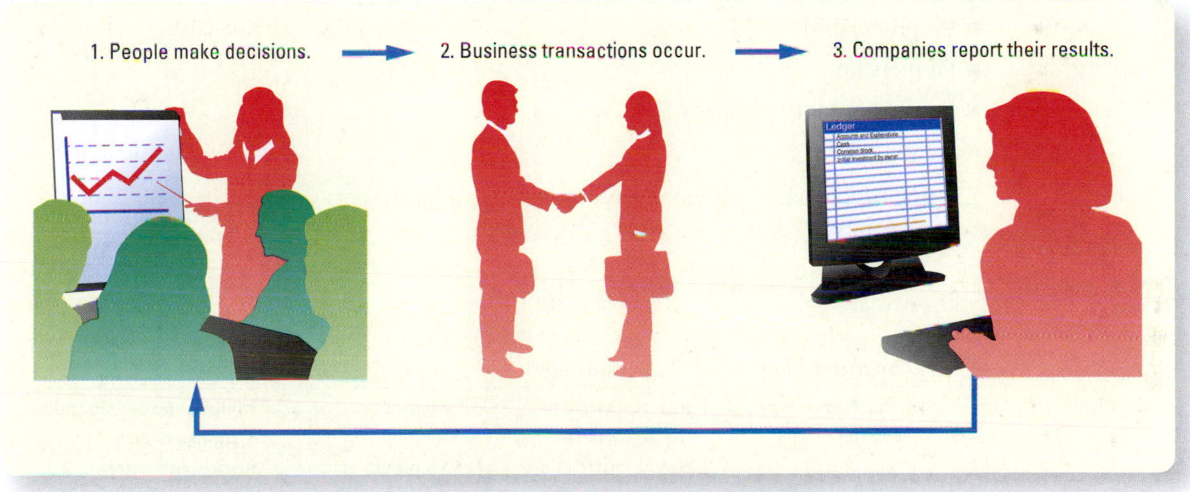

Describe the Decision Makers Who Use Accounting

Decision makers use many types of information. For example, a banker needs financial information from an applicant to decide whether to grant a loan request. Managers at Disney use revenue forecasts along with design-and-engineering plans to decide where to locate new theme parks and how large they will be. Let's explore how decision makers use accounting information.

- *Individuals.* People like you manage their personal bank accounts, decide whether to rent an apartment or buy a house, and calculate the monthly income and expenditures of their businesses. Accounting provides the information people need to make these decisions.
- *Investors and creditors.* Investors and creditors provide the money to finance The Walt Disney Company. Investors want to know how much income they can expect to earn on an investment. Creditors want to know when and how the company is going to pay them back. These decisions also require accounting information.
- *Regulatory bodies.* All kinds of regulatory bodies use accounting information. For example, the Internal Revenue Service (IRS) and various state and local governments require businesses, individuals, and other types of organizations to pay income, property, excise, and other taxes. The Securities and Exchange Commission (SEC) requires companies with

publicly-traded stock to provide it with many kinds of periodic financial reports. All of these reports contain accounting information.

- *Nonprofit organizations.* Churches, hospitals, and charities such as Habitat for Humanity and the Red Cross base many of their operating decisions on accounting data. These nonprofit organizations also have to file periodic financial reports with the IRS and state governments, even though they will owe no income taxes.

Describe the Two Types of Accounting and Who Uses Each Type

People inside *and* outside of an organization use accounting information. As a result, accounting has evolved into two branches: financial accounting and managerial accounting. **Financial accounting** provides relevant and accurate financial information to decision makers *outside* of an organization, such as investors, creditors, government agencies, and the public. This textbook focuses on financial accounting. **Managerial accounting** provides accurate and relevant information to people *inside* the organization, such as the managers of The Walt Disney Company. Examples of managerial accounting information include budgets, forecasts, and projections used to make strategic decisions. Managerial accounting is covered in a separate course that usually follows this one.

Explain How Businesses Are Organized

Accounting is used in every type of business. A business generally takes one of the following forms:

- Proprietorship
- Partnership
- Limited-liability company (LLC)
- Corporation

Exhibit 1-2 compares different ways to organize a business.

Exhibit 1-2 | The Various Forms of Business Organization

	Proprietorship	Partnership	LLC	Corporation
1. *Owner(s)*	Proprietor—one owner	Partners—two or more owners	Members	Stockholders—generally many owners
2. *Personal liability of owner(s) for business's debts*	Proprietor is personally liable	General partners are personally liable; limited partners are not	Members are *not* personally liable	Stockholders are *not* personally liable

Proprietorship. A **proprietorship** has a single owner. Proprietorships tend to be small retail stores or solo providers of services—physicians, attorneys, artists, electricians, or accountants. Legally, the business *is* the proprietor, and the proprietor is personally liable for all the business's debts. But for accounting purposes, a proprietorship is a distinct entity, separate from its proprietor. Thus, the business records should be kept separate from the proprietor's personal finances.

Partnership. A **partnership** has two or more parties as co-owners, and each owner is a partner. Individuals, corporations, partnerships, or other types of entities can be partners. Income and losses of the partnership "flow through" to the partners, and they recognize them based on their agreed-upon percentage interest in the business. The partnership does not pay taxes. Instead, each partner pays taxes based on that partner's individual or corporate rate. Many retail establishments, professional service firms (law, accounting, etc.), real estate, and oil and gas exploration companies operate as partnerships. Many partnerships are small or medium-sized, but some are gigantic, with thousands of partners.

Partnerships are governed by agreement, usually spelled out in writing in the form of a contract between the partners. In most partnerships, each partner can conduct business on behalf of the organization and can make agreements that legally bind all partners. Partnerships such as these are called *general partnerships*. They are risky because an irresponsible partner can create large debts for the other general partners without their knowledge or permission. This feature of general partnerships has led to the creation of limited-liability partnerships (LLPs). A *limited-liability partnership* is one in which a single partner cannot create a large liability for the other partners. In LLPs, each partner is liable for the partnership's debts only up to the extent of his or her investment in the partnership. However, each LLP must have one general partner with unlimited liability for all of the partnership debts.

Limited-Liability Company. A **limited-liability company (LLC)** is one in which the business (and not the owner) is liable for the company's debts. An LLC may have one owner or many owners, called *members*. Unlike a proprietorship or a general partnership, the members of an LLC have limited liability for the LLC's debts only up to the extent of their investment in the LLC. Similar to a partnership, the LLC's income "flows through" to the members, and they pay income taxes at their own tax rates. Because of these favorable features, many multiple-owner businesses are organized as LLCs.

Corporation. A **corporation** is a business owned by **stockholders**, or **shareholders**, who own **stock** representing shares of ownership in the corporation. Being able to raise large sums of capital by issuing shares of stock to the public is a major advantage of forming a corporation. All types of entities (individuals, partnerships, corporations, or other types) may be shareholders in a corporation. Even though proprietorships and partnerships are more numerous, corporations tend to be larger in terms of their assets, income, and number of employees. Most well-known companies, such as The Walt Disney Company, **Amazon.com, Inc.**, **Alphabet, Inc.** (parent company of **Google, Inc.**), **General Motors Company**, and **Apple Inc.**, are corporations. Unlike proprietorships and partnerships, a corporation must be formed under state law and is legally distinct from its owners. The corporation is like an artificial person and possesses many of the same rights that a person has. The stockholders have no personal obligation for the corporation's debts. So, stockholders of a corporation have limited liability, as do limited partners and members of an LLC. However, unlike partnerships or LLCs, a corporation pays a business income tax as well as many other types of taxes. So, the shareholders of a corporation are effectively taxed twice on distributions received from the corporation (called dividends): (1) when the corporation pays income taxes, and (2) when the shareholders pay taxes on the income distributed to them by the corporation. Thus, one of the major disadvantages of the corporate form of business is *double taxation of distributed profits*. The unique attributes of a corporation are covered in more detail in Chapter 10.

EXPLAIN AND APPLY UNDERLYING ACCOUNTING CONCEPTS, ASSUMPTIONS, AND PRINCIPLES

2 Explain and apply underlying accounting concepts, assumptions, and principles

Accountants follow professional standards for measuring and disclosing financial information. The most common set of standards are called **Generally Accepted Accounting Principles (GAAP)**. In the United States, the **Financial Accounting Standards Board (FASB)** formulates the standards for U.S. GAAP. The **International Accounting Standards Board (IASB)** sets **International Financial Reporting Standards (IFRS)**, as discussed later in this section.

Exhibit 1-3 gives an overview of the joint conceptual framework of accounting developed by the FASB and the IASB. Financial reporting standards (whether U.S. or international), at the bottom, follow this conceptual framework. The top frame shows that the overall *objective* of accounting is to provide financial information about the reporting entity that existing and potential investors, lenders, and other creditors can use to make decisions. The second level in the exhibit indicates that to be useful, the information must have two fundamental qualitative characteristics:

- relevance, and
- faithful representation.

Exhibit 1-3 Conceptual Foundation of Accounting

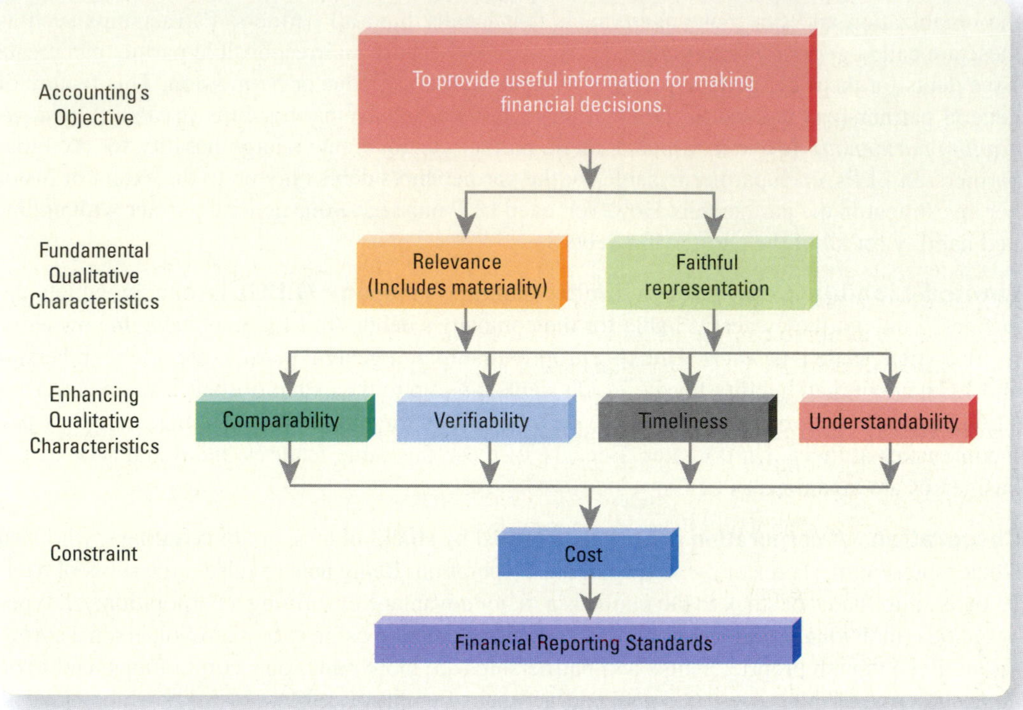

To be relevant, the information must be useful to decision makers in terms of helping them predict or confirm an organization's value. In addition, the information must be *material*, which means it must be important enough that, if it were omitted or incorrect, it would affect a user's decision. Only information that is material needs to be separately *disclosed* (listed or discussed) in financial statements. If it's not material, it can be combined with other information and not separately disclosed. To make a faithful representation, the information must be complete, neutral (free from bias), and free from error (accurate). Faithful representation makes the information *reliable* to users.

The third level in the exhibit indicates that accounting information must also have a number of *enhancing qualitative characteristics*. These include

- comparability,
- verifiability,
- timeliness, and
- understandability.

Comparability means that accounting information must be prepared in a way that allows it to be compared with information from other companies in the same period; the information should also be *consistent* with similar information for that company in previous periods. For example, the methods used to compute sales revenue should be consistent for each year presented in financial statements. *Verifiability* means that it must be possible to check the information for accuracy, completeness, and reliability. Verifiability enhances the reliability of information and thus makes the information more representative of economic reality. *Timeliness* means that the information must be made available to users early enough to help them make decisions. *Understandability* means the information must be transparent, or clear, enough so that it makes sense to reasonably informed users of the information (investors, creditors, regulatory agencies, and managers).

Cost is the fourth level in the exhibit. Because accounting information is costly to produce, the cost of disclosing it should not exceed its expected benefits to users. Managers must carefully decide what accounting costs the organization must incur to give users a good understanding of its financial situation and what accounting information is too costly to provide.

This course will expose you to U.S. GAAP as well as to relevant IFRS. We summarize U.S. GAAP in Appendix C and IFRS in Appendix D. In the following section, we briefly summarize some of the basic assumptions and principles that underlie these standards.

The Entity Assumption

The most basic accounting assumption (underlying idea) is the **entity**, which is any organization (or person) that stands apart as a separate economic unit. Sharp boundaries are drawn around each entity so as not to confuse its affairs with those of others.

Consider Robert A. Iger, Chairman and CEO of The Walt Disney Company. Iger likely owns several homes, automobiles, and other personal assets. In addition, he may owe money on some personal loans. All these assets and liabilities belong to Iger and have nothing to do with The Walt Disney Company. Likewise, Disney's cash, computers, and inventories belong to the company and not to Iger. Why? The entity assumption draws a sharp boundary around each entity. In this case, The Walt Disney Company is one entity, and Robert Iger is a second, separate entity.

Let's consider the various types of businesses that make up The Walt Disney Company. The company operates five types of businesses, called **segments**: media networks, parks and resorts, studio entertainment, consumer products, and interactive media (games and online services). Top managers evaluate the results of the parks and resorts businesses separately from those of media networks. If theme park revenues were falling, the company should identify the reason. But if revenue figures from all the businesses were combined in a single total, managers couldn't tell how differently each business segment was performing. To correct the problem, managers need accounting information for each business segment (entity) in the company. They also need separate information for each geographic region (such as country). To accomplish this, each type of business and each region keeps its own records so it can be evaluated separately.

The Continuity (Going-Concern) Assumption

When measuring and reporting accounting information, we assume that the entity will continue to operate long enough to sell its inventories, convert any receivables to cash, use other existing assets (such as land, buildings, equipment, and supplies) for their intended purposes, and settle its obligations in the normal course of business. This is called the **continuity (or going-concern) assumption**.

Consider the alternative to the **going-concern assumption**: the *quitting concern*, or going out of business assumption. An entity going out of business would have to sell all of its assets in the process. In that case, the most *relevant* measure of the value of the assets would be their liquidating values (or the amount the company can receive for the assets when sold in order to go out of business). But going out of business is the exception rather than the rule. Therefore, the continuity assumption says that a business should stay in business long enough to convert its inventories and receivables to cash and pay off its obligations in the ordinary course of business, and to continue this process of operating into the future.

The Historical Cost Principle

The **historical cost principle** states that assets should be recorded at their actual cost, measured on the date of purchase as the amount of cash paid plus noncash types of compensation given in exchange. For example, suppose The Walt Disney Company wants to purchase a building for a new Disney Store. The building's current owner is asking $6,000,000 for the building. Disney's managers believe the building is worth $5,850,000 and offer that amount. Two real estate professionals appraise the building at $6,100,000. The buyer and seller then compromise and agree on a price of $5,900,000. The historical cost principle requires Disney to initially record the building at its actual cost of $5,900,000—not at $5,850,000, $6,000,000, or $6,100,000, even though those amounts were what some people believed the building was worth. The $5,900,000 cost is both the *relevant* amount of the building's worth and the amount that *faithfully represents* a reliable figure for the price the company paid for it.

Based on the historical cost principle and the continuity assumption, The Walt Disney Company should continue to use historical cost to value the asset for as long as the business owns it. Why? Because cost is a *verifiable* measure that is relatively *free from bias*. Suppose that after the company has owned the building for six years, it can be sold for $6,500,000 because real estate prices have gone up. Should Disney increase the value of the building on the company's books to $6,500,000 at this point? No. According to the historical cost principle, the building remains on The Walt Disney Company's books at its historical cost of $5,900,000, less accumulated depreciation. According to the continuity assumption, Disney intends to stay in business and use the building—not sell it—so its historical cost is the most relevant and the most faithful representation of its value. It is also the most easily verifiable amount. Should the company decide to sell the building later at a price above or below its value, it will record the cash received, remove the value of the building from the books, and record a gain or a loss for the difference at that time.

Although the historical cost principle is used widely in the United States to value assets, accounting is moving in the direction of reporting more assets and liabilities at their fair values. **Fair value** is the amount that the business could sell the asset for, or the amount that the business could pay to settle the liability. The FASB has issued guidance for companies to report many assets and liabilities at fair values.[1] Moreover, in recent years, the FASB has agreed to "harmonize" U.S. GAAP with IFRS. IFRS generally allow more types of assets to be periodically adjusted to their fair values than U.S. GAAP. We will discuss the trend toward globalization of accounting standards in the following Global View feature, and we will illustrate it in later chapters throughout the book.

The Stable-Monetary-Unit Assumption

In the United States, we record transactions in dollars because that is our medium of exchange. British accountants record transactions in pounds sterling, Japanese in yen, and some continental Europeans in euros.

Unlike a liter or a mile, the value of a dollar changes over time. A rise in the general price level is called *inflation*. Inflation results in a dollar purchasing less food, less toothpaste, and less of other goods and services. When prices are stable—there is little inflation—a dollar's purchasing power is also stable.

Under the **stable-monetary-unit assumption**, accountants assume that the dollar's purchasing power is stable over time. We ignore inflation, and this allows us to add and subtract dollar amounts as though the dollar's purchasing power hasn't changed. This is important because businesses that report their financial information publicly usually report comparative financial information (that is, the current year along with one or more prior years). If we could not assume a stable monetary unit, assets and liabilities denominated in prior years' dollars would have to be adjusted to current-year price levels. In developed countries like the United States, inflation levels have been at very low levels for several decades and are expected to remain so for the foreseeable future. As a result, adjusting accounting information for inflation to make the information comparable over time isn't considered necessary.

[1] In 2013, the American Institute of Certified Public Accountants (AICPA) adopted a separate "financial reporting framework for small and medium-sized entities." The framework, which is called FRF-SME, avoids some of the complexities of full-blown GAAP. Many small-sized entities are owner managed and prepare financial statements mostly for the use of their bankers, who do not require all of the complex disclosures of GAAP. FRF-SME is less complicated than GAAP, and, while it requires accrual accounting, it emphasizes use of historical cost more than fair values for assets. Most of the principles we use in this text are applicable to both FRF-SME and GAAP. Accrual accounting is discussed in Chapter 3.

GLOBAL VIEW

International Financial Reporting Standards We live in a global economy: Investors in the United States can easily trade stocks on the Hong Kong, London, and Brussels stock exchanges over the Internet. Each year, American companies such as **Starbucks**, **The Gap**, **McDonald's**, **Microsoft**, and Disney conduct billions of dollars of business around the globe. Conversely, foreign companies such as **Nokia**, **Samsung**, **Toyota**, and **Nestlé** conduct billions of dollars of business in the United States. American companies have merged with foreign companies to create international conglomerates such as **Pearson** (the publisher of this textbook) and **Anheuser-Busch InBev** (producers of alcoholic beverages). No matter where your career starts, it is very likely that it will involve global markets.

At one time, the major developed countries in the world (the United States, the United Kingdom, Japan, Germany, etc.) all had their own versions of GAAP. This made it difficult and expensive for users to compare financial results across entities from different countries. Why? It compelled users to restate and convert accounting data from one country to the next in order to make them comparable.

This problem has been largely solved by the IASB, which has developed International Financial Reporting Standards (IFRS) that are now being used by most countries around the world. IFRS have not been adopted in the United States because existing U.S. GAAP have long been considered the strongest single set of accounting standards in the world. In addition, the application of U.S. GAAP for public companies in the United States has been overseen carefully by the SEC, a body that at present has no global counterpart. Although it has taken measures to permit some types of U.S. companies that operate globally to use IFRS, the SEC has stopped short of requiring it. Thus, it appears that the FASB and IASB will continue to co-exist in the future. The FASB and IFRS have ongoing projects to converge their standards. The goal is to adopt a rather uniform set of high-quality global accounting standards, although some major differences remain.

In chapters that cover concepts where major differences between U.S. GAAP and IFRS exist, we will briefly discuss those differences. Appendix D includes a table, cross-referenced by chapter, that summarizes all of these differences, as well as their impact on financial statements.

APPLY THE ACCOUNTING EQUATION TO BUSINESS ORGANIZATIONS

3 **Apply** the accounting equation to business organizations

The Walt Disney Company's financial statements tell us how the business is performing and where it stands. But how do we arrive at the financial statements? Let's examine the elements of financial statements, which are the building blocks from which statements are made.

Assets and Liabilities

The financial statements are based on the accounting equation. This equation presents the resources of a company and the claims to those resources.

- **Assets** are economic resources that are expected to produce a benefit in the future. The Walt Disney Company's cash, receivables, inventory, attractions, buildings, and equipment are examples of assets.

Claims on assets come from two sources:

- **Liabilities** are "outsider claims." They are debts owed to people and organizations outside of the business (creditors). For example, a creditor who has loaned money to The Walt Disney Company has a claim—a legal right—to a part of the company's assets until the company repays the debt.
- **Equity** (also called **capital, owners' equity,** or **stockholders' equity** for a corporation) represents the "insider claims" of a business. Equity means ownership, so The Walt Disney Company's equity is the stockholders' interest in the assets of the corporation. Throughout most of this book we will be discussing corporations, so the term stockholders' equity is most likely to be used.

The **accounting equation** shows the relationship among a company's assets, liabilities, and equity. Assets appear on the left side and liabilities and equity on the right. As Exhibit 1-4 shows, the two sides must be equal:

Exhibit 1-4 | The Accounting Equation

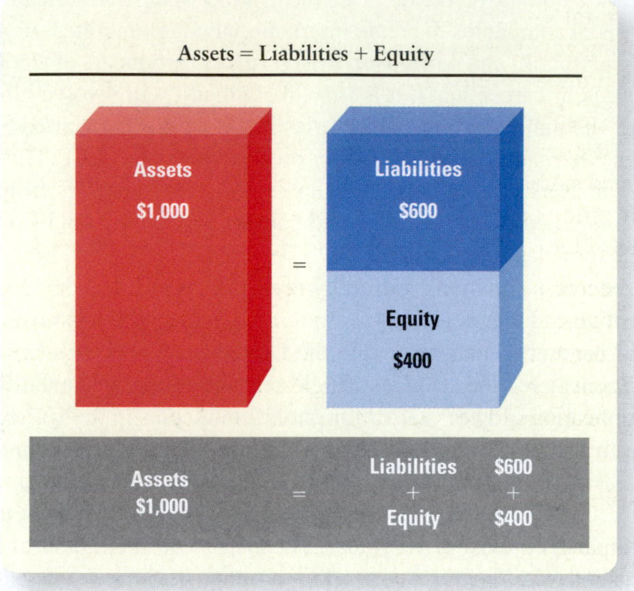

What are some of The Walt Disney Company's assets? As Exhibit 1-9 shows, the first asset is *cash and cash equivalents*. *Cash equivalents* are liquid assets that can be readily converted to cash. A certificate of deposit and a U.S. treasury bill are examples of cash equivalents. Another important asset is merchandise inventory (often called inventories)—the consumer products—Disney sells. The company also has assets in the form of parks, resorts, and equipment, or *fixed assets*. These are the long-lived assets the company uses to do business—theme park attractions (rides), buildings, computers, and other equipment.

The Walt Disney Company's liabilities include a number of payables, such as accounts payable and accrued liabilities. The word *payable* always signifies a liability. An account payable is a liability for goods or services purchased on credit. Accounts payable typically have to be paid within 30 to 60 days. **Long-term debt** (borrowings) is a liability that's payable beyond one year from the date of the financial statements. The *current portion of long-term debt* (*borrowings*) is the amount due within the next year, and it has to be disclosed separately in the current liabilities section.

Equity

The equity (owners' interests) of any business is its assets minus its liabilities. We can write the accounting equation to show that owners' equity is what's left over when we subtract liabilities from assets.

Assets − Liabilities = Equity

A corporation's equity—called stockholders' equity—has two main subparts:

- Paid-in capital
- Retained earnings

The accounting equation for a corporation can be written as

Assets = Liabilities + Stockholders' Equity
Assets = Liabilities + Paid-in Capital + Retained Earnings

- **Paid-in capital** is the amount the stockholders have invested in the corporation. The basic component of paid-in capital is **common stock**, which the corporation issues to the stockholders as evidence of their ownership. All corporations issue common stock.
- **Retained earnings** is the amount earned by income-producing activities and kept for use by the business. Three major types of transactions affect retained earnings: revenues, expenses, and dividends.
- **Revenues** are inflows of resources that increase retained earnings as a result of the company delivering goods or services to customers. For example, the entrance fees to Disney's theme parks bring in revenue and increase the company's retained earnings.
- **Expenses** are resource outflows that decrease a company's retained earnings due to operations. Expenses represent the costs of doing business; they are the opposite of revenues. The wages and salaries Disney pays its employees, the cost of the products and services it sells, and its utility and rent payments are expenses that decrease its retained earnings. The depreciation of Disney's attractions, buildings, and equipment are also expenses.
- **Dividends** decrease retained earnings, because they are distributions to stockholders of assets (usually cash) generated by a company's operating activities. A successful business may pay dividends to shareholders as a return on their investments. Remember: *dividends are not expenses, and they never affect a company's net income.* Instead of being subtracted from revenues to compute net income, dividends are recorded as direct reductions of retained earnings.

Businesses strive for *profits,* the excess of revenues over expenses.

- When a company's total revenues exceed total expenses, the result is called **net income**, **net earnings**, or **net profit**.
- When a company's total expenses exceed total revenues, the result is a **net loss**.
- Net income or net loss is the "bottom line" on an income statement. The Walt Disney Company's bottom line for the year ended October 1, 2016, was a net income of $9,391 million (line 16 on the Consolidated Statements of Income in Exhibit 1-7).

Exhibit 1-5 shows the relationships among the following:

- Retained earnings
- Revenues – Expenses = Net income (or net loss)
- Dividends

Exhibit 1-5 | The Components of Retained Earnings

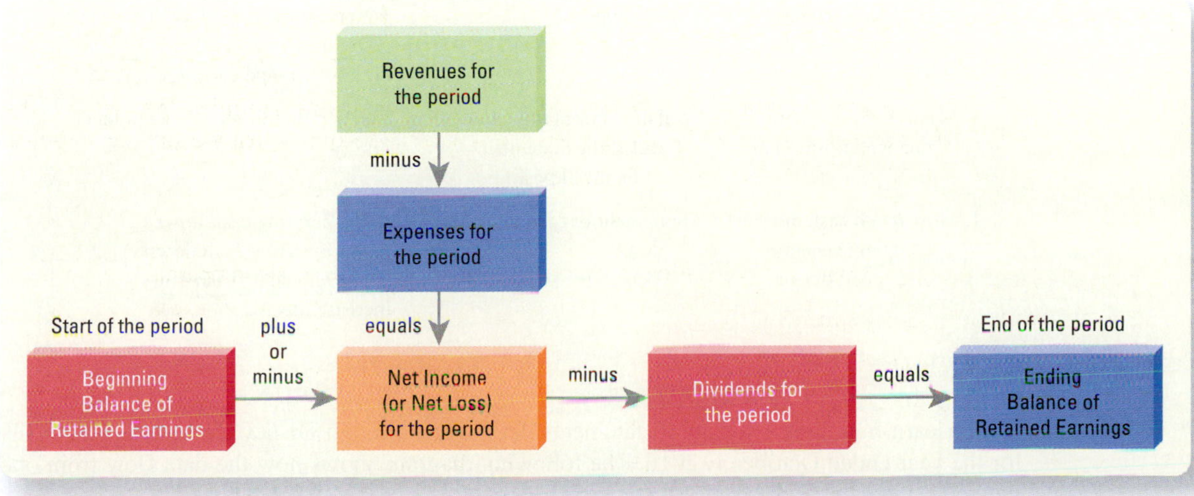

The equity of proprietorships and partnerships is different from that of corporations. Proprietorships and partnerships don't identify paid-in capital and retained earnings separately. Instead, they use a single heading: Capital. Examples include "Randall Waller, Capital" (for a proprietorship) and "Powers, Capital" and "Salazar, Capital" (for a partnership).

TRY IT

(Answers are given on page 59.)

(1) If the assets of a business are $480,000 and the liabilities are $160,000, how much is the equity?

(2) If the equity in a business is $160,000 and the liabilities are $100,000, how much are the assets?

(3) A company reported monthly revenues of $365,000 and monthly expenses of $225,000. What is the result of operations for the month?

(4) If the beginning balance of retained earnings is $180,000, revenue is $85,000, expenses total $35,000, and the company declares and pays a $20,000 dividend, what is the ending balance of retained earnings?

CONSTRUCT FINANCIAL STATEMENTS AND ANALYZE THE RELATIONSHIPS AMONG THEM

4 Construct financial statements and **analyze** the relationships among them

Financial statements present a company to the public in financial terms. Each financial statement relates to a specific date or time period. What would investors and other decision makers want to know about The Walt Disney Company at the end of its fiscal year? Exhibit 1-6 lists four questions they should ask. Each answer comes from one of the financial statements.

Exhibit 1-6 | Information Reported in the Financial Statements

Question	Financial Statement	Answer
1. How well did the company perform during the year?	Income statement (also called the Statement of operations)	Revenues − Expenses Net income (or Net loss)
2. Why did the company's retained earnings change during the year?	Statement of retained earnings	Beginning retained earnings + Net income (or − Net loss) − Dividends declared Ending retained earnings
3. What is the company's financial position at fiscal year end?	Balance sheet (also called the Statement of financial position)	Assets = Liabilities + Stockholders' Equity
4. How much cash did the company generate and spend during the year?	Statement of cash flows	Net Operating cash flows ± Net Investing cash flows ± Net Financing cash flows Increase (decrease) in cash

To learn how to use financial statements, let's work through Disney's financial statements for the year ended October 1, 2016. The following diagram shows how the data flow from one financial statement to the next. The order is important.

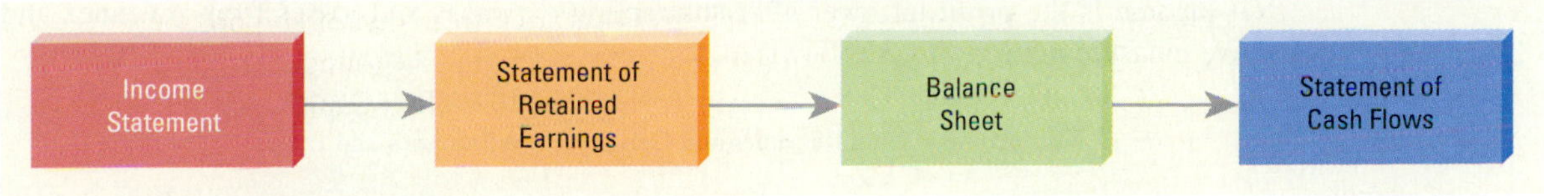

The Income Statement

Exhibit 1-7 shows Disney's **income statement**, or **statement of operations**, which reports revenues and expenses for the period. In other words, the income statement measures a company's operating performance. The bottom line in the statement is the net income or net loss for the period. At the top of Exhibit 1-7 is the company's name: The Walt Disney Company. On the second line is the term "Consolidated Statements of Income."

The Walt Disney Company is actually made up of several corporations owned by a common group of shareholders. Commonly controlled corporations like this are required to combine, or consolidate, all of their revenues, expenses, assets, liabilities, and stockholders' equity and to report them all as one.

Exhibit 1-7 | The Walt Disney Company, Consolidated Statements of Income

A1

	A	B	C	D	E
1	**The Walt Disney Company Consolidated Statements of Income**	**Fiscal 2016**	**Fiscal 2015**		
2		**12 Months Ended**			
3	**Adapted, in millions of $**	**Oct. 01, 2016**	**Oct. 03, 2015**		
4	Services revenue	$ 47,130	$ 43,894		
5	Products revenue	8,502	8,571		
6	Total revenues	55,632	52,465		
7	Cost of services	24,653	23,191		
8	Cost of products	5,340	5,173		
9	Selling, general, administrative and other	8,754	8,523		
10	Depreciation and amortization	2,527	2,354		
11	Total costs and expenses	41,274	39,241		
12	Income from operations	14,358	13,224		
13	Other items of income (expense), net	111	174		
14	Income before income taxes	14,469	13,398		
15	Income taxes	5,078	5,016		
16	Net income	$ 9,391	$ 8,382		
17					

Data from the U.S. Securities and Exchange Commission EDGAR Company Filings, www.sec.gov

The dates of The Walt Disney Company's Consolidated Statements of Income are 12 months ended October 1, 2016, and 12 months ended October 3, 2015. A *fiscal year* is a 52-week period used for accounting purposes and preparing financial statements that may or may not correspond to a calendar year. Companies often adopt a fiscal year that ends at the low point of their operations. Disney uses the 52 weeks ending closest to September 30 as its accounting year. This is because the summer vacation season is the busiest time of the year for the company, whereas September is typically a slower month, allowing the company time to get its books in order. **FedEx Corp.**'s fiscal year-end falls on May 31. Alternatively, about 60% of the largest companies, such as **Amazon.com, Inc.**, use a fiscal year corresponding to the calendar year.

The Walt Disney Company's Consolidated Statements of Income in Exhibit 1-7 report the results of its operations for two fiscal years in order to show trends for revenues, expenses, and net income. To avoid having to use a lot of zeros, the company reports its results in millions of dollars. Some relatively simple analyses of the company's consolidated statements of income will help us evaluate how well the company performed in fiscal 2016 versus fiscal 2015.

An income statement reports two main categories:

- Revenues and gains
- Expenses and losses

Net income is the profit left over after subtracting expenses and losses from revenues and gains. We measure net income as follows:

Net Income = Total Revenues and Gains − Total Expenses and Losses

Net income is the single most important item in the financial statements. During the fiscal year ended October 1, 2016, Disney earned total revenues of $55,632 million (line 6). The company earned net income (line 16) of $9,391 million.

Revenues. The Walt Disney Company earns significant revenues from performing services as well as selling products. Services revenue is generated in its media networks, parks and resorts, studio entertainment, and interactive divisions. Product sales revenue is generated in its consumer products division. To present a clearer picture of its results of operations, the company reports each of these revenue streams separately. For the fiscal year ended October 1, 2016, services revenue (line 4) comprised 84.7% of the company's total revenue ($47,130 million ÷ $55,632 million, on line 6). Products revenue (line 5) comprised 15.3% of total revenue for the year ($8,502 million ÷ $55,632 million). During the fiscal year ended October 1, 2016, services revenue increased about 7.4% over fiscal 2015, from $43,894 million to $47,130 million. Products revenue, however, fell by about 0.8% from fiscal 2015, from $8,571 million to $8,502 million. From these computations you can tell that the company's biggest revenue stream was its services revenue, and that its products revenue declined.

Expenses. Not all expenses have the word *expense* in their titles. For example, some of Disney's largest expenses are for cost of services and cost of products (lines 7 and 8, respectively). Line 7 shows Disney's direct cost of providing services (exclusive of depreciation and amortization) through its media networks, parks and resorts, studio entertainment, and interactive business segments. Examples of the cost of services include the labor and materials directly related to each service segment's revenue. The cost of services in fiscal 2016 was $24,653 million (up 6.3% from the fiscal 2015 cost of services of $23,191 million). Comparing the year-to-year increase in services revenue discussed in the preceding paragraph, we see that the company's service revenue in fiscal 2016 increased at a faster pace (about 7.4%) than the cost of those services. This means that the services business segments of The Walt Disney Company were more profitable in 2016 than they were in 2015.

Although it's not shown separately in Exhibit 1-7, you can calculate Disney's **gross profit** from services by subtracting the cost of services from services revenue. In fiscal 2016, the gross profit from services was $22,477 million ($47,130 million – $24,653 million). In fiscal 2015, the gross profit from services was $20,703 million ($43,894 million – $23,191 million). Thus, gross profit of the services segments rose by $1,774 million or 8.6%.

Line 8 reports that the cost of products in fiscal 2016 was $5,340 million, which was up $167 million, or 3.2%, from $5,173 million in fiscal 2015. When you compare this 3.2% increase in costs with the 0.8% decline in product revenue, you can see why the company's *gross profit* from the sale of products declined over the year. Gross profit from the sale of products (products revenue minus the related cost of those products) decreased from $3,398 million ($8,571 million – $5,173 million) in fiscal 2015 to $3,162 million ($8,502 million – $5,340 million) in fiscal 2016, a decrease of $236 million, or about 7%. In other words, over the year, services became more profitable, whereas products became less profitable. Expect some changes over the next several years in the products division of Walt Disney Company. Pat yourself on the back! You're beginning to understand financial statement analysis!

The Walt Disney Company has some other expense categories:

- **Selling, general, administrative and other expenses** (line 9) are the costs of everyday operations not directly related to performing services or selling products. Many expenses may be included in this category, including salaries paid to executives and administrative employees, information technology costs, warehousing expenses, and other general operating expenses. These expenses amounted to $8,754 million during fiscal 2016, up about 2.7% from fiscal 2015 ($8,523 million).

- **Depreciation and amortization** (line 10). The Walt Disney Company has invested billions of dollars in fixed assets. Examples are all of the buildings and attractions (rides) at Disney's theme parks, as well as the resorts and other properties it owns. These assets are reported at historical cost on the company's balance sheet (see Exhibit 1-9, line 11). **Depreciation** is a process that allocates a portion of the cost of these assets over their estimated useful lives against the revenues the assets help to generate. Depreciation is discussed in greater depth in Chapters 3 and 7. **Amortization** is a process similar to depreciation, except that it applies to certain other long-term tangible and intangible assets, as well as certain liabilities. These amounts are initially recorded as assets and liabilities on the balance sheet, and are allocated as amortization expenses to the time periods affected by them. Amortization is discussed in greater depth in Chapters 7 and 9. Depreciation and amortization was $2,527 million in fiscal 2016 and $2,354 million in fiscal 2015.
- **Income from operations** (line 12). The difference between all operating revenues and all operating expenses is called income from operations. This is a very important number on the income statement because it communicates whether a company's core business operations were profitable or not. Income from operations is the best predictor of the future profitability of the company. If income from operations is trending on a steady path upward, it is a positive sign that can help investors forecast continued profitability in the future. Disney's operating income grew by about 8.6% during fiscal 2016 (from $13,224 million to $14,358 million).
- **Other income (expense), net** (line 13) was $111 million for fiscal 2016 and $174 million for fiscal 2015. This line includes some items that are too small for the company to report separately, such as gains and losses from foreign currency transactions, as well as gains and losses from selling, exchanging, or otherwise disposing of fixed assets.
- **Income taxes** (line 15) are expenses levied on Disney's taxable income by the federal government. This is often one of a corporation's largest expenses. Disney's income tax expense for the 12 months ended October 1, 2016 was a whopping $5,078 million (35.1% of its net income before taxes)!
- **Net income** (line 16). The "bottom line" of the Consolidated Statements of Income (all revenues less all expenses) is net income. Those amounts were $9,391 million in fiscal 2016 and $8,382 million in fiscal 2015, reflecting an annual growth rate of about 12.0%.

Now let's examine the Statement of Retained Earnings in Exhibit 1-8.

Exhibit 1-8 | The Walt Disney Company, Consolidated Statements of Retained Earnings

	A	B
1	**The Walt Disney Company** **Consolidated Statements of Retained Earnings** **For the Two Years Ending October 1, 2016**	
2	**Adapted, in millions of $**	
3	Retained earnings, Sep. 27, 2014	$ 53,734
4	Net income, year ended October 3, 2015	8,382
5	Dividends declared, year ended October 3, 2015	(3,087)
6	Other reductions, year ended October 3, 2015	(1)
7	Retained earnings, October 3, 2015	59,028
8	Net income, year ended October 1, 2016	9,391
9	Dividends declared, year ended October 1, 2016	(2,328)
10	Other reductions, year ended October 1, 2016	(3)
11	Retained earnings, October 1, 2016	$ 66,088
12		

The Statement of Retained Earnings

The **statement of retained earnings** shows what a company did with its earnings. *Retained earnings* means exactly what the term implies: It is that portion of net income the company has retained, or kept, over a period of years, after making deductions for dividends to shareholders. If, historically, revenues exceed expenses, the result will be a positive balance in retained earnings. In contrast, if, historically, expenses have exceeded sales revenues, the accumulation of these losses will result in an accumulated **deficit** in retained earnings, which is usually shown in parentheses. Net income for The Walt Disney Company flows from the income statement (line 16 of Exhibit 1-7) to the statement of retained earnings (lines 4 and 8 in Exhibit 1-8).

Let's review The Walt Disney Company's Consolidated Statements of Retained Earnings for the two-year period ending October 1, 2016. This statement was excerpted from the company's Consolidated Statements of Stockholders' Equity, which analyze all of the increases and decreases in every account in the stockholders' equity section of the balance sheet. At the beginning of fiscal 2015 (September 27, 2014), Disney had $53,734 million in retained earnings (line 3). During fiscal 2015, the company earned net income of $8,382 million (line 4) and declared dividends of $3,087 million ($3,063 million in cash and $24 million in stock) to shareholders (line 5). Disney made another small negative adjustment to retained earnings of $1 million (line 6). The company ended the 2015 fiscal year with a retained earnings balance of $59,028 million, which carried over and became the beginning balance of retained earnings in fiscal 2016 (line 7).

During fiscal 2016, the company earned net income of $9,391 million (line 8). As shown on line 9, it then declared dividends to shareholders in the amount of $2,328 million. Of this amount, $2,313 million was distributed in cash, and another $15 million was distributed in the form of the company's common stock. We will discuss cash and stock dividends in greater depth in Chapter 10. After another small negative adjustment of $3 million, the company ended the 2016 fiscal year with $66,088 million in retained earnings (line 11).

Which item on the statement of retained earnings comes directly from the income statement? It is net income. Lines 4 and 8 of the retained earnings statement come directly from line 16 of the income statement (see Exhibit 1-7) for fiscal 2015 and 2016, respectively. Take a moment to trace this amount from one statement to the other. Then give yourself another pat on the back—You've learned more about how to analyze financial statements!

After a company earns net income, the **board of directors** decides whether or not to pay a dividend to the stockholders. Corporations are not obligated to pay dividends unless their boards decide to pay (i.e., declare) them. Usually, companies that are in a development stage or growth mode elect not to pay dividends, opting instead to plow resources back into the company to expand operations or purchase property, plant, and equipment. However, established companies like The Walt Disney Company usually have enough accumulated retained earnings (and cash) to pay dividends. Dividends decrease retained earnings because they represent a distribution of a company's assets (usually cash) to its stockholders.

The Balance Sheet

A company's **balance sheet**, also called the **statement of financial position**, reports three items: assets (line 14), liabilities (line 23), and equity (line 29). The Walt Disney Company's Consolidated Balance Sheets, shown in Exhibit 1-9, are dated at the *moment in time* when the accounting periods end (October 1, 2016, and October 3, 2015).

Assets. There are two main categories of assets: current and long-term. **Current assets** are assets expected to be converted to cash, sold, or consumed during the next 12 months or within the business's operating cycle if it's longer than a year. Disney's current assets at October 1, 2016, totaled $16,966 million (line 8). Let's examine each of the company's current assets.

- *Cash and cash equivalents* (line 4). Cash is a liquid asset, which means it can be immediately exchanged for goods and services. *Cash equivalents* include U.S. Treasury securities or other financial instruments that are easily convertible to cash. Disney owned $4,610 million in cash and cash equivalents at October 1, 2016. This was up from $4,269 million at October 3, 2015. We will explain this further when we discuss the statement of cash flows later.

Exhibit 1-9 | The Walt Disney Company, Consolidated Balance Sheets

	A	B	C	D
1	**The Walt Disney Company Consolidated Balance Sheets**	**Fiscal 2016**	**Fiscal 2015**	
2	**$ in Millions**	**Oct. 01, 2016**	**Oct. 03, 2015**	
3	**Current assets**			
4	Cash and cash equivalents	$ 4,610	$ 4,269	
5	Receivables	9,065	8,019	
6	Inventories	1,390	1,571	
7	Other current assets	1,901	2,899	
8	**Total current assets**	16,966	16,758	
9	Film and television costs	6,339	6,183	
10	Investments	4,280	2,643	
11	Parks, resorts and other property, net	27,349	25,179	
12	Intangible assets, net	34,759	34,998	
13	Other long-term assets	2,340	2,421	
14	**Total assets**	$ 92,033	$ 88,182	
15	**Current liabilities**			
16	Accounts payable and accrued liabilities	$ 9,130	$ 7,844	
17	Current portion of long-term borrowings	3,687	4,563	
18	Unearned royalties and other advances	4,025	3,927	
19	**Total current liabilities**	16,842	16,334	
20	Long-term borrowings	16,483	12,773	
21	Other long-term liabilities	11,385	10,420	
22	Contingent liabilities (Note 14)			
23	**Total liabilities**	44,710	39,527	
24	**Equity**			
25	Common stock, and additional paid-in capital	35,859	35,122	
26	Retained earnings	66,088	59,028	
27	Treasury stock, at cost	(54,703)	(47,204)	
28	Other equity, net*	79	1,709	
29	**Total equity**	47,323	48,655	
30	**Total liabilities and equity**	$ 92,033	$ 88,182	
31				

*Consists of items considered too advanced for this text

- *Receivables* (line 5) are monetary claims a company has against organizations and customers, acquired mainly by performing services for them, selling goods to them, or loaning money to them. For Disney, these claims include the amounts people and organizations owe for running ads on the company's television networks, booking vacations at Disney-owned resorts, and buying Disney's merchandise on credit to sell it, among many other things. Receivables are the largest single current asset of The Walt Disney Company as of October 1, 2016 ($9,065 million), up from $8,019 million the year before. The company expects to convert these receivables to cash within the next fiscal year.

- *Inventories* (line 6) are a merchandising company's most important, and often its largest, current asset. As we emphasized earlier, Disney's revenue comes mostly from services rather than sales of merchandise, so inventories are not the company's largest current asset. However, inventories are still significant, and totaled $1,390 million at October 1, 2016, down from $1,571 million at October 3, 2015. The company expects to sell these inventories and convert them to cash within the next fiscal year.

- *Other current assets* (line 7) may include *prepaid expenses*, which represent amounts paid in advance for advertising, rent, insurance, taxes, and supplies. These are current assets because the company will benefit from these expenditures within the next year. Disney owned $1,901 million in other current assets as of October 1, 2016, down from $2,899 million the previous year.

Long-term (non-current) assets are resources that are expected to benefit the company for long periods of time, beyond just the next fiscal year. Let's look at The Walt Disney Company's long-term assets.

- *Film and television costs* (line 9) include production costs such as labor, materials, and overhead for Disney's movies, television, and stage programs. As an example, consider the costs the company incurred to produce the films *Frozen* and *Star Wars: The Force Awakens*. Many of these costs are initially recorded ("capitalized") as assets of the company and are transferred over time to expenses through the process of amortization to be matched against the revenue recognized from the film in the same periods those revenues are earned. The amount of these unamortized costs was $6,339 million as of October 1, 2016, and $6,183 million as of October 3, 2015.
- *Investments* (line 10) represent mostly the amounts that Disney has in **equity method** *investments*, which are investments a company has made in other companies. Disney's investments in other media companies include stock the company owns in **A&E Television Networks**; **Seven TV**; **CTV Specialty Television**; **Hulu**; and **BAMTech**. These investments comprise 20% to 50% of the voting stock of other companies. The amount of Disney's equity investment in these companies was $4,280 million as of October 1, 2016, and $2,643 million as of October 3, 2015.
- *Parks, resorts, and other property, net* (line 11) includes the land, buildings, furniture, and equipment (*fixed assets*) that make up Disney's theme parks, resorts, hotels, and studios. The Walt Disney Company actually reports these assets on several lines on its balance sheet, and then reduces them by *accumulated depreciation,* which represents the amount of the historical cost of these assets that has been allocated to expenses in the income statement over time as the assets have been used to produce revenue. Thus, accumulated depreciation represents the used-up portion of the fixed asset. To save space, we have reported all of these assets on one line, *net* of accumulated depreciation. In other words, we have subtracted accumulated depreciation from the cost of parks, resorts, and other property to determine their net book values ($27,349 million at the end of fiscal 2016 and $25,179 million at the end of fiscal 2015 on line 11). We will discuss depreciation in more detail in Chapters 3 and 7.
- ***Intangible assets, net*** (line 12) are assets that have no physical substance. That is, you can neither see them nor touch them, but nevertheless they represent resources that have a future benefit to the company. Copyrights, trademarks, patents, franchises, and licenses are examples of intangible assets. Intangible assets were $34,759 million as of October 1, 2016, and $34,998 million as of October 3, 2015. Intangible assets are discussed in greater depth in Chapter 7.
- *Other long-term assets* (line 13) is a catchall category for assets that are difficult to classify. These primarily consist of long-term receivables and long-term prepaid expenses. Disney owned about $2,340 million of these assets as of October 1, 2016, compared with $2,421 million at October 3, 2015.
- Overall, The Walt Disney Company reported total assets (line 14) of $92,033 million at October 1, 2016, compared with $88,182 million at October 3, 2015.

Liabilities. Liabilities are also divided into current and long-term categories. **Current liabilities** (lines 16–18) are debts generally payable within one year of the balance sheet date. *Long-term liabilities* are payable after one year. Let's look at Disney's liabilities.

- *Accounts payable and accrued liabilities* (line 16) represent amounts owed to Disney's vendors and suppliers for the company's purchases of inventory, as well as for accrued liabilities (liabilities the company has incurred), such as salaries and taxes. These totaled $9,130 million at the end of fiscal 2016 and $7,844 million at the end of fiscal 2015.
- *Current portion of long-term borrowings* (line 17) represents the portion of long-term borrowings (usually notes payable) that the company will have to pay off within the next year. Notice on line 20 that, at October 1, 2016, the company had about $16,483 million in long-term borrowings, which was up from $12,773 million in fiscal 2015. In addition to that, another $3,687 million was due and payable within 12 months (line 17), resulting in a total

of $20,170 million in long-term borrowings. U.S. GAAP requires companies to segregate and report the portion of long-term debt due and payable within 12 months of the balance sheet date as a current liability, rather than a long-term liability. We'll discuss this in more depth in Chapters 8 and 9.

- *Unearned royalties and other advances* (line 18) represent amounts Disney has collected in advance from its customers for use of its corporate name, as well as for movie and television rights. Whenever cash is received in advance, in periods before services are rendered or goods are shipped, the amount received is required to be added to a liability account. In other words, the company is obligated to its customers to perform those services or ship those products in future periods. As of October 1, 2016, customers had paid Disney $4,025 million in advance for future services and shipment of goods. During fiscal 2017, the company will make adjusting entries to its books to transfer amounts from the unearned account to services revenue or products revenue as those services are performed or goods are shipped, which is the point at which revenues may be recognized as earned. We will discuss this topic in more depth in Chapters 3 and 8.
- At October 1, 2016, Disney's current liabilities totaled $16,842 million, up from $16,334 million as of October 3, 2015 (line 19). The company also owed $16,483 million in long-term borrowings (line 20) and $11,385 million in other long-term liabilities (line 21). These liabilities are due one year or more after the balance sheet date.
- At October 1, 2016, total liabilities were $44,710 million (line 23).

Equity (Stockholders' Equity). The accounting equation states that

$$\text{Assets} - \text{Liabilities} = \text{Equity}$$

Remember that a corporation's equity represents the stockholders' ownership of the business's assets. The Walt Disney Company's equity consists of the following:

- *Common stock and additional paid-in capital* (line 25), which consisted of shares issued to stockholders for about $35,859 million at October 1, 2016, and $35,122 million at October 3, 2015. This account represents the actual dollar amount printed on the stock certificates originally issued to Disney's shareholders when the company incorporated and they bought them. The account also includes *additional paid-in capital,* which consists of the additional amounts shareholders paid in excess of the printed value on the certificates. In other words, additional paid-in capital represents the value, or worth, of a company's shares above the par or stated value. We discuss these topics in greater depth in Chapter 10.
- *Retained earnings* (line 26) are $66,088 million and $59,028 million at the ends of fiscal 2016 and fiscal 2015, respectively. We saw these figures on the statement of retained earnings in Exhibit 1-8 (lines 7 and 11). Retained earnings' final resting place is the stockholders' equity section of the balance sheet.
- *Treasury stock, at cost* (line 27) represents amounts paid by the company to repurchase its own stock.
- *Other equity, net* (line 28) consists of items that are considered beyond the scope of this text and that are covered in depth in later accounting classes.
- At October 1, 2016, Disney's total equity was $47,323 million (line 29). We can now prove that the company's total assets (in millions) equaled its total liabilities and equity:

	Total assets (line 14)	$92,033	←
			Must equal
	Total liabilities (line 23)	$44,710	
+	Total equity (line 29)	$47,323	
	Total liabilities and equity (line 30)	$92,033	←

The statement of cash flows is the fourth required financial statement.

CASH FLOW

The Statement of Cash Flows

Companies engage in three basic types of activities:

- **Operating activities**
- **Investing activities**
- **Financing activities**

The **statement of cash flows** reports cash receipts and cash payments in each of these categories.

- *Companies operate by selling goods and services to customers.* **Operating activities** result in net income or net loss, and they either increase or decrease a company's cash. Whereas Disney's income statement reveals whether the company is profitable, its statement of cash flows reveals whether its operations increased the company's cash balance. Operating activities are most important, and they should be the company's main source of cash. Ongoing negative net cash flows from operations can bankrupt the company.
- *Companies invest in long-term assets.* The Walt Disney Company engages in **investing activities** by buying property for amusement parks and resorts, as well as other long-term assets. When these assets wear out, the company might sell them, which often increases the company's cash. Both purchases and sales of long-term assets result in outgoing and incoming cash flows from investments.
- *Companies need money for financing.* **Financing activities** include issuing stock, paying dividends, borrowing, and repaying borrowed funds. Disney issues stock to its shareholders and borrows from banks, which are cash inflows from financing activities. The company may also pay loans, pay dividends, and repurchase its own stock, which are cash outflows from financing activities.

Exhibit 1-10 | The Walt Disney Company, Consolidated Statements of Cash Flows

A1

	A	B	C	D	E
1	The Walt Disney Company Consolidated Statements of Cash Flows	Fiscal 2016	Fiscal 2015		
2	Adapted, in Millions of $	12 Months Ended			
3		Oct. 1, 2016	Oct. 3, 2015		
4	OPERATING ACTIVITIES				
5	Net income	$ 9,391	$ 8,382		
6	Adjustments to reconcile net income to net cash provided by operating activities	3,822	2,527		
7	Net cash provided by operating activities	13,213	10,909		
8	INVESTING ACTIVITIES				
9	Investments in parks, resorts, and other property	(4,773)	(4,265)		
10	Sales of investments/proceeds from dispositions	45	166		
11	Acquisitions and other investing activities	(1,030)	(146)		
12	Net cash used in investing activities	(5,758)	(4,245)		
13	FINANCING ACTIVITIES				
14	Net proceeds from borrowing	6,065	4,926		
15	Reductions of borrowings	(3,125)	(2,221)		
16	Repurchases of common stock	(7,499)	(6,095)		
17	Dividends	(2,313)	(3,063)		
18	Proceeds from exercise of stock options and other	(119)	939		
19	Net cash used in financing activities	(6,991)	(5,514)		
20	Effect of foreign exchange rate fluctuations on cash	(123)	(302)		
21	Net increase (decrease) in cash and cash equivalents	341	848		
22	Cash and cash equivalents at beginning of period	4,269	3,421		
23	Cash and cash equivalents at end of period	$ 4,610	$ 4,269		
24					

Overview. Each category of cash flows—operating, investing, and financing—either increases or decreases cash. On a statement of cash flows, cash receipts appear as positive amounts. Cash payments are negative amounts and are enclosed by parentheses.

Exhibit 1-10 shows The Walt Disney Company's Consolidated Statements of Cash Flows. Operating activities provided net cash of $13,213 million in the 12 months ended October 1, 2016 (line 7). Notice that this is $3,822 million more than net income ($9,391 million in line 5). Why is this so? This was caused primarily by depreciation and amortization expenses that were deducted from total revenues in order to compute Disney's net income. However, those expenses did not require an actual outlay of cash by the company. Investing activities for the fiscal year (mostly purchases of parks, resorts, and other property) required about a $5,758 million cash outlay (line 12). That indicates that Disney was expanding.

Financing activities used another $6,991 million (line 19). Examining the details, we find that The Walt Disney Company used a whopping $7,499 million in cash to repurchase its common stock from existing shareholders during the year (line 16). This was the largest single transaction reflected on the cash flow statement, besides net income. In addition, the company paid another $2,313 million in cash dividends to shareholders (line 17). We will discuss the reasons why companies repurchase stock from their shareholders and pay dividends in Chapter 10.

Overall, Disney's cash and cash equivalents increased by $341 million during the 12 months ended October 1, 2016 (line 21) and ended the year at $4,610 million (line 23). Trace the ending cash and cash equivalents back to the balance sheet in Exhibit 1-9 (line 4). Cash and cash equivalents links the statement of cash flows to the balance sheet. You've just performed more financial statement analysis!

Exhibit 1-11 summarizes the relationships among the financial statements of The Walt Disney Company for the fiscal year ending October 1, 2016. These statements are condensed, so the details of Exhibits 1-7 through 1-10 are omitted. Study the exhibit carefully because these relationships apply to all organizations. Specifically, note the following:

1. The income statement for the 12 months ended October 1, 2016:
   a. Reports total revenues and expenses of the year. Revenues and expenses are reported *only* on the income statement.
   b. Reports net income if total revenues exceed total expenses. If total expenses exceed total revenues, there is a net loss.
2. The statement of retained earnings for the 12 months ended October 1, 2016:
   a. Opens with the beginning retained earnings balance.
   b. Adds net income (or subtracts net loss). Net income comes directly from the income statement (arrow 1 in Exhibit 1-11).
   c. Subtracts dividends declared.
   d. In some cases, miscellaneous additions or reductions may occur. In fiscal 2016, the company subtracted $3 million of miscellaneous items.
   e. Reports the retained earnings balance at the end of the year.
3. The balance sheet at October 1, 2016, end of the accounting year:
   a. Reports assets, liabilities, and stockholders' equity at the end of the year. Only the balance sheet reports assets and liabilities.
   b. Reports that assets equal the sum of liabilities plus stockholders' equity. This balancing feature follows the accounting equation and gives the balance sheet its name.
   c. Reports ending retained earnings, which comes from the statement of retained earnings (arrow 2 in Exhibit 1-11).
4. The statement of cash flows for the 12 months ended October 1, 2016:
   a. Reports cash flows from operating, investing, and financing activities. Each category results in net cash provided (an increase) or used (a decrease).

b. Reports whether cash and cash equivalents increased (or decreased) during the year.

c. The statement shows the ending cash and cash equivalents balance, as reported on the balance sheet (arrow 3 in Exhibit 1-11).

Exhibit 1-11 | Relationships Among the Financial Statements (in millions of $)

	A	B	C	D	E
1	**The Walt Disney Company** **Consolidated Statement of Income (Adapted)** **12 Months Ended October 1, 2016**				
2	Total revenues	$ 55,743			
3	Total expenses	46,352			
4	Net income	$ 9,391			
5					

①

	A	B	C	D	E
1	**Consolidated Statement of Retained Earnings (Adapted)**				
2	Beginning retained earnings	$ 59,028			
3	Net income	9,391			
4	Dividends declared*	(2,328)			
5	Other reductions	(3)			
6	Ending retained earnings	$ 66,088			
7	*2,313 in cash plus 15 in stock				
8					

②

	A	B	C	D	E
1	**Consolidated Balance Sheet (Adapted)**				
2	Assets				
3	Cash and cash equivalents	$ 4,610			
4	All other assets	87,423			
5	Total assets	$ 92,033			
6	Liabilities				
7	Total liabilities	$ 44,710			
8	Equity				
9	Common stock and additional paid-in capital	35,859			
10	Retained earnings	66,088			
11	Other equity	(54,624)			
12	Total equity	47,323			
13	Total liabilities and equity	$ 92,033			
14					

③

	A	B	C	D	E
1	**Consolidated Statement of Cash Flows (Adapted)**				
2	Net cash provided by operating activities	$ 13,213			
3	Net cash used in investing activities	(5,758)			
4	Net cash used in financing activities	(6,991)			
5	Effect of foreign exchange rate fluctuations on cash	(123)			
6	Net increase (decrease) in cash and cash equivalents	341			
7	Cash and cash equivalents, beginning of year	4,269			
8	Cash and cash equivalents, end of year	$ 4,610			
9					

Decision Guidelines

IN EVALUATING A COMPANY, WHAT DO DECISION MAKERS LOOK FOR?

These Decision Guidelines illustrate how people use financial statements. Decision Guidelines appear throughout the book to show how accounting information aids decision making.

Suppose you are considering buying The Walt Disney Company's stock. How do you proceed? Where do you get the information you need? What do you look for?

Decision	Guidelines
1. Can the company sell its services or products?	**1.** Look at the net revenue on the income statement. Are revenues growing or falling?
2. What are the main income measures to watch for trends?	**2.** Look at the gross profit (sales – cost of goods sold), operating income (gross profit – operating expenses), and the net income (bottom line of the income statement). All three income measures should be increasing over time.
3. What percentage of revenue ends up as profit?	**3.** Divide net income by sales revenue. Examine the trend of the net income percentage from year to year.
4. Can the company collect its receivables?	**4.** From the balance sheet, compare the percentage increase in accounts receivable to the percentage increase in sales. If receivables are growing much faster than sales, collections may be too slow, and a cash shortage may result.
5. Can the company pay its a. current liabilities? b. current and long-term liabilities?	**5.** From the balance sheet, compare a. current assets to current liabilities. Current assets should be somewhat greater than current liabilities. b. total assets to total liabilities. Total assets must be somewhat greater than total liabilities.
6. Where is the company's cash coming from? How is cash being used?	**6.** On the cash flows statement, operating activities should provide the bulk of the company's cash during most years. Otherwise, the business will fail. Examine investing cash flows to see if the company is purchasing long-term assets—property, plant, and equipment and intangibles (this signals growth).

EVALUATE BUSINESS DECISIONS ETHICALLY

5 **Evaluate** business decisions ethically

Good business requires decision making, which in turn requires the exercise of good judgment, both at the individual and the corporate level. For example, you may work for or eventually run a company like Starbucks that has decided to plow back a portion of its profits to support social development projects in the communities that produce its coffee, tea, and cocoa. Can that be profitable in the long run?

Perhaps as an accountant, you may have to decide whether to report a $50,000 expenditure for a piece of equipment as an asset on the balance sheet or an expense on the income statement. Alternatively, as a sales manager for a company like **IBM**, you may have to decide whether

$25 million of goods and services shipped to customers in 2016 would be more appropriately recorded as revenue in 2016 or 2017. Depending on the type of business, the facts and circumstances surrounding accounting decisions may not always make them clear-cut, and yet the decision may determine whether the company shows a profit or a loss in a particular period! What are the factors that influence business and accounting decisions, and how should these factors be weighed? Generally, three types of factors influence business and accounting decisions: *economic, legal,* and *ethical*.

The *economic* factor states that the decision being made should *maximize the economic benefits* to the decision maker. Based on economic theory, every rational person faced with a decision will choose the course of action that maximizes his or her own welfare, without regard to how that decision impacts others. In summary, the combined outcome of each person acting in his or her own self-interest will maximize the benefits to society as a whole.

The *legal* factor is based on the proposition that free societies are governed by laws. Laws are written to provide clarity and to prevent abuse of the rights of individuals or society. Democratically enacted laws both contain and express society's moral standards. Legal analysis involves applying the relevant laws to each decision and then choosing the action that complies with those laws. A complicating factor for a global business may be that what is legal in one country might not be legal in another. In that case, it is usually best to abide by the laws of the most restrictive country.

The *ethical* factor recognizes that while certain actions might be both economically profitable and legal, they may still not be right. Therefore, most companies, and many individuals, have established standards for themselves to enforce a higher level of conduct than that imposed by law. These standards govern how we treat others and the way we restrain our selfish desires. This behavior and its underlying beliefs are the essence of ethics. **Ethics** are shaped by our cultural, socioeconomic, and religious backgrounds. An *ethical analysis* is needed to guide our judgments when making decisions.

The decision rule in an ethical analysis is to choose the action that fulfills ethical duties—responsibilities of the members of society to each other. The challenge in an ethical analysis is to identify specific ethical duties and stakeholders to whom you owe these duties. As with legal issues, a complicating factor in making global ethical decisions may be that what is considered ethical in one country is not considered ethical in another.

Among the questions you may ask in making an ethical analysis are the following:

- *Which options are most honest, open, and truthful?*
- *Which options are most kind and compassionate and will build a sense of community?*
- *Which options create the greatest good for the greatest number of stakeholders?*
- *Which options result in treating others as I would want to be treated?*

Ethical training starts at home and continues throughout our lives. It is reinforced by the teaching that we receive in our churches, synagogues, and mosques; by the schools we attend; and by the people and companies we associate with.

A thorough understanding of ethics requires more study than we can accomplish in this book. However, remember that when you are making accounting decisions, you should not check your ethics at the door!

In the business setting, ethics work best when modeled "from the top." The Ethisphere Institute (**http://www.ethisphere.com**) has established the Business Ethics Leadership Alliance (BELA), aimed at "reestablishing ethics as the foundation of everyday business practices." BELA members agree to embrace and uphold four core values that incorporate ethics and integrity into all their practices: (1) legal compliance, (2) transparency, (3) conflict identification, and (4) accountability.

Each year, the Ethisphere Institute publishes a list of the World's Most Ethical Companies. The 2016 list includes corporations like **Colgate-Palmolive Company**, **Cummins, Inc.**, **Deere & Company**, and **Levi Strauss & Co.** As you begin to make your decisions about future employers, put these companies on your list! It's easier to act ethically when you work for companies that recognize the importance of ethics in business practices. These companies have learned from experience that, in the long run, ethical conduct pays big rewards—not only socially, morally, and spiritually, but economically as well!

Decision Guidelines

DECISION FRAMEWORK FOR MAKING ETHICAL JUDGMENTS

Weighing tough ethical judgments in business and accounting requires a decision framework. Answering the following four questions will guide you through tough decisions:

Decision	Guidelines
1. What is the issue?	**1.** The issue will usually require making a judgment about an accounting measurement or disclosure that results in economic consequences, often to numerous parties.
2. Who are the stakeholders, and what are the consequences of the decision to each?	**2.** Stakeholders are anyone who might be impacted by the decision—you, your company, and potential users of the information (investors, creditors, and regulatory agencies) are all stakeholders. The consequences can be economic, legal, or ethical in nature.
3. Weigh the alternatives.	**3.** Analyze the impact of the decision on all stakeholders, using economic, legal, and ethical criteria. Ask "Who will be helped or hurt, whose rights will be exercised or denied, and in what way?"
4. Make the decision and be prepared to deal with the consequences.	**4.** Exercise the courage to either defend the decision or to change it, depending on its positive or negative impact. How does your decision make you feel afterward?

To simplify the analysis, ask yourself these three questions:

1. Is the action legal? If not, don't do it, unless you want to go to jail or pay monetary damages to injured parties. If the action is legal, go on to questions 2 and 3.
2. Who will be affected by the decision and how? Be as thorough about this analysis as possible, and analyze it from all three standpoints (economic, legal, and ethical).
3. How will this decision make me feel afterward? How would it make me feel if my family reads about it in the newspaper?

In later chapters throughout the book, we will apply this model to different accounting decisions.

American Institute of Certified Public Accountants Code of Professional Conduct

The decision framework for making ethical judgments provides general guidance for everyone, regardless of one's profession or industry. Many professional organizations, businesses, and other entities adopt their own ethical guidelines or codes of conduct so their members have more specific guidance.

The American Institute of Certified Public Accountants (AICPA) is one such organization. The AICPA has a code of professional conduct that applies to all of its members. Excerpts from the basic principles of the AICPA Code of Professional Conduct[2] are as follows:

- **Responsibilities principle.** In carrying out their responsibilities as professionals, members should exercise sensitive professional and moral judgments in all their activities.

As professionals, members perform an essential role in society. Consistent with that role, members of the American Institute of Certified Public Accountants have responsibilities to all those who use their professional services. Members also have a continuing responsibility to cooperate with each other to improve the art of accounting, maintain the public's confidence, and carry out the profession's special responsibilities for self-governance. The collective efforts of all members are required to maintain and enhance the traditions of the profession.

- **The public interest principle.** Members should accept the obligation to act in a way that will serve the public interest, honor the public trust, and demonstrate a commitment to professionalism.

  A distinguishing mark of a profession is acceptance of its responsibility to the public. The accounting profession's public consists of clients, credit grantors, governments, employers, investors, the business and financial community, and others who rely on the objectivity and integrity of members to maintain the orderly functioning of commerce. This reliance imposes a public interest responsibility on members. The public interest is defined as the collective well-being of the community of people and institutions that the profession serves.

  In discharging their professional responsibilities, members may encounter conflicting pressures from each of those groups. In resolving those conflicts, members should act with integrity, guided by the precept that when members fulfill their responsibility to the public, clients' and employers' interests are best served.

- **Integrity principle.** To maintain and broaden public confidence, members should perform all professional responsibilities with the highest sense of integrity.

  Integrity is an element of character fundamental to professional recognition. It is the quality from which the public trust derives and the benchmark against which a member must ultimately test all decisions. Integrity requires a member to be, among other things, honest and candid within the constraints of client confidentiality. Service and the public trust should not be subordinated to personal gain and advantage. Integrity can accommodate the inadvertent error and honest difference of opinion; it cannot accommodate deceit or subordination of principle.

  Integrity is measured in terms of what is right and just. In the absence of specific rules, standards, or guidance or in the face of conflicting opinions, a member should test decisions and deeds by asking: "Am I doing what a person of integrity would do? Have I retained my integrity?"

  Integrity requires a member to observe both the form and the spirit of technical and ethical standards; circumvention of those standards constitutes subordination of judgment.

- **Objectivity and independence principle.** A member should maintain objectivity and be free of conflicts of interest in discharging professional responsibilities. A member in public practice should be independent in fact and appearance when providing auditing and other attestation services.

  Objectivity is a state of mind, a quality that lends value to a member's services. It is a distinguishing feature of the profession. The principle of objectivity imposes the obligation to be impartial, intellectually honest, and free of conflicts of interest. Independence precludes relationships that may appear to impair a member's objectivity in rendering attestation services.

- **Due care principle.** A member should observe the profession's technical and ethical standards, strive continually to improve competence and the quality of services, and discharge professional responsibility to the best of the member's ability.

  The quest for excellence is the essence of due care. Due care requires a member to discharge professional responsibilities with competence and diligence. It imposes the obligation to perform professional services to the best of a member's ability, with concern for the best interest of those for whom the services are performed, and consistent with the profession's responsibility to the public.

  Competence is derived from a synthesis of education and experience. It begins with a mastery of the common body of knowledge required for designation as a certified public accountant. The maintenance of competence requires a commitment to learning and professional improvement that must continue throughout a member's professional life. It is a member's individual responsibility. In all engagements and in all responsibilities, each member should undertake to achieve a level of competence that will assure that the quality of the member's services meets the high level of professionalism required by these Principles.

Competence represents the attainment and maintenance of a level of understanding and knowledge that enables a member to render services with facility and acumen. It also establishes the limitations of a member's capabilities by dictating that consultation or referral may be required when a professional engagement exceeds the personal competence of a member or a member's firm. Each member is responsible for assessing his or her own competence of evaluating whether education, experience, and judgment are adequate for the responsibility to be assumed.

- **Scope and nature of services.** A member in public practice should observe the Principles of the Code of Professional Conduct in determining the scope and nature of services to be provided.

Even though you may not become an accounting major and may never be a member of the AICPA and covered by the AICPA Code of Professional Conduct, the basic principles contained in it can be applied to a wide range of professions and organizations. In addition, you may in your future career have interactions with CPAs. It is helpful to understand the code of conduct to which CPAs must adhere if they are members of the AICPA.

End-of-Chapter | Summary Problem

Alladin Travel, Inc., began operations on April 1, 2018. During April, the business provided services for customers. It is now April 30 and Starr Williams, majority shareholder and manager, is trying to determine how well Alladin Travel performed during its first month. Ms. Williams also wants to know the company's financial position at the end of April and its cash flows during the month.

The following data are listed in alphabetical order.

Accounts payable	$ 1,800	Land	$18,000
Accounts receivable	2,000	Payments of cash:	
Adjustments to reconcile net income to net cash provided by operating activities	(3,900)	Acquisition of land	40,000
		Dividends	2,100
Cash balance, April 1	0	Rent expense	1,100
Cash balance, April 30	?	Retained earnings, April 1	0
Cash receipts:		Retained earnings, April 30	?
Issuance (sale) of stock to owners	50,000	Salary expense	1,200
Sale of land	22,000	Service revenue	10,000
Common stock	50,000	Supplies	3,700
		Utilities expense	400

Requirements

1. Prepare the income statement, the statement of retained earnings, and the statement of cash flows for the month ended April 30, 2018, and the unclassified balance sheet at April 30, 2018. Draw arrows linking the statements.
2. Answer the following questions:

   a. How well did Alladin Travel perform during its first month of operations?
   b. Where does Alladin Travel stand financially at the end of April?

Answers

Requirement 1

Financial Statements of Alladin Travel, Inc.

A1

	A	B	C	D
1	**Alladin Travel, Inc. Income Statement Month Ended April 30, 2018**			
2	**Revenue:**			
3	Service revenue		$ 10,000	
4	**Expenses:**			
5	Salary expense	$ 1,200		
6	Rent expense	1,100		
7	Utilities expense	400		
8	Total expenses		2,700	
9	Net Income		$ 7,300	
10				

①

A1

	A	B	C	D
1	**Alladin Travel, Inc. Statement of Retained Earnings Month Ended April 30, 2018**			
2	Retained earnings, April 1, 2018		$ 0	
3	Net income for period		7,300	
4			$ 7,300	
5	Less dividends declared		(2,100)	
6	Retained earnings, April 30, 2018		$ 5,200	
7				

②

A1

	A	B	C	D
1	**Alladin Travel, Inc. Balance Sheet April 30, 2018**			
2	**Assets**		**Liabilities**	
3	Cash	$ 33,300	Accounts payable	$ 1,800
4	Accounts receivable	2,000	**Stockholders' equity**	
5	Supplies	3,700	Common Stock	50,000
6	Land	18,000	Retained earnings	5,200
7			Total stockholders' equity	55,200
8			Total liabilities and	
9	Total assets	$ 57,000	stockholders' equity	$ 57,000
10				

③

A1

	A	B	C
1	**Alladin Travel, Inc. Statement of Cash Flows Month Ended April 30, 2018**		
2	**Cash flows from operating activities:**		
3	Net income		$ 7,300
4	Adjustments to reconcile net income to net cash provided by operating activities		(3,900)
5	Net cash provided by operating activities		3,400
6	**Cash flows from investing activities:**		
7	Acquisition of land	$ (40,000)	
8	Sale of land	22,000	
9	Net cash used for investing activities		(18,000)
10	**Cash flows from financing activities:**		
11	Issuance (sale) of stock	$ 50,000	
12	Payment of dividends	(2,100)	
13	Net cash provided by financing activities		47,900
14	Net increase in cash		$ 33,300
15	Cash balance, April 1, 2018		0
16	Cash balance, April 30, 2018		$ 33,300
17			

Requirement 2

a. Alladin Travel performed rather well in April. Its service revenue was $10,000, and its net income was $7,300. The company was able to pay cash dividends of $2,100.

b. Alladin Travel ended April with cash of $33,300. Total assets of $57,000 far exceeded total liabilities of $1,800. The stockholders' equity of $55,200 provided a good cushion for borrowing. The business's financial position at April 30, 2018, was strong.

Try It in Excel®

If you've had a basic course in Excel, you can prepare financial statements easily using an Excel spreadsheet. In this chapter, you learned the accounting equation (see Exhibit 1-4 on page 10). In Exhibit 1-5 you learned the formulas for net income as well as how to compute the ending balance of retained earnings. Using the balance sheet for Alladin Travel, Inc., in the End-of-Chapter Summary Problem, it is easy to prepare an Excel template for a balance sheet by programming cells for total assets (cell B9) and total liabilities and stockholders' equity (cell D9). Then, as long as you know what accounts belong in each category, you can use the insert function to insert individual assets, liabilities, and stockholders' equity accounts from a list into various cells of the spreadsheet (don't forget to include both description and amounts). You can insert subtotals for current assets, non-current assets, current liabilities, non-current liabilities, and stockholders' equity. You can also build a basic Excel template for the income statement for Alladin Travel by listing and totaling revenues and listing and totaling expenses, then subtracting total expenses from total revenues to compute net income (cell C9). You can build an Excel template for the statement of retained earnings by programming a cell for the ending balance of retained earnings (beginning balance + net income (loss) − dividends) (cell C6). Then merely insert the individual amounts, and bingo, your spreadsheet does all the math for you.

Don't forget the proper order of financial statement preparation: (1) income statement, (2) statement of retained earnings, (3) balance sheet, and (4) statement of cash flows. If you have to prepare all four statements, it's best to follow that order so that you can link the income statement cell containing net income to the corresponding cell in the statement of retained earnings; link the value of the ending balance of retained earnings to the cell containing the retained earnings amount in the balance sheet; and link the ending balance of cash on the statement of cash flows to the balance of cash on the balance sheet as of the year-end. These links correspond to the amounts connected by arrows (1, 2, and 3) on page 28.

The beauty of this approach is that once you build a set of basic templates, you can save and use them over and over again as you progress through the course.

REVIEW | The Financial Statements

Accounting Vocabulary

accounting (p. 3) The information system that measures business activities, processes that turn data into reports and financial statements, and communicates results to decision makers.

accounting cycle (p. 3) The process by which financial statements are prepared.

accounting equation (p. 10) The most basic tool of accounting: Assets = Liabilities + Equity.

amortization (p. 15) Allocating the cost of an intangible asset to expense it over its useful life.

asset (p. 9) An economic resource that is expected to be of benefit in the future.

balance sheet (p. 16) A list of an entity's assets, liabilities, and equity as of a specific date. Also called the *statement of financial position*.

board of directors (p. 16) A group elected by a company's stockholders to set the policy of the corporation and to appoint its officers.

capital (p. 9) Another name for the *equity* of a business.

common stock (p. 11) The most basic form of capital stock.

continuity assumption (p. 7) See the going-concern assumption.

corporation (p. 5) A business owned by stockholders. A corporation is a legal entity, an "artificial person" in the eyes of the law.

current asset (p. 16) An asset that is expected to be converted to cash, sold, or consumed during the next 12 months, or within the business's normal operating cycle if it's longer than a year.

current liability (p. 18) A debt due to be paid within one year or within the entity's operating cycle if the cycle is longer than a year.

deficit (p. 16) A negative balance in retained earnings caused by net losses over a period of years.

depreciation (p. 15) The allocation of the cost of a plant asset to expense it over its useful life.

dividends (p. 11) Distributions (usually cash) by a corporation to its stockholders.

entity (p. 7) An organization or a section of an organization that, for accounting purposes, stands apart from other organizations and individuals as a separate economic unit.

equity (p. 9) The claim of the owners of a business to the assets of the business. Also called *capital, owners' equity, stockholders' equity,* or *net assets*.

equity method (p. 18) Method of accounting used to account for investments that are at least 20% but not more than 50% owned.

ethics (p. 24) Standards of right and wrong that transcend economic and legal boundaries. Ethical standards deal with the way we treat others and restrain our own actions because of the desires, expectations, or rights of others, or because of our obligations to them.

expenses (p. 11) Decreases in retained earnings that result from operations; the cost of doing business; the opposite of revenues.

fair value (p. 8) The amount that a business could sell an asset for, or the amount that a business could pay to settle a liability.

financial accounting (p. 4) The branch of accounting that provides relevant and accurate information to people outside the firm.

Financial Accounting Standards Board (FASB) (p. 5) The regulatory body in the United States that formulates generally accepted accounting principles (GAAP).

financial statements (p. 1) Business documents that report financial information about a business entity to decision makers.

financing activities (p. 20) Activities that obtain from investors and creditors the cash needed to launch and sustain the business; a section of the statement of cash flows.

generally accepted accounting principles (GAAP) (p. 5) Accounting guidelines formulated by the Financial Accounting Standards Board that govern how accounting is practiced.

going-concern assumption (p. 7) The assumption that an entity will remain in operation for the foreseeable future.

gross profit (p. 14) Revenue from a particular activity minus the direct costs associated with earning that revenue.

historical cost principle (p. 7) A principle that states that assets should be recorded at their actual cost.

income statement (p. 13) A financial statement listing an entity's revenues, expenses, and net income or net loss for a specific period. Also called the *statement of operations*.

intangible assets (p. 18) Assets with no tangible form that represent resources that have a value and future benefit.

International Financial Reporting Standards (IFRS) (p. 5) Accounting guidelines, formulated by the **International Accounting Standards Board** (IASB).

investing activities (p. 20) Activities that increase or decrease the long-term assets available to the business; a section of the statement of cash flows.

liability (p. 9) An economic obligation (a debt) payable to an individual or an organization outside the business.

limited-liability company (p. 5) A business organization in which the business (not the owner) is liable for the company's debts.

long-term assets (p. 18) Assets that are expected to benefit the entity for long periods of time, beyond the end of the next fiscal year. These usually include investments, property and equipment (plant assets), and intangible assets.

long-term debt (p. 10) A liability that falls due beyond one year from the date of the financial statements.

managerial accounting (p. 4) The branch of accounting that generates information for the internal decision makers of a business, such as top executives.

net earnings (p. 11) Another name for *net income*.

net income (p. 11) The excess of total revenues over total expenses. Also called *net earnings* or *net profit*.

net loss (p. 11) The excess of total expenses over total revenues.

net profit (p. 11) Another name for *net income*.

operating activities (p. 20) Activities that create revenue or expenses in the statement of cash flows. Operating activities affect the income statement.

owners' equity (p. 9) See equity and stockholders' equity.

paid-in capital (p. 11) The amount of stockholders' equity that stockholders have contributed to the corporation. Also called *contributed capital*.

partnership (p. 4) An association of two or more persons who co-own a business for profit.

proprietorship (p. 4) A business with a single owner.

retained earnings (p. 11) The amount of stockholders' equity a corporation has earned through profitable operations and has not given back to stockholders.

revenues (p. 11) Increases in retained earnings from delivering goods or services to customers or clients.

segment (p. 7) A division or subset of a business's operations.

shareholder (p. 5) Another name for a *stockholder*.

stable-monetary-unit assumption (p. 8) The assumption that because the purchasing power of the dollar has been relatively stable, inflation's effect on accounting records can be ignored.

statement of cash flows (p. 20) A statement that reports cash receipts and cash payments classified according to the entity's major activities: operating, investing, and financing.

statement of financial position (p. 16) Another name for the *balance sheet*.

statement of operations (p. 13) Another name for the *income statement*.

statement of retained earnings (p. 16) A summary of the changes in the retained earnings of a corporation during a specific period.

stock (p. 5) Shares into which the owners' equity of a corporation is divided.

stockholder (p. 5) A person who owns stock in a corporation. Also called a *shareholder*.

stockholders' equity (p. 9) The stockholders' ownership interest in the assets of a corporation.

Quick Check (Answers are given on page 59.)

1. Financial statements can be used by which of the following groups?

a. Individuals
b. Investors and creditors
c. Regulatory bodies
d. All of the above

2. Nicholas is a software engineer and is starting a consulting practice. What form of business organization limits his liability to the amount he has invested in the business?

a. Proprietorship
b. Partnership
c. Corporation
d. None of the above

3. Hoot Enterprises buys a warehouse for $590,000 to use for its East Coast distribution operations. On the date of the purchase, a professional appraisal shows a value of $650,000 for the warehouse. The seller had originally purchased the building for $480,000. Hoot has a similar warehouse on the West Coast that has a book value of $603,000. Under the historical cost principle, Hoot should record the building for

a. $650,000.
b. $480,000.
c. $590,000.
d. $603,000.

4. To be useful, information must have which of the following fundamental qualitative characteristics?

a. Relevance and faithful representation
b. Timeliness and affordability
c. Expediency and relevance
d. Faithful representation and diversity

5. Which of the following is a true statement about International Financial Reporting Standards?

a. They are considered to be the single strongest set of accounting standards in the world.
b. They are more exact (contain more rules) than U.S. generally accepted accounting principles.
c. They are converging gradually with U.S. standards.
d. They are not being applied anywhere in the world yet, but soon they will be.

6. The accounting equation can be expressed as

a. Assets = Liabilities – Equity.
b. Assets + Liabilities = Equity.
c. Assets – Liabilities = Equity.
d. Equity – Assets = Liabilities.

7. The costs of doing business are classified as:

a. assets.
b. liabilities.
c. revenues.
d. expenses.

8. Alliance Corporation holds cash of $8,000 and owes $27,000 on accounts payable. Alliance has accounts receivable of $47,000, inventory of $20,000, and land that cost $60,000. How much are Alliance's total assets and liabilities?

	Total Assets	*Liabilities*
a.	$75,000	$87,000
b.	$135,000	$27,000
c.	$135,000	$47,000
d.	$115,000	$47,000

9. During the year, ChemClean Corporation has $280,000 in revenues, $130,000 in expenses, and $10,000 in dividend declarations and payments. Net income for the year was:

a. $140,000.
b. $150,000.
c. $160,000.
d. $280,000.

10. How would the issuance of common stock for cash affect the accounting equation?

a. Increase assets and increase stockholders' equity
b. Increase liabilities and decrease stockholders' equity
c. Increase assets and increase liabilities
d. Decrease assets and decrease liabilities

11. Dynasty Company has current assets of $50,000 and long-term assets of $45,000. Its total liabilities equal $35,000. Stockholders' equity is:

a. $95,000.
b. $60,000.
c. $130,000.
d. $80,000.

12. Which financial statement would show how well a company performed over the past year?

a. Balance sheet
b. Income statement
c. Statement of cash flows
d. Statement of retained earnings

13. On which financial statement would the ending balance of the account "accounts receivable" be found?

a. Income statement
b. Statement of retained earnings
c. Balance sheet
d. Statement of cash flows

14. What item flows from the income statement to the statement of retained earnings?
- **a.** Cash
- **b.** Dividends
- **c.** Net income
- **d.** Inventory

15. What item flows from the statement of retained earnings to the balance sheet?
- **a.** Cash
- **b.** Dividends
- **c.** Net income
- **d.** Retained earnings

16. Which of the following is the most accurate statement regarding ethics as applied to decision making in accounting?
- **a.** Ethics involves making difficult choices under pressure and should be kept in mind in making every decision, including those involving accounting.
- **b.** Ethics has no place in accounting because accounting deals purely with numbers.
- **c.** It is impossible to learn ethical decision making because it is just something you decide to do or not to do.
- **d.** Ethics is becoming less and less important as a field of study in business.

Some of the following exercises and problems are available as Excel questions in **MyLab Accounting**.

ASSESS YOUR PROGRESS

Ethics Check

EC1-1. ***(Learning Objective 5: Identify ethical principle violated)*** LO 5

For each of the situations listed, identify which of three principles (integrity, objectivity and independence, or due care) from the AICPA Code of Professional Conduct is violated. Assume all persons listed in the situations are members of the AICPA. (Note: Refer to the AICPA Code of Professional Conduct contained on pages 25–27 for descriptions of the principles.)

- **a.** Erica is eager to please her supervisor and wants to earn a promotion at the CPA firm. When Erica puts together her firm's financial statements and related information for the past year, she buries unfavorable results deep in the report and presents the good news prominently. She figures that by making the firm look good, it will make her case for promotion stronger.
- **b.** Evan is in charge of putting together his company's financial statements, but does not understand the newest financial reporting standard that went into effect last year. He decides to do the best he can with interpreting and applying the new standard because he does not have time right now to learn about the new standard in depth.
- **c.** Jay receives a large year-end bonus if his company's sales grow by 8% this year. Sales only grew by 7.5% so Jay created false sales documentation to make it appear that the sales growth goal was met.
- **d.** This year Gabby's company incurred higher cost of goods sold than expected, which resulted in an overall net loss for the company. Gabby does not want the company to lose investors due to the net loss, so she adjusts cost of goods sold so that the company has a positive net income.

Short Exercises

LO 1 **S1-1.** ***(Learning Objective 1: Explain and differentiate between business organizations)*** Hudson Signs, Inc., needs funds, and Alley Hudson, the president, has asked you to consider investing in the business. Answer the following questions about the different ways that Hudson might organize the business. Explain each answer.

a. What forms of organization will enable the owners of Hudson Signs, Inc., to limit their risk of loss to the amounts they have invested in the business?

b. What form of business organization will give Alley Hudson the most freedom to manage the business as she wishes?

c. What form of organization will give creditors the maximum protection in the event that Hudson Signs, Inc., fails and cannot pay its debts?

LO 2 **S1-2.** ***(Learning Objective 2: Identify relevant accounting assumptions)*** Fallon Osmond is chairperson of the board of Simple Treats, Inc. Suppose Osmond has just founded Simple Treats, and assume that she considers her home and other personal assets as part of Simple Treats. Answer these questions about the evaluation of Simple Treats, Inc.

1. Which accounting assumption governs this situation?
2. How can the proper application of this accounting assumption give Osmond and others a realistic view of Simple Treats, Inc.? Explain in detail.

LO 2 **S1-3.** ***(Learning Objective 2: Identify underlying accounting concepts, assumptions, and principles)*** Identify the accounting concept, assumption, or principle that best applies to each of the following situations:

a. Inflation has been about 2.5% for some time. Village Realtors is considering measuring its land values in inflation-adjusted amounts.

b. You get an especially good buy on a laptop, paying only \$300 when it normally costs \$800. What is your accounting value for this laptop?

c. **Burger King**, the restaurant chain, sold a store location to **McDonald's**. How can Burger King determine the sale price of the store—by a professional appraisal, Burger King's original cost, or the amount actually received from the sale?

d. **General Motors** wants to determine which division of the company—Chevrolet or Cadillac—is more profitable.

LO 3 **S1-4.** ***(Learning Objective 3: Apply the accounting equation)*** Identify the missing amount for each of the following situations:

	Total Assets	=	Total Liabilities	+	Stockholders' Equity
a.	\$?		\$300,000		\$360,000
b.	85,000		50,000		?
c.	350,000		?		275,000

LO 3 **S1-5.** ***(Learning Objective 3: Apply the accounting equation)***

1. If you know the assets and the equity of a business, how can you measure its liabilities? Give the equation.
2. Use the accounting equation to show how to determine the amount of a company's stockholders' equity. How would your answer change if you were analyzing your own household?

LO 3 **S1-6.** ***(Learning Objective 3: Identify assets, liabilities, and stockholders' equity accounts)*** Classify the following items as an asset (A), a liability (L), or stockholders' equity (S) for **Target Corporation**, a large retailer:

a. _____ Land
b. _____ Accrued expenses payable
c. _____ Supplies
d. _____ Equipment
e. _____ Notes payable
f. _____ Long-term debt
g. _____ Retained earnings
h. _____ Prepaid expenses
i. _____ Accounts payable
j. _____ Accounts receivable
k. _____ Merchandise inventory
l. _____ Common stock

S1-7. ***(Learning Objective 3: Accounting equation)*** Accounting definitions are precise, and you must understand the vocabulary to properly use accounting. Sharpen your understanding of key terms by answering the following questions: LO 3

1. How do the assets and stockholders' equity of **Nike, Inc.**, differ from each other? Which one (assets or stockholders' equity) must be at least as large as the other? Which one can be smaller than the other?
2. How are Nike, Inc.'s, liabilities and stockholders' equity similar? Different?

S1-8. ***(Learning Objective 4: Identify income statement components)*** LO 4

1. Identify the two basic categories of items on an income statement.
2. What do we call the bottom line of the income statement?

S1-9. ***(Learning Objective 4: Identify appropriate financial statement)*** Suppose you are analyzing the financial statements of Corley, Inc. Identify each item with its appropriate financial statement, using the following abbreviations: Income statement (I), Statement of retained earnings (R), Balance sheet (B), and Statement of cash flows (C). Three items appear on two financial statements, and one item shows up on three statements. LO 4

a.	_____ Salary expense	**i.**	_____ Retained earnings
b.	_____ Dividends	**j.**	_____ Long-term debt
c.	_____ Accounts payable	**k.**	_____ Increase or decrease in cash
d.	_____ Net income	**l.**	_____ Net cash provided by operating activities
e.	_____ Common stock		
f.	_____ Inventory	**m.**	_____ Sales revenue
g.	_____ Interest revenue	**n.**	_____ Net cash used for financing activities
h.	_____ Cash		

S1-10. ***(Learning Objective 4: Explain aspects of financial statements)*** Apply your understanding of the relationships among the financial statements to answer these questions. LO 4

a. How can a business earn large profits but have a small balance of retained earnings?
b. Give two reasons why a business can have a steady stream of net income over a five-year period and still experience a cash shortage.
c. If you could pick a single source of cash for your business, what would it be? Why?
d. How can a business be unprofitable several years in a row and still have plenty of cash?

S1-11. ***(Learning Objective 4: Identify appropriate financial statement use)*** For each of the following questions, indicate which financial statement would most likely be used to provide the information. Use the following abbreviations: Income statement (I), Statement of retained earnings (R), Balance sheet (B), and Statement of cash flows (C). LO 4

a. What were the company's net sales for the year?
b. What assets does the company have?
c. How much cash was generated by operating activities?
d. Why did the company's retained earnings change during the year?
e. How much in total debt does the company have?
f. How well did the company perform during the year?
g. Did the company declare a dividend during the year?
h. How much cash did the company generate and spend during the year?
i. What is the company's financial position at the end of the year?

S1-12. ***(Learning Objective 4: Construct an income statement)*** MacKensie Services Corporation began 2018 with total assets of $230 million and ended 2018 with total assets of $365 million. During 2018, MacKensie earned revenues of $394 million and had expenses of $171 million. MacKensie declared and paid dividends of $27 million in 2018. Prepare the company's income statement for the year ended December 31, 2018, complete with an appropriate heading. LO 4

LO 4 **S1-13.** ***(Learning Objective 4: Construct a statement of retained earnings)*** Journey Corporation began 2018 with retained earnings of $270 million. Revenues during the year were $460 million, and expenses totaled $380 million. Journey declared dividends of $64 million. What was the company's ending balance of retained earnings? To answer this question, prepare Journey's statement of retained earnings for the year ended December 31, 2018, complete with its proper heading.

LO 4 **S1-14.** ***(Learning Objective 4: Construct a balance sheet)*** At December 31, 2018, Jackson Corporation has cash of $52 million, accounts receivable of $23 million, and long-term assets of $45 million. The company owes accounts payable of $21 million and has a long-term note payable of $31 million. Jackson has common stock of $28 million and retained earnings of $40 million. Prepare Jackson Corporation's balance sheet at December 31, 2018, complete with its proper heading.

LO 4 **S1-15.** ***(Learning Objective 4: Solve for retained earnings and construct a balance sheet)*** Sullivan Corporation ended its fiscal year on September 30, 2018, with cash of $78 million, accounts receivable of $27 million, property and equipment of $27 million, and other long-term assets of $21 million. The company's liabilities consist of accounts payable of $34 million and long-term notes payable of $17 million. Sullivan Corporation has total stockholders' equity of $102 million; of this total, common stock is $31 million. Solve for the company's ending retained earnings and then prepare Sullivan Corporation's balance sheet at September 30, 2018. Use a proper heading on the balance sheet.

LO 4 **S1-16.** ***(Learning Objective 4: Construct a statement of cash flows)*** Python Legal Services, Inc., ended 2017 with cash of $16,000. During 2018, Python earned net income of $115,000 and had adjustments to reconcile net income to net cash provided by operations totaling $9,000 (this is a negative amount). Python paid $20,000 to purchase equipment during 2018. During 2018, the company declared and paid dividends of $15,000. Prepare Python's statement of cash flows for the year ended December 31, 2018, complete with its proper heading.

LO 4 **S1-17.** ***(Learning Objective 4: Construct an income statement, statement of retained earnings, and balance sheet)*** Following are partially completed financial statements (income statement, statement of retained earnings, and balance sheet) for Shaker Corporation. Complete the financial statements. All amounts are in millions.

A1

	A	B	C	D	E
1	**Shaker Corporation** **Income Statement** **for Year Ended December 31, 2018**				
2	Net sales	$ 183			
3	Expenses	101			
4	Net income	$ a			
5					

A1

	A	B	C	D	E
1	**Shaker Corporation** **Statement of Retained Earnings** **for Year Ended December 31, 2018**				
2	Beginning retained earnings	$ 74			
3	Net income	b			
4	Cash dividends declared	(7)			
5	Ending retained earnings	$ c			
6					

	A	B	C	D	E
1	**Shaker Corporation** **Balance Sheet** **December 31, 2018**				
2	Assets				
3	Cash	$ 118			
4	All other assets	d			
5	Total assets	$ e			
6	Liabilities				
7	Total liabilities	$ 48			
8	Stockholders' equity				
9	Common stock	33			
10	Retained earnings	f			
11	Total stockholders' equity	g			
12	Total liabilities and stockholders' equity	$ h			
13					

S1-18. ***(Learning Objective 5: Evaluate business decisions ethically)*** Good business and accounting practices require the exercise of good judgment. How should ethics be incorporated into making accounting judgments? Why is ethics important? LO 5

S1-19. ***(Learning Objectives 1, 2, 3, 4, 5: Match vocabulary terms with definitions)*** LO 1, 2, 3, 4, 5

Match the following definitions with one of the terms listed here.

Asset	Expenses	Managerial accounting
Balance sheet	Financial accounting	Net income
Bookkeeping	Historical cost principle	Partnership
Corporation	Income statement	Proprietorship
Equity	Investors and creditors	Revenues
Ethical duties	Liability	Statement of cash flows

Item	Definition
a.	Total revenues less total expenses
b.	Provides information for decision makers outside of the organization
c.	Provides information for managers of the organization
d.	Responsibilities of the members of society to each other
e.	Inflows of resources resulting from delivering goods or services to customers
f.	Owned by stockholders whose liability is limited to the amount they have invested in the business
g.	A debt payable to an outsider
h.	Costs of doing business
i.	A business organization form with a single owner who is personally liable for all of the business's debts
j.	States that assets should be recorded at their actual cost on the date of purchase
k.	Mechanical part of accounting
l.	Also called the statement of financial position
m.	Economic resources that are expected to produce benefits in the future
n.	Entities that provide money to finance a company's operations
o.	Answers the question "How well did the company perform during the period?"
p.	Reports cash flows from operating, investing, and financing activities
q.	A business organization form with two or more owners who are each personally liable for all of the business's debts
r.	Insider claims of a business

Exercises MyLab Accounting

Group A

LO 3, 4

E1-20A. ***(Learning Objectives 3, 4: Apply the accounting equation; evaluate business operations)*** Compute the missing amount in the accounting equation for each company (amounts in billions):

	Assets	Liabilities	Stockholders' Equity
Smythe Real Estate	$?	$41	$32
Odessa Florals	26	?	15
Hometown Bank	29	14	?

Which company appears to have the strongest financial position? Explain your reasoning.

LO 3, 4

E1-21A. ***(Learning Objectives 3, 4: Apply the accounting equation; evaluate business operations)*** Willow, Inc., has current assets of $220 million; property, plant, and equipment of $320 million; and other assets totaling $130 million. Current liabilities are $160 million and long-term liabilities total $380 million.

Requirements

1. Use these data to write Willow's accounting equation.
2. How much in resources does Willow have to work with?
3. How much does Willow owe creditors?
4. How much of the company's assets do the Willow stockholders actually own?

LO 3, 4

E1-22A. ***(Learning Objectives 3, 4: Apply the accounting equation; evaluate business operations)*** Collinswood Company's comparative balance sheet at January 31, 2019, and 2018, reports the following (in millions):

	2019	2018
Total assets	$77	$47
Total liabilities	25	19

Requirements

The following are three situations related to Collinswood Company's issuance of stock and declaration and payment of dividends during the year ended January 31, 2019. For each situation, use the accounting equation and what you know from the chapter about stockholders' equity, common stock, and retained earnings to calculate the amount of Collinswood's net income or net loss during the year ended January 31, 2019.

1. Collinswood issued $11 million of stock and declared no dividends.
2. Collinswood issued no stock but declared dividends of $20 million.
3. Collinswood issued $15 million of stock and declared dividends of $75 million.

E1-23A. ***(Learning Objective 4: Identify financial statement by type of information)*** Butler Tech, Inc., is expanding into India. The company must decide where to locate and how to finance the expansion. Identify the financial statement where these decision makers can find the following information about Butler Tech, Inc. In some cases, more than one statement will report the needed data. LO 4

- **a.** Revenue
- **b.** Common stock
- **c.** Current liabilities
- **d.** Long-term debt
- **e.** Dividends
- **f.** Ending cash balance
- **g.** Adjustments to reconcile net income to net cash provided by operations
- **h.** Cash spent to acquire the building
- **i.** Income tax expense
- **j.** Ending balance of retained earnings
- **k.** Selling, general, and administrative expense
- **l.** Total assets
- **m.** Net income
- **n.** Income tax payable

E1-24A. ***(Learning Objective 4: Construct a balance sheet)*** At December 31, 2018, Landy Products has cash of $24,000, receivables of $18,000, and inventory of $80,000. The company's equipment totals $182,000. Landy owes accounts payable of $22,000 and long-term notes payable of $172,000. Common stock is $34,500. Prepare Landy's balance sheet at December 31, 2018, complete with its proper heading. Use the accounting equation to compute retained earnings. LO 4

E1-25A. ***(Learning Objectives 3, 4: Apply the accounting equation; construct a balance sheet)*** The following are the assets and liabilities of Jill Carlson Realty Company, as of January 31, 2018. Also included are revenue, expense, and selected stockholders' equity figures for the year ended on that date (amounts in millions): LO 3, 4

Total revenue	$ 25.7	Investment assets (long-term)	$ 79.4
Receivables	0.5	Property and equipment, net	1.6
Current liabilities	2.9	Other expenses	7.6
Common stock	39.2	Retained earnings, beginning	2.6
Interest expense	1.5	Retained earnings, ending	?
Salary and other employee expenses	13.7	Cash	57.2
Long-term liabilities	102.6	Other assets (long-term)	9.3

Requirement

1. Construct the balance sheet of Jill Carlson Realty Company at January 31, 2018. Use the accounting equation to compute ending retained earnings.

E1-26A. ***(Learning Objective 4: Construct an income statement and a statement of retained earnings)*** This exercise should be used with Exercise 1-25A. LO 4

Requirements

1. Prepare the income statement of Jill Carlson Realty Company for the year ended January 31, 2018.
2. What amount of dividends did Jill Carlson declare during the year ended January 31, 2018? (*Hint*: Prepare a statement of retained earnings.)

LO 4 **E1-27A.** ***(Learning Objective 4: Construct an income statement and a statement of retained earnings)*** Assume the Giada Coffee Roasters Corp. ended the month of August 2019 with these data:

Payments of cash:		Cash balance, August 1, 2019	$ 0
Acquisition of equipment	$201,500	Cash balance, August 31, 2019	5,300
Dividends	2,800	Cash receipts:	
Retained earnings August 1, 2019	0	Issuance (sale) of stock to owners	14,900
Retained earnings August 31, 2019	?	Rent expense	1,800
Utilities expense	5,100	Common stock	14,900
Adjustments to reconcile net income to net cash provided by operations	1,400	Equipment	201,500
		Office supplies	7,400
		Accounts payable	8,800
Salary expense	78,500	Service revenue	278,700

Requirement

1. Prepare the income statement and the statement of retained earnings for Giada Coffee Roasters Corp., for the month ended August 31, 2019.

LO 4 **E1-28A.** ***(Learning Objective 4: Construct a balance sheet)*** Refer to the data in Exercise 1-27A.

Requirement

1. Prepare the balance sheet of Giada Coffee Roasters Corp., for August 31, 2019.

LO 4 **E1-29A.** ***(Learning Objective 4: Construct a statement of cash flows)*** Refer to the data in Exercises 1-27A and 1-28A.

Requirement

1. Prepare the statement of cash flows of Giada Coffee Roasters Corp., for the month ended August 31, 2019. Using Exhibit 1-11 as a model, show with arrows the relationships among the income statement, statement of retained earnings, balance sheet, and statement of cash flows.

LO 4 **E1-30A.** ***(Learning Objective 4: Evaluate business operations through the financial statements)*** This exercise should be used in conjunction with Exercises 1-27A through 1-29A.

The owner of Giada Coffee Roasters Corp. seeks your advice as to whether he should cease operations or continue the business. Complete the report, giving him your opinion of net income, dividends, financial position, and cash flows during his first month of operations. Cite specifics from the financial statements to support your opinion. Conclude your memo with advice on whether to stay in business or cease operations.

LO 4 **E1-31A.** ***(Learning Objective 4: Construct an income statement, statement of retained earnings, and balance sheet)*** During 2018, Edwin Company earned revenues of $150 million. Edwin incurred, during that same year, salary expense of $34 million, rent expense of $23 million, and utilities expense of $16 million. Edwin declared and paid dividends of $16 million during the year. At December 31, 2018, Edwin had cash of $185 million, accounts receivable of $70 million, property and equipment of $35 million, and other long-term assets of $22 million. At December 31, 2018, the company owed accounts payable of $56 million and had a long-term note payable of $26 million. Edwin began 2018 with a balance in retained earnings of $73 million. At December 31, 2018, Edwin had total stockholders' equity of $230 million, which consisted of common stock and retained earnings. Edwin has a year-end of December 31. Prepare the following financial statements (with proper headings) for 2018:

1. Income statement,
2. Statement of retained earnings,
3. Balance sheet.

Group B

E1-32B. ***(Learning Objectives 3, 4: Apply the accounting equation; evaluate business operations)*** Compute the missing amount in the accounting equation for each company (amounts in billions): LO 3, 4

	Assets	Liabilities	Stockholders' Equity
Water Street Bank	$?	$43	$35
Pufferbelly Restaurant	30	?	23
Blake Gift Shop	34	7	?

Which company appears to have the strongest financial position? Explain your reasoning.

E1-33B. ***(Learning Objectives 3, 4: Apply the accounting equation; evaluate business operations)*** Brandeberry, Inc., has current assets of $240 million; property, plant, and equipment of $390 million; and other assets totaling $130 million. Current liabilities are $100 million, and long-term liabilities total $360 million. LO 3, 4

Requirements

1. Use these data to write Brandeberry's accounting equation.
2. How much in resources does Brandeberry have to work with?
3. How much does Brandeberry owe creditors?
4. How much of the company's assets do the Brandeberry stockholders actually own?

E1-34B. ***(Learning Objectives 3, 4: Apply the accounting equation; evaluate business operations)*** Pillser, Inc.'s, comparative balance sheet at January 31, 2019, and 2018, reports the following (in millions): LO 3, 4

	2019	2018
Total assets	$72	$49
Total liabilities	23	17

Requirements

The following are three situations related to Pillser's issuance of stock and declaration and payment of dividends during the year ended January 31, 2019. For each situation, use the accounting equation and what you know from the chapter about stockholders' equity, common stock, and retained earnings to calculate the amount of Pillser's net income or net loss during the year ended January 31, 2019.

1. Pillser issued $3 million of stock and declared no dividends.
2. Pillser issued no stock but declared dividends of $4 million.
3. Pillser issued $20 million of stock and declared dividends of $8 million.

E1-35B. ***(Learning Objective 4: Identify financial statement by type of information)*** Flurry, Inc., is expanding into China. The company must decide where to locate and how to finance the expansion. Identify the financial statement where these decision makers can find the following information about Flurry, Inc. In some cases, more than one statement will report the needed data. LO 4

a. Ending cash balance
b. Adjustments to reconcile net income to net cash provided by operations
c. Common stock
d. Total assets
e. Net income
f. Revenue
g. Income tax payable
h. Income tax expense
i. Current liabilities
j. Cash spent to acquire the building
k. Selling, general, and administrative expenses
l. Long-term debt
m. Dividends
n. Ending balance of retained earnings

LO 4

E1-36B. ***(Learning Objective 4: Construct a balance sheet)*** At December 31, 2018, Patterson Products has cash of $20,000, receivables of $17,600, and inventory of $78,000. The company's equipment totals $186,000. Patterson owes accounts payable of $22,000 and long-term notes payable of $173,000. Common stock is $28,500. Prepare Patterson's balance sheet at December 31, 2018, complete with its proper heading. Use the accounting equation to compute retained earnings.

LO 3, 4

E1-37B. ***(Learning Objectives 3, 4: Apply the accounting equation; construct a balance sheet)*** The following are the assets and liabilities of Mary Burke Realty Company, as of March 31, 2018. Also included are revenue, expense, and selected stockholders' equity figures for the year ended on that date (amounts in millions):

Total revenue	$ 40.4	Investment assets (long-term)	$135.1
Receivables	0.1	Property and equipment, net	1.4
Current liabilities	2.7	Other expenses	6.6
Common stock	27.9	Retained earnings, beginning	17.2
Interest expense	0.4	Retained earnings, ending	?
Salary and other employee expenses	15.2	Cash	1.6
Long-term liabilities	102.3	Other assets (long-term)	10.3

Requirement

1. Construct the balance sheet of Mary Burke Realty Company at March 31, 2018. Use the accounting equation to compute ending retained earnings.

LO 4

E1-38B. ***(Learning Objective 4: Construct an income statement and a statement of retained earnings)*** This exercise should be used with Exercise 1-37B.

Requirements

1. Prepare the income statement of Mary Burke Realty Company for the year ended March 31, 2018.
2. What amount of dividends did Mary Burke Realty Company declare during the year ended March 31, 2018? (*Hint*: Prepare a statement of retained earnings.)

LO 4

E1-39B. ***(Learning Objective 4: Construct an income statement and a statement of retained earnings)*** Assume Island Coffee Roasters Corporation ended the month of August 2019 with these data:

Payments of cash:		Cash balance, August 1, 2019	$ 0
Acquisition of equipment	$200,000	Cash balance, August 31, 2019	6,000
Dividends	2,700	Cash receipts:	
Retained earnings August 1, 2019	0	Issuance (sale) of stock to owners	13,700
Retained earnings August 31, 2019	?	Rent expense	1,800
Utilities expense	5,800	Common stock	13,700
Adjustments to reconcile net income to net cash provided by operations	1,400	Equipment	200,000
Salary expense	78,100	Office supplies	7,500
		Accounts payable	8,900
		Service revenue	279,300

Requirement

1. Prepare the income statement and the statement of retained earnings for Island Coffee Roasters Corporation for the month ended August 31, 2019.

E1-40B. ***(Learning Objective 4: Construct a balance sheet)*** Refer to the data in Exercise 1-39B. LO 4

Requirement

1. Prepare the balance sheet of Island Coffee Roasters Corporation at August 31, 2019.

E1-41B. ***(Learning Objective 4: Construct a statement of cash flows)*** Refer to the data in Exercises 1-39B and 1-40B. LO 4

Requirement

1. Prepare the statement of cash flows of Island Coffee Roasters Corporation for the month ended August 31, 2019. Using Exhibit 1-11 as a model, show with arrows the relationships among the income statement, statement of retained earnings, balance sheet, and statement of cash flows.

E1-42B. ***(Learning Objective 4: Evaluate business operations through the financial statements)*** This exercise should be used in conjunction with Exercises 1-39B through 1-41B. LO 4

The owner of Island Coffee Roasters Corporation now seeks your advice as to whether she should cease operations or continue the business. Complete the report giving her your opinion of net income, dividends, financial position, and cash flows during her first month of operations. Cite specifics from the financial statements to support your opinion. Conclude your memo with advice on whether to stay in business or cease operations.

E1-43B. ***(Learning Objective 4: Construct an income statement, statement of retained earnings, and balance sheet)*** During 2018, Brewster Company earned revenues of $146 million. Brewster incurred, during that same year, salary expense of $28 million, rent expense of $23 million, and utilities expense of $19 million. Brewster declared and paid dividends of $15 million during the year. At December 31, 2018, Brewster had cash of $175 million, accounts receivable of $85 million, property and equipment of $39 million, and other long-term assets of $25 million. At December 31, 2018, the company owed accounts payable of $56 million and had a long-term note payable of $33 million. Brewster began 2018 with a balance in retained earnings of $76 million. At December 31, 2018, Brewster had total stockholders' equity of $235 million, which consisted of common stock and retained earnings. Brewster has a year-end of December 31. Prepare the following financial statements (with proper headings) for 2018: LO 4

1. Income statement,
2. Statement of retained earnings, and
3. Balance sheet.

Quiz

Test your understanding of the financial statements by answering the following questions. Select the best choice from among the possible answers given.

Q1-44. An organization's investors and creditors will primarily use information provided by:

a. the organization's financial accounting system.
b. the organization's managerial accounting system.
c. the Internal Revenue Service.
d. the Financial Accounting Standards Board.

Q1-45. The *primary* objective of financial reporting is to provide information

a. useful for making investment and credit decisions.
b. on the cash flows of a company.
c. about the profitability of an enterprise.
d. to the federal government.

Q1-46. Which type of business organization provides the least amount of protection for bankers and other creditors of a company?

a. Partnership
b. Corporation
c. Proprietorship
d. Both a and c

Q1-47. Assets are usually reported at their

a. appraised value.
b. historical cost.
c. current market value.
d. none of the above

Q1-48. Assume that a business is headed for certain bankruptcy and it is evident that its liabilities greatly exceed its assets. Which principle would be violated if its financial statements were prepared using standard U.S. GAAP?

a. Entity assumption
b. Continuity assumption
c. Historical cost principle
d. Stable-monetary-unit assumption

Q1-49. During February, assets increased by $83,000 and liabilities increased by $23,000. Equity must have

a. increased by $60,000.
b. increased by $106,000.
c. decreased by $106,000.
d. decreased by $60,000.

Q1-50. The amount a company expects to collect from customers appears on the

a. balance sheet in the current assets section.
b. balance sheet in the stockholders' equity section.
c. statement of cash flows.
d. income statement in the expenses section.

Q1-51. Revenues are

a. decreases in liabilities resulting from paying off loans.
b. increases in retained earnings resulting from selling products or performing services.
c. increases in paid-in capital resulting from the owners investing in the business.
d. all of the above.

Q1-52. All of the following are current assets except

a. prepaid expenses.
b. accounts payable.
c. inventory.
d. accounts receivable.

Q1-53. The financial statement that reports revenues and expenses is called the

a. income statement.
b. statement of retained earnings.
c. statement of cash flows.
d. balance sheet.

Q1-54. Another name for the balance sheet is the

a. statement of operations.
b. statement of profit and loss.
c. statement of earnings.
d. statement of financial position.

Q1-55. Maynard Corporation began the year with cash of $135,000 and land that cost $25,000. During the year, Maynard earned service revenue of $260,000 and had the following expenses: salaries, $185,000; rent, $81,000; and utilities, $28,000. At year-end, Maynard's cash balance was down to $31,000. How much net income (or net loss) did Maynard experience for the year?

a. ($138,000)
b. $75,000
c. ($34,000)
d. ($6,000)

Q1-56. Moody Instruments had retained earnings of $300,000 at December 31, 2017. Net income for 2018 totaled $200,000, and dividends declared for 2018 were $55,000. How much retained earnings should Moody report at December 31, 2018?

a. $500,000
b. $445,000
c. $300,000
d. $355,000

Q1-57. Net income appears on which financial statement(s)?

a. Balance sheet
b. Income statement
c. Statement of retained earnings
d. Both b and c

Q1-58. Cash paid to purchase a building appears on the statement of cash flows among the

a. financing activities.
b. operating activities.
c. investing activities.
d. stockholders' equity.

Q1-59. The stockholders' equity of Kowalski Company at the beginning and end of 2018 totaled $122,000 and $140,000, respectively. Assets at the beginning of 2018 were $149,000. If the liabilities of Kowalski Company increased by $69,000 in 2018, how much were total assets at the end of 2018? Use the accounting equation.

a. $218,000
b. $62,000
c. $236,000
d. $220,000

Q1-60. Paulson Company had the following on the dates indicated:

	12/31/18	12/31/17
Total assets	$ 530,000	$ 350,000
Total liabilities	36,000	23,000

Paulson had no stock transactions in 2018, so the change in stockholders' equity for 2018 was due to net income and dividends. If dividends were $75,000, how much was Paulson's net income for 2018? Use the accounting equation and the statement of retained earnings.

a. $92,000
b. $242,000
c. $167,000
d. $317,000

Q1-61. Which of the following factors should influence business and accounting decisions?

a. Economic
b. Legal
c. Ethical
d. All of the above

Problems MyLab Accounting

Group A

LO 3, 4

P1-62A. ***(Learning Objectives 3, 4: Apply the accounting equation; evaluate business operations)*** Compute the missing amount (?) for each company. (Amounts are in millions.)

	Kennedy Corp.	Caring Co.	Childress, Inc.
Beginning			
Assets	$76	$ 30	$?
Liabilities	51	21	1
Common stock	7	7	6
Retained earnings	?	2	10
Ending			
Assets	$?	$ 48	$20
Liabilities	53	32	?
Common stock	7	?	8
Retained earnings	26	?	?
Income statement			
Revenues	$227	?	$22
Expenses	218	157	?
Net income	?	?	?
Statement of retained earnings			
Beginning RE	$ 18	$ 2	$10
+ Net income	?	8	4
− Dividends declared	(1)	(6)	(2)
= Ending RE	$ 26	$ 4	$12

At the end of the year, which company had the

- highest net income?
- highest percent of net income to revenues?

LO 3, 4

P1-63A. ***(Learning Objectives 3, 4: Apply the accounting equation; evaluate business operations; construct a balance sheet)*** The manager of City News, Inc., prepared the company's balance sheet as of May 31, 2018, while the company's accountant was ill. The balance sheet contains numerous errors. In particular, the manager knew that the balance sheet should balance, so she plugged in the stockholders' equity amount needed to achieve this balance. The stockholders' equity amount is *not* correct. All other amounts are accurate.

	A	B	C	D
1	**City News, Inc. Balance Sheet May 31, 2018**			
2	**Assets**		**Liabilities**	
3	Cash	$ 10,000	Notes receivable	$ 15,800
4	Equipment	35,600	Interest expense	2,100
5	Accounts payable	6,500	Office supplies	700
6	Utilities expense	1,400	Accounts receivable	2,600
7	Advertising expense	400	Note payable	50,000
8	Land	81,000	Total	71,200
9	Salary expense	3,000	**Stockholders' Equity**	
10			Stockholders' equity	66,700
11	Total assets	$ 137,900	Total liabilities	$ 137,900
12				

Requirements

1. Prepare the correct balance sheet and date it properly. Compute total assets, total liabilities, and stockholders' equity.
2. Is City News actually in better (or worse) financial position than the erroneous balance sheet reports? Give the reason for your answer.
3. Identify the accounts listed on the incorrect balance sheet that should not be reported on the balance sheet. State why you excluded them from the correct balance sheet you prepared for Requirement 1. On which financial statement should these accounts appear?

LO 2, 3, 4

P1-64A. ***(Learning Objectives 2, 3, 4: Apply underlying accounting concepts; evaluate business operations; construct a balance sheet)*** Brandon Hilton is a realtor. He organized his business as a corporation on June 16, 2019. The business received $65,000 cash from Hilton and issued common stock. Consider the following facts as of June 30, 2019:

a. Hilton has $15,000 in his personal bank account and $55,000 in the business bank account.
b. Hilton owes $3,400 on a personal charge account at a local department store.
c. Hilton acquired business furniture for $30,000 on June 24. Of this amount, the business owes $16,000 on accounts payable at June 30.
d. Office supplies on hand at the real estate office total $8,000.
e. Hilton's business owes $112,000 on a note payable for some land acquired for a total price of $165,000.
f. Hilton's business spent $20,000 for a Realty Universe franchise, which entitles him to represent himself as an agent. Realty Universe is a national affiliation of independent real estate agents. This franchise is a business asset.
g. Hilton owes $182,000 on a personal mortgage on his personal residence, which he acquired in 2014 for a total price of $334,000.

Requirements

1. Prepare the balance sheet of the real estate business of Brandon Hilton Realtor, Inc., at June 30, 2019.
2. Does it appear that the realty business can pay its debts? How can you tell?
3. Identify the personal items given in the preceding facts that should not be reported on the balance sheet of the business.

LO 3, 4

P1-65A. ***(Learning Objectives 3, 4: Evaluate business operations; construct and analyze an income statement, a statement of retained earnings, and a balance sheet)*** The assets and liabilities of Oak Hill Garden Supply, Inc., as of December 31, 2018, and revenues and expenses for the year ended on that date are as follows:

Equipment	$110,000	Land	$ 25,000
Interest expense	10,300	Note payable	99,600
Interest payable	2,700	Property tax expense	7,400
Accounts payable	26,000	Rent expense	41,200
Salary expense	108,400	Accounts receivable	84,900
Building	406,000	Service revenue	452,600
Cash	44,000	Supplies	6,300
Common stock	13,800	Utilities expense	8,800

Beginning retained earnings was $364,600, and dividends declared and paid totaled $107,000 for the year.

Requirements

1. Prepare the income statement of Oak Hill Garden Supply, Inc., for the year ended December 31, 2018.
2. Prepare the company's statement of retained earnings for the year.
3. Prepare the company's balance sheet as of December 31, 2018.
4. Analyze Oak Hill Garden Supply, Inc., by answering these questions:
   a. Was Oak Hill profitable during 2018? By how much?
   b. Did retained earnings increase or decrease? By how much?
   c. Which is greater, total liabilities or total stockholders' equity? Who has a greater claim to Oak Hill's assets: its creditors or its stockholders?

LO 3, 4

P1-66A. ***(Learning Objectives 3, 4: Evaluate business operations; construct a statement of cash flows)*** The following data come from the financial statements of Mitchell Company for the year ended March 31, 2019 (in millions):

Purchases of property, plant, and equipment for cash	$ 2,640	Other investing cash payments	$ 195
Net income	3,020	Accounts receivable	650
Adjustments to reconcile net income to net cash provided by operating activities	2,420	Payment of dividends	265
Revenues	60,100	Common stock	4,900
Cash, beginning of year	220	Issuance of common stock	190
end of year	2,775	Cash proceeds on sale of property, plant, and equipment	25
Cost of goods sold	37,550	Retained earnings	12,830

Requirements

1. Prepare Mitchell Company's cash flow statement for the year ended March 31, 2019. Not all items listed will appear on the cash flow statement.
2. What activities provided the largest source of cash? Is this a sign of financial strength or weakness?

LO 4 **P1-67A.** ***(Learning Objective 4: Construct financial statements)*** Summarized versions of Calabasa Corporation's financial statements for two recent years are as follows.

A1

	A	B	C	D
1				
2		2019	2018	
3	**Income Statement**	(in Thousands)		
4	Revenues	$ k	$ 14,750	
5	Cost of goods sold	11,100	a	
6	Other expenses	1,300	1,200	
7	Income before income taxes	1,520	1,870	
8	Income taxes (35%)	l	655	
9	Net income	$ m	$ b	
10	**Statement of Retained Earnings**			
11	Beginning balance	$ n	$ 2,680	
12	Net income	o	c	
13	Dividends declared	(92)	(70)	
14	Ending balance	$ p	$ d	
15	**Balance Sheet**			
16	**Assets**			
17	Cash	$ q	$ e	
18	Property, plant, and equipment	1,547	1,316	
19	Other assets	r	11,104	
20	Total assets	$ s	$ 13,600	
21	**Liabilities**			
22	Current liabilities	$ t	$ 5,660	
23	Long-term debt	4,350	3,370	
24	Other liabilities	35	180	
25	Total liabilities	$ 9,200	$ f	
26	**Stockholders' equity:**			
27	Common stock	$ 425	$ 425	
28	Retained earnings	u	g	
29	Other stockholders' equity	180	140	
30	Total stockholders' equity	v	4,390	
31	Total liabilities and stockholders' equity	$ w	$ h	
32	**Cash Flow Statement**			
33	Net cash provided by operating activities	$ x	$ 875	
34	Net cash used in investing activities	(270)	(425)	
35	Net cash used in financing activities	(520)	(520)	
36	Increase (decrease) in cash	(160)	i	
37	Cash at beginning of year	y	1,250	
38	Cash at end of year	$ z	$ j	
39				

Requirement

1. Complete Calabasa Corporation's financial statements by determining the missing amounts denoted by the letters. If necessary, round numbers up to the nearest whole dollar.

Group B

P1-68B. ***(Learning Objectives 3, 4: Apply the accounting equation; evaluate business operations)*** Compute the missing amount (?) for each company. (Amounts are in millions.) LO 3, 4

	Babble Co.	Floralties, Inc.	Drake Co.
Beginning			
Assets	$ 79	$35	$?
Liabilities	51	15	5
Common stock	1	5	2
Retained earnings	?	15	6
Ending			
Assets	$?	$53	$ 15
Liabilities	52	27	?
Common stock	1	?	5
Retained earnings	35	?	?
Income statement			
Revenues	$227	$?	$ 27
Expenses	218	153	?
Net income	?	?	?
Statement of retained earnings			
Beginning RE	$ 27	$15	$ 6
+ Net income	?	10	4
− Dividends declared	(1)	(11)	(4)
= Ending RE	$ 35	$14	$ 6

At the end of the year, which company had the

- highest net income?
- highest percent of net income to revenues?

P1-69B. ***(Learning Objectives 3, 4: Apply the accounting equation; evaluate business operations; construct a balance sheet)*** The manager of Parker Design, Inc., prepared the company's balance sheet as of March 31, 2018, while the company's accountant was ill. The balance sheet contains numerous errors. In particular, the manager knew that the balance sheet should balance, so she plugged in the stockholders' equity amount needed to achieve this balance. The stockholders' equity amount is *not* correct. All other amounts are accurate. LO 3, 4

A1

	A	B	C	D
1	**Parker Design, Inc. Balance Sheet March 31, 2018**			
2	**Assets**		**Liabilities**	
3	Cash	$ 8,000	Notes receivable	$ 13,000
4	Equipment	39,000	Interest expense	1,500
5	Accounts payable	3,500	Office supplies	1,400
6	Utilities expense	1,600	Accounts receivable	3,900
7	Advertising expense	400	Note payable	53,000
8	Land	86,000	Total	72,800
9	Salary expense	3,000	**Stockholders' Equity**	
10			Stockholders' equity	68,700
11	Total assets	$ 141,500	Total liabilities	$ 141,500
12				

Requirements

1. Prepare the correct balance sheet and date it properly. Compute total assets, total liabilities, and stockholders' equity.
2. Is Parker Design, Inc., in better (or worse) financial position than the erroneous balance sheet reports? Give the reason for your answer.
3. Identify the accounts listed on the incorrect balance sheet that should *not* be reported on the balance sheet. State why you excluded them from the correct balance sheet you prepared for Requirement 1. On which financial statement should these accounts appear?

LO **2, 3, 4**

P1-70B. ***(Learning Objectives 2, 3, 4: Apply underlying accounting concepts; evaluate business operations; construct a balance sheet)*** Hudson Alvarez is a realtor. He organized his business as a corporation on June 16, 2019. The business received $75,000 from Alvarez and issued common stock. Consider these facts as of June 30, 2019.

a. Alvarez has $17,000 in his personal bank account and $44,000 in the business bank account.

b. Alvarez owes $6,500 on a personal charge account with a local department store.

c. Alvarez acquired business furniture for $17,600 on June 24. Of this amount, the business owes $9,000 on accounts payable at June 30.

d. Office supplies on hand at the real estate office total $4,000.

e. Alvarez's business owes $102,000 on a note payable for some land acquired for a total price of $162,000.

f. Alvarez's business spent $16,000 for a Realty Experience franchise, which entitles him to represent himself as an agent. Realty Experience is a national affiliation of independent real estate agents. This franchise is a business asset.

g. Alvarez owes $179,000 on a personal mortgage on his personal residence, which he acquired in 2014 for a total price of $419,000.

Requirements

1. Prepare the balance sheet of the real estate business of Hudson Alvarez Realtor, Inc., at June 30, 2019.
2. Does it appear that the realty business can pay its debts? How can you tell?
3. Identify the personal items given in the preceding facts that should not be reported on the balance sheet of the business.

P1-71B. ***(Learning Objectives 3, 4: Evaluate business operations; construct and analyze an income statement, a statement of retained earnings, and a balance sheet)*** The assets and liabilities of Full Moon Products, Inc., as of December 31, 2018, and revenues and expenses for the year ended on that date are as follows: LO 3, 4

Equipment	$ 115,000	Land	$ 29,000
Interest expense	10,000	Note payable	99,200
Interest payable	2,800	Property tax expense	7,300
Accounts payable	25,000	Rent expense	41,000
Salary expense	108,900	Accounts receivable	85,000
Building	405,000	Service revenue	451,600
Cash	46,000	Supplies	6,200
Common stock	26,100	Utilities expense	8,100

Beginning retained earnings was $364,800, and dividends declared and paid totaled $108,000 for the year.

Requirements

1. Prepare the income statement of Full Moon Products, Inc., for the year ended December 31, 2018.
2. Prepare the company's statement of retained earnings for the year.
3. Prepare the company's balance sheet as of December 31, 2018.
4. Analyze Full Moon Products, Inc., by answering these questions:
   a. Was Full Moon profitable during 2018? By how much?
   b. Did retained earnings increase or decrease? By how much?
   c. Which is greater, total liabilities or total stockholders' equity? Who has a greater claim to Full Moon Products' assets: its creditors or its stockholders?

P1-72B. ***(Learning Objectives 3, 4: Evaluate business operations; construct a statement of cash flows)*** The following data come from the financial statements of Tidal Wave Company for the year ended March 31, 2019 (in millions): LO 3, 4

Purchases of property, plant, and equipment for cash	$ 3,500	Other investing cash payments	$ 200
Net income	3,050	Accounts receivable	550
Adjustments to reconcile net income to net cash provided by operating activities	2,380	Payment of dividends	360
Revenues	59,400	Common stock	4,830
Cash, beginning of year	270	Issuance of common stock	200
end of year	1,900	Cash proceeds on sale of property, plant, and equipment	60
Cost of goods sold	37,410	Retained earnings	12,900

Requirements

1. Prepare Tidal Wave Company's cash flow statement for the year ended March 31, 2019. Not all the items listed will appear on the cash flow statement.
2. Which activities provided the largest source of cash? Is this a sign of financial strength or weakness?

LO 4

P1-73B. ***(Learning Objective 4: Construct financial statements)*** Summarized versions of Weaverton Corporation's financial statements for two recent years are as follows.

	A	B	C	D
1				
2		2019	2018	
3	**Income Statement**	(in Thousands)		
4	Revenues	$ k	$ 16,175	
5	Cost of goods sold	11,020	a	
6	Other expenses	1,250	1,220	
7	Income before income taxes	1,530	1,840	
8	Income taxes (35%)	l	644	
9	Net income	$ m	$ b	
10	**Statement of Retained Earnings**			
11	Beginning balance	$ n	$ 2,670	
12	Net income	o	c	
13	Dividends declared	(98)	(140)	
14	Ending balance	$ p	$ d	
15	**Balance Sheet**			
16	**Assets**			
17	Cash	$ q	$ e	
18	Property, plant, and equipment	1,487	1,316	
19	Other assets	r	12,060	
20	Total assets	$ s	$ 14,466	
21	**Liabilities**			
22	Current liabilities	$ t	$ 5,610	
23	Long-term debt	4,450	3,360	
24	Other liabilities	995	1,140	
25	Total liabilities	$ 9,400	$ f	
26	**Stockholders' equity:**			
27	Common stock	$ 450	$ 450	
28	Retained earnings	u	g	
29	Other stockholders' equity	200	180	
30	Total stockholders' equity	v	4,356	
31	Total liabilities and stockholders' equity	$ w	$ h	
32	**Cash Flow Statement**			
33	Net cash provided by operating activities	$ x	$ 875	
34	Net cash used in investing activities	(300)	(575)	
35	Net cash used in financing activities	(510)	(500)	
36	Increase (decrease) in cash	(110)	i	
37	Cash at beginning of year	y	1,290	
38	Cash at end of year	$ z	$ j	
39				

Requirement

1. Complete Weaverton Corporation's financial statements by determining the missing amounts denoted by the letters. If necessary, round numbers up to the nearest whole dollar.

APPLY YOUR KNOWLEDGE

Serial Case

C1-74 *Analyze basic financial statement information (Learning Objectives 3, 4)* LO 3, 4

Note: This mini-case is the first part of The Cheesecake Factory serial case contained in every chapter in this textbook.

The Cheesecake Factory Incorporated (NASDAQ: CAKE) was started by Evelyn Overton when she sold cheesecakes from her basement in Detroit in the 1940s. Its first restaurant opened in Beverly Hills in 1978. Cheesecake Factory has been a publicly held corporation since 1993 and currently has 185 restaurants and two bakery facilities. Its fiscal year end is the Tuesday closest to December 31 each year.

To follow are Cheesecake Factory's four basic financial statements for its most recent year, the year ending January 3, 2017.[3]

The Cheesecake Factory Incorporated
Consolidated Statement of Income (Adapted for Educational Use)
For Year Ended January 3, 2017
(in thousands)

Revenues	$ 2,275,719
Costs and expenses:	
Cost of sales	526,628
Labor expenses	759,998
Depreciation and amortization expense	88,010
Other expenses	700,090
Total costs and expenses	2,074,726
Income from operations	200,993
Interest and other expense, net	(9,225)
Income before income taxes	191,768
Income tax expense	52,274
Net income	$ 139,494

Note: Information presented here should not be used for investment decisions.

Data from the U.S. Securities and Exchange Commission EDGAR Company Filings, www.sec.gov

The Cheesecake Factory Incorporated
Statement of Retained Earnings (Adapted for Educational Use)
For Year Ended January 3, 2017
(in thousands)

Retained earnings balance, 12/29/2015	$ 1,140,788
Add: Net income	139,494
Less: Dividends declared	(42,270)
Retained earnings balance, 1/3/2017	$ 1,238,012

Note: Information presented here should not be used for investment decisions.

Data from the U.S. Securities and Exchange Commission EDGAR Company Filings, www.sec.gov

[3] Please note that all statements have been adapted and condensed for educational use and should not be used for investment decisions.

The Cheesecake Factory Incorporated
Consolidated Balance Sheet (Adapted for Educational Use)
As of January 3, 2017
(in thousands)

Assets	
Current assets:	
Cash and cash equivalents	$ 53,839
Accounts receivable	15,632
Income tax receivable	–
Other receivables	64,592
Inventories	34,926
Prepaid expenses	52,438
Total current assets	221,427
Property and equipment, net	910,134
Other assets:	
Intangible assets, net	23,054
Prepaid rent	42,162
Other assets	96,542
Total other assets	161,758
Total assets	$ 1,293,319
Liabilities and Stockholders' Equity	
Current liabilities:	
Accounts payable	$ 41,564
Other accrued expenses	334,962
Total current liabilities	376,526
Noncurrent liabilities	313,586
Stockholder's equity:	
Preferred stock	–
Common stock	947
Additional paid-in capital	774,137
Retained earnings	1,238,012
Treasury stock	(1,409,889)
Total stockholder's equity	603,207
Total liabilities and stockholder's equity	$ 1,293,319

Note: Information presented here should not be used for investment decisions.

Data from the U.S. Securities and Exchange Commission EDGAR Company Filings, www.sec.gov

The Cheesecake Factory Incorporated
Statement of Cash Flows (Adapted for Educational Use)
For Year Ended January 3, 2017
(in thousands)

Cash flows provided by operating activities	$ 302,520
Cash flows used in investing activities	(159,461)
Cash flows used by financing activities	(133,074)
Net change in cash and cash equivalents	$ 9,985
Cash and cash equivalents at beginning of period	43,854
Cash and cash equivalents at end of period	$ 53,839

Note: Information presented here should not be used for investment decisions.

Data from the U.S. Securities and Exchange Commission EDGAR Company Filings, www.sec.gov

Cheesecake Factory's complete, unabridged financial statements can be found on its investor relations website.

Requirements

1. What form of business organization is The Cheesecake Factory? How do you know?
2. Identify what line item flows from the income statement to the statement of retained earnings.
3. Identify the line item that flows from the statement of retained earnings to the balance sheet.
4. Identify the line item that flows from the statement of cash flows to the balance sheet.
5. Did The Cheesecake Factory have net income or net loss for its fiscal year 2016? (The Cheesecake Factory's 2016 fiscal year end is January 3, 2017.) Over what period of time was this amount earned?
6. Write The Cheesecake Factory's accounting equation as of January 3, 2017.
7. How much in total resources does The Cheesecake Factory have to work with at January 3, 2017? How much does The Cheesecake Factory owe to creditors at January 3, 2017?

Decision Cases

C1-75. *(Learning Objectives 1, 4: Explain accounting language; evaluate business operations through financial statements)* Two businesses, Queens Service Corp. and Insley Sales Co., have sought business loans from you. To decide whether to make the loans, you have requested their balance sheets. LO 1, 4

	A	B	C	D
1	**Queens Service Corp.** **Balance Sheet** **August 31, 2019**			
2	**Assets**		**Liabilities**	
3	Cash	$ 5,000	Accounts payable	$ 50,000
4	Accounts receivable	10,000	Note payable	80,000
5	Land	75,000	Total liabilities	130,000
6	Furniture	15,000	**Stockholders' Equity**	
7	Equipment	45,000	Stockholders' equity	20,000
8			Total liabilities and	
9	Total assets	$ 150,000	stockholders' equity	$ 150,000
10				

	A	B	C	D
1	**Insley Sales Co.** **Balance Sheet** **August 31, 2019**			
2	**Assets**		**Liabilities**	
3	Cash	$ 5,000	Accounts payable	$ 6,000
4	Accounts receivable	10,000	Note payable	9,000
5	Merchandise inventory	15,000	Total liabilities	15,000
6	Building	35,000	**Stockholders' Equity**	
7			Stockholders' equity	50,000
8			Total liabilities and	
9	Total assets	$ 65,000	stockholders' equity	$ 65,000
10				

Requirement

1. Using only these balance sheets, to which entity would you be more comfortable lending money? Explain fully, citing specific items and amounts from the respective balance sheets. (Challenge)

LO 3, 4

C1-76. *(Learning Objectives 3, 4: Evaluate business operations through financial statements; correct errors; construct financial statements)* A year out of college, you have $10,000 to invest. A friend has started Flowers Unlimited, Inc., and he asks you to invest in his company. You obtain the company's financial statements, which are summarized at the end of the first year as follows:

	A	B	C
1	**Flowers Unlimited, Inc.** **Income Statement** **Year Ended December 31, 2018**		
2	Revenues		$ 100,000
3	Expenses		80,000
4	Net income		$ 20,000
5			

	A	B	C	D
1	**Flowers Unlimited, Inc.** **Balance Sheet** **December 31, 2018**			
2	Cash	$ 6,000	Liabilities	$ 60,000
3	Other assets	100,000	Stockholders' equity	46,000
4	Total assets	$ 106,000	Total liabilities and stockholders' equity	$ 106,000
5				

Visits with your friend turn up the following facts:

a. Flowers Unlimited delivered $140,000 of services to customers during 2018 and collected $100,000 from customers for those services.

b. Flowers Unlimited recorded a $50,000 cash payment for software as an asset. This cost should have been an expense.

c. To get the business started, your friend borrowed $10,000 from his parents at the end of 2017. The proceeds of the loan were used to pay salaries for the first month of 2018. Because the loan was from his parents, your friend did not reflect the loan or the salaries in the accounting records.

Requirements

1. Prepare corrected financial statements.
2. Use your corrected statements to evaluate Flowers Unlimited's results of operations and financial position. (Challenge)
3. Will you invest in Flowers Unlimited? Give your reason. (Challenge)

Ethical Issue

LO 5

C1-77. *(Learning Objective 5: Evaluate ethical decisions)* You are studying frantically for an accounting exam tomorrow. You are having difficulty in this course, and the grade you make on this exam can make the difference between receiving a final grade of B or C. If you receive a C, it will lower your grade point average to the point that you could lose your academic scholarship. An hour ago, a friend, also enrolled in the course but in a different section under the same professor, called you with some unexpected news. In her sorority test files, she has just found a copy of an old exam from the previous year. In looking at the exam, it appears to contain questions that come right from the class notes you have taken, even the very same numbers. She offers to make a copy for you and bring it over.

You glance at your course syllabus and find the following: "You are expected to do your own work in this class. Although you may study with others, giving, receiving, or obtaining information pertaining to an examination is considered an act of academic dishonesty, unless such action is authorized by the instructor giving the examination. Also, divulging the contents of an essay or objective examination designated by the instructor as an examination is considered an act of academic dishonesty. Academic dishonesty is considered a violation of the student honor code and will subject the student to disciplinary procedures, which can include suspension from the university." Although you have heard a rumor that fraternities and sororities have cleared their exam files with professors, you are not sure.

Requirements

1. What is the ethical issue in this situation?
2. Who are the stakeholders? What are the possible consequences to each?
3. Analyze the alternatives from the following standpoints: (a) economic, (b) legal, and (c) ethical.
4. What would you do? How would you justify your decision? How would your decision make you feel afterward?
5. How is this similar to a business situation?

Focus on Financials | Apple Inc.

LO 3, 4

C1-78. ***(Learning Objectives 3, 4: Apply the accounting equation; evaluate business operations)*** This and similar cases in succeeding chapters are based on the consolidated financial statements of **Apple Inc.** shown in Appendix A and online in the filings section of **www.sec.gov**.

Requirements

1. Go online and do some research on Apple Inc. and its industry. Use one or more popular websites such as Yahoo! Finance or Google Finance. Write a paragraph (about 100 words) that describes the industry, some current developments, and a projection for future growth.
2. Read Part I, Item 1 (Business) of Apple's annual report. What do you learn here and why is it important?
3. Name at least one of Apple's competitors. Why is this information important in evaluating Apple's financial performance?
4. Suppose you own stock in Apple. If you could pick one item on the company's Consolidated Statements of Operations to increase year after year, what would it be? Why is this item so important? Did this item increase or decrease during fiscal 2016? Is this good news or bad news for the company?
5. What was Apple's largest expense in 2014–2016? In your own words, explain the meaning of this item. Give specific examples of items that make up this expense. The chapter gives another title for this expense. What is it?
6. Use the Consolidated Balance Sheets of Apple in Appendix A to answer these questions: At the end of fiscal 2016, how much in total resources did Apple have to work with? How much did the company owe? How much of its assets did the company's stockholders actually own? Use these amounts to write Apple's accounting equation at September 24, 2016.
7. How much cash and cash equivalents did Apple have at September 26, 2015? How much cash and cash equivalents did Apple have at September 24, 2016?

Focus on Analysis | Under Armour, Inc.

LO 3, 4

C1-79. *(Learning Objectives 3, 4: Apply the accounting equation; evaluate business operations)* This and similar cases in each chapter are based on the 2016 consolidated financial statements of **Under Armour, Inc.** You can retrieve the 2016 Under Armour financial statements at **www.sec.gov** by clicking on Filings and then searching for "Under Armour" under Company Filings. When you see the list of filings for the company, select the Form 10-K for 2016. Be sure to retrieve the 2016 financial statements, not another year.

Requirements

1. Go online and do some research on Under Armour and its industry. Use one or more popular websites such as Yahoo! Finance or Google Finance. Write a paragraph (about 100 words) that describes the industry, some current developments, and a projection for where the industry is headed.
2. Read Note 1—(Description of Business) of Under Armour's annual report. What do you learn here and why is it important?
3. Name two of Under Armour's competitors. Why is this information important in evaluating Under Armour's financial performance?
4. Write Under Armour's accounting equation as of December 31, 2016 (express all items in millions and round to the nearest $1 million). Does Under Armour's financial condition look strong or weak? How can you tell?
5. What was the result of Under Armour's operations during 2016? Identify both the name and the dollar amount of the result of operations for 2016. Does an increase (or decrease) signal good news or bad news for the company and its stockholders?
6. Examine retained earnings in the Consolidated Statements of Stockholders' Equity. What caused retained earnings to increase during 2016?
7. Which statement reports cash and cash equivalents as part of Under Armour's financial position? Which statement tells *why* cash and cash equivalents increased (or decreased) during the year? Which activities caused the company's cash and cash equivalents to change during 2016, and how much did each activity provide or use?

Group Projects

Project 1. As instructed by your professor, obtain the annual report of a well-known company.

Requirements

1. Suppose you are a member of a loan committee at Bank of America. Assume a company has requested a loan from the bank. Analyze the company's financial statements and any other information you need to decide how much money you would be willing to lend the firm. Specify the following:
   a. The length of the loan period—that is, over what period will you allow the company to pay you back?
   b. The interest rate you will charge on the loan. Will you charge the prevailing interest rate, a lower rate, or a higher rate? Why?
   c. Any restrictions you will impose on the borrower as a condition for making the loan.

Note: The long-term debt note to the financial statements gives details of the company's existing liabilities.

2. Write your group decision in a report addressed to the bank's board of directors. Limit your report to two double-spaced typed pages (400 to 600 words).
3. If your professor directs, present your decision and your analysis to the class. Limit your presentation to 10 to 15 minutes.

Project 2. *You are the owner of a company that is about to "go public," that is, issue its stock to outside investors. You want to make your company look as attractive as possible to raise $1 million to expand the business. At the same time, you want to give potential investors a realistic picture of your company.*

Requirements

1. Design a prospectus (a report) to portray your company in a way that will enable outsiders to reach an informed decision as to whether to buy some of your stock. The prospectus should include the following:
   a. Name and location of your company.
   b. Nature of the company's business (be as detailed as possible).
   c. How you plan to spend the money you raise.
   d. The company's comparative income statement, statement of retained earnings, balance sheet, and statement of cash flows for two years: the current year and the preceding year. Make the data as realistic as possible with the intent of receiving $1 million.
2. Create your prospectus using Word, Pages, or other similar tool. Do not exceed five pages.
3. If directed by your professor, make a copy for each member of your class. Distribute copies to the class and present your case with the intent of interesting your classmates in investing in the company. Limit your presentation to 10 to 15 minutes.

Quick Check Answers

1. *d*
2. *c*
3. *c*
4. *a*
5. *c*
6. *c [This is not the typical way the accounting equation is expressed (Assets – Liabilities = Equity), but it may be rearranged this way.]*
7. *d*
8. *b [Total assets = $135,000 ($8,000 + $47,000 + $60,000 + $20,000). Liabilities = $27,000]*
9. *b ($280,000 – $130,000 = $150,000)*
10. *a*
11. *b ($60,000 = $50,000 + $45,000 – $35,000)*
12. *b*
13. *c*
14. *c*
15. *d*
16. *a*

Try It Solutions

Page 12:

1. $320,000 ($480,000 – $160,000)
2. $260,000 ($160,000 + $100,000)
3. Net income of $140,000 ($365,000 – $225,000); revenues minus expenses
4. $210,000 [$180,000 beginning balance + net income $50,000 ($85,000 – $35,000) – dividends $20,000]

2 Transaction Analysis

LEARNING OBJECTIVES

1. **Recognize** a business transaction and the various types of accounts in which it can be recorded
2. **Analyze** the impact of business transactions on the accounting equation
3. **Analyze** the impact of business transactions on accounts
4. **Journalize** transactions and post journal entries to the ledger
5. **Construct** a trial balance

SPOTLIGHT

The Walt Disney Company Records Millions of Transactions a Year!

Each time you purchase a ticket to a Disney theme park, it results in a business transaction. And that's just the tip of the iceberg. If you log on to Disney's website (**www.disney.com**), as millions of people do every day, you can buy a Disney cruise, purchase merchandise at Disney's online store, play Disney video games, view Disney movies that have been released, or download them to your phone with an app—all for a price. All of these actions result in business transactions.

As you learned in Chapter 1, **The Walt Disney Company** made $55.6 billion in revenues in 2016. The company also incurred $46.2 billion in expenses of various types, to earn net income of about $9.4 billion that year. Where did those figures come from? From millions and millions of business transactions. ●

Helen Sessions/Alamy Stock Photo

Chapter 1 introduced the financial statements. In Chapters 2 and 3, we discuss business transactions, how they are recorded, and the role they play in the accounting cycle and the preparation of financial statements.

The diagram below shows this chapter's learning objectives, which consist of the first 5 steps in that process:

The Accounting Cycle (Part I)

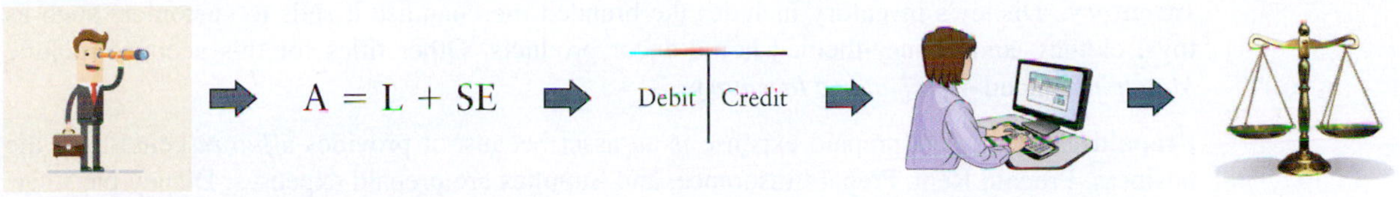

1. Recognize a business transaction
2. Analyze impact of transaction on accounting equation
3. Analyze impact of transaction on accounts
4. Journalize transaction and post to the ledger
5. Construct trial balance

Images: Dim Tik/Shutterstock; Ganna Rassadnikova/123RF; Michelangelus/Shutterstock.

RECOGNIZE A BUSINESS TRANSACTION AND THE VARIOUS TYPES OF ACCOUNTS IN WHICH IT CAN BE RECORDED

1 Recognize a business transaction and the various types of accounts in which it can be recorded

A **transaction** is any event that has a financial impact on a business and can be measured reliably. For example, The Walt Disney Company purchases fresh produce and meat for its restaurants and supplies for its hotels and resorts. The company also provides entertainment services through its television networks, sells Disney merchandise, borrows money, and repays the loans—all of which result in separate transactions.

But not all events qualify as transactions. A Disney cruise may be featured in a travel brochure, or a person planning a vacation may see a Disney theme park advertisement on TV. These events make people aware of Disney's products and services and, ultimately, may result in new business for the company. However, no transaction occurs until someone actually buys tickets to the theme park, stays as a guest at a Disney resort, purchases Disney products, or otherwise engages in an exchange with Disney.

Transactions are always two-sided:

1. Something is given.

and

2. Something is received in return.

In accounting, we always record both sides of a transaction. However, we must be able to measure the financial impact of the event on the accounts of a business before recording the transaction.

As you learned in Chapter 1, the basic accounting equation is as follows:

Assets = Liabilities + Stockholders' Equity

For each asset, each liability, and each element of stockholders' equity, we use a record called an account. An **account** is the record of all the changes in a particular asset, liability, or stockholders' equity during a period. Before we analyze some transactions, let's review some of the accounts companies use.

Assets

Assets are economic resources that provide a future benefit for a business. Most businesses use the following asset accounts:

Cash. A company's **cash** account includes money and any medium of exchange including the company's bank account balances, paper currency, coins, certificates of deposit, and checks.

Accounts Receivable. Sometimes when a business sells goods or services, it doesn't receive cash in exchange for them. Instead, the business receives a promise for a future cash payment in a number of days (usually 30 to 90). The accounts receivable account consists of these future payments owed to the business.

Notes Receivable. Notes receivable are amounts other parties must pay the business because they signed a promissory note to do so. A *promissory note* is a written promise to pay a certain amount of money by a certain date, with interest. These amounts owed appear in the business's notes receivable account.

Inventory. Disney's inventory includes the branded merchandise it sells to customers such as toys, clothes, and Disney-themed home décor products. Other titles for this account include *Merchandise* and *Merchandise Inventory*.

Prepaid Expenses. A prepaid expense is an asset because it provides a *future* benefit for the business. Prepaid Rent, Prepaid Insurance, and Supplies are prepaid expenses. Disney pays certain expenses in advance, such as insurance and rent.

Film and Television Costs. These costs include production costs, production overhead, interest, and development costs for Disney films and television programs. The outlays are accumulated in an asset account and eventually amortized as expenses as the films and television programs are shown. These costs are unique to media companies like The Walt Disney Company.

Investments. As explained in Chapter 1, The Walt Disney Company has invested in other companies that operate all over the world. Because these investments have a long-term future use to the company, they are listed among its long-term assets.

Parks, Resorts, and Other Property. This account shows the cost of the land, buildings, and equipment owned by Disney and used in its operations to earn revenue. Within this category, the company segregates each asset by type and eventually allocates much of the cost associated with the asset by depreciating it over the time periods it helps earn revenue. Most other companies call this account *Property, Plant, and Equipment*.

Liabilities

Recall that a *liability* is a debt. A payable is always a liability. The most common types of liabilities include the following:

Accounts Payable. Accounts payable are the direct opposite of accounts receivable. When Disney promises to pay a supplier, the amount appears in the company's accounts payable account.

Notes Payable (borrowings). The notes payable account includes the amounts Disney must *pay* because it signed notes promising to pay a future amount. Notes payable, like notes receivable in the assets section of the balance sheet, also bear interest.

Accrued Liabilities. An **accrued liability** is a liability for an expense you have not yet paid. Interest payable and salary payable are accrued liability accounts for most companies because they don't pay those expenses as soon as they are owed. Instead, the amounts are paid only periodically—every two weeks, every month, or every year, for example. Income tax payable is another accrued liability.

Stockholders' Equity

The owners' claims to the assets of a corporation are called *stockholders' equity*, *shareholders' equity*, or simply *equity*. A corporation such as The Walt Disney Company uses common stock, retained earnings, and dividend accounts to record the company's stockholders' equity. In a proprietorship, there is a single equity account. For a partnership, each partner has a separate equity account.

Common Stock. The common stock account shows the owners' investment in the corporation. The Walt Disney Company receives cash and issues common stock to its stockholders. A company's common stock is its most basic element of equity. All corporations have common stock.

Retained Earnings. The retained earnings account shows the cumulative net income earned by The Walt Disney Company over the company's lifetime, minus its cumulative net losses and dividends.

Dividends. Dividends are optional; they are decided (declared) by the board of directors. After profitable operations, Disney's board might decide to declare and pay a cash dividend. To do this the corporation would keep a separate account titled *dividends*, which indicates that the company's retained earnings are reduced after dividends have been declared and paid.

Revenues. Revenues increase stockholders' equity. A company can use as many revenue accounts as it needs. The Walt Disney Company uses a products revenue account for the revenue it earns from products, and a services revenue account for the revenue it earns by providing services to customers. A lawyer who provides legal services for clients also uses a service revenue account. A bank that loans money needs an interest revenue account. If a business rents a building to a tenant, the business needs a rent revenue account.

Expenses. The cost of operating a business is called an *expense*. Expenses *decrease* stockholders' equity, the opposite effect of revenues. A business needs a separate account for each type of expense, such as cost of goods or services sold, salary expense, rent expense, advertising expense, insurance expense, utilities expense, and income tax expense. Businesses strive to minimize expenses and thereby maximize net income.

TRY IT

(Answers are given on p. 119.)

Name two things that

(1) increase The Walt Disney Company's stockholders' equity, and

(2) decrease The Walt Disney Company's stockholders' equity.

ANALYZE THE IMPACT OF BUSINESS TRANSACTIONS ON THE ACCOUNTING EQUATION

Example: Alladin Travel, Inc.

2 Analyze the impact of business transactions on the accounting equation

To illustrate the accounting for transactions, let's return to Alladin Travel, Inc., which appeared in Chapter 1's End-of-Chapter Problem. Aladdin's primary shareholder and manager Starr Williams opened the business in April 2018.

We will consider 11 transactions and analyze each in terms of its effect on Alladin Travel. We will begin by using the accounting equation to build the financial statements in spreadsheet format. In the second half of the chapter, we will record transactions using the journal and ledger of the business.

Try It in Excel®

As you review the 11 transactions, build an Excel template. Use the accounting equation on page 61 as a model. Remember that each transaction has either an equal effect on both the left- and right-hand sides of the accounting equation, or an offsetting effect (both positive and negative) on the same side of the equation. Recreate the spreadsheet in Exhibit 2-1, Panel B (page 68), step by step, as you go along. In Excel, open a new blank spreadsheet.

Step 1 Format the worksheet. Label cell A2 "Trans." You will put transaction numbers corresponding to the transactions below in the cells in column A. Row 1 will contain the elements of the accounting equation. Enter "Assets" in cell D1. Enter an "=" sign in cell F1. Enter "Liabilities + Stockholders' Equity" in cell G1. Enter "Type of SE (abbreviation for stockholders' equity) Transaction" in cell J1. Highlight cells B1 through E1 and click "merge and center" on the top toolbar. Highlight cells G1 through I1 and click "merge and center." Now you will have a spreadsheet organized around the elements of the accounting equation: "Assets = Liabilities + Stockholders' Equity" and, for all transactions impacting stockholders' equity, you will be able to enter the type (common stock, revenue, expense, or dividends). This will be important later when you construct the financial statements (Exhibit 2-2, page 70).

Step 2 Continue formatting. In cells B2 through E2, enter the asset account titles that transactions 1–11 deal with. B2: Cash; C2: AR (an abbreviation for accounts receivable);

D2: Supplies; E2: Land. In cells G2 through I2, enter the liability and stockholders' equity account titles that Alladin Travel, Inc.'s, transactions deal with: G2: AP (an abbreviation for accounts payable); H2: C Stock (an abbreviation for common stock); and I2: RE (abbreviation for retained earnings; this is where all transactions impacting revenue, expenses, and dividends will go for now).

Step 3 In row 15, enter the formula to sum each column from B through E and G through I. For example, the formula in cell B15 should be "=sum(B3:B14)." In cell A15, enter "Bal." This will allow you to keep a running sum of the accounts in the balance sheet as you enter each transaction.

Step 4 In cell A16, enter "Totals." In cell C16, enter "=sum(B15:E15)." In cell H16, enter "=sum(G15:I15)." You can use the short cut symbol "∑" followed by highlighting the respective cells. Excel allows you to keep a running sum of the column totals on each side of the equation. You should find that the running sum of the column totals on the left-hand side of the equation always equals the running sum of the column totals on the right-hand side, so the accounting equation always stays in balance. As a final formatting step, highlight cells B3 through I16. Using the "number" tab on the toolbar at the top of the spreadsheet, select "Accounting" for format with no $ sign, and select "decrease decimal" to zero places. Now you're ready to process the transactions.

Transaction 1. On April 1, Starr Williams and a few friends invest $50,000 to open Alladin Travel, Inc., and the business issues common stock to the stockholders. The transaction increases both the company's cash and common stock:

Assets		Liabilities +	Stockholders' Equity	Type of Stockholders' Equity Transaction
Cash	=		Common Stock	
(1) + 50,000			+ 50,000	Issued common stock

Every transaction's net amount on the left side of the accounting equation must equal the net amount on the right side. If you're following along in Excel, enter 1 in cell A3 of the spreadsheet you are creating. Enter 50000 in cell B3 (under Cash) and 50000 in cell H3 (under C Stock). To the right of the transaction in cell J3 write "Issued common stock" to show the reason for the increase in stockholders' equity. You don't have to enter commas; Excel will do that for you. Notice that the sum of Cash (cell B15) is now 50,000 and the sum of Common Stock (cell H15) is also 50,000. The total of accounts on the left side of the accounting equation is 50,000 (cell C16) and it equals the total of accounts on the right side of the accounting equation (cell H16).

Every transaction affects the financial statements of the business. We can prepare financial statements after one, two, or any number of transactions have occurred. For example, after its first transaction, Alladin Travel could create the company's balance sheet shown here:

A1

	A	B	C	D	E	F
1	**Alladin Travel, Inc.** **Balance Sheet** **April 1, 2018**					
2	**Assets**			**Liabilities**		
3	Cash		$ 50,000	None		
4				**Stockholders' Equity**		
5				Common stock	$ 50,000	
6				Total stockholders' equity	50,000	
7				Total liabilities and		
8	Total assets		$ 50,000	stockholders' equity	$ 50,000	
9						

The balance sheet shows that the business has $50,000 in cash and owes no liabilities. A bank would look favorably on this balance sheet because the business has $50,000 cash and no debt—a strong financial position.

As a practical matter, most entities report their financial statements at the end of the accounting period, and not after each transaction. But an accounting system based on a structure similar to our Excel spreadsheet can produce statements whenever managers need to know where the business stands.

Transaction 2. Alladin purchases land for a new location and pays cash of $40,000. The effect of this transaction on the accounting equation is as follows:

	Assets				Liabilities + Stockholders' Equity	Type of Stockholders' Equity Transaction
	Cash	+	Land		Common Stock	
(1)	50,000			=	50,000	Issued common stock
(2)	− 40,000		+ 40,000			
Bal	10,000		40,000		50,000	
		50,000			50,000	

The purchase increases one asset (Land) and decreases another asset (Cash) by the same amount. If you're following along in Excel, enter a 2 in cell A4. Enter –40000 in cell B4 and 40000 in cell E4. The spreadsheet automatically updates, showing that after the transaction is completed, Alladin has cash of $10,000, land of $40,000, total assets of $50,000, and no liabilities. Stockholders' equity is unchanged at $50,000. Note that, as shown in cells C16 and H16, total assets must always equal total liabilities plus stockholders' equity.

Transaction 3. The business buys supplies on account, agreeing to pay $3,700 within 30 days. This transaction increases both the assets and the liabilities of the business. Its effect on the accounting equation follows:

	Assets						Liabilities	+	Stockholders' Equity
	Cash	+	Supplies	+	Land		Accounts Payable	+	Common Stock
Bal	10,000				40,000	=			50,000
(3)			+ 3,700				+ 3,700		
Bal	10,000		3,700		40,000		3,700		50,000
			53,700					53,700	

The new asset is Supplies, and the liability is an Account Payable. Alladin signs no formal promissory note, so the liability is an account payable, not a note payable. If you're following along in Excel, enter 3 in cell A5, 3700 in cell D5 under the account "Supplies," and 3700 in cell G5 under "AP" (accounts payable). Notice that the spreadsheet now reflects three assets in row 15: cash with a balance of $10,000 (cell B15), supplies with a balance of $3,700 (cell D15), and land with a balance of $40,000 (cell E15), for total assets of $53,700 (cell C16). On the right-hand side of the accounting equation, Alladin now has accounts payable (a liability) of $3,700 (cell G15) and common stock (cell H15) of $50,000, for a total of $53,700 (cell H16).

Transaction 4. Alladin earns $7,000 in revenue by providing services for customers. The business collects the cash. The effect on the accounting equation is an increase in the asset Cash and an increase in Retained Earnings, as follows:

	Assets				Liabilities + Stockholders' Equity			Type of Stockholders' Equity Transaction
	Cash	+ Supplies	+ Land		Accounts Payable	+ Common Stock	+ Retained Earnings	
Bal	10,000	3,700	40,000	=	3,700	50,000		
(4)	+7,000						+7,000	Service revenue
Bal	17,000	3,700	40,000		3,700	50,000	7,000	
	60,700				60,700			

In the Excel spreadsheet on line 6, we enter 7000 under Cash (cell B6) and 7000 under Retained Earnings (cell I6). In cell J6, we enter "Service revenue" to show where the $7,000 of increase in retained earnings came from. Our grand totals on the bottom of the spreadsheet now show $60,700 for total assets as well as $60,700 for total liabilities and stockholders' equity.

Transaction 5. Alladin performs services on account, which means that Alladin lets some customers pay later. Alladin earns revenue but doesn't receive the cash immediately. In transaction 5, Alladin arranges travel for several large corporate customers, and they agree to pay Alladin $3,000 within one month. This promise is an account receivable—an asset—of Alladin Travel. The transaction record is:

	Assets					Liabilities + Stockholders' Equity			Type of Stockholders' Equity Transaction
	Cash	+ Accounts Receivable	+ Supplies	+ Land		Accounts Payable	+ Common Stock	+ Retained Earnings	
Bal	17,000		3,700	40,000	=	3,700	50,000	7,000	
(5)		+3,000						+3,000	Service revenue
Bal	17,000	3,000	3,700	40,000		3,700	50,000	10,000	
	63,700					63,700			

It's performing the service that earns the revenue—not collecting the cash. Therefore, Alladin records revenue when it performs the service—regardless of whether Alladin receives cash now or later. In your Excel spreadsheet, enter 3000 under Accounts Receivable on the left-hand side (cell C7) and 3000 under Retained Earnings on the right-hand side (cell I7). Also enter "Service revenue" in cell J7 to keep a record of the type of transaction (revenue) that affects stockholders' equity (SE).

Transaction 6. During the month, Alladin pays $2,700 for the following expenses: rent, $1,100; employee salaries, $1,200; and utilities, $400. The effect on the accounting equation is:

	Assets					Liabilities + Stockholders' Equity			Type of Stockholders' Equity Transaction
	Cash	+ Accounts Receivable	+ Supplies	+ Land		Accounts Payable	+ Common Stock	+ Retained Earnings	
Bal	17,000	3,000	3,700	40,000		3,700	50,000	10,000	
(6)	−2,700				=			−1,100	Rent expense
								−1,200	Salary expense
								− 400	Utilities expense
Bal	14,300	3,000	3,700	40,000		3,700	50,000	7,300	
	61,000					61,000			

This transaction will take up lines 8, 9, and 10 of the Excel spreadsheet. Enter –2700 under Cash (cell B8); –1100 under Retained Earnings (cell I8); –1200 under Retained Earnings (cell I9);

and –400 under Retained Earnings (cell I10). Enter the type of transaction (rent expense, salary expense, or utilities expense) to account for the type of transaction impacting stockholders' equity (SE). These expenses decrease Alladin Travel, Inc.'s, Cash and Retained Earnings. List each expense separately to keep track of its amount and to help prepare the company's income statement later.

Transaction 7. Alladin pays $1,900 on account, which means the company makes a payment that reduces its account payable. In this transaction Alladin pays the store from which it purchased supplies in transaction 3. The transaction decreases Cash (cell B11 on the Excel spreadsheet) and also decreases Accounts Payable (cell G11):

	Assets					Liabilities +	Stockholders' Equity	
	Cash +	Accounts Receivable +	Supplies +	Land		Accounts Payable +	Common Stock +	Retained Earnings
Bal	14,300	3,000	3,700	40,000	=	3,700	50,000	7,300
(7)	−1,900					−1,900		
Bal	12,400	3,000	3,700	40,000		1,800	50,000	7,300
		59,100					59,100	

Transaction 8. Starr Williams, the major stockholder of Alladin Travel, paid $30,000 out of her personal (not business) bank account to remodel her home. This event is a personal transaction of the Williams family. It is not recorded by Alladin Travel, Inc. We focus solely on the business entity, not on its owners. This transaction illustrates the entity assumption from Chapter 1.

Transaction 9. In transaction 5, Alladin performed travel services for customers on account. The business now collects $1,000 from one of those customers. We say that Alladin *collects the cash on account*. Alladin will record the collection as an increase in Cash and a decrease in Accounts Receivable. This is not service revenue because Alladin already recorded the revenue in transaction 5. The effect of collecting cash on account is:

	Assets					Liabilities +	Stockholders' Equity	
	Cash +	Accounts Receivable +	Supplies +	Land		Accounts Payable +	Common Stock +	Retained Earnings
Bal	12,400	3,000	3,700	40,000	=	1,800	50,000	7,300
(9)	+1,000	−1,000						
Bal	13,400	2,000	3,700	40,000		1,800	50,000	7,300
		59,100					59,100	

This transaction is entered on line 12 of the Excel spreadsheet as an increase in Cash (cell B12) and a decrease in AR (cell C12).

Transaction 10. Alladin sells some land for $22,000, the amount the firm paid for it. Alladin receives $22,000 cash, and the effect on the accounting equation is:

	Assets					Liabilities +	Stockholders' Equity	
	Cash +	Accounts Receivable +	Supplies +	Land		Accounts Payable +	Common Stock +	Retained Earnings
Bal	13,400	2,000	3,700	40,000	=	1,800	50,000	7,300
(10)	+22,000			−22,000				
Bal	35,400	2,000	3,700	18,000		1,800	50,000	7,300
		59,100					59,100	

Note that the company did not sell all its land; Alladin still owns $18,000 worth of land. This transaction is entered in the Excel spreadsheet as an increase in Cash (cell B13) and a decrease in Land (cell E13).

Transaction 11. Alladin Travel, Inc., declares a dividend and pays its stockholders $2,100 cash. The effect on the accounting equation is:

	Assets					Liabilities +	Stockholders' Equity		Type of Stockholders' Equity Transaction
	Cash +	Accounts Receivable +	Supplies +	Land		Accounts Payable +	Common Stock +	Retained Earnings	
Bal	35,400	2,000	3,700	18,000	=	1,800	50,000	7,300	
(11)	−2,100							−2,100	Dividend
Bal	33,300	2,000	3,700	18,000		1,800	50,000	5,200	
	57,000					57,000			

The dividend decreases both Alladin's Cash (cell B14) and Retained Earnings (cell I14). However, dividends are not an expense. They are a separate type of reduction of stockholders' equity. Therefore, enter "Dividend" in cell J14. We should now have all of the transactions impacting stockholders' equity labeled properly, which will help us prepare Alladin's financial statements later.

Exhibit 2-1 | Transaction Analysis: Alladin Travel, Inc.

PANEL A—Transaction Details

(1) Received $50,000 cash and issued stock to the owners
(2) Paid $40,000 cash for land
(3) Bought $3,700 of supplies on account
(4) Received $7,000 cash from customers for services performed
(5) Performed services for customers on account, $3,000
(6) Paid cash expenses: rent, $1,100; employee salary, $1,200; utilities, $400
(7) Paid $1,900 on the account payable created in transaction 3
(8) Major stockholder paid personal funds to remodel home, *not* a transaction of the business
(9) Received $1,000 on account
(10) Sold land for cash at the land's cost of $22,000
(11) Declared and paid a dividend of $2,100 to the stockholders

PANEL B—Transaction Analysis

A1

	A	B	C	D	E	F	G	H	I	J
1		Assets				=	Liabilities+	Stockholders' Equity		Type of SE Transaction
2	Trans	Cash	AR	Supplies	Land		AP	C Stock	RE	
3	1	50,000						50,000		Issued common stock
4	2	(40,000)			40,000					
5	3			3,700			3,700			
6	4	7,000							7,000	Service revenue
7	5		3,000						3,000	Service revenue
8	6	(2,700)							(1,100)	Rent expense
9									(1,200)	Salary expense
10									(400)	Utilities expense
11	7	(1,900)					(1,900)			
12	9	1,000	(1,000)							
13	10	22,000			(22,000)					
14	11	(2,100)							(2,100)	Dividend
15	Bal	33,300	2,000	3,700	18,000		1,800	50,000	5,200	
16	Totals		57,000					57,000		
17										

Statement of Cash Flows Data (rows 3–15)

Income Statement Data (rows 6–10)

Statement of Retained Earnings Data (row 14)

Balance Sheet Data

Transactions and Financial Statements

Exhibit 2-1 summarizes the 11 transactions we just discussed. Panel A gives the details of the transactions. As you study the exhibit, note that every transaction maintains the equality:

$$\text{Assets} = \text{Liabilities} + \text{Stockholders' Equity}$$

If you prepared an Excel spreadsheet as you followed the 11 transactions, it should look very similar to Panel B in Exhibit 2-1. The transaction analysis in Panel B contains the data we need to prepare Alladin Travel's financial statements:

- *Income statement* data appear as revenues and expenses under Retained Earnings. The revenues increase retained earnings; the expenses decrease retained earnings.
- The *balance sheet* data are composed of the ending balances of the assets, liabilities, and stockholders' equities shown at the bottom of the exhibit. The accounting equation shows that total assets ($57,000) equal total liabilities plus stockholders' equity ($57,000).
- The *statement of retained earnings* repeats the net income (or net loss) from the income statement. Dividends are subtracted. Ending retained earnings is the final result.
- Data for the *statement of cash flows* appear under the Cash account. Cash receipts increase cash, and cash payments, which are shown in parentheses, decrease cash. *Note: We did not reproduce the statement of cash flows in Exhibit 2-2.*

Exhibit 2-2 shows Alladin Travel's income statement, statement of retained earnings, and balance sheet at the end of April, the company's first month of operations. Follow the flow of data and you will see the following:

1. The income statement reports revenues, expenses, and either a net income or a net loss for the period. During April, Alladin earned net income of $7,300. Panel B in Exhibit 2-1 shows that service revenue consists of the sum of cells I6 and I7 ($7,000 for cash and $3,000 on account). Expenses (salary $1,200 from cell I9, rent $1,100 from cell I8, and utilities $400 from cell I10) are listed separately in the income statement. The sum of these expenses is $2,700. Net income consists of the difference between service revenue and total expenses ($10,000 − $2,700 = $7,300). This is known as a "single-step" income statement: The revenue ($10,000) is shown as one number—as are all of the expenses ($2,700)—so only one step, a subtraction between the two numbers, is needed to calculate the company's net income ($7,300). With "multistep" income statements, that's not the case. You will learn more about single-step versus multistep income statements in Chapters 3 and 6.
2. The statement of retained earnings starts with the beginning balance of retained earnings (zero for a new business). Add net income for the period from the income statement (arrow ①), subtract dividends ($2,100 from cell I14 of the transaction analysis spreadsheet in Exhibit 2-1, Panel B), and compute the ending balance of retained earnings ($5,200).
3. The balance sheet lists the assets, liabilities, and stockholders' equity of the business at the end of the period. The assets consist of the totals of cash, accounts receivable, supplies, and land (see cells B15 through E15 in Exhibit 2-1, Panel B). Liabilities consist of only accounts payable (cell G15). Common stock carries over from cell H15. Also included in stockholders' equity is retained earnings, which comes from the statement of retained earnings (arrow ②). It has also been accumulated in cell I15 of Exhibit 2-1, Panel B.

Exhibit 2-2 | Financial Statements of Alladin Travel, Inc.

	A	B	C	D
1	**Alladin Travel, Inc.** **Income Statement** **Month Ended April 30, 2018**			
2	**Revenues**			
3	Service revenue ($7,000 + $3,000)		$ 10,000	
4	**Expenses**			
5	Salary expense	$ 1,200		
6	Rent expense	1,100		
7	Utilities expense	400		
8	Total expenses		2,700	
9	Net income		$ 7,300	
10				

①

	A	B	C	D
1	**Alladin Travel, Inc.** **Statement of Retained Earnings** **Month Ended April 30, 2018**			
2	Retained earnings, April 1, 2018		$ 0	
3	Add: Net income for the month		7,300	
4	Subtotal		7,300	
5	Less: Dividends declared		(2,100)	
6	Retained earnings, April 30, 2018		$ 5,200	
7				

②

	A	B	C	D	E	F
1	**Alladin Travel, Inc.** **Balance Sheet** **April 30, 2018**					
2	**Assets**			**Liabilities**		
3	Cash		$ 33,300	Accounts payable	$ 1,800	
4	Accounts receivable		2,000	**Stockholders' Equity**		
5	Supplies		3,700	Common stock	50,000	
6	Land		18,000	Retained earnings	5,200	
7				Total stockholders' equity	55,200	
8				Total liabilities and		
9	Total assets		$ 57,000	stockholders' equity	$ 57,000	
10						

Try It in Excel®

If you are familiar with Excel, a quick look at Exhibit 2-2 should convince you of how easy it is to prepare the income statement, statement of retained earnings, and balance sheet in Excel. If you have not already prepared them in Chapter 1 (see page 29), prepare three simple templates for each of these financial statements for Alladin Travel, Inc. You may use these templates again, and add to them, in Chapter 3 as you learn the adjusting entry process. Selected problems in MyLab Accounting have already prepared these templates for you. The mid-chapter summary problem will illustrate with another small company.

Let's put into practice what you have learned so far.

Mid-Chapter | Summary Problem

Marian Palomino opens a research service near a college campus. She names the corporation Palomino Researchers, Inc. During the first month of operations, July 2018, the business engages in these transactions:

a. Palomino Researchers, Inc., issues its common stock to Marian Palomino, who invests $25,000 to open the business.

b. The company purchases on account office supplies costing $350.

c. Palomino Researchers pays cash of $20,000 to acquire a lot next to the campus. The company intends to use the land as a building site for a business office.

d. Palomino Researchers performs research for clients and receives cash of $1,900.

e. Palomino Researchers pays $100 on the account payable that it created in transaction b.

f. Palomino pays $2,000 of personal funds for a vacation.

g. Palomino Researchers pays cash expenses for office rent ($400) and utilities ($100).

h. The business sells a small parcel of the land for its cost of $5,000.

i. The business declares and pays a cash dividend of $1,200.

Requirements

1. Using Excel, build a spreadsheet to analyze the preceding transactions in terms of their effects on the accounting equation of Palomino Researchers, Inc. Use Exhibit 2-1, Panel B, as a guide.
2. Using Excel, prepare the income statement, statement of retained earnings, and balance sheet of Palomino Researchers, Inc., after recording the transactions. Draw arrows linking the statements. Use Exhibit 2-2 as a guide. The balance sheet does not have to be classified.

Answers

Requirement 1

PANEL B—Transaction Analysis: Palomino Researchers, Inc.

A1

	A	B	C	D	E	F	G	H	I
1			Assets		=	Liabilities	+ Stockholders' Equity		Type of SE Transaction
2	Trans	Cash	Office Supplies	Land		AP	C Stock	RE	
3	a	25,000					25,000		Issued common stock
4	b		350			350			
5	c	(20,000)		20,000					
6	d	1,900						1,900	Service revenue
7	e	(100)				(100)			
8	f (n/a)								
9	g	(400)						(400)	Rent expense
10		(100)						(100)	Utilities expense
11	h	5,000		(5,000)					
12	i	(1,200)						(1,200)	Dividend
13	Bal	10,100	350	15,000		250	25,000	200	
14	Totals		25,450				25,450		
15									

Requirement 2

Palomino Researchers, Inc. **Income Statement** **Month Ended July 31, 2018**		
Revenues		
Service revenue		$ 1,900
Expenses		
Rent expense	$ 400	
Utilities expense	100	
Total expenses		500
Net income		$ 1,400

Palomino Researchers, Inc. **Statement of Retained Earnings** **Month Ended July 31, 2018**	
Retained earnings, July 1, 2018	$ 0
Add: Net income for the month	1,400
Subtotal	1,400
Less: Dividends declared	(1,200)
Retained earnings, July 31, 2018	$ 200

Palomino Researchers, Inc. **Balance Sheet** **July 31, 2018**			
Assets		**Liabilities**	
Cash	$ 10,100	Accounts payable	$ 250
Office supplies	350	**Stockholders' Equity**	
Land	15,000	Common stock	25,000
		Retained earnings	200
		Total stockholders' equity	25,200
		Total liabilities and	
Total assets	$ 25,450	stockholders' equity	$ 25,450

The analysis in the first half of this chapter can be used, but even in Excel, it can be cumbersome. The Walt Disney Company has hundreds of accounts and millions of transactions. The spreadsheet to account for The Walt Disney Company's transactions would be huge! In the second half of this chapter we discuss double-entry accounting as it is actually used in business.

ANALYZE THE IMPACT OF BUSINESS TRANSACTIONS ON ACCOUNTS

3 Analyze the impact of business transactions on accounts

You have learned that a business transaction is always two-sided. Accounting is, therefore, based on a double-entry system, which records these dual effects. Each transaction affects at least two accounts. For example, Alladin Travel, Inc., received $50,000 cash in exchange for issuing stock.

The transaction increased both Cash and Common Stock by $50,000. It would be incomplete to record only the increase in Cash or only the increase in Common Stock.

The T-Account

An account can be represented by the letter T. We call this a *T-account*. The vertical line in the letter T represents the division of the account into its left and right sides. The account title appears at the top of the T. For example, the T-account for Cash appears as follows:

Cash	
(Left side)	(Right side)
Debit	*Credit*

The left side of each account is called the **debit** side, and the right side is called the **credit** side. Often, students are confused by the words *debit* and *credit*. To become comfortable using these terms, remember that every business transaction involves both a debit and a credit. You should remember that *debit* means "left-hand side" and *credit* means "right-hand side."

Debit = Left side	Credit = Right side

Increases and Decreases in the Accounts: The Rules of Debit and Credit

The type of account determines how we record increases and decreases. Exhibit 2-3 outlines the rules for how debits and credits are recorded.

Exhibit 2-3 | The Accounting Equation and the Rules of Debit and Credit

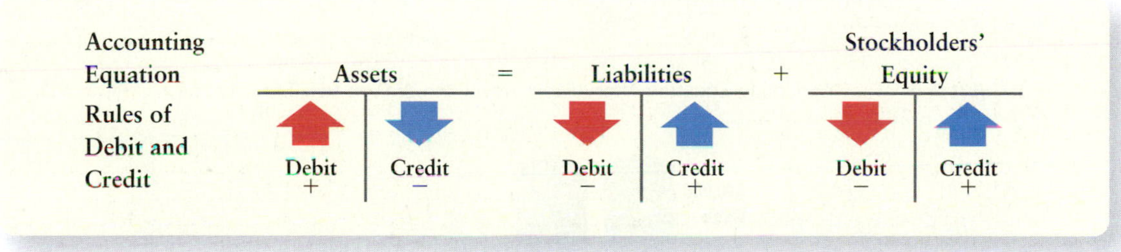

- Increases in assets are recorded on the left (debit) side of the account. Decreases in assets are recorded on the right (credit) side. You receive cash and debit the Cash account. You pay cash and credit the Cash account.
- Conversely, increases in liabilities *and* stockholders' equity are recorded by credits. Decreases in liabilities *and* stockholders' equity are recorded by debits.

To illustrate the ideas diagrammed in Exhibit 2-3, let's review the first transaction: Alladin Travel, Inc., received $50,000 and issued (gave) $50,000 in stock. Which accounts are affected? The Cash account and the Common Stock account.

The amount remaining in an account is called its *balance*. This first transaction gives Cash a $50,000 debit balance and Common Stock a $50,000 credit balance. Exhibit 2-4 shows this relationship.

Exhibit 2-4 | The Accounting Equation After Alladin Travel, Inc.'s, First Transaction

Cash	
Debit for increase, 50,000	

Common Stock	
	Credit for increase, 50,000

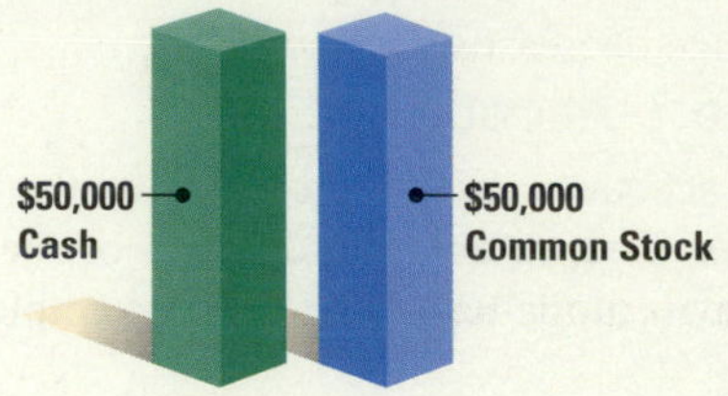

Alladin's second transaction is a $40,000 cash purchase of land. This transaction decreases Cash with a credit and increases Land with a debit, as shown in the following T-accounts (focus on Cash and Land):

Cash			
Bal	50,000	Credit for decrease, 40,000	
Bal	10,000		

Common Stock			
		Bal	50,000

Land			
Debit for increase, 40,000			
Bal	40,000		

After this transaction, Cash has a $10,000 debit balance, Land has a debit balance of $40,000, and Common Stock has a $50,000 credit balance, as shown in Exhibit 2-5.

Exhibit 2-5 | The Accounting Equation After Alladin Travel, Inc.'s, First Two Transactions

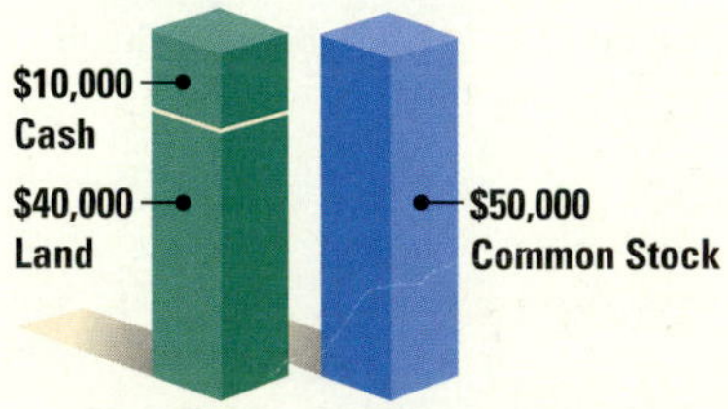

Additional Stockholders' Equity Accounts: Revenues and Expenses

Stockholders' equity also includes the two categories of income statement accounts, Revenues and Expenses:

- *Revenues* are increases in stockholders' equity that result from delivering goods or services to customers.
- *Expenses* are decreases in stockholders' equity due to the cost of operating the business.

Therefore, the accounting equation may be expanded as shown in Exhibit 2-6. Revenues and expenses appear in parentheses because their net effect—revenues minus expenses—equals net income, which increases stockholders' equity. If expenses exceed revenues, there is a net loss, which decreases stockholders' equity.

Exhibit 2-6 | The Expanded Accounting Equation

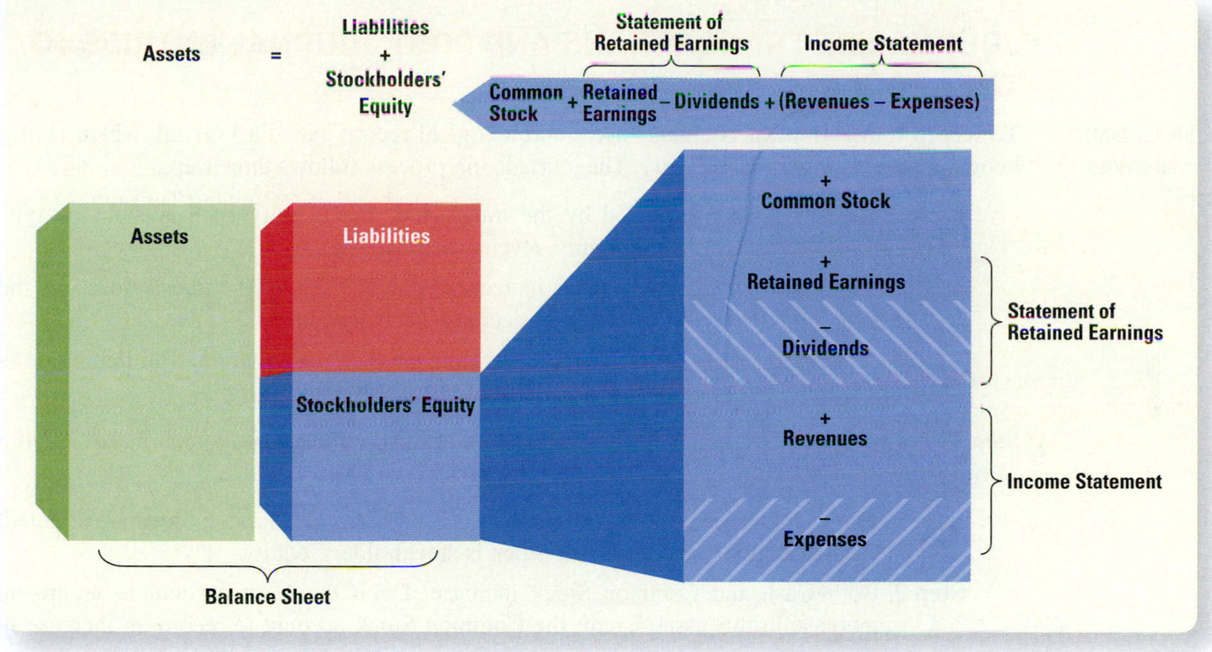

Exhibit 2-7 shows the final form of the rules of debit and credit. You should not proceed until you have learned these rules. For example, you must remember that

- a debit increases an asset account;
- a credit decreases an asset account.

Exhibit 2-7 | Final Form of the Rules of Debit and Credit

ASSETS = LIABILITIES + STOCKHOLDERS' EQUITY

Account	Debit	Credit
Assets	+	−
Liabilities	−	+
Common Stock	−	+
Retained Earnings	−	+
Dividends	+	−
Revenues	−	+
Expenses	+	−

Liabilities and stockholders' equity are the opposite.

- A credit increases a liability or stockholders' equity account.
- A debit decreases a liability or stockholders' equity account.

Dividends and Expense accounts are exceptions to the rule. Dividends and Expenses are equity accounts that are increased by a debit. Dividends and Expense accounts are negative (or *contra*) equity accounts. Revenues and expenses always appear below the other equity accounts, as Exhibit 2-7 shows.

JOURNALIZE TRANSACTIONS AND POST JOURNAL ENTRIES TO THE LEDGER

4 Journalize transactions and post journal entries to the ledger

To record transactions, accountants use a chronological record called a **journal**, which is also known as the *book of original entry*. The journalizing process follows three steps:

1. Specify each account affected by the transaction and classify each account by type (asset, liability, stockholders' equity, revenue, or expense).
2. Determine whether each account is increased or decreased by the transaction. Use the rules of debit and credit to increase or decrease each account.
3. Record the transaction in the journal, including a brief explanation. The debit side is entered on the left margin, and the credit side is indented to the right.

Step 3 is also called "journalizing the transaction." Let's use the steps to journalize Alladin Travel's first transaction.

Step 1 The business receives cash and issues stock. Cash and Common Stock are affected. Cash is an asset, and Common Stock is stockholders' equity.

Step 2 Both Cash and Common Stock increase. Debit the Cash account to record an increase in this asset. Credit the Common Stock account to record an increase in this equity account.

Step 3 Journalize the transaction:

	A	B	C	D	E	F
		JOURNAL				
1	Date	Accounts and Explanation	Debit	Credit		
2	Apr 1	Cash	50,000			
3		Common Stock		50,000		
4		*Issued common stock.*				
5						

When analyzing a transaction, first pinpoint the effects (if any) on Cash. Did Cash increase or decrease? Typically, it is easiest to identify Cash effects. Then identify the effects on the other accounts.

Posting from the Journal to the Ledger

The journal is a chronological record of all company transactions listed by date. But the journal does not indicate how much cash or accounts receivable the business has.

The **ledger** is a grouping of all the T-accounts, with their balances. For example, the balance of the Cash T-account shows how much cash the business has. The balance of Accounts Receivable shows the amount due from customers. Accounts Payable shows how much the business owes suppliers on open account, and so on.

In the phrase "keeping the books," *books* refers to the journals as well as the accounts in the ledger. In most accounting systems, the ledger is computerized. Exhibit 2-8 shows how asset, liability, and stockholders' equity accounts are grouped in the ledger. Revenue and expense accounts also appear in the general ledger, which can contain hundreds or even thousands of accounts.

Exhibit 2-8 | The Ledger (Asset, Liability, and Stockholders' Equity Accounts)

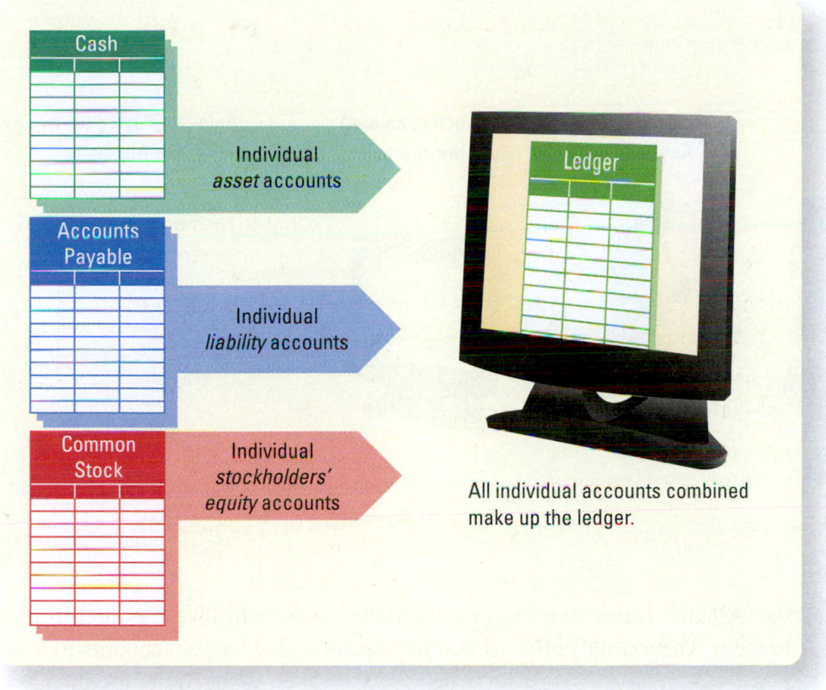

Entering a transaction in the journal does not get the data into the ledger. Data must be copied to the ledger—a process called **posting**. Debits in the journal are always posted as debits in the accounts, and credits are always posted as credits in the accounts. Exhibit 2-9 shows how Alladin's stock issuance transaction is posted to the accounts.

Exhibit 2-9 | Journal Entry and Posting to the Accounts

PANEL A—Journal Entry

A1

	A	B	C
1	**Accounts and Explanation**	**Debit**	**Credit**
2	Cash	50,000	
3	Common Stock		50,000
4	*Issued common stock.*		
5			

PANEL B—Posting to the Accounts

Cash	
50,000	

Common Stock	
	50,000

The Flow of Accounting Data

Exhibit 2-10 summarizes the flow of accounting data from a business transaction to the ledger. Let's look at the journal entries for the same 11 transactions we illustrated earlier for Alladin Travel. Each journal entry posted to the accounts is keyed by transaction number, which allows you to keep track of it.

Exhibit 2-10 | Flow of Accounting Data

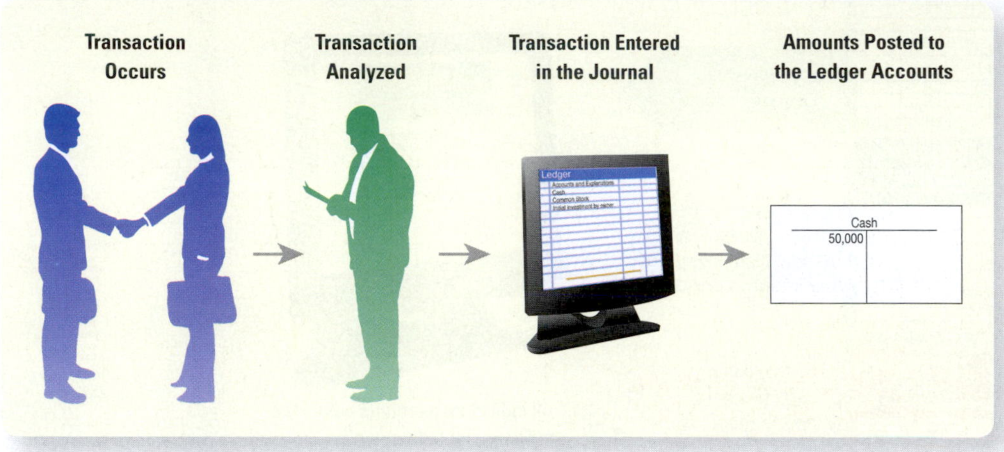

Transaction 1 Analysis. Alladin Travel, Inc., received $50,000 cash from investors and in turn issued common stock to them. The journal entry, accounting equation, and ledger accounts follow:

	A	B	C	D	E
1	Cash	50,000			
2	Common Stock		50,000		
3	*Issued common stock.*				
4					

	Assets	=	Liabilities	+	Stockholders' Equity
Accounting equation	+50,000	=	0	+	50,000

The ledger accounts

Cash	
(1) 50,000	

Common Stock	
	(1) 50,000

Transaction 2 Analysis. The business paid $40,000 cash for land. The purchase decreased cash; therefore, credit Cash. The purchase increased the asset land; to record this increase, debit Land.

	A	B	C	D	E
1	Land	40,000			
2	Cash		40,000		
3	*Paid cash for land.*				
4					

	Assets	=	Liabilities	+	Stockholders' Equity
Accounting equation	+ 40,000	=	0	+	0
	− 40,000				

The ledger accounts

Cash				Land	
(1) 50,000		(2) 40,000		(2) 40,000	

Transaction 3 Analysis. The business purchased supplies for $3,700 on accounts payable. The purchase increased Supplies, an asset, and Accounts Payable, a liability.

A1

	A	B	C	D	E
1	Supplies	3,700			
2	Accounts Payable		3,700		
3	*Purchased office supplies on account.*				
4					

	Assets	=	Liabilities	+	Stockholders' Equity
Accounting equation	+ 3,700	=	+ 3,700	+	0

The ledger accounts

Supplies		Accounts Payable	
(3) 3,700			(3) 3,700

Transaction 4 Analysis. The business performed services for clients and in return received cash of $7,000. The transaction increased cash and service revenue. To record the revenue, credit Service Revenue.

A1

	A	B	C	D	E
1	Cash	7,000			
2	Service Revenue		7,000		
3	*Performed services for cash.*				
4					

	Assets	=	Liabilities	+	Stockholders' Equity	+	Revenues
Accounting equation	+ 7,000	=	0			+	7,000

The ledger accounts

Cash		Service Revenue	
(1) 50,000	(2) 40,000		(4) 7,000
(4) 7,000			

Transaction 5 Analysis. Alladin performed services for other customers on account. These customers did not pay immediately, so Alladin billed them for $3,000. The transaction increased accounts receivable; therefore, debit Accounts Receivable. Service revenue also increased, so credit the Service Revenue account.

	A	B	C	D	E
1	Accounts Receivable	3,000			
2	Service Revenue		3,000		
3	*Performed services on account.*				
4					

	Assets	=	Liabilities	+	Stockholders' Equity	+	Revenues
Accounting equation	+ 3,000	=	0			+	3,000

The ledger accounts

Accounts Receivable			
(5)	3,000		

Service Revenue			
		(4)	7,000
		(5)	3,000

Transaction 6 Analysis. The business paid $2,700 for the following expenses: rent, $1,100; salaries, $1,200; and utilities, $400. Credit Cash for the sum of the expense amounts. The expenses increased, so debit each expense account separately.

	A	B	C	D	E
1	Rent Expense	1,100			
2	Salary Expense	1,200			
3	Utilities Expense	400			
4	Cash		2,700		
5	*Paid expenses.*				
6					

	Assets	=	Liabilities	+	Stockholders' Equity	−	Expenses
Accounting equation	− 2,700	=	0			−	2,700

The ledger accounts

Cash			
(1)	50,000	(2)	40,000
(4)	7,000	(6)	2,700

Rent Expense			
(6)	1,100		

Salary Expense			
(6)	1,200		

Utilities Expense			
(6)	400		

Transaction 7 Analysis. The business paid $1,900 on the account payable created in transaction 3. Credit Cash for the payment. The payment decreased a liability, so debit Accounts Payable.

	A	B	C	D	E
1	Accounts Payable	1,900			
2	Cash		1,900		
3	*Paid cash on account.*				
4					

	Assets	=	Liabilities	+	Stockholders' Equity
Accounting equation	− 1,900	=	− 1,900	+	0

The ledger accounts

Cash

(1)	50,000	(2)	40,000
(4)	7,000	(6)	2,700
		(7)	1,900

Accounts Payable

(7)	1,900	(3)	3,700

Transaction 8 Analysis. Starr Williams, the major stockholder of Alladin Travel, Inc., remodeled her personal residence. This is not a transaction of the business, so the business does not record the transaction.

Transaction 9 Analysis. The business collected $1,000 cash on account from the client in transaction 5. Cash increased, so debit Cash. The asset accounts receivable decreased; therefore, credit Accounts Receivable.

	A	B	C	D	E
1	Cash	1,000			
2	Accounts Receivable		1,000		
3	*Collected cash on account.*				
4					

	Assets	=	Liabilities	+	Stockholders' Equity
Accounting equation	+ 1,000	=	0	+	0
	− 1,000				

The ledger accounts

Cash

(1)	50,000	(2)	40,000
(4)	7,000	(6)	2,700
(9)	1,000	(7)	1,900

Accounts Receivable

(5)	3,000	(9)	1,000

Transaction 10 Analysis. The business sold land for its cost of $22,000, receiving cash for it. The asset cash increased; debit Cash. The asset land decreased; credit Land.

	A	B	C	D	E
1	Cash	22,000			
2	Land		22,000		
3	*Sold land.*				
4					

Accounting equation

Assets	=	Liabilities	+	Stockholders' Equity
+ 22,000	=	0	+	0
− 22,000				

The ledger accounts

Cash

(1)	50,000	(2)	40,000
(4)	7,000	(6)	2,700
(9)	1,000	(7)	1,900
(10)	22,000		

Land

(2)	40,000	(10)	22,000

Transaction 11 Analysis. Alladin Travel declared and paid its stockholders cash dividends of $2,100. Credit Cash for the payment. The transaction also decreased stockholders' equity and requires a debit to an equity account. Therefore, debit Dividends.

A1

	A	B	C	D	E
1	Dividends	2,100			
2	Cash		2,100		
3	*Declared and paid dividends.*				
4					

Accounting equation

Assets	=	Liabilities	+	Stockholders' Equity	−	Dividends
− 2,100	=	0			−	2,100

The ledger accounts

Cash

(1)	50,000	(2)	40,000
(4)	7,000	(6)	2,700
(9)	1,000	(7)	1,900
(10)	22,000	(11)	2,100

Dividends

(11)	2,100		

Accounts After Posting to the Ledger

Exhibit 2-11 shows the accounts after all journal entries have been posted to the ledger. Group the accounts under assets, liabilities, and stockholders' equity.

Exhibit 2-11 | Alladin Travel, Inc.'s, Ledger Accounts After Posting

Assets = Liabilities + Stockholders' Equity

Assets

Cash

(1)	50,000	(2)	40,000
(4)	7,000	(6)	2,700
(9)	1,000	(7)	1,900
(10)	22,000	(11)	2,100
Bal	33,300		

Accounts Receivable

(5)	3,000	(9)	1,000
Bal	2,000		

Supplies

(3)	3,700		
Bal	3,700		

Land

(2)	40,000	(10)	22,000
Bal	18,000		

Liabilities

Accounts Payable

(7)	1,900	(3)	3,700
		Bal	1,800

Stockholders' Equity

Common Stock

		(1)	50,000
		Bal	50,000

Dividends

(11)	2,100		
Bal	2,100		

Revenue

Service Revenue

		(4)	7,000
		(5)	3,000
		Bal	10,000

Expenses

Rent Expense

(6)	1,100		
Bal	1,100		

Salary Expense

(6)	1,200		
Bal	1,200		

Utilities Expense

(6)	400		
Bal	400		

Each account has a balance, denoted as Bal, which is the difference between the account's total debits and its total credits. For example, the Accounts Payable balance of \$1,800 is the difference between the credit (\$3,700) and the debit (\$1,900). Cash has a balance of \$33,300.

A horizontal line separates the journal entry amounts from the account's balance. If an account's debits exceed its total credits, that account has a debit balance, such as you see in the Cash account. If the sum of the credits is greater than the debits, the account has a credit balance, as you see in the Accounts Payable account.

CONSTRUCT A TRIAL BALANCE

5 Construct a trial balance

A **trial balance** lists all accounts with their balances—assets first, and then liabilities and stockholders' equity (including revenue and expense accounts). The trial balance summarizes all the account balances for the financial statements and proves that the total of accounts with debit balances equals the total of accounts with credit balances. A trial balance may be taken at any time, but the most common time is at the end of the period. Exhibit 2-12 is the trial balance of Alladin Travel, Inc., after all transactions have been journalized and posted at the end of April.

Exhibit 2-12 | Trial Balance

	A	B	C	D	E
1	**Alladin Travel, Inc.** **Trial Balance** **April 30, 2018**				
2		**Balance**			
3	**Account Title**	**Debit**	**Credit**		
4	Cash	$33,300			
5	Accounts receivable	2,000			
6	Supplies	3,700			
7	Land	18,000			
8	Accounts payable		$ 1,800		
9	Common stock		50,000		
10	Dividends	2,100			
11	Service revenue		10,000		
12	Rent expense	1,100			
13	Salary expense	1,200			
14	Utilities expense	400			
15	Total	$61,800	$61,800		
16					

The trial balance facilitates the preparation of the financial statements. We can prepare an income statement, statement of retained earnings, and balance sheet from the data shown in a trial balance such as the one in Exhibit 2-12. For Alladin Travel, Inc., the financial statements would appear exactly as shown in Exhibit 2-2 on page 70. However, the financial statements are normally not constructed at this point, because they do not yet contain end-of-period adjustments, which are covered in Chapter 3.

Try It in Excel®

A trial balance can be one of the most simple and useful applications of Excel. Try building Exhibit 2-12 in Excel. Open a new blank worksheet. Format the title (company name, trial balance, and date), and provide column headings (account title, balance, debit, and credit) exactly as shown in Exhibit 2-12. Then on successive lines enter account titles and amounts from the general ledger accounts, being careful to enter amounts in the proper debit or credit columns. Finally, sum both debit and credit columns. The total amounts of debits and credits should be equal.

Analyzing Accounts

You can often tell what a company did by analyzing its accounts. Managers who understand accounting possess powerful tools for analyzing the activity in their company's accounts. For example, if you know the beginning and ending balances of Cash, and if you know total cash receipts, you can compute total cash payments during the period.

In our chapter example, suppose Alladin Travel began May with cash of $1,000. During May, Alladin received cash of $8,000 and ended the month with a cash balance of $3,000. You can compute total cash payments by analyzing Alladin's Cash account:

Cash

			x = beginning balance + cash receipts − ending balance
Beginning balance	1,000		= 1,000 + 8,000 − 3,000
Cash receipts	8,000	Cash payments	x = 6,000
Ending balance	3,000		

Or, if you know Cash's beginning and ending balances and total payments, you can compute cash receipts during the period—for any company!

You can compute either sales on account or cash collections on account by analyzing the Accounts Receivable account. Here we determine collections on account (using assumed amounts).

Accounts Receivable

			x = beginning balance + sales on account − ending balance = 6,000 + 10,000 − 5,000
Beginning balance	6,000		
Sales on account	10,000	Collections on account	x = 11,000
Ending balance	5,000		

Also, you can determine how much you paid on account by analyzing Accounts Payable (using assumed amounts):

Accounts Payable

	x = beginning balance + purchases on account − ending balance = 9,000 + 6,000 − 11,000		
		Beginning balance	9,000
Payments on account	x = 4,000	Purchases on account	6,000
		Ending balance	11,000

Please master this powerful technique. It works for any company and for your personal finances! You will find this tool very helpful when you become a manager.

Correcting Accounting Errors

Accounting errors can occur even in computerized systems. Input data may be wrong, or they may be entered twice or not at all. A debit may be entered as a credit and vice versa. If an account balance is erroneously high, it is said to be *overstated*. If an account balance is erroneously low, it is said to be *understated*. You can detect the reason or reasons behind many out-of-balance conditions by computing the difference between total debits and total credits in the trial balance. Then perform one or more of the following actions:

1. Search the records for a missing account. Trace each account back and forth from the journal to the ledger. A $200 transaction may have been recorded incorrectly in the journal or posted incorrectly to the ledger. Search the journal for a $200 transaction.
2. Divide the out-of-balance amount by 2. A debit treated as a credit, or vice versa, doubles the amount of error. Suppose Alladin Travel, Inc., added $300 to Cash instead of subtracting $300. The out-of-balance amount is $600, and dividing by 2 identifies $300 as the amount of the transaction. Search the journal for the $300 transaction and trace to the account affected.
3. Divide the out-of-balance amount by 9. If the result is an integer (no decimals), the error may be one of the following:
   - a *slide error*—for example, writing $400 as $40. The accounts would be out of balance by $360 ($400 – $40 = $360). Dividing $360 by 9 yields $40. Scan the trial balance in Exhibit 2-12 for an amount similar to $40. Utilities Expense (balance of $400) is the misstated account.
   - a *transposition error*—for example, writing $2,100 as $1,200. The accounts would be out of balance by $900 ($2,100 – $1,200 = $900). Dividing $900 by 9 equals $100. Trace all amounts on the trial balance back to the T-accounts. The Dividends account, which has a balance of $2,100, is the misstated account in this example.

Chart of Accounts

As you know, the ledger contains the accounts grouped under these headings:

1. **Balance sheet accounts: Assets, Liabilities, and Stockholders' Equity**
2. **Income statement accounts: Revenues and Expenses**

Organizations use a **chart of accounts** to list all their accounts and account numbers. Account numbers are usually listed in numerical sequence and have two or more digits. For example, asset account numbers might begin with 1, liabilities with 2, stockholders' equity with 3, revenues with 4, and expenses with 5. The second, third, and higher digits in an account number indicate the position of the individual account within the category. For example, Cash might be account number 101, which is the first asset account. Accounts Payable might be number 201, the first liability. All accounts are numbered using this system.

Organizations with many accounts use lengthy account numbers. For example, Disney's chart of accounts might use 10-digit account numbers. The chart of accounts for Alladin Travel appears in Exhibit 2-13. The gap between account numbers 111 and 141 leaves room to add another category of receivables. For example, if Alladin needed to add Notes Receivable, it could be numbered 121.

Exhibit 2-13 | Chart of Accounts—Alladin Travel, Inc.

Balance Sheet Accounts

Assets		Liabilities		Stockholders' Equity	
101	Cash	201	Accounts Payable	301	Common Stock
111	Accounts Receivable	231	Notes Payable	311	Retained Earnings
141	Supplies			312	Dividends
151	Land				
191	Office Furniture				

Income Statement Accounts (Part of Stockholders' Equity)

Revenues		Expenses	
401	Service Revenue	501	Rent Expense
		502	Salary Expense
		503	Utilities Expense

Appendix B to this book gives two expanded charts of accounts that you will find helpful as you work through this course. The first chart lists the typical accounts that a service corporation, such as Alladin Travel, Inc., would have after a period of growth. The second chart is for a *merchandising* corporation, one that sells a product instead of a service.

The Normal Balance of an Account

An account's *normal balance* falls on the side of the account—debit or credit—where increases are recorded. The normal balance of assets is on the debit side, so assets are *debit-balance accounts*. Conversely, liabilities and stockholders' equity usually have a credit balance, so these are *credit-balance accounts*. Exhibit 2-14 illustrates the normal balances of all the assets, liabilities, and stockholders' equities, including revenues and expenses.

Exhibit 2-14 | Normal Balances of the Accounts

Assets	Debit	
Liabilities		Credit
Stockholders' Equity—overall		Credit
Common stock		Credit
Retained earnings		Credit
Dividends	Debit	
Revenues		Credit
Expenses	Debit	

As you have learned, stockholders' equity usually contains several accounts. Dividends and expenses carry debit balances because they represent decreases in stockholders' equity. In total, the normal balance for total stockholders' equity is a credit balance.

Now apply what you've learned. Study the Decision Guidelines, which summarize the chapter.

Decision Guidelines

HOW TO MEASURE RESULTS OF OPERATIONS AND FINANCIAL POSITION

The managers who operate a business, along with its owners, need to be able to determine whether the venture is profitable. To do this, they need to understand when transactions occur and how and where they should be recorded. Doing so will help ensure the business's financial statements are accurate and provide a good picture of its operational results and financial position. The following guidelines will help:

Decision	Guidelines
Has a transaction occurred?	If the event affects the entity's financial position and can be reliably recorded—Yes If either condition is absent—No
Where should the transaction be recorded?	In the journal, the chronological record of transactions
How should an increase or decrease in the following accounts be recorded?	The rules of debit and credit state:

	Increase	Decrease
Assets	Debit	Credit
Liabilities	Credit	Debit
Stockholders' equity	Credit	Debit
Revenues	Credit	Debit
Expenses	Debit	Credit

Decision	Guidelines
Where should all of the information for each account be stored?	In the ledger, the book of accounts
Where should all of the accounts and their balances be listed?	In the trial balance
Where should the following be reported:	
Results of operations?	In the income statement (Revenues – Expenses = Net income or net loss)
Financial position?	In the balance sheet (Assets = Liabilities + Stockholders' equity)

End-of-Chapter | Summary Problem

The trial balance of Dunn Service Center, Inc., on March 1, 2018, lists the entity's assets, liabilities, and stockholders' equity on that date.

	Balance	
Account Title	**Debit**	**Credit**
Cash	$26,000	
Accounts receivable	4,500	
Accounts payable		$ 2,000
Common stock		10,000
Retained earnings		18,500
Total	$30,500	$30,500

During March, the business completed the following transactions:

a. Borrowed $45,000 from the bank, with Dunn signing a note payable in the name of the business.

b. Paid cash of $40,000 to a real estate company to acquire land.

c. Performed a service for a customer and received cash of $5,000.

d. Purchased supplies on credit, $300.

e. Performed a service for a customer and earned $2,600 of revenue on account.

f. Paid $1,200 on account.

g. Paid the following cash expenses: salaries, $3,000; rent, $1,500; and interest, $400.

h. Received $3,100 on account.

i. Received a $200 utility bill that will be paid next week.

j. Declared and paid a dividend of $1,800.

Requirements

1. Use the T-account format to create the following accounts and balances:
   - Assets—Cash, $26,000; Accounts Receivable, $4,500; Supplies, no balance; Land, no balance
   - Liabilities—Accounts Payable, $2,000; Note Payable, no balance
   - Stockholders' Equity—Common Stock, $10,000; Retained Earnings, $18,500; Dividends, no balance
   - Revenues—Service Revenue, no balance
   - Expenses—(none have balances) Salary Expense, Rent Expense, Interest Expense, Utilities Expense
2. Journalize the preceding transactions. Key the journal entries by transaction letter.
3. Post the transactions from the journal to the ledger and compute the balance in each account after all the transactions have been posted.
4. Prepare the trial balance of Dunn Service Center, Inc., at March 31, 2018.
5. To determine the net income or net loss of the company during the month of March, prepare a single-step income statement for the month ended March 31, 2018. List the expenses in order from the largest to the smallest.

Answers

Requirement 1

Assets = Liabilities + Stockholders' Equity

Assets

Cash	
Bal 26,000	

Accounts Receivable	
Bal 4,500	

Supplies	

Land	

Liabilities

Accounts Payable	
	Bal 2,000

Note Payable	

Stockholders' Equity

Common Stock	
	Bal 10,000

Retained Earnings	
	Bal 18,500

Dividends	

Revenue

Service Revenue	

Expenses

Salary Expense	

Rent Expense	

Interest Expense	

Utilities Expense	

Requirement 2

Accounts and Explanation	Debit	Credit
a. Cash	45,000	
Note Payable		45,000
Borrowed cash on note payable.		
b. Land	40,000	
Cash		40,000
Purchased land for cash.		
c. Cash	5,000	
Service Revenue		5,000
Performed service and received cash.		
d. Supplies	300	
Accounts Payable		300
Purchased supplies on account.		
e. Accounts Receivable	2,600	
Service Revenue		2,600
Performed service on account.		
f. Accounts Payable	1,200	
Cash		1,200
Paid on account.		
g. Salary Expense	3,000	
Rent Expense	1,500	
Interest Expense	400	
Cash		4,900
Paid cash expenses.		
h. Cash	3,100	
Accounts Receivable		3,100
Received cash on account.		
i. Utilities Expense	200	
Accounts Payable		200
Received utility bill to be paid later.		
j. Dividends	1,800	
Cash		1,800
Declared and paid dividends.		

Requirement 3

Assets = Liabilities + Stockholders' Equity

Assets

Cash

Bal	26,000	(b)	40,000
(a)	45,000	(f)	1,200
(c)	5,000	(g)	4,900
(h)	3,100	(j)	1,800
Bal	31,200		

Accounts Receivable

Bal	4,500	(h)	3,100
(e)	2,600		
Bal	4,000		

Supplies

(d)	300		
Bal	300		

Land

(b)	40,000		
Bal	40,000		

Liabilities

Accounts Payable

(f)	1,200	Bal	2,000
		(d)	300
		(i)	200
		Bal	1,300

Note Payable

		(a)	45,000
		Bal	45,000

Stockholders' Equity

Common Stock

		Bal	10,000

Retained Earnings

		Bal	18,500

Dividends

(j)	1,800		
Bal	1,800		

Revenue

Service Revenue

		(c)	5,000
		(e)	2,600
		Bal	7,600

Expenses

Salary Expense

(g)	3,000		
Bal	3,000		

Rent Expense

(g)	1,500		
Bal	1,500		

Interest Expense

(g)	400		
Bal	400		

Utilities Expense

(i)	200		
Bal	200		

Requirement 4

	A	B	C	D	E
1	**Dunn Service Center, Inc.** **Trial Balance** **March 31, 2018**				
2		**Balance**			
3	**Account Title**	**Debit**	**Credit**		
4	Cash	$ 31,200			
5	Accounts receivable	4,000			
6	Supplies	300			
7	Land	40,000			
8	Accounts payable		$ 1,300		
9	Notes payable		45,000		
10	Common stock		10,000		
11	Retained earnings		18,500		
12	Dividends	1,800			
13	Service revenue		7,600		
14	Salary expense	3,000			
15	Rent expense	1,500			
16	Interest expense	400			
17	Utilities expense	200			
18	Total	$ 82,400	$ 82,400		
19					

Requirement 5

A1

	A	B	C	D	E
1	**Dunn Service Center, Inc.** **Income Statement** **Month Ended March 31, 2018**				
2	**Revenues**				
3	Service revenue		$ 7,600		
4					
5	**Expenses**				
6	Salary expense	$ 3,000			
7	Rent expense	1,500			
8	Interest expense	400			
9	Utilities expense	200			
10	Total expenses		5,100		
11	Net income		$ 2,500		
12					

REVIEW | Transaction Analysis

Accounting Vocabulary

account (p. 61) The record of the changes that have occurred in a particular asset, liability, or stockholders' equity during a period. The basic summary device of accounting.

accrued liability (p. 62) A liability for an expense that has not yet been paid by a business.

cash (p. 61) Money and any medium of exchange that a bank accepts at face value.

chart of accounts (p. 86) A list of a company's accounts and their account numbers.

credit (p. 73) The right side of an account.

debit (p. 73) The left side of an account.

journal (p. 76) The chronological accounting record of an entity's transactions.

ledger (p. 76) The book of accounts and their balances.

posting (p. 77) The process of copying amounts from the journal to the ledger.

transaction (p. 61) Any event that has a financial impact on the business and can be measured reliably.

trial balance (p. 83) A list of all the ledger accounts with their balances.

Quick Check (Answers are given on page 119.)

1. All of the following events at a sandwich shop are transactions *except*

a. A customer purchases a sandwich.
b. A delivery of coffee beans purchased on account from the local roaster is received.
c. A representative from the local university contacts the manager of the shop to get a list of catering services.
d. The accountant for the sandwich shop pays the electric bill.

2. Identify the asset from the following list of accounts:

a. Notes Payable
b. Common Stock
c. Retained Earnings
d. Inventory

3. Amounts owed to a company by its customers would be:
 a. Accounts Receivable.
 b. Accounts Payable.
 c. Inventory.
 d. Prepaid Expenses.

4. Thorpe Corporation purchases a new delivery truck and signs a note payable at the truck dealership for the total cost. The impact of this transaction on Thorpe Corporation
 a. increases assets and decreases stockholders' equity.
 b. decreases assets and increases liabilities.
 c. increases assets and increases liabilities.
 d. increases assets and increases stockholders' equity.

5. Adam Corporation issues stock to Cara Riley in exchange for $24,000 cash. The impact on Adam Corporation's assets from this transaction
 a. increases assets.
 b. decreases assets.
 c. does not have any impact on assets.
 d. Not enough information is provided to determine the impact on assets.

6. Blake Company completed a consulting job and billed the customer $5,000. The impact on Blake Company from this transaction
 a. increases assets and increases liabilities.
 b. increases liabilities and decreases stockholders' equity.
 c. decreases liabilities and increases stockholders' equity.
 d. increases assets and increases stockholders' equity.

7. Accounts Receivable will appear on which of the following financial statements?
 a. Income statement
 b. Statement of retained earnings
 c. Balance sheet
 d. Statement of cash flows

8. Accounts Payable had a normal beginning balance of $1,200. During the period, there were debit postings of $200 and credit postings of $800. What was the ending balance?
 a. $600 credit
 b. $1,800 debit
 c. $1,800 credit
 d. $600 debit

9. Which of the following debit and credit rules is correct?
 a. Increases in assets and liabilities are debited.
 b. Increases in liabilities and stockholders' equity are debited.
 c. Decreases in assets and liabilities are credited.
 d. Increases in liabilities and stockholders' equity are credited.

10. A company's beginning Cash balance was $8,000. At the end of the period, the balance was $6,000. If total cash paid out during the period was $28,000, the amount of cash receipts was
 a. $34,000.
 b. $30,000.
 c. $26,000.
 d. $36,000.

11. An attorney performs services of $1,100 for a client and receives $400 cash, with the remainder on account. The journal entry for this transaction would
 a. debit Cash, credit Service Revenue.
 b. debit Cash, credit Accounts Receivable, credit Service Revenue.
 c. debit Cash, debit Service Revenue, credit Accounts Receivable.
 d. debit Cash, debit Accounts Receivable, credit Service Revenue.

12. A doctor purchases medical supplies of $640 and pays $290 cash with the remainder on account. The journal entry for this transaction would be which of the following?
   a. *Debit* Supplies
   Credit Accounts Payable
   Credit Cash
   b. *Debit* Supplies
   Debit Accounts Payable
   Credit Cash
   c. *Debit* Supplies
   Credit Accounts Receivable
   Credit Cash
   d. *Debit* Supplies
   Debit Accounts Receivable
   Credit Cash

13. A credit entry to an account will
   a. increase assets.
   b. increase liabilities.
   c. increase expenses.
   d. decrease revenues.

14. In a double-entry accounting system,
   a. a debit entry is recorded on the left side of a T-account.
   b. half of all the accounts have a normal credit balance.
   c. liabilities, stockholders' equity, and revenue accounts all have normal debit balances.
   d. both a and b are correct.

15. Which is the correct sequence for recording transactions and preparing financial statements?
   a. Journal, ledger, trial balance, financial statements
   b. Ledger, journal, trial balance, financial statements
   c. Ledger, trial balance, journal, financial statements
   d. Financial statements, trial balance, ledger, journal

16. The following accounts have normal debit balances:
   a. Assets
   b. Liabilities
   c. Revenues
   d. All of the listed accounts have a normal debit balance.

Excel Project
Autograded Excel Project available in **MyLab Accounting**.

ASSESS YOUR PROGRESS

Ethics Check

EC2-1. Identify ethical principle violated

For each of the situations listed, identify which of three principles (integrity, objectivity and independence, or due care) from the AICPA Code of Professional Conduct is violated. Assume all persons listed in the situations are members of the AICPA. (Note: Refer to the AICPA Code of Professional Conduct contained on pages 25–27 in Chapter 1 for descriptions of the principles.)

   a. Jackie recently received a promotion and is required to do more complex journal entries than in her previous position. Since Jackie is embarrassed that she does not know how to do the journal entries, she does not attend a training session at her company. She figures that she can figure it out on her own; after all, the company promoted her.

b. Tim is in charge of entering accounts receivable journal entries. Tim is notorious for transposing the numbers in his journal entries, so his supervisor requires him to review his work at the end of each day. Tim is annoyed by this policy and leaves work without reviewing his journal entries.

c. Troy, the managing partner of a CPA firm, received two tickets to the upcoming Alabama versus Ohio State football game from an accounting software vendor. The CPA firm is currently conducting an audit of that accounting software vendor. These football tickets sell for over $500 each.

d. Paige sets up a fake supplier account and then creates false invoices and bills her company for work done by this fictitious supplier. Once the check is cut for the fake supplier, Paige deposits it in her own bank account.

Short Exercises

LO 1

S2-1. ***(Learning Objective 1: Identify transactions)*** For each of the following items, indicate whether that item would be considered to be a transaction at Gerbig Pet Grooming Corporation.

a. A customer, Layne Gracen, gives Gerbig a check for $620 to prepay for her dog's grooming appointments for the upcoming year.
b. Gerbig pays $310 for last month's electric bill.
c. Gerbig selects a new supplier for its shampoos and conditioners.
d. The controller for Gerbig pays the bill for a catered lunch at its annual training event for employees.
e. Gerbig files its articles of incorporation with the state.
f. Gerbig acquires a new stainless steel tub by signing a note payable with PetStar, a supplier of pet grooming supplies and products.
g. Maggie Cramer, a customer, signs a contract for next year's dog grooming with Gerbig.
h. Gerbig pays its employees an annual bonus on December 31.

LO 1

S2-2. ***(Learning Objective 1: Differentiate between different types of accounts)*** For each of the following accounts, identify whether that item is an asset, liability, or equity account.

a. Bonds payable
b. Equipment
c. Accounts payable
d. Salaries payable
e. Common stock
f. Retained earnings
g. Cash
h. Accounts receivable
i. Sales revenue
j. Inventory

LO 1

S2-3. ***(Learning Objective 1: Differentiate between different types of accounts)*** Dan Crater opened a software consulting firm that immediately paid $28,000 for a computer system. Was Crater's computer system an expense of the business? If not, explain.

LO 2

S2-4. ***(Learning Objective 2: Show the impact of transactions on the accounting equation)*** Dazzle Fashion is a clothing retailer. During August, the company completed a series of transactions. For each of the following items, give an example of a transaction that has the described effect on Dazzle's accounting equation.

a. Increase one asset and decrease another asset.
b. Increase an asset and increase stockholders' equity.
c. Increase an asset and increase a liability.
d. Decrease an asset and decrease stockholders' equity.
e. Decrease an asset and decrease a liability.

S2-5. ***(Learning Objective 2: Show the impact of transactions on the accounting equation)*** Complete the following chart to show the impact on the accounting equation from each transaction.

LO 2

		Assets		Liabilities		Stockholders' equity	
Date	**Description**	**Increase**	**Decrease**	**Increase**	**Decrease**	**Increase**	**Decrease**
Jan 2	Purchased office supplies on account for $500						
Jan 4	Issued common stock for cash for $5,000						
Jan 10	Performed services on account for $2,000						
Jan 15	Paid amount owed to vendor for the office supplies purchased on account on January 2						
Jan 18	Performed services for cash $200						
Jan 21	Received cash for payment on account from revenue on January 10						
Jan 31	Paid employees for monthly payroll $1,500						

S2-6. ***(Learning Objective 3: Analyze the impact of business transactions on accounts)*** Ford's Catering began with cash of $8,000. Ford then bought supplies for $2,500 on account. Separately, Ford paid $7,200 for equipment. Answer these questions.

LO 3

a. How much in total assets does Ford have?
b. How much in liabilities does Ford owe?

S2-7. ***(Learning Objective 3: Analyze the impact of business transactions on accounts)*** Fourth Investments, Inc., began by issuing common stock for cash of $200,000. The company immediately purchased computer equipment on account for $56,000.

LO 3

1. Set up the following T-accounts of Fourth Investments, Inc.: Cash, Computer Equipment, Accounts Payable, and Common Stock.
2. Record the first two transactions of the business directly in the T-accounts without using a journal.
3. Show that total debits equal total credits.

LO 3 **S2-8.** ***(Learning Objective 3: Analyze the impact of business transactions on accounts)*** Iris Baer, MD, opened a medical practice. The business completed the following transactions:

July 1	Baer invested $26,000 cash to start her medical practice. The business issued common stock to Baer.
2	Purchased medical supplies on account totaling $8,500.
3	Paid monthly office rent of $5,500.
6	Recorded $8,500 revenue (in cash) for service rendered to patients.

After these transactions, how much cash does the business have to work with? Use a T-account to show your answer.

LO 4 **S2-9.** ***(Learning Objective 4: Journalize transactions)*** After operating for several months, architect Donovan Freeman completed the following transactions during the latter part of July:

Jul 15	Borrowed $64,000 from the bank, signing a note payable.
22	Performed services on account for clients totaling $17,300.
28	Received $16,000 cash on account from clients.
29	Received and paid a utility bill of $1,800.
31	Paid monthly salaries of $10,000 to employees.

Journalize the transactions of Donovan Freeman, Architect. Include an explanation with each journal entry.

LO 4 **S2-10.** ***(Learning Objective 4: Journalize and post transactions)*** Consultant Mary Gervais purchased supplies on account for $4,300. Later Gervais paid $3,450 on account.

1. Journalize the two transactions on the books of Mary Gervais, Consultant. Include an explanation for each transaction.
2. Open a T-account for Accounts Payable and post to Accounts Payable. Compute the balance and denote it as Bal.
3. How much does the business owe after both transactions? In which account does this amount appear?

LO 4 **S2-11.** ***(Learning Objective 4: Journalize and post transactions)*** Orman Consulting performed services for a client who could not pay immediately. Orman expected to collect the $4,600 the following month. A month later, Orman received $2,100 cash from the client.

1. Record the two transactions on the books of Orman Consulting. Include an explanation for each transaction.
2. Post to these T-accounts: Cash, Accounts Receivable, and Service Revenue. Compute each account balance and denote it as Bal.

LO 4 **S2-12.** ***(Learning Objective 4: Journalize transactions)*** Journalize the following transactions. Include dates and a brief explanation for each journal entry.

July 1: Issued common stock for $13,000
July 5: Performed services on account for $8,000
July 9: Purchased office supplies on account for $600
July 10: Performed services for cash of $3,100
July 12: Received payment in full for services performed on account from July 5
July 24: Paid in full for office supplies purchased on July 9
July 25: Received and paid monthly electric bill of $450
July 30: Signed a note payable to purchase office furniture for $2,500
July 31: Paid monthly payroll of $3,100

LO 5

S2-13. ***(Learning Objective 5: Construct a trial balance)*** Assume that Harbor Marine Company reported the following summarized data at December 31, 2018. Accounts appear in no particular order; dollar amounts are in millions.

Other liabilities	$ 2	Revenues	$37
Other assets	20	Cash	4
Expenses	26	Accounts payable	6
Stockholders' equity	5		

Prepare the trial balance of Harbor Marine Company at December 31, 2018. List the accounts in their proper order. How much was the company's net income or net loss?

LO 5

S2-14. ***(Learning Objective 5: Use a trial balance)*** Purpleberry, Inc.'s, trial balance follows:

	A	B	C	D	E
1	**Purpleberry, Inc.** **Trial Balance** **December 31, 2018**				
2		**Balance**			
3	**Account Title**	**Debit**	**Credit**		
4	Cash	$ 4,500			
5	Accounts receivable	28,000			
6	Supplies	5,000			
7	Land	45,000			
8	Equipment	19,000			
9	Accounts payable		$ 39,000		
10	Note payable		22,000		
11	Common stock		12,000		
12	Retained earnings		11,000		
13	Service revenue		56,000		
14	Salary expense	27,000			
15	Rent expense	10,000			
16	Utilities expense	1,500			
17	Total	$ 140,000	$ 140,000		
18					

Calculate these amounts for the business:

1. Total assets
2. Total liabilities
3. Net income or net loss during December

LO 5

S2-15. ***(Learning Objective 5: Use a trial balance)*** Refer to Purpleberry, Inc.'s, trial balance in Short Exercise 2-14. The purpose of this exercise is to help you learn how to correct three common accounting errors.

Error 1. Slide. Suppose the trial balance lists Land as $4,500 instead of $45,000. Recalculate the column totals, take the difference, and divide by 9. The result is an integer (no decimals), which suggests that the error is either a transposition or a slide.

Error 2. Transposition. Assume the trial balance lists Accounts Receivable as $82,000 instead of $28,000. Recalculate the column totals, take the difference, and divide by 9. The result is an integer (no decimals), which suggests that the error is either a transposition or a slide.

Error 3. Mislabeling an item. Assume that Purpleberry, Inc., accidentally listed Accounts Receivable as a credit balance instead of a debit. Recalculate the trial balance totals for debits and credits. Then take the difference between total debits and total credits and divide the difference by 2. You get back to the original amount of Accounts Receivable.

LO 1, 2, 3, 4, 5

S2-16. ***(Learning Objectives 1, 2, 3, 4, 5: Define accounting terms)*** Accounting has its own vocabulary and basic relationships. Match the accounting terms at the left with the corresponding definition or meaning at the right.

______ **1.** Posting	**A.** The cost of operating a business; a decrease in stockholders' equity
______ **2.** Expense	**B.** Always an asset
______ **3.** Debit	**C.** Side of an account where increases are recorded
______ **4.** Trial balance	**D.** Lists a company's accounts and account numbers (no account balances in this item)
______ **5.** Equity	**E.** Copying data from the journal to the ledger
______ **6.** Net income	**F.** Assets – Liabilities
______ **7.** Receivable	**G.** Revenues – Expenses
______ **8.** Chart of accounts	**H.** Lists all accounts with their balances
______ **9.** Payable	**I.** Always a liability
______**10.** Journal	**J.** Record of transactions
______**11.** Normal balance	**K.** Left side of an account
______**12.** Ledger	**L.** The book of accounts and their balances

Exercises MyLab Accounting

Group A

LO 1, 2, 4

E2-17A. ***(Learning Objectives 1, 2, 4: Identify transactions, analyze impact on accounting equation, journalize transactions)*** Cedar Point is an amusement park in Sandusky, Ohio, owned by Cedar Fair Entertainment Company. Over 3.5 million people visit Cedar Point each year between May and October. It covers 364 acres and has more than 150 rides and attractions, including 16 roller coasters. Cedar Point is the second oldest continuously operating amusement park in the United States (the oldest is Lake Compounce in Connecticut.) Millions of events occur at Cedar Point each year. The following items are possible events:

- May 1: Sell admission tickets, $100,000, cash
- May 3: Purchase merchandise inventory, $5,000, on account
- May 6: Rent lockers to guests, $500, cash
- May 8: Sign a letter of intent to switch electric suppliers starting in June
- May 15: Pay employees, $75,000, cash
- May 18: Make an offer of employment for a new position in the Merchandise & Games office
- May 20: Borrow money from bank by signing a six-month note, $200,000

Requirements

1. What criteria does an event have to meet to qualify as a financial transaction? Identify which of the listed events are financial transactions.
2. Journalize each of the transactions.
3. Indicate how the company's assets, liabilities, and equity would be impacted by each transaction.

E2-18A. ***(Learning Objective 3: Analyze the impact of business transactions on accounts)*** Set up the following T-accounts: Cash, Accounts Receivable, Office Supplies, Office Furniture, Accounts Payable, Common Stock, Dividends, Service Revenue, Salary Expense, and Rent Expense. Record the following transactions directly in the T-accounts without using a journal. Use the letters to identify the transactions. Determine the ending balance in each account. LO 3

a. Brian Durham opened a law firm by investing $25,500 cash and office furniture with a fair value of $9,400. Organized as a professional corporation, the business issued common stock to Durham.
b. Paid monthly rent of $1,500.
c. Purchased office supplies on account, $700.
d. Paid employees' salaries of $2,900.
e. Paid $250 of the account payable created in transaction c.
f. Performed legal service on account, $11,000.
g. Declared and paid dividends of $2,000.

E2-19A. ***(Learning Objective 3: Analyze the impact of business transactions on accounts)*** The following selected events were experienced by either Smith Eldercare Services, Inc., a corporation, or Tony Smith, its major stockholder. State whether each event (1) increased, (2) decreased, or (3) had no effect on the total assets of the business. Identify any specific asset affected. LO 3

a. Paid $400 cash on accounts payable.
b. Made a cash purchase of land for a building site for the business, $89,000.
c. Sold land and received cash of $69,000 (the land was carried on the company's books at $69,000).
d. Received $15,400 cash from customers on account.
e. Purchased medical equipment and signed a $90,000 promissory note in payment.
f. Purchased a flat-screen TV for Smith's home.
g. Paid Smith a cash dividend of $4,000.
h. Purchased office supplies on account for $1,200.
i. Borrowed $62,000 from the bank for use in the business.
j. Received $12,000 cash and issued stock to a stockholder.

E2-20A. ***(Learning Objective 2: Show the impact of business transactions on the accounting equation)*** Dr. Helen Samoa opened a medical practice specializing in physical therapy. During the first month of operation (December), the business, titled Dr. Helen Samoa, Professional Corporation (P.C.), experienced the following events: LO 2

Dec	6	Samoa invested $150,000 in the business, which in turn issued its common stock to her.
	9	The business paid cash for land costing $64,000. Samoa plans to build an office building on the land.
	12	The business purchased medical supplies for $2,400 on account.
	15	Dr. Helen Samoa, P.C., officially opened for business.
	15–31	During the rest of the month, Samoa treated patients and earned service revenue of $9,800, receiving cash for half the revenue earned.
	15–31	The business paid cash expenses: employee salaries, $3,600; office rent, $900; utilities, $400.
	31	The business sold medical supplies to another physician for cost of $1,000 and received cash.
	31	The business borrowed $34,000, signing a note payable to the bank.
	31	The business paid $1,300 on account.

Requirements

1. Analyze the effects of these events on the accounting equation of the medical practice of Dr. Helen Samoa, P.C.

2. After completing the analysis, answer these questions about the business.
   a. How much are total assets?
   b. How much does the business expect to collect from patients?
   c. How much does the business owe in total?
   d. How much of the business's assets does Samoa really own?
   e. How much net income or net loss did the business experience during its first month of operations?

LO 4

E2-21A. ***(Learning Objective 4: Journalize transactions in the books)*** Refer to Exercise 2-20A.

Requirement

1. Record the transactions in the journal of Dr. Helen Samoa, P.C. List the transactions by date and give an explanation for each transaction.

LO 4, 5

E2-22A. ***(Learning Objectives 4, 5: Post journal entries and prepare a trial balance)*** Refer to Exercises 2-20A and 2-21A.

Requirements

1. After journalizing the transactions of Exercise 2-20A, post the entries to the ledger, using T-accounts. Key transactions by date. Determine the ending balance in each account.
2. Prepare the trial balance of Dr. Helen Samoa, P.C., at December 31, 2018.
3. From the trial balance, determine total assets, total liabilities, and total stockholders' equity on December 31.

LO 4

E2-23A. ***(Learning Objective 4: Journalize entries and calculate ending balances)*** The first seven transactions of Frontier Advertising, Inc., have been posted to the company's accounts:

Cash

(1)	8,500	(4)	13,000
(2)	9,000	(6)	310
(5)	45	(7)	3,900

Supplies

(3)	800	(5)	45

Land

(4)	38,000		

Equipment

(7)	3,900		

Accounts Payable

(6)	310	(3)	800

Note Payable

		(2)	9,000
		(4)	25,000

Common Stock

		(1)	8,500

Requirement

1. Prepare the journal entries that served as the sources for the seven transactions. Include an explanation for each entry. Determine the ending balance in each account. As Frontier moves into the next period, how much cash does the business have? How much does Frontier owe in total liabilities?

LO 5

E2-24A. ***(Learning Objective 5: Construct and use a trial balance)*** The accounts of Deluxe Patio Service, Inc., follow with their normal balances at April 30, 2018. The accounts are listed in no particular order.

Account	Balance	Account	Balance
Dividends	$ 3,300	Common stock	$ 16,700
Utilities expense	2,100	Accounts payable	4,600
Accounts receivable	5,900	Service revenue	20,700
Delivery expense	300	Equipment	30,600
Retained earnings	6,300	Note payable	21,500
Salary expense	8,300	Cash	19,300

Requirements

1. Prepare the company's trial balance at April 30, 2018, listing accounts in proper sequence, as illustrated in the chapter. For example, Accounts Receivable comes before Equipment. List the expense with the largest balance first, the expense with the next largest balance second, and so on.
2. Prepare the financial statement for the month ended April 30, 2018, which will show the company the results of operations for the month.

LO 5

E2-25A. ***(Learning Objective 5: Correct errors and prepare a trial balance)*** The trial balance of Addison, Inc., at September 30, 2018, does not balance:

Cash	$ 14,100	
Accounts receivable	12,700	
Inventory	16,900	
Supplies	800	
Land	59,000	
Accounts payable		$12,300
Common stock		47,100
Sales revenue		49,700
Salary expense	2,000	
Rent expense	1,000	
Utilities expense	300	
Total	$106,800	$109,100

The accounting records hold the following errors:

a. Recorded a $700 cash revenue transaction by debiting Accounts Receivable. The credit entry was correct.
b. Posted a $1,000 credit to Accounts Payable as $100.
c. Did not record utilities expense or the related account payable in the amount of $400.
d. Understated Common Stock by $200.
e. Omitted Insurance Expense of $3,400 from the trial balance.

Requirement

1. Prepare the corrected trial balance at September 30, 2018, complete with a heading. Journal entries are not required.

LO 5

E2-26A. ***(Learning Objective 5: Solve for cash and construct a trial balance)*** Assume that Old Center Company reported the following summarized data at September 30, 2018. Accounts appear in no particular order; dollar amounts are in millions.

Stockholders' equity, September 30, 2018*	$ 6	Revenues	$ 33
Accounts payable	8	Expenses	21
Other assets	23	Cash	?
Other liabilities	2		

*Stockholders' equity does not include the current period net income.

Requirements

1. Solve for Cash.
2. Prepare the trial balance of Old Center at September 30, 2018. List the accounts in their proper order. How much was Old Center Company's net income or net loss?

Group B

LO **1, 2, 4** E2-27B. ***(Learning Objectives 1, 2, 4: Identify transactions, analyze impact on accounting equation, journalize transactions)*** Cedar Point is an amusement park in Sandusky, Ohio, owned by Cedar Fair Entertainment Company. Over 3.5 million people visit Cedar Point each year between May and October. It covers 364 acres and has more than 150 rides and attractions, including 16 roller coasters. Cedar Point is the second oldest continuously operating amusement park in the United States (the oldest is Lake Compounce in Connecticut). Millions of events occur at Cedar Point each year. The following items are possible events:

- May 1: Sell admission tickets, $150,000, cash
- May 3: Purchase merchandise inventory, $9,000, on account
- May 6: Rent lockers to guests, $700, cash
- May 8: Sign a letter of intent to switch electric suppliers starting in June
- May 15: Pay employees, $92,000, cash
- May 18: Make an offer of employment for a new position in the Merchandise & Games office
- May 20: Borrow money from bank by signing a six-month note, $400,000

Requirements

1. What criteria does an event have to meet to qualify as a financial transaction? Identify which of the listed events are financial transactions.
2. Journalize each of the transactions.
3. Indicate how the company's assets, liabilities, and equity would be impacted by each transaction.

LO **3** E2-28B. ***(Learning Objective 3: Analyze the impact of business transactions on accounts)*** Set up the following T-accounts: Cash, Accounts Receivable, Office Supplies, Office Furniture, Accounts Payable, Common Stock, Dividends, Service Revenue, Salary Expense, and Rent Expense. Record the following transactions directly in the T-accounts without using a journal. Use the letters to identify the transactions. Determine the ending balance in each account.

a. Michael Dover opened a law firm by investing $23,500 cash and office furniture with a fair value of $8,600. Organized as a professional corporation, the business issued common stock to Dover.
b. Paid monthly rent of $1,100.
c. Purchased office supplies on account, $800.
d. Paid employee salaries of $2,800.
e. Paid $200 of the account payable created in transaction c.
f. Performed legal service on account, $10,700.
g. Declared and paid dividends of $2,900.

LO **3** E2-29B. ***(Learning Objective 3: Analyze the impact of business transactions on accounts)*** The following selected events were experienced by either Cardinal Industries, Inc., a corporation, or Larry Cardinal, the major stockholder. State whether each event (1) increased, (2) decreased, or (3) had no effect on the total assets of the business. Identify any specific asset affected.

a. Sold land and received a note receivable of $43,000 (the land was carried on the company's books at $43,000).
b. Purchased equipment for the business for $81,000 cash.
c. Cardinal used personal funds to purchase a pool table for his home.
d. Purchased land for a building site for the business and signed a $98,000 promissory note to the bank.
e. Received $140,000 cash and issued stock to a stockholder.
f. Earned $15,000 in revenue for services performed. The customer promises to pay Cardinal Industries in one month.
g. The business paid Cardinal a cash dividend of $4,500.
h. Paid $12,000 cash on accounts payable.
i. Received $37,000 cash from customers for services performed.
j. Purchased supplies on account for $4,000.

E2-30B. ***(Learning Objective 2: Show the impact of business transactions on the accounting equation)*** Dr. Char Morin opened a medical practice specializing in surgery. During the first month of operation (July), the business, titled Dr. Char Morin, Professional Corporation (P.C.), experienced the following events: LO 2

Jul	6	Morin invested $155,000 in the business, which in turn issued its common stock to her.
	9	The business paid cash for land costing $62,000. Morin plans to build an office building on the land.
	12	The business purchased medical supplies for $1,500 on account.
	15	Dr. Char Morin, P.C., officially opened for business.
	15–31	During the rest of the month, Morin treated patients and earned service revenue of $9,100, receiving cash for half the revenue earned.
	15–31	The business paid cash expenses: employee salaries, $3,300; office rent, $1,400; utilities, $400.
	31	The business sold medical supplies to another physician for cost of $500 and received cash.
	31	The business borrowed $33,000, signing a note payable to the bank.
	31	The business paid $600 on account.

Requirements

1. Analyze the effects of these events on the accounting equation of the medical practice of Dr. Char Morin, P.C.
2. After completing the analysis, answer these questions about the business.
   a. How much are total assets?
   b. How much does the business expect to collect from patients?
   c. How much does the business owe in total?
   d. How much of the business's assets does Morin really own?
   e. How much net income or net loss did the business experience during its first month of operations?

E2-31B. ***(Learning Objective 4: Journalize transactions in the books)*** Refer to Exercise 2-30B. LO 4

Requirement

1. Record the transactions in the journal of Dr. Char Morin, P.C. List the transactions by date and give an explanation for each transaction.

E2-32B. ***(Learning Objectives 4, 5: Post journal entries and prepare a trial balance)*** Refer to Exercises 2-30B and 2-31B. LO 4, 5

Requirements

1. Post the entries to the ledger, using T-accounts. Key transactions by date. Determine the ending balance in each account.
2. Prepare the trial balance of Dr. Char Morin, P.C., at July 31, 2018.
3. From the trial balance, determine total assets, total liabilities, and total stockholders' equity on July 31.

LO 4

E2-33B. ***(Learning Objective 4: Journalize entries and calculate ending balances)*** The first seven transactions of Gallagher Advertising, Inc., have been posted to the company's accounts:

Cash

	Debit		Credit
(1)	8,800	(4)	11,000
(2)	8,500	(6)	290
(5)	90	(7)	4,000

Supplies

	Debit		Credit
(3)	900	(5)	90

Land

	Debit		Credit
(4)	34,000		

Equipment

	Debit		Credit
(7)	4,000		

Accounts Payable

	Debit		Credit
(6)	290	(3)	900

Note Payable

	Debit		Credit
		(2)	8,500
		(4)	23,000

Common Stock

	Debit		Credit
		(1)	8,800

Requirement

1. Prepare the journal entries that served as the sources for the seven transactions. Include an explanation for each entry. Determine the ending balance in each account. As Gallagher moves into the next period, how much cash does the business have? How much does Gallagher owe in total liabilities?

LO 5

E2-34B. ***(Learning Objective 5: Construct and use a trial balance)*** The accounts of Specialty Deck Service, Inc., follow with their normal balances at April 30, 2018. The accounts are listed in no particular order.

Account	Balance	Account	Balance
Dividends	$ 3,100	Common stock	$ 16,200
Utilities expense	2,300	Accounts payable	4,300
Accounts receivable	5,300	Service revenue	20,500
Delivery expense	700	Equipment	30,800
Retained earnings	7,800	Note payable	21,000
Salary expense	8,400	Cash	19,200

Requirements

1. Prepare the company's trial balance at April 30, 2018, listing accounts in proper sequence, as illustrated in the chapter. For example, Accounts Receivable comes before Equipment. List the expense with the largest balance first, the expense with the next largest balance second, and so on.
2. Prepare the financial statement for the month ended April 30, 2018, which will show the company the results of operations for the month.

LO 5

E2-35B. ***(Learning Objective 5: Correct errors and prepare a trial balance)*** The trial balance of St. James, Inc., at September 30, 2018, does not balance.

Cash	$ 14,400	
Accounts receivable	13,300	
Inventory	17,500	
Supplies	300	
Land	55,600	
Accounts payable		$11,500
Common stock		47,900
Service revenue		46,400
Salary expense	1,900	
Rent expense	300	
Utilities expense	1,100	
Total	$104,400	$105,800

The accounting records hold the following errors:

- **a.** Recorded a $400 cash revenue transaction by debiting Accounts Receivable. The credit entry was correct.
- **b.** Posted a $4,000 credit to Accounts Payable as $400.
- **c.** Did not record utilities expense or the related account payable in the amount of $600.
- **d.** Understated Common Stock by $400.
- **e.** Omitted Insurance Expense of $5,400 from the trial balance.

Requirement

1. Prepare the corrected trial balance at September 30, 2018, complete with a heading. Journal entries are not required.

LO 5

E2-36B. ***(Learning Objective 5: Solve for cash and construct a trial balance)*** Assume that All Towne Company reported the following summarized data at September 30, 2018. Accounts appear in no particular order; dollar amounts are in millions.

Stockholders' equity, September 30, 2018*	$ 4	Revenues	$ 33
Accounts payable	5	Expenses	16
Other assets	21	Cash	?
Other liabilities	1		

*Stockholders' equity does not include the current period net income.

Requirements

1. Solve for Cash.
2. Prepare the trial balance of All Towne at September 30, 2018. List the accounts in their proper order. How much was All Towne Company's net income or net loss?

Serial Exercise

Exercise 2-37 begins an accounting cycle that will be completed in Chapter 3.

LO 4, 5

E2-37. ***(Learning Objectives 4, 5: Journalize and post transactions; construct and use a trial balance)*** Olivia Matthews, Certified Public Accountant, operates as a professional corporation (P.C.). The business completed these transactions during the first part of May 2018:

May 2	Received $12,000 cash from Matthews, and issued common stock to her.
2	Paid monthly office rent, $500.
3	Paid cash for a desktop computer, $1,800, with the computer expected to remain in service for five years.
4	Purchased office furniture on account, $6,000, with the furniture projected to last for five years.
5	Purchased supplies on account, $900.
9	Performed tax services for a client and received cash for the full amount of $600.
12	Received bill and paid utility expenses, $750.
18	Performed consulting services for a client on account, $3,100.

Requirements

1. Journalize the transactions for Olivia Matthews, Certified Public Accountant. Explanations are not required.
2. Post to the T-accounts. Key all items by date and determine the ending balance in each account. Denote an account balance on May 18, 2018, as Bal.
3. Prepare a trial balance at May 18, 2018. In the Serial Exercise of Chapter 3, we will add transactions for the remainder of May and will require a trial balance at May 31.

Quiz

Test your understanding of transaction analysis by answering the following questions. Select the best choice from among the possible answers.

Q2-38. Which of the following is an asset?

a. Common Stock
b. Service Revenue
c. Salary Expense
d. None of the listed accounts is an asset.

Q2-39. Which statement is false?

a. Liabilities are decreased by debits.
b. Assets are increased by debits.
c. Revenues are increased by credits.
d. Dividends are increased by credits.

Q2-40. The journal entry to record the acquisition of land and a building by issuing common stock

a. debits Land and credits Common Stock.
b. debits Land and Building and credits Common Stock.
c. debits Land, Building, and Common Stock.
d. debits Common Stock and credits Land and Building.

Q2-41. The journal entry to record the purchase of supplies on account

a. credits Supplies and debits Accounts Payable.
b. debits Supplies Expense and credits Supplies.
c. credits Supplies and debits Cash.
d. debits Supplies and credits Accounts Payable.

Q2-42. If the credit to record the purchase of supplies on account is not posted,

a. liabilities will be understated.
b. assets will be understated.
c. stockholders' equity will be understated.
d. expenses will be overstated.

Q2-43. The journal entry to record a payment on account will

a. debit Accounts Payable and credit Retained Earnings.
b. debit Expenses and credit Cash.
c. debit Cash and credit Expenses.
d. debit Accounts Payable and credit Cash.

Q2-44. If the credit to record the payment of an account payable is not posted,

a. cash will be overstated.
b. liabilities will be understated.
c. expenses will be understated.
d. cash will be understated.

Q2-45. Which statement is false?

a. A trial balance lists all the accounts with their current balances.
b. A trial balance can be taken at any time.
c. A trial balance can verify the equality of debits and credits.
d. A trial balance is the same as a balance sheet.

Q2-46. If a corporation purchases a delivery van for $35,000 cash, the net impact of this transaction will be

a. a decrease in total assets of $35,000.
b. an increase in total assets of $35,000.
c. an increase in both assets and liabilities of $35,000.
d. no impact on total assets.

Q2-47. Girard Unlimited, a new company, completed these transactions.

1. Stockholders invested $55,000 cash and inventory with a fair value of $30,000.
2. Sales on account, $25,000.

What will Girard's total assets equal?

a. $110,000
b. $85,000
c. $55,000
d. $80,000

Q2-48. An investment of cash by stockholders into the business will

a. decrease total assets.
b. increase stockholders' equity.
c. have no effect on total assets.
d. decrease total liabilities.

Q2-49. Purchasing a laptop computer on account will

a. have no effect on stockholders' equity.
b. increase total liabilities.
c. increase total assets.
d. All of the listed choices are correct.

Q2-50. Performing a service on account will

a. increase stockholders' equity.
b. increase total assets.
c. increase total liabilities.
d. accomplish both a and b.

Q2-51. Receiving cash from a customer on account will

a. increase total assets.
b. have no effect on total assets.
c. increase stockholders' equity.
d. decrease liabilities.

Q2-52. Purchasing computer equipment for cash will

a. increase both total assets and total liabilities.
b. decrease both total assets and stockholders' equity.
c. have no effect on total assets, total liabilities, or stockholders' equity.
d. decrease both total liabilities and stockholders' equity.

Q2-53. Purchasing a building for $115,000 by paying cash of $25,000 and signing a note payable for $90,000 will

a. decrease total assets and increase total liabilities by $25,000.
b. increase both total assets and total liabilities by $115,000.
c. decrease both total assets and total liabilities by $25,000.
d. increase both total assets and total liabilities by $90,000.

Q2-54. What is the effect on total assets and stockholders' equity of paying the telephone bill as soon as it is received each month?

Total assets	Stockholders' equity
a. No effect	No effect
b. Decrease	No effect
c. Decrease	Decrease
d. No effect	Decrease

Q2-55. Which of the following transactions will increase an asset and increase a liability?

a. Purchasing office equipment for cash
b. Buying equipment on account
c. Paying an account payable
d. Issuing stock

Q2-56. Which of the following transactions will increase an asset and increase stockholders' equity?

a. Performing a service on account for a customer
b. Borrowing money from a bank
c. Collecting cash from a customer on an account receivable
d. Purchasing supplies on account

Q2-57. Where is a transaction first recorded?

a. Trial balance
b. Account
c. Journal
d. Ledger

Problems MyLab Accounting

Group A

LO 5

P2-58A. ***(Learning Objective 5: Construct and use a trial balance)*** The trial balance of Baker Specialties, Inc., follows:

	A	B	C	D	E
1	**Baker Specialties, Inc.** **Trial Balance** **December 31, 2018**				
2	Cash	$ 13,000			
3	Accounts receivable	49,000			
4	Prepaid expenses	5,000			
5	Building	103,000			
6	Equipment	225,000			
7	Accounts payable		$ 50,400		
8	Note payable		94,000		
9	Common stock		65,000		
10	Retained earnings		174,600		
11	Dividends	20,000			
12	Service revenue		160,000		
13	Rent expense	55,000			
14	Advertising expense	3,000			
15	Wage expense	64,000			
16	Supplies expense	7,000			
17	Total	$ 544,000	$ 544,000		
18					

Veronica Gomez, your best friend, is considering investing in Baker Specialties, Inc. Veronica seeks your advice in interpreting the company's information. Specifically, she asks how to use this trial balance to compute the company's total assets, total liabilities, and net income or net loss for the year.

Requirement

1. Write a short note to answer Veronica's questions. In your note, state the amounts of Baker's total assets, total liabilities, and net income or net loss for the year. Also show how you computed each amount.

LO 2, 3

P2-59A. ***(Learning Objectives 2, 3: Analyze the impact of business transactions on the accounting equation and accounts)*** The following amounts summarize the financial position of Grueser Computing, Inc., on September 30, 2018:

	Assets							=	Liabilities	+	Stockholders' Equity		
	Cash	+	Accounts Receivable	+	Supplies	+	Equipment	=	Accounts Payable	+	Common Stock	+	Retained Earnings
Bal	2,500		3,250				12,200		8,300		6,300		3,350

During October 2018, Grueser Computing completed these transactions:

a. The company received cash of $3,700 and issued common stock.
b. Performed services for a customer and received cash of $6,700.
c. Paid $4,700 on accounts payable.
d. Purchased supplies on account, $800.
e. Collected cash from a customer on account, $1,300.
f. Consulted on the design of a computer system and billed the customer for services rendered, $4,700.
g. Recorded the following business expenses for the month: (1) paid office rent—$1,900; (2) paid advertising—$500.
h. Declared and paid a cash dividend of $3,400.

Requirements

1. Analyze the effects of the preceding transactions on the accounting equation of Grueser Computing, Inc.
2. Prepare the income statement of Grueser Computing, Inc., for the month ended October 31, 2018. List expenses in decreasing order by amount.
3. Prepare the entity's statement of retained earnings for the month ended October 31, 2018.
4. Prepare the balance sheet of Grueser Computing, Inc., at October 31, 2018.

P2-60A. ***(Learning Objective 4: Journalize transactions and calculate account balances)*** This problem can be used in conjunction with Problem 2-59A; see that problem for the relevant data. LO 4

Requirements

1. Journalize the transactions of Grueser Computing, Inc. Explanations are not required.
2. Prepare a T-account for each account. Insert in each T-account its September 30 balance as given (example: Cash $2,500). Then, post the October transactions to the T-accounts.
3. Compute the balance in each account.

P2-61A. ***(Learning Objectives 4, 5: Journalize and post transactions; prepare a trial balance)*** During the first month of operations, Cloutier Services, Inc., completed the following transactions: LO 4, 5

Aug	2	Cloutier Services received $69,000 cash and issued common stock to the stockholders.
	3	Purchased supplies, $500, and equipment, $11,800, on account.
	4	Performed services for a customer and received cash, $5,600.
	7	Paid cash to acquire land, $33,000.
	11	Performed services for a customer and billed the customer, $3,300. Cloutier expects to collect within one month.
	16	Paid for the equipment purchased August 3 on account.
	17	Paid for newspaper advertising, $560.
	18	Received partial payment from customer on account, $1,200.
	22	Received and paid the water and electricity bills, $390.
	29	Received $3,000 cash for servicing the heating unit of a customer.
	31	Paid employee salaries, $2,500.
	31	Declared and paid dividends of $2,000.

Requirements

1. Record each transaction in the journal. Be sure to record the date in each entry. Explanations are not required.
2. Post the transactions to the T-accounts, using transaction dates as posting references. Determine the ending balance in each account.
3. Prepare the trial balance of Cloutier Services, Inc., at August 31 of the current year.
4. Michael Cloutier, the manager, asks you how much in total resources the business has to work with, how much it owes, and whether August was profitable (and by how much).

LO 3, 5

P2-62A. ***(Learning Objectives 3, 5: Analyze the impact of business transactions on accounts and construct a trial balance)*** During the first month of operations (January 2018), Samuels Music Services Corporation completed the following selected transactions:

a. The business received cash of $41,000 and a building with a fair value of $110,000. The corporation issued common stock to the stockholders.
b. Borrowed $61,000 from the bank; signed a note payable.
c. Paid $46,000 for music equipment.
d. Purchased supplies on account, $340.
e. Paid employees' salaries, $6,300.
f. Received $3,700 for music services performed for customers.
g. Performed services for customers on account, $12,800.
h. Paid $200 of the account payable created in transaction d.
i. Received an $800 bill for utilities expense that will be paid in the near future.
j. Received cash on account, $1,500.
k. Paid the following cash expenses: (1) rent, $1,000; (2) advertising, $800.

Requirements

1. Record each transaction directly in the T-accounts without using a journal. Use the letters to identify the transactions. Determine the ending balance in each account.
2. Prepare the trial balance of Samuels Music Services Corporation at January 31, 2018.

Group B

LO 5

P2-63B. ***(Learning Objective 5: Construct and use a trial balance)*** The trial balance of Colby Design, Inc., follows:

	A	B	C	D	E
1	**Colby Design, Inc.** **Trial Balance** **December 31, 2018**				
2	Cash	$ 13,000			
3	Accounts receivable	55,000			
4	Prepaid expenses	6,500			
5	Building	104,000			
6	Equipment	235,000			
7	Accounts payable		$ 50,300		
8	Note payable		94,000		
9	Common stock		50,000		
10	Retained earnings		167,200		
11	Dividends	24,000			
12	Service revenue		200,000		
13	Rent expense	28,000			
14	Advertising expense	6,000			
15	Wage expense	85,000			
16	Supplies expense	5,000			
17	Total	$ 561,500	$ 561,500		
18					

Clara Lancey, your best friend, is considering making an investment in Colby Design, Inc. Clara seeks your advice in interpreting the company's information. Specifically, she asks how to use this trial balance to compute the company's total assets, total liabilities, and net income or net loss for the year.

Requirement

1. Write a short note to answer Clara's questions. In your note, state the amounts of Colby Design's total assets, total liabilities, and net income or net loss for the year. Also show how you computed each amount.

P2-64B. ***(Learning Objectives 2, 3: Analyze the impact of business transactions on the accounting equation and accounts)*** The following amounts summarize the financial position of Davis Computing, Inc., on September 30, 2018:

LO **2, 3**

	Assets							=	Liabilities	+	Stockholders' Equity		
	Cash	+	Accounts Receivable	+	Supplies	+	Equipment	=	Accounts Payable	+	Common Stock	+	Retained Earnings
Bal	2,400		3,450				11,700		7,900		5,500		4,150

During October 2018, Davis Computing completed these transactions:

a. The company received cash of $3,500 and issued common stock.
b. Performed services for a customer and received cash of $6,500.
c. Paid $4,400 on accounts payable.
d. Purchased supplies on account, $1,200.
e. Collected cash from a customer on account, $1,700.
f. Consulted on the design of a computer system and billed the customer for services rendered, $4,700.
g. Recorded the following expenses for the month: (1) paid office rent, $1,800; (2) paid advertising, $550.
h. Declared and paid a cash dividend of $2,700.

Requirements

1. Analyze the effects of the preceding transactions on the accounting equation of Davis Computing, Inc.
2. Prepare the income statement of Davis Computing, Inc., for the month ended October 31, 2018. List expenses in decreasing order by amount.
3. Prepare the statement of retained earnings of Davis Computing, Inc., for the month ended October 31, 2018.
4. Prepare the balance sheet of Davis Computing, Inc., at October 31, 2018.

P2-65B. ***(Learning Objective 4: Journalize transactions and calculate account balances)*** This problem can be used in conjunction with Problem 2-64B; see that problem for the relevant data.

LO **4**

Requirements

1. Journalize the transactions of Davis Computing, Inc. Explanations are not required.
2. Prepare a T-account for each account. Insert in each T-account its September 30 balance as given (example: Cash $2,400). Then, post the October transactions to the T-accounts.
3. Compute the balance in each account.

LO 4, 5

P2-66B. ***(Learning Objectives 4, 5: Journalize and post transactions; prepare a trial balance)*** During the first month of operations, Augusta Services, Inc., completed the following transactions:

Mar	2	Augusta received $68,000 cash and issued common stock to the stockholders.
	3	Purchased supplies, $900, and equipment, $12,000, on account.
	4	Performed services for a customer and received cash, $5,600.
	7	Paid cash to acquire land, $32,000.
	11	Performed services for a customer and billed the customer, $4,700. Augusta expects to collect within one month.
	16	Paid for the equipment purchased March 3 on account.
	17	Paid for newspaper advertising, $540.
	18	Received partial payment from customer on account, $2,600.
	22	Received and paid the water and electricity bills, $370.
	29	Received $3,000 cash for servicing the heating unit of a customer.
	31	Paid employee salaries, $2,500.
	31	Declared and paid dividends of $2,200.

Requirements

1. Record each transaction in the journal. Be sure to record the date in each entry. Explanations are not required.
2. Post the transactions to the T-accounts, using transaction dates as posting references. Determine the ending balance in each account.
3. Prepare the trial balance of Augusta Services, Inc., at March 31 of the current year.
4. Lauren Augusta, the manager, asks you how much in total resources the business has to work with, how much it owes, and whether March was profitable (and by how much).

LO 3, 5

P2-67B. ***(Learning Objectives 3, 5: Analyze the impact of business transactions on accounts and construct a trial balance)*** During the first month of operations (May 2018), Shreve Music Corporation completed the following selected transactions:

- **a.** The business received cash of $46,000 and a building with a fair value of $106,000. The corporation issued common stock to the stockholders.
- **b.** Borrowed $60,000 from the bank; signed a note payable.
- **c.** Paid $47,000 for music equipment.
- **d.** Purchased supplies on account, $530.
- **e.** Paid employees' salaries, $5,700.
- **f.** Received $3,710 for music services performed for customers.
- **g.** Performed services for customers on account, $12,900.
- **h.** Paid $300 of the account payable created in transaction d.
- **i.** Received a $700 bill for utilities expense that will be paid in the near future.
- **j.** Received cash on account, $1,200.
- **k.** Paid the following cash expenses: (1) rent, $1,100; (2) advertising, $800.

Requirements

1. Record each transaction directly in the T-accounts without using a journal. Use the letters to identify the transactions. Determine the ending balance in each account.
2. Prepare the trial balance of Shreve Music Corporation at May 31, 2018.

Challenge Exercises and Problem

LO 5

E2-68. *(Learning Objective 5: Analyzing accounts)* The manager of West Industries Furniture needs to compute the following amounts:

a. Total cash paid during December.
b. Cash collections from credit customers during December. Analyze Accounts Receivable.
c. Cash paid on a note payable during December. Analyze Notes Payable.

Here's the additional data you need to analyze the accounts:

Account	Balance Nov 30	Balance Dec 31	Additional Information for the Month of December
1. Cash	$14,500	$ 7,250	Cash receipts, $99,000
2. Accounts Receivable	29,000	27,000	Sales on account, $49,000
3. Notes Payable	15,500	23,500	New borrowing, $28,000

Requirement

1. Prepare a T-account to compute each amount, *a* through *c*.

LO 3, 5

E2-69. *(Learning Objectives 3, 5: Analyze the impact of business transactions on accounts; construct and use a trial balance)* The trial balance of Jubilee, Inc., at October 31, 2018, does not balance.

Cash	$ 4,100	Common stock	$23,900
Accounts receivable	7,300	Retained earnings	1,200
Land	31,700	Service revenue	9,800
Accounts payable	6,700	Salary expense	2,500
Note payable	5,400	Advertising expense	1,200

Requirements

1. Prepare a trial balance for the ledger accounts of Jubilee, Inc., as of October 31, 2018.
2. Determine the out-of-balance amount. The error lies in the Accounts Receivable account. Add the out-of-balance amount to, or subtract it from, Accounts Receivable to determine the correct balance of Accounts Receivable. After correcting Accounts Receivable, advise the top management of Jubilee, Inc., on the company's
   a. total assets.
   b. total liabilities.
   c. net income or net loss for October.

LO 3

E2-70. *(Learning Objective 3: Analyze the impact of business transactions on accounts)* This question concerns the items and the amounts that two entities, Marion Co. and Ashland Hospital, should report in their financial statements.

During November, Ashland provided Marion with medical exams for Marion employees and sent a bill for $48,000. On December 7, Marion sent a check to Ashland for $33,000. Marion began November with a cash balance of $51,000; Ashland began with cash of $0.

Requirements

1. For this situation, show everything that both Marion and Ashland will report on their November and December income statements and on their balance sheets at November 30 and December 31.
2. After showing what each company should report, briefly explain how the Marion and Ashland data relate to each other.

LO **2, 3, 4**

E2-71. ***(Learning Objectives 2, 3, 4: Analyze the impact of business transactions; analyze the impact of errors and compute correct amounts; journalize and post transactions in the books)*** Backline Advertising creates, plans, and handles advertising campaigns in a three-state area. Recently, Backline had to replace an inexperienced office worker in charge of bookkeeping because of some serious mistakes that had been uncovered in the accounting records. You have been hired to review these transactions to determine any corrections that might be necessary. In all cases, the bookkeeper made an accurate description of the transaction.

A1

	A	B	C	D
1	May 1	Accounts receivable	1,700	
2		Service revenue		1,700
3		*Collected an account receivable.*		
4				
5	2	Rent expense	4,000	
6		Cash		4,000
7		*Paid monthly rent, $400.*		
8				
9	5	Cash	3,400	
10		Accounts receivable		3,400
11		*Collected cash for services provided.*		
12				
13	10	Supplies	4,300	
14		Accounts payable		4,300
15		*Purchased office equipment on account.*		
16				
17	16	Dividends	5,500	
18		Cash		5,500
19		*Paid salaries.*		
20				
21	25	Accounts receivable	3,900	
22		Cash		3,900
23		*Paid for supplies purchased earlier on account.*		
24				

Requirements

1. For each of the preceding entries, indicate the effect of the error on cash, total assets, and net income. The answer for the first transaction has been provided as an example.

Date	Effect on Cash	Effect on Total Assets	Effect on Net Income
May 1	Understated $1,700	Overstated $1,700	Overstated $1,700

2. What is the correct balance of cash if the balance of cash on the books before correcting the preceding transactions was $6,300?
3. What is the correct amount of total assets if the total assets on the books before correcting the preceding transactions was $20,000?
4. What is the correct net income for May if the reported income before correcting the preceding transactions was $9,000?

APPLY YOUR KNOWLEDGE

Serial Case

C2-72 *(Learning Objectives 2, 4: Journalize transactions; analyze their impact on the accounting equation)* LO 2, 4

Note: This mini-case is part of The Cheesecake Factory serial case contained in every chapter in this textbook.

The Cheesecake Factory Incorporated (NASDAQ: CAKE) owns and operates over 200 restaurants, including The Cheesecake Factory, the Grad Lux Cafe, and the RockSugar Pan Asian Kitchen brand restaurants. It also operates two bakery production facilities. Millions of transactions occur at The Cheesecake Factory Incorporated each year. The following items are examples of hypothetical Cheesecake Factory transactions:

February 1: Received $15,000 in daily restaurant sales revenue, cash (ignore cost of sales entry)
February 2: Purchased sugar (inventory), $11,000, on account
February 8: Paid for February advertising in local newspapers, $2,000, cash
February 11: Paid employees, $75,000, cash, for the one-week pay period ending February 10
February 12: Borrowed money from bank by signing a six-month note payable, $80,000
February 15: Received and paid the electricity bill for administrative offices, $1,500
February 19: Paid $11,000 on account for the purchase of sugar on February 2
February 20: Sold Cheesecake Factory gift cards, $1,000, cash
February 27: Paid February rent for restaurant building, $3,500, cash

Requirements

1. What would be the journal entry for each of the listed transactions?
2. For each listed transaction, how would Cheesecake Factory's assets, liabilities, and equity be impacted?

Decision Cases

C2-73. *(Learning Objectives 3, 5: Analyze the impact of transactions on business accounts; construct a trial balance)* A friend named Lance Barton has asked what effect certain transactions will have on his company, Blast Networks, Inc. Time is short, so you cannot apply the detailed procedures of journalizing and posting. Instead, you must analyze the transactions without the use of a journal. Barton will continue the business only if he can expect to earn monthly net income of at least $5,000. The following transactions occurred this month: LO 3, 5

a. Barton deposited $7,000 cash in a business bank account, and the corporation issued common stock to him.
b. Borrowed $6,000 cash from the bank and signed a note payable due within 1 year.
c. Paid $1,300 cash for supplies.
d. Purchased advertising in the local newspaper for cash, $1,800.
e. Purchased office furniture on account, $5,400.
f. Paid the following cash expenses for one month: employee salary—$2,000; office rent—$1,200.
g. Earned revenue on account, $8,000.
h. Earned revenue and received $2,500 cash.
i. Collected cash from customers on account, $1,200.
j. Paid on account, $1,000.

Requirements

1. Set up the following T-accounts: Cash, Accounts Receivable, Supplies, Furniture, Accounts Payable, Notes Payable, Common Stock, Service Revenue, Salary Expense, Advertising Expense, and Rent Expense.

2. Record the transactions directly in the accounts without using a journal. Key each transaction by letter. Determine the ending balance in each account.
3. Construct a trial balance for Blast Networks, Inc., at the current date. List expenses with the largest amount first, the next largest amount second, and so on.
4. Compute the amount of net income or net loss for this first month of operations. Why would you or wouldn't you recommend that Barton continue in business?

LO 3

C2-74. ***(Learning Objective 3: Analyze the impact of transactions on accounts; correct erroneous financial statements; decide whether to expand a business)*** Joe Ferritto opened an Italian restaurant. Business has been good, and Ferritto is considering expanding the restaurant. Ferritto, who knows little accounting, produced the following financial statements for Romano Castle, Inc., at December 31, 2018, the end of the first month of operations:

	A	B	C
1	**Romano Castle, Inc.** **Income Statement** **Month Ended December 31, 2018**		
2	Sales revenue		$ 42,000
3	Common stock		10,000
4	Total revenue		52,000
5			
6	Accounts payable		8,000
7	Advertising expense		5,000
8	Rent expense		6,000
9	Total expenses		19,000
10	Net income		$ 33,000
11			

	A	B	C
1	**Romano Castle, Inc.** **Balance Sheet** **December 31, 2018**		
2	Assets		
3	Cash		$ 12,000
4	Cost of sales (expense)		22,000
5	Food inventory		5,000
6	Furniture		10,000
7	Total Assets		$ 49,000
8	Liabilities		
9	None		
10	Stockholders' Equity		$ 49,000
11			

In these financial statements all *amounts* are correct, except for Stockholders' Equity. Ferritto heard that total assets should equal total liabilities plus stockholders' equity, so he plugged in the amount of stockholders' equity at $49,000 to make the balance sheet come out even.

Requirement

1. Joe Ferritto has asked whether he should expand the restaurant. His banker says Ferritto may be wise to expand if (a) net income for the first month reached $10,000 and (b) total assets are at least $35,000. It appears that the business has reached these milestones, but Ferritto doubts whether the financial statements tell the true story. He needs your help in

making this decision. Prepare a corrected income statement and balance sheet. (Remember that Retained Earnings, which was omitted from the balance sheet, should equal net income for the first month; there were no dividends.) After preparing the statements, give Joe Ferritto your recommendation as to whether he should expand the restaurant.

Ethical Issues

C2-75. Shabby Fitch is the president and principal stockholder of Shabby's Bar & Grill, Inc. To expand, the business is applying for a $350,000 bank loan. To get the loan, Fitch is considering two options for beefing up the stockholders' equity of the business:

Option 1. Issue $200,000 of common stock for cash. A friend has wanted to invest in the company. This may be the right time to extend the offer.

Option 2. Transfer $200,000 of Fitch's personal land to the business, and issue common stock to Fitch. Then, after obtaining the loan, Fitch can transfer the land back to himself, and the balance in the common stock account will then equal $0.

Requirements

Use the ethical decision model in Chapter 1 to answer the following questions:

1. What is the ethical issue?
2. Who are the stakeholders? What are the possible consequences to each?
3. Analyze the alternatives from the following standpoints: (a) economic, (b) legal, and (c) ethical.
4. What would you do? How would you justify your decision? How would your decision make you feel afterward?

C2-76. Part a. You have received your grade in your first accounting course, and to your amazement, it is an A. You feel the instructor must have made a big mistake. Your grade was a B going into the final, but you are sure that you really "bombed" the exam, which is worth 30% of the final grade. In fact, you walked out after finishing only 50% of the exam, and the grade report says you made 99% on the exam!

Requirements

1. What is the ethical issue?
2. Who are the stakeholders? What are the possible consequences to each?
3. Analyze the alternatives from the following standpoints: (a) economic, (b) legal, and (c) ethical.
4. What would you do? How would you justify your decision? How would it make you feel afterward?

Part b. Now assume the same facts that were just provided, except that you have received your final grade for the course and the grade is a B. You are confident that you "aced" the final. In fact, you stayed to the very end of the period and checked every figure twice! You are confident that the instructor must have made a mistake grading the final.

Requirements

1. What is the ethical issue?
2. Who are the stakeholders and what are the consequences to each?
3. Analyze the alternatives from the following standpoints: (a) economic, (b) legal, and (c) ethical.
4. What would you do? How would you justify your decision? How would it make you feel?

Part c. How is this situation like a financial accounting misstatement? How is it different?

Focus on Financials | Apple Inc.

LO 4, 5 *(Learning Objectives 4, 5: Record transactions; compute net income)* Refer to **Apple Inc.**'s financial statements in Appendix A and online in the filings section of **www.sec.gov**. Assume that Apple completed the following selected transactions during 2016:

a. Made company sales (revenue) of $215,639 million, all on account (debit Accounts Receivable, net; credit Net Sales).
b. Collected cash on accounts receivable, $216,734 million.
c. Purchased inventories on account, $131,159 million (credit Accounts Payable).
d. Incurred cost of sales in the amount of $131,376 million. Debit the Cost of Sales (expense) account. Credit the Inventories account.
e. Paid accounts payable in cash, $129,355 million.
f. Paid operating expenses in cash, $24,239 million.
g. Received cash from Other Income/(Expense), net, $1,348 million.
h. Paid income taxes, $15,685 million in cash (debit Provision for Income Taxes).
i. Paid cash for other non-current assets, $3,335 million.
j. Paid cash of $4,539 million for purchase of Property, Plant, and Equipment, net.

Requirements

1. Set up T-accounts for beginning balances of Cash ($0* balance); Accounts Receivable, net (debit balance of $16,849 million); Inventories (debit balance of $2,349 million); Property, Plant, and Equipment, net (debit balance of $22,471 million); Other Non-Current Assets (debit balance of $5,422 million); Accounts Payable (credit balance of $35,490 million); Net Sales ($0 balance); Cost of Sales ($0 balance); Operating Expenses ($0 balance); Other Income/(Expense), net ($0 balance); Provision for Income Taxes ($0 balance).
2. Journalize Apple's transactions a–j. Explanations are not required.
3. Post to the T-accounts, and compute the balance for each account. Key postings by transaction letters a–j.
4. For each of the following accounts, compare your computed balance to Apple's actual balance as shown on its 2016 Consolidated Statement of Operations or Consolidated Balance Sheet in Appendix A at the end of the book. Your amounts should agree with the actual figures.
   a. Accounts Receivable, net
   b. Inventories
   c. Property, Plant, and Equipment, net (assume no other activity in these assets than given in the problem)
   d. Other Non-Current Assets
   e. Accounts Payable
   f. Net Sales
   g. Cost of Sales
   h. Operating Expenses
   i. Other Income/(Expense), net
   j. Provision for Income Taxes
5. Use the relevant accounts from requirement 4 to prepare a summary, single-step income statement for Apple for 2016. Compare the net income (loss) you computed to Apple's actual net income (loss). The two amounts should be equal.

Focus on Analysis | Under Armour, Inc.

LO 5 *(Learning Objective 5: Analyze financial statements)* Retrieve the 2016 Under Armour financial statements at **www.sec.gov** by clicking on Filings and then searching for "Under Armour" under Company Filings. When you see the list of filings for the company, select the Form 10-K for 2016. Be sure to retrieve the 2016 financial statements, not another year.

Suppose you are an investor considering buying Under Armour, Inc.'s, common stock. Answer the following questions. Show amounts in millions.

---

*To keep this exercise at an appropriate level of difficulty, we are using a hypothetical beginning balance of zero for Cash.

Requirements

1. Which was larger for Under Armour during 2016: (1) net revenues or (2) cash collected from customers? Why? Show computation. Assume all revenues are on credit.
2. Investors are vitally interested in a company's sales and profits and its trends of sales (net revenues) and profits over time. Consider Under Armour's net revenues and net income (net loss) during the period from 2014 through 2016. Compute the percentage increase or decrease in net revenues and also in net income (net loss) from 2014 to 2016. Which item grew faster during this two-year period—net revenues or net income (net loss)? Can you offer a possible explanation for these changes?

Group Projects

Project 1. You are promoting a concert in your area. Your purpose is to earn a profit. Assume you organize as a corporation.

Requirements

1. Make a detailed list of 10 factors you must consider as you establish the business.
2. Describe 10 things your business must do to promote and stage the concert.
3. Identify the transactions that your business can undertake to organize, promote, and stage the concert. Journalize the transactions, and post to the relevant T-accounts. Set up the accounts you need for your business ledger.
4. Prepare the income statement, statement of retained earnings, and balance sheet immediately after the concert—that is, before you have had time to pay all the business bills and to collect all receivables.
5. Assume that you will continue to promote concerts if the venture is successful. If it is unsuccessful, you will terminate the business within three months after the concert. Discuss how to evaluate the success of your venture and how to decide whether to continue in business.

Project 2. Contact a local business and arrange with the owner to learn what accounts the business uses.

Requirements

1. Obtain a copy of the business's chart of accounts.
2. Prepare the company's financial statements for the most recent month, quarter, or year. You may use either made-up account balances or balances supplied by the owner.

If the business has a large number of accounts within a category, combine the related accounts and report a single amount on the financial statements. For example, the company may have several cash accounts. Combine all cash amounts and report a single Cash amount on the balance sheet.

You will probably encounter numerous accounts that you have not yet learned. Deal with these as best you can. The charts of accounts given in Appendix B at the end of the book could be helpful.

Quick Check Answers

1. *c*
2. *d*
3. *a*
4. *c*
5. *a*
6. *d*
7. *c*
8. *c ($1,200 credit balance − $200 debits + $800 credits = $1,800 credit balance)*
9. *d*
10. *c* ($8,000 + x − $28,000 = $6,000; x = $26,000)
11. *d*
12. *a*
13. *b*
14. *a*
15. *a*
16. *a*

Try It Solutions

Page 63:

1. Increases in stockholders' equity: Sale of stock and net income (revenues greater than expenses).
2. Decreases in stockholders' equity: Dividends and net loss (expenses greater than revenues).

3 Accrual Accounting and Income

LEARNING OBJECTIVES

1. **Explain** how accrual accounting differs from cash-basis accounting
2. **Apply** the revenue and expense recognition principles
3. **Adjust** the accounts
4. **Construct** the financial statements
5. **Close** the books
6. **Analyze** and evaluate a company's debt-paying ability

SPOTLIGHT

September Is Busy at Walt Disney World Headquarters

The Walt Disney Company has chosen September as the last month in its fiscal year, so when September rolls around, things start to heat up at the company's world headquarters in Burbank, California. There's lots of work to be done. The millions of transactions reflecting the huge company's worldwide operations for the year will be compiled over the next 50 to 60 days and processed into the company's financial statements. The statements are included in the company's annual report (form 10-K) submitted to the Securities and Exchange Commission (SEC), during the last two weeks of November. Certain accounts must be adjusted in the financial statements to bring them up to date as of the last day of the last full week in September. The goal is to clearly and transparently reflect the company's financial position and operating results in accordance with U.S. Generally Accepted Accounting Principles (GAAP). Disney must also close its books for the year. ●

Dimitry Bobroff/Alamy Stock Photo

This chapter completes our examination of the accounting cycle and covers adjusting entries, constructing financial statements, and closing a company's books. It also covers three key calculations based on this information that you need to understand in order to determine whether a company's debt-paying ability is weak or strong. The following figure shows the final steps in the accounting cycle.

The Accounting Cycle (End of Year)

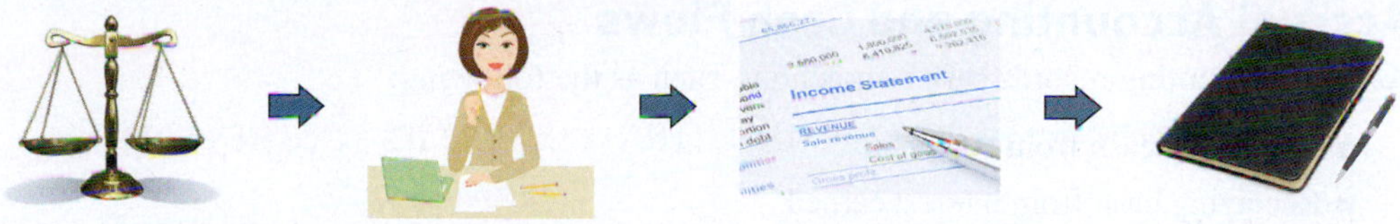

(from Chapter 2) Unadjusted trial balance → Adjust the accounts → Construct the financial statements → Close the books

Images: Michelangelus/Shutterstock; Neyro2008/123RF; Casper1774 Studio/Shutterstock; Billion Photos/Shutterstock

EXPLAIN HOW ACCRUAL ACCOUNTING DIFFERS FROM CASH-BASIS ACCOUNTING

1 Explain how accrual accounting differs from cash-basis accounting

Accrual accounting records the impact of a business transaction as it occurs. When the business performs a service, makes a sale, or incurs an expense, the accountant records the transaction, even if the business receives or pays no cash.

Cash-basis accounting records only cash transactions—cash receipts and cash payments. Cash receipts are treated as revenues, and cash payments are handled as expenses.

Generally Accepted Accounting Principles (GAAP) Require Accrual Accounting. Under accrual accounting, a business records revenues as they are earned and expenses as they are incurred—not necessarily when cash changes hands. Suppose you sell inventory that cost you $500, for $800 on account and then collect the $800 from the customer 30 days later. The sale and the subsequent cash collection are actually two separate transactions. Which transaction increases your wealth—making an $800 sale on account, or collecting the $800 cash 30 days later? Making the sale increases your wealth by $300 because you gave up inventory that cost you $500 and you got a receivable worth $800. Collecting cash later merely swaps your $800 receivable for $800 cash—no wealth is created by this transaction. Making the sale—not collecting the cash—increases your wealth.

People using cash-basis financial statements are making decisions based on incomplete information, which can lead to mistakes. For example, suppose your business makes a sale on account. The cash basis method does not record the sale because you received no cash. You may be thinking, "Let's wait until we collect cash and then record the sale. After all, we pay the bills with cash, so let's ignore transactions that don't affect cash."

What's wrong with this argument? There are two problems with the cash method. One occurs on the balance sheet and the other occurs on the income statement.

Incomplete Balance Sheet. If we fail to record a sale on account, the balance sheet reports no account receivable. Why is this so bad? The receivable represents a claim to receive cash in the future, which is an asset, and it should appear on the balance sheet. Without this information, assets are understated on the balance sheet.

Incomplete Income Statement. A sale on account provides revenue that increases the company's wealth. Ignoring the sale understates a company's revenue and net income on its income statement.

The take-away lessons from this discussion are as follows:

- Companies that use the cash basis of accounting do not follow U.S. GAAP. Their financial statements omit important information.
- Although accrual accounting is more complex, it is a more faithful representation of a company's financial picture than cash-basis accounting. Consequently, all but the smallest businesses use accrual accounting.

Accrual Accounting and Cash Flows

CASH FLOW

Accrual accounting records cash transactions, such as the following:

- Collecting cash from customers
- Receiving cash from interest earned
- Paying salaries, rent, and other expenses
- Borrowing money
- Paying off loans
- Issuing stock

But accrual accounting also records *noncash* transactions, such as the following:

- Sales on account
- Purchases of inventory on account
- Accrual of expenses incurred but not yet paid
- Depreciation expense
- Usage of prepaid rent, insurance, and supplies
- Earning of revenue when cash was collected in advance

Accrual accounting is based on the framework of concepts and principles that we discussed in Chapter 1 (Exhibit 1-3), as well as the time-period concept, the revenue principle, and the expense recognition principle, which we will discuss next.

The Time-Period Concept

The only way for a business to know for certain how well it performed is to shut down, sell its assets, pay its liabilities, and return any leftover cash to the owners. This process, called liquidation, means going out of business. Ongoing companies can't wait until they go out of business to measure their income. Instead, they need regular progress reports. Accountants, therefore, prepare financial statements for specific periods. The **time-period concept** ensures that accounting information is reported at regular intervals.

The basic accounting period is one year, and virtually all businesses prepare annual financial statements. Approximately 60% of large companies—including **Amazon.com, eBay**, and **Under Armour, Inc**.—use the calendar year from January 1 through December 31.

A *fiscal* year may end on a date other than December 31. Most retailers, including **Walmart, The Gap**, and **J.C. Penney**, use a fiscal year that ends on or near January 31 because the low point in their business activity falls in January, after Christmas. The Walt Disney Company uses a 52-week fiscal year that ends on the last day of the last full week in September.

Companies also prepare financial statements for interim periods of less than a year, such as a month, a quarter (three months), or a semiannual period (six months). However, most of the discussions in this text are based on an annual accounting period.

APPLY THE REVENUE AND EXPENSE RECOGNITION PRINCIPLES

2 Apply the revenue and expense recognition principles

The Revenue Principle

The **revenue principle** deals with two issues:

1. When to record (recognize) revenue
2. What amount of revenue to record

When should you record (or recognize) revenue? After it has been earned—and not before. In most cases, revenue is earned when a business has delivered goods to, or has performed a service for, a customer for an amount the business expects to receive in exchange for those goods or services.

Exhibit 3-1 provides guidance on when to record revenue for The Walt Disney Company. Suppose a person walks up to a ticket kiosk outside the Magic Kingdom and inserts a credit card to purchase a 1-day park pass. The transaction creates a contract that both parties are obligated to fulfill. Disney recognizes revenue when the ticket is dispensed, satisfying its contractual obligation and entitling it to collect cash. The customer receives the 1-day pass in exchange for the admission price, satisfying the customer's contractual obligation.

Exhibit 3-1 | When to Record Revenue

Helen Sessions/Alamy Stock Photo

By contrast, suppose a plumbing company (a service-type business) signs a contract to perform plumbing services for a building at Disney World. The value of the services is $50,000. In signing the contract, the plumbing company becomes obligated to complete the plumbing services by a certain date. Revenue may not be recognized until the plumbing company has substantially completed its obligation and has finished performing the services for the company.

The *amount* of revenue to record is the amount of cash or its equivalent that is transferred, or will be transferred, from the customer to the seller. For example, suppose The Disney Store runs a promotion and sells character dolls that regularly sell for $20 for the discount price of $15. How much revenue should The Disney Store record when a customer buys a doll? The answer is $15—the current fair (cash) value of the transaction. The amount of the sale, $15, is the amount of revenue earned—not the regular price of $20.

GLOBAL VIEW

Determining when and how to recognize revenue can be tricky, depending on the type of business. This text deals mostly with the retail industry, where businesses enter into relatively simple and straightforward contracts to purchase and sell largely finished goods and render services. In other industries, such as computer software development, long-term construction, motion pictures, natural resources, and real estate, contracts can be more complex, making the issue of how and when to recognize revenue more complicated.

Fortunately, the FASB (Financial Accounting Standards Board) and the IASB (International Accounting Standards Board) have issued a joint standard that provides a simple, globally consistent way to recognize revenue. The standard is based on the idea that all business transactions involve contracts that exchange goods or services for cash or claims to receive cash. The selling entity must do the following: (1) identify the contract with the customer, (2) identify the separate performance obligations in the contract, (3) determine the transaction price, (4) allocate the transaction price to the separate performance obligations in the contract, and (5) recognize revenue when (or as) the entity satisfies the performance obligation.

The Expense Recognition Principle

The **expense recognition principle** is the basis for recording expenses. Expenses are the costs of assets used up and of liabilities created in earning revenue. Expenses have no future benefit to the company. The expense recognition principle includes two steps:

1. Identify all the expenses incurred during the accounting period.
2. Measure the expenses and recognize them in the same period in which any related revenues are earned.

To *recognize* expenses along with related revenues means to subtract expenses from related revenues to compute a company's net income or net loss. Exhibit 3-2 illustrates the expense recognition principle. The expense recognition principle is also referred to as the *matching principle* because a company is essentially matching the period's expenses with the revenues the expenses generated during the period.

Exhibit 3-2 | The Expense Recognition Principle

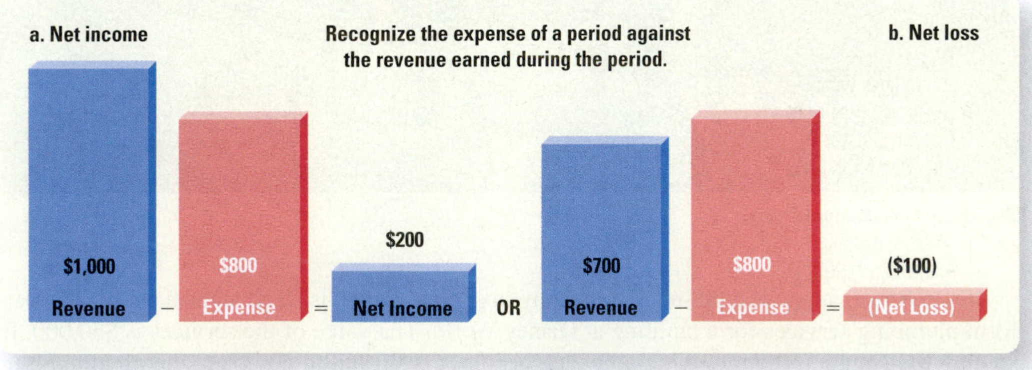

Some expenses are paid in cash. Other expenses arise from using up an asset such as supplies. Still other expenses occur when a company creates a liability. For example, The Walt Disney Company's salary expense occurs when employees work for the company. However, the company might not pay the expense right away. Instead, Disney might record the expense as a liability to be paid later, perhaps in two weeks. Either way, the company has incurred the expense. The critical event for recording it is the employees' working for the company, not the payment of cash to them.

TRY IT

(Answers are given on p. 200.)

(1) On March 15, a customer pays $3,133 for ten 4-day passes to Disney World for a vacation that will take place June 1–4. Did Disney earn the revenue on March 15?

(2) On July 1, The Walt Disney Company prepays $60,000 in rent for a Disney Store building for the next six months. Did Disney incur the expense on July 1? If not, when will the company recognize rent expense?

ADJUST THE ACCOUNTS

3 **Adjust** the accounts

At the end of the period, the business reports its financial statements. This process begins with the trial balance introduced in Chapter 2. We refer to this trial balance as "unadjusted" because many of the accounts are not yet ready for the financial statements. They must be brought up to date by recognizing certain revenues and expenses that have not yet been recognized. This process is known as "adjusting the accounts."

Which Accounts Need to Be Updated (Adjusted)?

Exhibit 3-3 shows the unadjusted trial balance of Alladin Travel, Inc., at June 30, 2018. Assume that Alladin wishes to prepare its financial statements as of the end of June.

Exhibit 3-3 Unadjusted Trial Balance

	A	B	C	D	E
1	**Alladin Travel, Inc. Unadjusted Trial Balance June 30, 2018**	**Debit**	**Credit**		
2	Cash	$36,800			
3	Accounts receivable	2,200			
4	Supplies	700			
5	Prepaid rent	3,000			
6	Land	18,000			
7	Equipment	24,000			
8	Accounts payable		$13,100		
9	Unearned service revenue		400		
10	Common stock		50,000		
11	Retained earnings		18,800		
12	Dividends	3,200			
13	Service revenue		7,000		
14	Salary expense	900			
15	Utilities expense	500			
16	Total	$89,300	$89,300		
17					

This trial balance reflects the same accounts as those in Chapter 2 (see Exhibit 2-12), except for some additional accounts. Exhibit 3-3 also reflects two additional months of transaction activity—May and June, 2018. Cash, Land, Equipment, Accounts Payable, Common Stock, and Dividends are up to date and need no adjustment at the end of the period. Why? Because the day-to-day transactions provide all the data needed for these accounts.

Accounts Receivable, Supplies, Prepaid Rent, and the other accounts are another story. These accounts are not yet up to date on June 30. Why? Because certain transactions have not yet been recorded. Consider Supplies. During June, Alladin Travel used cleaning supplies to clean its office building. But Alladin didn't make a journal entry for the supplies used every time it used them. That would waste time and money. Instead, Alladin waits until the end of the month and then records the supplies used up during the entire month.

The cost of supplies used up is an expense. An adjusting entry at the end of June updates both Supplies (an asset) and Supplies Expense. We must adjust all accounts whose balances are not yet up to date.

Categories of Adjusting Entries

Accounting adjustments fall into three basic categories: deferrals, depreciation, and accruals.

Deferrals. A **deferral** is an adjustment for the payment of an item or receipt of cash in advance. The Walt Disney Company purchases supplies for use in its operations. During the period, some supplies (assets) are used up and become expenses. At the end of the period, an adjustment is needed to decrease the Supplies account for the supplies used up. The amount of supplies used up goes into the Supplies Expense account. Prepaid Rent, Prepaid Insurance, and all other prepaid expenses require deferral adjustments.

There are also deferral adjustments for liabilities. The Walt Disney Company collects cash for park admissions several months in advance of earning the revenue. The collection results in a liability for Disney to provide future park admission to the customer. The liability is called Unearned (or deferred) Services Revenue. Then, each time the customers with paid admission tickets actually visit the park, the company earns Service Revenue as those tickets are scanned at the park entrance. This earning process requires an adjustment at the end of the period. The adjustment decreases the liability and increases the company's services revenue. The Walt Disney Company also collects royalties in advance for the use of its film and media products and earns that revenue later as those products are used by its customers. Consequently, Disney must make an adjusting entry at the end of the period, as those revenues are earned later.

Depreciation. **Depreciation** allocates the cost of a plant asset to expense over the asset's useful life. Depreciation is the most common long-term deferral. The Walt Disney Company buys buildings and equipment. As the company uses the assets, it records depreciation for wear and tear and obsolescence. The accounting adjustment increases Depreciation Expense and decreases the asset's book value over its life. The process is identical to a deferral-type adjustment; the only difference is the type of asset involved.

Accruals. An **accrual** is the opposite of a deferral. For an accrued *expense*, The Walt Disney Company records the expense before paying cash. For an accrued *revenue*, Disney records the revenue before collecting cash.

Salary Expense can create an accrual adjustment. As employees work for The Walt Disney Company, the company's salary expense accrues with the passage of time. At October 1, 2016, The Walt Disney Company owed employees some salaries to be paid after year-end. At October 1, The Walt Disney Company recorded Salary Expense and Salary Payable for the amount owed. Other examples of expense accruals include interest expense and income tax expense.

An accrued revenue is a revenue that the business has earned and will collect next year. At year-end, The Walt Disney Company must accrue the revenue. The adjustment debits a receivable and credits a revenue. For example, accrual of interest revenue debits Interest Receivable and credits Interest Revenue.

Let's see how the adjusting process works for Alladin Travel, Inc., at June 30. We start with prepaid expenses.

Prepaid Expenses

A **prepaid expense** is an expense paid in advance. Therefore, prepaid expenses are assets because they provide a future benefit for the owner. Let's make the adjustments for prepaid rent and supplies.

Prepaid Rent. Prepaying rent creates an asset for the renter, who can then use the rented item in the future. Suppose Alladin Travel prepays three months' store rent ($3,000) on June 1. The entry for the prepayment of three months' rent debits Prepaid Rent as follows:

	A	B	C	D	E	F
1	Jun 1	Prepaid Rent ($1,000 × 3)	3,000			
2		Cash		3,000		
3		*Paid three months' rent in advance.*				
4						

The accounting equation shows that one asset (Prepaid Rent) increases and another (Cash) decreases. Total assets are unchanged:

Assets	=	Liabilities	+	Stockholders' Equity
3,000	=	0	+	0
− 3,000				

After posting, the Prepaid Rent account appears as follows:

Prepaid Rent			
Jun 1	3,000		

Throughout June, the Prepaid Rent account carries the $3,000 beginning balance, as shown in Exhibit 3-3. The adjustment transfers $1,000 from Prepaid Rent to Rent Expense as follows:[1]

Adjusting entry a

	A	B	C	D	E	F
1	Jun 30	Rent Expense ($3,000 × 1/3)	1,000			
2		Prepaid Rent		1,000		
3		*To record rent expense.*				
4						

Both assets and stockholders' equity decrease.

Assets	=	Liabilities	+	Stockholders' Equity	−	Expenses
− 1,000	=	0				− 1,000

After posting, Prepaid Rent and Rent Expense appear as follows (with the adjustment highlighted):

Prepaid Rent					Rent Expense			
Jun 1	3,000	Jun 30	1,000	→	Jun 30	1,000		
Bal	2,000				Bal	1,000		

This adjusting entry illustrates application of the expense recognition principle. We record an expense when incurred in order to measure net income.

[1] See Exhibit 3-8 (p. 136) for a summary of adjustments a–g.

Supplies. Supplies are another type of prepaid expense. On June 2, Alladin Travel paid cash of $700 for cleaning supplies:

	A	B	C	D	E	F
1	Jun 2	Supplies	700			
2		Cash		700		
3		*Paid cash for supplies.*				
4						

Assets	=	Liabilities	+	Stockholders' Equity
700	=	0	+	0
− 700				

The cost of the supplies Alladin Travel used is Supplies Expense. To measure June's supplies expense, the business counts the supplies on hand at the end of the month. The count shows that $400 of supplies remain. Subtracting the $400 of supplies on hand from the supplies available ($700) measures the supplies expense for the month ($300):

Asset Available During the Period	−	Asset on Hand at the End of the Period	=	Asset Used (Expense) During the Period
$700	−	$400	=	$300

The June 30 adjusting entry debits the expense and credits the asset:

Adjusting entry b

	A	B	C	D	E	F
1	Jun 30	Supplies Expense ($700 − $400)	300			
2		Supplies		300		
3		*To record supplies expense.*				
4						

Assets	=	Liabilities	+	Stockholders' Equity	−	Expenses
− 300	=	0				− 300

After posting, the Supplies and Supplies Expense accounts appear as follows. The adjustment is highlighted for emphasis.

Supplies

Jun 2	700	Jun 30	300
Bal	400		

Supplies Expense

Jun 30	300		
Bal	300		

At the start of July, Supplies has a $400 balance, and the adjustment process is repeated each month.

TRY IT

(Answers are given on p. 200.)

At the beginning of the month, supplies were $5,000. During the month, $7,000 of supplies were purchased. At month's end, $3,000 of supplies are still on hand. What is the

- adjusting entry?
- ending balance in the Supplies account?

Depreciation of Plant Assets

Plant assets are long-lived tangible assets, such as land, buildings, furniture, and equipment. All plant assets except land decline in terms of their usefulness. This decline is an expense. Accountants spread the cost of each plant asset, except land, over its useful life. Depreciation is the process of allocating the cost of a long-term plant asset to expense.

Suppose that on June 3 Alladin Travel purchases equipment on account for $24,000:

	A	B	C	D	E	F
1	Jun 3	Equipment	24,000			
2		Accounts Payable		24,000		
3		*Purchased equipment on account.*				
4						

Assets	=	Liabilities	+	Stockholders' Equity
24,000	=	24,000	+	0

After posting, the Equipment account appears as follows:

Equipment		
Jun 3	24,000	

Alladin Travel records an asset when it purchases machinery and equipment. Then, as the asset is used, a portion of the asset's cost is transferred to Depreciation Expense. The machinery and equipment are being used to produce revenue. The cost of the machinery and equipment should be allocated (matched) against that revenue. This is another illustration of the expense recognition principle. Computerized accounting systems automatically enter the deprecation for each period.

Alladin Travel's equipment will remain useful for five years and then be worthless. One way to compute the amount of depreciation for each year is to divide the cost of the asset ($24,000 in our example) by its expected useful life (five years). This procedure—which is called the straight-line depreciation method—results in annual depreciation of $4,800. The depreciation amount is an estimate. (Chapter 7 covers plant assets and depreciation in more detail.)

Annual depreciation = $24,000/5 years = $4,800 per year

Depreciation for June is $400.

Monthly depreciation = $4,800/12 months = $400 per month

The Accumulated Depreciation Account. Alladin Travel's depreciation expense for June is recorded as follows:

Adjusting entry c

	A	B	C	D	E	F
1	Jun 30	Depreciation Expense—Equipment	400			
2		Accumulated Depreciation—Equipment		400		
3		*To record depreciation.*				
4						

Total assets decrease by the amount of the expense:

Assets	=	Liabilities	+	Stockholders' Equity	−	Expenses
− 400	=	0				− 400

The Accumulated Depreciation—Equipment account (not Equipment) is credited to preserve the original cost of the asset in the Equipment account. Managers can then refer to the Equipment account if they ever need to know how much the asset cost.

The **Accumulated Depreciation** account shows the sum of all depreciation expense from using the asset. Therefore, the balance in the Accumulated Depreciation account increases over the asset's life.

Accumulated Depreciation is a contra asset account—an asset account with a normal credit balance. A **contra account** has two distinguishing characteristics:

1. It always has a companion account.
2. Its normal balance is opposite that of the companion account.

In this case, Accumulated Depreciation—Equipment is the contra account to Equipment, so it appears directly after Equipment on the balance sheet. A business carries an accumulated depreciation account for each depreciable asset it owns. Accumulated Depreciation—Building and Accumulated Depreciation—Equipment are examples of this type of account.

After posting, the plant asset accounts of Alladin Travel are as follows—with the adjustment highlighted:

Equipment

Jun 3	24,000	
Bal	24,000	

Accumulated Depreciation—Equipment

		Jun 30	400
		Bal	400

Depreciation Expense—Equipment

Jun 30	400	
Bal	400	

Book Value. The net amount of a plant asset (cost minus accumulated depreciation) is called that asset's **book value**, or *carrying value.* Exhibit 3-4 shows how Alladin Travel would report the book value of its land and equipment at June 30.

Exhibit 3-4 | Plant Assets on the Balance Sheet of Alladin Travel

	A	B	C	D	E
1	**Alladin Travel, Inc.** **Plant Assets at June 30**				
2	Land		$18,000		
3	Equipment	$24,000			
4	Less: Accumulated Depreciation	(400)	23,600		
5					
6	Book value of plant assets		$41,600		
7					

At June 30, the book value of equipment is $23,600.

TRY IT

(Answers are given on p. 200.)

What will be the book value of Alladin's equipment at the end of July?

Exhibit 3-5 shows how The Walt Disney Company reports its parks, resorts, and other property, net, in its October 1, 2016, annual report. Line 8 shows the amount of accumulated depreciation, and line 11 shows the assets' book value ($27,349 million and $25,179 million at the end of the current and prior periods, respectively).

Exhibit 3-5 | The Walt Disney Corporation's Reporting of Parks, Resorts, and Other Property, Net (Adapted, in millions)

	A	B	C	D	E
1	**The Walt Disney Company** **Parks, Resorts and Other Property** **(Note 13 of 2016 Annual Report)**				
2	Adapted in millions of $	**October 1, 2016**	**October 3, 2015**		
3	Attractions, buildings, and improvements	$ 27,930	$ 21,556		
4	Leasehold improvements	830	769		
5	Furniture, fixtures and equipment	16,912	16,068		
6	Land improvements	4,598	4,352		
7		50,270	42,745		
8	Accumulated depreciation	(26,849)	(24,844)		
9	Projects in progress	2,684	6,028		
10	Land	1,244	1,250		
11	Parks, resorts and other property, net	$ 27,349	$ 25,179		
12					

Accrued Expenses

Businesses may incur expenses before they pay cash. The term **accrued expense** refers to a liability that arises from an expense that has been incurred but has not yet been paid. As we have explained, salary expense accrues as employees work before they are paid. Another example is interest expense on a note payable. Interest accrues as the clock ticks before the payment date.

Companies don't record accrued expenses daily or weekly. Instead, they wait until the end of the period and use an adjusting entry to update each expense (and related liability) for the financial statements. Let's look at salary expense.

Most companies pay their employees at set times. Suppose Alladin Travel, Inc., pays its employee a monthly salary of $1,800, half on the 15th and half on the last day of the month. The following calendar for June has the paydays circled:

June

Sun.	Mon.	Tue.	Wed.	Thur.	Fri.	Sat.
						1
2	3	4	5	6	7	8
9	10	11	12	13	14	(15)
16	17	18	19	20	21	22
23	24	25	26	27	28	29
(30)						

Assume that if a payday falls on a Sunday, Alladin Travel pays the employee on the following Monday. During June, Alladin Travel paid its employee the first half-month salary of $900 and made the following entry:

	A	B	C	D	E	F
1	Jun 15	Salary Expense	900			
2		Cash		900		
3		*To pay salary.*				
4						

Assets	=	Liabilities	+	Stockholders' Equity	−	Expenses
−900	=	0				−900

After posting, the Salary Expense account appears as follows:

Salary Expense		
Jun 15	900	

The trial balance at June 30 (Exhibit 3-3, p. 125) includes Salary Expense with its debit balance of $900. Because June 30, the second payday of the month, falls on a Sunday, the second half-month amount of $900 will be paid on Monday, July 1. At June 30, therefore, Alladin Travel adjusts for the additional salary expense and salary payable of $900:

Adjusting entry d

	A	B	C	D	E	F
1	Jun 30	Salary Expense	900			
2		Salary Payable		900		
3		*To accrue salary expense.*				
4						

An accrued expense increases liabilities and decreases stockholders' equity:

Assets	=	Liabilities	+	Stockholders' Equity	−	Expenses
0	=	900				− 900

After posting, the Salary Payable and Salary Expense accounts appear as follows (adjustment highlighted):

Salary Payable

		Jun 30	900
		Bal	900

Salary Expense

Jun 15	900		
Jun 30	900		
Bal	1,800		

The accounts now hold all of June's salary information. Salary Expense has a full month's salary, and Salary Payable shows the amount owed at June 30. All accrued expenses are recorded this way—debit the expense and credit the liability.

Accrued Revenues

Businesses often earn revenue before they receive the cash. Revenue that has been earned but not yet collected is called an **accrued revenue.**

Assume that on June 15 a luxury resort hotel agrees to pay Alladin Travel a commission of $600 for booking 100 clients into its hotel over the next 30 days. Alladin books 50 clients into the resort in June and 50 customers in July. During June, Alladin Travel will earn half a month's fee, $300, for work done June 15 through June 30. On June 30, Alladin makes the following adjusting entry:

Adjusting entry e

	A	B	C	D	E	F
1	Jun 30	Accounts Receivable ($600 × 1/2)	300			
2		Service Revenue		300		
3		*To accrue service revenue.*				
4						

Revenue increases both total assets and stockholders' equity:

Assets	=	Liabilities	+	Stockholders' Equity	+	Revenues
300	=	0				+ 300

Recall that Accounts Receivable has an unadjusted balance of $2,200, and Service Revenue's unadjusted balance is $7,000 (Exhibit 3-3, p. 125). This June 30 adjusting entry has the following effects (adjustment highlighted):

Accounts Receivable

	2,200		
Jun 30	300		
Bal	2,500		

Service Revenue

			7,000
		Jun 30	300
		Bal	7,300

All accrued revenues are accounted for similarly—debit a receivable and credit a revenue.

TRY IT

(Answers are given on p. 200.)

Suppose Alladin Travel, Inc., holds a note receivable as an investment. At the end of June, $100 of interest revenue has been earned. Journalize the accrued revenue adjustment at June 30.

Unearned Revenues

As discussed earlier, some businesses collect cash from customers before earning the revenue. This creates a liability called **unearned revenue**. Only when the job is completed does the business earn the revenue. Suppose the Disney World Resort in Orlando, Florida, contracts with a large group of travel agencies, including Alladin Travel, paying them commissions in advance to book clients in Disney resort hotels. Assume Disney World Resort pays Alladin Travel $400 monthly, beginning immediately, if it books up to eight clients into the resort within a 30-day period. If Alladin Travel collects the first amount on June 15, then it records this transaction as follows:

A1

	A	B	C	D	E	F
1	Jun 15	Cash	400			
2		Unearned Service Revenue		400		
3		*Received cash for revenue in advance.*				
4						

Assets	=	Liabilities	+	Stockholders' Equity
400	=	400	+	0

After posting, the liability account appears as follows:

Unearned Service Revenue	
	Jun 15 400

Unearned Service Revenue is a liability because Alladin Travel is obligated to perform services (i.e., book clients) for Disney World Resort. The June 30 unadjusted trial balance (Exhibit 3-3, p. 125) lists Unearned Service Revenue with a $400 credit balance. During the last 15 days of the month, Alladin Travel books four clients into Disney World Resort and earns one-half of the $400, or $200. On June 30, Alladin Travel, Inc., makes the following adjustment:

Adjusting entry f

A1

	A	B	C	D	E	F
1	Jun 30	Unearned Service Revenue ($400 × 1/2)	200			
2		Service Revenue		200		
3		*To record unearned service revenue that has been earned.*				
4						
5						

Assets	=	Liabilities	+	Stockholders' Equity	+	Revenues
0	=	−200				+200

This adjusting entry shifts $200 of the total amount received ($400) from liability to revenue. After posting, Unearned Service Revenue is reduced to $200, and Service Revenue is increased by $200, as follows (adjustment highlighted):

Unearned Service Revenue

Jun 30	200	Jun 15	400
		Bal	200

Service Revenue

			7,000
		Jun 30	300
		Jun 30	200
		Bal	7,500

All revenues collected in advance are accounted for this way. An unearned revenue is a liability, not a revenue.

One company's prepaid expense is the other company's unearned revenue. For example, Disney World Resort's prepaid expense is Alladin Travel's liability for unearned revenue.

Exhibit 3-6 outlines the timing of prepaids and accruals. Study prepaid expenses all the way across. Then study unearned revenues across, and so on.

Exhibit 3-6 Prepaid and Accrual Adjustments

PREPAIDS—Cash First

	First			Later		
Prepaid expenses	*Pay cash and record an asset:*			*Record an expense and decrease the asset:*		
	Prepaid Expense......	XXX		Expense............................	XXX	
	Cash..............		XXX	Prepaid Expense........		XXX
Unearned revenues	*Receive cash and record unearned revenue:*			*Record revenue and decrease unearned revenue:*		
	Cash.......................	XXX		Unearned Revenue	XXX	
	Unearned Revenue		XXX	Revenue		XXX

ACCRUALS—Cash Later

	First			Later		
Accrued expenses	*Accrue expense and a payable:*			*Pay cash and decrease the payable:*		
	Expense..................	XXX		Payable.............................	XXX	
	Payable..........		XXX	Cash..........................		XXX
Accrued revenues	*Accrue revenue and a receivable:*			*Receive cash and decrease the receivable:*		
	Receivable..............	XXX		Cash.................................	XXX	
	Revenue		XXX	Receivable.................		XXX

Summary of the Adjusting Process

Two purposes of the adjusting process are to

- measure income, and
- update the balance sheet.

Therefore, every adjusting entry affects both of the following:

- Revenue or expense—to measure income
- Asset or liability—to update the balance sheet

Exhibit 3-7 summarizes the standard adjustments.

Exhibit 3-7 | Summary of Adjusting Entries

	Type of Account	
Category of Adjusting Entry	Debit	Credit
Prepaid expense..................	Expense	Asset
Depreciation........................	Expense	Contra asset
Accrued expense.................	Expense	Liability
Accrued revenue..................	Asset	Revenue
Unearned revenue...............	Liability	Revenue

Exhibit 3-8 summarizes the adjustments of Alladin Travel, Inc., at June 30—the adjusting entries we've examined over the past few pages.

- Panel A repeats the data for each adjustment.
- Panel B shows the adjusting entries.
- Panel C shows the accounts after posting the adjusting entries. The adjustments are keyed by letter.

Exhibit 3-8 | The Adjusting Process of Alladin Travel, Inc.

PANEL A—Information for Adjustments at June 30, 2018	PANEL B—Adjusting Entries		
(a) Prepaid rent expired, $1,000.	(a) Rent Expense	1,000	
	Prepaid Rent		1,000
	To record rent expense.		
(b) Supplies used, $300.	(b) Supplies Expense....................................	300	
	Supplies...		300
	To record supplies used.		
(c) Depreciation on equipment, $400.	(c) Depreciation Expense—Equipment	400	
	Accumulated Depreciation—Equipment		400
	To record depreciation.		
(d) Accrued salary expense, $900.	(d) Salary Expense	900	
	Salary Payable....................................		900
	To accrue salary expense.		
(e) Accrued service revenue, $300.	(e) Accounts Receivable................................	300	
	Service Revenue..................................		300
	To accrue service revenue.		
(f) Amount of unearned service revenue that has been earned, $200.	(f) Unearned Service Revenue........................	200	
	Service Revenue..................................		200
	To record unearned revenue that has been earned.		
(g) Accrued income tax expense, $600.	(g) Income Tax Expense	600	
	Income Tax Payable............................		600
	To accrue income tax expense.		

PANEL C—Ledger Accounts

Assets

Cash

Bal 36,800	

Accounts Receivable

2,200	
(e) 300	
Bal 2,500	

Supplies

700	(b) 300
Bal 400	

Prepaid Rent

3,000	(a) 1,000
Bal 2,000	

Land

Bal 18,000	

Equipment

Bal 24,000	

Accumulated Depreciation—Equipment

	(c) 400
	Bal 400

Liabilities

Accounts Payable

	Bal 13,100

Salary Payable

	(d) 900
	Bal 900

Unearned Service Revenue

(f) 200	400
	Bal 200

Income Tax Payable

	(g) 600
	Bal 600

Stockholders' Equity

Common Stock

	Bal 50,000

Retained Earnings

	Bal 18,800

Dividends

Bal 3,200	

Revenue

Service Revenue

	7,000
	(e) 300
	(f) 200
	Bal 7,500

Expenses

Rent Expense

(a) 1,000	
Bal 1,000	

Salary Expense

900	
(d) 900	
Bal 1,800	

Supplies Expense

(b) 300	
Bal 300	

Depreciation Expense—Equipment

(c) 400	
Bal 400	

Utilities Expense

Bal 500	

Income Tax Expense

(g) 600	
Bal 600	

Exhibit 3-8 includes an additional adjusting entry that we have not yet discussed—the accrual of income tax expense. Like individual taxpayers, corporations must pay income taxes. A business typically accrues income tax expense and the related income tax payable as the final adjusting entry of the period. Alladin Travel accrues income tax expense with adjusting entry g:

Adjusting entry g

A1

	A	B	C	D	E	F
1	Jun 30	Income Tax Expense	600			
2		Income Tax Payable		600		
3		*To accrue income tax expense.*				
4						

The income tax accrual follows the pattern for accrued expenses.

The Adjusted Trial Balance

This chapter began with the unadjusted trial balance (see Exhibit 3-3, p. 125). After the adjustments are journalized and posted, the accounts appear as shown in Exhibit 3-8, Panel C. A useful step in preparing the financial statements is to list the accounts, along with their adjusted balances, on an **adjusted trial balance**. This document lists all the accounts from the ledger and their final balances in a single place.

Exhibit 3-9 shows a worksheet that can be a useful tool for preparing Alladin Travel, Inc.'s adjusted trial balance.

Exhibit 3-9 | Trial Balance Worksheet

A1

	A	B	C	D	E	F	G	H
1	**Alladin Travel, Inc.** **Trial Balance Worksheet** **June 30, 2018**							
2		**Trial Balance**		**Adjustments**		**Adjusted Trial Balance**		
3	**Account Title**	**Debit**	**Credit**	**Debit**	**Credit**	**Debit**	**Credit**	
4	Cash	36,800				36,800		
5	Accounts receivable	2,200		(e) 300		2,500		
6	Supplies	700			(b) 300	400		
7	Prepaid rent	3,000			(a) 1,000	2,000		
8	Land	18,000				18,000		
9	Equipment	24,000				24,000		
10	Accumulated depreciation–equipment				(c) 400		400	Balance sheet (*Exhibit 3-12*)
11	Accounts payable		13,100				13,100	
12	Salary payable				(d) 900		900	
13	Unearned service revenue		400	(f) 200			200	
14	Income tax payable				(g) 600		600	
15	Common stock		50,000				50,000	
16	Retained earnings		18,800				18,800	Statement of retained earnings (*Exhibit 3-11*)
17	Dividends	3,200				3,200		
18	Service revenue		7,000		(e) 300		7,500	
19					(f) 200			
20	Rent expense			(a) 1,000		1,000		Income statement (*Exhibit 3-10*)
21	Salary expense	900		(d) 900		1,800		
22	Supplies expense			(b) 300		300		
23	Depreciation expense–equipment			(c) 400		400		
24	Utilities expense	500				500		
25	Income tax expense			(g) 600		600		
26	Totals	89,300	89,300	3,700	3,700	91,500	91,500	
27								

Note how clearly this worksheet presents the data. The Account Title and the Trial Balance data come from the unadjusted trial balance. The two Adjustments columns summarize the adjusting entries. The Adjusted Trial Balance columns then give the final account balances. Each adjusted amount in Exhibit 3-9 is the unadjusted balance plus or minus the adjustments. For example, Accounts Receivable starts with a balance of $2,200. Then the $300 debit adjustment is added to get Accounts Receivable's ending balance of $2,500. Spreadsheets are designed for this type of analysis.

Try It in Excel®

Envision Exhibit 3-9 as an Excel spreadsheet. By preparing one, you can use it as a template to solve future problems just by changing the initial trial balance data. To prepare the template, follow these steps:

1. Open a blank Excel spreadsheet. Format the spreadsheet header and column headings exactly as you see in Exhibit 3-9.
2. Enter the account titles and account balances from the unadjusted trial balance (Exhibit 3-3).
3. Calculate a sum for both the debit and credit columns labeled "Trial Balance."

4. Enter adjusting journal entries (a) through (g) one at a time in the "adjustments" columns. For example, for adjusting journal entry (a), enter 1,000 in the debit column on the "Rent expense" line, and 1,000 in the credit column of the "Prepaid rent" line. Do not enter the letters (a) through (g); use only the amounts.
5. In the adjusted trial balance debit and credit columns, enter formulas as follows:
   - For asset, dividend, and expense accounts: = + (debit amounts from "Trial Balance" and "Adjustments" columns) – (credit amounts from "Adjustments" columns).
   - For contra asset, liability, common stock, retained earnings, and service revenue accounts: = + (credit amounts from "Trial Balance" and "Adjustments" columns) – (debit amounts from "Adjustments" columns)
6. Sum the Adjustments debit and credit columns.
7. Sum the Adjusted Trial Balance debit and credit columns.

Formatted spreadsheets for adjusting journal entries are provided for you in selected problems in MyLab Accounting.

CONSTRUCT THE FINANCIAL STATEMENTS

4 Construct the financial statements

The June financial statements of Alladin Travel, Inc., can be prepared from the adjusted trial balance. At the far right, Exhibit 3-9 shows how the accounts are distributed to the financial statements.

- The income statement (Exhibit 3-10) lists the revenue and expense accounts.
- The statement of retained earnings (Exhibit 3-11) shows the changes in retained earnings.
- The balance sheet (Exhibit 3-12) reports assets, liabilities, and stockholders' equity.

The arrows in Exhibits 3-10, 3-11, and 3-12 show the flow of data from one statement to the next.

Try It in Excel®

If you have already prepared Excel templates for the income statement, statement of retained earnings, and balance sheet for Alladin Travel, Inc., in Chapter 2 (see Exhibit 2-2), or Chapter 1 (see page 28), you may update these. You can do so by inserting additional amounts, and copying and pasting values from the cells in the worksheet in Exhibit 3-9 to the appropriate cells in the financial statements. The value of Excel is that once you have prepared the templates for the worksheet and financial statements, you can reuse them multiple times for different sets of facts.

Why is the income statement prepared first and the balance sheet prepared last?

1. The income statement reports a company's net income or net loss, which is then transferred to the statement of retained earnings and ultimately the balance sheet. The first arrow (1) tracks net income.
2. Retained Earnings is the final balancing element of the balance sheet. To solidify your understanding, trace the $18,500 retained earnings figure from Exhibit 3-11 to Exhibit 3-12. Arrow 2 tracks retained earnings.

Exhibit 3-10 | Income Statement

Alladin Travel, Inc. Income Statement Month ended June 30, 2018		
Revenue:		
Service revenue		$7,500
Expenses:		
Salary expense	$1,800	
Rent expense	1,000	
Utilities expense	500	
Depreciation expense—equipment	400	
Supplies expenses	300	4,000
Income before tax		3,500
Income tax expense		600
Net income		$2,900

Exhibit 3-11 | Statement of Retained Earnings

①

Alladin Travel, Inc. Statement of Retained Earnings Month ended June 30, 2018	
Retained earnings, May 31, 2018	$18,800
Add: Net income	2,900
Subtotal	21,700
Less: Dividends declared	(3,200)
Retained earnings, June 30, 2018	$18,500

Exhibit 3-12 | Balance Sheet

②

Alladin Travel, Inc. Balance Sheet June 30, 2018				
Assets			**Liabilities**	
Cash		$36,800	Accounts payable	$13,100
Accounts receivable		2,500	Salary payable	900
Supplies		400	Unearned service revenue	200
Prepaid rent		2,000	Income tax payable	600
Land		$18,000	Total liabilities	14,800
Equipment	$24,000			
Less: Accumulated depreciation	(400)	23,600	**Stockholders' Equity**	
			Common stock	50,000
			Retained earnings	18,500
			Total stockholders' equity	68,500
Total assets		$83,300	Total liabilities and stockholders' equity	$83,300

Mid-Chapter Summary Problem

The following trial balance for Badger Ranch Company pertains to December 31, 2018, which is the end of the company's year-long accounting period. The data needed to adjust the entries include:

a. Supplies on hand at year-end, $2,000.

b. Depreciation on furniture and fixtures, $20,000.

c. Depreciation on building, $10,000.

d. Salaries owed but not yet paid, $5,000.

e. Accrued service revenue, $12,000.

f. Of the $45,000 balance of unearned service revenue, $32,000 was earned during the year.

g. Accrued income tax expense, $35,000.

	A	B	C	D	E
1	**Badger Ranch Company Trial Balance December 31, 2018**				
2	Cash	$ 198,000			
3	Accounts receivable	370,000			
4	Supplies	6,000			
5	Building	250,000			
6	Accumulated depreciation—building		$ 130,000		
7	Furniture and fixtures	100,000			
8	Accumulated depreciation—furniture and fixtures		40,000		
9	Accounts payable		380,000		
10	Salary payable				
11	Unearned service revenue		45,000		
12	Income tax payable				
13	Common stock		100,000		
14	Retained earnings		193,000		
15	Dividends	65,000			
16	Service revenue		286,000		
17	Salary expense	172,000			
18	Supplies expense				
19	Depreciation expense—building				
20	Depreciation expense—furniture and fixtures				
21	Income tax expense				
22	Miscellaneous expense	13,000			
23	Total	$1,174,000	$1,174,000		
24					

Requirements

1. Open the ledger accounts with their unadjusted balances. Accounts Receivable is an example:

Accounts Receivable

Debit	Credit
370,000	

2. Journalize Badger Ranch Company's adjusting entries at December 31, 2018. Key the entries by letter, as in Exhibit 3-8 (p. 136).
3. Post the adjusting entries to the accounts.
4. Using an Excel spreadsheet, prepare a worksheet for the adjusted trial balance, as shown in Exhibit 3-9 (p. 138).
5. Prepare the income statement, the statement of retained earnings, and the balance sheet. Draw arrows linking these three financial statements.

Answers

Requirements 1 and 3

Assets

Cash

	Debit		Credit
Bal	198,000		

Accounts Receivable

	Debit		Credit
	370,000		
(e)	12,000		
Bal	382,000		

Supplies

	Debit		Credit
	6,000	(a)	4,000
Bal	2,000		

Building

	Debit		Credit
Bal	250,000		

Accumulated Depreciation—Building

	Debit		Credit
			130,000
		(c)	10,000
		Bal	140,000

Furniture and Fixtures

	Debit		Credit
Bal	100,000		

Accumulated Depreciation—Furniture and Fixtures

	Debit		Credit
			40,000
		(b)	20,000
		Bal	60,000

Liabilities

Accounts Payable

	Debit		Credit
		Bal	380,000

Salary Payable

	Debit		Credit
		(d)	5,000
		Bal	5,000

Unearned Service Revenue

	Debit		Credit
(f)	32,000		45,000
		Bal	13,000

Income Tax Payable

	Debit		Credit
		(g)	35,000
		Bal	35,000

Stockholders' Equity

Common Stock

	Debit		Credit
		Bal	100,000

Retained Earnings

	Debit		Credit
		Bal	193,000

Dividends

	Debit		Credit
Bal	65,000		

Revenues

Service Revenue

	Debit		Credit
			286,000
		(e)	12,000
		(f)	32,000
		Bal	330,000

Expenses

Salary Expense

	Debit		Credit
	172,000		
(d)	5,000		
Bal	177,000		

Supplies Expense

	Debit		Credit
(a)	4,000		
Bal	4,000		

Depreciation Expense—Building

	Debit		Credit
(c)	10,000		
Bal	10,000		

Depreciation Expense—Furniture and Fixtures

	Debit		Credit
(b)	20,000		
Bal	20,000		

Income Tax Expense

	Debit		Credit
(g)	35,000		
Bal	35,000		

Miscellaneous Expense

	Debit		Credit
Bal	13,000		

Requirement 2

A1

	A	B	C	D	E	F	G
1	(a)	Dec 31	Supplies Expense ($6,000 − $2,000)	4,000			
2			Supplies		4,000		
3			*To record supplies used.*				
4							
5	(b)	31	Depreciation Expense—Furniture and Fixtures	20,000			
6			Accumulated Depreciation—Furniture and Fixtures		20,000		
7			*To record depreciation expense on furniture and fixtures.*				
8							
9	(c)	31	Depreciation Expense—Building	10,000			
10			Accumulated Depreciation—Building		10,000		
11			*To record depreciation expense on building.*				
12							
13	(d)	31	Salary Expense	5,000			
14			Salary Payable		5,000		
15			*To accrue salary expense.*				
16							
17	(e)	31	Accounts Receivable	12,000			
18			Service Revenue		12,000		
19			*To accrue service revenue.*				
20							
21	(f)	31	Unearned Service Revenue	32,000			
22			Service Revenue		32,000		
23			*To record unearned service revenue that has been earned.*				
24							
25	(g)	31	Income Tax Expense	35,000			
26			Income Tax Payable		35,000		
27			*To accrue income tax expense.*				
28							

Requirement 4

	A	B	C	D	E	F	G
1	**Badger Ranch Company** **Trial Balance Worksheet** **December 31, 2018**						
2		**Trial Balance**		**Adjustments**		**Adjusted Trial Balance**	
3	**Account title**	**Debit**	**Credit**	**Debit**	**Credit**	**Debit**	**Credit**
4	Cash	198,000				198,000	
5	Accounts receivable	370,000		(e) 12,000		382,000	
6	Supplies	6,000			(a) 4,000	2,000	
7	Building	250,000				250,000	
8	Accumulated depreciation—building		130,000		(c) 10,000		140,000
9	Furniture and fixtures	100,000				100,000	
10	Accumulated depreciation—furniture and fixtures		40,000		(b) 20,000		60,000
11	Accounts payable		380,000				380,000
12	Salary payable				(d) 5,000		5,000
13	Unearned service revenue		45,000	(f) 32,000			13,000
14	Income tax payable				(g) 35,000		35,000
15	Common stock		100,000				100,000
16	Retained earnings		193,000				193,000
17	Dividends	65,000				65,000	
18	Service revenue		286,000		(e) 12,000		330,000
19					(f) 32,000		
20	Salary expense	172,000		(d) 5,000		177,000	
21	Supplies expense			(a) 4,000		4,000	
22	Depreciation expense—building			(c) 10,000		10,000	
23	Depreciation expense—furniture and fixtures			(b) 20,000		20,000	
24	Income tax expense			(g) 35,000		35,000	
25	Miscellaneous expense	13,000				13,000	
26		1,174,000	1,174,000	118,000	118,000	1,256,000	1,256,000
27							

Requirement 5

	A	B	C
1	**Badger Ranch Company Income Statement Year ended December 31, 2018**		
2	Revenue:		
3	Service revenue		$330,000
4	Expenses:		
5	Salary expense	$177,000	
6	Depreciation expense—furniture and fixtures	20,000	
7	Depreciation expense—building	10,000	
8	Supplies expense	4,000	
9	Miscellaneous expenses	13,000	224,000
10	Income before tax		106,000
11	Income tax expense		35,000
12	Net income		$ 71,000
13			

①

	A	B
1	**Badger Ranch Company Statement of Retained Earnings Year ended December 31, 2018**	
2	Retained earnings, December 31, 2017	$193,000
3	Add: Net income	71,000
4	Subtotal	264,000
5	Less: Dividends declared	(65,000)
6	Retained earnings, December 31, 2018	$199,000
7		

②

	A	B	C	D	E
1	**Badger Ranch Company Balance Sheet December 31, 2018**				
2	**Assets**			**Liabilities**	
3	Cash		$198,000	Accounts payable	$380,000
4	Accounts receivable		382,000	Salary payable	5,000
5	Supplies		2,000	Unearned service revenue	13,000
6	Building	$250,000		Income tax payable	35,000
7	Less: Accumulated			Total liabilities	433,000
8	depreciation	(140,000)	110,000		
9				**Stockholders' Equity**	
10	Furniture and fixtures	$100,000		Common stock	100,000
11	Less: Accumulated			Retained earnings	199,000
12	depreciation	(60,000)	40,000	Total stockholders' equity	299,000
13				Total liabilities and	
14	Total assets		$732,000	stockholders' equity	$732,000
15					

CLOSE THE BOOKS

5 **Close** the books

It is now June 30, the end of the month. Starr Williams, Alladin Travel's manager, will continue to run the company in July, August, and beyond. But wait—the revenue and the expense accounts still hold amounts for June. At the end of each month or accounting period, it is necessary to close the books in order to make an accurate measurement of revenue, expenses, and dividends for that period before proceeding to the next.

Closing the books means to prepare the accounts for the next period's transactions. The **closing entries** set the revenue, expense, and dividends balances back to zero at the end of the period. The idea is the same as setting the scoreboard back to zero after a game. The closing process is obviously handled by computers, but it must be carefully overseen by a company's accounting department managers.

Temporary Accounts. Because revenues and expenses relate to a limited period, they are called **temporary accounts**. The Dividends account is also temporary. The closing process applies only to temporary accounts (revenues, expenses, and dividends).

Permanent Accounts. Let's contrast the temporary accounts with the **permanent accounts**: assets, liabilities, and stockholders' equity. The permanent accounts are not closed at the end of the period because they carry over to the next period. Cash, Receivables, Equipment, Accounts Payable, Common Stock, and Retained Earnings are examples. Their ending balances for one period become the beginning balances of the next period.

Closing entries transfer revenue, expense, and dividends balances to Retained Earnings, where they will reside on a permanent basis. Here are the steps to close the books of a company such as The Walt Disney Company or Alladin Travel, Inc.:

1. Debit each revenue account for the amount of its credit balance. Credit Retained Earnings for the sum of the revenues. This process transfers the sum of all revenues into Retained Earnings, thereby increasing Retained Earnings.
2. Credit each expense account for the amount of its debit balance. Debit Retained Earnings for the sum of the expenses. This process transfers the sum of the expenses into Retained Earnings, thereby decreasing Retained Earnings.
3. Credit the Dividends account for the amount of its debit balance. Debit Retained Earnings. This entry places the dividends amount in the debit side of Retained Earnings. Remember that dividends are not expenses, but represent a permanent reduction of retained earnings.

Assume that Alladin Travel closes its books at the end of each month. Exhibit 3-13 illustrates the complete closing process for the business for the month of June. Panel A shows the closing journal entries, and Panel B shows the accounts after closing.

After closing the books, the Retained Earnings account of Alladin Travel, Inc., appears as follows (the data are from Exhibit 3-13):

Retained Earnings

		Beginning balance	18,800
Expenses	4,600	Revenues	7,500
Dividends	3,200		
		Ending balance	18,500

Exhibit 3-13 | Journalizing and Posting the Closing Entries

PANEL A—Journalizing the Closing Entries — Page 5

		Closing Entries		
①	Jun 30	Service Revenue	7,500	
		Retained Earnings		7,500
②	30	Retained Earnings	4,600	
		Rent Expense		1,000
		Salary Expense		1,800
		Supplies Expense		300
		Depreciation Expense–Equipment		400
		Utilities Expense		500
		Income Tax Expense		600
③	30	Retained Earnings	3,200	
		Dividends		3,200

PANEL B—Posting to the Accounts

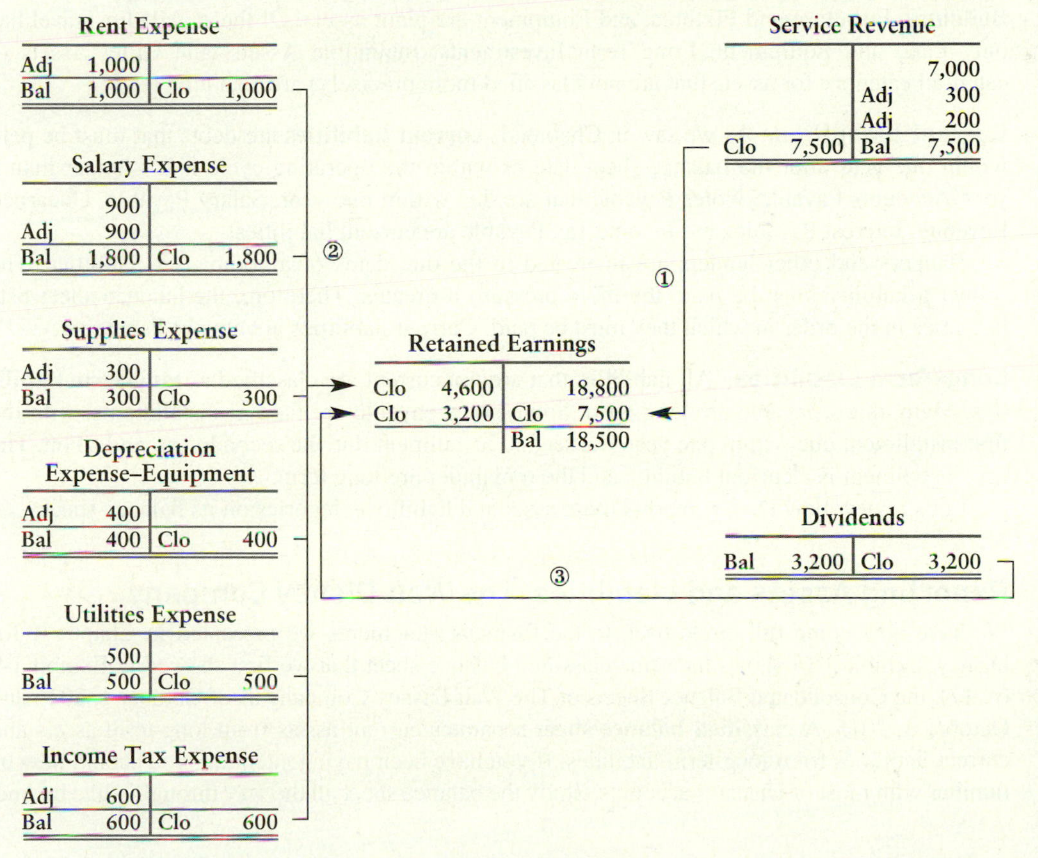

Adj = Amount posted from an adjusting entry
Clo = Amount posted from a closing entry
Bal = Balance
As arrow ② in Panel B shows, we can make a compound closing entry for all the expenses.

Classifying Assets and Liabilities

On the balance sheet, assets are classified as current or long term to indicate their relative liquidity. **Liquidity** measures how quickly an asset can be converted to cash and used to pay off liabilities that are due within the next year or operating cycle. Liquidity is an important measure because, as you have learned, even a profitable company can go out of business if it doesn't have enough cash on hand to pay its bills.

Cash is the most liquid asset. Accounts receivable are relatively liquid because cash collections usually follow quickly. Inventory is less liquid than accounts receivable because the company must first sell the goods. Equipment and buildings are even less liquid because these assets take even more time to sell and receive cash. A balance sheet lists assets and liabilities as either current or long-term.

Current Assets. As we saw in Chapter 1, **current assets** are the most liquid assets. They will be converted to cash, sold, or consumed during the next 12 months after the balance sheet date or within the business's normal operating cycle if it's longer than a year. The **operating cycle** is the time span over which a business pays cash to produce goods and services, which then are sold to bring cash back into the business.

For most businesses, the operating cycle is a few months. Cash, Short-Term Investments, Accounts Receivable, Merchandise Inventory, and Prepaid Expenses are the typical current assets.

Long-Term Assets. **Long-term assets** are all assets not classified as current assets. One category of long-term assets is plant assets, often labeled Property, Plant, and Equipment. Land, Buildings, Furniture and Fixtures, and Equipment are plant assets. Of these, Alladin Travel has only Land and Equipment. Long-Term Investments, Intangible Assets, and Other Assets (a catch-all category for assets that are not classified more precisely) are also long term.

Current Liabilities. As we saw in Chapter 1, **current liabilities** are debts that must be paid within one year after the balance sheet date or within the operating cycle if it's longer than a year. Accounts Payable, Notes Payable that are due within one year, Salary Payable, Unearned Revenue, Interest Payable, and Income Tax Payable are current liabilities.

Bankers and other lenders are interested in the due dates of a company's liabilities. The sooner a liability must be paid, the more pressure it creates. Therefore, the balance sheet lists liabilities in the order in which they must be paid. Current liabilities are always listed first.

Long-Term Liabilities. All liabilities that are not current are classified as **long-term liabilities**. Many notes payable are long term. Some notes payable are paid in installments, with the first installment due within one year, the second installment due the second year, and so on. The first installment is a current liability, and the remainder are long term.

Let's review how Disney reports these asset and liability categories on its balance sheet.

Reporting Assets and Liabilities: The Walt Disney Company

We have now come full circle back to the financial statements we presented in Chapter 1 for Disney. Exhibit 3-14 shows the same classified balance sheet that we first showed in Exhibit 1-9 (p. 17): the Consolidated Balance Sheets of The Walt Disney Company as of October 1, 2016 and October 3, 2015. A **classified balance sheet** separates current assets from long-term assets and current liabilities from long-term liabilities. If you have been paying attention, you should now be familiar with most of Disney's accounts. Study the balance sheet all the way through—line by line.

Formats for the Financial Statements

Companies can format their financial statements in different ways. Both the balance sheet and the income statement can be formatted in two basic ways.

Balance-Sheet Formats. The **report format** lists the assets at the top, followed by the liabilities and stockholders' equity below. The comparative Consolidated Balance Sheets of The Walt Disney Company in Exhibit 3-14 illustrate the report format. The report format is more popular, with approximately 60% of large companies using it.

Exhibit 3-14 | Classified Balance Sheet of The Walt Disney Company

A1

	A	B	C	D	E
1	**The Walt Disney Company Consolidated Balance Sheets**	**Fiscal 2016**	**Fiscal 2015**		
2	USD ($) in millions	**Oct. 01, 2016**	**Oct. 03, 2015**		
3	**Current assets:**				
4	Cash and cash equivalents	$ 4,610	$ 4,269		
5	Receivables	9,065	8,019		
6	Inventories	1,390	1,571		
7	Other current assets	1,901	2,899		
8	**Total current assets**	16,966	16,758		
9	Film and television costs	6,339	6,183		
10	Investments	4,280	2,643		
11	Parks, resorts and other property, net	27,349	25,179		
12	Intangible assets, net	34,759	34,998		
13	Other long-term assets	2,340	2,421		
14	**Total assets**	$ 92,033	$ 88,182		
15	**Current liabilities:**				
16	Accounts payable and accrued liabilities	$ 9,130	$ 7,844		
17	Current portion of long-term borrowings	3,687	4,563		
18	Unearned royalties and other advances	4,025	3,927		
19	**Total current liabilities**	16,842	16,334		
20	Long-term borrowings	16,483	12,773		
21	Other long-term liabilities	11,385	10,420		
22	Contingent liabilities (Note 14)				
23	**Total liabilities**	44,710	39,527		
24	**Equity:**				
25	Common stock, and additional paid-in capital	35,859	35,122		
26	Retained earnings	66,088	59,028		
27	Treasury stock at cost	(54,703)	(47,204)		
28	Other equity, net	79	1,709		
29	**Total equity**	47,323	48,655		
30	**Total liabilities and equity**	$ 92,033	$ 88,182		
31					

Source: Data from the U.S. Securities and Exchange Commission EDGAR Company Filings, www.sec.gov

ormat lists assets on the left and liabilities and stockholders' equity on the that a T-account does. Exhibit 3-12 (p. 140) shows an account format bal- vel, Inc. Either format is acceptable.

ts. A **single-step income statement** (statement of earnings) lists a heading such as Revenues, or Revenues and Gains. The le category titled Expenses, or Expenses and Losses. So, of Expenses and Losses from the sum of Revenues and pany's income before income tax expense. Alladin in Exhibit 3-10 (p. 140) appears in a single-step

r of subtotals to highlight important rela- states Exhibit 1-7 and shows The Walt f Income in a multistep format. We otal the cost of services and prod- 39 million for fiscal 2016, up from tant piece of information for a company amount of "pure profit" that results from rectly from the revenue generated by those

sei

A few extra quick computations can reveal some other valuable information. Disney's total gross profit for fiscal 2016 ($25,639 million) can be further separated and categorized as the gross profit from services of $22,477 million ($47,130 million – $24,653 million) and the gross profit from products of $3,162 million ($8,502 million – $5,340 million). We can then compute the gross profit percentage from both services and products (gross profit ÷ revenue) to reveal the percentage of each type of revenue dollar that represents profits. For services, the gross profit percentage is 47.7% ($22,477 million ÷ $47,130 million). For products, the gross profit percentage is 37.2% ($3,162 million ÷ $8,502 million). In other words, Disney's services business is more profitable than its products business. These ratios can be compared with those of the prior period as well as those of competitors to evaluate how well The Walt Disney Company is performing. We will cover the gross profit percentage in more detail in Chapter 6. Exhibit 3-15 also shows various levels of income, such as operating income, other income, income before taxes, and net income.

Exhibit 3-15 | The Walt Disney Company Income Statement in Multistep Format

A1

	A	B	C	D	E
1	**The Walt Disney Company Consolidated Statements of Income**	**Fiscal 2016**	**Fiscal 2015**		
2		**12 months ended**			
3	**Adapted, in millions of $**	**Oct. 01, 2016**	**Oct. 03, 2015**		
4	Services revenue	$ 47,130	$ 43,894		
5	Products revenue	8,502	8,571		
6	**Total revenues**	55,632	52,465		
7	Cost of services	(24,653)	(23,191)		
8	Cost of products	(5,340)	(5,173)		
9	**Total cost of services and products**	(29,993)	(28,364)		
10	**Gross profit on services and products**	25,639	24,101		
11	Selling, general, administrative and other	(8,754)	(8,523)		
12	Depreciation and amortization	(2,527)	(2,354)		
13	**Income from operations**	14,358	13,224		
14	Other items of income (expense), net	111	174		
15	**Income before income taxes**	14,469	13,398		
16	Income taxes	(5,078)	(5,016)		
17	**Net income**	$ 9,391	$ 8,382		
18					

Source: Data from the U.S. Securities and Exchange Commission EDGAR Company Filings, www.sec.gov

In particular, income from operations ($14,358 million) is separated from other types of income—more specifically, Other items of income (expense), net. This is income Disney did not earn by performing entertainment services or selling products. Operating income reflects the earnings from the company's core business activities. The other income consists mainly of interest income and other investment income.

Most companies' income statements do not conform to either a pure single-step format or a pure multistep format. Business operations are too complex for all companies to conform to rigid reporting formats.

ANALYZE AND EVALUATE A COMPANY'S DEBT-PAYING ABILITY

6 **Analyze** and evaluate a company's debt-paying ability

As you have learned, accounting provides information for decision making. A bank considering lending money must try to predict whether the borrower can repay the loan. If the borrower already has a lot of debt, the probability of repayment may be low. If the borrower owes little, the loan may go through. To analyze a company's financial position, decision makers use data and ratios computed from various items in the financial statements. Let's see how this process works.

Net Working Capital

Net working capital is a computed dollar amount that represents operating liquidity. Its computation is simple:

$$\text{Net working capital} = \text{Total current assets} - \text{Total current liabilities}$$

For The Walt Disney Company, at October 1, 2016 (amounts in millions in Exhibit 3-14),

$$\text{Net working capital} = \$16{,}966 - \$16{,}842 = \$124$$

Generally, to be considered liquid, a company should have a sufficient excess of current assets over current liabilities. The amount considered "sufficient" varies with the industry. The Walt Disney Company's current assets exceed its current liabilities by $124 million, meaning that after the company pays all of its current liabilities, it will still have about $124 million in cash and other assets that can be converted into cash. Thus, The Walt Disney Company is considered "liquid."

Current Ratio

Another way of expressing operating liquidity is with the **current ratio**, which divides total current assets by total current liabilities.

$$\text{Current ratio} = \frac{\text{Total current assets}}{\text{Total current liabilities}}$$

For The Walt Disney Company, at October 1, 2016 (amounts in millions from Exhibit 3-14),

$$\text{Current ratio} = \frac{\text{Total current assets}}{\text{Total current liabilities}} = \frac{\$16{,}966}{\$16{,}842} = 1.007$$

Like net working capital, the current ratio measures a company's ability to pay its current liabilities with its current assets. A company prefers a high current ratio, which means that the business has plenty of current assets to pay its current liabilities. An increasing current ratio from period to period indicates improvement in the company's liquidity.

As a rule of thumb, a strong current ratio is 1.50, which indicates that the company has $1.50 in current assets for every $1.00 in current liabilities. A company with a current ratio of 1.50 would probably have little trouble paying its current liabilities. Many successful businesses operate with current ratios between 1.20 and 1.50. A current ratio of less than 1.00 is considered low. That would mean that current liabilities exceed current assets.

Although The Walt Disney Company's current ratio of 1.007 is below the "benchmarks" mentioned in the previous paragraph, the company's current ratio isn't considered weak for several reasons. First, the computation of the current ratio assumes the worst-case scenario—that the company will have to liquidate all of its current assets (turn them into cash), pay off all its current liabilities at once, and go out of business. That is far from a realistic assumption for a company like The Walt Disney Company. Second, The Walt Disney Company generated a huge amount of cash through its operating activities (over $13.2 billion in fiscal 2016, according to its Consolidated Statements of Cash Flows in Exhibit 1-10 on page 20), which is more than enough to pay off its accounts payable and accrued liabilities ($9.1 billion) and the current portion of its long-term borrowings ($3.7 billion) as they become due. Disney's remaining current liabilities consists of unearned income, which has been collected in advance. In summary, it is necessary to evaluate each company on its own merits based on an understanding of its entire financial picture and a thorough knowledge of its business model, rather than attempt to adopt a "one size fits all" benchmark or a single ratio. In fact, lenders and investors use many ratios to evaluate a company.

Debt Ratio

Still another measure of a company's debt-paying ability is its **debt ratio**, which is the ratio of its total liabilities to its total assets.

$$\text{Debt ratio} = \frac{\text{Total liabilities}}{\text{Total assets}}$$

The debt ratio indicates the proportion of a company's assets that is financed with debt. This ratio measures a business's ability to pay both its current and long-term debts (total liabilities). The debt ratio for The Walt Disney Company, at October 1, 2016 (amounts in millions from Exhibit 3-14) was

$$\text{Debt ratio} = \frac{\text{Total liabilities}}{\text{Total assets}} = \frac{\$44{,}710}{\$92{,}033} = 0.49$$

A low debt ratio is safer than a high debt ratio. Why? A company with few liabilities has low required debt payments and is unlikely to get into financial difficulty. By contrast, a business with a high debt ratio may have trouble paying its liabilities, especially when its sales are low and its cash is scarce. Most bankruptcies result in part from high debt ratios. Companies that continue in this pattern are often forced out of business.

The Walt Disney Company's debt ratio of 49% (0.49) is low compared to most companies in the United States. The norm for the debt ratio ranges from 60% to 70%. This relatively low debt ratio indicates to creditors that the company is a low credit risk, meaning that there is a high probability that borrowed money will be paid back on time, along with interest.

How Do Transactions Affect the Ratios?

Companies such as The Walt Disney Company are aware of how transactions affect their ratios. Lending agreements often require that a company's current ratio not fall below a certain level. Another loan requirement is that the company's debt ratio may not rise above a threshold, such as 0.70. When a company fails to meet one of these conditions, it is said to default on its lending agreements. The penalty can be severe: The lender can require immediate payment of the loan. The Walt Disney Company has a sufficiently small amount of debt that the company is not in danger of default. But many companies are. To help keep debt ratios within normal limits, companies might use one or more of the following strategies:

- Increase revenue and decrease costs, thus increasing current assets, net income, and retained earnings without increasing liabilities
- Sell stock, thus increasing cash and stockholders' equity
- Choose to borrow less money

Let's use The Walt Disney Company to examine the effects of some transactions on the company's current ratio and debt ratio. As shown in the preceding section, Disney's ratios are as follows (dollar amounts in millions):[2]

$$\text{Current ratio} = \frac{\$16{,}966}{\$16{,}842} = 1.007$$

$$\text{Debt ratio} = \frac{\$44{,}710}{\$92{,}033} = 0.486$$

[2] Because of the relatively small amounts of these particular illustrative transactions compared to the original components, we have chosen to carry current ratio and debt ratio computations to three or four decimal places in order to illustrate the impact of individual transactions on the current ratio and debt ratio. The larger the individual transaction in comparison with the original components (for example, see the End-of-Chapter Summary Problem), the less necessary this will be.

The managers of any company would be concerned about how inventory purchases, payments on account, expense accruals, and depreciation would affect its ratios. Let's see how Disney would be affected by some typical transactions. For each transaction, the journal entry helps identify the effects on the company.

a. Issued stock and received cash of $50 million.

	A	B	C	D	E	F
1	*Journal entry:*	Cash	50			
2		Common Stock		50		
3						

Cash, a current asset, affects both the current ratio and the debt ratio as follows:

$$\text{Current ratio} = \frac{\$16{,}966 + \$50}{\$16{,}842} = 1.0103 \qquad \text{Debt ratio} = \frac{\$44{,}710}{\$92{,}033 + \$50} = 0.4855$$

Issuing stock improves both ratios slightly.

b. Paid cash to purchase buildings for $20 million.

	A	B	C	D	E	F
1	*Journal entry:*	Buildings	20			
2		Cash		20		
3						

Cash, a current asset, decreases, but total assets stay the same. Liabilities are unchanged.

$$\text{Current ratio} = \frac{\$16{,}966 - \$20}{\$16{,}842} = 1.006 \qquad \text{Debt ratio} = \frac{\$44{,}710}{\$92{,}033 + \$20 - \$20} = 0.486\text{; no change}$$

A cash purchase of a building hurts the current ratio but doesn't affect the debt ratio.

c. Made a $30 million sale on account.

	A	B	C	D	E	F
1	*Journal entry:*	Accounts Receivable	30			
2		Sales Revenue		30		
3						

The increase in Accounts Receivable increases current assets and total assets, as follows:

$$\text{Current ratio} = \frac{\$16{,}966 + \$30}{\$16{,}842} = 1.009 \qquad \text{Debt ratio} = \frac{\$44{,}710}{\$92{,}033 + \$30} = 0.4856$$

A sale on account improves both ratios slightly.

d. Collected the account receivable, $30 million.

	A	B	C	D	E	F
1	*Journal entry:*	Cash	30			
2		Accounts Receivable		30		
3						

This transaction has no effect on total current assets, total assets, or total liabilities. Both ratios are unaffected.

e. Accrued expenses at year-end, $40 million.

	A	B	C	D	E	F
1	*Journal entry:*	Expenses	40			
2		Expenses Payable		40		
3						

$$\text{Current ratio} = \frac{\$16{,}966}{\$16{,}842 + \$40} = 1.005 \qquad \text{Debt ratio} = \frac{\$44{,}710 + \$40}{\$92{,}033} = 0.4862$$

Most expenses hurt both ratios.

f. Recorded depreciation, $80 million.

	A	B	C	D	E	F
1	*Journal entry:*	Depreciation Expense	80			
2		Accumulated Depreciation		80		
3						

No current accounts are affected, so only the debt ratio is affected.

$$\text{Current ratio} = \frac{\$16{,}966}{\$16{,}842} = 1.007 \qquad \text{Debt ratio} = \frac{\$44{,}710}{\$92{,}033 - \$80} = 0.4862$$

Depreciation decreases total assets and therefore hurts the debt ratio.

g. Earned interest revenue and collected cash, $40 million.

	A	B	C	D	E	F
1	*Journal entry:*	Cash	40			
2		Interest Revenue		40		
3						

Cash, a current asset, affects both the current ratio and the debt ratio as follows:

$$\text{Current ratio} = \frac{\$16{,}966 + \$40}{\$16{,}842} = 1.0097 \qquad \text{Debt ratio} = \frac{\$44{,}710}{\$92{,}033 + \$40} = 0.4856$$

Revenue improves both ratios.

Now, let's wrap up the chapter by using net working capital, the current ratio, and the debt ratio for decision making. The Decision Guidelines feature offers some clues.

Decision Guidelines

EVALUATE A COMPANY'S DEBT-PAYING ABILITY USING ITS NET WORKING CAPITAL, THE CURRENT RATIO, AND THE DEBT RATIO

In general, a larger amount of net working capital is preferable to a smaller amount. Similarly, a high current ratio is preferable to a low current ratio. Increases in net working capital and increases in the current ratio improve a company's financial position. By contrast, a low debt ratio is preferable to a high debt ratio. A decrease in the debt ratio indicates a company's financial position has improved.

Let's apply what we have learned. Suppose you are a loan officer at Bank of America and The Walt Disney Company has asked you for a $20 million loan to launch a new theme park ride. How will you make this loan decision? The Decision Guidelines show how bankers and investors use two key ratios.

➤ USING NET WORKING CAPITAL AND THE CURRENT RATIO

Decision	Guidelines
How can you measure a company's ability to pay its current liabilities with its current assets?	Net working capital = Total current assets − Total current liabilities $\text{Current ratio} = \frac{\text{Total current assets}}{\text{Total current liabilities}}$
Who uses net working capital and the current ratio for decision making?	*Lenders and other creditors*, who must predict whether a borrower can pay its current liabilities. *Stockholders*, who know that a company that cannot pay its debts is not a good investment because it may go bankrupt. *Managers*, who must have enough cash to pay the company's current liabilities.
What are good values for net working capital and the current ratio?	There is no correct answer for this. It depends on the industry as well as the individual entity's ability to generate cash quickly and primarily from operations. A company with strong operating cash flow can operate successfully with a low amount of net working capital as long as cash comes in through operations at least as fast as the company's accounts payable become due. A current ratio of, say, 1.10–1.20 is sometimes sufficient. A company with relatively slow cash flow from operations needs a higher current ratio of, say, 1.30–1.50. Traditionally, a current ratio of 2.00 was considered ideal. Recently, acceptable values have decreased as companies have been able to operate more efficiently. Today, a current ratio of 1.50 is considered strong. Although not ideal, cash-rich companies like Disney can operate with a current ratio at or near 1.0.

➤ USING THE DEBT RATIO

Decision	Guidelines
How can you measure a company's ability to pay its total liabilities?	$\text{Debt ratio} = \dfrac{\text{Total liabilities}}{\text{Total assets}}$
Who uses the debt ratio for decision making?	*Lenders and other creditors*, who must predict whether a borrower can pay its debts. *Stockholders*, who know that a company that cannot pay its debts is not a good investment because it may go bankrupt. *Managers*, who must have enough assets to pay the company's debts.
What is a good value of the debt ratio?	It depends on the industry: A company with strong cash flow can operate successfully with a high debt ratio of, say, 0.70–0.80. A company with weak cash flow needs a lower debt ratio of, say, 0.50–0.60. Traditionally, a debt ratio of 0.50 was considered ideal. Recently, values have increased as companies have been able to operate more efficiently. Today, a normal value of the debt ratio is around 0.60–0.70.

End-of-Chapter | Summary Problem

Refer to the Mid-Chapter Summary Problem that begins on page 141. The adjusted trial balance appears on page 144.

Requirements

1. Make Badger Ranch Company's closing entries at December 31, 2018. Explain what they accomplish and why they are necessary.
2. Post the closing entries to Retained Earnings and compare Retained Earnings' ending balance with the amount reported on the balance sheet on page 145. The two amounts should be the same.
3. Prepare Badger Ranch Company's classified balance sheet to identify the company's current assets and current liabilities. (The company has no long-term liabilities.) Use the account format. Then compute the company's net working capital, current ratio, and debt ratio at December 31, 2018.
4. Badger Ranch Company's top managers have asked you for a $500,000 loan to expand the business and propose to pay off the loan over a 10-year period. Recalculate Badger Ranch Company's debt ratio assuming you make the loan. Use the company financial statements plus the ratio values to decide whether to grant the loan at an interest rate of 8%, 10%, or 12%. Badger Ranch Company's cash flow is strong. Give the reasoning underlying your decision.

Answers

Requirement 1

2018			
Dec 31	Service Revenue	330,000	
	Retained Earnings		330,000
31	Retained Earnings	259,000	
	Salary Expense		177,000
	Depreciation Expense—Furniture and Fixtures		20,000
	Depreciation Expense—Building		10,000
	Supplies Expense		4,000
	Income Tax Expense		35,000
	Miscellaneous Expense		13,000
31	Retained Earnings	65,000	
	Dividends		65,000

Explanation of Closing Entries

The closing entries set the balance of each revenue, expense, and dividend account back to zero for the start of the next accounting period. We must close these accounts because their balances relate only to one accounting period.

Requirement 2

Retained Earnings

			193,000
Clo	259,000	Clo	330,000
Clo	65,000		
		Bal	199,000

The balance in the Retained Earnings account agrees with the amount reported on the balance sheet, as it should.

Requirement 3

	A	B	C	D	E
1	**Badger Ranch Company Balance Sheet December 31, 2018**				
2	**Assets**			**Liabilities**	
3	Current assets:			Current liabilities:	
4	Cash		$198,000	Accounts payable	$380,000
5	Accounts receivable		382,000	Salary payable	5,000
6	Supplies		2,000	Unearned service revenue	13,000
7	Total current assets		582,000	Income tax payable	35,000
8	Building	$250,000		Total current liabilities	433,000
9	Less: Accumulated			**Stockholders' Equity**	
10	depreciation	(140,000)	110,000	Common stock	100,000
11	Furniture and fixtures	$100,000		Retained earnings	199,000
12	Less: Accumulated			Total stockholders' equity	299,000
13	depreciation	(60,000)	40,000	Total liabilities and	
14	Total assets		$732,000	stockholders' equity	$732,000
15					

$$\text{Net working capital} = \$582{,}000 - \$433{,}000 = \$149{,}000$$

$$\text{Current ratio} = \frac{\$582{,}000}{\$433{,}000} = 1.34$$

$$\text{Debt ratio} = \frac{\$433{,}000}{\$732{,}000} = 0.59$$

Requirement 4

$$\text{Debt ratio assuming the loan is made} = \frac{\$433{,}000 + \$500{,}000}{\$732{,}000 + \$500{,}000} = \frac{\$933{,}000}{\$1{,}232{,}000} = .76$$

Decision: Make the loan at 10%.

Reasoning: Prior to the loan, the company's financial position and cash flow are strong. The current ratio is in a middle range, and the debt ratio is not too high. Net income (from the income statement) is high in relation to total revenue. Therefore, the company should be able to repay the loan.

The loan will increase the company's debt ratio from 59% to 76%, which is more risky than the company's financial position at present. On this basis, a midrange interest rate appears reasonable—at least as the starting point for the negotiation between Badger Ranch Company and the bank.

REVIEW | Accrual Accounting and Income

Accounting Vocabulary

account format (p. 149) A balance-sheet format that lists assets on the left and liabilities and stockholders' equity on the right.

accrual (p. 126) An expense or a revenue that occurs before the business pays or receives cash. An accrual is the opposite of a deferral.

accrual accounting (p. 121) Accounting that records the impact of a business event as it occurs, regardless of whether the transaction affected cash.

accrued expense (p. 131) An expense incurred but not yet paid in cash.

accrued revenue (p. 133) A revenue that has been earned but not yet received in cash.

accumulated depreciation (p. 130) The cumulative sum of all depreciation expense from the date of acquiring a plant asset.

adjusted trial balance (p. 138) A list of all the ledger accounts with their adjusted balances.

book value (of a plant asset) (p. 130) The asset's cost minus accumulated depreciation.

cash-basis accounting (p. 121) Accounting that records only transactions in which cash is received or paid.

classified balance sheet (p. 148) A balance sheet that shows current assets separate from long-term assets and current liabilities separate from long-term liabilities.

closing the books (p. 146) The process of preparing the accounts to begin recording the next period's transactions. Closing the books consists of journalizing and posting the closing entries to set the balances of the revenue, expense, and dividends accounts to zero. Also called *closing the accounts*.

closing entries (p. 146) Entries that transfer the revenue, expense, and dividends balances from these respective accounts to the Retained Earnings account.

contra account (p. 130) An account that always has a companion account and whose normal balance is opposite that of the companion account.

current asset (p. 148) An asset that is expected to be converted to cash, sold, or consumed during the next 12 months or within the business's normal operating cycle if longer than a year.

current liability (p. 148) A debt due to be paid within one year or within the entity's operating cycle if the cycle is longer than a year.

current ratio (p. 151) Current assets divided by current liabilities, which measures a company's ability to pay its current liabilities with its current assets.

debt ratio (p. 152) The ratio of a company's total liabilities to its total assets, which indicates the proportion of the company's assets financed with debt.

deferral (p. 126) An adjustment for which a business paid or received cash in advance. Examples include prepaid rent, prepaid insurance, and supplies.

depreciation (p. 126) The allocation of the cost of a long-term plant asset to expense over its useful life.

expense recognition principle (p. 124) A principle that states that all expenses incurred during a period should be identified and measured to match them against revenues earned during that same period.

liquidity (p. 148) A measure of how quickly an item can be converted to cash.

long-term asset (p. 148) An asset that is not a current asset.

long-term liability (p. 148) A liability that is not a current liability.

multistep income statement (p. 149) An income statement that contains subtotals to highlight important relationships between revenues and expenses.

net working capital (p. 151) A measure of liquidity; current assets – current liabilities.

operating cycle (p. 148) Time span during which cash is paid for goods and services that are sold to customers who pay the business in cash.

permanent accounts (p. 146) Asset, liability, and stockholders' equity accounts that are not closed at the end of the period.

plant assets (p. 129) Long-lived assets, such as land, buildings, and equipment, used in the operation of the business. Also called *fixed assets*.

prepaid expense (p. 126) A category of miscellaneous assets that typically expire or get used up in the near future. Examples include prepaid rent, prepaid insurance, and supplies.

report format (p. 148) A balance-sheet format that lists assets at the top, followed by liabilities and stockholders' equity below.

revenue principle (p. 123) The basis for recording revenues; a principle that tells accountants when to record revenue and the amount of revenue to record.

single-step income statement (p. 149) An income statement that lists all the revenues together under a heading such as Revenues or Revenues and Gains. Expenses appear in a separate category called Expenses or perhaps Expenses and Losses.

temporary accounts (p. 146) Revenue and expense accounts that relate to a limited period and are closed at the end of the period. For a corporation, the Dividends account is also temporary.

time-period concept (p. 122) A concept that ensures that accounting information is reported at regular intervals.

unearned revenue (p. 134) A liability created when a business collects cash from customers in advance of earning the revenue. The obligation is to provide a product or a service in the future.

Quick Check (Answers are given on p. 199.)

1. If Oxbow Corporation does not record a sale made on account in December until a month later when the customer pays its invoice, how will Oxbow's December financial statements be impacted?

a. Assets will be understated on the balance sheet, while revenues will be overstated on the income statement.
b. Assets will be understated on the balance sheet, while revenues will be understated on the income statement.
c. Assets will be overstated on the balance sheet, while revenues will be overstated on the income statement.
d. Assets will be overstated on the balance sheet, while revenues will be understated on the income statement.

2. Which of the following transactions would be recorded if using the accrual basis of accounting but **not** if using the cash basis of accounting?

a. Borrowing money
b. Paying off loans
c. Purchasing inventory on account
d. Collecting customer payments

3. A physician performs medical services for a patient on October 20; the total bill for the medical services was $200. The patient makes a co-pay of $20 on October 20, and the insurance company pays the remaining balance of $180 on November 19. On what date(s) will the physician record the revenue for those medical services provided on October 20?

a. $200 of revenue on October 20
b. $20 of revenue on October 20 and $180 of revenue on November 19
c. $200 of revenue on November 19
d. $180 of revenue on October 20 and the remaining $20 on November 19

4. The Animal Adventure zoo gift shop sells stuffed animal toys. Its stuffed giraffe has a suggested retail price of $19.95. The zoo initially priced it at $17.99, but it is now marked down to $13.50. At other zoos, this same stuffed giraffe is priced at $15.99. An Animal Adventure zoo customer purchases the giraffe for $13.50 from the gift shop. At what price should Animal Adventure record the sale?

a. $13.50
b. $15.99
c. $17.99
d. $19.95

5. According to U.S. GAAP, when should revenue be recognized?

a. When cash is received from the customer
b. When the service is performed or the goods have been delivered to the customer
c. When the goods or services have been priced and offered for sale
d. At the stated date in the contract

6. All of the following are types of adjusting entries *except*

a. depreciation.
b. deferrals.
c. accruals.
d. transactions.

7. Alomar Corporation had a balance of $1,000 in Prepaid Supplies at the beginning of the year. The company purchased $700 of supplies during the year. At year end, Prepaid Supplies had a balance of $1,100. What is the amount of Supplies Expense that Alomar Corporation will recognize for the year?

a. $600
b. $700
c. $800
d. $1,100

8. What type of account is Unearned Revenue?

a. Asset
b. Liability
c. Revenue
d. Expense

9. What data flows from the statement of retained earnings to the balance sheet?

a. Net income
b. Cash
c. Ending retained earnings
d. Assets

10. Which financial statement reports assets, liabilities, and equity?

a. Income statement
b. Statement of retained earnings
c. Balance sheet
d. Statement of cash flows

11. A company's balance of retained earnings on January 1 was $35 million. During the year, sales revenue was $82 million, while expenses totaled $50 million. The company declared and paid $5 million in cash dividends during the year. What was the balance of retained earnings at the end of the year?

a. $62 million
b. $67 million
c. $72 million
d. $172 million

12. Which of the following accounts would need to be closed at the end of the period?

a. Cash
b. Supplies expense
c. Unearned revenue
d. Accounts receivable

13. All of the following accounts are temporary accounts *except* for

a. sales revenue.
b. salaries expense.
c. dividends.
d. prepaid insurance.

14. How are the assets and liabilities ordered on the balance sheet?

a. Alphabetical order
b. Based on liquidity (most liquid to least liquid)
c. Based on liquidity (least liquid to most liquid)
d. Random order

15. Which ratio measures the ability to pay current liabilities with current assets?

a. Debt ratio
b. Current ratio
c. Liability ratio
d. Asset ratio

16. Total assets are $12.0 million, with $4.0 million being long-term assets. Current liabilities are $2.5 million and total liabilities are $6.5 million. The current ratio would be closest to:

a. 1.6.
b. 1.8.
c. 3.2.
d. 4.8.

Excel Project
Autograded Excel Project available in **MyLab Accounting**.

ASSESS YOUR PROGRESS

Ethics Check

EC3-1. Identify ethical principle violated

For each of the situations listed, identify which of three principles (integrity, objectivity and independence, or due care) from the AICPA Code of Professional Conduct is violated. Assume all persons listed in the situations are members of the AICPA. (Note: Refer to the AICPA Code of Professional Conduct contained on pages 25–27 in Chapter 1 for descriptions of the principles.)

a. Drew purposely excludes a large amount of accrued salaries payable from this year's financial statements so his company's debt-to-equity ratio appears lower to investors.

b. Abbey's company determines year-end bonuses based on revenue growth. Abbey records the sales of gift cards during this month as revenue rather than as unearned revenue. None of these gift cards have been used by customers as of the end of the current month. By recording the gift card sales as revenue in the current period, revenue will be higher and Abbey's bonus will, as a result, be higher as well.

c. Debbie, a CPA, is an associate at a regional public accounting firm. Debbie's firm is auditing a local payroll company. Debbie does not disclose that her husband is a manager at the payroll company.

d. A new revenue recognition standard has been issued by the Financial Accounting Standards Board (FASB) and the International Accounting Standards Board (IASB). John does not attend training on the new revenue recognition standard because he is busy dealing with the accounting impact of a merger.

Short Exercises

LO 1

S3-1. ***(Learning Objective 1: Explain how accrual accounting differs from cash-basis accounting)*** Southeast Corporation made sales of $950 million during 2018. Of this amount, Southeast collected cash for $876 million. The company's cost of goods sold was $260 million, and all other expenses for the year totaled $275 million. Also during 2018, Southeast paid $410 million for its inventory and $250 million for everything else. Beginning cash was $75 million.

a. How much was Southeast's net income for 2018?

b. How much was Southeast's cash balance at the end of 2018?

LO 1

S3-2. ***(Learning Objective 1: Explain how accrual accounting differs from cash-basis accounting)*** Portage Corporation began 2018 owing notes payable of $4.0 million. During 2018, Portage borrowed $1.9 million on notes payable and paid off $1.7 million of notes payable from prior years. Interest expense for the year was $1.1 million, including $0.2 million of interest payable accrued at December 31, 2018.

Show what Portage should report for these facts on the following financial statements:

1. Income statement for 2018
   a. Interest expense

2. Balance sheet as of December 31, 2018
   a. Notes payable
   b. Interest payable

S3-3. ***(Learning Objective 2: Apply the revenue and expense recognition principles)*** As the controller of Chardon Consulting, you have hired a new employee, whom you must train. She objects to making an adjusting entry for accrued salaries at the end of the period. She reasons, "We will pay the salaries soon. Why not wait until payment to record the expense? In the end, the result will be the same." Write a reply to explain to the employee why the adjusting entry is needed for accrued salary expense. LO 2

S3-4. ***(Learning Objective 2: Apply the revenue and expense recognition principles)*** A large auto manufacturer sells large fleets of vehicles to auto rental companies, such as Budget and Hertz. Suppose Budget is negotiating with the auto manufacturer to purchase 1,000 vehicles. Write a short paragraph to explain to the auto manufacturer when the company should, and should not, record this sales revenue and the related expense for cost of goods sold. Mention the accounting principles that provide the basis for your explanation. LO 2

S3-5. ***(Learning Objective 2: Apply the revenue and expense recognition principles)*** Identify the accounting concept or principle that gives the most direction on how to account for each of the following situations: LO 2

a. A utility bill is received on December 27 and will be paid next year. When should the company record utility expense?

b. A physician performs a surgical operation and bills the patient's insurance company. It may take three months to collect from the insurance company. Should the physician record revenue now or wait until cash is collected?

c. March has been a particularly slow month, and the business will have a net loss for the second quarter of the year. Management is considering not following its customary practice of reporting quarterly earnings to the public.

d. Salary expense of $48,000 is accrued at the end of the period to measure income properly.

e. A construction company is building a highway system, which will take four years. When should the company record the revenue it earns?

S3-6. ***(Learning Objective 2: Apply the revenue and expense recognition principles)*** During 2018, Peoria Airlines paid salary expense of $40.8 million. At December 31, 2018, Peoria accrued salary expense of $2.3 million. Peoria then paid $2.6 million to its employees on January 3, 2019, the company's next payday after the end of the 2018 year. For this sequence of transactions, show what Peoria would report on its 2018 income statement and on its balance sheet at the end of 2018. LO 2

S3-7. ***(Learning Objective 3: Adjust the accounts)*** Answer the following questions about prepaid expenses: LO 3

a. On March 1, Meadow Tree Service prepaid $7,200 for six months' rent. Give the adjusting entry to record rent expense at March 31. Include the date of the entry and an explanation. Then post all amounts to the two accounts involved, and show their balances at March 31. Meadow adjusts the accounts only at March 31, the end of its fiscal year.

b. On March 1, Meadow Tree Service paid $1,050 for supplies. At March 31, Meadow has $400 of supplies on hand. Make the required journal entry at March 31. Then post all amounts to the accounts and show their balances at March 31. Assume no beginning balance in supplies.

S3-8. ***(Learning Objective 3: Adjust the accounts for depreciation)*** Suppose that on January 1 Sunbeam Travel Company paid cash of $50,000 for equipment that is expected to remain useful for four years. At the end of four years, the equipment's value is expected to be zero. LO 3

1. Make journal entries to record (a) the purchase of the equipment on January 1 and (b) annual depreciation on December 31. Include dates and explanations, and use the following accounts: Equipment, Accumulated Depreciation—Equipment, and Depreciation Expense—Equipment.
2. Post to the accounts and show their balances at December 31.
3. What is the equipment's book value at December 31?

LO 3

S3-9. ***(Learning Objective 3: Adjust the accounts for interest expense)*** Trent Restaurant borrowed $110,000 on October 1 by signing a note payable to Hometown Bank. The interest expense for each month is $825. The loan agreement requires Trent to pay interest on January 2 for October, November, and December.

1. Make Trent's adjusting entry to accrue monthly interest expense at October 31, at November 30, and at December 31. Date each entry and include its explanation.
2. Post all three entries to the Interest Payable account. You do not need to calculate the balance of the account at the end of each month.
3. Record the payment of three months' interest on January 2.

LO 3

S3-10. ***(Learning Objective 3: Adjust the accounts for interest revenue)*** Return to the situation in Short Exercise 3-9. Here you are accounting for the same transactions on the books of Hometown Bank, which lent the money to Trent Restaurant.

1. Make Hometown Bank's adjusting entry to accrue monthly interest revenue at October 31, at November 30, and at December 31. Date each entry and include its explanation.
2. Post all three entries to the Interest Receivable account. You do not need to calculate the balance of the account at the end of each month.
3. Record the receipt of three months' interest on January 2.

LO 3

S3-11. ***(Learning Objective 3: Adjust the accounts for unearned revenue)*** Write a paragraph to explain why unearned revenues are liabilities instead of revenues. In your explanation, use the following actual example: *The New York Times*, a national newspaper, collects cash from subscribers in advance and later provides news content via print newspapers and online access to subscribers over a one-year period. Explain what happens to the unearned revenue over the course of a year as *The New York Times* delivers papers and online content to subscribers. Into what account does the earned subscription revenue go as *The New York Times* delivers papers and online content? Give the journal entries that *The New York Times* would make to (a) collect $85,000 of subscription revenue in advance and (b) record earning $40,000 of subscription revenue. Include an explanation for each entry, as illustrated in the chapter.

LO 3

S3-12. ***(Learning Objective 3: Adjust the accounts for prepaid rent)*** Due to the terms of its lease, Hawke Services, Inc., pays the rent for its new office space in one annual payment of $26,800 on August 1, 2018. The lease covers the period of August 1, 2018, through July 31, 2019. Hawke Services has a year-end of December 31. Assume that Hawke Services had no other prepaid rent transactions, nor did it have a Prepaid Rent beginning balance in 2018. Give the journal entries that Hawke Services would make for (a) the annual rent payment of $26,800 on August 1 and (b) the adjusting entry for rent expense on December 31, 2018. What is the balance of Prepaid Rent at December 31, 2018?

LO 3

S3-13. ***(Learning Objective 3: Adjust the accounts for accrued and unearned revenue)*** Dexter, Inc., collects cash from customers in advance and from other customers after the sale. Journalize the following transactions for Dexter:

a. ***Accrued revenue.*** Some customers pay Dexter after Dexter has performed the service for the customer. During 2018, Dexter performed services for $22,000 on account and later received cash of $9,000 on account from these customers.

b. ***Unearned revenue.*** A few customers pay Dexter in advance, and Dexter later performs the service for the customer. During 2018, Dexter collected $4,500 cash in advance and later earned $3,000 of this amount.

S3-14. ***(Learning Objective 4: Construct the financial statements)*** Suppose Robin Sporting Goods Company reported the following data at July 31, 2018, with amounts in thousands: LO 4

Retained earnings, July 31, 2017	$ 31,500	Cost of goods sold	$136,800
Accounts receivable	34,000	Cash	50,000
Net revenues	191,000	Property and equipment, net	19,400
Total current liabilities	80,000	Common stock	26,000
All other expenses	29,000	Inventories	36,000
Other current assets	5,000	Long-term liabilities	11,700
Other assets	30,000	Dividends	0

Use these data to prepare Robin Sporting Goods Company's single-step income statement for the year ended July 31, 2018; statement of retained earnings for the year ended July 31, 2018; and classified balance sheet at July 31, 2018. Use the report format for the balance sheet. Draw arrows linking the three statements.

S3-15. ***(Learning Objective 5: Close the books)*** Use the Robin Sporting Goods Company data in Short Exercise 3-14 to make the company's closing entries at July 31, 2018. Then set up a T-account for Retained Earnings and post to that account. Compare Retained Earnings' ending balance to the amount reported on Robin's statement of retained earnings and balance sheet. What do you find? LO 5

S3-16. ***(Learning Objective 6: Analyze and evaluate liquidity and debt-paying ability)*** Robin Sporting Goods reported the following data at July 31, 2018, with amounts in thousands: LO 6

A1

	A	B	C	D	E
1	**Robin Sporting Goods Company** **Income Statement** **Year ended July 31, 2018**				
2	*(Amounts in thousands)*				
3	Net revenues	$191,000			
4	Cost of goods sold	136,800			
5	All other expenses	29,000			
6	Net income	$ 25,200			
7					

A1

	A	B	C	D	E
1	**Robin Sporting Goods Company** **Statement of Retained Earnings** **Year ended July 31, 2018**				
2	*(Amounts in thousands)*				
3	Retained earnings, July 31, 2017		$31,500		
4	Add: Net income		25,200		
5	Retained earnings, July 31, 2018		$56,700		
6					

	A	B	C	D	E
1	**Robin Sporting Goods Company** **Balance Sheet** **July 31, 2018**				
2	*(Amounts in thousands)*				
3	**Assets**				
4	Current:				
5	Cash	$ 50,000			
6	Accounts receivable	34,000			
7	Inventories	36,000			
8	Other current assets	5,000			
9	Total current assets	125,000			
10	Property and equipment, net	19,400			
11	Other assets	30,000			
12	Total assets	$174,400			
13	**Liabilities**				
14	Total current liabilities	$ 80,000			
15	Long-term liabilities	11,700			
16	Total liabilities	91,700			
17	**Stockholders' Equity**				
18	Common stock	26,000			
19	Retained earnings	56,700			
20	Total stockholders' equity	82,700			
21	Total liabilities and stockholders' equity	$174,400			
22					

1. Calculate Robin's net working capital.
2. Calculate Robin's current ratio. Round to two decimal places.
3. Calculate Robin's debt ratio. Round to two decimal places.

Do these values and ratios look strong, weak, or in between?

LO **5**

S3-17. ***(Learning Objective 5: Make closing entries and calculate net income)*** The adjusted trial balance of Amana Corporation at December 31 shows that sales revenue for the year was $513,000 and other revenue was $37,000. Cost of goods sold for that same period was $256,000, while other expenses totaled $185,000. The corporation declared and paid dividends of $12,000 during the year. The balance of retained earnings before closing entries was $457,000.

1. Prepare the closing entries for revenues, expenses, and dividends for the year.
2. What was net income for the year?
3. What is the ending balance of retained earnings after the closing entries are posted?

Exercises MyLab Accounting

Group A

LO **1, 2**

E3-18A. ***(Learning Objectives 1, 2: Explain how accrual accounting differs from cash-basis accounting; apply the revenue and expense recognition principles)*** During 2018, Able Network, Inc., which designs network servers, earned revenues of $820 million. Expenses totaled $520 million. Able collected all but $20 million of the revenues and paid $610 million on its expenses.

a. Under accrual accounting, what amount of revenue should Able report for 2018? How does the revenue principle help to answer this question?

b. Under accrual accounting, what amount of total expense should Able report for 2018? Which accounting principle helps to answer this question?

c. Redo parts a and b using the cash basis. Explain how the accrual basis differs from the cash basis.

d. Which financial statement reports revenues and expenses? Which statement reports cash receipts and cash payments?

E3-19A. ***(Learning Objectives 1, 3: Explain how accrual accounting differs from cash-basis accounting; adjust the accounts)*** An accountant made the following adjustments at December 31, the end of the accounting period:

LO **1, 3**

a. Prepaid insurance, beginning, $500. Payments for insurance during the period, $2,000. Prepaid insurance, ending, $400.
b. Interest revenue accrued, $2,500.
c. Unearned service revenue, beginning, $1,700. Unearned service revenue, ending, $300.
d. Depreciation on building, $5,600.
e. Employees' salaries owed for two days of a five-day work week; weekly payroll, $19,000.
f. Income before income tax, $21,000. Income tax rate is 35%.

Requirements

1. Journalize the adjusting entries.
2. Suppose the adjustments were not made. Calculate the overall overstatement or understatement of net income resulting from the omission of these adjustments.

E3-20A. ***(Learning Objectives 2, 3: Apply the revenue and expense recognition principles; adjust the accounts)*** Greenville Corporation experienced four situations for its supplies. Calculate the amounts that have been left blank for each situation. For situations 1 and 2, journalize the needed transaction. Consider each situation separately.

LO **2, 3**

Situation	1	2	3	4
Beginning supplies	$2,100	$1,100	$ 700	$ 500
Purchases of supplies during the year	?	400	?	500
Total amount to account for	3,500	?	?	1,000
Ending supplies	(1,100)	(800)	(600)	?
Supplies Expense	$2,400	$?	$1,500	$ 800

E3-21A. ***(Learning Objective 3: Adjust the accounts)*** Jenkins Rentals Company faced the following situations. Journalize the adjusting entry needed at December 31, 2020, for each situation. Consider each fact separately.

LO **3**

a. The business has interest expense of $3,100 that it must pay early in January 2021.
b. Interest revenue of $4,400 has been earned but not yet received.
c. On July 1, 2020, when the business collected $14,200 rent in advance, it debited Cash and credited Unearned Rent Revenue. The tenant was paying for two years' rent.
d. Salary expense is $5,700 per day—Monday through Friday—and the business pays employees each Friday. This year, December 31 falls on a Thursday.
e. The unadjusted balance of the Supplies account is $3,100. The total cost of supplies on hand is $1,200.
f. Equipment was purchased on January 1 of this year at a cost of $140,000. The equipment's useful life is five years. There is no residual value. Record depreciation for this year and then determine the equipment's book value.

E3-22A. ***(Learning Objectives 3, 4: Adjust the accounts for prepaid expenses; construct the financial statements)*** Dizzy Toys prepaid three years' rent ($36,000) on January 1, 2018. At December 31, 2018, Dizzy prepared a trial balance and then made the necessary adjusting entry at the end of the year. Dizzy adjusts its accounts once each year—on December 31.

LO **3, 4**

What amount appears for Prepaid Rent on

a. Dizzy's *unadjusted* trial balance at December 31, 2018?
b. Dizzy's *adjusted* trial balance at December 31, 2018?

What amount appears for Rent Expense on

c. Dizzy's *unadjusted* trial balance at December 31, 2018?
d. Dizzy's *adjusted* trial balance at December 31, 2018?

LO 4

E3-23A. ***(Learning Objective 4: Construct the financial statements)*** The adjusted trial balance of Pearl Industries, Inc., follows.

	A	B	C	D	E
1	**Pearl Industries, Inc. Adjusted Trial Balance December 31, 2018**				
2	*(Amounts in thousands)*				
3	**Account**	**Debit**	**Credit**		
4	Cash	$ 4,400			
5	Accounts receivable	1,600			
6	Inventories	2,700			
7	Prepaid expenses	1,800			
8	Property, plant, and equipment	16,500			
9	Accumulated depreciation—property, plant, and equipment		$ 2,400		
10	Other assets	9,700			
11	Accounts payable		7,900		
12	Income tax payable		400		
13	Other liabilities		2,700		
14	Common stock		14,500		
15	Retained earnings (beginning December 31, 2017)		5,700		
16	Dividends	1,600			
17	Sales revenue		43,200		
18	Cost of goods sold	25,100			
19	Selling, administrative, and general expenses	10,500			
20	Income tax expense	2,900			
21	Total	$76,800	$76,800		
22					

Requirement

1. Prepare Pearl Industries, Inc.'s single-step income statement and statement of retained earnings for the year ended December 31, 2018, and its balance sheet on that date.

LO 3, 4

E3-24A. ***(Learning Objectives 3, 4: Adjust the accounts; construct the financial statements)*** The adjusted trial balances of Patterson Corporation at August 31, 2018, and August 31, 2017, include these amounts (in millions):

	2018	2017
Accounts receivable	$430	$210
Prepaid insurance	330	400
Accrued liabilities payable (for other operating expenses)	710	640

Patterson Corporation completed these transactions (in millions) during the year ended August 31, 2018.

Collections from customers	$20,400
Payment of prepaid insurance	470
Cash payments for other operating expenses	4,000

Calculate the amount of sales revenue, insurance expense, and other operating expenses to report on the income statement for the year ended August 31, 2018. Assume all sales are on account.

E3-25A. ***(Learning Objective 5: Close the books)*** Prepare the closing entries from the following selected accounts from the records of North Pole Enterprises at December 31, 2018: LO 5

Cost of services sold	$14,800	Service revenue	$32,200
Accumulated depreciation	41,100	Depreciation expense	4,100
Selling, general, and administrative expenses	6,200	Other revenue	1,000
		Dividends declared	500
Retained earnings, December 31, 2017	2,000	Income tax expense	900
		Income tax payable	600

How much net income did North Pole Enterprises earn during 2018? Prepare a T-account for Retained Earnings to show the December 31, 2018, balance of Retained Earnings.

E3-26A. ***(Learning Objectives 3, 5: Adjust the accounts; close the books)*** The unadjusted trial balance and income statement amounts from the December 31 adjusted trial balance of Crawford Production Company follow. LO 3, 5

	A	B	C	D	E	F	G	H
1	**Crawford Production Company**							
2	**Account**	**Unadjusted Trial Balance**		**Adjustments**		**Adjusted Trial Balance**		
3	Cash	15,000						
4	Prepaid rent	1,000						
5	Equipment	42,000						
6	Accumulated depreciation—equipment		6,700					
7	Accounts payable		4,000					
8	Salary payable							
9	Unearned service revenue		8,600					
10	Income tax payable							
11	Notes payable, long-term		11,000					
12	Common stock		8,300					
13	Retained earnings		13,000					
14	Dividends	1,000						
15	Service revenue		13,300				18,300	
16	Salary expense	4,200				4,800		
17	Rent expense	1,700				2,100		
18	Depreciation expense—equipment					900		
19	Income tax expense					1,800		
20	Total	$ 64,900	$ 64,900			$ 9,600	$ 18,300	
21								

Requirement

1. Journalize the adjusting and closing entries of Crawford Production Company at December 31. There was only one adjustment to Service Revenue.

LO 4, 6

E3-27A. ***(Learning Objectives 4, 6: Construct the financial statements; analyze and evaluate liquidity and debt-paying ability)*** Refer to Exercise 3-26A.

Requirements

1. Use the data in the partial worksheet to prepare Crawford Production Company's classified balance sheet at December 31 of the current year. Use the report format. First you must calculate the adjusted balance for several of the balance-sheet accounts.
2. Calculate Crawford Production Company's net working capital, current ratio, and debt ratio at December 31. A year ago, net working capital was $5,000, the current ratio was 1.54, and the debt ratio was 0.59. Indicate whether the company's ability to pay its debts—both current and total—improved or deteriorated during the current year.

LO 6

E3-28A. ***(Learning Objective 6: Analyze and evaluate liquidity and debt-paying ability)*** Peyton Company reported these ratios at December 31, 2018 (dollar amounts in millions):

$$\text{Current ratio} = \frac{\$20}{\$10} = 2.00$$

$$\text{Debt ratio} = \frac{\$40}{\$70} = 0.57$$

Peyton Company completed these transactions during 2019:

a. Purchased equipment on account, $5
b. Paid long-term debt, $5
c. Collected cash from customers in advance, $4
d. Accrued interest expense, $3
e. Made cash sales, $7

Determine whether each transaction improved or hurt the company's current ratio and debt ratio.

Group B

LO 1, 2

E3-29B. ***(Learning Objectives 1, 2: Explain how accrual accounting differs from cash-basis accounting; apply the revenue and expense recognition principles)*** During 2018, Barron Network, Inc., which designs network servers, earned revenues of $740 million. Expenses totaled $560 million. Barron collected all but $26 million of the revenues and paid $610 million on its expenses.

a. Under accrual accounting, what amount of revenue should Barron report for 2018? How does the revenue principle help to answer this question?
b. Under accrual accounting, what amount of total expense should Barron report for 2018? Which accounting principle helps to answer this question?
c. Redo parts a and b using the cash basis. Explain how the accrual basis differs from the cash basis.
d. Which financial statement reports revenues and expenses? Which statement reports cash receipts and cash payments?

LO 1, 3

E3-30B. ***(Learning Objectives 1, 3: Explain how accrual accounting differs from cash-basis accounting; adjust the accounts)*** An accountant made the following adjustments at December 31, the end of the accounting period:

a. Prepaid insurance, beginning, $400. Payments for insurance during the period, $2,100. Prepaid insurance, ending, $600.
b. Interest revenue accrued, $2,400.
c. Unearned service revenue, beginning, $1,700. Unearned service revenue, ending, $400.
d. Depreciation on building, $5,300.
e. Employees' salaries owed for two days of a five-day work week; weekly payroll, $21,000.
f. Income before income tax, $30,000. Income tax rate is 35%.

Requirements

1. Journalize the adjusting entries.
2. Suppose the adjustments were not made. Calculate the overall overstatement or understatement of net income resulting from the omission of these adjustments.

LO 2, 3

E3-31B. ***(Learning Objectives 2, 3: Apply the revenue and expense recognition principles; adjust the accounts)*** Englewood Corporation experienced four situations for its supplies. Calculate the amounts that have been left blank for each situation. For situations 1 and 2, journalize the needed transaction. Consider each situation separately.

Situation	1	2	3	4
Beginning supplies	$1,500	$ 700	$ 700	$ 1,000
Purchases of supplies during the year	?	400	?	800
Total amount to account for	2,900	?	?	1,800
Ending supplies	(990)	(900)	(700)	?
Supplies Expense	$1,910	$?	$ 1,300	$ 1,600

LO 3

E3-32B. ***(Learning Objective 3: Adjust the accounts)*** Thornton Company faced the following situations. Journalize the adjusting entry needed at December 31, 2020, for each situation. Consider each fact separately.

a. The business has interest expense of $3,800 that it must pay early in January 2021.
b. Interest revenue of $4,300 has been earned but not yet received.
c. On July 1, 2020, when the business collected $12,600 rent in advance, it debited Cash and credited Unearned Rent Revenue. The tenant was paying for two years' rent.
d. Salary expense is $6,500 per day—Monday through Friday—and the business pays employees each Friday. This year, December 31 falls on a Thursday.
e. The unadjusted balance of the Supplies account is $3,300. The total cost of supplies on hand is $1,200.
f. Equipment was purchased on January 1 of this year at a cost of $60,000. The equipment's useful life is five years. There is no residual value. Record depreciation for this year and then determine the equipment's book value.

LO 3, 4

E3-33B. ***(Learning Objectives 3, 4: Adjust the accounts for prepaid expenses; construct the financial statements)*** Fairmount Co. prepaid three years' rent ($31,500) on January 1, 2018. At December 31, 2018, Fairmount prepared a trial balance and then made the necessary adjusting entry at the end of the year. Fairmount adjusts its accounts once each year—on December 31.

What amount appears for Prepaid Rent on

a. Fairmount's *unadjusted* trial balance at December 31, 2018?
b. Fairmount's *adjusted* trial balance at December 31, 2018?

What amount appears for Rent Expense on

c. Fairmount's *unadjusted* trial balance at December 31, 2018?
d. Fairmount's *adjusted* trial balance at December 31, 2018?

LO 4

E3-34B. ***(Learning Objective 4: Construct the financial statements)*** The adjusted trial balance of Sabrina, Inc., follows:

	A	B	C
1	**Sabrina, Inc.** **Adjusted Trial Balance** **December 31, 2018**		
2	*(Amounts in thousands)*		
3	**Account**	**Debit**	**Credit**
4	Cash	$ 4,300	
5	Accounts receivable	1,300	
6	Inventories	2,400	
7	Prepaid expenses	1,800	
8	Property, plant, and equipment	16,700	
9	Accumulated depreciation—property, plant, and equipment		$ 2,300
10	Other assets	9,400	
11	Accounts payable		7,700
12	Income tax payable		600
13	Other liabilities		2,200
14	Common stock		14,600
15	Retained earnings (beginning December 31, 2017)		5,900
16	Dividend	1,200	
17	Sales revenue		42,500
18	Cost of goods sold	25,600	
19	Selling, administrative, and general expenses	10,600	
20	Income tax expense	2,500	
21	Total	$ 75,800	$ 75,800
22			

Requirement

1. Prepare Sabrina's single-step income statement and statement of retained earnings for the year ended December 31, 2018, and its balance sheet on that date.

LO 3, 4

E3-35B. ***(Learning Objectives 3, 4: Adjust the accounts; construct the financial statements)*** The adjusted trial balances of Verne Corporation at August 31, 2018, and August 31, 2017, include these amounts (in millions):

	2018	2017
Accounts receivable	$490	$260
Prepaid insurance	330	450
Accrued liabilities payable (for other operating expenses)	730	640

Verne completed these transactions (in millions) during the year ended August 31, 2018.

Collections from customers	$20,800
Payment of prepaid insurance	480
Cash payments for other operating expenses	4,800

Calculate the amount of sales revenue, insurance expense, and other operating expenses to report on the income statement for the year ended August 31, 2018. Assume all sales are on account.

E3-36B. ***(Learning Objective 5: Close the books)*** Prepare the closing entries from the following selected accounts from the records of North Shore, Inc., at December 31, 2018: LO 5

Cost of services sold	$14,400	Service revenue	$31,700
Accumulated depreciation ...	41,400	Depreciation expense	4,600
Selling, general, and administrative expenses	6,400	Other revenue	100
		Dividends declared	500
Retained earnings, December 31, 2017	2,500	Income tax expense	800
		Income tax payable	400

How much net income did North Shore earn during 2018? Prepare a T-account for Retained Earnings to show the December 31, 2018, balance of Retained Earnings.

E3-37B. ***(Learning Objectives 3, 5: Adjust the accounts; close the books)*** The unadjusted trial balance and income statement amounts from the December 31 adjusted trial balance of Lauer Production Company follow: LO 3, 5

A1

	A	B	C	D	E	F	G
1	**Lauer Production Company**						
2	**Account**	**Unadjusted Trial Balance**		**Adjustments**		**Adjusted Trial Balance**	
3	Cash	18,000					
4	Prepaid rent	1,000					
5	Equipment	45,000					
6	Accumulated depreciation—equipment		6,100				
7	Accounts payable		4,300				
8	Salary payable						
9	Unearned service revenue		8,900				
10	Income tax payable						
11	Notes payable, long-term		15,000				
12	Common stock		8,100				
13	Retained earnings		15,400				
14	Dividends	1,500					
15	Service revenue		13,500				20,900
16	Salary expense	4,700				5,000	
17	Rent expense	1,100				1,800	
18	Depreciation expense—equipment					950	
19	Income tax expense					1,400	
20	Total	71,300	71,300			9,150	20,900
21							

Requirement

1. Journalize the adjusting and closing entries of Lauer Production Company at December 31. There was only one adjustment to Service Revenue.

E3-38B. ***(Learning Objectives 4, 6: Construct the financial statements; analyze and evaluate liquidity and debt-paying ability)*** Refer to Exercise 3-37B. LO 4, 6

Requirements

1. Use the data in the partial worksheet to prepare Lauer Production Company's classified balance sheet at December 31 of the current year. Use the report format. First you must calculate the adjusted balance for several of the balance-sheet accounts.
2. Calculate Lauer Production Company's net working capital, current ratio, and debt ratio at December 31. A year ago, the net working capital was $10,600, the current ratio was 2.40, and the debt ratio was 0.50. Indicate whether the company's ability to pay its debts—both current and total—improved or deteriorated during the current year.

LO 6

E3-39B. ***(Learning Objective 6: Analyze and evaluate liquidity and debt-paying ability)*** Burnes Consulting Company reported these ratios at December 31, 2018 (dollar amounts in millions):

$$\text{Current ratio} = \frac{\$20}{\$10} = 2.00 \qquad \text{Debt ratio} = \frac{\$30}{\$60} = 0.50$$

Burnes Consulting completed these transactions during 2019:

a. Purchased equipment on account, $4
b. Paid long-term debt, $7
c. Collected cash from customers in advance, $5
d. Accrued interest expense, $6
e. Made cash sales, $8

Determine whether each transaction improved or hurt the company's current ratio and debt ratio.

Serial Exercise

Exercise 3-40 continues the Olivia Matthews, Certified Public Accountant, Professional Corporation (P.C.), situation begun in Exercise 2-37 of Chapter 2.

LO 3, 4, 5, 6

E3-40. ***(Learning Objectives 3, 4, 5, 6: Adjust the accounts; construct the financial statements; close the books; analyze and evaluate liquidity and debt-paying ability)*** Refer to Exercise 2-37 of Chapter 2. Start from the trial balance and the posted T-accounts that Olivia Matthews, Certified Public Accountant, Professional Corporation (P.C.), prepared for her accounting practice at May 18, 2018. A professional corporation is not subject to income tax. Later in May, the business completed these transactions:

May 21	Received $2,400 in advance for tax work to be performed over the next 30 days.
22	Hired an assistant to be paid on the 15th day of each month.
26	Paid $900 for the supplies purchased on May 5.
28	Collected $3,100 from the client on May 18.
31	Declared and paid dividends of $1,200.

Requirements

1. Journalize the transactions of May 21 through 31.
2. Post the May 21 to 31 transactions to the T-accounts, keying all items by date.
3. Prepare an Excel spreadsheet showing the unadjusted trial balance at May 31. Set up the worksheet to prepare the adjusted trial balance as seen in Exhibit 3-9 on page 138.
4. At May 31, Matthews gathers the following information for the adjusting entries:
   a. Accrued service revenue, $2,000.
   b. Earned $800 of the service revenue collected in advance on May 21.
   c. Supplies on hand, $300.
   d. Depreciation expense equipment, $30; furniture, $100.
   e. Accrued expense for assistant's salary, $900.
   Refer to the Excel spreadsheet you prepared in Requirement 3. Make these adjustments in the adjustments columns and complete the adjusted trial balance at May 31.
5. Journalize and post the adjusting entries. Denote each adjusting amount as Adj and an account balance as Bal.
6. Prepare the single-step income statement and statement of retained earnings of Olivia Matthews, Certified Public Accountant, P.C., for the month ended May 31 and the classified balance sheet at that date.
7. Journalize and post the closing entries at May 31. Denote each closing amount as Clo and an account balance as Bal.
8. Calculate the net working capital, current ratio, and the debt ratio of Olivia Matthews, Certified Public Accountant, P.C., and determine if they indicate a strong or weak financial position.

Quiz

Test your understanding of accrual accounting by answering the following questions. Select the best choice from among the possible answers given.

Questions 41–43 are based on the following facts: Jenna Newbury began a music business in July 2018. Newbury prepares monthly financial statements and uses the accrual basis of accounting. The following transactions are Newbury Company's only activities during July through October:

Jul 14	Bought music on account for $65, with payment to the supplier due in 90 days.
Aug 3	Performed a job on account for Alanna Turner for $55, collectible from her in 30 days. Used up all the music purchased on July 14.
Sep 16	Collected the $55 receivable from Turner.
Oct 22	Paid the $65 owed to the supplier from the July 14 transaction.

Q3-41. In which month should Newbury record the cost of the music as an expense?

a. July
b. August
c. September
d. October

Q3-42. In which month should Newbury report the $55 revenue on its income statement?

a. September
b. August
c. October
d. July

Q3-43. If Newbury Company uses the *cash* basis of accounting instead of the accrual basis, in what month will Newbury report revenue and in what month will it report expense?

Revenue	Expense
a. August	October
b. September	July
c. August	August
d. September	October

Q3-44. Using the accrual basis, in which month should revenue be recorded?

a. In the month that cash is collected from the customer
b. In the month that goods are ordered by the customer
c. In the month that goods are shipped to the customer
d. In the month that the invoice is mailed to the customer

Q3-45. On January 1 of the current year, Oliver Company paid $2,100 rent to cover six months (January–June). Oliver recorded this transaction as follows:

	A	B	C	D	E	F
1		Journal Entry				
2	**Date**	**Accounts**	**Debit**	**Credit**		
3	Jan 1	Prepaid Rent	2,100			
4		Cash		2,100		
5						

Oliver adjusts the accounts at the end of each month. Based on these facts, the adjusting entry at the end of January should include

a. a credit to Prepaid Rent for $350.
b. a debit to Prepaid Rent for $1,750.
c. a credit to Prepaid Rent for $1,750.
d. a debit to Prepaid Rent for $350.

Q3-46. Assume the same facts as in question 3-45. Oliver's adjusting entry at the end of February should include a debit to Rent Expense in the amount of

a. $700.
b. $0.
c. $350.
d. $1,400.

Q3-47. What effect does the adjusting entry in question 3-46 have on Oliver's net income for February?

a. Net income will decrease by $350.
b. Net income will increase by $350.
c. Net income will increase by $700.
d. Net income will decrease by $700.

Q3-48. An adjusting entry recorded June salary expense that will be paid in July. Which statement best describes the effect of this adjusting entry on the company's accounting equation?

a. Assets are not affected, liabilities are increased, and stockholders' equity is decreased.
b. Assets are not affected, liabilities are increased, and stockholders' equity is increased.
c. Assets are decreased, liabilities are not affected, and stockholders' equity is decreased.
d. Assets are decreased, liabilities are increased, and stockholders' equity is decreased.

Q3-49. On April 1, 2018, Solutions Insurance Company sold a one-year insurance policy covering the year ended March 31, 2019. Solutions collected the full $2,700 on April 1, 2018. Solutions made the following journal entry to record the receipt of cash in advance:

A1

	A	B	C	D	E	F
1		**Journal Entry**				
2	**Date**	**Accounts**	**Debit**	**Credit**		
3	Apr 1	Cash	2,700			
4		Unearned Revenue		2,700		
5						

Nine months have passed, and Solutions has made no adjusting entries. Based on these facts, the adjusting entry needed at December 31, 2018, is

A1

	A	B	C	D	E	F
1	a.	Unearned Revenue	2,025			
2		Insurance Revenue		2,025		
3	b.	Insurance Revenue	2,025			
4		Unearned Revenue		2,025		
5	c.	Unearned Revenue	675			
6		Insurance Revenue		675		
7	d.	Insurance Revenue	675			
8		Unearned Revenue		675		
9						

Q3-50. The Unearned Revenue account of Melrose Incorporated began 2018 with a normal balance of $5,500 and ended 2018 with a normal balance of $16,000. During 2018, the Unearned Revenue account was credited for $19,000 that Melrose will earn later. Based on these facts, how much revenue did Melrose earn in 2018?

a. $8,500
b. $19,000
c. $29,500
d. $0

Q3-51. What is the effect on the financial statements of recording depreciation on equipment?

a. Assets are decreased, but net income and stockholders' equity are not affected.
b. Net income is not affected, but assets and stockholders' equity are decreased.
c. Net income, assets, and stockholders' equity are all decreased.
d. Net income and assets are decreased, but stockholders' equity is not affected.

Q3-52. For 2018, Broadview Company had revenues in excess of expenses. Which statement describes Broadview's closing entries at the end of 2018? (Assume there is only one closing entry for both revenue and expenses.)

a. Revenues will be credited, expenses will be debited, and retained earnings will be credited.
b. Revenues will be debited, expenses will be credited, and retained earnings will be debited.
c. Revenues will be credited, expenses will be debited, and retained earnings will be debited.
d. Revenues will be debited, expenses will be credited, and retained earnings will be credited.

Q3-53. Which of the following accounts would *not* be included in the closing entries?

a. Service Revenue
b. Depreciation Expense
c. Retained Earnings
d. Accumulated Depreciation

Q3-54. A major purpose of preparing closing entries is to

a. update the Retained Earnings account.
b. adjust the asset accounts to their correct current balances.
c. close out the Supplies account.
d. zero out the liability accounts.

Q3-55. Selected data for the Rubio Company follow:

Current assets	$ 31,200	Current liabilities	$ 26,000
Long-term assets	185,000	Long-term liabilities	110,000
Total revenues	199,000	Total expenses	160,000

Based on these facts, what are Rubio's current ratio and debt ratio?

Current ratio	Debt ratio
a. 1.200	0.629
b. 1.590	0.629
c. 8.315	0.833
d. 1.244	0.236

Q3-56. Unadjusted net income equals $5,500. Calculate what net income will be after the following adjustments:

1. Salaries payable to employees, $510
2. Interest due on note payable at the bank, $90
3. Unearned revenue that has been earned, $850
4. Supplies used, $200

Q3-57. Salary Payable at the beginning of the month totals $26,000. During the month, salaries of $125,000 were accrued as expense. If ending Salary Payable is $10,000, what amount of cash did the company pay for salaries during the month?

a. $141,000
b. $136,000
c. $89,000
d. $161,000

Problems MyLab Accounting

Group A

LO 1 **P3-58A.** ***(Learning Objective 1: Explain how accrual accounting differs from cash-basis accounting)*** Berkley Consulting had the following selected transactions in July:

July	1	Prepaid insurance for July through September, $3,900.
	4	Purchased office furniture for cash, $3,000.
	5	Performed services and received cash, $1,800.
	8	Paid advertising expense, $300.
	11	Performed service on account, $3,100.
	19	Purchased computer on account, $1,600.
	24	Collected for July 11 service.
	26	Paid account payable from July 19.
	29	Paid salary expense, $1,100.
	31	Adjusted for July insurance expense (see July 1).
	31	Earned revenue of $400 that was collected in advance back in June.
	31	Recorded July depreciation expense on all fixed assets, $408.

Requirements

1. Show how each transaction would be handled (in terms of recognizing revenues and expenses) using the cash basis and the accrual basis.
2. Calculate July income (loss) before tax under each accounting method.
3. Indicate which measure of net income or net loss is preferable. Use the transactions on July 11 and July 24 to explain.

LO 3 **P3-59A.** ***(Learning Objective 3: Adjust the accounts)*** Journalize the adjusting entry needed on December 31, the end of the current accounting period, for each of the following independent cases affecting Castaway Corporation. Include an explanation for each entry.

a. The details of Prepaid Insurance are as follows:

Prepaid Insurance		
Jan 1 Bal	2,900	
Mar 31	4,000	

Castaway prepays insurance on March 31 each year. At December 31, $1,700 is still prepaid.

b. Castaway pays employees each Friday. The amount of the weekly payroll is $6,100 for a five-day work week. The current accounting period ends on a Wednesday.

c. Castaway has a note receivable. During the current year, Castaway has earned accrued interest revenue of $700 that it will collect next year.

d. The beginning balance of supplies was $3,000. During the year, Castaway purchased supplies costing $6,200, and at December 31 supplies on hand total $2,200.

e. Castaway is providing services for Blue Whale Investments, and the owner of Blue Whale paid Castaway an annual service fee of $10,500. Castaway recorded this amount as Unearned Service Revenue. Castaway estimates that it has earned 60% of the total fee during the current year.

f. Depreciation for the current year includes Office Furniture, $3,800, and Equipment, $5,400.

P3-60A. ***(Learning Objectives 3, 4: Adjust the accounts; construct the financial statements)*** Consider the unadjusted trial balance of Princess, Inc., at December 31, 2020, and the related month-end adjustment data.

LO **3, 4**

A1

	A	B	C	D	E	F	G
1	**Princess, Inc.** **Trial Balance Worksheet** **December 31, 2020**						
2		**Trial Balance**		**Adjustments**		**Adjusted Trial Balance**	
3	**Account**	**Debit**	**Credit**	**Debit**	**Credit**	**Debit**	**Credit**
4	Cash	9,400					
5	Accounts receivable	2,200					
6	Prepaid rent	1,200					
7	Supplies	2,600					
8	Furniture	48,000					
9	Accumulated depreciation—furniture		3,900				
10	Accounts payable		3,800				
11	Salary payable						
12	Common stock		6,000				
13	Retained earnings		32,210				
14	Dividends	3,800					
15	Service revenue		25,100				
16	Salary expense	3,300					
17	Rent expense						
18	Utilities expense	510					
19	Depreciation expense—furniture						
20	Supplies expense						
21	Total	71,010	71,010				
22							

Adjustment data at December 31, 2020:

a. Accrued service revenue at December 31, $2,980.

b. Prepaid rent expired during the month. The unadjusted prepaid balance of $1,200 relates to the period December 1, 2020, through February 28, 2021.

c. Supplies used during December, $2,160.

d. Depreciation on furniture for the month. The estimated useful life of the furniture is five years.

e. Accrued salary expense at December 31 for Monday, Tuesday, and Wednesday. The five-day weekly payroll of $15,000 will be paid on Friday.

Requirements

1. Prepare the adjusted trial balance of Princess, Inc., at December 31, 2020. Key each adjusting entry by letter.
2. Prepare the single-step monthly income statement, the statement of retained earnings, and the classified balance sheet. Draw arrows linking the three statements.

LO 3

P3-61A. ***(Learning Objective 3: Adjust the accounts)*** Appletree Rental Company's unadjusted and adjusted trial balances at June 30, 2018, follow.

	A	B	C	D	E
1	**Appletree Rental Company** **Trial Balance Worksheet** **June 30, 2018**				
2		**Trial Balance**		**Adjusted Trial Balance**	
3	**Account**	**Debit**	**Credit**	**Debit**	**Credit**
4	Cash	$ 8,400		$ 8,400	
5	Accounts receivable	6,100		6,880	
6	Interest receivable			600	
7	Note receivable	4,400		4,400	
8	Supplies	1,500		200	
9	Prepaid insurance	3,100		1,800	
10	Building	68,000		68,000	
11	Accumulated depreciation—building		$ 7,800		$ 9,200
12	Accounts payable		7,000		7,000
13	Wages payable				870
14	Unearned rental revenue		1,900		1,400
15	Common stock		16,000		16,000
16	Retained earnings		44,500		44,500
17	Dividends	3,300		3,300	
18	Rental revenue		19,350		20,630
19	Interest revenue		1,050		1,650
20	Depreciation expense—building			1,400	
21	Supplies expense			1,300	
22	Utilities expense	700		700	
23	Wage expense	1,700		2,570	
24	Property tax expense	400		400	
25	Insurance expense			1,300	
26	Total	$97,600	$97,600	$101,250	$101,250
27					

Requirements

1. Make the adjusting entries that account for the differences between the two trial balances.
2. Calculate Appletree's total assets, total liabilities, net income, and total equity.

P3-62A. ***(Learning Objectives 4, 6: Construct the financial statements; analyze and evaluate debt-paying ability)*** The adjusted trial balance for the year of Sunray Corporation at March 31, 2018, follows. LO 4, 6

	A	B	C
1	**Sunray Corporation** **Adjusted Trial Balance** **March 31, 2018**		
2	**Account**	**Debit**	**Credit**
3	Cash	$ 13,000	
4	Accounts receivable	19,300	
5	Supplies	2,900	
6	Prepaid rent	1,600	
7	Equipment	37,200	
8	Accumulated depreciation—equipment		$ 4,200
9	Accounts payable		9,000
10	Interest payable		500
11	Unearned service revenue		1,100
12	Income tax payable		2,100
13	Note payable		18,600
14	Common stock		12,000
15	Retained earnings		2,000
16	Dividends	12,000	
17	Service revenue		105,000
18	Depreciation expense—equipment	1,500	
19	Salary expense	40,400	
20	Rent expense	10,100	
21	Interest expense	2,700	
22	Insurance expense	4,300	
23	Supplies expense	2,400	
24	Income tax expense	7,100	
25	Total	$ 154,500	$ 154,500
26			

Requirements

1. Prepare Sunray Corporation's 2018 single-step income statement, statement of retained earnings, and balance sheet. Draw arrows linking the three financial statements.
2. Sunray's lenders require that the company maintain a debt ratio no higher than 0.50. Calculate Sunray's debt ratio at March 31, 2018, to determine whether the company is in compliance with this debt restriction. If not, suggest a way that Sunray could have avoided this difficult situation.

LO 5

P3-63A. *(Learning Objective 5: Close the books, and evaluate retained earnings)* The accounts of Valley Services, Inc., at January 31, 2018, are listed in alphabetical order.

Accounts payable	$14,000	Interest expense	$ 400
Accounts receivable	5,000	Note payable, long term	15,400
Accumulated depreciation, equipment	7,000	Other assets, long-term	14,400
Advertising expense	10,800	Prepaid expenses	6,600
Cash	26,000	Retained earnings, January 31, 2017	13,600
Common stock	4,500	Salary expense	26,300
Current portion of long-term note payable	1,000	Salary payable	2,300
Depreciation expense—equipment	2,100	Service revenue	96,000
Dividends declared	15,000	Supplies	2,400
Equipment	43,000	Supplies expense	4,500
		Unearned service revenue	2,700

Requirements

1. All adjustments have been journalized and posted, but the closing entries have not yet been made. Journalize Valley's closing entries at January 31, 2018.
2. Set up a T-account for Retained Earnings and post to that account. Then calculate Valley's net income for the year ended January 31, 2018. What is the ending balance of Retained Earnings?
3. Did Retained Earnings increase or decrease during the fiscal year? What caused the increase or the decrease?

LO 4, 6

P3-64A. *(Learning Objectives 4, 6: Construct the financial statements; analyze and evaluate liquidity and debt-paying ability)* Refer back to Problem 3-63A.

Requirements

1. Use the Valley Services data in Problem 3-63A to prepare the company's classified balance sheet at January 31, 2018.
2. Calculate Valley's net working capital, current ratio, and debt ratio at January 31, 2018, rounding to two decimal places. At January 31, 2017, net working capital was $19,500, the current ratio was 1.80, and the debt ratio was 0.15. Did Valley's ability to pay both current and total debts improve or deteriorate during the fiscal year? Evaluate Valley's debt position as strong or weak and give your reason.

LO 6

P3-65A. ***(Learning Objective 6: Analyze and evaluate liquidity and debt-paying ability)*** Bellwood Company's condensed and adapted balance sheet at December 31, 2018, follows:

	(In millions)
Total current assets	$15.2
Property, plant, equipment, and other assets	15.9
	$31.1
Total current liabilities	$ 9.4
Total long-term liabilities	5.9
Total stockholders' equity	15.8
	$31.1

Assume that during the first quarter of the following year, 2019, Bellwood completed the following transactions:

a. Earned revenue, $2.6 million, on account.
b. Borrowed $5.0 million in long-term debt.
c. Paid half of the current liabilities.
d. Paid selling expense of $1.0 million.
e. Accrued general expense of $0.7 million. Credit General Expense Payable, a current liability.
f. Purchased equipment for $4.4 million, paying cash of $1.7 million, and signing a long-term note payable for $2.7 million.
g. Recorded depreciation expense of $0.9 million.

Requirements

1. Calculate Bellwood's current ratio and debt ratio at December 31, 2018. Round to two decimal places.
2. Consider each transaction separately. Calculate Bellwood's current ratio and debt ratio after each transaction during 2019—that is, seven times. Round ratios to two decimal places.
3. Complete the following statements with either "increase" or "decrease":
   a. Revenues usually ____________ the current ratio.
   b. Revenues usually ____________ the debt ratio.
   c. Expenses usually ____________ the current ratio. (*Note:* Depreciation is an exception to this rule.)
   d. Expenses usually ____________ the debt ratio.
   e. If a company's current ratio is greater than 1.0, as it is for Bellwood, paying off a current liability will always ____________ the current ratio.
   f. Borrowing money on long-term debt will always ____________ the current ratio and the debt ratio.

Group B

LO 1

P3-66B. ***(Learning Objective 1: Explain how accrual accounting differs from cash-basis accounting)*** Westchester Consulting had the following selected transactions in May:

May	1	Prepaid insurance for May through July, $2,250.
	4	Purchased office furniture for cash, $4,000.
	5	Performed services and received cash, $1,000.
	8	Paid advertising expense, $300.
	11	Performed service on account, $3,500.
	19	Purchased computer on account, $2,000.
	24	Collected for May 11 service.
	26	Paid account payable from May 19.
	29	Paid salary expense, $1,000.
	31	Adjusted for May insurance expense (see May 1).
	31	Earned revenue of $1,000 that was collected in advance back in April.
	31	Recorded May depreciation expense on all fixed assets, $108.

Requirements

1. Show how each transaction would be handled (in terms of recognizing revenues and expenses) using the cash basis and the accrual basis.
2. Calculate May income (loss) before tax under each accounting method.
3. Indicate which measure of net income or net loss is preferable. Use the transactions on May 11 and May 24 to explain.

LO 3

P3-67B. ***(Learning Objective 3: Adjust the accounts)*** Journalize the adjusting entry needed on December 31, the end of the current accounting period, for each of the following independent cases affecting Rowling Corp. Include an explanation for each entry.

a. The details of Prepaid Insurance are as follows:

Prepaid Insurance

Jan	1	Bal	2,100	
Mar 31			3,300	

Rowling prepays insurance on March 31 each year. At December 31, $200 is still prepaid.

b. Rowling pays employees each Friday. The amount of the weekly payroll is $5,900 for a five-day work week. The current accounting period ends on Monday.

c. Rowling has a note receivable. During the current year, Rowling has earned accrued interest revenue of $400 that it will collect next year.

d. The beginning balance of supplies was $2,700. During the year, Rowling purchased supplies costing $6,400, and at December 31 supplies on hand total $2,100.

e. Rowling is providing services for Lion Investments, and the owner of Lion paid Rowling an annual service fee of $10,600. Rowling recorded this amount as Unearned Service Revenue. Rowling estimates that it has earned 70% of the total fee during the current year.

f. Depreciation for the current year includes Office Furniture, $3,400, and Equipment, $6,100.

LO 3, 4

P3-68B. ***(Learning Objectives 3, 4: Adjust the accounts; construct the financial statements)*** Consider the unadjusted trial balance of Royal, Inc., at December 31, 2020, and the related month-end adjustment data.

	A	B	C	D	E	F	G
1	**Royal, Inc.** **Trial Balance Worksheet** **December 31, 2020**						
2		**Trial Balance**		**Adjustments**		**Adjusted Trial Balance**	
3	**Account**	**Debit**	**Credit**	**Debit**	**Credit**	**Debit**	**Credit**
4	Cash	9,400					
5	Accounts receivable	1,900					
6	Prepaid rent	3,300					
7	Supplies	2,600					
8	Furniture	72,000					
9	Accumulated depreciation—furniture		3,100				
10	Accounts payable		3,400				
11	Salary payable						
12	Common stock		12,000				
13	Retained earnings		58,620				
14	Dividends	4,200					
15	Service revenue		19,300				
16	Salary expense	2,500					
17	Rent expense						
18	Utilities expense	520					
19	Depreciation expense—furniture						
20	Supplies expense						
21	Total	96,420	96,420				
22							

Adjustment data at December 31, 2020, include the following:

- **a.** Accrued service revenue at December 31, $3,850.
- **b.** Prepaid rent expired during the month. The unadjusted prepaid balance of $3,300 relates to the period December 1, 2020, through February 28, 2021.
- **c.** Supplies used during December, $2,120.
- **d.** Depreciation on furniture for the month. The furniture's expected useful life is five years.
- **e.** Accrued salary expense at December 31 for Monday, Tuesday, and Wednesday. The five-day weekly payroll is $14,000 and will be paid on Friday.

Requirements

1. Prepare the adjusted trial balance of Royal, Inc., at December 31, 2020. Key each adjusting entry by letter.
2. Prepare the single-step income statement, the statement of retained earnings, and the classified balance sheet. Draw arrows linking the three statements.

LO 3

P3-69B. ***(Learning Objective 3: Adjust the accounts)*** Crossway Rental Company's unadjusted and adjusted trial balances at June 30, 2018, follow:

	A	B	C	D	E
1	**Crossway Rental Company** **Trial Balance Worksheet** **June 30, 2018**				
2		**Trial Balance**		**Adjusted Trial Balance**	
3	**Account**	**Debit**	**Credit**	**Debit**	**Credit**
4	Cash	$ 8,400		$ 8,400	
5	Accounts receivable	6,100		6,850	
6	Interest receivable			1,000	
7	Note receivable	4,800		4,800	
8	Supplies	1,800		200	
9	Prepaid insurance	3,000		2,000	
10	Building	66,600		66,600	
11	Accumulated depreciation—building		$ 7,300		$ 8,700
12	Accounts payable		7,000		7,000
13	Wages payable				780
14	Unearned rental revenue		1,600		1,300
15	Common stock		16,000		16,000
16	Retained earnings		41,600		41,600
17	Dividends	3,000		3,000	
18	Rental revenue		20,600		21,650
19	Interest revenue		1,100		2,100
20	Depreciation expense—building			1,400	
21	Supplies expense			1,600	
22	Utilities expense	100		100	
23	Wage expense	1,200		1,980	
24	Property tax expense	200		200	
25	Insurance expense			1,000	
26	Total	$ 95,200	$ 95,200	$ 99,130	$ 99,130
27					

Requirements

1. Make the adjusting entries that account for the differences between the two trial balances.
2. Calculate Crossway's total assets, total liabilities, net income, and total equity.

P3-70B. ***(Learning Objectives 4, 6: Construct the financial statements; analyze and evaluate debt-paying ability)*** The adjusted trial balance for the year of Nelson Corporation at July 31, 2018, follows:

LO 4, 6

	A	B	C
1	**Nelson Corporation** **Adjusted Trial Balance** **July 31, 2018**		
2	**Account**	**Debit**	**Credit**
3	Cash	$ 17,000	
4	Accounts receivable	19,200	
5	Supplies	2,100	
6	Prepaid rent	1,600	
7	Equipment	36,800	
8	Accumulated depreciation—equipment		$ 5,000
9	Accounts payable		9,000
10	Interest payable		800
11	Unearned service revenue		700
12	Income tax payable		2,200
13	Note payable		18,600
14	Common stock		10,000
15	Retained earnings		4,000
16	Dividends	12,000	
17	Service revenue		106,600
18	Depreciation expense—equipment	1,200	
19	Salary expense	40,200	
20	Rent expense	11,100	
21	Interest expense	3,000	
22	Insurance expense	3,500	
23	Supplies expense	2,000	
24	Income tax expense	7,200	
25	Total	$ 156,900	$ 156,900
26			

Requirements

1. Prepare Nelson Corporation's 2018 single-step income statement, statement of retained earnings, and balance sheet. Draw arrows linking the three financial statements.
2. Nelson's lenders require that the company maintain a debt ratio no higher than 0.50. Calculate Nelson's debt ratio at July 31, 2018, to determine whether the company is in compliance with this debt restriction. If not, suggest a way Nelson Corporation could have avoided this difficult situation.

LO 5

P3-71B. ***(Learning Objective 5: Close the books, evaluate retained earnings)*** The accounts of Meadowbrook Service, Inc., at January 31, 2018, are listed in alphabetical order.

Accounts payable	$ 10,000	Interest expense	$ 200
Accounts receivable	1,000	Note payable, long-term	15,600
Accumulated depreciation, equipment	7,100	Other assets, long-term	13,900
Advertising expense	11,200	Prepaid expenses	5,000
Cash	22,000	Retained earnings, January 31, 2017	13,700
Common stock	1,500	Salary expense	27,800
Current portion of long term note payable	2,200	Salary payable	2,000
Depreciation expense—equipment	2,100	Service revenue	95,500
Dividends declared	13,000	Supplies	6,400
Equipment	43,000	Supplies expense	5,000
		Unearned service revenue	3,000

Requirements

1. All adjustments have been journalized and posted, but the closing entries have not yet been made. Journalize Meadowbrook's closing entries at January 31, 2018.
2. Set up a T-account for Retained Earnings and post to that account. Then calculate Meadowbrook's net income for the year ended January 31, 2018. What is the ending balance of Retained Earnings?
3. Did Retained Earnings increase or decrease during the fiscal year? What caused the increase or decrease?

LO 4, 6

P3-72B. ***(Learning Objectives 4, 6: Construct the financial statements; analyze and evaluate liquidity and debt-paying ability)*** Refer back to Problem 3-71B.

Requirements

1. Use the Meadowbrook Services data in Problem 3-71B to prepare the company's classified balance sheet at January 31, 2018.
2. Calculate Meadowbrook's net working capital, current ratio, and debt ratio at January 31, 2018, rounding to two decimal places. At January 31, 2017, the net working capital was $16,700, the current ratio was 1.75, and the debt ratio was 0.25. Did Meadowbrook's ability to pay both current and total liabilities improve or deteriorate during the fiscal year? Evaluate Meadowbrook's debt position as strong or weak and give your reason.

P3-73B. ***(Learning Objective 6: Analyze and evaluate liquidity and debt-paying ability)*** LO 6
McClain Company's condensed and adapted balance sheet at December 31, 2018, follows:

	(In millions)
Total current assets	$15.9
Property, plant, equipment, and other assets	16.2
	$32.1
Total current liabilities	$ 9.6
Total long-term liabilities	5.5
Total shareholders' equity	17.0
	$32.1

Assume that during the first quarter of the following year, 2019, McClain completed the following transactions:

a. Earned revenue of $2.8 million, on account.
b. Borrowed $7.0 million in long-term debt.
c. Paid half of the current liabilities.
d. Paid selling expense of $0.6 million.
e. Accrued general expense of $0.8 million. Credit General Expense Payable, a current liability.
f. Purchased equipment for $4.6 million, paying cash of $1.9 million and signing a long-term note payable for $2.7 million.
g. Recorded depreciation expense of $0.4 million.

Requirements

1. Calculate McClain's current ratio and debt ratio at December 31, 2018. Round to two decimal places.
2. Consider each transaction separately. Calculate McClain's current ratio and debt ratio after each transaction during 2019—that is, seven times. Round ratios to two decimal places.
3. Complete the following statements with either "increase" or "decrease":
   a. Revenues usually ____________ the current ratio.
   b. Revenues usually ____________ the debt ratio.
   c. Expenses usually ____________ the current ratio. (*Note:* Depreciation is an exception to this rule.)
   d. Expenses usually ____________ the debt ratio.
   e. If a company's current ratio is greater than 1.0, as for McClain, paying off a current liability will always ____________ the current ratio.
   f. Borrowing money on long-term debt will always ____________ the current ratio and the debt ratio.

Challenge Exercises and Problems

LO 6

E3-74. ***(Learning Objective 6: Analyze and evaluate liquidity and debt-paying ability)*** Saginaw Corporation reported the following current accounts at December 31, 2018 (amounts in thousands):

Cash	$1,400
Receivables	5,200
Inventory	2,400
Prepaid expenses	1,400
Accounts payable	2,400
Unearned revenue	1,300
Accrued expenses payable	2,000

During January 2019, Saginaw completed these selected transactions:

- Sold services on account, $9,400
- Depreciation expense, $200
- Paid for expenses, $7,400
- Collected from customers on account, $7,800
- Accrued expenses, $300
- Paid on account, $1,100
- Used up prepaid expenses, $1,000

Calculate Saginaw's net working capital and current ratio at December 31, 2018, and again at January 31, 2019. Did the net working capital and current ratio improve or deteriorate during January 2019? Comment on the level of the company's net working capital and current ratio.

LO 3, 4

E3-75. ***(Learning Objectives 3, 4: Adjust the accounts; calculate financial statement amounts)*** The accounts of Huntley Digital Services Company prior to the year-end adjustments follow:

Cash	$ 7,200	Common stock	$ 10,000
Accounts receivable	7,700	Retained earnings	46,000
Supplies	4,600	Dividends declared	12,000
Prepaid insurance	3,400	Service revenue	158,000
Building	105,000	Salary expense	36,000
Accumulated depreciation—building	16,200	Depreciation expense—building	
Land	57,000	Supplies expense	
Accounts payable	6,600	Insurance expense	
Salary payable		Advertising expense	7,100
Unearned service revenue	5,400	Utilities expense	2,200

Adjusting data at the end of the year include the following:

a. Unearned service revenue that has been earned, $1,620
b. Accrued service revenue, $31,600
c. Supplies used in operations, $3,500
d. Accrued salary expense, $3,000
e. Prepaid insurance expired, $1,500
f. Depreciation expense—building, $2,700

Alison Sikes, the principal stockholder, has received an offer to sell Huntley Digital Services Company. She needs to know the following information:

a. Net income for the year covered by these data
b. Total assets
c. Total liabilities
d. Total stockholders' equity
e. Proof that Total assets = Total liabilities + Total stockholders' equity after all items are updated

Requirement

Without opening any accounts, making any journal entries, or using a work sheet, provide Sikes with the requested information. The business is not subject to income tax.

LO 4

P3-76. ***(Learning Objective 4: Construct a balance sheet from given financial data)*** Crystal Detailing Company provides mobile auto detailing to its customers. The Income Statement for the month ended January 31, 2019, the Balance Sheet for December 31, 2018, and details of postings to the Cash account in the general ledger for the month of January 2019 follow:

	A	B	C	D	E
1	**Crystal Detailing Company** **Income Statement** **Month ended January 31, 2019**				
2	Revenue:				
3	Detailing revenue	$35,000			
4	Gift certificates redeemed	1,200	$36,200		
5	Expenses:				
6	Salary expense	$7,000			
7	Depreciation expense—equipment	7,000			
8	Supplies expense	3,700			
9	Advertising expense	2,400	20,100		
10	Net income		$ 16,100		
11	(Assume all revenue is on account.)				

	A	B	C	D	E	F
1			**Crystal Detailing Company** **Balance Sheet** **December 31, 2018**			
2	**Assets**			**Liabilities**		
3	Cash		$ 800	Accounts payable	$ 4,000	
4	Accounts receivable		1,800	Salary payable	1,400	
5	Supplies		1,300	Unearned service revenue	1,100	
6	Equipment	$35,000		Total liabilities	6,500	
7	Less: Accumulated			**Stockholders' Equity**		
8	depreciation	(7,000)	28,000	Common stock	14,000	
9				Retained earnings	11,400	
10				Total stockholders' equity	25,400	
11				Total liabilities and		
12	Total assets		$31,900	stockholders' equity	$31,900	
13						

Cash

Bal 12/31/2018	800		
Cash collections from customers	37,700	Salaries paid	8,000
Issuance of common stock	8,000	Dividends paid	800
		Purchase of equipment	3,500
		Payments of accounts payable	6,100
		Advertising paid	2,200
Bal 1/31/2019	?		

The following additional information is also available:

1. $1,500 of the cash collected from customers in January 2019 was for gift certificates for detailing services to be performed in the future. As of January 31, 2019, $1,400 of gift certificates were still outstanding.
2. $3,100 of supplies were purchased on account.
3. Employees are paid monthly during the first week after the end of the pay period.

Requirement

Based on these statements, prepare the Balance Sheet for January 31, 2019.

APPLY YOUR KNOWLEDGE

Serial Case

C3-77 *(Learning Objectives 3, 4: Analyze basic financial statement information)* LO **3, 4**

Note: This case is part of The Cheesecake Factory serial case contained in every chapter in this textbook.

The Cheesecake Factory Incorporated (NASDAQ: CAKE) is publicly held and uses U.S. Generally Accepted Accounting Principles (GAAP) to prepare its financial statements. Its fiscal year-end is the 52- or 53-week period ending on the Tuesday closest to December 31. In 2016, its fiscal year end was January 3, 2017.

At fiscal year-end, Cheesecake Factory makes several adjusting entries so that its assets, liabilities, income and expenses are recorded properly and in the correct time period. Here is a partial list of some accounts that require adjusting entries:

Prepaid Expenses: This current asset could include the cost of supplies used at the restaurants, including napkins, straws, tablecloths, dishes, flatware, and a variety of other items needed to stock its restaurants. The balance of these prepaid expense items at December 29, 2015, was $13,378. A physical count of the prepaid expense items performed on January 3, 2017, revealed that $12,580 of prepaid expense items remained on hand. Assume that purchases of napkins, straws, tablecloths, dishes, flatware, and other items during 2016 totaled $63,500.

Prepaid Rent: The Cheesecake Factory rents all of its locations. Some of its leases require payment of the lease in advance. At December 29, 2015, Cheesecake Factory's prepaid rent balance was $5,236. Assume that it paid a total of $47,700 in prepaid rent throughout 2016. An analysis of the prepaid rent lease agreements at the end of 2016 reveals that Cheesecake Factory had $16,072 in prepaid rent as of January 3, 2017.

Gift Cards: The Cheesecake Factory sells gift cards to customers. As of December 29, 2015, it had $153,629 in outstanding, unredeemed gift cards. Assume that during 2016, it sold $379,000 in gift cards. (When Cheesecake Factory sells a gift card, it increases (debit) Cash and increases (credit) Gift Cards, a current liability.) As of January 3, 2017, Cheesecake Factory had $123,619 in unredeemed gift cards.

Salaries and Wages Payable: The balance of Salaries and Wages Payable at December 29, 2015, was $31,570; this balance represented salaries and wages earned by Cheesecake Factory employees in 2015 that were then paid in January 2016. When Cheesecake Factory paid the $31,570 in January 2016, it reduced (debited) Salaries and Wages Payable and reduced (credited) Cash. As of January 3, 2017, Cheesecake Factory employees had earned salaries and wages of $39,401 that would be paid in early January 2017.

Requirements

1. Create the adjusting journal entry necessary at January 3, 2017, for:
   a. Prepaid Expenses
   b. Prepaid Rent
   c. Gift Cards
   d. Salaries and Wages Payable
2. If these adjusting journal entries had not been made for 2016, what would have been the impact on Cheesecake Factory's operating income?

Decision Cases

LO **3, 6**

C3-78. ***(Learning Objectives 3, 6: Adjust the accounts; analyze and evaluate liquidity)*** The unadjusted trial balance of Stone Park Services, Inc., at January 31, 2019, does not balance. The list of accounts and their balances follows. The trial balance needs to be prepared and adjusted before the financial statements at January 31, 2019, can be prepared. The manager of Stone Park Services also needs to know the business's current ratio.

Cash	$ 8,000
Accounts receivable	4,200
Supplies	800
Prepaid rent	1,200
Land	43,000
Accounts payable	12,000
Salary payable	0
Unearned service revenue	700
Note payable, due in three years	23,400
Common stock	5,000
Retained earnings	9,300
Service revenue	9,100
Salary expense	3,400
Rent expense	0
Advertising expense	900
Supplies expense	0

Requirements

1. How much *out of balance* is the trial balance? Notes Payable (the only error) is understated.
2. Stone Park Services needs to make the following adjustments at January 31:
   - **a.** Supplies of $400 were used during January.
   - **b.** The balance of prepaid rent was paid on January 1 and covers the entire calendar year of 2019. No adjustment was made on January 31.
   - **c.** At January 31, Stone Park Services owed employees $1,000.
   - **d.** Unearned service revenue of $500 was earned during January.

Prepare a corrected, adjusted trial balance. Give Notes Payable its correct balance.

3. After the error is corrected and after these adjustments are made, calculate and analyze the current ratio of Stone Park Services, Inc. Analyze this current ratio.

C3-79. ***(Learning Objectives 4, 6: Construct the financial statements; analyze and evaluate liquidity and debt-paying ability)*** On October 1, 2018, Elise Pulito opened Tree City Cafe, Inc. Pulito is now at a crossroads. The October financial statements paint a glowing picture of the business, and Pulito has asked you whether she should expand the business. To expand the business, she wants to be earning net income of $10,000 per month and have total assets of $50,000. Pulito believes she is meeting both goals. LO **4, 6**

To start the business, Pulito invested $25,000, not the $15,000 amount reported as "Common stock" on the balance sheet. The business issued $25,000 of common stock to Pulito. The bookkeeper "plugged" the $15,000 "Common stock" amount into the balance sheet to make it balance. The bookkeeper made some other errors, too. Pulito shows you the following financial statements that the bookkeeper prepared:

	A	B	C	D	E
1	**Tree City Cafe, Inc.** **Income Statement** **Month ended October 31, 2018**				
2	**Revenue:**				
3	Investments by owner	$25,000			
4	Unearned banquet sales revenue	3,000			
5			$28,000		
6	**Expenses:**				
7	Wages expense	$ 5,000			
8	Rent expense	4,000			
9	Dividends	3,000			
10	Depreciation expense—fixtures	1,000			
11			13,000		
12	**Net income**		$ 15,000		
13					

	A	B	C	D	E
1		**Tree City Cafe, Inc.** **Balance Sheet** **October 31, 2018**			
2	**Assets**		**Liabilities**		
3	Cash	$ 8,000	Accounts payable	$ 7,000	
4	Prepaid insurance	1,000	Sales revenue	32,000	
5	Insurance expense	1,000	Accumulated depreciation—		
6	Food inventory	5,000	fixtures	1,000	
7	Cost of goods sold (expense)	12,000		40,000	
8	Fixtures (tables, chairs, etc.)	24,000	**Stockholders' Equity**		
9	Dishes and silverware	4,000	Common stock	15,000	
10		$55,000		$55,000	
11					

Requirement

1. Prepare corrected financial statements for Tree City Cafe: single-step Income Statement, Statement of Retained Earnings, and Balance Sheet. Then, based on Pulito's goals and your corrected statements, recommend to Pulito whether or not she should expand the coffee shop.

LO 3, 4

C3-80. ***(Learning Objectives 3, 4: Adjust the accounts; construct the financial statements; evaluate a business based on financial statements)*** Teresa Gardner has owned and operated Gardner Advertising, Inc., since it began ten years ago. Recently, Gardner mentioned that she would consider selling the company for the right price.

Assume that you are interested in buying this business. You obtain its most recent monthly trial balance, which follows. Revenues and expenses vary little from month to month, and June is a typical month. Your investigation reveals that the trial balance does not include the effects of monthly revenues of $4,000 and expenses totaling $1,100. If you were to buy Gardner Advertising, you would hire a manager so you could devote your time to other duties. Assume that your manager would require a monthly salary of $5,000.

	A	B	C
1	**Gardner Advertising, Inc.** **Trial Balance** **June 30, 2018**		
2	Cash	$ 12,000	
3	Accounts receivable	6,900	
4	Prepaid expenses	3,200	
5	Land	158,000	
6	Plant assets	125,000	
7	Accumulated depreciation—plant assets		$ 81,500
8	Accounts payable		13,800
9	Salary payable		
10	Unearned advertising revenue		58,700
11	Common stock		50,000
12	Retained earnings		93,000
13	Dividends	9,000	
14	Advertising revenue		22,000
15	Rent expense		
16	Salary expense	4,000	
17	Utilities expense	900	
18	Depreciation expense—plant assets		
19	Supplies expense		
20	Total	$319,000	$319,000
21			

Requirements

1. Assume that the most you would pay for the business is 16 times the amount of monthly net income *you could expect to earn* from it. Calculate this possible price.
2. Gardner states that the least she will take for the business is two times its stockholders' equity on June 30. Calculate this amount.
3. Under these conditions, how much should you offer Gardner? Give your reason. (Challenge)

Ethical Issues

C3-81. Blue Vistas Energy Co. is in its third year of operations, and the company has grown. To expand the business, Blue Vistas borrowed $15 million from Bank of Forest Lake. As a condition for making this loan, the bank required that Blue Vistas maintain a current ratio of at least 1.50 and a debt ratio of no more than 0.50. If Blue Vistas does not maintain at least the minimum level of these two ratios, it will have to pay back its loan immediately.

Business recently has been worse than expected. Expenses have brought the current ratio down to 1.47 and the debt ratio up to 0.51 at December 15. Danielle Preston, the general manager, is thinking about what will happen if this current ratio is reported to the bank. Preston is considering recording some revenue on account this year that Blue Vistas will actually earn next year. The contract for this job has been signed, and Blue Vistas will deliver the natural gas during January of next year. If this revenue is recorded just one month early, Blue Vistas will be in compliance with the bank's ratio requirements.

Requirements

1. Journalize the revenue transaction (without dollar amounts), and indicate how recording this revenue in December would affect the current ratio and the debt ratio.
2. Analyze this transaction according to the Decision Framework for Making Ethical Judgments in Chapter 1:
   a. What is the issue?
   b. Who are the stakeholders, and what are the alternatives? Weigh them from the standpoint of economic, legal, and ethical implications.
   c. What decision would you make?
3. Propose an ethical course of action for Blue Vistas.

C3-82. The net income of Summit Photography Company decreased sharply during 2018. Anette Summit, the owner of the company, anticipates the need for a bank loan in 2019. Late in 2018, Summit instructed Tim Loftus, the company's controller, to record a $15,000 sale of portraits to the Summit family, even though the photos will not be shot until January 2019. Summit also told Loftus *not* to make the following December 31, 2018, adjusting entries:

Salaries owed to employees	$14,000
Prepaid insurance that has expired	$2,000

Requirements

1. Calculate the overall effect of these transactions on the company's reported income for 2018. Is reported net income overstated or understated?
2. Why did Summit take these actions? Are they ethical? Give your reason, identifying the parties helped and the parties harmed by Summit's action. Consult the Decision Framework for Making Ethical Judgments in Chapter 1. Which factor (economic, legal, or ethical) seems to be taking precedence? Identify the stakeholders and the potential consequences to each.
3. What advice would you give to Loftus?

Focus on Financials | Apple Inc.

LO **3, 4, 6**

(Learning Objectives 3, 4, 6: Adjust the accounts; construct financial statements; evaluate debt-paying ability) **Apple Inc.**—like all other businesses—adjusts its accounts prior to year-end to get correct amounts for the financial statements. Examine Apple's Consolidated Balance Sheets in Appendix A and online in the filings section of **www.sec.gov**. Pay particular attention to "Accrued expenses."

Requirements

1. Why does a company have accrued expenses payable at year-end?
2. See Apple's Consolidated Balance Sheets for 2015 and 2016. What was the balance of Accrued expenses at the end of each of those balance sheet years? What type of account is "Accrued expenses"?
3. Calculate net working capital, the current ratio, and the debt ratio for Apple at September 26, 2015, and September 24, 2016. Did the amount of net working capital and ratio values improve, deteriorate, or hold steady during fiscal 2016? Do Apple's ratio values indicate relative financial strength or weakness?

Focus on Analysis | Under Armour, Inc.

LO 1 *(Learning Objective 1: Explain accruals and deferrals)* Refer to the consolidated financial statements of **Under Armour, Inc.**, online in the filings section of **www.sec.gov**. You can retrieve the 2016 Under Armour financial statements at **www.sec.gov** by clicking on Filings and then searching for "Under Armour" under Company Filings. When you see the list of filings for the company, select the Form 10-K for 2016. Be sure to retrieve the 2016 financial statements, not another year.

During 2016, the company reported net revenues of more than $4,825 million in its consolidated statement of income. In addition, the company had numerous accruals and deferrals. (Note that all amounts in this activity are rounded to the nearest million.)

Requirements

1. Examine Note 2, Summary of Significant Accounting Policies. Explain the company's policy for recognizing each type of revenue that is included in the Consolidated Statements of Income.
2. Examine Under Armour's, consolidated balance sheets at December 31, 2016, and December 31, 2015, as well as Note 2, Summary of Significant Accounting Policies. Ending net accounts receivable for 2015 (beginning balance for 2016) were $434 million. Ending net receivables for 2016 were $623 million (all amounts are rounded to the nearest million). Explain the source of these receivables. Were all of these amounts considered collectible (see Allowance for Doubtful Accounts under Note 2)? Why or why not?
3. Refer to Under Armour, Inc.'s, consolidated balance sheets at December 31, 2016, and December 31, 2015, and examine the balances of the account entitled "Prepaid expenses and other current assets." What specific accounts might be included in this balance sheet line item? The beginning balance is $152 million, and the ending balance is $175 million. Construct a journal entry or entries that might account for the change.
4. View Note 3, Property and Equipment, Net. Notice that accumulated depreciation and amortization stood at $293 million at the end of 2015 and at $397 million at year-end 2016. Assume that depreciation and amortization expense for 2016 was $144 million. Explain what must have happened to account for the remainder of the change in the accumulated depreciation account during 2016. (Challenge)
5. In Note 2, Summary of Significant Accounting Policies, locate the paragraph entitled "Accrued Expenses." What are the primary categories of items in Accrued Expenses? What type of account is Accrued Expenses? Did the company's Accrued Expenses increase, decrease, or stay the same from 2015 to 2016? How would this change have impacted the company's overall net income in 2016?

Group Project

After completing his electrical technology degree program, Jason Whitmer accepted a position as an electrician's assistant for a large electrical repair company. After working for three years, Jason earned a master electrician's license and decided to open his own business. He had saved $10,000, which he invested in the business, transferring the money from his personal savings account. His attorney advised him to set up the business as a corporation. He received 10,000 shares of common stock in exchange for his investment.

On October 1, 2018, Jason purchased a used panel truck for $6,000 cash and some used tools for $1,200 cash. That same day, he signed a lease on a small shop building and paid $3,000 in advance for the first six months' rent. Also on October 1, 2018, he obtained an iPhone on a two-year contract, paying a $100 deposit, which he will get back at the end of the contract term. He also placed a small advertisement on Craigslist that day. Finally, Jason opened the doors of Whitmer Electronics, Inc., on October 1, 2018. After one month of operations, he hired an assistant.

At the end of the year, prompted in part by concern about his income tax situation (corporations have to pay taxes as well as their employees) and partly by a $15,000 bank loan application for shop expansion, Jason realizes that he needs to prepare financial statements. He gathers the following information for the three months ended December 31, 2018:

- Bank account deposits for collections from customers for services totaled $33,000.
- Services billed to customers but not yet collected totaled $3,000.
- Checks written included: Jason's salary, $5,000; his assistant's salary, $3,500 (he still owes the assistant $500); payroll taxes, $575; supplies purchased, $9,500 (the count of supplies still on hand on December 31 is $1,000); fuel and maintenance on truck, $1,200; insurance, $700; utilities including telephone, $825; and advertising, $600 (he still owes $100).
- According to the Internal Revenue Service, the estimated life of the truck is five years and the estimated life of the tools is three years. These assets have no estimated salvage value and you recommend that Jason use the straight-line method of depreciation.
- Jason has put Whitmer Electronics's revenue and expenses for the quarter into a spreadsheet and calculated an estimated quarterly income tax payable of $1,680.

Requirements

1. Analyze the paragraphs above for evidence of business transactions. As you do so, prepare an Excel spreadsheet that includes every financial statement account involved (e.g., cash, accounts receivable, supplies, property & equipment, etc.). (*Hint:* To make sure you enter the transactions correctly and completely, number the transactions consecutively as you recognize them.)
2. From the spreadsheet you created in Requirement 1, prepare the single-step income statement of Whitmer Electronics, Inc., using generally accepted accounting principles, for the three months ended December 31, 2018.
3. From the spreadsheet you created in Requirement 1, prepare the statement of retained earnings of Whitmer Electronics, Inc., for the three months ended December 31, 2018.
4. From the spreadsheet you created in Requirement 1, prepare the balance sheet for Whitmer Electronics, Inc., as of December 31, 2018.
5. Analyze the account "cash" that you created in Requirement 1, and prepare a statement of cash flows for Whitmer Electronics, Inc., for the three months ended December 31, 2018. Divide the various increases and decreases to the account into three categories: operating, investing, and financing. What do each of these categories mean? (Challenge)
6. Thoroughly analyze Whitmer Electronics, Inc.'s, creditworthiness for the bank loan. For this purpose, assume that the term of the loan is 5 years and that the principal balance is not due and payable until the end of the term of the loan. Only interest is payable yearly. Use all of the ratios you have learned so far. Consider not only Whitmer's present position but also its position should the loan be granted. Do you think the bank will approve Whitmer's request for the loan? Why or why not?

Quick Check Answers

1. *b*
2. *c*
3. *a*
4. *a*
5. *b*
6. *d*
7. *a [$1,000 + $700 – $1,100 =$600]*
8. *b*
9. *c*
10. *c*
11. *a*
12. *b*
13. *d*
14. *b*
15. *b*
16. *c [($12.0 – $4.0) / $2.5 = 3.2]*

Try It Solutions

Page 125

1. No. The Walt Disney Company received the cash in March but will not perform the services until June. The company will earn the revenue when the customers go through the gates and a park employee scans the barcode on the tickets on June 1, 2, 3, and 4. Until this happens, The Walt Disney Company must recognize a liability to the customer for 4 days of admission to Disney World (unearned revenue).

2. No. The Walt Disney Company has paid cash for rent in advance. No expense has yet been incurred because the company has not yet occupied the space. This prepaid rent is an asset because Disney has acquired the use of a store location in the future. Rent expense in the amount of $10,000 will be recognized during each of the next six months as the store is occupied.

Page 129

A1

	A	B	C	D	E	F
1		Supplies Expense ($5,000 + $7,000 − $3,000)	9,000			
2		Supplies		9,000		
3						
4		Ending balance of supplies = $3,000 (the supplies				
5		still on hand)				
6						

Page 131

$24,000 − $400 − $400 = $23,200.

Page 134

A1

	A	B	C	D	E	F
1	Jun 30	Interest Receivable	100			
2		Interest Revenue		100		
3		*To accrue interest revenue.*				
4						

4 Internal Control and Cash

LEARNING OBJECTIVES

1. **Describe** fraud and its impact
2. **Explain** the objectives and components of internal control
3. **Evaluate** internal controls over cash receipts and cash payments
4. **Prepare** a bank reconciliation
5. **Report** cash on the balance sheet

SPOTLIGHT

Cooking the Books at Green Valley Coffee Company: $10 million Is a Lot of Beans!

Although a fictional company is used in the following vignette, it is based on a true story:

Green Valley Coffee Company, based in Littleton, Colorado, had achieved a worldwide reputation over its 40-year history for its premium roasted and uniquely flavored coffees as well as syrups, candies, and confections. Starting with just one small store in 1988, the company had grown rapidly, achieving meteoric sales growth between 1995 and 2016. By that time, it operated over 100 stores in upscale shopping areas along interstate highways across the midwestern United States. The company's store sales more than doubled from $20,000,000 in 2012, to over $50,000,000 in 2016. The company's Internet sales of coffee products brought in an additional $10,000,000 in 2016. ●

PondPond/Shutterstock

However, in early 2017, the company's top management began to suspect that something was amiss. They noticed that between 2011 and 2016, the company's cash balances and profits had declined. Eventually, they traced the problem back to Joe Johnson, the company controller, who had been one of Green Valley Coffee Company's most trusted employees since 2005.

As controller, Johnson was given the job of writing checks to company vendors (suppliers). He also had access to the supply of unused company checks, the electronic signature of Frank Roberts, the CEO, and the accounting records. Johnson discovered that this combination of incompatible duties gave him an opportunity to embezzle money from the company. He stole $5 million over a nine-year period, using the following scheme: Johnson would run up vast amounts of charges (often exceeding $50,000 per month) on his personal credit cards. In spite of his relatively modest salary of $100,000 per year, the credit cards allowed Johnson to maintain a lavish lifestyle that included a mountain vacation home, a multimillion dollar watch and jewelry collection, numerous luxury automobiles, and a 600-bottle wine collection. When the credit card bills came to his house, Johnson would take them to the office and pay them with company checks made out to the banks. Almost 900 such checks were written. Roberts had never bothered to review the checks that had gone out under his electronic signature. Johnson also had the responsibility of reconciling the company's bank statement, giving him a convenient way to make sure the month-end bank statements always agreed with the books, even if Johnson had to manipulate the outstanding checks list to make it balance.

Green Valley Coffee Company fired Johnson and filed criminal charges against him. He was convicted and sentenced to 10 years in prison. The company also reformed its internal controls. A separate staff with no access to cash now oversees the company's accounts payable records. Only approved vendors can be paid with company checks. The controller's department no longer has access to the supply of unused checks or to the CEO's electronic signature.

Once vendors' checks are prepared, they are sent to the treasurer's department for final review, along with supporting documentation, which must include a purchase order, receiving report, and approved vendor invoice. People processing the checks with Roberts's electronic signature review the supporting documents to determine that all documents are in order before affixing the signature. Checks exceeding $10,000 require dual signatures of Roberts and another company executive.

Once a check is signed, the supporting documents are marked "paid" to prevent them from being reused to support the writing of another check. Signed checks are mailed out directly from the treasurer's department to vendors, rather than being returned to the controller's office. Another employee, who has neither cash handling nor customer bookkeeping responsibilities, reconciles Green Valley Coffee Company's monthly bank statement and reconciles the total checks written with the total amount of approved vendors' invoices processed.

Paying personal bills with company funds is a type of fraud known as "misappropriation of assets." Although it doesn't take a genius to accomplish, it is more likely to occur when a company's internal accounting control system is weak.

This chapter begins with a discussion of fraud, its types, and common characteristics. We then discuss internal controls, which are the primary means by which fraud, as well as unintentional financial statement errors, are prevented. We also discuss how to account for cash. These three topics—fraud, internal control, and cash—go together. Internal controls help prevent fraud. Cash is the asset that is most often misappropriated through fraud.

DESCRIBE FRAUD AND ITS IMPACT

1 Describe fraud and its impact

Fraud is the intentional misrepresentation of facts, designed to persuade another party to act in a way that causes injury or damage to that party. Fraud is a huge problem and is becoming more extensive, not only in the United States but across the globe. A 2016 report by the Association for Certified Fraud Examiners (ACFE) revealed the following statistics about fraud:[1]

- A typical organization loses 5% of its revenue each year to fraud. This translates to a worldwide projected annual fraud loss of over $3.7 trillion.
- The median loss in occupational fraud cases is $150,000; these tend to be cases involving employee theft.
- Of reported fraud cases, 23% percent have caused losses of at least $1 million; these larger cases tended to involve misleading financial statements.
- The longer a perpetrator has worked for an organization, the higher the fraud losses tend to be.
- Most reported frauds (77%) are perpetrated by employees in one of six departments: accounting, operations, sales, executive/upper management, customer service, and purchasing.
- Most occupational fraudsters are one-time offenders with clean employment histories.
- In most reported cases, fraudsters exhibit one or more behavioral red flags, including (a) living beyond one's means; (b) financial difficulties; and (c) unusually close associations with vendors or customers.

Fraud has exploded with the expansion of e-commerce via the Internet. In addition, studies have shown that the percentage of losses related to fraud from transactions originating in third-world, or developing, countries via the Internet is even higher than in economically developed countries.

There are many types of fraud. Some of the most common types are insurance fraud, check forgery, Medicare fraud, credit card fraud, and identity theft. The two most common types of fraud that impact financial statements are the following:

- **Misappropriation of assets.** This type of fraud occurs when employees steal money from their companies and cover it up by falsifying accounting records. The Green Valley Coffee Company case is an example. Other examples of asset misappropriation include theft of inventory, bribery or kickback schemes involving purchasing department employees, or overstatement of expense reimbursement requests.
- **Fraudulent financial reporting.** This type of fraud is committed by company managers who make false and misleading accounting entries to try to make their company's financial results appear better than they actually are. The purpose of this type of fraud is to deceive investors and creditors into investing or loaning money to the company when they might not have done so otherwise.

[1] *Report to the Nations 2016 Global Fraud Study*. Published by Association of Certified Fraud Examiners. Austin, TX: ACFE, 2016. www.acfe.com/rttn2016/resources/downloads.aspx

Both of these types of fraud involve making false or misleading entries in the books of a company. We call this *cooking the books*. Of these two types, asset misappropriation is the most common, but fraudulent financial reporting is by far the most expensive. Two of the most notorious cases of fraudulent financial reporting in recent history in the United States involved Enron Corporation in 2001 and WorldCom Inc. in 2002. These two scandals alone rocked the U.S. economy and impacted financial markets across the world. Enron committed fraudulent financial reporting by overstating its profits through bogus sales of nonexistent assets with inflated values. When Enron's banks found out, they stopped loaning the company money to operate, causing it to go out of business almost overnight. WorldCom (discussed in Chapter 7) reported expenses as plant assets and overstated both profits and assets. The company's internal auditor blew the whistle on WorldCom, resulting in the company's eventual collapse.

The combined effects of fraud on the business world usually involve losses in billions of dollars and thousands of jobs. Widespread media coverage usually sparks adverse market reaction, loss of confidence in the financial reporting system, and losses through declines in stock values.

Exhibit 4-1 explains in graphic form the elements that make up virtually every fraud. We call it the **fraud triangle**.

Exhibit 4-1 | The Fraud Triangle

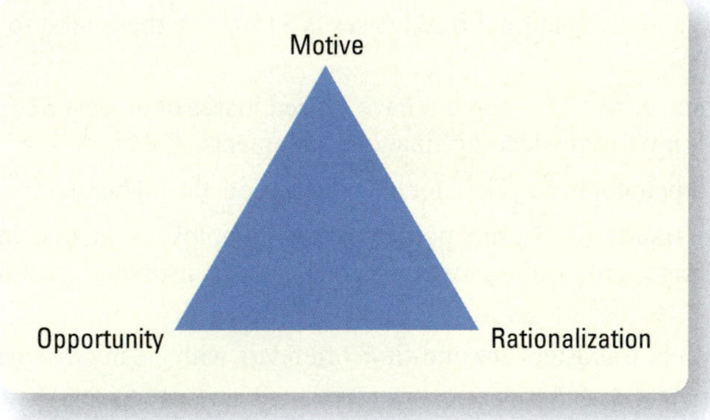

The first element in the fraud triangle is *motive*. This usually results from either critical need or greed on the part of the person who commits the fraud (the perpetrator). Although the perpetrator of the fraud might have a legitimate financial need, such as a medical emergency, he or she uses illegitimate means to meet that need.

The second element in the fraud triangle is *opportunity*. As in the case of Green Valley Coffee Company, the opportunity to commit fraud usually results from weak controls. Improperly segregating the job duties of employees and/or giving them improper access to the company's assets are examples of weak controls. Or it might result from a weak control environment, such as a domineering CEO, a weak or conflicted board of directors, or lax ethical practices, which allow top managers to override a company's controls.

The third element in the triangle is *rationalization*. The perpetrator engages in distorted thinking, such as "I deserve this"; "Nobody treats me fairly"; "No one will ever know"; "Just this once, I won't let it happen again"; or "Everyone else is doing it."

Fraud and Ethics

As we pointed out in our decision model for making ethical accounting and business judgments introduced in Chapter 1, the decision to engage in fraud is an act with economic, legal, and ethical implications. The perpetrators of fraud usually do so for their own short-term economic gain, while others incur economic losses that may far outstrip the gains of the fraudsters. Moreover, fraud is illegal. Those who are found guilty of it ultimately face penalties that include imprisonment, fines, and monetary damages. Finally, from an ethical standpoint, fraud violates the rights of many for the temporary betterment of a few and for the ultimate betterment of no one. At the end of the day, everyone loses. Fraud is the ultimate unethical act in business.

EXPLAIN THE OBJECTIVES AND COMPONENTS OF INTERNAL CONTROL

2 Explain the objectives and components of internal control

The primary way that fraud, as well as unintentional accounting errors, is prevented, detected, or corrected in an organization is through a proper system of internal control. **Internal control** is a plan of organization and a system of procedures implemented by company management and the board of directors designed to accomplish the following five objectives:

1. *Safeguard assets.* A company must safeguard its assets against waste, inefficiency, and fraud.
2. *Encourage employees to follow company policies.* A proper system of controls provides clear policies that result in the fair treatment of both customers and employees.
3. *Promote operational efficiency.* Effective controls minimize waste, which lowers costs and increases profits.
4. *Ensure accurate, reliable accounting records.* Without proper controls, the records may be unreliable, making it impossible to tell which part of the business is profitable and which part needs improvement.
5. *Comply with legal requirements.* Effective internal controls help ensure a company complies with the law and avoids legal difficulties.

How critical are internal controls? They're so critical that the U.S. Congress has passed the Sarbanes-Oxley Act (SOX), which applies to public companies (i.e., companies that sell their stock to the public). Among other things, SOX requires these companies to maintain systems of internal controls that are adequate to prevent material misstatements in the companies' financial statements. In addition, each public company CEO and chief financial officer (CFO) must certify in writing that their company's annual and quarterly reports are accurate and complete, and that their internal controls are adequate to prevent material misstatements in the financial statements. Stiff penalties and prison time await violators—25 years in prison for securities fraud and 20 years for an executive making false sworn statements. Exhibit 4-2 is an excerpt from a typical public company's annual report expressing management's certification of its internal controls.

Exhibit 4-2 | Excerpt from a Public Company's Management Report on the Company's Internal Controls

> Management is responsible for establishing and maintaining adequate internal control over financial reporting. . . . The Company's internal control over financial reporting includes the maintenance of records that . . . accurately and fairly reflect the transactions and . . . assets of the Company . . . provide reasonable assurance that transactions are recorded as necessary to permit preparation of financial statements in accordance with generally accepted accounting principles, and that receipts and expenditures of the Company are being made only in accordance with authorizations of management and directors of the Company. . . .
>
> Under the supervision and with the participation of management, including our principal executive officer and principal financial officer, we conducted an evaluation of the effectiveness of our internal control over financial reporting. . . . Based on our evaluation . . . management concluded that our internal control over financial reporting was effective as of December 31, 2018.

Exhibit 4-3 shows that internal controls act as a barrier to protect an organization and its assets from fraud, waste, and inefficiency. Internal controls also help ensure companies do business in a trustworthy way the public can count on—an extremely important element in maintaining the stability of financial markets around the world.

Exhibit 4-3 | The Function of an Internal Control System

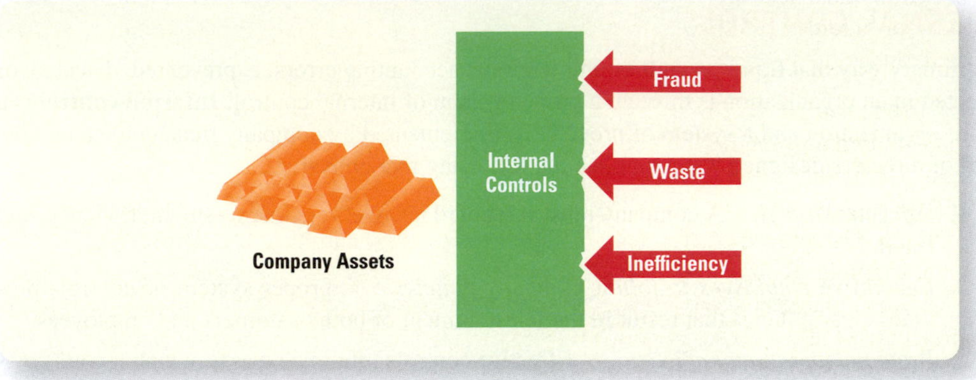

How does a business achieve good internal controls? The next section identifies the components of internal control.

The Components of Internal Control

A system of internal controls consists of five components:

- Control environment
- Risk assessment
- Information system
- Control procedures
- Monitoring of controls

Exhibit 4-4 diagrams the components of internal control.

Exhibit 4-4 | The Components of an Internal Control System

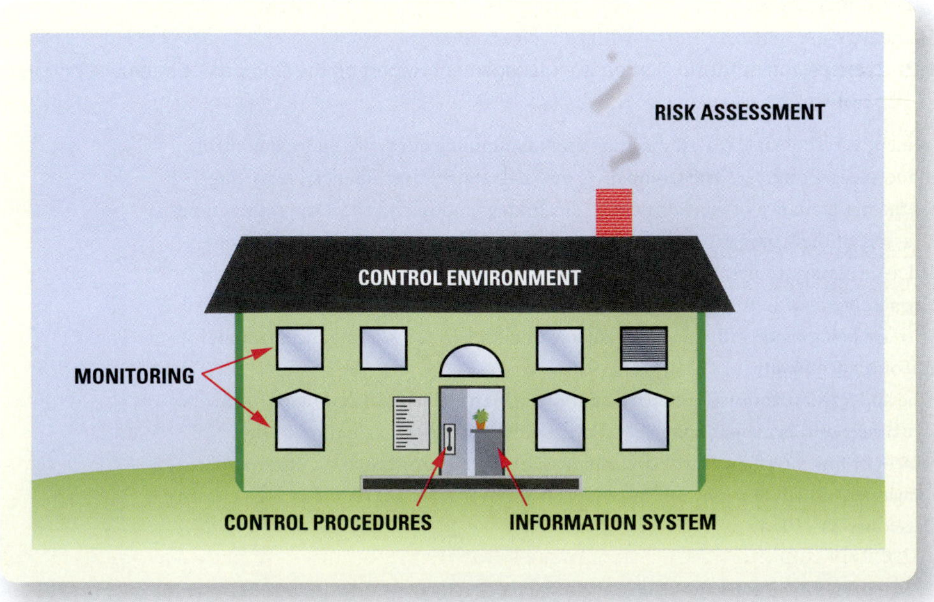

Control Environment. The control environment, which is symbolized by the roof over the building in Exhibit 4-4, is the "tone at the top" of the business. It starts with the owner and the top managers. They must behave honorably to set a good example for the company's employees. The owner must demonstrate the importance of internal controls if he or she expects employees to take the controls seriously. A key ingredient in the control environment of many companies is a corporate code of ethics, which includes provisions such as prohibition against giving or taking bribes or kickbacks from customers or suppliers, prohibition of transactions that involve conflicts of interest, and provisions that encourage good citizenship and corporate social responsibility.

Risk Assessment. Risk assessment is symbolized by the smoke rising from the chimney in Exhibit 4-4. Perhaps you have heard the saying, "Where there's smoke, there's fire." Assessing the risks a company faces offers hints (represented by the smoke) of where mistakes or fraud might arise (that is, where a "fire" might occur). A company must be able to identify its business risks and establish procedures for dealing with those risks to minimize their impacts on the company. For example, **Kraft Foods** faces the risk that its food products may sicken people. **Southwest Airlines'** planes may crash. And all companies face the risk of bankruptcy. Companies have to identify these risks and do what they can to prevent them from causing financial or other harm to the company, its customers, employees, owners, and creditors.

Information System. Symbolized by the door of the building, the information system is the way that accounting information enters and exits a business. The owner of a business needs accurate information to keep track of assets and measure profits and losses. Every system within the business that processes accounting data should be able to capture transactions as they occur, record (journalize) those transactions in an accurate and timely manner, and summarize (post) them in the books (ledgers) so they are reflected in the business's account balances and financial statements.

Control Procedures. Also symbolized by the door, control procedures built into the control environment and information system are the way companies gain access to the five objectives of internal controls discussed previously. Examples include the proper separation of employees' duties, comparison and other checks, adequate records, proper approvals, and physical safeguards to protect assets from theft. The next section discusses internal control procedures.

Monitoring of Controls. Symbolized by the windows of the building, monitoring provides "eyes and ears" so that no one person or group of persons can process a transaction completely without being seen and checked by another person or group. Much of the monitoring of a company's day-to-day activities is done by computer programs that automatically track cash receipts and disbursements and generate exception reports. **Exception reporting** is the process of identifying data that is not within "normal limits" so managers can follow up on it and take corrective action. For example, if an abnormally large transaction occurred, an exception report would be generated. In addition, companies hire auditors to monitor their controls. Auditors are discussed more fully in the next section.

Internal Control Procedures

Whether the business is Green Valley Coffee Company, **Microsoft**, or a Disney Store, it needs to have the following internal control procedures.

Smart Hiring Practices and Separation of Duties. Good internal controls start with a company's hiring practices, which should include clearly defined job descriptions that ensure all important jobs get done. For instance, the company's **treasurer** should be in charge of handling cash as well as signing checks. Warehouse personnel should be in charge of storing and keeping track of inventory. Background checks should be conducted on job candidates prior to their being hired. Once hired, to ensure they become competent and remain with the company, employees should be properly trained and supervised as well as paid competitive salaries.

An extremely important aspect of internal control is separating three key accounting duties: asset handling, record keeping, and transaction approval. Accountants must not handle cash, and cash handlers must not have access to the accounting records. If one employee has both cash-handling and accounting duties, that person can steal cash and conceal the theft. This is what happened at Green Valley Coffee Company. Separating the handling of cash from keeping the vendor accounts payable records would have made it impossible for Joe Johnson to have engaged in fraud at Green Valley Coffee Company. If he had been denied access to signed company checks, he would not have been able to use them to pay his own bills.

For companies that are too small to hire separate employees to do all of these functions, the key to good internal control is getting the owner involved. For example, the owner might approve all large transactions, make bank deposits, or reconcile the company's monthly bank account.

Comparisons and Compliance Monitoring. No person or department should be able to completely process a transaction from beginning to end without being cross-checked by another person or department. For example, one division of the treasurer's department should be responsible for signing checks. The **controller** is the chief accounting officer of a business. The controller's department should be responsible for recording company purchases and payments to suppliers. A third and separate employee who reconciles the bank statement should compare canceled (paid) checks with supporting invoices, payments recorded in the journal, and payments posted to individual vendor accounts payable by the controller's department.

One of the most effective tools for monitoring compliance with management's policies is the use of budgets. A **budget** is a quantitative financial plan that helps control a company's day-to-day management activities to keep its profits and cash flow in line with management's plans. Managers prepare budgets on a yearly, quarterly, monthly, or more frequent basis. **Operating budgets** are budgets for the net income of future periods. The operating budgets project a company's future revenue and expenses. **Cash budgets** are budgets for the cash receipts and cash disbursements of future periods.

Exception reporting is used in conjunction with operating and cash budgets. Exception reporting shows by how much each account varies from its budgeted amount. Department managers are required to explain the variances and to take corrective actions to keep the budgets in line with expectations.

To validate their accounting records and monitor their compliance with company policies, most companies have an audit. An **audit** is an examination of a company's financial statements and its accounting system, including its controls. Audits can be internal or external. *Internal auditors* are employees of the business. They ensure that employees are following company policies and that operations are running efficiently. Internal auditors also determine whether the company is following legal requirements.

External auditors are usually certified public accountants (CPAs) who are completely independent of the business. They are hired to determine whether the company's financial statements are prepared in accordance with generally accepted accounting principles. Auditors examine the client's financial statements and the underlying transactions to form a professional opinion on the accuracy and reliability of the company's financial statements.

Adequate Records. Accounting records provide the details of business transactions. The general rule is that all major groups of transactions should be supported by either hard copy documents or electronic records. Examples include sales invoices, shipping records, customer remittance advices, purchase orders, vendor invoices, receiving reports, and canceled (paid) checks.

If you have a checking account, you know that all of the checks in your checkbook are prenumbered. If you discover one of the checks in the sequence is missing, you know you have a problem: Either you forgot to record having written the check or the check could have been stolen. Similarly, the documents a company produces should be prenumbered. This ensures that all of the transactions related to them are processed and recorded. It also helps prevent theft. A gap in the numbered document sequence indicates that a transaction might not have been processed or a theft may have occurred.

Limited Access. To complement the segregation of duties, a company should limit the access employees have to assets based on their job responsibilities. For example, the access to cash should be limited to employees in the treasurer's department, and the supply of unused checks should be kept under lock and key. The access to inventory should be limited to warehouse personnel and employees responsible for shipping and receiving functions. Likewise, employees who have record-keeping responsibilities should be the only people allowed to access a company's accounting records. Individual computers in the business should be protected by user identification and password. Electronic data files should be encrypted (processed through a special code) to prevent their recognition if accessed by a "hacker" or other unauthorized person.

Proper Approvals. No transaction should be processed without management's general or specific approval. The bigger the transaction, the more specific approval it should have. For individual small transactions, management might delegate approval to a specific department. For example, sales to customers on account should all be approved by a separate credit department that first reviews customers' creditworthiness. Similarly, purchases the company makes on credit should be approved by a separate purchasing department that specializes in that function. Among other things, the purchasing department should only buy from approved vendors, on the basis of competitive bids, to ensure that the company gets the highest quality products for the most competitive prices.

What's an easy way to remember the basic control procedures for any class of transactions? Look at the first letters of each of the headings in this section:

Smart hiring practices and **S**eparation of duties

Comparisons and compliance monitoring

Adequate records

Limited access to both assets and records

Proper approvals (either general or specific) for each class of transaction

Remembering SCALP and how to apply each of these principles will help you establish good internal controls in your business.

Information Technology

Information technology (IT) has automated a great deal of record keeping, asset handling, and monitoring. For example, bar codes monitor the flow of inventory, speed up the checkout process, and more accurately tally the amount of transactions. Electronic sensors that trigger alarms and are attached to merchandise help prevent theft.

Alpa Prod/Shutterstock

However, computers have to be correctly programmed to prevent corruption of data. It is therefore important to hire experienced and competent people to run a company's IT department. Personnel in the IT department should check data entered into and retrieved from the computers for accuracy and completeness, and test and retest programs on a regular basis. In addition, only authorized personnel should be given access to sensitive data and the company's IT background systems.

Safeguard Controls

Businesses keep important documents in fireproof vaults. Burglar alarms safeguard buildings, and security cameras safeguard other property. Retailers might also hire security guards who help detect whether merchandise is being stolen by customers or employees, and who train personnel to spot suspicious activity.

Employees who handle cash are in a tempting position. Many businesses purchase fidelity bonds on cashiers. A **fidelity bond** is an insurance policy that reimburses the company for any losses due to employee theft. Before issuing a fidelity bond, the insurance company investigates the employee's background. Rotating employees into different job positions and requiring them to take mandatory vacations also improves internal control. Why? Knowing someone else will be doing your job keeps you honest. People who commit fraud are often caught by their coworkers when they notice improprieties in their work.

Internal Controls for E-Commerce

E-commerce creates its own risks. Hackers may gain access to confidential information such as account numbers and passwords. E-commerce pitfalls include

- stolen credit card numbers,
- malware, and
- phishing expeditions.

Stolen Credit Card Numbers. IT employees need to safeguard a company's computer systems from hackers. Cyber criminals are experts at hacking into databases of businesses and banks and stealing personal data such as credit card and social security numbers. Amateur hacker Carlos Salgado, Jr., used his home computer to steal 100,000 credit card numbers with a combined limit exceeding $1 billion. Salgado was caught when he tried to sell the numbers to an undercover FBI agent.

Malware. IT employees also need to safeguard a company's computer systems from *malware,* which is short for "malicious software." There are many different types of malware. Viruses, worms, spyware, ransomware, and Trojan horses are examples. Malware can destroy or alter data, make bogus calculations, infect files, and steal information. Malware circulates on the Internet, can be placed on websites, and can even be embedded in legitimate software products unbeknownst to their developers. Most companies have found malware in their systems at some point.

Phishing Expeditions. Thieves **phish** by creating bogus websites, such as AOL4Free.com and AmericaBank.com. The almost-authentic-sounding website attracts lots of visitors, and the thieves obtain account numbers and passwords from unsuspecting people. The thieves then use the data for illicit purposes.

Security Measures

To address the risks posed by e-commerce, companies have devised a number of security measures, including

- encryption and
- firewalls.

Encryption. One technique for protecting customer data is **encryption**, which rearranges messages by a mathematical process. The encrypted message can't be read by those who don't know the code. An accounting example uses check-sum digits for account numbers: In other words, each account number has its last digit equal to the sum of the previous digits. For example, consider Customer Number 2237, where $2 + 2 + 3 = 7$. Any account number that fails this test triggers an error message.

Firewalls. **Firewalls** limit unauthorized access to an organization's computer network. Members can access the network but nonmembers can't. At the point of entry, passwords, personal identification numbers (PINs), and signatures are required. Usually, several firewalls are built into the system. Think of a fortress with multiple walls protecting the company's computerized records in the center. More sophisticated firewalls are placed deeper in the network.

EVALUATE INTERNAL CONTROLS OVER CASH RECEIPTS AND CASH PAYMENTS

3 **Evaluate** internal controls over cash receipts and cash payments

Cash requires some specific internal controls because it is relatively easy to steal and it is easy to convert to other forms of wealth. Moreover, most transactions ultimately affect cash. Let's look at the internal controls companies use for cash receipts.

Cash Receipts over the Counter

Consider the transactions at a **Whole Foods Market** store. The point-of-sale terminal (or cash register) provides control over the cash receipts, while also recording the sale and reducing the inventory for the appropriate cost of the goods sold. For each transaction, the Whole Foods sales associate issues a receipt to the customer as proof of purchase. The cash drawer opens when the sales associate enters a transaction, and the machine electronically transmits a record of the sale to the store's main computer. At the end of each shift, the sales associate delivers the cash drawer to the office, where it is combined with cash from all other terminals and delivered by armored car to the bank for deposit. Later, a separate employee in the accounting department reconciles the electronic record of the sales for each terminal to the record of the cash turned in. These measures, coupled with oversight by a manager, discourage theft.

Exhibit 4-5 | Cash Receipts over the Counter

Monkeybusinessimages/iStock/Getty Images

Point-of-sale terminals also provide effective control over inventory. For example, in a restaurant, these devices track sales by menu item and total sales by cash, type of credit card, gift card redeemed, etc. They create the daily sales journal for that restaurant, which, in turn, interfaces with the general ledger. Managers can use records produced by point-of-sale terminals to check inventory levels and compare them against sales records for accuracy. For example, in a restaurant, an effective way to monitor the sales of expensive wine is for a manager to perform a quick count of the bottles on hand at the end of the day and compare it with the count at the end of the previous day. The count at the end of the previous day, plus the record of bottles purchased, minus the count at the end of the current day should equal the amount sold.

Cash Receipts by Mail

Many companies receive cash by mail. Exhibit 4-6 shows how companies control the cash they receive by mail. All incoming mail is opened by a mailroom employee. The mailroom then sends all customer checks to the treasurer, who has the cashier deposit the checks in the bank. The remittance advices go to the accounting department for journal entries to Cash and customer Accounts Receivable. As a final step, the controller compares the following two records for the day:

1. The amount of the bank deposit prepared by the treasurer
2. The debit to Cash made by the accounting department

The debit to Cash should equal the amount deposited in the bank. All cash receipts are safe in the bank, and the company's books are up-to-date.

Exhibit 4-6 | Cash Receipts by Mail

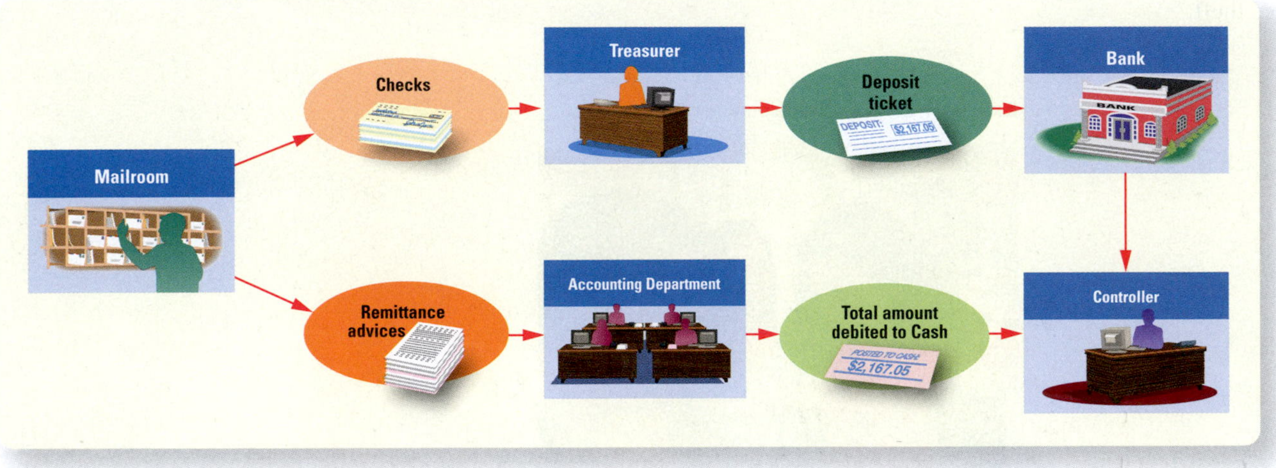

To further prevent the theft of cash, many companies accept electronic funds transfers from their customers. An **electronic funds transfer (EFT)** is a transfer of cash that occurs electronically rather than by paper documents. When a customer receives an invoice and approves it for payment, the customer authorizes its bank to make an EFT to the seller's bank. The seller's bank then sends the seller a detailed record of all of the funds it received, by customer. The seller then posts the collections to Accounts Receivable. Internal control is tight because company personnel never touch the incoming cash.

Controls over Payments Made by Check or EFT

Companies make most payments by check or with an EFT, which provides a record of the payment. The check must be signed by an authorized official. The EFT must be approved by an authorized official. Before signing the check or authorizing the EFT, the official should study the evidence supporting the payment.

Controls over Purchase and Payment. To illustrate the internal control over cash payments by check, suppose Green Valley Coffee Company buys some of its flavoring syrup from Sysco Foods. The purchasing and payment process follows the steps shown in Exhibit 4-7. Start with the box for Green Valley Coffee Company on the left side.

Exhibit 4-7 | Cash Payments by Check or EFT

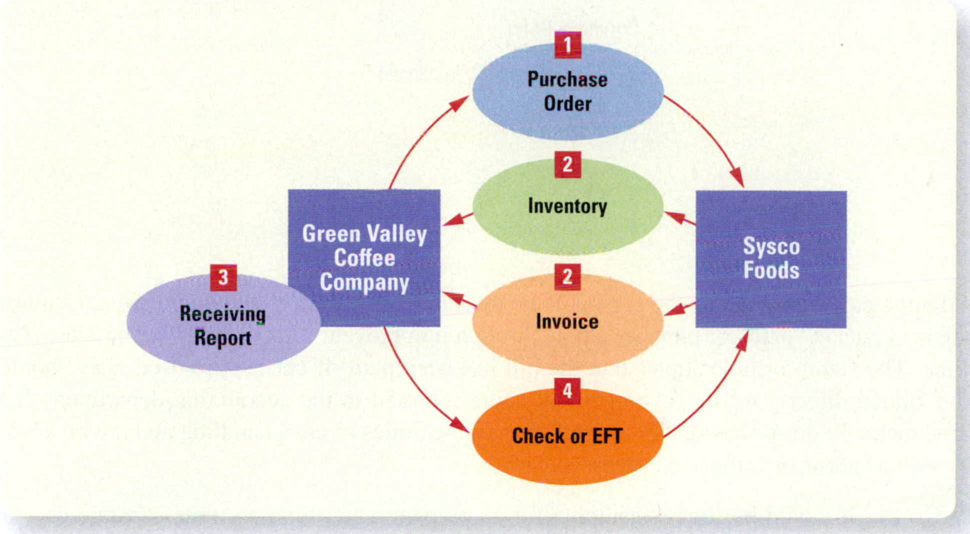

1. Green Valley Coffee Company faxes or e-mails an electronic purchase order to Sysco Foods for 2,000 16-ounce bottles of syrup.
2. Sysco ships 2,000 bottles of syrup and sends an electronic or paper invoice back to Green Valley Coffee Company.
3. Green Valley Coffee Company receives 2,000 16-ounce bottles of syrup and prepares a *receiving report* to list the inventory received.
4. After making sure all documents agree and approving the payment, Green Valley sends a check to Sysco or authorizes an EFT directly from its bank to Sysco's bank.

For good internal control, the purchasing agent should neither receive the goods nor approve the payment. If these duties aren't separated, a purchasing agent could buy goods and have them shipped to his or her home. Or a purchasing agent could spend too much on purchases, approve the payment, and split the excess with the supplier. To avoid these problems, companies split the following duties among different employees:

- Purchasing goods
- Receiving goods
- Preparing check or EFT for payment
- Approval of the payment

Exhibit 4-8 shows Green Valley Coffee Company's payment packet of documents. The accounting department should match the purchase order, receiving report, and invoice to make sure that all quantities agree. The accounting department can then prepare the check, but may not sign it. Rather, the packet should be sent to the treasurer's department for signing. Before signing the check or approving the EFT, the treasurer's department should examine the packet again to prove that all the documents agree. Only then does the company know that

1. it received the goods ordered, and
2. it is paying only for the goods received.

Exhibit 4-8 | Payment Packet

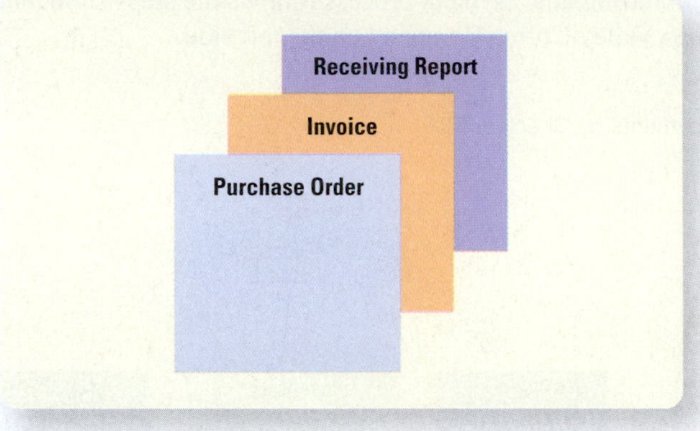

After the payment is made, the person in the treasurer's department who authorized it stamps the payment packet "paid" or punches a hole through it to prevent it from being submitted a second time. The stamp or hole shows that the bill has been paid. If checks are used, they should then be mailed directly to the payee without being returned to the accounting department that prepared them. To do so would violate separation of the duties of cash handling and record keeping, as well as allow unauthorized access to cash.

Petty Cash. It would be time consuming for a company's treasurer to write separate checks for small amounts of money the company spends. Instead, companies keep a **petty cash** fund. The word *petty* means "small." That's what petty cash is—a small cash fund kept by a single employee for the purpose of making such on-the-spot minor purchases. For example, petty cash might be used to reimburse an employee for doughnuts he purchased for a morning meeting or to pay a postal employee a few cents due on a letter received by the company.

The petty cash fund is opened with a particular amount of cash. A check for that amount is then issued to the custodian of the petty cash fund (the person who has custody of it). He or she is solely responsible for accounting for it. Assume that on February 28, **Cisco Systems**, the worldwide leader in networks for the Internet, establishes a petty cash fund of $500 in a sales department by writing a check to the designated custodian. The custodian of the petty cash fund cashes the check and places $500 in the fund, which may be a cash box or other device.

For each petty cash payment, the custodian prepares a petty cash voucher to list the item purchased. The sum of the cash in the petty cash fund plus the total of the paid vouchers in the cash box should equal the opening balance at all times—in this case, $500. The petty cash account keeps its $500 balance at all times. Maintaining the petty cash account at a particular balance (cash plus vouchers) is referred to as an **imprest system**. An imprest system serves as an internal control because the amount for which the custodian is responsible is always the same.

Company-issued debit cards are taking the place of petty cash systems in many organizations. Employees who use the cards turn in the receipts for their purchases; these receipts are then compared to the amounts debited on the company's bank statement.

The Limitations of Internal Control—Costs and Benefits

Unfortunately, most internal controls can be circumvented. Collusion—two or more people working together—can beat internal controls. Consider Green Valley Coffee Company's situation. Even if Roberts (the CEO) were to hire a new person to approve cash payments, if that person conspired with Johnson, they could design a scheme identical to the one Johnson designed, and split what they stole. Another way to circumvent a good system of internal controls is for a top manager to override them. Human limitations such as fatigue and negligence can also circumvent a good system, or it can gradually deteriorate over time if control procedures are neglected. In other words, internal controls cannot overcome every type of breakdown. The best a company can do is to exercise care in hiring honest people who have no conflicts of interest with existing employees and to exercise constant diligence in monitoring the internal control system to ensure it continues to work properly.

The stricter the internal control system, the more it costs. An overly complex system of internal control can strangle the business with red tape. How tight should the controls be? Internal controls must be judged based on their costs and benefits. Here is an example of a good cost/benefit relationship: A part-time security guard at a **Walmart** store costs about $28,000 a year. On average, each part-time guard prevents about $50,000 of theft. The net savings to Walmart is $22,000.

Mid-Chapter | Summary Problem

Requirement

For each of the five situations that follow, state the reasons for the requirement. What error(s) or fraudulent practice is the control designed to prevent?

1. Drayton University requires that all tickets to its home football games be bar-coded. Ticket takers are stationed at all gates of the stadium with electronic devices to scan the tickets as fans enter the stadium. Once admitted, if a fan exits the stadium, he or she may not re-enter.
2. **Publix Supermarket** has a strict policy that requires employees who run check-out terminals to hand each customer a receipt for his or her purchases.
3. The server staff at the Elite Restaurant are each assigned to particular stations for particular shifts during the day. Servers take customers' orders on pre-numbered sales checks (invoices) based on prices from a printed menu. Each item on the menu is assigned a unique number in the company's food and beverage accounting system. Once orders are taken, servers enter the items from sales checks (invoices) by number on touch-screen terminals and serve them to customers as the kitchen or bar completes the order. As customers finish their meals or drinks, servers prepare the checks (invoices), in duplicate. Customers are asked to sign and return one copy and pay with cash or a credit or debit card and to take the other copy with them as they exit.
4. The Larson Manufacturing Company prepares prenumbered written purchase orders in quadruplicate for each item purchased. The original purchase order is sent to the vendor. One copy of the purchase order, with quantities deleted, is sent to Larson's central receiving department. Another copy of the purchase order is sent to Larson's accounting department. The fourth copy is filed in Larson's purchasing department. As goods are received from particular vendors, the receiving department is required to count the goods and to prepare a separate receiving report in triplicate. One copy of the receiving report is sent to the accounting department. Another copy is sent to purchasing. The third copy is filed in the receiving department.
5. After the treasurer of the Fargo Company signs checks, the supporting documents are marked "paid" and returned to the accounting department to be filed. Checks are mailed directly to vendors from the treasurer's department and cannot be returned to the accounting department.

Answers

1. By bar-coding all tickets, the university makes a separate record of all authorized ticketholders, as well as tickets used and unused for each game. Scanning the tickets ensures that only authorized paid ticketholders are admitted to games, and that, once the ticket is scanned, fans are not permitted to leave ("stub out") and allow unauthorized ticket-holders to return using their tickets. The system also results in accurate records of game attendance and ticket revenues.
2. This system helps ensure that all sales are recorded, and it prevents employees from stealing items from the store or stealing cash remitted for items sold. The customer acts as the check on the sales clerk. The computer system keeps an independent record, by item, of sales, as well as the cost of inventory sold. At the end of the shift, the cash drawer from the register is reconciled with the cash (including debit and credit card receipts) turned in and the recorded amount of sales from the register. Managers can trace any cash shortages back to the terminals where the sales originated, and ultimately to the employees who rang up the sales.
3. Similar to (2), this system helps ensure that the restaurant records all sales, at the correct amounts. It helps prevent employee theft of cash or inventory, because managers can compare the totals of customer checks (invoices) with the cash (including debit and credit card receipts) turned in at the end of each shift, as well as inventory of food and liquor.
4. Requiring multiple copies of purchase orders and receiving reports creates independent records of each of these functions for comparison later in the process. Deleting the quantities from the copy of the purchase order sent to the receiving department forces the employees in the receiving department to count the goods and prepare an independent record of items received. Ordinarily, the accounting department receives one copy of the purchase order, as well as a copy of the receiving report supporting each purchase. The accounting department then matches these two documents with the purchase invoice received from the vendor. This matching should occur before the accounting department approves the vendor's invoice for payment. These procedures help ensure that the company received the goods ordered and it is only paying for the goods received. These procedures also prevent employees from stealing inventory by ordering goods and having them delivered to an offsite location for their unauthorized personal use or sale.
5. Separating the bookkeeping function (which occurs in the accounting department) from the cash handling function (which occurs in the treasurer's department) is essential to prevent employees from stealing cash. Marking the supporting documents "paid" as checks are signed prevents those documents from being resubmitted for payment a second time.

PREPARE A BANK RECONCILIATION

4 Prepare a bank reconciliation

Keeping cash in a bank account helps control cash because banks have established practices for safeguarding customers' money. The documents used to control a bank account include

- a signature card,
- a deposit ticket,
- a check,
- a bank statement, and
- a bank reconciliation.

Signature Card

Banks require each person authorized to sign on an account to provide a *signature card*. When a check or other document is submitted for payment, the signature on it is compared to the one on the card. The two signatures must match to ensure someone other than an authorized account holder hasn't signed the document. This protects against forgery.

Deposit Ticket

Banks supply standard forms such as *deposit tickets*. The customer fills in the amount of each deposit on the ticket. As proof of the transaction, the customer receives a deposit receipt.

Check

To pay cash, the depositor can write a **check**, which tells the bank to pay the designated party a specified amount. There are three parties to a check:

- The maker, who signs the check
- The payee, to whom the check is paid
- The bank on which the check is drawn

Exhibit 4-9 shows a check created by Green Valley Coffee Company, the maker. The check is written to Superior Office Products, which is the payee. The check has two parts, the check itself and the remittance advice**.** The **remittance advice** is an optional attachment to a check that indicates the payer, date, and amount of the cash payment. Sometimes the remittance advice is a perforated tear-off document and other times it can be electronically scanned. The optional attachment is used as the source document for posting to Green Valley's account receivable in Superior Office Products' records.

Exhibit 4-9 | Check with Remittance Advice

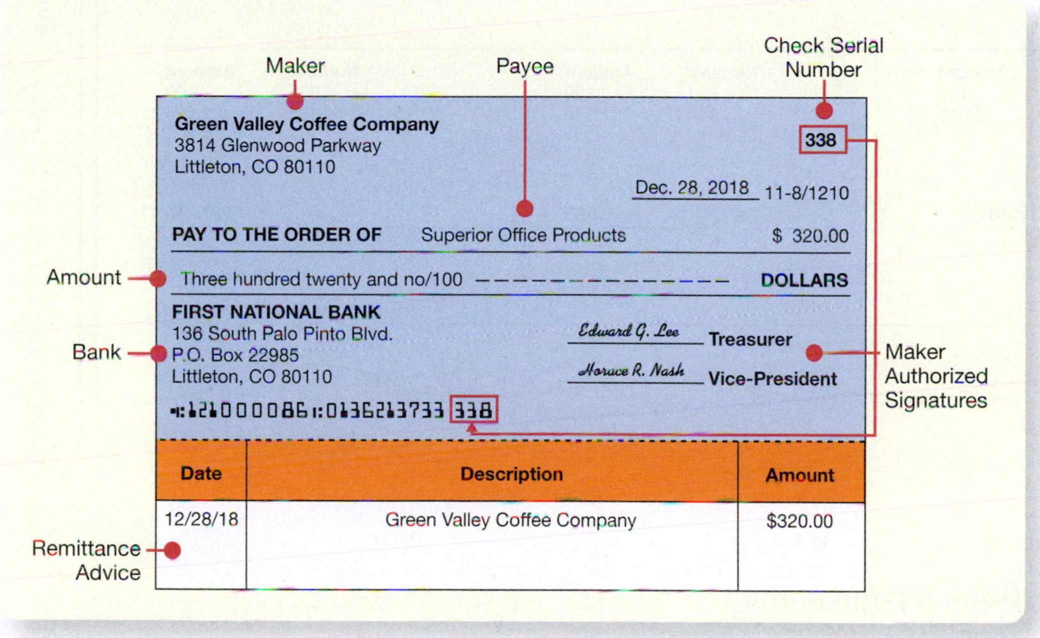

Bank Statement

Banks usually send monthly statements to their commercial or business customers. A **bank statement** reports what the bank did with the customer's cash. The statement shows the account's beginning and ending balances, cash receipts, and payments. Included with the statement is a list, and often visual images, of the maker's *canceled checks* (actual paid checks). Most large companies have multiple bank accounts in different banks. Exhibit 4-10 shows the December bank statement for one of Green Valley Coffee Company's smaller bank accounts at the First National Bank.

Exhibit 4-10 | Bank Statement

BANK STATEMENT

FIRST NATIONAL BANK
136 South Palo Pinto Pkwy. P.O. BOX 22985 Littleton, CO 80110

Green Valley Coffee Company
3814 Glenwood Parkway
Littleton, CO 80110

CHECKING ACCOUNT 136–213733
December 31, 2018

BEGINNING BALANCE	TOTAL DEPOSITS	TOTAL WITHDRAWALS	SERVICE CHARGES	ENDING BALANCE
6,550	4,370	5,000	20	5,900

TRANSACTIONS

DEPOSITS	DATE	AMOUNT
Deposit	12/04	1,150
Deposit	12/08	190
EFT—Receipt of cash dividend	12/17	900
Bank Collection	12/26	2,100
Interest	12/31	30

CHARGES	DATE	AMOUNT
Service Charge	12/31	20

CHECKS

Number	Amount	Number	Amount	Number	Amount
307	100	333	150	335	100
332	3,000	334	100	336	1,100

OTHER DEDUCTIONS	DATE	AMOUNT
NSF	12/04	50
EFT—Insurance	12/20	400

Bank Reconciliation

There are two records of a business's cash:

1. The Cash account in the company's general ledger. Exhibit 4-11 shows that Green Valley Coffee Company's ending cash balance in the company's checking account at First National Bank is $3,340.
2. The bank statement for the same checking account, which shows the cash receipts and payments transacted through this account at the bank. Exhibit 4-10 shows that Green Valley Coffee Company's ending balance for this account is $5,900.

Exhibit 4-11 | Cash Records of Green Valley Coffee Company

General Ledger:

ACCOUNT Cash: Checking Account First National Bank				
Date	**Item**	**Debit**	**Credit**	**Balance**
2018				
Dec 1	Balance			6,550
2	Cash receipt	1,150		7,700
7	Cash receipt	190		7,890
31	Cash payments		6,150	1,740
31	Cash receipt	1,600		3,340

Cash Payments:

	A	B	C	D
1	Check No.	Amount	Check No.	Amount
2	332	$3,000	337	$ 280
3	333	510*	338	320
4	334	100	339	250
5	335	100	340	490
6	336	1,100	Total	$6,150
7				

*Correct amount of check #333 is $150. See bank reconciliation in Exhibit 4–12 for correction.

At this point you are probably wondering why the two amounts are different. In fact, it is normal for a company's books and its bank statement to show different cash balances. The differences occur because of a time lag in recording transactions. Here are some examples:

- When you write a check, you usually deduct it immediately in your checkbook. But the bank does not subtract the amount of the check from your account until the bank pays the item a few days later. Likewise, you immediately add to your checkbook all your deposits or EFT credits. But it may take a day or two for the bank to add them to your balance.
- Your EFT payments and cash receipts may be added to your account by your bank before you learn about them.

To ensure accurate cash records, you need to update your cash record—either online or after you receive your bank statement. The result of this updating process creates a **bank reconciliation**, which you must prepare. The bank reconciliation explains all the differences between your cash records and your bank balance. The person who prepares the bank reconciliation should have no other cash duties. Otherwise, he or she can steal cash and manipulate the reconciliation to conceal the theft.

The bank reconciliation for Green Valley Coffee Company is presented in Panel B of Exhibit 4-12. Panel A of Exhibit 4-12 lists all the items used to prepare the bank reconciliation.

Exhibit 4-12 Bank Reconciliation

PANEL A—Reconciling Items

Bank side:

1. Deposit in transit, $1,600.
2. Bank error: The bank deducted $100 for a check written by another company. Add $100 to the bank balance.
3. Outstanding checks—total of $1,340.

	A	B
1	**Check No.**	**Amount**
2	337	$280
3	338	320
4	339	250
5	340	490
6		

Book side:

4. EFT receipt of your dividend revenue earned on an investment, $900.
5. Bank collection of your account receivable, $2,100.
6. Interest revenue earned on your bank balance, $30.
7. Book error: You recorded check no. 333 for $510. The amount you actually paid on account was $150. Add $360 to your book balance.
8. Bank service charge, $20.
9. NSF check from a customer, $50. Subtract $50 from your book balance.
10. EFT payment of insurance expense, $400.

PANEL B—Bank Reconciliation

	A	B	C	D	E	F
1	**Green Valley Coffee Company Bank Reconciliation: First National Bank Checking Account December 31, 2018**					
2	**Bank**			**Books**		
3	**Balance, December 31**		**$ 5,900**	**Balance, December 31**		**$ 3,340**
4	Add:			Add:		
5	1. Deposit in transit		1,600	4. EFT receipt of dividend revenue		900
6	2. Correction of bank error		100	5. Bank collection of account		
7			7,600	receivable		2,100
8				6. Interest revenue earned on		
9				bank balance		30
10				7. Correction of book error—		
11				overstated our check no. 333		360
12	Less:					$ 6,730
13	3. Outstanding checks					
14	No. 337	$280		Less:		
15	No. 338	320		8. Service charge	$ 20	
16	No. 339	250		9. NSF check	50	
17	No. 340	490	(1,340)	10. EFT payment of insurance expense	400	(470)
18	**Adjusted bank balance**		**$ 6,260**	**Adjusted book balance**		**$ 6,260**
19						

These amounts should agree.

SUMMARY OF THE VARIOUS RECONCILING ITEMS:

BANK BALANCE—ALWAYS

- *Add* deposits in transit.
- *Subtract* outstanding checks.
- *Add* or *subtract* corrections of bank errors.

BOOK BALANCE—ALWAYS

- *Add* bank collections, interest revenue, and EFT receipts.
- *Subtract* service charges, NSF checks, and EFT payments.
- *Add* or *subtract* corrections of book errors.

Preparing the Bank Reconciliation

Panel B of Exhibit 4-12 illustrates Green Valley Coffee Company's bank reconciliation. It lists items that account for the cash differences between the bank balance and the company's book balance (the balance on the company's books).

Bank Side of the Reconciliation

1. The left side of Panel A in Exhibit 4-12 lists the items to show on the Bank side of the reconciliation. They include the following:
   a. **Deposits in transit** (outstanding deposits). You have recorded these deposits, but the bank has not. Add deposits in transit on the bank reconciliation.
   b. **Outstanding checks**. You have recorded these checks, but the bank has not yet paid them. Subtract outstanding checks.
   c. **Bank errors**. Correct all bank errors on the Bank side of the reconciliation. For example, the bank may erroneously subtract from your account a check written by someone else.

Book Side of the Reconciliation

1. The right side of Panel A in Exhibit 4-12 lists the items to show on the Book side of the bank reconciliation. They include the following:
   a. **Bank collections.** Bank collections are cash receipts the bank has recorded for your account, but you haven't recorded the cash receipt yet. An example is a bank collecting an account or note receivable for you. Add bank collections on the bank reconciliation.
   b. **Electronic funds transfers (EFT)**. The bank may receive or pay cash on your behalf. An EFT may be a cash receipt or a cash payment. Add EFT receipts and subtract EFT payments.
   c. **Service charge**. This cash payment is the bank's fee for processing your transactions. Subtract service charges.
   d. **Interest revenue on your checking account**. On certain types of bank accounts, you earn interest if you keep enough cash in your account. Add interest revenue.
   e. **Nonsufficient funds (NSF) checks**. A **nonsufficient funds (NSF) check** is a check for which the payer's bank account has insufficient money to pay the check. NSF checks received from customers of a business represent worthless cash receipts. They are sometimes referred to as "hot" checks or "bounced" checks. On your bank reconciliation, subtract NSF checks from customers because you don't receive the funds for these checks.
   f. **The cost of printed checks**. This cash payment is handled like a service charge. Subtract this cost.
   g. **Book errors**. Correct all book errors on the Book side of the reconciliation. For example, you may have recorded a $150 check that you wrote as $510. Book errors can be added or subtracted.

Journalizing Transactions from the Bank Reconciliation. The bank reconciliation in Exhibit 4-12 requires Green Valley Coffee Company to make journal entries to bring its Cash account up to date. The numbers in red in the exhibit correspond to the reconciling items listed in Panel A, the Book side. All items on the Book side of a bank reconciliation require journal entries.

	A	B	C	D	E
1	4.	Dec 31	Cash	900	
2			Dividend Revenue		900
3			*Receipt of dividend revenue earned on investment.*		
4					
5	5.	31	Cash	2,100	
6			Accounts Receivable		2,100
7			*Account receivable collected by bank.*		
8					
9	6.	31	Cash	30	
10			Interest Revenue		30
11			*Interest earned on bank balance.*		
12					
13	7.	31	Cash	360	
14			Accounts Payable		360
15			*Correction of check no. 333.*		
16					
17	8.	31	Miscellaneous Expense[1]	20	
18			Cash		20
19			*Bank service charge.*		
20					
21	9.	31	Accounts Receivable	50	
22			Cash		50
23			*NSF check returned by bank.*		
24					
25	10.	31	Insurance Expense	400	
26			Cash		400
27			*Payment of monthly insurance.*		
28					

[1]Miscellaneous Expense is debited for the bank service charge because the service charge pertains to no particular expense category.

The entry for the NSF check (entry 9) requires explanation. Upon learning that a customer's $50 check was not good, the company must credit Cash to update the Cash account. Unfortunately, there is still a receivable from the customer, so Accounts Receivable must be debited to reinstate the receivable.

Online Banking

Online banking allows you to pay bills and view your account electronically. You don't have to wait until the end of the month to get a bank statement. With online banking, you can reconcile transactions at any time and keep your account current whenever you wish. Exhibit 4-13 shows a page from the account history of Toni Anderson's bank account.

Exhibit 4-13 | Online Banking—Account History

Account History for Toni Anderson Checking # 5401-632-9
as of Close of Business 07/27/2018

Account Details

Current Balance $4,136.08

Date	Description	Withdrawals	Deposits	Balance
	Current Balance			**$ 4,136.08**
07/27/18	DEPOSIT		1,170.35	4,136.08
07/26/18	28 DAYS INTEREST		2.26	2,965.73
07/25/18	Check #6131 View Image	443.83		2,963.47
07/24/18	Check #6130 View Image	401.52		3,407.30
07/23/18	EFT PYMT CINGULAR	61.15		3,808.82
07/22/18	EFT PYMT CITICARD PAYMENT	3,172.85		3,869.97
07/20/18	Debit card payment, Anthropologie Stores	550.00		7,042.82
07/19/18	Debit card payment, CEPCO Convenience Stores	50.00		7,592.82
07/16/18	Debit card payment, Haverty's Furniture Stores	2,056.75		7,642.82
07/15/18	Debit card payment, Dillard's Department Stores	830.00		9,699.57
07/13/18	Debit card payment, HEB Stores	150.00		10,529.57
07/11/18	ATM 4900 SANGER AVE	200.00		10,679.57
07/09/18	Debit card payment, CEPCO Convenience Stores	30.00		10,879.57
07/05/18	Debit card payment, Warren University	2,500.00		10,909.57
07/04/18	ATM 4900 SANGER AVE	100.00		13,409.57
07/01/18	DEPOSIT		9,026.37	13,509.57
07/01/18	Beginning Balance			**$ 4,483.20**

E-Mail

The account history—like a bank statement—lists deposits, checks, EFT payments, ATM withdrawals, and interest earned on your bank balance. It also often lists the running balance in the account (the updated balance after each addition and subtraction).

TRY IT

(Answers are given on p. 247.)

A company's bank statement balance is $4,500 and shows a service charge of $15, interest earned of $5, and an NSF check for $300. Deposits in transit total $1,200; outstanding checks are $575. The company's bookkeeper erroneously recorded a check received from a customer as a $152 check when it was actually a $125 check. This created a book error of $27.

(1) What is the adjusted bank balance?

(2) What was the book balance of cash before the reconciliation?

REPORT CASH ON THE BALANCE SHEET

5 Report cash on the balance sheet

Most companies have numerous bank accounts, but they usually combine all cash amounts into a single total called "Cash and Cash Equivalents." **Cash equivalents** include liquid assets such as time deposits, certificates of deposit, and high-grade U.S. or foreign government securities that are very close to maturity (three months or less at the time of purchase). Time deposits are interest-bearing accounts that can be withdrawn for immediate use. Although they are slightly less liquid than cash, cash equivalents are sufficiently similar to be reported along with cash. The balance sheet of Green Valley Coffee Company reported the following:

	A	B	C
1	**Green Valley Coffee Company** **Balance Sheet (Excerpts, adapted)** **December 31, 2018**		
2	**Assets**		
3	Cash and cash equivalents		$ 6,000,000
4			

Most public companies include additional information about cash and cash equivalents in the footnotes to their financial statements. For example, Note 1 (Summary of Significant Accounting Policies) of Apple Inc.'s 2016 financial statements contains the following brief comment about the company's cash equivalents:

Cash equivalents . . .

All highly liquid investments with maturities of three months or less at the date of purchase are classified as cash equivalents.

Source: Data from the Securities and Exchange Commission EDGAR Company Filings, www.sec.gov

End-of-Chapter | Summary Problem

The cash account of Ayers Associates at February 28, 2018, is as follows:

Cash

Feb 1	Bal 3,995	Feb 3	400
6	800	12	3,100
15	1,800	19	1,100
23	1,100	25	500
28	2,400	27	900
Feb 28	Bal 4,095		

Ayers Associates received the following bank statement on February 28, 2018 (negative amounts are in parentheses):

	A	B	C
1	**Bank Statement for February 2018**		
2	Beginning balance		$ 3,995
3	Deposits:		
4	Feb 7	$ 800	
5	15	1,800	
6	24	1,100	3,700
7	Checks (total per day):		
8	Feb 8	$ 400	
9	16	3,100	
10	23	1,100	(4,600)
11	Other items:		
12	Service charge		(10)
13	NSF check from M. E. Crown		(700)
14	Bank collection of note receivable for the company		1,000
15	EFT—monthly rent expense		(330)
16	Interest revenue earned on account balance		15
17	Ending balance		$ 3,070
18			

Ayers deposits all cash receipts in the bank and makes all payments by check.

Requirements

1. Prepare the bank reconciliation for Ayers Associates at February 28, 2018.
2. Journalize the entries based on the bank reconciliation.

Answers

Requirement 1

	A	B	C
1	**Ayers Associates** **Bank Reconciliation** **February 28, 2018**		
2	**Bank:**		
3	Balance, February 28, 2018		$ 3,070
4	Add: Deposit of February 28 in transit		2,400
5			5,470
6			
7	Less: Outstanding checks issued on Feb 25 ($500)		
8	and Feb 27 ($900)		(1,400)
9	Adjusted bank balance, February 28, 2018		$ 4,070
10			
11	**Books:**		
12	Balance, February 28, 2018		$ 4,095
13	Add: Bank collection of note receivable		1,000
14	Interest revenue earned on bank balance		15
15			5,110
16	Less: Service charge	$ 10	
17	NSF check	700	
18	EFT—Rent expense	330	(1,040)
19	Adjusted book balance, February 28, 2018		$ 4,070
20			

equal

Requirement 2

	A		C	D	G
1	Feb	28	Cash	1,000	
2			Note Receivable		1,000
3			*Note receivable collected by bank.*		
4					
5		28	Cash	15	
6			Interest Revenue		15
7			*Interest earned on bank balance.*		
8					
9		28	Miscellaneous Expense	10	
10			Cash		10
11			*Bank service charge.*		
12					
13		28	Accounts Receivable–M.E. Crown	700	
14			Cash		700
15			*NSF check returned by bank.*		
16					
17		28	Rent Expense	330	
18			Cash		330
19			*Monthly rent expense.*		
20					

REVIEW | Internal Control and Cash

Accounting Vocabulary

audit (p. 208) A periodic examination of a company's financial statements and the accounting systems, controls, and records that produce them. Audits may be either external or internal. External audits are usually performed by certified public accountants (CPAs).

bank collections (p. 221) The collection of money by a bank on behalf of a depositor.

bank reconciliation (p. 219) A document a company prepares to explain the differences in the amount of cash it has on its books versus its bank's records.

bank statement (p. 217) A document showing the beginning and ending balances of a particular bank account along with the month's transactions that affected the account.

budget (p. 208) A quantitative financial plan that helps control a company's day-to-day activities to keep its profits and cash flow in line with management's plans.

cash budget (p. 208) A budget that projects a company's future cash receipts and cash disbursements.

cash equivalent (p. 224) Investments such as time deposits, certificates of deposit, or high-grade government securities that are considered so similar to cash that they are combined with cash for financial disclosure purposes on the balance sheet.

check (p. 217) Document instructing a bank to pay the designated person or business the specified amount of money.

controller (p. 208) The chief accounting officer of a business.

deposits in transit (p. 221) Deposits recorded by a company but not yet by its bank.

electronic funds transfer (EFT) (p. 212) A system that transfers cash by electronic communication rather than by paper documents.

encryption (p. 210) Mathematical rearranging of data within an electronic file to prevent unauthorized access to information.

exception reporting (p. 207) The process of identifying data that is not within "normal limits" so that managers can follow up and take corrective action. Exception reporting is used to monitor operating and cash budgets to keep a company's profits and cash flow in line with management's plans.

fidelity bond (p. 210) An insurance policy that reimburses a company for any losses due to employee theft.

firewall (p. 211) An electronic barrier that prevents unauthorized access to a company's computer network.

fraud (p. 203) An intentional misrepresentation of facts, made for the purpose of persuading another party to act in a way that causes injury or damage to that party.

fraud triangle (p. 204) The three elements that are present in almost all cases of fraud. These elements are motive, opportunity, and rationalization on the part of the perpetrator.

fraudulent financial reporting (p. 203) Fraud perpetrated by management by preparing misleading financial statements.

imprest system (p. 214) A way to account for petty cash by maintaining a constant balance in the petty cash account. The cash in the account plus vouchers must always total the same amount.

internal control (p. 205) A plan of organization and a system of procedures designed to safeguard a company's assets, encourage adherence to the company's policies, promote operational efficiency, ensure accurate and reliable accounting records, and ensure compliance with legal requirements.

misappropriation of assets (p. 203) Fraud committed by employees stealing assets from a company.

nonsufficient funds (NSF) check (p. 221) A "hot" or "bounced" check for which the payer's bank account has insufficient money to pay the check. NSF checks are cash receipts that turn out to be worthless.

operating budget (p. 208) A budget of a company's future net income. The operating budget projects a company's future revenue and expenses.

outstanding check (p. 221) A check issued by a company and recorded on its books but not yet paid by its bank.

petty cash (p. 214) A fund containing a small amount of cash a company can use to pay minor amounts.

phish (p. 210) Creating bogus websites for the purpose of stealing unauthorized data, such as names, addresses, Social Security numbers, and bank account and credit card numbers.

remittance advice (p. 217) An optional attachment to a check (sometimes a perforated tear-off document and sometimes capable of being electronically scanned) that indicates the payer, date, and amount of the cash payment. A company often uses the remittance advice as the source documents for recording cash receipts.

treasurer (p. 207) In a large company, the individual in charge of the department responsible for cash handling and cash management. The duties of the treasurer's department include cash budgeting, cash collections, writing checks, investing excess funds, and making proposals for raising additional cash when needed.

Quick Check (Answers are given on page 247.)

1. A weak internal control system is which element in the fraud triangle?

   a. Motive
   b. Attitude
   c. Opportunity
   d. Rationalization

2. Which of the following items is *not* true about fraud?

   a. It can cause injury or damage to another party.
   b. It is an intentional misrepresentation of facts.
   c. Its damages must exceed a threshold of $150,000.
   d. It is designed to persuade another party to act in a way that causes injury or damage to that party.

3. Fictitious accounting entries are recorded that cause revenue to be overstated by $5 million for the year; the accounting manager was trying to make the company's income look better on the company's upcoming loan application. This type of fraud is:

   a. asset misappropriation.
   b. fraudulent financial reporting.
   c. GAAP disordering.
   d. IFRS misalignment.

4. Each of the following represents an internal control procedure except for:

   a. separation of duties.
   b. limited access to both assets and records.
   c. compliance monitoring.
   d. clear lines of authority and communication.

5. As part of a strong internal control system, which of the following accounting duties needs to be separated from cash handling?

   a. Record keeping
   b. Filing
   c. Transaction approval
   d. Both a and c need to be separated from cash handling.

6. Having a corporate code of ethics that prohibits employees from accepting gifts from customers or vendors is an example of which component of internal control?

   a. Control environment
   b. Risk assessment
   c. Control procedures
   d. Information system

7. Which law or regulation requires that public companies must maintain strong internal control systems?

   a. Dodd-Frank Act
   b. Sarbanes-Oxley Act
   c. Securities and Exchange Act of 1933
   d. Treadway Commission

8. Why does cash require some specific internal controls?

   a. Most transactions ultimately affect cash.
   b. Cash is relatively easy to steal.
   c. Cash is easy to convert to other forms of wealth.
   d. All of the above.

9. Each of the following documents is a control for a bank account *except*

   a. signature card.
   b. geographic location of ATMs.
   c. bank statement.
   d. bank reconciliation.

10. A journal entry would need to be made for which of the following adjustments on a bank reconciliation?

    a. Bank service charges
    b. Outstanding checks
    c. Deposits in transit
    d. Bank error to be corrected by the bank

11. The bookkeeper for Maxwell Company wrote a check for $300 to pay for furnace maintenance. The check was incorrectly recorded in the general journal as $30. The entry to correct this error would be:
   - **a.** increase Repairs and Maintenance Expense by $270.
   - **b.** increase Repairs and Maintenance Expense by $300.
   - **c.** increase Cash by $270.
   - **d.** decrease Cash by $300.

12. All of the following items are included on the balance sheet as Cash and Cash Equivalents *except*
   - **a.** certificates of deposit.
   - **b.** time deposits.
   - **c.** 4-week U.S. Treasury bills.
   - **d.** All of the above are included.

Excel Project
Autograded Excel Project available in **MyLab Accounting**.

ASSESS YOUR PROGRESS

Ethics Check

EC4-1. Identify ethical principle violated

For each of the situations listed, identify which of three principles (integrity, objectivity and independence, or due care) from the AICPA Code of Professional Conduct is violated. Assume all persons listed in the situations are members of the AICPA. (Note: Refer to the AICPA Code of Professional Conduct contained on pages 25–27 in Chapter 1 for descriptions of the principles.)

- **a.** Reggie, the managing partner of an audit firm, has the authority to approve all transactions. As a result, he uses firm funds to purchase a new couch for his home.
- **b.** Taylor is a first-year auditor for a large public accounting firm. She is assigned to audit Bike Global, a regional travel agency specializing in bike tours. Taylor does not disclose to her firm that her mother is a co-owner of Bike Global, since Taylor knows that she will not allow herself to be influenced by her mom.
- **c.** Rick has been working for his company for ten years and is required to attend internal control training annually. Rick does not attend the training this year because he feels he already understands the policies. Significant policy updates have occurred during the past year.
- **d.** Brooke, an accounts payable clerk, must have her manager sign off on all checks over $10,000. Her manager is out of the office this week, so Brooke forges her manager's signature to make sure the check is sent out on time.

Short Exercises

S4-1. ***(Learning Objective 1: Define fraud and its components)*** Define "fraud." List and briefly discuss the three major components of the fraud triangle. LO 1

S4-2. ***(Learning Objective 1: Describe fraud and its impact)*** Donna Franks, an accountant for Southern Technologies Corporation, discovers that her supervisor, Elise Silverton, made several errors last year. Overall, the errors overstated the company's net income by 40%. It is not clear whether the errors were deliberate or accidental. What should Franks do? LO 1

S4-3. ***(Learning Objective 2: Describe objectives and components of internal control)*** List the components of internal control. Briefly describe each component. LO 2

S4-4. ***(Learning Objective 2: Explain the objectives and components of internal control)*** Explain why separation of duties is often described as the cornerstone of internal control for safeguarding assets. Describe what can happen if the same person has custody of an asset and also accounts for the asset. LO 2

S4-5. ***(Learning Objective 2: Explain the objectives and components of internal control)*** Identify the other control procedures usually found in a company's system of internal control besides separation of duties, and tell why each is important. LO 2

LO 3 **S4-6.** ***(Learning Objective 3: Evalue internal controls over cash)*** Cash may be a small item on the financial statements. Nevertheless, internal control over cash is very important. Why is this true?

LO 3 **S4-7.** ***(Learning Objective 3: Evaluate internal controls over cash payments)*** Fireball Company requires that all documents supporting a check (purchase order, invoice, and receiving report) be canceled by punching a hole through the packet. Why is this practice required? What might happen if it were not?

LO 3 **S4-8.** ***(Learning Objective 3: Evaluate internal control over cash receipts and cash payments)*** James Cooper sells memberships to the Atlanta Symphony Association. The Association's procedure requires that Cooper prepare and give each customer a receipt for each membership sold. The receipt forms are prenumbered. Cooper is having personal financial problems, and he kept the $500 cash received from a customer for a new membership. To hide his theft, Cooper destroyed the Association's copy of the receipt that he gave to the customer. What will alert manager Terry Reynolds that something is wrong?

LO 3 **S4-9.** ***(Learning Objective 3: Evaluate internal control over cash receipts and cash payments)*** Answer the following questions about internal control over cash payments:

1. Payment by check includes three controls over cash. What are they?
2. Suppose a purchasing agent receives the goods that she purchases and also approves payment for those goods. How could a dishonest purchasing agent cheat the company? How do companies avoid this internal control weakness?

LO 4 **S4-10.** ***(Learning Objective 4: Prepare a bank reconciliation)*** The Cash account of Reese Corporation had a balance of $3,540 at October 31, 2018. Included were outstanding checks totaling $1,800 and an October 31 deposit of $300 that did not appear on the bank statement. The bank statement, which came from Turnstone State Bank, listed an October 31 balance of $5,570. Included in the bank balance was an October 30 collection of $600 on account from a customer who pays the bank directly. The bank statement also showed a $30 service charge, $10 of interest revenue that Reese earned on its bank balance, and an NSF check for $50.

Prepare a bank reconciliation to determine how much cash Reese actually had at October 31.

LO 4 **S4-11.** ***(Learning Objective 4: Prepare a bank reconciliation)*** After preparing Reese Corp.'s bank reconciliation in Short Exercise 4-10, make the company's journal entries for transactions that arise from the bank reconciliation. Date each transaction October 31, 2018, and include an explanation with each entry.

LO 4 **S4-12.** ***(Learning Objective 4: Prepare a bank reconciliation)*** Constance Hermaine manages Springfield Manufacturing. Hermaine fears that a trusted employee has been stealing from the company. This employee receives cash from clients and also prepares the monthly bank reconciliation. To check up on the employee, Hermaine prepares her own bank reconciliation, as follows:

	A	B	C	D	E
1	**Springfield Manufacturing Bank Reconciliation May 31, 2018**				
2	**Bank**		**Books**		
3	Balance, May 31	$ 4,200	Balance, May 31		$ 4,120
4	Add:		Add:		
5	Deposits in transit	700	Bank collections		1200
6			Interest revenue		10
7	Less:		Less:		
8	Outstanding checks	(860)	Service charge		(40)
9	Adjusted bank balance	$ 4,040	Adjusted book balance		$ 5,290
10					

Does it appear that the employee has stolen from the company? If so, how much? Explain your answer. Which side of the bank reconciliation shows the company's true cash balance?

S4-13. ***(Learning Objective 5: Report cash on the balance sheet)*** Describe the types of assets that are typically included under the heading "cash and cash equivalents" on the balance sheet. What is a "cash equivalent"? LO 5

S4-14. ***(Learning Objectives 1, 2, 3, 4, 5: Match definitions with vocabulary terms)*** Use these terms to complete the statements that follow. You can use a term more than once or not at all. LO 1, 2, 3, 4, 5

Bank reconciliation	Firewall	Misappropriation of assets
Cash equivalents	Fraud triangle	Outstanding check
Controller	Fraudulent financial reporting	Phishing
Deposits in transit	Imprest system	Remittance advice
Fidelity bond	Internal control	Treasurer

a. When a company has recorded a deposit but the bank has not yet processed it, this item is a/an ________.

b. ________ occurs when management prepares misleading financial statements.

c. A/An ________ is an optional attachment to a check that lists the payer, date, and amount of the payment.

d. An organization's system of procedures designed to safeguard its assets and encourage adherence to the company's policies is called the system of ________.

e. When a company has issued a check but the check has not yet been processed or paid by the bank, this item is a/an ________.

f. The ________ is responsible for the accounting systems in an organization.

g. A/An ________ is an electronic barrier that prevents unauthorized access to an organization's computer network.

h. The ________ is typically responsible for cash handling and cash management.

i. A/An ________ is prepared to explain the difference between the cash on the books versus the bank cash balance.

j. Investments such as time deposits and certificates of deposit are ________.

k. Petty cash can be accounted for using a/an ________.

l. An insurance policy that reimburses a company for any losses due to employee theft is a/an ________.

m. Motive, opportunity, and rationalization are elements of the ________.

n. The fraudulent practice of creating bogus websites or sending fake e-mails to get individuals to share personal information such as birthdays, passwords, and credit card numbers is called ________.

o. When employees steal assets from an organization, it is called ________.

Exercises MyLab Accounting

Group A

LO 1, 2, 3

E4-15A. ***(Learning Objectives 1, 2, 3: Describe fraud and its impact; explain the objectives and components of internal control; evaluate internal controls over cash payments and receipts)*** Identify the internal control weakness in the following situations. State how the person can hurt the company.

a. Emily Chen is the purchasing agent for Wilson Industries. Chen prepares purchase orders based on requests from division managers of the company. She faxes the purchase order to suppliers, who then ship the goods to Wilson. Chen receives each incoming shipment and checks it for agreement with the purchase order and the related invoice. She then routes the goods to the respective division managers and sends the receiving report and the invoice to the accounting department for payment.

b. Chris Frabotta works as a security guard at PARKFAST parking in St. Louis. Frabotta has a master key to the cash box where customers pay for parking. Each night Frabotta prepares the cash report that shows (a) the number of cars that parked on the lot and (b) the day's cash receipts. Holly Van, the PARKFAST bookkeeper, checks Frabotta's figures by multiplying the number of cars by the parking fee per car. Van then deposits the cash in the bank.

LO 3

E4-16A. ***(Learning Objective 3: Evaluate internal controls over cash receipts and cash payments)*** The following situations describe two cash payment situations and two cash receipt situations. In each pair, one set of internal controls is better than the other. Evaluate the internal controls in each situation as strong or weak, and give the reason for your answer.

Cash receipts:

a. At Samson Carpet Mill, cash received by mail goes straight to the bookkeeper, who debits Cash and credits Accounts Receivable to record the collections from customers. The bookkeeper then deposits the cash in the bank.

b. Cash received by mail at Liberty Dermatology Clinic goes to the mailroom, where a mail clerk opens envelopes and totals the cash receipts for the day. The mail clerk forwards customer checks to the cashier for deposit in the bank and forwards the remittance advices to the accounting department for posting credits to customer accounts.

Cash payments:

a. Scott Construction policy calls for construction supervisors to request the equipment needed for their jobs. The home office then purchases the equipment and has it shipped to the construction site.

b. Remington Home Construction's policy calls for project supervisors to purchase the equipment needed for jobs. The supervisors then submit the paid receipts to the home office for reimbursement. This policy enables supervisors to get the equipment quickly and keep construction jobs moving.

LO 3

E4-17A. ***(Learning Objective 3: Evaluate internal control over cash payments)*** Lander Company manufactures a popular line of work clothes. Lander employs 125 workers and keeps time sheets that show how many hours the employees work each week. On Friday the shop foreman collects the time sheets, checks them for accuracy, and delivers them to the payroll department so it can prepare paychecks. The treasurer signs the paychecks and returns them to the payroll department for distribution to the employees.

Identify the main internal control weakness in this situation, state how the weakness can hurt Lander, and propose a way to correct the weakness.

E4-18A. ***(Learning Objectives 1, 2, 3: Describe fraud and its impact; explain the objectives and components of internal control; evaluate internal controls over cash receipts and cash payments)*** Ruth Bixby served as executive director of Uptown Allentown, an organization created to revitalize Allentown, Pennsylvania. Over the course of 13 years, Bixby embezzled $543,000 through a variety of methods. Bixby deposited the organization's cash receipts in her own bank account. She wrote Uptown Allentown checks to herself, and she also created phony entities to which Uptown Allentown wrote checks. LO 1, 2, 3

Uptown Allentown was led by a board of directors comprised of civic leaders. Bixby's embezzlement went undetected until the organization couldn't pay its bills.

Give four ways Bixby's embezzlement could have been prevented.

E4-19A. ***(Learning Objective 4: Prepare a bank reconciliation)*** Sangreen Company's checkbook lists the following: LO 4

Date	Check No.	Item	Check	Deposit	Balance
5/1					$ 505
4	622	Two Sisters Catering	$ 30		475
9		Dividends received		$ 150	625
13	623	City Tire Co.	115		510
14	624	Jiffy Lube	28		482
18	625	Cash	30		452
26	626	American Diabetes Association	40		412
28	627	Riverbend Apartments	125		287
31		Paycheck		1,235	1,522

The May bank statement shows:

Balance			$505
Add: Deposits			150
Debit checks: No.	Amount		
622	$30		
623	115		
624	82*		
625	30		(257)
Other charges:			
NSF check		$45	
Service charge		20	(65)
Balance			$333

*This is the correct amount for check number 624.

Requirement

1. Prepare Sangreen's bank reconciliation at May 31, 2019.

E4-20A. ***(Learning Objective 4: Use a bank reconciliation)*** Jim Patrick operates a roller skating center, Skatetown USA. He has just received the company's monthly bank statement at March 31 from Ringley National Bank, and the statement shows an ending balance of $710. Listed on the statement are an EFT rent collection of $315, a service charge of $10, two NSF checks totaling $100, and an $11 charge for printed checks. In reviewing his cash records, Patrick identifies outstanding checks totaling $615 and a March 31 deposit in transit of $1,775. During March, he recorded a $210 check for the salary of a part-time employee as $21. Patrick's Cash account shows a March 31 cash balance of $1,865. How much cash does Patrick actually have at March 31, 2018? LO 4

E4-21A. ***(Learning Objective 4: Use a bank reconciliation)*** Use the data from Exercise 4-20A to make the journal entries that Patrick should record on March 31 to update his Cash account. Include an explanation for each entry. LO 4

Group B

LO 1, 2, 3

E4-22B. ***(Learning Objectives 1, 2, 3: Describe fraud and its impact; explain the objectives and components of internal control; evaluate internal control over cash payments and receipts)*** Identify the internal control weakness in the following situations. State how the person can hurt the company.

a. Katie Parker is the purchasing agent for Salem Sports Equipment. Parker prepares purchase orders based on requests from division managers of the company. Parker faxes the purchase order to suppliers, who then ship the goods to Salem. She receives each incoming shipment and checks it for agreement with the purchase order and the related invoice. She then routes the goods to the respective division managers and sends the receiving report and the invoice to the accounting department for payment.

b. Melissa Makers works as a security guard at RAPID parking in Kansas City. Makers has a master key to the cash box where customers pay for parking. Each night Makers prepares the cash report that shows (a) the number of cars that parked on the lot and (b) the day's cash receipts. Julie Gibbons, the RAPID treasurer, checks Makers' figures by multiplying the number of cars by the parking fee per car. Gibbons then deposits the cash in the bank.

LO 3

E4-23B. ***(Learning Objective 3: Evaluate internal controls over cash receipts and cash payments)*** The following situations describe two cash payment situations and two cash receipt situations. In each pair, one set of internal controls is better than the other. Evaluate the internal controls in each situation as strong or weak, and give the reason for your answer.

Cash receipts:

a. At Franklin Carpet Mill, cash received by mail goes straight to the bookkeeper, who debits Cash and credits Accounts Receivable to record the collections from customers. The bookkeeper then deposits the cash in the bank.

b. Cash received by mail at Mayfield Heart Clinic goes to the mailroom, where a mail clerk opens envelopes and totals the cash receipts for the day. The mail clerk forwards customer checks to the cashier for deposit in the bank and forwards the remittance slips to the accounting department for posting credits to customer accounts.

Cash payments:

a. Garber Construction policy calls for construction supervisors to request the equipment needed for their jobs. The home office then purchases the equipment and has it shipped to the construction site.

b. Tuttle Home Construction's policy calls for project supervisors to purchase the equipment needed for jobs. The supervisors then submit the paid receipts to the home office for reimbursement. This policy enables supervisors to get the equipment quickly and keep construction jobs moving.

LO 3

E4-24B. ***(Learning Objective 3: Evaluate internal control over cash payments)*** Harper Company manufactures a popular brand of footballs. Harper employs 147 workers and keeps time sheets that show how many hours the employees work each week. On Friday the shop foreman collects the time sheets, checks them for accuracy, and delivers them to the payroll department so it can prepare paychecks. The treasurer signs the paychecks and returns them to the payroll department for distribution to the employees.

Identify the main internal control weakness in this situation, state how the weakness can hurt Harper, and propose a way to correct the weakness.

LO 1, 2, 3

E4-25B. ***(Learning Objectives 1, 2, 3: Describe fraud and its impact; explain the objectives and components of internal control; evaluate internal controls over cash receipts and cash payments)*** Mary Jenson served as executive director of Downtown Bridgeport, an organization created to revitalize Bridgeport, Oregon. Over the course of 14 years, Jenson embezzled $295,000 through a variety of methods. Jenson deposited the organization's cash receipts in her own bank account. She wrote Downtown Bridgeport checks to herself, and she also created phony entities to which Downtown Bridgeport wrote checks.

Downtown Bridgeport was led by a board of directors comprised of civic leaders. Jenson's embezzlement went undetected until the organization couldn't pay its bills.

Give four ways Jenson's embezzlement could have been prevented.

E4-26B. ***(Learning Objective 4: Prepare a bank reconciliation)*** Lexitech Company's checkbook lists the following: LO 4

Date	Check No.	Item	Check	Deposit	Balance
1/1					$ 505
4	622	Tuscan Sandwiches	$ 60		445
9		Dividends received		$ 120	565
13	623	Hartford Co.	120		445
14	624	FastMobil	78		367
18	625	Cash	45		322
26	626	Red Cross	70		252
28	627	Brookside Apartments	140		112
31		Paycheck		1,240	1,352

The January bank statement shows:

Balance				$505
Add: Deposits				120
Debit checks:	No.	Amount		
	622	$60		
	623	120		
	624	87*		
	625	45		(312)
Other charges:				
NSF check			$20	
Service charge			25	(45)
Balance				$268

*This is the correct amount for check number 624.

Requirement

1. Prepare Lexitech's bank reconciliation at January 31, 2018.

E4-27B. ***(Learning Objective 4: Use a bank reconciliation)*** Harry McCall operates a roller skating center, McCall Rinks. He has just received the company's monthly bank statement at February 28 from Ridgeway National Bank, and the statement shows an ending balance of $755. Listed on the statement are an EFT rent collection of $305, a service charge of $7, two NSF checks totaling $120, and a $9 charge for printed checks. In reviewing his cash records, McCall identifies outstanding checks totaling $612 and a February 28 deposit in transit of $1,775. During February, he recorded a $270 check for the salary of a part-time employee as $27. McCall's Cash account shows a February 28 cash balance of $1,992. How much cash does McCall actually have at February 28, 2018? LO 4

E4-28B. ***(Learning Objective 4: Use a bank reconciliation)*** Use the data from Exercise 4-27B to make the journal entries that McCall should record on February 28 to update his Cash account. Include an explanation for each entry. LO 4

Quiz

Test your understanding of internal control and cash by answering the following questions. Answer each question by selecting the best choice from among the options given.

Q4-29. All of the following are objectives of internal control *except*

a. to ensure accurate and reliable accounting records.
b. to comply with legal requirements.
c. to maximize net income.
d. to safeguard assets.

Q4-30. All of the following are internal control procedures *except*

a. Sarbanes-Oxley reforms.
b. assignment of responsibilities.
c. adequate records.
d. internal and external audits.

Q4-31. Requiring that an employee with no access to cash do the accounting is an example of which characteristic of internal control?

a. Separation of duties
b. Assignment of responsibility
c. Competent and reliable personnel
d. Monitoring of controls

Q4-32. All of the following are controls for cash received over the counter *except*

a. a printed receipt must be given to the customer.
b. the cash drawer should open only when the sales clerk enters an amount on the keys.
c. the customer should be able to see the amounts entered into the cash register.
d. the sales clerk must have access to the cash register tape.

Q4-33. In a bank reconciliation, an outstanding check is

a. deducted from the book balance.
b. deducted from the bank balance.
c. added to the bank balance.
d. added to the book balance.

Q4-34. In a bank reconciliation, an EFT cash payment is

a. deducted from the bank balance.
b. added to the bank balance.
c. added to the book balance.
d. deducted from the book balance.

Q4-35. If a bookkeeper mistakenly recorded a $73 deposit as $37, the error would be shown on the bank reconciliation as a

a. $36 deduction from the book balance.
b. $37 addition to the book balance.
c. $36 addition to the book balance.
d. $37 deduction from the book balance.

Q4-36. If a bank reconciliation included a deposit in transit of $790, the entry to record this reconciling item would include

a. a credit to Cash for $790.
b. a credit to Prepaid insurance for $790.
c. a debit to Cash for $790.
d. No entry is required.

Q4-37. In a bank reconciliation, interest revenue earned on your bank balance is

a. added to the book balance.
b. deducted from the book balance.
c. deducted from the bank balance.
d. added to the bank balance.

Q4-38. Before paying an invoice for goods received on account, the controller or treasurer should ensure that

a. the company is paying for the goods it actually received.
b. the company is paying for the goods it ordered.
c. the company has not already paid this invoice.
d. all of the above.

Q4-39. Which of the following is an example of poor internal control in an organization?

a. The company rotates employees through various jobs.
b. The accounting department compares goods received with the related purchase order.
c. The mailroom clerk records daily cash receipts in the journal.
d. Employees must take vacations.

Q4-40. Which of the following assets are *not* included in "cash equivalents" in a typical balance sheet?

a. Foreign government securities
b. Certain very low-risk equity securities
c. U.S. government securities
d. Time deposits
e. All of the above might be included in "cash equivalents."

Problems MyLab Accounting

Group A

LO 1, 3

P4-41A. ***(Learning Objectives 1, 3: Describe fraud and its impact; evaluate internal controls over cash receipts and cash payments)*** Italian Imports buys furniture and décor items from Italy and sells them to retailers. Amelia Rossi is the general manager of the company. Rossi employs two other people in the business. Marcia Moretti serves as the buyer for the company. Moretti travels throughout Italy to find interesting new products. When Moretti finds a new product, she arranges for Italian Imports to purchase and pay for the item. She helps the artisans prepare their invoices and then faxes the invoices to Rossi in the company office.

Rossi operates out of an office in Boston, Massachusetts. The office is managed by Alexa DeLuca, who handles the mail, keeps the accounting records, makes bank deposits, and prepares the monthly bank reconciliation. Virtually all of the company's cash receipts arrive by mail—from sales made to **Target**, **Pier 1 Imports**, and specialty shops.

DeLuca also prepares checks for payment based on invoices that come in from the suppliers that have been contacted by Moretti. To maintain control over cash payments, Rossi examines the paperwork and signs all checks.

Requirement

1. Identify all the major internal control weaknesses in Italian Imports' system and explain how they could hurt the company. Also state how to correct each weakness.

LO 2, 3

P4-42A. ***(Learning Objectives 2, 3: Explain the objectives and components of internal control; evaluate internal controls)*** Each of the following situations reveals an internal control weakness:

- **a.** Jake Bates has been an employee of the city of Elmhurst for many years. Because the city is small, Bates performs all of its accounting duties, in addition to opening the mail and preparing bank deposits and bank reconciliations.
- **b.** A purchasing agent for Mark Manufacturing is responsible for buying diamonds for use in the company's manufacturing process, approving the invoices for payment, and signing the checks. No supervisor reviews the purchasing agent's work.
- **c.** Bailey Price owns an architectural firm. Price's staff consists of 16 professional architects, and Price manages the office. Often her work requires her to travel to meet with clients. During the past six months, Price has observed that when she returns from a business trip, the architecture jobs in the office have not progressed satisfactorily. She learns that when she is away, two of her senior architects take over office management and neglect their normal duties. One employee could manage the office.

Requirements

1. Identify the missing internal control characteristic in each situation.
2. Identify each organization's possible problem.
3. Propose a solution to the problem.

LO 3

P4-43A. ***(Learning Objective 3: Evaluate internal controls)*** Mark Kershey, a former Smucker employee, was charged with defrauding the **J.M. Smucker Company** of more than $4.1 million over a 16-year period. Charges were filed in October 2014. In 2015, Kershey was sentenced to nearly five years in prison. Kershey was the chief airplane mechanic at the company's hangar at the Akron-Canton Airport in Ohio from 1990 until he was discharged by Smucker in 2013. From 1997 until the time he left Smucker, Kershey invoiced Smucker for more than $4.1 million by using a fictitious entity he created. He billed Smucker for nonexistent parts and/or work that he himself actually performed as part of his duties as a salaried employee. Most of these invoices were for less than $10,000, which Kershey himself was authorized to approve. A supervisor to Kershey approved the few invoices that were for more than $10,000 based on his trust in Kershey. To carry out his false billing scheme, Kershey set up a post office box in Lake Township, Ohio, using the fictitious entity name of Aircraft Parts Services Co. (APS). He (as APS) would then invoice Smucker using nonsequential invoice numbers, so it looked like APS was invoicing other companies too. Kershey used the proceeds to purchase and maintain two planes and several automobiles, and to make payments on his house.

Kershey was eventually caught in late 2012 when three checks written by Smucker to APS totaling $44,000 were not cashed. When a Smucker employee questioned Kershey about the uncashed checks, Kershey indicated that APS had been sold to another Smucker vendor. The false billing scheme began to unravel and Kershey was fired.

Requirements

1. What internal controls could have been used to prevent Kershey from carrying out the false billing scheme?
2. What factors might have contributed to the weak internal control environment that allowed this scheme to exist for 16 years?

LO 4

P4-44A. ***(Learning Objective 4: Prepare a bank reconciliation)*** The cash data of Duffy Automotive for May 2018 follow:

Cash — Account No. 101

Date	Item	Jrnl. Ref.	Debit	Credit	Balance
May 1	Balance				7,150
30		CR6	9,751		16,901
30		CP11		10,308	6,593

Cash Receipts (CR)		Cash Payments (CP)	
Date	**Cash Debit**	**Check No.**	**Cash Credit**
May 2	$ 2,728	3113	$ 1,522
8	512	3114	1,759
10	1,693	3115	1,930
16	832	3116	63
22	427	3117	805
29	982	3118	87
30	2,577	3119	476
Total	$9,751	3120	1,049
		3121	257
		3122	2,360
		Total	$10,308

Duffy Automotive received the following bank statement on May 31, 2018:

Bank Statement for May 2018

Beginning balance			$ 7,150
Deposits and other additions:			
May	1	$ 700 EFT	
	4	2,728	
	9	512	
	12	1,693	
	17	832	
	22	427	
	23	1,325 BC	8,217
Checks and other deductions:			
May	7	$ 1,522	
	13	1,390	
	14	492 US	
	15	1,759	
	18	63	
	21	316 EFT	
	26	805	
	30	87	
	30	10 SC	(6,444)
Ending balance			$ 8,923

Explanation: BC—bank collection of note receivable from customer, EFT—electronic funds transfer, US—unauthorized signature, SC—service charge

Additional data for the bank reconciliation include the following:

a. The EFT deposit was a receipt of monthly rent. The EFT debit was a monthly insurance payment.

b. The unauthorized signature check was received from a customer and returned by the bank unpaid.

c. The correct amount of check number 3115, a payment on account, is $1,390. (Duffy Automotive's accountant mistakenly recorded the check as $1,930.)

Requirements

1. Prepare Duffy Automotive's bank reconciliation at May 31, 2018.
2. Prepare the journal entries required at May 31, 2018.
3. Describe how a bank account and the bank reconciliation help the general manager control Duffy Automotive's cash.

Group B

P4-45B. ***(Learning Objectives 1, 3: Describe fraud and its impact; evaluate internal controls over cash receipts and cash payments)*** Parisian Imports buys furniture and décor items from France and sells them to retailers. Erin Moreland is the general manager of the company. Moreland employs two other people in the business. Nadine Mast serves as the buyer for the company. Mast travels throughout France to find interesting new products. When Mast finds a new product, she arranges for Parisian Imports to purchase and pay for the item. She helps the artisans prepare their invoices and then faxes the invoices to Moreland in the company office. LO **1, 3**

Moreland operates out of an office in Brooklyn, New York. The office is managed by Sandy Richter, who handles the mail, keeps the accounting records, makes bank deposits, and prepares the monthly bank reconciliation. Virtually all of the company's cash receipts arrive by mail—from sales made to **Target**, **Crate and Barrel**, and **Williams-Sonoma**.

Richter also prepares checks for payment based on invoices that come in from the suppliers that have been contacted by Mast. To maintain control over cash payments, Moreland examines the paperwork and signs all checks.

Requirement

1. Identify all the major internal control weaknesses in Parisian Imports' system and explain how they could hurt the company. Also state how to correct each weakness.

LO 2, 3

P4-46B. ***(Learning Objectives 2, 3: Explain the objectives and components of internal control; evaluate internal controls)*** Each of the following situations reveals an internal control weakness:

a. Tom Dickens has been an employee of the city of Fulton for many years. Because the city is small, Dickens performs all of its accounting duties, in addition to opening the mail and preparing bank deposits and bank reconciliations.

b. A purchasing agent for Sampson Manufacturing is responsible for buying diamonds for use in the company's manufacturing process, approving the invoices for payment, and signing the checks. No supervisor reviews the purchasing agent's work.

c. Pam Silk owns an architectural firm. Silk's staff consists of 19 professional architects, and Silk manages the office. Often, her work requires her to travel to meet with clients. During the past six months, Silk has observed that when she returns from a business trip, the architecture jobs in the office have not progressed satisfactorily. She learns that when she is away, two of her senior architects take over office management and neglect their normal duties. One employee could manage the office.

Requirements

1. Identify the missing internal control characteristic in each situation.
2. Identify each organization's possible problem.
3. Propose a solution to the problem.

LO 3

P4-47B. ***(Learning Objective 3: Evaluate internal controls)*** Beaumont Independent School District (BISD) is a public school district in Beaumont, Texas. It has three high schools, six middle schools, and 16 elementary schools, serving approximately 21,000 students. In February, 2015, Patricia Lambert, former BISD Assistant Superintendent, was indicted for theft connected with her position in the school district. Lambert allegedly defrauded the school district for more than $750,000. Lambert was sentenced for federal charges of theft in 2016 to 40 months in prison and ordered to pay back $500,000 in restitution.

The story of Lambert at BISD begins in 2002, when Lambert was hired by the district as a teacher. She would eventually be promoted several times, finally to assistant superintendent, a position in which she remained until her retirement in 2014. During the course of her employment, she is charged with embezzling more than $750,000 from BISD. Here are descriptions of the schemes in which she participated/orchestrated:

- **Booster Club funds:** Lambert took control of the Booster Club from the parents who had been running it. She gained full access to the booster club's funds, which were not subject to BISD oversight or audits. She began taking money from the booster club; she wrote checks for more than $24,381 payable to her children or herself from the booster club funds. Lambert also purchased clothing, clothing accessories, and electronics for her own personal use from the booster club funds.
- **Student activity fees:** During Lambert's tenure at the school district, she also directed that certain student activity fees be paid to the booster club where she had control of the funds. For students to obtain copies of their official transcripts, they had to pay a small fee, usually less than $5. Those transcript fees were directed to the booster club account by Lambert where she had access, without audit or supervision, to the funds.
- **Booster club reimbursement for travel:** Lambert also wrote checks out of the booster club account to reimburse herself for school district travel, even though she had already been reimbursed by BISD for the travel.
- **Cash fund:** Students in the district would have to pay a $10 fine when found with a cell phone in class or when they lost their student ID. These fines went into a cash fund. In addition, there was a snack area set up near the cafeteria where students could purchase candy and chips. The inventory of candy and chips was paid for by the booster club. A portion of all of these cash fees and sales were deposited into Lambert's personal bank account.

As a side note, before she joined BISD in 2002 as a teacher, Lambert was convicted of extortion in Louisiana after running a kickback scheme with teachers for whom she secured pay raises and job promotions.

Requirements

1. For each of the four schemes allegedly run by Lambert, comment on what internal control principles would likely have been violated.
2. For each of the four schemes listed, describe controls that could have been put into place to prevent the type of fraud that Lambert is charged with committing.

LO 4

P4-48B. ***(Learning Objective 4: Prepare a bank reconciliation)*** The cash data of Eddy Automotive for October 2018 follow:

Cash					Account No. 101
Date	**Item**	**Jrnl. Ref.**	**Debit**	**Credit**	**Balance**
October 1	Balance				7,950
31		CR 6	9,330		17,280
31		CP 11		10,122	7,158

Cash Receipts (CR)		Cash Payments (CP)	
Date	**Cash Debit**	**Check No.**	**Cash Credit**
October 2	$ 2,828	3113	$ 1,542
8	597	3114	1,729
10	1,652	3115	1,830
16	837	3116	47
22	360	3117	782
29	904	3118	169
30	2,152	3119	478
Total	$9,330	3120	1,023
		3121	234
		3122	2,288
		Total	$10,122

Eddy Automotive received the following bank statement on October 31, 2018:

Bank Statement for October 2018

Beginning balance			$ 7,950
Deposits and other additions:			
October	1	$ 600 EFT	
	4	2,828	
	9	597	
	12	1,652	
	17	837	
	22	360	
	23	1,500 BC	8,374
Checks and other deductions:			
October	7	$1,542	
	13	1,380	
	14	419 US	
	15	1,729	
	18	47	
	21	441 EFT	
	26	782	
	30	169	
	30	10 SC	(6,519)
Ending balance			$ 9,805

Explanation: BC—bank collection of note receivable from customer, EFT—electronic funds transfer, US—unauthorized signature, SC—service charge

Additional data for the bank reconciliation include the following:

a. The EFT deposit was a receipt of monthly rent. The EFT debit was a monthly insurance payment.

b. The unauthorized signature check was received from a customer and returned by the bank unpaid.

c. The correct amount of check number 3115, a payment on account, is $1,380. (Eddy Automotive's accountant mistakenly recorded the check as $1,830.)

d. The bank collected a note receivable for Eddy Automotive.

Requirements

1. Prepare Eddy Automotive's bank reconciliation at October 31, 2018.
2. Prepare the journal entries required at October 31, 2018.
3. Describe how a bank account and the bank reconciliation help the general manager control Eddy Automotive's cash.

Challenge Exercises and Problem

LO 1, 3

E4-49. ***(Learning Objectives 1, 3: Describe fraud and its impact; evaluate internal controls over cash receipts and cash payments)*** Janet Black, the owner of Janet's Catering, has delegated the management of the business to Danielle Vale, a friend. Black drops by to meet customers and check up on cash receipts, but Vale buys the merchandise and handles cash payments. Business has been very good lately, and cash receipts have kept pace with the apparent level of sales. However, for a year or so, the amount of cash on hand has been too low. When asked about this, Vale explains that suppliers are charging more for goods than in the past. During the past year, Vale has taken two expensive vacations, and Black wonders how Vale can afford these trips on her $52,000 annual salary and commissions.

List at least three ways Vale could be defrauding Black of cash. In each instance, also identify how Black can determine whether Vale's actions are ethical. Limit your answers to the store's cash payments. The business pays all suppliers by check (no EFTs).

LO 4

P4-50. ***(Learning Objective 4: Prepare a bank reconciliation)*** The president of The Peterson Company suspects the bookkeeper is embezzling cash from the company. She asks you, confidentially, to look over the bank reconciliation that the bookkeeper has prepared to see if you discover any discrepancies between the books and the bank statement. She provides you with the Cash account from the general ledger, the bank statement, and the bank reconciliation as of December 31. You learn from the November bank reconciliation that the following checks were outstanding on November 30: No. 1560 for $187, No. 1880 for $542, No. 1882 for $119, and No. 1883 for $460. There was one deposit in transit on November 30 for $1,284. An examination of the actual deposit slips revealed no bank errors. Assume the cash deposit of $2,450 on December 24 is the correct amount. The January bank statement showed that a $610 deposit cleared the bank on January 2.

A1

	A	B	C	D	E	F
1	**Peterson Company Bank Reconciliation December 31**					
2	**Bank**			**Books**		
3	Balance, 12/31		$ 4,065	Balance, 12/31		$ 11,755
4	Add:			Add:		
5	Deposits in transit		3,110	EFT receipt from customer		53
6	Subtotal		7,175	Interest revenue		6
7	Less:			Subtotal		11,814
8	Outstanding checks			Less:		
9	No. 1560	$ 187		Book error	$ 5,000	
10	No. 1901	847		NSF check	100	
11	No. 1902	162	(1,196)	EFT payment of utilities	735	(5,835)
12	Adjusted bank balance		$ 5,979	Adjusted book balance		$ 5,979
13						

General Ledger
Cash

Bal 12/1	6,266		
Cash receipt 12/7	1,500		
Cash receipt 12/15	4,195		
Cash receipt 12/23	7,450		
Cash receipt 12/30	610	No. 1884	1,287
		No. 1885	1,323
		No. 1886	750
		No. 1887	2,439
		No. 1888	1,025
		No. 1889	433
		No. 1901	847
		No. 1902	162
Bal 12/31	11,755		

Bank Statement for December 31

Bal 12/1		$ 3,790
Deposits		
Dec 1	$ 1,284	
8	1,500	
16	4,195	
24	2,450	
Interest 31	6	
EFT 31	53	
Total deposits		9,488
Checks and other debits:		
No. 1880	542	
No. 1882	119	
No. 1883	460	
No. 1884	1,287	
No. 1885	1,323	
No. 1886	750	
No. 1887	2,439	
No. 1888	1,025	
No. 1889	433	
NSF	100	
EFT	735	
Total checks and other debits		(9,213)
Bal 12/31		$ 4,065

Explanation: EFT—electronic funds transfer, NSF—nonsufficient funds

Requirement

1. Prepare a corrected bank reconciliation. Show the unexplained difference as an adjustment to the book balance. Include in your analysis the amount of the theft and how the bookkeeper attempted to conceal the theft.

APPLY YOUR KNOWLEDGE

Serial Case

LO 3

C4-51. ***(Learning Objective 3: Analyze internal controls in place at a restaurant)***

Note: This case is part of The Cheesecake Factory serial case contained in every chapter in this textbook.

The Cheesecake Factory must implement and enforce an effective internal control system to both comply with financial reporting regulations and protect its assets. Let's look at a description of a typical day for a server at a Cheesecake Factory restaurant.

Each shift starts with $250 cash in the cash register. Upon arriving and starting a shift, a designated server counts the cash in the cash register and records the amount of cash and the time. If the count entered does not match what the computer system has as the current cash level ($250), the manager must record an explanation before proceeding.

The server is now ready to begin his or her shift and start waiting on customers. When taking a customer's order, the server writes the menu items ordered on an order ticket. After leaving the table, the server then enters the order into the computer system. The kitchen receives the order from the computer system once it is entered. No food or beverages can be produced until the order is entered into the computer system.

When the order is ready, the kitchen staff marks the order as complete in the computer system and the server is notified that the order is ready. The server then picks up the food and takes it out to the customer. Once the diners are finished eating, the server clears the table, prints the check from the computer system, and brings the check to the table.

If a price adjustment is necessary due to an error, the server must get a manager's approval to override the price in the computer system. Prior to authorizing an override, the manager visits the table to speak with the customer to ensure the person is satisfied.

At the end of the shift, the cash drawer is reconciled and set to equal the amount needed at the start of the next shift, $250. The manager counts and reconciles the drawer in the presence of another employee. All cash collected during the shift, less the $250, is removed from the register and taken to the bank for deposit by the manager.

The computer system sales totals for the shift are reconciled with the cash deposit by an accounting staff member in The Cheesecake Factory's headquarters each day. Any discrepancies trigger a phone call from headquarters and a possible investigation of that restaurant.

Requirements

1. Identify the internal controls present in this situation.
2. Which asset do the controls primarily protect?

Decision Cases

LO 1, 3, 4

C4-52. ***(Learning Objectives 1, 3, 4: Describe fraud and its impact; evaluate internal controls over cash receipts and cash payments; prepare a bank reconciliation)*** Nashville Motels, Inc., has poor internal controls. Recently, Rick Colby, the manager, has suspected the bookkeeper of stealing. Details of the company's cash position at September 30 follow.

a. The Cash account shows a balance of $10,402. This amount includes a September 30 deposit of $3,794 that does not appear on the September 30 bank statement.

b. The September 30 bank statement shows a balance of $8,224. The bank statement lists a $200 bank collection, an $8 service charge, and a $36 NSF check. The bookkeeper has not recorded any of these items.

c. At September 30, the following checks are outstanding:

Check No.	Amount
154	$116
256	150
278	853
291	990
292	206
293	145

d. The bookkeeper receives all incoming cash and makes the bank deposits. He also reconciles the monthly bank statement. Here is his September 30 reconciliation:

Balance per books, September 30		$10,402
Add: Outstanding checks		1,460
Bank collection................................		200
Subtotal...		12,062
Less: Deposits in transit............................	$3,794	
Service charge	8	
NSF check.......................................	36	(3,838)
Balance per bank, September 30................		$ 8,224

Requirement

1. Colby has asked you to determine whether the bookkeeper has stolen cash from the business and, if so, how much. He also asks you to explain how the bookkeeper attempted to conceal the theft. To make this determination, you perform a proper bank reconciliation. There are no bank or book errors. Colby also asks you to evaluate the internal controls and to recommend any changes needed to improve them.

C4-53. ***(Learning Objectives 1, 3: Describe fraud and its impact; evaluate internal controls over cash receipts and cash payments)*** This case is based on an actual situation experienced by one of the authors. Augusta Construction, headquartered in Topeka, Kansas, built a motel in Kansas City. The construction foreman, Pete Garcia, hired the workers for the project. Garcia had his workers fill out the necessary tax forms and sent the employment documents to the home office. LO 1, 3

Work on the motel began on May 1 and ended in December. Each Thursday evening, Garcia filled out a time card that listed the hours worked by each employee during the five-day work week that ended at 5 p.m. on Thursday. Garcia faxed the time sheets to the home office, which prepared the payroll checks on Friday morning. Garcia drove to the home office after lunch on Friday, picked up the payroll checks, and returned to the construction site. At 5 p.m. on Friday, Garcia distributed the paychecks to the workers.

a. Describe in detail the internal control weakness in this situation. Specify what negative result could occur because of the internal control weakness.

b. Describe what you would do to correct the weakness.

Ethical Issues

C4-54. For each of the following situations, answer the following questions:

1. What is the ethical issue in this situation?
2. What are the alternatives?
3. Who are the stakeholders? What are the possible consequences to each? Analyze from the following standpoints: (a) economic, (b) legal, and (c) ethical.
4. Place yourself in the role of the decision maker. What would you do? How would you justify your decision?

Issue 1. Daylight Bank recently appointed the accounting firm of Jones, Gilroy, and Franks as the bank's auditor. Daylight quickly became one of Jones, Gilroy, and Franks' largest clients. Because it is subject to banking regulations, Daylight must accrue for any expected losses on notes receivable that Daylight may not collect in full.

During the course of the audit, Jones, Gilroy, and Franks determined that three large notes receivable seemed questionable. The auditors discussed these loans with Lisa Smith, the controller of Daylight. Smith assured the auditors that these notes were good and that the makers of the notes would be able to pay their notes after the economy improves.

Jones, Gilroy, and Franks stated that Daylight must record a loss for a portion of these notes receivable to account for the likelihood that Daylight may never collect their full amount. Smith objected and threatened to dismiss the auditors if they demanded that the bank record the loss. Jones, Gilroy, and Franks wants to keep Daylight as a client. In fact, the firm was counting on the revenue from the Daylight audit to finance an expansion.

Issue 2. Cari Morris is executive vice president of University Bank. Active in community affairs, Morris serves on the board of directors of The Salvation Army. The Salvation Army is expanding rapidly and is considering relocating. At a recent meeting, The Salvation Army decided to buy 250 acres of land on the edge of town. The owner of the property is Oliver West, a major depositor in University Bank. West is completing a bitter divorce, and Morris knows that West is eager to sell his property. In view of West's difficult situation, Morris believes West would accept a low offer for the land. Realtors have appraised the property at $3.6 million.

Issue 3. University Bank has a loan receivable from Stevenson Chocolates. Stevenson is six months late in making payments to the bank, and Joan Gus, a University Bank vice president, is helping Stevenson restructure its debt.

Gus learns that Stevenson is depending on landing a contract with Twix Foods, another University Bank client. Gus also serves as Twix Foods' loan officer at the bank. She is aware that Twix is considering bankruptcy. No one else outside Twix Foods knows this. Gus has been a great help to Stevenson, and Stevenson's owner is counting on Gus's expertise in loan workouts to advise the company through this difficult process. To help the bank collect on this large loan, Gus has a strong motivation to alert Stevenson of Twix's financial difficulties.

Focus on Financials | Apple Inc.

LO 5 *(Learning Objective 5: Report cash on the balance sheet)* Refer to the **Apple Inc.** consolidated financial statements in Appendix A and online in the filings section of **www.sec.gov**. The cash and cash equivalents section of the Consolidated Balance Sheet shows a balance of $20,484 million as of September 24, 2016.

Requirements

1. What are the general criteria for an asset to be classified as a cash equivalent?
2. Refer to the Financial Instruments section of Note 1—Summary of Significant Accounting Policies. What types of assets does the company generally include in the category of cash equivalents?
3. Does the company include any more detailed description of cash equivalents? Where? Describe the categories.

Focus on Analysis | Under Armour, Inc.

LO **2, 5**

(Learning Objectives 2, 5: Analyze internal controls and cash flows) Refer to the **Under Armour, Inc.**, Financial Statements online in the filings section of **www.sec.gov**. You can retrieve the 2016 Under Armour financial statements at **www.sec.gov** by clicking on Filings and then searching for "Under Armour" under Company Filings. When you see the list of filings for the company, select the Form 10-K for 2016. Be sure to retrieve the 2016 financial statements, not another year.

Requirements

1. Focus on cash and cash equivalents. Why did cash and cash equivalents change during 2016? The statement of cash flows holds the answer to this question. Analyze the seven largest *individual* items on the statement of cash flows (not the summary subtotals such as "net cash provided by operating activities"). For each of the seven individual items, state how Under Armour's actions affected cash. Show amounts in millions and round to the nearest $1 million. (Challenge)
2. Refer to Exhibit 4-2 on page 205 that contains the Management Report on Internal Controls. Under Armour, Inc. has a similar report included in its annual report. Show how this report corresponds to the objectives of internal control included in this chapter. (Challenge)

Group Project

You are holding a concert in your area. Assume you organize as a partnership, with each member of your group contributing $5,000 in exchange for an ownership interest and a share of the profits. Therefore, each of you is risking some money on this venture. Assume it is April 1 and that the concert will be performed on June 30. Your promotional activities begin immediately, and ticket sales start on May 1. You expect to sell all of the partnership's assets, pay all the liabilities, and distribute all remaining cash to the group members by July 31.

Requirements

Write an internal control manual that will help to safeguard the assets of the business. The manual should address the following aspects of internal control:

1. Assign responsibilities among the group members.
2. Authorize individuals, including group members and any outsiders that you need to hire, to perform specific jobs.
3. Separate duties among the group and any employees.
4. Describe all documents needed to account for and safeguard the company's assets.

Quick Check Answers

1. *c*	5. *d*	9. *b*
2. *c*	6. *a*	10. *a*
3. *b*	7. *b*	11. *a*
4. *d*	8. *d*	12. *d*

Try It Answers

Page 223

1. $5,125 ($4,500 + $1,200 − $575).
2. $5,462 ($5,125 + $15 − $5 + $300 + $27). The adjusted book and bank balances are the same. The answer can be determined by working backward from the adjusted balance.

5 Receivables and Revenue

LEARNING OBJECTIVES

1 **Apply** GAAP for proper revenue recognition

2 **Account for** Sales Returns and Allowances

3 **Account for** Sales Discounts

4 **Account for** accounts receivable

5 **Evaluate** collectibility using the allowance for uncollectible accounts

6 **Account for** notes receivable and interest revenue

7 **Evaluate** liquidity using three new ratios

SPOTLIGHT

Apple's Accounts Receivable Are Small Compared to the Company's Net Sales Revenue and Are Mostly Collectible

Apple Inc., is a U.S.-based multinational corporation that designs, manufactures, and markets highly innovative and reliable consumer electronics and related peripheral equipment and software. The company sells products and services worldwide through its retail stores, online store, and direct sales force, as well as through third-party cellular network carriers, wholesalers, and retailers. As reflected in the excerpt from the company's Consolidated Statements of Operations on page 249, Apple's superior products and marketing efforts generated $215.6 billion in net sales for the company in fiscal 2016, most of it in cash. Also reflected in the excerpt from Apple's Consolidated Balance Sheets (page 249), is the fact that the company held $15.7 billion in net accounts receivable from customers as of September 24, 2016 (only 7.3% of net sales), and that its allowance for doubtful accounts (i.e., accounts the company may not be able to collect) is only $53 million—just two-hundredths of one percent of total net sales. Notice from the balance sheet that, as of September 24, 2016, the company owns $67.2 billion in cash and near-cash liquid assets (short-term marketable securities). That makes Apple Inc.'s revenue cycle a cash-generating machine. ●

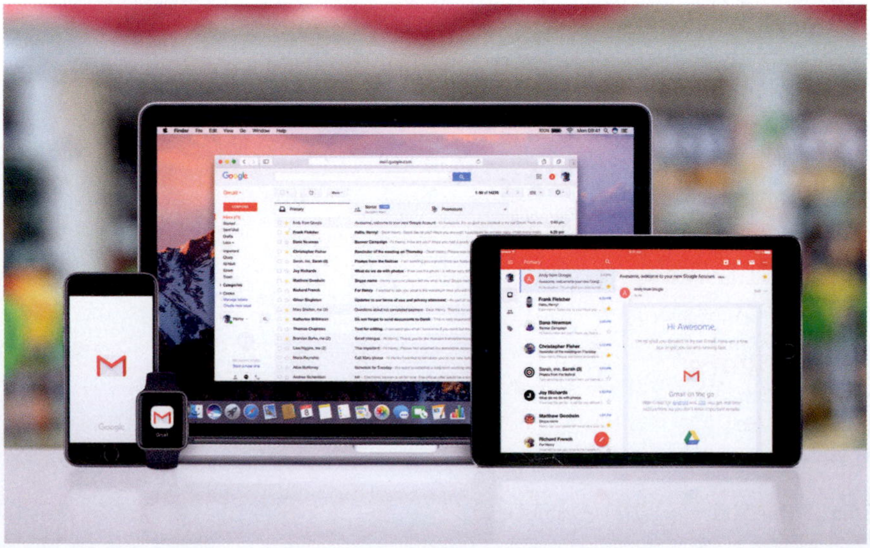

Alexey Boldin/Shutterstock

	A	B	C	D
1	**Apple Inc. Balance Sheet (Excerpt, Adapted)**			
2	**(In Millions of $)**	**Sep. 24, 2016**	**Sep. 26, 2015**	
3	**Current assets:**			
4	Cash and cash equivalents	$ 20,484	$ 21,120	
5	Short-term marketable securities	46,671	20,481	
6	Accounts receivable, less allowances of $53 and $63, respectively	15,754	16,849	
7	Inventories	2,132	2,349	
8	Vendor non-trade receivables	13,545	13,494	
9	Other current assets	8,283	15,085	
10	Total current assets	106,869	89,378	
11				
12	**Consolidated Statements of Operations (Excerpt)**			
13	Net sales	$ 215,639	$ 233,715	
14	Receivables to net sales	7.3%	7.2%	
15				

Data from the U.S. Securities and Exchange Commission EDGAR Company Filings, www.sec.gov

Try It in Excel®

You can access the most current annual report of Apple Inc., in Excel format at **www.sec.gov**. Using the "FILINGS" link on the toolbar at the top of the home page, select "Company Filings Search." This will take you to the "EDGAR Company Filings" page. Type "Apple" in the company name box, and select "Search." This will produce the "EDGAR Search Results" page showing the company name. Click on the "CIK" link beside the company name. This will pull up a list of the reports the company has filed with the SEC. Under the "Filing Type" box, type "10-K," and click on the search box. Form 10-K is the SEC form for the company's annual report. Find the year that you wish to view. Click on the "Interactive Data" box, which takes you to the "View Filing Data" page. Find and click on the "View Excel Document" link at the top of this page. You may choose to either open or download the Excel files containing the company's most recent financial statements.

All types of organizations, large and small, rely on the revenue cycle to generate cash, which is the life-blood of most businesses. However, most companies experience a time lag between earning revenue and collecting the cash for it. This chapter shows how businesses account for their receivables and the cash the companies hope to ultimately collect for them. The chapter also discusses how businesses deal with receivables they *can't* collect. Even if a business's receivables are high, the organization can find itself in a bind if it can't convert those receivables to cash. The chapter also discusses three additional ratios that use receivables to measure an organization's financial health: the quick (acid-test) ratio, accounts receivable turnover, and days' sales outstanding (DSO).

APPLY GENERALLY ACCEPTED ACCOUNTING PRINCIPLES (GAAP) FOR PROPER REVENUE RECOGNITION

1 Apply GAAP for proper revenue recognition

The revenue recognition principle is the basis for measurement and reporting in the revenue cycle. Recall from Chapters 1 and 3 that **revenue** is the inflow of resources (or reduction of liabilities) resulting from delivering goods to or rendering services for customers. Revenue should be recognized when it is earned, and not before.

The core principle for revenue recognition is that revenue should be recognized when an entity transfers goods or services to customers in an amount that reflects the cash or fair market value of other assets that the entity expects to receive in exchange for those goods or services. The process of revenue recognition is based on contracts that a business has with outsiders. A **contract** is an agreement (either written or oral) between two parties that creates enforceable rights or performance obligations. Use the following five-step model to determine when and how much revenue to recognize:

1. Identify the contract(s) with the customer.
2. Identify the performance obligation(s) in the contract.
3. Determine the transaction price.
4. Allocate the transaction price to the performance obligation(s) in the contract.
5. Recognize revenue when (or as) the entity satisfies its performance obligation(s).

To satisfy a performance obligation means that the seller of goods or provider of services has done everything required to earn the revenue. If the sale of products is involved, the performance obligation is generally satisfied when the goods have been transferred to the customer and when the customer has assumed ownership and control over the goods. When services are involved, the performance obligation is generally satisfied when the provider has substantially completed the service for the customer. In addition, the price of the goods or services must be fixed or determinable, and the collection of the amount must be reasonably assured. The amount of the revenue to be recognized by the seller is the amount of cash or fair market value of other assets the seller expects to receive from the buyer to satisfy the buyer's obligation to purchase the goods or services.

Sometimes revenue recognition occurs as the result of a simple contract that may not even be written. For example, retailers sell groceries over the counter to customers who pay cash to purchase them. No contract is signed. Instead, the contract is implied based on the customer taking the products and paying cash to the retailer for them. The seller has a single performance obligation: to transfer goods in exchange for cash received. Revenue is recognized when that event takes place. However, business transactions are often not that simple. Large businesses often engage in complex, multifaceted contracts, some of which have multiple performance obligations to deliver multiple products and/or services for prices that may be variable or contingent on future events. In these cases, application of the revenue recognition model can become quite complex and might require the exercise of a great deal of judgment on the part of management. This text deals only with simple and straightforward contracts with single performance obligations. The more complex applications of the revenue recognition model are reserved for more advanced courses in accounting.

Exhibit 5-1 shows an excerpt from Apple's financial statements that describes the company's revenue recognition policy. The first two paragraphs state the company's relatively simple policy for recognizing revenue related to the sale of products alone. The company records revenue at the point the products are shipped to the customer. The last paragraph describes how the company records revenue from contracts with multiple deliverables, including hardware, software, and service and support contracts. These types of revenues are more complex in nature, requiring more computations and the exercise of more judgment on the part of management. We do not discuss these types of revenues in this text.

Exhibit 5-1 | Excerpt from Apple Inc.'s Financial Statements Describing Its Revenue Recognition Policy

Net sales consist primarily of revenue from the sale of hardware, software, digital content and applications, accessories and service and support contracts. The Company recognizes revenue when persuasive evidence of an arrangement exists, delivery has occurred, the sales price is fixed or determinable and collection is probable. Product is considered delivered to the customer once it has been shipped and title, risk of loss and rewards of ownership have been transferred. For most of the Company's product sales, these criteria are met at the time the product is shipped. For online sales to individuals, for some sales to education customers in the U.S., and for certain other sales, the Company defers revenue until the customer receives the product because the Company retains a portion of the risk of loss on these sales during transit.

...

The Company records reductions to revenue for estimated commitments related to price protection and other customer incentive programs. For transactions involving price protection, the Company recognizes revenue net of the estimated amount to be refunded... The Company also records reductions to revenue for expected future product returns based on the Company's historical experience...

Revenue Recognition for Arrangements with Multiple Deliverables

For multi-element arrangements that include hardware products containing software essential to the hardware product's functionality, undelivered software elements that relate to the hardware product's essential software, and undelivered non-software services, the Company allocates revenue to all deliverables based on their relative selling prices...

Source: Data from the U.S. Securities and Exchange Commission EDGAR Company Filings, www.sec.gov

Let's look at a simple example. Suppose Apple enters into a contract to deliver a truckload of iPhones to an **AT&T Wireless** warehouse in Florida. On the truck are 30,000 iPhones, each of which Apple sells to AT&T Wireless for $100 on account. Each phone costs Apple $60 to produce. Let's apply the five-step revenue recognition model to this set of facts.

1. Identify the contract. Apple agrees to ship 30,000 iPhones to AT&T, its customer, in exchange for a promise from AT&T to pay cash for the phones within 30 days.
2. Identify the performance obligations. Apple Inc.'s only obligation in this contract is to ship the products to AT&T, which, on receipt, will then package them with various service contracts and sell them to its customers.
3. Determine the transaction price. Recall that the price is the amount of cash or fair market value of other property the seller expects to receive from the buyer to satisfy the buyer's obligation. That amount can vary from customer to customer, depending on the terms of the individual contract. Large customers with excellent credit histories and cash flows often get **trade discounts** for making large purchases. A trade discount is a reduction in the price of a product or service as an incentive to a business customer to buy it. Trade discounts are a way to change prices for certain customers without publishing a new price list, or to disguise real prices from competitors. Suppose Apple's original price of a phone was $125. With a 20% trade discount for being a favored customer, AT&T would only pay $100 [$125 × (1 − .20)] per phone.
4. Allocate the transaction price to the performance obligation(s) in the contract. The transaction price of each phone is $100. The total transaction price is $100 times the number of phones sold.
5. Recognize revenue as the performance obligation is fulfilled. According to Apple's revenue recognition policy in Exhibit 5-1, when the company ships the phones to AT&T, it performs its obligation to supply them. Simultaneously, AT&T Wireless assumes ownership of them and acquires the obligation to pay for them.

Apple Inc., records the sales transaction on account to AT&T Wireless with two entries[1]:

	A	B	C	D
1		Accounts Receivable	3,000,000	
2		Sales Revenue ($100 × 30,000)		3,000,000
3		*To record sale of 30,000 iPhones for $100 each on account*		
4				

	A	B	C	D
1		Cost of Goods Sold	1,800,000	
2		Inventory		1,800,000
3		*To record cost of products sold ($60 × 30,000)*		
4				

Shipping Terms

The **shipping terms** in a sales contract dictate the date on which the title, or ownership, of the goods transfers to the buyer. A common shipping term you will see is **FOB (free on board),** which indicates the point at which the seller is free of ownership of the goods. After this point, the buyer owns them and is responsible for losses if they get damaged, lost, or stolen.

When goods are shipped *FOB shipping point*, ownership changes hands and revenue is recognized when the goods leave the seller's shipping dock. When goods are shipped *FOB destination*, ownership changes hands and revenue is recognized at the point of delivery to the customer. Exhibit 5-1 indicates that Apple records most of its product sales as FOB shipping point, which means that the company recognizes revenue and records the cost of goods sold at the point the goods leave its shipping dock.

Collection

When AT&T fulfills its obligation to pay for the phones, Apple records collection as follows:

	A	B	C	D
1		Cash	3,000,000	
2		Accounts Receivable		3,000,000
3		*To record collection of credit sale*		
4				
5				

Speeding up the Cash Flow from Sales

All companies want speedy cash receipts. Rapid cash flow means companies have the ability to pay off their current liabilities faster, as well as to finance new products, research, and development. Consequently, companies develop strategies to shorten the credit cycle and collect cash more quickly. For example, they might offer sales discounts for early payment, as discussed later. They might also charge interest on customer accounts that have not been paid after a certain period of time.

For retailers, yet another way to speed up cash collections is to accept credit card or debit card sales. This strategy can increase sales dramatically, but the added revenue comes at a cost,

[1] We assume that Apple Inc., uses a perpetual inventory system, which requires continual accounting for all inventories purchased and sold as those transactions take place. Consequently, every sales transaction requires two entries: (1) to record the receivable and sale at the gross amount the company expects to collect and (2) to record the cost of goods sold (an expense) and to reduce (credit) inventory for the cost of the products. Inventory and cost of goods sold are the subjects of Chapter 6.

which is typically about 2% to 3% of the total amount of the sale. Let's see how credit cards and debit cards work from the seller's perspective.

Suppose Apple Inc., sells a computer and peripheral devices for $5,000 at one of its stores, and the customer pays with a VISA card. VISA's fee is 2%. Apple Inc., records the sale, ignoring cost of goods sold:

	A	B	C
1	Cash	4,900	
2	Credit Card Discount Expense	100	
3	Sales Revenue		5,000
4	*Recorded bankcard sales.*		
5			

Assets	=	Liabilities	+	Stockholders' Equity	+	Revenues	−	Expenses
+4,900	=	0	+			+5,000		−100

The Apple Store enters the transaction in its accounting system via a point-of-sale terminal. The terminal, linked to a VISA server, automatically credits Apple Inc.'s bank account for a discounted portion, say $4,900, of the $5,000 sale amount. Two percent ($100) goes to VISA. To Apple Inc., the credit card discount is reported on the income statement as interest expense.

ACCOUNT FOR SALES RETURNS AND ALLOWANCES

2 **Account for** Sales Returns and Allowances

Customers usually have a right to return unsatisfactory or damaged merchandise to sellers for refund, credit, or exchange. This is called a **sales return** or **allowance**. If they paid cash, customers are entitled to cash refunds for merchandise they return. When a customer returns a product purchased on credit, the seller will issue a **credit memo**, which is a document authorizing a credit to the customer's account receivable on the seller's books.

Companies are required to estimate expected future returns as a part of the end-of-period adjusting entry process. Look back at Apple's revenue recognition policy in Exhibit 5-1. Notice the following sentence in the second paragraph: *"The Company also records reductions to revenue for expected future product returns based on the Company's historical experience."* This requires the company to (1) increase sales returns as well as recognize an accrued liability for the sales prices of items expected to be returned; and (2) adjust the inventory and cost of goods sold accounts for the cost of the items expected to be returned.

Let's illustrate with an example. Suppose Apple's historical experience is that 1% of the items it sells eventually are returned for one reason or another. Let's assume that Apple's sales revenue for the month of June 2018 is $200 million. To estimate its sales returns and adjust its inventory, Apple would record the following two entries at June 30 (assuming cost of goods sold is 60% of sales):

	A	B	C	D
1		**Debit**	**Credit**	
2				
3	Sales Returns and Allowances (200,000,000 × .01)	2,000,000		
4	Sales Refunds Payable		2,000,000	
5	*To record estimated refunds for June*			
6				
7	Inventory Returns Estimated (2,000,000 × .6)	1,200,000		
8	Cost of Goods Sold		1,200,000	
9	*To record cost of estimated returns for June*			
10				

As items are actually returned in the future, the company reduces its sales refund payable account for the amount of cash or accounts receivable credit it gives back to customers. Apple also debits its inventory account for items that are returned and put back into inventory, and credits the company's inventory returns estimated account by the same amount. Assume that in July 2018, Apple customers actually return $1,800,000 of inventory. Using the same cost of goods sold percentage (.60), the company would make the following entries:

	A	B	C	D
1		Debit	Credit	
2				
3	Sales Refunds Payable	1,800,000		
4	Cash (or Accounts Receivable)		1,800,000	
5	*To record refunds or credits for returned goods*			
6				
7	Inventory (1,800,000 × 0.6)	1,080,000		
8	Inventory Returns Estimated		1,080,000	
9	*To record cost of items returned in July*			
10				

ACCOUNT FOR SALES DISCOUNTS

3 Account for Sales Discounts

The typical credit cycle for most sales on account is 30 days. This means that sellers typically expect customers to pay their accounts in full within 30 days of receiving the goods or services. Sometimes in order to speed up the cash flow from credit sales, some businesses offer customers a percentage discount off the sales price if they agree to pay their accounts earlier than 30 days. These incentives are called **sales discounts**. A typical sales discount might be stated as *2/10, n/30.* This expression means that the seller is willing to discount the order by 2% if the buyer pays the invoice within 10 days of the invoice date. If the buyer doesn't pay within 10 days, it must pay the full, or net, amount within 30 days. (The *n* in n/30 stands for *net.*)

Let's consider an example. **Ace Hardware** makes sales of building materials to several large construction companies. To encourage customers to pay within 10 days, Ace Hardware offers its customers a 2/10, n/30 discount on all sales. On June 30, Ace sells $100,000 of lumber on account to Sorrells Construction Company, and the lumber is delivered that day. The cost of the lumber to Ace is $75,000. How should Ace record the sale?

Step 3 of the revenue recognition model requires that the seller set the price of the sale at the amount the seller *expects to receive* from the customer. The problem for Ace is deciding what amount this is. The decision is usually based on a company's past experience with customers.

Let's assume that, in the construction industry, Ace does not expect its customers to take advantage of sales discounts, but does offers discounts when they do pay in full within the discount period (10 days). In this case, Ace would record the sale to Sorrells as follows:[2]

	A	B	C	D
1	**June 30, 2018**	Debit	Credit	
2				
3	Accounts Receivable-Sorrells Construction Company	100,000		
4	Sales		100,000	
5	*To record sale of lumber on account*			
6				
7	Cost of Goods Sold	75,000		
8	Inventory		75,000	
9	*To record cost of lumber sold*			
10				

[2] This method of recording sales discounts is called the *gross method.* We assume the gross method is used in this chapter, as well as end-of-chapter exercises and problems. An alternative method for recording sales discounts is the *net method,* which assumes that all customers will pay within the discount period. With the net method, all sales are recorded at the net amounts (in our illustration, $98,000), with adjustments being required later for customers that fail to pay early. The net method is covered in more detail in later accounting courses.

Now assume that Sorrells Construction pays its invoice in full, less the sales discount, on July 10 (within 10 days). Ace makes the following entry to record the collection:

	A	B	C	D
1	**July 10, 2018**	**Debit**	**Credit**	
2				
3	Cash	$98,000		
4	Sales Discounts	2,000		
5	Accounts Receivable-Sorrells Construction Company		$100,000	
6	*To record collection of Sorrells Construction account*			
7	*receivable, less 2% discount*			
8				

Disclosure of Net Revenues on the Income Statement

Retailers, wholesalers, and manufacturers typically disclose sales revenue at the *net* amount, which means after sales discounts and sales returns and allowances have been subtracted. Apple Inc.'s net sales revenue for 2016, compared with the last two years, was:

	A	B	C	D
1	**Apple Inc.** **Statements of Operations (Excerpt, Adapted)** **Year Ending September 24, 2016**			
2		2016	2015	2014
3	Net revenue (in millions)	$ 215,639	$ 233,715	$ 182,795
4				

Cooking the Books

OCZ Technology Group

Research sponsored by a federal agency has shown that over 60% of all financial statement frauds over the past three decades have involved improper revenue recognition.[3] Revenue can be improperly recognized in a number of ways, including the following:

1. Fictitious sales (sales to fictitious customers that do not exist)
2. Sales recorded at inflated amounts
3. Unrecorded sales returns
4. Misclassification of sales discounts
5. Channel stuffing (shipping goods to customers without their approval or their having ordered them)
6. Improper application of FOB terms

An example of one company that used these schemes is **OCZ Technology Group, Inc.**

OCZ Technology Group, Inc., based in San Jose, California, was a computer memory storage and power-supply device distributor. OCZ primarily sold solid state drives, a new generation of computer storage drives the company promoted as being superior to traditional

[3] Source: https://www.coso.org/documents/FraudStudyOverview_000.pdf.

hard drives. OCZ was founded in 2002 by Ryan Petersen, its CEO, and became a publicly traded company in 2006, about the same time that Arthur Knapp became its chief financial officer. From 2010 through 2012, OCZ raised over $200 million by selling its shares to investors.

In filings with the SEC, Knapp and Petersen made statements to investors that emphasized OCZ's improvements in its revenue growth and gross margin (revenue minus cost of goods sold). The company also made predictions about future revenues and gross margins, which securities analysts relied upon to value the company's stock.

In late 2011, OCZ began negotiating with another technology company about the possible sale of OCZ. Revenue growth and gross margin improvements were important metrics to the potential acquiring company. Negotiations continued through the spring of 2012. In June 2012, Petersen expressed in an email to Knapp concerns about the acquiring company's focus on revenues and gross profits. He stated, "[i]f we don't have numbers that look reasonable on a high revenue growth and good gross profit margins for the first quarter, we will be lucky to trade over cash value, and I am sure they will withdraw their offer completely."

Under extreme pressure to boost sales and gross profit margins, Knapp took the following fraudulent actions, among other things:

1. OCZ's stated shipping terms for revenue recognition purposes were FOB destination. However, the company started recognizing revenue to all customers FOB shipping point, thus accelerating revenue recognition on all shipments by several days, and recognizing revenue before it was earned.
2. OCZ understated product returns. As a result, they were only about 20% of the value they should have been.
3. OCZ purposely understated sales discounts to customers by misclassifying them as marketing expenses in the operating expense section of its income statement, rather than as direct deductions from sales.
4. Knapp made several other deliberate misstatements of ending inventory, which understated OCZ's cost of goods sold and overstated its gross margins.

Between the second quarter of fiscal 2011 and the first quarter of fiscal 2013, the fraudulent accounting practices overstated OCZ's revenue by over $102 million and its gross margin by almost $120 million. During this time, both Knapp and Petersen took large bonuses from the company and sold some of their shares of OCZ stock at inflated prices.

OCZ eventually filed for bankruptcy and went out of business. Both Knapp and Petersen were forced to pay back all of the bonuses they had received from the company as well as fines. Each of them was also barred from ever being an officer or director of a public company again.

ACCOUNT FOR ACCOUNTS RECEIVABLE

4 Account for accounts receivable

Receivables are the third most-liquid asset—after cash and short-term investments. The rest of this chapter shows how to account for receivables.

Types of Receivables

Receivables are monetary claims against others. Accounts receivable, which are current assets, are sometimes called *trade receivables* or merely *receivables*. They arise from credit sales of goods or services to customers in the normal course of business. Notes receivable arise from loaning money to others.

The journal entries to record accounts receivable and notes receivable are:

Performing a Service on Account			Lending Money on a Note Receivable		
Accounts Receivable	XXX		Notes Receivable	XXX	
Service (or Sales) Revenue		XXX	Cash		XXX
Performed a service (or sold goods) on account.			*Loaned money to another company.*		

The Accounts Receivable account in the general ledger shows the total amount receivable from all customers. Companies also keep another accounts receivable ledger called a *subsidiary ledger*. The subsidiary ledger shows the separate accounts for each individual customer:

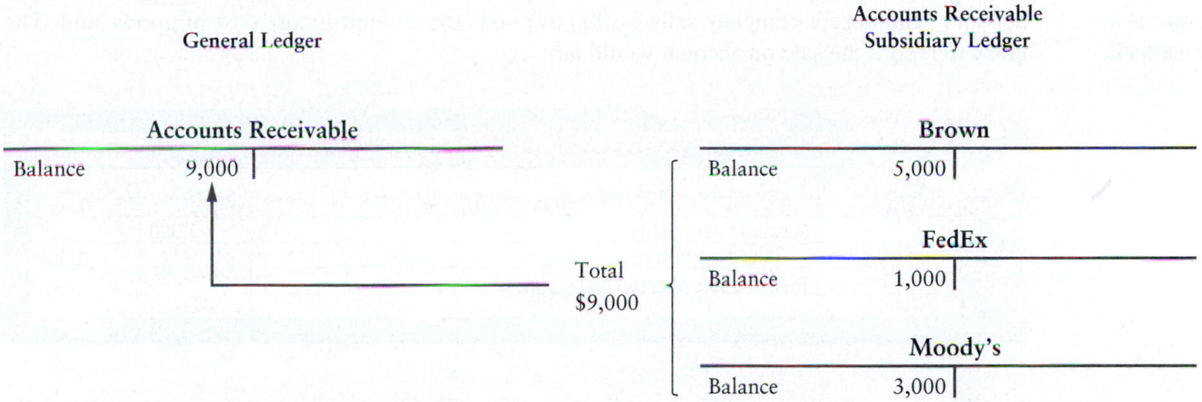

Notes receivable are more formal contracts than accounts receivable. For a note, the borrower signs a written promise to pay the lender a definite sum at a certain date, plus interest. This is why notes are also called *promissory notes*. The note may require the borrower to pledge *security*, or *collateral*, which are assets the lender can claim if the borrower fails to pay the amount due.

Other receivables is a miscellaneous category for all receivables other than accounts receivable and notes receivable. Examples include interest receivable and advances to employees.

Managing and Accounting for Receivables

By selling on credit, companies run the risk of not collecting some receivables. Unfortunately, some customers don't pay their debts. The prospect of failing to collect from a customer provides the biggest challenge in accounting for receivables. The Decision Guidelines address this challenge.

Decision Guidelines

HOW CAN THE RISK OF NOT COLLECTING RECEIVABLES BE MANAGED?

A company faces management and accounting issues when it extends credit to customers. Suppose you open a health club near your college. Assume you let customers use the club and bill them later for their monthly dues. Let's look at the issues you will encounter by extending credit to your customers as well as the plan of action you can use to resolve each issue:

Issue	Plan of Action
1. What are the benefits and the costs of extending credit to customers?	**1.** The benefits are increased sales. The costs are the risk of not collecting the amounts owed to the business.
2. How do you know which customers to extend credit to?	**2.** Run credit checks on prospective customers. Extend credit only to creditworthy customers.
3. How do we keep employees from stealing customer payments?	**3.** Separate cash handling and record-keeping responsibilities. See Chapter 4.
4. How can we maximize cash flow from customer payments?	**4.** Keep a close eye on customers' payment habits. Send second and third statements to slow-paying customers, if necessary. Better solution: Have customers sign agreements for automatic payment by electronic funds transfers (EFTs) from their bank accounts each month. (See Chapter 4.)

EVALUATE COLLECTIBILITY USING THE ALLOWANCE FOR UNCOLLECTIBLE ACCOUNTS

5 Evaluate collectibility using the allowance for uncollectible accounts

A company acquires an account receivable only when it sells its product or service on credit (on account). Suppose a company sells $1,000 of goods on account Ignore cost of goods sold. The entry to record the sale on account would be:

	A	B	C	D
1		Accounts Receivable	1,000	
2		Sales Revenue		1,000
3		*To record sale of goods on account*		
4				

Ideally, the company would like to collect cash for all of its receivables. But suppose it is only able to collect $950 of the $1,000. The entry to record the cash would be as follows:

	A	B	C	D
1		Cash	950	
2		Accounts Receivable		950
3		*Collection on account.*		
4				

In fact, companies rarely collect all of their accounts receivable. Consequently, they must account for their uncollectible accounts, which is $50 in this example. Accountants label this cost **uncollectible-account expense**, **doubtful-account expense**, or **bad-debt expense**.

Apple Inc., reports accounts receivable as follows on its 2016 balance sheet (in millions):

	Sept. 24, 2016	Sep. 26, 2015
Accounts receivable, less allowances of $53 and $63, respectively	$15,754	$16,849

The phrase "less allowances" means that a relatively small amount ($53 million) has been subtracted from Apple's total accounts receivable. This is the amount Apple does *not* expect to collect.[4] Sometimes the amount of the allowance is not considered sufficiently material to separately disclose it in the line item for accounts receivable, so it is disclosed in an explanatory financial statement footnote. In this case, the line item in the balance sheet simply reads "accounts receivable, net."

Apple Inc.'s net amount of the receivables ($15,754 million) is the amount the company *does* expect to collect. Notice that Apple's net amount of receivables decreased by about 7% compared to the previous year (from $16,849 million to $15,754 million). In contrast, the allowance for doubtful accounts decreased by about 16% over the year (from $63 million to $53 million).

[4] Apple Inc., like many other large manufacturing and marketing companies, makes allowances for sales returns (see discussion on pages 253) as well as uncollectible accounts. In the discussion of the computation of the allowance for uncollectible accounts in the pages that follow, as well as related exercise and problem material, we assume that the figures used for both accounts receivable and sales have already been reduced by allowances for sales returns. Combining sales returns allowances with the allowance for uncollectible accounts is outside the scope of this text and is covered in more advanced accounting courses.

Allowance Method

The best way to measure uncollectible accounts expense (bad debts) is by the **allowance method**. This method records losses from the failure to collect receivables based on an estimate developed from the company's collection experience. Apple has calculated this estimate. Consequently, it doesn't wait to see which customers will not pay. Instead, it records the estimated amount as Uncollectible-Account Expense at the end of each accounting period, which appears on the income statement. On the balance sheet, Apple also sets up a contra-account to Accounts Receivable called **Allowance for Uncollectible Accounts**. This account shows the amount of receivables the business expects *not* to collect. Other titles for this account are **Allowance for Doubtful Accounts** and **Allowance for Bad Debts**. The Allowance for Uncollectible Accounts reduces Apple's gross receivables to their *net realizable value*, which is the amount of receivables the company realistically expects to collect.

In Chapter 3 we used the Accumulated Depreciation account to show the amount of a plant asset's cost that has been expensed—the portion of the asset that's no longer a benefit to the company. The Allowance for Uncollectible Accounts serves a similar purpose for Accounts Receivable. The allowance shows the amount of receivables that is not expected to be collected. The following excerpt from a company's balance sheet provides an example. Customers owe this company $10,000, but it expects to collect only $9,100. The net realizable value of the receivables is therefore $9,100.

Equipment	$100,000	Accounts receivable	$10,000
Less: Accumulated depreciation	(40,000)	Less: Allowance for uncollectible accounts	(900)
Equipment, net	60,000	Accounts receivable, net	9,100

Another way to report these receivables is as follows:

Accounts receivable, less allowance of $900	$9,100

Decision Guidelines

HOW SHOULD UNCOLLECTIBLE RECEIVABLES BE MEASURED AND REPORTED?

The main issues and action plans related to accounting for receivables that may be uncollectible are as follows. (Assume the amounts in the "Plan of Action" column are for the health club you started, referenced in the Decision Guidelines on page 257.)

Issue	Plan of Action
1. How do you measure and report receivables on the balance sheet?	**1.** Report them at their net realizable value, which is the amount you expect to collect for them.
2. How do you measure and report the expense associated with the failure to collect receivables?	**2.** Report it on the income statement as *uncollectible-account expense* (or *doubtful-account expense* or *bad-debt expense*).

Report receivables at net realizable value:

Balance sheet

Receivables	$1,000
Less: Allowance for uncollectible accounts	(80)
Receivables, net	$ 920

Measure the expense of not collecting from customers:

Income statement

Sales (or service) revenue	$8,000
Expenses:	
Uncollectible-account expense	190

»TRY IT

(Answers are given on p. 304.)

Refer to the Apple Inc., balance sheet at the beginning of the chapter. At September 24, 2016, how much in total did customers owe Apple? How much did Apple expect to collect and *not* to collect on September 24, 2016? What was the net realizable value of Apple Inc.'s receivables on September 24, 2016?

The best way to estimate uncollectibles uses the company's history of collections from customers. There are two basic ways to estimate uncollectibles:

- Percent-of-sales method
- Aging-of-receivables method

Percent-of-Sales. The **percent-of-sales method** estimates a business's uncollectible-account expense as a percent of the company's revenue.[5] This method is considered an income-statement approach because it focuses on the amount of expense to be reported on the income statement. Assume it is September 24, 2016, and Apple Inc.'s accounts have these balances *before year-end adjustments* (amounts in millions):

Accounts Receivable	
15,807	

Allowance for Uncollectible Accounts	
	5

Suppose Apple's credit department estimates that, on the basis of its past experience with credit customers, uncollectible-account expense is 0.0002 (1/50 of 1%) of total revenues. Total revenues are $215,639 million, so uncollectible accounts expense is $43 million (.0002 × $215,639 million). The entry that records Apple's uncollectible-account expense for the year also updates the allowance as follows:

	A	B	C	D
1	Sep. 24	Uncollectible-Account Expense ($215,639 × .0002)	43	
2		Allowance for Uncollectible Accounts		43
3		*Recorded uncollectible account expense for the year.*		
4		*(Calculations rounded to nearest million.)*		
5				

The expense decreases Apple Inc.'s assets, as shown by the accounting equation.

Assets	=	Liabilities	+	Stockholders' Equity	−	Expenses
−43	=	0			−	43

The percent-of-sales method uses the expense recognition (matching) concept to estimate, probably on a monthly or quarterly basis, the cost that has been incurred in order to earn a certain amount of revenue and to recognize both in the same time period.

Accounts Receivable	
15,807	

Allowance for Uncollectible Accounts		
	Beg Bal	5
	Adj	43
	End Bal	48

Uncollectible-Account Expense	
43	

Net accounts receivable, $15,759

[5] In this text, we assume that all sales are on account, unless it is specifically stated that they are in cash.

Using the percent-of-sales method, the net realizable value of accounts receivable, or the amount ultimately expected to be collected from customers, would be $15,759 million ($15,807 million – $48 million). This method will usually produce a different result than the aging method, discussed next.

Aging-of-Receivables. The other popular method for estimating uncollectibles is called the **aging-of-receivables** method. The aging method is a balance-sheet approach because it focuses on what should be the most relevant and faithful representation of accounts receivable as of the balance-sheet date. In the aging method, individual receivables from specific customers are analyzed based on how long they have been outstanding.

Suppose it is September 24, 2016, and Apple Inc.'s Accounts Receivable shows the following *before* the year-end adjustment (amounts in millions):

Accounts Receivable			Allowance for Uncollectible Accounts	
15,807				5

These accounts are not yet ready for the financial statements because the allowance balance is not realistic.

Apple Inc.'s accounting software system ages the company's accounts receivable. Exhibit 5-2 shows a representative aging schedule at September 24, 2016. Apple Inc.'s gross receivables total $15,807 million. Of this amount, the aging schedule shows that the company will *not* collect $53 million (lower right corner).

Exhibit 5-2 | Aging Accounts Receivable of Apple Inc.

	Age of Account (Dollar amounts rounded to the nearest million)				
Customer	1–30 Days	31–60 Days	61–90 Days	Over 90 Days	Total Balance
Best Buy					
Walmart					
Totals	$14,943	$ 600	$ 200	$ 64	$15,807
Estimated percent uncollectible	× 0.2075%	× 1%	× 5%	× 10%	
Allowance for Uncollectible Accounts balance should be	$ 31* +	$ 6 +	$ 10 +	$ 6* =	$ 53

*Computations are rounded

The aging method will bring the balance of the allowance account—$5 million—to the needed amount as determined by the aging schedule—$53 million. The lower right corner of the aging schedule gives the needed balance in the allowance account. To update the allowance, Apple would make this adjusting entry at year-end:

	A	B	C	D
1	2016	**(in millions)**		
2	Sep. 24	Uncollectible-Account Expense	48	
3		Allowance for Uncollectible Accounts ($53 – $5)		48
4		*Recorded uncollectible accounts expense for the year.*		
5				

The expense decreases Apple Inc.'s assets and net income, as shown by the accounting equation.

Assets	=	Liabilities	+	Stockholders' Equity	−	Expenses
− 48	=	0			−	48

Now the balance sheet can report the amount that Apple actually expects to collect from customers: $15,754 million ($15,807 million − $53 million). This is the net realizable value of Apple's accounts receivable.

Accounts Receivable

15,807	

Allowance for Uncollectible Accounts

	Beg. Bal.	5
	Adj.	48
	End Bal	53

Uncollectible-Account Expense

48	

Net accounts receivable, $15,754

Writing Off Uncollectible Accounts. Assume that at the beginning of fiscal 2017, Apple Inc., had these accounts receivable (amounts in millions):

Accounts Receivable—RS

9	

Accounts Receivable—TM

3	

Allowance for Uncollectible Accounts

	53

Accounts Receivable—Other

15,795	

Total Accounts Receivable = $15,807

Allowance = $53

Accounts Receivable, Net = $15,754

Suppose that, early in fiscal 2017, Apple's credit department determines that the company cannot collect from customers RS and TM. It then writes off the receivables from these customers with the following entry:

A1

	A	B	C	D
1	2016	**(in millions)**		
2	Oct 31	Allowance for Uncollectible Accounts	12	
3		Accounts Receivable—RS		9
4		Accounts Receivable—TM		3
5		*Wrote off uncollectible receivables.*		
6				

Assets	=	Liabilities	+	Stockholders' Equity
+ 12 − 12	=	0	+	0

After the write-off, Apple Inc.'s accounts show these amounts:

Accounts Receivable—RS	
9	9

Accounts Receivable—TM	
3	3

Allowance for Uncollectible Accounts	
12	53
	41

Accounts Receivable—Other	
15,795	

Total Accounts Receivable = $15,795 | Allowance = $41

Accounts Receivable, Net = $15,754

The accounting equation shows that the write-off of uncollectibles has no effect on any of the following: Apple's total assets, current assets, or net accounts receivable. Notice that Accounts Receivable, Net is still $15,754 million. There is no effect on net income either. Why is there no effect on net income? Net income is unaffected because the write-off of uncollectibles affects no expense account. If the company uses the allowance method, as discussed in the previous section, expenses *would* have been properly recognized in the period they were incurred, which is the same period in which the related sales took place.

Combining the Percent-of-Sales and the Aging Methods. Most companies use the percent-of-sales and aging-of-accounts methods together:

- For monthly and quarterly statements, companies often use the percent-of-sales method because it is easier and quicker to apply. The percent-of-sales method focuses on the uncollectible-account *expense*, but that is not enough.
- At the end of the year, companies use the aging method to fine-tune their allowances for uncollectibles and ensure their Accounts Receivable are reported at net realizable values on the balance sheet.
- Using the two methods together provides good measures of both the expense and the asset related to a company's receivables. Exhibit 5-3 compares the two methods.

Exhibit 5-3 | Comparing the Percent-of-Sales and Aging Methods for Estimating Uncollectible Accounts

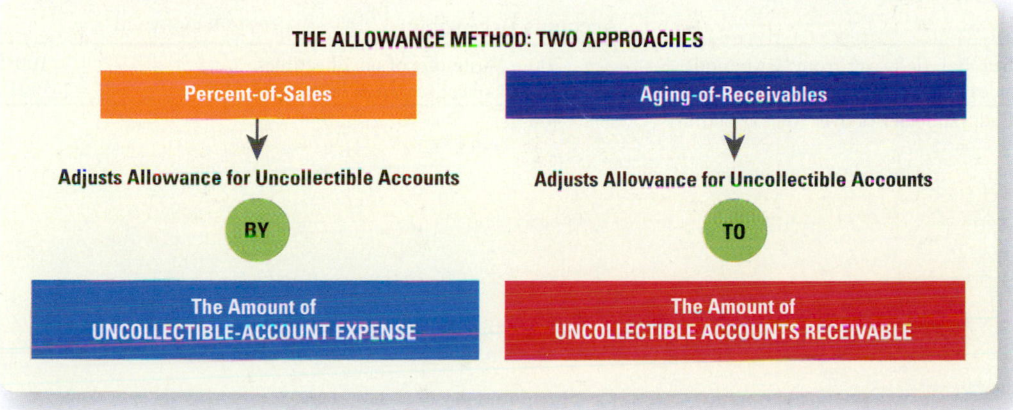

Direct Write-Off Method

There is another, less preferable way to account for uncollectible receivables. Under the **direct write-off method**, the company waits until a specific customer's receivable proves uncollectible. Then, the accountant writes off the customer's account and records Uncollectible-Account Expense (using assumed data):

	A	B	C	D
1	2016			
2	Oct 31	Uncollectible-Account Expense	12	
3		Accounts Receivable—RS		9
4		Accounts Receivable—TM		3
5		*Wrote off uncollectible accounts by direct write-off method.*		
6				

The direct write-off method is not considered as being in keeping with U.S. GAAP for financial statement purposes, for two reasons:

1. It uses no allowance for uncollectibles. As a result, receivables are always reported at their full amount, which is more than the business expects to collect. Assets on the balance sheet may be overstated.
2. It fails to recognize the expense of uncollectible accounts in the same period in which the related sales revenue is earned. In this example, Apple made the sales to RS and TM in fiscal year 2016, and should have recorded the uncollectible-account expense during fiscal year 2016—not in fiscal year 2017 when it wrote off the accounts.

The direct write-off method is the *required* method of accounting for uncollectible accounts for federal income tax purposes. It is one of several sources of timing differences that may arise between net income for financial reporting purposes and net income for federal income tax purposes.

Computing Cash Collections from Customers

Collections from customers are the single most important source of cash for any business. You can compute a company's collections from customers by analyzing its Accounts Receivable account. Receivables typically hold only five items, as reflected in the five elements of the following T-account for a business's Accounts Receivable (amounts assumed):

Accounts Receivable

Beg. Bal. (left over from last period)	200	Write-offs of uncollectibles	100**
Sales (or service) revenue on account	1,800*	Collections from customers	X = 1,500†
End. Bal. (carries over to next period)	400		

The following are the coded journal entries that affect Accounts Receivable in this example.

*The journal entry that places revenue into the accounts receivable account is:

	A	B	C
1	Accounts Receivable	1,800	
2	Sales (or Service) Revenue		1,800
3			

**The journal entry for write-offs of uncollectible accounts is:

	A	B	C
1	Allowance for Uncollectible Accounts	100	
2	Accounts Receivable		100
3			

†The journal entry that records cash collections of accounts receivable is:

	A	B	C
1	Cash	1,500	
2	Accounts Receivable		1,500
3			

Suppose you know all these amounts *except* collections from customers. You can compute collections by solving for *X* in the T-account.[6] Often, write-offs are unknown and must be omitted. Then the computation of collections becomes an approximation.

ACCOUNT FOR NOTES RECEIVABLE AND INTEREST REVENUE

6 Account for notes receivable and interest revenue

As you have learned, notes receivable are more formal than accounts receivable. Before exploring how notes receivable are accounted for, let's define some key terms:

Creditor. The party to whom money is owed. The creditor is also called the *lender*.

Debtor. The party that borrowed and owes money on the note. The debtor is also called the *maker* of the note or the *borrower*.

Interest. Interest is the cost of borrowing money. The interest is stated as an annual percentage rate.

Maturity date. The date on which the debtor must pay the note.

Maturity value. The sum of principal and interest on the note.

Principal. The amount of money borrowed by the debtor and lent by the creditor.

Term. The length of time from when the note was signed by the debtor to when the debtor must pay the note.

There are two parties to a note:

- The *creditor* has a note receivable.
- The *debtor* has a note payable.

[6] An equation may help you solve for *X*. The equation is \$200 + \$1,800 − *X* − \$100 = \$400. *X* = \$1,500.

Exhibit 5-4 is an example of a promissory note.

Exhibit 5-4 | Promissory Note

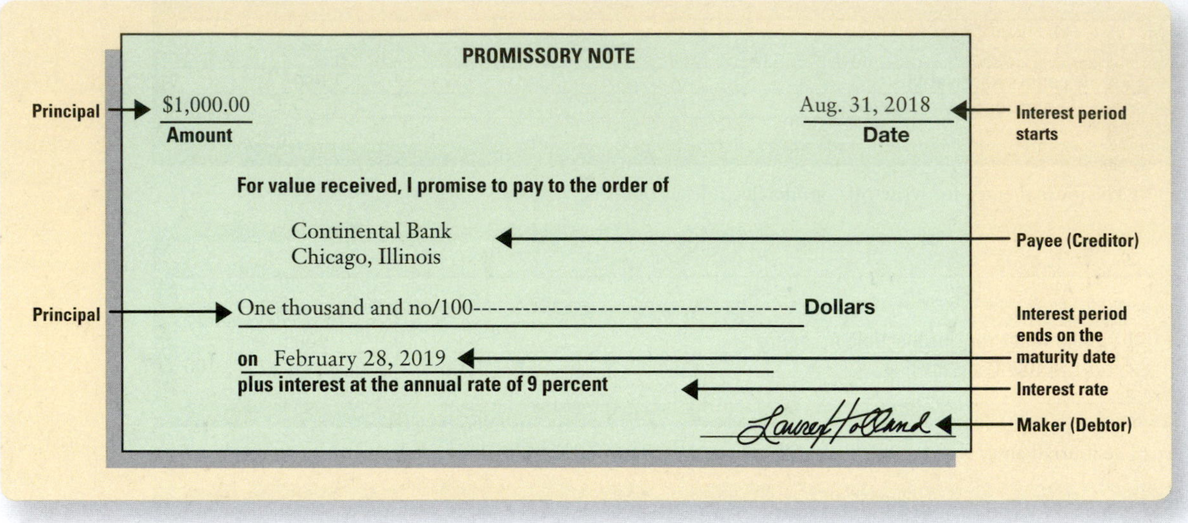

The principal amount of the note ($1,000) is the amount borrowed by the debtor and lent by the creditor. This six-month note receivable runs from August 31, 2018, to February 28, 2019, when Lauren Holland (the maker) promises to pay Continental Bank (the creditor) the principal of $1,000 plus 9% interest. Interest is revenue to the creditor (Continental Bank, in this case).

Accounting for Notes Receivable

Notes receivable due within one year or operating cycle, whichever is longer, are current assets. Notes due beyond one year, or one operating cycle, whichever is longer, are long-term receivables and are reported as long-term assets. Some notes receivable are collected in installments. The portion due within one year or operating cycle, whichever is longer, is a current asset, and the remainder is a long-term asset.

Consider the promissory note in Exhibit 5-4. After Lauren Holland signs the note, Continental Bank gives her $1,000 cash. The bank's entries follow, assuming a December 31 year-end for Continental Bank:

A1

	A	B	C	D
1	2018			
2	Aug 31	Note Receivable—L. Holland	1,000	
3		Cash		1,000
4		*Made a loan.*		
5				

Note Receivable—
L. Holland

1,000	

The bank gives one asset, cash, in exchange for another asset, a note receivable; so total assets do not change.

Continental Bank earns interest revenue during September, October, November, and December. At December 31, 2018, the bank accrues 9% interest revenue for four months:

	A	B	C	D
1	2018			
2	Dec 31	Interest Receivable ($1,000 × .09 × 4/12)	30	
3		Interest Revenue		30
4		*Accrued interest revenue.*		
5				

The bank's assets and revenues increase.

Continental Bank reports these amounts in its financial statements at December 31, 2018:

Balance sheet	
Current assets:	
Note receivable	$1,000
Interest receivable...............	30
Income statement	
Interest revenue..................	$ 30

The bank collects the note on February 28, 2019, and records the following:

	A	B	C	D
1	2019			
2	Feb 28	Cash	1,045	
3		Note Receivable—L. Holland		1,000
4		Interest Receivable		30
5		Interest Revenue ($1,000 × .09 × 2/12)		15
6		*Collected note at maturity.*		
7				

This entry zeroes out the Note Receivable and Interest Receivable accounts and also records the interest revenue earned in 2019.

Note Receivable—L. Holland		Interest Receivable	
1,000	1,000	30	30

In its financial statements for the year ended December 31, 2019, the only item that Continental Bank will report is the interest revenue of $15 that was earned in 2019. There's no note receivable or interest receivable on the balance sheet because those accounts were zeroed out when the bank collected the note at maturity.

Three aspects of the interest computation deserve mention:

1. Interest rates are always for an annual period, unless stated otherwise. In this example, the annual interest rate is 9%. At December 31, 2018, Continental Bank accrues interest revenue for four months. The interest computation is:

Principal	×	Interest Rate	×	Time	=	Amount of Interest
$1,000	×	.09	×	4/12	=	$30

2. The time element (4/12) is the fraction of the year that the note has been in force during 2018.
3. Interest is often computed for a number of days. For example, suppose you loaned out $10,000 on April 10. The note receivable runs for 90 days, and the interest rate is 8%.

   a. Interest starts accruing on April 11 and ends 90 days later on the due date, July 9:

Month	Number of Days That Interest Accrues
April	20
May	31
June	30
July	9
Total	90

   b. The interest computation is

$$\$10,000 \times 0.08 \times 90/365 = \$197$$

Some companies sell goods and services on notes receivable (versus selling on accounts receivable). This often occurs when the payment term extends beyond the customary accounts receivable period of 30 to 60 days.

Suppose that on March 20, 2019, Apple sells a large number of iPads to **Walmart**. Apple gets Walmart's three-month promissory note plus 10% annual interest. At the outset, Apple would debit Notes Receivable and credit Sales Revenue.

A company may also accept a note receivable from a customer whose account receivable is past due. The company then debits Notes Receivable and credits Accounts Receivable.

EVALUATE LIQUIDITY USING THREE NEW RATIOS

7 **Evaluate** liquidity using three new ratios

We introduced the current ratio in Chapter 3. Next, let's look at some other ratios investors and creditors use to evaluate a business's financial health.

Quick (Acid-Test) Ratio

The balance sheet lists assets in the order of their relative liquidity:

1. Cash and cash equivalents
2. Short-term investments
3. Accounts (or notes) receivable

Apple Inc.'s balance sheet in the chapter-opening story lists these accounts in order.

Managers, stockholders, and creditors care about the liquidity of a company's assets. The current ratio measures an organization's ability to pay its current liabilities with its current assets. A more stringent measure of the ability to pay current liabilities is the **quick ratio (or *acid-test*)**. The quick ratio measures a company's ability to pay its current liabilities with its shorter-term assets—cash and other current assets that are only one step away from cash—marketable securities and net receivables. The following equation shows how Apple's quick ratio is calculated:

(Dollars in millions, taken from Apple Inc.'s balance sheet)

$$\text{Quick (acid-test) ratio} = \frac{\text{Cash and cash equivalents} + \text{Short-term investments} + \text{Net current receivables}}{\text{Total current liabilities}} = \frac{\$20{,}484 + \$46{,}671 + \$15{,}754}{\$79{,}006} = 1.05$$

The higher the quick ratio, the easier it is to pay an organization's current liabilities. A benchmark for the quick ratio is 1:1, which means that the company can cover every dollar's worth of current liabilities by cashing in its quick assets. Apple Inc.'s quick ratio of 1.05 means that it has $1.05 of quick assets to pay each $1 of current liabilities, which is considered to be healthy.

What is considered an acceptably high quick ratio? The answer depends on the industry. For example, auto dealers can operate smoothly with a quick ratio of 0.20. They can survive with so low a quick ratio because the auto manufacturers they work with help finance their inventory. The dealers don't have to pay in full for the vehicles before they sell them to consumers. Instead, the dealers can wait until the vehicles are sold to pay the manufacturers the full amounts they owe them.

Accounts Receivable Turnover and Days' Sales Outstanding

The **accounts receivable turnover ratio** shows the number of times per year a company completely collects its average accounts receivable. The accounts receivable turnover ratio indicates how effective a company is at collecting cash from customers that bought products on credit. The ratio does so by measuring the business's ratio of net credit sales to its average net accounts receivable. The result is expressed as a decimal fraction. A larger number is better than a smaller number for this ratio.

Once the turnover ratio is computed, it is converted to the **days' sales outstanding (DSO) ratio** by dividing it into 365 (days per year). For DSO, shorter is better because it shows that cash is coming in quickly. Notice that high turnover translates to a smaller number for DSO, and low turnover translates to a larger number for DSO.

Apple Inc.'s accounts receivable turnover and days' sales outstanding (DSO) for fiscal 2016 are computed as follows:

(Dollars in millions, taken from Apple Inc.'s financial statements)

$$\text{Accounts receivable turnover} = \frac{\text{Net credit sales}}{\text{Average net accounts receivable}}$$

$$= \frac{\$215{,}639}{(\$15{,}754 + \$16{,}849)/2}$$

$$= 13.23 \text{ times}$$

$$\text{Days' sales outstanding (DSO)} = \frac{365}{13.23} = 27.6 \text{ days}$$

Apple's accounts receivable turnover was 13.23 times per year. This means the company converted its average accounts receivable to cash 13.23 times during fiscal 2016. Converted to days, it took Apple an average of 27.6 days (365 ÷ 13.23) to collect the average customer account.

To evaluate Apple Inc.'s DSO, we need to compare 27.6 days to the credit terms that Apple Inc., offers customers when the company makes a sale, as well as the number of days on average that creditors typically allow Apple Inc., to pay them without penalty. Suppose Apple sells on "net 30" terms, which means that its customers should pay Apple within 30 days of the sale. That makes Apple Inc.'s DSO quite acceptable in comparison to its credit terms. With regard to its credit terms for payables, if Apple Inc.'s short-term creditors expect payment of their accounts payable within 30 days, Apple Inc.'s DSO is also acceptable.

Companies watch their collection periods closely. Whenever collections slow down, the business must find other sources of financing, such as borrowing or selling receivables. During recessions, customers pay more slowly and a longer collection period may be unavoidable.[7]

---

[7] Another way to compute DSO is to follow two logical steps. First, compute the company's average daily sales (or average revenue for one day). Then divide the average daily sales into average net receivables for the period. Following this method, we can calculate days' sales in receivables for Apple Inc., as follows:

(Dollars in millions, taken from Apple Inc.'s financial statements)

Days' Sales in Receivables		(In millions)
1. Average daily sales	$= \dfrac{\text{Net credit sales}}{365 \text{ days}}$	$\dfrac{\$215{,}639}{365 \text{ days}} = \$590.79$ per day
2. Days' sales in receivables	$= \dfrac{\text{Average net receivables*}}{\text{Average daily sales}}$	$\dfrac{\$16{,}301.50^*}{\$590.79 \text{ per day}} = 27.6$ days

$$\text{*Average net receivables} = \frac{\text{Beginning net receivables} + \text{Ending net receivables}}{2} = \frac{\$15{,}754 + \$16{,}849}{2} = \$16{,}301.50$$

You can see that this method merely rearranges the equations in the body of the text, "going through the back door" to achieve the same result.

End-of-Chapter | Summary Problem

Excelsior Technical Resources' (ETR's) balance sheet at December 31, 2018, reported the following:

	(In millions)
Accounts receivable	$382
Allowance for doubtful accounts	(52)

ETR uses both the percent-of-sales and the aging methods to account for uncollectible receivables.

Requirements

1. How much of the December 31, 2018, balance of accounts receivable did ETR expect to collect? Stated differently, what was the net realizable value of ETR's receivables?

2. Journalize, without explanations, the following 2019 entries for ETR:
   a. Estimated doubtful-account expense of $40 million, based on the percent-of-sales method, all during the year.
   b. Write-offs of uncollectible accounts receivable total $58 million. Prepare a T-account for Allowance for Doubtful Accounts and post the write-offs and the doubtful-account expense from part a. to this account. Show its unadjusted balance at December 31, 2019.
   c. On December 31, 2019, an aging-of-receivables, indicates that $47 million of the total receivables of $409 million is uncollectible at year-end. Record doubtful-account expense at December 31, 2019. Post this amount to Allowance for Doubtful Accounts, and show its adjusted balance at December 31, 2019.
3. Show how ETR's receivables and the related allowance will appear on the December 31, 2019, balance sheet.
4. Show what ETR's income statement for the year ending December 31, 2019, will report for these transactions.

Answers

Requirement 1

	(In millions)
Net realizable value of receivables ($382 − $52)	$330

Requirement 2

	A	B	C	D
1			(In millions)	
2	a.	Doubtful-Account Expense	40	
3		Allowance for Doubtful Accounts		40
4				
5	b.	Allowance for Doubtful Accounts	58	
6		Accounts Receivable		58
7				

Allowance for Doubtful Accounts

		Dec 31, 2018	52
2019 Write-offs	58	2019 Expense	40
		Unadjusted balance at Dec 31, 2019	34

	A	B	C	D
1			(In millions)	
2	c.	Doubtful-Account Expense ($47 − $34)	13	
3		Allowance for Doubtful Accounts		13
4				

Allowance for Doubtful Accounts

		Dec 31, 2019 Unadj bal	34
		2019 Expense	13
		Dec 31, 2019 Adj bal	47

Requirement 3

	(In millions)
Accounts receivable	$409
Allowance for doubtful accounts	(47)
Accounts receivable, net	$362

Requirement 4

	(In millions)
Expenses: Doubtful-account expense for 2019 ($40 + $13)	$53

REVIEW | Receivables and Revenue

Accounting Vocabulary

accounts receivable turnover ratio (p. 269) Net credit sales divided by average net accounts receivable.

acid-test ratio (p. 268) Another name for the *quick ratio.*

aging-of-receivables (p. 261) A way to estimate bad debts by analyzing individual accounts receivable according to the length of time they have been receivable from the customer.

Allowance for Bad Debts (p. 259) Another name for *Allowance for Uncollectible Accounts.*

Allowance for Doubtful Accounts (p. 259) Another name for *Allowance for Uncollectible Accounts.*

Allowance for Uncollectible Accounts (p. 259) The estimated amount of collection losses on accounts receivable. Another name for *Allowance for Doubtful Accounts* and *Allowance for Bad Debts.*

allowance method (p. 259) A method of recording collection losses based on estimates of how much money the business will not collect from its credit customers.

bad-debt expense (p. 258) Another name for *Uncollectible-Account Expense.*

contract (p. 250) An agreement between two parties that creates enforceable rights or obligations.

credit memo (p. 253) A document issued to a credit customer for merchandise returned, authorizing a credit to the customer's account receivable for the amount of the sale.

creditor (p. 265) The party to whom money is owed.

days' sales outstanding (DSO) ratio (p. 269) 365 ÷ accounts receivable turnover. Indicates how many days' sales remain in Accounts Receivable awaiting collection. Also called *days' sales in receivables* or the *collection period.*

debtor (p. 265) The party who owes money.

direct write-off method (p. 264) A method of accounting for bad debts in which the company waits until a customer's account receivable proves uncollectible and then debits Uncollectible-Account Expense and credits the customer's Account Receivable.

doubtful-account expense (p. 258) Another name for *Uncollectible-Account Expense.*

FOB (p. 252) Acronym for "free on board"; it indicates the shipment point at which the seller is free of ownership of the goods it sold. See also *shipping terms.*

interest (p. 265) The borrower's cost of renting money from a lender. Interest is revenue for the lender and expense for the borrower.

maturity date (p. 265) The date on which the debtor must pay the note.

maturity value (p. 265) The sum of principal and interest on the note.

percent-of-sales method (p. 260) A method that computes a business's Uncollectible-Account Expense as a percentage of the organization's net credit sales. Also called the *income-statement approach* because it focuses on the amount of expense to be reported on the income statement.

principal (p. 265) The amount borrowed by a debtor and lent by a creditor.

quick ratio (p. 268) The ratio of the sum of a business's cash plus short-term investments and net current receivables to total current liabilities. The ratio indicates whether the business can pay all its current liabilities if they come due immediately. Also called the *acid-test ratio.*

receivables (p. 256) Monetary claims against a business or an individual, acquired mainly by selling goods or services and by lending money.

revenue (p. 250) Inflows of resources to an entity that result from delivering goods or rendering services to customers.

sales discount (p. 254) A percentage reduction of the sales price by a seller as an incentive for early payment before the due date. A typical way to express a sales discount is "2/10, n/30." This means the seller will grant a 2% discount if the invoice is paid within 10 days, and the entire amount is due within 30 days.

sales return (or allowance) (p. 253) Credits or refunds given to customers who return merchandise.

shipping terms (p. 252) Terms provided by the seller of merchandise that dictate the date on which title transfers to the buyer. A typical way to express shipping terms is through FOB terms. *FOB destination* means title to the goods passes to the buyer when the goods are delivered and the buyer assumes control over them. *FOB shipping point* means title passes on the date the goods are shipped from the seller's warehouse.

term (p. 265) The length of time from a note's inception to its maturity.

trade discounts (p. 251) Special discounts offered to business customers to entice them to purchase merchandise or services. The discounts are another way to quote prices of goods or services to select customers without other customers knowing it.

uncollectible-account expense (p. 258) Cost to the seller of extending credit. Arises from the failure to collect from credit customers. Also called *doubtful-account expense* or *bad-debt expense*.

Quick Check (Answers are given on page 304.)

1. A doctor for the Benson Family Practice performs a sports physical exam for Allison Smythe on February 1. The charge for the exam is $100; Smythe's insurance company, Cardinal Health, is billed for the entire $100 on February 1. Cardinal Health receives the invoice on February 2, and enters the amount into its payment system on February 4. Benson Family Practice receives the $100 payment from Cardinal Health on February 20. On which date would Benson Family Practice recognize the revenue for Smythe's physical?
   a. February 1
   b. February 2
   c. February 4
   d. February 20

2. On March 15, Maxwell Plush sold and shipped merchandise on account for $6,000 to Kittson Amusement Park, terms FOB shipping point, n/30. Maxwell's cost of goods sold is 40% of sales. How is Maxwell impacted by this sale on March 15?
   a. Its assets will increase, while its equity remains the same.
   b. Its assets will increase, as will its equity.
   c. Its assets will remain the same, while its equity increases.
   d. Its assets will remain the same, while its equity decreases.

3. When a customer returns a product to Hartville Equipment that the customer purchased on account, Hartville will issue a ____________ to authorize a credit to the customer's account receivable on Hartville's books:
   a. return authorization
   b. refund note
   c. credit memo
   d. manager approval

4. What is the financial impact on a company when a customer returns a product for a refund?
   a. Sales revenue will decrease because sales revenue will be debited.
   b. Sales revenue will not be impacted because the company has already accrued for estimated refunds and returns.
   c. Sales revenue will increase because sales revenue will be credited.
   d. Returns expense will increase because returns expense will be debited.

5. Washington Products offers credit terms of 3/10, n/45. Which of the following statements is correct?
   a. The customer can take a 3% discount if the bill is paid within 45 days of the invoice date.
   b. The total amount of the invoice must be paid within 10 days of the invoice date.
   c. A discount of 3% can be taken if the invoice is paid within 10 days of the invoice date.
   d. No discount is offered for early payment.

6. Which of the following statements is true?

a. Credit sales increase receivables.
b. Collections on account decrease receivables.
c. Write-offs of accounts decrease receivables.
d. All of these statements are true.

7. Duncan Corporation began 2018 with a balance in Accounts Receivable of $500,000. Service revenue, all on account, for the year totaled $2,600,000. The company ended the year with a balance in Accounts Receivable of $700,000. Duncan's bad-debt write-offs are nonexistent. How much cash did the company collect from customers in 2018?

a. $3,300,000
b. $2,600,000
c. $2,800,000
d. $2,400,000

Use the following information to answer questions 8–12.
Jackson Company had the following information in 2018:

Accounts receivable 12/31/18	$ 8,000
Allowance for uncollectible-accounts credit balance 12/31/18 (before adjustment)	900
Credit service revenue during 2018	39,000
Cash service revenue during 2018	20,000
Collections from customers on account during 2018	40,000

8. Uncollectible accounts are determined by the percent-of-sales method to be 3% of credit sales. How much is uncollectible-account expense for 2018?

a. $1,010
b. $900
c. $320
d. $1,170

9. Uncollectible account expense for 2018 is $1,615. What is the adjusted balance in the Allowance account at year-end for 2018?

a. $650
b. $2,515
c. $1,615
d. $900

10. If uncollectible accounts are determined by the aging-of-receivables method to be $1,260, the uncollectible-account expense for 2018 would be

a. $2,160.
b. $1,260.
c. $360.
d. $900.

11. Refer to Question 10. Using the aging-of-receivables method, the balance of the Allowance account after the adjusting entry at year-end 2018 would be

a. $1,260.
b. $2,160.
c. $360.
d. $9,260.

12. Refer to Question 10. Using the aging-of-receivables method, the net realizable value of accounts receivable on the December 31, 2018, balance sheet would be

a. $9,260.
b. $8,640.
c. $8,000.
d. $6,740.

13. Accounts Receivable has a debit balance of $2,500, and the Allowance for Uncollectible Accounts has a credit balance of $500. A $70 account receivable is written off. What is the amount of net receivables (net realizable value) after the write-off?

a. $2,430
b. $1,930
c. $2,000
d. $2,070

14. Swan Corporation received a four-month, 8%, $1,650 note receivable on March 1. The adjusting entry on March 31 will include

a. a debit to Interest Receivable for $44.
b. a credit to Interest Revenue for $11.
c. a debit to Cash for $132.
d. a debit to Interest Receivable for $132.

15. What is the maturity value of a $30,000, 12%, six-month note?

a. $28,200 **c.** $30,000
b. $33,600 **d.** $31,800

16. If the adjusting entry to accrue interest on a note receivable is omitted, then

a. liabilities are understated, net income is overstated, and stockholders' equity is overstated.
b. assets, net income, and stockholders' equity are understated.
c. assets, net income, and stockholders' equity are overstated.
d. assets are overstated, net income is understated, and stockholders' equity is understated.

17. Net credit sales total $1,264,800. Beginning and ending accounts receivable are $38,000 and $43,600, respectively. Calculate the days' sales outstanding.

a. 12 days **c.** 13 days
b. 18 days **d.** 9 days

18. From the following list of accounts, calculate the quick ratio.

Cash	$ 2,000	Accounts payable	$ 5,000
Accounts receivable	7,000	Salary payable	9,000
Inventory	17,000	Notes payable (due in two years)	8,000
Prepaid insurance	1,000	Short-term investments	5,000

a. 1.5 **c.** 1.8
b. 1.0 **d.** 2.3

Excel Project
Autograded Excel Project available in **MyLab Accounting**.

ASSESS YOUR PROGRESS

Ethics Check

EC5-1. Identify ethical principle violated

For each of the situations listed, identify which of three principles (integrity, objectivity and independence, or due care) from the AICPA Code of Professional Conduct is violated. Assume all persons listed in the situations are members of the AICPA. (Note: Refer to the AICPA Code of Professional Conduct contained on pages 25–27 in Chapter 1 for descriptions of the principles.)

a. April, a staff accountant for Rogers & Co., is confused by the process for estimating uncollectible-accounts expense using an aging schedule; she struggled with this topic when she was in her accounting program in college. When she is given the responsibility for reviewing the entries related to her company's uncollectible-accounts expense and the aging schedule, she compares this period to the prior period and does not do any further review or analysis as is needed.

b. Will is on the audit staff of Monroe & Co, CPAs. He is assigned to the audit of Lafayette Holdings, a fast-growing technology firm that is run by his stepmother. He is excited to be assigned to this exciting audit because he feels it will help to advance his career. He does not disclose the relationship to anyone, nor does his stepmother.

c. Shana is the treasurer of Oxford Company. She knows that her company plans to keep its investment in **Google** stock for several years. (It has actually been pledged as collateral for a loan that Oxford has at a local bank.) However, she decides to classify the Google stock as a short-term security. Classifying the Google stock as a short-term security makes it a current asset and increases Oxford's current ratio, making the company look more favorable to investors.

d. Conway Corporation has a large number of customers who buy on credit. Nick, the controller for Conway, deliberately underestimates the amount of uncollectible account expense this year so that the company's income will achieve the targeted income figure. If the company's income reaches or exceeds the target, monetary performance bonuses for all members of management, including Nick, will be awarded.

Short Exercises

LO 1

S5-1. ***(Learning Objective 1: Apply GAAP for proper revenue recognition)*** On December 23, 2018, Silverman Sports Manufacturing sells a truckload of merchandise to the Baseball World store in Cincinnati, Ohio. The terms of the sale are FOB destination. The truck runs into bad weather on the way to Cincinnati and doesn't arrive until January 2, 2019. Silverman's invoice totals $160,000. The company's year-end is December 31. What amount should Silverman reflect in its 2018 income statement for this sale?

LO 1

S5-2. ***(Learning Objective 1: Record a credit card sale)*** Maple Woodworking accepts credit cards at its store. Maple's credit card processor charges a fee of 2% of the total amount of any credit sale. Assume that Ralph Stone purchases $9,000 of custom furniture and pays with a VISA card. Make the entry that Maple would make to record the sale to Stone. (You do not need to make the cost of goods sold entry in this exercise.)

LO 1, 2

S5-3. ***(Learning Objectives 1, 2: Apply GAAP for proper revenue recognition; account for sales returns)*** In August, Joplin Designs sold $510,000 of merchandise; all sales were in cash. The cost of sales for August was $400,000. Based on past experience, Joplin uses an estimated return rate of 3% of sales. Record the journal entries for the monthly sales, cost of sales, estimated returns, and cost of estimated returns for August.

LO 1, 3

S5-4. ***(Learning Objectives 1, 3: Apply GAAP for proper revenue recognition; account for sales discounts)*** On April 3, Hamilton Company sold $50,000 of merchandise on account to Ranger Corporation, terms 5/10, n/30, FOB shipping point. Hamilton's cost of sales for this merchandise was $34,000. The merchandise left Hamilton's facility on April 4 and arrived at Ranger on April 10. Ranger paid the invoice for the merchandise on April 11.

Requirements

1. Prepare the journal entries for Hamilton Company for the sale of the merchandise, the cost of the sale, and the related receipt of payment from Ranger Corporation. Assume that Ranger Corporation takes the discount if payment is within the discount period.
2. Indicate which company (Hamilton or Ranger) owns the merchandise at the end of each of the following dates:
   a. April 3
   b. April 4
   c. April 10

LO 3

S5-5. ***(Learning Objective 3: Account for sales discounts)*** Roswell Company purchases inventory from Clear Pool Supplies on June 1. The sales terms on the invoice from Clear Pool Supplies are 3/10, n/30. What does this mean? What is Roswell's potential savings, if any? How much time does the company have to take advantage of these savings?

S5-6. ***(Learning Objective 4: Account for accounts receivable)*** Perform the following accounting tasks for the receivables of Able and Bowman, a law firm, at December 31, 2018. LO 4

Requirements

1. Set up T-accounts for Cash, Accounts Receivable, and Service Revenue. Start with the beginning balances as follows: Cash $28,000; Accounts Receivable $103,000; and Service Revenue $0. Post the following 2018 transactions to the T-accounts:
   a. Service revenue of $705,000, all on account
   b. Collections on account, $713,000
2. What are the ending balances of Cash, Accounts Receivable, and Service Revenue?

S5-7. ***(Learning Objective 5: Evaluate collectibility using the allowance for uncollectible accounts)*** During its first year of operations, Spring Garden, Inc., had sales of $439,000, all on account. Industry experience suggests that Spring Garden's uncollectibles will amount to 4% of credit sales. At December 31, 2018, accounts receivable total $59,000. The company uses the allowance method to account for uncollectibles. LO 5

1. Make Spring Garden's journal entry for uncollectible-account expense using the percent-of-sales method.
2. Show how Spring Garden should report accounts receivable on its balance sheet at December 31, 2018.

S5-8. ***(Learning Objective 5: Evaluate collectibility using the allowance for uncollectible accounts)*** At the end of the current year (before adjusting entries), Autumn Corporation had a balance of $76,000 in Accounts Receivable and a credit balance of $11,000 in Allowance for Uncollectible Accounts. Service revenue (all on credit) for the year totaled $490,000. LO 5

Requirements

Consider each of the following two independent situations.

1. Using the percent-of-sales method, calculate the amount of Uncollectible-Account Expense if Autumn Corporation estimates its uncollectible-account expense using a rate of 2% of credit sales. What is the ending balance of the Allowance for Uncollectible-Accounts under this scenario?
2. Now assume that Autumn Corporation uses the aging-of-receivables method. Autumn Corporation estimates that its Allowance for Uncollectible Accounts should have a credit balance of $21,000. Calculate the amount of its Uncollectible-Account Expense. What is the ending balance of the Allowance for Uncollectible Accounts under this scenario?

S5-9. ***(Learning Objective 6: Account for notes receivable)*** LO 6

1. Compute the amount of interest during 2018, 2019, and 2020 for the following note receivable: On May 31, 2018, Wyoming State Bank loaned $240,000 to Lindsey Weston on a two-year, 8% note.
2. Which party has a/an
   a. note receivable?
   b. note payable?
   c. interest revenue?
   d. interest expense?
3. How much in total would Wyoming State Bank collect if Lindsey Weston paid off the note early on November 30, 2018?

S5-10. ***(Learning Objective 6: Account for notes receivable)*** On August 31, 2018, Betsy Totten borrowed $1,000 from Iowa State Bank. Totten signed a note payable, promising to pay the bank principal plus interest on August 31, 2019. The interest rate on the note is 6%. The accounting year of Iowa State Bank ends on June 30, 2019. Journalize Iowa State Bank's (a) lending money on the note receivable at August 31, 2018, (b) accrual of interest at June 30, 2019, and (c) collection of principal and interest at August 31, 2019, the maturity date of the note. LO 6

LO 6

S5-11. ***(Learning Objective 6: Account for notes receivable)*** Car title lenders are considered to be predatory lenders, since they charge high rates of interest to those individuals who can least afford it. Various laws in recent years have attempted to curb the high interest rates and these practices. Car title lenders still operate and some would argue that they fill a need in society. Individuals using car title lender services typically are poor and have no other way to borrow funds. An *LA Times* report in 2015 stated that about 1 out of 9 car title loans end in the borrower's car being repossessed.

An NBC report found that the average car title loan is $950, and borrowers take an average of 10 months to repay the loan. Typically, consumers can borrow up to 26% of the value of their cars and the lender charges 25% per month. This interest rate means a consumer borrowing $950 would pay about $238 per month in interest, or $2,375 over the 10-month period that the $950 was borrowed.

One consumer lender is LoanMax, which loans cash in exchange for a car title. The potential borrower brings in a free and clear car title (i.e., has no liens on it), the vehicle, and his/her photo ID to a LoanMax location. LoanMax determines how much cash it will loan the person based on the value of the vehicle. The borrower signs paperwork and departs LoanMax with cash in hand. No credit check is performed. Loans range from $100 to $10,000. Cars can be repossessed if the borrower does not pay.

Requirements

1. Let's say an individual borrows $500 cash from LoanMax. Does LoanMax have a receivable or a payable when it hands over the cash to the borrower?
2. When LoanMax disburses the cash at the time of borrowing, how are its assets, liabilities, and equity impacted?
3. Do you think the car title loan process is ethical? Explain your point of view.

LO 7

S5-12. ***(Learning Objective 7: Evaluate liquidity using the quick [acid-test] ratio and days' sales in receivables)*** Northern Products reported the following amounts in its 2019 financial statements. The 2018 amounts are given for comparison.

	2019		2018	
Current assets:				
Cash		$ 9,500		$ 9,500
Short-term investments		10,500		7,000
Accounts receivable	$86,500		$70,100	
Less: Allowance for uncollectibles	(7,500)	79,000	(5,500)	64,600
Inventory		189,000		190,000
Prepaid insurance		2,200		2,200
Total current assets		290,200		273,300
Total current liabilities		99,000		106,000
Net sales (all on account)		1,077,000		734,000

Requirements

1. Compute Northern's quick (acid-test) ratio at the end of 2019. Round to two decimal places. How does the quick ratio compare with the industry average of 0.92?
2. Compare days' sales outstanding for 2019 with the company's credit terms of net 30 days.

Exercises MyLab Accounting

Group A

E5-13A. ***(Learning Objectives 1, 2: Apply GAAP for proper revenue recognition; account for sales allowances)*** Lakewood Jewelry sells to retailers who then resell the products. Lakewood does not offer sales discounts for early payment; it asks that customers pay in full within 15 days or at the point of sale with a credit card. The company had the following selected transactions during July: LO 1, 2

July 2	Sold $50,000 of merchandise to Oceanside Jewels on account.
July 3	Sold $10,000 of merchandise to Brilliant Crystals, which paid by credit card. The credit card company charges Lakewood a fee of 2% on credit card sales.
July 16	Oceanside Jewels paid the balance of what it owed for the purchase on July 2.
July 17	Sold $65,000 of merchandise to Precious Stones on account.
July 19	Precious Stones noticed that some of the merchandise received was damaged, so it returned $5,000 worth of merchandise to Lakewood.
July 30	Precious Stones paid the balance of what it owed for the purchase on July 17.

Requirements

1. Journalize Lakewood's July transactions. (You do not need to record the cost of goods sold.)
2. Calculate the gross sales revenue for the month.

E5-14A. ***(Learning Objectives 1, 3: Apply GAAP for proper revenue recognition; account for sales discounts)*** At Hometown Arts, gross sales for the month included: LO 1, 3

Sales on account (2/10, n/30)	$150,000
Credit card sales (3% credit card fee)	$200,000

Half of the sales on account were paid within the discount period; the other accounts were paid in full by the end of the month.

Requirements

1. Journalize the sales on account, the credit card sales, and the cash payments on account received during the month.
2. Calculate the net sales revenue for the month.

E5-15A. ***(Learning Objectives 1, 2, 3: Apply GAAP for proper revenue recognition; account for sales allowances; account for sales discounts)*** Main Street Tours provides historical guided tours of several U.S. cities. The company charges $250 per person for the eight-hour tour. For groups of four or more, a group discount of $50 per person is offered. Here is a selection of transactions during June: LO 1, 2, 3

June 2	Marlene booked a tour of Boston for June 5. She and three friends would be going on the tour; Marlene booked the tour for the entire group. Main Street Tours asks that payment for the tour be made in full within ten days after the tour; it offers a 5% discount for payment within that ten-day period.
June 5	Marlene and her friends went on the tour of Boston. Near the end of the tour, the tour guide tripped on a step and twisted her ankle. Since the tour guide was unable to walk, the tour ended after seven hours instead of the full eight hours.
June 7	Since the tour was shorter than planned, Marlene called the customer service representative for Main Street Tours and requested a discount. The representative agreed to give a discount of $200 in total for the tour.
June 14	Marlene paid for the group tour.

Requirement

1. Journalize all transactions for Main Street Tours.

LO **1, 2, 3**

E5-16A. ***(Learning Objectives 1, 2, 3: Apply GAAP for sales, sales returns, and sales discounts)*** Antique Interiors reported the following transactions in October:

Oct 2	Sold merchandise on account to Tim Hinkel, $1,200, terms 1/10, n/30.
10	Sold merchandise on account to Ben Hoffman, $2,600, terms 2/10, n/30.
11	Collected payment from Hinkel for the October 2 sale.
15	Hoffman returned $2,000 of the merchandise purchased on October 10.
19	Collected payment from Hoffman for the balance of the October 10 sale.

Requirements

1. Record the foregoing transactions in the journal of Antique Interiors using the gross method. (You do not need to make the cost of sales journal entries; assume that these entries will be made by the company when it makes its other adjusting entries at period end.)
2. Calculate the amount of gross sales minus sales discounts for the month of October.

LO **4, 5**

E5-17A. ***(Learning Objectives 4, 5: Account for accounts receivable and uncollectible accounts)*** Perform the following accounting for the receivables of Andrews and Johnson, a law firm, at December 31, 2018.

Requirements

1. Set up T-accounts and start with the beginning balances for these T-accounts:
   - Accounts Receivable, $100,000
   - Allowance for Uncollectible Accounts, $14,000

   Post the following 2018 transactions to the T-accounts:

   a. Service revenue of $697,000, all on account
   b. Collections on account, $714,000
   c. Write-offs of uncollectible accounts, $8,000
   d. Uncollectible-account expense (allowance method), $11,000
2. What are the ending balances of Accounts Receivable and Allowance for Uncollectible Accounts?
3. Show how Andrews and Johnson will report accounts receivable on its balance sheet at December 31, 2018.

LO **5**

E5-18A. ***(Learning Objective 5: Apply GAAP for uncollectible receivables)*** At December 31, 2018, Waco Travel Agency has an Accounts Receivable balance of $93,000. Allowance for Uncollectible Accounts has a credit balance of $870 before the year-end adjustment. Service revenue (all on account) for 2018 was $800,000. Waco estimates that its uncollectible-account expense for the year is 1% of service revenue. Make the year-end entry to record uncollectible-account expense. Show how Accounts Receivable and Allowance for Uncollectible Accounts are reported on the balance sheet at December 31, 2018.

LO **4, 5**

E5-19A. ***(Learning Objectives 4, 5: Account for accounts receivable and uncollectible receivables)*** On June 30, Premier Party Planners had a $35,000 balance in Accounts Receivable and a $2,752 credit balance in Allowance for Uncollectible Accounts. During July, Premier made credit sales of $193,000. July collections on account were $164,000, and write-offs of uncollectible receivables totaled $2,870. Uncollectible-accounts expense is estimated as 3% of credit sales. No sales returns are expected. Ignore cost of goods sold.

Requirements

1. Journalize sales, collections, write-offs of uncollectibles, and uncollectible-account expense by the allowance method during July. Explanations are not required.
2. Show the ending balances in Accounts Receivable, Allowance for Uncollectible Accounts, and *Net* Accounts Receivable at July 31. How much does Premier expect to collect?
3. Show how Premier Party Planners will report accounts receivable and net sales on its July 31 balance sheet and income statement for the month ended July 31.

LO 5

E5-20A. ***(Learning Objective 5: Apply GAAP to uncollectible receivables)*** At December 31, 2018, before any year-end adjustments, the Accounts Receivable balance of Alpha Company, Inc., is $390,000. The Allowance for Uncollectible Accounts has a $15,500 credit balance. Alpha prepares the following aging schedule for Accounts Receivable:

	Age of Accounts			
Total Balance	1–30 Days	31–60 Days	61–90 Days	Over 90 Days
$390,000	$160,000	$120,000	$80,000	$30,000
Estimated uncollectible	0.6%	2.0%	5.0%	40.0%

Requirements

1. Based on the aging of Accounts Receivable, is the unadjusted balance of the allowance account adequate? Too high? Too low?
2. Make the entry required by the aging schedule. Prepare a T-account for the allowance.
3. Show how Alpha will report Accounts Receivable on its December 31 balance sheet.

LO 5

E5-21A. ***(Learning Objective 5: Apply GAAP to uncollectible accounts)*** Walnut Foods, Inc., experienced the following revenue and accounts receivable write-offs:

		Accounts Receivable Write-Offs in Month			
Month	Service Revenue	February	March	April	Totals
February	$ 3,400	$51	$ 87		$138
March	4,100		100	$37	137
April	4,000			118	118
	$11,500	$51	$187	$155	$393

Suppose Walnut estimates that 4% of (gross) revenues will become uncollectible. Assume all revenues are on credit.

Requirement

1. Journalize service revenue (all on account), uncollectible-accounts expense, and write-offs during April. Include explanations.

LO 6

E5-22A. ***(Learning Objective 6: Apply GAAP for notes receivable)*** Record the following note receivable transactions in the journal of Mediterranean Services. How much interest revenue did Mediterranean earn this year? *Use a 365-day year* for interest computations, and round interest amounts to the nearest dollar. Mediterranean Services has a December 31 fiscal year-end.

Oct 1	Loaned $21,000 cash to Brandy Shields on a one-year, 10% note.
Dec 6	Performed service for Lawn Pro, receiving a 90-day, 9% note for $5,000.
16	Received a $4,000, six-month, 11% note on account from Peabody Company.
31	Accrued interest revenue for the year.

LO **1, 7** E5-23A. *(Learning Objectives 1, 7: Show how to speed up cash flow from receivables; evaluate liquidity through ratios)* Moore Corporation reported the following items at December 31, 2018, and 2017:

	A	B	C	D	E	F
1	**Balance Sheets (Summarized)**					
2						
3		**Year-end**			**Year-end**	
4		**2018**	**2017**		**2018**	**2017**
5	**Current assets:**			**Current liabilities:**		
6	Cash	$ 18,000	$ 14,000	Accounts payable	$ 19,000	$ 20,500
7	Marketable securities	20,000	9,000	Other current liabilities	108,000	110,000
8	Accounts receivable, net	53,000	67,000	Long-term liabilities	20,000	21,000
9	Inventory	190,000	186,000			
10	Other current assets	3,000	3,000	Stockholders' equity	137,000	137,500
11	Long-term assets		10,000			
12	Total assets	$ 284,000	$ 289,000	Total liabilities and equity	$ 284,000	$ 289,000
13						
14	**Income statement (partial):**	**2018**				
15	Sales Revenue	$ 900,000				
17						

Requirements

1. Compute the company's (a) quick (acid-test) ratio and (b) days' sales outstanding for 2018. Evaluate each ratio value as strong or weak. All sales are on account with terms of net 30 days.
2. Recommend two ways for Moore to speed up its cash flow from receivables.

LO **1, 7** E5-24A. *(Learning Objectives 1, 7: Show how to speed up cash flow from receivables; evaluate liquidity through ratios)* Geneva Co., Inc., an electronics and appliance chain, reported these figures in millions of dollars:

	2019	2018
Net sales	$523,125	$543,125
Receivables at end of year	3,860	4,510

Requirements

1. Compute Geneva's days' sales in receivables or days' sales outstanding (DSO) during 2019. (For this exercise, use "net sales" for "net credit sales" when calculating ratios.)
2. Is Geneva's DSO long or short? Kurzwel Networks takes 39 days to collect its average level of receivables. Domarko Freight, the overnight shipper, takes 33 days. What causes Geneva's collection period to be so different?

Group B

E5-25B. ***(Learning Objectives 1, 2: Apply GAAP for proper revenue recognition; account for sales allowances)*** Niagara Jewelry sells to retailers who then resell the products. Niagara does not offer sales discounts for early payment; it asks that customers pay in full within 15 days or at the point of sale with a credit card. The company had the following selected transactions during July:

LO **1, 2**

July 2	Sold $150,000 of merchandise to Lakeside Jewels on account.
July 3	Sold $12,000 of merchandise to Superior Crystals, which paid by credit card. The credit card company charges Niagara a fee of 2% on credit card sales.
July 16	Lakeside Jewels paid the balance of what it owed for the purchase on July 2.
July 17	Sold $185,000 of merchandise to Shining Stones on account.
July 19	Shining Stones noticed that some of the merchandise received was damaged, so it returned $17,000 worth of merchandise to Niagara.
July 30	Shining Stones paid the balance of what it owed for the purchase on July 17.

Requirements

1. Journalize Niagara's July transactions. (You do not need to record the cost of goods sold)
2. Calculate the gross sales revenue for the month.

E5-26B. ***(Learning Objectives 1, 3: Apply GAAP for proper revenue recognition; account for sales discounts)*** At Uptown Arts, gross sales for the month included:

LO **1, 3**

Sales on account (2/10, n/30)	$350,000
Credit card sales (2% credit card fee)	$250,000

Half of the sales on account were paid within the discount period; the other accounts were paid in full by the end of the month.

Requirements

1. Journalize the sales on account, the credit card sales, and the cash payments on account received during the month.
2. Calculate the net sales revenue for the month.

E5-27B. ***(Learning Objectives 1, 2, 3: Apply GAAP for proper revenue recognition; account for sales allowances; account for sales discounts)*** Town Center Tours provides historical guided tours of several U.S. cities. The company charges $175 per person for the eight-hour tour. For groups of four or more, a group discount of $25 per person is offered. Here is a selection of transactions during June:

LO **1, 2, 3**

June 2	Laura booked a tour of San Francisco for June 5. She and three friends would be going on the tour; Laura booked the tour for the entire group. Town Center Tours asks that payment for the tour be made in full within ten days after the tour; it offers a 3% discount for payment within that ten-day period.
June 5	Laura and her friends went on the tour of San Francisco. Near the end of the tour, the tour guide tripped on a step and twisted her ankle. Since the tour guide was unable to walk, the tour ended after seven hours instead of the full eight hours.
June 7	Since the tour was shorter than planned, Laura called the customer service representative for Town Center Tours and requested a discount. The representative agreed to give a discount of $100 in total for the tour.
June 14	Laura paid for the group tour.

Requirement

1. Journalize all transactions for Town Center Tours.

LO **1, 2, 3**

E5-28B. ***(Learning Objectives 1, 2, 3: Apply GAAP for sales, sales returns, and sales discounts)*** Pastel Interiors reported the following transactions in June:

June 2	Sold merchandise on account to Elisa Birch, $700, terms 1/10, n/30.
10	Sold merchandise on account to Melissa Movens, $2,400, terms 1/10, n/30.
11	Collected payment from Elisa Birch for June 2 sale.
15	Movens returned $1,400 of the merchandise purchased on June 10.
19	Collected payment from Movens for the balance of the June 10 sale.

Requirements

1. Record the foregoing transactions in the journal of Pastel Interiors using the gross method. (You do not need to make the cost of sales journal entries; assume that these entries will be made by the company when it makes its other adjusting entries at period end.)
2. Calculate the amount of gross sales minus sales discounts for the month of June.

LO **4, 5**

E5-29B. ***(Learning Objectives 4, 5: Account for accounts receivable and uncollectible accounts)*** Perform the following accounting for the receivables of Hawkins and Harris, a CPA firm, at December 31, 2018.

Requirements

1. Set up T-accounts and start with the beginning balances for these T-accounts:
   - Accounts Receivable, $104,000
   - Allowance for Uncollectible Accounts, $12,000

   Post the following 2018 transactions to the T-accounts:

   a. Service revenue of $695,000, all on account
   b. Collections on account, $720,000
   c. Write-offs of uncollectible accounts, $8,000
   d. Uncollectible-account expense (allowance method), $15,000
2. What are the ending balances of Accounts Receivable and Allowance for Uncollectible Accounts?
3. Show how Hawkins and Harris will report accounts receivable on its balance sheet at December 31, 2018.

LO **5**

E5-30B. ***(Learning Objective 5: Apply GAAP for uncollectible receivables)*** At December 31, 2018, Concord Travel Agency has an Accounts Receivable balance of $87,000. Allowance for Uncollectible Accounts has a credit balance of $880 before the year-end adjustment. Service revenue (all on account) for 2018 was $800,000. Concord estimates that its uncollectible-account expense for the year is 3% of service revenue. Make the year-end entry to record uncollectible-account expense. Show how Accounts Receivable and Allowance for Uncollectible Accounts are reported on the balance sheet at December 31, 2018.

LO **4, 5**

E5-31B. ***(Learning Objectives 4, 5: Account for accounts receivable and uncollectible receivables)*** On November 30, Palmer Party Planners had a $41,000 balance in Accounts Receivable and a $3,584 credit balance in Allowance for Uncollectible Accounts. During December, Palmer made credit sales of $200,000. December collections on account were $168,000, and write-offs of uncollectible receivables totaled $2,910. Uncollectible-account expense is estimated as 1% of credit sales. No sales returns are expected. Ignore cost of goods sold.

Requirements

1. Journalize sales, collections, write-offs of uncollectibles, and uncollectible-account expense by the allowance method during December. Explanations are not required.
2. Show the ending balances in Accounts Receivable, Allowance for Uncollectible Accounts, and *Net* Accounts Receivable at December 31. How much does Palmer expect to collect?
3. Show how Palmer Party Planners will report Accounts Receivable and net sales on its December 31 balance sheet and income statement for the month ended December 31.

Exhibit 3-14 | Classified Balance Sheet of The Walt Disney Company

The Walt Disney Company Consolidated Balance Sheets	Fiscal 2016	Fiscal 2015
USD ($) in millions	Oct. 01, 2016	Oct. 03, 2015
Current assets:		
Cash and cash equivalents	$ 4,610	$ 4,269
Receivables	9,065	8,019
Inventories	1,390	1,571
Other current assets	1,901	2,899
Total current assets	16,966	16,758
Film and television costs	6,339	6,183
Investments	4,280	2,643
Parks, resorts and other property, net	27,349	25,179
Intangible assets, net	34,759	34,998
Other long-term assets	2,340	2,421
Total assets	$ 92,033	$ 88,182
Current liabilities:		
Accounts payable and accrued liabilities	$ 9,130	$ 7,844
Current portion of long-term borrowings	3,687	4,563
Unearned royalties and other advances	4,025	3,927
Total current liabilities	16,842	16,334
Long-term borrowings	16,483	12,773
Other long-term liabilities	11,385	10,420
Contingent liabilities (Note 14)		
Total liabilities	44,710	39,527
Equity:		
Common stock, and additional paid-in capital	35,859	35,122
Retained earnings	66,088	59,028
Treasury stock at cost	(54,703)	(47,204)
Other equity, net	79	1,709
Total equity	47,323	48,655
Total liabilities and equity	$ 92,033	$ 88,182

Source: Data from the U.S. Securities and Exchange Commission EDGAR Company Filings, www.sec.gov

The **account format** lists assets on the left and liabilities and stockholders' equity on the right in the same way that a T-account does. Exhibit 3-12 (p. 140) shows an account format balance sheet for Alladin Travel, Inc. Either format is acceptable.

Income Statement Formats. A **single-step income statement** (statement of earnings) lists all the revenues together under a heading such as Revenues, or Revenues and Gains. The expenses are listed together in a single category titled Expenses, or Expenses and Losses. So, only one step, the subtraction of the sum of Expenses and Losses from the sum of Revenues and Gains, needs to be done to determine a company's income before income tax expense. Alladin Travel, Inc.'s single-step statement of earnings in Exhibit 3-10 (p. 140) appears in a single-step format.

A **multistep income statement** reports a number of subtotals to highlight important relationships between revenues and expenses. Exhibit 3-15 restates Exhibit 1-7 and shows The Walt Disney Company's comparative Consolidated Statements of Income in a multistep format. We have modified Exhibit 3-15 slightly from Exhibit 1-7 to subtotal the cost of services and products and to show the company's total gross profit ($25,639 million for fiscal 2016, up from $24,101 million for fiscal 2015). Gross profit is an important piece of information for a company like The Walt Disney Company, because it shows the amount of "pure profit" that results from subtracting the cost of services and products directly from the revenue generated by those services and products, respectively.

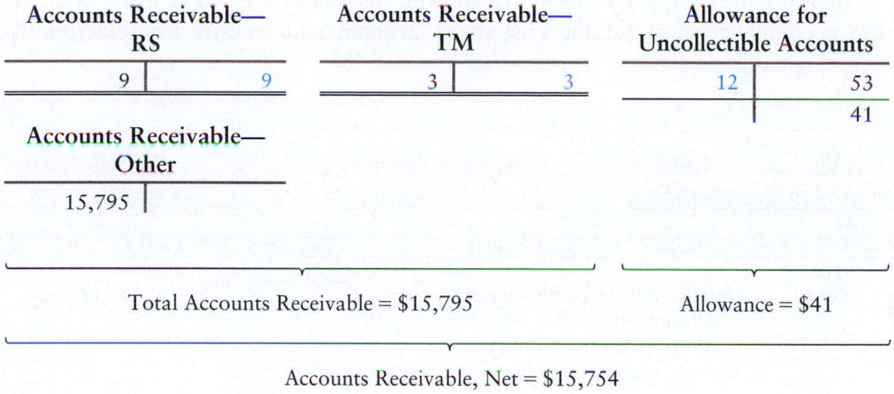LO 5

E5-32B. ***(Learning Objective 5: Apply GAAP to uncollectible receivables)*** At December 31, 2018, before any year-end adjustments, the Accounts Receivable balance of Hampton Company, Inc., is $330,000. The Allowance for Uncollectible Accounts has a $15,400 credit balance. Hampton prepares the following aging schedule for Accounts Receivable:

	Age of Accounts			
Total Balance	1–30 Days	31–60 Days	61–90 Days	Over 90 Days
$330,000	$130,000	$100,000	$70,000	$30,000
Estimated uncollectible	0.6%	3.0%	5.0%	40.0%

Requirements

1. Based on the aging of Accounts Receivable, is the unadjusted balance of the allowance account adequate? Too high? Too low?
2. Make the entry required by the aging schedule. Prepare a T-account for the allowance.
3. Show how Hampton will report Accounts Receivable on its December 31 balance sheet.

LO 5

E5-33B. ***(Learning Objective 5: Apply GAAP to uncollectible accounts)*** Aspen Foods, Inc., experienced the following revenue and accounts receivable write-offs:

		Accounts Receivable Write-Offs in Month			
Month	Service Revenue	January	February	March	Totals
January	$ 4,300	$48	$ 94		$142
February	3,200		104	$ 27	131
March	3,500			109	109
	$11,000	$48	$198	$136	$382

Suppose Aspen estimates that 4% of (gross) revenues will become uncollectible. Assume all revenues are on credit.

Requirement

1. Journalize service revenue (all on account), uncollectible-accounts expense, and write-offs during March. Include explanations.

LO 6

E5-34B. ***(Learning Objective 6: Apply GAAP for notes receivable)*** Record the following note receivable transactions in the journal of Windham Golf. How much interest revenue did Windham earn this year? *Use a 365-day year* for interest computations, and round interest amounts to the nearest dollar. Windham Golf has a December 31 fiscal year-end.

Oct 1	Loaned $17,000 cash to Jill Wateman on a one-year, 8% note.
Dec 6	Performed service for Fairway Pro, receiving a 90-day, 10% note for $14,000.
16	Received a $5,000, six-month, 5% note on account from Paulson Company.
31	Accrued interest revenue for the year.

LO 1, 7

E5-35B. ***(Learning Objectives 1, 7: Show how to speed up cash flow from receivables; evaluate liquidity through ratios)*** Swenson Corporation reported the following items at December 31, 2018, and 2017:

	A	B	C	D	E	F
1	**Balance Sheets (Summarized)**					
2						
3		**Year-end**			**Year-end**	
4		**2018**	**2017**		**2018**	**2017**
5	**Current assets:**			**Current liabilities:**		
6	Cash	$ 12,000	$ 8,000	Accounts payable	$ 18,000	$ 19,500
7	Marketable securities	23,000	12,000	Other current liabilities	105,000	107,000
8	Accounts receivable, net	55,000	69,000	Long-term liabilities	20,000	21,000
9	Inventory	191,000	187,000			
10	Other current assets	2,000	2,000	Stockholders' equity	140,000	140,500
11	Long-term assets		10,000			
12	Total assets	$ 283,000	$ 288,000	Total liabilities and equity	$ 283,000	$ 288,000
13						
14	**Income statement (partial):**	**2018**				
15	Sales Revenue	$ 868,000				
16						

Requirements

1. Compute the company's (a) quick (acid-test) ratio and (b) days' sales outstanding for 2018. Evaluate each ratio value as strong or weak. All sales are on account with terms of net 30 days.
2. Recommend two ways for Swenson to speed up its cash flow from receivables.

LO 1, 7

E5-36B. ***(Learning Objectives 1, 7: Show how to speed up cash flow from receivables; evaluate liquidity through ratios)*** Norfolk Co., Inc., an electronics and appliance chain, reported these figures in millions of dollars:

	2019	2018
Net sales	$398,500	$418,500
Receivables at end of year	3,860	4,110

Requirements

1. Compute Norfolk's days' sales in receivables or days' sales outstanding (DSO) during 2019. (For this exercise, use "net sales" for "net credit sales" when calculating ratios.)
2. Is Norfolk's DSO long or short? Nico Networks takes 39 days to collect its average level of receivables. Divencenzo, the overnight shipper, takes 33 days. What causes Norfolk's collection period to be so different?

Quiz

Test your understanding of receivables and revenue recognition by answering the following questions. Select the best choice from among the possible answers given.

Q5-37. Fairmont Company has shipped goods to Willowbook Recreation FOB shipping point. Fairmont will recognize sales revenue when:

a. the goods leave Fairmont's shipping dock.
b. Fairmont and Willowbrook agree that the revenue should be recognized.
c. the customer has paid the invoice.
d. Willowbrook has received the goods.

Q5-38. Which of the following statements regarding contracts is incorrect?
a. Identifying the contract with the customer is the first step of the revenue recognition model.
b. A contract must be written to be valid.
c. For a business that provides services, the performance obligation is generally satisfied when the service provider has substantially completed the service for the customer.
d. A contract is an agreement between two parties that creates enforceable rights or performance obligations.

Q5-39. Which of the following statements is correct?
a. Sales returns and allowances increase a company's profit.
b. If a customer returns a product, sales revenue will be credited.
c. The performance obligation in a sale of products is generally satisfied when the customer orders the products.
d. A company must accrue for estimated future returns at the end of the period in which the related sales revenue is recognized.

Q5-40. On April 3, a customer returned $600 of merchandise that had been purchased with cash to Ryan Supplies. Ryan's cost of the goods returned was $200. Which journal entry or entries should Ryan prepare? (No sales discount was offered for early payment.)
a. One entry to debit Cash and credit Sales Refunds Payable for $600; another entry to debit Inventory Returns Estimated and credit Inventory for $200.
b. One entry to debit Sales Refunds Payable and credit Cash for $600; another entry to debit Inventory and credit Inventory Returns Estimated for $200.
c. One entry to debit Sales Revenue for $600 and credit Cash for $600.
d. One entry to debit Sales Revenue for $400, debit Refund Expense for $200, and credit Cash for $600.

Q5-41. Maple Grove Legal Association performs legal services for Weymouth Construction for $5,000 on account with credit terms of 2/10, n/30. If Weymouth pays the invoice within the discount period, Maple Grove will record a debit to Cash in the amount of:
a. $5,100.
b. $100.
c. $5,000.
d. $4,900.

Q5-42. Under the allowance method for uncollectible receivables, the entry to record uncollectible-account expense has what effect on the financial statements?
a. Decreases assets and has no effect on net income
b. Increases expenses and increases stockholders' equity
c. Decreases net income and decreases assets
d. Decreases stockholders' equity and increases liabilities

Q5-43. Sprague Company uses the aging method to adjust the allowance for uncollectible accounts at the end of the period. At December 31, 2018, the balance of accounts receivable is $250,000 and the allowance for uncollectible accounts has a credit balance of $4,000 (before adjustment). An analysis of accounts receivable produced the following age groups:

Current	$150,000
60 days past due	90,000
Over 60 days past due	10,000
	$250,000

Based on past experience, Sprague estimates that the percentage of accounts that will prove to be uncollectible within the three age groups is 2% of the current balance, 8% of the 60 days past due balance, and 18% of the over 60 days past due balance. Based on these facts, the adjusting entry for uncollectible accounts should be made in the amount of
a. $8,000.
b. $12,000.
c. $17,000.
d. $16,000.

Q5-44. Refer to **Q5-43**. The net receivables on the balance sheet as of December 31, 2018, are ___________.

Q5-45. Milford Company uses the percent-of-sales method to estimate uncollectibles. Net credit sales for the current year amount to $140,000, and management estimates 2% will be uncollectible. The Allowance for Uncollectible Accounts prior to adjustment has a credit balance of $3,000. The amount of expense to report on the income statement will be

a. $1,500.
b. $2,800.
c. $8,400.
d. $5,800.

Q5-46. Refer to Q5-45. The balance of Allowance for Uncollectible Accounts, after adjustment, will be

a. $5,200.
b. $5,800.
c. $1,500.
d. $2,800.

Q5-47. Refer to questions 5-45 and 5-46. The following year, Milford Company wrote off $2,800 of old receivables as uncollectible. What is the balance in the Allowance account now?

Questions 5-48 through 5-51 use the following data:

On August 1, 2018, Avonette, Inc., sold equipment and accepted a six-month, 9%, $50,000 note receivable. Avonette's year-end is December 31.

Q5-48. How much interest revenue should Avonette accrue on December 31, 2018?

a. $4,500
b. $2,425
c. $1,875
d. $2,250

Q5-49. If Avonette fails to make an adjusting entry for the accrued interest on December 31, 2018,

a. net income will be understated and liabilities will be overstated.
b. net income will be understated and assets will be understated.
c. net income will be overstated and assets will be overstated.
d. net income will be overstated and liabilities will be understated.

Q5-50. How much interest does Avonette expect to collect on the maturity date (February 1, 2019)?

a. $3,050
b. $2,250
c. $375
d. $4,500

Q5-51. Which of the following accounts will Avonette credit in the journal entry at maturity on February 1, 2019, assuming collection in full?

a. Cash
b. Note Payable
c. Interest Payable
d. Interest Receivable

Q5-52. Which of the following is included in the calculation of the quick (acid-test) ratio?

a. Inventory and short-term investments
b. Inventory and prepaid expenses
c. Cash and accounts receivable
d. Prepaid expenses and cash

Q5-53. A company with net credit sales of $960,000, beginning net receivables of $70,000, and ending net receivables of $90,000 has days' sales outstanding closest to:

a. 37 days.
b. 30 days.
c. 34 days.
d. 41 days.

Q5-54. A company sells on credit terms of 2/10, n/30 and has days' sales in accounts receivable of 30.2 days. Its days' sales outstanding is

a. too low.
b. too high.
c. about right.
d. not able to be evaluated from the data given.

Problems MyLab Accounting

Group A

P5-55A. ***(Learning Objectives 1, 2: Apply GAAP for proper revenue recognition; account for sales returns and allowances)*** Treno Industries sells to wholesalers. Customers must pay within 15 days or at the point of sale using a credit card. Treno's cost of goods sold is 40% of sales. The company had the following selected transactions during March:

LO 1, 2

March	3	Sold $15,000 of merchandise to Whittier Company on account.
March	4	Sold $2,000 of merchandise to Yeller Corp., who paid by credit card. The credit card company charges Treno a fee of 2% on credit card sales.
March	5	Whittier Company returned $500 of the merchandise from March 3.
March	7	Sold $600 of merchandise to Madison, Inc., on account.
March	15	Whittier Company paid the balance of what it owed for the purchase on March 3.
March	19	Sold $22,000 of merchandise to Zucca Co. on account.
March	21	Zucca reported that some of the merchandise received was scratched and returned $1,000 worth of merchandise to Treno.
March	23	Sold $32,000 of merchandise to Nichols Co. on account.
March	25	Zucca paid the balance of what it owed for the purchase on March 19.
March	31	Treno made the adjusting entries for the month to accrue for estimated future returns. Treno estimates that 5% of total sales will be returned.

Requirements

1. Record Treno's transactions, including the cost of goods sold entry for each sale.
2. Calculate the gross sales revenue for the month.

P5-56A. ***(Learning Objectives 1, 3: Apply GAAP for proper revenue recognition; account for sales discounts)*** Preston Industrial Supply offers terms of 2/10, n/30 to its wholesale customers. Preston's cost of goods sold is 25% of sales. The company had the following transactions during October:

LO 1, 3

October	1	Sold $6,000 of merchandise to Penzey Co. on account.
October	3	Sold $2,000 of merchandise to Brownlee Corporation, who paid by credit card. The credit card company charges Preston a fee of 2% on credit card sales.
October	7	Sold $23,000 of merchandise to Marigold Company on account.
October	8	Penzey paid the balance of what it owed for the purchase on October 1.
October	12	Sold $13,000 of merchandise to Wolf Enterprises on account.
October	16	Marigold paid the balance of what it owed for the purchase on October 7.
October	31	Wolf paid the balance of what it owed for the purchase on October 12.

Requirements

1. Record Preston's transactions, including the cost of goods sold entry for each sale.
2. Calculate the net sales revenue for the month.

LO **1, 4, 5, 6**

P5-57A. ***(Learning Objectives 1, 4, 5, 6: Apply GAAP for revenue, receivables, collections, and uncollectibles using the percent-of-sales method; account for notes receivable)*** Lincoln Delivery Corporation is an overnight shipper. Since it sells on credit, the company cannot expect to collect 100% of its accounts receivable. At December 31, 2018, and 2019, respectively, Lincoln reported the following on its balance sheet (in millions of dollars):

	December 31, 2019	December 31, 2018
Accounts receivable	$4,300	$3,900
Less: Allowance for uncollectible accounts	(190)	(210)
Accounts receivable, net	$4,110	$3,690

During the year ended December 31, 2019, Lincoln earned service revenue and collected cash from customers. Assume uncollectible-account expense for the year was 3% of service revenue on account and that Lincoln wrote off uncollectible receivables and made other adjustments as necessary (see below). At year-end, Lincoln ended with the foregoing December 31, 2019, balances.

Requirements

1. Prepare T-accounts for Accounts Receivable and Allowance for Uncollectible Accounts, and insert the December 31, 2018, balances as given.
2. Journalize the following transactions of Lincoln for the year ended December 31, 2019 (explanations are not required):
   a. Service revenue was $32,600 million, of which 15% is cash and the remainder is on account.
   b. Collections from customers on account were $26,364 million.
   c. Uncollectible-account expense was 3% of service revenue on account.
   d. Write-offs of uncollectible accounts receivable were $851 million.
   e. On December 1, Lincoln received a 2-month, 9%, $135 million note receivable from a large corporate customer in exchange for the customer's past due account; Lincoln made the proper year-end adjusting entry for the interest on this note.
   f. Lincoln's December 31, 2019, year-end bank statement reported $40 million of non-sufficient funds (NSF) checks from customers.
3. Post your entries to the Accounts Receivable and the Allowance for Uncollectible Accounts T-accounts.
4. Compute the ending balances for Accounts Receivable and the Allowance for Uncollectible Accounts and compare your balances to the actual December 31, 2019, amounts. They should be the same. How much does Lincoln expect to collect from its customers after December 31, 2019?
5. Show the net effect of these transactions on Lincoln Delivery's net income for the year ended December 31, 2019.

LO **5**

P5-58A. ***(Learning Objective 5: Apply GAAP for uncollectible receivables)*** The September 30, 2019, records of New York Communications include these accounts:

Accounts Receivable	$244,000
Allowance for Doubtful Accounts	(8,000)

During the year, New York Communications estimates Uncollectible-account expense at 1% of credit sales. At year-end (December 31), the company ages its receivables and adjusts the balance in Allowance for Uncollectible Accounts to correspond to the following aging schedule.

	Age of Accounts			
Accounts Receivable	1–30 Days	31–60 Days	61–90 Days	Over 90 Days
$238,000	$144,000	$49,000	$17,000	$28,000
Estimated percent uncollectible	0.2%	2%	15%	35%

During the last quarter of 2019, the company completed the following selected transactions:

Nov 30	Wrote off as uncollectible the $1,300 account receivable from Clupper Carpets and the $500 account receivable from Medina Antiques.
Dec 31	Adjusted the Allowance for Uncollectible Accounts and recorded uncollectible-account expense at year-end, based on the aging of receivables.

Requirements

1. Record the transactions for the last quarter of 2019 in the journal. Explanations are not required.
2. Prepare a T-account for Allowance for Uncollectible Accounts with the appropriate beginning balance. Post the entries from requirement 1 to that account.
3. Show how New York Communications will report its accounts receivable in a comparative balance sheet for 2018 and 2019. (Use the three-line reporting format.) At December 31, 2018, the company's Accounts Receivable balance was $212,000, and the Allowance for Uncollectible Accounts stood at $4,300.

P5-59A. ***(Learning Objectives 5, 7: Apply GAAP for uncollectible receivables; evaluate liquidity through ratios)*** Wronkovich & Sells, an accounting firm, advises Off the Boat Seafood that its financial statements must be changed to conform to GAAP. At December 31, 2018, Off the Boat's accounts include the following: LO 5, 7

Cash	$83,000
Accounts receivable	40,000
Inventory	57,000
Prepaid expenses	18,000
Total current assets	$198,000
Accounts payable	$62,000
Other current liabilities	42,000
Total current liabilities	$104,000

The accounting firm advised Off the Boat of the following:

- Off the Boat has been using the direct write-off method to account for uncollectible receivables. During 2018, the company wrote off bad receivables of $4,500. The aging of Off the Boat's receivables at year-end indicated uncollectibles of $28,500.
- Off the Boat reported net income of $93,000 in 2018.

Requirements

1. Restate Off the Boat's current accounts to conform to GAAP. (Challenge)
2. Compute the company's current ratio and quick (acid-test) ratio both before and after your correction.
3. Determine the company's correct net income for 2018. (Challenge)

LO 6

P5-60A. ***(Learning Objective 6: Apply GAAP for notes receivable)*** Markley Foods completed the following selected transactions.

2018	
Oct 31	Sold goods to Basic Foods, receiving a $30,000, three-month, 5.25% note. (You do not need to make the cost of goods sold journal entry for this transaction.)
Dec 31	Made an adjusting entry to accrue interest on the Basic Foods note.
2019	
Jan 31	Collected the Basic Foods note.
Nov 11	Loaned $15,800 cash to Strafford Shops, receiving a 90-day, 10.0% note.
Dec 31	Accrued the interest on the Strafford Shops note.

Requirements

1. Record the transactions in Markley Foods' journal. Assume that no sales returns are expected. Round all amounts to the nearest dollar. Explanations are not required.
2. Show what Markley Foods will report on its comparative classified balance sheet at December 31, 2019, and December 31, 2018, for Notes Receivable and Interest Receivable.

LO 1, 7

P5-61A. ***(Learning Objectives 1, 7: Show how to speed up cash flow from receivables; evaluate liquidity using ratios)*** The comparative financial statements of Sunset Pools, Inc., for 2020, 2019, and 2018 included the following select data:

	(In millions)		
	2020	2019	2018
Balance sheet			
Current assets:			
Cash	$ 85	$ 60	$ 40
Investment in trading securities	160	175	110
Receivables, net of allowance for uncollectible accounts of $7, $6, and $4, respectively	270	260	240
Inventories	360	335	320
Prepaid expenses	60	45	70
Total current assets	$ 935	$ 875	$ 780
Total current liabilities	$ 620	$ 635	$ 670
Income statement			
Net sales (all on account)	$7,685	$5,500	$5,110

Requirements

1. Compute the following ratios for 2020 and 2019:
   a. Current ratio
   b. Quick (acid-test) ratio
   c. Days' sales outstanding
2. Which ratios improved from 2019 to 2020 and which ratios deteriorated? Are each of the trends favorable or unfavorable?
3. Recommend two ways for Sunset Pools to improve cash flows from receivables.

P5-62A. ***(Learning Objectives 1, 2, 3, 4, 5: Apply GAAP for proper revenue recognition; account for sales allowances; account for sales discounts; account for accounts receivable; write off account; estimate uncollectible account expense)*** LO **1, 2, 3, 4, 5**

Bowerston Variety Store had the following balances as of November 1:

Accounts Receivable	$5,100
Allowance for Uncollectible Accounts	$360

The following selected transactions occurred at Bowerston Variety Store during the month of November:

November	3	Sold $300 of merchandise to Martino's Inc., which paid for the items in cash. The items cost Bowerston $120.
November	5	Sold $600 of merchandise to Liberty Co., which paid by credit card. The credit card company charges Bowerston a fee of 2% on credit card sales. Bowerston's cost of this merchandise was $245.
November	10	Sold $1,300 of merchandise to Willow Creek on account. Terms were 2/10, net 30. Bowerston's cost of this merchandise was $500.
November	11	Sold $2,000 of merchandise to Amherst Shoppes on account. Terms were 2/10, net 30. Bowerston's cost of this merchandise was $900.
November	12	Sold $900 of merchandise to Black River Inc., on account. Terms were 2/10, net 30. Bowerston's cost of this merchandise was $387.
November	18	Willow Creek reported that some of the merchandise received was in a different color than ordered so it returned $150 of the merchandise. The cost to Bowerston was $58.
November	20	Amherst Shoppes paid the balance of what it owed for the purchase on November 11.
November	22	Black River Inc., returned $200 of the merchandise for a refund. Bowerston's cost of the returned merchandise was $86.
November	22	Black River Inc., paid the remaining balance owed for the purchase on November 12.
November	23	Sold $5,000 of merchandise to Charleston Co. on account. Terms were 2/10, net 30. Bowerston's cost of this merchandise was $2,000.
November	25	Willow Creek paid the balance of what it owed for the purchase on November 10.
November	26	Discovered that Etna Enterprises, a customer owing $150 from a July transaction, declared bankruptcy and there is no chance of collection. Wrote off the balance of Etna's account.
November	27	Sold $700 of merchandise to Denis's One-Stop-Shop on account. Terms were 2/10, net 30. Bowerston's cost of this merchandise was $245.
November	1–30	Sales on account during the month of November for transactions not listed individually totaled $7,200. Cost of goods sold for these sales totaled $3,000.
November	1–30	Credit card sales on account during the month of November for transactions not listed individually totaled $2,500. The credit card company charges Bowerston a fee of 2% on credit card sales. Cost of goods sold for these sales totaled $900.
November	1–30	Cash collections on account during the month of November for transactions not listed individually totaled $4,500. (No discounts were taken by these customers.)
November	30	Bowerston made the adjusting entries for the month to accrue for estimated future returns. Bowerston estimates that 5% of total sales will be returned. Bowerston assumes that cost of goods sold is 40% of sales.
November	30	Bowerston made an adjusting entry to estimate uncollectible account expense for the month of November. Bowerston estimates its uncollectible-account expense as 1% of total credit (on account) sales for the month.

Requirements

1. Record Bowerston's November transactions, including the cost of goods sold entries for each sale.
2. Calculate the net realizable value of accounts receivable as of November 30.

Group B

LO 1, 2

P5-63B. ***(Learning Objectives 1, 2: Apply GAAP for proper revenue recognition; account for sales returns and allowances)*** Dearborn Industries sells to wholesalers. Customers must pay within 15 days or at the point of sale using a credit card. Dearborn's cost of goods sold is 35% of sales. The company had the following selected transactions during March:

March 3	Sold $25,000 of merchandise to Greenleaf Company on account.
March 4	Sold $4,000 of merchandise to Yardley Corp., who paid by credit card. The credit card company charges Dearborn a fee of 2% on credit card sales.
March 5	Greenleaf Company returned $5,000 of the merchandise from March 3.
March 7	Sold $1,000 of merchandise to Athens, Inc., on account.
March 15	Greenleaf Company paid the balance of what it owed for the purchase on March 3.
March 19	Sold $12,000 of merchandise to Zurich Co. on account.
March 21	Zurich reported that some of the merchandise received was scratched and returned $500 worth of merchandise to Dearborn.
March 23	Sold $38,000 of merchandise to Niles Co. on account.
March 25	Zurich paid the balance of what it owed for the purchase on March 19.
March 31	Dearborn made the adjusting entries for the month to accrue for estimated future returns. Dearborn estimates that 4% of total sales will be returned.

Requirements

1. Record Dearborn's transactions, including the cost of goods sold entry for each sale.
2. Calculate the gross sales revenue for the month.

LO 1, 3

P5-64B. ***(Learning Objectives 1, 3: Apply GAAP for proper revenue recognition; account for sales discounts)*** Marshall Industrial Supply offers terms of 2/10, n/30 to its wholesale customers. Marshall's cost of goods sold is 30% of sales. The company had the following transactions during October:

October 1	Sold $8,000 of merchandise to Pez Co. on account.
October 3	Sold $1,000 of merchandise to Omaha Corporation, who paid by credit card. The credit card company charges Marshall a fee of 2% on credit card sales.
October 7	Sold $32,000 of merchandise to Magnolia Company on account.
October 8	Pez paid the balance of what it owed for the purchase on October 1.
October 12	Sold $17,000 of merchandise to Wexler Enterprises on account.
October 16	Magnolia paid the balance of what it owed for the purchase on October 7.
October 31	Wexler paid the balance of what it owed for the purchase on October 12.

Requirements

1. Record Marshall's transactions, including the cost of goods sold entry for each sale.
2. Calculate the net sales revenue for the month.

P5-65B. ***(Learning Objectives 1, 4, 5, 6: Apply GAAP for revenue, receivables, collections, and uncollectibles using the percent-of-sales method; account for notes receivable)*** Hopewell Shipping Corporation is an overnight shipper. Since it sells on credit, the company cannot expect to collect 100% of its accounts receivable. At October 31, 2018, and 2019, respectively, Hopewell reported the following on its balance sheet (in millions of dollars):

LO 1, 4, 5, 6

	October 31, 2019	October 31, 2018
Accounts receivable	$4,200	$4,000
Less: Allowance for uncollectible accounts	(170)	(160)
Accounts receivable, net	$4,030	$3,840

During the year ended October 31, 2019, Hopewell earned service revenue and collected cash from customers. Assume uncollectible-account expense for the year was 5% of service revenue on account and Hopewell wrote off uncollectible receivables and made other adjustments as necessary (see below). At year-end, Hopewell ended with the foregoing October 31, 2019, balances.

Requirements

1. Prepare T-accounts for Accounts Receivable and Allowance for Uncollectible Accounts, and insert the October 31, 2018, balances as given.
2. Journalize the following transactions of Hopewell for the year ended October 31, 2019 (explanations are not required):
   a. Service revenue was $32,500 million, of which 8% is cash and the remainder is on account.
   b. Collections from customers on account were $28,123 million. No sales discounts were taken.
   c. Uncollectible-account expense was 5% of service revenue on account.
   d. Write-offs of uncollectible accounts receivable were $1,485 million.
   e. On October 1, Hopewell received a 2-month, 9%, $135 million note receivable from a large corporate customer in exchange for the customer's past due account; Hopewell made the proper year-end adjusting entry for the interest on this note.
   f. Hopewell's October 31, 2019, year-end bank statement reported $43 million of non-sufficient funds (NSF) checks from customers.
3. Post your entries to the Accounts Receivable and Allowance for Uncollectible Accounts T-accounts.
4. Compute the ending balances for Accounts Receivable and Allowance for Uncollectible Accounts and compare your balances to the actual October 31, 2019, amounts. They should be the same. How much does Hopewell expect to collect from its customers after October 31, 2019?
5. Show the net effect of these transactions on Hopewell's net income for the year ended October 31, 2019.

LO 5

P5-66B. ***(Learning Objective 5: Apply GAAP for uncollectible receivables)*** The September 30, 2019, records of West Point Communications include these accounts:

Accounts Receivable	$249,000
Allowance for Doubtful Accounts	(8,000)

During the year, West Point Communications estimates Uncollectible-account expense at 1% of credit sales. At year-end (December 31), the company ages its receivables and adjusts the balance in Allowance for Uncollectible Accounts to correspond to the following aging schedule:

	Age of Accounts			
Accounts Receivable	1–30 Days	31–60 Days	61–90 Days	Over 90 Days
$235,000	$132,000	$52,000	$15,000	$36,000
Estimated percent uncollectible	0.5%	2%	15%	35%

During the last quarter of 2019, the company completed the following selected transactions:

Nov 30	Wrote off as uncollectible the $1,200 account receivable from Looper Carpets and the $800 account receivable from Williams Antiques.
Dec 31	Adjusted the Allowance for Uncollectible Accounts and recorded uncollectible-account expense at year-end, based on the aging of receivables.

Requirements

1. Record the transactions for the last quarter of 2019 in the journal. Explanations are not required.
2. Prepare a T-account for Allowance for Uncollectible Accounts with the appropriate beginning balance. Post the entries from requirement 1 to that account.
3. Show how West Point Communications will report its accounts receivable in a comparative balance sheet for 2018 and 2019. (Use the three-line reporting format.) At December 31, 2018, the company's Accounts Receivable balance was $212,000 and the Allowance for Uncollectible Accounts stood at $4,800.

LO 5, 7

P5-67B. ***(Learning Objectives 5, 7: Apply GAAP for uncollectible receivables; evaluate liquidity through ratios)*** McClinton and Jefferson, an accounting firm, advises Lakeside Seafood that its financial statement must be changed to conform to GAAP. At December 31, 2018, Lakeside's accounts include the following:

Cash	$77,000
Accounts receivable	39,000
Inventory	59,000
Prepaid expenses	9,000
Total current assets	$184,000
Accounts payable	$62,000
Other current liabilities	42,000
Total current liabilities	$104,000

The accounting firm advised Lakeside of the following:

- Lakeside has been using the direct write-off method to account for uncollectible receivables. During 2018, the company wrote off bad receivables of $8,500. The aging of Lakeside's receivables at year-end indicated uncollectibles of $23,500.
- Lakeside reported net income of $93,000 for 2018.

Requirements

1. Restate Lakeside's current accounts to conform to GAAP. (Challenge)
2. Compute the company's current ratio and quick (acid-test) ratio both before and after your correction.
3. Determine the company's correct net income for 2018. (Challenge)

P5-68B. ***(Learning Objective 6: Apply GAAP for notes receivable)*** Garrett Meals completed the following selected transactions: LO 6

2018		
Oct	31	Sold goods to Rose Foods, receiving a $32,000, three-month 5.5% note. (You do do not need to make the cost of goods sold journal entry for this transaction.)
Dec	31	Made an adjusting entry to accrue interest on the Rose Foods note.
2017		
Jan	31	Collected the Rose Foods note.
Nov	11	Loaned $15,800 to Franklin Shops, receiving a 90-day, 9.75% note.
Dec	31	Accrued the interest on the Franklin Shops note.

Requirements

1. Record the transactions in Garrett Meals' journal. Assume that no sales returns are expected. Round all amounts to the nearest dollar. Explanations are not required.
2. Show what Garrett Meals will report on its comparative classified balance sheet at December 31, 2019, and December 31, 2018, for Notes Receivable and Interest Receivable.

P5-69B. ***(Learning Objectives 1, 7: Show how to speed up cash flow from receivables; evaluate liquidity using ratios)*** The comparative financial statements of Diamond Pools, Inc., for 2020, 2019, and 2018 included the following select data: LO 1, 7

	(In millions)		
	2020	2019	2018
Balance sheet			
Current assets:			
Cash	$ 90	$ 95	$ 60
Investment in trading securities	150	180	115
Receivables, net of allowance for uncollectible accounts of $7, $6, and $4, respectively	270	280	230
Inventories	340	355	325
Prepaid expenses	50	40	35
Total current assets	$ 900	$ 950	$ 765
Total current liabilities	$ 550	$ 640	$ 650
Income statement			
Net sales (all on account)	$7,700	$5,355	$4,745

Requirements

1. Compute the following ratios for 2020 and 2019:
   a. Current ratio
   b. Quick (acid-test) ratio
   c. Days' sales outstanding
2. Which ratios improved from 2019 to 2020 and which ratios deteriorated? Are each of the trends favorable or unfavorable?
3. Recommend two ways for Diamond Pools to improve cash flows from receivables.

LO 1, 2, 3, 4, 5

P5-70B. ***(Learning Objectives 1, 2, 3, 4, 5: Apply GAAP for proper revenue recognition; account for sales allowances; account for sales discounts; account for accounts receivable; write off account; estimate uncollectible account expense)***

Baker Variety Store had the following balances as of November 1:

Accounts Receivable	$10,100
Allowance for Uncollectible Accounts	$760

The following selected transactions occurred at Baker Variety Store during the month of November:

November 3	Sold $500 of merchandise to Maxwell's Inc., which paid for the items in cash. The items cost Baker $200.
November 5	Sold $1,600 of merchandise to Lemmon Co., which paid by credit card. The credit card company charges Baker a fee of 2% on credit card sales. Baker's cost of this merchandise was $592.
November 10	Sold $1,500 of merchandise to Rapid City on account. Terms were 2/10, net 30. Baker's cost of this merchandise was $500.
November 11	Sold $20,000 of merchandise to Appalachian Shoppes on account. Terms were 2/10, net 30. Baker's cost of this merchandise was $8,400.
November 12	Sold $800 of merchandise to Ontario Inc., on account. Terms were 2/10, net 30. Baker's cost of this merchandise was $344.
November 18	Rapid City reported that some of the merchandise received was in a different color than ordered so it returned $100 of the merchandise. The cost to Baker was $38.
November 20	Appalachian Shoppes paid the balance of what it owed for the purchase on November 11.
November 22	Ontario Inc., returned $300 of the merchandise for a refund. Baker's cost of the returned merchandise was $129.
November 22	Ontario Inc., paid the remaining balance owed for the purchase on November 12.
November 23	Sold $7,000 of merchandise to Carlsbad Co. on account. Terms were 2/10, net 30. Baker's cost of this merchandise was $2,800.
November 25	Rapid City paid the balance of what it owed for the purchase on November 10.
November 26	Discovered that Eagle Enterprises, a customer owing $125 from a July transaction, declared bankruptcy and there is no chance of collection. Wrote off the balance of Eagle's account.
November 27	Sold $1,300 of merchandise to Dave's One-Stop-Shop on account. Terms were 2/10, net 30. Baker's cost of this merchandise was $245.
November 1–30	Sales on account during the month of November for transactions not listed individually totaled $9,200. Cost of goods sold for these sales totaled $3,895.
November 1–30	Credit card sales on account during the month of November for transactions not listed individually totaled $5,000. The credit card company charges Baker a fee of 2% on credit card sales. Cost of goods sold for these sales totaled $1,800.
November 1–30	Cash collections on account during the month of November for transactions not listed individually totaled $7,000. (No discounts were taken by these customers.)
November 30	Baker made the adjusting entries for the month to accrue for estimated future returns. Baker estimates that 5% of total sales will be returned. Baker assumes that cost of goods sold is 40% of sales.
November 30	Baker made an adjusting entry to estimate uncollectible account expense for the month of November. Baker estimates its uncollectible-account expense as 1% of total credit (on account) sales for the month.

Requirements

1. Record Baker's November transactions, including the cost of goods sold entries for each sale.
2. Calculate the net realizable value of accounts receivable as of November 30.

Challenge Exercises and Problem

LO 1

E5-71. ***(Learning Objective 1: Show how to speed up cash from receivables)*** Patterson Shirt Company sells on credit and manages its own receivables. Average experience for the past three years has been the following:

	Cash	Credit	Total
Sales	$250,000	$250,000	$500,000
Cost of goods sold	125,000	125,000	250,000
Uncollectible-account expense	—	18,000	18,000
Other expenses	82,500	82,500	165,000

The owner of Patterson is considering whether to accept credit cards (VISA and MasterCard) instead of granting credit to customers. If Patterson were to accept credit cards, the owner expects total sales to increase by 10% but cash sales to remain unchanged. Further, if Patterson were to accept credit cards, the business can save $9,000 on other expenses, but the credit card processors charge 3% on credit card sales.

Requirement

1. Should Patterson Shirt Company start accepting credit cards? Show the computations of net income under the present plan and under the credit card plan. (Ignore estimated sales returns and refunds for this exercise.)

LO 4, 5

E5-72. ***(Learning Objectives 4, 5: Apply GAAP for receivables and uncollectible receivables)*** Suppose Easton, Inc., reported net receivables of $2,582 million and $2,260 million at January 31, 2019, and 2018, respectively, after subtracting allowances of $72 million and $67 million at these respective dates. Easton earned total revenue of $43,333 million (all on account) and recorded uncollectible-account expense of $13 million for the year ended January 31, 2019.

Requirement

1. Use this information to measure the following amounts for the year ended January 31, 2019:
   a. Write-offs of uncollectible receivables
   b. Collections from customers

LO 1, 2, 3, 4, 5

P5-73. ***(Learning Objectives 1, 2, 3, 4, 5: Account for and evaluate accounts receivable including returns, sales discounts, and uncollectible accounts)*** The balance sheet of Aqua, Inc., a world leader in the design and sale of telescopic equipment, reported the following information on its balance sheets for 2018 and 2017 (figures are in thousands):

(In thousands)	December 31, 2018	December 31, 2017
Accounts receivable (net of allowance of $1,080 and $940, respectively)	$8,300	$8,560

In 2018, Aqua recorded $15,700 (gross) in sales (all on account), of which $700 (gross) was returned for credit. The cost of sales was $7,700; the cost of the merchandise returned was $400. Aqua offers its customers credit terms of 2/10, n/30. Ninety percent of collections on accounts receivable were made within the discount period. Aqua wrote off uncollectible accounts receivable in the amount of $120 (gross) during 2018. Sales returns are estimated to be 4% of sales.

Requirements

1. Calculate the amount of uncollectible accounts expense recorded by Aqua in 2018.
2. Calculate Aqua's cash collections from customers in 2018.
3. Open T-accounts for Accounts Receivable and Allowance for Uncollectible Accounts. Enter the beginning balances into each of these accounts. Prepare summary journal entries to record the transactions and post the transactions to the T-accounts for the following for 2018:
   a. Sales revenue
   b. Cost of goods sold
   c. Estimated returns inventory
   d. Cost of estimated returns
   e. Merchandise returned
   f. Cost of merchandise returned
   g. Collections
   h. Write-offs of uncollectible accounts
   i. Uncollectible-accounts expense

APPLY YOUR KNOWLEDGE

Serial Case

LO 4

C5-74. *(Learning Objective 4: Analyze accounts receivable for a company in the restaurant industry)*

Note: This case is part of The Cheesecake Factory serial case contained in every chapter in this textbook.

The Cheesecake Factory Incorporated (NASDAQ: CAKE) operates two bakeries in the United States where it makes over 70 desserts for its own restaurants. In addition, the Cheesecake Factory bakeries sell selected desserts to a variety of foodservice operators and retailers, including **Sam's Club, Walmart, Target, BJ's Wholesale Club,** and **Barnes & Noble** Cafés.

The Cheesecake Factory has accounts receivable on its financial statements. The primary source of its accounts receivable is its sales to bakery customers.

Requirements

1. Identify the financial statement where The Cheesecake Factory accounts receivable would be found. What is the balance of The Cheesecake Factory's accounts receivable as of January 3, 2017? Did its accounts receivable balance increase or decrease since its 2015 fiscal year?
2. Assume that BJ's Wholesale Club places an order with The Cheesecake Factory bakery for 1,000 Cheesecake Factory Original Cheesecakes on account (FOB shipping point) for a total cost of $7,500. No discount was offered for early payment. Write the journal entry, if any, which would be made on each of the following dates by The Cheesecake Factory (ignore the cost of sales journal entry here):
   a. Order date
   b. Shipment date
   c. Payment date
3. How will The Cheesecake Factory's assets, liabilities, and equity be impacted on each of the previous dates related to BJ's Wholesale Club order?

Decision Cases

C5-75. ***(Learning Objectives 1, 4, 5: Apply GAAP for revenue, accounts receivable, and uncollectible receivables)*** A fire during 2018 destroyed most of the accounting records of Lyons Entertainment, Inc. The only accounting data for 2018 that Lyons can come up with are the following balances at December 31, 2018. The general manager also knows that uncollectible-account expense should be 5% of its service revenue on credit.

LO 1, 4, 5

Accounts receivable, December 31, 2018	$180,000
Less: Allowance for bad debts	(22,000)
Total expenses, excluding bad-debt expense	670,000
Collections from customers	840,000
Write-offs of bad receivables	30,000
Accounts receivable, December 31, 2017	110,000

Prepare a summary income statement for Lyons Entertainment, Inc., for the year ended December 31, 2018. The stockholders want to know whether the company was profitable in 2018. Use a T-account for Accounts Receivable to compute service revenue. Assume that all revenues are on credit.

C5-76. ***(Learning Objectives 5, 7: Apply GAAP for uncollectible receivables; evaluate liquidity through ratios)*** Suppose you work in the loan department of Third National Bank. Byron Blakely, the owner of Byron's Beauty Solutions, has come to you seeking a loan for $500,000 to expand operations. He proposes to use accounts receivable as collateral for the loan and has provided you with the following information from the company's most recent financial statements:

LO 5, 7

	2019	2018	2017
	(In thousands)		
Sales (all on account)	$1,475	$1,001	$902
Cost of goods sold	876	647	605
Gross profit	599	354	297
Other expenses	518	287	253
Net profit or (loss) before taxes	$ 81	$ 67	$ 44
Accounts receivable	$ 128	$ 107	$ 94
Allowance for doubtful accounts	13	11	9

Requirement

1. Analyze the trends of sales, days' sales outstanding, and cash collections from customers for 2019 and 2018. Would you make the loan to Blakely? Support your decision with facts and figures. Assume there are no write-offs in 2018 and 2019.

Ethical Issue

C5-77. Strasburg Loan Company is in the consumer loan business. Strasburg borrows from banks and loans out the money at higher interest rates. Strasburg's bank requires Strasburg to submit quarterly financial statements to keep its line of credit. Strasburg's main asset is Notes Receivable. Therefore, Uncollectible-Account Expense and Allowance for Uncollectible Accounts are important accounts for the company.

Raquel Lanser, the company's owner, prefers that net income reflect a steady increase in a smooth pattern, rather than an increase in some periods and a decrease in other periods. To report smoothly increasing net income, Lanser underestimates uncollectible-account expense in some periods. In other periods, Lanser overestimates the expense. She reasons that the income overstatements roughly offset the income understatements over time.

Requirements

1. What is the ethical issue in this situation?
2. Who are the stakeholders? What are the possible consequences to each?
3. Analyze the alternatives from the following standpoints: (a) economic, (b) legal, (c) ethical.
4. What would you do? How would you justify your decision?

Focus on Financials | Apple Inc.

LO **1, 7**

(Learning Objectives 1, 7: Apply GAAP for proper revenue recognition; calculate ratios) Refer to **Apple Inc.'s** consolidated financial statements in Appendix A and online in the filings section of **www.sec.gov**.

Requirements

1. Using the Revenue Recognition section of Note 1 as a reference, describe how Apple Inc., recognizes revenue. From what types of activities does Apple earn its revenue?
2. The third account listed on Apple's Consolidated Balance Sheet is called "Accounts receivable, less allowances." To what does the "allowances" refer?
3. Refer to the Accounts Receivable section of Note 2. What kinds of accounts receivable are included in Apple Inc.'s receivables?
4. How much is the allowance for uncollectible accounts in 2016 and 2015?
5. Calculate the current ratio, quick (acid-test) ratio, and net working capital for Apple Inc., for 2016 and 2015. Evaluate Apple Inc.'s liquidity trend over the two years. What other information might be helpful in evaluating these statistics?

Focus on Analysis | Under Armour, Inc.

LO 1, 4, 7

(Learning Objectives 1, 4, 7: Apply GAAP for revenue recognition; account for and control accounts receivable; calculate ratios) This case is based on **Under Armour, Inc.'s**, consolidated balance sheets, consolidated statements of income, and Note 2 of its financial statements (Significant Accounting Policies) found online in the filings section of **www.sec.gov**. You can retrieve the 2016 Under Armour financial statements at **www.sec.gov** by clicking on Filings and then searching for "Under Armour" under Company Filings. When you see the list of filings for the company, select the Form 10-K for 2016. Be sure to retrieve the 2016 financial statements, not another year.

Requirements

1. Describe Under Armour, Inc.'s, revenue recognition policy. According to the Concentration of Credit Risk section of Note 2, from what sources does it earn most of its revenue?
2. Since Under Armour, Inc., is a consumer retail business, most of its retail sales are cash sales. However, accounts receivable still comprise about 18% ($280/$1,549) of its current assets. What type of customers do business with Under Armour, Inc., on account? Why is this necessary? Use Note 2, Concentration of Credit Risk section.
3. Compute the following for 2016:
   a. Average daily sales, using total revenues.
   b. Days' sales outstanding. Assume all sales are on account.
4. Calculate the current ratio, quick (acid-test) ratio, and net working capital for Under Armour, Inc., for 2016 and 2015. Evaluate the two-year trend in Under Armour, Inc.'s, liquidity. What other information might be helpful in evaluating these statistics?

Group Project

Jillian Michaels and Dee Childress worked for several years as sales representatives for **Xerox Corporation**. During this time, they became close friends as they acquired expertise with the company's full range of copying and printing equipment. Now they see an opportunity to put their expertise to work and fulfill lifelong desires to establish their own business. Navarro Community College, located in their city, is expanding, and there is no copy center within five miles of the campus. Business in the area is booming, office buildings and apartments are springing up, and the population of the Navarro section of the city is growing.

Michaels and Childress want to open a printing, copying, and shipping center, similar to **FedEx Kinko's**, near the Navarro campus. A small shopping center across the street from the college has a vacancy that would fit their needs. Michaels and Childress each have $35,000 to invest in the business, but they forecast the need for $200,000 to renovate the store and purchase some equipment. Xerox Corporation will lease two large printers to them at a total monthly rental of $6,000. With enough cash to see them through the first six months of operation, they are confident they can make the business succeed. The two women work very well together, and both have excellent credit ratings. Michaels and Childress must borrow $130,000 to start the business, advertise its opening, and keep it running for its first six months.

Requirements

Assume two roles: (1) Michaels and Childress, the partners who will own Navarro Copy Center; and (2) loan officers at Synergy Bank.

1. As a group, visit a copy center to familiarize yourselves with its operations. If possible, interview the manager or another employee. Then write a loan request that Michaels and Childress will submit to Synergy Bank with the intent of borrowing $130,000 to be paid back over three years. The loan will be a personal loan to the partnership of Michaels and Childress, not to Navarro Copy Center. The request should specify all the details of the plan that will motivate the bank to grant the loan. Include a budget for each of the first six months of operation of the proposed copy center.
2. As a group, interview a loan officer in a bank. Write Synergy Bank's reply to the loan request. Specify all the details that the bank should require as conditions for making the loan.
3. If necessary, modify the loan request or the bank's reply in order to reach agreement between the two parties.

Quick Check Answers

1. *a*
2. *b*
3. *c*
4. *b*
5. *c*
6. *d*
7. *d ($500,000 + $2,600,000 − $700,000 = $2,400,000)*
8. *d ($39,000 × 0.03 = $1,170)*
9. *b ($900 + $1,615 = $2,515)*
10. *c ($1,260 − $900 = $360)*
11. *a*
12. *d ($8,000 − $1,260 = $6,740)*
13. *c ($2,500 − $70 = $2,430; $500 − $70 = $430; $2,430 − $430 = $2,000)*
14. *b [($1,650 × 0.08 × 1/12) = $11]*
15. *d [$30,000 + ($30,000 × 0.12 × 6/12) = $31,800]*
16. *b*
17. *a [$1,264,800 / {($38,000 + $43,600)/2}] = 31; 365 / 31 = 12 days (rounded)*
18. *b ($2,000 + $7,000 + $5,000) / ($5,000 + $9,000) = 1.0*

Try It Solutions

Page 260

	Millions
Customers owed Apple Inc.	$15,807 ($15,754 + $53)
Apple Inc. expected not to collect the allowance of.....	(53)
Apple Inc. expected to collect—net realizable value	$15,754

Notice that to determine the *total,* or *gross* amount, customers owed, you have to add the amount of the allowance back to the net realizable value ($15,754 million + $53 million = $15,807 million). Of this amount, $53 million was expected not to be collected, leaving $15,754 million that the company expected to collect (its net realizable value). Although the gross amount is not shown in the financial statements, it is useful for analysis purposes, as shown on page 259.

6 Inventory and Cost of Goods Sold

LEARNING OBJECTIVES

1. **Show** how to account for inventory
2. **Apply and compare** various inventory cost methods
3. **Explain and apply** underlying U.S. GAAP for inventory
4. **Compute and evaluate** gross profit (margin) percentage, inventory turnover, and days' inventory outstanding (DIO)
5. **Use** the cost-of-goods-sold (COGS) model to make management decisions
6. **Analyze** effects of inventory errors

SPOTLIGHT

Under Armour, Inc.'s Performance Slips

Under Armour, Inc.'s, products are sold worldwide and are worn by athletes at all levels, from youth to professional, on playing fields around the globe, as well as by consumers with active lifestyles. In the past, Under Armour's stock has been a high performer. However, in 2016 the company's stock price fell dramatically. Why?

We can answer this question by examining some trends on the company's Consolidated Statements of Income (page 306). Net revenues in 2016 (line 3) were about \$4.83 billion, an increase of about 21.8% over the previous year (about \$3.96 billion). At first glance, this percentage increase looks great. However, 2016's increase was far less than the 28.5% increase in net revenues Under Armour experienced in 2015 from 2014 (\$3.96 billion vs. \$3.08 billion).

At the same time, Cost of Goods Sold, the largest expense on the Consolidated Statements of Income (line 4), increased by about 25.6%—from \$2.06 billion in 2015 to \$2.58 billion in 2016. This is almost 4% more than the percentage increase in sales, which is not a good sign. Consequently, the company's gross profit (net revenues – cost of goods sold) of \$2.24 billion in 2016 was up by only about 17.6% over 2015 (\$1.91 billion).

Under Armour's gross profit percentage (gross profit ÷ net sales) slipped from 48.1% (\$1.91 billion ÷ \$3.96 billion) in 2015 to slightly more than 46.4% (\$2.24 billion ÷ \$4.83 billion) in 2016. That means the company earned 1.7% less profit on its products in 2016 than it did in 2015. Another potentially troublesome sign: Under Armour's 2016 Consolidated Balance Sheets (page 306) show that the company's inventory balances as of December 31, 2016 (\$917.5 million), were up by 17.2% over their 2015 levels (\$783 million).

In summary, Under Armour experienced big problems with its sales and gross profit growth in 2016, and its unsold inventory level climbed. This helps explain why the company's stock price lost 78% of its value between April 2016 and March 2017. ●

	A	B	C	D
1	**Under Armour, Inc. Consolidated Balance Sheets (partial)**	**Dec. 31, 2016**	**Dec. 31, 2015**	**% change**
2	**In Thousands of $**			
3	**Assets**			
4				
5	Cash and cash equivalents	$ 250,470	$ 129,852	
6	Accounts receivable, net	622,685	433,638	
7	Inventories	917,491	783,031	17.20%
8	Prepaid expenses and other current assets	174,507	152,242	
9	**Total current assets**	1,965,153	1,498,763	
10	Property and equipment, net	804,211	538,531	
11	Goodwill	563,591	585,181	
12	Intangible assets, net	64,310	75,686	
13	Deferred income taxes	136,862	92,157	
14	Other long term assets	110,204	75,652	
15	**Total assets**	$ 3,644,331	$ 2,865,970	
16				

Source: Data from the U.S. Securities and Exchange Commission EDGAR Company Filings, www.sec.gov

	A	B	C	D
1	**Under Armour, Inc. Consolidated Statements of Income**		**12 Months Ended**	
2	**In Thousands of $**	**Dec. 31, 2016**	**Dec. 31, 2015**	**Dec. 31, 2014**
3	Net revenues	$ 4,825,335	$ 3,963,313	$ 3,084,370
4	Cost of goods sold	2,584,724	2,057,766	1,572,164
5	Gross profit	2,240,611	1,905,547	1,512,206
6	Selling, general and administrative expenses	1,823,140	1,497,000	1,158,251
7	Income from operations	417,471	408,547	353,955
8	Interest expense, net	(26,434)	(14,628)	(5,335)
9	Other expense, net	(2,755)	(7,234)	(6,410)
10	Income before income taxes	388,282	386,685	342,210
11	Provision for income taxes	131,303	154,112	134,168
12	Net income	$ 256,979	$ 232,573	$ 208,042
13	% change in Net revenues 2015 to 2016	21.8%		
14	% change in Cost of goods sold 2015 to 2016	25.6%		
15	% change in Gross profit	17.6%		
16	Gross profit % (Gross profit/Net revenues)	46.4%	48.1%	
17				

Source: Data from the U.S. Securities and Exchange Commission EDGAR Company Filings, www.sec.gov

Companies that sell goods rather than services generally carry inventory, or merchandise, on their balance sheets. Cost of goods sold is the largest and most important expense on the income statements of companies such as these. This chapter explains how inventory and cost of goods sold are accounted for and how they affect a business's profit measures. The chapter also discusses inventory turnover measures, which indicate how fast products are sold. All of these are important measures of success for a merchandising company.

Try It in Excel®

You can access the most current annual report of Under Armour, Inc., in Excel format at www.sec.gov. Using the "FILINGS" link on the toolbar at the top of the page, select "Company Filings Search." This will take you to the "EDGAR Company Filings" page. Type "Under Armour" in the company name box, and select "Search." This will produce the "EDGAR Search Results" page showing the company name. Click on the "CIK" link beside the company name. This will pull up a list of the reports that the company has filed with the SEC. Under the "Filing Type" box, type "10-K." Form 10-K is the SEC form for the company's annual report. Find the year that you wish to view. Click on the "Interactive Data" box, which takes you to the "View Filing Data" page. You may choose to either open or download the Excel files containing the company's selected financial statements.

SHOW HOW TO ACCOUNT FOR INVENTORY

1 Show how to account for inventory

How do the financial statements of a merchandiser such as Under Armour, Inc., differ from those of a service company such as **Century 21 Real Estate**? The financial statements in Exhibit 6-1 highlight how service entities differ from merchandisers.

Exhibit 6-1 Contrasting a Service Company with a Merchandising Company

Service Company

	A	B
1	**Century 21 Real Estate Income Statement Year Ended December 31, 2016**	
2	*Service revenue*	$ XXX
3	*Expenses:*	
4	Salary expense	X
5	Depreciation expense	X
6	Income tax expense	X
7	Net income	$ X
8		

Merchandising Company

	A	B
1	**Under Armour, Inc. Income Statement Year Ended December 31, 2016**	
2	*Sales revenue*	$ XXX
3	*Cost of goods sold*	XXX
4	Gross profit	XXX
5	Operating expenses:	
6	Salary expense	X
7	Depreciation expense	X
8	Income tax expense	X
9	Net income (net loss)	$ X
10		

	A	B
1	**Century 21 Real Estate Balance Sheet (Partial) December 31, 2016**	
2	**Assets**	
3		
4	Current assets	
5	Cash	$ X
6	Accounts receivable, net	X
7	Prepaid expenses	X
8		

	A	B
1	**Under Armour, Inc. Balance Sheet (Partial) December 31, 2016**	
2	**Assets**	
3		
4	Current assets	
5	Cash	$ X
6	Accounts receivable	X
7	*Inventory*	X
8	Prepaid expenses	X
9		

Merchandisers have two accounts that service entities don't need:

- Cost of goods sold on the income statement
- Inventory on the balance sheet

The basic concept of accounting for merchandise inventory can be illustrated with an example. Suppose that an outlet store has in stock 300 men's Under Armour fleece hoodies that cost $30 each. The store marks each hoodie up by $20 and sells 200 of the hoodies for $50 each. After the sale of 200 hoodies:

- The store's balance sheet reports the 100 hoodies that the company still holds in inventory.
- The income statement reports both the revenue from and the cost of the 200 hoodies sold, as shown in Exhibit 6-2.

Exhibit 6-2 | Relationship Between Inventory and Cost of Goods Sold

Balance Sheet (partial)		Income Statement (partial)	
Current assets		Sales revenue	
Cash	$XXX	(200 hoodies @ $50 each)	$10,000
Accounts receivable	XXX	Cost of goods sold	
Inventory (100 hoodies @ $30 each)	3,000	(200 hoodies @ $30 each)	6,000
Prepaid expenses	XXX	Gross profit	$ 4,000

Here is the basic concept of how we distinguish **inventory**, the asset, from **cost of goods sold**, the expense. The cost of the inventory sold shifts from asset to expense when the seller fulfills its contract with the customer, delivers the goods to the buyer and recognizes revenue.

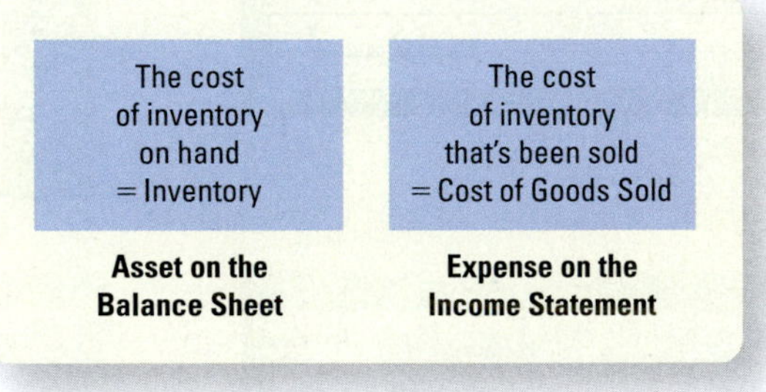

Sales Price versus Cost of Inventory

Note the difference between the sales price, also called the selling price, of inventory and the cost of inventory. In our example,

- sales revenue is based on the *sales price* of the inventory sold ($50 per hoodie);
- cost of goods sold is based on the *cost* of the inventory sold ($30 per hoodie);
- inventory on the balance sheet is based on the *cost* of the inventory still on hand ($30 per hoodie).

Exhibit 6-2 shows these items.

Gross profit, also called *gross margin,* is the excess of sales revenue over a business's cost of goods sold. The word *gross* indicates that operating expenses have not yet been subtracted from the sales revenue—only the cost of the goods sold has been subtracted at this point. Exhibit 6-3 shows actual inventory and cost-of-goods-sold data adapted from the financial statements of Under Armour, Inc.

Exhibit 6-3 | Under Armour, Inc., Inventories and Cost of Goods Sold

	A	B	C
1	**Under Armour, Inc.** **Consolidated Balance Sheet (Partial, Adapted)** **December 31, 2016**		
2	**Assets**		
3	**(in millions)**		
4	Current assets		
5	Cash and cash equivalents		$ 250.5
6	Accounts receivable, net		622.7
7	Inventories		917.5
8			

	A	B	C
1	**Under Armour, Inc.** **Consolidated Statement of Income (Partial, Adapted)** **Year Ended December 31, 2016**		
2	**(In millions)**		
3	Net (sales) revenues		$ 4,825.3
4	Cost of goods sold		2,584.7
5	Gross profit (margin)		$ 2,240.6
6			

Source: Data from the U.S. Securities and Exchange Commission EDGAR Company Filings, www.sec.gov

Under Armour's inventory of $917.5 million represents

Inventory (balance sheet)	=	Number of units of inventory *on hand*	×	Cost per unit of inventory

Under Armour's cost of goods sold ($2,584.7 million) represents

Cost of goods sold (income statement)	=	Number of units of inventory *sold*	×	Cost per unit of inventory

Let's see what "units of inventory" and "cost per unit" mean.

Number of Units of Inventory. The number of inventory units on hand is determined by a physical count of the goods at year-end. In these counts, companies have to be careful to include only goods they legally own. For this purpose, a retail business is required to *exclude* from its inventory all items that are held on **consignment**. Consignment inventory consists of items that other companies still own but that the retailer is willing to sell (for a fee). Consignment inventory is reported on the balance sheet of the owner, not the company holding the inventory. In addition, a company might have to include items that are in transit from its suppliers or in transit to its customers, depending on the terms of shipment. Recall from Chapter 5 that a contract's shipping terms, otherwise known as *FOB (free on board) terms*, indicate who owns the goods at a particular point in time. When the sales contract specifies FOB shipping point (the most common business practice), legal title to the goods passes from the seller to the buyer when the inventory leaves the seller's place of business; therefore the buyer would include the goods in inventory when the inventory leaves the seller. When the contract specifies FOB destination, the title to the goods does not pass from the seller to the buyer until the goods arrive at the buyer's receiving dock; these goods would remain in the inventory of the seller until arriving at their destination.

Cost per Unit of Inventory. The cost per unit of inventory poses a challenge because companies purchase goods at different prices throughout the year. Which unit costs go into ending inventory? Which unit costs go into cost of goods sold?

Starting on page 313, we discuss how the selection between different accounting methods determines reported amounts on the balance sheet and the income statement. First, however, let's take a step back and look at how inventory accounting systems work.

Periodic versus Perpetual Inventory Systems

There are two main types of inventory accounting systems: the periodic system and the perpetual system. The **periodic inventory system**, which is discussed in more detail in Appendix 6A, is a system whereby goods are counted by hand and then priced at certain intervals (monthly, quarterly, or yearly). For example, a small local hardware store that has been in business for many years might not keep a running record of every board or nail it sells. Instead, the store might count and price its inventory periodically—at least once a year—to determine inventory quantities. The store would also keep a record of inventory purchased. It would then calculate Cost of Goods Sold using the following formula:

$$\text{Beginning Inventory} + \text{Purchases} - \text{Ending Inventory} = \text{Cost of Goods Sold}$$

In contrast, a **perpetual inventory system** uses computer software and barcodes to keep a running record of inventory on hand, purchased, and sold. When a business purchases inventory, employees run items through a scanner which reads the barcode on them and adds them to the inventory account as well as to accounts payable. When items of inventory are sold, they are scanned again. The company's computer system records the sale, the cost of goods sold, and updates the inventory, removing the item from the company's records, all in one step. By keeping a running record of all items purchased as well as sold, in addition to beginning and ending inventories, a company always has a record of how much inventory *should be* on hand. Then, by taking periodic physical counts of inventory actually on hand, the business can compare the counts with the perpetual records. This helps the business track down inventory errors as well as theft. Because computers have simplified the process of keeping track of inventories, most businesses today use perpetual inventory systems.

Recording Transactions in the Perpetual System. All accounting systems record each purchase of inventory. When an Under Armour outlet store makes a sale, two entries are needed in the perpetual system:

- The company records the sale—debits Cash or Accounts Receivable and credits Sales Revenue for the sales price of the goods.
- The Under Armour outlet store also debits Cost of Goods Sold and credits Inventory for the cost of the inventory sold.

Exhibit 6-4 shows the accounting for inventory in a perpetual system. Panel A shows the journal entries and the T-accounts, and Panel B shows the income statement and the balance sheet. All amounts are assumed. (Appendix 6A shows how these same transactions are accounted for using a periodic inventory system.)

Exhibit 6-4 | Recording and Reporting Inventory—Perpetual System

PANEL A—Recording Transactions and the T-accounts (All amounts are assumed)

Journal Entry

A1

	A		C	D	G
1	1.	Inventory		560,000	
2		Accounts Payable			560,000
3		*Purchased inventory on account.*			
4					
5	2.	Accounts Receivable		900,000	
6		Sales Revenue			900,000
7		*Sold inventory on account.*			
8		Cost of Goods Sold		540,000	
9		Inventory			540,000
10		*Recorded cost of goods sold.*			
11					

Inventory

Beginning balance	100,000*		
Purchases	560,000	Cost of goods sold	540,000
Ending balance	120,000		

*Beginning inventory was $100,000

Cost of Goods Sold

Cost of goods sold	540,000		

PANEL B—Reporting in the Financial Statements

Income Statement (partial)

Sales revenue	$900,000
Cost of goods sold	540,000
Gross profit	$360,000

Ending Balance Sheet (partial)

Current assets:	
Cash	$ XXX
Short-term investments	XXX
Accounts receivable	XXX
Inventory	120,000
Prepaid expenses	XXX

In Exhibit 6-4 (panel A), the first entry to Inventory summarizes in one entry what, in practice, may actually be several entries. The cost of the inventory, $560,000, is the *net* amount of the store's inventory purchases, which are determined as follows (using assumed amounts):

Purchase price of the inventory	$600,000
+ **Freight in** (the cost to transport the goods from the seller to the buyer)	4,000
− **Purchase returns** for unsuitable goods returned to the seller	(25,000)
− **Purchase allowances** granted by the seller	(5,000)
− **Purchase discounts** for early payment by the buyer	(14,000)
= Net purchases of inventory—Cost to the buyer	$560,000

Freight in is the transportation cost, paid by the buyer under terms FOB shipping point, to move goods from the seller to the buyer. Freight in is accounted for as part of the cost of inventory. Although it's not shown in the exhibit, the cost a business pays to ship goods to its customers is referred to as **freight out**. Freight out is not part of the cost of inventory. Instead, freight out is considered a delivery expense. It is the seller's expense of delivering merchandise to customers.

A **purchase return** occurs when a buyer returns goods to the seller (vendor). A purchase return represents a decrease in inventory for the buyer and a corresponding decrease in its accounts payable because the company no longer owes the seller for them. A **purchase allowance** is a decrease in the cost of a purchase because the seller has granted the buyer a deduction (an allowance) from the amount owed. The buyer keeps the inventory but decreases its cost by the amount of the allowance. These terms are similar to the concepts of a seller's *sales return* and *sales allowance* discussed in Chapter 5.

To document the approval of a purchase return, the buyer issues a **debit memorandum** to the seller informing the business that the buyer debited its accounts payable (reduced it) by the amount of the item(s) returned. The offsetting credit is to inventory because the goods are shipped back to the seller. Purchase returns and allowances are usually confirmed on the final invoice the seller sends the buyer. Throughout this book, we often refer to net purchases simply as *purchases*.

A **purchase discount** (which is similar to the concept of a sales discount discussed in Chapter 5) is a decrease in the buyer's cost of inventory earned by paying quickly. Many companies offer payment terms of "2/10 n/30." This means the buyer can take, and the seller grants, a 2% discount for payment within 10 days, with the final amount due within 30 days. Another common credit term is "net 30," which tells the customer to pay the full amount within 30 days. In summary,

Net purchases = Purchases
− Purchase returns and allowances
− Purchase discounts
+ Freight in

The journal entries for purchase returns and purchase discounts are as follows (assuming a purchase return of \$500 in merchandise and a purchase of \$1,000 in merchandise with terms of 2/10, n/30):

	A	B	C	D
1		**Purchase returns:**	**Debit**	**Credit**
2		Accounts payable	500	
3		Inventory		500
4		*To record purchase return of merchandise that cost \$500.*		
5				
6		**Purchase discounts:**		
7		Original purchase, terms 2/10, n/30:		
8		Inventory (1,000 × 1)	1,000	
9		Accounts payable (1,000 × 1)		1,000
10		*To record a gross purchase of \$1,000 in merchandise.*		
11				
12		**Payment 10 days later (within discount period):**		
13		Accounts payable	1,000	
14		Inventory		20
15		Cash		980
16		*To record payment for merchandise within 10 days at 2% discount.*		
17				

Note that the cost of inventory on the balance sheet represents all the costs that the company incurred to bring its inventory to the point of sale. The following cost principle applies to all assets:

The cost of any asset, such as inventory, is the sum of all the costs incurred to bring the asset to its intended use, less any discounts.

The cost of inventory includes its basic purchase price, plus freight in, insurance while in transit, and any fees or taxes paid to get the inventory ready to sell, less returns, allowances, and discounts.

After an Under Armour t-shirt is sitting on the shelf in the store, other costs, such as advertising and sales commissions, are *not* included as the cost of inventory. Advertising, sales commissions, and delivery costs are selling expenses that go in the income statement rather than in the balance sheet.

APPLY AND COMPARE VARIOUS INVENTORY COST METHODS

2 Apply and compare various inventory cost methods

The accounting method a company selects will affect the profits it reports, the amount of income tax to be paid, and the values of the inventory turnover and gross margin percentage ratios derived from the financial statements.

Apply the Various Inventory Costing Methods

Determining the cost of inventory is easy when the unit cost remains constant over time, as in Exhibit 6-2. But the unit cost of merchandise usually fluctuates over time. For example, the prices of products sometimes rise along with fuel prices that increase the transportation costs to ship merchandise. The t-shirt that cost Under Armour, Inc., $10 in January may cost $14 in June and $18 in October. Suppose an Under Armour outlet store sells 1,000 t-shirts in November. How many of them cost $10, how many cost $14, and how many cost $18?

To compute the cost of goods sold and the cost of ending inventory still on hand, we must assign a unit cost to the items. To do so, a company can use any of the following inventory methods:

- **Specific-identification method**
- **Average-cost method**
- **First-in, first-out (FIFO) method**
- **Last-in, first-out (LIFO) method**

These methods can have very different effects on reported profits, income taxes, and cash flow. Therefore, companies select their inventory method with great care.

Specific Identification Method. Some businesses deal in unique inventory items, such as automobiles, antique furniture, jewels, and real estate. These businesses cost their inventories at the specific cost of the particular unit. This inventory costing method is referred to as the **specific identification method**. For instance, a **Toyota** dealer may have two vehicles in the showroom—a base model that cost the dealer $19,000 and a luxury sport model that cost the dealer $30,000. If the dealer sells the luxury sport model, the cost of goods sold is $30,000. The base model vehicle will be the only unit left in inventory, and so ending inventory is $19,000. The specific identification method is too expensive to use when a company sells large numbers of lower-cost goods that are nearly identical to one another, such as bushels of wheat, gallons of paint, or auto tires. Accounting for each unit separately would be too time consuming and costly.

The other inventory accounting methods do not use the specific cost of a particular unit. Instead, they assign different costs to units sold and units remaining in inventory based on an assumed *flow* of inventory. To illustrate the differences in the methods, we use the information in Exhibit 6-5.

Exhibit 6-5 | Inventory Data for an Under Armour Outlet Store

Inventory				
Beg bal	(10 units @ $10)	100		
Purchases:			Cost of goods sold	
No. 1	(25 units @ $14)	350	(40 units @ ?)	?
No. 2	(25 units @ $18)	450		
End bal	(20 units @ ?)	?		

Assume that an Under Armour outlet store began the period with 10 t-shirts that cost $10 each; the beginning inventory was therefore $100. During the period, the store bought 50 more t-shirts, sold 40 t-shirts, and ended the period with 20 t-shirts.

Goods Available		Number of Units	Total Cost
Goods available	=	10 + 25 + 25 = 60 units	$100 + $350 + $450 = $900
Cost of goods sold	=	40 units	?
Ending inventory	=	20 units	?

The big accounting questions are as follows:

1. What is the cost of goods sold for the income statement?
2. What is the cost of the ending inventory for the balance sheet?

The answers to these questions depend on which inventory method Under Armour uses. Let's look at average costing first.

Average-Cost Method. The **average-cost method**, sometimes called the **weighted-average method**, is based on the average cost of inventory during the period. Using data from Exhibit 6-5, the average cost per unit is determined as:

$$\text{Average cost per unit} = \frac{\text{Cost of goods available}^{1}}{\text{Number of units available}} = \frac{\$900}{60} = \$15$$

The store's cost of goods sold is:

$$\begin{aligned}\text{Cost of goods sold} &= \text{Number of units sold} \times \text{Average cost per unit}\\ &= 40 \text{ units} \times \$15 = \$600\end{aligned}$$

The balance of the store's ending inventory is:

$$\begin{aligned}\text{Ending inventory} &= \text{Number of units on hand} \times \text{Average cost per unit}\\ &= 20 \text{ units} \times \$15 = \$300\end{aligned}$$

The following diagram illustrates the average-cost method:

Average costing

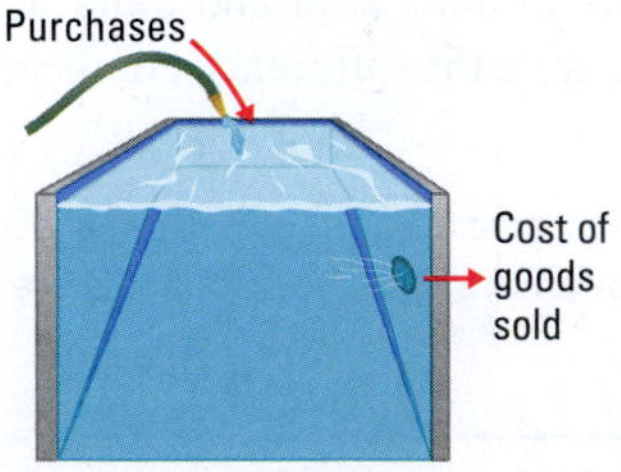

The following T-account shows the effects of average costing:

Inventory (at Average Cost)

Beg bal	**(10 units @ $10)**	**100**	
Purchases:			
No. 1	**(25 units @ $14)**	**350**	
No. 2	**(25 units @ $18)**	**450**	**Cost of goods sold (40 units @ average cost of $15 per unit) 600**
End bal	**(20 units @ average cost of $15 per unit)**	**300**	

[1]Cost of Goods Available (used synonymously with Cost of Goods Available for Sale throughout the chapter) = Beginning inventory + Purchases.

FIFO Method. Under the **FIFO (first-in, first-out) method**, the first costs into inventory are the first costs assigned to the cost of goods sold—hence the name *first-in, first-out*. The following diagram illustrates the effect of FIFO costing.

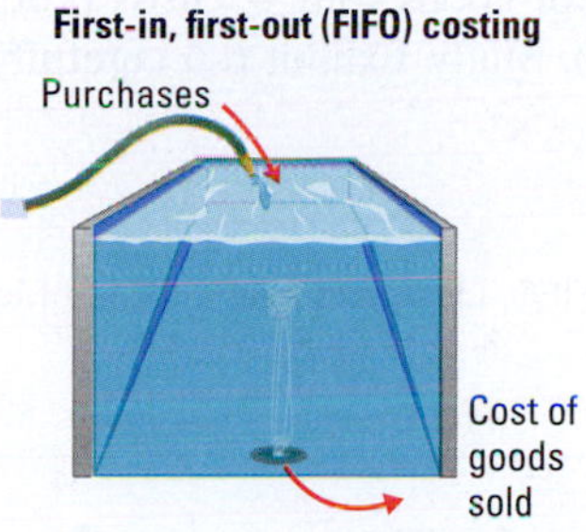

The following T-account shows how to compute the store's cost of goods sold and ending inventory under FIFO (data from Exhibit 6-5):

Inventory (at FIFO cost)

Beg bal	(10 units @ $10)	100			
Purchases:			Cost of goods sold (40 units):		
No. 1	(25 units @ $14)	350	(10 units @ $10)	100	
No. 2	(25 units @ $18)	450	(25 units @ $14)	350	540
			(5 units @ $18)	90	
End bal	(20 units @ $18)	360			

Under FIFO, the cost of ending inventory is always based on the latest costs incurred—in this case, $18 per unit.

LIFO Method. The **LIFO (last-in, first-out) method** of costing is the opposite of FIFO. Under LIFO, the last costs into inventory go immediately to the cost of goods sold, as illustrated in the following diagram.

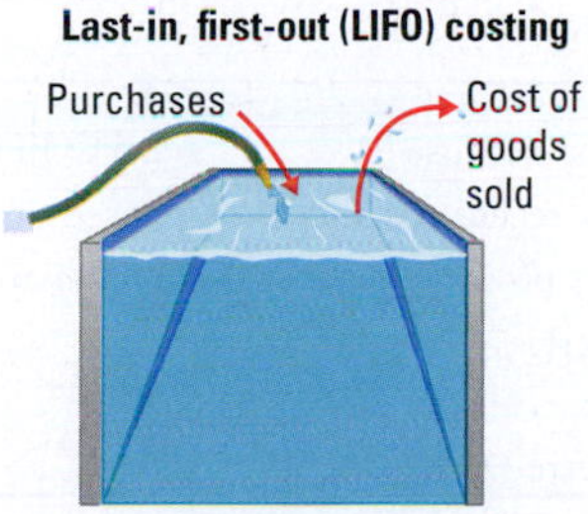

The following T-account shows how to compute the LIFO inventory amounts for the Under Armour t-shirts (data from Exhibit 6-5):

Inventory (at LIFO cost)

Beg bal	(10 units @ $10)	100			
Purchases:			Cost of goods sold (40 units):		
No. 1	(25 units @ $14)	350	(25 units @ $18)	450	660
No. 2	(25 units @ $18)	450	(15 units @ $14)	210	
End bal	(10 units @ $10)	240			
	(10 units @ $14)				

Under LIFO, the cost of ending inventory is always based on the oldest costs—from beginning inventory plus the earliest purchases of the period—$10 and $14 per unit.

Compare the Effects of the FIFO, LIFO, and Average-Cost Methods on Gross Profit and Ending Inventory

Because they produce differences in cost of goods sold, the different inventory methods also lead to differences in a company's gross profit and ending inventory balance. Exhibit 6-6 summarizes the income effects (Sales − Cost of goods sold = Gross profit) of the three inventory methods (remember that prices are rising). Study Exhibit 6-6 carefully, focusing on cost of goods sold and gross profit.

Exhibit 6-6 | Income Effects of the FIFO, LIFO, and Average-Cost Methods

	FIFO	LIFO	Average
Sales revenue (assumed)	$1,000	$1,000	$1,000
Cost of goods sold	540 (lowest)	660 (highest)	600
Gross profit	$ 460 (highest)	$ 340 (lowest)	$ 400

Exhibit 6-7 shows the impact of both the FIFO and LIFO costing methods when inventory costs are increasing (Panel A) and inventory costs are decreasing (Panel B). Study this exhibit carefully; it will help you *really* understand FIFO and LIFO.

Exhibit 6-7 | Effects of the FIFO and LIFO Methods on Cost of Goods Sold and Ending Inventory

PANEL A—When Inventory Costs Are Increasing

	Cost of Goods Sold (COGS)	Ending Inventory (EI)
FIFO	FIFO COGS is lowest because it's based on the oldest costs, which are low. Gross profit is, therefore, the highest.	FIFO EI is highest because it's based on the most recent costs, which are high.
LIFO	LIFO COGS is highest because it's based on the most recent costs, which are high. Gross profit is, therefore, the lowest.	LIFO EI is lowest because it's based on the oldest costs, which are low.

PANEL B—When Inventory Costs Are Decreasing

	Cost of Goods Sold (COGS)	Ending Inventory (EI)
FIFO	FIFO COGS is highest because it's based on the oldest costs, which are high. Gross profit is, therefore, the lowest.	FIFO EI is lowest because it's based on the most recent costs, which are low.
LIFO	LIFO COGS is lowest because it's based on the most recent costs, which are low. Gross profit is, therefore, the highest.	LIFO EI is highest because it's based on the oldest costs, which are high.

Financial analysts searching for companies with good prospects for income growth sometimes need to compare the net income of a company that uses LIFO with the net income of a company that uses FIFO. Appendix 6B, at the end of this chapter, shows how to convert a LIFO company's net income to the FIFO basis in order to compare the companies.

The Tax Advantage of LIFO

The Internal Revenue Service requires all U.S. companies to use the same method of costing inventories for tax purposes that they use for financial reporting purposes. Consequently, the inventory method a company chooses directly affects its income taxes. When costs are rising, LIFO results in the lowest taxable income and thus the lowest income taxes. Let's use the gross profit data in Exhibit 6-6 to illustrate:

	FIFO	LIFO
Gross profit (from Exhibit 6–6)	$460	$340
Operating expenses (assumed)	260	260
Income before income tax	$200	$ 80
Income tax expense (40%)	$ 80	$ 32

Income tax expense is lowest under LIFO by $48 ($80 − $32). This is the most attractive feature of LIFO—low income tax payments—which is why about one-third of all U.S. companies use LIFO. During periods of high inflation, companies that can justify it may switch to LIFO for its tax and cash-flow advantages. Because the switch can have a big effect on the financial statements of a company, it needs to restate them for prior years using LIFO so they are comparable from year to year. The company also must disclose the change. Let's compare the FIFO and LIFO inventory methods from a couple of different standpoints.

1. *Measuring cost of goods sold.* How well does each method match inventory expense—cost of goods sold—against revenue? LIFO results in the most realistic net income figure because LIFO matches the most recent inventory costs to the most recent revenue the company earned. In contrast, FIFO matches old inventory costs against the most recent revenue the company earned. FIFO income is therefore less realistic than LIFO income.
2. *Measuring ending inventory.* Which method reports the most up-to-date inventory cost on the balance sheet? FIFO. LIFO can value inventory at very old costs because LIFO leaves the oldest costs in ending inventory.

LIFO and Managing Reported Income. LIFO allows managers to manipulate net income by timing their purchases of inventory. When inventory costs are rising rapidly and a company wants to show less income (in order to pay less taxes), managers can buy a large amount of inventory near the end of the year. Under LIFO, these high inventory costs go straight to cost of goods sold. As a result, net income is decreased.

If the business is having a bad year, the company might wish to report higher income. The business can do so by delaying the purchase of high-cost inventory until the next year. In the process, the company draws down its inventory quantities.

LIFO Liquidation. A *LIFO liquidation* occurs when a business draws down its inventory to the point where the quantity of its ending inventory falls below the level of the previous period. The company is therefore using some of its lower-cost, older inventory to compute the cost of goods sold for the business. The result is higher net income as well as higher income taxes. To avoid this result, managers generally try to avoid LIFO liquidations.

GLOBAL VIEW

International Perspective on LIFO. Many U.S. companies that currently use LIFO for their U.S. operations must use another method if they have operations in foreign countries. Why? International Financial Reporting Standards (IFRS) do not permit the use of LIFO, although they do permit FIFO and other methods.

These differences can create problems for financial analysts when they compare a U.S. company to a foreign competitor. If U.S. Generally Accepted Accounting Principles (GAAP) and the International Financial Reporting Standards (IFRS) were to become fully integrated in the future, U.S. companies that use LIFO might be forced to use another method. This could substantially increase the net income as well as income taxes many U.S. companies must pay, including some small- and medium-sized businesses that can least afford it. We will cover other key differences between U.S. GAAP and IFRS in later chapters. Appendix D summarizes many of these differences.

Mid-Chapter Summary Problem

Suppose a division of **Texas Instruments Incorporated** that sells computer microchips has these inventory records for January 2018:

Date	Item	Quantity	Unit Cost	Total Cost
Jan 1	Beginning inventory	100 units	$ 8	$ 800
6	Purchase	60 units	9	540
21	Purchase	150 units	9	1,350
27	Purchase	90 units	10	900

The company's accounting records show 310 units were sold for revenue of $6,770. Operating expense for January was $1,900.

Requirements

1. Prepare the company's January, multistep income statement. Calculate income using the LIFO, average-cost, and FIFO methods. Label the bottom line "Operating income." Round the average cost per unit to three decimal places and all other figures to whole-dollar amounts. Show your computations.
2. Suppose you are the financial vice president of Texas Instruments. Which inventory method will you use if your motive is to

   a. minimize income taxes?

   b. report the highest operating income?

   c. report operating income between the extremes of FIFO and LIFO?

   d. report inventory on the balance sheet at the most current cost?

   e. attain the best measure of net income for the income statement?

   State the reason for each of your answers.

Answers

Requirement 1

	A	B	C	D
1	**Texas Instruments Incorporated** **Income Statement for Microchip** **Month Ended January 31, 2018**			
2		**LIFO**	**Average**	**FIFO**
3	Sales revenue	$ 6,770	$ 6,770	$ 6,770
4	Cost of goods sold	2,870	2,782	2,690
5	Gross profit	3,900	3,988	4,080
6	Operating expenses	1,900	1,900	1,900
7	Operating income	$ 2,000	$ 2,088	$ 2,180
8				

Cost of goods sold computations:

LIFO: (90 @ \$10) + (150 @ \$9) + (60 @ \$9) + (10 @ \$8) = \$2,870

Average: 310 × \$8.975* = \$2,782

FIFO: (100 @ \$8) + (60 @ \$9) + (150 @ \$9) = \$2,690

$$^{*}\ \frac{(\$800 + \$540 + \$1{,}350 + \$900)}{(100 + 60 + 150 + 90)} = \$8.975$$

Requirement 2

a. Use LIFO to minimize income taxes. Operating income under LIFO is lowest when inventory unit costs are increasing, as they are in this case (from $8 to $10). (If inventory costs were decreasing, income under FIFO would be lowest.)

b. Use FIFO to report the highest operating income. Income under FIFO is highest when inventory unit costs are increasing, as in this situation.

c. Use the average-cost method to report an operating income amount between the FIFO and LIFO extremes. This is true in this situation and in others when inventory unit costs are increasing or decreasing.

d. Use FIFO to report the inventory on the balance sheet at the most current cost. The oldest inventory costs are expensed as cost of goods sold, leaving in ending inventory the most recent (most current) costs of the period.

e. Use LIFO to attain the best measure of net income. LIFO produces the best current expense recognition by matching the most current expense with current revenue. The most recent (most current) inventory costs are expensed as cost of goods sold.

EXPLAIN AND APPLY UNDERLYING U.S. GAAP FOR INVENTORY

3 Explain and apply underlying U.S. GAAP for inventory

Several accounting principles have special relevance to inventories:

- Consistency
- Disclosure
- Representational faithfulness

Disclosure Principle

The **disclosure principle** states that a company's financial statements should report enough information for outsiders to make informed decisions about the company. The company should report *relevant* and *representationally faithful* information about itself. That means properly disclosing the business's inventory accounting methods as well as the substance of all material transactions that affect the proper valuation of the inventory. The disclosure principle also requires companies to use *comparable* methods to ensure the *consistency* of the information presented from period to period. This is why, for example, a company that decides to switch from LIFO to FIFO or vice versa must disclose this information. Otherwise, a creditor or investor who isn't provided with this information could make an unwise lending or investment decision.

Lower-of-Cost-or-Market Rule

The **lower-of-cost-or-market (LCM) rule** is a U.S. GAAP requirement based on the principles of relevance and representational faithfulness. LCM requires that inventory be reported in the financial statements at whichever is lower—the inventory's historical cost or its market value.

Applied to inventories, *market value* generally means *net realizable value, which equals selling price minus disposal costs.* If the market value of the inventory thus defined is below its historical cost, the business must write down the value of the goods to their market value because it is the most relevant and representationally faithful measure of the inventory's true worth to the business. The business reports its ending inventory at its LCM value on the balance sheet. How is the write-down accomplished?

Suppose Under Armour, Inc., paid $3,000,000 for inventory on November 1. By December 31, its fiscal year-end, the company determines that the market value of the inventory has fallen to $2,000,000. Under Armour's year-end balance sheet must report the inventory at the LCM value of $2,000,000. Exhibit 6-8 shows the effects of LCM on the balance sheet and the income statement. Before any LCM effect, cost of goods sold is $9,000,000. An LCM write-down decreases Inventory and increases Cost of Goods Sold:

A1

	A	B	C	D
1	Dec. 31	Cost of Goods Sold	1,000,000	
2		Inventory		1,000,000
3		*Wrote inventory down to market value.*		
4				

Exhibit 6-8 | Lower-of-Cost-or-Market (LCM) Effects on Inventory and Cost of Goods Sold

Balance Sheet

Current assets:	
Cash	$ XXX,XXX
Short-term investments	XXX,XXX
Accounts receivable	XXX,XXX
Inventories, at market (which is lower than $3,000,000 cost)	2,000,000
Prepaid expenses	XXX,XXX
Total current assets	$X,XXX,XXX

Income Statement

Sales revenue	$21,000,000
Cost of goods sold ($9,000,000 + $1,000,000)	10,000,000
Gross profit	$11,000,000

If the market value of Under Armour's inventory had been above its cost, the company would have simply reported it at its cost and made no LCM adjustment.

Cooking the Books

Logitech International

In the fourth quarter of 2010, **Logitech International** released the Revue, a TV set-top box designed to integrate cable and satellite TV with Internet content. The Revue's Google search bar allowed users to find content on the Internet and project that content to their TV screens. The Revue was manufactured by contract manufacturers, not Logitech itself. In the arrangement with the contract manufacturers, Logitech authorized the manufacturers to purchase about $11 million of parts before the production of the Revue began. The company was gearing up for high sales during the 2010 holiday season.

However, in the fourth quarter of 2010, only 165,000 units were sold—far less than the 350,000 units Logitech expected to sell. The Revue's price was high, and the device contained numerous software bugs. Networks such as Hulu, CBS, and ABC blocked its access to their content. Less than one year after it hit the market, the Revue was discontinued.

As a result, Logitech was stuck with millions of dollars in excess inventory of component parts for the Revue. Despite knowing that the component parts would not be used to manufacture other Logitech products and that the market value of the parts was minimal, the lower-of-cost-or-market inventory write-down that Logitech made to its books fell far short of the actual decline in the parts' market value.

In 2016, the U.S. Securities and Exchange Commission (SEC) alleged that some of Logitech's executives and accounting staff committed accounting fraud. The SEC asserted that the improper inventory accounting contributed to an overstatement of Logitech's operating income in 2011 of more than 27%, or $30.7 million. Logitech paid a fine of $7.5 million to settle a lawsuit with the SEC over the improper inventory recording issues. Individuals from Logitech, including its former CFO, paid fines ranging from $25,000 to $50,000.

GLOBAL VIEW

Another IFRS Difference. Recall that IFRS does not allow the use of LIFO inventories. For companies that use the FIFO or average costing methods, IFRS and U.S. GAAP both define "market value" as "net realizable value," which, for inventories, is their selling price minus their disposal costs. However, U.S. GAAP requires that companies using LIFO inventories define "market value" as "current replacement cost."

Under U.S. GAAP, inventory write-downs can never be reversed. In contrast, under IFRS, some LCM write-downs can be reversed, and the inventory can be subsequently written up again, not to exceed original cost. This may cause more fluctuations than we currently see in the reported incomes of companies that sell merchandise.

COMPUTE AND EVALUATE GROSS PROFIT (MARGIN) PERCENTAGE, INVENTORY TURNOVER, AND DAYS' INVENTORY OUTSTANDING (DIO)

4 Compute and evaluate gross profit (margin) percentage, inventory turnover, and days' inventory outstanding (DIO)

Owners, managers, and investors use ratios to evaluate a business. Three ratios relate directly to inventory: gross profit percentage, inventory turnover, and days' inventory outstanding (DIO).

Gross Profit Percentage

Gross profit—sales minus cost of goods sold—is a key indicator of a company's ability to sell inventory at a profit. Merchandisers strive to increase the **gross profit percentage**, also called the *gross margin percentage.* The gross profit percentage is a business's gross profit stated as a percentage of its net sales. Under Armour's gross profit percentage is computed as follows for the year ended December 31, 2016. Figures (in thousands) are taken from the company's Consolidated Statements of Income on page 306.

$$\text{Gross profit percentage} = \frac{\text{Gross profit}}{\text{Net sales revenue}} = \frac{\$2{,}240{,}611}{\$4{,}825{,}335} = 0.464 = 46.4\%$$

The gross profit percentage is watched carefully by managers and investors. A 46.4% gross profit percentage means that each dollar of sales generates about $0.46 of gross profit. Therefore, on average, cost of goods sold consumes $0.54 ($1.00 − $0.46) of each sales dollar. For most companies, the gross profit percentage changes little from year to year, so a small downturn may signal trouble, and an upturn by a small percentage can mean millions of dollars in additional profits. Under Armour's, gross profit percentages for fiscal years 2014, 2015, and 2016 were 49.0%, 48.1%, and 46.4%, respectively. These figures reflect steady decreases, which is a disturbing trend. The 2.6% decrease from 2014 through 2016, when multiplied by 2016 sales of $4.8 billion means that Under Armour's gross profit was about $124 million less in 2016 than it would have been had the company's gross profit percentage remained at its 2014 level of 49.0%. So, even though Under Armour's gross profit in absolute dollars increased over the three years, the percentage of profit it earned on its products continued to fall.

Is Under Armour's gross profit percentage strong, weak, or average compared to a competitor? **Nike** is a very big player in the athletic wear market, and its size gives it tremendous leverage and buying power over its competitors. While Under Armour's gross profit percentage steadily declined over the 3-year period from 2014 through 2016, Nike's gross profit percentage increased from 44.8% to 46.2%[2].

Exhibit 6-9 shows the 2016 gross profit percentage of Under Armour, Inc. versus Nike, Inc. Knowing a few more facts can help you figure out why the 3-year trend in Under Armour's gross profit percentage has been negative. Under Armour has only been a public company since 2005. A large percentage of its customer base is made up of specialty retail stores across North America, like **Dick's Sporting Goods**, **Sports Authority**, **Foot Locker**, and **Modell's**. These chains consist of relatively small stores that sell specialized (and higher priced) athletic wear. Two of the chains have recently experienced financial difficulty and have filed for bankruptcy, thus negatively impacting Under Armour's sales and gross profits. Also, Under Armour has only recently (2006) entered the high-style (and relatively high gross margin) athletic shoe market, which has been dominated by Nike for years.

In contrast, Nike is a much more mature company in terms of its global market penetration, years in business, and diversity of product offerings and price ranges than Under Armour. Although Nike sells competing products to specialty stores, it has a much larger customer base than Under Armour. Nike also sells some lower-end branded products to budget retailers like **Walmart**, **Target**, and **Dollar General Stores**. Thus, Nike would be expected to have a slightly lower gross profit percentage than Under Armour. However, because of its volume of sales ($32.4 billion in fiscal 2016) and greater diversity of customers (discount chains as well as specialty athletic wear retailers), Nike generates a larger amount of gross profit in terms of absolute dollars (about $15 billion) than Under Armour.

---

[2] These computations came from data from the U.S. Securities and Exchange Commission EDGAR Company Filings, www.sec.gov for Nike, Inc.'s comparative financial statements for 2014 through 2016 (not shown).

Exhibit 6-9 | Gross Profit Percentages of Under Armour, Inc. and Nike, Inc. in 2016

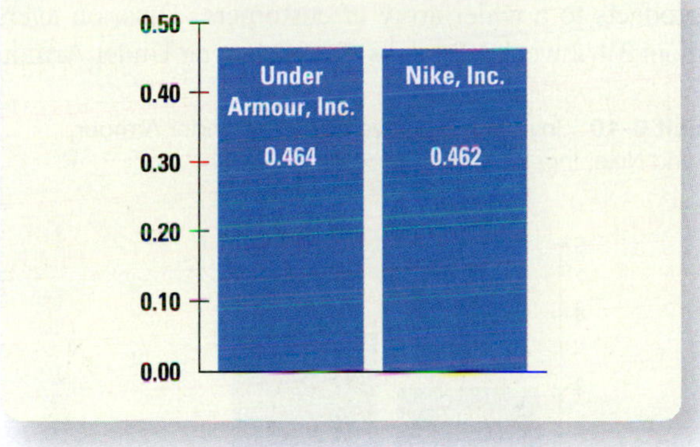

Data from the U.S. Securities and Exchange Commission EDGAR Company Filings, www.sec.gov

Inventory Turnover and Days Inventory Outstanding (DIO)

Companies strive to sell their inventory as quickly as possible because the goods generate no profit until they're sold. The faster the sales, the higher the income. The reverse is true for slow-moving goods. Ideally, a business could operate with zero inventory, but most businesses, especially retailers, must keep some goods on hand. **Inventory turnover**, the ratio of cost of goods sold to average inventory, indicates how rapidly inventory is sold. The comparative inventory turnover statistics for 2016 and 2015 for Under Armour, Inc., follow (data in thousands from the Consolidated Balance Sheets and Statements of Income) on page 306:

$$\text{Inventory turnover} = \frac{\text{Cost of goods sold}}{\text{Average inventory}} = \frac{\text{Cost of goods sold}}{\left(\begin{array}{c}\text{Beginning}\\ \text{inventory}\end{array} + \begin{array}{c}\text{Ending}\\ \text{inventory}\end{array}\right) \div 2}$$

for year ended December 31, 2016:

$$= \frac{\$2{,}584{,}724}{(\$917{,}491 + \$783{,}031)/2} = 3.04 \text{ times per year}$$

DIO for 2016: $= 365/3.04 = 120$ days

for year ended December 31, 2015:

$$= \frac{\$2{,}057{,}766}{(\$783{,}031 + \$536{,}714^*)/2} = 3.12 \text{ times per year}$$

DIO for 2015: $= 365/3.12 = 117$ days

*Beginning inventory for 2015 from 2015 annual report (not shown)

Source: Data from the U.S. Securities and Exchange Commission EDGAR Company Filings, www.sec.gov.

The inventory turnover ratio shows how many times the company sold (or turned over) its average level of inventory during the year. Inventory turnover varies from industry to industry and company to company. During the year ended December 31, 2016, Under Armour, Inc.'s, inventory turned over 3.04 times. Inventory turnover can be converted to **days' inventory outstanding (DIO)** by dividing it into 365. Therefore, DIO during 2016 was 120 days. This means that, on average, Under Armour's items in inventory sat on the shelves for 120 days in 2016 before being sold.

Are these results strong or weak? Let's compare them to the preceding year. Using the DIO calculation, we can also determine Under Armour's inventory turnover for the year ended December 31, 2015. It was 3.12 times, or every 117 days. Therefore, 2016's turnover of 3.04 (120 days) is rather slow, and it is still slower than 2015's ratio of 3.12 (117 days). On average, it took three more days to sell an item of inventory in 2016 than it did in 2015. Therefore, 2016's results were weaker than those of 2015.

Another way to evaluate Under Armour's inventory turnover is to compare it with a competitor. Exhibit 6-10 graphs the rate of inventory turnover for Under Armour, Inc., for 2016 against that of Nike, Inc. In 2016, Nike turned its inventory over 3.79 times (every 96 days); Under Armour turned its inventory over 3.04 times (every 120 days). Although Nike's gross profit percentage is roughly the same as Under Armour's, Nike is a much larger company. It also sells a greater variety and higher volume of products to a wider array of customers. Thus, on average, a Nike product moves off the shelves about 3 1/2 weeks (24 days) faster than an Under Armour product.

Exhibit 6-10 | Inventory Turnover Rates of Under Armour, Inc. and Nike, Inc. in 2016

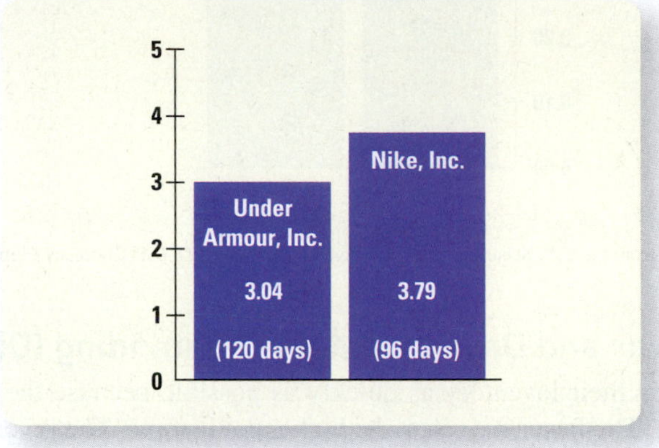

Data from the U.S. Securities and Exchange Commission EDGAR Company Filings, www.sec.gov

TRY IT

(Answers are given on p. 362.)

Examine Exhibits 6-9 and 6-10. What do those ratio values say about the relative success of Under Armour, Inc., vs. Nike, Inc.?

USE THE COST-OF-GOODS-SOLD (COGS) MODEL TO MAKE MANAGEMENT DECISIONS

5 Use the cost-of-goods-sold (COGS) model to make management decisions

Exhibit 6-11 presents the **cost-of-goods-sold (COGS) model**. The COGS model is used by all companies, regardless of their accounting systems. The model is extremely powerful because it captures all the inventory information for an entire accounting period. Study this model carefully (all amounts are assumed).

Exhibit 6-11 | The Cost-of-Goods-Sold Model

	A	B
1	**Cost of goods sold (in thousands):**	
2	Beginning inventory	$1,200
3	+ Purchases	6,300
4	= Cost of goods available	7,500
5	− Ending inventory	(1,500)
6	= Cost of goods sold	$6,000
7		

Source: Data from the U.S. Securities and Exchange Commission EDGAR Company Filings, www.sec.gov

Assume that Exhibit 6-11 represents the cost of goods sold for an Under Armour outlet store. Because the outlet store's sales prices are discounted, the gross profit percentage is 35% rather than 46% as reflected in the company's overall consolidated statement of income, illustrated earlier. Let's see how the store manager can use the COGS model to manage the business effectively.

Computing Budgeted Purchases

1. What's the single most important question for the Under Armour outlet store to address?
   - Which merchandise should the store offer to its customers? This is a marketing question that requires market research. If the store continually stocks up on the wrong merchandise, sales will suffer and profits will drop.
2. What's the second most important question for the Under Armour outlet store?
   - How much inventory should the store buy? This is an accounting question faced by all merchandisers. If the store buys too much merchandise, it will have to lower prices, the gross profit percentage will suffer, and the store may lose money. Buying the right quantity of inventory is critical for success. This question can be answered with the COGS model. Let's see how it works.

We must rearrange the COGS model illustrated in Exhibit 6-11. Then we can help the store's manager know how much inventory to buy, as follows (using amounts from Exhibit 6-11):

1 Cost of goods sold (based on the plan for the next period)	$6,000
2 + Ending inventory (based on the plan for the next period)	1,500
3 = Cost of goods available as planned	7,500
4 − Beginning inventory (actual amount left over from the prior period)	(1,200)
5 = Purchases (how much inventory the manager needs to buy)	$6,300

In this case, the manager should buy $6,300 of merchandise to implement the plan for the upcoming period.

Estimating Inventory Using the Gross Profit Method

Sometimes a business may need to estimate the value of its ending inventory. For example, suppose a fire destroys the business's warehouse, inventory, and all records. The insurance company requires an estimate of the loss. In this case, the business must estimate the cost of ending inventory because the records have been destroyed.

The **gross profit method**, also known as the *gross margin method,* is widely used to estimate ending inventory. This method uses the familiar COGS model (amounts are assumed).

Beginning inventory	$ 4,000
+ Purchases	16,000
= Cost of goods available	20,000
− Ending inventory	(5,000)
= Cost of goods sold	$15,000

For the gross profit method, we rearrange ending inventory and cost of goods sold as follows:

Beginning inventory	$ 4,000
+ Purchases	16,000
= Cost of goods available	20,000
− Cost of goods sold	(15,000)
= Ending inventory	$ 5,000

Suppose a fire destroys some of the Under Armour outlet store's inventory as well as the computer system on which the records are kept, which prevents the manager from physically reconstructing the records of the inventory lost. To collect insurance, the company must estimate the cost of the ending inventory destroyed. Because the manager of the store knows its gross profit percentage is 35%, the manager can estimate the store's cost of goods sold. Then the manager can subtract cost of goods sold from cost of goods available to estimate the amount of ending inventory. Exhibit 6-12 shows the calculations for the gross profit method, with new amounts assumed for the illustration.

Exhibit 6-12 | Gross Profit Method of Estimating Inventory

	A	B	C
1	Beginning inventory		$ 38,000
2	Purchases		72,000
3	Cost of goods available		110,000
4	Estimated cost of goods sold:		
5	Net sales revenue	$ 100,000	
6	Less estimated gross profit percentage of 35%	35,000	
7	Estimated cost of goods sold		65,000
8	Estimated cost of ending inventory lost		$ 45,000
9			

You can also use the gross profit method to test the overall reasonableness of an ending inventory amount. This method also helps to detect large errors.

TRY IT

(Answers are given on p. 362)

A company's beginning inventory is $70,000, net purchases total $365,000, and net sales are $500,000. With a normal gross profit rate of 40% of sales (cost of goods sold = 60%), how much is ending inventory?

ANALYZE EFFECTS OF INVENTORY ERRORS

6 Analyze effects of inventory errors

Inventory errors sometimes occur. An error in ending inventory creates errors for two accounting periods. In Exhibit 6-13, start with period 1 in which ending inventory is overstated by $10,000 and cost of goods sold is therefore understated by $10,000. Then compare period 1 with period 3, which is correct. *Period 1 should look exactly like period 3.*

Exhibit 6-13 | Inventory Errors: An Example

	A	B	C	D	E	F	G
1		Period 1 Ending Inventory Overstated by $10,000		Period 2 Beginning Inventory Overstated by $10,000		Period 3 Correct	
2	Sales revenue		$ 100,000		$100,000		$ 100,000
3	Cost of goods sold:						
4	Beginning inventory	$ 10,000		$ 20,000		$ 10,000	
5	Purchases	50,000		50,000		50,000	
6	Cost of goods available	60,000		70,000		60,000	
7	Ending inventory	(20,000)		(10,000)		(10,000)	
8	Cost of goods sold		40,000		60,000		50,000
9	Gross profit		$ 60,000		$ 40,000		$ 50,000
10							
11				$ 100,000			
12							

Inventory errors counterbalance in two consecutive periods. Why? Recall that period 1's ending inventory becomes period 2's beginning amount. Thus, the period 1 error carries over into period 2. Trace the ending inventory of $20,000 from period 1 to period 2. Then compare periods 2 and 3. *All three periods should look exactly like period 3.* The Exhibit 6-13 amounts in color are incorrect.

Beginning inventory and ending inventory have opposite effects on cost of goods sold (beginning inventory is added; ending inventory is subtracted). Therefore, after two periods, an inventory error washes out (counterbalances). Notice that total gross profit is correct for periods 1 and 2 combined ($100,000) even though each year's gross profit is off by $10,000. The correct gross profit is $50,000 for each period, as shown in period 3.

We must have accurate information for all periods. Exhibit 6-14 summarizes the effects of inventory accounting errors.

Exhibit 6-14 | Effects of Inventory Errors

	A	B	C	D	E
1		Period 1 Cost of Goods Sold	Period 1 Gross Profit and Net Income	Period 2 Cost of Goods Sold	Period 2 Gross Profit and Net Income
2	Period 1				
3	Ending inventory overstated	Understated	Overstated	Overstated	Understated
4	Period 1				
5	Ending inventory understated	Overstated	Understated	Understated	Overstated
6					

The following Decision Guidelines summarize the situations that call for (a) a particular inventory system and (b) the motivation for using each costing method.

Decision Guidelines

ACCOUNTING FOR INVENTORY

Suppose a **Williams-Sonoma** store stocks two basic categories of merchandise:

- High-end cookware, small electric appliances, cutlery, and kitchen furnishings
- Small items of low value, such as cup holders and bottle openers, which are located near the checkout area.

The store manager is considering how accounting will affect the business. Let's examine several decisions the manager must make to properly account for the store's inventory.

Decision	Guidelines	System or Method
Which inventory system to use?	• Expensive merchandise • Cannot control inventory by visual inspection	→ Perpetual system for high-unit-cost items
	• Can control inventory by visual inspection	→ Periodic system for the small, low-value items
	• Unique inventory items	→ Specific unit cost for one-of-a-kind objects because they are unique
Which costing method to use?	• Most current cost of ending inventory • Maximizes reported income when costs are rising	→ FIFO
	• Most current measure of cost of goods sold and net income • Minimizes income tax when costs are rising	→ LIFO
	• Middle-of-the-road approach for income tax and reported income	→ Average

End-of-Chapter | Summary Problem

The Gift Horse began in 2018 with 60,000 units of inventory that cost $36,000. During 2018, The Gift Horse purchased merchandise on account for $352,500:

Purchase 1	100,000 units costing	$ 65,000
Purchase 2	270,000 units costing	175,500
Purchase 3	160,000 units costing	112,000

Cash payments on account totaled $326,000 during the year (ignore purchase discounts).

The Gift Horse's sales during 2018 consisted of 520,000 units of inventory for $660,000, all on account. The company uses the FIFO inventory method.

Cash collections from customers were $630,000. Operating expenses totaled $240,500, of which The Gift Horse paid $211,000 in cash. The Gift Horse credited Accrued Liabilities for the remainder. At December 31, The Gift Horse accrued income tax expense at the rate of 35% of income before tax.

Requirements

1. Show how The Gift Horse would compute its cost of goods sold for 2018. Follow the FIFO example on page 315.
2. Prepare The Gift Horse's income statement for 2018. Show subtotals for the gross profit and income before tax.
3. Make summary journal entries to record The Gift Horse's transactions for the year, assuming the company uses a perpetual inventory system. Explanations are not required.
4. Determine the FIFO cost of The Gift Horse's ending inventory at December 31, 2018, two ways:
   a. Use a T-account.
   b. Multiply the number of units on hand by the unit cost.
5. Determine The Gift Horse's gross profit percentage, rate of inventory turnover, and net income as a percentage of sales for the year. In The Gift Horse's industry, a gross profit percentage of 40%, an inventory turnover of six times per year, and a net income percentage of 7% are considered excellent. How well does The Gift Horse compare to these industry averages?

Answers

Requirement 1

Cost of goods sold (520,000 units):	
60,000 units costing	$ 36,000
100,000 units costing	65,000
270,000 units costing	175,500
90,000 units costing $0.70 each*	63,000
Cost of goods sold	$339,500

*From Purchase 3: $112,000/160,000 units = $0.70 per unit.

Requirement 2

	A	B	C
1	**The Gift Horse** **Income Statement** **Year Ended December 31, 2018**		
2	Sales revenue	$ 660,000	
3	Cost of goods sold	339,500	
4	Gross profit	320,500	
5	Operating expenses	240,500	
6	Income before tax	80,000	
7	Income tax expense (35%)	28,000	
8	Net income	$ 52,000	
9			

Requirement 3

	A	B	C	D
1		Inventory ($65,000 + $175,500 + $112,000)	352,500	
2		Accounts Payable		352,500
3				
4		Accounts Payable	326,000	
5		Cash		326,000
6				
7		Accounts Receivable	660,000	
8		Sales Revenue		660,000
9				
10		Cost of Goods Sold (see Requirement 1)	339,500	
11		Inventory		339,500
12				
13		Cash	630,000	
14		Accounts Receivable		630,000
15				
16		Operating Expenses	240,500	
17		Cash		211,000
18		Accrued Liabilities		29,500
19				
20		Income Tax Expense (see Requirement 2)	28,000	
21		Income Tax Payable		28,000
22				

Requirement 4

Inventory

Beg bal	36,000		
Purchases	352,500	Cost of goods sold	339,500
End bal	49,000		

Number of units in ending inventory (60,000 + 100,000 + 270,000 + 160,000 − 520,000).............	70,000
Unit cost of ending inventory at FIFO ($112,000 ÷ 160,000 from Purchase 3).....	× $ 0.70
FIFO cost of ending inventory......................	$49,000

Requirement 5

		Industry Average
Gross profit percentage:	$320,500 ÷ $660,000 = 48.6%	40%
Inventory turnover:	$\frac{\$339{,}500}{(\$36{,}000 + \$49{,}000)/2} = 8$ times	6 times
Net income as a percent of sales:	$52,000 ÷ $660,000 = 7.9%	7%

The Gift Horse's statistics are better than the industry averages.

REVIEW | Inventory and Cost of Goods Sold

Accounting Vocabulary

average-cost method (p. 314) An inventory costing method based on the average cost of inventory during the period. Average cost is determined by dividing the cost of goods available by the number of units available. Also called the *weighted-average method*.

consignment (p. 309) An inventory arrangement where the seller sells inventory that belongs to another party. The seller does not include consigned merchandise on hand in its balance sheet, because the seller does not own this inventory.

cost of goods sold (p. 308) The cost of the inventory a business has sold to customers.

cost-of-goods-sold (COGS) model (p. 324) A formula that brings together all the inventory data for the entire accounting period: Beginning inventory + Purchases = Cost of goods available (i.e., cost of goods available for sale). Cost of goods available − Ending inventory = Cost of goods sold.

days' inventory outstanding (DIO) (p. 323) A measure that converts inventory turnover to days to show how many days an average item of inventory remains on shelves before being sold. The DIO is calculated as 365 ÷ inventory turnover.

debit memorandum (p. 312) A document issued to the seller (vendor) when an item of inventory that is unwanted or damaged is returned. The document informs the seller that the buyer debited its accounts payable (reduced it) by the amount of the return.

disclosure principle (p. 320) A principle that states that a business's financial statements must report enough information for outsiders to make knowledgeable decisions about the business. The company should report relevant and representationally faithful information about its financial affairs.

first-in, first-out (FIFO) method (p. 315) An inventory costing method by which the first costs into inventory are the first costs out to cost of goods sold. Ending inventory is based on the costs of the most recent purchases.

freight in (p. 311) The transportation cost, paid by the buyer to move goods from the seller to the buyer.

freight out (p. 311) The seller's expense of delivering merchandise to customers.

gross margin (p. 308) Another name for *gross profit*.

gross margin method (p. 325) Another name for the *gross profit method*.

gross margin percentage (p. 322) Another name for the *gross profit percentage*.

gross profit (p. 308) Sales revenue minus cost of goods sold. Also called *gross margin*.

gross profit method (p. 325) A way to estimate ending inventory based on a rearrangement of the cost-of-goods-sold model: Beginning inventory + Net purchases = Cost of goods available − Cost of goods sold = Ending inventory. Also called the *gross margin method*.

gross profit percentage (p. 322) Gross profit divided by net sales revenue. Also called the *gross margin percentage*.

inventory (p. 308) The merchandise that a company sells to customers.

inventory turnover (p. 323) The ratio of cost of goods sold to average inventory. The ratio indicates how rapidly (in terms of times per year) inventory is sold.

last-in, first-out (LIFO) cost method (p. 315) An inventory costing method that assumes the last costs into inventory are the first costs out to cost of goods sold. This method leaves the oldest costs—those of beginning inventory and the earliest purchases of the period—in ending inventory.

lower-of-cost-or-market (LCM) rule (p. 320) A U.S. GAAP rule that requires inventory be reported in financial statements at whichever is lower—its historical cost or its market value.

periodic inventory system (p. 310) An inventory system that does not keep a continuous record of the inventory on hand. Instead, the business records inventory purchased. At the end of the period, it makes a physical count of the inventory on hand and applies the appropriate unit costs to the items to determine the cost of the ending inventory. Then, cost of goods sold is determined by applying the model for cost of goods sold.

perpetual inventory system (p. 310) An inventory system that keeps a continuous record of each inventory item on hand at all times.

purchase allowance (p. 311) A decrease in the cost of purchases because the seller has granted the buyer a subtraction (an allowance) from the amount owed.

purchase discount (p. 312) A decrease in the cost of purchases earned by making an early payment to the vendor.

purchase return (p. 311) A decrease in the cost of purchases because the buyer returned the goods to the seller.

specific identification method (p. 313) An inventory cost method based on the specific cost of particular units of inventory.

weighted-average method (p. 314) Another name for the *average-cost method*.

Quick Check (Answers are given on page 362.)

1. Ravenna Candles recently purchased candleholders for resale in its shops. Which of the following costs would be part of the cost of the candleholder inventory?
   a. Advertising costs
   b. Freight in
   c. Freight out
   d. Purchasing agent wages

2. Which inventory system maintains a running record of inventory on hand, purchased, and sold?
   a. Accrued
   b. Periodic
   c. Consigned
   d. Perpetual

3. How is cost of goods sold classified in the financial statements?
   a. As a revenue
   b. As an expense
   c. As an asset
   d. As a liability

Questions 4–7 use the following data of Snyder Company:

	Units	Unit Cost	Total Cost
Beginning inventory	20	$100	$2,000
Purchase on July 3	60	120	7,200
Sales	65	?	?

4. Snyder's total cost of goods available for sale would be:

a. $2,000. **b.** $7,200. **c.** $8,000. **d.** $9,200.

5. Snyder's cost of goods sold using the average-cost method would be:

a. $1,725. **b.** $6,500. **c.** $7,475. **d.** $9,200.

6. Snyder's ending inventory using the FIFO method would be:

a. $1,500. **b.** $1,800. **c.** $7,400. **d.** $9,200.

7. Snyder's cost of goods sold using the LIFO method would be:

a. $7,200. **b.** $7,400. **c.** $7,475. **d.** $7,700.

8. Which U.S. GAAP principle or rule would apply if the net realizable value of a company's inventory is below its original cost?

a. Lower-of-cost-or-market rule **b.** Consistency principle **c.** Disclosure principle **d.** Historical cost principle

Use the following information for questions 9–12.

Corrigan Corporation had beginning inventory of $20,000 and ending inventory of $24,000. Its net sales were $164,000 and net purchases were $81,000.

9. Corrigan's cost of goods sold for the period is

a. $63,000. **b.** $77,000. **c.** $85,000. **d.** $79,000.

10. Corrigan's gross profit for the period is

a. $79,000. **b.** $83,000. **c.** $87,000. **d.** $164,000.

11. What is Corrigan's gross profit percentage (rounded to the nearest whole percentage)?

a. 53% **b.** 51% **c.** 48% **d.** 47%

12. What is Corrigan's rate of inventory turnover?

a. 3.2 times **b.** 3.9 times **c.** 3.5 times **d.** 4.0 times

13. A company's beginning inventory is $150,000, its net purchases are $230,000, and its net sales total $440,000. Its normal gross profit percentage is 30% of sales. Using the gross profit method, how much is ending inventory?

a. $132,000 **b.** $72,000 **c.** $210,000 **d.** $228,000

14. An understatement of ending inventory by $2 million in one period results in

a. an overstatement of gross profit by $2 million in the next period.

b. an understatement of gross profit by $2 million in the next period.

c. no effect on net income of the next period.

d. an overstatement of the beginning inventory by $2 million in the next period.

Excel Project
Autograded Excel Project available in **MyLab Accounting**.

ASSESS YOUR PROGRESS

Ethics Check

EC6-1 Identify ethical principle violated

For each of the situations listed, identify which of three principles (integrity, objectivity and independence, or due care) from the AICPA Code of Professional Conduct is violated. Assume all persons listed in the situations are members of the AICPA. (Note: Refer to the AICPA Code of Professional Conduct contained on pages 25–27 in Chapter 1 for descriptions of the principles.)

a. Maureen's company is switching to FIFO, after using the LIFO method for several years. Maureen does not remember how to apply the FIFO method, but is too busy to review the technique. She figures the auditors will catch anything she does wrong.

b. Elyse is an auditor at a public accounting firm. She is auditing one of her firm's largest clients. Her aunt is the CEO of this client. Elyse does not mention the relationship to her manager.

c. A fire at Steve's company has destroyed most of the accounting records and a significant amount of inventory. He finds some partial records he can use to estimate the amount of inventory the company had on hand using the gross profit method. He knows that the quantity on hand was much lower than what he claims on the insurance form he submits, but rationalizes that his company has paid insurance premiums for many years.

d. Wei is the chief accountant for a furniture manufacturer. Two years ago, Wei changed the company's inventory method to FIFO. This year, Wei is changing back to LIFO. The motivation for the changes is solely to manipulate net income.

Short Exercises

S6-1. ***(Learning Objective 1: Show how to account for inventory transactions)*** Jasmine Corporation purchased inventory costing $125,000 and sold 75% of the goods for $163,750. All purchases and sales were on account. Jasmine later collected 25% of the accounts receivable. Assume that sales returns are nonexistent. LO 1

1. Journalize these transactions for Jasmine, which uses the perpetual inventory system.
2. For these transactions, show what Jasmine will report for inventory, revenues, and expenses on its financial statements at the end of the month. Report gross profit on the appropriate statement. Assume beginning inventory is $0.

S6-2. ***(Learning Objective 1: Show how to account for inventory transactions)*** Beavercreek Company sold 14,000 jars of its organic honey in the most current year for $15 per jar. The company had paid $10.50 per jar of honey. (Assume that sales returns are nonexistent.) Calculate the following: LO 1

1. Sales revenue
2. Cost of goods sold
3. Gross profit

LO 1 **S6-3.** ***(Learning Objective 1: Show how to account for inventory transactions)*** Marshall Company made total purchases of $260,000 in the most current year. It paid freight in of $3,500 on its purchases. Freight out, the cost to deliver the merchandise when it was sold to Marshall's customers, totaled $7,500. Of the total purchases Marshall made during the period, it returned $25,500 of the merchandise. Marshall took advantage of $2,800 of purchase discounts offered by its vendors. What was Marshall's cost of inventory?

LO 2 **S6-4.** ***(Learning Objective 2: Apply the average-cost, FIFO, and LIFO methods)*** Carson Print Supplies, Inc., sells laser printers and supplies. Assume Carson started the year with 100 containers of ink (average cost of $8.90 each, FIFO cost of $9.00 each, LIFO cost of $7.80 each). During the year, the company purchased 800 containers of ink at $9.80 and sold 600 units for $21.50 each. Carson paid operating expenses throughout the year, a total of $4,000. Ignore income taxes for this exercise.

Prepare Carson's income statement for the current year ended December 31 using the average-cost, FIFO, and LIFO inventory costing methods. Include a complete statement heading.

LO 2 **S6-5.** ***(Learning Objective 2: Compare income tax effects of the inventory costing methods)*** This exercise should be used in conjunction with S6-4. Carson Print Supplies, Inc., is a corporation subject to a 25% income tax. Compute the company's income tax expense under the average-cost, FIFO, and LIFO inventory costing methods. Which method would you select to (a) maximize income before tax and (b) minimize income tax expense?

Short Exercises S6-6 through S6-8 use the following data of Sandy Corporation:

A1

	A	B	C	D
1		**Quantity**	**Unit Cost**	**Total**
2	Beginning inventory	90	$ 4.00	$ 360
3	Purchases	180	$ 7.00	$ 1,260
4	Goods available for sale	270		
5	Ending inventory	80		
6	Cost of goods sold	190		
7				

LO 2 **S6-6.** ***(Learning Objective 2: Apply the average-cost method)*** Using the average-cost method, calculate the cost of ending inventory and cost of goods sold for Sandy Corporation.

LO 2 **S6-7.** ***(Learning Objective 2: Apply the FIFO method)*** Using the FIFO method, calculate the cost of ending inventory and cost of goods sold for Sandy Corporation.

LO 2 **S6-8.** ***(Learning Objective 2: Apply the LIFO method)*** Using the LIFO method, calculate the cost of ending inventory and cost of goods sold for Sandy Corporation.

LO 2 **S6-9.** ***(Learning Objective 2: Compare income, tax, and other effects of the inventory methods)*** This exercise tests your understanding of the four inventory methods. List the name of the inventory method that best fits the description. Assume that the cost of inventory is rising.

1. Results in a cost of ending inventory that is close to the current cost of replacing the inventory
2. Used to account for automobiles, jewelry, and art objects
3. Generally associated with saving income taxes
4. Provides a middle-ground measure of ending inventory and cost of goods sold
5. Maximizes reported income
6. Enables a company to keep reported income from dropping lower by liquidating older layers of inventory (assume rising prices)
7. Writes inventory down when its net realizable value drops below its historical cost
8. Results in an old measure of the cost of ending inventory
9. Matches the most current cost of goods sold against sales revenue
10. Enables a company to buy high-cost inventory at year-end and thereby decrease reported income and income tax

LO 3

S6-10. ***(Learning Objective 3: Apply the lower-of-cost-or-market rule to inventory)*** It is December 31, the end of the year, and the controller of Reed Corporation is applying the lower-of-cost-or-market (LCM) rule to inventories. Before any year-end adjustments, the company reports the following data:

Cost of goods sold..	$450,000
Historical cost of ending inventory, as determined by a physical count..............	66,000

Reed determines that the net realizable value of ending inventory is $42,000. Show what Reed should report for ending inventory and for cost of goods sold. Identify the financial statement where each item appears.

LO 4

S6-11. ***(Learning Objective 4: Compute ratio data to evaluate operations)*** Fairbanks Company made sales of $24,600 million during 2018. Cost of goods sold for the year totaled $9,840 million. At the end of 2017, Fairbanks' inventory stood at $1,000 million, and Fairbanks ended 2018 with inventory of $1,400 million. Compute Fairbanks' gross profit percentage and rate of inventory turnover for 2018.

LO 5

S6-12. ***(Learning Objective 5: Estimate ending inventory by the gross profit method)*** Volcano Technology began the year with inventory of $275,000 and purchased $1,850,000 of goods during the year. Sales for the year are $2,600,000, and Volcano Technology's gross profit percentage is 40% of sales. Compute Volcano Technology's estimated cost of ending inventory by using the gross profit method.

LO 6

S6-13. ***(Learning Objective 6: Analyze the effect of an inventory error on two years)*** Warner Supply's $3.5 million cost of inventory at the end of last year was understated by $1.9 million.

1. Was last year's reported gross profit of $3.1 million overstated, understated, or correct? What was the correct amount of gross profit last year?
2. Is this year's gross profit of $3.4 million overstated, understated, or correct? What is the correct amount of gross profit for the current year?
3. Was last year's reported cost of goods sold of $5.2 million overstated, understated, or correct? What was the correct amount of cost of goods sold last year?
4. Is this year's cost of goods sold of $5.3 million overstated, understated, or correct? What is the correct amount of cost of goods sold for this year?

LO 6

S6-14. ***(Learning Objective 6: Analyze the effect of an inventory error on multiple years)*** Here is the original schedule of cost of goods sold for Talladega Company for the years of 2016 through 2019:

A1

	A	B	C	D	E
1		2019	2018	2017	2016
2	Beginning inventory	$ 750	$ 600	$ 650	$ 700
3	+ Purchases	950	1,150	1,250	900
4	= Cost of goods available	$ 1,700	$ 1,750	$ 1,900	$ 1,600
5	− Ending inventory	300	750	600	650
6	= Cost of goods sold	$ 1,400	$ 1,000	$ 1,300	$ 950
7					

During the preparation of its 2019 financial statements, Talladega Company discovered that its 2017 ending inventory was understated by $400. Make the correction to the 2017 ending inventory and all other numbers in the schedule of cost of goods sold for any years affected.

1. What is the corrected cost of goods sold for 2017?
2. Did the understatement of ending inventory in 2017 cause the 2017 cost of goods sold to be overstated or understated?
3. What is the corrected cost of goods sold for 2018?
4. Did the understatement of ending inventory in 2017 cause the 2018 cost of goods sold to be overstated or understated?
5. Were any other years impacted by the 2017 $400 understatement of ending inventory? Why or why not?

Exercises MyLab Accounting

Group A

LO 1, 2

E6-15A. ***(Learning Objectives 1, 2: Show how to account for inventory transactions; apply the FIFO cost method)*** Accounting records for Jubilee Corporation yield the following data for the year ended June 30, 2018 (assume sales returns are non-existent):

Inventory, June 30, 2017	$ 7,000
Purchases of inventory (on account)	61,000
Sales of inventory—77% on account; 23% for cash (cost $49,000)	100,000
Inventory at FIFO, June 30, 2018	19,000

Requirements

1. Journalize Jubilee's inventory transactions for the year under the perpetual system.
2. Report ending inventory, sales, cost of goods sold, and gross profit on the appropriate financial statement.

LO 1, 2

E6-16A. ***(Learning Objectives 1, 2: Show how to account for inventory transactions; apply the FIFO cost method)*** Griffin Company's inventory records for its retail division show the following at December 31:

Dec 1	Beginning inventory	9 units @ $165	=	$1,485
15	Purchase	5 units @ 166	=	$ 830
26	Purchase	13 units @ 175	=	$2,275

At December 31, 11 of these units are on hand. Journalize the following for Griffin Company under the perpetual system:

1. Total December purchases in one summary entry. All purchases were on credit.
2. Total December sales and cost of goods sold in two summary entries. The selling price was $500 per unit, and all sales were on credit. Assume that Griffin uses the FIFO inventory method.
3. Under FIFO, how much gross profit would Griffin earn for the month ending December 31? What is the FIFO cost of Griffin Company's ending inventory?

LO 2

E6-17A. ***(Learning Objective 2: Compare ending inventory and cost of goods sold using four methods)*** Use the data for Griffin Company in E6-16A to answer the following.

Requirements

1. Compute cost of goods sold and ending inventory, using each of the following methods:
   a. Specific identification, with seven $165 units and four $175 units still on hand at the end
   b. Average cost
   c. FIFO
   d. LIFO
2. Which method produces the highest cost of goods sold? Which method produces the lowest cost of goods sold? What causes the difference in cost of goods sold?

LO 2

E6-18A. ***(Learning Objective 2: Compare the tax advantage of LIFO over FIFO)*** Use the data for Griffin Company in E6-16A to illustrate Griffin's income tax advantage from using LIFO over FIFO. Sales revenue is $8,000, operating expenses are $2,000, and the income tax rate is 30%. How much in taxes would Griffin Company save by using the LIFO method versus FIFO?

LO 2

E6-19A. ***(Learning Objective 2: Apply the average, FIFO, and LIFO methods)*** Selma Company's inventory records for the most recent year contain the following data:

A1

	A	B	C
1		Quantity	Unit Cost
2	Beginning inventory	4,000	$ 8.00
3	Purchases during year	16,000	$ 12.00
4			

Selma Company sold a total of 18,500 units during the year.

Requirements

1. Using the average-cost method, compute the cost of goods sold and ending inventory for the year.
2. Using the FIFO method, compute the cost of goods sold and ending inventory for the year.
3. Using the LIFO method, compute the cost of goods sold and ending inventory for the year.

LO 2

E6-20A. ***(Learning Objective 2: Compare ending inventory and cost of goods sold—FIFO vs. LIFO)*** Woody's specializes in sound equipment. Company records indicate the following data for a line of speakers:

Date	Item	Quantity	Unit Cost	Sale Price
Mar 1	Balance..................	11	$46	
2	Purchase................	7	68	
7	Sale	6		$91
13	Sale	4		91

Requirements

1. Determine the amounts that Woody's should report for cost of goods sold and ending inventory two ways:
   a. FIFO
   b. LIFO
2. Woody's uses the FIFO method. Prepare the company's income statement for the month ended March 31, 2018, reporting gross profit. Operating expenses totaled $330, and the income tax rate was 35%.

LO 2

E6-21A. ***(Learning Objective 2: Compare gross profit—FIFO vs. LIFO—falling prices)*** Suppose a Walmart store in Fillmore, Missouri, ended January 2018 with 900,000 units of merchandise that cost $5 each. Suppose the store then sold 50,000 units for $510,000 during February. Further, assume the store made two large purchases during February as follows:

Feb 10	10,000 units @ $3.10	=	$31,000
21	25,000 units @ $2.20	=	$55,000

Requirements

1. Calculate the store's gross profit under both FIFO and LIFO at February 28.
2. What caused the FIFO and LIFO gross profit figures to differ?

LO 3

E6-22A. ***(Learning Objective 3: Apply the lower-of-cost-or-market rule to inventories)*** Oak Ridge Garden Supplies uses a perpetual inventory system. The company has these account balances at May 31, 2018, prior to making the year-end adjustments:

Inventory		Cost of Goods Sold		Sales Revenue	
Beg bal 10,000					
End bal 13,000		Bal 71,000			Bal 120,000

A year ago, the net realizable value of ending inventory was $11,500, which exceeded the cost of $10,000. Oak Ridge has determined that the net realizable value of the May 31, 2018, ending inventory is $12,000.

Requirement

1. Prepare the company's 2018 income statement through gross profit to show how the company would apply the lower-of-cost-or-market rule to its inventories.

LO 5

E6-23A. ***(Learning Objective 5: Compute cost of goods sold and gross profit)*** Supply the missing income statement amounts for each of the following companies:

Company	Net Sales	Beginning Inventory	Net Purchases	Ending Inventory	Cost of Goods Sold	Gross Profit
Sutherland	$100,000	$20,000	$59,000	$16,000	(a)	(b)
Crossen	125,000	28,000	(c)	45,000	(d)	52,000
Williams	(e)	(f)	52,000	20,000	60,000	36,000
Scott	88,000	7,000	29,000	(g)	33,000	(h)

Requirement

1. Prepare the income statement for Sutherland Company for the year ended December 31, 2018. Use the cost-of-goods-sold model to compute cost of goods sold. Sutherland's operating and other expenses for the year were $36,000. Ignore income tax.

Note: E6-24A builds on E6-23A with a profitability analysis of these companies.

LO 4

E6-24A. ***(Learning Objective 4: Evaluate profitability and inventory turnover)*** Refer to the data in E6-23A. Compute all ratio values to answer the following questions:

- Which company has the highest and which company has the lowest gross profit percentage?
- Which company has the highest and which has the lowest rate of inventory turnover?

Based on your figures, which company appears to be the most profitable?

LO 4

E6-25A. ***(Learning Objective 4: Compute and evaluate gross profit percentage and inventory turnover)*** The Blue Heron Shop had the following inventory data:

	2017	2018
Ending inventory at:		
FIFO Cost	$15,160	$ 30,040
LIFO Cost	12,440	18,520
Cost of goods sold at:		
FIFO Cost		$ 81,360
LIFO Cost		92,880
Sales revenue		144,000

Company managers need to know the company's gross profit percentage and rate of inventory turnover for 2018 under

1. FIFO.
2. LIFO.

Which method produces a higher gross profit percentage? A higher inventory turnover?

LO 5

E6-26A. ***(Learning Objective 5: Use the COGS model to make management decisions)*** McGuire Industries prepares budgets to help manage the company. McGuire is budgeting for the fiscal year ended January 31, 2018. During the preceding year ended January 31, 2017, sales totaled $9,200 million and cost of goods sold was $6,300 million. At January 31, 2017, inventory was $1,700 million. During the upcoming 2018 year, suppose McGuire expects cost of goods sold to increase by 12%. The company budgets next year's ending inventory at $2,000 million.

Requirement

1. One of the most important decisions a manager makes is how much inventory to buy. How much inventory should McGuire purchase during the upcoming year to reach its budget?

LO 5

E6-27A. ***(Learning Objective 5: Use the COGS model to make management decisions)*** Valentine Antiques, Inc., began May with inventory of $49,300. The business made net purchases of $50,200 and had net sales of $81,300 before a fire destroyed the company's inventory. For the past several years, Valentine's gross profit percentage has been 45%. Estimate the cost of the inventory destroyed by the fire. Identify another reason that owners and managers use the gross profit method to estimate inventory.

LO 6

E6-28A. ***(Learning Objective 6: Analyze the effect of an inventory error)*** Banta Tile & Marble Corporation reported the following comparative income statements for the years ended November 30, 2018, and 2017:

A1

	A	B	C	D	E
1	**Banta Tile & Marble Corporation Income Statements For the Years Ended November 30, 2018 and 2017**				
2		**2018**		**2017**	
3	Sales revenue		$ 138,000		$ 125,000
4	Cost of goods sold:				
5	Beginning inventory	$ 15,000		$ 14,500	
6	Net purchases	78,000		66,000	
7	Cost of goods available	93,000		80,500	
8	Ending inventory	(18,500)		(15,000)	
9	Cost of goods sold		74,500		65,500
10	Gross profit		63,500		59,500
11	Operating expenses		31,000		29,000
12	Net income		$ 32,500		$ 30,500
13					

Banta's president and shareholders are thrilled by the company's boost in sales and net income during 2018. Then the accountants for the company discover that ending 2017 inventory was understated by $8,500. Prepare the corrected comparative income statements for the two-year period, complete with a heading for the statements. How well did Banta really perform in 2018 as compared with 2017?

Group B

LO 1, 2

E6-29B. ***(Learning Objectives 1, 2: Show how to account for inventory transactions; apply the FIFO cost method)*** Accounting records for Allegheny Corporation yield the following data for the year ended June 30, 2018:

Inventory, June 30, 2017	$ 13,000
Purchases of inventory (on account)	53,000
Sales of inventory—82% on account; 18% for cash (cost $46,000)	73,000
Inventory at FIFO, June 30, 2018	20,000

Requirements

1. Journalize Allegheny's inventory transactions for the year under the perpetual system.
2. Report ending inventory, sales, cost of goods sold, and gross profit on the appropriate financial statement.

LO 1, 2

E6-30B. ***(Learning Objectives 1, 2: Show how to account for inventory transactions; apply the FIFO cost method)*** Spear Corporation's inventory records for its retail division show the following at May 31:

May 1	Beginning inventory	10 units @ $160	=	$1,600
15	Purchase	5 units @ 161	=	805
26	Purchase	14 units @ 170	=	2,380

At May 31, 11 of these units are on hand. Journalize the following for Spear Corporation under the perpetual system:

1. Total May purchases in one summary entry. All purchases were on credit.
2. Total May sales and cost of goods sold in two summary entries. The selling price was $560 per unit, and all sales were on credit. Assume that Spear uses the FIFO inventory method.
3. Under FIFO, how much gross profit would Spear earn for the month ending May 31? What is the FIFO cost of Spear Corporation's ending inventory?

LO 2

E6-31B. ***(Learning Objective 2: Compare ending inventory and cost of goods sold using four methods)*** Use the data for Spear Corporation in E6-30B to answer the following.

Requirements

1. Compute cost of goods sold and ending inventory using each of the following methods:
   a. Specific identification, with seven $160 units and four $170 units still on hand at the end
   b. Average cost
   c. FIFO
   d. LIFO
2. Which method produces the highest cost of goods sold? Which method produces the lowest cost of goods sold? What causes the difference in cost of goods sold?

E6-32B. ***(Learning Objective 2: Compare the tax advantage of LIFO over FIFO)*** Use the data for Spear Corporation in E6-30B to illustrate Spear's income tax advantage from using LIFO over FIFO. Sales revenue is $10,080, operating expenses are $800, and the income tax rate is 25%. How much in taxes would Spear Corporation save by using the LIFO method versus FIFO? LO 2

E6-33B. ***(Learning Objective 2: Apply the average, FIFO, and LIFO methods)*** Sherwood Company's inventory records for the most recent year contain the following data: LO 2

	A	B	C
1		Quantity	Unit Cost
2	Beginning inventory	2,000	$ 4.00
3	Purchases during year	18,000	$ 6.00
4			

Sherwood Company sold a total of 19,800 units during the year.

Requirements

1. Using the average-cost method, compute the cost of goods sold and ending inventory for the year.
2. Using the FIFO method, compute the cost of goods sold and ending inventory for the year.
3. Using the LIFO method, compute the cost of goods sold and ending inventory for the year.

E6-34B. ***(Learning Objective 2: Compare ending inventory and cost of goods sold—FIFO vs. LIFO)*** Paulson's specializes in sound equipment. Company records indicate the following data for a line of speakers: LO 2

Date	Item	Quantity	Unit Cost	Sale Price
Jun 1	Balance..................	18	$49	
2	Purchase................	3	64	
7	Sale	7		$115
13	Sale	6		103

Requirements

1. Determine the amounts that Paulson's should report for cost of goods sold and ending inventory two ways:
   a. FIFO
   b. LIFO
2. Paulson's uses the FIFO method. Prepare the company's income statement for the month ended June 30, 2018, reporting gross profit. Operating expenses totaled $340, and the income tax rate was 35%.

E6-35B. ***(Learning Objective 2: Compare gross profit—FIFO vs. LIFO—falling prices)*** Suppose a **Target** store in Chicago, Illinois, ended November 2018 with 500,000 units of merchandise that cost $8.00 each. Suppose the store then sold 110,000 units for $960,000 during December. Further, assume the store made two large purchases during December as follows: LO 2

Dec 8	35,000 units @ $6.10	=	$213,500
28	50,000 units @ $5.20	=	$260,000

Requirements

1. Calculate the store's gross profit under FIFO and LIFO at December 31.
2. What caused the FIFO and LIFO gross profit figures to differ?

LO 3

E6-36B. ***(Learning Objective 3: Apply the lower-of-cost-or-market rule to inventories)*** Huron Garden Supplies uses a perpetual inventory system. The company has these account balances at October 31, 2018, prior to making the year-end adjustments:

Inventory		Cost of Goods Sold		Sales Revenue	
Beg bal 10,500					
End bal 15,500		Bal 73,000			Bal 119,000

A year ago, the net realizable value of ending inventory was $12,800, which exceeded the cost of $10,500. Huron has determined that the net realizable value of the October 31, 2018, ending inventory is $11,000.

Requirement

1. Prepare the company's 2018 income statement through gross profit to show how the company would apply the lower-of-cost-or-market rule to its inventories.

LO 5

E6-37B. ***(Learning Objective 5: Compute cost of goods sold and gross profit)*** Supply the missing amounts for each of the following companies:

Company	Net Sales	Beginning Inventory	Net Purchases	Ending Inventory	Cost of Goods Sold	Gross Profit
Altieri	$115,000	$26,000	$63,000	$20,000	(a)	(b)
Malbasa	150,000	31,000	(c)	29,000	(d)	57,000
Hoffman	(e)	(f)	55,000	23,000	69,000	31,000
Hinkel	80,000	11,000	26,000	(g)	32,000	(h)

Requirement

1. Prepare the income statement for Altieri Company for the year ended December 31, 2018. Use the cost-of-goods-sold model to compute cost of goods sold. Altieri's operating and other expenses for the year were $34,000. Ignore income tax.

Note: E6-38B builds on E6-37B with a profitability analysis of these companies.

LO 4

E6-38B. ***(Learning Objective 4: Evaluate profitability and inventory turnover)*** Refer to the data in E6-37B. Compute all ratio values to answer the following questions:

- Which company has the highest and which company has the lowest gross profit percentage?
- Which company has the highest and which has the lowest rate of inventory turnover?

Based on your figures, which company appears to be the most profitable?

LO 4

E6-39B. ***(Learning Objective 4: Compute and evaluate gross profit percentage and inventory turnover)*** The Red Wagon Shop had the following inventory data:

	2017	2018
Ending inventory at:		
FIFO Cost	$27,920	$ 30,500
LIFO Cost	12,510	20,150
Cost of goods sold at:		
FIFO Cost		$ 87,630
LIFO Cost		97,980
Sales revenue		138,000

Company managers need to know the company's gross profit percentage and rate of inventory turnover for 2018 under

1. FIFO.
2. LIFO.

Which method produces a higher gross profit percentage? A higher inventory turnover?

LO 5

E6-40B. ***(Learning Objective 5: Use the COGS model to make management decisions)*** Spicer Industries prepares budgets to help manage the company. Spicer is budgeting for the fiscal year ended January 31, 2018. During the preceding year ended January 31, 2017, sales totaled $9,700 million and cost of goods sold was $6,400 million. At January 31, 2017, inventory was $1,500 million. During the upcoming 2018 year, suppose Spicer expects cost of goods sold to increase by 12%. The company budgets next year's ending inventory at $1,800 million.

Requirement

1. One of the most important decisions a manager makes is how much inventory to buy. How much inventory should Spicer purchase during the upcoming year to reach its budget?

LO 5

E6-41B. ***(Learning Objective 5: Use the COGS model to make management decisions)*** Sokol Antiques, Inc., began June with inventory of $48,400. The business made net purchases of $51,300 and had net sales of $104,000 before a fire destroyed the company's inventory. For the past several years, Sokol's gross profit percentage has been 35%. Estimate the cost of the inventory destroyed by the fire. Identify another reason that owners and managers use the gross profit method to estimate inventory.

LO 6

E6-42B. ***(Learning Objective 6: Analyze the effect of an inventory error)*** Simon Granite & Stone Corporation reported the following comparative income statements for the years ended September 30, 2018, and 2017:

	A	B	C	D	E
1	**Simon Granite & Stone Corporation Income Statements For the Years Ended September 30, 2018 and 2017**				
2		**2018**		**2017**	
3	Sales revenue		$ 140,000		$ 121,000
4	Cost of goods sold:				
5	Beginning inventory	$ 13,000		$ 12,000	
6	Net purchases	78,000		74,000	
7	Cost of goods available	91,000		86,000	
8	Ending inventory	(16,000)		(13,000)	
9	Cost of goods sold		75,000		73,000
10	Gross profit		65,000		48,000
11	Operating expenses		29,000		19,000
12	Net income		$ 36,000		$ 29,000
13					

Simon's president and shareholders are thrilled by the company's boost in sales and net income during 2018. Then the accountants for the company discover that ending 2017 inventory was understated by $6,000. Prepare the corrected comparative income statements for the two-year period, complete with a heading for the statements. How well did Simon really perform in 2018 as compared with 2017?

Quiz

Test your understanding of accounting for inventory by answering the following questions. Select the best choice from among the possible answers given.

Q6-43. When does the cost of inventory become an expense?

a. When cash is collected from the customer
b. When inventory is delivered to a customer
c. When payment is made to the supplier
d. When inventory is purchased from the supplier

Q6-44. Lakeside Software began January with $3,900 of merchandise inventory. During January, Lakeside made the following entries for its inventory transactions:

	A	B	C	D
1		Inventory	6,000	
2		Accounts Payable		6,000
3				
4		Accounts Receivable	7,500	
5		Sales Revenue		7,500
6				
7		Cost of Goods Sold	5,600	
8		Inventory		5,600
9				

How much was Lakeside's inventory at the end of January?

a. $4,300 **c.** $ – 0 –
b. $9,900 **d.** $6,000

Q6-45. What was Lakeside's gross profit for January?

a. $7,500 **c.** $1,900
b. $ – 0 – **d.** $5,600

Q6-46. The word *market* as used in "the lower of cost or market" generally means

a. net realizable value. **c.** retail market price.
b. liquidation price. **d.** original cost.

Q6-47. The sum of ending inventory and cost of goods sold is

a. net purchases.
b. beginning inventory.
c. cost of goods available (or cost of goods available for sale).
d. gross profit.

The next two questions use the following facts. The Corner Frame Shop wants to know the effect of different inventory costing methods on its financial statements. Inventory and purchases data for June are:

		Units	Unit Cost	Total Cost
Jun 1	Beginning inventory	2,500	$11.00	$27,500
4	Purchase	1,800	$11.80	21,240
9	Sale	(1,900)		

Q6-48. If The Corner Frame Shop uses the FIFO method, the cost of the ending inventory will be

a. $21,200. **c.** $21,240.
b. $20,900. **d.** $27,840.

Q6-49. If The Corner Frame Shop uses the LIFO method, cost of goods sold will be

a. $21,200. **c.** $20,900.
b. $21,240. **d.** $22,340.

Q6-50. In a period of rising prices,

a. cost of goods sold under LIFO will be less than under FIFO.
b. gross profit under FIFO will be higher than under LIFO.
c. LIFO inventory will be greater than FIFO inventory.
d. net income under LIFO will be higher than under FIFO.

Q6-51. The income statement for Gilmore Uniforms shows gross profit of $143,000, operating expenses of $130,000, and cost of goods sold of $219,000. What is the amount of net sales revenue?

a. $362,000 **c.** $273,000
b. $492,000 **d.** $349,000

Q6-52. The following data come from the inventory records of Albrecht Company:

Net sales revenue	$623,000
Beginning inventory	65,000
Ending inventory	47,000
Net purchases	400,000

Based on these facts, the gross profit for Albrecht Company is

a. $120,000. **c.** $195,000.
b. $223,000. **d.** $205,000.

Q6-53. Pineview Company ended the month of March with inventory of $26,000. Pineview expects to end April with inventory of $14,000 after selling goods with a cost of $98,000. How much inventory must Pineview purchase during April in order to accomplish these results?

a. $112,000 **c.** $138,000
b. $110,000 **d.** $86,000

Q6-54. An error understated Golden Flash Company's December 31, 2018, ending inventory by $27,000. What effect will this error have on net income for 2019?

a. Understate it
b. Have no effect on it
c. Overstate it

Q6-55. Two financial ratios that clearly distinguish a discount chain such as Walmart from a high-end retailer such as **Gucci** are the gross profit percentage and the rate of inventory turnover. Which set of relationships is most likely for Gucci?

Gross profit percentage	Inventory turnover
a. Low	High
b. High	Low
c. High	High
d. Low	Low

Q6-56. A company's sales are $550,000 and cost of goods sold is $350,000. Beginning and ending inventories are $27,000 and $38,000, respectively. How many times did the company turn its inventory over during this period?

a. 10.8 times **c.** 7.4 times
b. 6.2 times **d.** 16.9 times

Q6-57. Roswell Corporation reported the following data:

Freight in	$ 22,000	Dividends	$ 5,000
Purchases	206,000	Purchase returns	6,000
Beginning inventory	51,000	Sales revenue	440,000
Purchase discounts	4,500	Ending inventory	45,000

Roswell's gross profit percentage is

a. 49.2.
b. 50.8.
c. 56.0.
d. 48.2.

Q6-58. Scott Equine Supplies had the following beginning inventory, net purchases, net sales, and gross profit percentage for the first quarter of 2018:

Beginning inventory, $51,000	Net purchases, $73,000
Net sales revenue, $94,000	Gross profit rate, 20%

By the gross profit method, the ending inventory should be

a. $75,200.
b. $48,800.
c. $105,200.
d. $124,000.

Q6-59. An error understated Power Corporation's December 31, 2018, ending inventory by $54,000. What effect will this error have on total assets and net income for 2018?

Assets	**Net income**
a. Understate	Understate
b. Understate	No effect
c. No effect	Overstate
d. No effect	No effect

Problems MyLab Accounting

Group A

LO **1, 2**

P6-60A. ***(Learning Objectives 1, 2: Show how to account for inventory in a perpetual system using the average-costing method)*** Eastern Trading Company purchases inventory in crates of merchandise; each crate of inventory is a unit. The fiscal year of Eastern Trading ends each January 31. Assume you are dealing with a single Eastern Trading store in San Diego, California. The San Diego store began the year with an inventory of 24,000 units that cost a total of $1,272,000. During the year, the store purchased merchandise on account as follows:

Jul (29,000 units at $55)	$1,595,000
Nov (49,000 units at $59)	2,891,000
Dec (59,000 units at $65)	3,835,000
Total purchases	$8,321,000

Cash payments on account totaled $7,993,000. During fiscal year 2018, the store sold 149,000 units of merchandise for $15,272,500, of which $4,700,000 was for cash and the balance was on account. Eastern Trading and all of its stores use the average-cost method for inventories. The San Diego store's operating expenses for the year were $4,250,000. It paid 70% in cash and accrued the rest as accrued liabilities. The store accrued income tax at the rate of 40%.

Requirements

1. Make summary journal entries to record the store's transactions for the year ended January 31, 2018. Eastern Trading and all of its stores use a perpetual inventory system. Round average cost per unit to two decimal places and round all other amounts to the nearest dollar.
2. Prepare a T-account to show the activity in the Inventory account.
3. Prepare the store's income statement for the year ended January 31, 2018. Show totals for gross profit, income before tax, and net income.

P6-61A. ***(Learning Objective 2: Apply various inventory costing methods)*** A Gold Medal Sports outlet store began August 2018 with 42 pairs of running shoes that cost the store $31 each. The sales price of these shoes was $63. During August, the store completed these inventory transactions:

LO 2

		Units	Unit Cost	Unit Sales Price
Aug 2	Sale	16	$31	$63
9	Purchase......	81	33	
13	Sale	26	31	63
18	Sale	13	33	64
22	Sale	36	33	64
29	Purchase......	18	35	

Requirements

1. The preceding data are taken from the store's perpetual inventory records. Which cost method does the store use? Explain how you arrived at your answer.
2. Determine the store's cost of goods sold for August. Also compute gross profit for August.
3. What is the cost of the store's August 31 inventory of running shoes?

P6-62A. ***(Learning Objective 2: Compare inventory by three methods)*** Navy Surplus began July 2018 with 80 stoves that cost $10 each. During the month, the company made the following purchases at cost:

LO 2

July 6	90 stoves @ $20 =	$1,800
18	100 stoves @ $25 =	2,500
26	30 stoves @ $30 =	900

The company sold 250 stoves, and at July 31, the ending inventory consisted of 50 stoves. The sales price of each stove was $52.

Requirements

1. Determine the cost of goods sold and ending inventory amounts for July under the average-cost, FIFO, and LIFO costing methods. Round the average cost per unit to two decimal places, and round all other amounts to the nearest dollar.
2. Explain why cost of goods sold is highest under LIFO. Be specific.
3. Prepare the Navy Surplus income statement for July. Report gross profit. Operating expenses totaled $3,250. The company uses average costing for inventory. The income tax rate is 40%.

LO 2

P6-63A. ***(Learning Objective 2: Compare various inventory costing methods)*** The records of Atlanta Aviation include the following accounts for inventory of aviation parts at July 31 of the current year:

Inventory

Aug 1	Balance	800 units @ $5.00	$ 4,000	
Nov 5	Purchase	500 units @ $6.80	3,400	
Jan 24	Purchase	8,000 units @ $7.00	56,000	
Apr 8	Purchase	700 units @ $8.00	5,600	

Sales Revenue

	Jul 31	9,090 units	$128,169

Requirements

1. Prepare a partial income statement through gross profit under the average-cost, FIFO, and LIFO methods. Round average cost per unit to two decimal places and all other amounts to the nearest dollar.
2. Which inventory method would you use to minimize income tax? Explain why this method causes income tax to be the lowest.

LO 3

P6-64A. ***(Learning Objective 3: Explain GAAP and apply the lower-of-cost-or-market rule to inventories)*** Anderson Trade Mart has recently had lackluster sales. The rate of inventory turnover has dropped, and the merchandise is gathering dust. At the same time, competition has forced Anderson's suppliers to lower the prices that Anderson will pay when it replaces its inventory. It is now December 31, 2018, and the net realizable value of Anderson's ending inventory is $55,000 below what the company actually paid for the goods, which was $265,000. Before any adjustments at the end of the period, the Cost of Goods Sold account has a balance of $820,000.

a. What accounting action should Anderson take in this situation?
b. Give any journal entry required.
c. At what amount should the company report Inventory on the balance sheet?
d. At what amount should the company report Cost of Goods Sold on the income statement?
e. Discuss the accounting principle or concept that is most relevant to this situation.

LO 4

P6-65A. ***(Learning Objective 4: Compute and evaluate gross margin and inventory turnover)*** Crispy Donut, Inc., and Calhoun Coffee Corporation are both specialty food chains. The two companies reported these figures, in millions:

A1

	A	B	C
1	**Crispy Donut, Inc. Income Statements (Adapted) Years Ended December 31**		
2	**(Amounts in millions)**	**2018**	**2017**
3	Revenues:		
4	Net sales	$ 600	$ 710
5			
6	Costs and Expenses:		
7	Cost of goods sold	540	602
8	Selling, general, and administrative expenses	64	53
9			

	A	B	C
1	**Crispy Donut, Inc.** **Balance Sheets (Adapted)** **December 31**		
2	**(Amounts in millions)**	**2018**	**2017**
3	**Assets**		
4	Current assets:		
5	Cash and cash equivalents	$ 13	$ 29
6	Receivables	23	38
7	Inventories	15	25
8			

	A	B	C
1	**Calhoun Coffee Corporation** **Income Statements (Adapted)** **Years Ended December 31**		
2	**(Amounts in millions)**	**2018**	**2017**
3	Net sales	$ 7,000	$ 6,399
4	Cost of goods sold	6,370	2,610
5	Selling, general, and administrative expenses	250	2,363
6			

	A	B	C
1	**Calhoun Coffee Corporation** **Balance Sheets (Adapted)** **December 31**		
2	**(Amounts in millions)**	**2018**	**2017**
3	**Assets**		
4	Current assets:		
5	Cash and temporary investments	$ 317	$ 177
6	Receivables, net	228	190
7	Inventories	700	600
8			

Requirements

1. Compute the gross margin percentage and the rate of inventory turnover for Crispy Donut and Calhoun Coffee for 2018.
2. Based on these statistics, which company looks more profitable? Why?

LO 4, 5

P6-66A. ***(Learning Objectives 4, 5: Compute gross profit; estimate inventory using the gross profit method)*** Cleveland Company, a camera store, lost some inventory in a fire on October 15. To file an insurance claim, the company must estimate its October 15 inventory using the gross profit method. For the past two years, Cleveland Company's gross profit has averaged 41% of net sales. Its inventory records reveal the following data:

Inventory, October 1	$ 57,700
Transactions October 1–15:	
Purchases	490,800
Purchase discounts	17,000
Purchase returns	70,900
Sales	660,000

Requirements

1. Estimate the cost of the lost inventory using the gross profit method.
2. Prepare the income statement for October 1 to October 15 for this product through gross profit. Show the detailed computations of cost of goods sold in a separate schedule.

LO 5

P6-67A. ***(Learning Objective 5: Use the COGS model to make management decisions, and estimate amount of inventory to purchase)*** Ricky's Convenience Stores' income statement for the year ended December 31, 2017, and its balance sheet as of December 31, 2017, are as follows:

	A	B
1	**Ricky's Convenience Stores Income Statement Year Ended December 31, 2017**	
2	Sales	$ 955,000
3	Cost of sales	719,000
4	Gross profit	236,000
5	Operating expenses	111,000
6	Net income	$ 125,000
7		

	A	B	C	D
1	**Ricky's Convenience Stores Balance Sheet December 31, 2017**			
2	**Assets**		**Liabilities and Capital**	
3	Cash	$ 39,000	Accounts payable	$ 30,000
4	Inventories	67,000	Note payable	195,000
5	Land and		Total liabilities	225,000
6	buildings, net	265,000	Owner, capital	146,000
7			Total liabilities	
8	Total assets	$ 371,000	and capital	$ 371,000
9				

The business is organized as a proprietorship, so it pays no corporate income tax. The owner is budgeting for 2018 and expects sales and cost of goods sold to increase by 7%. To meet customer demand, ending inventory will need to be $80,000 at December 31, 2018. The owner hopes to earn a net income of $152,000 next year.

Requirements

1. One of the most important decisions a manager makes is the amount of inventory to purchase. Show how to determine the amount of inventory to purchase in 2018.
2. Prepare the store's budgeted income statement for 2018 to reach the target net income of $152,000. To reach this goal, operating expenses must decrease by $10,480.

LO 6

P6-68A. ***(Learning Objective 6: Analyze the effects of inventory errors)*** The accounting records of Timberlake Home Store show these data (in millions):

	2018		2017		2016	
Net sales revenue		$40		$37		$34
Cost of goods sold:						
Beginning inventory	$ 11		$ 10		$ 9	
Net purchases	29		27		25	
Cost of goods available	40		37		34	
Less ending inventory	(12)		(11)		(10)	
Cost of goods sold		28		26		24
Gross profit		12		11		10
Operating expenses		3		3		3
Net income		$ 9		$ 8		$ 7

The shareholders are very happy with Timberlake's steady increase in net income. However, auditors discovered that the ending inventory for 2016 was understated by $5 million and that the ending inventory for 2017 was understated by $8 million. The ending inventory at December 31, 2018, was correct.

Requirements

1. Show corrected income statements for each of the three years.
2. How much did these assumed corrections add to or take away from Timberlake's total net income over the three-year period? How did the corrections affect the trend of net income?
3. Will Timberlake's shareholders still be happy with the company's trend of net income? Explain.

Group B

LO 1, 2

P6-69B. ***(Learning Objectives 1, 2: Show how to account for inventory in a perpetual system using the average-costing method)*** Western Trading Company purchases inventory in crates of merchandise; each crate of inventory is a unit. The fiscal year of Western Trading ends each January 31. Assume you are dealing with a single Western Trading store in Nashville, Tennessee. The Nashville store began the year with an inventory of 20,000 units that cost a total of $1,060,000. During the year, the store purchased merchandise on account as follows:

July (29,000 units at $59)	$1,711,000
November (49,000 units at $63)	3,087,000
December (59,000 units at $69)	4,071,000
Total purchases	$8,869,000

Cash payments on account totaled $8,541,000. During fiscal year 2018, the store sold 155,000 units of merchandise for $15,887,500, of which $4,900,000 was for cash and the balance was on account. Eastern Trading and all of its stores use the average-cost method for inventories. The Nashville store's operating expenses for the year were $2,250,000. It paid 70% in cash and accrued the rest as accrued liabilities. The store accrued income tax at the rate of 40%.

Requirements

1. Make summary journal entries to record the store's transactions for the year ended January 31, 2018. Western Trading and all of its stores use a perpetual inventory system. Round average cost per unit to two decimal places and round all other amounts to the nearest dollar.
2. Prepare a T-account to show the activity in the Inventory account.
3. Prepare the store's income statement for the year ended January 31, 2018. Show totals for gross profit, income before tax, and net income.

LO 2

P6-70B. ***(Learning Objective 2: Apply various inventory costing methods)*** A Swoosh Sports outlet store began December 2018 with 47 pairs of running shoes that cost the store $34 each. The sales price of these shoes was $63. During December, the store completed these inventory transactions:

			Units	Unit Cost	Unit Sale Price
Dec	2	Sale	20	$34	$63
	9	Purchase......	82	36	
	13	Sale	27	34	63
	18	Sale	11	36	64
	22	Sale	31	36	64
	29	Purchase......	27	38	

Requirements

1. The preceding data are taken from the store's perpetual inventory records. Which cost method does the store use? Explain how you arrived at your answer.
2. Determine the store's cost of goods sold for December. Also compute gross profit for December.
3. What is the cost of the store's December 31 inventory of running shoes?

LO 2

P6-71B. ***(Learning Objective 2: Compare inventory by three methods)*** SWAT Surplus began March 2018 with 100 tents that cost $10 each. During the month, the company made the following purchases at cost:

Mar	6	110 tents @ $20	=	$2,200
	18	120 tents @ $25	=	3,000
	26	40 tents @ $30	=	1,200

The company sold 318 tents, and at March 31, the ending inventory consisted of 52 tents. The sales price of each tent was $52.

Requirements

1. Determine the cost of goods sold and ending inventory amounts for March under the average-cost, FIFO, and LIFO costing methods. Round the average cost per unit to two decimal places, and round all other amounts to the nearest dollar.
2. Explain why cost of goods sold is highest under LIFO. Be specific.
3. Prepare the SWAT Surplus income statement for March. Report gross profit. Operating expenses totaled $3,250. The company uses average costing for inventory. The income tax rate is 36%.

LO 2

P6-72B. ***(Learning Objective 2: Compare various inventory costing methods)*** The records of Eaton Aviation include the following accounts for inventory of aviation parts at July 31 of the current year:

Inventory

Aug	1	Balance	800 units @ $7.00	$ 5,600	
Nov	5	Purchase	500 units @ $7.10	3,550	
Jan	24	Purchase	8,100 units @ $7.50	60,750	
Apr	8	Purchase	600 units @ $8.50	5,100	

Sales Revenue

	Jul 31	9,030 units	$130,935

Requirements

1. Prepare a partial income statement through gross profit under the average-cost, FIFO, and LIFO methods. Round average cost per unit to two decimal places and all other amounts to the nearest whole dollar.
2. Which inventory method would you use to minimize income tax? Explain why this method causes income tax to be the lowest.

LO 3

P6-73B. ***(Learning Objective 3: Explain GAAP and apply the lower-of-cost-or-market rule to inventories)*** Freshwater Trade Mart has recently had lackluster sales. The rate of inventory turnover has dropped, and the merchandise is gathering dust. At the same time, competition has forced Freshwater's suppliers to lower the prices that Freshwater will pay when it replaces its inventory. It is now December 31, 2018, and the net realizable value of Freshwater's ending inventory is $60,000 below what the company actually paid for the goods, which was $210,000. Before any adjustments at the end of the period, the Cost of Goods Sold account has a balance of $820,000.

a. What accounting action should Freshwater take in this situation?
b. Give any journal entry required.
c. At what amount should the company report Inventory on the balance sheet?
d. At what amount should the company report Cost of Goods Sold on the income statement?
e. Discuss the accounting principle or concept that is most relevant to this situation.

LO 4

P6-74B. ***(Learning Objective 4: Compute and evaluate gross margin and inventory turnover)*** Sprinkle Top, Inc., and Coffee Shop Corporation are both specialty food chains. The two companies reported these figures, in millions:

	A	B	C
1	**Sprinkle Top, Inc. Income Statements (Adapted) Years Ended December 31**		
2	**(Amounts in millions)**	**2018**	**2017**
3	Revenues:		
4	Net sales	$ 450	$ 701
5			
6	Costs and Expenses:		
7	Cost of goods sold	360	598
8	Selling, general, and administrative expenses	64	50
9			

	A	B	C
1	**Sprinkle Top, Inc. Balance Sheets (Adapted) December 31**		
2	**(Amounts in millions)**	**2018**	**2017**
3	**Assets**		
4	Current assets:		
5	Cash and temporary investments	$ 15	$ 32
6	Receivables	28	31
7	Inventories	10	30
8			

A1		
Coffee Shop Corporation Income Statements (Adapted) Years Ended December 31		
(Amounts in millions)	**2018**	**2017**
Net sales	$ 8,000	$ 6,370
Cost of goods sold	6,500	2,620
Selling, general, and administrative expenses	2,950	2,330

A1		
Coffee Shop Corporation Balance Sheets (Adapted) December 31		
(Amounts in millions)	**2018**	**2017**
Assets		
Current assets:		
Cash and temporary investments	$ 314	$ 171
Receivables, net	228	194
Inventories	780	470

Requirements

1. Compute the gross margin percentage and the rate of inventory turnover for Sprinkle Top and Coffee Shop for 2018.
2. Based on these statistics, which company looks more profitable? Why?

LO 4, 5

P6-75B. ***(Learning Objectives 4, 5: Compute gross profit; estimate inventory using the gross profit method)*** Ross Company, a camera store, lost some inventory in a fire on December 15. To file an insurance claim, the company must estimate its December 15 inventory using the gross profit method. For the past two years, Ross Company's gross profit has averaged 44% of net sales. Its inventory records reveal the following data:

Inventory, December 1	$ 57,700
Transactions December 1–15:	
Purchases	490,500
Purchase discounts	15,000
Purchase returns	70,500
Sales	664,000

Requirements

1. Estimate the cost of the lost inventory using the gross profit method.
2. Prepare the income statement for December 1 through December 15 for this product through gross profit. Show the detailed computation of cost of goods sold in a separate schedule.

LO 5

P6-76B. ***(Learning Objective 5: Use the COGS model to make management decisions, and estimate amount of inventory to purchase)*** Eddie's Convenience Stores' income statement for the year ended December 31, 2017, and its balance sheet as of December 31, 2017, are as follows:

	A	B
1	**Eddie's Convenience Stores** **Income Statement** **Year Ended December 31, 2017**	
2	Sales	$ 958,000
3	Cost of sales	717,000
4	Gross profit	241,000
5	Operating expenses	108,000
6	Net income	$ 133,000
7		

	A	B	C	D
1	**Eddie's Convenience Stores** **Balance Sheet** **December 31, 2017**			
2	**Assets**		**Liabilities and Capital**	
3	Cash	$ 39,000	Accounts payable	$ 28,000
4	Inventories	65,000	Note payable	185,000
5	Land and		Total liabilities	213,000
6	buildings, net	266,000	Owner, capital	157,000
7			Total liabilities	
8	Total assets	$ 370,000	and capital	$ 370,000
9				

The business is organized as a proprietorship, so it pays no corporate income tax. The owner is budgeting for 2018 and expects sales and cost of goods sold to increase by 9%. To meet customer demand, ending inventory will need to be $84,000 at December 31, 2018. The owner hopes to earn a net income of $156,000 next year.

Requirements

1. One of the most important decisions a manager makes is the amount of inventory to purchase. Show how to determine the amount of inventory to purchase in 2018.
2. Prepare the store's budgeted income statement for 2018 to reach the target net income of $156,000. To reach this goal, operating expenses must decrease by $1,310.

LO 6

P6-77B. ***(Learning Objective 6: Analyze the effects of inventory errors)*** The accounting records of Boston Home Store show these data (in millions):

	2018		2017		2016	
Net sales revenue		$41		$38		$35
Cost of goods sold:						
Beginning inventory	$ 9		$ 8		$ 7	
Net purchases	31		29		27	
Cost of goods available	40		37		34	
Less ending inventory	(10)		(9)		(8)	
Cost of goods sold		30		28		26
Gross profit		11		10		9
Operating expenses		3		3		3
Net income		$ 8		$ 7		$ 6

The shareholders are very happy with Boston's steady increase in net income. However, auditors discovered that the ending inventory for 2016 was understated by $6 million and that the ending inventory for 2017 was understated by $7 million. The ending inventory at December 31, 2018, was correct.

Requirements

1. Show corrected income statements for each of the three years.
2. How much did these assumed corrections add to or take away from Boston's total net income over the three-year period? How did the corrections affect the trend of net income?
3. Will Boston's shareholders still be happy with the company's trend of net income? Explain.

Challenge Exercises and Problem

LO 2

E6-78. ***(Learning Objective 2: Apply various inventory methods to make decisions)*** For each of the following situations, identify the inventory method that you would use; or, given the use of a particular method, state the strategy that you would follow to accomplish your goal.

a. Inventory costs are increasing, and the company prefers to report high income.

b. Inventory costs have been stable for several years, and you expect costs to remain stable for the indefinite future. (Give the reason for your choice of method.)

c. Inventory costs are decreasing, and your company's board of directors wants to minimize income taxes.

d. Your company prefers to use an inventory costing method that avoids extremes.

e. Inventory costs are increasing. Your company uses LIFO and is having an unexpectedly good year. It is near year-end, and you need to keep net income from increasing too much in order to save on income tax.

f. The supplier of your inventory is experiencing a labor strike, which could make it difficult for you to obtain inventory. Your income taxes could increase as a result.

LO 2

E6-79. ***(Learning Objective 2: Measure the effect of a LIFO liquidation)*** Suppose Chic Fashions, a specialty retailer, had these records for evening gowns during 2018:

Beginning inventory (41 @ $1,025)	$ 42,025
Purchase in February (17 @ $1,050)	17,850
Purchase in June (47 @ $1,175)	55,225
Purchase in December (33 @ $1,200)	39,600
Cost of goods available for sale	$154,700

Assume that Chic sold 112 gowns during 2018 and uses the LIFO method to account for inventory. Chic's income tax rate is 35%.

Requirements

1. Compute Chic's cost of goods sold for evening gowns in 2018.
2. Compute what cost of goods sold would have been if Chic had purchased enough inventory in December—at $1,200 per evening gown—to keep year-end inventory at the same level it was at the beginning of the year.

LO 4

E6-80. ***(Learning Objective 4: Evaluate profitability)*** Westpark Video, Inc., declared bankruptcy. The company reported these figures:

	A	B	C	D	E
1	**Westpark Video, Inc.** **Statements of Income** **Years Ended December 31**				
2	**Millions**	**2018**	**2017**	**2016**	**2015**
3	Sales	$ 36.2	$ 35.2	$ 34.3	
4	Cost of sales	28.7	27.5	26.7	
5	Selling expenses	8.1	6.4	5.6	
6	Other expenses	0.1	0.9	0.7	
7	Net income (net loss)	$ (0.7)	$ 0.4	$ 1.3	
8	Additional data:				
9	Ending inventory	$ 8.0	$ 7.6	$ 7.0	$ 6.4
10					

Requirement

1. Evaluate the trend of Westpark Video's results of operations during 2016 through 2018. Consider the trends of sales, gross profit, and net income. Track the gross profit percentage and the rate of inventory turnover in each year. Also discuss the role that selling expenses must have played in the company's recent history.

LO 1, 2, 4

P6-81. ***(Learning Objectives 1, 2, 4: Account for inventory; analyze two companies that use different inventory methods)*** Pickering Financial Management believes that the biotechnology industry is a good investment and is considering investing in one of two companies. However, one company, BrightWorld, Inc., uses the FIFO method of inventory, and another company, BioTech, Inc., uses LIFO. Because the companies use two different methods and because BioTech is a much larger company, it is difficult to compare their net incomes to see which is a better investment. The following information about the two companies is available from their annual reports:

BrightWorld, Inc.	2018	2017
Inventory	$ 96,000	$ 80,000
Cost of goods sold	1,144,000	913,000
Sales	1,760,000	1,660,000
Net income	197,000	190,000

BioTech, Inc.	2018	2017
Inventory (See Note)	$ 344,000	$ 299,000
Cost of goods sold	3,864,000	4,224,000
Sales	7,360,000	7,040,000
Net income	830,000	730,000

Notes to the Financial Statement. If BioTech had used the FIFO method, inventory would have been $21,000 higher at the end of 2017 and $26,000 higher at the end of 2018.

To better compare the two companies, Pickering wants you to prepare the following analysis.

Requirements

1. Show the computation of BioTech's cost of goods sold in 2018 using the LIFO method. Refer to Appendix 6B for an illustration.
2. Prepare summary journal entries for 2018 for BioTech's purchases of inventory (assume all purchases are on account), sales (assume all are on account), and cost of goods sold. Prepare a T-account for inventory and post these transactions into the T-account. The company uses the perpetual inventory method.
3. Show the computation of BioTech's cost of goods sold for 2018 using the FIFO method.
4. Compute the gross profit percentage for 2018 for both BrightWorld and BioTech using FIFO figures for both.
5. Compute the inventory turnover for 2018 for both BrightWorld and BioTech using FIFO figures for both.
6. Which company appears stronger? Support your answer.

APPLY YOUR KNOWLEDGE

Serial Case

LO 1, 4

C6-82 *(Learning Objectives 1,4: Analyze inventory and gross profit of a company in the restaurant industry)*

Note: This case is part of The Cheesecake Factory serial case contained in every chapter in this textbook.

The Cheesecake Factory Incorporated (NASDAQ: CAKE) operates over 200 restaurants and two bakeries in the United States. In its two bakeries, it bakes and prepares more than 70 desserts, both for its own use in its restaurants and for sale to a wide variety of wholesalers and retailers. The Cheesecake Factory's inventories consist of restaurant food and supplies, bakery raw materials, and bakery finished goods. To account for its inventory, the company uses the average-cost method at its restaurants and the FIFO method at its bakeries.

The Cheesecake Factory Incorporated's financial statements from its 2016 Form 10-K are as follows:

	A	B	C
1	**The Cheesecake Factory Incorporated** **Consolidated Balance Sheets: Condensed and adapted for educational use** ***(in thousands, except share data)***		
2		**January 3, 2017**	**December 29, 2015**
3	**Assets**		
4	Current assets:		
5	Cash and cash equivalents	$ 53,839	$ 43,854
6	Accounts receivable	15,632	14,159
7	Income tax receivable	-	18,739
8	Other receivables	64,592	72,658
9	Inventories	34,926	34,010
10	Prepaid expenses	52,438	41,976
11	Total current assets	221,427	225,396
12	Property and equipment, net	910,134	892,191
13	Other assets:		
14	Intangible assets, net	23,054	21,972
15	Prepaid rent	42,162	46,881
16	Other assets	96,542	46,906
17	Total other assets	161,758	115,759
18	Total assets	$ 1,293,319	$ 1,233,346
19			
20	**Liabilities and Stockholders' Equity**		
21	Current liabilities:		
22	Accounts payable	$ 41,564	$ 47,770
23	Other accrued expenses	334,962	302,456
24	Total current liabilities	376,526	350,226
25	Noncurrent liabilities	313,586	294,581
26	Stockholders' equity:		
27	Preferred stock	-	-
28	Common stock	947	931
29	Additional paid-in-capital	774,137	710,242
30	Retained earnings	1,238,012	1,140,788
31	Treasury stock	(1,409,889)	(1,263,422)
32	Total stockholders' equity	603,207	588,539
33	Total liabilities and stockholders' equity	$ 1,293,319	$ 1,233,346
34			
35	*Note: Financial information presented here should not be used for investment decisions.*		
36			

Source: Data from the U.S. Securities and Exchange Commission EDGAR Company Filings, www.sec.gov

	A	B	C	D
1	**The Cheesecake Factory Incorporated** **Consolidated Statements of Income: Condensed and adapted for educational use** ***(in thousands)***			
2				
3			**Fiscal Year**	
4		**2016**	**2015**	**2014**
5	Revenues	$ 2,275,719	$ 2,100,609	$ 1,976,624
6	Costs and expenses:			
7	Cost of sales	526,628	504,031	490,306
8	Labor expenses	759,998	684,818	646,102
9	Depreciation and amortization expense	88,010	85,563	82,835
10	Other expenses	700,090	660,951	612,650
11	Total costs and expenses	2,074,726	1,935,363	1,831,893
12	Income from operations	200,993	165,246	144,731
13	Interest and other expense, net	(9,225)	(5,894)	(6,187)
14	Income before income taxes	191,768	159,352	138,544
15	Income tax expense	52,274	42,829	37,268
16	Net income	$ 139,494	$ 116,523	$ 101,276
17				
18	*Note: Financial information presented here should not be used for investment decisions.*			
19				

Source: Data from the U.S. Securities and Exchange Commission EDGAR Company Filings, www.sec.gov

The preceding financial statements have been condensed and adapted for educational use and should not be used for investment decisions.

Requirements

1. Give an example of an item that could be found in each of the following types of inventory for The Cheesecake Factory:
   a. Restaurant food and supplies
   b. Bakery finished goods and work in progress inventory
   c. Bakery raw materials and supplies
2. In which financial statement is The Cheesecake Factory's inventory found? What is the balance of the company's inventory at January 3, 2017? At December 29, 2015?
3. In which financial statement is The Cheesecake Factory's cost of sales found? What is its cost of sales for fiscal year ended January 3, 2017? For fiscal year ended December 29, 2015? For fiscal year ended December 30, 2014?
4. Calculate The Cheesecake Factory's gross profit percentages for 2016 and 2015. Did its gross profit percentage improve or deteriorate from 2015 to 2016?
5. Calculate The Cheesecake Factory's inventory turnover for 2016 and 2015. (The Cheesecake Factory's inventory balance as of December 30, 2014, was $33,255 thousand.) Did the company's inventory turnover speed up or slow down from 2015 to 2016?
6. Next, calculate the days' inventory outstanding for 2016 and 2015. Do the number of days' inventory outstanding make sense for The Cheesecake Factory? Why or why not?

Decision Cases

LO 2

C6-83. ***(Learning Objective 2: Apply and compare various inventory methods, and assess the impact of a year-end purchase of inventory)*** Jasper Corporation is nearing the end of its first year of operations. Jasper made inventory purchases of $745,000 during the year, as follows:

January	1,000 units @	$100.00 =	$100,000
July	4,000	121.25	485,000
November	1,000	160.00	160,000
Totals	6,000		$745,000

Sales for the year are 5,000 units for $1,200,000 of revenue. Expenses other than cost of goods sold and income taxes total $200,000. The president of the company is undecided about whether to adopt the FIFO method or the LIFO method for inventories. The company's income tax rate is 40%.

Requirements

1. Prepare income statements for the company under FIFO and under LIFO.
2. Compare the net income under FIFO with the net income under LIFO. Which method produces the higher net income? What causes this difference? Be specific.

LO 2, 3

C6-84. ***(Learning Objectives 2, 3: Apply and compare various inventory cost methods; apply underlying GAAP for inventory)*** The inventory costing method a company chooses can affect its financial statements and the decisions of the people who use those statements.

Requirements

1. Company A uses the LIFO inventory method and discloses its use in the notes to the financial statements. Company B uses the FIFO method to account for its inventory. Company B does *not* disclose which inventory method it uses. Company B reports a higher net income than Company A. In which company would you prefer to invest? Give your reason.
2. Representational faithfulness is an accepted accounting concept. If you were a shareholder or a creditor of a company, would you want it to faithfully represent its accounting for inventory? Give your reason.

Ethical Issue

C6-85. During 2016, Coalmont, Inc., changed to the LIFO method. Suppose that during 2017, Coalmont changed back to the FIFO method. In 2018, the company switched back to LIFO again.

Requirements

1. What would you think of a company's ethics if it changed accounting methods every year?
2. What accounting principle would changing methods every year violate?
3. Who can be harmed and how when a company changes its accounting methods too often?

Focus on Financials | Apple Inc.

LO 1, 4

(Learning Objectives 1, 4: Show how to account for inventories; compute and evaluate gross profit and inventory turnover) This case will help you learn to use a company's inventory notes. The notes are part of the financial statements. They give details that would clutter the financial statements themselves. Refer to **Apple Inc.**'s consolidated financial statements and related notes in Appendix A and online in the filings section of **www.sec.gov** and answer the following questions:

Requirements

1. How much was Apple's merchandise inventory at September 24, 2016? At September 26, 2015? Does Apple include all inventory that it handles in the inventory account on its balance sheet?
2. Refer to Note 1, Summary of Significant Accounting Policies, Inventories section. How does Apple value its inventories? Which cost method does the company use?
3. Using the cost-of-goods-sold model, compute Apple's purchases of inventory during the year ended September 24, 2016.

4. Did Apple's gross profit percentage on company sales improve or deteriorate in the year ended September 24, 2016, compared to the previous year?
5. Assume that ending inventory on September 27, 2014, was $2,111 million. (Remember that the ending inventory in one period becomes the beginning inventory in the next period.) Compute Apple's inventory turnover for 2016 and 2015. Is Apple's rate of inventory turnover for the years ended September 24, 2016, and September 26, 2015, fast or slow compared to most other companies in its industry? Explain your answer.
6. Go to the SEC's website (**www.sec.gov**). Find Apple's consolidated balance sheet and consolidated statement of operations for the fiscal year ended September 30, 2017. What has happened to the company's inventory turnover and gross profit percentages since September 24, 2016? Why have they changed? Where would you find the company's explanations for the changes? (Challenge)

Focus on Analysis | Under Armour, Inc.

LO 1, 2, 4

(Learning Objectives 1, 2, 4: Show how to account for inventory; explain GAAP for inventory; compute and evaluate gross profit and inventory turnover) Retrieve the 2016 Under Armour financial statements at **www.sec.gov** by clicking on Filings and then searching for "Under Armour" under Company Filings. When you see the list of filings for the company, select the Form 10-K for 2016. Be sure to retrieve the 2016 financial statements, not another year. Show amounts in millions and round to the nearest $1 million.

Requirements

1. Three important pieces of inventory information are (a) the cost of inventory on hand, (b) the cost of goods sold, and (c) the cost of inventory purchases. Identify or compute each of these items for Under Armour at December 31, 2016.
2. Which item in requirement 1 is most directly related to cash flow? Why? (Challenge)
3. Assume that all inventory purchases were made on account and that only inventory purchases increased Accounts Payable. Compute Under Armour, Inc.'s, cash payments for inventory during 2016.
4. See Note 2 Summary of Significant Accounting Policies, Inventories section. How does Under Armour value its inventories? Which costing method does Under Armour use?
5. Did Under Armour's gross profit percentage and rate of inventory turnover improve or deteriorate in 2016 (versus 2015)? Consider the overall effect of these two ratios. Did Under Armour improve its performance during 2016? How did these factors affect the net income for 2016? (Note: Under Armour's inventories totaled $537 million at the end of fiscal 2014.) Round answers to three decimal places.

Group Project

LO 4

(Learning Objective 4: Evaluate inventory turnover ratios) Obtain the annual reports of ten companies, two from each of five different industries. Most companies' financial statements can be downloaded from their websites.

Requirements

1. Compute each company's gross profit percentage and rate of inventory turnover for the most recent two years.
2. For the industries of the companies you are analyzing, obtain the industry averages for gross profit percentage and inventory turnover by searching online for: (1) *industry averages for gross profit percentage* and (2) *industry averages for inventory turnover.* Be sure to cite your source for industry averages. Alternatively, you may be able to find the averages from one of the following sources in your school's library: Robert Morris Associates, *Annual Statement Studies;* Dun and Bradstreet, *Industry Norms and Key Business Ratios;* or Leo Troy, *Almanac of Business and Industrial Financial Ratios.*
3. How well does each of your companies compare to the other company in its industry? How well do your companies compare to the average for their industry? What insight about your companies can you glean from these ratios?
4. Write a report summarizing your findings and state whether or not your group would invest in each of the companies it analyzed.

Quick Check Answers

1. *b*
2. *d*
3. *b*
4. *d* [(20 × \$100) + (60 × \$120) = \$9,200]
5. *c* [(\$2,000 + \$7,200)/(20 + 60) = \$115; \$115 × 65 = \$7,475]
6. *b* (15 × \$120 = \$1,800)
7. *d* [(60 × \$120) + (5 × \$100) = \$7,700]
8. *a*
9. *b* (\$20,000 + \$81,000 − \$24,000 = \$77,000)
10. *c* [\$20,000 + \$81,000 − \$24,000 = \$77,000; \$164,000 − \$77,000 = \$87,000]
11. *a* [\$87,000 gross profit (see Question 10) / \$164,000]
12. *c* [\$77,000 ÷ ([\$20,000 + \$24,000]/2)]
13. *b* [\$150,000 + \$230,000 − [\$440,000 × (1 − 0.30)]]
14. *a*

Try It Solutions

Page 324

Nike, Inc. is a much larger company than Under Armour, Inc., with a wider global distribution network for its products. Although gross profit percentages for the two companies are almost identical, Nike has a faster rate of inventory turnover, making it more profitable than Under Armour.

Page 326

\$135,000 = [\$70,000 + \$365,000 − (0.60 × \$500,000)]

APPENDIX 6A

ACCOUNTING FOR INVENTORY IN THE PERIODIC SYSTEM

In the periodic inventory system, the business keeps no running record of the merchandise. Instead, at the end of the period, the business counts inventory on hand and applies the unit costs to determine the cost of ending inventory. This inventory figure appears on the balance sheet and is used to compute cost of goods sold.

Recording Transactions in the Periodic System

In the periodic system, the Inventory account carries the beginning balance left over from the preceding period throughout the current period. The business records purchases of inventory in the Purchases account (an expense). Then, at the end of the period, the Inventory account must be updated for the financial statements. A journal entry removes the beginning balance by crediting Inventory and debiting Cost of Goods Sold. A second journal entry sets up (debits) the ending inventory balance, based on the physical count, and credits Cost of Goods Sold. The final entry in this sequence transfers the amount of Purchases to Cost of Goods Sold, crediting Purchases and debiting Cost of Goods Sold. These end-of-period entries can be made during the closing process.

Exhibit 6A-1 illustrates the accounting in the periodic system. After the process is complete, Inventory has its correct ending balance of \$120,000, and Cost of Goods Sold shows \$540,000.

Exhibit 6A-1 | Recording and Reporting Inventories—Periodic System (All amounts assumed)

PANEL A—Recording Transactions and the T-accounts (All amounts are assumed)

	A	B	C	D
1	1.	Purchases	560,000	
2		Accounts Payable		560,000
3		*Purchased inventory on account.*		
4				
5	2.	Accounts Receivable	900,000	
6		Sales Revenue		900,000
7		*Sold inventory on account.*		
8				
9	3.	End-of-period entries to update Inventory and record Cost of Goods Sold:		
10	a.	Cost of Goods Sold	100,000	
11		Inventory (beginning balance)		100,000
12		*Transferred beginning inventory to COGS.*		
13				
14	b.	Inventory (ending balance)	120,000	
15		Cost of Goods Sold		120,000
16		*Set up ending inventory based on physical count.*		
17				
18	c.	Cost of Goods Sold	560,000	
19		Purchases		560,000
20		*Transferred purchases to COGS.*		
21				

The T-accounts show the following:

Inventory

Debit	Credit
100,000*	100,000
120,000	

*Beginning inventory was $100,000

Cost of Goods Sold

Debit	Credit
100,000	120,000
560,000	
540,000	

PANEL B—Reporting in the Financial Statements

Income Statement (Partial)

Sales revenue		$900,000
Cost of goods sold:		
Beginning inventory	$ 100,000	
Purchases	560,000	
Cost of goods available	660,000	
Ending inventory	(120,000)	
Cost of goods sold		540,000
Gross profit		$360,000

Ending Balance Sheet (Partial)

Current assets:	
Cash	$ XXX
Short-term investments	XXX
Accounts receivable	XXX
Inventory	120,000
Prepaid expenses	XXX

APPENDIX ASSIGNMENTS

Short Exercises

S6A-1. ***(Record inventory transactions in the periodic system)*** Wexton Technologies began the year with inventory of $560. During the year, Wexton purchased inventory costing $1,160 and sold goods for $2,600, with all transactions on account. Wexton ended the year with inventory of $640. Journalize all the necessary transactions under the periodic inventory system.

S6A-2. ***(Compute cost of goods sold and prepare the income statement—periodic system)*** Use the data in S6A-1 to do the following for Wexton Technologies.

➤ Requirements

1. Post to the Inventory and Cost of Goods Sold accounts.
2. Compute cost of goods sold by the cost-of-goods-sold model.
3. Prepare the income statement of Wexton Technologies through gross profit.

Exercises

E6A-3. ***(Compute amounts for the GAAP inventory methods—periodic system)*** Suppose Synthetix Corporation's inventory records for a particular computer chip indicate the following at October 31:

Oct	1	Beginning inventory	4 units @ $60 = $240
	8	Purchase...............................	3 units @ $60 = 180
	15	Purchase...............................	12 units @ $70 = 840
	26	Purchase...............................	1 units @ $80 = 80

The physical count of inventory at October 31 indicates that five units of inventory are on hand.

➤ Requirements

Compute ending inventory and cost of goods sold, using each of the following methods:

1. Specific unit cost, assuming three $60 units and two $70 units are on hand
2. Average cost (round average unit cost to the nearest cent)
3. First-in, first-out
4. Last-in, first-out

E6A-4. ***(Journal inventory transactions in the periodic system; compute cost of goods sold)*** Use the data in E6A-3.

➤ Requirements

Journalize the following for the periodic system:

1. Total October purchases in one summary entry. All purchases were on credit.
2. Total October sales in a summary entry. Assume that the selling price was $275 per unit and that all sales were on credit.
3. October 31 entries for inventory. Synthetix uses LIFO. Post to the Cost of Goods Sold T-account to show how this amount is determined. Label each item in the account.
4. Show the computation of cost of goods sold by the cost-of-goods-sold model.

Problems

P6A-5. ***(Compute cost of goods sold and gross profit on sales—periodic system)*** Assume a Championship outlet store began July 2018 with 52 units of inventory that cost $18 each. The sales price of these units was $75. During July, the store completed these inventory transactions:

			Units	Unit Cost	Unit Sale Price
July	3	Sale	18	$18	$75
	8	Purchase......	86	19	77
	11	Sale	34	18	75
	19	Sale	2	19	77
	24	Sale	33	19	77
	30	Purchase......	22	20	78
	31	Sale	3	19	77

➤ Requirements

1. Determine the store's cost of goods sold for July under the periodic inventory system. Assume the FIFO method.
2. Compute the store's gross profit for July.

P6A-6. ***(Record transactions in the periodic system; report inventory items in the financial statements)*** Accounting records for Just Desserts, Inc., show the following data for the year ended December 31, 2018 (amounts in thousands):

Inventory, Dec 31, 2017	$ 510
Purchases of inventory (on account)	1,180
Sales of inventory—80% on account, 20% for cash	3,400
Inventory at the lower of FIFO cost or market, Dec 31, 2018	690

➤ Requirements

1. Journalize Just Desserts' inventory transactions for the year under the periodic system. Show all amounts in thousands.
2. Report ending inventory, sales, cost of goods sold, and gross profit on the appropriate financial statement (amounts in thousands). Show the computation of cost of goods sold.

APPENDIX 6B

THE LIFO RESERVE—CONVERTING A LIFO COMPANY'S NET INCOME TO THE FIFO BASIS

Suppose you are a financial analyst and it is your job to recommend stocks for your clients to purchase as investments. You have narrowed your choice to Mega-Mart Stores, Inc. (a hypothetical company) and **Kohl's Corporation**. Assume that Mega-Mart uses the LIFO method for inventories, and Kohl's uses FIFO. The two companies' net incomes are not comparable because they use different inventory methods. To compare the two companies, you need to place them on the same footing.

The Internal Revenue Service allows companies to use LIFO for income tax purposes only if they use LIFO for financial reporting. Companies that use LIFO inventories also report supplemental FIFO inventory information in the footnotes to the financial statements, allowing the investor to convert a company's net income from the LIFO basis to what the income would have been if the business had used FIFO. Companies that use LIFO usually report the FIFO cost, as well as a LIFO Reserve, in the footnotes of their financial statements. The LIFO Reserve[3] is the difference between the LIFO cost of an inventory and what the cost of that inventory would be under FIFO. In our example, assume that our hypothetical Mega-Mart reports the following amounts:

Mega-Mart Stores, Inc. Uses LIFO	(In millions) 2017	2016
From the Mega-Mart balance sheet:		
Inventories (approximate FIFO cost)	$ 25,056	$22,749
Less LIFO reserve	(165)	(135)
LIFO cost	24,891	22,614
From the Mega-Mart income statement:		
Cost of goods sold	$191,838	
Net income	8,039	
Income tax rate	35%	

[3]The LIFO Reserve account is widely used in practice even though the word *reserve* is poor terminology.

Converting Mega-Mart's 2017 net income to the FIFO basis focuses on the LIFO Reserve because the reserve captures the difference between Mega-Mart's ending inventory costed at LIFO and at FIFO. Observe that during each year, the FIFO cost of ending inventory exceeded the LIFO cost. During 2017, the LIFO Reserve increased by $30 million ($165 million − $135 million). *The LIFO Reserve can increase only when inventory costs are rising.* Recall that during a period of rising costs, LIFO produces the highest cost of goods sold and the lowest net income. Therefore, for 2017, Mega-Mart's cost of goods sold would have been lower if the company had used the FIFO method for inventories. Mega-Mart's net income would have been higher, as the following computations show:

If Mega-Mart Had Used FIFO in 2017

	(In millions)
Cost of goods sold, as reported under LIFO	$191,838
− Increase in LIFO Reserve ($165 − $135)	(30)
= Cost of goods sold, if Mega-Mart had used FIFO	$191,808
Lower cost of goods sold → Higher pretax income by	$ 30
Minus income taxes (35%)	11
Higher net income under FIFO	19
Net income as reported under LIFO	8,039
Net income Mega-Mart would have reported for 2017 if using FIFO	$ 8,058

Now you can compare Mega-Mart's net income with that of Kohl's Corporation. All the ratios used for the analysis—current ratio, inventory turnover, and so on—can be compared between the two companies as long as we use the FIFO figures for Cost of Goods Sold and Inventories for Mega-Mart.

The LIFO Reserve provides another opportunity for managers and investors to answer a key question about a company.

How much income tax has the company saved over its lifetime by using the LIFO method to account for inventory?

Using Mega-Mart as an example, the computation at the end of 2017 is as follows (amounts in millions):

Income tax saved by using LIFO	=	LIFO Reserve	×	Income tax rate
$58	=	$165	×	.35

With these price changes, by the end of 2017, Mega-Mart has saved a total of $58 million by using the LIFO method to account for its merchandise inventory. Had Mega-Mart used the FIFO method, Mega-Mart would have almost $58 million less cash to invest in the opening of new stores.

In recent years, some companies have experienced declines in the value of their inventories, either due to decreasing physical quantities or decreasing unit prices. When this happens, LIFO reserves can decline or even reverse. This ultimately makes gross profit and net income less under FIFO than LIFO. The details of this topic are reserved for more advanced accounting classes.

7 Plant Assets, Natural Resources, and Intangibles

LEARNING OBJECTIVES

1 **Explain** how to account for the cost of plant assets

2 **Distinguish** a capital expenditure from an immediate expense

3 **Explain** how to account for depreciation on plant assets

4 **Analyze** the effect of a plant asset disposal

5 **Apply** GAAP for natural resources and intangible assets

6 **Explain** the effect of an asset impairment on the financial statements

7 **Analyze** the rate of return on assets

8 **Analyze** the cash flow impact of long-lived asset transactions

SPOTLIGHT

FedEx Corporation

If you need a document or package delivered across the country overnight or any of a number of other business services, FedEx can handle it. **FedEx Corporation** sets a high standard for quick delivery, as well as other transportation, e-commerce, and business services. For this reason, FedEx has, for more than a decade, consistently made *Fortune*

Lee Snider/Alamy

magazine's "World's Most Admired Companies" list. As you can see from the company's Consolidated Balance Sheets below, FedEx moves packages using property and equipment, such as aircraft, package-handling equipment, computers, and vehicles. These are FedEx's most important resources (lines 10–14). The company owned over $47 billion of property and equipment as of May 31, 2016 (line 15), which was actually almost $1 billion more than its total assets (line 22)! How can this be?

Notice that over the estimated useful lives of these assets, the company built up accumulated depreciation of about $22.7 billion (line 16), indicating that the assets were almost half used up as of that date ($22,734/$47,018 = 48.4%). The net book value of FedEx's property and equipment was about $24.3 billion (line 17). The company also owned about $9.8 billion in goodwill and other tangible and intangible long-term assets (line 21). When you complete this chapter, you will understand better what these terms and concepts mean.

	A	B	C
1	**FedEx Corporation Consolidated Balance Sheets (Partial, Adapted)**		
2	**(in millions of $)**	**May 31, 2016**	**May 31, 2015**
3	**CURRENT ASSETS**		
4	Cash and cash equivalents	$ 3,534	$ 3,763
5	Receivables, less allowances of $178 and $185	7,252	5,719
6	Spare parts, supplies and fuel, less allowances of $218 and $207	496	498
7	Prepaid expenses and other	707	355
8	Total current assets	11,989	10,335
9	**PROPERTY AND EQUIPMENT, AT COST**		
10	Aircraft and related equipment	17,499	16,186
11	Package handling and ground support equipment	7,961	6,725
12	Computer and electronic equipment	5,149	5,208
13	Vehicles	6,422	5,816
14	Facilities and other	9,987	8,929
15	Gross property and equipment	47,018	42,864
16	Less accumulated depreciation and amortization	(22,734)	(21,989)
17	Net property and equipment	24,284	20,875
18	**OTHER LONG-TERM ASSETS**		
19	Goodwill	6,747	3,810
20	Other assets	3,044	1,511
21	Total other long-term assets	9,791	5,321
22	TOTAL ASSETS	$ 46,064	$ 36,531
23			

Data from the U.S. Securities and Exchange Commission EDGAR Company filings, www.sec.gov

This chapter covers the measurement and reporting principles for long-term tangible fixed assets (also known as *plant assets* or *property and equipment*), as well as intangible assets. Unlike inventories, which are typically bought, manufactured, and sold, fixed tangible and intangible assets are used in the business to earn a profit. This chapter also briefly covers measurement and reporting principles for natural resources, which begin as long-term assets. Then, as they are extracted or depleted, their cost is transferred to the income statement as an expense. The latter part of the chapter covers the rate of return on total assets, an important ratio that measures how profitably a company employs its assets.

Try It in Excel®

You can access the most current annual report of FedEx Corporation in Excel format at **www.sec.gov**. Using the "FILINGS" link on the toolbar at the top of the home page, select "Company Filings Search." This will take you to the "EDGAR Company Filings" page. Type "FedEx" in the company name box, and select "Search." This will produce the "EDGAR Search Results" page showing the company name. Click on the "CIK" link beside the company name. Doing so will pull up a list of the reports the company has filed with the SEC. Under the "Filing Type" box, type "10-K" and click the search box. Form 10-K is the SEC form for the company's annual report. Find the year that you wish to view. Click on the "Interactive Data" box, which takes you to the "View Filing Data" page. Find and click on the "View Excel Document" link at the top of this page. You can choose to either open or download the Excel files containing the company's most recent financial statements.

Businesses use several types of long-lived assets. We show these assets in Exhibit 7-1, along with the expense account that is typically associated with each one.

Exhibit 7-1 | Long-Lived Assets and Related Expense Accounts

Asset Account (Balance Sheet)	Related Expense Account (Income Statement)
Plant Assets	
Land	None
Buildings, Machinery, and Equipment	Depreciation Expense
Furniture and Fixtures	Depreciation Expense
Land Improvements	Depreciation Expense
Natural Resources	Depletion Expense (through cost of goods sold)
Intangible Assets	Amortization Expense

- ***Plant assets*** (also known as *property, plant, and equipment* or *fixed assets*) are long-lived assets that are tangible. Land, buildings, and equipment are examples. The expense associated with plant assets is called *depreciation expense*. Of the plant assets, land is unique. Land is not expensed over time because its usefulness does not decrease. Most companies report plant assets as property, plant, and equipment on the balance sheet. FedEx uses the heading Property and Equipment in its balance sheet, which is shown on page 368 (lines 9–17).
- *Natural resources* such as oil and gas reserves, coal mines, or stands of timber, are accounted for as long-term assets when they are purchased or developed. As the natural resource is extracted, its cost is transferred to inventory. Later, as the inventory is sold, its cost is transferred to the cost of goods sold in a manner similar to that described in Chapter 6.
- *Intangible assets* are useful because of the special rights they carry. They have no physical form. Patents, copyrights, and trademarks are intangible assets, as is goodwill. Accounting for intangibles is similar to accounting for plant assets. FedEx reports its intangible assets on its balance sheet as Goodwill and Other Assets (lines 19–21).

EXPLAIN HOW TO ACCOUNT FOR THE COST OF PLANT ASSETS

1 Explain how to account for the cost of plant assets

Recall from Chapter 6 that the basic working rule for measuring the cost of an asset is as follows:

The cost of any asset is the sum of all the costs incurred to bring the asset to its intended use.

The cost of a plant asset includes its purchase price, plus any taxes, commissions, and other amounts paid to make the asset ready for use. The specific costs differ for the various types of plant assets.

Land

The cost of land includes its purchase price (cash plus any note payable given); brokerage commission, survey fees, legal fees; and any back property taxes the purchaser pays. The cost also includes expenditures for grading and clearing the land and for removing unwanted buildings.

The cost of land does *not* include the cost of fencing, paving, security systems, and lighting. These are separate plant assets—called *land improvements*—and they are subject to depreciation.

Suppose FedEx signs a $300,000 note payable to purchase 20 acres of land for a new shipping site. FedEx also pays $10,000 for real estate commission, $8,000 of back property tax, $5,000 for removal of an old building, a $1,000 survey fee, and $260,000 to pave the parking lot—all in cash. What is FedEx's cost of this land?

Purchase price of land		$300,000
Add related costs:		
Real estate commission	$10,000	
Back property tax	8,000	
Removal of building	5,000	
Survey fee	1,000	
Total related costs		24,000
Total cost of land		$324,000

Note that the cost to pave the parking lot, $260,000, is *not* included in the land's cost, because the pavement is a land improvement. FedEx would record the purchase of the land as follows:

	A	B	C	D
1		Land	324,000	
2		Note Payable		300,000
3		Cash		24,000
4				

Assets	=	Liabilities	+	Stockholders' Equity
+324,000 − 24,000	=	+300,000	+	0

The purchase of land increases both assets and liabilities but has no effect on equity.

Buildings, Machinery, and Equipment

The cost of constructing a building includes architectural fees, building permits, contractors' charges, and payments for material, labor, and overhead. If a company borrows money to finance the construction, the cost of the building will also include the interest on the loan.

When an existing building (new or old) is purchased, its cost includes the purchase price, brokerage commission, sales and other taxes paid, and all expenditures to repair and renovate the building for its intended purpose.

The cost of FedEx's package-handling equipment includes its purchase price (less any discounts), plus transportation from the seller to FedEx, insurance while in transit, sales and other taxes, purchase commission, installation costs, and any expenditures to test the asset before it's placed in service. The equipment cost will also include the cost of any special platforms. Then, after the asset is up and running, insurance, taxes, and maintenance costs are recorded as expenses, not as part of the asset's cost.

Land Improvements and Leasehold Improvements

For a FedEx shipping terminal, the cost to pave a parking lot ($260,000) would be recorded in a separate account entitled Land Improvements. This account includes costs for other items such as driveways, signs, fences, and sprinkler systems. Although these assets are located on the land, they are subject to decay, and their cost should therefore be depreciated.

FedEx leases some of its airplanes and other assets such as trucks and customizes these assets for its special needs. For example, FedEx paints its logo on delivery trucks. These improvements, which are referred to as *leasehold improvements,* are assets of FedEx even though the company does not own the trucks. The cost of a leasehold improvement should be depreciated over the shorter of the useful life of the improvement or the term of the lease. Most companies call the depreciation on leasehold improvements **amortization**, which is a similar concept to depreciation.

Lump-Sum (or Basket) Purchases of Assets

Businesses often purchase several types of fixed assets as a group, or a "basket," for a single lump-sum amount. For example, FedEx might pay one price for land and a building. In this case, it is necessary to identify the cost of each asset, because different accounting rules might apply to each of the different assets in the group. For example, buildings are depreciated, while land is not, so the two assets have to be accounted for separately. The total cost is divided among the assets according to their relative sales (or market) values. This technique is called the *relative-sales-value method.*

Suppose FedEx purchases land and a building in Denver. The building sits on two acres of land, and the combined purchase price of land and building is $2,800,000. An appraisal indicates the land's market value is $300,000 and the building's market value is $2,700,000.

FedEx first figures the ratio of each asset's market value to the total market value. The total appraised value is $2,700,000 + $300,000 = $3,000,000. Thus, the land, valued at $300,000, is 10% of the total market value. The building's appraised value is 90% of the total. These percentages are then used to determine the cost of each asset:

Asset	Market (Sales) Value		Total Market Value		Percentage of Total Market Value		Total Cost	Cost of Each Asset
Land	$ 300,000	÷	$3,000,000	=	10%	×	$2,800,000	$ 280,000
Building	2,700,000	÷	3,000,000	=	90%	×	$2,800,000	2,520,000
Total	$3,000,000				100%			$2,800,000

If FedEx pays cash, the entry to record the purchase of the land and building is

	A	B	C	D
1		Land	280,000	
2		Building	2,520,000	
3		Cash		2,800,000
4				

Assets	=	Liabilities	+	Stockholders' Equity
+ 280,000	=			
+ 2,520,000	=	0	+	0
− 2,800,000	=			

Total assets don't change—the transaction is merely an exchange of cash for two fixed assets.

TRY IT

(Answers are given on p. 435.)

How would FedEx divide a $120,000 lump-sum purchase price for land, building, and equipment with estimated market values of $40,000, $95,000, and $15,000, respectively?

DISTINGUISH A CAPITAL EXPENDITURE FROM AN IMMEDIATE EXPENSE

2 **Distinguish** a capital expenditure from an immediate expense

When a company spends money on a plant asset, it must decide whether to record it as an asset or an expense. Examples of these expenditures range from FedEx's purchase of an airplane to tires for a FedEx truck.

Expenditures that increase an asset's capacity or extend its useful life are called **capital expenditures**. For example, the cost of a major overhaul that extends the useful life of a FedEx truck is a capital expenditure. Capital expenditures are said to be *capitalized,* which means the cost is added to an asset account and not expensed immediately. A major decision in accounting for plant assets is whether to capitalize or to expense a certain cost.

Costs that do not extend the asset's capacity or its useful life, but merely maintain the asset or restore it to working order, are recorded as expenses. For example, Repair Expense is reported on the income statement and matched against revenue. The costs of repainting a FedEx delivery truck, repairing a dented fender, and replacing tires are also expensed immediately. Exhibit 7-2 shows different types of capital expenditures vs. those that should be immediately expensed.

Exhibit 7-2 | Capital Expenditures vs. Immediate Expenses

Record an Asset for Capital Expenditures	Record Repair and Maintenance Expense (Not an Asset) for an Expense
Extraordinary repairs:	**Ordinary repairs:**
Major engine overhaul	Repair of transmission or other mechanism
Modification of body for new use of truck	Oil change, lubrication, and so on
Addition to storage capacity of truck	Replacement of tires and windshield, or a paint job

The distinction between a capital expenditure (a long-term asset) and an immediate expense requires judgment: Does the cost extend the asset's usefulness or its useful life? If so, record an asset. If the cost merely maintains the asset in its present condition or returns it to its prior condition, then record an expense.

Most companies expense all small (immaterial) costs (say, below $1,000) regardless of whether the costs are capital in nature. For larger (material) costs, companies follow the capitalization rule stated in the previous paragraph. Conservative financial managers avoid overstating their companies' assets and profits.

Accounting errors sometimes occur when plant-asset costs are recorded. For example, a company may

- expense a cost that should have been capitalized. This error overstates expenses and understates net income in the year of the error.
- capitalize a cost that should have been expensed. This error understates expenses and overstates net income in the year of the error.

A company, as well as its executives, that deliberately overstate its assets and net income may eventually be charged with fraudulent financial reporting.

Cooking the Books

WorldCom

It is one thing to accidentally capitalize a plant asset instead of expensing it, but quite another to do it intentionally. Doing so deliberately overstates a company's assets, understates its expenses, and overstates its net income. One notorious company committed one of the biggest financial statement frauds in U.S. history in this way.

In 2002, **WorldCom, Inc.**, was one of the largest telecommunications service providers in the world. The company had grown rapidly from a small, regional telephone company in 1983 to a giant corporation in 2002 by acquiring an ever-increasing number of other telecommunications companies. But 2002 was a bad year for WorldCom, as well as for many others in the telecom industry. The United States was reeling from the effects of a deep economic recession after the "dot-com" bubble burst in 2000 and terrorist attacks on U.S. soil in 2001 intensified the recession. Wall Street was looking high and low for positive signs, pressuring public companies to keep profits trending upward in order to support share prices, without much success, at least for the honest companies.

Bernard J. ("Bernie") Ebbers, WorldCom's chief executive officer, was worried. He began to press his chief financial officer, Scott Sullivan, to find a way to make the company's income statement look healthier. After all legitimate attempts to improve earnings failed, Sullivan concocted a scheme to cook the books.

Like all telecommunications companies, WorldCom had signed contracts with other telephone companies, paying them fees so that WorldCom's customers could use their lines for telephone calls and Internet activity. Generally accepted accounting principles (GAAP) require these fees to be expensed rather than capitalized. WorldCom overestimated the growth of its business and incurred billions of dollars in such costs, about 15% more than its customers would ever use.

In direct violation of GAAP, Sullivan rationalized that the excessive amounts WorldCom had spent on line costs would eventually lead to the company's recognizing revenue in future years. He directed the accountants working under him to reclassify line costs as property, plant, and equipment assets, rather than as expenses, and to depreciate (spread) the costs over several years rather than to expense them in the periods in which they were incurred. Over several quarters, Mr. Sullivan and his assistants transferred a total of $3.1 billion in such charges from operating expense accounts to property, plant, and equipment, resulting in the transformation of what would have been a net loss for all of 2001 and the first quarter of 2002 into a sizeable profit. It was the largest single fraud in U.S. history to that point.

Sullivan's fraudulent scheme was discovered by the company's internal auditing staff during a routine spot-check of the company's records for capital expenditures. The staff members reported Sullivan's fraudulent activities to the head of the company's audit committee and its external auditor, setting in motion a chain of events that resulted in Ebbers and Sullivan being fired and the company eventually declaring bankruptcy. The shareholders of WorldCom lost billions of dollars, and more than 500,000 people lost their jobs. Ebbers, Sullivan, and several of their assistants went to prison for their participation in this fraudulent scheme.

The WorldCom scandal rocked the financial world, causing global stock markets to plummet from a lack of confidence. This prompted Congress and President George W. Bush to enact the Sarbanes-Oxley Act of 2002 (see Chapter 4), the most significant piece of shareholder protection legislation since the Great Depression in the 1930s.

EXPLAIN HOW TO ACCOUNT FOR DEPRECIATION ON PLANT ASSETS

3 Explain how to account for depreciation on plant assets

As you have learned, a plant asset is reported on the balance sheet at its book value, which is calculated as follows:

Book Value of a Plant Asset = Cost − Accumulated Depreciation

Plant assets wear out, grow obsolete, and lose value over time. To account for this process, we allocate a plant asset's cost to expense over its life—a process called depreciation. The depreciation process follows the expense recognition principle discussed in Chapter 3. Depreciation apportions the cost of a fixed asset over time by allocating a portion of that cost against the revenue the asset helps earn each period. Exhibit 7-3 illustrates the accounting for the cost of a Boeing 737 jet by FedEx.

Exhibit 7-3 | Depreciation: Allocating Costs to Periods in Which Revenues Are Generated

Recall that depreciation expense (not accumulated depreciation) is reported on the income statement. Accumulated depreciation is reported on the balance sheet.

Only land has an unlimited life and is not depreciated for accounting purposes. For most plant assets, depreciation is caused by one of the following:

- *Physical wear and tear.* For example, physical deterioration takes its toll on the usefulness of FedEx's airplanes, equipment, delivery trucks, and buildings.
- *Obsolescence.* Computers and other electronic equipment may become obsolete before they deteriorate. An asset is obsolete when another asset can do the job more efficiently. An asset's useful life may be shorter than its physical life. FedEx and other companies depreciate their computers over a short period of time—perhaps four years—even though the computers will remain in working condition much longer.

Suppose FedEx buys a computer for use in tracking packages. FedEx believes it will get four years of service from the computer, after which it will be worthless. Under straight-line depreciation, FedEx expenses one-quarter of the asset's cost in each of its four years of use.

You've just seen what depreciation is. Let's see what depreciation is *not*.

1. *Depreciation is not a process of valuation.* Businesses do *not* record depreciation based on changes in the market value of their plant assets. Instead, businesses allocate the asset's *cost* to the periods of its useful life.
2. *Depreciation does not mean setting aside cash to replace assets as they wear out.* Any cash fund is entirely separate from depreciation.

How to Measure Depreciation

To measure depreciation for a plant asset, we must know three things about it:

1. Cost
2. Estimated useful life
3. Estimated residual value

We have discussed cost, which is a known amount. The other two factors must be estimated.

Estimated useful life is the length of service expected from using the asset, which can be expressed in years, units of output, miles, or some other measure. For example, the useful life of a building is stated in years. The useful life of a FedEx airplane or delivery truck may be expressed as the number of miles the vehicle is expected to travel. Companies base these estimates on their experience and on trade publications.

Estimated residual value—also called *scrap value* or *salvage value*—is the expected cash value of an asset at the end of its useful life. For example, FedEx may believe that a package-handling machine will be useful for seven years. After that time, the company may expect to sell the machine as scrap metal. The amount FedEx believes it can get for the machine at disposal is the estimated residual value, which in this case is the scrap value. The estimated residual value is *not* depreciated because FedEx expects to receive this amount from selling the asset. If there's no expected residual value, the full cost of the asset is depreciated. A plant asset's **depreciable cost** is measured as follows:

$$\text{Depreciable Cost} = \text{Asset's cost} - \text{Estimated residual value}$$

Depreciation Methods

There are three main depreciation methods:

- Straight-line method
- Units-of-production method
- Double-declining balance method

These methods allocate different amounts of depreciation to each period. However, they all result in the same total amount of depreciation, which is the asset's depreciable cost. Exhibit 7-4 shows the data we use to illustrate the depreciation computations for a FedEx truck.

Exhibit 7-4 | Depreciation Computation Data

Data Item	Amount
Cost of truck	$41,000
Less: Estimated residual value	(1,000)
Depreciable cost	$40,000
Estimated useful life:	
Years	5 years
Units of production	100,000 units [miles]

Straight-Line Method. With the **straight-line method**, an equal amount of depreciation is assigned to each year (or period) of asset use. The depreciable cost is divided by the asset's useful life in years to determine the annual depreciation expense. Applied to the FedEx truck data from Exhibit 7-4, straight-line depreciation is

$$\text{Straight-line depreciation per year} = \frac{\text{Cost} - \text{Residual value}}{\text{Useful life, in years}}$$

$$= \frac{\$41{,}000 - \$1{,}000}{5}$$

$$= \$8{,}000$$

The entry to record the depreciation in a given year is

	A	B	C	D
1		Depreciation Expense—Truck	8,000	
2		Accumulated Depreciation—Truck		8,000
3				

Assets	=	Liabilities	+	Stockholders' Equity	−	Expenses
− 8,000	=	0				− 8,000

Observe that depreciation decreases the asset (through Accumulated Depreciation) and also decreases equity (through Depreciation Expense). Let's assume that FedEx purchased this truck on January 1, 2015. Assume that FedEx's accounting year ends on December 31. Exhibit 7-5 shows the straight-line depreciation schedule for the truck. The final column of the exhibit shows the asset's book value, which is the asset's cost less accumulated depreciation.

Exhibit 7-5 Straight-Line Depreciation Schedule for Truck

	A	B	C	D	E	F	G
1	Date	Cost	Rate*	Depreciable Cost	Yearly Expense	Accum. Deprec.	Book Value
2	1/1/2015	41,000		40,000			41,000
3	12/31/2015		0.2	40,000	8,000	8,000	33,000
4	12/31/2016		0.2	40,000	8,000	16,000	25,000
5	12/31/2017		0.2	40,000	8,000	24,000	17,000
6	12/31/2018		0.2	40,000	8,000	32,000	9,000
7	12/31/2019		0.2	40,000	8,000	40,000	1,000
8							

*1/years of useful life = 1/5 = 0.2

As an asset is used in operations,

- accumulated depreciation increases.
- the book value of the asset decreases.

You can estimate the age (or the "used up" amount) of a plant asset by calculating the ratio between accumulated depreciation on a straight-line basis and cost. For example, if accumulated depreciation is $500,000 and cost is $1,000,000, the plant asset is approximately half used up. An asset's final book value is its residual value ($1,000, as shown in Exhibit 7-5). At the end of its useful life, the asset is said to be *fully depreciated*.

Try It in Excel®

Building depreciation schedules such as the one in Exhibit 7-5 is easy with Excel. Use the information in Exhibit 7-4 and the formula on page 376 to help you program the cells. To construct Exhibit 7-5 in Excel:

1. Open a new workbook. In cells A1 through G1, insert column headings to correspond to those of Exhibit 7-5. You will have to adjust the column width of your spreadsheet to accommodate the headings.
2. In cells B2 and G2 (asset cost and book value), type in the original gross cost (41,000). The remainder of the cells in column B should be blank.
3. In cell A2, type in the original purchase date (1/1/2015). In cells A3 through A7, type in the year-end dates of 12/31/2015 through 12/31/2019, respectively. Change the formatting of these cells to "date."
4. In cells C3 through C7, enter the depreciation rate for each year, which is the reciprocal of the asset's useful life (1/5, or 20%). Enter .2 in cell C3 and copy this value down through cell C7.
5. In cell D2, calculate the depreciable cost of $40,000. Enter = B2–1000. Copy this value down through cell D7.
6. In cell E3, enter the formula = C3*D3. The value $8,000 should appear. Copy this formula to cells E4 through E7.
7. Column F keeps a running sum of accumulated depreciation. Start with cell F3. Enter the formula = F2 + E3. $8,000 (accumulated depreciation at the end of year 1) should appear. Copy cell F3 down to cells F4 through F7. You should get the same values as you see in Exhibit 7-5.
8. Column G keeps a running calculation of the declining net book value of the asset. Start with cell G3. Freeze the value of the original cost of the asset ($41,000) in cell G2 by entering "$" before both the column and row. Then subtract the value of accumulated depreciation (cell F3). The formula in cell G3 becomes = G2–F3. The result should be $33,000 ($41,000 – $8,000). Copy cell G3 down through cell G7.

TRY IT

(Answers are given on p. 435.)

A FedEx sorting machine that cost $10,000 with a useful life of five years and a residual value of $2,000 was purchased on January 1. What is straight-line depreciation for each year?

Units-of-Production Method. With the **units-of-production (UOP) method**, a fixed amount of depreciation is assigned to each unit of output, or unit of service, produced by the asset. The depreciable cost is divided by the asset's useful life—in units of production—to determine this amount. The per-unit depreciation expense is then multiplied by the number of units produced each period to compute depreciation. The units-of-production depreciation per unit of output (mile) for the FedEx truck data in Exhibit 7-4 is

$$\text{Units-of-production depreciation per unit of output} = \frac{\text{Cost} - \text{Residual value}}{\text{Useful life, in units of production}}$$

$$= \frac{\$41{,}000 - \$1{,}000}{100{,}000 \text{ miles}} = \$0.40 \text{ per mile}$$

Assume that FedEx expects to drive the truck 20,000 miles during the first year, 30,000 during the second year, 25,000 during the third year, 15,000 during the fourth year, and 10,000 during the fifth year. Exhibit 7-6 shows the UOP depreciation schedule.

Exhibit 7-6 | Units-of-Production (UOP) Depreciation Schedule for Truck

	A	B	C	D	E	F	G
1	Date	Cost	Rate per unit	Number Units	Yearly Expense	Accum. Deprec.	Book Value
2	1/1/2015	41,000					41,000
3	12/31/2015		0.4	20,000	8,000	8,000	33,000
4	12/31/2016		0.4	30,000	12,000	20,000	21,000
5	12/31/2017		0.4	25,000	10,000	30,000	11,000
6	12/31/2018		0.4	15,000	6,000	36,000	5,000
7	12/31/2019		0.4	10,000	4,000	40,000	1,000
8							

The amount of UOP depreciation varies each period with the number of units the asset produces, not the amount of time it is used. In our example, the total number of units (miles) produced is 100,000.

Try It in Excel®

If you built the straight-line depreciation schedule in Exhibit 7-5 with Excel, changing the spreadsheet for units-of-production depreciation is a snap. Steps 1–3 and 6–8 are identical. Only steps 4 and 5, dealing with columns C and D, change. You might want to start by opening the straight-line schedule you prepared and saving it under another name: "units-of-production depreciation." Next, change the column headings for column C and column D. Column C should be labeled "Rate per unit." Column D should be labeled "Number Units." Assuming you do this, here are the modified steps 4 and 5 of the process we used before:

4. In column C, calculate a per unit (rather than per year as we did with straight-line) depreciation rate by dividing the depreciable cost ($41,000 – $1,000 in Exhibit 7-4) by the number of units (100,000 miles) to get a fixed depreciation rate per mile ($0.40). Enter .4 in cell C3 and copy down through cell C7.
5. In cells D3 through D7, respectively, enter the number of miles driven in years one through five of the asset's useful life. These numbers are 20,000, 30,000, 25,000, 15,000, and 10,000, respectively.

All of the other amounts in the table will automatically recalculate to reflect units-of-production depreciation, exactly as shown in Exhibit 7-6.

Double-Declining-Balance Method. The **double-declining-balance (DDB) method** is an **accelerated depreciation method** because it writes off a larger amount of an asset's cost in the early years of its useful life. The method computes annual depreciation by multiplying the asset's declining book value at the beginning of the year by a constant percentage that is two times the straight-line depreciation rate. DDB rates are computed as follows:

$$\text{DDB depreciation rate per year} = \frac{1}{\text{Useful life, in years}} \times 2$$

$$= \frac{1}{5 \text{ years}} \times 2$$

$$= 20\% \times 2 = 40\%$$

1. Compute the straight-line depreciation rate per year. A truck with a 5-year useful life has a straight-line depreciation rate of 1/5, or 20%, each year. An asset with a 10-year useful life has a straight-line depreciation rate of 1/10, or 10%, and so on.
2. Multiply the straight-line rate by 2 to compute the DDB rate. For a 5-year asset, the DDB rate is 40% (20% × 2). A 10-year asset has a DDB rate of 20% (10% × 2). The DDB rate for the FedEx truck in our example (p. 375) is 40%.
3. Multiply the DDB rate by the period's *beginning* asset book value (cost less accumulated depreciation). Under the DDB method, ignore the residual value of the asset in computing depreciation, except during the last year.
4. Determine the final year's depreciation amount, that is, the amount needed to reduce the asset's book value to its residual value. In Exhibit 7-7, the fifth and final year's DDB depreciation expense is $4,314—the asset's book value of $5,314 at end of year (2018) less the $1,000 residual value. The residual value should not be depreciated but should remain on the books until the asset is disposed of.

Exhibit 7-7 | Double-Declining-Balance (DDB) Depreciation Schedule for Truck

A1

	A	B	C	D	E	F
1	**Date**	**Cost**	**DDB Rate**	**Yearly Expense**	**Accum. Deprec.**	**Book Value**
2	1/1/2015	41,000				41,000
3	12/31/2015		0.4	16,400	16,400	24,600
4	12/31/2016		0.4	9,840	26,240	14,760
5	12/31/2017		0.4	5,904	32,144	8,856
6	12/31/2018		0.4	3,542	35,686	5,314
7	12/31/2019		0.4	4,314*	40,000	1,000
8						

* Final-year depreciation is a plug amount needed to reduce asset book value to estimated salvage value

Try It in Excel®

If you built the straight-line and UOP depreciation schedules in Exhibits 7-5 and 7-6 with Excel, changing the spreadsheet for double-declining-balance (DDB) depreciation is easy. Steps 1–3 and 7–8 are identical. The other steps differ only slightly. You might want to start by opening the straight-line schedule you prepared and saving it under another name: "DDB depreciation." Next, change the column heading for column C to "DDB Rate." Right-click on column D (labeled "depreciable cost" in Exhibit 7-5) and delete the entire column. This moves the "yearly expense" over to column D. Here are modified steps 4 and 5 of the process we used for the straight-line rate, which replace steps 4–6 for the straight-line method:

4. In column C, calculate a new depreciation rate that is double the straight-line rate. In our example, the straight-line rate is 20% per year. The DDB rate is 40% (2 × 20%). Enter .4 in cell C3 and copy down through cell C7.
5. Column D now contains a calculated amount for yearly depreciation expense. The yearly depreciation expense is the product of the previous book value of the asset (in column F) times the DDB rate (in column C). For 2015, depreciation expense is $16,400, which is calculated in Excel as = F2*C3. Enter this formula in cell D3. Your result should be $16,400. Copy this formula down through cell D6 (*not* cell D7, for reasons explained shortly).

All of the other amounts in the table through line 6 will automatically recalculate to reflect DDB depreciation, exactly as shown in Exhibit 7-7.

The DDB method differs from the other methods in two ways:

1. Residual value is ignored initially; first-year depreciation is computed on the asset's full cost.
2. Depreciation expense in the final year is the "plug" amount needed to reduce the asset's book value to the residual amount. For this reason, depreciation expense in cell D7 of your Excel table should be 4,314, which is the amount needed to reduce the final book value to the residual amount of $1,000.

TRY IT

(Answers are given on p. 435.)

What is the DDB depreciation each year for the asset in the Try It on page 377?

Comparing Depreciation Methods

Let's compare the three methods in terms of the yearly amount of depreciation. The yearly amount varies by method, but the total $40,000 depreciable cost is the same under all methods.

	Amount of Depreciation per Year		
Year	Straight-Line	Units-of-Production	Accelerated Method Double-Declining Balance
1	$ 8,000	$ 8,000	$16,400
2	8,000	12,000	9,840
3	8,000	10,000	5,904
4	8,000	6,000	3,542
5	8,000	4,000	4,314
Total	$40,000	$40,000	$40,000

GAAP requires expense recognition in such a way as to match an asset's depreciation against the revenue the asset produces. For a plant asset that generates revenue evenly over time, the straight-line method best meets the expense recognition principle. The units-of-production method best meets the principle for those assets that wear out because of physical use rather than obsolescence. The accelerated method (DDB) best meets the principle for those assets that generate more revenue earlier in their useful lives and less in later years.

Exhibit 7-8 graphs annual depreciation amounts for the straight-line, units-of-production, and accelerated depreciation (DDB) methods. The graph of straight-line depreciation is flat through time because annual depreciation is the same in all periods. Units-of-production depreciation follows no particular pattern because annual depreciation depends on the use of the asset. Accelerated depreciation is greatest in the first year and less in the later years.

Exhibit 7-8 | Depreciation Patterns Through Time

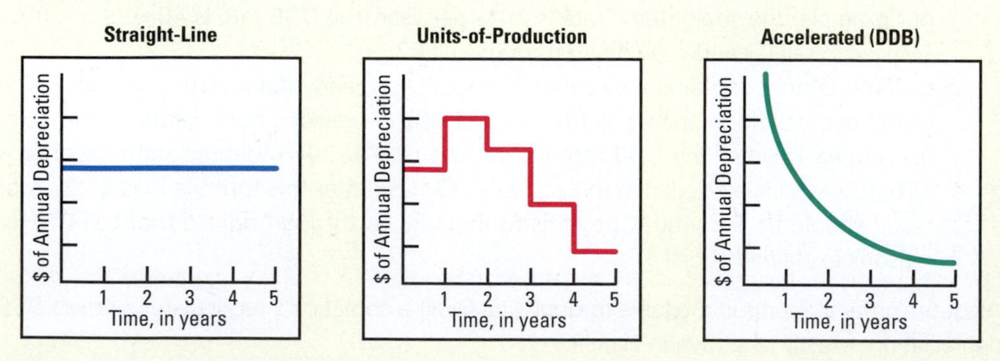

Exhibit 7-9 shows the percentage of companies that use each depreciation method based on a recent survey of 600 companies conducted by the American Institute of Certified Public Accountants (AICPA).

Exhibit 7-9 | Depreciation Methods Used by 600 Companies

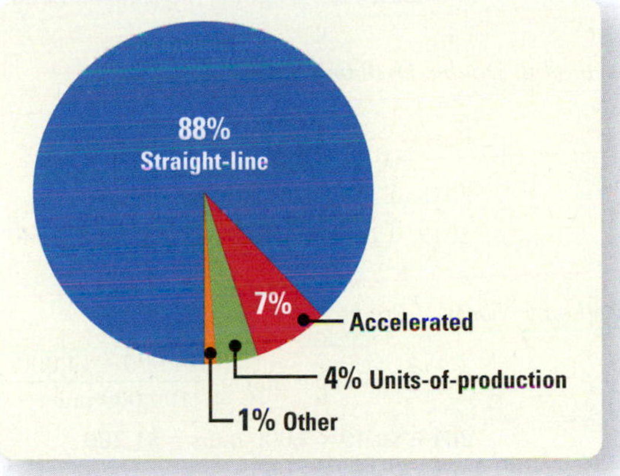

For reporting in the financial statements, straight-line depreciation is the most popular method. However, accelerated depreciation is most popular for income tax purposes.

Mid-Chapter | Summary Problem

Suppose FedEx purchased equipment on January 1, 2018, for $44,000. The expected useful life of the equipment is 10 years or 100,000 units of production, and its residual value is $4,000. Under three depreciation methods, the annual depreciation expense and the balance of accumulated depreciation at the end of 2018 and 2019 are

	Method A		*Method B*		*Method C*	
Year	Annual Depreciation Expense	Accumulated Depreciation	Annual Depreciation Expense	Accumulated Depreciation	Annual Depreciation Expense	Accumulated Depreciation
2018	$4,000	$4,000	$8,800	$ 8,800	$1,200	$1,200
2019	4,000	8,000	7,040	15,840	5,600	6,800

Requirements

1. Identify the depreciation method used in each instance, and show the equation and computation for each; round to the nearest dollar.
2. Determine the annual depreciation expense, accumulated depreciation, and book value of the equipment for 2018 through 2020 under each method, assuming 12,000 units of production in 2020.

Answers

Requirement 1

Method A: Straight-Line

$$\text{Depreciable cost} = \$40{,}000(\$44{,}000 - \$4{,}000)$$
$$\text{Each year: } \$40{,}000/10 \text{ years} = \$4{,}000$$

Method B: Double-Declining-Balance

$$\text{Rate} = \frac{1}{10 \text{ years}} \times 2 = 10\% \times 2 = 20\%$$
$$2018\text{: } 0.20 \times \$44{,}000 = \$8{,}800$$
$$2019\text{: } 0.20 \times (\$44{,}000 - \$8{,}800) = \$7{,}040$$

Method C: Units-of-Production

$$\text{Depreciation per unit} = \frac{\$44{,}000 - \$4{,}000}{100{,}000 \text{ units}} = \$0.40$$
$$2018\text{: } \$0.40 \times 3{,}000 \text{ units} = \$1{,}200$$
$$2019\text{: } \$0.40 \times 14{,}000 \text{ units} = \$5{,}600$$

Requirement 2

Method A: Straight-Line

Year	Annual Depreciation Expense	Accumulated Depreciation	Book Value
Start			$44,000
2018	$4,000	$ 4,000	40,000
2019	4,000	8,000	36,000
2020	4,000	12,000	32,000

Method B: Double-Declining-Balance

Year	Annual Depreciation Expense	Accumulated Depreciation	Book Value
Start			$44,000
2018	$8,800	$ 8,800	35,200
2019	7,040	15,840	28,160
2020	5,632	21,472	22,528

Method C: Units-of-Production

Year	Annual Depreciation Expense	Accumulated Depreciation	Book Value
Start			$44,000
2018	$1,200	$ 1,200	42,800
2019	5,600	6,800	37,200
2020	4,800	11,600	32,400

Computations for 2020

Straight-line	$40,000/10 years = $4,000
Double-declining-balance	$28,160 × 0.20 = $5,632
Units-of-production	12,000 units × $0.40 = $4,800

Other Issues in Accounting for Plant Assets

Plant assets are complex because

- they have long lives.
- depreciation affects income taxes.
- companies may have gains or losses when they sell plant assets.

Depreciation for Tax Purposes

CASH FLOW

FedEx and most other companies use straight-line depreciation on their financial statements. However, for income tax purposes, they also keep a separate set of depreciation records, based on accelerated depreciation methods in the Internal Revenue Code (IRC) developed by the Internal Revenue Service (IRS). Using accelerated depreciation methods is legal, ethical, and honest; U.S. tax law not only permits it, but also expects it. The reason that different methods are typically used for financial statement and income tax purposes is that the objectives of GAAP are different from the tax-reporting objectives of the IRC. The objective of GAAP is to provide useful information to help stockholders and creditors make economic decisions. The objective of the IRC is to raise a sufficient amount of revenue to pay for federal government expenditures.

Suppose you are a business manager and the IRS allows an accelerated depreciation method. Why do FedEx managers prefer accelerated over straight-line depreciation for income tax purposes? Accelerated depreciation provides the fastest tax deductions, thus decreasing a company's immediate tax payments. FedEx can reinvest the tax savings back into the business.

To understand the relationships among cash flow, depreciation, and income tax, recall our depreciation example of a FedEx truck:

- First-year depreciation is $8,000 under the straight-line method, and $16,400 under the double-declining-balance (DDB) method.
- DDB is permitted for income tax purposes.

Assume that this FedEx office has $400,000 in revenue, $300,000 in cash operating expenses during the truck's first year, and an income tax rate of 30%. The cash flow analysis appears in Exhibit 7-10.

Exhibit 7-10 | The Cash Flow Advantage of Accelerated Depreciation for Tax Purposes

		SL	Accelerated
1	Cash revenue	$400,000	$400,000
2	Cash operating expenses	300,000	300,000
3	Net cash provided by operations before income tax	100,000	100,000
4	Depreciation expense (a noncash expense)	8,000	16,400
5	Income before income tax	$ 92,000	$ 83,600
6	Income tax expense (30%)	$ 27,600	$ 25,080
	Cash-flow analysis:		
7	Net cash provided by operations before tax	$100,000	$100,000
8	Income tax expense	27,600	25,080
9	Net cash provided by operations	$ 72,400	$ 74,920
10	Extra cash available for investment if DDB is used ($74,920 – $72,400)		$ 2,520

You can see that, for income tax purposes, accelerated depreciation helps conserve cash for the business. That's why virtually all companies use accelerated depreciation to compute their income taxes.

There is a special depreciation method—used only for income tax purposes—called the **Modified Accelerated Cost Recovery System (MACRS)**. Under MACRS, each fixed asset is classified into one of eight classes, depending on the type of asset. (See Exhibit 7-11.) Depreciation for the first four classes is computed using the double-declining-balance method. Depreciation for 15-year assets and 20-year assets is computed using the 150% declining-balance method. Under 150% DB, annual depreciation is computed by multiplying the straight-line rate by 1.50 (instead of 2.00, as for DDB). For a 20-year asset, the straight-line rate is 0.05 per year (1/20 = 0.05), so the annual MACRS depreciation rate is 0.075 (0.05 × 1.50). The business computes the annual depreciation of the asset by multiplying its book value at the beginning of the year by 0.075 in a way that's similar to how the DDB is calculated.

Exhibit 7-11 | Modified Accelerated Cost Recovery System (MACRS)

Class Identified by Asset Life (years)	Representative Assets	Depreciation Method
3	Race horses	DDB
5	Automobiles, light trucks, computers	DDB
7	Office furniture, fixtures	DDB
10	Other equipment	DDB
15	Sewage-treatment plants	150% DB
20	Certain real estate	150% DB
27½	Residential rental property	SL
39	Nonresidential rental property	SL

The IRC permits several other accelerated depreciation methods. Some of the methods allow a company to take an additional "bonus depreciation" on "tangible personal property" (fixed assets that are not real estate) for tax purposes in the year of initial purchase. In other cases, a certain amount of investment in these types of fixed assets can be deducted entirely from the business's taxable income rather than capitalized and depreciated. All of these methods are intended to provide incentives for businesses to continually reinvest in new plant and equipment, saving them cash in tax outlays while stimulating the U.S. economy.

Most real estate is depreciated using the straight-line method (see the last two categories in Exhibit 7-11).

Depreciation for Partial Years

Companies purchase plant assets whenever they need them, not just at the beginning of the year. Therefore, companies must compute *depreciation for partial years*. Suppose FedEx purchases a warehouse building on September 1 for $500,000. The building's estimated life is 20 years, and its estimated residual value is $80,000. FedEx's accounting year ends on May 31. Let's consider how FedEx computes the asset's depreciation for September through May.

1. Compute the depreciation for a full year (unless you are using the units-of-production method, which automatically adjusts for partial periods by merely accounting for the number of units produced in the period).
2. Multiply the full-year depreciation by the fraction of the year that you held the asset—in this case, 9/12. If the straight-line method is used, the partial year's depreciation for the building is $15,750. It is calculated as follows:

$$\text{Full-year depreciation} \quad \frac{\$500{,}000 - \$80{,}000}{20} = \$21{,}000$$

$$\text{Partial year depreciation} \quad \$21{,}000 \times 9/12 = \$15{,}750$$

What if FedEx bought the asset on September 18? Many businesses record no monthly depreciation on assets purchased after the 15th of the month, and they record a full month's depreciation on an asset bought on or before the 15th.

Most companies use computerized systems to account for fixed assets. Each asset has a unique identification number, and the system will automatically calculate and update the asset's depreciation expense. The system will also automatically calculate and update Accumulated Depreciation.

Changing the Useful Life of a Depreciable Asset

After an asset is in use, managers may change its useful life on the basis of experience and new information. The Walt Disney Company made such a change, called a *change in accounting estimate,* several years ago. The company recalculated the depreciation on several of its theme park assets based on their revised useful lives. The following note in the company's financial statements that year reported this change in accounting estimate:

> **Note 5**
> **... [T]he Company extended the estimated useful lives of certain theme park ride and attraction assets based upon historical data and engineering studies. The effect of this change was to decrease depreciation by approximately $8 million (an increase in net income of approximately $4.2 million...).**
>
> *Source: From Disney Enterprises, Inc.'s Financial Statements, 2014.*

Assume that a Disney hot dog stand cost $50,000 and that the company originally believed the asset had a 10-year useful life with no residual value. Using the straight-line method, the company would record $5,000 in depreciation each year ($50,000 ÷ 10 years = $5,000). Suppose Disney used the asset for four years. Accumulated depreciation reached $20,000, leaving a remaining depreciable book value (cost less accumulated depreciation less residual value) of $30,000 ($50,000 – $20,000). From its experience, management believes the asset will remain useful for an additional 10 years. The company would spread the remaining depreciable book value over the asset's remaining life as follows:

Asset's remaining depreciable book value	÷	(New) Estimated useful life remaining	=	(New) Annual depreciation
$30,000	÷	10 years	=	$3,000

The yearly depreciation entry based on the new estimated useful life is as follows:

	A	C	D	G
1		Depreciation Expense—Hot Dog Stand	3,000	
2		Accumulated Depreciation—Hot Dog Stand		3,000
3				

Depreciation decreases both assets and equity.

Assets	=	Liabilities	+	Stockholders' Equity	− Expenses
−3,000	=	0			−3,000

Cooking the Books

Waste Management

Since plant assets usually involve relatively large amounts and relatively large numbers of assets, sometimes a seemingly subtle change in the way they are accounted for can have a tremendous impact on the financial statements. When these changes are made in order to cook the books, the results can be devastating.

Waste Management, Inc., is North America's largest integrated waste service company, providing collection, transfer, recycling, disposal, and waste-to-energy services for commercial, industrial, municipal, and residential customers from coast to coast.

Starting in 1992, six top executives of the company, including its founder and chairman of the board, its chief financial officer, its corporate controller, its top lawyer, and its vice president of finance, decided that the company's profits were not growing fast enough to meet "earnings targets," which were tied to their executive bonuses. Among several fraudulent financial tactics these executives used to cook the books were (1) assigning unsupported and inflated salvage values to garbage trucks, (2) unjustifiably extending the estimated useful lives of their garbage trucks, and (3) assigning arbitrary salvage values to other fixed assets that previously had no salvage values. All of these tactics had the effect of decreasing the amount of depreciation expense in Waste Management's income statements and increasing the company's net income by a corresponding amount. Although practices like this might seem relatively subtle and even insignificant when performed on an individual asset, remember that there were thousands of trash trucks and dumpsters involved, so the dollar amount grew huge in a short time. In addition, the company continued these practices for five years, overstating Waste Management's earnings by $1.7 billion.

When the fraud was disclosed, Waste Management shareholders lost over $6 billion in the market value of their investments as the stock price plummeted by more than 33%. The company and these officers eventually settled civil lawsuits for approximately $700 million because of the fraud.

Fully Depreciated Assets

Recall that a fully depreciated asset is one that has reached the end of its estimated useful life. Suppose FedEx has fully depreciated some equipment with zero residual value. The equipment's cost was $60,000. FedEx accounts will appear as follows:

Equipment			Accumulated Depreciation			Book value
60,000		−		60,000	=	$0

The equipment's book value is zero, but that doesn't mean the equipment is worthless. FedEx might use the equipment for a few more years, but the company will not record any more depreciation on the asset because it is already fully depreciated.

When FedEx disposes of the equipment, the company will remove both the asset's cost ($60,000) and its accumulated depreciation ($60,000) from the books. The next section shows how to account for plant asset disposals.

ANALYZE THE EFFECT OF A PLANT ASSET DISPOSAL

4 Analyze the effect of a plant asset disposal

Eventually, a plant asset ceases to serve a company's needs. The asset may wear out or become obsolete. Before accounting for the disposal of the asset, the business should bring depreciation up to date to

- measure the asset's final book value, and
- record the expense up to the date of disposal.

Disposing of a Fully Depreciated Asset for No Proceeds

To account for an asset's disposal, remove it and its related accumulated depreciation from the books. Suppose the final year's depreciation expense has just been recorded for a machine that cost $60,000 and is estimated to have zero residual value. The machine's accumulated depreciation thus totals $60,000. Assuming that this asset is junked, the entry to record its disposal is as follows:

	A	C	D	G
1		Accumulated Depreciation—Machinery	60,000	
2		Machinery		60,000
3		*To dispose of a fully depreciated machine.*		
4				

Assets	=	Liabilities	+	Stockholders' Equity
+ 60,000 − 60,000	=	0	+	0

There is no gain or loss on this disposal, and there's no effect on total assets, liabilities, or equity.

If assets are disposed of for no proceeds before being fully depreciated, the company incurs a loss on the disposal in the amount of the asset's net book value. Suppose FedEx disposes of equipment that cost $60,000. This asset's accumulated depreciation is $50,000, and book value is, therefore, $10,000. Junking this equipment results in a loss equal to the book value of the asset:

	A	C	D	G
1		Accumulated Depreciation—Equipment	50,000	
2		Loss on Disposal of Equipment	10,000	
3		Equipment		60,000
4		*To dispose of equipment.*		
5				

Assets	=	Liabilities	+	Stockholders' Equity	−	Losses
+ 50,000 − 60,000	=	0				− 10,000

FedEx disposed of an asset with $10,000 book value and received nothing. The result is a $10,000 loss, which decreases both total assets and equity.

The Loss on Disposal of Equipment is reported as Other income (expense) on the income statement. Losses decrease net income exactly as expenses do. Gains increase net income the same as revenues do.

Selling a Plant Asset

Suppose FedEx sells equipment on September 30, 2018, for $7,300 cash. The equipment cost $10,000 when purchased on January 1, 2015, and has been depreciated using the straight-line method. FedEx estimated the equipment has a 10-year useful life and no residual value. Prior to recording the sale, FedEx's accountants must update the asset's depreciation. Assume that FedEx uses the calendar year as its accounting period. Partial-year depreciation must be recorded for the asset's depreciation from January 1, 2018, to the sale date. The straight-line depreciation entry at September 30, 2018, is

	A	C	D	G
1	Sep 30	Depreciation Expense ($10,000/10 years × 9/12)	750	
2		Accumulated Depreciation—Equipment		750
3		*To update depreciation.*		
4				

The Equipment account and the Accumulated Depreciation—Equipment account appear as follows. The equipment's book value is $6,250 ($10,000 − $3,750):

Equipment

Jan 1, 2015	10,000	

−

Accumulated Depreciation—Equipment

	Dec 31, 2015	1,000
	Dec 31, 2016	1,000
	Dec 31, 2017	1,000
	Sep 30, 2018	750
	Balance	3,750

= Book value $6,250

The gain on the sale of the equipment for $7,300 is $1,050, computed as follows:

Cash received from sale of the asset		$7,300
Book value of asset sold:		
Cost	$10,000	
Less: Accumulated depreciation	(3,750)	6,250
Gain on sale of the asset		$1,050

The entry to record sale of the equipment is

	A	C	D	G
1	Sep 30	Cash	7,300	
2		Accumulated Depreciation—Equipment	3,750	
3		Equipment		10,000
4		Gain on Sale of Equipment		1,050
5		*To sell equipment.*		
6				

Total assets increase, and so does equity—by the amount of the gain.

Assets	=	Liabilities	+	Stockholders' Equity	+	Gains
+ 7,300						
+ 3,750	=	0			+	1,050
−10,000						

Gains and losses on asset disposals appear as Other income (expense), or Other gains (losses), on the income statement.

Exchanging a Plant Asset

Managers often trade in old assets for new ones. This is called a *nonmonetary exchange*. The accounting for nonmonetary exchanges is based on the fair values of the assets involved. Thus, the cost of an asset like plant and equipment received in a nonmonetary exchange is equal to the fair values of the assets given up (including the old asset and any cash paid). Any difference between the fair value of the old asset and its book value is recognized as a gain (if the fair value of the old asset exceeds its book value) or a loss (if the book value of the old asset exceeds its fair value) on the exchange. For example, assume **Papa John's Pizza**'s

- old delivery car cost $9,000 and has accumulated depreciation of $8,000. Thus, the old car's book value is $1,000.

Assume Papa John's trades in the old automobile for a new one with a fair market value of $15,000 and pays cash of $10,000. Thus, the implied fair value of the old car is $5,000 ($15,000 – $10,000). This amount is treated as cash received by the business for the old vehicle.

- The cost of the new delivery car is $15,000 (fair value of the old asset, $5,000, plus cash paid, $10,000).

The pizzeria records the exchange transaction:

	A	C	D	G
1		Delivery Auto (new)	15,000	
2		Accumulated Depreciation—Delivery Auto (old)	8,000	
3		Delivery Auto (old)		9,000
4		Cash		10,000
5		Gain on Exchange of Delivery Auto		4,000
6		*Traded in old delivery car for new auto.*		
7				

Assets	=	Liabilities	+	Stockholders' Equity	+	Gains
+15,000						
+ 8,000	=	0			+	4,000
− 9,000						
−10,000						

There was a net increase in total assets of $4,000 and a corresponding increase in stockholders' equity to reflect the gain on the exchange. Notice that this amount represents the excess of the fair value of the old asset ($5,000) over its book value ($1,000). Some special rules may apply in this situation, but they are reserved for more advanced courses.

T-Accounts for Analyzing Plant Asset Transactions

You can perform quite a bit of analysis if you know how transactions affect the plant asset accounts. Here are the accounts with descriptions of the activity in each account.

Building (or Equipment)	
Beg bal Cost of assets purchased	Cost of assets disposed of
End bal	

Accumulated Depreciation	
Accumulated depreciation of assets disposed of	Beg bal Depreciation expense for the current period
	End bal

Cash	
Cash proceeds for assets disposed of	Cash paid for assets purchased

Long-Term Debt	
	New Debt incurred for assets purchased

Depreciation Expense	
Depreciation expense for the current period	

Gain on Sale of Building (or Equipment)	
	Gain on sale

Loss on Sale of Building (or Equipment)	
Loss on sale	

You can analyze transactions as they flow through these accounts to answer very useful questions such as the amount of cash paid to purchase new plant assets, the amount of cash proceeds from disposal of plant assets, the cost of assets purchased, and the gross cost as well as net book value of assets disposed of.

Example: Suppose you started the year with buildings that cost $100,000. During the year, you bought another building for $150,000 and ended the year with buildings that cost $180,000. What was the cost of the building you sold?

Building

Beg bal	100,000		
Cost of assets purchased	150,000	Cost of assets sold	X = 70,000*
End bal	180,000		

*X = 100,000 + 150,000 − 180,000

GLOBAL VIEW

Valuing and Depreciating Assets Under GAAP versus IFRS. One of the most significant differences between U.S. GAAP and International Financial Reporting Standards (IFRS) is the reported carrying values allowed for property, plant, and equipment. Recall from Chapter 1 that under U.S. GAAP, the historical cost principle is most appropriate for plant assets because it results in a more objective (nonbiased) and therefore a more reliable (auditable) figure. It also supports the continuity assumption, which states that we expect the entity to remain in business long enough to recover the cost of its plant assets through depreciation.

Historical cost is the primary basis of accounting under IFRS too. However, IFRS allows plant assets to be periodically revalued at their fair market value. The primary justification for this position is that the historical cost of plant assets purchased years ago does not properly reflect their current values. Thus, the amounts shown on the balance sheet for these assets do not reflect a relevant measure of what the assets are worth.

For example, suppose a business bought a building in downtown Orlando, Florida, in 1960 for $1 million. Assume that this year the building has been appraised for $20 million. IFRS would permit the company periodically to revalue the building on its balance sheet. In this case, the building account would be debited for $19 million, and an offsetting credit would be made to Revaluation Surplus, which is a separate account in stockholders' equity. Depreciation from this point forward would be based on the revalued amount in the asset's account. If in the future, the fair value of the building goes down, the building account could be credited, and the revaluation surplus would be reduced by an offsetting amount.

The primary objection to the use of fair values on the balance sheet for plant assets is that these values are subjective and subject to change, sometimes quite rapidly. Consider, for example, residential and commercial real estate in California during the housing and credit crisis of 2008 and 2009. The fair market values of residential and commercial real estate dropped by double-digit percentages in a period of less than one year. If the assets had been valued at fair market values on the books of the companies that held them, the assets would have to have been adjusted accordingly, causing the balance sheet amounts to fluctuate wildly. The depreciation expense and accumulated depreciation related to the assets would also have fluctuated wildly and would have had to be adjusted more frequently.

IFRS also differs substantially from U.S. GAAP with respect to accounting for depreciation. Whereas GAAP depreciates each asset as a composite whole (a building, manufactured equipment, an aircraft, etc.), IFRS uses a "components" approach. For example, suppose a company builds and owns a building that it is using for its operations. The total cost of the building, including all components (air-conditioning systems, roofing, duct work, plumbing, lighting systems, etc.) is $15 million. U.S. GAAP usually treats the building as a single composite asset within the class of buildings, with an estimated useful life of about 40 years that it depreciates using straight-line depreciation (about $375,000 per year).

In contrast, IFRS does not view the building as a single composite asset, but recognizes the separate components of it—each with a different useful life and potentially accounted for with a different depreciation method. Thus, the frame of the building, the roof, air-conditioning system, duct work, plumbing, light fixtures, and all other major components of the building each might have a different useful life (most being far less than 40 years) and be depreciated using a different method over shorter periods of time. Each has to be set up on the books as a separate component asset with separate amounts of depreciation expense and accumulated depreciation. Converting a large enterprise's accounting system to a component approach for depreciation requires a massive one-time expenditure in information technology, as well as more extensive ongoing record-keeping requirements.

APPLY GAAP FOR NATURAL RESOURCES AND INTANGIBLE ASSETS

Accounting for Natural Resources

5 Apply GAAP for natural resources and intangible assets

Natural resources are long-term assets of a special type, such as iron ore, petroleum (oil), and timber. These resources are often called *wasting assets* because, in contrast to property and equipment, they are actually physically used up over time. The process by which this occurs is called **depletion**. Depletion is distinctively different from depreciation because it involves actually tracking the flow of a natural resource from its raw state, through inventory to the cost of goods sold or some other expense on the income statement. When an area with natural resources is acquired, the business acquiring it follows the cost principle used to account for a plant asset. Then, when the natural resource is extracted, the business follows an approach much like the units-of-production depreciation method to account for the production. If all of the resource extracted is immediately sold, like oil is after being extracted by a drilling and exploration company, the amount depleted is transferred directly from the company's long-term assets to its income statement in the form of an expense (such as Depletion Expense). However, if a portion of the extracted resource is not immediately sold, it becomes saleable inventory (a current asset). This is what occurs when an oil company drills as well as refines oil before selling it. Then, as the inventory of refined oil is sold, its cost is transferred to an expense such as cost of goods sold, as discussed in Chapter 6.

For example, suppose **ExxonMobil** buys an oil reserve that costs $100,000,000 and contains an estimated 10,000,000 barrels of oil. ExxonMobil is an integrated oil company, meaning it both drills for oil and refines it, so the company retains some inventory rather than selling all it produces. When it purchases the oil reserve (assuming the company paid cash), ExxonMobil makes the following entry:

A1

	A	C	D	G
1		Oil Reserve	100,000,000	
2		Cash		100,000,000
3				

The depletion rate is $10 per barrel ($100,000,000 ÷ 10,000,000 barrels). If 3,000,000 barrels are extracted and 1,000,000 barrels are sold, the company's different divisions might make the following entries. First, the oil reserve (long-term asset) is depleted by $30,000,000 (3,000,000 barrels × $10 per barrel) and $30,000,000 is transferred to inventory. The depletion entry is:

	A	C	D	G
1		Oil Inventory (3,000,000 barrels × $10)	30,000,000	
2		Oil Reserve		30,000,000
3				

Suppose the following week, ExxonMobil sells one third of the oil. The company makes the following entry to Cost of Oil Sold (ignore entry to sales revenue).

	A	C	D	G
1		Cost of Oil Sold (1,000,000 barrels × $10)	10,000,000	
2		Oil Inventory		10,000,000
3				

This would assign $10 million to Cost of Oil Sold (an expense) and leave $20 million in Oil Inventory (a current asset). The net book value of the oil reserve (the long-term asset) after these entries is $70 million ($100 million – $30 million).

Accounting for Intangible Assets

Recall that **intangible assets** are long-lived assets with no physical form. Patents, copyrights, trademarks, franchises, and goodwill are examples of intangible assets:

- **Patents** are federal government grants that give the holder the exclusive right for 20 years to produce and sell an invention. The invention may be a product or a process—for example, the **Sony** Blu-Ray disc players and the **Dolby Laboratories** surround-sound process.
- **Copyrights** are exclusive rights to reproduce and sell a book, musical composition, film, or other work of art. Copyrights also protect computer software programs, such as **Microsoft**'s Windows and Excel. Issued by the federal government, copyrights extend 70 years beyond the author's (composer's, artist's, or programmer's) life.
- **Trademarks** and **trade names** (or *brand names*) are distinctive identifications of products or services. The "eye" symbol that flashes across our television screens is the trademark that identifies the **CBS** television network. You are probably also familiar with **NBC**'s peacock. Advertising slogans that are legally protected include **American Airlines**' "AAdvantage" program and **CocaCola Co.**'s "Taste the Feeling" slogan. These are distinctive identifications of products or services, marked with the symbol ™ or ®.
- **Franchises** and **licenses** are privileges granted by a private business or a government to sell a product or service in accordance with specified conditions. The **Chicago Cubs** baseball organization is a franchise granted to its owner by the **National League**. **McDonald's** restaurants and **Holiday Inns** are popular franchises.
- **Goodwill** has a very specific meaning in accounting:

Goodwill is defined as the excess of the cost of purchasing another company over the sum of the market values of the acquired company's net assets (assets minus liabilities).

Put another way, goodwill is the abnormal earning power a company has due to factors including having good brands, good customer and employee relations, or superior products and technology. The purchasers of a company are willing to pay extra for goodwill.

Like buildings and equipment, intangible assets are recorded at their acquisition costs. Intangibles are the most valuable assets of high-tech companies and those that depend on research and development. The residual value of most intangibles is zero.

Intangible assets fall into one of two categories:

- Intangibles with *finite lives* that can be measured. Because patents and copyrights legally expire after a certain number years, they are intangible assets with finite lives. These intangibles are amortized over either their legal or useful lives—whichever is shorter. Amortization Expense is the title of the expense account associated with these intangibles, and the expense is recorded annually and usually computed on a straight-line basis. Amortization can also be credited directly to the asset account.
- Intangibles with *indefinite lives*. Goodwill is the most prominent example of an intangible asset with an indefinite life. Record no amortization for these intangibles. Instead, check them annually for any loss in value (impairment, which is discussed later in the chapter). Record a loss when it occurs.

Accounting for Specific Intangibles

Each type of intangible asset is unique, so the accounting can vary from one intangible asset to another.

Patents. A patent may be either developed internally by a company or purchased. Under GAAP, the only costs of an internally developed patent that can be capitalized are legal and registration costs. Other costs of development are treated as research and development costs, and must be expensed as incurred (see discussion below). In contrast, patents that are purchased from another company may be capitalized and amortized. Suppose Sony Corporation pays $170,000 to acquire a patent on January 1, and the business believes the expected useful life of the patent is 5 years—not the entire 20-year period. Amortization expense is $34,000 per year ($170,000 ÷ 5 years). Sony records the acquisition and amortization for this patent:

A1

	A	C	D	G
1	Jan 1	Patents	170,000	
2		Cash		170,000
3		*To acquire a patent.*		
4				

A1

	A	C	D	G
1	Dec 31	Amortization Expense—Patents ($170,000/5)	34,000	
2		Patents		34,000
3		*To amortize the cost of a patent.*		
4				

Assets	=	Liabilities	+	Stockholders' Equity	−	Expenses
− 34,000	=	0				− 34,000

You can see that we credited the Patents account directly (and not the Accumulated Amortization account). The amortization of an intangible asset decreases a business's assets and equity exactly like depreciation does.

Copyrights. The cost of obtaining a copyright from the government is low, but a company may pay a large sum to purchase an existing copyright from the owner. For example, a publisher may pay the author of a popular novel $1 million or more for the book's copyright. Because the useful life of a copyright is usually no longer than two or three years, each period's amortization amount is a high proportion of the copyright's cost. Accounting for copyrights is similar to that of patents.

Trademarks and Trade Names. Some trademarks may have a definite useful life set by contract. We should amortize the cost of this type of trademark over its useful life. In this case, the accounting for a trademark is similar to that of patents and copyrights. But some trademarks or trade names may have an indefinite life and not be amortized. For example, McDonald's can continue to use its golden-arches trademark indefinitely because the company originally developed it (didn't buy it).

Franchises and Licenses. The useful lives of many franchises and licenses are indefinite and, therefore, are not amortized.

Goodwill. Because of the definition of goodwill (the excess of cost over fair market value of net assets acquired), accounting for goodwill is somewhat different from that for the intangibles discussed above. Suppose FedEx acquires Europa Company at a cost of $10 million. Europa's assets have a market value of $9 million, and the market value of its liabilities total $2 million, so Europa's net assets total $7 million at current market value. Consequently, FedEx paid $3 million for the goodwill:

Purchase price paid for Europa Company		$10 million
Sum of the market values of Europa Company's assets	$9 million	
Less: Market values of Europa Company's liabilities	(2 million)	
Market value of Europa Company's net assets		7 million
Excess is called *goodwill*		$ 3 million

FedEx's entry to record the acquisition of Europa Company, including its goodwill, would be

	A	C	D	G
1		Assets (Cash, Receivables, Inventories, Plant Assets,		
2		all at market value)	9,000,000	
3		Goodwill	3,000,000	
4		Liabilities		2,000,000
5		Cash		10,000,000
6				

Goodwill in accounting has special features:

1. Goodwill is recorded *only* when it is purchased in the acquisition of another company. A purchase transaction provides objective evidence of the value of goodwill. Companies never record the goodwill they create for their own business.
2. According to GAAP, goodwill is not amortized because for many entities, it increases in value over time. Instead, each year, companies with goodwill on their financial statements are required to perform a special impairment test for goodwill, which is similar (but not identical) to the impairment test for other long-term assets described in the next section. If the test shows that goodwill is impaired, it must be written down to the impaired value. The details of this impairment test are beyond the scope of this text and are reserved for later courses.

Accounting for Research and Development Costs

Research and development (R&D) costs are costs incurred to develop and create new products. R&D represents perhaps the most valuable activity many companies engage in, particularly companies in the software, technology, aerospace, pharmaceutical, and consumer products industries. For example, **Apple Inc.**, our focus company featured in Appendix A of this text, spent over $10 billion in its fiscal 2016 year on R&D. Accounting for R&D costs is one of the most difficult issues in accounting. In general, U.S. companies do not report R&D as assets on their balance sheets, because under U.S. GAAP, these costs do not possess sufficient probability of producing future economic benefits to qualify as assets. Instead, under U.S. GAAP, R&D costs must be classified as expenses on the income statement as they are incurred.

EXPLAIN THE EFFECT OF AN ASSET IMPAIRMENT ON THE FINANCIAL STATEMENTS

6 Explain the effect of an asset impairment on the financial statements

Generally accepted accounting principles require companies to test both their tangible and intangible long-term assets for impairment yearly. **Impairment** occurs when the expected future cash flows (which approximate the expected future benefits) from a long-term asset fall below the asset's net book (carrying) value (cost minus accumulated depreciation or amortization). Generally the fall in value is due to the abrupt damage or obsolescence of the asset. For example, suppose a pharmaceutical company with a patent for a new drug suddenly discovers that people experience toxic effects when taking it. Obviously the value of this patent is greatly decreased following the discovery, so the asset is impaired.

If an asset is impaired, the company is required to adjust the carrying value downward from its book value to its **fair value**. In this case, fair value is based not on the expected future cash flows, but on the asset's estimated market value at the date of the impairment test. Exhibit 7-12 displays both the normal relationship and an impaired relationship among the net book value, future cash flows, and fair value of an asset.

Exhibit 7-12 | Normal Relationship and Impaired Relationship Among Values of an Asset

Normal		Impaired	
Largest:	Future cash flows	Largest:	Net book value
Middle:	Fair value	Middle:	Future cash flows
Smallest:	Net book value	Smallest:	Fair value

In a normal relationship, estimated future cash flows represent the largest of the three amounts, followed by fair value, and then net book value. An impaired relationship exists if an asset's net book value exceeds its estimated future cash flows. The process of accounting for asset impairment requires two steps:

Step 1 Test the asset for impairment.
- **If net book value > Estimated future cash flows, then the asset is impaired.**

Step 2 If the asset is impaired under step 1, compute the impairment loss.
- **Impairment loss = Net book value – Fair value**

To illustrate, let's assume that FedEx has a long-term asset with the following information as of May 31, 2016:

- **Net book value $100 million**
- **Estimated future cash flows $80 million**
- **Fair (market) value $70 million**

The two-stage impairment process is

Step 1 Impairment test: Is net book value ($100) > estimated future cash flows ($80)? (Answer: Yes, so the asset is impaired.)

Step 2 Impairment loss = Net book value ($100) – Fair value ($70) = $30

FedEx will make the following entry (in millions):

	A	C	D	G
1	2016			
2	May 31	Impairment Loss on Long-term Asset ($100 – $70)	30	
3		Long-term Asset		30
4				

Assets	=	Liabilities	+	Stockholders' Equity	–	Losses
– 30	=	0				– 30

Both long-term assets and equity decrease (through the Loss account). Under U.S. GAAP, once a long-term asset has been written down because of impairment, it may never again be written back up, should it increase in value.

GLOBAL VIEW

Asset Impairments. IFRS require that tests of impairment for long-lived assets be based on a one-step impairment process. The details of this process are covered in more advanced accounting courses. Unlike U.S. GAAP, asset impairments under IFRS can be reversed in future periods for some types of long-term assets, in the event that the market price of an asset recovers. Thus, under IFRS, a company can record an impairment loss on certain long-term assets in one period and then write the asset back up with a corresponding gain in a later period.

R&D Costs. Accounting for research and development (R&D) costs represents another prominent difference between U.S. GAAP and IFRS. Whereas under U.S. GAAP, both research and development costs are expensed as incurred, under IFRS, the costs associated with the creation of the assets are classified into research-phase costs and development-phase costs. Costs in the research phase are always expensed. However, costs in the development phase are capitalized (put on the balance sheet and depreciated) if a company can demonstrate meeting various criteria, including the technical feasibility of completing the intangible asset, the ability to use or sell it, and the asset's future economic benefits. Because development costs are not all immediately expensed, the reported incomes for companies using IFRS will be higher than they are under GAAP.

Internally generated intangibles. Still another difference between U.S. GAAP and IFRS relates to internally generated intangible assets such as brand names and patents. U.S. GAAP only permits capitalization of these costs when they are purchased from a source outside the company. The cost of internally generated brand names and patents must be expensed on the income statement. In contrast, IFRS allows internally generated intangible assets like these to be capitalized as long as it is probable (i.e., more likely than not) that the company will receive future benefits from them. Finite life intangible assets are amortized over their useful lives. Indefinite life intangible assets are not amortized but are tested for impairment annually.

ANALYZE THE RATE OF RETURN ON ASSETS

7 Analyze the rate of return on assets

Evaluating a company's performance is a key goal of financial statement analysis. Shareholders and creditors entrust managers to develop business strategies that utilize a company's assets in a way that both effectively and efficiently generates a profit. One way to evaluate how well managers have performed in this regard is to examine the company's **return on assets (ROA)**.

ROA, also known as the *rate of return* on assets, measures how well company assets have been used to generate net income (profit). The basic formula for the ROA ratio is

$$\text{ROA} = \frac{\text{Net income}^1}{\text{Average total assets}}$$

where Average total assets = (Beginning total assets + Ending total assets)/2

ROA measures how much the entity earned for each dollar of assets invested by both stockholders and creditors. Companies with a high ROA have both selected the right assets and managed them more successfully than companies with a low ROA. ROA is often computed on a divisional or product-line basis to help identify less profitable business segments and improve their performance.

DuPont Analysis: A More Detailed View of ROA

To better understand why ROA increased or decreased over time, companies often perform a **DuPont Analysis**,[2] which breaks ROA down into two component ratios that drive it:

$$\text{Net profit margin ratio} = \frac{\text{Net income}}{\text{Net sales}}$$

$$\text{Total asset turnover} = \frac{\text{Net sales}}{\text{Average total assets}}$$

A business's **net profit margin ratio** measures how much every sales dollar generates in profit. In other words, the ratio shows how much of every dollar of sales a company gets to keep as earnings. A company can increase its net profit margin ratio in one of three ways: (1) by increasing its sales volume, or the amount of goods sold or services performed; (2) by increasing its sales prices; or (3) by decreasing its cost of goods sold and operating expenses.

Total asset turnover measures how many sales dollars are generated for each dollar of assets invested. This is a measure of how efficiently the company manages its assets. Total asset turnover can be increased by (1) increasing sales in the ways just described; (2) keeping less inventory on hand; or (3) closing unproductive or low-performing facilities, selling idle assets, and consolidating operations to fewer places to reduce the amount of plant assets needed and focus efforts on the more profitable areas of the business.

ROA is the product of a company's net profit margin ratio and total asset turnover:

$$\text{ROA} = \text{Net profit margin ratio} \times \text{Total asset turnover}$$

$$\text{ROA} = \frac{\text{Net income}}{\text{Net sales}} \times \frac{\text{Net sales}}{\text{Average total assets}} = \frac{\text{Net income}}{\text{Average total assets}}$$

By influencing the drivers of net profit margin ratio and total asset turnover, management devises strategies to improve each one, thus increasing ROA. Successful companies often choose between a mixture of two different strategies: *product differentiation* or *low cost.* A company with a high product differentiation strategy usually spends a great deal on research and development and advertising to convince customers that the company's products (usually higher priced) are worth the investment. For example, Apple Inc., follows a product differentiation strategy: The company introduces innovative and attractive products in the marketplace before

[1] For companies with a significant amount of debt, some analysts may add interest expense to net income. While it is theoretically correct to do so, in order to illustrate DuPont analysis, we do not. Adding back interest makes a material difference to ROA only when a company's interest expense is relatively high compared to the business's net income.

[2] The full DuPont Analysis model actually illustrates a way to compute Return on Common Stockholders' Equity (ROE), which is the product of three component ratios: net profit margin ratio, total asset turnover, and leverage. In this chapter, we discuss a partial version of the full DuPont model, ROA, which is the product of the first two component ratios. In Chapter 9 we introduce the third component ratio (leverage) and in Chapter 10 we illustrate how the leverage ratio is used to convert ROA to ROE.

any other competitor does and always sells them at a higher price. Alternatively, a low-cost strategy usually relies on efficiently managing a business's inventory and productive assets to produce a high asset turnover. **Dell, Inc.,** a competitor of Apple's, follows a low-cost strategy. Of course, all companies would like to have the best of both worlds and maximize both their net profit margin ratio and their total asset turnover ratio. However, some companies have to settle for one or the other.

To illustrate, let's look at FedEx's ROA, using DuPont analysis.

FedEx Corporation
Selected (Adapted) Financial Data

(Amounts in millions)	2015	2016
Net sales	$47,453	$50,365
Net income	1,050	1,820
Average total assets	34,801	41,297

FedEx Corporation
DuPont Analysis

	Net profit margin ratio × (Net income/Net sales)	×	Total asset turnover (Net sales/Average total assets)	=	ROA (Net income/Average total assets)
2015	$\frac{\$1,050}{\$47,453}$	×	$\frac{\$47,453}{\$34,801}$	=	3.0%
2016	$\frac{\$1,820}{\$50,365}$	×	$\frac{\$50,365}{\$41,297}$	=	4.4%

In 2015, the company's net profit margin ratio was 2.21% ($1,050 million ÷ $47,453 million), which means that for each dollar of net sales, the company earned 2.21 cents in net profit (income). Its asset turnover was 1.364 ($47,453 million ÷ $34,801 million), meaning that it earned $1.364 of sales revenue for every $1 of assets invested. In 2016, the company improved its net profit margin ratio to 3.61% ($1,820 million ÷ $50,365 million) by increasing sales while holding operating and other expenses down. At the same time, FedEx's asset turnover slowed to 1.2196 ($50,365 million ÷ $41,297 million). FedEx purchased proportionately more property and equipment during that year than the increase it experienced in net sales. Thus, the company was more effective (profitable) in 2016 than 2015, but its efficiency declined slightly during the same period. Fortunately, the increase in profits outweighed the decrease in efficiency, so ROA increased from 3.0% to 4.4%.

ROA is the first of several ratios we will introduce over the next few chapters to show how analysts dissect financial statements to get behind the numbers, discover management's strategies, and evaluate their performance. In Chapters 9 and 10 we will add the component of financial leverage to the DuPont Analysis model and explain how it is combined with ROA to calculate return on common stockholders' equity (ROE).

ANALYZE THE CASH FLOW IMPACT OF LONG-LIVED ASSET TRANSACTIONS

8 Analyze the cash flow impact of long-lived asset transactions

Three main types of long-lived asset transactions appear on the statement of cash flows:

- acquisitions,
- sales, and
- depreciation (as well as amortization).

CASH FLOW

Acquiring and selling long-term assets are *investing* activities. Capital expenditures, which increase an asset's capacity or extend its useful life, are examples of investing activities (outflows) that appear on the statement of cash flows. The disposition of plant and other long-term assets results in a cash inflow in the investing activities section. Sometimes cash outflows and inflows from various investing activities are netted, as illustrated in Exhibit 7-13, which excerpts data from the cash flow statement of FedEx Corporation. Depreciation, acquisitions, capital expenditures, and sales (dispositions) of long-term capital assets are denoted in color (lines 7, 11, and 12).

Exhibit 7-13 | Reporting Investing Activities on FedEx Corporation's Statement of Cash Flows

	A	B
1	**FedEx Corporation** **Statement of Cash Flows (Partial, Adapted)** **Year Ended May 31, 2016**	
2		**(In millions)**
3	**Cash Flows from Operating Activities:**	
4	Net income	$ 1,820
5	Adjustments to reconcile net income	
6	to net cash provided by operating activities:	
7	Depreciation and amortization	2,631
8	Other items (summarized)	1,257
9	Net cash provided by operating activities	5,708
10	**Cash Flows from Investing Activities:**	
11	Capital expenditures, net	(4,818)
12	Other asset acquisitions and dispositions, net	(4,628)
13	Net cash (used in) investing activities	(9,446)
14	**Cash Flows from Financing Activities:**	
15	Net cash provided by financing activities	3,611
16	Effect of exchange rate changes on cash	(102)
17	**Net (decrease) in cash and cash equivalents**	(229)
18	**Cash and cash equivalents, beginning of period**	3,763
19	**Cash and cash equivalents, end of period**	$ 3,534
20		

Data from the U.S. Securities and Exchange Commission EDGAR Company Filings, www.sec.gov

Let's examine FedEx's investing activities first. During 2016, FedEx invested $4,818 million in capital expenditures (line 11). FedEx also engaged in the net acquisition and disposition of other long-term assets, spending another $4,628 million (line 12). FedEx's statement of cash flows reports Depreciation and amortization (line 7) of $2,631 million. Observe that Depreciation and amortization is listed as a positive item under Adjustments to reconcile net income to net cash provided by operating activities. Since depreciation and amortization do not affect cash, you may be wondering why these amounts appear on the statement of cash flows. In this format, the operating activities section of the statement of cash flows starts with net income (line 4) and reconciles to net cash provided by operating activities (line 9). Depreciation and amortization decrease net income but do not affect cash. Depreciation and amortization are therefore added back to net income to measure cash flow from operations. The add-back of depreciation and amortization to net income offsets the earlier subtraction of these expenses. The sum of net income plus depreciation and amortization, therefore, helps to reconcile net income (on the accrual basis) to net cash flow from operations (a cash-basis amount). We revisit this topic in the full context of the statement of cash flows in Chapter 11.

FedEx's cash flows for fiscal 2016 were strong. Net cash provided by operating activities exceeded net income by $3,888 million ($5,708 million – $1,820 million). With this excess, the company made sizeable capital expenditures, signaling that it invested in new plant and equipment and other long-term assets needed to expand and run its business. In addition, as reflected in the financing activities section, the company issued additional long-term debt as well as made payments to shareholders in the amount of $3,611 million. Although cash and cash equivalents decreased by $229 million from 2015, the company's cash and cash equivalents position at the end of fiscal 2016, in the amount of $3,534 million, was still very strong.

Decision Guidelines

PLANT ASSETS AND RELATED EXPENSES

FedEx Corporation, like all other companies, must make some decisions about how to account for its plant assets and intangibles. Let's review some of these decisions.

Decision	**Guidelines**
Capitalize or expense:	General rule: Capitalize all costs that provide future benefit for the business such as a new package-handling system. Expense all costs that provide no future benefit, such as a repair to an airplane.
• A cost associated with a new asset?	Capitalize all costs that bring the asset to its intended use, including the purchase price, transportation charges, and taxes paid to acquire the asset.
• A cost associated with an existing asset?	Capitalize only those costs that add to the asset's capacity or to its useful life. Expense all other costs as maintenance or repairs.
Which depreciation method to use:	
• For financial reporting?	Use the method that best allocates the cost of an asset through depreciation expense against the revenues produced by the asset. Most companies use the straight-line method.
• For income tax?	Use the method that produces the fastest tax deductions (MACRS). A company can use different depreciation methods for financial reporting and for income tax purposes. In the United States, this practice is both legal and ethical.
How to account for natural resources?	Capitalize the asset's acquisition cost and all later costs that add to the natural resource's future benefit. Record depletion by the units-of-production method by transferring the amount extracted to inventory and eventually to cost of goods sold.
How to account for intangibles?	Capitalize the asset's acquisition cost and all later costs that add to its future benefit. For intangibles with finite lives, record amortization expense. For intangibles with indefinite lives, measure the impairment in value and record a loss for that amount.
How to record impairments in long-term assets?	Every year, conduct a two-step impairment process for most long-term assets: STEP 1: Compare the net book value with expected cash flows from the asset. If net book value > expected cash flows, the asset is impaired. Otherwise, the asset is not impaired. STEP 2: For all impaired assets under step 1, reduce the carrying value of the asset from net book value to fair value. Record a loss for the difference.
How profitable is the company?	Return on assets (ROA) = Net profit margin ratio × Total asset turnover = (Net income/Net sales) × (Net sales/Average total assets)

End-of-Chapter | Summary Problem

The figures that follow appear in the Answers to the Mid-Chapter Summary Problem, Requirement 2, on page 382.

Equipment, Purchase date: January 1, 2018
Cost: $44,000; Expected useful life: 10 years; Expected residual value: $4,000

	Method A: Straight-Line			*Method B: Double-Declining-Balance*		
Year	Annual Depreciation Expense	Accumulated Depreciation	Book Value	Annual Depreciation Expense	Accumulated Depreciation	Book Value
Start			$44,000			$44,000
2018	$4,000	$ 4,000	40,000	$8,800	$ 8,800	35,200
2019	4,000	8,000	36,000	7,040	15,840	28,160
2020	4,000	12,000	32,000	5,632	21,472	22,528

Requirements

1. Suppose the income tax authorities permitted a choice between these two depreciation methods. Which method would FedEx select for income tax purposes? Why?
2. Suppose FedEx purchased the equipment described in the table on January 1, 2018, and depreciated the equipment using the double-declining-balance method. On July 1, 2020, FedEx sold the equipment for $27,000 cash.

   Record depreciation for 2020 and the sale of the equipment on July 1, 2020.

Answers

Requirement 1

For tax purposes, most companies select an accelerated depreciation method because it results in the most depreciation in the earliest years of the asset's life. Accelerated depreciation minimizes a company's income tax payments and maximizes the business's cash in the early years of the asset's life.

Requirement 2

Entries to record depreciation to date of sale, and then the sale of the equipment, follow:

A1

	A	B	C	D
1	2020			
2	Jul 1	Depreciation Expense—Equipment ($5,632 X 1/2 year)	2,816	
3		Accumulated Depreciation—Equipment		2,816
4		*To update depreciation.*		
5				
6	Jul 1	Cash	27,000	
7		Accumulated Depreciation—Equipment		
8		($15,840 + $2,816)	18,656	
9		Equipment		44,000
10		Gain on Sale of Equipment		1,656
11		*To record sale of equipment.*		
12				

REVIEW | Plant Assets, Natural Resources, and Intangibles

Accounting Vocabulary

accelerated depreciation method (p. 378) A depreciation method that writes off a relatively larger amount of the asset's cost nearer the start of its useful life than the straight-line method does.

amortization (p. 371) Allocating the cost of an intangible asset to expense over the period of its useful life.

capital expenditure (p. 372) An expenditure that increases an asset's capacity or extends its useful life. Capital expenditures are debited to an asset account.

copyright (p. 392) The exclusive right to reproduce and sell a book, musical composition, film, other work of art, or computer program. Issued by the federal government, copyrights extend 70 years beyond the author's, composer's, artist's, or programmer's life.

depletion (p. 391) That portion of a natural resource's cost that is used up in a particular period. Depletion expense is computed in the same way as units-of-production depreciation. A depleted asset usually flows into inventory and eventually to the cost of goods sold as the resource is sold.

depreciable cost (p. 375) The cost of a plant asset minus its estimated residual value.

double-declining-balance (DDB) method (p. 378) An accelerated depreciation method that computes annual depreciation by multiplying the asset's decreasing book value at the beginning of the year by a constant percentage that is two times the straight-line rate.

DuPont Analysis (p. 397) A detailed approach to measuring the rate of return on equity (see Chapter 10). In this chapter, we confine our discussion to return on assets, comprising the first two components of return on equity, which are calculated as follows: Net profit margin ratio (Net income/Net sales) × Total asset turnover (Net sales/Average total assets).

estimated residual value (p. 375) The expected cash value of an asset at the end of its useful life. Also called *residual value, scrap value*, or *salvage value*.

estimated useful life (p. 375) The length of service a business expects to get from an asset, which may be expressed in years, units of output, miles, or other measures.

fair value (p. 395) An asset's estimated market value at a particular date.

franchises and licenses (p. 392) Privileges granted by a private business or a government to sell a product or service in accordance with specified conditions.

goodwill (p. 392) The excess of the cost of an acquired company over the sum of the market values of its net assets (assets minus liabilities).

impairment (p. 395) The condition that exists when the carrying amount of a long-lived asset exceeds the amount of the future cash flows from the asset. Whenever long-term assets have been impaired, they have to be written down to fair values using a two-step process. Under GAAP, once impaired, the carrying value of a long-lived asset may never again be increased. Under IFRS, if the fair value of impaired assets recovers in the future, the values may be increased.

intangible asset (p. 392) An asset with no physical form—a special right to current and expected future benefits.

Modified Accelerated Cost Recovery System (MACRS) (p. 384) A special depreciation method used only for income tax purposes. Assets are grouped into classes, and for a given class, depreciation is computed using the double-declining-balance method, the 150% declining-balance method, or, for most real estate, the straight-line method.

natural resources (p. 391) Assets such as oil and gas reserves, coal mines, or stands of timber, accounted for as long-term assets when purchased or extracted; their cost is transferred to expense through a process called depletion.

net profit margin ratio (p. 397) A ratio computed by the formula Net income/Net sales. The ratio measures how much every sales dollar generates in profit.

patent (p. 392) A federal government grant giving the holder the exclusive right for 20 years to produce and sell an invention.

plant assets (p. 369) Long-lived assets, such as land, buildings, and equipment, used in the operation of the business. Also called *fixed assets* or *property and equipment*.

return on assets (ROA) (p. 396) Also known as the *rate of return on assets*, it measures how effectively and how efficiently a company has used its assets to generate net income (profit).

straight-line method (p. 376) A depreciation method in which an equal amount of depreciation expense is assigned to each year of an asset's use.

total asset turnover (p. 397) A measure of efficiency in usage of total assets. The ratio measures how many sales dollars are generated for each dollar of assets invested. Formula: Net sales/Average total assets. Also known as *asset turnover*.

trademark, trade name (p. 392) A distinctive identification of a product or service. Also called a *brand name*.

units-of-production (UOP) method (p. 377) Depreciation method by which a fixed amount of depreciation is assigned to each unit of output produced by the plant asset.

Quick Check (Answers are given on page 435.)

1. Smatter Corporation purchased land for a new building. Which of the following costs would not be included in the cost of the land?
   a. Purchase price of the land
   b. Cost of demolishing an old garage located on the land
   c. Cost of a new parking lot constructed on the land
   d. Brokerage commission paid to the real estate agent who handled the land transaction

2. Carlos Company purchased a building and land for $400,000 in total. Individually, the land appraised for $84,000 and the building appraised for $336,000. How much of the purchase price should be allocated to the cost of the land?
   a. $75,000
   b. $80,000
   c. $84,000
   d. $400,000

3. Whitmore Corporation purchased a new delivery van on the last day of its fiscal year. The cost of the delivery van will appear on Whitmore's ____________ in the year of purchase.
   a. Income statement
   b. Statement of retained earnings
   c. Balance sheet
   d. Statement of stockholders' equity

4. When a company expenses the cost of maintenance for its heating and cooling system, that cost will appear on its
   a. Income statement.
   b. Statement of retained earnings.
   c. Balance sheet.
   d. Statement of stockholders' equity.

5. Capitalizing a cost involves increasing what type of account?
   a. Liability
   b. Expense
   c. Stockholders' equity
   d. Asset

6. Planter Company purchased a delivery van for $30,000 on January 1. The van has an estimated 5-year life with a residual value of $5,000. What would the depreciation expense for this van be in the first year if Planter uses the straight-line method?
   a. $5,000
   b. $6,000
   c. $25,000
   d. $30,000

7. Bixby Corporation purchased a forklift for $40,000 on July 1. The forklift has an estimated useful life of 20,000 usage hours with a residual value of $8,000. Bixby uses the units-of-production method for depreciation. If Bixby uses the forklift for 6,400 hours during the first year, the depreciation expense on the forklift would be
   a. $8,000.
   b. $10,240.
   c. $12,800.
   d. $40,000.

8. On the first day of its fiscal year, Spearhead Company purchased a new computer system for a total cost of $50,000. The computer system is expected to have a life of 5 years with a residual value of $5,000. If the company uses the double-declining-balance method, its depreciation expense for this computer system in the first year will be
   a. $9,000.
   b. $10,000.
   c. $18,000.
   d. $20,000.

9. The depreciation method that does not initially use the residual value in depreciation calculations is the
   a. straight-line method.
   b. units-of-production method.
   c. double-declining balance method.
   d. direct method.

10. Sokolsky Excavating purchased a used dump truck for $90,000 on January 1, 2018. The company has depreciated the dump truck using the straight-line method over its estimated 10-year life with a $6,000 residual value. Sokolsky sold the dump truck on January 1, 2021, for $68,700. Total accumulated depreciation on the dump truck on the date of sale was $25,200. What gain or loss should be recorded on the sale?

a. A gain of $3,900
b. A loss of $3,900
c. A loss of $21,300
d. A gain of $21,300

11. Barron Fuel purchased an oil well for $200,000. The well is estimated to contain 50,000 barrels, have an eight-year life, and have no residual value. If the company extracts and sells 2,000 barrels of oil in the first year, how much in cost of sales should be recorded?

a. $8,000
b. $20,000
c. $25,000
d. $100,000

12. Which of the following is an intangible asset?

a. Land
b. Leasehold improvements
c. Equipment
d. Copyright

13. Which of the following situations indicates that an asset is impaired?

a. The net book value of the asset is less than the asset's estimated future cash flows.
b. The net book value of the asset is more than the asset's estimated future cash flows.
c. The fair market value of the asset is less than the asset's net book value.
d. The fair market value of the asset is more than the asset's net book value.

14. Which of the following is a measure of profitability?

a. Quick (acid-test) ratio
b. Net sales
c. Inventory turnover
d. Return on assets (ROA)

15. Total asset turnover has increased at the O'Neil Company since last year. This increase must mean that

a. the company has become more efficient.
b. the company has become more effective and more efficient.
c. the company has become more effective.
d. the company has become neither more effective nor more efficient.

16. The purchase of new equipment with cash would appear on the statement of cash flows as a/an

a. operating cash flow.
b. investing cash flow.
c. financing cash flow.
d. depreciating cash flow.

Excel Project
Autograded Excel Project available in **MyLab Accounting**.

ASSESS YOUR PROGRESS

Ethics Check

EC7-1. Identify ethical principle violated

For each of the situations listed, identify which of three principles (integrity, objectivity and independence, or due care) from the AICPA Code of Professional Conduct is violated. Assume all persons listed in the situations are members of the AICPA. (Note: Refer to the AICPA Code of Professional Conduct contained on pages 25–27 in Chapter 1 for descriptions of the principles.)

a. Dominick is an audit manager at a local auditing firm. The firm wants to outsource its payroll function. Dominick strongly urges his firm to select the ABC Payroll Company, but does not disclose that his son is a co-owner of the company.

b. Currently, NorthernWay Airlines uses the straight-line method of depreciation to depreciate its airplanes. Julie's boss would like to see if switching to the units-of-production method would be a tax savings strategy for the company. Julie does not remember how to calculate depreciation using the units-of-production method, so she makes up numbers to show her boss based on what she thinks might be right.

c. In order to increase the tax benefits to her company, Tamika categorizes the survey fees and grading and clearing expenditures associated with getting a plot of land ready for building as land improvements instead of including those expenditures in the cost of the land.

d. Samuel is aware that his company will receive tax benefits for recording depreciation expense. He depreciates a new asset using the double-declining-balance method in the first year. In the second year, he switches to the units-of-production method, but does not account for the depreciation he already expensed last year. As a result, the company will recognize a higher amount of depreciation expense on its tax return in the second year than if Samuel had done the depreciation calculation correctly.

Short Exercises

S7-1. ***(Learning Objective 1: Measure the cost and book value of a company's plant assets)*** Examine the excerpt of a footnote from Albrecht Corporation's September 30, 2018, annual report to follow. LO 1

A1

	A	B	C
1	**Balances of Major Classes of Property and Equipment Are as Follows (in thousands)**		
2		**Sep. 30, 2018**	**Sep. 30, 2017**
3	Land	$ 76,592	$ 48,923
4	Buildings and leasehold improvements	2,219,765	1,958,612
5	Capitalized real estate leases	24,872	24,263
6	Fixtures and equipment	1,580,325	1,408,779
7	Construction in progress and equipment not yet in service	55,236	114,599
8		3,956,790	3,555,176
9	Less accumulated depreciation and amortization	(1,877,967)	(1,700,010)
10		$ 2,078,823	$ 1,855,166
11			

1. What are Albrecht's largest two categories of property and equipment as of September 30, 2018? Describe in general terms the types of expenditures included in these categories.
2. What was Albrecht's gross cost of property and equipment at September 30, 2018? What was the book value of property and equipment on this date? Why is book value less than cost?

S7-2. ***(Learning Objective 1: Measure and record the cost of individual assets in a lump-sum purchase of assets)*** Lexington Garden Supply pays $280,000 for a group purchase of land, building, and equipment. At the time of acquisition, the land has a current market value of $124,000, the building's current market value is $31,000, and the equipment's current market value is $155,000. Prepare a schedule allocating the purchase price of $280,000 to each of the individual assets purchased based on their relative market values, then journalize the lump-sum purchase of the three assets. The business signs a note payable for the purchase price. LO 1

LO 2

S7-3. ***(Learning Objective 2: Distinguish a capital expenditure from an immediate expense)*** Identify each of the following items as a capital expenditure, an immediate expense, or neither.

1. Constructed a new parking lot on leased property for $300,000.
2. Paid property taxes of $75,000 for the first year a new administrative services building was occupied.
3. Paid dividends of $40,000.
4. Paid interest on a six-month note payable that financed the construction of a new plant building, $550,000.
5. Purchased equipment for a new manufacturing plant, $6,000,000.
6. Paid $90,000 for the installation of the equipment in (5.)
7. Repaired plumbing in existing manufacturing plant, paying $27,000.
8. Paid $148,000 to tear down an old building on a new manufacturing plant site.
9. Purchased new network servers for $29,000.
10. Paid maintenance costs of $31,000 on the equipment in (5) during its first year of use.

LO 2

S7-4. ***(Learning Objective 2: Distinguish a capital expenditure from an immediate expense)*** **LimeBike**, located in San Mateo, California, is a startup founded in 2017. Its mission is to make shared bicycles accessible and affordable. The company has taken the basic idea of shared bicycles and eliminated the need to return the bike to a docking station, which may not be near the cyclist's destination. LimeBike charges $1 per 30 minutes of riding, or $0.50 per ride for students.

To use LimeBike, you first use the LimeBike app to locate one of the citrus-colored bikes near your location. Once you are at the bike, you scan the QR code on the bike or enter the bike's plate number into the app to unlock the bike. When you are finished using the bike, you park the bike by a bike rack or post—anywhere that is legal and visible. Once you press down the back-wheel lock, the trip is finalized and your payment is processed by LimeBike's app.

LimeBike does not depend on government funding, making it appealing to cities with tight budgets. In mid-2017 the company raised $12 million from investors to expand its operations. It is set to begin operating in as-of-yet undisclosed cities sometime in 2017 or 2018.

Assume that LimeBike has officially begun operating its bike sharing program.

1. For each of the following items, identify whether the cost of the item would be expensed or capitalized at LimeBike:
   - **a.** Customized bikes from **Trek** and **Specialized**
   - **b.** Development costs of LimeBike's app for locating, paying, and returning bikes
   - **c.** Salary of the salesperson who works to get cities to adopt LimeBike's program
   - **d.** Replacement tires for bikes
   - **e.** Routine bike maintenance including chain lubrication, brake pad replacement, and drivetrain cleaning
   - **f.** Electricity and other utilities in the company's administrative offices
2. Why does it matter whether a cost item is expensed or capitalized? Explain.

LO 3

S7-5. ***(Learning Objective 3: Compute depreciation and book value by three methods—first year only)*** On January 1, 2017, Northeast Transportation Company purchased a used aircraft at a cost of $58,900,000. Northeast expects the plane to remain useful for five years (7,200,000 miles) and to have a residual value of $4,900,000. Northeast expects to fly the plane 750,000 miles the first year, 1,375,000 miles each year during the second, third, and fourth years, and 2,325,000 miles the last year.

1. Compute Northeast's depreciation for the first two years on the plane using the following methods:
   - **a.** Straight-line method
   - **b.** Units-of-production method (round depreciation per mile to the closest cent)
   - **c.** Double-declining-balance method
2. Show the airplane's book value at the end of the first year under each depreciation method.

S7-6. ***(Learning Objective 3: Select the best depreciation method for income tax purposes)*** This exercise uses the Northeast data from S7-5. Assume Northeast is trying to decide which depreciation method to use for income tax purposes. The company can choose from among the following methods: (a) straight-line, (b) units-of-production, or (c) double-declining-balance methods. LO 3

1. Which depreciation method offers the highest tax advantage for the first year? Describe the nature of the tax advantage.
2. How much income tax will Northeast save for the first year of the airplane's use under the method you just selected as compared with using the straight-line depreciation method? The company's income tax rate is 34%. Ignore any earnings from investing the extra cash.

The following data should be used for S7-7 through S7-9.
Grafton Company purchased a new car for use in its business on January 1, 2017. It paid $29,000 for the car. Grafton expects the car to have a useful life of four years with an estimated residual value of zero. Grafton expects to drive the car 40,000 miles during 2017, 75,000 miles during 2018, 90,000 miles in 2019, and 85,000 miles in 2020, for total expected miles of 290,000.

S7-7. ***(Learning Objective 3: Compute depreciation using straight-line method with a residual value of zero)*** Using the straight-line method of depreciation, calculate the following amounts for the car for each of the four years of its expected life: LO 3

a. Depreciation expense
b. Accumulated depreciation balance
c. Book value

S7-8. ***(Learning Objective 3: Compute depreciation using units-of-production method with a residual value of zero)*** Using the units-of-production method of depreciation (with miles as the production unit), calculate the following amounts for the car for each of the four years of its expected life: LO 3

a. Depreciation expense
b. Accumulated depreciation balance
c. Book value

S7-9. ***(Learning Objective 3: Compute depreciation using double-declining-balance method with a residual value of zero)*** Using the double-declining-balance method of depreciation, calculate the following amounts for the car for each of the four years of its expected life: LO 3

a. Depreciation expense
b. Accumulated depreciation balance
c. Book value

The following data should be used for S7-10 through S7-12.
FlavorRite purchased a used van for use in its business on January 1, 2017. It paid $17,000 for the van. FlavorRite expects the van to have a useful life of four years, with an estimated residual value of $1,400. FlavorRite expects to drive the van 16,000 miles during 2017, 19,000 miles during 2018, 17,000 miles in 2019, and 48,000 miles in 2020, for total expected miles of 100,000.

S7-10. ***(Learning Objective 3: Compute depreciation using straight-line method with residual value)*** Using the straight-line method of depreciation, calculate the following amounts for the van for each of the four years of its expected life: LO 3

a. Depreciation expense
b. Accumulated depreciation balance
c. Book value

LO 3 **S7-11.** ***(Learning Objective 3: Compute depreciation using units-of-production method with residual value)*** Using the units-of-production method of depreciation (with miles as the production unit), calculate the following amounts for the van for each of the four years of its expected life (do not round here; use three decimal places for the depreciation cost per mile):

a. Depreciation expense
b. Accumulated depreciation balance
c. Book value

LO 3 **S7-12.** ***(Learning Objective 3: Compute depreciation using double-declining-balance method with residual value)*** Using the double-declining-balance method of depreciation, calculate the following amounts for the van for each of the four years of its expected life:

a. Depreciation expense
b. Accumulated depreciation balance
c. Book value

LO 3 **S7-13.** ***(Learning Objective 3: Compute partial year depreciation, and select the best depreciation method)*** Assume that on September 30, 2017, EuroAir, an international airline based in Germany, purchased a Jumbo aircraft at a cost of €45,000,000 (€ is the symbol for the euro). EuroAir expects the plane to remain useful for four years (4,000,000 miles) and to have a residual value of €6,000,000. EuroAir will fly the plane 350,000 miles during the remainder of 2017. Compute EuroAir's depreciation on the plane for the year ended December 31, 2017, using the following methods:

a. Straight-line
b. Units-of-production
c. Double-declining-balance

Which method would produce the highest net income for 2017? Which method produces the lowest net income?

LO 3 **S7-14.** ***(Learning Objective 3: Compute and record depreciation after a change in useful life of the asset)*** Fun Town Amusement Park paid $500,000 for a concession stand. Fun Town started out depreciating the building using the straight-line method over 25 years with a residual value of zero. After using the concession stand for four years, Fun Town determines that the building will remain useful for only five more years. Record Fun Town's depreciation on the concession stand for year five using the straight-line method.

LO 3, 4 **S7-15.** ***(Learning Objectives 3, 4: Compute depreciation; record a gain or loss on disposal)*** On January 1, 2017, Worldwide Manufacturing purchased a machine for $810,000 that it expected to have a useful life of four years. The company estimated that the residual value of the machine was $50,000. Worldwide Manufacturing used the machine for two years and sold it on January 1, 2019, for $350,000. As of December 31, 2018, the accumulated depreciation on the machine was $380,000.

1. Calculate the gain or loss on the sale of the machinery.
2. Record the sale of the machine on January 1, 2019.

LO 5 **S7-16.** ***(Learning Objective 5: Account for the depletion of a company's natural resources)*** Jackson Petroleum, a giant oil company, holds reserves of oil and gas assets. At the end of 2018, assume the cost of Jackson's oil reserves totaled $180 billion, representing 10 billion barrels of oil in the ground.

1. Which depreciation method is similar to the depletion method that Jackson and other oil companies use to compute their annual depletion expense for the oil removed from the ground?
2. Suppose the company removed 1,000 million barrels of oil during 2019. Record this event. Show amounts in billions.
3. Assume that, of the amount removed in (2), the company sold 800 million barrels. Make the cost of sales entry.

LO 5

S7-17. ***(Learning Objective 5: Measure and record goodwill)*** Munchies, Inc., dominates the snack-food industry with its Salty Chip brand. Assume that Munchies purchased Sweet Snacks Company for $5.4 million cash. The market value of Sweet Snacks' assets is $10 million, and Sweet Snacks has liabilities with a market value of $7.1 million.

Requirements

1. Compute the cost of the goodwill purchased by Munchies.
2. Explain how Munchies will account for goodwill in future years.

LO 6

S7-18. ***(Learning Objective 6: Explain the effect of asset impairment on financial statements)*** For each of the following scenarios, indicate whether a long-term asset has been impaired (Y for yes and N for no) and, if so, the amount of the loss that should be recorded.

Asset	Book Value	Estimated Future Cash Flows	Fair Value	Impaired? (Y or N)	Amount of Loss
a. Equipment	$190,000	$157,000	$135,000		
b. Trademark	$420,000	$540,000	$485,000		
c. Land	$60,000	$38,000	$32,000		
d. Factory building	$10 million	$10 million	$8 million		

LO 7

S7-19. ***(Learning Objective 7: Calculate return on assets)*** In 2018, Ambrosia Corporation reported $100 million in sales, $18 million in net income, and average total assets of $200 million. What is Ambrosia's return on assets in 2018?

LO 7

S7-20. ***(Learning Objective 7: Calculate return on assets)*** Oscar Optical Corporation provides a full line of designer eyewear to consumers. Oscar reported the following information for 2018 and 2017:

	2018	2017
Sales revenue	$500,000	$410,000
Net income	$ 43,700	$ 34,650
Average total assets	$230,000	$210,000

Compute return on assets (ROA) for 2018 and 2017. Using the DuPont model, identify the components and state whether each improved or worsened from 2017 to 2018.

LO 8

S7-21. ***(Learning Objective 8: Analyze the cash flow impact of investing activities on the statement of cash flows)*** During 2018, Silverspring Systems, Inc., purchased two other companies for $10 million in cash. Also during 2018, Silverspring made capital expenditures of $8.6 million in cash to expand its market share. During the year, Silverspring sold its North American operations, receiving cash of $8.4 million. Overall, Silverspring reported a net income of $6.9 million during 2018.

Show what Silverspring would report for cash flows from investing activities on its statement of cash flows for 2018. Report a total amount for net cash provided by (used in) investing activities.

Exercises MyLab Accounting

Group A

LO 1 E7-22A. ***(Learning Objective 1: Measure the cost of plant assets)*** Murphy Self Storage purchased land, paying $160,000 cash as a down payment and signing a $185,000 note payable for the balance. Murphy also had to pay delinquent property tax of $2,000, title insurance costing $6,000, and $11,000 to level the land and remove an unwanted building. The company paid $58,000 to add soil for the foundation and then constructed an office building at a cost of $700,000. It also paid $52,000 for a fence around the property, $11,000 for the company sign near the property entrance, and $3,000 for lighting of the grounds. What is the capitalized cost of each of Murphy's land, land improvements, and building?

LO 1, 4 E7-23A. ***(Learning Objectives 1, 4: Allocate costs to assets acquired in a lump-sum purchase; dispose of a plant asset)*** Sugar Ridge Manufacturing bought three used machines in a $167,000 lump-sum purchase. An independent appraiser valued the machines as shown:

Machine No.	Appraised Value
1	$ 38,250
2	73,100
3	58,650

What is each machine's individual cost? Immediately after making this purchase, Sugar Ridge sold Machine No. 3 for its appraised value. What is the result of the sale? (Round decimals to three places when calculating proportions, and use your computed percentages in all calculations.)

LO 2 E7-24A. ***(Learning Objective 2: Distinguish capital expenditures from expenses)*** Assume Karo Products, Inc., purchased conveyor-belt machinery. Classify each of the following expenditures as a capital expenditure or an immediate expense related to machinery:

a. Periodic lubrication after the machinery is placed in service
b. Special reinforcement to the machinery platform
c. Major overhaul to extend the machinery's useful life by five years
d. Training of personnel for initial operation of the machinery
e. Purchase price
f. Income tax paid on income earned from the sale of products manufactured by the machinery
g. Ordinary repairs to keep the machinery in good working order
h. Transportation and insurance while machinery is in transit from seller to buyer
i. Sales tax paid on the purchase price
j. Lubrication of the machinery before it is placed in service
k. Installation of the conveyor-belt machinery

LO 1, 3 E7-25A. ***(Learning Objectives 1, 3: Measure, depreciate, and report plant assets)*** During 2018, Chang's Book Store paid $481,000 for land and built a store in Newark, New Jersey. Prior to construction, the city of Newark charged Chang's $1,200 for a building permit, which Chang's paid. Chang's also paid $15,200 for architect's fees. The construction cost of $679,900 was financed by a long-term note payable, with interest costs of $28,180 paid at the completion of the project. The building was completed June 30, 2018. Chang's depreciates the building using the straight-line method over 35 years, with estimated residual value of $335,000.

1. Journalize transactions for the following (explanations are not required):
   a. Purchase of the land
   b. All the costs chargeable to the building in a single entry
   c. Depreciation on the building for 2018
2. Report Chang's plant assets on the company's balance sheet at December 31, 2018.
3. What will Chang's income statement for the year ended December 31, 2018, report for these facts?

E7-26A. ***(Learning Objective 3: Determine depreciation amounts by three methods)*** Presley Pizza bought a used Ford delivery van on January 2, 2018, for $22,000. The van was expected to remain in service for four years (80,000 miles). At the end of its useful life, Presley management estimated that the van's residual value would be $2,000. The van traveled 32,000 miles the first year, 28,000 miles the second year, 15,000 miles the third year, and 5,000 miles in the fourth year. LO 3

Requirements

1. Prepare a schedule of depreciation expense per year for the van under the three depreciation methods discussed in this chapter. (For units-of-production and double-declining-balance methods, round to the nearest two decimal places after each step of the calculation.)
2. Which method best tracks the wear and tear on the van?
3. Which method would Presley prefer to use for income tax purposes? Explain your reasoning in detail.

E7-27A. ***(Learning Objectives 1, 3, 8: Report plant assets, depreciation, and investing cash flows)*** On January 1, 2018, Little City Bar & Grill purchased a building, paying $58,000 cash and signing a $110,000 note payable. The company paid another $62,000 to remodel the building. Furniture and fixtures cost $55,000, and dishes and supplies—a current asset—were obtained for $9,400. All expenditures were for cash. Assume that all of these expenditures occurred on January 1, 2018. LO 1, 3, 8

Little City is depreciating the building over 25 years using the straight-line method, with an estimated residual value of $51,000. The furniture and fixtures will be replaced at the end of five years and are being depreciated using the double-declining-balance method, with a residual value of zero. At the end of the first year, the company still had dishes and supplies worth $1,300.

Show what the company reported for supplies, plant assets, and cash flows at the end of the first year on its

- income statement,
- balance sheet, and
- statement of cash flows (investing only).

Note: The purchase of dishes and supplies is an operating cash flow because supplies are a current asset.

E7-28A. ***(Learning Objective 3: Change a plant asset's useful life)*** Fresno Consultants purchased a building for $440,000 and depreciated it on a straight-line basis over 40 years. The estimated residual value was $82,000. After using the building for 20 years, Fresno realized that the building would remain useful only 14 more years. Starting with the 21st year, Fresno began depreciating the building over a revised total life of 34 years and decreased the residual value to $14,600. Record depreciation expense on the building for years 20 and 21. LO 3

E7-29A. ***(Learning Objectives 3, 4: Compute depreciation; record a gain or loss on disposal)*** On January 1, 2017, Stockton Manufacturing purchased a machine for $910,000. The company expected the machine to remain useful for eight years and to have a residual value of $80,000. Stockton Manufacturing uses the straight-line method to depreciate its machinery. Stockton Manufacturing used the machine for four years and sold it on January 1, 2021, for $350,000. LO 3, 4

1. Compute accumulated depreciation on the machine at January 1, 2021 (same as December 31, 2020).
2. Record the sale of the machine on January 1, 2021.

E7-30A. ***(Learning Objectives 3, 4: Measure DDB depreciation; analyze the effect of a sale of a plant asset)*** On January 2, 2018, Ellet Furniture purchased display shelving for $8,900 cash, expecting the shelving to remain in service for five years. Ellet depreciated the shelving on a double-declining-balance basis, with $1,100 estimated residual value. On August 31, 2019, the company sold the shelving for $2,800 cash. Record both the depreciation expense on the shelving for 2019 and its sale in August. Also show how to compute the gain or loss on the disposal of the shelving. LO 3, 4

LO **1, 3, 4** E7-31A. ***(Learning Objectives 1, 3, 4: Measure a plant asset's cost; calculate UOP depreciation; analyze the effect of a used asset trade-in)*** Concord Truck Company is a large trucking company. The company uses the units-of-production (UOP) method to depreciate its trucks.

To follow are facts about one Mack truck in the company's fleet. When this truck was acquired in 2018, the tractor-trailer rig had cost $420,000 and was expected to remain in service for 10 years or 1,000,000 miles. Its estimated residual value was $100,000. During 2018, the truck was driven 77,000 miles; during 2019, 175,000 miles; and during 2020, 190,000 miles. After the truck was driven 45,000 miles in 2021, the company traded in the Mack truck for a Freightliner truck with a fair market value of $270,000. In addition to the trade-in of the Mack truck, Concord Truck Company paid cash of $31,000 for the Freightliner truck. Determine Concord's gain or loss on the transaction. Prepare the journal entry to record the trade-in of the old truck for the new one. Use two decimal places for depreciation cost per mile.

LO **5** E7-32A. ***(Learning Objective 5: Record natural resource assets and depletion)*** Mineral Mines paid $425,000 for the right to extract ore from a 250,000-ton mineral deposit. In addition to the purchase price, Mineral Mines paid a $110 filing fee to the country recorder, a $2,000 license fee to the state of Colorado, and $55,390 for a geologic survey. Because the company purchased the rights to the minerals only, it expects this mineral rights asset to have a residual value of zero when it is fully depleted. During the first year of production, Mineral Mines removed 35,000 tons of ore, of which it sold 29,000 tons. Make journal entries to record (a) purchase of the mineral rights, (b) payment of fees and other costs, (c) depletion for first-year production, and (d) cost of the ore sold. Round depletion per unit to the closest cent.

LO **5, 6** E7-33A. ***(Learning Objectives 5, 6: Record intangibles, amortization, and impairment)*** Sweitzer Printers incurred external costs of $400,000 for a patent for a new laser printer. Although the patent gives legal protection for 20 years, it was expected to provide Sweitzer with a competitive advantage for only ten years due to expected technological advances in the industry. Sweitzer uses the straight-line method of amortization.

After using the patent for five years, Sweitzer learned at an industry trade show that Kaytown Printers has patented a more efficient printer and will be selling this printer next quarter. Because of this new information, Sweitzer determined that the expected future cash flows from its patent were now only $130,000. The fair value of Sweitzer's patent on the open market was now zero.

Requirements

1. Write the journal entries to record (a) the purchase of the patent and (b) amortization for year 1.
2. Once Sweitzer learned of the competing printer and adjusted the expected future cash flows from its original patent, was this asset impaired? If so, make the impairment adjusting entry.

LO **5, 6** E7-34A. ***(Learning Objectives 5, 6: Compute and account for goodwill and impairment)*** Assume Kaledan Company paid $15 million to acquire Roeder Industries. Assume further that Roeder had the following summarized data at the time of the Kaledan acquisition (amounts in millions):

Roeder Industries			
Assets		**Liabilities and Equity**	
Current assets	$18	Total liabilities	$23
Long-term assets	20	Stockholders' equity	15
	$38		$38

Roeder's current assets had a current market value of $18 million, long-term assets had a current market value of only $14 million, and liabilities had a market value of $23 million.

Requirements

1. Compute the cost of goodwill purchased by Kaledan Company.
2. Journalize Kaledan's purchase of Roeder Industries.
3. Explain how Kaledan will account for goodwill.

LO 7

E7-35A. ***(Learning Objective 7: Calculate return on assets)*** Handley Grocery Corporation reported the following information in its comparative financial statements for the fiscal year ended January 31, 2018:

	January 31, 2018	January 31, 2017
Net sales	$50,000	$48,350
Net earnings	$ 2,200	$ 2,100
Average total assets	$40,000	$39,300

Requirements

1. Compute the net profit margin ratio for the years ended January 31, 2018, and 2017. Did it improve or worsen in 2018?
2. Compute asset turnover for the years ended January 31, 2018, and 2017. Did it improve or worsen in 2018?
3. Compute return on assets for the years ended January 31, 2018, and 2017. Did it improve or worsen in 2018? Which component—net profit margin ratio or asset turnover—was mostly responsible for the change in the company's return on assets?

LO 8

E7-36A. ***(Learning Objective 8: Report cash flows for plant assets)*** Assume Alfonso Corporation completed the following transactions:

- **a.** Sold a store building for $670,000. The building had cost Alfonso $1,600,000, and at the time of the sale, its accumulated depreciation totaled $930,000.
- **b.** Lost a store building in a fire. The building cost $300,000 and had accumulated depreciation of $220,000. The insurance proceeds received by Alfonso totaled $200,000.
- **c.** Renovated a store at a cost of $140,000 (cash).
- **d.** Purchased store fixtures for $110,000 (cash). The fixtures are expected to remain in service for ten years and then be sold for $110,000. Alfonso uses the straight-line depreciation method.

For each transaction, show what Alfonso would report for investing activities on its statement of cash flows. Show negative amounts in parentheses.

Group B

LO 1

E7-37B. ***(Learning Objective 1: Measure the cost of plant assets)*** Belvidere Self Storage purchased land, paying $170,000 cash as a down payment and signing a $180,000 note payable for the balance. Belvidere also had to pay delinquent property tax of $2,000, title insurance costing $2,500, and $3,000 to level the land and remove an unwanted building. The company paid $57,000 to add soil for the foundation and then constructed an office building at a cost of $600,000. It also paid $55,000 for a fence around the property, $14,000 for the company sign near the property entrance, and $5,000 for lighting of the grounds. What is the capitalized cost of each of Belvidere's land, land improvements, and building?

LO 1, 4

E7-38B. ***(Learning Objectives 1, 4: Allocate costs to assets acquired in a lump-sum purchase; dispose of a plant asset)*** Portland Manufacturing bought three used machines in a $209,000 lump-sum purchase. An independent appraiser valued the machines as shown:

Machine No.	Appraised Value
1	$73,100
2	$120,400
3	$21,500

What is each machine's individual cost? Immediately after making this purchase, Portland sold Machine No. 3 for its appraised value. What is the result of the sale? (Round decimals to three places when calculating proportions, and use your computed percentages in all calculations.)

LO 2 **E7-39B.** ***(Learning Objective 2: Distinguish capital expenditures from expenses)*** Assume Byron Athletic Products, Inc., purchased conveyor-belt machinery. Classify each of the following expenditures as a capital expenditure or an immediate expense related to machinery:

a. Purchase price
b. Installation of conveyor-belt machinery
c. Special reinforcement to the machinery platform
d. Ordinary repairs to keep the machinery in good working order
e. Lubrication of the machinery before it is placed in service
f. Sales tax paid on the purchase price
g. Major overhaul to extend the machinery's useful life by four years
h. Training of personnel for initial operation of the machinery
i. Income tax paid on income earned from the sale of products manufactured by the machinery
j. Periodic lubrication after the machinery is placed in service
k. Transportation and insurance while machinery is in transit from seller to buyer

LO 1, 3 **E7-40B.** ***(Learning Objectives 1, 3: Measure, depreciate, and report plant assets)*** During 2018, Ming's Book Store paid $486,000 for land and built a store in Naperville, Illinois. Prior to construction, the city of Naperville charged Ming's $1,000 for a building permit, which Ming's paid. Ming's also paid $15,000 for architect's fees. The construction cost of $670,000 was financed by a long-term note payable, with interest costs of $28,020 paid at the completion of the project. The building was completed June 30, 2018. Ming's depreciates the building using the straight-line method over 35 years, with estimated residual value of $330,000.

1. Journalize transactions for the following (explanations are not required):
a. Purchase of the land
b. All the costs chargeable to the building in a single entry
c. Depreciation on the building for 2018
2. Report Ming's plant assets on the company's balance sheet at December 31, 2018.
3. What will Ming's income statement for the year ended December 31, 2018, report for this situation?

LO 3 **E7-41B.** ***(Learning Objective 3: Determine depreciation amounts by three methods)*** Lima Pizza bought a used Toyota delivery van on January 2, 2018, for $18,600. The van was expected to remain in service for four years (57,000 miles). At the end of its useful life, Lima management estimated that the van's residual value would be $1,500. The van traveled 20,500 miles the first year, 16,000 miles the second year, 15,400 miles the third year, and 5,100 miles in the fourth year.

Requirements

1. Prepare a schedule of depreciation expense per year for the van under the three depreciation methods discussed in this chapter. (For units-of-production and double-declining-balance methods, round to the nearest two decimal places after each step of the calculation.)
2. Which method best tracks the wear and tear on the van?
3. Which method would Lima prefer to use for income tax purposes? Explain your reasoning in detail.

E7-42B. ***(Learning Objectives 1, 3, 8: Report plant assets, depreciation, and investing cash flows)*** On January 1, 2018, Black Iron Bar & Grill purchased a building, paying $56,000 cash and signing a $101,000 note payable. The company paid another $60,000 to remodel the building. Furniture and fixtures cost $51,000, and dishes and supplies—a current asset—were obtained for $9,600. All expenditures were for cash. Assume that all of these expenditures occurred on January 1, 2018. LO 1, 3, 8

Black Iron is depreciating the building over 25 years using the straight-line method, with an estimated residual value of $52,000. The furniture and fixtures will be replaced at the end of five years and are being depreciated using the double-declining-balance method, with a residual value of zero. At the end of the first year, the company still had dishes and supplies worth $1,600.

Show what the company reported for supplies, plant assets, and cash flows at the end of the first year on its

- income statement,
- balance sheet, and
- statement of cash flows (investing only).

Note: The purchase of dishes and supplies is an operating cash flow because supplies are a current asset.

E7-43B. ***(Learning Objective 3: Change a plant asset's useful life)*** Chester Consultants purchased a building for $430,000 and depreciated it on a straight-line basis over 40 years. The estimated residual value was $70,000. After using the building for 20 years, Chester realized that the building would remain useful only 14 more years. Starting with the 21st year, Chester began depreciating the building over the newly revised total life of 34 years and decreased the estimated residual value to $12,980. Record depreciation expense on the building for years 20 and 21. LO 3

E7-44B. ***(Learning Objectives 3, 4: Compute depreciation; record a gain or loss on disposal)*** On January 1, 2017, Lincoln Manufacturing purchased a machine for $930,000. The company expected the machine to remain useful for eight years and to have a residual value of $110,000. Lincoln Manufacturing uses the straight-line method to depreciate its machinery. Lincoln Manufacturing used the machine for four years and sold it on January 1, 2021, for $250,000. LO 3, 4

1. Compute accumulated depreciation on the machine at January 1, 2021 (same as December 31, 2020).
2. Record the sale of the machine on January 1, 2021.

E7-45B. ***(Learning Objectives 3, 4: Measure DDB depreciation; analyze the effect of a sale of a plant asset)*** On January 2, 2018, Drake Furnishings purchased display shelving for $8,100 cash, expecting the shelving to remain in service for five years. Drake depreciated the shelving on a double-declining-balance basis, with $1,300 estimated residual value. On September 30, 2019, the company sold the shelving for $2,400 cash. Record both the depreciation expense on the shelving for 2019 and its sale in September. Also show how to compute the gain or loss on the disposal of the shelving. LO 3, 4

E7-46B. ***(Learning Objectives 1, 3, 4: Measure a plant asset's cost; calculate UOP depreciation; analyze the effect of a used asset trade-in)*** Canyon Truck Company is a large trucking company. The company uses the units-of-production (UOP) method to depreciate its trucks. LO 1, 3, 4

To follow are facts about one Mack truck in the company's fleet. When this truck was acquired in 2018, the tractor-trailer had cost $450,000 and was expected to remain in service for 10 years or 1,000,000 miles. Its estimated residual value was $20,000. During 2018, the truck was driven 80,000 miles; during 2019, 175,000 miles; and during 2020, 185,000 miles. After the truck was driven 40,000 miles in 2021, the company traded in the Mack truck for a Freightliner truck with a fair market value of $250,000. In addition to the trade-in of the Mack truck, Canyon paid cash of $30,000 for the Freightliner truck. Determine Canyon's gain or loss on the transaction. Prepare the journal entry to record the trade-in of the old truck for the new one. Use two decimal places for depreciation cost per mile.

LO 5

E7-47B. ***(Learning Objective 5: Record natural resource assets and depletion)*** Bearcreek Mines paid $433,000 for the right to extract ore from a 450,000-ton mineral deposit. In addition to the purchase price, Bearcreek Mines paid a $155 filing fee to the county recorder, a $2,800 license fee to the state of Utah, and $95,045 for a geologic survey. Because the company purchased the rights to the minerals only, it expects this mineral rights asset to have a residual value of zero when it is fully depleted. During the first year of production, Bearcreek Mines removed 75,000 tons of ore, of which it sold 72,000 tons. Make journal entries to record (a) purchase of the mineral rights, (b) payment of fees and other costs, (c) depletion for first-year production, and (d) cost of the ore sold. Round depletion per unit to the closest cent.

LO 5, 6

E7-48B. ***(Learning Objectives 5, 6: Record intangibles, amortization, and impairment)***

1. Milton Printers incurred external costs of $700,000 for a patent for a new laser printer. Although the patent gives legal protection for 20 years, it was expected to provide Milton with a competitive advantage for only eight years due to expected technological advances in the industry. Milton uses the straight-line method of amortization.
2. After using the patent for four years, Milton learned at an industry trade show that Anderson Printers has patented a more efficient printer and will begin selling the new printer next quarter. Because of this new information, Milton determined that the expected future cash flows from its patent were now only $270,000. The fair value of Milton's patent on the open market was now zero.

Requirements

1. Write the journal entries to record (a) the purchase of the patent and (b) amortization for year 1.
2. Once Milton learned of the competing printer and adjusted the expected future cash flows from its original patent, was this asset impaired? If so, make the impairment adjusting entry.

LO 5, 6

E7-49B. ***(Learning Objectives 5, 6: Compute and account for goodwill and impairment)*** Assume Voltron Company paid $22 million to acquire Brighton Industries. Assume further that Brighton had the following summarized data at the time of the Voltron acquisition (amounts in millions):

Brighton Industries

Assets		Liabilities and Equity	
Current assets	$11	Total liabilities	$23
Long-term assets	26	Stockholders' equity	14
	$37		$37

Brighton's current assets had a current market value of $11 million, long-term assets had a current market value of only $19 million, and liabilities had a market value of $23 million.

Requirements

1. Compute the cost of goodwill purchased by Voltron.
2. Journalize Voltron's purchase of Brighton Industries.
3. Explain how Voltron will account for goodwill.

LO 7

E7-50B. ***(Learning Objective 7: Calculate return on assets)*** Hometown Supply Company reported the following information in its comparative financial statements for the fiscal year ended January 31, 2018:

	January 31, 2018	January 31, 2017
Net sales	$84,000	$82,600
Net earnings	$ 4,200	$ 4,050
Average total assets	$70,000	$69,450

Requirements

1. Compute the net profit margin ratio for the years ended January 31, 2018, and 2017. Did it improve or worsen in 2018?
2. Compute asset turnover for the years ended January 31, 2018, and 2017. Did it improve or worsen in 2018?
3. Compute return on assets for the years ended January 31, 2018, and 2017. Did it improve or worsen in 2018? Which component—net profit margin ratio or asset turnover—was mostly responsible for the change in the company's return on assets?

LO 8

E7-51B. ***(Learning Objective 8: Report cash flows for plant assets)*** Assume Howard Manufacturing Corporation completed the following transactions:

- **a.** Sold a store building for $690,000. The building had cost Howard Manufacturing $1,200,000, and at the time of the sale, its accumulated depreciation totaled $510,000.
- **b.** Lost a store building in a fire. The building cost $300,000 and had accumulated depreciation of $250,000. The insurance proceeds received by Howard Manufacturing totaled $240,000.
- **c.** Renovated a store at a cost of $120,000 (cash).
- **d.** Purchased store fixtures for $80,000 (cash). The fixtures are expected to remain in service for ten years and then be sold for $80,000. Howard Manufacturing uses the straight-line depreciation method.

For each transaction, show what Howard Manufacturing would report for investing activities on its statement of cash flows. Show negative amounts in parentheses.

Quiz

Test your understanding of accounting for plant assets, natural resources, and intangibles by answering the following questions. Select the best choice from among the possible answers given.

Q7-52. A capital expenditure

- **a.** adds to an asset.
- **b.** is expensed immediately.
- **c.** is a credit like capital (equity).
- **d.** records additional capital.

Q7-53. Which of the following items should be accounted for as a capital expenditure?

- **a.** The monthly rental cost of an office building
- **b.** Costs incurred to repair leaks in a building's roof
- **c.** Maintenance fees paid with funds provided by the company's capital
- **d.** Taxes paid in conjunction with the purchase of office equipment

Q7-54. Suppose you buy land for \$2,800,000 and spend \$1,100,000 to develop the property. You then divide the land into lots as follows:

Category	Sale Price per Lot
15 Hilltop lots................	\$510,000
15 Valley lots	\$240,000

How much did each Hilltop lot cost you?

a. \$176,800
b. \$83,200
c. \$510,000
d. \$36,667

Q7-55. Which statement about depreciation is false?

a. A major objective of depreciation accounting is to allocate the cost of using an asset against the revenues it helps to generate.
b. Depreciation should not be recorded in years in which the market value of the asset has increased.
c. Obsolescence as well as physical wear and tear should be considered when determining the period over which an asset should be depreciated.
d. Depreciation is a process of allocating the cost of an asset to expense over its useful life.

Q7-56. At the beginning of last year, Bratworth Corporation purchased a piece of heavy equipment for \$99,000. The equipment has a life of five years or 100,000 hours. The estimated residual value is \$9,000. Bratworth used the equipment for 21,000 hours last year and 27,000 hours this year. Depreciation expense for year two using double-declining-balance (DDB) and units-of-production methods would be as follows:

	DDB	UOP
a.	\$23,760	\$26,730
b.	\$21,600	\$26,730
c.	\$21,600	\$24,300
d.	\$23,760	\$24,300

Q7-57. Madison Corporation acquired a machine for \$27,000 and has recorded depreciation for two years using the straight-line method over a five-year life and \$8,000 residual value. At the start of the third year of use, Madison revised the estimated useful life to a total of 10 years. Estimated residual value declined to \$0.

How much depreciation should Madison record in each of the asset's last eight years (that is, year 3 through year 10), following the revision?

a. \$2,700
b. \$10,800
c. \$2,425
d. Some other amount

Q7-58. Kline Company failed to record depreciation of equipment. How does this omission affect Kline's financial statements?

a. Net income is overstated and assets are understated.
b. Net income is overstated and assets are overstated.
c. Net income is understated and assets are overstated.
d. Net income is understated and assets are understated.

Q7-59. Acton, Inc., uses the double-declining-balance method for depreciation on its computers. Which item is *not* needed to compute depreciation for the first year?

a. Estimated residual value
b. Expected useful life in years
c. Original cost
d. All the items listed are needed.

Q7-60. Which of the following costs are reported on a company's income statement and balance sheet?

	Income statement	Balance sheet
a.	Cost of goods sold	Accumulated depreciation
b.	Accumulated deprecation	Land
c.	Gain on sale of land	Cost of goods sold
d.	Goodwill	Accounts payable

Use the following information to answer questions 7-61 through 7-62.
Taylor Company purchased a machine for $9,800 on January 1, 2016. The machine has been depreciated using the straight-line method assuming it has a five-year life with a $1,400 residual value. Taylor sold the machine on January 1, 2018, for $7,600.

Q7-61. What is the book value of the machine on December 31, 2017?

a. $2,100
b. $6,440
c. $8,400
d. $9,800

Q7-62. What gain or loss should Taylor record on the sale?

a. Gain, $800
b. Loss, $1,160
c. Loss, $520
d. Gain, $1,160

Q7-63. A company purchased mineral assets holding approximately 240,000 tons of ore for $960,000. The estimated residual value of the assets is zero. During the first year, 40,000 tons are extracted and sold. What is the amount of depletion for the first year?

a. $10,000
b. $160,000
c. $240,000
d. Cannot be determined from the data given

Q7-64. Suppose Speedy Delivery pays $62 million to buy Lone Star Overnight. The fair value of Lone Star's assets is $80 million, and the fair value of its liabilities is $24 million. How much goodwill did Speedy Delivery purchase in its acquisition of Lone Star Overnight?

a. $42 million
b. $24 million
c. $38 million
d. $6 million

Q7-65. Harlem, Inc., was reviewing its assets for impairment at the end of the current year. Information about one of its assets is as follows:

Net book value..........................	$ 1,300,000
Estimated future cash flows......	$ 1,050,000
Fair (market) value..................	$ 1,025,000

Harlem should report an impairment loss for the current year of

a. $275,000.
b. $25,000.
c. $0.
d. $250,000.

Q7-66. Text World, Inc., reported sales revenue of $450,000, net income of $54,000, and average total assets of $360,000. Text World's return on assets is

a. 12.0%.
b. 1.25%.
c. 15.0%.
d. 80.0%.

Problems MyLab Accounting

Group A

LO **1, 2, 3**

P7-67A. ***(Learning Objectives 1, 2, 3: Measure and account for plant assets; distinguish a capital expenditure from an expense; measure and record depreciation)*** Becker Supply, Inc., opened an office in White Bear Lake, Minnesota. Becker incurred the following costs in acquiring land, making land improvements, and constructing and furnishing the new sales building:

a. Purchase price of land, including an old building that will be used for a garage (land market value is $310,000; building market value is $90,000)	$340,000
b. Grading (leveling) land	8,800
c. Fence around the land	31,400
d. Attorney fee for title search on the land	1,100
e. Delinquent real estate taxes on the land to be paid by Becker Supply	5,800
f. Company signs at entrance to the property	1,900
g. Building permit for the sales building	700
h. Architect fee for the design of the sales building	87,800
i. Masonry, carpentry, and roofing of the sales building	518,000
j. Renovation of the garage building	37,100
k. Interest cost on construction loan for sales building	9,900
l. Landscaping (trees and shrubs)	6,100
m. Parking lot and concrete walks on the property	52,200
n. Lights for the parking lot and walkways	7,500
o. Salary of construction supervisor (84% to sales building; 10% to land improvements; and 6% to garage building renovations)	40,000
p. Office furniture for the sales building	79,000
q. Transportation and installation of furniture	1,000

The company depreciates buildings over 30 years, land improvements over 15 years, and furniture over 12 years, all on a straight-line basis with residual values of zero.

Requirements

1. Identify the proper account (Land, Land Improvements, Sales Building, Garage Building, or Furniture) for each of the costs listed in the problem. Calculate the total cost of each asset.
2. All construction was complete and the assets were placed in service on April 2. Record depreciation for the year ended December 31. Round to the nearest dollar.
3. Why would a manager need to understand the concepts covered in this problem?

LO **1, 3**

P7-68A. ***(Learning Objectives 1, 3: Measure and account for the cost of plant assets; measure and record depreciation under DDB)*** Forest Lake Resort reported the following on its balance sheet at December 31, 2018:

Property, plant, and equipment, at cost:	
Land	$ 149,000
Buildings	706,000
Less: Accumulated depreciation	(342,000)
Equipment	406,000
Less: Accumulated depreciation	(269,000)

On July 1, 2019, the resort expanded operations and purchased additional equipment for cash at a cost of $109,000. The company depreciates buildings using the straight-line method over 20 years with residual values of $81,000. Due to expected obsolescence, the equipment has a useful life of only 10 years and is being depreciated using the double-declining-balance method with a residual value of zero.

Requirements

1. Journalize Forest Lake Resort's plant asset purchase and depreciation transactions for 2019.
2. Report plant assets on the December 31, 2019, balance sheet.

LO 1, 3, 4

P7-69A. ***(Learning Objectives 1, 3, 4: Measure and account for the cost of plant assets and depreciation; analyze and record a plant asset disposal)*** Blair, Inc., has the following plant asset accounts: Land, Buildings, and Equipment, with a separate accumulated depreciation account for each of these except Land. Blair completed the following transactions:

Jan 3	Traded in equipment with accumulated depreciation of $63,000 (cost of $130,000) for similar new equipment with a cash cost of $171,000. Received a trade-in allowance of $71,000 on the old equipment and paid $100,000 in cash.
Jun 30	Sold a building that had a cost of $635,000 and had accumulated depreciation of $170,000 through December 31 of the preceding year. Depreciation is computed on a straight-line basis. The building has a 40-year useful life and a residual value of $295,000. Blair received $135,000 cash and a $325,750 note receivable.
Oct 31	Purchased land and a building for a single price of $340,000 cash. An independent appraisal valued the land at $108,900 and the building at $254,100.
Dec 31	Recorded depreciation as follows: Equipment has an expected useful life of five years and an estimated residual value of 5% of cost. Depreciation is computed using the double-declining-balance method. Depreciation on buildings is computed using the straight-line method. The new building carries a 40-year useful life and a residual value equal to 10% of its cost.

Requirement

1. Record the transactions in Blair's journal.

LO 1, 3, 8

P7-70A. ***(Learning Objectives 1, 3, 8: Measure and account for the cost of a plant asset; measure depreciation by three methods; identify the cash flow advantage of accelerated depreciation for tax purposes)*** On January 3, 2018, Pawnee Company paid $230,000 for a computer system. In addition to the basic purchase price, the company paid a setup fee of $1,000, sales tax of $6,000, and $28,000 for a special platform on which to place the computer. Pawnee's management estimates that the computer will remain in service for five years and have a residual value of $15,000. The computer will process 30,000 documents the first year, with annual processing decreasing by 2,500 documents during each of the next four years (that is, 27,500 documents in 2019; 25,000 documents in 2020; and so on). For help with deciding which depreciation method to use, the company president has requested a depreciation schedule for each of the three depreciation methods. If rounding is necessary, use two decimal places for the depreciation amount per document.

Requirements

1. For each of the generally accepted depreciation methods, prepare a depreciation schedule showing asset cost, depreciation expense, accumulated depreciation, and asset book value.
2. For financial reporting purposes, Pawnee uses the depreciation method that maximizes reported income in the early years of an asset's use. For income tax purposes, the company uses the depreciation method that minimizes income tax payments in those early years. Consider the first year Pawnee Co. uses the computer. Identify the depreciation methods that meet Pawnee's objectives, assuming the income tax authorities permit the use of any of the methods.
3. Net cash provided by operations before income tax is $157,000 for the computer's first year. The company's income tax rate is 40%. For the two depreciation methods identified in requirement 2, compare the net income and net cash provided by operations (cash flow). Show which method gives the net income advantage and which method gives the cash flow advantage.

LO **1, 3, 4, 6, 8**

P7-71A. ***(Learning Objectives 1, 3, 4, 6, 8: Analyze plant asset transactions from a company's financial statements)*** Savanaugh Stores, Inc., sells electronics and appliances. The excerpts that follow are adapted from Savanaugh's financial statements for 2018 and 2017.

Balance Sheet (dollars in millions)	March 31, 2018	March 31, 2017
Assets		
Total current assets	$7,986	$6,906
Property, plant, and equipment	4,833	4,196
Less: Accumulated depreciation	2,129	1,723
Goodwill	552	512

Statement of Cash Flows (dollars in millions)	Year Ended March 31, 2018	Year Ended March 31, 2017
Operating activities:		
Net income	$1,149	$989
Noncash items affecting net income:		
Depreciation	473	460
Gain on sale of property, plant and equipment	(142)	0
Investing activities:		
Additions to property, plant, and equipment	(712)	(616)
Sale of property, plant and equipment	150	0

Requirements

1. How much was Savanaugh's cost of plant assets at March 31, 2018? How much was the book value of plant assets? Show computations.
2. The financial statements provide three pieces of evidence that Savanaugh purchased plant assets and goodwill during fiscal year 2018. What are they?
3. Prepare T-accounts for Property, Plant, and Equipment; Accumulated Depreciation; and Goodwill. Then fill in the T-accounts with information from the comparative balance sheets and cash flow statements. Label each increase or decrease and give its dollar amount.
4. Prepare the journal entry for the sale of property, plant, and equipment in 2018.

LO **5**

P7-72A. ***(Learning Objective 5: Account for natural resources)*** Pacific Energy Company's balance sheet includes the asset Iron Ore Rights. Pacific Energy paid $3.0 million cash for the right to work a mine that contained an estimated 240,000 tons of ore. The company paid $70,000 to remove unwanted buildings from the land and $79,000 to prepare the surface for mining. Pacific Energy also signed a $38,200 note payable to a landscaping company to return the land surface to its original condition after the rights to work the mine end. During the first year, Pacific Energy removed 35,500 tons of ore, of which it sold 28,500 tons on account for $39 per ton. Operating expenses for the first year totaled $258,000, all paid in cash. In addition, the company accrued income tax at the tax rate of 40%.

Requirements

1. Record all of Pacific Energy's transactions for the year. Round depletion per unit to the closest cent.
2. Prepare the company's single-step income statement for its iron ore operations for the first year. Evaluate the profitability of the company's operations.
3. What balances should appear from these transactions on Pacific Energy's balance sheet at the end of its first year of operations?

P7-73A. ***(Learning Objectives 1, 4, 8: Analyze the effect of a plant asset addition and disposal; report plant asset transactions on the financial statements)*** At the end of 2017, Stretch Energy had total assets of $17.3 billion and total liabilities of $9.7 billion. Included among the assets were property, plant, and equipment with a cost of $4.9 billion and accumulated depreciation of $2.7 billion. Stretch Energy completed the following selected transactions during 2018: The company earned total revenues of $26 billion and incurred total expenses of $21.6 billion, which included depreciation of $1.6 billion. During the year, Stretch Energy paid $2.1 billion for new property, plant, and equipment and sold old plant assets for $0.7 billion. The cost of the assets sold was $1.2 billion, and their accumulated depreciation was $0.8 billion. LO **1, 4, 8**

Requirements

1. Explain how to determine whether Stretch Energy had a gain or loss on the sale of old plant assets during the year. What was the amount of the gain or loss, if any?
2. Show how Stretch Energy would report property, plant, and equipment on the balance sheet at December 31, 2018, after all the year's activity. What was the book value of property, plant, and equipment?
3. Show how Stretch Energy would report its operating activities and investing activities on its statement of cash flows for 2018. Ignore gains and losses.

P7-74A. ***(Learning Objective 7: Calculate return on assets)*** One Stop Shop Corporation operates general merchandise and food discount stores in the United States. The company reported the following information for the three years ending December 31, 2017: LO **7**

	A	B	C	D
1	**One Stop Shop Corporation** **Consolidated Statements of Operations (Adapted)**			
2		**For the year ended December 31**		
3	**In millions of USD**	**2017**	**2016**	**2015**
4	Total net revenue	$ 60,000	$ 50,000	$ 48,500
5	Cost of sales	21,600	17,500	16,975
6	Selling, general and administrative expenses	31,520	26,790	23,785
7	Net income from operations	6,880	5,710	7,740
8	Other revenue (expense)	(750)	(850)	(780)
9	Net income before income taxes	6,130	4,860	6,960
10	Income tax expense	(2,230)	(1,260)	(660)
11	Net income	$ 3,900	$ 3,600	$ 6,300
12				

	A	B	C	D
1	**One Stop Shop Corporation** **Partial Balance Sheets (Condensed)**			
2	**In millions of USD**	**Dec. 31, 2017**	**Dec. 31, 2016**	**Dec. 31, 2015**
3	Total current assets	$ 28,880	$ 27,000	$ 10,990
4	Property, plant and equipment, net	28,700	25,100	25,600
5	Other assets	870	800	810
6	Total assets	$ 58,450	$ 52,900	$ 37,400
7				

Requirements

1. Compute the net profit margin ratio for One Stop Shop for the years ended December 31, 2017, and December 31, 2016.
2. Compute asset turnover for One Stop Shop for the years ended December 31, 2017, and December 31, 2016.
3. Compute return on assets for One Stop Shop for the years ended December 31, 2017, and December 31, 2016.
4. What factors contributed to the change in return on assets during the year?

LO 4, 8

P7-75A. ***(Learning Objectives 4, 8: Analyze the effect of a plant asset disposal and the cash flow impact of long-lived asset transactions)*** Parker Corporation reported the following related to property and equipment (all in millions):

From the balance sheets:

	12/31/2018	12/31/2017
Property and equipment	$27,490	$25,670
Accumulated depreciation	(18,770)	(17,530)

From the investing activities section of the 2018 cash flow statement:

Cash used to purchase property and equipment	($2,640)
Proceeds from sale of property and equipment	50

From the 2018 income statement:

Depreciation expense	$1,690
Gain or loss on the sale of equipment	??

Requirements

1. Draw T-accounts for Property and Equipment and Accumulated Depreciation. Enter the information as presented and solve for the unknown in each account. (*Hint*: Recall the types of transactions that make each of the two accounts increase and decrease. You are solving for the cost of Property and Equipment sold and the Accumulated Depreciation on those assets.)
2. Based on your calculations in requirement 1, calculate the book value of assets sold during 2018. What is the difference between the sales price and the book value?
3. Prepare the journal entry for the sale of property and equipment during 2018. Describe the effect of this transaction on the financial statements. Compare the sales price and the book value in the journal entry, and compare this to the difference you calculated in requirement 2. Describe briefly.
4. Prepare a T-account for Property and Equipment, Net. Repeat requirement 1.

Group B

P7-76B. ***(Learning Objectives 1, 2, 3: Measure and account for plant assets; distinguish a capital expenditure from an expense; measure and record depreciation)*** Lancey Supply, Inc., opened an office in Ypsilanti, Michigan. Lancey incurred the following costs in acquiring land, making land improvements, and constructing and furnishing the new sales building: LO 1, 2, 3

a. Purchase price of land, including an old building that will be used for a garage (land market value is $310,000; building market value is $90,000)	$340,000
b. Grading (leveling) land	8,700
c. Fence around the land	31,500
d. Attorney fee for title search on the land	1,000
e. Delinquent real estate taxes on the land to be paid by Lancey Supply	5,100
f. Company signs at entrance to the property	1,700
g. Building permit for the sales building	500
h. Architect fee for the design of the sales building	31,480
i. Masonry, carpentry, and roofing of the sales building	510,000
j. Renovation of the garage building	40,140
k. Interest cost on construction loan for sales building	9,000
l. Landscaping (trees and shrubs)	6,200
m. Parking lot and concrete walks on the property	52,400
n. Lights for the parking lot and walkways	7,900
o. Salary of construction supervisor (81% to sales building; 11% to land improvements; and 8% to garage building renovations)	42,000
p. Office furniture for the sales building	79,800
q. Transportation and installation of furniture	2,600

The company depreciates buildings over 50 years, land improvements over 20 years, and furniture over 12 years, all on a straight-line basis with residual values of zero.

Requirements

1. Identify the proper account (Land, Land Improvements, Sales Building, Garage Building, or Furniture) for each of the costs listed in the problem. Calculate the total cost of each asset.
2. All construction was complete and the assets were placed in service on April 2. Record depreciation for the year ended December 31. Round to the nearest dollar.
3. Why would a manager need to understand the concepts covered in this problem?

P7-77B. ***(Learning Objectives 1, 3: Measure and account for the cost of plant assets; measure and record depreciation under DDB)*** Greco Lake Resort reported the following on its balance sheet at December 31, 2018: LO 1, 3

Property, plant, and equipment, at cost:	
Land	$ 142,000
Buildings	705,000
Less: Accumulated depreciation	(342,000)
Equipment	403,000
Less: Accumulated depreciation	(269,000)

On July 1, 2019, the resort expanded operations and purchased additional equipment for cash at a cost of $109,000. The company depreciates buildings using the straight-line method over 20 years with residual values of $86,000. Due to expected obsolescence, the equipment has a useful life of only 10 years and is being depreciated using the double-declining-balance method with a residual value of zero.

Requirements

1. Journalize Greco Lake Resort's plant asset purchase and depreciation transactions for 2019.
2. Report plant assets on the December 31, 2019, balance sheet.

LO **1, 3, 4**

P7-78B. ***(Learning Objectives 1, 3, 4: Measure and account for the cost of plant assets and depreciation; analyze and record a plant asset disposal)*** Mayfield, Inc., has the following plant asset accounts: Land, Buildings, and Equipment, with a separate accumulated depreciation account for each of these except Land. Mayfield completed the following transactions:

Jan 3	Traded in equipment with accumulated depreciation of $65,000 (cost of $132,000) for similar new equipment with a cash cost of $180,000. Received a trade-in allowance of $72,000 on the old equipment and paid $108,000 in cash.
Jun 30	Sold a building that had a cost of $660,000 and had accumulated depreciation of $135,000 through December 31 of the preceding year. Depreciation is computed using the straight-line method. The building has a 40-year useful life and a residual value of $220,000. Mayfield received $105,000 cash and a $414,500 note receivable.
Oct 31	Purchased land and a building for a single price of $370,000 cash. An independent appraisal valued the land at $147,000 and the building at $273,000.
Dec 31	Recorded depreciation as follows: Equipment has an expected useful life of ten years and an estimated residual value of 12% of cost. Depreciation is computed using the double-declining-balance method. Depreciation on buildings is computed using the straight-line method. The new building carries a 40-year useful life and a residual value equal to 20% of its cost.

Requirement

1. Record the transactions in Mayfield's journal.

LO **1, 3, 8**

P7-79B. ***(Learning Objectives 1, 3, 8: Measure and account for the cost of a plant asset; measure depreciation by three methods; identify the cash flow advantage of accelerated depreciation for tax purposes)*** On January 2, 2018, Jupiter Company paid $270,000 for a computer system. In addition to the basic purchase price, the company paid a setup fee of $1,800, sales tax of $6,900, and $31,300 for a special platform on which to place the computer. Jupiter's management estimates that the computer will remain in service for five years and have a residual value of $35,000. The computer will process 30,000 documents the first year, with annual processing decreasing by 2,500 documents during each of the next four years (that is, 27,500 documents in year 2019, 25,000 documents in year 2020, and so on). For help with deciding which depreciation method to use, the company president has requested a depreciation schedule for each of the three depreciation methods. If rounding is necessary, use two decimal places for the depreciation amount per document.

Requirements

1. For each of the generally accepted depreciation methods, prepare a depreciation schedule showing asset cost, depreciation expense, accumulated depreciation, and asset book value.
2. For financial reporting purposes, Jupiter uses the depreciation method that maximizes reported income in the early years of an asset's use. For income tax purposes, the company uses the depreciation method that minimizes income tax payments in those early years. Consider the first year Jupiter uses the computer. Identify the depreciation methods that meet Jupiter's objectives, assuming the income tax authorities permit the use of any of the methods.
3. Net cash provided by operations before income tax is $154,000 for the computer's first year. The company's income tax rate is 35%. For the two depreciation methods identified in requirement 2, compare the net income and net cash provided by operations (cash flow). Show which method gives the net income advantage and which method gives the cash flow advantage.

P7-80B. ***(Learning Objectives 1, 3, 4, 6, 8: Analyze plant asset transactions from a company's financial statements)*** Caribbean Sales, Inc., sells electronics and appliances. The excerpts that follow are adapted from Caribbean's financial statements for 2018 and 2017: LO 1, 3, 4, 6, 8

Balance Sheet (dollars in millions)	April 30, 2018	2017
Assets		
Total current assets	$7,989	$6,909
Property, plant and equipment	4,834	4,193
Less: Accumulated depreciation	2,128	1,730
Goodwill	554	519

Statement of Cash Flows (dollars in millions)	Year Ended April 30, 2018	2017
Operating activities:		
Net income	$1,143	$981
Noncash items affecting net income:		
Depreciation	463	453
Gain on sale of property, plant and equipment	(134)	0
Investing activities:		
Additions to property, plant and equipment	(714)	(617)
Sale of property, plant and equipment	142	0

Requirements

1. How much was Caribbean's cost of plant assets at April 30, 2018? How much was the book value of plant assets? Show computations.
2. The financial statements provide three pieces of evidence that Caribbean purchased plant assets and goodwill during fiscal year 2018. What are they?
3. Prepare T-accounts for Property, Plant, and Equipment; Accumulated Depreciation; and Goodwill. Then fill in the T-accounts with information from the comparative balance sheets and cash flow statements. Label each increase or decrease and give its dollar amount.
4. Prepare the journal entry for the sale of property, plant, and equipment in 2018.

P7-81B. ***(Learning Objective 5: Account for natural resources)*** Atlantic Energy Company's balance sheet includes the asset Iron Ore Rights. Atlantic Energy paid $2.9 million cash for the right to work a mine that contained an estimated 225,000 tons of ore. The company paid $68,000 to remove unwanted buildings from the land and $78,000 to prepare the surface for mining. Atlantic Energy also signed a $38,750 note payable to a landscaping company to return the land surface to its original condition after the rights to work the mine end. During the first year, Atlantic Energy removed 35,000 tons of ore, of which it sold 28,500 tons on account for $38 per ton. Operating expenses for the first year totaled $256,000, all paid in cash. In addition, the company accrued income tax at the tax rate of 40%. LO 5

Requirements

1. Record all of Atlantic Energy's transactions for the year. Round depletion per unit to the closest cent.
2. Prepare the company's single-step income statement for its iron ore operations for the first year. Evaluate the profitability of the company's operations.
3. What balances should appear from these transactions on Atlantic Energy's balance sheet at the end of its first year of operations?

LO 1, 4, 8

P7-82B. ***(Learning Objectives 1, 4, 8: Analyze the effect of a plant asset addition and disposal; report plant asset transactions on the financial statements)*** At the end of 2017, Solar Power had total assets of $17.8 billion and total liabilities of $9.1 billion. Included among the assets were property, plant, and equipment with a cost of $4.5 billion and accumulated depreciation of $3.4 billion.

Solar Power completed the following selected transactions during 2018: The company earned total revenues of $27.1 billion and incurred total expenses of $22.1 billion, which included depreciation of $1.0 billion. During the year, Solar Power paid $1.4 billion for new property, plant, and equipment and sold old plant assets for $0.5 billion. The cost of the assets sold was $0.8 billion, and their accumulated depreciation was $0.7 billion.

Requirements

1. Explain how to determine whether Solar Power had a gain or loss on the sale of old plant assets during the year. What was the amount of the gain or loss, if any?
2. Show how Solar Power would report property, plant, and equipment on the balance sheet at December 31, 2018, after all the year's activity. What was the book value of property, plant, and equipment?
3. Show how Solar Power would report its operating activities and investing activities on its statement of cash flows for 2018. Ignore gains and losses.

LO 7

P7-83B. ***(Learning Objective 7: Calculate return on assets)*** Bargain Basement Corporation operates general merchandise and food discount stores in the United States. The company reported the following information for the three years ending December 31, 2017:

	A	B	C	D
1	**Bargain Basement Corporation** **Consolidated Statements of Operations (Adapted)**			
2	**In millions of USD**	**For the year ended December 31,**		
3		**2017**	**2016**	**2015**
4	Total net revenue	$ 80,000	$ 62,000	$ 60,000
5	Cost of sales	28,800	21,700	21,000
6	Selling, general and administrative expenses	41,220	32,206	35,450
7	Net income from operations	9,980	8,094	3,550
8	Other revenue (expense)	(730)	(810)	(780)
9	Net income before income taxes	9,250	7,284	2,770
10	Income tax expense	(1,050)	(914)	(720)
11	Net income	$ 8,200	$ 6,370	$ 2,050
12				

	A	B	C	D
1	**Bargain Basement Corporation** **Partial Balance Sheets (Condensed)**			
2	**In millions of USD**	**Dec. 31, 2017**	**Dec. 31, 2016**	**Dec. 31, 2015**
3	Total current assets	$ 20,930	$ 5,710	$ 1,140
4	Property, plant and equipment, net	25,200	25,400	25,000
5	Other assets	870	890	860
6	Total assets	$ 47,000	$ 32,000	$ 27,000
7				

Requirements

1. Compute the net profit margin ratio for Bargain Basement Corporation for the years ended December 31, 2017, and December 31, 2016.
2. Compute asset turnover for Bargain Basement Corporation for the years ended December 31, 2017, and December 31, 2016.
3. Compute return on assets for Bargain Basement Corporation for the years ended December 31, 2017, and December 31, 2016.
4. What factors contributed to the change in return on assets during the year?

LO 4, 8

P7-84B. ***(Learning Objectives 4, 8: Analyze the effect of a plant asset disposal and the cash flow impact of long-lived asset transactions)*** Walker Corporation reported the following related to property and equipment (all in millions):

From the balance sheets:

	12/31/2018	12/31/2017
Property and equipment	$24,510	$22,630
Accumulated depreciation	(16,770)	(15,840)

From the investing activities section of the 2018 cash flow statement:

Cash used to purchase property and equipment	($2,360)
Proceeds from sale of property and equipment	48

From the 2018 income statement:

Depreciation expense	$1,250
Gain or loss on the sale of equipment	??

Requirements

1. Draw T-accounts for Property and Equipment and Accumulated Depreciation. Enter the information as presented and solve for the unknown in each account. (*Hint*: Recall the types of transactions that make each of the two accounts increase and decrease. You are solving for the cost of Property and Equipment sold and the Accumulated Depreciation on those assets.)
2. Based on your calculations in requirement 1, calculate the book value of assets sold during 2018. What is the difference between the sales price and the book value?
3. Prepare the journal entry for the sale of property and equipment during 2018. Describe the effect of this transaction on the financial statements. Compare the sales price and the book value in the journal entry, and compare this to the difference you calculated in requirement 2. Describe briefly.
4. Prepare a T-account for Property and Equipment, Net. Repeat requirement 1.

Challenge Exercises and Problem

LO 3

E7-85. ***(Learning Objective 3: Determine the effect on net income of a change in the depreciation method)*** Borzani Corporation reported net income of $52 million for 2018. Depreciation expense for the year totaled $18 million. Borzani depreciates plant assets over eight years using the straight-line method with residual values of zero.

Borzani paid $144 million for plant assets at the beginning of 2018. At the start of 2019, the company changed its method of accounting for depreciation to the double-declining-balance method. The year 2019 is expected to be the same as 2018, except for the change in depreciation method. If Borzani had been using the double-declining-balance method of depreciation all along, how much net income could the company expect to earn during 2019? Ignore income taxes.

LO 2

E7-86. ***(Learning Objective 2: Distinguish a capital expenditure from an expense, and measure the financial statement effects of an expensing error)*** Transcontinental is a major telecommunication conglomerate. Assume that early in 2018, Transcontinental purchased equipment at a cost of 6 million euros (€6 million). Management expects the equipment to remain in service for four years and the estimated residual value to be negligible. Transcontinental uses the straight-line depreciation method. Because of an accounting error, Transcontinental expensed the entire cost of the equipment at the time of purchase. Because Transcontinental operates as a partnership, it pays no income taxes.

Requirements

Prepare a schedule to show the overstatement or understatement in the following items at the end of each year over the four-year life of the equipment:

1. Total current assets
2. Equipment, net
3. Net income

LO 4 **P7-87.** ***(Learning Objective 4: Determine plant and equipment transactions for an actual company)*** ShipFaster Corporation provides a broad portfolio of transportation, e-commerce, and business services. ShipFaster reported the following information in its most recent annual report:

	A	B	C
1	**ShipFaster Corporation Partial Consolidated Balance Sheets**		
2		**May 31**	
3	(in millions)	**2018**	**2017**
4	**PROPERTY AND EQUIPMENT, AT COST**		
5	Aircraft and related equipment	$ 10,550	$ 10,150
6	Package handling and ground support equipment	4,510	4,670
7	Computer and electronic equipment	4,330	4,080
8	Vehicles	2,760	2,500
9	Facilities and other	6,720	6,560
10	Gross property and equipment	28,870	27,960
11	Less accumulated depreciation and amortization	(18,140)	(17,900)
12	Net property and equipment	$ 10,730	$ 10,060
13			

	A	B	C
1	**ShipFaster Corporation Partial Statements of Cash Flows**		
2	(In millions)	**May 31**	
3		**2018**	**2017**
4	**Investing Activities**		
5	Capital expenditures	$ (3,440)	$ (2,940)
6	Business acquisitions	(117)	(96)
7	Proceeds from asset dispositions and other	514	103
8	Cash used in investing activities	$ (3,043)	$ (2,933)
9			

NOTE 1: DESCRIPTION OF BUSINESS AND SUMMARY OF SIGNIFICANT ACCOUNTING POLICIES

Property and equipment (excerpted):

For financial reporting purposes, we record depreciation and amortization of property and equipment on a straight-line basis over the asset's service life or related lease term, if shorter. For income tax purposes, depreciation is computed using accelerated methods when applicable… Depreciation expense, excluding gains and losses on sales of property and equipment used in operations, was $2 billion in 2017 and 2016, and $1.5 billion in 2015.

In June 2017, we retired from service seven Boeing MD11 aircraft and 12 related engines, four Airbus A310-300 aircraft and three related engines, three Airbus A300-600 aircraft and three related engines and one Boeing MD10-10 aircraft and three related engines, and related parts. As a consequence of this decision, impairment and related charges of $250 million … were recorded in the fourth quarter.

Requirements

1. Using the information provided from the balance sheet and statement of cash flows for ShipFaster, reconstruct the Property and Equipment and Accumulated Depreciation accounts. You will not have to account for individual asset categories, but only for the gross cost of property and equipment and accumulated depreciation. You will have to solve for the original gross cost and accumulated depreciation of the plant and equipment sold. Ignore business acquisitions for this part.
2. Prepare the journal entries to record total capital expenditures and total depreciation expense.

APPLY YOUR KNOWLEDGE

Serial Case

C7-88 *(Learning Objective 3: Calculate depreciation for a new location of a company in the restaurant industry)* LO 3

Note: This case is part of The Cheesecake Factory serial case contained in every chapter in this textbook.

In 2016, **The Cheesecake Factory Incorporated** (NASDAQ: CAKE) opened its first New York City restaurant. The new Cheesecake Factory is in Queens and is 8,850 square feet and seats 240 guests.

Rather than selling franchises, Cheesecake Factory owns and operates all of its U.S. restaurants, which at last count numbered more than 200. It typically has a long-term lease for each restaurant location and depreciates the cost of building a restaurant over the life of the lease.

Planning for this NYC Cheesecake Factory started a few years ago when the former facility in this location, **Children's Place**, closed. Cheesecake Factory officials had been searching for a suitable location for some time and this Queens location seemed to be a good fit. Prior to building, Cheesecake Factory had to have architects draw up building plans to be approved by the city. In addition, Cheesecake Factory had to obtain the City's permission to operate a sidewalk cafe. Its plans called for outdoor dining during good weather; large windows can be closed in times of inclement weather. The last roadblock, the permit for a sidewalk cafe, was granted in March 2016. Construction started soon thereafter and the restaurant officially opened seven months later in late October 2016.

In Cheesecake Factory's Form 10-K for 2016, it indicates that its average cost to build and equip a new restaurant is approximately $900 per interior square foot. Furnishings and equipment would typically include booths, chairs, grills, ovens, refrigerators, plates, glasses, and the like. Leasehold improvements could include walls, flooring, ceilings, windows, doors, lighting, heating and cooling systems, and similar items. Combined, the estimated cost of this new location is $7.965 million. For the purpose of this analysis, assume that 75% of the estimated cost covers leasehold improvements, with the remainder covering furnishings and equipment.

The Cheesecake Factory's fiscal year end is the closest Tuesday to December 31 each year. Partial year depreciation would be calculated based on the number of whole months out of twelve months that the asset is in service the first year. For this analysis, estimate the salvage value of Cheesecake Factory's plant and equipment as 10% of the original cost.

To follow are excerpts from Cheesecake Factory's 2016 Form 10-K related to its property and equipment.

> *We currently lease all of our restaurants and utilize capital for leasehold improvements and furnishings, fixtures and equipment ("FF&E") to build out our restaurant premises. Total costs are targeted at approximately $900 per interior square foot for The Cheesecake Factory restaurants. (Source: Page 4, Description of Business)*
>
> *We record property and equipment at cost less accumulated depreciation. Improvements are capitalized while repairs and maintenance costs are expensed as incurred. The useful life of property and equipment and the determination as to what constitutes a capitalized cost versus a repair and maintenance expense involve judgment by management, which may produce materially different amounts of repairs and maintenance or depreciation expense than if different assumptions were used. (Source: Page 39, Critical Accounting Policies in Management's Discussion and Analysis)*
>
> *We record property and equipment at cost less accumulated depreciation. Improvements are capitalized while repairs and maintenance costs are expensed as incurred. Depreciation and amortization are calculated using the straight-line method over the estimated useful life of the assets or the lease term, whichever is shorter. Leasehold*

improvements include the cost of our internal development and construction department. Depreciation and amortization periods[3] are as follows:

- *Buildings and land improvements 25 to 30 years*
- *Leasehold improvements 10 to 30 years*
- *Furnishings, fixtures and equipment 3 to 15 years*
- *Computer software and equipment 3 to 5 years*

Gains and losses related to property and equipment disposals are recorded in interest and other expenses, net. (Source: Page 51, Notes to Consolidated Financial Statements)

Data from the U.S. Securities and Exchange Commission EDGAR Company Filings, www.sec.gov

Requirements

1. Assume that the Cheesecake Factory paid cash for all costs of building and equipping its new restaurant in NYC. How would its assets, liabilities, and equity each be impacted by the construction and opening of this restaurant in 2016? (Ignore the impact of depreciation when answering this question.)
2. On which 2016 financial statement would you find the costs of building and equipping this new restaurant?
3. Which financial statement(s) would be impacted by depreciation on the new restaurant and its furniture and fixtures?
4. Calculate the total depreciation expense related to this new restaurant's property and equipment for:
   a. 2016 (assume two months of depreciation in 2016)
   b. 2017
5. What would the net book value of the NYC Queens restaurant's property and equipment be at the end of fiscal year 2017?

Decision Cases

LO 3

C7-89. ***(Learning Objective 3: Measure profitability based on different inventory and depreciation methods)*** Suppose you are considering investing in two businesses, Bahama Bakery and Burgers Galore. The two companies are virtually identical, and both began operations at the beginning of the current year. During the year, each company purchased the following inventory:

Jan	4	10,000 units at $4 =	40,000
Apr	6	5,000 units at 5 =	25,000
Aug	9	7,000 units at 6 =	42,000
Nov	27	10,000 units at 7 =	70,000
Totals		32,000	$177,000

During the first year, both companies sold 25,000 units of inventory.

In early January, both companies purchased equipment costing $150,000 that had a 10-year estimated useful life and a $20,000 residual value. Bahama Bakery uses the inventory and depreciation methods that maximize reported income. By contrast, Burgers Galore uses the inventory and depreciation methods that minimize income tax payments. Assume that both companies' trial balances at December 31 included the following:

Sales revenue	$350,000
Operating expenses*	50,000

*Does not include depreciation expense

The income tax rate for both companies is 40%.

[3] For the purpose of this case analysis, use the midpoint of the range of years when calculating depreciation for a given category of property and equipment.

Requirements

1. Prepare both companies' multiple-step income statements.
2. Which company appears to be more profitable? Which company has more cash to invest in promising projects? If prices continue rising over the long term, which company would you prefer to invest in? Why? (Challenge)

C7-90. ***(Learning Objectives 2, 5: Distinguish between capital expenditures and expense; account for plant assets and intangible assets)*** The following questions are unrelated except that they all apply to plant assets and intangible assets: LO **2, 5**

1. The manager of Wallace Manufacturing regularly buys plant assets and debits the cost to Repairs and Maintenance Expense. Why would she do that, since she knows this action violates GAAP?
2. The manager of Arbor Homes debits the cost of repairs and maintenance of plant assets to Plant and Equipment. Why would he do that, since he knows he is violating GAAP?
3. It has been suggested that because many intangible assets have no value except to the company that owns them, they should be valued at $1.00 or zero on the balance sheet. Many accountants disagree with this view. Which view do you support? Why?

Ethical Issue

C7-91. Toledo National Bank purchased land and a building for the lump sum of $6 million. To get the maximum tax deduction, the bank's managers allocated 80% of the purchase price to the building and only 20% to the land. A more realistic allocation would have been 60% to the building and 40% to the land.

Requirements

1. What is the ethical issue in this situation?
2. Who are the stakeholders? What are the possible consequences to each?
3. Analyze the alternatives from the following standpoints: (a) economic, (b) legal, and (c) ethical.
4. What would you do? How would you justify your decision?

Focus on Financials | Apple Inc.

(Learning Objectives 1, 2, 3, 5: Analyze activity in plant assets) Refer to Apple Inc.'s Consolidated Financial Statements in Appendix A and online in the filings section of **www.sec.gov**, and answer the following questions: LO **1, 2, 3, 5**

Requirements

1. Refer to Note 1 and Note 3 of the Notes to Consolidated Financial Statements. What kinds of assets are included in the Property, Plant and Equipment of Apple Inc.?
2. Refer to Note 1, Property, Plant and Equipment section. Which depreciation method does Apple use for reporting to stockholders and creditors in the financial statements? What type of depreciation method does the company probably use for income tax purposes? Why is this method preferable for tax purposes?
3. Depreciation expense is embedded in operating expense accounts listed on the income statement, so you can't break out the actual figure for depreciation in that way. Refer to the section on Property, Plant and Equipment in Note 1. How much was Apple's depreciation and amortization expense on plant assets during 2016? What did this figure include? Now refer to Note 3—Consolidated Financial Statement Details. How much was Apple's accumulated depreciation on fixed assets at the end of 2016? Explain why accumulated depreciation exceeds depreciation expense for the current year.
4. Refer to Notes 1 and 4 of the Notes to Consolidated Financial Statements. What are Apple's intangible assets? How does the company account for each of these intangibles over its lifetime?

Focus on Analysis | Under Armour, Inc.

LO **1, 3, 5, 7, 8**

(Learning Objectives 1, 3, 5, 7, 8: Measure the cost of plant assets; explain plant asset activity; apply GAAP for intangible assets, explain an asset impairment, analyze rate of return on assets; analyze the cash flow impact of long-lived asset transactions) Retrieve the 2016 **Under Armour** financial statements at **www.sec.gov** by clicking on Filings and then searching for "Under Armour" under Company Filings. When you see the list of filings for the company, select the Form 10-K for 2016. Be sure to retrieve the 2016 financial statements, not another year. This case leads you through an analysis of the activity for some of Under Armour's long-term assets, as well as the calculation of its rate of return on total assets.

Requirements

1. On the statement of cash flows, how much did Under Armour pay for property and equipment during 2016? In what section of the cash flows statement do you find this amount?
2. Which depreciation method does Under Armour use? Over what range of useful lives does Under Armour depreciate various types of fixed assets? You can find discussions of this in Note 2 (Summary of Significant Accounting Policies).
3. Review the information in Note 3 (Property and Equipment, Net). List the categories of Under Armour's property and equipment as of December 31, 2016, and December 31, 2015. How much depreciation expense is included in the calculation of net income for these two fiscal years? Does it appear that Under Armour's property and equipment was proportionately newer or older at the end of 2016 (vs. 2015)? Explain your answer. (Challenge)
4. Examine Note 4 (Goodwill and Intangible Assets, Net) and Note 2. Briefly describe Under Armour's accounting for goodwill and other intangible assets. What other types of intangible assets did Under Armour own as of December 31, 2016?
5. Using DuPont Analysis, calculate Under Armour's rate of return on total assets for fiscal 2016 and fiscal 2015. Total assets at December 31, 2014 (the end of its 2014 fiscal year) were $2,095 million. Did the company perform better or worse in 2016 than in 2015? Use millions for ratios.

Group Project

Visit a local business and do the following.

Requirements

1. List all its plant assets.
2. If possible, interview the manager. Gain as much information as you can about the business's plant assets. For example, try to determine the assets' costs, the depreciation method the company is using, and the estimated useful life of each asset category. If an interview is impossible, then develop your own estimates of the assets' costs, useful lives, and book values, assuming an appropriate depreciation method.
3. Determine whether the business has any intangible assets. If so, list them and gain as much information as possible about their nature, cost, and estimated useful lives.
4. Write a detailed report of your findings and be prepared to present your results to the class.

Quick Check Answers

1. *c*
2. *b [$84,000 / ($84,000 + $336,000)] × $400,000 = $80,000*
3. *c*
4. *a*
5. *d*
6. *a [($30,000 − $5,000) / 5 = $5,000]*
7. *b [($40,000 − $8,000) / 20,000] × 6,400 = $10,240*
8. *d [$50,000 × (2 / 5)] = $20,000*
9. *c*
10. *a [($90,000 − $6,000) / 10] × 3 = $25,200; [$68,700 – ($90,000 – $25,200)] = $3,900 gain*
11. *a [($200,000 / 50,000) × 2,000 = $8,000]*
12. *d*
13. *b*
14. *d*
15. *a*
16. *b*

Try It Solutions

Page 372

	Estimated Market Value	Percentage of Total Market Value	×	Total Cost	=	Cost of Each Asset
Land.................	$ 40,000	26.7%*	×	$120,000	=	$ 32,040
Building............	95,000	63.3%	×	$120,000	=	75,960
Equipment.........	15,000	10.0%	×	$120,000	=	12,000
Total................	$150,000	100.0%				$120,000

*$40,000/$150,000 = 0.267, and so on

Page 377

$1,600 = ($10,000 – $2,000)/5

Page 380

Yr. 1: $4,000 ($10,000 × 40%)
Yr. 2: $2,400 ($6,000 × 40%)
Yr. 3: $1,440 ($3,600 × 40%)
Yr. 4: $160 ($10,000 – $4,000 – $2,400 – $1,440 – $2,000 = $160)*
Yr. 5: $0

*The asset is not depreciated below residual value of $2,000.

8 Current and Contingent Liabilities

LEARNING OBJECTIVES

1 **Distinguish** between current and long-term liabilities

2 **Account for** accounts payable and **analyze** accounts payable turnover

3 **Account for** notes payable and accrued interest

4 **Account for** accrued liabilities and unearned revenue

5 **Account for** contingent liabilities

SPOTLIGHT

Amazon.com Moves a Lot of Merchandise and Incurs Many Liabilities

Amazon.com is the largest virtual store on the globe. Since its inception as primarily a bookseller in 1995, the company has become synonymous with Internet retailing, expanding its lines of merchandise to cover almost every conceivable consumer item: books, movies, music, games, computer hardware and software, electronics, home and garden supplies, groceries, health and beauty products, apparel, sports gear, auto and industrial tools, and on and on. One of the things that differentiates Amazon.com from its competitors is that, in addition to selling its own products, the company allows other retailers and manufacturers to market their own products on its website.

Digital products are delivered instantaneously, of course, but the company offers same-day delivery on many physical products, including groceries. One of the company's most recent product innovations is the Echo Show, a wireless smart speaker with a video touchscreen activated through a voice control system called Alexa. Using voice recognition software and touchscreens, consumers can search the Web, shop online, make phone calls, and activate all sorts of popular smart-home devices (garage door openers, heating and air conditioning system controls, appliances, lights, etc.).

Amazon.com took the grocery business by storm in 2017 with its purchase of **Whole Foods, Inc.** for $13.7 billion in cash. This deal marked the beginning of an era in which the e-commerce giant entered the brick-and-mortar world. The company passed this milestone after it announced plans to launch Amazon Go, a checkout-free grocery store in Seattle, Washington. Customers register with their smart phones and get an app through their Amazon.com account. The new store's integrated software called "Just Walk Out" automatically detects when products are taken off the shelf (or replaced). After customers leave the store, Amazon.com sends them a virtual receipt.

Matthew Horwood/Alamy Stock Photo

Amazon.com processes billions of transactions a year. In addition to purchasing inventory through its accounts payable system, the company also has about 340,000 employees whose salaries and wages have to be paid. Their payroll taxes, insurance premiums, and retirement benefits must be paid as well. This requires the company to maintain a massive payroll database through which the company accrues and pays its payroll related liabilities. Amazon.com offers a membership service called Amazon Prime. Members who prepay a yearly subscription fee obtain free two-day shipping on all orders, plus a wide variety of special services such as video-on-demand, streaming music, and special rates on Kindle books. The company warranties its popular Kindle reader and Echo devices against defects for one year from the date of purchase. It also employs attorneys to defend it against legal claims brought by other companies. All of these functions require accounting for current liabilities. Examine the liability section of Amazon.com's fiscal 2016 selected financial data in the figure below. Notice that Amazon.com, Inc. classified over 68% ($43,816 million/$64,117 million) of its liabilities as of December 31, 2016, as current. This chapter covers accounting for current liabilities. ●

	A	B	C
1	**Amazon.com, Inc.** **Selected balance sheet and income statement data (Adapted)**	**Fiscal 2016**	**Fiscal 2015**
2	**in millions of $**	**Dec. 31, 2016**	**Dec. 31, 2015**
3	**Current assets:**		
4	Cash and cash equivalents	$ 19,334	$ 15,890
5	Marketable securities	6,647	3,918
6	Accounts receivable, net and other	8,339	5,654
7	Inventories	11,461	10,243
8	**Total current assets**	45,781	35,705
9	Non-current assets (net)	37,621	29,042
10	**TOTAL ASSETS**	$ 83,402	$ 64,747
11	**Current liabilities:**		
12	Accounts payable	$ 25,309	$ 20,397
13	Accrued expenses and other	13,739	10,372
14	Unearned revenue	4,768	3,118
15	**Total current liabilities**	43,816	33,887
16	Long-term debt	7,694	8,227
17	Other long-term liabilities	12,607	9,249
18	Commitments and contingencies (Note 7)		
19	**TOTAL LIABILITIES**	**64,117**	**51,363**
20	Stockholders' Equity	19,285	13,384
21	**TOTAL LIABILITIES AND STOCKHOLDERS' EQUITY**	$ 83,402	$ 64,747
22			
23	Net sales	$ 135,987	$ 107,006
24	Cost of sales	88,265	71,651
25	Gross profit	$ 47,722	$ 35,355
26			

Data from the U.S. Securities and Exchange Commission EDGAR Company Filings, www.sec.gov

Try It in Excel®

You can access the most current annual report of Amazon.com, Inc. in Excel at **www.sec.gov**. Using the "FILINGS" link on the toolbar at the top of the home page, select "Company Filings Search." This will take you to the "Edgar Company Filings" page. Type "Amazon" in the company name box, and select "Search." This will produce the "EDGAR Search Results" page showing the company name. Click on the "CIK" link beside the company name. Doing so will pull up a list of the reports the company has filed with the SEC. Under the "Filing Type" box, type "10-K" and click the search box. Form 10-K is the SEC form for the company's annual report. Find the year that you wish to view. Click on the "Interactive Data" box, which takes you to the "View Filing Data" page. Find and click on the "View Excel Document" link at the top of this page. You may choose to either open or download the Excel files containing the company's most recent financial statements.

DISTINGUISH BETWEEN CURRENT AND LONG-TERM LIABILITIES

1 Distinguish between current and long-term liabilities

As you have learned, current liabilities are debts generally payable in cash within one year (or operating cycle if longer) of a company's balance sheet date. Current liabilities are usually associated with various day-to-day operating activities. The most frequently used current liabilities are accounts payable, notes payable, accrued liabilities, current portion of long-term borrowings, and unearned (deferred) revenue. Exhibit 8-1 matches various types of current liabilities with the operating activities associated with them.

Exhibit 8-1 | Operating Activities and Current Liabilities

Operating Activity	Current Liability
Purchasing inventory, supplies, paying operating expenses	Accounts payable
Borrowing money for operations	Notes payable and accrued interest payable
Paying employees	Accrued salaries, wages and related payroll taxes payable
Paying income taxes	Accrued income tax payable
Fulfilling warranty claims	Accrued warranties payable
Processing advance cash payments from customers	Unearned (deferred) revenue

In contrast, long-term liabilities are incurred mostly for financing activities, such as the construction of buildings, purchases of property, plant, and equipment, and purchases of other companies. Accounting for long-term liabilities is the subject of Chapter 9.

ACCOUNT FOR ACCOUNTS PAYABLE AND ANALYZE ACCOUNTS PAYABLE TURNOVER

2 Account for accounts payable and **analyze** accounts payable turnover

Amounts owed for products or services purchased on account are *accounts payable*. Amazon.com, Inc.'s Accounts Payable at December 31, 2016 was $25,309 million (line 12 on page 437). For example, the company purchases all its inventory as well as pays most of its operating expenses through accounts payable. We have seen many accounts payable examples in preceding chapters.

Accounts Payable Turnover. An important measure of liquidity for a retail business is a ratio called **accounts payable turnover**, which measures the number of times a year the company is able to pay its accounts payable. The ratio is computed as follows:

Accounts payable turnover (T/O) = Purchases from suppliers (assumed all on credit) ÷ Average accounts payable

Turnover expressed in days = 365 ÷ T/O (computed above)

The hard part about computing the ratio is that "purchases from suppliers" is not normally reflected by any number on a company's financial statements. Therefore, the purchases must be computed. For a merchandising company, inventory purchases can be computed by analyzing the activity in the business's inventory account and solving for them as follows:

Inventory	
Beginning balance (from balance sheet)	Cost of goods sold (cost of sales)
Purchases from suppliers*	
Ending balance (from balance sheet)	

*Purchases from suppliers (assumed all on credit) = Cost of goods sold (or cost of sales, from income statement) + Ending inventory (from comparative balance sheet) − Beginning inventory (from comparative balance sheet)

If there is not a material difference between the company's beginning inventory and ending inventory (i.e., if they haven't increased or decreased very much during the year), it is not necessary to adjust for inventory amounts because the difference has little or no effect on the turnover ratio. This makes the computation easier; simply divide the cost of goods sold by the business's average accounts payable to compute the company's accounts payable turnover. Then divide 365 by the turnover ratio. Doing so expresses the turnover ratio in terms of the average number of days it took the business to pay its suppliers' invoices, or **days' payable outstanding (DPO)**. For fiscal years 2016 and 2015, Amazon.com's accounts payable turnover ratio and DPO were as follows (using figures from selected financial data on page 437):

A1

	A	B	C
1		**2016**	**2015**
2	Cost of Goods Sold	$ 88,265	$ 71,651
3	Add: ending inventory	11,461	10,243
4	Less: beginning inventory	(10,243)	(8,299)*
5	Purchases	89,483	73,595
6	÷ Average accounts payable	22,853	18,428*
7	= Accounts payable turnover ratio	3.92	3.99
8	Days' Payable Outstanding (DPO)		
9	= 365 ÷ Accounts Payable Turnover Ratio	93.11	91.48
10			

*Amounts for inventory and accounts payable as of 12/31/2014 were taken from 12/31/2014 balance sheet (not included in text).

For 2016, Amazon.com's accounts payable turned over 3.92 times, which translates to a DPO of 93.1 days (365/3.92). This means it took Amazon.com. an average of 93 days to pay a supplier in 2016, which was up slightly from 91.5 days for the same period in 2015.

Does this seem to be a long or short period of time? Here are comparative 2016 DPO statistics for Amazon.com's competitors, **Walmart Stores, Inc.**, and **Target Corp.**

	Walmart Stores, Inc.	Target Corp.
Days' payable outstanding (365/turnover)	40.5 days	55.1 days

Walmart pays its accounts payable in about 40.5 days, whereas Target takes 55 days to pay its accounts payable. If you were a supplier of any of these three giant companies, which would you rather do business with, on the basis of this ratio? If cash collections are important to you in order to pay your own bills, the obvious answer is Walmart, based strictly on this ratio.

What makes an accounts payable turnover ratio strong or weak in the eyes of creditors and investors? Generally, a high turnover ratio (short period in days) is better than a low turnover ratio. Companies with shorter payment periods are generally better credit risks than those with longer payment periods. A typical credit period is 30 days. However, the three companies we just discussed—Amazon.com, Walmart, and Target—have DPO numbers that are longer than 30 days. These huge companies strategically stretch out their DPOs by withholding payments for as long as possible in order to maximize the returns on their excess cash. Having to wait so long to get paid can be tough on suppliers. However, because of their size, market share, and buying power, few suppliers can afford *not* to do business with Amazon.com, Walmart, and Target.

ACCOUNT FOR NOTES PAYABLE AND ACCRUED INTEREST

3 Account for notes payable and accrued interest

As you learned in Chapter 5, a note is a written promise to pay a certain amount of money at a given date in the future along with interest. **Short-term notes payable** are notes payable due within one year (or operating cycle if longer). Short-term notes payable to banks are often used to finance business operations. For example, a company might sign a short-term note payable to finance the purchase of inventory or to pay operating expenses.

The following sequence of entries covers the purchase of inventory on January 1, 2018, in the amount of $8,000, in exchange for a short-term note payable, due in one year, with interest at 10%. It also covers accrual of interest expense and payment of the short-term note payable at the end of one year's time.

	A	B	C	D
1	2018			
2	Jan 1	Inventory	8,000	
3		Note Payable, Short-Term		8,000
4		*Purchase of inventory by issuing a note payable.*		
5				

This transaction increases both an asset and a liability.

Assets	=	Liabilities	+	Stockholders' Equity
+ 8,000	=	+ 8,000	+	0

Assume the company's fiscal year ends each September 30. At year-end, the company must accrue interest expense at 10% for January through September:

	A	B	C	D
1	Sep 30	Interest Expense ($8,000 × 0.10 × 9/12)	600	
2		Interest Payable		600
3		*Accrual of interest expense at year-end.*		
4				

Liabilities increase and equity decreases because of the expense.

Assets	=	Liabilities	+	Stockholders' Equity	−	Expenses
0	=	+ 600				− 600

The balance sheet at year-end will report the Note Payable, Short-Term of $8,000 and the related Interest Payable of $600 as current liabilities. The income statement will report the $600 interest expense.

The following entry records the company's payment of the short-term note payable at maturity on January 1, 2019:

	A	B	C	D
1	2019			
2	Jan 1	Note Payable, Short-Term	8,000	
3		Interest Payable	600	
4		Interest Expense ($8,000 × 0.10 × 3/12)	200	
5		Cash [$8,000 + ($8,000 × 0.10)]		8,800
6		*Payment of a note payable and interest at maturity.*		
7				
8				

The debits zero out the short-term note payable as well as the interest payable account and also record the company's interest expense for October, November, and December.

Current Portion of Long-Term Debt. Recall that companies usually incur long-term debt to make long-term investments in assets such as property and equipment or equity investments in other companies. Long-term notes payable and bonds payable are examples of long-term debt, which we cover in Chapter 9. However, most long-term debt agreements are structured to be paid in installments. The **current portion of long-term debt** (also called *current maturity* or *current installment*) is the amount of the principal that is payable within one year (or operating cycle if longer). Because it's due in one year (or operating cycle if longer), the current portion is considered a short-term liability. At the end of each year, a company reclassifies (from long-term debt to a current liability) the portion of its long-term debt principal payments that must be paid in the next year.

Amazon.com, Inc. reported long-term debt in the amount of $7,694 million as of December 31, 2016 (line 16 on page 437). According to the financial statement footnotes (not shown), this debt consists of a series of long-term notes due in installments through the year 2044. The amount shown in the company's long-term liability section of its balance sheet excludes the current maturities of these notes, which amounted to $1,056 million at December 31, 2016. So, the total amount of long-term debt was actually $8,750 million ($7,694 million + $1,056 million). However, the current portion of the debt was reclassified into current liabilities and included in the "accrued expenses and other" current liabilities line item (which totaled $13,739 million at December 31, 2016).

ACCOUNT FOR ACCRUED LIABILITIES AND UNEARNED REVENUE

4 Account for accrued liabilities and unearned revenue

As we discussed in Chapter 3, the accrual method of accounting requires that expenses be recognized as they are incurred and matched against revenues earned in the same period. Liabilities associated with these expenses are called **accrued liabilities**. Some accrued liabilities such as sales taxes and commissions are incurred at the point of sale and must be recognized in the same period as those sales are made. Other liabilities such as accrued salaries and rent are recognized at the end of a period in the form of adjustments to the financial statements.

Amazon.com includes accrued liabilities in a current liability line item called "accrued expenses and other." The amount of this account is $13,739 million at December 31, 2016, which is the company's second-largest liability classification. According to footnote 1, "accrued expenses and other" includes liabilities for "unredeemed gift cards, leases and asset retirement obligations, current debt, acquired digital media content, and other operating expenses."[1] We will discuss the following as examples of accrued liabilities:

- Sales taxes payable
- Payroll liabilities (salaries and wages, payroll taxes)
- Accrued Warranties Payable

[1] Data from the U.S. Securities and Exchange Commission EDGAR Company filings, www.sec.gov.

Sales Taxes Payable. Most states levy a sales tax on retail sales. Retailers collect the tax from customers and thus owe the state for the sales tax collected. Suppose one Saturday's sales at a **Home Depot** store totaled $200,000 (assume this is all in cash). Home Depot collected an additional 5% ($10,000) of sales tax. The store would record that day's sales as follows:

	A	B	C
1	Cash ($200,000 × 1.05)	210,000	
2	Sales Revenue		200,000
3	Sales Tax Payable ($200,000 × 0.05)		10,000
4	*To record cash sales and the related sales tax.*		
5			

Assets, liabilities, and equity all increase—equity because of the revenues:

Assets	=	Liabilities	+	Stockholders' Equity	+	Revenues
+ 210,000	=	+ 10,000				+ 200,000

Within a day or two, the $10,000 liability to the state government will be paid by issuing a check to the state treasurer. That will leave just the $200,000 increase in cash and the $200,000 in revenue on Home Depot's books.

Payroll Liabilities. **Payroll**, also called *employee compensation*, is a major operating expense.

For service organizations—such as law firms, real estate companies, and airlines—compensation is *the* major operating expense, just as cost of goods sold is the largest expense for a merchandising company.

Employee compensation takes many different forms. A *salary* is employee pay stated at a monthly or yearly rate. A *wage* is employee pay stated at an hourly rate. Sales employees earn a *commission*, which is a percentage of the sales the employee has made. A *bonus* is an amount over and above regular compensation. Accounting for all forms of compensation follows the pattern illustrated below (using assumed figures):

	A	B	C
1	Salary Expense	10,000	
2	Employee Income Tax Payable		1,200
3	FICA Tax Payable		800
4	Salary Payable [take-home pay]		8,000
5	*To record salary expense.*		
6			

Salary Expense represents *gross pay* (that is, employee pay before subtractions for taxes and other deductions). Salary Expense creates several payroll liabilities:

- *Employee Income Tax Payable* is the employees' income tax that has been withheld from paychecks.
- *FICA Tax Payable* includes the employees' Social Security tax and Medicare tax, which also are withheld from paychecks. (FICA stands for the Federal Insurance Contributions Act, which created the Social Security tax. The rate for FICA is currently 6.2% of gross salaries and wages up to $127,200 per person. In addition, employees must pay 1.45% of their gross salaries as Medicare tax.)
- *Salary Payable* is employees' net (take-home) pay.

Companies must also pay some *employer* payroll taxes and expenses for employee benefits. For example, employers must match employee contributions for FICA and Medicare taxes. Employers must contribute a certain percentage of the gross salaries and wages they pay to their employees to federal and state governments for unemployment insurance. Accounting for these expenses is similar to the illustration above.

Every expense accrual, including payroll, has the same effect: Liabilities increase and equity decreases because of the expense. The accounting equation shows these effects for our payroll example:

Assets	=	Liabilities	+	Stockholders' Equity	−	Expenses
		+ 1,200				− 10,000
0	=	+ 800				
		+ 8,000				

Accrued Warranties Payable. Many companies provide warranties with their products. A *warranty* guarantees that a company will repair or replace a product or provide a refund for it if it is found to be defective within a certain period of time. Automobile companies—like **General Motors, BMW**, and **Toyota**—accrue liabilities for estimated vehicle warranties. Amazon.com warranties its own products such as Kindle readers and Echo devices.

Regardless of the warranty period, the expense recognition (matching) principle requires a company to record the *warranty expense* for a product in the same period that the business records the product's sales revenue. After all, the warranty motivates customers to buy products, so the company must record the warranty expenses related to the products when they are sold. At the time of the sale, however, the company doesn't know which products are defective. The exact amount of warranty expense cannot be known with certainty, so the business must estimate warranty expense and the related accrued liability.

Suppose that this year, **Black & Decker**, which manufactures power tools, made sales of \$100,000 subject to product warranties. Assume that in past years between 2% and 4% of products were defective. Black & Decker could estimate that 3% of sales will require replacement of the items. In this case, Black & Decker would estimate its warranty expense to be \$3,000 (\$100,000 × 0.03) for the year and make the following accrual entry:

A1

	A	B	C	D
1		Warranty Expense	3,000	
2		Accrued Warranties Payable		3,000
3		*To accrue warranty expense.*		
4				

Accrued Warranties Payable

	3,000

However, suppose the defects add up to only \$2,800. Black & Decker will replace the defective products and then record the following entry:

A1

	A	B	C	D
1		Accrued Warranties Payable	2,800	
2		Inventory		2,800
3		*To replace defective products sold under warranty.*		
4				

Accrued Warranties Payable

2,800	3,000
	Bal 200

At the end of the year, Black & Decker will report Accrued Warranties Payable of $200 as a current liability. The income statement reports Warranty Expense of $3,000 for the year. Then, next year Black & Decker will repeat this process. The Accrued Warranties Payable account probably won't ever zero out. If Black & Decker paid cash to satisfy the warranty, then the credit would be to Cash rather than to Inventory.

Unearned Revenues. *Unearned revenues* are also called *deferred revenues* or *revenues collected in advance*. These are cash amounts a business has received from customers before earning the revenue. In other words, unearned revenues represent prepayments by customers for goods and services. When the cash is collected, the company incurs a liability—an obligation to provide goods or services to the customer—in the future.

According to its selected balance sheet data on page 437, Amazon.com, Inc. had $4,768 million of unearned revenue as of December 31, 2016, compared with $3,118 million as of December 31, 2015. Footnote 1 (Accounting policies) describes the contents of Amazon.com's unearned revenue as follows: "Unearned revenue is recorded when payments are received in advance of performing our service obligations and is recognized over the service period. Unearned revenue primarily relates to prepayments of Amazon Prime memberships and AWS (Amazon Web Service) services."[2]

Suppose that on June 30, 2018, Amazon.com collected $3 million for one-year memberships to Amazon Prime. The company records the cash collection and related liability as follows:

A1

	A	B	C	D
1	2018			
2	June 30	Cash	3,000,000	
3		Unearned Revenue		3,000,000
4		*Received cash in advance for 1-year memberships*		
5		*to Amazon Prime.*		
6				

Unearned Revenue

	3,000,000

On December 31, Amazon.com needs to recognize that one-half of the one-year service period has passed, and thus, one-half of the revenue should be recorded. Therefore, the company will record the following adjusting journal entry to recognize the service revenue that has been earned.

A1

	A	B	C	D
1	2018			
2	Dec 31	Unearned Revenue	1,500,000	
3		Service Revenue ($3 million × 1/2)		1,500,000
4		*Earned revenue that was collected in advance.*		
5				

Unearned Revenue

1,500,000	3,000,000
	Bal 1,500,000

Service Revenue

	1,500,000

[2] Data from the U.S. Securities and Exchange Commission EDGAR Company filings, www.sec.gov.

The liability decreases and the revenue increases.

At year-end, Amazon.com reports the following amounts:

- $1.5 million of Unearned Revenue on the balance sheet, and
- $1.5 million of Service Revenue on the income statement.

ACCOUNT FOR CONTINGENT LIABILITIES

5 Account for contingent liabilities

A **contingent liability** is a potential liability that depends on the future outcome of past events. Examples of contingent liabilities are future financial obligations that may arise because of lawsuits, tax disputes, or alleged violations of environmental protection laws. Although contingent liabilities can be classified as either current or long-term, we have chosen to cover contingent liabilities in this chapter, because accrued liabilities—one of the ways that a contingent liability may be accounted for—are covered here. Recall from Chapter 1 that the principle of representational faithfulness requires that companies disclose their financial positions and operational results in a way that is as transparent and complete as possible. With liabilities, that principle implies: "When in doubt, disclose the liability. When necessary, accrue the liability." The Financial Accounting Standards Board (FASB) provides these guidelines to account for contingent liabilities:

1. *Accrue* (i.e., make an adjusting journal entry for) a contingent liability if, in management's opinion, it is probable that the loss (or expense) will occur and that the amount of the loss can be reasonably estimated. For example, if a company determines it will probably lose a lawsuit and have to pay estimated damages of $1 million, the business would accrue the liability.
2. *Disclose* a contingency in a financial statement note if it is reasonably possible (less than probable but more than remote) that a loss (or expense) will occur. Lawsuits in progress are a prime example. Probable loss contingencies that cannot be reasonably estimated should also be disclosed.

   The following is a note Amazon.com included in its 2016 financial statements to report a contingent liability from an ongoing patent infringement lawsuit it was involved in:

Note 7. Commitments and Contingencies (Legal Proceedings)

The Company is subject to various legal proceedings [...] including [...] In May 2009, Big Baboon, Inc. filed a complaint against Amazon.com, Inc. and Amazon Payments, Inc. for patent infringement in the United States District Court for the Central District of California. The complaint alleges, among other things, that our third-party selling and payments technology infringes patents owned by Big Baboon, Inc. ... and seeks injunctive relief, monetary damages, treble damages, costs, and attorneys' fees. In February 2011, the court entered an order staying the lawsuit pending the outcome of the United States Patent and Trademark Office's re-examination of the patent. We dispute the allegations of wrongdoing and intend to defend ourselves vigorously in this matter. The outcomes of our legal proceedings are inherently unpredictable, subject to significant uncertainties, and could be material to our operating results and cash flows for a particular period. In addition, for some matters for which a loss is probable or reasonably possible, an estimate of the amount of loss or range of losses is not possible and we may be unable to estimate the possible loss or range of losses that could potentially result from the application of non-monetary remedies.

Source: Data from the U.S. Securities and Exchange Commission EDGAR Company Filings, www.sec.gov

3. There is no need to report a contingent loss that is unlikely to occur. Instead, wait until an actual transaction clears up the situation. For example, suppose **Del Monte Foods**, a U.S. company, grows vegetables in Nicaragua, and the Nicaraguan government threatens to confiscate the assets of all foreign companies. Del Monte will report nothing about the contingency if the probability of a loss is considered remote.

GLOBAL VIEW

Contingent Liabilities. The IFRS accounting standard for contingent liabilities contains different language and different requirements than U.S. GAAP. Under IFRS, the term *contingency* is defined as a possible obligation that arises from a past event and whose existence will be confirmed only by the occurrence or nonoccurrence of one or more future events that are beyond the control of a business. Because, by definition, they are only "possible," contingencies are considered less than 50% likely to occur. They are not accrued, but only disclosed in a company's financial statement footnotes.

If it is "more likely than not" (i.e., greater than a 50% probability) that an obligation is going to arise, and if an estimate can be made of the amount, IFRS requires that a "provision" be recorded by making an accrual journal entry. Therefore, the circumstances for the accrual of possible obligations are slightly different under IFRS than under U.S. GAAP. Further details on this concept are covered in more advanced accounting texts. Appendix D summarizes the differences between the two standards and is cross-referenced by chapter.

Volkswagen Cooks its Engines

Volkswagen AG, based in Germany, manufactures the iconic Beetle in addition to other models including the Passat and the Jetta, as well as **Audi** and **Porsche** vehicles. In 2015, Volkswagen was caught by the U.S. Environmental Protection Agency (EPA) rigging its emissions testing on about 500,000 2.0-liter four-cylinder diesel models in the United States and an estimated 11 million models worldwide. The EPA has since cited approximately 85,000 2009–2016 models fitted with 3.0-liter V6 diesel engines from Audi, Porsche, and Volkswagen, all owned by Volkswagen AG, as not complying with emissions regulations.

The software in these cars is programmed to detect if the car is undergoing emissions testing by monitoring the car's speed, its engine operation, air pressure in the engine area, and the position of the steering wheel. If the software detects a "testing" situation, the software adjusts engine performance to be within emissions tolerances, causing the emissions to be much lower than with normal engine performance. If the car were to be driven using the lower adjustments, its driving performance would be greatly reduced. These emissions adjustments are not minor. The offending engines emit nitrogen oxide pollutants up to 40 times above what is allowed in the United States.

In the United States, Volkswagen, AG has reached settlements with federal officials to fix or buy back all affected vehicles, on top of compensating owners for having misled them about their cars' emissions. In June 2016, the company stated it would spend about $10 billion to buy back the roughly 475,000 Volkswagens and Audi A3 models that have 2-liter engines. The company also agreed to fix or buy back 80,000 vehicles with 3-liter engines. It will try to fix a majority of those to be compliant with emissions standards, but some owners will be offered a buyback option outright. VW agreed to buy back or fix affected vehicles by December 2018. The Environmental Protection Agency (EPA) in the United States has the power to fine the company $37,500 for each vehicle that does not meet emissions standards. Additionally, the Internal Revenue Service (IRS) can fine VW for the tax credits that were awarded to car purchasers (the cars originally qualified for certain fuel-efficiency credits, but would not meet the tax credit standards with the true emissions levels). In October 2016, Volkswagen reached a settlement agreement with the EPA that gives owners the option of having their cars repaired or, if not satisfied, the company will repurchase the cars. In addition, in January 2017, six high-level Volkswagen employees were indicted by a grand jury for criminal misconduct. The company admitted criminal wrongdoing. Over 2015 and 2016, provisions for costs related to penalties and vehicle repairs have reached €22.6 billion ($25.3 billion).

The potential costs are still mounting. VW is facing multiple class action lawsuits. Some of these lawsuits are seeking damages from the reduced resale value of VW cars affected by the emissions scandal. Others are related to reduced efficiency and increased ecological footprints of the vehicles. The Federal Bureau of Investigation (FBI) has opened a criminal probe of the VW emissions matter. In addition, several European regulatory agencies are investigating VW for violations.

Questions

1. Volkswagen AG's financial statements are governed by IFRS rather than U.S. GAAP. How does the IFRS definition of *contingent liability* differ from the definition contained in U.S. GAAP?
2. Sort the facts as you read them in the VW emissions scandal into two categories: (a) those that are probable and (b) those that are not. (For the purpose of this question, *probable* is defined as "more likely than not," which means that the chance is more than 50% that this contingent event will occur.) For those facts in category (a), what will the company have to do? For those facts in category (b), what will the company have to do?

Answers

1. Under IFRS, contingent liabilities are recorded if they meet the test of "more likely than not to occur." If a potential liability reaches the level of "more likely than not" (greater than a 50% probability) and if the amount is estimable, the company has to record a "provision" for the liability (i.e., accrue the liability). Under U.S. GAAP, "probable" has a significantly higher threshold than IFRS's threshold of "more likely than not." As a result, fewer contingencies are accrued under U.S. GAAP than IFRS.
2. (a) The company rigged the computers on many of its vehicles to falsely adjust engine performance in "testing mode" to make it seem that the company was in compliance with emissions guidelines. When out of "testing mode" the computer adjusted engine settings to make the cars perform better and get better mileage, but not in compliance with emissions guidelines. It is more likely than not that the company will incur losses for vehicle repairs, vehicle buybacks and penalties. As a result, the company has accrued "provisions" for losses in the amount of €22.6 billion (about $25.3 billion) spread between the company's 2015 and 2016 financial statements. (b) Additional civil and criminal penalties may occur in the future as a result of ongoing class action investigations, as well as those of the FBI, IRS, and various other governmental agencies worldwide. The outcome of these investigations as well as the estimated future costs to the company are still unknown. The company has disclosed these facts as "contingencies" in the footnotes to its financial statements (labeled "the diesel matter"), and will have to continue to do so for several years to come.

End-of-Chapter | Summary Problem

Assume that the **Estée Lauder Companies, Inc.**, faced the following liability situations at June 30, 2018, the end of the company's fiscal year. Show how Estée Lauder would report these liabilities on its balance sheet at June 30, 2018.

a. Salary expense for the last payroll period of the year was $900,000. Of this amount, employees' withheld income tax totaled $88,000 and FICA taxes were $61,000. These amounts will be paid in early July.

b. The company estimates that its warranty expense for the fiscal year will be 2% of its $400 million in sales. One year ago, at June 30, 2017, Accrued Warranty Payable stood at $3 million. Warranty payments were $9 million during the year ended June 30, 2018.

c. The company pays royalties on its purchased trademarks. Royalties for the trademarks are equal to a percentage of Estée Lauder's sales. Assume that the company's $400 million in sales for fiscal year 2018 were subject to a royalty rate of 3%. At June 30, 2018, Estée Lauder owes two-thirds of the year's royalty, to be paid in July.

d. Long-term debt, outstanding since 2016, totaled $100 million and is payable in annual installments of $10 million each. The interest rate on the debt is 7%, and the interest is paid each December 31.

e. The company recognizes a contingent liability for additional federal income taxes due to ongoing IRS audits of the company's 2016 and 2017 corporate income tax returns conducted in 2018. As of the date of issuance of the 2018 financial statements, the IRS audits are incomplete. The company's management estimates that it is possible that additional amounts of income taxes will be due pending the eventual outcome of these audits, but is unable to make an estimate of the amounts. However, the amounts are not expected to be material to the company's financial position or results of operations for 2018.

Answer

Liabilities at June 30, 2018:	
a. Current liabilities:	
Salary payable ($900,000 − $88,000 − $61,000)	$ 751,000
Employee income tax payable	88,000
FICA tax payable	61,000
b. Current liabilities:	
Accrued warranty payable	2,000,000
[$3,000,000 + ($400,000,000 × 0.02) − $9,000,000]	
c. Current liabilities:	
Royalties payable ($400,000,000 × 0.03 × 2/3)	8,000,000
d. Current liabilities:	
Current installment of long-term debt	10,000,000
Interest payable ($100,000,000 × 0.07 × 6/12)	3,500,000
Long-term debt ($100,000,000 − $10,000,000)	90,000,000
e. The company will add a footnote to its 2018 financial statements explaining the IRS audits, the fact that as of the date of issuance of the 2018 financial statements, the audits are incomplete, and the fact that the amount of additional income tax liability is not expected to be material to the company's financial position as of June 30, 2018.	

REVIEW | Current and Contingent Liabilities

Accounting Vocabulary

accounts payable turnover (page 438) The number of times per year a company pays off its accounts payable.

contingent liability (p. 445) A potential liability that depends on the future outcome of past events.

current portion of long-term debt (p. 441) The amount of the principal of a long-term note that is payable within one year (or operating cycle if longer).

days' payable outstanding (DPO) (p. 439) Accounts payable turnover expressed in days (365/accounts payable turnover).

payroll (p. 442) Employee compensation, a major expense of many businesses

short-term notes payable (p. 440) Notes payable that are due within one year (or operating cycle if longer).

Quick Check (Answers are given on page 467.)

1. All of the following are reported as current liabilities except:

a. interest payable.
b. bonds payable due in 18 months.
c. salaries payable.
d. sales tax payable.

2. Which of the following is *not* a liability?

a. Income taxes payable
b. Accrued warranties payable
c. Accrued vacation pay
d. Allowance for bad debts

3. Accounts payable turnover for Blue Industries increased from 10 to 12 during 2018. Which of the following statements best describes what this means?

a. The company paid its accounts payable more quickly in 2018, signaling a stronger liquidity position.
b. The company paid its accounts payable more slowly in 2018, signaling a weaker liquidity position.
c. Inventory turned over faster in 2018, meaning sales increased.
d. Not enough information is provided to form a conclusion.

4. What is accounts payable turnover?

a. Purchases on account divided by average accounts payable
b. A measure of liquidity
c. A measure of the number of times a year a company is able to pay its accounts payable
d. All of the listed answers are correct.

5. Edger & Company has an accounts payable turnover of 5.6, while Salerno Industries has an accounts payable turnover of 8.9. Which company is more liquid?

a. Edger & Company
b. Salerno Industries
c. Both are equally liquid.
d. Unknown because accounts payable turnover is not a measure of liquidity.

6. Nicholas Corporation accrues the interest expense on a short-term note payable at the end of its fiscal year. Due to this transaction

a. current liabilities will decrease and stockholders' equity will decrease.
b. current liabilities will increase and stockholders' equity will decrease.
c. current liabilities will increase and current assets will increase.
d. current liabilities will increase and stockholders' equity will increase.

7. Phoebe Corporation signed a six-month note payable on October 23, 2018. What accounts relating to the note payable will be reported on its financial statements for the fiscal year ending December 31, 2018?

a. Notes payable and interest payable will be reported on the balance sheet.
b. Notes payable will be reported on the balance sheet and interest payable will be reported on the income statement.
c. Notes payable, interest payable, and interest expense will be reported on the balance sheet.
d. Interest receivable will be reported on the balance sheet and notes payable will be reported on the income statement.

8. The current pay period ends on Friday, January 2, yet the company's fiscal year-end is on Wednesday, December 31. If the company does not make the proper adjusting entry to accrue payroll expenses at year-end, what would be the impact?

a. Assets will be understated.
b. Operating income will be overstated.
c. Stockholders' equity will be understated.
d. Liabilities will be overstated.

9. Backpack Co. was organized to sell a single product that carries a 45-day warranty against defects. Engineering estimates indicate that 2% of the units sold will prove defective and require an average repair cost of $60 per unit. During Backpack's first month of operations, total sales were 900 units; by the end of the month, five defective units had been repaired. The liability for product warranties at month-end should be

a. $1,380.
b. $300.
c. $1,080.
d. $780.

10. When a company receives cash from customers before earning the revenue, __________ will be credited.

a. accounts receivable
b. estimated cash
c. unearned revenue
d. accounts payable

11. Potential liabilities that depend on future events arising out of past events are called

a. contingent liabilities.
b. estimated liabilities.
c. current liabilities.
d. long-term liabilities.

12. A contingent liability should be recorded in the accounts

a. if the amount can be reasonably estimated.
b. if the amount is due in cash within one year.
c. if the related future event will probably occur.
d. both b and c
e. both a and c

Excel Project
Autograded Excel Project available at **MyLab Accounting**

ASSESS YOUR PROGRESS

Ethics Check

EC8-1. Identify ethical principle violated

For each of the situations listed, identify which of three principles (integrity, objectivity and independence, or due care) from the AICPA Code of Professional Conduct is violated. Assume all persons listed in the situations are members of the AICPA. (Note: Refer to the AICPA Code of Professional Conduct contained on pages 25–27 in Chapter 1 for descriptions of the principles.)

a. Lance recently graduated with an accounting degree and found a job in the payables department of Sawyer Sneaker Company. Lance is in charge of adjusting entries for accrued liabilities that have been paid, but he does not remember how to treat these entries because he has not seen them since one of his courses from his junior year in college. Lance assumes the accrued liabilities for this month are the same amounts as last month so he does not enter in the new accrual entries for this month and does not reverse last month's entries.

b. Frankie Candle Co. is a small, family-owned company that only employs one accountant, Jenny. Since Jenny is in charge of all areas of accounting and knows she will not get caught, she decides to create fictitious accounts payable entries at Frankie Candle Co. for the company she owns, Candle Supply Inc.

c. April is a newly hired auditor for Penny & Blake, a CPA firm. Her father owns E&E Veterinary Supply. April is excited to be assigned to work on the account of E&E since she understands the business well from working part-time during summers there when she was growing up. April does not disclose that her father owns E&E because she knows she will not have any bias.

d. Anne works in the payables department of Yellow Steel, Inc. She noticed that her company's current ratio is a little lower than the industry average. In an attempt to improve the current ratio, she decides not to accrue wages payable for this month.

Short Exercises

S8-1. ***(Learning Objective 1: Identify the current liabilities associated with operating activities)*** LO 1
Identify the current liability associated with each of the following operating activities:

1. Perform work on a warranty claim
2. Pay income taxes
3. Purchase supplies
4. Pay payroll taxes
5. Borrow money for operations using a short-term note
6. Process cash received in advance from customers
7. Purchase inventory
8. Pay employee salaries

S8-2. ***(Learning Objective 2: Calculate purchases by analyzing inventory account activity)*** LO 2
On Willow Grove Department Stores' most recent balance sheet, the balance of its inventory at the beginning of the year was $12,000. At the end of the year, the inventory balance was $14,500. During that year, its cost of goods sold was $55,000. All purchases of inventory throughout the year were on account. What was the total of Willow Grove's purchases during the year?

S8-3. ***(Learning Objective 2: Calculate days' payable outstanding)*** The balance of Landy Corporation's accounts payable at the beginning of the most recent year was $50,000. At the end of the year, the accounts payable balance was $54,000. Landy's sales revenue for the year was $3,105,000, while its cost of goods sold for the year was $1,508,000. Calculate Landy's days' payable outstanding (DPO) for the year. Assume inventory levels are constant throughout the year. If the credit terms from Landy's suppliers are n/30, how would you interpret Landy's DPO? LO 2

S8-4. ***(Learning Objective 3: Account for a short-term note payable)*** On June 1, 2019, Franklin Company purchased inventory costing $90,000 by signing an 8%, nine-month, short-term note payable. Franklin will pay the entire note (principal and interest) on the note's maturity date. Journalize the company's (a) purchase of inventory and (b) accrual of interest on the note payable on December 31, 2019. LO 3

S8-5. ***(Learning Objective 3: Account for a short-term note payable)*** Jamison Sports Authority purchased inventory costing $25,000 by signing a 12%, six-month, short-term note payable. The purchase occurred on January 1, 2018. Jamison will pay the entire note (principal and interest) on the note's maturity date of July 1, 2018. Journalize the company's (a) purchase of inventory and (b) payment of the note plus interest on July 1, 2018. LO 3

S8-6. ***(Learning Objective 4: Account for warranty expense and accrued warranty payable)*** LO 4
North Boulder USA, a tire manufacturer, guarantees its tires against defects for five years or 60,000 miles, whichever comes first. Suppose North Boulder USA can expect warranty costs during the five-year period to add up to 3% of sales. Assume that a North Boulder USA dealer in Denver, Colorado, made sales of $641,000 during 2018. North Boulder USA received cash for 15% of the sales and took notes receivable for the remainder. Payments to satisfy customer warranty claims totaled $18,500 during 2018.

1. Record the sales, warranty expense, and warranty payments for North Boulder USA. Ignore cost of goods sold.
2. Post to the Accrued Warranty Payable T-account. The beginning balance was $14,000. At the end of 2018, how much in accrued warranty payable does North Boulder USA owe to its customers?

S8-7. ***(Learning Objective 4: Report warranties in the financial statements)*** Refer to the data given in S8-6. What amount of warranty expense will North Boulder USA report during 2018? Which accounting principle addresses this situation? Does the warranty expense for the year equal the year's cash payments for warranties? Explain the relevant accounting principle as it applies to measuring warranty expense. LO 4

LO 4

S8-8. ***(Learning Objective 4: Account for accrued payroll)*** Fitzgerald Company pays its employees every other Friday. December 31, 2017, was a Sunday. On Friday, January 5, 2018, Fitzgerald paid wages of $112,000, which covered the 14-day period from December 20, 2017, through January 2, 2018. Wages were earned evenly across all days, including Saturdays and Sundays. Employee income taxes withheld for this payroll period totaled $15,610, while the FICA tax withheld was $12,600. (Ignore the employer payroll taxes in this exercise.) Prepare the entry to accrue the company's wages and payroll taxes at December 31, 2017.

LO 5

S8-9. ***(Learning Objective 5: Interpret a company's contingent liabilities)*** Martinson Cycles, Inc., a motorcycle manufacturer, included the following note in its annual report:

NOTES TO CONSOLIDATED FINANCIAL STATEMENTS
7 (In Part): **Commitments and Contingencies**
The Company self-insures its product liability losses in the United States up to $3.8 million (catastrophic coverage is maintained for individual claims in excess of $3.8 million up to $26.3 million). Outside the United States, the Company is insured for product liability up to $26.3 million per individual claim and in the aggregate.

1. Why are these *contingent* (versus *real*) liabilities?
2. In the United States, how can the contingent liability become a real liability for Martinson? What are the limits to the company's product liabilities in the United States?
3. How can a contingency outside the United States become a real liability for the company? How does Martinson's potential liability differ for claims outside the United States?

Exercises

Group A

LO 1, 2

E8-10A. ***(Learning Objectives 1, 2: Analyze current and long-term liabilities; evaluate accounts payable turnover)*** EnviroFriend Structures, Inc., builds environmentally sensitive structures. The company's 2018 revenues totaled $2,780 million. At December 31, 2018, and 2017, the company had, respectively, $656 million and $591 million in current assets. The December 31, 2018, and 2017, balance sheets and income statements reported the following amounts:

A1

	A	B	C
1	**At year-end (In millions)**	**2018**	**2017**
2	Liabilities and stockholders' equity		
3	Current liabilities		
4	Accounts payable	$ 148	$ 184
5	Accrued expenses	149	177
6	Accrued employee compensation and benefits	14	30
7	Current portion of long-term debt	3	20
8	Total current liabilities	314	411
9	Long-term debt	1,485	1,313
10	Post-retirement benefits payable	134	131
11	Other liabilities	5	23
12	Total stockholders' equity	1,844	1,584
13	Total liabilities and stockholders' equity	$ 3,782	$ 3,462
14	Year-end (in millions)		
15	Cost of goods sold	$ 2,656	$ 2,046
16			

Requirements

1. Describe each of EnviroFriend Structures, Inc.'s, liabilities and state how the liability arose.
2. What were the company's total assets at December 31, 2018?
3. Assume that beginning and ending inventories for both periods did not differ by a material amount. Accounts payable at the end of 2016 was $188 million. Calculate accounts payable turnover as a ratio and days' payable outstanding (DPO) for 2017 and 2018. Calculate current ratios for 2017 and 2018 as well. Evaluate whether the company improved or deteriorated from the standpoint of its ability to cover accounts payable and current liabilities over the year.

E8-11A. ***(Learning Objective 2: Analyze accounts payable turnover)*** Wicker Sales, Inc.'s, comparative income statements and balance sheets show the following selected information for 2017 and 2018: LO 2

	2018	2017
Cost of goods sold	$2,850,000	$2,900,000
Ending inventory	$ 650,000	$ 400,000
Beginning inventory	$ 400,000	$ 250,000
Average accounts payable	$ 285,000	$ 240,000

Requirements

1. Calculate the company's accounts payable turnover and days' payable outstanding (DPO) for 2017 and 2018.
2. On the basis of this computation alone, has the company's liquidity position improved or deteriorated during 2018?

E8-12A. ***(Learning Objective 3: Purchase inventory, accrue interest, and pay a short-term note)*** On August 1, 2019, The Shoppes at Mill Lake, Inc., purchased inventory costing $40,000 by signing a 6%, six-month, short-term note payable. The company will pay the entire note (principal and interest) on the note's maturity date. LO 3

Requirements

1. Journalize the company's purchase of inventory.
2. Make the adjusting entry for accrual of interest on the note payable on December 31, 2019.
3. At December 31, 2019, what is reported on the balance sheet related to this note payable?
4. Record the payment of the note payable (principal and interest) on its maturity date.

E8-13A. ***(Learning Objective 3: Record note payable transactions)*** Dean Sales Company completed the following note payable transactions: LO 3

2018	
Jul 1	Purchased delivery truck costing $58,000 by issuing a one-year, 4% note payable.
Dec 31	Accrued interest on the note payable.
2019	
Jul 1	Paid the note payable at maturity.

Requirements

1. How much interest expense must be accrued at December 31, 2018? (Round your answer to the nearest whole dollar.)
2. Determine the amount of Dean Sales' final payment on July 1, 2019.
3. How much interest expense will Dean Sales report for 2018 and for 2019? (If needed, round your answer to the nearest whole dollar.)

LO 3 **E8-14A.** ***(Learning Objective 3: Account for a short-term note payable)*** Quimby Sports Authority purchased inventory costing $30,000 by signing a 6% short-term, one-year note payable. The purchase occurred on July 31, 2018. Quimby pays annual interest each year on July 31. Journalize the company's (a) purchase of inventory; (b) accrual of interest expense on April 30, 2019, which is the company's fiscal year-end; and (c) payment of the note plus interest on July 31, 2019. (Round your answers to the nearest whole number.) (d) Show what the company would report for liabilities on its balance sheet at April 30, 2019, and on its income statement for the year ended on that date.

LO 4 **E8-15A.** ***(Learning Objective 4: Account for warranty expense and the related liability)*** The accounting records of Artie's Appliances included the following balances at the end of the period:

Accrued Warranty Payable		Sales Revenue		Warranty Expense	
	Beg bal 3,500		110,000		

In the past, Artie's warranty expense has been 8% of sales. During the current period, the business paid $7,500 to satisfy the warranty claims.

Requirements

1. Journalize Artie's warranty expense for the period and the company's cash payments to satisfy warranty claims. Explanations are not required.
2. Show what Artie's will report on its income statement and balance sheet for this situation at the end of the period.
3. Which data item from requirement 2 will affect the current ratio? Will Artie's current ratio increase or decrease due to this item?

LO 4 **E8-16A.** ***(Learning Objective 4: Record and report current liabilities)*** Travis Publishing completed the following transactions for one subscriber during 2018:

Oct 1	Sold a one-year subscription, collecting cash of $1,800, plus sales tax of 10%. The subscription will begin on October 1.
Nov 15	Remitted (paid) the sales tax to the state of South Carolina.
Dec 31	Made the necessary adjustment at year-end.

Requirement

1. Journalize these transactions (explanations not required). Then report any liability on the company's balance sheet at December 31, 2018.

LO 4 **E8-17A.** ***(Learning Objective 4: Account for payroll expense and liabilities)*** Key West has an annual payroll of $150,000. In addition, the company incurs payroll tax expense of 10% of the annual payroll. At December 31, Key West owes salaries of $8,000 and FICA and other payroll tax of $1,000. The company will pay these amounts early next year. Show what Key West will report for the foregoing on its income statement for the year and on its year-end balance sheet.

LO 1, 2, 3, 4 **E8-18A.** ***(Learning Objectives 1, 2, 3, 4: Report current and long-term liabilities)*** Robson Electronics completed these selected transactions during March 2018:

a. Sales of $2,050,000 are subject to an accrued warranty cost of 9%. The accrued warranty payable at the beginning of the year was $32,000, and warranty payments for the year totaled $53,000.

b. On March 1, Robson Electronics signed a $55,000 note payable that requires annual payments of $11,000 plus 3% interest on the unpaid balance beginning March 1, 2019.

c. Barnard, Inc., a chain of discount stores, ordered $125,000 worth of wireless speakers and related products. With its order, Barnard, Inc., sent a check for $125,000 in advance, and Robson shipped $90,000 of the goods. Robson will ship the remainder of the goods on April 3, 2018.

d. Robson's March payroll of $280,000 is subject to employee withheld income tax of $30,500 and FICA tax of 7.65%. On March 31, Robson pays employees their take-home pay and accrues all tax amounts.

Requirement

1. Report these items on Robson Electronics' balance sheet at March 31, 2018.

E8-19A. ***(Learning Objective 5: Report a contingent liability)*** Pine Systems' revenues for 2018 totaled $27.1 million. As with most companies, Pine is a defendant in lawsuits related to its products. Note 14 of the Pine annual report for 2018 reported the following: LO **5**

> **14. Contingencies**
> The company is involved in various legal proceedings.... It is the Company's policy to accrue for amounts related to these legal matters if it is probable that a liability has been incurred and an amount is reasonably estimable.

Requirements

1. Suppose Pine's lawyers believe that a significant legal judgment against the company is reasonably possible. How should Pine report this situation in its financial statements?
2. Suppose Pine's lawyers believe it is probable that a $2.1 million judgment will be rendered against the company. In general terms, how would this situation be reported in Pine's financial statements (using U.S. GAAP)?

Group B

E8-20B. ***(Learning Objectives 1, 2: Analyze current and long-term liabilities; evaluate accounts payable turnover)*** Green Earth Homes, Inc., builds environmentally sensitive structures. The company's 2018 revenues totaled $2,770 million. At December 31, 2018, and 2017, the company had, respectively, $663 million and $613 million in current assets. The December 31, 2018, and 2017, balance sheets and income statements reported the following amounts: LO **1, 2**

	A	B	C
1	**At year-end (In millions)**	**2018**	**2017**
2	Liabilities and stockholders' equity		
3	Current liabilities		
4	Accounts payable	$ 110	$ 174
5	Accrued expenses	149	167
6	Accrued employee compensation and benefits	37	16
7	Current portion of long-term debt	12	4
8	Total current liabilities	308	361
9	Long-term debt	1,578	1,324
10	Post-retirement benefits payable	129	125
11	Other liabilities	18	19
12	Total stockholders' equity	2,420	1,273
13	Total liabilities and stockholders' equity	$ 4,453	$ 3,102
14	Year-end (in millions)		
15	Cost of goods sold	$ 1,704	$ 1,239
16			

Requirements

1. Describe each of Green Earth Homes, Inc.'s, liabilities and state how the liability arose.
2. What were the company's total assets at December 31, 2018?
3. Assume that beginning and ending inventories for both periods did not differ by a material amount. Accounts payable at the end of 2016 was $180 million. Calculate accounts payable turnover as a ratio and days' payable outstanding (DPO) for 2017 and 2018. Calculate current ratios for 2017 and 2018 as well. Evaluate whether the company improved or deteriorated from the standpoint of its ability to cover accounts payable and current liabilities over the year.

LO 2

E8-21B. ***(Learning Objective 2: Analyze accounts payable turnover)*** Barnacle Sales, Inc.'s, comparative income statements and balance sheets show the following selected information for 2017 and 2018:

	2018	2017
Cost of goods sold	$2,850,000	$2,700,000
Ending inventory	$ 800,000	$ 600,000
Beginning inventory	$ 600,000	$ 400,000
Average accounts payable	$ 305,000	$ 255,000

Requirements

1. Calculate the company's accounts payable turnover and days' payable outstanding (DPO) for 2017 and 2018.
2. On the basis of this computation alone, has the company's liquidity position improved or deteriorated during 2018?

LO 3

E8-22B. ***(Learning Objective 3: Purchase inventory, accrue interest, and pay a short-term note)*** On September 1, 2019, The Shoppes at Forest Lake, Inc., purchased inventory costing $63,000 by signing an 8%, six-month, short-term note payable. The company will pay the entire note (principal and interest) on the note's maturity date.

Requirements

1. Journalize the company's purchase of inventory.
2. Make the adjusting entry for accrual of interest on the note payable on December 31, 2019.
3. At December 31, 2019, what is reported on the balance sheet related to this note payable?
4. Record the payment of the note payable (principal and interest) on its maturity date.

LO 3

E8-23B. ***(Learning Objective 3: Record note payable transactions)*** Cape Cod Sales Company completed the following note payable transactions:

2018	
Apr 1	Purchased delivery truck costing $56,000 by issuing a one-year, 7% note payable.
Dec 31	Accrued interest on the note payable.
2019	
Apr 1	Paid the note payable at maturity.

Requirements

1. How much interest expense must be accrued at December 31, 2018? (Round your answer to the nearest whole dollar.)
2. Determine the amount of Cape Cod Sales' final payment on April 1, 2019.
3. How much interest expense will Cape Cod Sales report for 2018 and for 2019? (If needed, round your answer to the nearest whole dollar.)

LO 3

E8-24B. ***(Learning Objective 3: Account for a short-term note payable)*** Sherlock Sports Authority purchased inventory costing $30,000 by signing a 4%, short-term, one-year note payable. The purchase occurred on July 31, 2018. Sherlock pays annual interest each year on July 31. Journalize the company's (a) purchase of inventory; (b) accrual of interest expense on April 30, 2019, which is the company's fiscal year-end; and (c) payment of the note plus interest on July 31, 2019. (Round your answers to the nearest whole number.) (d) Show what the company would report for liabilities on its balance sheet at April 30, 2019, and on its income statement for the year ended on that date.

E8-25B. ***(Learning Objective 4: Account for warranty expense and the related liability)*** The accounting records of Carmen Appliances included the following balances at the end of the period: LO 4

Accrued Warranty Payable		Sales Revenue		Warranty Expense	
	Beg bal 5,500		104,000		

In the past, Carmen's warranty expense has been 8% of sales. During the current period, the business paid $7,500 to satisfy the warranty claims.

Requirements

1. Journalize Carmen's warranty expense for the period and the company's cash payments to satisfy warranty claims. Explanations are not required.
2. Show what Carmen will report on its income statement and balance sheet for this situation at the end of the period.
3. Which data item from requirement 2 will affect the current ratio? Will Carmen's current ratio increase or decrease due to this item?

E8-26B. ***(Learning Objective 4: Record and report current liabilities)*** Centennial Publishing completed the following transactions for one subscriber during 2018: LO 4

Oct 1	Sold a one-year subscription, collecting cash of $2,100, plus sales tax of 6%. The subscription will begin on October 1.
Nov 15	Remitted (paid) the sales tax to the state of Nebraska.
Dec 31	Made the necessary adjustment at year-end.

Requirement

1. Journalize these transactions (explanations not required). Then report any liability on the company's balance sheet at December 31, 2018.

E8-27B. ***(Learning Objective 4: Account for payroll expense and liabilities)*** Buckeye has an annual payroll of $170,000. In addition, the company incurs payroll tax expense of 9% of the annual payroll. At December 31, Buckeye owes salaries of $7,800 and FICA and other payroll tax of $850. The company will pay these amounts early next year. LO 4

Show what Buckeye will report for the foregoing on its income statement for the year and on its year-end balance sheet.

E8-28B. ***(Learning Objectives 1, 2, 3, 4: Report current and long-term liabilities)*** Western Electronics completed these selected transactions during March 2018: LO 1, 2, 3, 4

- **a.** Sales of $2,400,000 are subject to an accrued warranty cost of 9%. The accrued warranty payable at the beginning of the year was $37,000, and warranty payments for the year totaled $59,000.
- **b.** On March 1, Western signed a $20,000 note payable that requires annual payments of $4,000 plus 6% interest on the unpaid balance beginning March 1, 2019.
- **c.** Urban, Inc., a chain of discount stores, ordered $140,000 worth of wireless speakers and related products. With its order, Urban, Inc., sent a check for $140,000, and Western shipped $55,000 of the goods. Western will ship the remainder of the goods on April 3, 2018.
- **d.** Western's March payroll of $260,000 is subject to employee withheld income tax of $30,500 and FICA tax of 7.65%. On March 30, Western pays employees their take-home pay and accrues all tax amounts.

Requirement

1. Report these items on Western Electronics' balance sheet at March 31, 2018.

LO 5

E8-29B. ***(Learning Objective 5: Report a contingent liability)*** Diamond Security Systems' revenues for 2018 totaled $27.5 million. As with most companies, Diamond is a defendant in lawsuits related to its products. Note 14 of the Diamond annual report for 2018 reported the following:

> **14. Contingencies**
> The company is involved in various legal proceedings.... It is the Company's policy to accrue for amounts related to these legal matters if it is probable that a liability has been incurred and an amount is reasonably estimable.

Requirements

1. Suppose Diamond's lawyers believe that a significant legal judgment against the company is reasonably possible. How should Diamond report this situation in its financial statements?
2. Suppose Diamond's lawyers believe it is probable that a $2.8 million judgment will be rendered against the company. In general terms, how would this situation be reported in Diamond's financial statements (using U.S. GAAP)?

Quiz

Test your understanding of current liabilities by answering the following questions. Select the best choice from among the possible answers given.

Q8-30. Notes payable due in six months are reported as

a. current liabilities on the balance sheet.
b. current liabilities on the income statement.
c. contra-assets on the income statement.
d. long-term liabilities on the balance sheet.

Q8-31. For the purpose of classifying liabilities as current or noncurrent, the term *operating cycle* refers to

a. the time period between the date the sale is made and the date the related revenue is collected.
b. the time period between the purchase of merchandise and the conversion of this merchandise back to cash.
c. a period of one year.
d. the average time period between business recessions.

Q8-32. A company reports purchases of $388,000, a beginning accounts payable balance of $27,000, and an ending accounts payable balance of $48,000. All purchases were on account. The company's accounts payable turnover would be closest to:

a. 7.26
b. 8.33
c. 10.33
d. 14.06

Q8-33. Failure to accrue interest expense results in

a. an overstatement of net income and an understatement of liabilities.
b. an understatement of net income and an overstatement of liabilities.
c. an understatement of net income and an understatement of liabilities.
d. an overstatement of net income and an overstatement of liabilities.

Q8-34. Gravel Corporation borrowed $250,000 from a bank on January 1, 2019, by signing a 10%, six-month note. The journal entry made by Gravel on January 1, 2019, will debit

a. Interest Expense for $25,000 and credit Interest Payable for $25,000.
b. Cash for $225,000 and credit Notes Payable for $225,000.
c. Interest Expense for $25,000 and credit Cash for $25,000.
d. Cash for $250,000 and credit Notes Payable for $250,000.

Q8-35. Lexter Corporation borrows cash by signing a $90,000, 8%, eight-month note on December 1 with its local bank. The total cash paid for interest (only) at the maturity of the note by Lexter will be

a. $600.
b. $3,600.
c. $4,800.
d. $7,200.

Q8-36. Jackson Bank lends Jabbour Clothing Company $125,000 on September 1. Jabbour signs a $125,000, 6%, six-month note. The journal entry made by Jabbour on December 31, its fiscal year-end, is

a. debit Interest Payable and credit Interest Expense for $2,500.
b. debit Interest Expense and credit Interest Payable for $2,500.
c. debit Interest Payable and credit Cash for $2,500.
d. debit Interest Expense and credit Cash for $2,500.

Q8-37. Connors Company paid $700 cash to make a repair on equipment it sold under a one-year warranty in the prior year. The entry to record the payment will debit

a. Accrued Warranty Payable and credit Cash.
b. Operating Expense and credit Cash.
c. Warranty Expense and credit Cash.
d. Repair Expense and credit Cash.

Q8-38. Swisher Company sold inventory with a selling price of $5,000 to customers for cash. It also collected sales taxes of $250. The journal entry to record this information includes a

a. credit to Sales Tax Expense $250.
b. credit to Sales Revenue $5,250.
c. debit to Sales Tax Payable $250.
d. debit to Cash of $5,250.

Q8-39. Tennis Shoe Warehouse operates in a state with a 6.5% sales tax. For convenience, Tennis Shoe Warehouse credits Sales Revenue for the total amount (selling price plus sales tax) collected from each customer. If Tennis Shoe Warehouse fails to make an adjustment for sales taxes,

a. net income will be understated and liabilities will be overstated.
b. net income will be overstated and liabilities will be overstated.
c. net income will be overstated and liabilities will be understated.
d. net income will be understated and liabilities will be understated.

Q8-40. What kind of account is Unearned Revenue?

a. Liability account
b. Asset account
c. Expense account
d. Revenue account

Q8-41. An end-of-period adjusting entry that debits Unearned Revenue most likely will credit

a. a revenue.
b. an asset.
c. a liability.
d. an expense.

Q8-42. Blue Jay, Inc., manufactures and sells computer monitors with a three-year warranty. Warranty costs are expected to average 7% of sales during the warranty period. The following table shows the sales and actual warranty payments during the first two years of operations:

Year	Sales	Warranty Payments
2018	$650,000	$ 5,850
2019	850,000	42,500

Based on these facts, what amount of warranty liability should Blue Jay, Inc., report on its balance sheet at December 31, 2019?

a. $48,350
b. $56,650
c. $105,000
d. $42,500

Q8-43. Which of the following statements is false?

a. A contingent liability should be disclosed in the notes to the financial statements if there is a reasonable possibility that a loss (or expense) will occur.
b. All contingent liabilities should be reported as liabilities on the financial statements, even those that are unlikely to occur.
c. A contingent liability is a potential obligation that depends on the future outcome of past events.
d. A contingent liability should be accrued if the loss is probable and the amount of the loss can be reasonably estimated.

Problems MyLab Accounting

Group A

LO 1, 2, 3, 4

P8-44A. ***(Learning Objective 1, 2, 3, 4: Measure and report current liabilities)*** Sea Air Marine experienced these events during the current year.

a. December revenue totaled $120,000; and, in addition, Sea Air collected sales tax of 5%. The tax amount will be sent to the state of Florida early in January.

b. On August 31, Sea Air signed a six-month, 6% note payable to purchase a boat costing $86,000. The note requires payment of principal and interest at maturity.

c. On August 31, Sea Air received cash of $2,400 in advance for service revenue. This revenue will be earned evenly over six months.

d. Revenues of $850,000 were covered by Sea Air's service warranty. At January 1, accrued warranty payable was $11,800. During the year, Sea Air recorded warranty expense of $34,000 and paid warranty claims of $34,500.

e. Sea Air owes $90,000 on a long-term note payable. At December 31, 10% interest for the year plus $30,000 of this principal are payable within one year.

Requirement

1. For each item, indicate the account and the related amount to be reported as a current liability on the Sea Air Marine balance sheet at December 31.

LO 1, 2, 3, 4

P8-45A. ***(Learning Objective 1, 2, 3, 4: Record liability-related transactions)*** The following transactions of Smooth Sounds Music Company occurred during 2018 and 2019:

2018	
Mar 3	Purchased a piano (inventory) for $65,000, signing a six-month, 8% note payable.
May 31	Borrowed $105,000 on an 6% one-year note payable.
Sep 3	Paid the six-month, 8% note at maturity.
Dec 31	Accrued warranty expense, which is estimated at 1.5% of sales of $193,000.
31	Accrued interest on the outstanding note payable.
2019	
May 31	Paid the outstanding note payable at maturity.

Requirement

1. Record the transactions in Smooth Sounds' journal. Explanations are not required.

LO 1, 2, 3, 4

P8-46A. ***(Learning Objectives 1, 2, 3, 4: Measure and report current liabilities)*** At December 31, 2018, Filbert Corporation's adjusted trial balance shows the following balances:

Accrued Warranty Payable	$ 58,000
4% Notes Payable, due April 30, 2019	150,000
Unearned Service Revenue	48,000
Accounts Payable	225,000
Employee Income Tax Payable	27,000
Accounts Receivable	279,000
Interest Payable	29,000
8% Bonds Payable, due December 31, 2023	500,000
Accumulated Depreciation	75,000
Treasury Stock	164,000
Salaries Payable	84,000
5% Notes Payable, due December 31, 2019	200,000
Sales Tax Payable	67,000
FICA Tax Payable	7,000

Filbert Corporation provides multi-year warranties with its products. Half of the Accrued Warranty Liability relates to warranty liabilities that will be paid in 2019, while the other half relates to warranty liabilities to be paid in 2020. The Unearned Service Revenue pertains to a service contract that will be performed during 2019. $100,000 of the 8% bonds payable due December 31, 2023, is due on December 31, 2019.

Requirement

1. Prepare the current liability section of Filbert Corporation's balance sheet at December 31, 2018.

LO 4, 5

P8-47A. ***(Learning Objectives 4, 5: Account for estimated warranties payable; account for contingent liabilities)*** Randall Go-Karts sells motorized go-karts. Randall Go-Karts are motorized and are typically purchased by amusement parks and other recreation facilities, but are also occasionally purchased by individuals for their own personal use. The company uses a perpetual inventory system. Selected transactions in the month of December follow:

December 1	Randall sold 10 go-karts on account. The selling price of each go-kart was $1,000; the cost of goods sold for each was $250.
5	Randall received notice of a class-action lawsuit being filed against it. The lawsuit claims that Randall's go-karts have engine defects that appear after the warranty period expires. The plaintiffs want Randall to replace the defective engines and pay damages for the owners' loss of use. The cost of replacing the engines would be approximately $400,000 (not including any damages). Randall's attorney believes that it is reasonably possible that Randall will lose the case, but the attorney cannot provide a dollar estimate of the potential loss amount.
20	Randall performed repairs due to product warranty complaints for two go-karts sold earlier in the year. Randall's cost of the repairs, paid in cash, was $500.
22	An individual claims that he suffered emotional distress from a high-speed ride on a Randall Go-Kart and is seeking $500,000 in damages. Randall's attorney believes the case is frivolous because it does not have any legal merit.
27	Another customer is suing Randall for $200,000 because a defect in the customer's Randall Go-Kart engine started a fire and destroyed the customer's garage. Randall's attorney believes the customer will probably win the case and receive $200,000. (Use the following account names: Loss from Lawsuit and Accrued Liability from Lawsuit.)
31	Randall estimates that the warranty expense is 5% of gross sales. Randall's gross sales for the period totaled $700,000.

Requirements

1. Prepare the journal entries to record the transactions shown. Omit explanations.
2. Describe how each of the contingent liabilities in the selected December transactions would be treated in Randall's financial statements for 2019.

Group B

LO **1, 2, 3, 4**

P8-48B. ***(Learning Objectives 1, 2, 3, 4: Measure and report current liabilities)*** Big Wave Marine experienced these events during the current year.

a. December revenue totaled $110,000; and, in addition, Big Wave collected sales tax of 7%. The tax amount will be sent to the state of Delaware early in January.

b. On August 31, Big Wave signed a six-month, 9% note payable to purchase a boat costing $94,000. The note requires payment of principal and interest at maturity.

c. On August 31, Big Wave received cash of $3,600 in advance for service revenue. This revenue will be earned evenly over six months.

d. Revenues of $850,000 were covered by Big Wave's service warranty. At January 1, accrued warranty payable was $11,800. During the year, Big Wave recorded warranty expense of $34,000 and paid warranty claims of $34,600.

e. Big Wave owes $100,000 on a long-term note payable. At December 31, 10% interest for the year plus $30,000 of this principal are payable within one year.

Requirement

1. For each item, indicate the account and the related amount to be reported as a current liability on the Big Wave Marine balance sheet at December 31.

LO **1, 2, 3, 4**

P8-49B. ***(Learning Objectives 1, 2, 3, 4: Record liability-related transactions)*** The following transactions of Melody Music Company occurred during 2018 and 2019:

2018	
Mar 3	Purchased a piano (inventory) for $45,000, signing a six-month, 10% note payable.
May 31	Borrowed $100,000 on a 5% one-year note payable.
Sep 3	Paid the six-month, 10% note at maturity.
Dec 31	Accrued warranty expense, which is estimated at 2% of sales of $202,000.
31	Accrued interest on the outstanding note payable.
2019	
May 31	Paid the outstanding note payable at maturity.

Requirement

1. Record the transactions in Melody Music Company's journal. Explanations are not required.

LO **1, 2, 3, 4**

P8-50B. ***(Learning Objectives 1, 2, 3, 4: Measure and report current liabilities)*** At December 31, 2018, Jackson Corporation's adjusted trial balance shows the following balances:

Accrued Warranty Payable	$ 48,000
3% Notes Payable, due April 30, 2019	180,000
Unearned Service Revenue	64,000
Accounts Payable	187,000
Employee Income Tax Payable	23,000
Accounts Receivable	312,000
Interest Payable	23,000
7% Bonds Payable, due December 31, 2023	1,000,000
Accumulated Depreciation	57,000
Treasury Stock	77,000
Salaries Payable	93,000
4% Notes Payable, due December 31, 2019	150,000
Sales Tax Payable	41,000
FICA Tax Payable	8,000

Jackson Corporation provides multi-year warranties with its products. Half of the Accrued Warranty Liability relates to warranty liabilities that will be paid in 2019, while the other half relates to warranty liabilities to be paid in 2020. The Unearned Service Revenue pertains to a service contract that will be performed during 2019. $200,000 of the 7% bonds payable due December 31, 2023, is due on December 31, 2019.

Requirement

1. Prepare the current liability section of Jackson Corporation's balance sheet at December 31, 2018.

P8-51B. ***(Learning Objectives 4, 5: Account for estimated warranties payable; account for contingent liabilities)*** Bennett Go-Karts sells motorized go-karts. Bennett Go-Karts are motorized and are typically purchased by amusement parks and other recreation facilities, but are also occasionally purchased by individuals for their own personal use. The company uses a perpetual inventory system. Selected transactions in the month of December follow: LO 4, 5

December 1	Bennett sold 12 go-karts on account. The selling price of each go-kart was $1,100; the cost of goods sold for each was $300.
5	Bennett received notice of a class-action lawsuit being filed against it. The lawsuit claims that Bennett's go-karts have engine defects that appear after the warranty period expires. The plaintiffs want Bennett to replace the defective engines and pay damages for the owners' loss of use. The cost of replacing the engines would be approximately $300,000 (not including any damages). Bennett's attorney believes that it is reasonably possible that Bennett will lose the case, but the attorney cannot provide a dollar estimate of the potential loss amount.
20	Bennett performed repairs due to product warranty complaints for two go-karts sold earlier in the year. Bennett's cost of the repairs, paid in cash, was $700.
22	An individual claims that he suffered emotional distress from a high-speed ride on a Bennett Go-Kart and is seeking $200,000 in damages. Bennett's attorney believes the case is frivolous because it does not have any legal merit.
27	Another customer is suing Bennett for $100,000 because a defect in the customer's Bennett Go-Kart engine started a fire and destroyed the customer's garage. Bennett's attorney believes the customer will probably win the case and receive $100,000. (Use the following account names: Loss from Lawsuit and Accrued Liability from Lawsuit.)
31	Bennett estimates that the warranty expense is 4% of gross sales. Bennett's gross sales for the period totaled $800,000.

Requirements

1. Prepare the journal entries to record the transactions shown. Omit explanations.
2. Describe how each of the contingent liabilities in the selected December transactions would be treated in Bennett's financial statements for 2019.

Challenge Exercise

LO 1 E8-52. *(Learning Objective 1: Report current liabilities; evaluate liquidity)* The top management of Flashline Services examines the following company accounting records at July 29, immediately before the end of the year, July 31:

Total current assets	$ 324,500
Noncurrent assets	1,086,000
	$1,410,500
Total current liabilities	$ 173,500
Noncurrent liabilities	253,400
Stockholders' equity	983,600
	$1,410,500

Requirement

1. Suppose Flashline's management wants to achieve a current ratio of 3. How much in current liabilities should the company pay off within the next two days in order to achieve its goal?

APPLY YOUR KNOWLEDGE

Serial Case

LO 5 **C8-53.** *(Learning Objective 5: Analyze contingent liabilities of a company in the restaurant industry)*

Note: This case is part of The Cheesecake Factory serial case contained in every chapter in this textbook.

Like many other large companies, **The Cheesecake Factory Incorporated** has several legal actions pending against it at any given time. It must accrue for and/or disclose certain contingent liabilities, such as pending or possible legal actions, in its financial statements and notes to its financial statements. The necessary reporting depends on the specific circumstances of the situations and the company's attorneys' assessment of the potential outcomes.

To follow are four *hypothetical* legal situations that might face The Cheesecake Factory.

Situation A: A former restaurant employee filed a class-action lawsuit alleging that The Cheesecake Factory violated the local law when it required employees to purchase their work uniforms. Legal counsel has indicated that the case will probably be settled for $2,500.

Situation B: A customer filed a lawsuit alleging that The Cheesecake Factory was negligent when she slipped and fell on a wet floor near the bar area in a Cheesecake Factory in Topeka, Kansas. Legal counsel has indicated that the company will most likely settle this case, but counsel is unable to estimate the dollar amount of the settlement.

Situation C: A customer filed a lawsuit alleging that The Cheesecake Factory caused her severe emotional distress when her favorite dessert was out of stock for her birthday dinner at the restaurant. Legal counsel has indicated that the chance of losing this lawsuit is remote.

Situation D: A former restaurant hourly employee filed a class-action lawsuit for $200,000 alleging that The Cheesecake Factory violated the local law by failing to pay overtime. Legal counsel has stated that it is reasonably possible, but not probable, that The Cheesecake Factory could lose the lawsuit.

Requirement

1. Describe the accounting treatment for each of the contingent liabilities listed. Support your answers.

Decision Cases

LO 2

C8-54. ***(Learning Objective 2: Calculate and analyze accounts payable turnover for two companies in the toy and game industry)*** **Hasbro, Inc.** (NASDAQ: HAS) and **Mattel, Inc.** (NASDAQ: MAT) are two companies in the toy and game industry. Hasbro's products include Monopoly board games, G.I. Joe dolls, Furby electronic stuffed animals, Transformers mechanical toys, and the My Little Pony toys. Mattel's products include Fisher-Price toys, Barbie dolls, Hot Wheels cars, American Girl dolls, Apples to Apples games, and Blokus games.

To follow are selected data for both Hasbro and Mattel from their Form 10-Ks for the years 2012–2016.

Hasbro, Inc.
Selected financial data from Form 10-K
(in thousands)

	12/25/2016	12/27/2015	12/28/2014	12/29/2013	12/30/2012
Inventory	$ 387,675	$ 384,492	$ 339,572	$ 348,794	$ 316,049
Accounts payable	319,525	241,210	212,549	198,799	139,906
Cost of sales* (for year)	1,905,474	1,677,033	1,698,372	1,672,901	1,671,980

Mattel, Inc.
Selected financial data from Form 10-K
(in thousands)

	12/31/2016	12/31/2015	12/31/2014	12/31/2013	12/31/2012
Inventory	$ 613,798	$ 587,521	$ 562,047	$ 568,843	$ 465,057
Accounts payable	664,857	651,681	430,259	375,328	385,375
Cost of sales* (for year)	2,902,259	2,896,255	3,022,797	3,006,009	3,011,684

**Both Hasbro and Mattel refer to their cost of goods sold as "cost of sales."*

For this case, assume that both companies make all purchases on account.

Requirements

1. Calculate accounts payable turnover for both Hasbro and Mattel for 2013 through 2016.
2. Is Hasbro's accounts payable turnover improving or deteriorating? Explain.
3. Is Mattel's accounts payable turnover improving or deteriorating? Explain.
4. Describe factors that might be causing the trends in the accounts payable turnover for both companies.

LO **5** **C8-55.** *(Learning Objective 5: Analyze a contingent liability at an automobile manufacturer)* **Ford Motor Company** produces and sells the Ford Mustang Shelby GT350, which Ford markets as a track-ready car built to reach and sustain high speeds.

Three of the 2016 Ford Mustang Shelby GT350 owners have filed a class action suit against Ford, alleging that these cars are not track-ready. The owners claim that the car goes into "limp mode" at high speeds due to high differential and trans temperatures. The limp mode slows the car down to a greatly reduced speed. The slowdown of the engine occurs after 15 minutes or less of high-speed driving.

Ford has reacted to the reports of limp mode by telling owners to purchase transmission and differential coolers (at the owner's expense, not Ford's).

The 2017 model now includes transmission and differential coolers.

An estimated 3,991 Shelby 350GTs could be covered by this class-action lawsuit.

Requirements

1. What is a contingent liability?
2. What factors should Ford consider when deciding how to treat the Ford Mustang Shelby GT350 contingent liability?
3. In your opinion, how do you think Ford should handle this contingent liability in its financial reports (accrue, disclose, or do nothing)? Explain.

Ethical Issue

C8-56. **Microsoft Corporation** is the defendant in numerous lawsuits claiming unfair trade practices. Microsoft has strong incentives not to disclose these contingent liabilities. However, U.S. GAAP requires that companies report their contingent liabilities.

Requirements

1. Why would a company prefer not to disclose its contingent liabilities?
2. Identify the parties involved in the decision and the potential consequences to each.
3. Analyze the issue of whether to report contingent liabilities from lawsuits from the following standpoints:
   - **a.** Economic
   - **b.** Legal
   - **c.** Ethical
4. What impact could future changes in accounting standards, both at the U.S. level and the international level, likely have on the issue of disclosure of loss contingencies?

Focus on Financials | Apple Inc.

LO **1, 2, 5** *(Learning Objectives 1, 2, 5: Analyze current liabilities; evaluate accounts payable turnover; evaluate contingent liabilities)* Refer to **Apple Inc.**'s consolidated financial statements in Appendix A and online in the filings section of **www.sec.gov**.

Requirements

1. Did accounts payable for Apple increase or decrease in 2016? Calculate Apple's accounts payable turnover for 2016. How many days does it take Apple to pay an average account payable? Comment on the length of the period in days.
2. Examine Note 5—Income Taxes—in the Notes to Consolidated Financial Statements. Income tax provision is another title for income tax expense. What was Apple's income tax provision in 2016? Is the income tax provision likely to be equal to the amount Apple paid for its taxes in 2016? Why or why not? What was the company's effective tax rate in 2016?
3. Examine Note 10—Commitments and Contingencies—in the Notes to Consolidated Financial Statements. Describe some of Apple Inc.'s commitments and contingent liabilities as of September 24, 2016. Are any of these amounts included in the numbers in the balance sheet line items?

Focus on Analysis | Under Armour, Inc.

LO 1, 2, 5

(Learning Objectives 1, 2, 5: Analyze current liabilities; evaluate accounts payable turnover; evaluate contingent liabilities) Retrieve the 2016 **Under Armour** financial statements at **www.sec.gov** by clicking on Filings and then searching for "Under Armour" under Company Filings. When you see the list of filings for the company, select the Form 10-K for 2016. Be sure to retrieve the 2016 financial statements, not another year. These financial statements report a number of liabilities.

Requirements

1. The current liability section of Under Armour's Consolidated Balance Sheet as of December 31, 2016, lists four different liabilities. List them and give a brief description of each one.
2. For 2016, calculate accounts payable turnover, both as a ratio and in number of days. Describe what this ratio means. Also compute the following other ratios for 2016 (if you have already computed them as part of your work in previous chapters, refer to them): (1) current ratio, (2) quick ratio, (3) days' sales outstanding, and (4) days' inventory outstanding. How would you combine the information in these ratios to assess Under Armour's current debt-paying ability?
3. Refer to the note entitled "Commitments and Contingencies." Describe the contents of the "Other" subsection in the note. Are any of these items included in the liabilities recorded in either the current or long-term section of the balance sheet? Why or why not?
4. Now download Under Armour's most recent financial statements from **www.sec.gov**. What has happened to Under Armour's accounts payable turnover since the end of 2016?

Group Project

Consider three different businesses:

1. A bank
2. A magazine publisher
3. A department store

For each business, list all of its liabilities—both current and long-term. Then compare the three lists to identify the liabilities that the three businesses have in common. Also identify the liabilities that are unique to each type of business.

Quick Check Answers

1. *b*
2. *d*
3. *a*
4. *d*
5. *b*
6. *b*
7. *a*
8. *b*
9. *d* $[(900 \times .02) \times \$60] = \$1{,}080;\ \$1{,}080 - (\$60 \times 5) = \$780$
10. *c*
11. *a*
12. *e*

9 Long-Term Liabilities

LEARNING OBJECTIVES

1 **Account for** bonds payable and interest expense with straight-line amortization

2 **Account for** bonds payable and interest expense with effective-interest amortization

3 **Account for** other features of bonds payable

4 **Describe** other long-term liabilities

5 **Analyze** the impact of leverage on the financial statements

6 **Report** long-term liabilities on the financial statements

SPOTLIGHT

Southwest Airlines Is Flying High

Southwest Airlines has gained a reputation for providing reliable, low-cost travel from smaller airports that are convenient for many business commuters and vacationers. As of December 31, 2016, Southwest was the largest domestic air carrier in the United States in terms of passengers boarded (over 100 million a year). Utilizing a fleet of more than 700 airplanes (all **Boeing** 737s), the company served more than 100 destinations—including cities in Puerto Rico, Mexico, Jamaica, the Bahamas, Aruba, the Dominican Republic, Belize, Costa Rica, and Cuba.

Despite the fact that the airlines industry is very volatile, Southwest Airlines has managed to remain consistently profitable for most of its history, in part, by keeping its expenses low. In 2016, the company earned $2.2 billion after taxes on operating revenue of $20.4 billion.

Like other airlines, Southwest finances many of its aircraft and ground facilities with long-term debt. As shown on its consolidated balance sheet on page 469, as of December 31, 2016, the company owed a total of $3,387 million in long-term debt, which consisted of notes payable and bonds payable. $2,821 million of this debt was classified as long term, and $566 million was classified as current maturities, the portion of long-term debt due and payable in 2017. In addition, the company owed $3,374 million in deferred income taxes, had construction obligations of $1,078 million, and $728 million in other noncurrent liabilities. Of $14,845 million in total liabilities, $8,001 million (53.9%) was classified as noncurrent.

E.J. Baumeister Jr./Alamy Stock Photo

	A	B	C
1	**Southwest Airlines Co.**		
2	**Consolidated Balance Sheet (Adapted)**	**12/31/16**	**12/31/15**
3	**(in millions of $)**		
4	**Assets**		
5	Current assets	$ 4,498	$ 4,024
6	Property, plant, and equipment, net	17,044	15,601
7	Other assets	1,744	1,687
8	TOTAL ASSETS	$ 23,286	$ 21,312
9	**Liabilities and Stockholders' Equity**		
10	Current liabilities:		
11	Accounts payable	$ 1,178	$ 1,188
12	Accrued liabilities	1,985	2,591
13	Air traffic liability	3,115	2,990
14	Current maturities of long-term debt	566	637
15	Total current liabilities	6,844	7,406
16	Long-term debt less current maturities	2,821	2,541
17	Deferred income taxes	3,374	2,490
18	Construction obligation	1,078	757
19	Other noncurrent liabilities	728	760
20	Total noncurrent liabilities	8,001	6,548
21	TOTAL LIABILITIES	14,845	13,954
22	TOTAL STOCKHOLDERS' EQUITY	8,441	7,358
23	TOTAL LIABILITIES AND STOCKHOLDERS' EQUITY	$ 23,286	$ 21,312
24			

Data from the U.S. Securities and Exchange Commission EDGAR Company filings, www.sec.gov

This chapter shows how to account for long-term liabilities, both those on the face of the balance sheet and those that are merely footnote disclosures. We begin with bonds payable.

Try It in Excel®

You can access the most current annual report of Southwest Airlines Company in Excel format at **www.sec.gov**. Using the "FILINGS" link on the toolbar at the top of the home page, select "Company Filings Search." This will take you to the "Edgar Company Filings" page. Type "Southwest Airlines" in the company name box, and select "Search." This will produce the "EDGAR Search Results" page showing the company name. Click on the "CIK" link beside the company name. Doing so will pull up a list of the reports the company has filed with the SEC. Under the "Filing Type" box, type "10-K" and click the search box. Form 10-K is the SEC form for the company's annual report. Find the year that you wish to view. Click on the "Interactive Data" box, which takes you to the "View Filing Data" page. Find and click on the "View Excel Document" link at the top of this page. You may choose to either open or download the Excel files containing the company's most recent financial statements.

ACCOUNT FOR BONDS PAYABLE AND INTEREST EXPENSE WITH STRAIGHT-LINE AMORTIZATION

1 Account for bonds payable and interest expense with straight-line amortization

Large companies such as Southwest Airlines, **Apple Inc.**, and **Toyota** cannot borrow billions of dollars from a single lender. So how do corporations borrow huge amounts? They issue (sell) bonds or long-term notes to the public. We treat bonds payable and notes payable together because the accounting for each is virtually identical.

Bonds payable are groups of debt securities issued to multiple lenders, called *bondholders*. Southwest Airlines needs airplanes, ground facilities, and other long-term assets. The company can finance the purchase of these assets by issuing bonds to thousands of individual and institutional investors. Bonds payable are debts of the issuing company. Purchasers of bonds receive a bond certificate, which carries the issuing company's name. The certificate also states the *principal*, which is typically stated in units of $1,000; principal is also called the bond's *face value*, *maturity value*, or *par value*. The bond obligates the issuing company to pay the debt at a specific future time called the *maturity date*.

Interest is the fee paid by a borrower for the use of someone else's money. The bond certificate states the interest rate the issuer will pay the holder and the dates the interest payments are due (generally, twice a year).

Issuing bonds usually requires the services of a securities firm, such as **JP Morgan Chase & Co.** or **Bank of America**, to act as the underwriter of the bond issue. The **underwriter** purchases the bonds from the issuing company and resells them to its clients, and earns a commission on the sale. Underwriters' commissions are deducted from the proceeds of a bond issuance and are treated as part of its cost.

Types of Bonds. All the bonds in a particular issuance may mature at the same time (**term bonds**) or in installments over a period of time (**serial bonds**). Serial bonds are like installment notes payable. Some of Southwest Airlines' long-term debts are serial in nature because they are payable in installments.

Secured, or *mortgage*, *bonds* give the bondholder the right to assume ownership of certain assets of a company if it defaults on the bonds—that is, fails to pay the interest or principal owed on them. *Unsecured bonds*, called **debentures**, are backed only by the borrower's promise to pay. Debentures carry a higher rate of interest than secured bonds because debentures are riskier investments.

Bond Prices. Once bonds are issued publicly, they trade in the open (secondary) market, just like shares of stock. This secondary market has no impact on the issuing company's financial statements. Bond prices fluctuate daily, just like prices of a company's stock. Bond prices are quoted at a percentage of their maturity (also called face or par) value. For example,

- a $1,000 bond quoted at 100 is bought or sold for $1,000, which is 100% of its face value.
- The same bond quoted at 101.5 has a market price of $1,015 (101.5% of face value = $1,000 × 1.015).
- A $1,000 bond quoted at 88.375 is priced at $883.75 ($1,000 × 0.88375).

Bond Premiums and Bond Discounts. A bond issued at a price above its face (par) value is said to be issued at a **premium**, and a bond issued at a price below face (par) value is said to be issued at a **discount**. Premium on Bonds Payable has a *credit* balance and Discount on Bonds Payable carries a *debit* balance. Discount on Bonds Payable is therefore a contra liability account.

As a bond nears maturity, its market price moves toward face (par) value. Therefore, the price of a bond issued at a

- premium decreases toward face or maturity value.
- discount increases toward face or maturity value.

On the maturity date, a bond's market value exactly equals its face value because the company that issued the bond pays that amount to retire the bond.

The Time Value of Money. Appendix F to this text covers the time value of money. We recommend that you become familiar with this material because it shows in detail how the time value of money impacts the price of a financial asset or liability.

Interest Rates and Bond Prices. Bonds are always sold at their market price, which is the amount investors will pay for the bond. The market price of a bond depends in part on the bond's present value. The **present value** is today's value of a future payment or series of future payments, assuming that those payments include interest.

The market value of a bond equals the present value of the principal payment of the bond at the end of its term plus the present value of the stream of cash interest payments from the date the bond was issued until its maturity date. Interest is usually paid semiannually (twice a year). Some companies pay interest annually or quarterly.

Two interest rates work to set the price of a bond:

- The **stated interest rate**, also called the coupon rate, is the interest rate printed on the bond certificate. The stated interest rate determines the amount of cash interest the borrower pays—and the investor receives—each year. For example, suppose Southwest Airlines bonds have a stated interest rate of 9%. Southwest would pay $9,000 of interest annually on $100,000 of bonds. Each semiannual payment would be $4,500 ($100,000 × 0.09 × 6/12).
- The **market interest rate**, or *effective-interest rate*, is the rate that investors demand for loaning their money. The market interest rate varies by the minute.

A company may issue bonds with a stated interest rate that differs from the prevailing market interest rate. In fact, because market interest rates can fluctuate daily, the two interest rates usually differ.

Exhibit 9-1 shows how the stated interest rate and the market interest rate interact to determine the issue price of a bond payable for three separate cases.

Exhibit 9-1 How Stated Interest Rates and Market Interest Rates Interact to Determine the Price of a Bond

Issue Price of Bonds Payable

Case A:				
Stated interest rate on a bond payable	equals	Market interest rate	Therefore,	Price of face (par, or maturity) value
Example: 9%	=	9%	→	*Par: $1,000 bond issued for $1,000*
Case B:				
Stated interest rate on a bond payable	less than	Market interest rate	Therefore,	Discount price (price below face value)
Example: 9%		10%	→	*Discount: $1,000 bond issued for a price below $1,000*
Case C:				
Stated interest rate on a bond payable	greater than	Market interest rate	Therefore,	Premium price (price above face value)
Example: 9%		8%	→	*Premium: $1,000 bond issued for a price above $1,000*

For example, Southwest Airlines could issue 9% bonds when the market rate has risen to 10%. Will the Southwest 9% bonds attract investors in this market? No, because investors can earn 10% on other bonds of similar risk. Therefore, investors will purchase Southwest bonds only at a price less than their face value, or at a discount (Case B in Exhibit 9-1). Conversely, if the market interest rate is 8%, Southwest's 9% bonds will be so attractive that investors will pay more than face value to purchase them at a premium (Case C in Exhibit 9-1).

Issuing Bonds Payable at Par (Face Value)

We start with the most straightforward situation—issuing bonds at their par value (Case A in Exhibit 9-1). There is no premium or discount on these bonds payable.

Suppose Southwest Airlines issues $100,000 of 9% bonds payable that mature in five years. Assume that Southwest issues these bonds at par on January 1, 2018. This means that the stated rate of interest on the bonds exactly equals the market rate on January 1, 2018. The issuance entry is as follows:

	A	B	C	D
1	2018			
2	Jan 1	Cash	100,000	
3		Bonds Payable		100,000
4		*To issue bonds at par.*		
5				

Bonds Payable

	100,000

Assets and liabilities increase when a company issues bonds payable.

Assets	=	Liabilities	+	Stockholders' Equity
+ 100,000	=	+ 100,000	+	0

Southwest, the borrower, makes a one-time entry to record the receipt of cash and the issuance of bonds. Afterward, individual investors buy and sell the bonds to each other through the bond markets. These later buy-and-sell transactions between outside investors do *not* involve Southwest at all.

Interest payments occur each January 1 and July 1. Southwest's entry to record the first semiannual interest payment is as follows:

	A	B	C	D
1	2018			
2	Jul 1	Interest Expense ($100,000 × 0.09 × 6/12)	4,500	
3		Cash		4,500
4		*To pay semiannual interest.*		
5				

The payment of interest expense decreases Southwest's assets and equity. The Bonds Payable account is not affected.

Assets	=	Liabilities	+	Stockholders' Equity	−	Expenses
− 4,500	=	0	+			− 4,500

At year-end, Southwest accrues interest expense and interest payable for six months (July through December), as follows:

	A	B	C	D
1	2018			
2	Dec 31	Interest Expense ($100,000 × 0.09 × 6/12)	4,500	
3		Interest Payable		4,500
4		*To accrue interest.*		
5				

Liabilities increase, and equity decreases.

Assets	=	Liabilities	+	Stockholders' Equity	−	Expenses
0	=	+ 4,500	+			− 4,500

On January 1, 2019, Southwest will pay the interest, debiting Interest Payable and crediting Cash. This process continues throughout the five-year term of the bonds.

On the maturity date (January 1, 2023), Southwest pays off the bonds and makes the following entry:

	A	B	C	D
1	2023			
2	Jan 1	Bonds Payable	100,000	
3		Cash		100,000
4		*To pay bonds payable at maturity.*		
5				

Bonds Payable

100,000	100,000
	Bal 0

Assets	=	Liabilities	+	Stockholders' Equity
− 100,000	=	− 100,000		

Issuing Bonds Payable at a Discount

Sometimes market conditions force a company to issue bonds at a discount. Suppose Southwest Airlines issues $100,000 of 9%, five-year bonds when the market interest rate is 10%. Interest payments occur semiannually, each January 1 and July 1. The market price of the bonds drops from 100 to 96.15 (96.15% of par value), and Southwest receives $96,150[1] when the bonds are issued ($100,000 × 0.9615). The transaction is recorded as follows:

	A	B	C	D
1	2018			
2	Jan 1	Cash	96,150	
3		Discount on Bonds Payable	3,850	
4		Bonds Payable		100,000
5		*To issue bonds at a discount.*		
6				

Assets	=	Liabilities	+	Stockholders' Equity
+ 96,150	=	− 3,850	+	0
		+ 100,000		

The Bonds Payable accounts have an initial carrying value of $96,150 as follows:

Bonds Payable		−	Discount on Bonds Payable		=	Initial carrying value of bonds payable
	100,000		3,850			$96,150

[1] The example in Appendix F on page 807 shows how to determine the price of this bond as follows: (1) the present value of $100,000 paid 10 periods in the future, discounted at the market rate of 5% (0.10 annual rate ÷ 2), plus (2) the present value of an ordinary annuity, a stream of ten interest payments of $4,500 each (100,000 × face rate of 0.045 each period) discounted at 5%. The price is $96,149. To simplify computations in this example, we round up to $96,150.

Immediately after the bonds are issued, Southwest's balance sheet at January 1, 2018 would report the following:

Total current liabilities		$ XXX
Long-term liabilities:		
Bonds payable, 9%, due 2023	$100,000	
Less: Discount on bonds payable	(3,850)	96,150

Discount on Bonds Payable is a contra account to Bonds Payable and decreases the company's liabilities. Subtracting the discount from Bonds Payable yields the carrying value of the bonds, which is the difference between the face value of the bonds and the premium or discount they were sold at. The initial carrying value of the bonds issued by Southwest is $96,150 ($100,000 − $3,850).

Each semiannual cash interest payment is set by the terms stated on the face of the bond contract and therefore remains constant over the life of the bonds:

$$\text{Semiannual cash interest payment} = \$100{,}000 \times 0.09 \times 6/12$$
$$= \$4{,}500$$

However, Southwest's interest expense must be increased each period in order to account for the fact that the bonds were issued at a discount, which represents an additional cost of borrowing. This discount must be amortized over the term of the bonds, assigning a portion to each interest period as additional interest expense.

The *straight-line amortization method* divides a bond discount into equal amounts over the bond's term. The amount of interest expense is therefore the same for each interest period. Let's apply the straight-line amortization method to the Southwest Airlines bonds issued at a price of 96.150:

	Semiannual cash interest payment ($100,000 × 0.09 × 6/12)	$4,500
+	Semiannual amortization of discount ($3,850 ÷ 10)...........................	385
=	Estimated semiannual interest expense	$4,885

(Remember that the "10" in the calculation is the number of periods that interest will be paid for these bonds. The Southwest Airlines bonds are five-year bonds that pay interest semiannually, or twice per year. Therefore, the number of periods is 5 years × 2, or 10.) The straight-line amortization method uses these same amounts every period over the term of the bonds. Southwest's entry to record interest expense on July 1, 2018 (the first interest payment period) using the straight-line amortization method is as follows:

A1

	A	B	C	D
1	2018			
2	Jul 1	Interest Expense	4,885	
3		Discount on Bonds Payable		385
4		Cash		4,500
5		*To pay semiannual interest and amortize bond discount.*		
6				

After this entry is posted, the bonds would have a carrying value of $96,535, calculated as follows:

Bonds Payable − **Discount on Bonds Payable** = Carrying value 96,535

Bonds Payable (Dr)	Bonds Payable (Cr)		Discount (Dr)		Discount (Cr)	
	01/01/18	100,000	01/01/18	3,850	07/01/18	385
			Bal.	3,465		

Each interest period, the discount on bonds payable is decreased by $385, and the carrying value of the bonds correspondingly increases by $385 until the carrying value of the bond reaches $100,000 face value at maturity, and the bonds are paid off with cash.

Issuing Bonds Payable at a Premium

Suppose instead that Southwest Airlines issues its bonds at a price of 103.85. In this case, the stated rate of interest of the bonds is greater than the market rate, producing a bond premium. Each bond sells for 103.85% of par value, or $1,038.50. The initial carrying value of the bonds is $103,850, which is comprised of $100,000 in face value of Bonds Payable plus $3,850 in Premium on Bonds Payable.

Bonds Payable		+	Premium on Bonds Payable		=	Initial carrying value
	01/01/18 $100,000			01/01/18 $3,850		$103,850

Using the straight-line method, amortization of the premium over the term of the bonds is computed exactly the same way as discount amortization. However, as the premium is amortized, it reduces the amount of interest expense recognized each period because the issue price was greater than the face value of the bonds. The bond premium is reduced, as is the carrying value of the bonds, until it reaches the face amount at maturity. Each semiannual interest payment remains at $4,500 as computed before. However, one-tenth of the bond premium ($385) must be amortized each interest payment date, resulting in interest expense of $4,115 ($4,500 – $385). Again, 10 periods are used in the calculation because the bonds are five-year bonds paying interest twice per year, or 5 × 2 = 10. The entry to record the first interest payment on July 1, 2018, is:

	A	B	C	D
1	2018			
2	Jul 1	Interest Expense	4,115	
3		Premium on Bonds Payable	385	
4		Cash		4,500
5		*To pay semi-annual interest and amortize bond premium.*		
6				

After the first interest payment is posted to the accounts, the Premium on Bonds Payable account is reduced to $3,465, and the bonds' carrying value is reduced to $103,465.

Bonds Payable			+	Premium on Bonds Payable				=	Carrying value
	01/01/18	100,000		07/01/18	385	01/01/18	3,850		103,465
						Bal.	3,465		

The Premium on Bonds Payable is decreased by $385 each interest payment date, and the carrying value of the bonds is correspondingly reduced by $385 for 10 periods until finally the carrying value of the bonds reaches its $100,000 face amount at maturity, and the bonds are paid off with cash.

The following graph shows the carrying value of bonds originally issued at (1) a discount price of 96.15, shown by the red line, and (2) a premium price of 103.85, shown by the blue line. Notice how in both scenarios, the carrying values eventually converge to par or face value at maturity (the green line) as the bonds are amortized. Of course, if the bonds were issued at par or face value, their carrying value would remain constant.

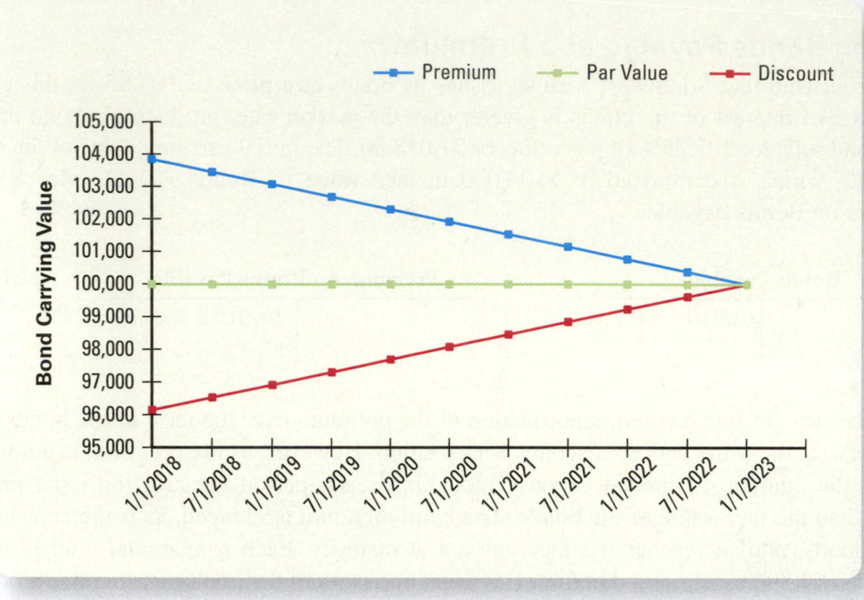

ACCOUNT FOR BONDS PAYABLE AND INTEREST EXPENSE WITH EFFECTIVE-INTEREST AMORTIZATION

2 Account for bonds payable and interest expense with effective-interest amortization

Generally accepted accounting principles (GAAP) allow businesses to use the straight-line amortization method only when the amounts calculated do not differ significantly from the amounts calculated using the effective-interest method. The **effective-interest method** is the most theoretically correct way to amortize bond discount and premium because it recognizes the impact that the time value of money has on the interest expense recognized each interest-payment period. When the effective-interest method is used, a company's interest expense will be different in each payment period, not the same like it is when the straight-line method is used.

To calculate a company's interest expense using the effective-interest method, follow these steps:

1. Determine the exact price of the bonds at issuance, taking into account the market rate of interest, the periodic interest payments based on the face value multiplied by the face interest rate, and the maturity value of the bonds. This step can be performed most efficiently by using the present value (PV) function of Excel, as explained in Appendix F.
2. Build an amortization table showing the bond's interest payments, interest expense, discount or premium amortization, discount or premium balance, and carrying value of the bonds. Again, Excel is the recommended tool to create an amortization table.

Issuing Bonds Payable at a Discount

Panel A of Exhibit 9-2 repeats the Southwest Airlines bond data we've been using when the bonds are issued at a discount. Panel B is an amortization table that does two things:

- It shows the periodic interest expense (column C).
- It shows the bonds' carrying value (column F).

Exhibit 9-2 | Amortization of Bond Discount

Panel A—Bond Data

	A	B
1	Issue date—January 1, 2018	Maturity date—January 1, 2023
2	Face (par or *maturity*) value—$100,000	Market interest rate at time of issue—10% annually, 5% semiannually
3	Stated interest rate—9%	Issue price—$96,149
4	Interest paid—4 1/2% semiannually, $4,500 = $100,000 × 0.09 × 6/12	
5	Interest paid—Jan. 1 and July 1	
6		

Panel B—Amortization Table

	A	B	C	D	E	F
1	Semiannual Interest Date	Int Pmt (0.045* Maturity Value)	Interest Expense (0.05* Preceding Bond Carrying Value)	Discount Amortization (C – B)	Discount Account Balance (Preceding E – D)	Bond Carrying Value ($100,000 – E)
2	1/1/2018				3,851	96,149
3	7/1/2018	4,500	4,807	307	3,544	96,456
4	1/1/2019	4,500	4,823	323	3,221	96,779
5	7/1/2019	4,500	4,839	339	2,882	97,118
6	1/1/2020	4,500	4,856	356	2,526	97,474
7	7/1/2020	4,500	4,874	374	2,152	97,848
8	1/1/2021	4,500	4,892	392	1,760	98,240
9	7/1/2021	4,500	4,912	412	1,348	98,652
10	1/1/2022	4,500	4,933	433	915	99,085
11	7/1/2022	4,500	4,954	454	461	99,539
12	1/1/2023	4,500	4,961**	461	0	100,000
13						

*Indicates multiplication in Excel.
**Adjusted for the effects of rounding.

Try It in Excel®

Bond amortization tables are a snap when you prepare them in Excel. Open a blank Excel spreadsheet.

- In line 1, label the columns as shown in Panel B of Exhibit 9-2.
- Column A. Starting in line 2, enter the issue date (1/1/2018) followed by each of the semiannual interest payment dates. This will continue through line 12 with the last interest payment on January 1, 2023. Highlight all cell values in rows 2 through 12 of column A, and click on the drop-down box in the "number" field on the ruler at the top of the spreadsheet. Choose the "date" category and click OK to change all cell values in Column A to the date format.
- Line 2, column E (bond discount). Enter 3851 in cell E2. Enter the formula =100000–E2 in cell F2. The calculated value of 96149 should appear in cell F2, representing the initial carrying value of the bond.
- Line 3, column B (semiannual cash interest payments, fixed by contract). Enter formula =.045*100000 in cell B3. A calculated value of 4500 should appear, representing the amount of the first cash interest payment.

- Line 3, column C (interest expense, calculated as the market rate of 5% × the previous period's carrying value of the bond). In cell C3, enter formula =.05*F2. A calculated value of 4807 should appear, representing the calculated amount of interest expense. If the cell shows a decimal fraction, use the "decrease decimal" command in the "number" field of the toolbar to reduce the decimals to none. This will round the value to the nearest dollar.
- Line 3, column D (discount amortization, which is the excess of interest expense in column C over the interest payment in column B). In cell D3, enter formula =C3–B3. A value of 307 should appear, representing the amount of discount amortization included in interest expense on the first interest payment date.
- Line 3, column E (unamortized discount account balance, which decreases as it is amortized). In cell E3, enter formula =E2–D3. A value of 3544 should appear, representing the unamortized discount remaining after the first interest payment.
- Line 3, column F (bond carrying value). In cell F3, enter formula =100000–E3. A value of 96456 should appear, representing the adjusted carrying value of the bond after the first interest payment.
- For columns B through F, copy line 3 down through line 12. All of the numbers in the table should fill in. Line 12 will have to be adjusted for rounding by taking the remaining unamortized discount from cell E11 (461) and substituting that value in cell D12 (discount amortization). Also, substitute 4961 for interest expense in cell C12. This will adjust the final bond carrying value to the maturity value of $100,000 and the unamortized discount to 0.
- Highlight cells B2 through F12, and insert commas to make the table easier to read. When you insert the commas, Excel automatically inserts two decimals and zeros, so use the "decrease decimal" key to format the table to whole dollars.

Interest Expense on Bonds Issued at a Discount

In Exhibit 9-2, Southwest Airlines borrowed $96,149 cash but must pay $100,000 when the bonds mature. What happens to the $3,851 discount account balance (column E) over the life of the bond issue?

The $3,851 is additional interest expense to Southwest over and above the stated interest the company pays each six months. Exhibit 9-3 graphs the interest expense (column C in Exhibit 9-2) and the interest payment (column B in Exhibit 9-2) on the Southwest bonds over their lifetime. Notice that the semiannual interest payment is fixed—by contract—at $4,500. But the amount of interest expense increases as the discount bond marches upward toward maturity.

Exhibit 9-3 Interest Expense on Bonds Payable Issued at a Discount

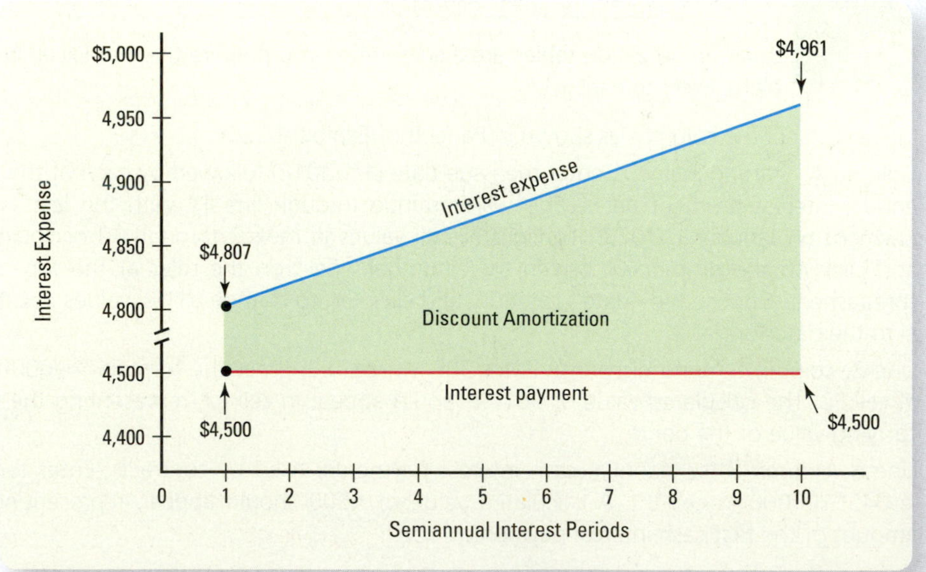

The discount is allocated to interest expense through amortization over the term of the bonds. Exhibit 9-4 shows the amortization of the bond discount, so the carrying value of the bonds increases from $96,149 at the start to $100,000 at maturity, as shown in column F of Exhibit 9-2 (p. 477).

Exhibit 9-4 | Amortizing a Discount on Bonds Payable

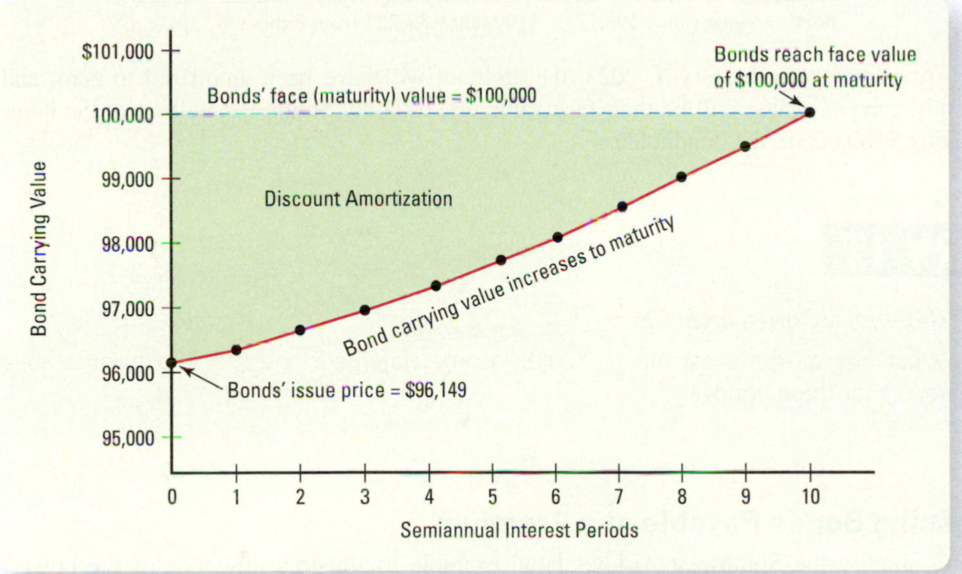

Now let's see how Southwest would account for these bonds each interest payment period. Southwest issues its bonds on January 1, 2018. On July 1, Southwest makes the first semiannual interest payment. But Southwest's interest expense is greater than its payment of $4,500. Southwest's journal entry to record the interest expense and the interest payment for the first six months is as follows (with all amounts taken from Exhibit 9-2):

	A	B	C	D
1	2018			
2	Jul 1	Interest Expense	4,807	
3		Discount on Bonds Payable		307
4		Cash		4,500
5		*To pay semiannual interest and amortize bond discount.*		
6				

The credit to Discount on Bonds Payable accomplishes two purposes:

- It adjusts the carrying value of the bonds as they march upward toward maturity value.
- It amortizes the discount to interest expense.

At December 31, 2018, Southwest accrues interest and amortizes the bond discount for July through December with this entry (amounts from Exhibit 9-2, page 477):

	A	B	C	D
1	2018			
2	Dec 31	Interest Expense	4,823	
3		Discount on Bonds Payable		323
4		Interest Payable		4,500
5		*To accrue semiannual interest and amortize bond discount.*		
6				

At December 31, 2018, Southwest's bond accounts appear as follows:

Bonds Payable		Discount on Bonds Payable	
	100,000	3,851	307
			323
		Bal 3,221	

Bond carrying value, \$96,779 = \$100,000 − \$3,221 from Exhibit 9-2, page 477.

At maturity on January 1, 2023, the discount will have been amortized to zero, and the bonds' carrying value will be their face value of \$100,000. Southwest will retire the bonds by paying \$100,000 to the bondholders.

TRY IT

(Answers are given on p. 521.)

What would Southwest Airlines' 2018 income statement and year-end balance sheet report for these bonds?

Issuing Bonds Payable at a Premium

Let's modify the Southwest Airlines bond example to illustrate issuance of the bonds at a premium. Assume that on January 1, 2018, Southwest issues \$100,000 of five-year, 9% bonds that pay interest semiannually. If the 9% bonds are issued when the market interest rate is 8%, their issue price is \$104,100.[2] The premium on these bonds is \$4,100, and Exhibit 9-5 shows how to amortize the premium on bonds using the effective-interest method. In practice, bond premiums are rare because few companies issue their bonds to pay cash interest above the market interest rate.

Southwest's entry to record the bond issue on January 1, 2018, is as follows:

	A	B	C	D
1	2018			
2	Jan 1	Cash	104,100	
3		Bonds Payable		100,000
4		Premium on Bonds Payable		4,100
5		*To issue bonds at a premium.*		
6				

When the bonds are issued, Southwest's liability is \$104,100—not \$100,000. The accounting equation makes this clear:

Assets	=	Liabilities	+	Stockholders' Equity
+ 104,100	=	+ 100,000	+	0
		+ 4,100		

[2] You can use the same concepts as those in the example in Appendix F to determine the price of this bond.

Exhibit 9-5 | Amortization of Bond Premium

Panel A—Bond Data

A1

	A	B
1	Issue date—January 1, 2018	Maturity date—January 1, 2023
2	Face (par or *maturity*) value—$100,000	Market interest rate at time of issue—8% annually, 4% semiannually
3	Stated interest rate—9%	Issue price—$104,100
4	Interest paid—4 1/2% semiannually, $4,500 = $100,000 × 0.09 × 6/12	
5	Interest paid—Jan. 1 and July 1	
6		

Panel B—Amortization Table

A1

	A	B	C	D	E	F
1	**Semiannual Interest Date**	**Int Pmt (0.045* Maturity Value)**	**Interest Expense (0.04* Preceding Bond Carrying Value)**	**Premium Amortization (B − C)**	**Premium Account Balance (Preceding E − D)**	**Bond Carrying Value ($100,000 + E)**
2	1/1/2018				4,100	104,100
3	7/1/2018	4,500	4,164	336	3,764	103,764
4	1/1/2019	4,500	4,151	349	3,415	103,415
5	7/1/2019	4,500	4,137	363	3,052	103,052
6	1/1/2020	4,500	4,122	378	2,674	102,674
7	7/1/2020	4,500	4,107	393	2,281	102,281
8	1/1/2021	4,500	4,091	409	1,872	101,872
9	7/1/2021	4,500	4,075	425	1,447	101,447
10	1/1/2022	4,500	4,058	442	1,005	101,005
11	7/1/2022	4,500	4,040	460	545	100,545
12	1/1/2023	4,500	3,955**	545	0	100,000
13						

*Indicates multiplication in Excel.
**Adjusted for the effects of rounding.

Try It in Excel®

If you prepared a debt amortization table for a bond discount with Excel (Exhibit 9-2), it's easy to prepare an amortization table for a bond premium. Open a blank Excel spreadsheet.

- In line 1, label the columns as shown in Panel B of Exhibit 9-5.
- Column A. Starting in line 2, enter the issue date (1/1/2018) followed by each of the semiannual interest payment dates. This will continue through line 12 with the last interest payment on January 1, 2023. Highlight all cell values in rows 2 through 12 of column A, and click on the drop-down box in the "number" field on the ruler at the top of the spreadsheet. Choose the "date" category and click OK to change all cell values in Column A to the date format.
- Line 2, column E (bond premium). Enter 4100 in cell E2. Enter the formula =100000+E2 in cell F2. The calculated value of 104100 should appear in cell F2, representing the initial carrying value of the bond.
- Line 3, column B (semiannual interest payments, fixed by contract). In cell B3, enter formula =.045*100000. A calculated value of 4500 should appear, representing the first cash interest payment.

- Line 3, column C (interest expense, calculated as the market rate of 4% × previous period's carrying value of the bond). In cell C3, enter formula =.04*F2. A calculated value of 4164 should appear, representing the interest expense recognized on the first interest payment date. If the cell shows a decimal fraction, use the "decrease decimal" command in the "number" field of the toolbar to reduce the decimals to none. This will round the value to the nearest dollar.
- Line 3, column D (premium amortization, which is the excess of interest payment in column B over the interest expense in column C). In cell D3, enter formula = B3–C3. A value of 336 should appear, representing the amount of premium amortization deducted from interest expense on the first interest payment date.
- Line 3, column E (unamortized premium account balance, which decreases as it is amortized). In cell E3, enter formula = E2–D3. A value of 3764 should appear, representing the remaining unamortized premium after the first interest payment.
- Line 3, column F (bond carrying value). In cell F3, enter formula =100000+E3. A value of 103764 should appear, representing the adjusted carrying value of the bond after the first interest payment.
- For columns B to F, copy line 3 down through line 12. All of the numbers in the table should fill in. Line 12 will have to be adjusted for rounding by taking the remaining unamortized premium from cell E11 (544) and substituting that value in cell D12 (premium amortization). Also, substitute 3955 for interest expense in cell C12. This will adjust the final bond carrying value to the maturity value of $100,000 and the unamortized premium to 0. Your Excel table may be $1 off in some places because of rounding.
- Highlight cells B2 through F12 and format them for commas but no decimals, as you did for Exhibit 9-2.

Immediately after issuing the bonds at a premium on January 1, 2018, Southwest would report the bonds payable on the balance sheet as follows:

Total current liabilities		$ XXX
Long-term liabilities:		
Bonds payable	$100,000	
Premium on bonds payable	4,100	104,100

A premium is added to the balance of bonds payable to determine the carrying value.

In Exhibit 9-5, Southwest borrowed $104,100 cash but must pay back only $100,000 at maturity. Amortization of the $4,100 premium will result in a reduction in Southwest's interest expense over the term of the bonds. The first interest payment on July 1, 2018, follows:

A1

	A	B	C	D
1	2018			
2	Jul 1	Interest Expense (from Exhibit 9-5)	4,164	
3		Premium on Bonds Payable	336	
4		Cash		4,500
5		*To pay semiannual interest and amortize bond premium.*		
6				

This entry shows that amortization of the premium over the first six months results in reducing the company's interest expense to $4,164 ($4,500 − $336) while the cash interest paid remains at $4,500. Exhibit 9-6 graphs Southwest's interest payments (column B from Exhibit 9-5) and interest expense (column C).

Exhibit 9-6 | Interest Expense on Bonds Payable Issued at a Premium

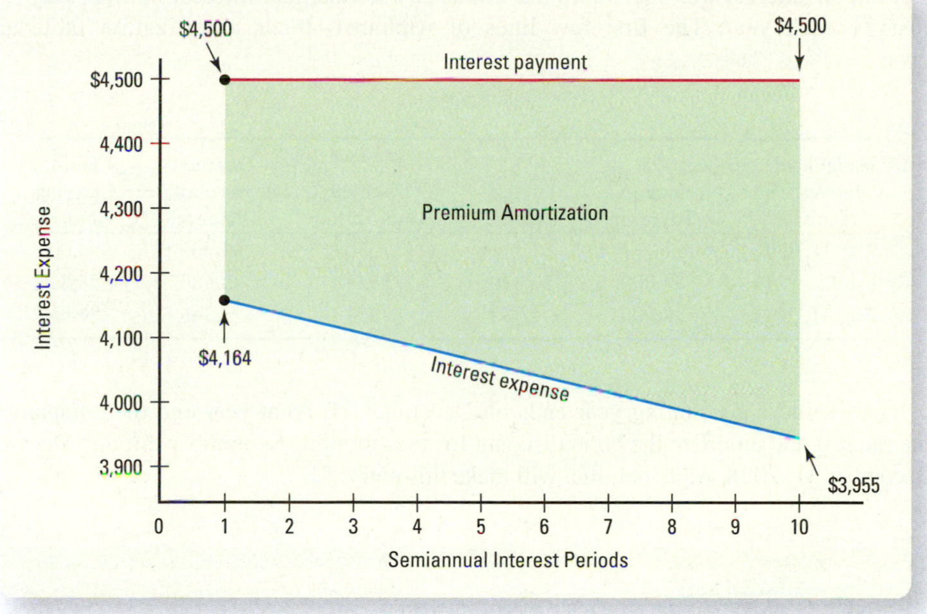

Amortization of the premium decreases interest expense each period over the term of the bonds. Exhibit 9-7 shows the amortization of the bond premium so the carrying value of the bonds decreases from their issue price of $104,100 to maturity value of $100,000. All amounts are taken from Exhibit 9-5.

Exhibit 9-7 | Amortizing Premium on Bonds Payable

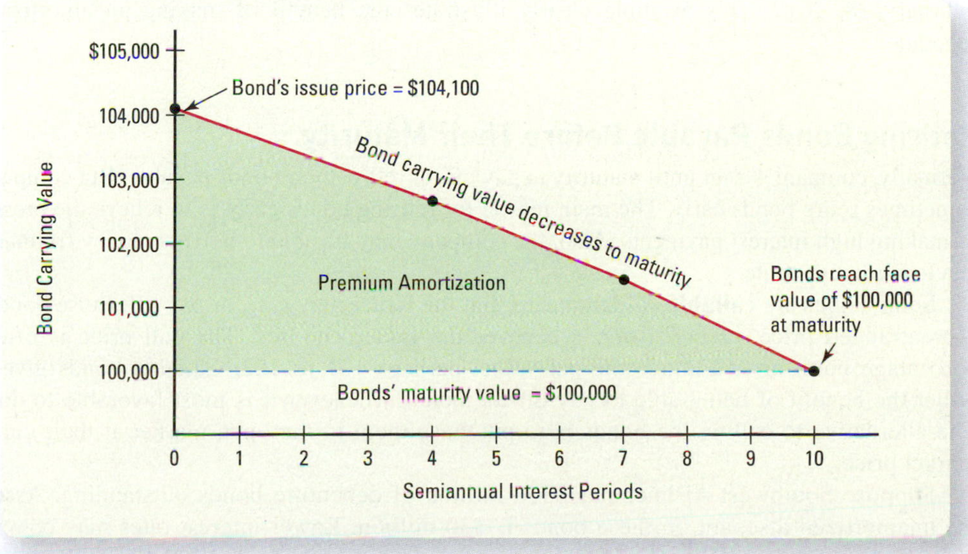

ACCOUNT FOR OTHER FEATURES OF BONDS PAYABLE

3 Account for other features of bonds payable

Accounting for Partial-Period Interest Amounts

Companies don't always issue bonds at the beginning or the end of their accounting year. They issue bonds when market conditions are most favorable, and that may be on May 16, August 1, or any other date. To illustrate partial-period interest, assume **Alphabet, Inc.**, the parent of **Google**, issues $100,000 of 8% bonds payable at $96 on August 31, 2018. The market rate of interest was 9%, and these bonds pay semiannual interest on February 28 and August 31 each year. The first few lines of Alphabet, Inc.'s amortization table are as follows:

Semiannual Interest Date	4% Interest Payment	4 ½% Interest Expense	Discount Amortization	Discount Account Balance	Bond Carrying Amount
Aug 31, 2018				$4,000	$96,000
Feb 28, 2019	$4,000	$4,320	$320	3,680	96,320
Aug 31, 2019	4,000	4,334	334	3,346	96,654

Alphabet, Inc.'s accounting year ends on December 31, so at year-end the company must accrue interest and amortize the bond discount for four months (September through December). At December 31, 2018, Alphabet, Inc. will make this entry:

	A	B	C	D
1	2018			
2	Dec 31	Interest Expense ($4,320 × 4/6)	2,880	
3		Discount on Bonds Payable ($320 × 4/6)		213
4		Interest Payable ($4,000 × 4/6)		2,667
5		*To accrue interest and amortize discount at year-end.*		
6				

The year-end entry at December 31, 2018, uses 4/6 of the upcoming semiannual amounts at February 28, 2019. This example clearly illustrates the benefit of making an amortization schedule.

Retiring Bonds Payable Before Their Maturity

Normally, companies wait until maturity to pay off, or retire, their bonds payable. But companies sometimes retire bonds early. The main reason for retiring bonds early is to relieve the pressure of making high interest payments. Also, the company may be able to borrow money (refinance) at a lower interest rate.

Some bonds are **callable**, which means that the issuer may *call*, or pay off, those bonds at a prearranged price, or *call price*, whenever the issuer chooses. The call price is often a percentage point or two above the par value, perhaps 101 or 102. Callable bonds give the issuer the benefit of being able to pay off the bonds whenever it is most favorable to do so. The alternative to calling the bonds is to purchase them in the open market at their current market price.

Suppose Southwest Airlines has $300 million of debenture bonds outstanding. Assume the unamortized discount on these bonds is $30 million. Lower interest rates may convince the company to pay off the bonds now. Assume that the bonds are callable at 101. If the market price of the bonds is 99, will Southwest call the bonds at 101 or purchase them for 99 in the open market? Paying the market price is the better choice because it is lower than the call price. Retiring the bonds at 99 results in a loss of $27 million, which is computed as follows:

	Millions
Par value of bonds being retired	$300
Less: Unamortized discount	(30)
Carrying value of the bonds being retired	270
Market price ($300 × 0.99)	297
Loss on retirement of bonds payable	$ 27

Gains and losses on early retirement of bonds payable are reported as Other income (loss) on the income statement.

Accounting for Convertible Bonds and Notes

Some corporate bonds can be converted into the issuing company's common stock. These bonds are called **convertible bonds**, or **convertible notes**. For investors, convertible bonds combine the safety of (a) assured receipt of interest and principal on the bonds with (b) the opportunity for gains on the stock. The conversion feature is so attractive that investors usually accept lower interest rates on convertible bonds than they do on nonconvertible bonds. The lower cash interest payments benefit the issuer. If the market price of the issuing company's stock gets high enough, the bondholders will convert the bonds into stock.

Suppose Southwest Airlines has convertible notes payable of $100 million. If Southwest's stock price rises high enough, the note holders will convert the notes into the company's common stock. The conversion of the notes payable into stock will decrease Southwest's liabilities and increase its equity.

Assume the note holders convert the notes into four million shares of Southwest Airlines common stock on May 14, and that the par value of the stock is $1. Southwest makes the following entry:

A1

	A	B	C	D
1	May 14	Convertible Notes Payable	100,000,000	
2		Common Stock (4,000,000 × $1 par)		4,000,000
3		Paid-in Capital in Excess of Par—Common		96,000,000
4		*To record conversion of notes payable.*		
5				

The accounting equation shows that liabilities decrease and stockholders' equity increases.

Assets	=	Liabilities	+	Stockholders' Equity
0	=	(100,000,000)		+ 4,000,000 + 96,000,000

The carrying value of the notes ($100 million) ceases to be debt and becomes stockholders' equity. Common Stock is recorded at its par value, which is a dollar amount assigned to each share of stock. In this case, the credit to Common Stock is $4,000,000 (4,000,000 shares × $1 par value per share). The extra carrying value of the notes payable ($96,000,000) is credited to another stockholders' equity account, Paid-in Capital in Excess of Par—Common. We'll be using this account in various ways in the next chapter.

DESCRIBE OTHER LONG-TERM LIABILITIES

4 Describe other long-term liabilities

Southwest Airlines Co. has several other long-term liabilities recorded as line items on its balance sheet. In addition, some commitments and obligations are reported in the financial statement footnotes, but are not required to be recorded as line items in the liability section on the balance sheet. Accounting for these liabilities can be very complex. For simplicity, we will skip many of the details because they are covered in later courses. We will briefly discuss deferred income taxes, commitments, and leases, because they are prominent in Southwest Airlines Company's financial statements.

Deferred Income Taxes

Southwest Airlines, like most public companies, maintains two sets of accounting records. Both sets of records reflect the same transactions, but measurement and reporting of these transactions follow two different sets of rules: one for the purpose of financial reporting and the other for reporting the company's taxes. Having two sets of records and rules is not illegal; in fact, it is a legal requirement.

For financial accounting purposes, the company must follow U.S. generally accepted accounting principles (GAAP), the objective of which is to provide useful economic information for making business decisions. *Income tax expense (or provision for federal income taxes)* on a company's income statement helps measure net income and is based on GAAP. Southwest Airlines Co.'s income tax expense (provision) on its Consolidated Statement of Income for fiscal 2016 was $1,303 million (which was 36.7% of its net income before taxes).

However, for tax reporting purposes, the company must follow the rules and regulations set forth by the Internal Revenue Code (IRC). The purpose behind the IRC and related regulations is to raise sufficient revenues to pay for government expenditures. Tax laws are written to encourage certain taxpayer behaviors (such as providing businesses with economic incentives to re-invest frequently in fixed assets in order to keep the economy moving).

Income taxes payable, a current liability on the balance sheet, represents the amount of income tax Southwest will pay to the federal government based on tax reporting rules. The allocation of revenues and expenses to various time periods can be different for financial accounting and tax purposes, producing a difference between a company's income tax expense on its income statement and income tax payable on its balance sheet in any one period.

Let's consider a simple example. Suppose Southwest Airlines' income tax expense and income tax payable are the same. Therefore, there are no timing differences between the company's book income and taxable income. Let's assume that the company's pretax accounting income is $2,500 million, and that its income tax rate is 40%. On December 31, 2018, the company would record its income tax expense and income tax payable as equal amounts, as follows:

	A	B	C	D
1	2018	(in millions)		
2	Dec. 31	Income tax expense ($2,500 x .4)	1,000	
3		Income tax payable		1,000
4		*To record income tax for the year.*		
5				

Southwest Airlines Co.'s financial statements (partial) for fiscal 2018 would report these figures (in millions):

	A	B	C	D
1	**Income Statement (in millions)**		**Balance sheet (in millions)**	
2	Income before income tax	$ 2,500	Current liabilities:	
3	Income tax expense	1,000	Income tax payable	$ 1,000
4	Net income	$ 1,500		
5				

For almost all companies, income tax expense and income tax payable differ. This occurs because there are many types of revenue and expense transactions that affect income in different periods for accounting purposes and tax purposes. These are called temporary differences because they reverse themselves as time passes. The most common temporary difference between accounting income and taxable income occurs when a corporation uses straight-line depreciation in its financial statements and the Modified Accelerated Cost Recovery System (MACRS) depreciation for the tax return. These differences were discussed in Chapter 7.

As a hypothetical example, suppose that for fiscal 2017, Southwest Airlines owns 30 airplanes that originally cost \$50 million each, for a total investment of \$1,500 million. The GAAP book value of the planes is \$1,200 million. However, for tax purposes, the book value of the planes is \$1,000 million. The \$200 million difference is a timing difference, the result of Southwest Airlines using

- straight-line depreciation for accounting purposes, and
- MACRS depreciation for tax purposes.

Using this simplified example, as of the end of fiscal 2017, Southwest Airlines has been able to delay (or defer) paying federal income taxes by reporting \$200 million more depreciation expense on its tax return than it reported on its income statement. Assuming that Southwest's corporate tax rate is 40%, the amount of the deferred tax liability account for 2017 for the 30 planes is \$80 million (\$200 million × .4). If there are no other deferred tax items, Southwest Airlines would report a deferred tax liability of \$80 million for 2017.

At the end of 2018, Southwest Airlines Co. will again compare the GAAP book value of the 30 planes to the tax book value. Assume that their GAAP book value is now \$1,100 million, and the tax book value is now \$800 million. The timing difference between GAAP book value and tax book value is now \$300 million (\$1,100 million − \$800 million). This timing difference results in a deferred tax liability of \$120 million (\$300 million × .4), an increase of \$40 million from fiscal 2017.

Assume the company completes its tax return in 2018 and determines that it has taxable income of \$2,500 million. Assuming a tax rate of 40%, therefore, the company owes \$1,000 million in federal income tax (\$2,500 million × .40). The income tax expense reported under GAAP is the amount needed to complete a journal entry to record (1) the accrual for the amount for the 2018 taxes (a current liability) for \$1,000 million, plus (2) the increase in the deferred tax liability account (a long-term liability) of \$40 million. The entry to record the tax accrual for 2018 is:

A1

	A	B	C	D
1	2018	(in millions)		
2	Dec. 31	Income tax expense	1,040	
3		Income tax payable (\$2,500 x .4)		1,000
4		Deferred income taxes payable (\$120 - \$80)		40
5		*To record income taxes.*		
6				

Some transactions produce taxable income that exceeds book income (the opposite of our example). When that occurs, the company debits a deferred tax asset account rather than credits a deferred tax liability. For financial statement disclosure purposes, deferred tax assets may offset deferred tax liabilities.

In the footnotes to its actual 2016 financial statements, Southwest Airlines Co. reported gross deferred tax liabilities of \$4,860 million as of December 31, 2016, mostly due to accelerated depreciation on its planes and ground facilities. The company also reported gross deferred tax assets from various other types of transactions in the amount of \$1,486 million. The net amount (a deferred tax liability) on the company's balance sheet was therefore \$3,374 million (\$4,860 million − \$1,486 million).

The details of accounting for deferred taxes are quite complex and are reserved for later courses. At this point, all you need to understand is that deferred tax assets and deferred tax liabilities arise because of temporary timing differences for recording certain revenues and expenses between the income statement and the tax return. Each temporary difference has an impact on the company's income statement in one accounting period and the company's tax return in another period.

Commitments

Commitments are contractual promises to make transactions in the future that create financial obligations for a company. Note 4 of Southwest Airlines Company's 2016 financial statements (the same note that describes contingencies) also includes a chart that describes the company's contractual purchase commitments to take delivery of 478 new Boeing 737 aircraft from 2017 through 2027. It would not be proper to accrue future commitments as long-term liabilities on the balance sheet because the transactions have not yet occurred. However, because of the substantial amount of money required to fulfill these commitments and their impact on the company's financial statements in future years, Southwest is obligated to disclose them to shareholders and creditors in the footnotes to its financial statements.

In addition, Southwest Airlines has entered into agreements with several municipalities in Florida, Texas, and California to oversee and manage the construction of airport terminals, other airport infrastructure, and international facilities for the company's international flights. The projects are funded by the municipalities. Southwest accounts for these commitments much like it does its long-term finance leases (discussed in the next section). During construction of the facilities, the company records the expenditures as Assets Constructed for Others in the fixed asset section of its Consolidated Balance Sheet. As the company receives reimbursements from the various municipalities, it records them as increases to the account entitled Construction Obligation in the long-term liability section. As of December 31, 2016, the company had recorded $1,078 million in this account, and about an equal amount in the fixed assets section of the balance sheet. The details of this type of accounting are considered beyond the scope of this text.

Leases

A **lease** allows a business to use a fixed asset without having to make the large up-front payment to purchase it. For this reason, many large companies lease, rather than purchase, fixed assets of all kinds—buildings, vehicles, operating equipment, furniture, fixtures, and more. Accountants distinguish between two types of leases: finance leases and operating leases.

A **finance lease** enables the company leasing the asset to own it after a period of time. In other words, a finance lease is actually a mechanism for financing a purchase. A lease agreement that meets any one of the following criteria is considered a finance lease:

1. The lease transfers ownership of the asset to the **lessee** by the end of the lease term.
2. The lease grants the lessee an option to purchase the asset that the lessee is reasonably certain to exercise.
3. The lease term is for the major part of the remaining economic life of the asset.
4. The present value[3] of the sum of lease payments and any residual value guaranteed by the lessee that is not already reflected in lease payments equals or exceeds substantially all of the fair value of the asset.
5. The asset is of such a specialized nature that it is expected to have no alternative use to the **lessor** (property owner) at the end of the lease term.

If the lease agreement contains none of the above criteria, it is considered an operating lease. An **operating lease** allows the company leasing the asset to use it but not eventually own it.

In 2016, the Financial Accounting Standards Board adopted a new standard for measuring and reporting leases, which goes into effect for public companies in December 2018 (2019 for nonpublic companies). The new standard requires *both* finance and operating leases that are longer than 12 months to be placed on the balance sheet. The leased asset is capitalized in the

[3] See Appendix F.

fixed asset section of the balance sheet, and the related obligation for future lease payments is recorded as a long-term liability.

To understand the importance of the new lease standard, you have to understand how lease agreements were treated before the new standard was issued and how the new standard affects leased assets and lease liabilities. The previous standard, like the new one, classified leases that did not meet any of the criteria as an operating lease. However, under the previous standard, with an operating lease, a company wasn't required to recognize the related leased assets and lease liabilities in the body of its balance sheet. Instead, an operating lease was treated like rent expense, and the future amount of the lease payments was only required to be disclosed in the footnotes to the financial statements.

Capitalizing a lease (putting it on a company's balance sheet) can significantly increase a company's long-term debt as well as its total assets. This, in turn, will increase the company's debt ratio and decrease its return on assets (ROA), potentially making it a less attractive credit or investment candidate.

Southwest Airlines leases some of its aircraft and most of its ground facilities. Let's look at how it accounted for its leased assets as of December 31, 2016, before the new standard took effect. Then, let's estimate the impact of the new standard on Southwest's debt and ROA ratios.

At December 31, 2016, Southwest Airlines Co. reported its financing (capital) leases in Note 7 of its financial statements, as follows:

Note 7 Leases (partial)
The Company's fleet included 51 aircraft on capital lease as of December 31, 2016, compared with 28 aircraft on capital lease, including one B717, as of December 31, 2015. Amounts applicable to these aircraft that are included in property and equipment were:

(in millions)	2016	2015
Flight equipment	$ 923	$ 435
Less: accumulated amortization	82	29
	$ 841	$ 406

Source: Data from the U.S. Securities and Exchange Commission EDGAR Company filings, www.sec.gov

The company capitalized the cost of the 51 aircraft in fixed assets and included the obligation for their future lease payments in long-term liabilities.

Now let's look at how the company accounted for its operating leases in 2016. Another excerpt from Note 7 of Southwest's 2016 financial statements reads as follows:

Note 7 Leases (partial)
Total rental expense for operating leases, both aircraft and other, charged to operations in 2016, 2015, and 2014 was $932 million, $909 million, and $931 million, respectively. The majority of the Company's terminal operations space, as well as 83 aircraft, were under operating leases at December 31, 2016. For aircraft operating leases and for terminal operations leases, expense is recorded on a straight-line basis and included in Aircraft rentals and in Landing fees and other rentals, respectively, in the Consolidated Statement of Income. Future minimum lease payments under noncancelable operating leases, net of subleases revenue, with initial or remaining terms in excess of one year at December 31, 2016, were:

(in millions)	Operating leases, net
2017	$ 592
2018	485
2019	419
2020	325
2021	217
Thereafter	1,297
Total	$ 3,335

Source: Data from the U.S. Securities and Exchange Commission EDGAR Company filings, www.sec.gov

In 2016, the company recorded $932 million of rental expense. However, Southwest has an obligation to pay more than $3.3 billion for several years to the companies with which it has operating leases. Neither these obligations nor the associated assets are included in Southwest Airlines Co.'s Consolidated Balance Sheet as of December 31 2016.

Let's make a rough approximation of what would have happened to Southwest's debt ratio and ROA if the operating leases had been capitalized and the corresponding long-term liabilities had been recognized as of December 31, 2016, as the new standard requires.

	A	B	C	D	E	F
1					**Operating Leases as Stated**	**Operating Leases under New Standard**
2						
3			Total Liabilities		$ 14,845	$14,845 + $3,335
4	Debt ratio	=	Total Assets	=	$ 23,286	$23,286 + $3,335
5						
6				=	63.8%	68.3%
7						
8	Return on Assets (ROA)	=	Net income		$ 2,244	$ 2,244
9			Average Total assets	=	$ 22,299	$ 25,876
10						
11				=	10.1%	8.7%
12						

Note that capitalizing the operating leases increases Southwest's debt ratio from 63.8% to 68.3%, and decreases its ROA from 10.1% to 8.7%. Southwest Airlines Company is in better financial condition than many U.S. companies, so it appears that adoption of the new lease standard will not affect the company's debt or ROA ratios that severely. However, the balance sheets of other companies with significant operating leases will be impacted in a much more significant way. For example, **Walgreen Boots Alliance** (the parent company of Walgreens) had about $70 billion in average total assets and about $40 billion in total liabilities on its balance sheet at the end of its 2016 fiscal year (a debt ratio of about 57%). It also had $33 billion in operating lease agreements that were not recorded in either assets or liabilities. The company had about $4.2 billion in net income. Adding $33 billion in both assets and liabilities to Walgreens' balance sheet would increase its debt ratio from about 57% to about 71% ($73 billion / $103 billion). Walgreens' ROA would fall by one-third, from about 6% ($4.2 billion/$70 billion) to about 4% ($4.2 billion / $103 billion).

ANALYZE THE IMPACT OF LEVERAGE ON THE FINANCIAL STATEMENTS

5 **Analyze** the impact of leverage on the financial statements

As you have learned, financing with debt can be advantageous, but a company must be careful not to incur too much debt. Chapter 3 discussed the debt ratio, which measures the proportion of a company's total liabilities to its total assets:

$$\text{Debt ratio} = \frac{\text{Total debt (liabilities)}}{\text{Total assets}}$$

The Leverage Ratio

We can rearrange the relationship among total assets, total liabilities, and stockholders' equity differently to illustrate the impact that **leverage** (debt) can have on a business's profitability. The **leverage ratio** is calculated as follows:

$$\text{Leverage ratio} = \frac{\text{Average total assets}}{\text{Average common stockholders' equity}}$$

Also known as the **equity multiplier**, the leverage ratio shows a company's average total assets per dollar of average common stockholders' equity. A leverage ratio of exactly 1.0 would mean a company has no debt, because total assets would exactly equal total stockholders' equity. However, virtually all companies have liabilities and, therefore, have leverage ratios in excess of 1.0. The more debt a company accumulates, the smaller is the relative amount of total assets that are financed with stockholders' equity; thus, the denominator of the fraction decreases, increasing the leverage ratio. As you have learned, having a healthy amount of debt can actually enhance a company's profitability, in terms of the shareholders' investment.

The leverage ratio is the third element of the *DuPont Analysis* model, introduced earlier in the discussion of return on assets (ROA) (in Chapter 7).[4] The higher the leverage ratio (the more money a company borrows), the more it magnifies the return on stockholders' equity (Net income/Average stockholders' equity, or ROE). If net income is positive, return on assets (ROA) is positive. The leverage ratio magnifies a positive return, making the return on equity (ROE) even more positive. However, if earnings are negative (losses), ROA is negative, so the leverage ratio makes ROE even more negative.

Let's focus on understanding the meaning of the leverage ratio by looking at Southwest Airlines in comparison with one of its competitors, United Continental Holdings (the parent company of United Airlines). Here are the leverage ratios and debt ratios for the two companies at the end of 2016:

(In millions) for 2016	Southwest	United Continental
1. Average total assets	$22,299	$40,476
2. Average common stockholders' equity	$ 7,900	$ 8,785
3. Leverage ratio (1 ÷ 2)	2.82	4.61
4. Total liabilities (debt)	$14,845	$31,485
5. Total assets	$23,286	$40,091
6. Debt ratio (4 ÷ 5)	63.8%	78.5%

Source: Data from the U.S. Securities and Exchange Commission EDGAR Company filings, www.sec.gov

These figures show that Southwest has a leverage ratio of 2.82. (The company owns $2.82 of average total assets for each dollar of average stockholders' equity.) Southwest's debt ratio is 63.8%, which we learned in Chapter 3 is about normal for many companies, and relatively low for the airline industry. In comparison, United Continental has a leverage ratio of 4.61 and a debt ratio of 78.5%, which is much higher. Southwest is likely to be regarded as a less risky borrower from the standpoint of potential creditors than United Continental on the basis of these ratios because its leverage and debt ratios are lower. United Continental's leverage ratio is higher, so it relies on borrowed capital more than Southwest does. However, with its higher leverage ratio, if United Continental has a positive ROA, its ROE will be enhanced more than that of Southwest Airlines Company.

The Times-Interest-Earned Ratio

Analysts use a second ratio—the **times-interest-earned ratio**—to relate operating income to interest expense. To compute this ratio, we divide a company's *operating income* (also called *income from operations*) by its interest expense. This ratio measures the number of times that operating income can *cover* interest expense. The times-interest-earned ratio is also called the **interest-coverage ratio**. A high times-interest-earned ratio indicates it's easy for a company to pay interest expense with operating income; a low value suggests it is difficult.

[4] The DuPont analysis model provides a detailed analysis of return on equity (ROE). It is the product of three elements: (Net income/Net sales) × (Net sales/Average total assets) × (Average total assets/Average common stockholders' equity). Notice that elements cross-cancel so that the model reduces to Net income/Average common stockholders' equity. See Chapter 10 for a more complete discussion of ROE.

Let's see how Southwest and United Continental compare on the times-interest-earned ratio (dollar amounts in millions taken from the companies' 2016 financial statements):

$$\text{Times-interest-earned ratio} = \frac{\text{Operating income}}{\text{Interest expense}}$$

$$\text{Southwest} \quad \frac{\$3{,}760}{\$122} = 30.8 \text{ times}$$

$$\text{United Continental} \quad \frac{\$4{,}338}{\$614} = 7.1 \text{ times}$$

Data from the U.S. Securities and Exchange Commission EDGAR Company filings, www.sec.gov

Southwest's income from operations covers its interest expense 30.8 times, which is quite strong, indicating it is a highly profitable company fully capable of servicing its debt. In contrast, United Continental can cover its interest expense 7.1 times, which is still comfortable, but not as strong as Southwest.

REPORT LONG-TERM LIABILITIES ON THE FINANCIAL STATEMENTS

6 Report long-term liabilities on the financial statements

Reporting on the Balance Sheet

This chapter began with the liabilities reported on the consolidated balance sheets of Southwest Airlines. Exhibit 9-8 shows a standard way for Southwest to report its current liabilities and long-term debt.

Exhibit 9-8 Reporting the Liabilities of Southwest Airlines Company

A1

	A	B	C	D	E
1	**Southwest Airlines Co. Consolidated Balance Sheet (Partial, Adapted)**	**Dec. 31, 2016**		**Note 6 Long-Term Debt (In millions) (Adapted)**	**Dec. 31, 2016**
2	**Liabilities (in millions)**				
3	Current Liabilities:			Term loans due 2019–26	$ 1,446
4	Accounts payable	$ 1,178		Pass-through certificates due 2022	324
5	Accrued liabilities	1,985		Fixed rate aircraft notes	829
6	Air traffic liability	3,115		7 3/8% debentures due 2027	130
7	Current maturities of			Capital leases	681
8	long-term debt	566		Total long-term debt	3,410
9	Total current liabilities	6,844		Less current maturities	(566)
10	Long-term debt, less current			Less debt discounted and	
11	maturities	2,821		issuance costs	(23)
12	Other long-term liabilities	5,180		Long-term debt	$ 2,821
13					
14	Total liabilities	$ 14,845			
15					

Exhibit 9-8 includes Note 6 from Southwest's consolidated financial statements. The note gives additional details about the company's liabilities. Note 6 shows the interest rates and the maturity dates of Southwest's long-term debt. Investors need this information to evaluate the company. The note also reports

- current maturities of long-term debt ($566 million) as a current liability.
- long-term debt (less current maturities) of $2,821 million.

Trace these amounts from the note to the balance sheet. Working back and forth between the financial statements and the related notes is an important part of financial analysis. You now have the tools to understand the liabilities reported on an actual balance sheet.

Disclosing the Fair Value of Long-Term Debt

Generally accepted accounting principles encourage companies to report the fair value of their long-term debt. At December 31, 2016, Southwest Airlines' Note 11 included this excerpt (adapted, details omitted):

> The estimated fair value of the Company's long-term debt, excluding current maturities, was $2,787 million.

Overall, the fair value of Southwest's long-term debt, excluding current maturities, is about $34 million less than its carrying amount on the books ($2,821 million). Fair values of publicly traded debt are based on quoted market prices, which fluctuate with interest rates and overall market conditions. Therefore, at any one time, fair values for various obligations can either exceed or be less than their carrying amounts.

Reporting Financing Activities on the Statement of Cash Flows

CASH FLOW

Let's examine Southwest's financing activities as reported on its statement of cash flows. Exhibit 9-9 is an excerpt from Southwest's consolidated statement of cash flows.

Exhibit 9-9 | Consolidated Statement of Cash Flows (partial, adapted) for Southwest Airlines Co.

	A	B
1	**Southwest Airlines Co. Consolidated Statement of Cash Flows (Adapted)**	
2	**(In millions)**	**Year Ended December 31, 2016**
3	Cash Flow from Operating Activities:	
4	Net cash provided by operating activities	$ 4,293
5	Cash Flow from Investing Activities:	
6	Net cash used for investing activities	(2,272)
7	Cash Flow from Financing Activities:	
8	Payments of long-term debt and capital lease obligations	(523)
9	Repurchase of common stock	(1,750)
10	Proceeds from issuance of long-term debt	515
11	Payments of cash dividends	(222)
12	Other financing sources (net)	56
13	Net cash used for financing activities	(1,924)
14	Net change in cash and cash equivalents	$ 97
15		

Southwest provided about $4.3 billion more cash from operations than it used in 2016. The company has a long history of good financial management, and it is one of the most liquid and profitable airline companies in the industry. With the excess cash generated from operations, Southwest had net investing activities of about $2.27 billion in property and equipment and investments of various types. In contrast, the company borrowed $515 million in long-term debt and spent $523 million in payments on long-term debt and capital lease obligations. It spent $1,750 million repurchasing common stock and paid $222 million in dividends, topics we will cover in Chapter 10. Southwest has borrowed rather heavily in order to finance its growth and refurbish its fleet of aircraft. This is evident in the long-term debt footnote in Exhibit 9-8. Much of that debt had not yet come due as of the end of 2016. About $2.8 billion of the debt still remained, with current maturities of about $566 million and the remainder extending to 2027. Over the next several years, the company will have to pay the debt off as it comes due, in installments, with cash provided by its operations.

End-of-Chapter | Summary Problem

The Cessna Aircraft Company has issued 4% convertible bonds that mature October 1, 2026. Suppose the bonds are issued October 1, 2018, and pay interest each April 1 and October 1.

Bond Data

Maturity (face) value—$100,000

Stated interest rate—4%

Interest paid—2% semiannually, $2,000 ($100,000 × 0.04 × 6/12)

Market interest rate at the time of issue—5% annually, $2^{1}/_{2}$% semiannually

Requirements

1. Assume the bonds are issued at a price of 93.5. Using the straight-line method to amortize the bond discount:
   a. Calculate the company's interest expense on bonds payable for each semiannual interest payment period. Use two decimal places.
   b. Calculate the amount of accrued interest payable on the company's December 31, 2018, financial statements.
   c. Prepare the journal entry required as of December 31, 2018, to accrue interest on the bonds payable.
2. Use Excel to build an amortization table through October 1, 2020. Use Excel to obtain the issue price. Use the effective-interest method of amortization. Round to the nearest dollar.
3. Using the amortization table, record the following transactions:
   a. The issuance of the bonds on October 1, 2018.
   b. The accrual of interest and amortization of the bond discount on December 31, 2018.
   c. The payment of interest and amortization of the bond discount on April 1, 2019.
   d. The conversion of one-third of the bonds payable into stock on October 2, 2020. For the stock, transfer the bond carrying value into the Common Stock account. There is no Additional Paid-in Capital account.
   e. The retirement of two-thirds of the bonds payable on October 2, 2020. The purchase price of the bonds is based on their call price of 102.

Answers

Requirement 1

	A B	C	D	E
1	1 (a):			
2	(a) Face amount of bonds		$ 100,000	
3	× Issue price		×.935	
4	(b) Proceeds		$ 93,500	
5	(c) Discount ((a) – (b))		$ 6,500	
6	Number of semiannual interest payment periods (8 × 2)		16	
7	Straight-line amortization per interest period ($6,500/16)		$ 406.25	
8	Interest paid each interest period (.02 × $100,000)		$2,000.00	
9	Total interest expense each interest period		$2,406.25	
10	1 (b):			
11	Accrued interest payable as of 12/31/2018:			
12	Interest paid each interest period (.02 × $100,000)		$2,000.00	
13	× portion of period between 10/1/2018 and 12/31/2018		× 3/6	
14	Accrued interest payable as of 12/31/2018		$1,000.00	
15	1(c):			
16	Interest Expense ($2,406.25 × .5)		1,203.13	
17	Discount on Bonds Payable ($406.25 × .5)			203.13
18	Interest Payable ($2,000 × .5)			1,000.00
19				

Requirement 2

A1

	A	B	C	D	E	F
1	**Amortization Table Cessna Aircraft Company**					
2	**Semiannual Interest Payment Date**	**Interest Payment (2% of Maturity Value)**	**Interest Expense (2.5% of Preceding Bond Carrying Value)***	**Discount Amortization (C – B)***	**Discount Account Balance (Preceding E – D)***	**Bond Carrying Value ($100,000 – E)***
3	10/1/2018				$ 6,528	$ 93,472
4	4/1/2019	$ 2,000	$ 2,337	$ 337	$ 6,191	$ 93,809
5	10/1/2019	$ 2,000	$ 2,345	$ 345	$ 5,846	$ 94,154
6	4/1/2020	$ 2,000	$ 2,354	$ 354	$ 5,492	$ 94,508
7	10/1/2020	$ 2,000	$ 2,363	$ 363	$ 5,129	$ 94,871
8						
9	Issue price	$ 93,472				
10						

*Amounts may vary by $1 because of rounding.

Requirement 3

	A	B	C	D	E
1		2018		**Debit**	**Credit**
2	a.	Oct 1	Cash	93,472	
3			Discount on Bonds Payable	6,528	
4			Bonds Payable		100,000
5			*To issue bonds at a discount.*		
6					
7	b.	Dec 31	Interest expense (2,337 × 3/6)	1,169	
8			Discount on Bonds Payable (337 × 3/6)		169
9			Interest Payable (2,000 × 3/6)		1,000
10			*To accrue interest and amortize bond discount.*		
11		2019			
12	c.	Apr 1	Interest expense (2,337 × 3/6)	1,168	
13			Interest payable	1,000	
14			Discount on Bonds Payable (337 × 3/6)		168
15			Cash		2,000
16			*To pay semiannual interest, part of which*		
17			*was accrued, and amortize bond discount.*		
18					
19	d.	2020			
20		Oct 2	Bonds Payable (100,000 × 1/3)	33,333	
21			Discount on Bonds Payable (5,129 × 1/3)		1,710
22			Common Stock (94,871 × 1/3)		31,623
23			*To convert one-third of bonds to common stock.*		
24					
25	e.	Oct 2	Bonds Payable (100,000 × 2/3)	66,667	
26			Loss on Retirement of Bonds	4,752	
27			Discount on Bonds Payable (5,129 × 2/3)		3,419
28			Cash (100,000 × 2/3 × 1.02)		68,000
29			*To retire bonds payable before maturity at 102.*		
30					

REVIEW | Long-Term Liabilities

Accounting Vocabulary

bonds payable (p. 470) Groups of debt securities issued to multiple lenders called *bondholders*.

callable bond (p. 484) Bonds that are paid off early at a specified price at the option of the issuer.

convertible bonds (or notes) (p. 485) Bonds or notes that may be converted into the issuing company's common stock at the investor's option.

debentures (p. 470) Unsecured bonds—bonds backed only by the good faith of the borrower.

discount (on a bond) (p. 470) Excess of a bond's face (par) value over its issue price.

effective-interest method (p. 476) Amortization method for debt premium or discount that takes into account the time value of money.

equity multiplier (p. 491) Another name for *leverage ratio.*

finance lease (p. 488) Lease agreement in which the lessee assumes, in substance, the risks and rewards of asset ownership. In the United States, a lease is assumed to be a finance lease if it meets any one of five criteria: (1) The lease transfers ownership of the asset to the lessee by the end of the lease term. (2) The lease grants the lessee an option to purchase the asset that the lessee is reasonably certain to exercise; (3) The lease term is for the major part of the remaining economic life of the asset; (4) The present value[5] of the sum of lease payments and any residual value guaranteed by the lessee that is not already reflected in lease payments equals or exceeds substantially all of the fair value of the asset; (5) The asset is of such a specialized nature that it is expected to have no alternative use to the lessor at the end of the lease term.

[5] See Appendix F.

interest-coverage ratio (p. 491) Another name for the *times-interest-earned ratio*.

lease (p. 488) Rental agreement in which the tenant (lessee) agrees to make rent payments to the property owner (lessor) in exchange for the use of the asset.

lessee (p. 488) Tenant in a lease agreement.

lessor (p. 488) Property owner in a lease agreement.

leverage (p. 490) Using borrowed funds to increase the return on equity. Successful use of leverage means earning more income on borrowed money than the related interest expense, thereby increasing the earnings for the owners of the business. Also called *trading on the equity*.

leverage ratio (p. 490) The ratio of average total assets ÷ average total common stockholders' equity, showing the proportion of average total assets to average total common stockholders' equity. This ratio, like the debt ratio introduced in Chapter 3, tells the mixture of a company's debt and equity financing and is useful in calculating rate of return on stockholders' equity (ROE) through the DuPont Model.

market interest rate (p. 471) Interest rate that investors demand for loaning their money. Also called *effective interest rate*.

operating lease (p. 488) A lease in which the lessee does not assume the risks or rewards of asset ownership, and one that does not meet any of the criteria for a finance lease.

premium (on a bond) (p. 470) Excess of a bond's issue price over its face (par) value.

present value (p. 470) Today's value of a future payment or series of future payments, assuming that those payments include interest at the current market rate.

serial bonds (p. 470) Bonds that mature in installments over a period of time.

stated interest rate (p. 471) Interest rate that determines the amount of cash interest the borrower pays and the investor receives each year.

term bonds (p. 470) Bonds that all mature at the same time for a particular issue.

times-interest-earned ratio (p. 491) Ratio of income from operations to interest expense. Measures the number of times that operating income can cover interest expense. Also called the *interest-coverage ratio*.

underwriter (p. 470) Organization that purchases the bonds from an issuing company and resells them to its clients or sells the bonds for a commission, agreeing to buy all unsold bonds.

Quick Check (Answers are given on page 521.)

1. Brownlee Company issued $525,000, 8%, six-year bonds for 110, with interest paid annually. Assuming straight-line amortization, what is the carrying value of the bonds after one year?

a. $573,125
b. $577,500
c. $586,250
d. $568,750

2. A bond with a face value of $250,000 and a quoted price of 98 has a selling price of

a. $250,098.
b. $245,000.
c. $255,102.
d. $250,000.

3. Mission Furniture issued $500,000 in bonds payable at par. The journal entry to record a semiannual interest payment on these bonds would

a. debit Cash and credit Interest Payable.
b. debit Cash and credit Interest Expense.
c. debit Interest Expense and credit Bonds Payable.
d. debit Interest Expense and credit Cash.

4. Bonds with an 8% stated interest rate were issued when the market rate of interest was 5%. This bond was issued at

a. face value.
b. par value.
c. a premium.
d. a discount.

5. Brimfest Corporation issued $2,400,000, 10-year, 6% bonds for $2,352,000 on January 1, 2019. Interest is paid semiannually on January 1 and July 1. The corporation uses the straight-line method of amortization. Brimfest's fiscal year ends on December 31. The amount of discount amortization on July 1, 2019, would be

a. $2,400.
b. $4,800.
c. $48,000.
d. $144,000.

6. The Discount on Bonds Payable account

a. is an expense account.
b. is a contra account to Bonds Payable.
c. is expensed at the bond's maturity.
d. is a miscellaneous revenue account.

7. The discount on a bond payable becomes

a. additional interest expense in the year the bonds are sold.
b. a reduction of interest expense in the year the bonds mature.
c. a reduction in interest expense over the life of the bonds.
d. additional interest expense over the life of the bonds.

8. The carrying value of Bonds Payable equals

a. Bonds Payable plus Discount on Bonds Payable.
b. Bonds Payable minus Discount on Bonds Payable.
c. Bonds Payable minus Premium on Bonds Payable.
d. Bonds Payable plus Accrued Interest.

9. If bonds are issued at a discount and the effective-interest method is used, the amount of interest expense

a. remains the same over the term of the bonds.
b. is less than the cash interest payment.
c. increases each period as the bonds approach maturity.
d. decreases each period as the bonds approach maturity.

10. When the effective-interest method is used, the amount of bond discount amortized each interest period is equal to the

a. amount of interest expense less the cash paid for interest.
b. amount of interest expense plus the cash paid for interest.
c. face value of the bond times the market interest rate at the date of issue.
d. face value of the bond times the stated interest rate.

11. Ellison Corporation issued $300,000, 8%, five-year bonds on January 1, 2019, for $325,591 when the market interest rate was 6%. Interest is paid semiannually on January 1 and July 1. The corporation uses the effective-interest method to amortize bond discounts and premiums. The total amount of bond interest expense recognized on July 1, 2019, would be closest to

a. $9,000.
b. $9,768.
c. $12,000.
d. $24,000.

12. When a company retires bonds early, the gain or loss on the retirement is the difference between the cash paid and the

a. face value of the bonds.
b. maturity value of the bonds.
c. carrying value of the bonds.
d. original selling price of the bonds.

13. Which type of lease will *not* increase a company's assets or long-term liabilities?

a. A one-year operating lease
b. A finance lease
c. A lease for an asset of a specialized nature with no alternative use at the end of the lease term
d. A lease that transfers ownership of the asset to the lessee by the end of the lease term

14. Dart Corporation's leverage ratio increased from 2.5 in 2017 to 3.0 in 2018. Without looking at the financial statements, which statement best describes what may have occurred?

a. The company incurred new equity financing in 2018, but it may or may not have been more profitable.
b. The company incurred new debt financing in 2018, making it more profitable.
c. The company incurred new debt financing in 2018, but it may or may not have been more profitable.
d. The company incurred new equity financing in 2018, making it less profitable.

15. The debt ratio is calculated by dividing:

a. total assets by total debt.
b. total debt by total assets.
c. total assets by long-term liabilities.
d. long-term liabilities by total assets.

16. Merryweather Corporation reported net income of $150,000, income before taxes of $240,000 and interest expense of $32,000. What is the times-interest-earned ratio? (Round your final answer to two decimal places.)

a. 4.69
b. 5.69
c. 7.50
d. 8.50

17. Bonds with a face value of $450,000 are issued at 105. The statement of cash flows would report a cash inflow of:

a. $450,000 in the financing activities section.
b. $472,500 in the financing activities section.
c. $22,500 in the financing activities section.
d. $450,000 in the investing activities section.

Excel Project
Autograded Excel Project available in **MyLab Accounting**

ASSESS YOUR PROGRESS

Ethics Check

EC9-1. Identify ethical principle violated

For each of the situations listed, identify which of three principles (integrity, objectivity and independence, or due care) from the AICPA Code of Professional Conduct is violated. Assume all persons listed in the situations are members of the AICPA. (Note: Refer to the AICPA Code of Professional Conduct contained on pages 25–27 in Chapter 1 for descriptions of the principles.)

a. Susan, a CPA, works in the accounting department of Majestic Industries. She noticed that the company's debt ratio is a little higher than its bank agreement allows. In an attempt to decrease the debt ratio, she decides to record revenue from services that will be performed the first week of the next period. She reasons that the revenue is going to be recognized anyway; her entry simply accelerates it.

b. Zachary, a CPA, accepted a position in the accounting department of Fairless State Bank. Zachary is in charge of making the bank's bond amortization adjusting entries each month. He does not remember how to make these entries because he has not used the effective-interest method since his junior year in college. Zachary assumes the amortization entry for this month is the same amount as last month and uses that total rather than calculating the current amortization amount.

c. Thompson Pools is a small, family-owned company that employs one accountant, Andrew Poling, CPA. Andrew performs all of the accounting functions at Thompson Pools. He writes checks payable to the bank for loan payments. Some of the checks are duplicate loan payments; Andrew cashes these checks at the bank and pockets the cash.

d. Isabelle is an auditor for Roeder & McFarland, a CPA firm. Her mother owns Hartville Plumbing Supply. Isabelle is excited to be assigned to work on the Hartville account because she understands the business well from working part-time for Hartville during college summer breaks. Isabelle does not disclose that her mother owns Hartville because she knows she will be impartial.

Short Exercises

S9-1. ***(Learning Objective 1: Review of bonds issued at a discount)*** Read each statement below, indicate if it is true or false, and give a brief explanation of your answer. LO 1

1. When a bond is issued at a discount, the semiannual amount of interest expense will be greater than the cash payment for interest.
2. When a bond is sold at a discount, the maturity value is less than the present value of the principal and interest payments, based on the market rate of interest on the date of issue.
3. When a bond is issued at a discount, the semiannual cash interest payments are calculated using the market interest rate on the date of issue.
4. When a bond is sold at a discount, the cash received is less than the present value of the future cash flows from the bond, which are based on the market rate of interest on the date of issue.

5. When the year-end accrual of interest and amortization of discount is recorded, the carrying value of Bonds Payable on the balance sheet will increase.
6. The amortization of the discount on a bond payable results in additional interest expense recorded over the life of the bond.

LO 1

S9-2. ***(Learning Objective 1: Determine bond prices at par, discount, or premium)*** Determine whether the following bonds payable will be issued at par value, at a premium, or at a discount.

a. Evergreen Company issued bonds payable that pay stated interest of $6^1/_4$%. On the date of issuance, the market interest rate was $6^3/_4$%.

b. Seven Hills, Inc., issued 3% bonds payable when the market rate was $3^3/_4$%.

c. Flagstaff Corporation issued 5% bonds when the market interest rate was 5%.

d. The market interest rate is 4%. Rainforest Corp. issues bonds payable with a stated rate of $5^1/_2$%.

LO 1

S9-3. ***(Learning Objective 1: Journalize basic bond payable transactions and bonds issued at par)*** Yancy Corp. issued 6% seven-year bonds payable with a face amount of $110,000 when the market interest rate was 6%. Yancy's fiscal year-end is December 31. The bonds pay interest on January 1 and July 1. Journalize the following transactions for Yancy. Include an explanation for each entry.

a. Issuance of the bonds payable at par on July 1, 2018

b. Accrual of interest expense on December 31, 2018

c. Payment of cash interest on January 1, 2019

d. Payment of the bonds payable at maturity (give the date)

LO 1

S9-4. ***(Learning Objective 1: Determine bonds payable amounts with a discount; amortize bonds using the straight-line method)*** Starlight Drive-Ins Ltd. borrowed money by issuing $5,000,000 of 7% bonds payable at 95.5 on July 1, 2018. The bonds are 10-year bonds and pay interest each January 1 and July 1.

1. How much cash did Starlight receive when it issued the bonds payable? Journalize this transaction.
2. How much must Starlight pay back at maturity? When is the maturity date?
3. How much cash interest will Starlight pay each six months?
4. How much interest expense will Starlight report each six months? Use the straight-line amortization method. Journalize the entries for the accrual of interest and amortization of discount on December 31, 2018, and the payment of interest on January 1, 2019.

LO 1

S9-5. ***(Learning Objective 1: Determine bonds payable amounts with a premium; amortize bonds using the straight-line method)*** Windsor Company borrowed money by issuing $3,000,000 of 6% bonds payable at 102.9 on July 1, 2018. The bonds are five-year bonds and pay interest each January 1 and July 1.

1. How much cash did Windsor receive when it issued the bonds payable? Journalize this transaction.
2. How much must Windsor pay back at maturity? When is the maturity date?
3. How much cash interest will Windsor pay each six months?
4. How much interest expense will Windsor report each six months? Use the straight-line amortization method. Journalize the entries for the accrual of interest and the amortization of premium on December 31, 2018, and the payment of interest on January 1, 2019.

LO 2

S9-6. ***(Learning Objective 2: Issue bonds payable at a discount and amortize bonds using the effective-interest method)*** Pearce Corporation issued $580,000 of 6%, 10-year bonds payable on March 31, 2019. The market interest rate at the date of issuance was 10%, and the bonds pay interest semiannually. Pearce Corporation's year-end is March 31.

1. Using the PV function in Excel, calculate the issue price of the bonds.
2. Prepare an effective-interest amortization table for the bonds through the first three interest payments. Round amounts to the nearest dollar.
3. Record Pearce Corporation's issuance of the bonds on March 31, 2019, and payment of the first semiannual interest amount and amortization of the bond discount on September 30, 2019. Explanations are not required.

S9-7. ***(Learning Objective 2: Account for bonds payable issued at a discount using the effective-interest method)*** Use the amortization table that you prepared for Pearce Corporation's bonds in S9-6 to answer the following questions: LO 2

1. How much cash did Pearce Corporation borrow on March 31, 2019? How much cash will the company pay back at maturity on March 31, 2029?
2. How much cash interest will the company pay each six months?
3. How much interest expense will Pearce Corporation report on September 30, 2019, and on March 31, 2020? Why does the amount of interest expense increase each period?

S9-8. ***(Learning Objective 2: Issue bonds payable at a premium and amortize bonds using the effective-interest method)*** Leon Corporation issued $400,000 of 10%, 10-year bonds payable on January 1, 2019. The market interest rate at the date of issuance was 8%, and the bonds pay interest semiannually (on June 30 and December 31). Leon Corporation's year-end is June 30. LO 2

1. Using the PV function in Excel, calculate the issue price of the bonds.
2. Prepare an effective-interest amortization table for the bonds through the first three interest payments. Round amounts to the nearest dollar.
3. Record Leon Corporation's issuance of the bonds on January 1, 2019, and payment of the first semiannual interest amount and amortization of the bond premium on June 30, 2019. Explanations are not required.

S9-9. ***(Learning Objective 2: Account for bonds payable issued at a premium using the effective-interest method)*** Use the amortization table that you prepared for Leon Corporation's bonds in S9-8 to answer the following questions: LO 2

1. How much cash did Leon Corporation borrow on January 1, 2019? How much cash will Leon Corporation pay back at maturity?
2. How much cash interest will Leon Corporation pay each six months?
3. How much interest expense will Leon Corporation report on June 30, 2019, and on December 31, 2019? Does the amount of interest expense increase or decrease each period? Why?

S9-10. ***(Learning Objective 3: Account for a bond payable retirement before maturity)*** Jamison Corporation has $300 million of debenture bonds outstanding that have an unamortized discount of $30 million. Lower interest rates convinced the company to pay off the bonds now by purchasing them on the market where the price of the bonds is 98. What is Jamison's gain or loss on the retirement of the bonds? How would this gain or loss be shown in the financial statements? LO 3

S9-11. ***(Learning Objectives 4, 5: Deferred income tax, commitments, lease, and ratio vocabulary terms)*** Complete the following statements with one of the terms listed here. LO 4, 5

Commitment	Finance lease	Leverage ratio
Debt ratio	Income tax payable	Operating lease
Deferred income taxes payable	Lessee	Times-interest-earned ratio

1. The ____________ measures the proportion of a company's total liabilities to its total assets.
2. ____________ is usually a long-term liability arising from the temporary timing differences for revenues and expense recognition between GAAP accounting rules and the U.S. tax code.
3. A ____________ enables a company leasing an asset to own it after a period of time.
4. A high ____________ indicates ease in paying interest expense.
5. ____________ is a current liability and represents the amount of income taxes a company must pay to the federal government based on tax reporting rules.
6. A(n) ____________ covering twelve months or less is the only type of lease that is not required to be included on the balance sheet.
7. A company's average total assets per dollar of average common stockholders' equity is its ____________.
8. A contractual promise to make transactions in the future that create financial obligations for a company is a ____________.
9. The tenant in a lease arrangement is also known as the ____________.

LO 5 **S9-12.** ***(Learning Objective 5: Compute and evaluate three ratios)*** Tolbert Plumbing Products Ltd. reported the following data in 2018 (in millions):

	2018
Net operating revenues	$ 28.9
Operating expenses	24.2
Operating income	4.7
Nonoperating items:	
Interest expense	(0.8)
Other	(0.2)
Net income	$ 3.7
Total assets	$150.0
Total common stockholders' equity	57.0

Compute Tolbert's leverage ratio, debt ratio, and times-interest-earned ratio, and write a sentence to explain what those ratio values mean. Use year-end figures in place of averages where needed for the purpose of calculating the ratios. Would you be willing to lend Tolbert $1 million? Why or why not?

LO 5 **S9-13.** ***(Learning Objective 5: Calculate the leverage ratio, debt ratio, and times-interest-earned ratio, and evaluate debt-paying ability)*** Examine the following selected financial information for The Deal Corporation and Simple Stores, Inc., as of the end of their fiscal years ending in 2018:

(In millions)	The Deal Corporation	Simple Stores, Inc.
1. Total assets	$16,870	$203,130
2. Total common stockholders' equity	$ 3,080	$ 71,310
3. Operating income	$ 1,400	$ 26,930
4. Interest expense	$ 87	$ 2,050
5. Leverage ratio		
6. Total debt		
7. Debt ratio		
8. Times interest earned		

1. Complete the table, calculating all the requested information for the two companies. Use year-end figures in place of averages where needed for the purpose of calculating the ratios in this exercise.
2. Evaluate each company's long-term debt-paying ability (strong, medium, weak).

LO 6 **S9-14.** ***(Learning Objective 6: Report liabilities)*** Regal, Inc., includes the following selected accounts in its general ledger at December 31, 2018:

Bonds payable (excluding current portion)	$400,000
Equipment	113,000
Current portion of bonds payable	51,000
Notes payable, long-term	275,000
Interest payable (due March 1, 2019)	2,000
Accounts payable	37,000
Discount on bonds payable (all long-term)	12,000
Accounts receivable	32,000

Prepare the liabilities section of Regal's balance sheet at December 31, 2018, to show how the company would report these items. Report total current liabilities and total liabilities.

Exercises

Group A

LO 1

E9-15A. ***(Learning Objective 1: Issue bonds payable (discount), pay and accrue interest, and amortize bond discount using the straight-line method)*** On January 31, 2018, Dunkin Logistics, Inc., issued five-year, 3% bonds payable with a face value of $8,000,000. The bonds were issued at 93 and pay interest on January 31 and July 31. Dunkin Logistics amortizes bond discounts using the straight-line method. Record (a) the issuance of the bonds on January 31, 2018, (b) the semiannual interest payment and amortization of the bond discount on July 31, 2018, and (c) the interest accrual and discount amortization on December 31, 2018.

LO 1

E9-16A. ***(Learning Objective 1: Measure cash amounts for a bond payable (premium); amortize bond premium using the straight-line method)*** Perry Bank has $450,000 of 9% debenture bonds outstanding. The bonds were issued at 105 in 2018 and mature in 2038. The bonds have annual interest payments.

Requirements

1. How much cash did Perry Bank receive when it issued these bonds?
2. How much cash in *total* will Perry Bank pay the bondholders through the maturity date of the bonds?
3. Calculate the difference between your answers to requirements 1 and 2. This difference represents Perry Bank's total interest expense over the life of the bonds.
4. Compute Perry Bank's annual interest expense using the straight-line amortization method. Multiply this amount by 20. Your 20-year total should be the same as your answer to requirement 3.

LO 2

E9-17A. ***(Learning Objective 2: Issue bonds payable (discount); record interest payments and the related bond amortization using the effective-interest method)*** Winter Ltd. is authorized to issue $2,500,000 of 4%, 10-year bonds payable. On December 31, 2018, when the market interest rate is 5%, the company issues $2,000,000 of the bonds. Winter amortizes bond discount using the effective-interest method. The semiannual interest dates are June 30 and December 31.

Requirements

1. Use the PV function in Excel to calculate the issue price of the bonds.
2. Prepare a bond amortization table for the term of the bonds using Excel.
3. Record the issuance of the bonds payable on December 31, 2018; the first semiannual interest payment on June 30, 2019; and the second payment on December 31, 2019.

LO 2

E9-18A. ***(Learning Objective 2: Issue bonds payable (premium); record interest payment and the related bond amortization using the effective-interest method)*** On June 30, 2018, the market interest rate is 9%. Ramsey Corporation issues $550,000 of 12%, 20-year bonds payable. The bonds pay interest on June 30 and December 31. The company amortizes bond premium using the effective-interest method.

Requirements

1. Use the PV function in Excel to calculate the issue price of the bonds.
2. Prepare a bond amortization table for the term of the bonds using Excel.
3. Record the issuance of bonds payable on June 30, 2018; the payment of interest on December 31, 2018; and the payment of interest on June 30, 2019.

LO 1, 3

E9-19A. ***(Learning Objectives 1, 3: Account for bonds payable retired prior to maturity)*** On January 1, 2017, Kittle Corporation issued five-year, 4% bonds payable with a face value of $2,500,000. The bonds were issued at 95 and pay interest on January 1 and July 1. Kittle amortizes bond discounts using the straight-line method. On December 31, 2019, Kittle retired the bonds early by purchasing them at a market price of 97. The company's fiscal year ends on December 31.

Requirements

1. Journalize the issuance of the bonds on January 1, 2017.
2. Record the semiannual interest payment and amortization of bond discount on July 1, 2017.
3. Record the interest accrual and discount amortization on December 31, 2017.
4. Calculate the carrying value of the bonds payable on December 31, 2019, prior to their retirement.
5. Calculate the gain or loss on the retirement of the bonds payable on December 31, 2019. Indicate where this gain or loss will appear in the financial statements.

LO 4

E9-20A. ***(Learning Objective 4: Account for deferred taxes payable)*** Fresno Transportation owns a fleet of 50 semi-trucks. The original cost of the fleet was $7,500,000. Fresno uses straight-line depreciation for the fleet for accounting purposes, and MACRS depreciation for tax purposes. The company had a deferred tax liability balance of $220,000 at the end of fiscal year 2017 related to the fleet.

At the end of fiscal year 2018, the GAAP book value of the fleet was $6,230,000, while the tax book value was $5,610,000. Fresno's taxable income for fiscal year 2018 was $6,400,000. Its tax rate was 40%.

Requirements

1. Calculate the deferred tax liability related to the fleet as of the end of fiscal year 2018.
2. Record the tax accrual for 2018 as of the end of fiscal year 2018.

LO 5

E9-21A. ***(Learning Objective 5: Evaluate debt-paying ability)*** Companies that operate in different industries may have very different financial ratio values. These differences may grow even wider when we compare companies located in different countries.

Compare three fictitious companies (Albertson, Millstone, and Raleigh) by calculating the following ratios: current ratio, debt ratio, leverage ratio, and times-interest-earned ratio. Use year-end figures in place of averages where needed for calculating the ratios in this exercise.

	A	C	D	E
1	**(Amounts in millions or billions)**	**Albertson**	**Millstone**	**Raleigh**
2	Income data			
3	Total revenues	$ 9,723	¥ 7,311	€ 136,384
4	Operating income	291	222	5,584
5	Interest expense	41	26	655
6	Net income	21	16	441
7	**Assets and liability data**			
8	**(Amounts in millions or billions)**			
9	Total current assets	434	4,832	126,700
10	Long-term assets	96	573	68,297
11	Total current liabilities	247	2,237	72,400
12	Long-term liabilities	97	2,303	110,897
13	Common stockholders' equity	186	865	11,700
14				

Based on your computed ratios, which company looks the least risky?

LO 4, 5

E9-22A. ***(Learning Objectives 4, 5: Analyze current and long-term liabilities; evaluate debt-paying ability)*** EnviroFriend Structures, Inc., builds environmentally sensitive structures. The company's 2018 revenues totaled $2,780 million. At December 31, 2018, and 2017, the company had, respectively, $656 million and $591 million in current assets. The company's balance sheets and income statements reported the following amounts:

	A	B	C
1	**At year-end (In millions)**	**2018**	**2017**
2	Liabilities and stockholders' equity		
3	Current liabilities		
4	Accounts payable	$ 148	$ 184
5	Accrued expenses	149	177
6	Employee compensation and benefits	14	30
7	Current portion of long-term debt	3	20
8	Total current liabilities	314	411
9	Long-term bonds payable	1,485	1,313
10	Deferred income taxes payable	134	131
11	Leases payable	5	23
12	Common stockholders' equity	1,844	1,584
13	Total liabilities and stockholders' equity	$ 3,782	$ 3,462
14	Year-end (in millions)		
15	Cost of goods sold	$ 2,656	$ 2,046
16			

Requirements

1. Describe each of EnviroFriend's long-term liabilities and state how the liability arose.
2. What were the company's total assets at December 31, 2018? Evaluate the company's leverage and debt ratios at the end of 2017 and 2018. Use year-end figures in place of averages where needed for calculating the ratios in this exercise. Did the company improve, deteriorate, or remain about the same over the year?

LO 1, 6

E9-23A. ***(Learning Objectives 1, 6: Account for bonds payable; report long-term liabilities)*** Robson Corporation issued 5%, 10-year bonds with a face value of $1,000,000 at a price of 98 on July 1, 2018. The bonds pay interest each January 1 and July 1. Robson uses the straight-line amortization method for all bond premiums and discounts. The company has a fiscal year-end of December 31.

Requirements

1. Record the issuance of the bonds on July 1, 2018.
2. Record the accrual for the cash interest payable on the bonds and the amortization of any premium or discount on the bonds on December 31, 2018.
3. Show how the accounts related to the bonds issued on July 1, 2018, would be reported on Robson's balance sheet as of December 31, 2018.

Group B

LO 1

E9-24B. ***(Learning Objective 1: Issue bonds payable (discount); pay and accrue interest; amortize bond discount using the straight-line method)*** On January 31, 2018, Pristar Logistics, Inc., issued 10-year, 5% bonds payable with a face value of $5,000,000. The bonds were issued at 95 and pay interest on January 31 and July 31. Pristar Logistics amortizes bond discounts using the straight-line method. Record (a) the issuance of the bonds on January 31, 2018, (b) the semiannual interest payment and amortization of the bond discount on July 31, 2018, and (c) the interest accrual and discount amortization on December 31, 2018.

LO 1 **E9-25B.** ***(Learning Objective 1: Measure cash amounts for a bond payable (premium); amortize bond premium using the straight-line method)*** Town Bank has $100,000 of 4% debenture bonds outstanding. The bonds were issued at 106 in 2018 and mature in 2038. The bonds have annual interest payments.

Requirements

1. How much cash did Town Bank receive when it issued these bonds?
2. How much cash in *total* will Town Bank pay the bondholders through the maturity date of the bonds?
3. Calculate the difference between your answers to requirements 1 and 2. This difference represents Town Bank's total interest expense over the life of the bonds.
4. Compute Town Bank's annual interest expense using the straight-line amortization method. Multiply this amount by 20. Your 20-year total should be the same as your answer to requirement 3.

LO 2 **E9-26B.** ***(Learning Objective 2: Issue bonds payable (discount); record interest payments and the related bond amortization using the effective-interest method)*** Energy Ltd. is authorized to issue $3,000,000 of 1%, 10-year bonds payable. On December 31, 2018, when the market interest rate is 8%, the company issues $2,400,000 of the bonds. Energy amortizes bond discount using the effective-interest method. The semiannual interest dates are June 30 and December 31.

Requirements

1. Use the PV function in Excel to calculate the issue price of the bonds.
2. Prepare a bond amortization table for the term of the bonds using Excel.
3. Record the issuance of the bonds payable on December 31, 2018; the first semiannual interest payment on June 30, 2019; and the second payment on December 31, 2019.

LO 2 **E9-27B.** ***(Learning Objective 2: Issue bonds payable (premium); record interest payment and the related bond amortization using the effective-interest method)*** On June 30, 2018, the market interest rate is 9%. Randall Corporation issues $600,000 of 10%, 15-year bonds payable. The bonds pay interest on June 30 and December 31. The company amortizes bond premium using the effective-interest method.

Requirements

1. Use the PV function in Excel to calculate the issue price of the bonds.
2. Prepare a bond amortization table for the term of the bonds using Excel.
3. Record the issuance of bonds payable on June 30, 2018; the payment of interest on December 31, 2018; and the payment of interest on June 30, 2019.

LO 1, 3 **E9-28B.** ***(Learning Objectives 1, 3: Account for bonds payable retired prior to maturity)*** On January 1, 2017, Ditchey Corporation issued five-year, 6% bonds payable with a face value of $3,500,000. The bonds were issued at 96 and pay interest on January 1 and July 1. Ditchey amortizes bond discounts using the straight-line method. On December 31, 2019, Ditchey retired the bonds early by purchasing them at a market price of 99. The company's fiscal year ends on December 31.

Requirements

1. Journalize the issuance of the bonds on January 1, 2017.
2. Record the semiannual interest payment and amortization of bond discount on July 1, 2017.
3. Record the interest accrual and discount amortization on December 31, 2017.
4. Calculate the carrying value of the bonds payable on December 31, 2019, prior to their retirement.
5. Calculate the gain or loss on the retirement of the bonds payable on December 31, 2019. Indicate where this gain or loss will appear in the financial statements.

LO 4

E9-29B. ***(Learning Objective 4: Account for deferred taxes payable)*** Coldwell Transportation owns a fleet of 60 semi-trucks. The original cost of the fleet was $9,000,000. Coldwell uses straight-line depreciation for the fleet for accounting purposes, and MACRS depreciation for tax purposes. The company had a deferred tax liability balance of $248,000 at the end of fiscal year 2017 related to the fleet.

At the end of fiscal year 2018, the GAAP book value of the fleet was $7,680,000, while the tax book value was $6,980,000. Coldwell's taxable income for fiscal year 2018 was $950,000. Its tax rate was 40%.

Requirements

1. Calculate the deferred tax liability related to the fleet as of the end of fiscal year 2018.
2. Record the tax accrual for 2018 as of the end of fiscal year 2018.

LO 5

E9-30B. ***(Learning Objective 5: Evaluate debt-paying ability)*** Companies that operate in different industries may have very different financial ratio values. These differences may grow even wider when we compare companies located in different countries.

Compare three fictitious companies (Biltmore, Mackey, and Victory) by calculating the following ratios: current ratio, debt ratio, leverage ratio, and times-interest-earned ratio. Use year-end figures in place of averages where needed for calculating the ratios in this exercise.

A1

	A	B	C	D
1	**(Amounts in millions or billions)**	**Biltmore**	**Mackey**	**Victory**
2	Income data			
3	Total revenues	$ 9,731	¥ 7,313	€ 136,253
4	Operating income	292	222	5,603
5	Interest expense	41	30	655
6	Net income	26	12	441
7	**Assets and liability data**			
8	**(Amounts in millions or billions)**			
9	Total current assets	422	5,774	160,560
10	Long-term assets	98	564	54,154
11	Total current liabilities	187	2,187	72,000
12	Long-term liabilities	107	2,313	110,507
13	Common stockholders' equity	226	1,838	32,207
14				

Based on your computed ratios, which company looks the least risky?

LO **4, 5**

E9-31B. ***(Learning Objectives 4, 5: Analyze current and long-term liabilities; evaluate debt-paying ability)*** Green Earth Homes, Inc., builds environmentally sensitive structures. The company's 2018 revenues totaled $2,770 million. At December 31, 2018 and 2017, the company had, respectively, $663 million and $613 million in current assets. The company's balance sheets and income statements reported the following amounts:

	A	B	C
1	**At year-end (In millions)**	**2018**	**2017**
2	Liabilities and stockholders' equity		
3	Current liabilities		
4	Accounts payable	$ 110	$ 174
5	Accrued expenses	149	167
6	Employee compensation and benefits	37	16
7	Current portion of long-term debt	12	4
8	Total current liabilities	308	361
9	Long-term bonds payable	1,578	1,324
10	Deferred income taxes payable	129	125
11	Leases payable	18	19
12	Common stockholders' equity	2,420	1,273
13	Total liabilities and stockholders' equity	$ 4,453	$ 3,102
14	Year-end (in millions)		
15	Cost of goods sold	$ 1,704	$ 1,239
16			

Requirements

1. Describe each of Green Earth's long-term liabilities and state how the liability arose.
2. What were the company's total assets at December 31, 2018? Evaluate the company's leverage and debt ratios at the end of 2017 and 2018. Use year-end figures in place of averages where needed for calculating the ratios in this exercise. Did the company improve, deteriorate, or remain about the same over the year?

LO **1, 6**

E9-32B. ***(Learning Objectives 1, 6: Account for bonds payable; report long-term liabilities)*** Holloway Corporation issued 8%, 10-year bonds with a face value of $2,000,000 at a price of 96 on July 1, 2018. The bonds pay interest each January 1 and July 1. Holloway uses the straight-line amortization method for all bond premiums and discounts. The company has a fiscal year-end of December 31.

Requirements

1. Record the issuance of the bonds on July 1, 2018.
2. Record the accrual for the cash interest payable on the bonds and the amortization of any premium or discount on the bonds on December 31, 2018.
3. Show how the accounts related to the bonds issued on July 1, 2018, would be reported on Holloway's balance sheet as of December 31, 2018.

Quiz

Test your understanding of long-term liabilities by answering the following questions. Select the best choice from among the possible answers given.

Q9-33. A bond with a face amount of $12,000 has a current price quote of 107.15. What is the bond's price?

a. $12,107.15
b. $1,285.80
c. $12,858.00
d. $128,580

Q9-34. The carrying value on bonds equals Bonds Payable

a. minus Premium on Bonds Payable.
b. plus Discount on Bonds Payable.
c. plus Premium on Bonds Payable.
d. minus Discount on Bonds Payable.
e. both a and b
f. both c and d

Q9-35. What type of account is Discount on Bonds Payable, and what is its normal balance?

a. Adjusting account; Credit
b. Reversing account; Debit
c. Contra liability account; Debit
d. Contra liability account; Credit

Questions 36–37 use the following data:

Cheyenne Company sells $400,000 of 14%, 10-year bonds for 92.613 on April 1, 2018. The market rate of interest on that day is 15.5%. Interest is paid each year on April 1.

Q9-36. The entry to record the sale of the bonds on April 1 would be as follows:

	A	B	C	D
1	a.	Cash	370,452	
2		Discount on Bonds Payable	29,548	
3		Bonds Payable		400,000
4				
5	b.	Cash	400,000	
6		Discount on Bonds Payable		29,548
7		Bonds Payable		370,452
8				
9	c.	Cash	370,452	
10		Bonds Payable		370,452
11				
12	d.	Cash	400,000	
13		Bonds Payable		400,000
14				

Q9-37. Cheyenne Company uses the straight-line amortization method. The amount of interest expense for each year will be

a. $64,955.
b. $58,955.
c. $56,000.
d. $19,815.
e. none of these.

Q9-38. Amortizing the discount on bonds payable

a. increases the recorded amount of interest expense.
b. reduces the semiannual cash payment for interest.
c. reduces the carrying value of the bond liability.
d. is necessary only if the bonds were issued at more than face value.

Q9-39. The journal entry on the maturity date to record the retirement of bonds with a face value of $2,500,000 that were issued at a $90,000 discount includes

a. a debit to Discount on Bonds Payable for $90,000.
b. a credit to Cash for $2,590,000.
c. a debit to Bonds Payable for $2,500,000.
d. all of the above.

Q9-40. Mcdonaugh Corporation issued $250,000 of 5%, 10-year bonds payable on January 1, 2019. The market interest rate when the bonds were issued was 8%. Interest is paid semiannually on January 1 and July 1. The first interest payment is July 1, 2019. Using the effective-interest amortization method, how much interest expense will Mcdonaugh record on July 1, 2019? Use Excel to calculate the issue price.

a. $4,976
b. $7,961
c. $1,711
d. $10,000
e. $6,250

Q9-41. Using the facts in the preceding question, Mcdonaugh's entry to record the interest expense on July 1, 2019, will include a

a. debit to Premium on Bonds Payable.
b. credit to Discount on Bonds Payable.
c. debit to Bonds Payable.
d. credit to Interest Expense.

Q9-42. Maridell's Fashions has a debt that has been properly reported as a long-term liability up to the present year (2018). Some of this debt comes due in 2018. If Maridell's Fashions continues to report the current position as a long-term liability, the effect will be to

a. understate the debt ratio.
b. understate total liabilities.
c. overstate the current ratio.
d. overstate net income.

Q9-43. On January 1, 2020, Fergus Corporation issued $800,000, 10%, 5-year bonds. The bond interest is payable on January 1 and July 1. The bonds sold for $864,887. The market rate of interest when the bonds were issued was 8%. Under the effective-interest method, the interest expense for the six months ending July 1, 2020, would be closest to

a. $40,000.
b. $32,000.
c. $80,000.
d. $34,595.

Q9-44. Josselle Corporation retires its bonds at 106 on January 1, after the payment of interest. The face value of the bonds is $750,000. The carrying value of the bonds at retirement is $775,600. The entry to record the retirement will include a

a. debit of $19,400 to Premium on Bonds Payable.
b. credit of $19,400 to Premium on Bonds Payable.
c. debit of $25,600 to Premium on Bonds Payable.
d. credit of $25,600 to Premium on Bonds Payable.

Q9-45. Corporate bonds that can be exchanged for shares of the corporation's common stock if certain conditions are met are called

a. callable bonds.
b. equity bonds.
c. convertible bonds.
d. exchangeable bonds.

Q9-46. Which of the following items is most likely a short-term liability?

a. Deferred income taxes
b. Finance lease covering 30-year term
c. Bonds payable
d. Accounts payable

Q9-47. Cases Unlimited reported operating income of $780,000, interest expense of $120,000, and net income of $575,000. The weighted-average number of shares of common stock outstanding during the year was 100,000 shares. What is the times-interest-earned ratio? (Round your final answer to two decimal places.)

a. 4.79
b. 5.79
c. 6.50
d. 7.50

Q9-48. The leverage ratio is equal to average total ________ divided by average ________.

a. long-term debt; common stockholders' equity
b. assets; common stockholders' equity
c. debt; total assets
d. debt; common stockholders' equity

Q9-49. Apollo Corporation issued $300,000, five-year bonds at 98 on January 1, 2016. On December 31, 2020, the bonds matured. The payment of the bonds at maturity would be reported on the statement of cash flows as a cash outflow of

- **a.** $294,000 in the financing activities section.
- **b.** $294,000 in the investing activities section.
- **c.** $300,000 in the financing activities section
- **d.** $300,000 in the investing activities section.

Problems MyLab Accounting

Group A

LO 1, 6

P9-50A. ***(Learning Objectives 1, 6: Record bond transactions at par; report bonds payable on the balance sheet)*** The board of directors of Canterbury Plus authorized the issue of $9,000,000 of 7%, 15-year bonds payable. The semiannual interest dates are May 31 and November 30. The bonds are issued on May 31, 2018, at par.

Requirements

1. Journalize the following transactions:
   - **a.** Issuance of half of the bonds on May 31, 2018
   - **b.** Payment of interest on November 30, 2018
   - **c.** Accrual of interest on December 31, 2018
   - **d.** Payment of interest on May 31, 2019
2. Report interest payable and bonds payable as they would appear on the company's balance sheet at December 31, 2018.

LO 1, 6

P9-51A. ***(Learning Objectives 1, 6: Issue bonds at a discount; amortize using the straight-line method; report bonds payable and accrued interest payable on the balance sheet)*** On February 28, 2018, Dolphin Corp. issued 10%, 20-year bonds payable with a face value of $2,100,000. The bonds pay interest on February 28 and August 31. The company amortizes bond discount using the straight-line method.

Requirements

1. If the market interest rate is 9% when Dolphin Corp. issues its bonds, will the bonds be priced at par, at a premium, or at a discount? Explain.
2. If the market interest rate is 11% when Dolphin Corp. issues its bonds, will the bonds be priced at par, at a premium, or at a discount? Explain.
3. Assume that the issue price of the bonds is 94. Journalize the following bonds payable transactions.
   - **a.** Issuance of the bonds on February 28, 2018
   - **b.** Payment of interest and amortization of the bond discount on August 31, 2018
   - **c.** Accrual of interest and amortization of the bond discount on December 31, 2018 (fiscal year-end)
   - **d.** Payment of interest and amortization of the bond discount on February 28, 2019
4. Report interest payable and bonds payable as they would appear on Dolphin Corp.'s balance sheet at December 31, 2018.

LO 1

P9-52A. ***(Learning Objective 1: Account for bonds payable at a discount; amortize using the straight-line method)***

Requirements

1. Journalize the following transactions of Laporte Communications, Inc.:

2018		
Jan	1	Issued $4,000,000 of 7%, 10-year bonds payable at 94. Interest payment dates are July 1 and January 1.
Jul	1	Paid semiannual interest and amortized bond discount by the straight-line method on the 7% bonds payable.
Dec	31	Accrued semiannual interest expense and amortized the bond discount by the straight-line method on the 7% bonds payable.
2019		
Jan	1	Paid semiannual interest.
2028		
Jan	1	Paid the 7% bonds at maturity.

2. At December 31, 2018, after all year-end adjustments have been made, determine the carrying amount of Laporte's bonds payable, net.
3. For the six months ended July 1, 2018, determine the following for Laporte:
   a. Interest expense
   b. Cash interest paid
   What causes interest expense on the bonds to exceed cash interest paid?

LO 2, 6

P9-53A. ***(Learning Objectives 2, 6: Analyze a company's long-term debt; report long-term debt on the balance sheet [effective-interest method])*** The notes to the Thorson Ltd. financial statements reported the following data on December 31, Year 1 (end of the fiscal year):

Note 6. Indebtedness		
Bonds payable, 1% due on December 31, Year 8...	$3,500,000	
Less: Discount..........	?	?
Notes payable, 6%, payable in $45,000 annual installments starting in Year 5..........		$270,000

Thorson amortizes bond discounts using the effective-interest method and pays all interest amounts at December 31.

Requirements

1. Assume the market interest rate is 6% on January 1 of year 1, the date the bonds are issued.
   a. Using the PV function in Excel, what is the issue price of the bonds?
   b. What is the maturity value of the bonds?
   c. What is Thorson's annual cash interest payment on the bonds?
   d. What is the carrying amount of the bonds at December 31, year 1?
2. Prepare an amortization table through the maturity date for the bonds using Excel. (Round all amounts to the nearest dollar.) How much is Thorson's interest expense on the bonds for the year ended December 31, Year 4?
3. Show how Thorson would report these bonds and notes at December 31, Year 4.

P9-54A. ***(Learning Objectives 2, 3, 6: Issue convertible bonds at a discount, amortize using the effective-interest method, and convert bonds; report bonds payable on the balance sheet)*** On December 31, 2018, Mainland Corporation issues 6%, 10-year convertible bonds payable with a face value of $4,000,000. The semiannual interest dates are June 30 and December 31. The market interest rate is 8%. Mainland amortizes bond discounts using the effective-interest method. LO **2, 3, 6**

Requirements

1. Use the PV function in Excel to calculate the issue price of the bonds.
2. Prepare an effective-interest method amortization table for the term of the bonds using Excel.
3. Journalize the following transactions:
   a. Issuance of the bonds on December 31, 2018. Credit Convertible Bonds Payable.
   b. Payment of interest and amortization of the bond discount on June 30, 2019.
   c. Payment of interest and amortization of the bond discount on December 31, 2019.
   d. Conversion by the bondholders on July 1, 2020, of bonds with a total face value of $1,600,000 into 80,000 shares of Mainland's $1-par common stock.
4. Show how Mainland would report the remaining bonds payable on its balance sheet at December 31, 2020.

P9-55A. ***(Learning Objectives 4, 5, 6: Report liabilities on the balance sheet; calculate the leverage ratio, debt ratio, and times-interest-earned ratio)*** The accounting records of Burgess Foods, Inc., include the following items at December 31, 2018: LO **4, 5, 6**

Mortgage note payable, current portion	$ 86,000	Total assets	$5,400,000
Leases payable (long-term)	445,000	Accumulated depreciation, equipment	162,000
Bonds payable, long-term	250,000	Discount on bonds payable (all long-term)	21,000
Mortgage note payable, long-term	315,000	Operating income	360,000
Bonds payable, current portion	300,000	Equipment	747,000
Interest expense	227,000	Long-term investments (market value)	400,000
		Interest payable	70,000

Requirements

1. Show how each relevant item would be reported on the Burgess Foods classified balance sheet. Include headings and totals for current liabilities and long-term liabilities.
2. Answer the following questions about Burgess Food's financial position at December 31, 2018:
   a. What is the carrying amount of the bonds payable (combine the current and long-term amounts)?
   b. Why is the interest-payable amount so much less than the amount of interest expense?
3. How many times did Burgess Foods cover its interest expense during 2018?
4. Assume that all of the existing liabilities are included in the information provided. Calculate the leverage ratio and debt ratio of the company. Use year-end figures in place of averages where needed for the purpose of calculating ratios in this problem. Evaluate the health of the company from a leverage point of view. Assume the company only has common stock issued and outstanding. What other information would be helpful in making your evaluation?
5. Independent of your answer to (4), assume that Footnote 8 of the financial statements includes commitments for long-term operating leases over the next 15 years in the amount of $4,000,000. If the company had to capitalize these leases in 2018, how would it change the leverage ratio and the debt ratio? How would this impact your assessment of the company's health from a leverage point of view?

Group B

LO 1, 6

P9-56B. ***(Learning Objectives 1, 6: Record bond transactions at par; report bonds payable on the balance sheet)*** The board of directors of Mailroom Plus authorized the issue of $8,000,000 of 6%, 10-year bonds payable. The semiannual interest dates are May 31 and November 30. The bonds are issued on May 31, 2018, at par.

Requirements

1. Journalize the following transactions:
   a. Issuance of half of the bonds on May 31, 2018
   b. Payment of interest on November 30, 2018
   c. Accrual of interest on December 31, 2018
   d. Payment of interest on May 31, 2019
2. Report interest payable and bonds payable as they would appear on the company's balance sheet at December 31, 2018.

LO 1, 6

P9-57B. ***(Learning Objectives 1, 6: Issue bonds at a discount; amortize using the straight-line method; report bonds payable and accrued interest payable on the balance sheet)*** On February 28, 2018, Shark Corp. issued 10%, 10-year bonds payable with a face value of $1,500,000. The bonds pay interest on February 28 and August 31. The company amortizes bond discount using the straight-line method.

Requirements

1. If the market interest rate is 9% when Shark Corp. issues its bonds, will the bonds be priced at par, at a premium, or at a discount? Explain.
2. If the market interest rate is 11% when Shark Corp. issues its bonds, will the bonds be priced at par, at a premium, or at a discount? Explain.
3. Assume that the issue price of the bonds is 94. Journalize the following bond transactions.
   a. Issuance of the bonds on February 28, 2018
   b. Payment of interest and amortization of the bond discount on August 31, 2018
   c. Accrual of interest and amortization of the bond discount on December 31, 2018 (fiscal year-end)
   d. Payment of interest and amortization of the bond discount on February 28, 2019
4. Report interest payable and bonds payable as they would appear on Shark Corp.'s balance sheet at December 31, 2018.

LO 1

P9-58B. ***(Learning Objective 1: Account for bonds payable at a discount; amortize using the straight-line method)***

Requirements

1. Journalize the following transactions of Lyons Communications, Inc.:

2018	
Jan 1	Issued $3,000,000 of 6%, 10-year bonds payable at 95. Interest payment dates are July 1 and January 1.
Jul 1	Paid semiannual interest and amortized the bond discount by the straight-line method on the 6% bonds payable.
Dec 31	Accrued semiannual interest expense and amortized the bond discount by the straight-line method on the 6% bonds payable.
2019	
Jan 1	Paid semiannual interest.
2028	
Jan 1	Paid the 6% bonds at maturity.

2. At December 31, 2018, after all year-end adjustments have been made, determine the carrying amount of Lyons' bonds payable, net.
3. For the six months ended July 1, 2018, determine the following for Lyons:
   a. Interest expense
   b. Cash interest paid

   What causes interest expense on the bonds to exceed cash interest paid?

P9-59B. ***(Learning Objectives 2, 6: Analyze a company's long-term debt; report long-term debt on the balance sheet [effective-interest method])*** The notes to the Alliance Ltd. financial statements reported the following data on December 31, Year 1 (end of the fiscal year): LO 2, 6

Note 6. Indebtedness		
Bonds payable, 3% due December 31, Year 8........	$2,000,000	
Less: Discount..	?	?
Notes payable, 7%, payable in $50,000 annual installments starting in Year 5..............		300,000

Alliance amortizes bond discounts using the effective-interest method and pays all interest amounts at December 31.

Requirements

1. Assume the market interest rate is 7% on January 1 of year 1, the date the bonds are issued.
   a. Using the PV function in Excel, what is the issue price of the bonds?
   b. What is the maturity value of the bonds?
   c. What is Alliance's annual cash interest payment on the bonds?
   d. What is the carrying amount of the bonds at December 31, Year 1?
2. Prepare an amortization table through the maturity date for the bonds using Excel. How much is Alliance's interest expense on the bonds for the year ended December 31, Year 4?
3. Show how Alliance would report these bonds and notes payable at December 31, Year 4.

P9-60B. ***(Learning Objectives 2, 3, 6: Issue convertible bonds at a discount; amortize using the effective interest method; convert bonds; report bonds payable on the balance sheet)*** On December 31, 2018, Herndon Corporation issues 6%, 10-year convertible bonds payable with a face value of $1,000,000. The semiannual interest dates are June 30 and December 31. The market interest rate is 7%. Herndon amortizes bond discounts using the effective-interest method. LO 2, 3, 6

Requirements

1. Use the PV function in Excel to calculate the issue price of the bonds.
2. Prepare an effective-interest method amortization table for the term of the bonds using Excel.
3. Journalize the following transactions:
   a. Issuance of the bonds on December 31, 2018. Credit Convertible Bonds Payable.
   b. Payment of interest and amortization of the bond discount on June 30, 2019.
   c. Payment of interest and amortization of the bond discount on December 31, 2019.
   d. Conversion by the bondholders on July 1, 2020, of bonds with a total face value of $400,000 into 120,000 shares of Herndon $1-par common stock.
4. Show how Herndon would report the remaining bonds payable on its balance sheet at December 31, 2020.

LO 4, 5, 6

P9-61B. ***(Learning Objectives 4, 5, 6: Report liabilities on the balance sheet; calculate the leverage ratio, debt ratio, and times-interest-earned ratio)*** The accounting records of Brigham Foods, Inc., include the following items at December 31, 2018:

Mortgage note payable, current portion	$ 98,000	Total assets	$4,500,000
Leases payable (long-term)	445,000	Accumulated depreciation, equipment	163,000
Bonds payable, long-term	325,000	Discount on bonds payable (all long-term)	21,000
Mortgage note payable, long-term	311,000	Operating income	360,000
Bonds payable, current portion	50,000	Equipment	744,000
Interest expense	229,000	Long-term investments (market value)	400,000
		Interest payable	76,000

Requirements

1. Show how each relevant item would be reported on the Brigham Foods classified balance sheet. Include headings and totals for current liabilities and long-term liabilities.
2. Answer the following questions about Brigham Food's financial position at December 31, 2018:
   - **a.** What is the carrying amount of the bonds payable (combine the current and long-term amounts)?
   - **b.** Why is the interest-payable amount so much less than the amount of interest expense?
3. How many times did Brigham Foods cover its interest expense during 2018?
4. Assume that all of the existing liabilities are included in the information provided. Calculate the leverage ratio and debt ratio of the company. Use year-end figures in place of averages where needed for the purpose of calculating ratios in this problem. Evaluate the health of the company from a leverage point of view. Assume the company only has common stock issued and outstanding. What other information would be helpful in making your evaluation?
5. Independent of your answer to (4), assume that Footnote 8 of the financial statements includes commitments for long-term operating leases over the next 15 years in the amount of $3,800,000. If the company had to capitalize these leases in 2018, how would it change the leverage ratio and the debt ratio? How would this impact your assessment of the company's health from a leverage point of view?

Challenge Exercise and Problem

LO 5, 6

E9-62. ***(Learning Objectives 5, 6: Report current and long-term liabilities; evaluate leverage)*** The top management of Palermo Marketing Services examines the following company accounting records at August 29, immediately before the end of the company's year, August 31:

Total current assets	$ 324,500
Noncurrent assets	1,086,000
	$1,410,500
Total current liabilities	$ 173,500
Noncurrent liabilities	253,400
Common stockholders' equity	983,600
	$1,410,500

1. Suppose Palermo's management wants to achieve a current ratio of 3. How much in current liabilities should Palermo pay off within the next two days in order to achieve its goal?
2. Calculate Palermo's leverage ratio and debt ratio ignoring Requirement 1. Use year-end figures in place of averages where needed for the purpose of calculating ratios in this exercise. Evaluate the company's debt position. Is it low, high, or about average? What other information might help you to make a decision?

LO 4, 5

P9-63. ***(Learning Objectives 4, 5: Understand how structuring debt transactions can affect a company)*** The Juice Company reported the following comparative information at December 31, 2018, and December 31, 2017 (amounts in millions and adapted):

	2018	2017
Current assets	$21,100	$16,800
Total assets	71,800	47,800
Current liabilities	18,500	13,100
Total stockholders' equity	30,300	24,600
Net sales	34,600	29,600
Net income	11,575	7,170

Requirements

1. Calculate the following ratios for 2018 and 2017:
   a. Current ratio
   b. Debt ratio
2. During 2018, The Juice Company issued $1,640 million of long-term debt that was used to retire short-term debt. What would the current ratio and debt ratio have been if this transaction had not been made?
3. The Juice Company reports that its lease payments under operating leases will total $910 million in the future and $160 million will occur in the next year (2019). What would the current ratio and debt ratio have been in 2018 if these leases had been capitalized?

APPLY YOUR KNOWLEDGE

Serial Case

LO 5

C9-64. ***(Learning Objective 5: Calculate modified debt ratios for a company in the restaurant industry)***

Note: This case is part of The Cheesecake Factory serial case contained in every chapter in this textbook.

Near the end of 2016, **The Cheesecake Factory** entered into a new loan agreement with its creditors. This new four-year agreement provided loan commitments totaling up to $200 million. The commitments enable The Cheesecake Factory to borrow funds as needed at specified rates and terms. As of January 3, 2017, The Cheesecake Factory had not borrowed any funds associated with the commitment, so its long-term debt related to the new loan agreement was zero.

As part of the loan agreement, The Cheesecake Factory agreed to maintain a *maximum* "Net Adjusted Leverage Ratio" of 4.0 and a *minimum* "EBITDAR Ratio" of 1.9. Roughly, the Net Adjusted Leverage Ratio is a measure using specific debt balances divided by specific earnings items, while the EBITDAR Ratio is a measure of specific earnings items before interest, taxes, and other items divided by interest and rental expenses. As of December 29, 2015, The Cheesecake Factory's Net Adjusted Leverage Ratio was 2.4 and its EBITDAR Ratio was 3.1.

Suppose that The Cheesecake Factory borrows $30 million on July 1, 2018. Assume also that the interest rate in effect during 2018 is 1.5% for this loan and that The Cheesecake Factory does not make any principal payments on the loan during 2018 and had no other loans outstanding from this loan agreement during the year. Assume further that the loan terms call for monthly interest payments due on the 1st of the month for the month just ended. Monthly interest payments will begin on August 1, 2018.

Requirements

1. When the new loan agreement was made at the end of 2016, would The Cheesecake Factory have recorded the loan agreement in its general ledger? Would this new loan agreement have impacted The Cheesecake Factory's balance sheet in 2016? Explain.
2. What entry would The Cheesecake Factory make on July 1, 2018, to record its borrowing? How would the new borrowing impact its assets, liabilities, and equity on that date?
3. How much interest expense related to the hypothetical borrowing would The Cheesecake Factory need to accrue at its fiscal 2018 year-end? (Assume that fiscal year end for 2018 is December 31, 2018.) How would the adjusting entry for interest expense impact The Cheesecake Factory's assets, liabilities, and equity?
4. What would be the total interest expense related to the hypothetical borrowing for 2018?
5. Would the hypothetical borrowing in 2018 cause the Net Adjusted Leverage Ratio to increase, decrease, or stay the same? Explain.
6. Would the hypothetical borrowing in 2018 cause the EBITDAR Ratio to increase, decrease, or stay the same? Explain.

Decision Cases

LO 5

C9-65. ***(Learning Objective 5: Explore an actual bankruptcy; calculate leverage ratio, ROA, debt ratio, and times-interest-earned ratio)*** In 2002, **Enron Corporation** filed for Chapter 11 bankruptcy protection, shocking the business community: How could a company so large and successful go bankrupt? This case explores the causes and the effects of Enron's bankruptcy.

At December 31, 2000, and for the four years ended on that date, Enron reported the following (amounts in millions):

Balance Sheet (summarized)				
Total assets				$65,503
Total liabilities				54,033
Total common stockholders' equity				11,470
Income Statements (excerpts)				
	2000	1999	1998	1997
Net income	$ 979*	$893	$703	$105
Revenues	100,789			

*Operating income = $1,953
Interest expense = $838

Unknown to investors and lenders, Enron also controlled hundreds of partnerships that owed vast amounts of money. These special-purpose entities (SPEs) did not appear on the Enron financial statements. Assume that the SPEs' assets totaled $7,000 million and their liabilities stood at $6,900 million; assume a 10% interest rate on these liabilities.

During the four-year period up to December 31, 2000, Enron's stock price shot up from $17.50 to $90.56. Enron used its escalating stock price to finance the purchase of the SPEs by guaranteeing lenders that Enron would give them Enron stock if the SPEs could not pay their loans.

In 2001, the SEC launched an investigation into Enron's accounting practices. It was alleged that Enron should have been including the SPEs in its financial statements all along. Enron then restated net income for the years up to 2000, wiping out nearly $600 million of total net income (and total assets) for this four-year period. Assume that $300 million of this loss applied to 2000. Enron's stock price tumbled, and the guarantees to the SPEs' lenders added millions to Enron's liabilities (assume the full amount of the SPEs' debt was included). To make matters worse, the assets of the SPEs lost much of their value; assume that their market value is only $500 million.

Requirements

1. Compute the debt ratio that Enron reported at the end of 2000. By using the DuPont Model, compute Enron's return on total assets (ROA) for 2000. For this purpose, use only total assets at the end of 2000, rather than the average of 1999 and 2000.
2. Compute Enron's leverage ratio for 2000. Use total assets and total stockholders' equity at the end of 2000. Now compute Enron's return on equity (ROE) by multiplying the ROA computed in Part 1 by the leverage ratio. Can you see anything unusual in these ratios that might have caused you to question them? Why or why not?
3. Add the asset and liability information about the SPEs to the reported amounts provided in the table. Recompute all ratios after including the SPEs in Enron's financial statements. Also compute Enron's times-interest-earned ratio both ways for 2000. Assume that the changes to Enron's financial position occurred during 2000.
4. Why does it appear that Enron failed to include the SPEs in its financial statements? How do you view Enron after including the SPEs in the company's financial statements? (Challenge)

Focus on Financials | Apple Inc.

(Learning Objectives 4, 5, 6: Analyze current and long-term liabilities; evaluate debt-paying ability) Refer to **Apple Inc.**'s consolidated financial statements in Appendix A and online in the filings section of **www.sec.gov**. LO **4, 5, 6**

Requirements

1. Examine Note 5—Income Taxes—in the Notes to Consolidated Financial Statements. Income tax provision is another title for income tax expense. What was Apple's income tax provision in 2016? Is the income tax provision likely to be equal to the amount Apple paid for its taxes in 2016? Why or why not? What was the company's effective tax rate in 2016?
2. Examine Note 6—Debt. Did Apple borrow more or pay off more long-term debt during 2016? How can you tell? What was the company's effective interest rate on its long-term debt? Why do you think the rate was so low? (Challenge)
3. How would you rate Apple's overall debt position—risky, safe, or average? Compute three ratios at September 24, 2016, and September 26, 2015, that help answer this question.

Focus on Analysis | Under Armour, Inc.

LO **4, 5, 6** ***(Learning Objectives 4, 5, 6: Analyze current liabilities and long-term debt; calculate ratios)*** Retrieve the 2016 **Under Armour** financial statements at **www.sec.gov** by clicking on Filings and then searching for "Under Armour" under Company Filings. When you see the list of filings for the company, select the Form 10-K for 2016. Be sure to retrieve the 2016 financial statements, not another year. These financial statements report a number of liabilities.

Requirements

1. Refer to Note 5—Credit Facility and Other Long Term Debt. What is Under Armour's weighted average interest rate on outstanding borrowings for 2016? How much in long-term debt obligations does Under Armour currently owe for 2017?
2. Refer to the note entitled "Commitments and Contingencies." Describe its contents. Are any of these items included in the liabilities recorded in either the current or long-term section of the balance sheet? Why or why not?
3. Refer to Note 6—Commitments and Contingencies, under *Obligations Under Operating Leases.* Describe the company's commitments under its operating lease arrangements. Calculate the impact the operating leases would have had on Under Armour's ROA and debt ratios at the end of 2016 if the leases had been capitalized.
4. For 2016, compute the company's debt ratio, leverage ratio, and times-interest-earned ratio. Would you evaluate Under Armour as risky, safe, or average in terms of these ratios?
5. Access Under Armour's, most recent financial statements from **www.sec.gov**. What has happened to Under Armour's, debt position since the end of 2016? (Challenge)

Quick Check Answers

1. *d [$525,000 × 1.10 = $577,500; $52,500 ÷ 6 = $8,750; $577,500 – $8,750 = $568,750]*
2. *b [$250,000 × 0.98 = $245,000]*
3. *d*
4. *c*
5. *a [$2,400,000 – $2,352,000 = $48,000 discount; $48,000 ÷ 10 years × 6/12 = $2,400 discount amortization per period]*
6. *b*
7. *d*
8. *b*
9. *c*
10. *a*
11. *b [$325,591 × 3% = $9,768]*
12. *c*
13. *a*
14. *c*
15. *b*
16. *d [($240,000 + $32,000) ÷ $32,000 = 8.50]*
17. *b*

Try It Solutions

Page 480

Income Statement for 2018		
Interest expense ($4,807 + $4,823)		$ 9,630
Balance Sheet at December 31, 2018		
Current liabilities:		
Interest payable		$ 4,500
Long-term liabilities:		
Bonds payable	$100,000	
Less: Discount on bonds payable	(3,221)	96,779

10 Stockholders' Equity

LEARNING OBJECTIVES

1. **Explain** the features of a corporation
2. **Account** for the issuance of stock
3. **Explain** how treasury stock affects a company
4. **Account** for retained earnings, dividends, and stock splits
5. **Evaluate** a company's performance using new ratios
6. **Report** stockholders' equity transactions in the financial statements

SPOTLIGHT

The Home Depot: Building Toward Success

The Home Depot, Inc., is the world's largest home improvement specialty retailer, with more than 2,200 retail stores in the United States, its territories, Canada, and Mexico. During its 2016 fiscal year, The Home Depot reported net sales of $94.6 billion, up 6.9% from fiscal year 2015. This healthy increase in sales occurred in spite of a widely publicized security breach in 2014 in the company's payment data system, causing the business to incur millions of dollars in expenses from 2014 through 2016 to investigate and fix the problem. Net income for fiscal 2016 was about $8 billion. Basic earnings per share on the company's common stock increased 17.9% over fiscal 2015 to $6.47 per share. The company ended the year with 1.2 billion common shares outstanding (that is, shares in the hands of shareholders), and paid $3.4 billion in dividends ($2.76 per common share outstanding).

In 2016 the company's dividend payout ratio (cash dividends as a percent of net income) was 42.8%. In addition, over the 3-year period from February 2, 2014 to January 29, 2017, the company returned about $21 billion in cash to shareholders through repurchases of its stock. The company has a goal to maintain a high return on stockholders' equity (ROE). ROE reached an astounding 149.4% for the year ended January 29, 2017. The Home Depot has done this by maintaining a high level of return on assets (ROA), to be sure, but also by having

Niloo/Shutterstock

a very high level of leverage. Below, you'll find the company's Consolidated Balance Sheets as of January 29, 2017 and January 31, 2016. ●

	A	B	C
1	**The Home Depot, Inc. Consolidated Balance Sheets (Adapted)**	**Jan. 29, 2017**	**Jan. 31, 2016**
2	$ in millions, unless otherwise specified		
3	Current Assets:		
4	Total Current Assets	$ 17,724	$ 16,484
5	Net Property and Equipment	21,914	22,191
6	Other Assets	3,328	3,298
7	Total Assets	$ 42,966	$ 41,973
8	Current Liabilities	$ 14,133	$ 12,524
9	Long-Term Liabilities	24,500	23,133
10	Total Liabilities	38,633	35,657
11	**STOCKHOLDERS' EQUITY**		
12	Common Stock, par value $0.05; authorized: 10 billion shares;	88	88
13	issued: 1.776 billion shares at January 29, 2017 and		
14	1.772 billion shares at January 31, 2016;		
15	outstanding: 1.203 billion shares at January 29, 2017		
16	and 1.252 billion shares at January 31, 2016		
17	Paid-In Capital	9,787	9,347
18	Retained Earnings	35,519	30,973
19	Accumulated Other Comprehensive Loss	(867)	(898)
20	Treasury Stock, at cost, 573 million shares at January 29, 2017	(40,194)	(33,194)
21	and 520 million shares at January 31, 2016		
22	Total Stockholders' Equity	4,333	6,316
23	Total Liabilities and Stockholders' Equity	$ 42,966	$ 41,973
24			

Data from the U.S. Securities and Exchange Commission EDGAR Company Filings, www.sec.gov

In this chapter, we focus on stockholders' equity. We'll show you how to account for the issuance of corporate capital stock to investors. We'll also cover the other elements of stockholders' equity—Additional Paid-in Capital, Retained Earnings, and Treasury Stock, plus dividends and stock splits. We'll show you how to use a DuPont Analysis to calculate the rate of return on common shareholders' equity (ROE), using its component ratios of rate of return on assets (ROA) and leverage, which were covered in Chapters 7 and 9, respectively. We'll calculate earnings per share (EPS) and the price/earnings ratio as well as the dividend yield percentage. We'll conclude the chapter with a discussion of the impact of stockholders' equity transactions on cash flows, and the Statement of Stockholders' Equity, in which we analyze the changes in all of the component accounts in the stockholders' equity section of the balance sheet.

Try It in Excel®

You can access the most current annual report of The Home Depot, Inc., in Excel format at **www.sec.gov**. Using the "FILINGS" link on the toolbar at the top of the home page, select "Company Filings Search." This will take you to the "Edgar Company Filings" page. Type "Home Depot" in the company name box, and select "Search." This will produce the "EDGAR Search Results" page showing the company name. Click on the "CIK" link beside the company name. Doing so will pull up a list of the reports the company has filed with the SEC. Under the "Filing Type" box, type "10-K" and click the search box. Form 10-K is the SEC form for the company's annual report. Find the year that you wish to view. Click on the "Interactive Data" box, which takes you to the "View Filing Data" page. Find and click on the "View Excel Document" link at the top of this page. You can choose to either open or download the Excel files containing the company's most recent financial statements.

Let's begin with the organization of a corporation.

EXPLAIN THE FEATURES OF A CORPORATION

1 **Explain** the features of a corporation

As we pointed out in Chapter 1, corporations differ from proprietorships and partnerships in several ways. Let's review some of the most important attributes of the typical corporate business model.

Separate Legal Entity. A corporation is a business entity formed under state law. It is a distinct entity—an artificial person that exists apart from its owners, the **stockholders**, or **shareholders**. The corporation has many of the rights that a person has. For example, a corporation can buy, own, and sell property. The business's assets and liabilities belong to the corporation and not to its owners. The corporation can also enter into contracts, sue, and be sued.

Continuous Life and Transferability of Ownership. Unlike sole proprietorships and partnerships, corporations have continuous lives regardless of changes in their ownership. The stockholders of a corporation can buy more of the stock, sell the stock to another person, give it away, or bequeath it in a will. The transfer of the stock from one person to another does not affect the continuity of the corporation. In contrast, proprietorships and partnerships terminate when their ownership changes.

Limited Liability. Stockholders have **limited liability** for the corporation's debts. They have no personal obligation for corporate liabilities. The most that a stockholder can lose on an investment in a corporation's stock is the cost of the investment. Limited liability is one of the most attractive features of the corporate form of organization. It enables corporations to raise more capital from a wider group of investors than proprietorships and partnerships can. By contrast, proprietors and partners are personally liable for all the debts of their businesses.[1]

Separation of Ownership and Management. Stockholders own the corporation, but the business's **board of directors**—each of whom is elected by the stockholders—appoints officers to manage the business. The goal of the corporation's managers is to maximize the company's value for the stockholders through appreciation of its share price. But the separation between owners and managers can create problems. Without safeguards, corporate officers might try to run the business for their own benefit and not for the benefit of the stockholders. They might engage in fraudulent financial reporting or misappropriate assets. Proper corporate governance practices can help prevent this type of behavior. These practices include having internal and

[1] Unless the business is organized as a limited-liability company (LLC) or a limited-liability partnership (LLP).

external auditors examine the corporation's financial statements as well as electing independent board members who have no business dealings with the company that could create conflicts of interest.

Corporate Taxation. Corporations are separate taxable entities. They pay several taxes not borne by proprietorships or partnerships, including annual franchise taxes levied by their states. Corporations also pay federal and state income taxes.

Corporate earnings are subject to **double taxation** to the extent they are distributed to shareholders in the form of dividends.

- First, corporations pay income taxes on their corporate income.
- Second, stockholders pay income tax on the cash dividends received from corporations.

In contrast, proprietorships and partnerships pay no business income tax. Instead, the business tax falls solely on the owners.

Government Regulation. Because stockholders have only limited liability for a corporation's debts, outsiders doing business with the corporation can look no further than the corporation if it fails to pay. To protect a corporation's creditors and stockholders, both federal and state governments monitor corporations. The regulations mainly ensure that corporations disclose the information investors and creditors need to make informed decisions. Accounting provides much of this information.

Exhibit 10-1 summarizes the advantages and disadvantages of the corporate form of business organization.

Exhibit 10-1 | Advantages and Disadvantages of a Corporation

Advantages	Disadvantages
1. Can raise more capital than a proprietorship or partnership can	1. Separation of ownership and management
2. Continuous life	2. Double taxation of distributed profits
3. Ease of transferring ownership	3. Government regulation
4. Limited liability of stockholders	

Organizing a Corporation

The creation of a corporation begins when its organizers, called the *incorporators*, obtain a charter from the state. The charter includes the authorization for the corporation to issue a certain number of shares of stock. A share of stock is the basic unit of ownership for a corporation. The incorporators

- pay fees,
- sign the charter,
- file documents with the state, and
- agree to a set of **bylaws**, which act as the constitution for governing the company.

The corporation then comes into existence.

The ultimate control of the corporation rests with the stockholders by virtue of the board of directors they elect. The board members set company policy and appoint officers. The board elects a **chairperson**, who usually is the most powerful person in the organization and often also has the title of Chief Executive Officer (CEO). The board also appoints the **president**, who is the chief operating officer (COO) in charge of day-to-day operations. Although they are generally not chosen by the board, most corporations also have vice presidents in charge of sales, manufacturing, accounting and finance (the chief financial officer, or CFO), and other key areas. Exhibit 10-2 shows the authority structure in a corporation.

Exhibit 10-2 | Authority Structure of a Corporation

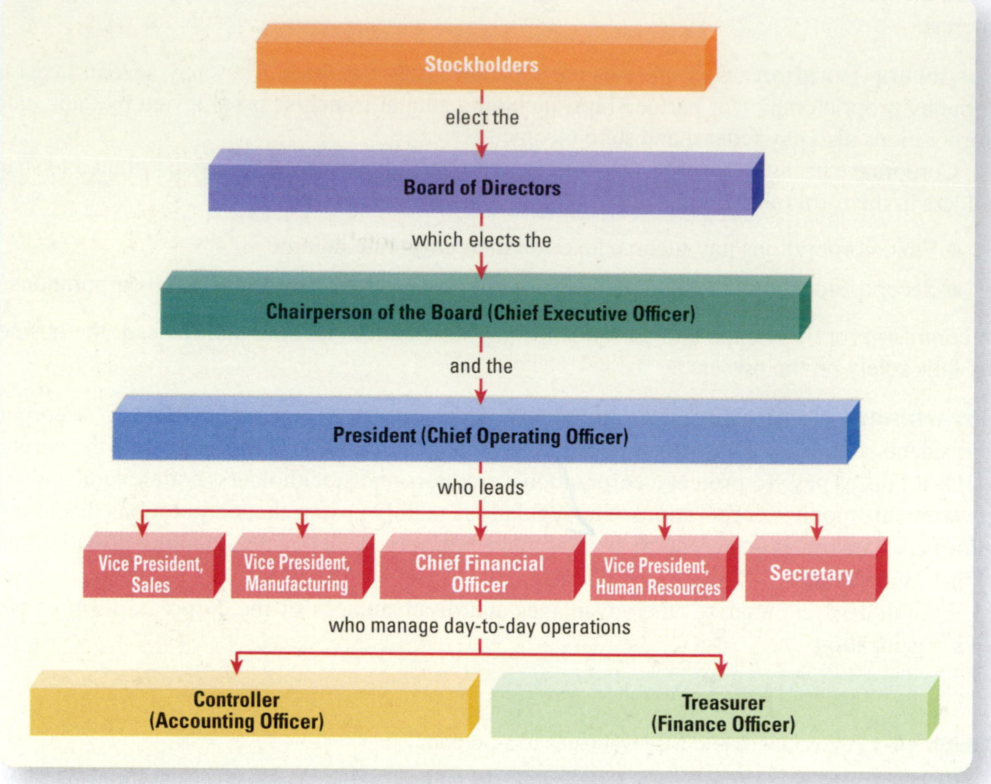

Stockholders' Rights

The ownership of stock entitles stockholders to the following four basic rights:

1. *Vote.* The right to participate in management by voting on matters that come before the stockholders. This is the stockholder's sole voice in the management of the corporation. A stockholder gets one vote for each share of stock owned.
2. *Dividends.* The right to receive a proportionate part of any dividend. Each share of stock in a particular class receives an equal dividend.
3. *Liquidation.* The right to receive a proportionate share of any assets remaining after the corporation liquidates. When a company liquidates, it goes out of business, sells its assets, pays all liabilities, and distributes any remaining cash to the stockholders.
4. *Preemption.* The right to maintain one's proportionate ownership in the corporation. Suppose you own 5% of a corporation's stock with preemptive rights. If the corporation issues 100,000 new shares, it must offer you the opportunity to buy 5% (5,000) of the new shares. While not automatic, the preemptive right may be granted to certain shareholders who own large percentages of the corporation's stock.

Stockholders' Equity

As we saw in Chapter 1, **stockholders' equity** represents the stockholders' ownership interest in the assets of a corporation. Stockholders' equity is divided into two main parts:

1. **Paid-in capital**, also called **contributed capital**. This is the amount of stockholders' equity the stockholders have contributed to the corporation. Paid-in capital includes the stock accounts and any additional paid-in capital.
2. **Retained earnings**. This is the amount of stockholders' equity the corporation has earned through profitable operations and has not used for dividends.

Corporations report stockholders' equity by source. They report paid-in capital separately from retained earnings because most states prohibit companies from paying cash dividends from their paid-in capital accounts. Instead, companies generally pay cash dividends using retained earnings.

The owners' equity of a corporation is divided into shares of **stock**. A corporation issues *stock certificates* to its owners when the company receives their investment in the business—usually cash. Because stock represents the corporation's capital, it is often called *capital stock*. The basic unit of capital stock is a *share*. Exhibit 10-3 shows a stock certificate for one share of a hypothetical corporation's common stock. A corporation can issue a stock certificate for any number of shares—1, 100, or any other number—but the total number of shares that the firm can sell is limited by the corporation's charter.

Exhibit 10-3 | Hypothetical Corporate Stock Certificate

Classes of Stock

Corporations issue different types of stock to appeal to a variety of investors. The stock of a corporation may be either

- common stock or preferred stock, and
- par value stock or no-par value stock.

Common Stock or Preferred Stock. Every corporation issues **common stock**, the basic form of capital stock. Unless designated otherwise, the word *stock* is understood to mean "common stock." Common stockholders have the four basic rights of stock ownership, unless a right is specifically withheld. The common stockholders are the owners of the corporation. They stand to benefit the most if the corporation succeeds because they take the most risk by investing in common stock.

Preferred stock gives its owners certain advantages over common stockholders. Preferred stockholders receive dividends before the common stockholders and they also receive assets before the common stockholders if the corporation liquidates. Owners of preferred stock also have the four basic stockholder rights, unless a right is specifically withheld. Companies can issue different classes of preferred stock (Class A and Class B or Series A and Series B, for example). Each class of stock is recorded in a separate account. In most cases, the most preferred stockholders can expect to earn on their investments is a fixed dividend because preferred stock typically does not appreciate in value like common stock does.

Preferred stock is a hybrid between common stock and long-term debt. Like interest on debt, preferred stock pays a fixed dividend, which is a dividend set to a certain amount. But, unlike interest on debt, the dividend is not required to be paid unless the board of directors declares the dividend.

Preferred stock is rare. A recent survey of 600 corporations reveals that only 9% of them have issued preferred stock. In contrast, all corporations issue common stock. The balance sheet of The Home Depot (p. 523) does not show any preferred stock issued.

Exhibit 10-4 shows some of the similarities and differences among common stock, preferred stock, and long-term debt.

Exhibit 10-4 | Comparison of Common Stock, Preferred Stock, and Long-Term Debt

	Common Stock	Preferred Stock	Long-Term Debt
1. Obligation to repay principal	No	No	Yes
2. Dividends/interest	Dividends are not tax-deductible	Dividends are not tax-deductible	Interest expense is tax-deductible
3. Obligation to pay dividends/interest	Only after declaration	Only after declaration	At fixed rates and dates

Par Value Stock or No-Par Value Stock. Stock may be par value stock or no-par value stock. **Par value stock** has an arbitrary amount assigned to each share when it is originally authorized by the corporate charter. Most states require companies to maintain a minimum amount of stockholders' equity for the protection of creditors. This minimum is often called the corporation's **legal capital**, which amounts to the par value of all of the shares issued. Most companies set the par value of their common stock low—sometimes as low as 1 cent—to avoid legal difficulties later.

The par value of **PepsiCo** common stock is $0.0166 (1⅔ cents) per share. **Best Buy**'s and **Southwest Airlines Company**'s common stock have a par value of $1 per share. The Home Depot's common stock has a par value of $0.05 per share.

No-par value stock (no-par stock) does not have a par value per share but may have a **stated value**, which is an arbitrary amount assigned to it. This makes the stock similar to par-value stock. In a recent survey, only 9% of the companies had no-par stock. **Krispy Kreme Doughnuts, Inc.** and **Sony Corporation** have no-par stock.

ACCOUNT FOR THE ISSUANCE OF STOCK

2 Account for the issuance of stock

Large corporations such as The Home Depot, Inc., **Alphabet, Inc.** (parent of **Google**), and **Microsoft** sometimes need to raise huge amounts of money for specific purposes, such as operations or paying off long-term debt. The first time a private company issues stock to the public, it makes an **initial public offering (IPO)** of shares of its stock. The corporation usually uses the service of an *underwriter*, such as the investment banking firms **JP Morgan Chase & Co.** and **Goldman Sachs**, to market its shares. To attract investors, companies often advertise the IPOs of their stock in the financial media, such as the *Wall Street Journal*. Let's see how a stock issuance works.

Common Stock

Common Stock at Par. Assume that The Home Depot wants to raise $100 million by issuing stock. Suppose The Home Depot's common stock has a par value equal to its issuing price of $10 per share. The entry for issuing 10 million shares of stock at par would be:

	A	B	C	D
1	Jan 8	Cash (10,000,000 × \$10)	100,000,000	
2		Common Stock		100,000,000
3		*To issue common stock.*		
4				

The Home Depot's assets and stockholders' equity increase by the same amount.

Assets	=	Liabilities	+	Stockholders' Equity
+ 100,000,000	=	0		+ 100,000,000

Common Stock Issued Above Par Value. Most corporations set their par values low and issue common stock for a price well above par. Rather than \$10 as in the example above, suppose The Home Depot's common stock has a par value of \$0.05 per share. The \$9.95 difference between the stock's issue price (\$10) and par value (\$0.05) is called Paid-in Capital. Other names for this account are Additional Paid-in Capital or Paid-in Capital in Excess of Par. Both the par value of the stock and the additional amount are part of paid-in capital in the company's balance sheet.

The Home Depot's actual entry to record the common stock issued would look something like this:

	A	B	C	D
1	Jul 23	Cash (10,000,000 × \$10)	100,000,000	
2		Common Stock (10,000,000 × \$0.05)		500,000
3		Paid-in Capital		
4		(10,000,000 × \$9.95)		99,500,000
5		*To issue common stock.*		
6				

Both assets and stockholders' equity increase by the same amount.

Assets	=	Liabilities	+	Stockholders' Equity
+ 100,000,000	=	0		+ 500,000
				+ 99,500,000

The Paid-in Capital account is listed in the stockholders' equity section of the balance sheet immediately after the type of stock to which it relates (in the case of The Home Depot, common stock). Hypothetically, then, after the last entry above, the Stockholders' Equity section of The Home Depot, Inc.'s, Balance Sheet might appear as follows (figures assumed):

	A	B
1	**Stockholders' Equity**	
2	Common stock, \$.05 par, 10 billion shares	
3	authorized, 10 million shares issued and outstanding	\$ 500,000
4	Paid-in Capital	99,500,000
5	Total paid-in capital	100,000,000
6	Retained earnings	500,000,000
7	Total stockholders' equity	\$ 600,000,000
8		

Because The Home Depot is dealing with its own stockholders, a sale of stock does not result in a gain, income, or profit to the corporation. This situation illustrates one of the fundamentals of accounting:

A company neither earns a profit nor incurs a loss when it sells its stock to, or buys its stock from, its own stockholders.

All the transactions in this section include a receipt of cash by the corporation as it issues *new* stock. The transactions are different from those reported in the daily financial press. In those transactions, one stockholder is selling stock to another investor. The corporation doesn't record those transactions because they were between two outside parties.

TRY IT

(Answers are given on p. 593.)

Examine The Home Depot's consolidated balance sheet at January 29, 2017 (p. 523). Answer these questions about its actual stock transactions:

(1) What was The Home Depot's total paid-in capital at January 29, 2017?

(2) How many shares of common stock had The Home Depot issued through January 29, 2017?

(3) What was the average issue price of The Home Depot's common stock that had been issued through January 29, 2017?

No-Par Common Stock. To record the issuance of no-par stock, the company debits the asset received and credits the Common Stock account for the cash or fair market value of the asset received. Suppose that, on April 1, 2017, **Krispy Kreme Doughnuts, Inc.**, issues 63,069 million shares of no-par common stock for $266,724,000. Krispy Kreme's stock issuance entry is:

A1

	A	B	C	D
1	Apr. 1	Cash	266,724,000	
2		Common Stock		266,724,000
3		To issue no-par common stock.		
4				

Assets	=	Liabilities	+	Stockholders' Equity
+266,724,000	=	0		+266,724,000

Krispy Kreme's charter authorizes the company to issue 300 million shares of no-par stock, and the company has an accumulated deficit of $10,584 million in retained earnings. After the prior journal entry, Krispy Kreme Doughnuts, Inc., reports stockholders' equity on its balance sheet as follows (in millions):

A1

	A	B
1	**Stockholders' Equity**	
2	**(in millions)**	
3	Common stock, no par, 300,000,000 shares	
4	authorized, 63,069,000 shares issued and outstanding	$ 266,724,000
5	Accumulated deficit	(10,584,000)
6	Total stockholders' equity	$ 256,140,000
7		

You can see that a company with true no-par stock has no Additional Paid-in Capital account.

No-Par Common Stock with a Stated Value. Accounting for no-par stock with a stated value is identical to accounting for par-value stock. The excess paid over the stated value is credited to Additional Paid-in Capital, or Paid-in Capital in Excess of Stated Value—Common.

Common Stock Issued for Assets Other Than Cash. When a corporation issues stock and receives assets other than cash, the company records the assets received at their current market value and credits the Common Stock and Additional Paid-in Capital accounts accordingly. The assets' prior book values aren't relevant because the stockholder will demand stock equal to the market value of the assets given. On November 12, Kahn Corporation issued 15,000 shares of its $1 par common stock for equipment with a market value of $4,000 and a building with a market value of $120,000. Kahn's entry is

	A	B	C	D
1	Nov 12	Equipment	4,000	
2		Building	120,000	
3		Common Stock (15,000 × $1)		15,000
4		Paid-in Capital in Excess of Par—Common		
5		($124,000 – $15,000)		109,000
6		*To issue $1-par common stock in exchange for*		
7		*equipment and a building.*		
8				

Assets and equity both increase by $124,000.

Assets	=	Liabilities	+	Stockholders' Equity
+ 4,000 + 120,000	=	0		+ 15,000 + 109,000

Common Stock Issued for Services. Sometimes a corporation will issue shares of common stock in exchange for services rendered, either by employees or outsiders. In this case, no cash is exchanged. However, the transaction is recognized at fair market value. The corporation usually recognizes an expense for the fair market value of the services rendered. Common stock is increased by its par value (if any), and additional paid-in capital is increased for any difference. For example, assume that Kahn Corporation hires an attorney to represent the company on a legal matter. The attorney's bill is $25,000. Instead of a cash payment, she agrees to accept 2,500 shares of $1 par common stock in settlement of the fee. The fair market value of the stock is $10 per share. The journal entry to record the transaction is

	A	B	C	D
1		Legal Expense	25,000	
2		Common Stock (2,500 × $1 par)		2,500
3		Paid-in Capital in Excess of Par—Common		
4		($25,000 – $2,500)		22,500
5				

In this case, the company's retained earnings (stockholders' equity) is eventually decreased by the $25,000 legal expense. Paid-in capital (stockholders' equity) is increased by the same amount.

How an "Other Than Cash" Stock Issuance Can Create an Ethical Challenge

Generally accepted accounting principles require a company to record the issuance of its stock at the fair market value of whatever the corporation receives in exchange for the stock. When the corporation receives cash, there is clear evidence of the value of the stock because cash is worth its face amount. But when the corporation receives an asset other than cash, the value of the asset can create an ethical challenge.

For example, suppose a computer whiz starts a new company and develops a new type of software. The software may be market-tested or it may not be. It may be worth millions, or it may be worthless. The corporation must record the asset received and the stock issued with a journal entry such as the following (assuming no-par stock is issued):

	A	B	C	D
1	Software		500,000	
2	Common Stock			500,000
3	*Issued stock in exchange for software.*			
4				

If the software is really worth $500,000, the accounting records are accurate. However, if the software has not yet been tested, both the company's assets and stockholders' equity may be overstated.

Suppose your computer-whiz friend invites you to invest in the new business and shows you this balance sheet:

	A	B	C	D
1	**Gee-Whiz Computer Solutions, Inc. Balance Sheet December 31, 2018**			
2	**Assets**		**Liabilities and Stockholders' Equity**	
3	Computer software	$ 500,000	Total liabilities	$ -0-
4			**Stockholders' Equity**	
5			Common stock	500,000
6	Total assets	$ 500,000	Total liabilities and stockholders' equity	$ 500,000
7				

Companies like to report large asset and equity amounts on their balance sheets. That makes them look prosperous and creditworthy. Gee-Whiz Computer Solutions appears to be debt free and to have a valuable asset. Will you invest in this new business? Here are two takeaway lessons:

- Some accounting values are more solid than others.
- Not all financial statements mean exactly what they say—unless they are audited by independent CPAs.

Preferred Stock

Accounting for preferred stock follows the same pattern we illustrated for common stock. When a company issues preferred stock, it credits Preferred Stock at its par value, with any excess credited to Paid-in Capital in Excess of Par—Preferred.

There may be separate accounts for paid-in capital in excess of par for preferred and common stock, but not necessarily. Some companies combine paid-in capital in excess of par from both preferred and common stock transactions into one account. Accounting for no-par preferred stock follows the same pattern as no-par common stock. When reporting stockholders' equity on the balance sheet, a corporation lists its accounts in this order:

- Preferred stock
- Common stock
- Additional paid-in capital
- Retained earnings

In Chapter 9, we saw how to account for convertible bonds or notes payable (p. 485). Companies also issue convertible preferred stock. The convertible preferred stock can usually be converted to the company's common stock at the discretion of the preferred stockholders, as the price of the common stock, as well as its dividend, rises to an attractive level in the future. Here are some representative journal entries for the issuance and conversion of convertible preferred stock, using assumed amounts:

- The sale of 50,000 shares of convertible preferred stock issued at par value of $1:

	A	B	C	D
1	2018	Cash	50,000	
2		Convertible Preferred Stock		50,000
3		*Issued convertible preferred stock.*		
4				

- The conversion of preferred stock to common stock at the rate of 6.25 to 1 (8,000 shares of $1 par-value common stock issued in exchange for 50,000 shares of preferred stock):

	A	B	C	D
1	2018	Convertible Preferred Stock	50,000	
2		Common Stock		8,000
3		Paid-in Capital in Excess of Par—Common		42,000
4		*Investors converted preferred into common.*		
5				

As you can see, we simply remove Convertible Preferred Stock from the books and assign the new Common Stock the prior book value of the preferred stock.

Mid-Chapter Summary Problem

1. Test your understanding of the first half of this chapter by deciding whether each of the following statements is true or false.
   a. The policy-making body in a corporation is called the board of directors.
   b. The owner of 100 shares of preferred stock has greater voting rights than the owner of 100 shares of common stock.
   c. Par-value stock is worth more than no-par value stock.
   d. Issuing 1,000 shares of $5 par-value stock at $12 increases contributed capital by $12,000.
   e. Issuing no-par value stock with a stated value is fundamentally different from issuing par-value stock.
   f. A corporation issues its preferred stock in exchange for land and a building with a combined market value of $200,000. This transaction increases the corporation's stockholders' equity by $200,000 regardless of the assets' prior book values.
   g. Preferred stock is a riskier investment than common stock.

2. Adolfo Company has two classes of common stock. Only the Class A common stockholders are entitled to vote. The company's balance sheet includes the following information:

	A	B
1	**Stockholders' Equity**	
2	Capital stock:	
3	Class A common stock, voting, $1 par value,	
4	authorized, issued, and outstanding 1,260,000 shares	$ 1,260,000
5	Class B common stock, nonvoting, no par value,	
6	authorized, issued, and outstanding 46,200,000 shares	11,000,000
7		12,260,000
8	Additional paid-in capital	2,011,000
9	Retained earnings	872,403,000
10	Total stockholders' equity	$ 886,674,000
11		

Requirements

a. Record the issuance of the Class A common stock for cash. Use Adolfo's account titles.

b. Record the issuance of the Class B common stock for cash. Use Adolfo's account titles.

c. How much of Adolfo's stockholders' equity was contributed by the stockholders? How much was provided by profitable operations? Does this division of equity suggest that the company has been successful? Why or why not?

d. Write a sentence to describe what Adolfo's stockholders' equity means.

Answers

1. a. True; b. False; c. False; d. True; e. False; f. True; g. False

2. a.

	A	B	C	D
1		Cash	3,271,000	
2		Class A Common Stock		1,260,000
3		Additional Paid-in Capital		2,011,000
4		*To record issuance of Class A common stock.*		
5				

b.

	A	B	C	D
1		Cash	11,000,000	
2		Class B Common Stock		11,000,000
3		*To record issuance of Class B common stock.*		
4				

c. Contributed by the stockholders: $14,271,000 ($12,260,000 + $2,011,000). Provided by profitable operations: $872,403,000. This division suggests that the company has been successful because most of its stockholders' equity has come from profitable operations.

d. Adolfo's stockholders' equity of $886,674,000 means that the company's stockholders own $886,674,000 of the business's assets.

Authorized, Issued, and Outstanding Stock

It is important to distinguish among three distinctly different numbers of a company's stock. The following examples use The Home Depot's actual data from page 523.

- **Authorized stock** is the maximum number of shares the company can issue under its charter. As of January 29, 2017, The Home Depot was authorized to issue 10 billion shares of common stock.
- **Issued stock** is the number of shares the company has issued to its stockholders. This is a cumulative total from the company's beginning up through the current date, less any shares permanently retired. As of January 29, 2017, The Home Depot had issued 1.776 billion common shares.
- **Outstanding stock** is the number of shares that the stockholders own (that is, the number of shares outstanding in the hands of the stockholders). Outstanding stock is issued stock minus treasury stock (discussed next). At January 29, 2017, The Home Depot had 1.203 billion shares of common stock outstanding, computed as

Issued shares (line 13, in billions)	1.776
Less: Treasury shares (line 20, in billions)	(0.573)
Outstanding shares (in billions)	1.203

Now let's learn about treasury stock.

EXPLAIN HOW TREASURY STOCK AFFECTS A COMPANY

3 Explain how treasury stock affects a company

A company's own stock that it has issued and later reacquired is called **treasury stock.**[2] In effect, the corporation holds this stock in its treasury. Many public companies spend billions of dollars each year to buy back their own stock. Corporations purchase their own stock for several reasons:

1. The company has issued all its authorized stock and needs some stock to distribute to employees under stock purchase plans or compensation plans.
2. The business wants to increase its net assets by buying its stock low and hoping to resell it for a higher price.
3. Management wants to avoid a takeover by an outside party.
4. Management wants to increase its reported earnings per share (EPS) of common stock (net income ÷ number of common shares outstanding). Purchasing shares removes them from outstanding shares, which decreases the denominator of this fraction and increases EPS. We cover the computation of EPS in more depth on page 547.
5. Management wants to use a repurchase program to return excess cash to shareholders who are willing to sell their shares back to the company as an alternative to receiving a cash dividend.

How Is Treasury Stock Recorded?

Treasury stock is recorded at its cost—which is the market value of the stock on the date it is purchased—without regard to the stock's par value. Treasury stock is a *contra stockholders' equity* account; therefore, the treasury-stock account carries a debit balance, the opposite of the other equity accounts. It is reported beneath the Retained Earnings account on the balance sheet as a negative amount.

[2] In this text, we illustrate the *cost* method of accounting for treasury stock because it is used most widely. Other methods are presented in intermediate accounting courses.

To understand the way treasury-stock transactions work, it is helpful to analyze the changes that occur in the treasury-stock account during the year. Let's start with The Home Depot's stockholders' equity at the end of the previous year, January 31, 2016 (we use rounded amounts in millions, except for shares):

	A	B
1	**The Home Depot, Inc. Stockholders' Equity January 31, 2016**	
2	**(in millions)**	
3	Common stock	88
4	Paid-in capital	9,347
5	Retained earnings	30,973
6	Accumulated other comprehensive loss	(898)
7	Treasury stock (520,000,000 shares)	(33,194)
8	Total stockholders' equity	$ 6,316
9		

Data from the U.S. Securities and Exchange Commission EDGAR Company filings, www.sec.gov

Notice that as of January 31, 2016, The Home Depot had spent $33,194 million to repurchase 520 million shares of its own stock. The average price it had paid for its shares through that date was about $63.83 per share ($33,194 million ÷ 520 million).

Repurchasing shares of stock provides a way for public companies to return cash to shareholders other than through dividends. The disadvantage to the shareholder of a share repurchase plan is that in order to receive cash, the shareholder has to surrender (dilute) his or her ownership in the company. Note 5 of The Home Depot's financial statements gives more information about the company's accelerated share repurchase (ASR) program:

> The Company enters into an Accelerated Share Repurchase ("ASR") agreement from time to time with a third-party financial institution to repurchase shares of the Company's common stock. Under the ASR agreement, the Company pays a specified amount to the financial institution and receives an initial delivery of shares. This initial delivery of shares represents the minimum number of shares that the Company may receive under the agreement. Upon settlement of the ASR agreement, the financial institution delivers additional shares, with the final number of shares delivered determined with reference to the volume weighted average price per share of the Company's common stock over the term of the agreement, less a negotiated discount. The transactions are accounted for as equity transactions and are included in Treasury Stock when the shares are received, at which time there is an immediate reduction in the weighted average common shares calculation for basic and diluted earnings per share.

The Consolidated Statements of Stockholders' Equity (Exhibit 10-8) shows that a total of 53 million shares were purchased for $7 billion. The average purchase price of these shares was $132.08 per share ($7 billion ÷ 53 million). The entry to record the aggregate of these purchases is

	A	B	C	D
1	2016	Treasury Stock	7,000,000,000	
2	Various	Cash		7,000,000,000
3		*Purchased treasury stock.*		
4				

Assets	=	Liabilities	+	Stockholders' Equity
− 7,000,000,000	=	0		− 7,000,000,000

Notice that treasury stock is recorded at cost, which is the market price of the stock on the various days that The Home Depot purchased it. The financial statement impact of these transactions is decreased cash as well as stockholders' equity. As of January 29, 2017, The Home Depot's balance sheet reported that the company owned 573 million shares of treasury stock for a total cost of $40,194 million (an average cost of $70.15 per share).

Retirement of Treasury Stock

A corporation may purchase its own stock and retire it by canceling the stock certificates. Retired stock cannot be reissued. Once the shares are repurchased, neither total assets nor total liabilities are affected, and a memorandum entry is made decreasing the number of shares issued in stockholders' equity.

Resale of Treasury Stock

Reselling treasury stock for cash grows a company's assets and stockholders' equity in exactly the same way as issuing new stock does. However, a company never records gains or losses on transactions involving its own treasury stock. Rather, amounts received in excess of the amounts originally paid for treasury stock are recorded as Paid-in Capital from Treasury Stock Transactions and appear on the balance sheet, not the income statement. If the amounts received from the resale of treasury stock were less than the amounts shareholders originally paid for the stock, the difference would be debited to Paid-in Capital from Treasury Stock Transactions to the extent of that balance, and after that, to Retained Earnings. The Home Depot did not resell any of its treasury stock in fiscal 2016, but suppose that on July 22, 2016, it had resold a million shares of treasury stock for $90 per share. Assuming the average cost of treasury shares is $70.15 (calculated above), the journal entry to record the resale of treasury shares would have been

A1

	A	B	C	D
1	2016			
2	Jul 22	Cash ($90 x 1,000,000)	90,000,000	
3		Treasury Stock ($70.15 x 1,000,000)		70,150,000
4		Paid-in Capital from Treasury Stock Transactions		19,850,000
5		*Sold treasury stock.*		
6				

Assets	=	Liabilities	+	Stockholders' Equity
+ 90,000,000	=	0		+ 70,150,000
				+ 19,850,000

Issuing Stock for Employee Compensation

Sometimes companies supplement employee salaries by granting shares of stock rather than giving cash. Sometimes they use treasury shares for this purpose and sometimes they grant newly issued shares for various reasons. The Consolidated Statements of Stockholders' Equity (Exhibit 10-8 on page 551) shows that during the year ended January 29, 2017, The Home Depot issued 4 million new (not treasury) shares in conjunction with its employee stock compensation plan. In addition, employees exercised options previously granted to them by the company to purchase additional stock. The total amount of these transactions ($76 million + $97 million + $267 million = $440 million) was treated as compensation. Because the par value of the shares is only $0.05, the common stock account was impacted by only $200,000 (4,000,000 shares × 0.05 par value per share). Paid-in capital was credited for the remainder. The entry the company made was

	A	B	C	D
1			**Debit**	**Credit**
2		Compensation Expense	440,000,000	
3		Common Stock (4,000,000 × .05)		200,000
4		Paid-in Capital		439,800,000
5		*To record stock-based compensation plan.*		
6				

Since items on the Statement of Stockholders' Equity are rounded to the nearest million, the impact on the common stock account is reflected as zero, and the entire credit ($440 million, rounded to the nearest million) is shown as an increase in paid-in capital.

Now let's take a look at The Home Depot's stockholders' equity as of January 29, 2017. For now, focus only on the treasury-stock account:

	A	B
1	**The Home Depot, Inc. Stockholders' Equity January 29, 2017**	
2	(in millions)	
3	Common stock	88
4	Paid-in capital	9,787
5	Retained earnings	35,519
6	Accumulated other comprehensive income (loss)	(867)
7	Less Treasury stock (at cost) 573 million shares	(40,194)
8	Total stockholders' equity	$ 4,333
9		

Data from the U.S. Securities and Exchange Commission EDGAR Company filings, www.sec.gov

After the company's treasury-stock transactions for the year ended January 29, 2017, have been recorded, the new number of treasury shares is 573 million. The balance in the treasury-stock account is $40,194 ($33,194 million + $7,000 million). Notice that the treasury stock account actually exceeds retained earnings by almost $5 billion. This means that, as of January 29, 2017, the company has returned more money to shareholders through share repurchases than it has accumulated in the form of undistributed earnings.

Summary of Treasury-Stock Transactions

The types of treasury-stock transactions we have reviewed are as follows:

- Buying treasury stock. Assets and equity *decrease* by an amount equal to the cost of treasury stock purchased.
- Reselling treasury stock. Assets and equity *increase* by an amount equal to the sale price of the treasury stock sold.
- Retiring treasury stock. Treasury stock is removed from both common stock and the treasury.
- Issuing stock for employee compensation. Expenses are increased, capital stock is increased for the par value of the shares, and additional paid-in capital is increased for the difference.

ACCOUNT FOR RETAINED EARNINGS, DIVIDENDS, AND STOCK SPLITS

4 Account for retained earnings, dividends, and stock splits

The Retained Earnings account contains the balance of the business's net income, less its net losses, and less any declared dividends that have been accumulated over the corporation's lifetime. *Retained* means "held on to." Successful companies grow by reinvesting in the business the assets they generate through profitable operations. Then the companies return cash to shareholders through either dividends or repurchases of outstanding shares. The Home Depot is an excellent example of a corporation that has returned significant amounts to its shareholders by both of these means.

The Retained Earnings account is not a reservoir of cash for paying dividends to the stockholders. In fact, the corporation may have a large balance in Retained Earnings but not have enough cash to pay a dividend. Cash and Retained Earnings are two entirely separate accounts with no particular relationship. Retained Earnings says nothing about the company's cash balance.

A *credit* balance in Retained Earnings is normal, indicating that the corporation's lifetime earnings exceed its lifetime losses and dividends. A *debit* balance in Retained Earnings, which is called a **deficit**, arises when a corporation's lifetime losses and dividends exceed its lifetime earnings. Deficits are subtracted to determine total stockholders' equity.

Should the Company Declare and Pay Cash Dividends?

A **dividend** is a distribution by a corporation to its stockholders, usually based on the company's earnings. Dividends usually take one of three forms:

- Cash
- Stock
- Noncash assets

In this section we focus on cash dividends and stock dividends because the distribution of noncash assets, such as inventory or property and equipment, as dividends is extremely rare.

Cash Dividends

Most dividends are cash dividends. To pay a dividend, a company must have both

- enough retained earnings to *declare* the dividend, and
- enough cash to *pay* the dividend.

A corporation declares a dividend before paying it. Only the board of directors has the authority to declare a dividend. The corporation has no obligation to pay a dividend until the board declares one, but once declared, the dividend becomes a legal liability of the corporation. There are three relevant dates for dividends (using assumed dates and amounts):

1. *Declaration date, June 19.* On the declaration date, the board of directors announces the dividend. Declaration of the dividend creates a liability for the corporation. It is recorded by debiting Retained Earnings and crediting Dividends Payable. Assume a $50,000 dividend is declared.

A1

	A	B	C	D
1	Jun 19	Retained Earnings[3]	50,000	
2		Dividends Payable		50,000
3		*Declared a cash dividend.*		
4				

[3]In the early part of this book, we debited a Dividends account to clearly identify the purpose of the payment. From here on, we follow the more common practice of debiting the Retained Earnings account when a dividend is declared.

Liabilities increase and stockholders' equity decreases.

Assets	=	Liabilities	+	Stockholders' Equity
0	=	+ 50,000		− 50,000

2. *Date of record, July 1.* As part of the declaration, the corporation announces the record date, which is the date on which the company looks to see who its stockholders are. Only those who are stockholders on the date of record will receive the dividend. The date of record follows the declaration date by a few weeks. There is no journal entry for the date of record.
3. *Payment date, July 10.* The payment of the dividend usually follows the record date by a week or two. The payment is recorded by debiting Dividends Payable and crediting Cash.

	A	B	C	D
1	Jul 10	Dividends Payable	50,000	
2		Cash		50,000
3		*Paid cash dividend.*		
4				

Both assets and liabilities decrease.

Assets	=	Liabilities	+	Stockholders' Equity
− 50,000	=	− 50,000		

The net effect of a dividend declaration and its payment, as shown in steps 1, 2, and 3, is a decrease in assets and a corresponding decrease in stockholders' equity.

Analyzing the Stockholders' Equity Accounts

If you understand accounting, you can look at a company's comparative year-to-year financial statements and tell a lot about what the company did during the current year. For example, at January 29, 2017, The Home Depot reported the following for Retained Earnings (in millions):

	Jan. 29, 2017	Jan. 31 2016
Retained Earnings	$35,519	$30,973

Data from the U.S. Securities and Exchange Commission EDGAR Company filings, www.sec.gov

What do these figures tell you about The Home Depot's results of operations during the fiscal year? Did the company earn net income or a net loss? How can you tell? Remember that

- net income is the only item that increases retained earnings;
- net losses decrease retained earnings;
- dividends declared decrease retained earnings; and
- other adjustments to retained earnings are usually relatively minor and relatively rare.

In most cases, if you know the amount of either a company's net income or dividends, but not both, and if you know both the beginning and ending balances of its retained earnings, you can figure out the amount you don't know by analyzing the Retained Earnings account.

Let's analyze The Home Depot's Retained Earnings account on January 29, 2017. As shown previously, the balance of Retained Earnings was $30,973 million on January 31, 2016. Net income for the year ended January 29, 2017, according to the company's consolidated statement of income, was $7,957 million. If there were no other changes in Retained Earnings besides dividends, how much in dividends did the company declare?

You can compute The Home Depot's dividend declarations during the year ended January 29, 2017, by analyzing the changes in the Retained Earnings account as follows (in millions):

Retained earnings

Other adjustments	7	Beg bal	30,973
Dividends	*X*	Net income	7,957
		End bal	35,519

During the year, the company had a minor nonrecurring negative adjustment of $7 million to retained earnings, which happens from time to time. Knowing this, we can calculate dividends as $3,404 million ($30,973 million + $7,957 million − $7 million − *X* = $35,519 million).

The two major elements that affect retained earnings are net income (loss) and dividends, so most of the time, the computation of dividends is as simple as analyzing the retained earnings account.

Dividends on Preferred Stock

When a company has issued both preferred and common stock, the preferred stockholders receive their dividends first. The common stockholders receive dividends only if the total dividend is large enough to pay the preferred stockholders first. Dividends on preferred stock are stated either as

- a percent of par value, or
- a dollar amount per share.

For example, preferred stock may be "6% preferred," which means that owners of the preferred stock receive an annual dividend equal to 6% of the stock's par value. If par value is $100 per share, preferred stockholders receive an annual cash dividend of $6 per share (6% of $100). Alternatively, the preferred stock may be "$3 preferred," which means that the preferred stockholders receive an annual dividend of $3 per share regardless of the stock's par value. The dividend rate on no-par preferred stock is stated as a dollar amount per share.

Consider the following hypothetical example: Avant Garde, Inc., has 100,000 shares of $1.50 preferred stock outstanding in addition to its common stock. The $1.50 designation means that the preferred stockholders receive an annual cash dividend of $1.50 per share, or a total of $150,000. In 2018, Avant Garde declares an annual dividend of $500,000. The allocation to preferred and common stockholders is:

Preferred dividend (100,000 shares × $1.50 per share)............	$150,000
Common dividend (remainder: $500,000 − $150,000)	350,000
Total dividend..	$500,000

If Avant Garde declares only a $200,000 dividend, preferred stockholders receive $150,000, and the common stockholders get the remainder, $50,000 ($200,000 − $150,000).

Dividends on Cumulative and Noncumulative Preferred Stock. The balance-sheet classification of preferred stock, as well as the allocation of dividends, can be complex if the preferred stock is *cumulative*. The owners of **cumulative preferred stock** must receive all dividends in arrears plus the current year's dividend before any dividends go to the common stockholders. In most states, preferred stock is cumulative unless it is specifically labeled as noncumulative. Corporations sometimes fail to pay a dividend to cumulative preferred stockholders. This is called *passing the dividend*, and the passed dividends are said to be *in arrears*. Although cumulative dividends must be paid before other dividends, they must still be declared by the company's board of directors.

Here's an example of how cumulative dividends work. Let's assume that the preferred stock of Avant Garde, Inc., is cumulative. Suppose Avant Garde passed the preferred dividend of $150,000 in 2017. Before paying dividends to the company's common stockholders in 2018, Avant Garde must first pay preferred dividends of $150,000 for both 2017 and 2018—a total of $300,000. On September 6, 2018, Avant Garde declares a $500,000 dividend. The entry to record the declaration is as follows:

	A	B	C	D
1	Sep 6	Retained Earnings	500,000	
2		Dividends Payable, Preferred ($150,000 × 2)		300,000
3		Dividends Payable, Common ($500,000 − $300,000)		200,000
4		*To declare a cash dividend.*		
5				

If the preferred stock is noncumulative, the corporation is not obligated to pay passed dividends.

Stock Dividends

A **stock dividend** is a proportional distribution by a corporation of its own stock to its stockholders. Stock dividends increase the Common Stock account, the Paid-in Capital in Excess of Par—Common, and decrease Retained Earnings. Total equity is unchanged, and no asset or liability is affected.

The corporation distributes stock dividends to stockholders in proportion to the number of shares they already own. If you own 300 shares of The Home Depot common stock and the corporation distributes a 10% common stock dividend, you get 30 (300 × 0.10) additional shares. You would then own 330 shares of the common stock. All other The Home Depot stockholders would also receive 10% more shares, leaving the proportionate ownership of all common stockholders unchanged.

When a company distributes a stock dividend, the corporation gives up no assets. As we indicated, total equity is unchanged, and no asset or liability is affected. Why, then, do companies issue stock dividends?

A corporation might choose to distribute stock dividends for these reasons:

1. *To continue dividends but conserve cash.* A company may need to conserve cash and yet wish to continue dividends in some form. So, instead of cash, the corporation may distribute a stock dividend. Stockholders pay no income tax on stock dividends.
2. *To reduce the per-share market price of its stock.* Distributing a stock dividend usually causes the stock's market price to fall because of the increased number of outstanding shares that result from it. The objective is to make the stock less expensive and therefore more attractive to more investors.

Generally accepted accounting principles (GAAP) consider a stock dividend of 25% or less of outstanding common shares to be small and require that the dividend be recorded at the market value of the shares distributed. Suppose The Home Depot declared and distributed a 10% common stock dividend on February 3, 2017. At the time, The Home Depot had approximately 1,203 million shares of common stock outstanding, and the corporation's stock was trading for $140 per share. The Home Depot would have recorded this stock dividend as follows:

	A	B	C	D
1	2017	Retained Earnings[4] (1,203,000,000 shares of		
2	Feb. 3	common outstanding × 0.10 stock dividend × $140		
3		market value per share of common)	16,842,000,000	
4		Common Stock (1,203,000,000 × 0.10 × $0.05		
5		par value per share)		6,015,000
6		Paid-in Capital		16,835,985,000
7		*Declared and distributed a 10% stock dividend.*		
8				

[4]Many companies debit Additional Paid-in Capital for their stock dividends.

The accounting equation clearly shows that a stock dividend has no effect on total assets, liabilities, or equity. The increases in equity offset the decrease, and the net effect is zero.

Assets	=	Liabilities	+	Stockholders' Equity
0	=	0		− 16,842,000,000
				+ 6,015,000
				+ 16,835,985,000

GAAP identifies stock dividends above 25% of outstanding common shares as large and permits large stock dividends to be recorded at par value. So, for a large stock dividend, The Home Depot, Inc., would debit Retained Earnings and credit Common Stock for the par value of the shares distributed in the dividend.

Stock Splits

A **stock split** is an increase in the number of shares of stock issued and outstanding, coupled with a proportionate reduction in the stock's par value. For example, if the company splits its stock 2 for 1, the number of outstanding shares is doubled and each share's par value is halved. A stock split, like a large stock dividend, decreases the market price of the stock—with the goal of making the stock more attractive in the market. Most leading companies in the United States—including **International Business Machines Corp., PepsiCo, Inc., Apple Inc.,** and The Home Depot, Inc.—have split their stock. The Home Depot's, stock price has split 13 times since the company's IPO in 1978.

Assume the market price of a share of The Home Depot, Inc.'s common stock is approximately $200 per share and that the company wants to decrease the market price to approximately $100 per share. The Home Depot can split its common stock 2 for 1, and the stock price will fall to around $100. A 2-for-1 stock split means that

- the company will have twice as many shares of stock issued and outstanding after the split as it had before, and
- each share's par value will be cut in half.

Suppose that before the split, The Home Depot had approximately 500 million shares of $0.10 (10 cents) par common stock issued and outstanding. Compare The Home Depot, Inc.'s, stockholders' equity before and after a 2-for-1 stock split (numbers are assumed, not actual):

	A	B	C	D
1	**The Home Depot, Inc., Stockholders' Equity (Adapted, Assumed Numbers)**			
2	**Before 2-for-1 Stock Split**	**(In millions)**	**After 2-for-1 Stock Split**	**(In millions)**
3	Common stock, $0.10 par, 1,000		Common stock, $0.05 par, 1,000	
4	shares authorized, 500 shares		shares authorized, 1,000 shares	
5	issued and outstanding	$ 50	issued and outstanding	$ 50
6	Additional paid-in capital	643	Additional paid-in capital	643
7	Retained earnings	4,304	Retained earnings	4,304
8	Other equity	260	Other equity	260
9	Total stockholders' equity	$ 5,257	Total stockholders' equity	$ 5,257
10				

All account balances are the same after the stock split as before. Only three items are affected:

- The par value per share drops from $0.10 to $0.05.
- Shares *issued* double from 500 to 1,000 (both in millions).
- Shares *outstanding* double from 500 to 1,000 (both in millions).

Total equity doesn't change, nor do any assets or liabilities.

Summary of the Effects on Assets, Liabilities, and Stockholders' Equity

We've seen how to account for the basic stockholders' equity transactions:

- Issuance of stock—common and preferred (pp. 528–533)
- Purchase and sale of treasury stock (pp. 535–538)
- Cash dividends (pp. 539–542)
- Stock dividends and stock splits (pp. 542–543)

How do these transactions affect assets, liabilities, and equity? Exhibit 10-5 provides a helpful summary.

Exhibit 10-5 | Effects of Stock Transactions

	Effect on Total				
Transaction	**Assets**	=	**Liabilities**	+	**Stockholders' Equity**
Issuance of stock—common and preferred	Increase		No effect		Increase
Purchase of treasury stock	Decrease		No effect		Decrease
Sale of treasury stock	Increase		No effect		Increase
Declaration of cash dividend	No effect		Increase		Decrease
Payment of cash dividend	Decrease		Decrease		No effect
Stock dividend—large and small	No effect		No effect		No effect*
Stock split	No effect		No effect		No effect

*The stock accounts increase and retained earnings decrease by offsetting amounts that net to zero.

EVALUATE A COMPANY'S PERFORMANCE USING NEW RATIOS

5 Evaluate a company's performance using new ratios

Business analysts use a great deal of information in the stockholders' equity section to evaluate company performance and make informed investment and credit decisions. In this section, we discuss the following ratios: (1) Return on equity (ROE) and the elements that comprise it; (2) Earnings per share (EPS); (3) Price/earnings (P/E) ratio (multiple); and (4) Dividend yield.

ROE: Relating Profitability to Stockholder Investment

One of the best ways to measure the performance of a company is to determine its profitability as a percentage of the amount invested in them. Companies that have a high rate of return per dollar invested are usually more valuable in terms of their stock prices. As you have learned, two ratios that measure profitability per dollar invested are

- return on assets (ROA, discussed in Chapter 7), which measures profitability as a percentage of a company's total asset investment by both creditors and shareholders; and
- return on equity (ROE), which measures profitability in comparison with just the shareholders' investment.

As the following diagram shows, a DuPont Analysis (discussed in Chapters 7 and 9) is a convenient way to analyze the various elements of profitability:

ROA			×	Leverage Ratio	=	ROE
Net Profit Margin Ratio	×	Asset Turnover Ratio	×	Leverage Ratio	=	Return on Equity
$\frac{\text{Net income*}}{\text{Net sales}}$	×	$\frac{\text{Net sales}}{\text{Average total assets}}$	×	$\frac{\text{Average total assets}}{\text{Average common stockholders' equity}}$	=	$\frac{\text{Net income*}}{\text{Average common stockholders' equity}}$

*minus preferred dividends

The left-hand side of the diagram shows that rate of return on total assets or return on assets (ROA) is the product of two drivers: the *net profit margin ratio* and *asset turnover ratio.* The net profit margin ratio measures how effectively the company has earned revenue while controlling costs. The asset turnover ratio measures how efficiently the company has managed its assets. We discussed strategies that management uses to improve these ratios in Chapter 7 (pp. 397). In Chapter 9 (pp. 490–491), we also introduced the *leverage ratio*, or *equity multiplier*, which shows the impact of the use of debt, or leverage, to magnify ROA. Together, the three ratios combine to measure the rate of return on common stockholders' equity, or return on equity (ROE), in the last column on the right-hand side of the diagram.

ROE shows the relationship between net income and common stockholders' equity. Return on equity is computed only on common stock because the return to preferred stockholders is usually known because the dividends they get—that is, their returns—are specified (for example, 5%), so there is no need to calculate them. The numerator of ROE is net income minus preferred dividends, if any. The denominator is *average common stockholders' equity*—the average of total stockholders' equity minus the average equity of any preferred stock. However, because most companies do not have preferred stock, such adjustments are usually not necessary.

Let's use the DuPont Analysis model to analyze The Home Depot, Inc.'s, ROE as of January 29, 2017. All balance sheet computations in this paragraph are based on figures taken from the company's comparative Consolidated Balance Sheets on page 523. You should re-compute the ratios and confirm the computations as you read. From its consolidated statements of earnings (www.sec.gov) (not reproduced in this chapter) we find that The Home Depot earned $7,957 million net income on $94,595 million in net sales for the year ended January 29, 2017, for a net profit margin ratio of 8.412%. This ratio is then combined with the balance-sheet information (in millions) to compute ROA and ROE as follows:

ROA			×	Leverage Ratio	=	ROE
Net Profit Margin Ratio	×	Asset Turnover Ratio	×	Leverage Ratio	=	Return on Equity
$\frac{\text{Net income*}}{\text{Net sales}}$	×	$\frac{\text{Net sales}}{\text{Average total assets}}$	×	$\frac{\text{Average total assets}}{\text{Average common stockholders' equity}}$	=	$\frac{\text{Net income*}}{\text{Average common stockholders' equity}}$
$\frac{\$7,957}{\$94,595}$	×	$\frac{\$94,595}{\$42,470}$	×	$\frac{\$42,470}{\$5,325}$	=	$\frac{\$7,957}{\$5,325}$
{8.412%}	×	{2.227}	×	{7.9756}	=	{149.4%}
{ROA = 18.73%}						

* minus preferred dividends

Each dollar of sales has resulted in about 8.412 cents of net profit. The company's asset turnover was 2.227, meaning that it earned $2.227 in sales for each average dollar invested in total assets. A leverage ratio of 7.9756 to 1 means that the company owns about $7.9756 of assets for each dollar of stockholders' equity invested. The Home Depot has chosen to finance itself with a high proportion of debt compared to equity. Average total liabilities are $37,145 million, so the debt ratio for the company (based on average total liabilities to average total assets) is about 87.5% ($37,145/$42,470). The leverage ratio of 7.9756, multiplied by ROA of 18.73%, magnifies the profitability on shareholder investment to 149.4%.

Are these returns strong, weak, or somewhere in between? To answer that question, we need other information, such as

- comparative returns for The Home Depot, Inc., for prior years and
- comparative returns for other companies in the same industry.

For example, the following diagram compares The Home Depot, Inc.'s, ROE for fiscal 2016, 2015, and 2014. The diagram also compares fiscal 2016 ROE for The Home Depot versus **Lowes Companies, Inc**.

	Net Profit Margin Ratio	×	Asset Turnover Ratio	×	Leverage Ratio	=	Return on Equity
The Home Depot, Inc. 2016	8.412%	×	2.227	×	7.9756	=	149.4%
The Home Depot, Inc. 2015	7.91%	×	2.16	×	5.23	=	89.4%
The Home Depot, Inc. 2014	7.63%	×	2.07	×	3.68	=	58.1%
Lowes Companies, Inc. 2016	4.30%	×	1.88	×	3.57	=	28.9%

Compared with fiscal 2015, The Home Depot, Inc.'s, ROE for fiscal 2016 is substantially higher. The company's net profit margin ratio in fiscal 2016 rose to 8.412% from 7.91% in fiscal 2015, meaning the company earned more profit on each dollar of sales. One-half of one percent improvement may not seem like much at first, but when multiplied by almost $95 billion in sales, it calculates to an extra $475 million in net profit. In addition, asset turnover increased from 2.16 to 2.227 times, which means the company earned more in sales per dollar invested in 2016 and was therefore more efficient than in fiscal 2015.

However, the really big story is the increase in the company's leverage ratio. As we discussed earlier in this chapter, the company has been repurchasing massive amounts of its common stock over the past few years. This has greatly increased The Home Depot's treasury stock, thus greatly decreasing the company's stockholders' equity, and greatly increasing the proportion of its total assets financed with debt. The leverage ratio increased to 7.9756 during fiscal 2016 from 5.23 during fiscal 2015, indicating the company was using proportionately more debt financing in fiscal 2016 than in any previous year. With interest rates at all-time lows, the period from 2014 through 2016 was a good period to incur debt, as long as it could be repaid in a timely manner and as long as the company was earning more on the borrowed funds than those funds cost in terms of interest. In summary, the company has been more effective (profitable), more efficient (a smaller relative investment in assets), and more highly leveraged (proportionate debt financing) in the past three years than ever before. All of this activity combined boosted ROE to an astounding 149.4% in fiscal 2016—good news for investors, and good news for the company's share price, which increased from $104.43 at February 1, 2015 to $138.47 at January 31, 2017.

Compared to ROE data for Lowes, The Home Depot's results in fiscal 2016 were higher in every dimension. Its net profit margin ratio (8.412%) bested Lowes by almost double, meaning The Home Depot stores were about twice as profitable per dollar of sales. The likely explanation for this is that The Home Depot's costs per dollar of sales were lower. The Home Depot also turned assets over more efficiently than Lowes in fiscal 2016 (2.227 times vs. 1.88 times). Finally, The Home Depot has significantly more leverage in its capital structure (7.9756 times vs. 3.57 times), thus magnifying its ROA from 18.73% to an ROE of 149.4% compared to an ROE of only 28.9% for Lowes.

What is a good rate of return on total assets? Ten percent is considered a strong benchmark in most industries. However, rates of return on assets vary by industry because the components of ROA are different across industries. Some high-technology companies earn much higher returns than do utility companies, grocery stores, and manufacturers of consumer goods such as toothpaste and paper towels. Companies that are efficient, generating a large amount of sales per dollar of assets invested, or companies that can differentiate their products and earn higher gross profit margins on them, have a higher ROA than companies that do not have these attributes.

You can see by studying the DuPont model that whenever ROA is positive, ROE is always higher than ROA because of the "multiplier" effect of the leverage ratio. This also makes sense from an economic standpoint. Stockholders take a lot more investment risk than creditors, so the stockholders demand that ROE exceed ROA. They also expect the return on their investment to exceed the cost of borrowed funds.

Investors and creditors compare the ROE of companies in much the same way they compare ROA. The higher the rate of return, the more successful the company. In many industries, 20% is considered a good ROE. The Home Depot's ROE of 149.4% for fiscal 2016 was exceptionally high, mostly due to its high degree of leverage relative to total assets.

Earnings Per Share (EPS)

Earnings per share (EPS) is the net income attributable to each share of a company's outstanding common stock. EPS is a key measure of a corporation's business success. Because net income (profit) is measured per share of common stock, EPS is a standard measure of operating performance that can be used to compare the profitability of companies of different sizes in different industries. EPS is used to help determine the market value of a share of the company's common stock, as well as its market capitalization, as we will see in the next section. Because of its importance in measuring business profitability, one of management's key objectives of a business is to maximize EPS. The formula for EPS is:

$$\text{Earnings per share} = \frac{\text{Net income} - \text{Preferred dividends}}{\text{Weighted-average number of shares of common stock outstanding}}$$

Notice that if a company has preferred stock outstanding, the preferred dividends must be subtracted from total net income in order to calculate the net income available to common shareholders.

Consider the EPS calculation of The Home Depot, Inc. Net income (the bottom line on the company's Consolidated Statement of Earnings) for the 2016 fiscal year was $7,957 million. This amount has also been designated as "Income Available to Common Shareholders." The Home Depot has no other classes of stock except common stock, so there is no deduction for preferred dividends. According to the Consolidated Balance Sheet on page 523, the company had 1,203 million shares of stock outstanding as of January 29, 2017. However, the EPS calculation requires the company to compute the weighted average number of shares outstanding for the year. Since the company repurchased 53 million shares during the year, the weighted average number of shares outstanding is slightly higher (1,229 million shares outstanding for the "basic" computation; from annual report.) The company has some contingent agreements that potentially could give rise to the issuance of 5 million additional shares (a total of 1,234 million shares), thus "diluting" the earnings per share. Consequently, the company computes both "basic" and "diluted" EPS. We show the computation for basic EPS only.

Weighted-average number of shares—basic..................................	1,229 million
Earnings per share—basic ($7,957 million/1,229 million).............	$6.47

The repurchase of treasury shares is a common practice among public companies to bolster reported EPS. For example, **Caterpillar Corporation** repurchased 31.6 million of its shares for $4.2 billion in 2014, accounting in part for a reported increase in EPS of $0.13 per share.

Effect of Preferred Dividends on Earnings Per Share. For illustrative purposes only, suppose that The Home Depot, Inc., had 5,000,000 shares of $100 par value 5% preferred stock outstanding. The preferred stockholders would be entitled to receive a $5 dividend per share, and the amount of net income attributable to the preferred stock would be $25 million (5,000,000 shares × $5). This amount is subtracted from net income, resulting in the following EPS:

Basic earnings per share of common stock:

$$\frac{\$7{,}957 \text{ million} - \$25 \text{ million preferred stock dividends}}{1{,}229 \text{ million common shares outstanding}} = \$6.45$$

Effect of Equity Financing on EPS

Managers must decide how to get the money they need to pay for assets that are to be used in their businesses. There are three main ways to finance an asset purchase:

- through profitable operations (with retained earnings).
- by issuing equity (stock)
- by issuing bonds (or notes) payable

Each strategy has its advantages and disadvantages

1. *Financing with retained earnings* means that the company has enough cash from operating profitably to purchase needed assets. There's no need to issue more stock or borrow money. This strategy is low risk to the company.
2. *Issuing equity (stock)* creates no liabilities or interest expense and is less risky to the issuing corporation. However, by issuing more shares of stock, the percentage amount of ownership and control exercised by each outstanding share declines (is diluted). In addition, EPS declines (is diluted).
3. *Issuing bonds or notes payable* does not result in more stockholders, so it does not dilute control of the corporation. It also usually results in higher EPS. In addition, interest expense on borrowed money is tax deductible, whereas dividend distributions to stockholders are not. But creating more debt increases the risk of the company.

To illustrate, suppose Home Depot needs $500 million to expand its operations. Assume for purposes of this illustration only that Home Depot has net income of $300 million and 100 million shares of common stock outstanding. Management is considering two financing plans. Plan 1 is to issue $500 million of 6% bonds payable, and plan 2 is to issue 50 million shares of common stock for $500 million. Management believes the new cash can be invested in a project to earn income of $200 million before interest and taxes.

Exhibit 10-6 shows the relative earnings-per-share advantage of borrowing. As you can see, Home Depot's EPS amount is higher if the company borrows by issuing bonds (compare lines 11 and 12). Home Depot's expected project net income of $102,000,000 (line 8) as a result of issuing the bonds is more than the $30,000,000 interest it pays on them (line 5). Using bonds or other debt to increase a company's earnings per share of common stock is called **trading on the equity**, or using **leverage**.

Exhibit 10-6 | Effect of Equity Financing on EPS

A1

	A	B	C	D	E
1		**Plan 1**		**Plan 2**	
2		**Borrow $500 million at 6%**		**Issue 50 million shares of Common Stock for $500 million**	
3	Net income before expansion		$ 300,000,000		$ 300,000,000
4	Expected project income before interest and income tax	$ 200,000,000		$ 200,000,000	
5	Less interest expense ($500,000,000 x 0.06)	(30,000,000)		–	
6	Expected project income before income tax	170,000,000		200,000,000	
7	Less income tax expense (40%)	(68,000,000)		(80,000,000)	
8	Expected project net income		102,000,000		120,000,000
9	Total company net income		$ 402,000,000		$ 420,000,000
10	Earnings per share after expansion				
11	Plan 1 Borrow ($402,000,000/100,000,000 shares)		$ 4.02		
12	Plan 2 Issue Stock ($420,000,000/150,000,000 shares)				$ 2.80
13					

In this example, borrowing results in higher EPS than issuing stock. In addition, interest on debt is tax deductible, whereas dividends on stock are not. Borrowing has its disadvantages, however. Borrowing increases a company's debt ratio, which can become so high that creditors may be unwilling to loan the company additional cash. In addition, a company's interest expense may be high enough to eliminate its net income and lead to losses. Also, borrowing creates liabilities that must be paid during bad years as well as good years. In contrast, a company that issues stock can decide not to pay dividends during a bad year.

Market Capitalization and the Price-Earnings Ratio

A company's **market capitalization** *(market cap)* is the value of the company as measured by the market price of one share of its common stock at a given date, multiplied by the number of shares of common stock the company has outstanding as of that date. As of January 29, 2017, The Home Depot reported 1,203 million shares of common stock outstanding (1,776 million shares issued − 573 million shares in treasury). Therefore, the market capitalization of The Home Depot was approximately $166,579 million: 1,203 million shares × $138.47 (the market price per share).

In almost all cases, stockholders are more concerned about the **market value**, or price, of a stock than any other value. Of course, the market value of a share varies with the corporation's net income, financial position, and future prospects, and with general economic conditions. The overall market assessment of the value, or price, of a share of common stock is reflected by the stock's **price-earnings (P/E) ratio**, or **multiple.** The P/E ratio is the market price of a share of common stock divided by the company's earnings per share of common stock:

$$\text{Price-earnings ratio} = \frac{\text{Market price of one share of common stock}}{\text{Earnings per share of common stock}}$$

For example, on January 29, 2017, the market price of one share of The Home Depot, Inc.'s, common stock was $138.47. The earnings per common share (basic) on its consolidated statement of earnings for the year ended January 29, 2017 was $6.45. Therefore, its price-earnings ratio (multiple) on January 29, 2017 was 21.47 ($138.47 ÷ $6.45).

A high P/E multiple indicates that the market is optimistic about the future earnings potential for a company. P/E multiples vary from company to company and industry to industry, but usually are in the range of 15 to 20 times earnings. By these standards, it appears that the market is optimistic about The Home Depot's ability to increase its earnings in the future because the stock's P/E ratio was 21.47. Companies whose future earnings investors expect to be higher ("growth companies") generally have higher P/E multiples than more established companies, or companies whose future earnings are expected to decline. Alternatively, companies with low P/E multiples might be undervalued by the market and might be considered a good buy by "value investors." We will cover this concept further in Chapter 12.

Dividend Yield. **Dividend yield** is the ratio of dividends per share of stock to the stock's market price per share. This ratio measures the percentage of a stock's market value returned annually to the stockholders as dividends. Although dividends are never guaranteed, some well-established companies have continued to pay dividends even through turbulent economic times. Preferred stockholders pay special attention to the ratio because they invest primarily to receive dividends. However, certain companies, such as The Home Depot, Inc., **General Electric, Merck Pharmaceuticals**, IBM, or Apple, also pay attractive dividends on their common stock. In periods of low interest rates on certificates of deposit or money-market funds, dividend-paying stocks become attractive alternatives for conservative investors.

The Home Depot has paid dividends on its common stock for many years. For fiscal 2016, The Home Depot, Inc. paid $2.76 per common share in dividends. Based on the Home Depot's stock price of $138.47 on January 29, 2017, the dividend yield for shareholders on the company's common stock on that date was

Formula		For The Home Depot, Inc. January 29, 2017
Dividend yield on common stock*	= $\dfrac{\text{Dividend per share of common stock}}{\text{Market price per share of common stock}}$	$\dfrac{\$2.76}{\$138.47} = .02\ (2\%)$

*Dividend yields may also be calculated for preferred stock in a similar manner.

A dividend of about 2% is quite attractive, given prevailing interest rates on alternative investments. Investors in The Home Depot have come to expect both profits and dividends from their investment in the company's stock. They have not been disappointed.

REPORT STOCKHOLDERS' EQUITY TRANSACTIONS IN THE FINANCIAL STATEMENTS

6 Report stockholders' equity transactions in the financial statements

The details of transactions impacting the various stockholders' equity accounts are reported on the statement of cash flows as well as on the statement of stockholders' equity.

Statement of Cash Flows

CASH FLOW

Many of the transactions we've covered are reported on the statement of cash flows. Equity transactions are financing activities. Financing transactions that affect both cash and equity fall into three main categories:

- Issuance of stock
- Treasury stock
- Dividends

Financing activities from the Consolidated Statement of Cash Flows for The Home Depot, Inc., for the year ended January 29, 2017, are reported in Exhibit 10-7.

Exhibit 10-7 | The Home Depot, Inc.'s, Financing Activities Related to Stockholders' Equity

A1

	A	B
1	**Cash Flows from Financing Activities**	**(In millions)**
2	Repurchases of common stock	(6,880)
3	Proceeds from sale of common stock	218
4	Cash Dividends Paid to Stockholders	(3,404)
5		

Issuances of Stock. The Home Depot, Inc., received cash of $218 million by issuing new common stock during fiscal 2016.

Treasury Stock. During fiscal 2016, The Home Depot, Inc., spent about $6.9 billion in cash to repurchase shares of treasury stock and reported the payment as a financing activity.

Dividends. Most mature companies, including The Home Depot, Inc., pay cash dividends to their stockholders. Dividend payments are a type of financing transaction because the company is paying its stockholders for the use of their money. During fiscal 2016, The Home Depot paid $3,404 million in cash dividends. Stock dividends are not reported on the statement of cash flows because their distribution does not involve cash.

In Exhibit 10-7, cash payments for the purchase of treasury stock and dividends appear as negative amounts, as denoted by parentheses. The issuance of stock appears as a positive amount.

Statement of Stockholders' Equity

Exhibit 10-8 contains the Consolidated Statements of Stockholders' Equity for The Home Depot, Inc., for the two fiscal years ended January 29, 2017.

Exhibit 10-8 The Home Depot, Inc.'s, Consolidated Statements of Stockholders' Equity

A1

	A	B	C	D	E	F	G	H	I
1	**The Home Depot, Inc. Consolidated Statements of Stockholders' Equity (Adapted)**								
2	**In Millions**	**Total**	**Common Stock**	**Shares**	**Paid-in Capital**	**Retained Earnings**	**Accumulated Other Comprehensive Income (Loss)**	**Treasury Stock**	**Shares**
3	**BALANCE at Feb. 1, 2015**	$ 9,322	$ 88	1,768	$ 8,885	$ 26,995	$ (452)	$ (26,194)	461
4	Net Earnings	7,009				7,009			
5	Shares Issued Under Employee Stock Plans, shares	73		4	73				
6	Tax Effect of Stock-Based Compensation	145			145				
7	Foreign-Currency Translation Adjustments	(412)					(412)		
8	Cash Flow Hedges, net of tax	(34)					(34)		
9	Stock Options, Awards and Amortization of Restricted Stock	244			244				
10	Repurchases of Common Stock	(7000)						(7000)	59
11	Cash Dividends	(3,031)				(3,031)			
12	Other								
13	**BALANCE at January 31, 2016**	$ 6,316	$ 88	1,772	$ 9,347	$ 30,973	$ (898)	$ (33,194)	520
14	Net Earnings	7,957				7,957			
15	Shares Issued Under Employee Stock Plans, shares	76		4	76				
16	Tax Effect of Stock-Based Compensation	97			97				
17	Foreign-Currency Translation Adjustments	(3)					(3)		
18	Cash Flow Hedges, net of tax	34					34		
19	Stock Options, Awards and Amortization of Restricted Stock	267			267				
20	Repurchases of Common Stock	(7,000)						(7,000)	53
21	Cash Dividends	(3,404)				(3,404)			
22	Other	(7)				(7)			
23	**BALANCE at January 29, 2017**	$ 4,333	$ 88	1,776	$ 9,787	$ 35,519	$ (867)	$ (40,194)	573
24									

Data from the U.S. Securities and Exchange Commission EDGAR Company filings, www.sec.gov

Notice that the Statement of Stockholders' Equity presents a detailed vertical analysis of the activity in each separate account in the Stockholders' Equity section over multiple years (usually three years, although, for space purposes, our illustration covers only two). There are separate columns for each account in stockholders' equity: Common Stock (both dollar amounts and number of shares); Paid-in Capital; Retained Earnings; and Treasury Stock (both dollar amounts and number of shares). The statement also contains another column called Accumulated Other Comprehensive Income (Loss), which summarizes changes in the few elements of income that are permitted to bypass the income statement. These elements include unrealized gains or losses on available-for-sale debt securities, and foreign-currency translation adjustments resulting from consolidating the accounting of a company's foreign subsidiaries. Accounting for available-for-sale debt securities is covered briefly in Appendix E. Foreign-currency translation adjustments are considered beyond the scope of this text and are covered in later courses.

A Detailed Stockholders' Equity Section of the Balance Sheet

One of the most important skills you will take from this course is the ability to understand the financial statements of real companies. Exhibit 10-9 presents a side-by-side comparison of the stockholders' equity section of the balance sheet using our general teaching format and the format you are likely to encounter in real-world balance sheets, such as that of The Home Depot, Inc. All amounts are assumed for this illustration.

Exhibit 10-9 Formats for Reporting Stockholders' Equity

	A	B	C	D
1	**General Teaching Format**		**Real-World Format**	
2	**Stockholders' Equity**		**Stockholders' Equity**	
3				
4	Paid-in capital:		Preferred stock, 8%, $10 par, 30,000	
5	Preferred stock, 8%, $10 par, 30,000		shares authorized, issued, and outstanding	$ 330,000
6	shares authorized, issued, and outstanding	$ 300,000	Common stock, $1 par, 100,000 shares	
7	Paid-in capital in excess of		authorized, 60,000 shares issued,	60,000
8	par—preferred	30,000	58,600 shares outstanding	
9	Common stock, $1 par, 100,000 shares		Additional paid-in capital	2,150,000
10	authorized, 60,000 shares issued,	60,000	Retained earnings	1,500,000
11	58,600 shares outstanding		Less: treasury stock, common	
12	Paid-in capital in excess of		(1,400 shares at cost)	(40,000)
13	par—common	2,100,000	Accumulated other comprehensive income	200,000
14	Paid-in capital from treasury stock		Total stockholders' equity	$ 4,200,000
15	transactions	20,000		
17	Paid-in capital from retirement of			
18	preferred stock	30,000		
19	Total paid-in capital	2,540,000		
20	Retained earnings	1,500,000		
21	Subtotal	4,040,000		
22	Less: treasury stock, common			
23	(1,400 shares at cost)	(40,000)		
24	Accumulated other comprehensive income	200,000		
25	Total stockholders' equity	$ 4,200,000		
26				

In general,

- Preferred stock (whenever it exists) comes first and is usually reported as a single amount.
- Common stock lists the par value per share, the number of shares authorized, the number of shares issued, and the number of shares outstanding. The balance of the Common Stock account is determined as

  Common stock = Number of shares *issued* × Par value per share

- Additional paid-in capital combines Paid-in capital in excess of par plus Paid-in capital from other sources. Additional paid-in capital belongs to the common stockholders.
- Outstanding stock equals issued stock minus treasury stock.
- Retained earnings comes after the paid-in capital accounts.
- Treasury stock is reported, usually at cost, as a deduction.
- Accumulated other comprehensive income is added (or accumulated other comprehensive loss is deducted). This account may be listed either before or after Treasury Stock.

Decision Guidelines

INVESTING IN STOCK

Suppose you've saved $5,000 to invest. You visit a nearby **Edward Jones** office, where the broker probes for your risk tolerance. Are you investing mainly for dividends or for growth in the stock price? These guidelines offer suggestions for what to consider when investing in stock.

Investor Decision	Guidelines
Which category of stock to buy for:	
• A safe investment?	Preferred stock is safer than common, but for even more safety, invest in high-grade corporate bonds or government securities.
• Steady dividends?	Cumulative preferred stock. However, the company is not obligated to declare preferred dividends, and the dividends are unlikely to increase.
• Increasing dividends?	Common stock, as long as the company's net income is increasing and the company has adequate cash flow to pay a dividend after meeting all obligations and other cash demands.
• Increasing stock price?	Common stock, but again only if the company's net income and cash flow are increasing.
• How to identify a good stock to buy?	There are many ways to pick stock investments. One strategy that works reasonably well is to invest in companies that consistently earn higher rates of return on assets and on equity than competing firms in the same industry. Another, called "value investing," is to invest in companies that have high earnings but relatively low price/earnings multiples compared to other companies in the same industry. Still another is to select companies with solid earnings in industries that are expected to grow.

End-of-Chapter | Summary Problems

1. The balance sheet of Newline Corp. reported the following at December 31, 2018.

A1

	A	B
1	Stockholders' Equity	
2	Preferred stock, 4%, $10 par, 10,000 shares authorized, issued,	
3	and outstanding	$ 100,000
4	Common stock, no-par, $5 stated value, 100,000 shares	
5	authorized, 50,000 shares issued, 49,000 shares outstanding	250,000
6	Paid-in capital in excess of stated value—Common	239,500
7	Retained earnings	395,000
8	Less: Treasury stock, common (1,000 shares)	(8,000)
9	Total stockholders' equity	$ 976,500
10		

Requirements

a. Is the preferred stock cumulative or noncumulative? How can you tell?
b. What is the total amount of the annual preferred dividend?
c. How many shares of common stock are outstanding?
d. Assume that Newline Corp. earns net income of $100,000. Calculate the corporation's earnings per common share of stock.
e. Assume Newline Corp.'s common stock's closing market price on December 31, 2018, is $51.04 per share. Calculate its price/earnings multiple and the corporation's market capitalization.
f. Assume Newline's board of directors declares a $1 dividend per share on its common stock. What is the stock's dividend yield?
g. Suppose you have gathered the following information from Newline Corp's financial statements for 2018 and 2017:

(1) Net profit margin ratio:	2018: 6.8%	2017: 6.3%
(2) Asset turnover:	2018: 2.3 times	2017: 2.1 times
(3) Leverage ratio:	2018: 3.8	2017: 3.5

Compute Newline Corp.'s return on assets (ROA) and return on equity (ROE) for both 2018 and 2017 and explain the trends.

2. Use the following accounts and related balances to prepare the classified balance sheet of Whittenwing, Inc., at September 30, 2018. Use the account format of the balance sheet.

Common stock, $1 par, 50,000 shares authorized, 20,000 shares issued	$ 20,000	Long-term note payable	$ 80,000
Dividends payable	4,000	Inventory	85,000
Cash	9,000	Property, plant, and equipment, net	226,000
Accounts payable	28,000	Accounts receivable, net	23,000
Paid-in capital in excess of par—common	115,000	Preferred stock, $3.75, no-par, 10,000 shares authorized, 2,000 shares issued	24,000
Treasury stock, common, 1,000 shares at cost	6,000	Accrued liabilities	3,000
		Retained earnings	75,000

Answers

1. **a.** The preferred stock is cumulative because it is not specifically labeled otherwise.
b. The total annual preferred dividend declared and paid: $4,000 ($100,000 × 0.04).
c. Common shares outstanding: 49,000 (50,000 issued − 1,000 treasury).
d. Earnings per share of common stock:

Earnings per share of common stock:

$$\frac{\text{Net income} - \text{preferred dividends}}{\text{Shares of common stock outstanding}} = \frac{\$100{,}000 - \$4{,}000}{49{,}000} = \$1.96$$

e. Price/earnings multiple and market capitalization:

Price/earnings multiple:

$$\frac{\text{Market price per share}}{\text{Earnings per share}} = \frac{\$51.04}{\$1.96} = 26$$

Market capitalization:

Market price per share × Number of shares outstanding
$51.04 × 49,000 = $2,500,960

f. Dividend yield:

$$\text{Dividend yield: } \frac{\text{Dividend per share}}{\text{Market price per share}} = \frac{\$1.00}{\$51.04} = .02\ (2\%)$$

g. Analysis of ROA trends using DuPont analysis:

	Net Profit Margin Ratio	×	Asset Turnover	=	ROA
2017	.063	×	2.1	=	.132
2018	.068	×	2.3	=	.156

The company's ROA increased from 2017 to 2018.

Analysis of ROE trends using DuPont analysis:

	Net Profit Margin Ratio	×	Asset Turnover	×	Leverage	=	ROE
2017	.063	×	2.1	×	3.5	=	.463
2018	.068	×	2.3	×	3.8	=	.594

- The company was more profitable in 2018 than 2017 (a .068 net profit margin ratio versus a .063 net profit margin ratio).
- The company was more efficient in 2018 than 2017 (2.3 versus 2.1 times asset turnover).
- The company was more highly levered in 2018 than 2017 (3.8 times versus 3.5 times).
- All of these trends raised ROE from 46.3% in 2017 to 59.4% in 2018.

2.

A1

	A	B	C	D	E
1	**Whittenwing, Inc. Balance Sheet September 30, 2018**				
2	**Assets**		**Liabilities**		
3	Current Assets		Current Liabilities		
4	Cash	$ 9,000	Account payable		$ 28,000
5	Accounts receivable, net	23,000	Dividends payable		4,000
6	Inventory	85,000	Accrued liabilities		3,000
7	Total current assets	117,000	Total current liabilities		35,000
8	Property, plant, and		Long-term note payable		80,000
9	equipment, net	226,000	Total liabilities		115,000
10					
11			**Stockholders' Equity**		
12			Preferred stock, $3.75, no par,		
13			10,000 shares authorized,		
14			2,000 shares issued and		
15			outstanding	$ 24,000	
16			Common stock, $1 par,		
17			50,000 shares authorized,		
18			20,000 shares issued,		
19			19,000 shares outstanding	20,000	
20			Paid-in capital in excess of		
21			par—common	115,000	
22			Retained earnings	75,000	
23			Treasury stock, common,		
24			1,000 shares at cost	(6,000)	
25			Total stockholders' equity		228,000
26			Total liabilities and		
27	Total assets	$ 343,000	stockholders' equity		$ 343,000
28					

REVIEW | Stockholders' Equity

Accounting Vocabulary

authorized stock (p. 535) The maximum number of shares a corporation can issue under its charter.

board of directors (p. 524) A group elected by the stockholders to set policy for a corporation and to appoint its officers.

bylaws (p. 525) The constitution for governing a corporation.

chairperson (p. 525) A person elected by a corporation's board of directors; usually the most powerful person in the corporation.

common stock (p. 527) The most basic form of capital stock. The common stockholders own a corporation.

contributed capital (p. 526) The amount of stockholders' equity stockholders have contributed to the corporation. Also called *paid-in capital.*

cumulative preferred stock (p. 541) Preferred stock whose owners must receive all dividends in arrears plus the current year's dividends before the corporation can pay dividends to the common stockholders.

deficit (p. 539) A debit balance in the Retained Earnings account.

dividend (p. 539) A distribution (usually cash) by a corporation to its stockholders.

dividend yield (p. 549) Ratio of the dividend per share of stock divided by the market price of stock.

double taxation (p. 525) The process of taxing the income of corporations as well as their stockholders, who must pay personal income taxes on the cash dividends they receive from the corporations.

earnings per share (EPS) (p. 547) The amount of earnings attributable to each share of common stock a company has outstanding.

initial public offering (IPO) (p. 528) The first time a corporation issues stock to the public, which causes the number of issued and outstanding shares of stock to increase.

issued stock (p. 535) The number of shares a corporation has issued to its stockholders.

legal capital (p. 528) Minimum amount of stockholders' equity that a corporation must maintain for the protection of creditors. For corporations with par-value stock, legal capital is the par value of the stock issued.

leverage (p. 548) Using debt financing to increase return on invested capital.

limited liability (p. 524) No personal obligation of an owner for the business entity's debts. An owner can therefore lose no more on an investment than the cost of the investment in the entity.

market capitalization (p. 549) The market price of one share of common stock × the total number of common shares outstanding a company has on a particular date.

market value (of a stock) (p. 549) The price for which a person can buy or sell a share of stock.

no-par value stock (p. 528). Stock that does not have a stated par value.

outstanding stock (p. 535) Stock in the hands of stockholders.

paid-in capital (p. 526) The amount of stockholders' equity that stockholders have contributed to the corporation. Also called *contributed capital.*

par value stock (p. 528) Arbitrary amount assigned by a company to a share of its stock.

preferred stock (p. 527) Stock that gives its owners certain advantages, such as the priority to receive dividends before the common stockholders and the priority to receive assets before the common stockholders if the corporation liquidates.

president (p. 525) The chief operating officer in charge of managing the day-to-day operations of a corporation.

price-earnings (P/E) ratio (multiple) (p. 549) The ratio of the market price of a share of common stock to its earnings per common share.

retained earnings (p. 526) The amount of stockholders' equity that the corporation has earned through profitable operation of the business and has not paid back to stockholders in the form of dividends.

shareholders (p. 524) People or other entities that own stock in a corporation. Also called *stockholders.*

stated value (p. 528) An arbitrary amount assigned to no-par stock; similar to par value.

stock (p. 527) Shares into which the owners' equity of a corporation is divided.

stock dividend (p. 542) A proportional distribution by a corporation of its own stock to its stockholders.

stock split (p. 543) An increase in the number of issued and outstanding shares of stock coupled with a proportionate reduction in the stock's par value.

stockholder (p. 524) A person who owns stock in a corporation. Also called a *shareholder.*

stockholders' equity (p. 526) The stockholders' ownership interest in the assets of a corporation.

trading on the equity (p. 548) See *leverage.*

treasury stock (p. 535) A corporation's own stock that it has issued and later reacquired.

Quick Check (Answers are given on page 593.)

1. The two main categories of stockholders' equity are

   a. assets and liabilities.
   b. retained earnings and common stock.
   c. common stock and preferred stock.
   d. retained earnings and paid-in capital.

2. Which of the following is *not* considered to be an advantage of a corporation?

   a. Limited liability of stockholders for the corporation's debts
   b. Continuous life
   c. Double taxation
   d. Ability to raise more capital than a partnership or proprietorship

3. Stockholders of a corporation directly elect the

   a. chairperson of the board.
   b. board of directors.
   c. president of the corporation.
   d. chief financial officer.

4. The par value of a share of common stock

   a. is determined by the stock market.
   b. must be recorded as a journal entry.
   c. changes every time stock is sold.
   d. is stated in the charter.

5. Shilling Company reports the following information for its fiscal year end of March 31, 2019:

Common stock, $0.01 par value per share	$57 million
Paid-in capital in excess of par - Common	300 million
Retained earnings	400 million
Total stockholders' equity	$757 million

   What is the total paid-in capital for Shilling Company at March 31, 2019?

   a. $57 million
   b. $300 million
   c. $357 million
   d. $757 million

6. If a corporation issues 1,000 shares of $1 par value common stock for $12,000, the journal entry would include a credit to

   a. Common Stock for $1,000.
   b. Retained Earnings for $1,000.
   c. Common Stock for $12,000.
   d. Paid-in Capital in Excess of Par—Common for $12,000.

7. A company might purchase treasury stock for all of the following reasons except

   a. it wants to increase its net assets by buying its stock low and reselling it at a higher price.
   b. management wants to decrease the earnings per share of common stock.
   c. management wants to avoid a takeover by an outside party.
   d. the company needs the stock to distribute to employees as part of its employee stock purchase plans.

8. Sandusky Corporation purchased 3,000 shares of its own $1 par value common stock for $143,000. As a result of this transaction, the company's stockholders' equity

   a. decreased by $143,000.
   b. increased by $140,000.
   c. increased by $143,000.
   d. increased by $3,000.

9. Graves Corporation issued 50,000 shares of $1 par value common stock. Later that year, Graves purchased 12,000 shares of its own common stock. Two months later, it reissued 2,000 shares. How many shares are issued and outstanding?

   a. 50,000 issued and 50,000 outstanding
   b. 52,000 issued and 40,000 outstanding
   c. 62,000 issued and 60,000 outstanding
   d. 50,000 issued and 40,000 outstanding

10. How does the declaration of a cash dividend affect a company's assets, liabilities, and equity?

a. It results in an increase to liabilities and a decrease to stockholders' equity, while assets remain the same.

b. It results in an increase to liabilities and a decrease to assets, while stockholders' equity remains the same.

c. It results in an increase to assets and a decrease to liabilities, while stockholders' equity remains the same.

d. It results in an increase to stockholders' equity and a decrease to assets, while liabilities remain the same.

11. For cash dividends, the journal entry on the date of record

a. debits Retained Earnings and credits Dividends Payable.

b. debits Dividends Payable and credits Cash.

c. debits Dividends and credits Cash.

d. No journal entry is required on the date of record.

12. A stock split

a. has no effect on total stockholders' equity.

b. increases assets and stockholders' equity.

c. increases assets and decreases stockholders' equity.

d. decreases assets and increases stockholders' equity.

13. The ____________ per share is the amount of income attributable to each share of common stock.

a. earnings

b. market value

c. book value

d. preferred value

14. Equator Corporation has the following data available on December 31 for the year just ended:

Average total assets for the year	$ 800,000
Total stockholders' equity at the beginning of the year	525,000
Total stockholders' equity at the end of the year	600,000
Net Income	250,000
Interest expense	30,000
Preferred dividends	50,000

The company's return on assets for the year is closest to

a. 21.25%.

b. 25.00%.

c. 31.25%.

d. 44.44%.

15. Return on equity

a. is a measure of the ratio of net income to dividends declared.

b. is calculated for preferred stock only.

c. is calculated by dividing net income plus preferred dividends by average common stockholders' equity.

d. is a measure used to compare companies of different sizes.

16. The purchase of treasury stock is reported on the statement of cash flows as a

a. negative cash flow in the financing activities section.

b. negative cash flow in the investing activities section.

c. positive cash flow in the financing activities section.

d. positive cash flow in the investing activities section.

Excel Project
Autograded Excel Project available in **MyLab Accounting**

ASSESS YOUR PROGRESS

Ethics Check

EC10-1. Identify ethical principle violated

For each of the situations listed, identify which of three principles (integrity, objectivity and independence, or due care) from the AICPA Code of Professional Conduct is violated. Assume all persons listed in the situations are members of the AICPA. (Note: Refer to the AICPA Code of Professional Conduct contained on pages 25–27 in Chapter 1 for descriptions of the principles.)

a. Shontelle's company, Hollow Technologies, recently decided to repurchase stock from its shareholders. Shontelle is in charge of booking the entries for this new treasury stock. However, she does not know how to record treasury stock transactions, so she just deducts the amount repurchased from Common Stock.

b. Haylee is a senior auditor for Leonarda & Calloway and has worked on its client, Blue Iron, Inc., for the past few years. A few months ago, Blue Iron, Inc., offered Haylee a position in its internal audit department. Haylee accepted the position and works very closely with the external auditors. In fact, she often prepares the work papers for the external auditor since she knows the systems better than the new auditors.

c. Andrew is a senior manager at Ford & Hill, a regional public accounting firm. Ford & Hill recently obtained a new client, Vista, Inc. Andrew's sister is the CEO of Vista, a fact that he did not disclose to the board.

d. Connor is the CFO for Tree Street Coffee Corporation and is going to take the company public within the next six months. In an effort to make the stock look more appealing and therefore sell at a higher price, Connor overrides the system controls and records fictitious sales entries.

Short Exercises

S10-1. ***(Learning Objective 1: Explain advantages and disadvantages of a corporation)*** LO 1
What are two main advantages that a corporation has over a proprietorship and a partnership? What are two main disadvantages of a corporation? Describe the authority structure of a corporation. Who holds ultimate power?

S10-2. ***(Learning Objective 1: Describe characteristics of preferred and common stock)*** LO 1
Answer the following questions about the characteristics of a corporation's stock:

1. Who are the real owners of a corporation?
2. What privileges do preferred stockholders have over common stockholders?
3. Which class of stockholders reaps greater benefits from a highly profitable corporation? Explain your answer.

S10-3. ***(Learning Objective 2: Describe the effect of a stock issuance on paid-in capital)*** LO 2
Saltwell Industries received $11,500,000 for the issuance of its stock on May 14. The par value of the Saltwell stock was only $11,500. Was the excess amount of $11,488,500 a profit to Saltwell? If not, what was it?

Suppose the par value of the Saltwell stock had been $2 per share, $4 per share, or $7 per share. Would a change in the par value of the company's stock affect Saltwell's total paid-in capital? Give the reason for your answer.

LO 2 **S10-4.** ***(Learning Objective 2: Issue stock—par-value stock and no-par stock)*** At the end of fiscal year 2018, Hammond Legal Services and Delectable Doughnuts reported these adapted amounts on their balance sheets (all amounts in millions except for par value per share):

	A	B	C
1		Hammond Legal Services:	
2		Common stock, $0.01 par value, 2,600 shares issued	$ 26
3		Additional paid-in capital	17,400
4			

	A	B	C
1		Delectable Doughnuts:	
2		Common stock, no par value, 68 shares issued	$ 296
3			

Assume each company issued its stock in a single transaction. Journalize each company's issuance of its stock, using its actual account titles. Explanations are not required.

LO 2 **S10-5.** ***(Learning Objective 2: Record issuance of stock for cash and for services)*** Attorney Kristen Maloney invoiced Dunn for $20,400 and has agreed to accept 1,500 shares of its $0.01 par-value common stock in full payment for this invoice. Dunn issued the common stock to Attorney Maloney on January 29. Record the stock-issuance transaction for Dunn.

LO 2 **S10-6.** ***(Learning Objective 2: Issue stock to finance the purchase of assets)*** This short exercise demonstrates the similarity and the difference between two ways to acquire plant assets.

Case A – Issue stock and buy the assets in separate transactions:

Wolford Company issued 12,000 shares of its $35 par common stock for cash of $950,000. In a separate transaction, Wolford used the cash to purchase a building for $560,000 and equipment for $390,000. Journalize the two transactions.

Case B – Issue stock to acquire the assets in a single transaction:

Wolford Company issued 12,000 shares of its $35 par common stock to acquire a building with a market value of $560,000 and equipment with a market value of $390,000. Journalize the transaction.

Compare the balances in all the accounts after making both sets of entries. Are the account balances the same or different?

LO 3 **S10-7.** ***(Learning Objective 3: Account for the purchase and sale of treasury stock)*** On January 10, 2019, Mahlon Design Services purchased treasury stock at a cost of $26 million. On July 3, 2019, Mahlon resold some of the treasury stock for $11 million; this resold treasury stock had cost the company $4 million. Record the purchase and resale of Mahlon's treasury stock. Overall, how much did stockholders' equity increase or decrease as a result of the two treasury-stock transactions?

LO 3

S10-8. ***(Learning Objective 3: Explain purchase of treasury stock to fight off a takeover of the corporation)*** Krugman Exports, Inc., is located in Clancy, New Mexico. The company does business with specialty stores such as **Neiman Marcus**. Krugman's recent success has made the company a prime target for a takeover. The investment group Creston is attempting to buy 52% of Krugman's outstanding stock against the wishes of Krugman's board of directors. Board members are convinced that Creston would sell the most desirable pieces of the business and leave little of value. At the most recent board meeting, several suggestions for fighting off the hostile takeover were made. The one with the most promise is to purchase a huge quantity of treasury stock. Krugman has the cash to carry out this plan.

Requirements

1. Suppose you are a significant stockholder of Krugman Exports, Inc. Write a memorandum to explain to the board how the purchase of treasury stock would make it difficult for Creston to take over Krugman. Explain the effect that purchasing treasury stock would have on stock outstanding and on the size of the corporation.
2. Suppose Krugman is successful in fighting off the takeover bid and later sells the treasury stock at prices greater than the purchase price. Explain what effect these sales will have on assets, stockholders' equity, and net income.

LO 4

S10-9. ***(Learning Objective 4: Account for cash dividends)*** On February 5, 2018, Festival Rental Corporation's board of directors declared a dividend of $0.30, to be paid on March 18, 2018, to the shareholders of record as of the close of business on March 9, 2018. Festival has 5,000,000 shares of $0.01 par-value common stock authorized with 1,600,000 shares issued and outstanding. The company has no preferred stock. Record the declaration of the dividend and the payment of the dividend. Include the proper dates with each journal entry.

LO 4

S10-10. ***(Learning Objective 4: Account for cash dividends)*** Glenmore Corporation earned net income of $90,000 during the year ended December 31, 2018. On December 15, Glenwood declared the annual cash dividend on its 1% preferred stock (13,000 shares with total par value of $130,000) and a $0.45 per share cash dividend on its common stock (65,000 shares with total par value of $650,000). Glenwood then paid the dividends on January 4, 2019.

Journalize the following for Glenwood:

- **a.** Declaring the cash dividends on December 15, 2018
- **b.** Paying the cash dividends on January 4, 2019

Did retained earnings increase or decrease during 2018? By how much?

LO 4

S10-11. ***(Learning Objective 4: Divide cash dividends between preferred and common stock)*** Alloy Corporation has 25,000 shares of $1.40 preferred stock outstanding in addition to its common stock. The $1.40 designation means that the preferred stockholders receive an annual cash dividend of $1.40 per share. In 2018, Alloy declares an annual dividend of $500,000. The allocation to preferred and common stockholders is:

Preferred dividend (25,000 shares × $1.40 per share)...............	$ 35,000
Common dividend (remainder: $500,000 − $35,000)	465,000
Total dividend..	$500,000

Answer these questions about Alloy's cash dividends.

1. How much in dividends must Alloy declare each year before the common stockholders receive any cash dividends for the year?
2. Suppose Alloy declares cash dividends of $200,000 for 2018. How much of the dividends goes to preferred shareholders? How much goes to common shareholders?
3. Is Alloy's preferred stock cumulative or noncumulative? How can you tell?
4. Alloy passed the preferred dividend in 2017 and 2018. Then in 2019, Alloy declares cash dividends of $800,000. How much of the dividends goes to preferred shareholders? How much goes to common shareholders?

LO 4 **S10-12.** ***(Learning Objective 4: Record a small stock dividend)*** Hometown Bancshares has 40,000 shares of $3 par value common stock outstanding. Suppose Hometown declares and distributes a 5% stock dividend when the market value of its stock is $15 per share.

1. Journalize Hometown's declaration and distribution of the stock dividend on May 11. An explanation is not required.
2. What was the overall effect of the stock dividend on Hometown's total assets? On total liabilities? On total stockholders' equity?

LO 6 **S10-13.** ***(Learning Objective 6: Prepare the stockholders' equity section of a balance sheet)*** The financial statements of Ridgeline Employment Services, Inc., reported the following accounts:

Paid-in capital in excess of par	$334,000	Total revenues	$1,600,000
Notes payable (short-term)	50,000	Accounts payable	100,000
Common stock, $0.01 par,		Retained earnings	660,000
600,000 shares issued	6,000	Other current liabilities	200,000
Long-term debt	25,000	Total expenses	1,000,000

Prepare the stockholders' equity section of Ridgeline's balance sheet. Net income has already been closed to Retained Earnings.

LO 5 **S10-14.** ***(Learning Objective 5: Use stockholders' equity data)*** Refer to the data in S10-13. Using only year-end figures rather than averages, calculate the following for Ridgeline:

a. Net income
b. Total liabilities
c. Total assets (use the accounting equation)
d. Net profit margin ratio
e. Asset turnover
f. Leverage ratio
g. Return on equity

What additional information do you need before you can use this data to make decisions?

LO 5 **S10-15.** ***(Learning Objective 5: Calculate book value per share)*** Petrov Gold, Inc., has the following stockholders' equity:

Preferred stock, 7%, $8 par, 33,000 shares authorized and issued	$ 264,000
Common stock, $1 par, 100,000 shares authorized, 62,000 shares issued	62,000
Additional paid-in capital—Common	2,190,000
Retained earnings	1,900,000
Less treasury stock, common (1,200 shares at cost)	(41,000)
Total stockholders' equity	$4,375,000

The company has not paid any preferred dividends for three years, including the current year. Calculate the book value per share of the company's common stock. Book value per share of common stock is calculated as [(Total stockholders' equity − Preferred equity) / Number of common shares outstanding].

LO 5 **S10-16.** ***(Learning Objective 5: Calculate and explain return on assets and return on equity)*** Give the DuPont model formula for computing (a) rate of return on total assets (ROA) and (b) rate of return on common stockholders' equity (ROE). Then answer these questions about the rate-of-return computations.

1. Explain the meaning of the component driver ratios in the computation of ROA.
2. What impact does the leverage ratio have on ROE?
3. Under what circumstances will ROE be higher than ROA? Under what circumstances would ROE be lower than ROA?

S10-17. ***(Learning Objective 5: Calculate return on assets and return on equity for a leading company)*** Toyama Corporation's 2018 financial statements reported the following information, with 2017 figures shown for comparison (adapted, and in millions): LO **5**

	A	B	C	D
1			**2018**	**2017**
2		**Balance Sheet**		
3		Total assets	¥ 10,618	¥ 9,509
4		Total liabilities	¥ 7,402	¥ 6,627
5		Total stockholders' equity (all common)	3,216	2,882
6		Total liabilities and stockholders' equity	¥ 10,618	¥ 9,509
7				
8		**Income Statement**		
9		Net sales revenue	¥ 7,635	
10		Operating expense	7,291	
11		Interest expense	32	
12		Other expense	193	
13		Net income	¥ 119	
14				

Use the DuPont model to calculate Toyama's return on assets and return on common equity for 2018. Evaluate the rates of return as strong or weak. What additional information would be helpful in making this decision? (¥ is the symbol for the Japanese yen.)

S10-18. ***(Learning Objective 5: Calculate earnings-per-share effects of financing with bonds versus stock)*** Waketown Marina needs to raise $2.0 million to expand the company. The company is considering issuing either: LO **5**

- $2,000,000 of 6% bonds payable to borrow the money; or
- 100,000 shares of common stock at $20 per share.

Before any new financing, Waketown expects to earn net income of $500,000, and the company already has 100,000 shares of common stock outstanding. Waketown believes the expansion will increase income before interest and income tax by $400,000. The company's income tax rate is 30%.

Prepare an analysis to determine which plan is likely to result in the higher earnings per share. Based solely on the earnings-per-share comparison, which financing plan would you recommend for Waketown?

S10-19. ***(Learning Objective 2, 5: Define and use various stock values)*** Zanzibar Corporation is conducting a special meeting of its board of directors to address some concerns raised by the stockholders. Stockholders have submitted the following questions. Answer each question. LO **2, 5**

1. What are the differences between common stock and preferred stock?
2. Suzanne Gibson, a Zanzibar shareholder, proposes to transfer some land she owns to the company in exchange for shares of Zanzibar stock. What value should Zanzibar use to determine the number of shares of stock to issue for the land?
3. Preferred shares generally are preferred with respect to dividends and in the event of liquidation. Why would investors buy Zanzibar common stock when preferred stock is available?
4. What is the difference between return on assets (ROA) and return on equity (ROE)?
5. What items can Zanzibar Corporation focus on to improve the company's ROE? (Hint: Use the DuPont model to answer this question.)

LO 6 **S10-20.** ***(Learning Objective 6: Measure cash flows from financing activities)*** During 2018, Smokey Corporation earned net income of $5.4 billion and paid off $2.5 billion of long-term notes payable. Smokey raised $1.1 billion by issuing common stock, paid $3.7 billion to purchase treasury stock, and paid cash dividends of $1.3 billion. Report Smokey's *cash flows from financing* activities on the statement of cash flows for 2018.

LO 6 **S10-21.** ***(Learning Objective 6: Analyze a basic statement of stockholders' equity)*** Use the following statement of stockholders' equity to answer the following questions about Flannery Corporation:

	A	B	C	D	E	F
1	**Flannery Corporation Statement of Stockholders' Equity For the Year Ended December 31, 2018**					
2		**Common Stock $2 Par**	**Additional Paid-in Capital**	**Retained Earnings**	**Treasury Stock**	**Total Stockholders' Equity**
3	Balance, December 31, 2017	$ 20,000	$ 17,000	$ 225,000	$ (28,000)	$ 234,000
4	Issuance of stock	64,000	500,000			564,000
5	Net income			70,000		70,000
6	Cash dividends			(27,000)		(27,000)
7	Purchase of treasury stock				(9,000)	(9,000)
8	Sale of treasury stock		1,000		8,500	9,500
9	Balance, December 31, 2018	$ 84,000	$ 518,000	$ 268,000	$ (28,500)	$ 841,500
10						

1. How much cash did the issuance of common stock bring in during 2018?
2. How much in dividends did Flannery declare during 2018?
3. What was the effect of the dividends on Flannery's retained earnings? On total paid-in capital? On total stockholders' equity? On total assets?
4. What was the cost of the treasury stock that Flannery purchased during 2018?
5. What was the cost of the treasury stock that Flannery sold during the year? For how much did Flannery sell the treasury stock during 2018?
6. How much was Flannery's net income?
7. What is Flannery's total stockholders' equity as of December 31, 2018?

LO 6 **S10-22.** ***(Learning Objective 6: Analyze a statement of stockholders' equity including stock dividends and other comprehensive income)*** The statement of stockholders' equity for Bailey Corporation follows.

	A	B	C	D	E	F	G
1	**Bailey Corporation Statement of Stockholders' Equity For the Year Ended December 31, 2018**						
2		**Common Stock $2 Par**	**Additional Paid-in Capital**	**Retained Earnings**	**Treasury Stock**	**Accumulated Other Comprehensive Income**	**Total Stockholders' Equity**
3	Balance, December 31, 2017	$ 20,000	$ 19,000	$ 125,000	$ (21,000)	$ 8,000	$ 151,000
4	Issuance of stock	64,000	530,000				594,000
5	Net income			94,000			94,000
6	Cash dividends			(21,000)			(21,000)
7	Stock dividends—10%	8,400	49,600	(58,000)			0
8	Purchase of treasury stock				(10,000)		(10,000)
9	Sale of treasury stock		6,000		3,000		9,000
10	Other comprehensive income					3,750	3,750
11	Balance, December 31, 2018	$ 92,400	$ 604,600	$ 140,000	$ (28,000)	$ 11,750	$ 820,750
12							

Use Bailey Corporation's statement to answer these questions:

1. How much cash did the issuance of common stock bring in during 2018?
2. What was the effect of the stock dividends on Bailey's retained earnings? On total paid-in capital? On total stockholders' equity? On total assets?
3. What was the cost of the treasury stock that Bailey purchased during 2018? What was the cost of the treasury stock that the company sold during the year? For how much did Bailey sell the treasury stock during 2018?

Exercises MyLab Accounting

Group A

E10-23A. ***(Learning Objective 1: Identify key terms associated with corporations)*** Complete each of the following statements with one of the terms listed here. LO 1

Board of directors	Charter	Common stock
Corporation	Legal capital	Limited liability
Liquidation	Par value	Preemption
Preferred stock	Retained earnings	Stockholders' equity

a. The right to maintain one's proportionate ownership in the corporation is the right of ____________.

b. The right to receive a proportionate share of any assets remaining after the corporation goes out of business, sells its assets, and pays off its liabilities is the right of ____________.

c. The stockholders' ownership interest in the assets of the corporation is called ____________.

d. ____________ is the legal concept that means stockholders can lose no more than the cost of their investment in the company.

e. The authorization from the state to issue a certain number of shares of stock is granted through the corporation's ____________.

f. The arbitrary amount assigned to each share of stock when it is originally authorized is its ____________.

g. ____________ is a hybrid form of capital stock resembling both equity and debt that pays a fixed dividend.

h. ____________ is the basic form of capital stock.

i. The ____________ is elected by stockholders.

j. The business entity formed under state law that has a separate legal identity from its owners is a ____________.

k. The total of the par value of all of the shares issued is the corporation's ____________.

l. ____________ represents the amount of stockholders' equity that the corporation has earned through profitable operations less any dividends declared.

E10-24A. ***(Learning Objectives 2, 6: Account for issuance of stock; prepare the stockholders' equity section of a balance sheet)*** Pickering Stores is authorized to issue 11,000 shares of common stock. During a two-month period, Pickering completed these stock transactions: LO 2, 6

Jan	23	Issued 1,000 shares of $6.00 par common stock for cash of $14.00 per share.
Feb	12	Received inventory with a market value of $11,000 and equipment with market value of $44,000 for 3,800 shares of the $6.00 par common stock.

Requirements

1. Journalize the transactions.
2. Prepare the stockholders' equity section of Pickering's balance sheet for the transactions. The company's Retained Earnings account has a balance of $41,000.

LO 2

E10-25A. ***(Learning Objective 2: Measure paid-in capital of a corporation)*** Excursion Publishing was recently organized as a corporation. The company issued common stock to an attorney who provided legal services worth $24,000 to help with the incorporation. Excursion also issued common stock to an inventor in exchange for her patent with a market value of $80,000. In addition, Excursion received cash both for the issuance of 10,000 shares of its preferred stock at $120 per share and for the issuance of 18,000 of its common shares at $4 per share. During the first year of operations, Excursion earned net income of $94,000 and declared a cash dividend of $30,000. Without making journal entries, determine the total paid-in capital created by these transactions.

LO 2, 6

E10-26A. ***(Learning Objective 2, 6: Prepare the stockholders' equity section of a balance sheet)*** The financial statements of Mountainview Employment Services, Inc., reported the following accounts (adapted, with dollar amounts in thousands except for par value):

Paid-in capital in excess of par	$197	Total revenues......................	$1,340
Other stockholders' equity (negative)........	(22)	Accounts payable	460
Common stock, $0.01 par,		Retained earnings................	648
1,100,000 shares issued........................	11	Other current liabilities	2,569
Long-term debt	24	Total expenses......................	804

Net income has already been closed to Retained Earnings. Prepare the stockholders' equity section of Mountainview's balance sheet.

LO 3, 6

E10-27A. ***(Learning Objectives 3, 6: Show how treasury stock affects a company; prepare the stockholders' equity section of a balance sheet)*** Bretton Software had the following selected account balances at December 31, 2018 (all numbers and amounts are in thousands, except par value per share):

Inventory......................................	$ 653	Common stock, $1.75 par	
Property, plant, and		per share, 1,000 shares	
equipment, net	854	authorized, 250 shares	
Paid-in capital in excess of par	902	issued	$ 438
Treasury stock,		Retained earnings...............	2,222
130 shares at cost......................	1,820	Accounts receivable, net......	200
Accumulated other		Notes payable	1,100
comprehensive income (loss)	(730)*		

*Debit balance

Requirements

1. Prepare the stockholders' equity section of Bretton's balance sheet (in thousands).
2. How can Bretton have a larger balance of treasury stock than the sum of Common Stock and Paid-in Capital in Excess of Par?

LO 3

E10-28A. ***(Learning Objective 3: Account for the purchase and sale of treasury stock)*** Wishtown Marketing Corporation reported the following stockholders' equity at December 31 (adapted and in millions):

Common stock................................	$ 281
Additional paid-in capital.................	245
Retained earnings............................	2,199
Treasury stock.................................	(691)
Total stockholders' equity	$2,034

During the next year, Wishtown purchased treasury stock at a cost of $28 million and resold treasury stock for $14 million (this treasury stock had cost the company $5 million). Record the purchase and resale of Wishtown's treasury stock. Overall, how much did stockholders' equity increase or decrease from the two transactions?

E10-29A. ***(Learning Objectives 2, 3, 4: Account for issuance of stock; show how treasury stock affects a company; account for dividends)*** At December 31, 2018, Atlantic Corporation reported the stockholders' equity accounts shown here (with dollar amounts in millions, except per-share amounts). LO **2, 3, 4**

Common stock $3.00 par value per share,	
21 million shares issued....................	$ 63
Paid-in capital in excess of par value.....	32
Retained earnings................................	245
Treasury stock, at cost	(20)
Total stockholders' equity..................	$320

Atlantic's 2019 transactions included

a. Net income, $440 million
b. Issuance of 4 million shares of common stock for $14.00 per share
c. Purchase of 5 million shares of treasury stock for $60 million
d. Sold 2 million of the treasury shares purchased in part c for $28 million
e. Declaration and payment of cash dividends of $32 million

Requirements

1. Journalize Atlantic's transactions in parts b, c, d, and e. Explanations are not required.
2. What was the overall effect of these transactions (parts a–e) on Atlantic's stockholders' equity?

E10-30A. ***(Learning Objective 6: Report stockholders' equity after a sequence of transactions)*** Use the Atlantic Corporation data in E10-29A to prepare the stockholders' equity section of the company's balance sheet at December 31, 2019. LO **6**

E10-31A. ***(Learning Objectives 2, 3, 4, 6: Infer transactions from a company's comparative stockholders' equity)*** Omega Products Company reported the following stockholders' equity on its balance sheet: LO **2, 3, 4, 6**

	A	B	C
1	**Stockholders' Equity** **(Dollars and shares in millions except for par value)**	**December 31, 2019**	**2018**
2	Convertible preferred stock—$2.50 par value; authorized 25 shares;		
3	issued and outstanding:		
4	2019 and 2018—6 and 12 shares, respectively	$ 15	$ 30
5	Common stock—$3.00 per share par value; authorized		
6	1,300 shares; issued: 2019 and 2018—300		
7	and 200 shares, respectively	900	600
8	Additional paid-in capital	1,500	855
9	Retained earnings	6,270	4,950
10	Treasury stock, common—at cost		
11	2019—20 shares; 2018—10 shares	(440)	(180)
12	Total stockholders' equity	8,245	6,255
13	Total liabilities and stockholders' equity	$ 48,870	$ 45,130
14			

Requirements

1. What caused Omega's preferred stock to decrease during 2019? Cite all possible causes.
2. What caused the company's common stock to increase during 2019? Identify all possible causes.
3. How many shares of Omega's common stock were outstanding at December 31, 2019?
4. Omega's net income during 2019 was $1,430 million. How much were the company's dividends during the year?
5. During 2019, Omega sold no treasury stock. What average price per share did the company pay for the treasury stock that it purchased during the year?

LO 4

E10-32A. *(Learning Objective 4: Calculate dividends on preferred and common stock)* Ontario Manufacturing, Inc., reported the following at December 31, 2018, and December 31, 2019:

	A	B
1	**Stockholders' Equity**	
2	Preferred stock, cumulative, $4.00 par, 5%, 70,000 shares issued	$ 280,000
3	Common stock, $0.05 par, 9,250,000 shares issued	462,500
4		

Ontario Manufacturing has paid all preferred dividends only through 2015.

Requirement

1. Calculate the total amounts of dividends to both preferred and common stockholders for 2018 and 2019 if total dividends are $90,000 in 2018 and $189,000 in 2019.

LO 4, 6

E10-33A. *(Learning Objectives 4, 6: Record a stock dividend and report stockholders' equity)* The stockholders' equity section of the balance sheet for Warren Corporation on August 16, 2019, follows:

	A	B
1	**Stockholders' Equity**	
2	Common stock, $0.50 par, 2,700,000 shares	
3	authorized, 300,000 shares issued	$ 150,000
4	Paid-in capital in excess of par—common	645,760
5	Retained earnings	7,750,000
6	Accumulated other comprehensive income (loss)	(185,000)
7	Total stockholders' equity	$ 8,360,760
8		

On August 16, 2019, the market price of Warren common stock was $20 per share. Warren declared and distributed a 10% stock dividend on this date.

Requirements

1. Journalize the declaration and distribution of the stock dividend.
2. Prepare the stockholders' equity section of the balance sheet after the stock dividend.
3. Why is total stockholders' equity unchanged by the stock dividend?
4. Suppose Warren had a cash balance of $530,000 on August 17, 2019. What is the maximum amount of cash dividends the company can declare?

LO 2, 3, 4

E10-34A. *(Learning Objectives 2, 3, 4: Measure the effects of stock issuance, dividends, splits, and treasury-stock transactions)* Identify the effects—both the direction and the dollar amount—of these transactions on the total stockholders' equity of Niles Corporation. Each transaction is independent.

a. Declaration of cash dividends of $85 million.
b. Payment of the cash dividend in (a).
c. A 5% stock dividend. Before the dividend, 68 million shares of $1.00 par common stock were outstanding; the market value was $13.87 at the time of the dividend.
d. A 25% stock dividend. Before the dividend, 68 million shares of $1.00 par common stock were outstanding; the market value was $17.25 at the time of the dividend.
e. Purchase of 1,600 shares of treasury stock (par value $1.00) at $16.25 per share.
f. Sale of 800 shares of the treasury stock for $18.00 per share. Cost of the treasury stock was $16.25 per share.
g. A 3-for-1 stock split. Prior to the split, 68 million shares of $1.00 par common stock were outstanding.

E10-35A. ***(Learning Objective 5: Calculate and interpret ratios)*** Data from the financial statements of Eclectic Candle Company included the following: LO 5

Average total assets	$50,000
Average common stockholders' equity	20,000
Net sales	100,000
Net income	7,500

The company had no preferred stock.

Requirements

1. Calculate the following ratios:
   - **a.** Net profit margin
   - **b.** Asset turnover ratio
   - **c.** Leverage ratio
   - **d.** Return on assets (ROA)
   - **e.** Return on equity (ROE)
2. Which is higher, ROA or ROE? Does this make sense for stockholders? Why or why not?

E10-36A. ***(Learning Objective 4, 6: Analyze alternative plans for raising money)*** United Financial Services is considering two plans for raising $800,000 to expand operations. Plan A is to borrow at 10%, and plan B is to issue 200,000 shares of common stock at $4.00 per share. Before any new financing, United has net income of $500,000 and 200,000 shares of common stock outstanding. Assume you own most of United's existing stock. Management believes the company can use the new funds to earn additional income of $800,000 before interest and taxes. United's income tax rate is 30%. LO 4, 6

Requirements

1. Analyze United's situation to determine which plan will result in higher earnings per share.
2. Which plan allows you to retain control of the company? Which plan creates more financial risk for the company? Which plan do you prefer? Why?

E10-37A. ***(Learning Objective 5: Evaluate profitability)*** Carolina Company included the following items in its financial statements for 2018, the current year (amounts in millions): LO 5

Payment of long-term debt	$17,100	Dividends paid	$ 215
Proceeds from issuance		Net sales:	
of common stock	8,500	Current year	60,000
Total liabilities:		Preceding year	92,000
Current year-end	32,319	Net income:	
Preceding year-end	38,023	Current year	2,200
Total stockholders' equity:		Preceding year	2,005
Current year-end	23,479	Operating income:	
Preceding year-end	14,033	Current year	4,880
Long-term liabilities	6,585	Preceding year	4,006

Requirements

1. Use DuPont Analysis to calculate Carolina's return on assets and return on common equity during 2018 (the current year). The company has no preferred stock outstanding.
2. Do the company's rates of return look strong or weak? Give your reason.
3. What additional information do you need to make the decision in requirement 2?

E10-38A. ***(Learning Objective 6: Report cash flows from financing activities)*** Use the Carolina Company data in E10-37A to show how the company reported cash flows from financing activities during 2018 (the current year). LO 6

LO 6

E10-39A. *(Learning Objective 6: Use a company's statement of stockholders' equity)* Lakeside Company reported the following items on its statement of shareholders' equity for the year ended December 31, 2018 (amounts in thousands of dollars):

	$3.50 Par Common Stock	Additional Paid-in Capital	Retained Earnings	Accumulated Other Comprehensive Income	Total Shareholders' Equity
Balance, December 31, 2017	$370	$2,630	$6,000	$15	$9,015
Net earnings			1,370		
Other comprehensive income				5	
Issuance of stock	245	155			
Cash dividends			(70)		
Balance, December 31, 2018					

Requirements

1. Determine the December 31, 2018, balances in Lakeside's shareholders' equity accounts and total shareholders' equity.
2. Lakeside's total liabilities on December 31, 2018, are $7,800. What is the company's debt ratio on this date?
3. Was there a profit or a loss for the year ended December 31, 2018? How can you tell?
4. At what price per share did Lakeside issue common stock during 2018?

Group B

LO 1

E10-40B. *(Learning Objective 1: Identify key terms associated with corporations)* Complete each of the following statements with one of the terms listed here.

Charter	Corporation	Double taxation
Limited liability	Liquidation	Paid-in capital
Par value	Preemption	Preferred stock
Retained earnings	Share of capital stock	Stockholders

a. ____________ represents the amount of stockholders' equity that the corporation has earned through profitable operations less any dividends declared.
b. The owners of the corporation are called ____________.
c. One disadvantage of the corporate form of organization is ____________.
d. ____________ is a hybrid form of capital stock resembling both equity and debt that pays a fixed dividend.
e. The basic unit of ownership for a corporation is one ____________.
f. The authorization from the state to issue a certain number of shares of stock is granted through the corporation's ____________.
g. The right to receive a proportionate share of any assets remaining after the corporation goes out of business, sells its assets, and pays off its liabilities is the right of ____________.
h. The business entity formed under state law that has a separate legal identity from its owners is a ____________.
i. The amount of stockholders' equity that the stockholders have contributed to the corporation is called ____________.
j. The arbitrary amount assigned to each share of stock when it is originally authorized is its ____________.
k. ____________ is the legal concept that means stockholders can lose no more than the cost of their investment in the company.
l. The right to maintain one's proportionate ownership in the corporation is the right of ____________.

E10-41B. ***(Learning Objectives 2, 6: Account for issuance of stock; prepare the stockholders' equity section of a balance sheet)*** Caribbean Imports is authorized to issue 16,000 shares of common stock. During a two-month period, Caribbean completed these stock transactions: LO **2, 6**

Apr	23	Issued 3,200 shares of $2.00 par common stock for cash of $16.00 per share.
May	12	Received inventory with a market value of $11,000 and equipment with market value of $44,000 for 3,700 shares of the $2.00 par common stock.

Requirements

1. Journalize the transactions.
2. Prepare the stockholders' equity section of Caribbean's balance sheet for the transactions. The company's Retained Earnings account has a balance of $51,000.

E10-42B. ***(Learning Objective 2: Measure paid-in capital of a corporation)*** Coastal Publishing was recently organized as a corporation. The company issued common stock to an attorney who provided legal services worth $25,000 to help with the incorporation. Coastal also issued common stock to an inventor in exchange for her patent with a market value of $75,000. In addition, Coastal received cash both for the issuance of 10,000 shares of its preferred stock at $100 per share and for the issuance of 21,000 shares of its common shares at $5 per share. During the first year of operations, Coastal earned net income of $50,000 and declared a cash dividend of $28,000. Without making journal entries, determine the total paid-in capital created by these transactions. LO **2**

E10-43B. ***(Learning Objective 2, 6: Prepare the stockholders' equity section of a balance sheet)*** The financial statements of Noble Employment Services, Inc., reported the following accounts (adapted, with dollar amounts in thousands except for par value): LO **2, 6**

Paid-in capital in excess of par	$196	Total revenues	$1,330
Other stockholders' equity (negative)	(22)	Accounts payable	510
Common stock, $0.01 par, 800,000 shares issued	8	Retained earnings	644
		Other current liabilities	2,569
Long-term debt	25	Total expenses	931

Net income has already been closed to Retained Earnings. Prepare the stockholders' equity section of Noble's balance sheet.

E10-44B. ***(Learning Objectives 3, 6: Show how treasury stock affects a company; prepare the stockholders' equity section of a balance sheet)*** Beluga Software had the following selected account balances at December 31, 2018 (all numbers and amounts are in thousands, except par value per share): LO **3, 6**

Inventory	$ 654	Common stock, $1.50 par per share, 1,100 shares authorized, 360 shares issued	$ 540
Property, plant, and equipment, net	900	Retained earnings	2,220
Paid-in capital in excess of par	901	Accounts receivable, net	200
Treasury stock, 160 shares at cost	2,560	Notes payable	1,274
Accumulated other comprehensive income (loss)	(727)*		

*Debit balance

Requirements

1. Prepare the stockholders' equity section of Beluga Software's balance sheet (in thousands).
2. How can Beluga have a larger balance of treasury stock than the sum of Common Stock and Paid-in Capital in Excess of Par?

LO **3**

E10-45B. ***(Learning Objective 3: Account for the purchase and sale of treasury stock)*** Allenton Marketing Corporation reported the following stockholders' equity at December 31 (adapted and in millions):

Common stock	$ 243
Additional paid-in capital	231
Retained earnings	2,149
Treasury stock	(601)
Total stockholders' equity	$2,022

During the next year, Allenton purchased treasury stock at a cost of $22 million and resold treasury stock for $10 million (this treasury stock had cost the company $2 million). Record the purchase and resale of Allenton's treasury stock. Overall, how much did stockholders' equity increase or decrease from the two transactions?

LO **2, 3, 4**

E10-46B. ***(Learning Objectives 2, 3, 4: Account for issuance of stock; show how treasury stock affects a company; account for dividends)*** At December 31, 2018, Creator Corporation reported the stockholders' equity accounts shown here (with dollar amounts in millions, except per-share amounts).

Common stock $2.00 par value per share, 23 million shares issued	$ 46
Paid-in capital in excess of par value	58
Retained earnings	285
Treasury stock, at cost	(70)
Total stockholders' equity	$319

Creator's 2019 transactions included

a. Net income, $451 million
b. Issuance of 22 million shares of common stock for $14.50 per share
c. Purchase of 10 million shares of treasury stock for $130 million
d. Sold 3 million of the treasury shares purchased in part c for $45 million
e. Declaration and payment of cash dividends of $28 million

Requirements

1. Journalize Creator's transactions in parts b, c, d, and e. Explanations are not required.
2. What was the overall effect of these transactions (parts a through e) on Creator's stockholders' equity?

LO **6**

E10-47B. ***(Learning Objective 6: Report stockholders' equity after a sequence of transactions)*** Use the Creator Corporation data in E10-46B to prepare the stockholders' equity section of the company's balance sheet at December 31, 2019.

E10-48B. ***(Learning Objectives 2, 3, 4, 6: Infer transactions from a company's comparative stockholders' equity)*** Optical Products Company reported the following stockholders' equity on its balance sheet:

LO **2, 3, 4, 6**

	A	B	C
		December 31,	
1	**Stockholders' Equity (Dollars and shares in millions except for par value)**	**2019**	**2018**
2	Convertible preferred stock—$2.50 par value; authorized 50 shares;		
3	issued and outstanding:		
4	2019 and 2018—6 and 12 shares, respectively	$ 15	$ 30
5	Common stock—$3.00 per share par value; authorized		
6	1,300 shares; issued: 2019 and 2018—300		
7	and 200 shares, respectively	900	600
8	Additional paid-in capital	1,500	855
9	Retained earnings	6,200	5,066
10	Treasury stock, common—at cost		
11	2019—26 shares; 2018—6 shares	(546)	(102)
12	Total stockholders' equity	8,069	6,449
13	Total liabilities and stockholders' equity	$ 48,594	$ 43,449
14			

Requirements

1. What caused Optical's preferred stock to decrease during 2019? Cite all possible causes.
2. What caused the company's common stock to increase during 2019? Identify all possible causes.
3. How many shares of Optical's common stock were outstanding at December 31, 2019?
4. Optical's net income during 2019 was $1,470 million. How much were the company's dividends during the year?
5. During 2019, Optical sold no treasury stock. What average price per share did the company pay for the treasury stock that it purchased during the year?

E10-49B. ***(Learning Objective 4: Calculate dividends on preferred and common stock)*** Huron Manufacturing, Inc., reported the following at December 31, 2018, and December 31, 2019:

LO **4**

	A	B
1	**Stockholders' Equity**	
2	Preferred stock, cumulative, $3.00 par, 4%, 55,000 shares issued	$ 165,000
3	Common stock, $0.35 par, 9,170,000 shares issued	3,209,500
4		

Huron Manufacturing has paid all preferred dividends only through 2015.

Requirement

1. Calculate the total amounts of dividends to both preferred and common stockholders for 2018 and 2019 if total dividends are $40,000 in 2018 and $120,000 in 2019.

LO 4, 6

E10-50B. ***(Learning Objectives 4, 6: Record a stock dividend and report stockholders' equity)*** The stockholders' equity section of the balance sheet for Yarrow Yogurt Company on August 12, 2019, follows:

	A	B
1	**Stockholders' Equity**	
2	Common stock, $0.20 par, 2,600,000 shares	
3	authorized, 500,000 shares issued	$ 100,000
4	Paid-in capital in excess of par—common	1,076,267
5	Retained earnings	7,144,000
6	Accumulated comprehensive income (loss)	(180,000)
7	Total stockholders' equity	$ 8,140,267
8		

On August 12, 2019, the market price of Yarrow common stock was $18 per share. Yarrow declared and distributed a 10% stock dividend on this date.

Requirements

1. Journalize the declaration and distribution of the stock dividend.
2. Prepare the stockholders' equity section of the balance sheet after the stock dividend.
3. Why is total stockholders' equity unchanged by the stock dividend?
4. Suppose Yarrow had a cash balance of $540,000 on August 13, 2019. What is the maximum amount of cash dividends the company can declare?

LO 2, 3, 4

E10-51B. ***(Learning Objectives 2, 3, 4: Measure the effects of stock issuance, dividends, splits, and treasury-stock transactions)*** Identify the effects—both the direction and the dollar amount—of these transactions on the total stockholders' equity of Cadberry Corporation. Each transaction is independent.

a. Declaration of cash dividends of $75 million.
b. Payment of the cash dividend in (a).
c. A 25% stock dividend. Before the dividend, 74 million shares of $1.00 par common stock were outstanding; the market value was $19.18 at the time of the dividend.
d. A 40% stock dividend. Before the dividend, 74 million shares of $1.00 par common stock were outstanding; the market value was $18.50 at the time of the dividend.
e. Purchase of 1,700 shares of treasury stock (par value $1.00) at $14.25 per share.
f. Sale of 900 shares of the treasury stock for $19.00 per share. Cost of the treasury stock was $14.25 per share.
g. A 2-for-1 stock split. Prior to the split, 74 million shares of $1.00 par common stock were outstanding.

LO 5

E10-52B. ***(Learning Objective 5: Calculate and interpret ratios)*** Data from the financial statements of Glowing Candle Company included the following:

Average total assets	$60,000
Average common stockholders' equity	25,000
Net sales	120,000
Net income	9,000

The company had no preferred stock.

Requirements

1. Calculate the following ratios:
   a. Net profit margin
   b. Asset turnover ratio
   c. Leverage ratio
   d. Return on assets (ROA)
   e. Return on equity (ROE)
2. Which is higher, ROA or ROE? Does this make sense for stockholders? Why or why not?

E10-53B. ***(Learning Objective 5: Analyze alternative plans for raising money)*** Bondwell Financial Services is considering two plans for raising $500,000 to expand operations. Plan A is to borrow at 6%, and plan B is to issue 100,000 shares of common stock at $5.00 per share. Before any new financing, Bondwell has net income of $200,000 and 100,000 shares of common stock outstanding. Assume you own most of Bondwell's existing stock. Management believes the company can use the new funds to earn additional income of $400,000 before interest and taxes. Bondwell's income tax rate is 30%. LO 5

Requirements

1. Analyze Bondwell's situation to determine which plan will result in the higher earnings per share.
2. Which plan allows you to retain control of the company? Which plan creates more financial risk for the company? Which plan do you prefer? Why?

E10-54B. ***(Learning Objective 5: Evaluate profitability)*** Virginia Company included the following items in its financial statements for 2018, the current year (amounts in millions): LO 5

Payment of long-term debt	$ 17,045	Dividends paid	$ 225
Proceeds from issuance		Net sales:	
of common stock	8,475	Current year	20,000
Total liabilities:		Preceding year	81,000
Current year-end	32,313	Net income:	
Preceding year-end	38,029	Current year	6,488
Total stockholders' equity:		Preceding year	2,009
Current year-end	23,471	Operating income:	
Preceding year-end	14,045	Current year	9,980
Long-term liabilities	6,665	Preceding year	3,996

Requirements

1. Use DuPont Analysis to calculate Virginia's return on assets and return on common equity during 2018 (the current year). The company has no preferred stock outstanding.
2. Do the company's rates of return look strong or weak? Give your reason.
3. What additional information do you need to make the decision in requirement 2?

E10-55B. ***(Learning Objective 6: Report cash flows from financing activities)*** Use the Virginia data in E10-54B to show how the company reported cash flows from financing activities during 2018 (the current year). LO 6

LO 6

E10-56B. ***(Learning Objective 6: Use a company's statement of stockholders' equity)*** Riverside Company reported the following items on its statement of shareholders' equity for the year ended December 31, 2018 (amounts in thousands of dollars):

	$3.50 Par Common Stock	Additional Paid-in Capital	Retained Earnings	Accumulated Other Comprehensive Income	Total Shareholders' Equity
Balance, December 31, 2017	$400	$2,200	$6,000	$8	$8,608
Net earnings			1,370		
Other comprehensive income				5	
Issuance of stock	140	160			
Cash dividends			(65)		
Balance, December 31, 2018					

Requirements

1. Determine the December 31, 2018, balances in Riverside's shareholders' equity accounts and total shareholders' equity.
2. Riverside's total liabilities on December 31, 2018, are $7,000. What is the company's debt ratio on this date?
3. Was there a profit or a loss for the year ended December 31, 2018? How can you tell?
4. At what price per share did Riverside issue common stock during 2018?

Quiz

Test your understanding of stockholders' equity by answering the following questions. Select the best choice from among the possible answers given.

Q10-57. Which of the following is a characteristic of a corporation?

a. No income tax
b. Limited liability of stockholders
c. Mutual agency
d. Both b and c

Q10-58. The basic form of capital stock is

a. par value stock.
b. the corporate charter.
c. a share of preferred stock.
d. a share of common stock.

Q10-59. Spirit World, Inc., issued 250,000 shares of no-par common stock for $5 per share. The journal entry to record the issuance would be:

	A	B	C	D
1	a.	Cash	1,250,000	
2		Common Stock		250,000
3		Gain on the Sale of Stock		1,000,000
4				
5	b.	Cash	250,000	
6		Common Stock		250,000
7				
8	c.	Cash	1,250,000	
9		Common Stock		1,250,000
10				
11	d.	Cash	1,250,000	
12		Common Stock		500,000
13		Paid-in Capital in Excess of Par		750,000
14				

Q10-60. Preferred stock is least likely to have which of the following characteristics?

a. Preference as to assets on liquidation of the corporation
b. The right of the holder to convert the shares to common stock
c. Preference as to voting
d. Preference as to dividends

Q10-61. Which of the following classifications represents the most shares of common stock?

a. Unissued shares
b. Issued shares
c. Treasury shares
d. Outstanding shares
e. Authorized shares

Use the following information for questions Q10-62 to Q10-64:
These account balances at December 31 relate to Sportplace, Inc.:

Accounts Payable	$ 51,700	Paid-in Capital in Excess of Par—Common	$240,000
Accounts Receivable	81,050	Preferred Stock, 10%, $100 Par	85,000
Common Stock	313,000	Retained Earnings	71,900
Treasury Stock	5,700	Notes Receivable	12,800
Bonds Payable	3,300		

Q10-62. What is total paid-in capital for Sportplace? (Assume that treasury stock does not reduce total paid-in capital.)

a. $632,300
b. $709,900
c. $643,700
d. $638,000
e. None of the above

Q10-63. What is total stockholders' equity for Sportplace, Inc.?

a. $709,900
b. $704,200
c. $638,000
d. $715,600
e. None of the above

Q10-64. Sportplace's net income for the period is $119,600 and its average common stockholders' equity is $699,415. Sportplace's return on common stockholders' equity is closest to

a. 17.1%.
b. 17.2%.
c. 18.4%.
d. 17.3%.

Q10-65. Quill Corporation paid $28 per share to purchase 900 shares of its common stock as treasury stock. The stock was originally issued at $12 per share. Which of the following would be the journal entry that Quill would make to record the purchase of the treasury stock?

A1

	A	B	C	D
1	a.	Treasury Stock	25,200	
2		Cash		25,200
3				
4	b.	Treasury Stock	10,800	
5		Retained Earnings	14,400	
6		Cash		25,200
7				
8	c.	Common Stock	25,200	
9		Cash		25,200
10				
11	d.	Treasury Stock	10,800	
12		Paid-in Capital in Excess of Par	14,400	
13		Cash		25,200
14				

Q10-66. When treasury stock is sold for less than its cost, the entry should include a debit to

a. Gain on Sale of Treasury Stock.
b. Loss on Sale of Treasury Stock.
c. Retained Earnings.
d. Paid-in Capital in Excess of Par.

Q10-67. Stockholders are eligible for a dividend if they own the stock on the date of

a. declaration.
b. record.
c. payment.
d. issuance.

Q10-68. Marvin's Foods has outstanding 400 shares of 2% preferred stock, $100 par value; and 1,500 shares of common stock, $15 par value. Marvin's declares dividends of $13,800. Which of the following is the correct entry?

	A	B	C	D
1	a.	Dividends Expense	13,800	
2		Cash		13,800
3				
4	b.	Retained Earnings	13,800	
5		Dividends Payable, Preferred		800
6		Dividends Payable, Common		13,000
7				
8	c.	Dividends Payable, Preferred	800	
9		Dividends Payable, Common	13,000	
10		Cash		13,800
11				
12	d.	Retained Earnings	13,800	
13		Dividends Payable, Preferred		6,900
14		Dividends Payable, Common		6,900
15				

Q10-69. A corporation has 100,000 shares of 4% preferred stock outstanding. Also, there are 100,000 shares of common stock outstanding. Par value for each is $100. If a $825,000 dividend is paid, how much goes to the preferred stockholders?

a. None
b. $400,000
c. $412,500
d. $33,000
e. $825,000

Q10-70. Assume the same facts as in Q10-69. What is the amount of dividends per share on common stock?

a. $8.25
b. $4.25
c. $4.33
d. $0.33
e. None of these

Q10-71. A company declares a 5% stock dividend. The debit to Retained Earnings is an amount equal to

a. the market value of the shares to be issued.
b. the par value of the shares to be issued.
c. the book value of the shares to be issued.
d. the excess of the market price over the original issue price of the shares to be issued.

Q10-72. Which of the following statements is *not* true about a 3-for-1 stock split?

a. Total stockholders' equity increases.
b. A stockholder with 10 shares before the split owns 30 shares after the split.
c. Retained Earnings remains the same.
d. The market price of each share of stock will decrease.
e. Par value is reduced to one-third of what it was before the split.

Q10-73. Amir Company's net income and net sales are $18,000 and $1,100,000, respectively, and average total assets are $100,000. What is Amir's return on assets?

a. 20.0%
b. 18.0%
c. 3.7%
d. 7.0%

Q10-74. In a DuPont analysis, what are the components of return on assets?

a. Net Profit Margin Ratio and Debt Ratio
b. Net Profit Margin Ratio and Leverage Ratio
c. Net Profit Margin Ratio and Asset Turnover Ratio
d. Asset Turnover Ratio and Leverage Ratio

Q10-75. The issuance of common stock in exchange for cash is reported in:

a. the operating activities section of the statement of cash flows.
b. the investing activities section of the statement of cash flows.
c. the financing activities section of the statement of cash flows.
d. the noncash financing section of the statement of cash flows.

Problems MyLab Accounting

Group A

P10-76A. ***(Learning Objectives 2, 6: Account for stock issuance; report stockholders' equity)*** The partners who own Jefferson Rafts Co. wished to avoid the unlimited personal liability of the partnership form of business, so they incorporated as Jefferson Rafts, Inc. The charter from the state of Vermont authorizes the corporation to issue 200,000 shares of $15 par common stock. In its first month, Jefferson Rafts, Inc., completed the following transactions: LO 2, 6

Jan	6	Issued 900 shares of common stock to the promoter for assistance with issuance of the common stock. The promotional fee was $27,000. Debit Organization Expense.
	9	Issued 4,000 shares of common stock to Lindsey Crow and 14,000 shares to Jackie Jefferson in return for cash equal to the stock's market value of $20 per share. The two women were partners in Jefferson Rafts Co.
	26	Issued 1,600 shares of common stock for $25 cash per share.

Requirements

1. Record the transactions in the journal.
2. Prepare the stockholders' equity section of the Jefferson Rafts, Inc., balance sheet at March 31, 2019. The ending balance of Retained Earnings is $55,000.

LO 6

P10-77A. ***(Learning Objective 6: Report stockholders' equity)*** Lima Corp. has the following stockholders' equity information:

Lima's charter authorizes the company to issue 4,000 shares of 11% preferred stock with par value of $200 and 700,000 shares of no-par common stock. The company issued 1,000 shares of the preferred stock at $200 per share. It issued 350,000 shares of the common stock for a total of $512,000. The company's retained earnings balance at the beginning of 2018 was $75,000, and net income for the year was $100,000. During 2018, Lima declared the specified dividend on preferred and a $0.10 per-share dividend on common. Preferred dividends for 2017 were in arrears.

Requirement

1. Prepare the stockholders' equity section of Lima Corp.'s balance sheet at December 31, 2018. Show the computation of all amounts. Journal entries are not required.

LO 2, 4

P10-78A. ***(Learning Objectives 2, 4: Analyze stockholders' equity and dividends of a corporation)*** Seasonal Outdoor Furniture Company included the following stockholders' equity on its year-end balance sheet at March 31, 2019:

Stockholders' Equity	
Preferred stock, 3.5% cumulative—par value $10 per share; authorized 140,000 shares in each class	
Class A—issued 70,000 shares	$ 700,000
Class B—issued 98,000 shares	980,000
Common stock—$5 par value: authorized 1,000,000 shares, issued 270,000 shares	1,350,000
Additional paid-in capital—common	5,540,000
Retained earnings	8,310,000
	$16,880,000

Requirements

1. Identify the different issues of stock that Seasonal Outdoor Furniture Company has outstanding.
2. Give the summary entries to record the issuance of all the Seasonal stock. Assume that all the stock was issued for cash. Explanations are not required.
3. Suppose Seasonal passed its preferred dividends for three years. Would the company have to pay those dividends in arrears before paying dividends to the common stockholders? Give your reason.
4. What amount of preferred dividends must Seasonal declare and pay each year to avoid having preferred dividends in arrears?
5. Assume that preferred dividends are in arrears for 2017. Journalize the declaration of an $860,000 dividend on March 31, 2019. An explanation is not required.

LO **2, 3, 4**

P10-79A. ***(Learning Objectives 2, 3, 4: Account for stock issuance, dividends, and treasury stock)*** Jubilee Jewelry Company reported the following summarized balance sheet at December 31, 2018:

Assets	
Current assets	$ 32,200
Property and equipment, net	89,000
Total assets	$121,200
Liabilities and Equity	
Liabilities	$ 36,500
Stockholders' equity:	
$0.70 cumulative preferred stock, $5 par, 800 shares issued	4,000
Common stock, $6 par, 6,700 shares issued	40,200
Paid-in capital in excess of par—common	18,500
Retained earnings	22,000
Total liabilities and equity	$121,200

During 2019, Jubilee Jewelry completed these transactions that affected stockholders' equity:

Feb 13	Issued 5,400 shares of common stock for $9 per share.
Jun 7	Declared the regular cash dividend on the preferred stock.
24	Paid the cash dividend.
Aug 9	Declared and distributed a 20% stock dividend on the common stock. Market price of the common stock was $12 per share.
Oct 26	Reacquired 600 shares of common stock as treasury stock, paying $14 per share.
Nov 20	Sold 300 shares of the treasury stock for $18 per share.
Dec 31	Declared a cash dividend of $0.25 per share on the outstanding common stock; dividends will be paid in January, 2020.

Requirements

1. Journalize Jubilee Jewelry's transactions. Explanations are not required.
2. Prepare the company's stockholders' equity section of the balance sheet at December 31, 2019. Net income for 2019 was $23,000.

LO **2, 3, 4, 6**

P10-80A. ***(Learning Objectives 2, 3, 4, 6: Measure the effects of stock-related transactions on a company)*** Assume Dessert Corner, Inc., completed the following transactions during 2018, the company's 10th year of operations:

Feb 3	Issued 20,000 shares of common stock ($2.00 par) for cash of $520,000.
Mar 19	Purchased 2,900 shares of the company's own common stock at $19 per share.
Apr 24	Sold 2,500 shares of treasury common stock for $32 per share.
Aug 15	Declared a cash dividend on the 16,000 shares of $0.20 no-par preferred stock.
Sep 1	Paid the cash dividends.
Nov 22	Declared and distributed a 15% stock dividend on the 95,000 shares of $2.00 par common stock outstanding. The market value of the common stock was $24 per share.

Requirements

1. Analyze each transaction in terms of its effect on the accounting equation of Dessert Corner.
2. What impact did each transaction have on cash flows?

LO 4, 5, 6

P10-81A. *(Learning Objectives 4, 5, 6: Prepare a corporation's balance sheet; measure profitability)* The following accounts and related balances of Eagle Designers, Inc., as of December 31, 2018, are arranged in no particular order:

Cash	$ 45,000	Interest expense	$ 16,100
Accounts receivable, net	28,000	Property, plant, and equipment, net	363,000
Paid-in capital in excess of par—common	17,000	Common stock, $1 par, 700,000 shares authorized, 121,000 shares issued	121,000
Accrued liabilities	27,000	Prepaid expenses	20,000
Long-term note payable	90,000	Common stockholders' equity, December 31, 2017	224,000
Inventory	98,000	Net income	12,000
Dividends payable	13,000	Total assets, December 31, 2017	497,000
Retained earnings	?	Treasury stock, 26,000 shares at cost	31,000
Accounts payable	130,000	Net sales	900,000
Trademarks, net	5,000		
Goodwill	17,000		

Requirements

1. Prepare Eagle's classified balance sheet in the account format at December 31, 2018.
2. Use a DuPont Analysis to calculate rate of return on total assets and rate of return on common stockholders' equity for the year ended December 31, 2018.
3. Do these rates of return suggest strength or weakness? Give your reason. What additional information might help you make your decision?

LO 5

P10-82A. *(Learning Objective 5: Differentiate financing with debt vs. equity)* Sullivan Medical Goods is embarking on a massive expansion. Assume plans call for opening 20 new stores during the next two years. Each store is scheduled to be 30% larger than the company's existing locations, offering more items of inventory and with more elaborate displays. Management estimates that company operations will provide $1.0 million of the cash needed for expansion. Sullivan Medical must raise the remaining $5.5 million from outsiders.

The board of directors is considering obtaining the $5.5 million either by borrowing at 6% or by issuing an additional 250,000 shares of common stock. This year the company has earned $4 million before interest and taxes and has 250,000 shares of $1-par common stock outstanding. The market price of the company's stock is $22.00 per share. Assume that income before interest and taxes is expected to grow by 10% each year for the next two years. The company's marginal income tax rate is 35%.

Requirements

1. Use Excel to evaluate the effect the two financing alternatives will have on Sullivan's net income and earnings per share two years from now.
2. Write a memo to Sullivan's management discussing the advantages and disadvantages of borrowing and of issuing common stock to raise the needed cash. Which method of raising the funds would you recommend?

P10-83A. ***(Learning Objective 6: Analyze a statement of stockholders' equity)*** Ahuja Specialties, Inc., reported the following statement of stockholders' equity for the year ended October 31, 2018:

LO 6

	A	B	C	D	E	F
1	**Ahuja Specialties, Inc.** **Statement of Stockholders' Equity** **For the Year Ended October 31, 2018**					
2	**(In millions)**	**Common Stock**	**Additional Paid-in Capital**	**Retained Earnings**	**Treasury Stock**	**Total**
3	**Balance, October 31, 2017**	$ 430	$ 1,610	$ 913	$ (118)	$ 2,835
4	Net income			480		480
5	Cash dividends			(195)		(195)
6	Issuance of stock (100 shares)	10	320			330
7	Stock dividend	44	160	(204)		—
8	Sale of treasury stock		11		9	20
9	**Balance, October 31, 2018**	$ 484	$ 2,101	$ 994	$ (109)	$ 3,470
10						

Requirements

Answer these questions about Ahuja's stockholders' equity transactions.

1. What is the par value of the company's common stock?
2. At what price per share did Ahuja issue its common stock during the year?
3. What was the cost of treasury stock sold during the year? What was the selling price of the treasury stock sold? What was the increase in total stockholders' equity?
4. Ahuja's statement of stockholders' equity lists the stock transactions in the order in which they occurred. What was the percentage of the stock dividend? Round to the nearest percentage. (Ignore treasury stock in answering this question.)

Group B

P10-84B. ***(Learning Objectives 2, 6: Account for stock issuance; report stockholders' equity)*** The partners who own Crew Kayaks Co. wished to avoid the unlimited personal liability of the partnership form of business, so they incorporated as Crew Kayaks, Inc. The charter from the state of Nevada authorizes the corporation to issue 125,000 shares of $15 par common stock. In its first month, Crew Kayaks, Inc., completed the following transactions:

LO 2, 6

Oct	6	Issued 600 shares of common stock to the promoter for assistance with issuance of common stock. The promotional fee was $12,000. Debit Organization Expense.
	9	Issued 10,000 shares of common stock to Lucy Littleton and 18,000 shares to Danielle Dunaway in return for cash equal to the stock's market value of $18 per share. The two women were partners in Crew Kayaks Co.
	26	Issued 900 shares of common stock for $21 cash per share.

Requirements

1. Record the transactions in the journal.
2. Prepare the stockholders' equity section of the Crew Kayaks, Inc., balance sheet at January 31, 2019. The ending balance of Retained Earnings is $95,000.

LO 6

P10-85B. ***(Learning Objective 6: Report stockholders' equity)*** Doorman Corp. has the following stockholders' equity information:

Doorman's charter authorizes the company to issue 9,000 shares of 8% preferred stock with par value of $120 and 700,000 shares of no-par common stock. The company issued 1,800 shares of the preferred stock at $120 per share. It issued 140,000 shares of the common stock for a total of $513,000. The company's retained earnings balance at the beginning of 2018 was $77,000, and net income for the year was $94,000. During 2018, Doorman declared the specified dividend on preferred and a $0.20 per-share dividend on common. Preferred dividends for 2017 were in arrears.

Requirement

1. Prepare the stockholders' equity section of Doorman Corp.'s balance sheet at December 31, 2018. Show the computation of all amounts. Journal entries are not required.

LO 2, 4

P10-86B. ***(Learning Objectives 2, 4: Analyze stockholders' equity and dividends of a corporation)*** Superior Outdoor Furniture Company included the following stockholders' equity on its year-end balance sheet at February 28, 2019:

Stockholders' Equity	
Preferred stock, 7.5% cumulative—par value $25 per share;	
authorized 130,000 shares in each class	
Class A—issued 79,000 shares	$ 1,975,000
Class B—issued 94,000 shares	2,350,000
Common stock—$10 par value:	
authorized 1,600,000 shares,	
issued 260,000 shares	2,600,000
Additional paid-in capital—common	5,580,000
Retained earnings	8,360,000
	$20,865,000

Requirements

1. Identify the different issues of stock that Superior Outdoor Furniture Company has outstanding.
2. Give the summary entries to record the issuance of all the Superior stock. Assume that all the stock was issued for cash. Explanations are not required.
3. Suppose Superior passed its preferred dividends for three years. Would the company have to pay those dividends in arrears before paying dividends to the common stockholders? Give your reasons.
4. What amount of preferred dividends must Superior declare and pay each year to avoid having preferred dividends in arrears?
5. Assume that preferred dividends are in arrears for 2017. Journalize the declaration of an $900,000 dividend on February 28, 2019. An explanation is not required.

P10-87B. ***(Learning Objectives 2, 3, 4: Account for stock issuance, dividends, and treasury stock)*** Madrid Jewelry Company reported the following summarized balance sheet at December 31, 2018:

LO 2, 3, 4

Assets	
Current assets	$ 33,400
Property and equipment, net	106,600
Total assets	$140,000
Liabilities and Equity	
Liabilities	$ 37,000
Stockholders' equity:	
$0.80 cumulative preferred stock, $10 par, 400 shares issued	4,000
Common stock, $9 par, 6,500 shares issued	58,500
Paid-in capital in excess of par—common	18,500
Retained earnings	22,000
Total liabilities and equity	$140,000

During 2019, Madrid Jewelry completed these transactions that affected stockholders' equity:

Feb	13	Issued 5,300 shares of common stock for $12 per share.
Jun	7	Declared the regular cash dividend on the preferred stock.
	24	Paid the cash dividend.
Aug	9	Declared and distributed a 20% stock dividend on the common stock. Market price of the common stock was $17 per share.
Oct	26	Reacquired 700 shares of common stock as treasury stock, paying $20 per share.
Nov	20	Sold 300 shares of the treasury stock for $24 per share.
Dec	31	Declared a cash dividend of $0.25 per share on the outstanding common stock; dividends will be paid in January, 2020.

Requirements

1. Journalize Madrid Jewelry's transactions. Explanations are not required.
2. Prepare the company's stockholders' equity section of the balance sheet at December 31, 2019. Net income for 2019 was $30,000.

P10-88B. ***(Learning Objectives 2, 3, 4, 6: Measure the effects of stock-related transactions on a company)*** Assume Dotty Cakes, Inc., completed the following transactions during 2018, the company's 10th year of operations:

LO 2, 3, 4, 6

Feb	3	Issued 14,000 shares of common stock ($3.00 par) for cash of $406,000.
Mar	19	Purchased 2,500 shares of the company's own common stock at $19 per share.
Apr	24	Sold 1,900 shares of treasury stock for $25 per share.
Aug	15	Declared a cash dividend on the 19,000 shares of $0.10 no-par preferred stock.
Sep	1	Paid the cash dividends.
Nov	22	Declared and distributed an 8% stock dividend on the 91,000 shares of $3.00 par common stock outstanding. The market value of the common stock was $26 per share.

Requirements

1. Analyze each transaction in terms of its effect on the accounting equation of Dotty Cakes.
2. What impact did each transaction have on cash flows?

LO 4, 5, 6

P10-89B. ***(Learning Objectives 4, 5, 6: Prepare a corporation's balance sheet; measure profitability)*** The following accounts and related balances of Cardinal Designers, Inc., as of December 31, 2018, are arranged in no particular order:

Cash	$45,000	Interest expense	$ 16,300
Accounts receivable, net	21,000	Property, plant, and equipment, net	358,000
Paid-in capital in excess of par—common	16,000	Common stock, $1 par, 1,500,000 shares authorized, 117,000 shares issued	117,000
Accrued liabilities	29,000	Prepaid expenses	24,000
Long-term note payable	90,000	Common stockholders' equity, December 31, 2017	221,000
Inventory	89,000	Net income	90,000
Dividends payable	4,000	Total assets, December 31, 2017	496,000
Retained earnings	?	Treasury stock, 20,000 shares at cost	35,000
Accounts payable	135,000	Net sales	750,000
Trademarks, net	9,000		
Goodwill	20,000		

Requirements

1. Prepare Cardinal's classified balance sheet in the account format at December 31, 2018.
2. Use a DuPont Analysis to calculate rate of return on total assets and rate of return on common stockholders' equity for the year ended December 31, 2018.
3. Do these rates of return suggest strength or weakness? Give your reason. What additional information might help you make your decision?

LO 5

P10-90B. ***(Learning Objective 5: Differentiate financing with debt vs. equity)*** Orchard Medical Goods is embarking on a massive expansion. Assume the plans call for opening 20 new stores during the next two years. Each store is scheduled to be 30% larger than the company's existing locations, offering more items of inventory and with more elaborate displays. Management estimates that company operations will provide $1.0 million of the cash needed for expansion. Orchard Medical must raise the remaining $4.75 million from outsiders.

The board of directors is considering obtaining the $4.75 million either by borrowing at 4% or by issuing an additional 200,000 shares of common stock. This year the company has earned $5 million before interest and taxes and has 200,000 shares of $1-par common stock outstanding. The market price of the company's stock is $23.75 per share. Assume that income before interest and taxes is expected to grow by 30% each year for the next two years. The company's marginal income tax rate is 30%.

Requirements

1. Use Excel to evaluate the effect the two financing alternatives will have on Orchard's net income and earnings per share two years from now.
2. Write a memo to Orchard's management discussing the advantages and disadvantages of borrowing and of issuing common stock to raise the needed cash. Which method of raising the funds would you recommend?

P10-91B. ***(Learning Objective 6: Analyze a statement of stockholders' equity)*** Patterson Specialties, Inc., reported the following statement of stockholders' equity for the year ended October 31, 2018: LO 6

Patterson Specialties, Inc.
Statement of Stockholders' Equity
For the Year Ended October 31, 2018

(In millions)	Common Stock	Additional Paid-in Capital	Retained Earnings	Treasury Stock	Total
Balance, October 31, 2017	$ 400	$ 1,680	$ 906	$ (113)	$ 2,873
Net income			360		360
Cash dividends			(193)		(193)
Issuance of stock (100 shares)	50	220			270
Stock dividend	45	170	(215)		—
Sale of treasury stock		18		14	32
Balance, October 31, 2018	$ 495	$ 2,088	$ 858	$ (99)	$ 3,342

Requirements

Answer these questions about Patterson's stockholders' equity transactions.

1. What is the par value of the company's common stock?
2. At what price per share did Patterson issue its common stock during the year?
3. What was the cost of treasury stock sold during the year? What was the selling price of the treasury stock sold? What was the increase in total stockholders' equity?
4. Patterson's statement of stockholders' equity lists the stock transactions in the order in which they occurred. What was the percentage of the stock dividend? Round to the nearest percentage. (Ignore treasury stock in answering this question.)

Challenge Exercises and Problem

E10-92. ***(Learning Objectives 2, 3, 4: Reconstruct transactions from the financial statements)*** Parker Networking Solutions began operations on January 1, 2018, and immediately issued its stock, receiving cash. Parker's balance sheet at December 31, 2018, reported the following stockholders' equity: LO 2, 3, 4

Common stock, $1 par	$ 59,000
Additional paid-in capital	473,500
Retained earnings	40,000
Treasury stock, 300 shares	(3,600)
Total stockholders' equity	$568,900

During 2018, Parker

a. issued stock for $9 per share.
b. purchased 800 shares of treasury stock, paying $12 per share.
c. resold some of the treasury stock.
d. declared and paid cash dividends.

Requirement

1. Journalize all of Parker's stockholders' equity transactions during the year. Parker's entry to close net income to Retained Earnings was

	A	B	C	D
1		Revenues	172,000	
2		Expenses		110,000
3		Retained Earnings		62,000
4				

LO 6

E10-93. ***(Learning Objective 6: Report financing activities on the statement of cash flows)*** Use the Parker Networking Solutions data in E10-92 to show how the company reported cash flows from financing activities during 2018.

LO 2, 3, 4

E10-94. ***(Learning Objectives 2, 3, 4: Account for issuance of stock and treasury stock; explain the changes in stockholders' equity)*** Hubble Corporation reported the following stockholders' equity data (all dollars in millions except par value per share):

	A	B	C
		December 31,	
1		2018	2017
2	Preferred stock	$ 606	$ 738
3	Common stock, $1 par value	910	888
4	Additional paid-in capital—common	1,526	1,482
5	Retained earnings	20,602	19,112
6	Treasury stock, common	(2,765)	(2,643)
7			

Hubble earned net income of $2,930 during 2018. For each account except Retained Earnings, one transaction explains the change from the December 31, 2017, balance to the December 31, 2018, balance. Two transactions affected Retained Earnings. Give a full explanation, including the dollar amount, for the change in each account.

LO 2, 3, 4

E10-95. ***(Learning Objectives 2, 3, 4: Account for issuance of stock, treasury stock, and other changes in stockholders' equity)*** Pueblo, Inc., ended 2018 with 8 million shares of $1 par common stock issued and outstanding. On December 31, 2018, additional paid-in capital was $16 million, and retained earnings totaled $38 million.

- In April 2019, Pueblo issued 6 million shares of common stock at a price of $3 per share.
- In June, the company declared and distributed a 10% stock dividend at a time when Pueblo's common stock had a market value of $13 per share.
- Then in September, Pueblo's stock price dropped to $1 per share and the company purchased 6 million shares of treasury stock.
- For the year, Pueblo earned net income of $26 million and declared cash dividends of $15 million.

Requirement

1. Complete the following tabulation to show what Pueblo, Inc., should report for stockholders' equity at December 31, 2019. Journal entries are not required.

(Amounts in millions)	Common Stock	+	Additional Paid-In Capital	+	Retained Earnings	−	Treasury Stock	=	Total Equity
Balance, Dec 31, 2018	$8		$16		$38		0		$62
Issuance of stock									
Stock dividend									
Purchase of treasury stock									
Net income									
Cash dividends									
Balance, Dec 31, 2019									

P10-96. ***(Learning Objectives 2, 3, 4, 6: Analyze information from stockholders' equity)*** The stockholders' equity of Bowling Green Uniforms as of December 31, 2018 and 2017, follows: LO **2, 3, 4, 6**

	2018	2017
Common stock, 1,700,000 shares authorized, 850,000 and 650,000 shares issued, respectively	$ 340,000	$ 260,000
Paid-in capital in excess of par	34,170,000	26,470,000
Paid-in capital-treasury stock transactions	57,000	56,000
Retained earnings	71,087,500	60,000,000
Treasury stock, at cost, 50,000 and 55,000 shares, respectively	(2,290,000)	(2,519,000)
Total stockholders' equity	$103,364,500	$84,267,000

Requirements

1. What is the par value of the common stock?
2. How many shares of common stock were outstanding at the end of 2018?
3. As of December 31, 2018, what was the average price that stockholders paid for all common stock when issued?
4. Prepare a summary journal entry to record the change in common stock during the year.
5. What was the average price that stockholders paid for the common stock issued in 2018?
6. What was the average price paid by Bowling Green Uniforms for the treasury stock at December 31, 2018?
7. Prepare a summary journal entry to record the change in treasury stock during the year.
8. Assuming net income for 2018 was $13,000,000, prepare a summary journal entry to record the dividends declared during 2018.

APPLY YOUR KNOWLEDGE

Serial Case

LO **2, 3, 4**

C10-97. *(Learning Objectives 2, 3, 4: Calculate impact of stock transactions on a company in the restaurant industry)*

Note: This case is part of The Cheesecake Factory serial case contained in every chapter in this textbook.

The Cheesecake Factory Incorporated (NASDAQ: CAKE) is publicly held and had more than 93 million common shares outstanding as of the end of the 2016 fiscal year. The company has preferred stock authorized but did not have any preferred stock issued.

During fiscal year 2016, The Cheesecake Factory declared and paid cash dividends of $0.88 per share, totaling approximately $42.3 million. During that same year, it purchased 2.9 million shares of its own common stock at an approximate cost of $146.5 million.

Requirements

1. What impact, if any, would the cash dividend have had on The Cheesecake Factory's assets, liabilities, and equity during 2016?
2. What impact, if any, would the cash dividend have had on The Cheesecake Factory's revenues and expenses during 2016?
3. On which financial statement(s) would the cash dividends be listed for 2016?
4. What impact, if any, would the purchase of the common stock have had on The Cheesecake Factory's assets, liabilities, and equity during 2016?
5. What impact, if any, would the purchase of the common stock have had on The Cheesecake Factory's revenues and expenses during 2016?
6. On which financial statement(s) would the repurchase of the common stock be listed for 2016?

Decision Cases

LO **2, 6**

C10-98. *(Learning Objectives 2, 6: Evaluate alternative ways of raising capital)*
Nick Sullivan and Donna James have written a computer program for a virtual reality video game system; it is expected to be more popular than any other gaming system currently on the market. They need additional capital to market the product, and they plan to incorporate their business. Sullivan and James are considering alternative capital structures for the corporation. Their primary goal is to raise as much capital as possible without giving up control of the business. Sullivan and James plan to receive 50,000 shares of the corporation's common stock in return for the net assets of their old business. After the old company's books are closed and the assets are adjusted to current market value, Sullivan's and James's capital balances will each be $25,000.

The corporation's plans for a charter include an authorization to issue 10,000 shares of preferred stock and 500,000 shares of $1 par common stock. Sullivan and James are uncertain about the most desirable features for the preferred stock. Prior to incorporating, they are discussing their plans with two investment groups. The corporation can obtain capital from outside investors under either of the following plans:

- *Plan 1.* Group 1 will invest $80,000 to acquire 800 shares of 6%, $100 par, nonvoting, preferred stock.
- *Plan 2.* Group 2 will invest $55,000 to acquire 500 shares of $5, no-par preferred stock and $35,000 to acquire 35,000 shares of common stock. Each preferred share receives 50 votes on matters that come before the stockholders.

Requirements

Assume that the corporation is chartered.

1. Journalize the issuance of common stock to Sullivan and James. Debit each person's capital account for its balance.
2. Journalize the issuance of stock to the outside investors under both plans.
3. Assume that the company's net income for the first year is $120,000 and total dividends are $30,000. Prepare the stockholders' equity section of the corporation's balance sheet under both plans.
4. Recommend one of the plans to Sullivan and James. Give your reasons. (Challenge)

C10-99. *(Learning Objective 5: Evaluate alternative ways of raising capital)* Business is going well for Air Parking Unlimited (APU), a company that operates remote parking lots near major airports. The board of directors of the family-owned company believes that APU could earn an additional $1.5 million income before interest and taxes by expanding into new markets. However, the $5 million that the business needs for growth cannot be raised within the family. The directors, who strongly wish to retain family control of the company, must consider issuing securities to outsiders. The directors are considering three financing plans.

LO 5

Plan A is to borrow at 6%. Plan B is to issue 100,000 shares of common stock. Plan C is to issue 100,000 shares of nonvoting, $3.75 preferred stock ($3.75 is the annual dividend paid on each share of preferred stock). APU presently has net income of $3.5 million and 1 million shares of common stock outstanding. The company's income tax rate is 35%.

Requirements

1. Prepare an analysis to determine which plan will result in the highest earnings per share of common stock.
2. Recommend a plan to the board of directors. Give your reasons.

Ethical Issues

C10-100. (*Note:* This case is based on a real situation.) George Campbell paid $50,000 for a franchise that entitled him to market Success Associates software programs in the countries of the European Union. Campbell intended to sell individual franchises for the major language groups of western Europe—German, French, English, Spanish, and Italian. Naturally, investors considering buying a franchise from Campbell asked to see the financial statements of his business.

Believing the value of the franchise to be greater than $50,000, Campbell sought to capitalize his own franchise at $500,000. The law firm of McDonald & LaDue helped Campbell form a corporation chartered to issue 500,000 shares of common stock with par value of $1 per share. Attorneys suggested the following chain of transactions:

a. A third party borrows $500,000 and purchases the franchise from Campbell.
b. Campbell pays the corporation $500,000 to acquire all its stock.
c. The corporation buys the franchise from the third party, who repays the loan.

In the final analysis, the third party is debt-free and out of the picture. Campbell owns all of the corporation's stock, and the corporation owns the franchise. The corporation balance sheet lists a franchise acquired at a cost of $500,000. This balance sheet is Campbell's most valuable marketing tool.

Requirements

1. What is the ethical issue in this situation?
2. Who are the stakeholders in the suggested transaction?
3. Analyze this case from the following standpoints: (a) economic, (b) legal, and (c) ethical. What are the consequences to each stakeholder?
4. How should the transaction be reported?

C10-101. St. Genevieve Petroleum Company is an independent oil producer in Baton Parish, Louisiana. In February, company geologists discovered a pool of oil that tripled the company's proven reserves. Prior to disclosing the new oil to the public, St. Genevieve quietly bought most of its stock as treasury stock. After the discovery was announced, the company's stock price increased from $6 to $27.

Requirements

1. What is the ethical issue in this situation? What accounting principle is involved?
2. Who are the stakeholders?
3. Analyze the facts from the following standpoints: (a) economic, (b) legal, and (c) ethical. What is the impact on each stakeholder?
4. What decision would you have made?

Focus on Financials | Apple Inc.

LO **2, 3, 4, 5** ***(Learning Objectives 2, 3, 4, 5: Analyze common stock, retained earnings, return on equity, and return on assets)*** **Apple Inc.'s** consolidated financial statements appear in Appendix A and online in the filings section of **www.sec.gov**.

Requirements

1. Refer to Apple's Consolidated Balance Sheets and Note 7 (Shareholders' Equity). Describe the class of stock that Apple has authorized. How many shares of that stock had been issued as of September 24, 2016? How many shares were outstanding as of that date?
2. Refer to the Consolidated Balance Sheets and the Consolidated Statements of Stockholders' Equity. How many shares of treasury stock did the company purchase during the year ended September 24, 2016? What was the cost of the treasury stock? How much per share?
3. Examine Apple's Consolidated Statement of Stockholders' Equity. Analyze the change that occurred in the company's Retained Earnings account during the year ended September 24, 2016. Can you trace the change to any of its other financial statements? Is this a good thing or a bad thing?
4. Use DuPont Analysis to calculate Apple's return on equity and return on assets for 2016. Pick a company that is a competitor of Apple and calculate these ratios for the competitor. Which ratios are similar? Which are different? Which company do you think is more profitable? Explain.

Focus on Analysis | Under Armour, Inc.

LO **2, 3, 4** ***(Learning Objectives 2, 3, 4: Analyze treasury stock and retained earnings)*** Retrieve the 2016 **Under Armour** financial statements at **www.sec.gov** by clicking on Filings and then searching for "Under Armour" under Company Filings. When you see the list of filings for the company, select the Form 10-K for 2016. Be sure to retrieve the 2016 financial statements, not another year. In particular, this case uses Under Armour, Inc.'s, Consolidated Balance Sheets and Consolidated Statements of Stockholders' Equity for the year 2016.

Requirements

1. As of the end of December 31, 2016, how many shares of common stock does Under Armour, Inc., have authorized? Issued? Outstanding?
2. Refer to Note 7—Stockholders' Equity and the Consolidated Statement of Stockholders' Equity for the year 2016. What is the difference between Under Armour's Class A Common Stock and Class B Convertible Common Stock? Are there any restrictions on who can own Class B stock?
3. Did Under Armour, Inc., issue any new shares of Class A Common Stock during 2016? How can you tell? (Challenge)
4. Prepare a T-account to show the beginning and ending balances plus all the activity in Retained Earnings for 2016.

Group Project in Ethics

The global economic recession that started in 2007 has impacted every business. The recession was especially hard on banks, automobile manufacturing, and retail companies. Banks were largely responsible for the recession. Some of the biggest banks made excessively risky investments collateralized by real estate mortgages, and many of these investments soured when the real estate markets collapsed. When banks had to write these investments down to market values, the regulatory authorities notified them that they had inadequate capital ratios on their balance sheets to operate. Banks stopped lending money. Because stock prices were depressed, companies could not raise capital by selling stock. With both debt and stock financing frozen, many businesses had to close their doors.

Fearing collapse of the whole economy, the central governments of the United States and several European nations loaned money to banks to prop up their capital ratios and keep them open. The government also loaned massive amounts to the largest insurance company in the United States (**AIG**) as well as to **General Motors** and **Chrysler** to help them stay in business. When asked why, many in government replied, "these businesses were too important to fail." In several cases, the U.S. government has taken an "equity stake" in some banks and businesses by taking preferred stock in exchange for the cash infusion.

Because of the recession, corporate downsizing has occurred on a massive scale throughout the world. Although companies in the retail sector provide more jobs than the banking and automobile industry combined, the government has not chosen to "bail out" any retail businesses. Each company or industry mentioned in this book has pared down plant and equipment, laid off employees, or restructured operations. Some companies have been forced out of business altogether.

Requirements

1. Identify all the stakeholders of a corporation. A *stakeholder* is a person or a group who has an interest (that is, a stake) in the success of the organization.
2. Do you believe that some entities are "too important to fail"? Should the federal government help certain businesses to stay afloat during economic recessions and allow others to fail?
3. Identify several measures by which a company may be considered deficient and in need of downsizing. How can downsizing help to solve this problem?
4. Debate the bailout issue. One group of students takes the perspective of the company and its stockholders, and another group of students takes the perspective of the other stakeholders of the company (the community in which the company operates and society at large).
5. What is the problem with the government taking an equity position such as preferred stock in a private enterprise?

Quick Check Answers

1. *d*
2. *c*
3. *b*
4. *d*
5. *c [$57 million + $300 million = $357 million]*
6. *a*
7. *b*
8. *a*
9. *d*
10. *a*
11. *d*
12. *a*
13. *a*
14. *b [(Net income $250,000 − Preferred Dividends $50,000) ÷ Average total assets $800,000 = 25.00%]*
15. *d*
16. *a*

Try It Solutions

Page 530

	January 29, 2017
1. Total paid-in capital (in millions)	$88 + $9,787 = $9,875
2. Number of shares of common stock issued (in millions)	1,776

3.

$$\frac{\text{Average issue price of common stock through January 29, 2017}}{} = \frac{\text{Total received from issuance of common stock (in millions)}}{\text{Common shares issued (in millions)}} = \frac{\$88 + \$9{,}787 = \$9{,}875}{1{,}776}$$

$$= \$5.56 \text{ per share}$$

The Home Depot has issued its common stock at an average price of $5.56 per share.

11 The Statement of Cash Flows

LEARNING OBJECTIVES

1 **Identify** the purposes of the statement of cash flows

2 **Distinguish** among operating, investing, and financing activities

3 **Prepare** a statement of cash flows using the indirect method

4 **Prepare** a statement of cash flows using the direct method

SPOTLIGHT

Google: The Ultimate Answer (and Cash) Machine

What Internet search engine do you use? When you're looking for an answer to a question, you probably "just Google it." Google is the world's most popular search engine. It was created by Larry Page and Sergey Brin when they were students at Stanford University. Google has grown from a small startup to a global technology leader by transforming the way people obtain all sorts of information. The company generates revenue primarily by delivering cost-effective online advertising on the billions of web pages it makes available via its search engine.

Google may be the ultimate "answer machine," but it's a cash machine as well. In 2015, Page and Brin established a holding company named Alphabet, Inc. (A holding company is a company that owns other businesses but doesn't conduct operations itself.) Google is Alphabet's largest subsidiary. Alphabet, Inc.'s stock has been a hit on Wall Street since its initial public offering (IPO). Recently, a share of Alphabet, Inc. stock traded at over $1,000 per share.

Stillfx/Fotolia

In 2016, Alphabet, Inc.'s net cash provided by operating activities exceeded its net income by over $16.5 billion, and the company finished the year with about $12.9 billion in cash and cash equivalents on its books.

	A	B	C
1	**Alphabet, Inc. Consolidated Statements of Cash Flows**	**12 Months Ended**	
2	**(In millions of $)**	**Dec. 31, 2016**	**Dec. 31, 2015**
3	**Operating activities**		
4	Net income	$ 19,478	$ 16,348
5	Adjustments:		
6	Depreciation and impairment of property and equipment	5,267	4,132
7	Amortization and impairment of intangible assets	877	931
8	Stock-based compensation expense	6,703	5,203
9	Deferred income taxes	(38)	(179)
10	Other (gains) and losses	449	546
11	Changes in assets and liabilities, net of effects of acquisitions:		
12	Accounts receivable	(2,578)	(2,094)
13	Income taxes, net	3,125	(179)
14	Prepaid revenue share, expenses and other assets	312	(318)
15	Accounts payable	110	203
16	Accrued expenses and other liabilities	1,515	1,597
17	Accrued revenue share	593	339
18	Deferred revenue	223	43
19	Net cash provided by operating activities	36,036	26,572
20	**Investing activities**		
21	Purchases of property and equipment	(10,212)	(9,950)
22	Proceeds from disposals of property and equipment	240	35
23	Purchases of marketable securities	(84,509)	(74,368)
24	Maturities and sales of marketable securities	66,895	62,905
25	Purchases of other investments, net	(3,579)	(2,333)
26	Net cash used in investing activities	(31,165)	(23,711)
27	**Financing activities**		
28	Net payments related to stock-based award activities	(3,304)	(2,375)
29	Adjustment Payment to Class C capital stockholders	–	(47)
30	Repurchases of capital stock	(3,693)	(1,780)
31	Proceeds from issuance of debt, net of costs	8,729	13,705
32	Repayments of debt	(10,064)	(13,728)
33	Net cash used in financing activities	(8,332)	(4,225)
34	Effect of exchange rate changes on cash and cash equivalents	(170)	(434)
35	Net decrease in cash and cash equivalents	$ (3,631)	$ (1,798)
36	Cash and cash equivalents at beginning of period	16,549	18,347
37	Cash and cash equivalents at end of period	$ 12,918	$ 16,549
38	Supplemental disclosures of cash flow information		
39	Cash paid for taxes, net of refunds	$ 1,643	$ 3,651
40	Cash paid for interest	$ 84	$ 96
41			

Data from the U.S. Securities and Exchange Commission EDGAR Company filings, www.sec.gov

Previous chapters covered cash flows as they related to various topics: receivables, plant assets, and so on. In this chapter, we show you how to prepare and use the statement of cash flows. We begin with the statement format used by the vast majority of companies, the *indirect method*. We end with the alternate format of the statement of cash flows, the *direct method*, which is used by a minority of companies but is considered by many to be more informative. After working through this chapter, you will be able to analyze the cash flows of actual companies using two different methods.

This chapter has three sections:

- ▶ Introduction, consisting of Learning Objectives 1 and 2, beginning on this page.
- ▶ Preparing the Statement of Cash Flows: Indirect Method (Learning Objective 3), pages 600–609.
- ▶ Preparing the Statement of Cash Flows: Direct Method (Learning Objective 4), pages 612–621.

Try It in Excel®

You can access the most current annual report of Alphabet, Inc. in Excel format at **www.sec.gov**. Using the "FILINGS" link on the toolbar at the top of the home page, select "Company Filings Search." This will take you to the "Edgar Company Filings" page. Type "Alphabet" in the company name box, and select "Search." This will produce the "EDGAR Search Results" page showing the company name. Click on the "CIK" link beside the company name. Doing so will pull up a list of the reports the company has filed with the SEC. Under the "Filing Type" box, type "10-K" and click the search box. Form 10-K is the SEC form for the company's annual report. Find the year that you wish to view. Click on the "Interactive Data" box, which takes you to the "View Filing Data" page. Find and click on the "View Excel Document" link at the top of this page. You can choose to either open or download the Excel files containing the company's most recent financial statements.

IDENTIFY THE PURPOSES OF THE STATEMENT OF CASH FLOWS

1 Identify the purposes of the statement of cash flows

The balance sheet reports a company's financial position. Balance sheets from two periods show whether cash increased or decreased. But that doesn't explain *why* the cash balance changed. The income statement reports net income and offers clues about cash, but it doesn't tell *why* cash increased or decreased. We need a third financial statement.

The **statement of cash flows** shows where cash came from (receipts) and how it was spent (payments). The statement covers a span of time and therefore is dated "Year Ended December 31, 2018" or "Month Ended June 30, 2018." Exhibit 11-1 illustrates the relative timing of the four basic statements.

Exhibit 11-1 | Timing of the Financial Statements

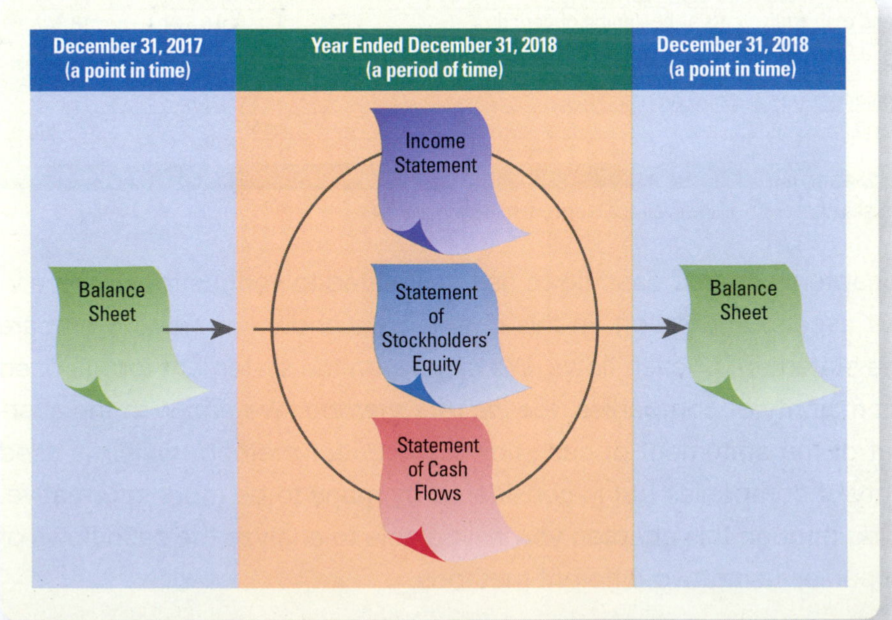

The statement of cash flows:

1. *Predicts future cash flows.* Past cash receipts and payments are reasonably good predictors of future cash flows.
2. *Evaluates management decisions.* Businesses that make wise decisions prosper, and those that make unwise decisions suffer losses. The statement of cash flows reports how managers got cash and how they used cash to run the business.
3. *Determines a company's ability to pay dividends and interest.* Stockholders want dividends on their investments. Creditors demand interest and principal on their loans. The statement of cash flows reports on the ability to make these payments.
4. *Shows the relationship of net income to cash flows.* Usually, high net income eventually leads to an increase in cash, and vice versa. But cash flow can suffer even when net income is high.

On a statement of cash flows, *cash* means more than just cash in the bank. It includes cash equivalents. Recall that cash equivalents are highly liquid short-term investments that can be converted into cash immediately. Examples include money-market accounts and investments in U.S. government securities. Throughout this chapter, the term *cash* refers to cash and cash equivalents.

How's Your Cash Flow? Telltale Signs of Financial Difficulty

Companies want to earn net income because profit measures success. Without net income, a business sinks. There will be no dividends, and the stock price is likely to suffer. High net income attracts investors, but you can't pay bills with net income. That requires cash.

A company needs both net income and strong cash flow. Income and cash flow usually move together because net income eventually generates cash. Sometimes, however, a company's net income and cash flow take different paths. To illustrate, consider Fastech Company:

A1

	A	B
1	**Fastech Company** **Income Statement** **Year Ended December 31, 2018**	
2	Sales revenue	$ 100,000
3	Cost of goods sold	30,000
4	Operating expenses	10,000
5	Net income	$ 60,000
6		

A1

	A	B	C	D
1	**Fastech Company** **Balance Sheet** **December 31, 2018**			
2	Cash	$ 3,000	Total current liabilities	$ 50,000
3	Receivables	37,000	Long-term liabilities	20,000
4	Inventory	40,000		
5	Plant assets, net	60,000	Stockholders' equity	70,000
6	Total assets	$ 140,000	Total liabilities and equity	$ 140,000
7				

What can we glean from Fastech's income statement and balance sheet?

- Fastech is profitable. Its net income is 60% of its revenue. Fastech's profitability looks outstanding.
- Fastech's current ratio is 1.6, and its debt ratio is only 50%. These measures suggest the company should have little trouble in paying bills.

However, Fastech is on the verge of bankruptcy. Can you see what is causing the problem? Three trouble spots leap out to a financial analyst:

1. The cash balance is very low. For a company with sales of $100,000, $3,000 isn't enough cash to pay the bills.
2. Fastech isn't selling inventory fast enough. Fastech turned over its inventory only 0.75 times during the year ($30,000 cost of goods sold ÷ $40,000 inventory). As we saw in Chapter 6, inventory turnover rates of 3–8 times a year are common. A turnover ratio of 0.75 times means that it takes Fastech far too long to sell its inventory, and that delays its cash collections.
3. Fastech's days' sales in receivables is 135 days [365 ÷ ($100,000 sales revenue /$37,000 receivables)]. Very few companies can wait that long to collect from their customers.

The takeaway lesson from this discussion is that a business needs both net income and strong cash flow to succeed.

Let's turn now to the different categories of cash flows.

DISTINGUISH AMONG OPERATING, INVESTING, AND FINANCING ACTIVITIES

2 Distinguish among operating, investing, and financing activities

A business engages in three types of business activities:

- Operating activities
- Investing activities
- Financing activities

Alphabet, Inc.'s statement of cash flows reports cash flows under these three headings, as shown on page 595.

Operating activities create revenues, expenses, gains, and losses—*net income*, which is a product of accrual basis accounting. Operating activities are the most important of the three categories because they reflect the core business activities of the organization. A successful business must generate most of its cash from operating activities.

Investing activities increase and decrease a company's long-term assets, such as its computers, land, buildings, equipment, and investments in other companies. Purchases and sales of these assets are investing activities. Investing activities are important, but they are less critical than operating activities.

Financing activities are related to a firm's long-term liabilities and stockholders' equity. These activities include obtaining cash from investors and creditors by issuing stock and borrowing money. Paying off a loan, buying and selling treasury stock, and paying cash dividends are other examples of financing activities. Exhibit 11-2 shows how operating, investing, and financing activities relate to the various parts of the balance sheet.

Exhibit 11-2 | How Operating, Investing, and Financing Activities Affect the Balance Sheet

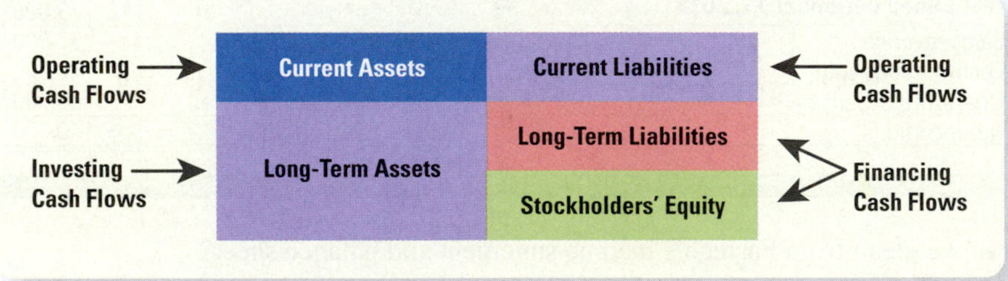

Examine Alphabet, Inc.'s statement of cash flows on page 595. Focus on the final line of each section: Operating, Investing, and Financing. Alphabet, Inc. has very strong cash flows. During 2016, the company's operating activities provided about \$36 billion of cash (line 19). Of that cash, about \$19.5 billion came from net income (line 4). We will explain the other adjustments later. Then, Alphabet, Inc. invested in the following: about \$10.2 billion in property and equipment (line 21); about \$84.5 billion in marketable securities (line 23); and about \$3.6 billion in other investments (line 25). The company sold another \$66.9 billion in marketable securities or received the proceeds of their maturity values (line 24). Finally, it used about $8.3 billion in net financing: It paid out cash related to stock-based compensation in the amount of about $3.3 billion, borrowed $8.7 billion, and repaid $10 billion of debt (lines 28, 31, and 32, respectively). These figures show that

- *operations* are Alphabet, Inc.'s largest source of cash. The company's core business activities are profitable and generate a surplus of cash that the company uses for other activities.
- the company is *investing* in the future by purchasing property, plant and equipment as well as investments in other companies.
- other companies, banks, and individuals are willing to *finance* the activities of Alphabet, Inc. by loaning money to the company. Also, the company has been successful in paying off creditors as well as returning cash to the stockholders by the repurchase of their stock.

Two Formats for Operating Activities

The two ways to format operating activities on the statement of cash flows are the indirect method and the direct method:

- The **indirect method** starts with net income, which is then converted to the net cash provided or used by operating activities. The method does so by adjusting for accrual-basis items, such as depreciation, which don't actually affect cash but do affect net income.
- The **direct method** requires computation of all of the individual cash receipts (collections from customers and receipts of interest and dividends) and cash disbursements (payments to suppliers and employees, and payments for interest and income taxes) to directly determine the net cash provided or used by a company's operating activities.

The two methods use different computations, but as the following table shows, they produce the same figure for Net cash provided by operating activities:

Indirect Method		Direct Method	
Net income	$600	Collections from customers	$2,000
Adjustments:		*Deductions:*	
Depreciation, etc.	300	Payments to suppliers, etc.	(1,100)
Net cash provided by operating activities	$900	Net cash provided by operating activities	$ 900

same

The two methods do not affect the reporting of investing or financing activities on the statement of cash flows. These sections on the statement of cash flows read the same regardless of how a company formats the operating activities section (using the direct or indirect method).

PREPARE A STATEMENT OF CASH FLOWS USING THE INDIRECT METHOD

3 Prepare a statement of cash flows using the indirect method

To explain how to prepare a company's statement of cash flows using the indirect method, we use The Red Roadster Superstore (TRRS), a dealer in auto parts for sports cars. Let's take it step by step.

Step 1 Lay out the template as shown in Part 1 of Exhibit 11-3. The exhibit is comprehensive. The diagram in Part 2 of Exhibit 11-3 (p. 601) provides an illustration of the components of the statement.

Step 2 Use the comparative balance sheets to determine the increase or decrease in cash during the period. The change in cash is the "check figure" for the statement of cash flows. Exhibit 11-4 (p. 601) shows The Red Roadster Superstore's (TRRS's) comparative balance sheets, with Cash highlighted. TRRS's cash decreased by $8,000 during 2018. Why? The statement of cash flows will provide the answer.

Exhibit 11-3 | Part 1: Template of the Statement of Cash Flows: Indirect Method

A1

	A
1	**The Red Roadster Superstore (TRRS)** **Statement of Cash Flows** **Year Ended December 31, 2018**
2	**Cash flows from operating activities:**
3	Net income
4	Adjustments to reconcile net income to net cash provided by operating activities:
5	+ Depreciation/depletion/amortization expense
6	+ Loss on sale of long-term assets
7	− Gain on sale of long-term assets
8	− Increases in current assets other than cash
9	+ Decreases in current assets other than cash
10	+ Increases in current liabilities
11	− Decreases in current liabilities
12	Net cash provided by (used for) operating activities
13	**Cash flows from investing activities:**
14	+ Sales of long-term assets (investments, land, building, equipment, and so on)
15	− Purchases of long-term assets
16	+ Collections of notes receivable
17	− Loans to others
18	Net cash provided by (used for) investing activities
19	**Cash flows from financing activities:**
20	+ Issuance of stock
21	+ Sale of treasury stock
22	− Purchase of treasury stock
23	+ Borrowing (issuance of notes or bonds payable)
24	− Payment of notes or bonds payable
25	− Payment of dividends
26	Net cash provided by (used for) financing activities
27	**Net increase (decrease) in cash during the year**
28	+ Cash at December 31, 2017
29	= Cash at December 31, 2018
30	

Exhibit 11-3 | Part 2: Positive and Negative Items on the Statement of Cash Flows: Indirect Method

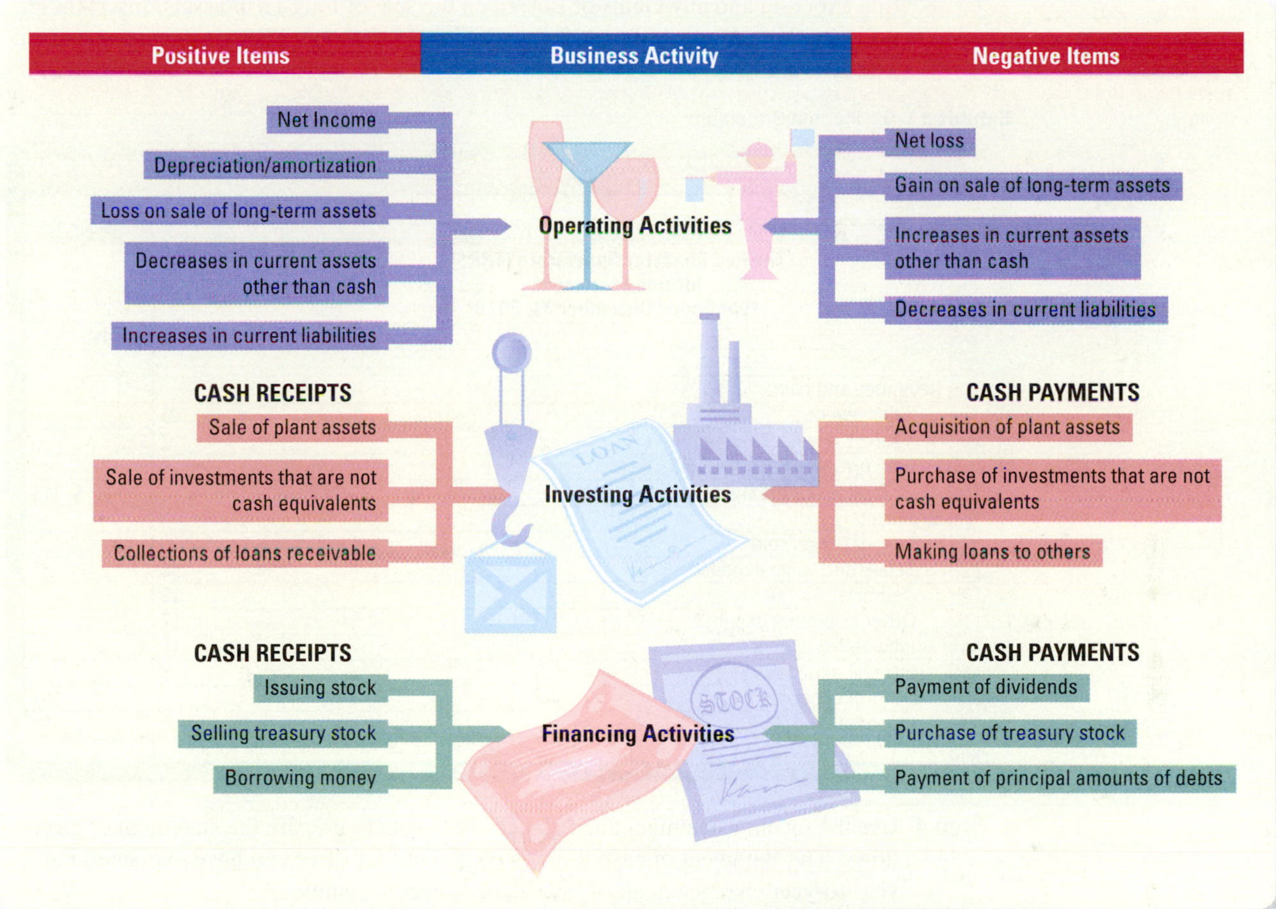

Exhibit 11-4 | Comparative Balance Sheets

A1

	A	B	C	D
1	**The Red Roadster Superstore (TRRS) Comparative Balance Sheets December 31, 2018 and 2017**			
2	**(In thousands)**	**2018**	**2017**	**Increase (Decrease)**
3	**Assets**			
4	Current:			
5	Cash	$ 34	$ 42	$ (8)
6	Accounts receivable	96	81	15
7	Inventory	35	38	(3)
8	Prepaid expenses	8	7	1
9	Plant assets, net of depreciation	343	219	124
10	Notes receivable	21	—	21
11	Total	$ 537	$ 387	$ 150
12	**Liabilities**			
13	Current:			
14	Accounts payable	$ 91	$ 57	$ 34
15	Salary and wage payable	4	6	(2)
16	Accrued liabilities	1	3	(2)
17	Long-term debt	160	77	83
18	**Stockholders' Equity**			
19	Common stock	162	158	4
20	Retained earnings	119	86	33
21	Total	$ 537	$ 387	$ 150
22				

Changes in current assets—Operating (rows 6–8)

Changes in noncurrent assets—Investing (rows 9–10)

Changes in current liabilities—Operating (rows 14–16)

Changes in long-term liabilities and paid-in capital accounts—Financing (rows 17–19)

Change due to net income—Operating
Change due to dividends—Financing (row 20)

Step 3 From the income statement, take Net income; Depreciation, depletion, and amortization expense; and any Gains or Losses on the sale of long-term assets. Insert these items on the statement of cash flows. Exhibit 11-5 shows TRRS's income statement. The relevant items are highlighted.

Exhibit 11-5 | Income Statement

	A	B	C
1	**The Red Roadster Superstore (TRRS) Income Statement Year Ended December 31, 2018**		
2		**(In thousands)**	
3			
4	Revenues and gains:		
5	Sales revenue	$ 303	
6	Interest revenue	2	
7	Gain on sale of plant assets	8	
8	Total revenues and gains		$ 313
9	Expenses:		
10	Cost of goods sold	$ 150	
11	Salary and wage expense	56	
12	Depreciation expense	18	
13	Other operating expense	17	
14	Income tax expense	15	
15	Interest expense	7	
16	Total expenses		263
17	Net income		$ 50
18			

Step 4 Use the income statement and balance-sheet data to prepare the statement of cash flows. The statement of cash flows is complete only after you have explained the year-to-year changes in all of the balance-sheet accounts.

Cash Flows from Operating Activities

Operating activities are related to the transactions that make up net income. Go to "Cash Flows from Operating Activities" in Exhibit 11-6.

The operating section of the Statement of Cash Flows (Exhibit 11-6) begins with Net income, which is taken from the Income Statement (Exhibit 11-5), and is followed by "Adjustments to reconcile net income to net cash provided by operating activities." Let's discuss these adjustments.

Exhibit 11-6 | Statement of Cash Flows—Operating Activities—Indirect Method

	A	B	C
1	**The Red Roadster Superstore (TRRS) Partial Statement of Cash Flows (Indirect Method) For the Year Ended December 31, 2018**		
2		**(In thousands)**	
3	**Cash flows from operating activities:**		
4	Net income		$ 50
5	Adjustments to reconcile net income to net cash		
6	provided by operating activities:		
7	Ⓐ Depreciation	$ 18	
8	Ⓑ Gain on sale of plant assets	(8)	
9	Ⓒ Increase in accounts receivable	(15)	
10	Ⓒ Decrease in inventory	3	
11	Ⓒ Increase in prepaid expenses	(1)	
12	Ⓒ Increase in accounts payable	34	
13	Ⓒ Decrease in salary and wage payable	(2)	
14	Ⓒ Decrease in accrued liabilities	(2)	27
15	Net cash provided by operating activities		$ 77
16			

Ⓐ Depreciation, Depletion, and Amortization Expenses. These expenses are added back to net income to convert it to cash flow. Let's see why. Depreciation is recorded as Depreciation Expense and has no effect on cash. But depreciation, like all other expenses, decreases net income. Therefore, to convert net income to cash flow, we add depreciation back to net income. The add-back cancels the earlier deduction.

	A	B	C
1	Depreciation Expense	18,000	
2	Accumulated Depreciation		18,000
3			

Example: Suppose you had only two transactions, a $1,000 cash sale and depreciation expense of $300. Net cash flow from operations is $1,000, and Net income is $700 ($1,000 – $300). To go from net income ($700) to cash flow ($1,000), we add back the depreciation ($300). Depletion and amortization are treated like depreciation.

Ⓑ Gains and Losses on the Sale of Long-Term Assets. Sales of long-term assets are investing activities, and there's often a gain or loss on the sale of these assets. On the statement of cash flows, the gain or loss is an adjustment to net income. Exhibit 11-6 includes an adjustment for a gain. During 2018, The Red Roadster Superstore sold equipment for $62,000. The book value was $54,000, so there was a gain of $8,000.

The $62,000 cash received from the sale is an investing activity (Exhibit 11-7, page 604), and the $62,000 includes the $8,000 gain. Net income also includes the gain, so we must subtract the gain from the net cash provided by operations so that it can be added to the net book value of equipment sold in the investing section ($54,000 + $8,000 = $62,000). We explain investing activities in the next section.

A loss on the sale of plant assets also creates an adjustment in the operating section. Because the cash received from the sale of a long-term asset at a loss is less than the asset's book value, the amount of cash received reflects the loss. Losses are deducted from net income. Therefore, in order to show the amount of cash received from the sale of the asset in the investing section, losses are *added back* to net income in the operating section to compute Net cash flow from operations.

Ⓒ Changes in the Current Asset and Current Liability Accounts, Excluding Cash. Most current assets and current liabilities result from operating activities. For example, accounts receivable result from sales, inventory relates to cost of goods sold, and so on. Except for cash, changes in the current accounts are adjustments to net income on the cash flow statement. The reasoning is as follows:

1. *An increase in a noncash current asset decreases cash.* It takes cash to acquire assets. Suppose you make a sale on account. Accounts receivable are increased, but cash isn't affected yet. Exhibit 11-4 (p. 601) reports that during 2018, The Red Roadster Superstore's Accounts Receivable increased by $15,000. To compute TRRS's cash flow from operations, we must subtract the $15,000 increase in Accounts Receivable, as shown in Exhibit 11-6. The reason is this: We have *not* collected this $15,000 in cash. Similar logic applies to all the other current assets. If they increase, cash decreases.
2. *A decrease in a noncash current asset increases cash.* Suppose TRRS's Accounts Receivable balance decreased by $4,000. Cash receipts caused Accounts Receivable to decrease, so we add decreases in Accounts Receivable and the other current assets to net income.
3. *A decrease in a current liability decreases cash.* Paying a current liability decreases both cash and the liability, so we subtract decreases in current liabilities from net income. In Exhibit 11-6, the $2,000 decrease in Accrued Liabilities is *subtracted* to compute Net cash provided by operations.
4. *An increase in a current liability increases cash.* The Red Roadster Superstore's Accounts Payable increased. That can occur only if cash was not spent to pay this debt. Cash payments are therefore less than expenses, and TRRS has more cash on hand. Thus, increases in current liabilities increase cash.

Evaluating Cash Flows from Operating Activities. Let's step back and evaluate The Red Roadster Superstore's operating cash flows during 2018. TRRS's operations provided net cash flow of $77,000. This amount exceeds net income, which is one sign of a healthy company. Now let's examine TRRS's investing and financing activities, as reported in Exhibit 11-7.

Exhibit 11-7 Statement of Cash Flows—Indirect Method

	A	B	C
1	**The Red Roadster Superstore (TRRS) Statement of Cash Flows (Indirect Method) For the Year Ended December 31, 2018**		
2		**(In thousands)**	
3	**Cash flows from operating activities:**		
4	Net income		$ 50
5	Adjustments to reconcile net income to net cash		
6	provided by operating activities:		
7	Ⓐ Depreciation	$ 18	
8	Ⓑ Gain on sale of plant assets	(8)	
9	Ⓒ Increase in accounts receivable	(15)	
10	Ⓒ Decrease in inventory	3	
11	Ⓒ Increase in prepaid expenses	(1)	
12	Ⓒ Increase in accounts payable	34	
13	Ⓒ Decrease in salary and wage payable	(2)	
14	Ⓒ Decrease in accrued liabilities	(2)	27
15	Net cash provided by operating activities		77
16	**Cash flows from investing activities:**		
17	Acquisition of plant assets	$ (196)	
18	Loan to another company	(21)	
19	Proceeds from sale of plant assets	62	
20	Net cash used for investing activities		(155)
21	**Cash flows from financing activities:**		
22	Proceeds from issuance of long-term debt	$ 94	
23	Proceeds from issuance of common stock	4	
24	Payment of long-term debt	(11)	
25	Payment of dividends	(17)	
26	Net cash provided by financing activities		70
27	**Net (decrease) in cash**		$ (8)
28	Cash balance, December 31, 2017		42
29	Cash balance, December 31, 2018		$ 34
30			

Cash Flows from Investing Activities

Investing activities affect long-term assets, such as plant assets and long-term investments including the debt and equity securities of other companies a business owns. Increases in these accounts represent purchases of these assets and are offset by decreases to cash. Decreases to these accounts represent sales of these assets and are offset by increases to cash. Data needed to complete the investing activities section are computed by analyzing changes in non-current assets accounts on the balance sheet.

Computing Purchases and Sales of Plant Assets. Companies keep a separate account for each plant asset. But for computing cash flows, it is helpful to combine all the plant assets into a single summary account because it's easier to work with. Also, we subtract accumulated depreciation and use the net figure.

To illustrate, observe that The Red Roadster Superstore's

- balance sheet reports beginning plant assets, net of accumulated depreciation, of $219,000. The ending balance is $343,000 (Exhibit 11-4).
- income statement shows depreciation expense of $18,000 and an $8,000 gain on the sale of plant assets (Exhibit 11-5).

Assume that TRRS's purchases of plant assets using cash total $196,000 (take this amount as given; see Exhibit 11-7). How much, then, are the proceeds from the sale of plant assets? First, we must determine the book value of the plant assets sold:

Plant Assets, Net

Beginning balance	+	Acquisitions	−	Depreciation expense	−	Book value of assets sold	=	Ending balance
$219,000	+	$196,000	−	$18,000		−X	=	$343,000
						−X	=	$343,000 − $219,000 − $196,000 + $18,000
						X	=	$54,000

The sale proceeds are $62,000, which are determined as follows:

Sale proceeds	=	Book value of assets sold	+	Gain	−	Loss
X	=	$54,000	+	$8,000	−	$0
X	=	$62,000				

Notice that the $8,000 gain *added to* the $54,000 net book value of assets sold in the investing section is the same gain that was *subtracted from* net income in the operating section, as discussed above. Since the gain represents excess cash received from the sale, it is appropriate to reflect it in the investing section of the cash flow statement rather than the operating section. Trace the sale proceeds of $62,000 to the statement of cash flows in Exhibit 11-7. The Plant Assets T-account provides another look at the computation of the book value of the assets sold.

Plant Assets, Net

Beginning balance	219,000	Depreciation expense	18,000
Acquisitions	196,000	Book value of assets sold	54,000
Ending balance	343,000		

If the sale had resulted in a loss of $3,000, the sale proceeds would be $51,000 ($54,000 – $3,000), and the statement of cash flows would report $51,000 as a cash receipt from this investing activity. That same loss would have been *added back* to net income in the operating section, so that it could be *subtracted from* the net book value of the assets sold in the investing section.

Computing Purchases and Sales of Investments, and Loans and Collections. The cash amounts of investment transactions can be computed the same way that cash amounts from plant assets are computed. However, computing investments is easier because, unlike plant assets, there is no depreciation. TRRS does not have investments, but we will assume it does to illustrate this example:

Investments (amounts assumed for illustration only)

Beginning balance	+	Purchases	−	Book value of investments sold	=	Ending balance
$100,000	+	$50,000		−X	=	$140,000
				−X	=	$140,000 − $100,000 − $50,000
				X	=	$10,000

The Investments T-account provides another look (amounts assumed):

Investments

Beginning balance	100,000		
Purchases	50,000	Book value of investments sold	10,000
Ending balance	140,000		

The Red Roadster Superstore has a long-term receivable, and the cash flows from loan transactions on notes receivable can be determined as follows (data from Exhibit 11-4):

Notes Receivable

Beginning balance	+	New loans made	−	Collections	=	Ending balance
$0	+	X		−0	=	$21,000
		X			=	$21,000

Notes Receivable

Beginning balance	0		
New loans made	21,000	Collections	0
Ending balance	21,000		

Refer to the investing section of the Statement of Cash Flows (Exhibit 11-7) to see all the investing activities listed together for TRRS. Exhibit 11-8 summarizes the cash flows from investing activities, which are highlighted in color.

Exhibit 11-8 Computing Cash Flows from Investing Activities

Receipts									
From sale of plant assets	Beginning plant assets, net	+	Acquisition cost	−	Depreciation expense	−	Book value of assets sold	=	Ending plant assets, net
	Cash received	=	Book value of assets sold	+ or −	Gain on sale / Loss on sale				
From sale of investments	Beginning investments	+	Purchase cost of investments	−	Book value of investments sold	=	Ending investments		
	Cash received	=	Book value of investments sold	+ or −	Gain on sale / Loss on sale				
From collection of notes receivable	Beginning notes receivable	+	New loans made	−	Collections	=	Ending notes receivable		
Payments									
For acquisition of plant assets	Beginning plant assets, net	+	Acquisition cost	−	Depreciation expense	−	Book value of assets sold	=	Ending plant assets, net
For purchase of investments	Beginning investments	+	Purchase cost of investments	−	Book value of investments sold	=	Ending investments		
For new loans made	Beginning notes receivable	+	New loans made	−	Collections	=	Ending notes receivable		

Cash Flows from Financing Activities

Financing activities affect liabilities and stockholders' equity accounts, such as Notes Payable, Bonds Payable, Long-Term Debt, Common Stock, Paid-in Capital in Excess of Par, and Retained Earnings. Most of the data come from the balance sheet. Increases in these accounts, excluding Retained Earnings, are offset by increases in cash. Decreases in these accounts are offset by decreases in cash.

Computing Issuances and Payments of Long-Term Debt. The beginning and ending balances of Long-Term Debt, Notes Payable, or Bonds Payable come from the balance sheet. If either new issuances or payments are known, the other amount can be computed. Assume that the proceeds from The Red Roadster Superstore's new long-term debt issuances (which increase cash) total $94,000 (take this amount as given in Exhibit 11-7). Debt payments (which decrease cash) are computed by performing an analysis of the Long-Term Debt account (see Exhibit 11-4).

Long-Term Debt (Notes Payable, Bonds Payable)

Beginning balance	+	Issuance of new debt	−	Payments of debt	=	Ending balance
$77,000	+	$94,000		−X	=	$160,000
				−X	=	$160,000 − $77,000 − $94,000
				X	=	$11,000

Long-Term Debt

		Beginning balance	**77,000**
Payments	11,000	**Issuance of new debt**	**94,000**
		Ending balance	**160,000**

Computing Issuances of Stock and Purchases of Treasury Stock. These cash flows can be determined from the stock accounts. For example, cash received from issuing common stock is computed from Common Stock and Paid-in Capital in Excess of Par. We use a single summary Common Stock account as we do for plant assets. The Red Roadster Superstore data are:

Common Stock

Beginning balance	+	Issuance of new stock	=	Ending balance
$158,000	+	$4,000	=	$162,000

Common Stock

		Beginning balance	**158,000**
		Issuance of new stock	4,000
		Ending balance	**162,000**

Increases in common stock and related additional paid-in capital are represented by offsetting increases in cash.

The Red Roadster Superstore has no treasury stock, but cash flows from purchasing treasury stock can be computed as follows (using assumed amounts):

Treasury Stock (amounts assumed for illustration only)

Beginning balance	+	Purchase of treasury stock	=	Ending balance
$16,000	+	$3,000	=	$19,000

Treasury Stock

Beginning balance	**16,000**		
Purchase of treasury stock	3,000		
Ending balance	**19,000**		

Increases (purchases) of treasury stock are represented by offsetting decreases in cash. If treasury stock is reissued for cash, the decrease in treasury stock is offset by an increase in cash.

Computing Dividend Declarations and Payments. If dividend declarations and payments are not given elsewhere, they can be computed. For The Red Roadster Superstore, this computation is as follows:

Retained Earnings

Beginning balance	+	Net income	−	Dividend declarations and payments	=	Ending balance
$86,000	+	$50,000		−X	=	$119,000
				X	=	$119,000 − $86,000 − $50,000
				X	=	$17,000

The T-account also shows the dividend computation. Dividends paid decrease retained earnings and are offset by decreases in cash.

Retained Earnings

Dividend declarations and payments	17,000	Beginning balance	86,000
		Net income	50,000
		Ending balance	119,000

Refer to the financing section of the Statement of Cash Flows (Exhibit 11-7) to see all the financing activities listed together for TRRS.

Exhibit 11-9 summarizes the cash flows from TRRS's financing activities, which are highlighted in color.

Exhibit 11-9 | Computing Cash Flows from Financing Activities

Receipts	
From borrowing—issuance of long-term debt (notes payable)	Beginning long-term debt (notes payable) + Cash received from issuance of long-term debt − Payment of debt = Ending long-term debt (notes payable)
From issuance of stock	Beginning stock + Cash received from issuance of new stock = Ending stock
Payments	
Of long-term debt	Beginning long-term debt (notes payable) + Cash received from issuance of long-term debt − Payment of debt = Ending long-term debt (notes payable)
To purchase treasury stock	Beginning treasury stock + Purchase cost of treasury stock = Ending treasury stock
Of dividends	Beginning retained earnings + Net income − Dividend declarations and payments = Ending retained earnings

TRY IT

(Answers are given on p. 667.)

Classify each of the following as an operating activity, an investing activity, or a financing activity as reported on the statement of cash flows prepared using the *indirect* method.

a. Issuance of stock
b. Borrowing long term
c. Sales revenue
d. Payment of dividends
e. Purchase of land with cash
f. Purchase of treasury stock
g. Paying bonds payable
h. Interest expense
i. Sale of equipment
j. Cost of goods sold
k. Purchase of another company with cash
l. Making a loan

Noncash Investing and Financing Activities

Companies make investments that do not require cash. They also obtain financing other than cash. Our examples have included none of these transactions. Now suppose The Red Roadster Superstore issued common stock valued at $300,000 to acquire a warehouse. TRRS would journalize this transaction as

A1

	A	B	C
1	Warehouse Building	300,000	
2	Common Stock		300,000
3			

This transaction would not be reported as a cash payment because TRRS paid no cash. But the investment in the warehouse and the issuance of stock are important. These noncash investing and financing activities should be reported in a separate schedule under the statement of cash flows. Exhibit 11-10 illustrates TRRS's noncash investing and financing activities (all amounts are assumed).

Exhibit 11-10 | Noncash Investing and Financing Activities

	A	B
1		**Thousands**
2		
3	**Noncash investing and financing activities:**	
4	Acquisition of building by issuing common stock	$ 300
5	Acquisition of land by issuing note payable	70
6	Payment of long-term debt by issuing common stock	100
7	Total noncash investing and financing activities	$ 470
8		

Mid-Chapter | Summary Problem

Luckas Company reported the following income statement and comparative balance sheets, along with transaction data for 2018:

	A	B	C
1	**Luckas Company Income Statement Year Ended December 31, 2018**		
2	Sales revenue		$ 662,000
3	Cost of goods sold		560,000
4	Gross profit		102,000
5	Operating expenses		
6	Salary expenses	$ 46,000	
7	Depreciation expense—equipment	7,000	
8	Amortization expense—patent	3,000	
9	Rent expense	2,000	
10	Total operating expenses		58,000
11	Income from operations		44,000
12	Other items:		
13	Loss on sale of equipment		(2,000)
14	Income before income tax		42,000
15	Income tax expense		16,000
16	Net income		$ 26,000
17			

	A	B	C	D	E	F
1	**Luckas Company Comparative Balance Sheets December 31, 2018 and 2017**					
2	**Assets**	**2018**	**2017**	**Liabilities**	**2018**	**2017**
3	Current:			Current:		
4	Cash and cash equivalents	$ 19,000	$ 3,000	Accounts payable	$ 35,000	$ 26,000
5	Accounts receivable	22,000	23,000	Accrued liabilities	7,000	9,000
6	Inventories	34,000	31,000	Income tax payable	10,000	10,000
7	Prepaid expenses	1,000	3,000	Total current liabilities	52,000	45,000
8	Total current assets	76,000	60,000	Long-term note payable	44,000	—
9	Equipment, net	67,000	52,000	Bonds payable	40,000	53,000
10	Long-term investments	18,000	10,000	**Stockholders' Equity**		
11	Patent, net	44,000	10,000	Common stock	52,000	20,000
12				Retained earnings	27,000	19,000
13				Less: Treasury stock	(10,000)	(5,000)
14	Total assets	$ 205,000	$ 132,000	Total liabilities and stockholders' equity	$ 205,000	$ 132,000
15						

Transaction Data for 2018:

Purchase of equipment with cash	$ 98,000	Issuance of long-term note payable to purchase patent	$ 37,000
Payment of cash dividends	18,000	Issuance of long-term note payable to borrow cash	7,000
Issuance of common stock to retire bonds payable	13,000	Issuance of common stock for cash	19,000
Purchase of long-term investment with cash	8,000	Proceeds from sale of equipment (book value, $76,000)	74,000
Purchase of treasury stock	5,000		

Requirement

1. Prepare Luckas Company's statement of cash flows (using the indirect method) for the year ended December 31, 2018. Take the four steps outlined below. For Step 4, prepare a T-account to show the transaction activity in each long-term balance-sheet account. For each plant asset, use a single account, net of accumulated depreciation (for example: Equipment, Net).

   Step 1 Lay out the template of the statement of cash flows.

   Step 2 From the comparative balance sheets, determine the increase in cash and cash equivalents during the year, $16,000.

   Step 3 From the income statement, take net income, depreciation, amortization, and the loss on sale of equipment to the statement of cash flows.

   Step 4 Complete the statement of cash flows. Account for the year-to-year change in each balance-sheet account.

Answer:

A1			
	A	**B**	**C**
1	**Luckas Company** **Statement of Cash Flows** **Year Ended December 31, 2018**		
2	**Cash flows from operating activities:**		
3	Net income		$ 26,000
4	Adjustments to reconcile net income to		
5	net cash provided by operating activities:		
6	Depreciation	$ 7,000	
7	Amortization	3,000	
8	Loss on sale of equipment	2,000	
9	Decrease in accounts receivable	1,000	
10	Increase in inventories	(3,000)	
11	Decrease in prepaid expenses	2,000	
12	Increase in accounts payable	9,000	
13	Decrease in accrued liabilities	(2,000)	19,000
14	Net cash provided by operating activities		45,000
15	**Cash flows from investing activities:**		
16	Purchase of equipment	$ (98,000)	
17	Sale of equipment	74,000	
18	Purchase of long-term investment	(8,000)	
19	Net cash used for investing activities		(32,000)
20	**Cash flows from financing activities:**		
21	Issuance of common stock	$ 19,000	
22	Payment of cash dividends	(18,000)	
23	Issuance of long-term note payable	7,000	
24	Purchase of treasury stock	(5,000)	
25	Net cash provided by financing activities		3,000
26	**Net increase in cash and cash equivalents**		16,000
27	Cash and cash equivalents balance, December 31, 2017		3,000
28	Cash and cash equivalents balance, December 31, 2018		$ 19,000
29	**Noncash investing and financing activities:**		
30	Issuance of long-term note payable to purchase patent		$ 37,000
31	Issuance of common stock to retire bonds payable		13,000
32	Total noncash investing and financing activities		$ 50,000
33			

Equipment, Net

Bal	52,000		
	98,000		76,000
			7,000
Bal	67,000		

Long-Term Investments

Bal	10,000		
	8,000		
Bal	18,000		

Patent, Net

Bal	10,000		
	37,000		3,000
Bal	44,000		

Long-Term Note Payable

		Bal	0
			37,000
			7,000
		Bal	44,000

Bonds Payable

		Bal	53,000
	13,000		
		Bal	40,000

Common Stock

		Bal	20,000
			13,000
			19,000
		Bal	52,000

Retained Earnings

		Bal	19,000
	18,000		26,000
		Bal	27,000

Treasury Stock

Bal	5,000		
	5,000		
Bal	10,000		

PREPARE A STATEMENT OF CASH FLOWS USING THE DIRECT METHOD

4 Prepare a statement of cash flows using the direct method

The Financial Accounting Standards Board (FASB) and the International Accounting Standards Board (IASB) prefer the direct method of reporting operating cash flows because it provides clearer information about the sources and uses of cash. However, only a very small percentage of companies use this method because it requires more computations than the indirect method. Investing and financing cash flows are unaffected by the method used.

To illustrate the statement of cash flows, we use The Red Roadster Superstore (TRRS), a dealer in auto parts for sports cars. To prepare the statement of cash using the direct method, proceed as follows:

Step 1 Lay out the template of the statement of cash flows using the direct method, as shown in Part 1 of Exhibit 11-11. Part 2 (p. 613) provides an illustration of the components of the statement.

Step 2 Use the comparative balance sheets to determine the increase or decrease in cash during the period. The change in cash is the "check figure" for the statement of cash flows. The Red Roadster Superstore's comparative balance sheets show that cash decreased by $8,000 during 2018 (Exhibit 11-4, p. 601). *Why* did cash decrease during 2018? The statement of cash flows explains.

Exhibit 11-11 | Part 1: Template of the Statement of Cash Flows—Direct Method

	A
1	**The Red Roadster Superstore (TRRS)** **Statement of Cash Flows** **Year Ended December 31, 2018**
2	**Cash flows from operating activities:**
3	Receipts:
4	Collections from customers
5	Interest received on notes receivable
6	Dividends received on investments in stock
7	Total cash receipts
8	Payments:
9	To suppliers
10	To employees
11	For interest
12	For income tax
13	Total cash payments
14	Net cash provided by (used for) operating activities
15	**Cash flows from investing activities:**
16	+ Sales of long-term assets (investments, land, building, equipment, and so on)
17	− Purchases of long-term assets
18	+ Collections of notes receivable
19	− Loans to others
20	Net cash provided by (used for) investing activities
21	**Cash flows from financing activities:**
22	+ Issuance of stock
23	+ Sale of treasury stock
24	− Purchase of treasury stock
25	+ Borrowing (issuance of notes or bonds payable)
26	− Payment of notes or bonds payable
27	− Payment of dividends
28	Net cash provided by (used for) financing activities
29	**Net increase (decrease) in cash during the year**
30	+ Cash at December 31, 2017
31	= Cash at December 31, 2018
32	

Exhibit 11-11 | Part 2: Cash Receipts and Cash Payments on the Statement of Cash Flows—Direct Method

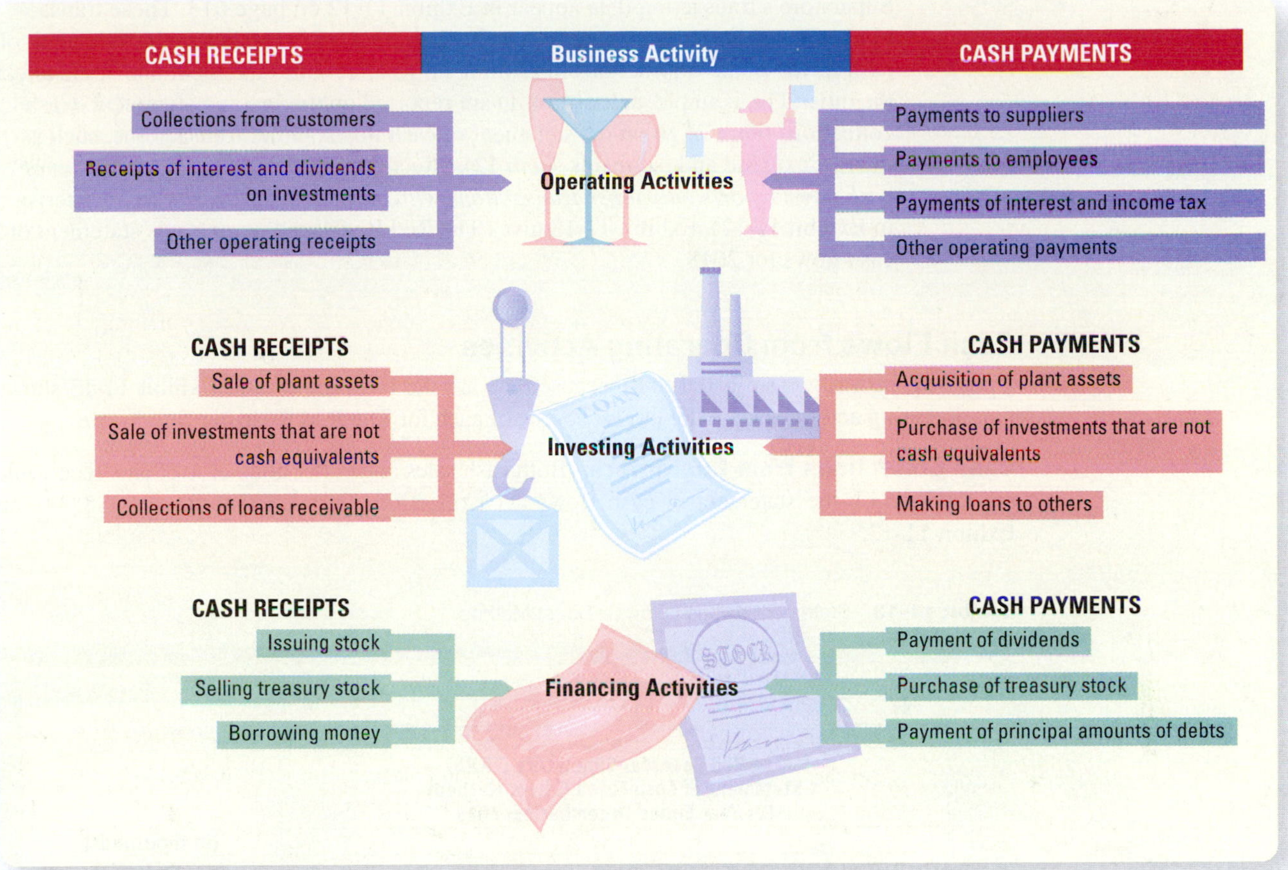

Exhibit 11-12 | Summary of The Red Roadster Superstore's 2018 Transactions

Operating Activities

1. Sales on credit, $303,000
*2. Collections from customers, $288,000
*3. Interest revenue and receipts, $2,000
4. Cost of goods sold, $150,000
5. Purchases of inventory on credit, $147,000
*6. Payments to suppliers, $133,000
7. Salary and wage expense, $56,000
*8. Payments of salary and wages, $58,000
9. Depreciation expense, $18,000
10. Other operating expense, $17,000
*11. Income tax expense and payments, $15,000
*12. Interest expense and payments, $7,000

Investing Activities

*13. Cash payments to acquire plant assets, $196,000
*14. Loan to another company, $21,000
*15. Proceeds from sale of plant assets, $62,000, including $8,000 gain

Financing Activities

*16. Proceeds from issuance of long-term debt, $94,000
*17. Proceeds from issuance of common stock, $4,000
*18. Payment of long-term debt, $11,000
*19. Declaration and payment of cash dividends, $17,000

*Indicates a cash flow to be reported on the statement of cash flows.
Note: Income statement data are taken from Exhibit 11-16, page 617.

Step 3 Use the available data to prepare the statement of cash flows. The Red Roadster Superstore's transaction data appear in Exhibit 11-12 on page 613. These transactions affected both the income statement (Exhibit 11-5, p. 602) and the statement of cash flows. Some transactions in Exhibit 11-12 affect one statement and some affect the other. For example, sales (item 1) are reported on the income statement. Cash collections (item 2) go on the statement of cash flows. Other transactions, such as interest expense and payments (item 12), affect both statements. *The statement of cash flows reports only those transactions with cash effects* (those with an asterisk in Exhibit 11-12). Exhibit 11-13 gives The Red Roadster Superstore's statement of cash flows for 2018.

Cash Flows from Operating Activities

Operating cash flows are listed first because they are the most important. Exhibit 11-13 shows that operating activities were the largest source of cash for The Red Roadster Superstore.

Cash Collections from Customers. Both cash sales and collections of accounts receivable are reported on the statement of cash flows as "Collections from customers ... $288,000" in Exhibit 11-13.

Exhibit 11-13 | Statement of Cash Flows—Direct Method

	A	B	C
1	**The Red Roadster Superstore (TRRS)** **Statement of Cash Flows (Direct Method)** **For Year Ended December 31, 2018**		
2		**(In thousands)**	
3	**Cash flows from operating activities:**		
4	Receipts:		
5	Collections from customers	$ 288	
6	Interest received	2	
7	Total cash receipts		$ 290
8	Payments:		
9	To suppliers	$ (133)	
10	To employees	(58)	
11	For income tax	(15)	
12	For interest	(7)	
13	Total cash payments		(213)
14	Net cash provided by operating activities		77
15	**Cash flows from investing activities:**		
16	Acquisition of plant assets	$ (196)	
17	Loan to another company	(21)	
18	Proceeds from sale of plant assets	62	
19	Net cash used for investing activities		(155)
20	**Cash flows from financing activities:**		
21	Proceeds from issuance of long-term debt	$ 94	
22	Proceeds from issuance of common stock	4	
23	Payment of long-term debt	(11)	
24	Payment of dividends	(17)	
25	Net cash provided by financing activities		70
26	**Net (decrease) in cash**		(8)
27	Cash balance, December 31, 2017		42
28	Cash balance, December 31, 2018		$ 34
29			

Cash Receipts of Interest and Dividends. The income statement reports interest revenue and dividend revenue. Only the cash receipts of interest and dividends appear on the statement of cash flows—$2,000 of interest received in Exhibit 11-13. The Red Roadster Superstore received no revenue from dividends in 2018.

Payments to Suppliers. Suppliers are businesses that provide a company with inventory or other goods and services, such as advertising, utilities, and office supplies used in the business's operating activities Exhibit 11-13 shows that The Red Roadster Superstore paid its suppliers $133,000 in 2018.

Payments to Employees. This category includes salaries, wages, and other forms of employee pay. Accrued amounts are excluded because they have not yet been paid. The statement of cash flows reports only the cash payments made to employees, which amounted to $58,000.

Payments for Interest Expense and Income Tax Expense. Interest and income tax payments are reported separately. The Red Roadster Superstore paid cash for all its interest and income taxes. Both amounts go on the statement of cash flows because the payments affect TRRS's cash.

Depreciation, Depletion, and Amortization Expense

These expenses are *not* listed on the direct-method statement of cash flows because they do not affect cash.

Cash Flows from Investing Activities

Investments are critical because they affect a company's future. Large investments in plant assets signal a company is expanding. Meager investments signal a company is not growing.

Purchasing Plant Assets and Investments and Making Loans to Other Companies. The Red Roadster Superstore's first investing activity in Exhibit 11-13 is the acquisition of plant assets ($196,000). TRRS also made a $21,000 loan and thus got a note receivable. These cash payments were made to acquire long-term assets.

Proceeds from Selling Plant Assets and Investments and from Collecting Notes Receivable. These cash receipts are also investing activities. The sale of the plant assets needs some explanation: The Red Roadster Superstore received $62,000 cash from the sale of plant assets, and there was an $8,000 gain on this transaction. What is the appropriate amount to show on the cash flow statement? It is $62,000, the cash received from the sale, not the $8,000 gain.

Investors are often reluctant to invest in companies that sell large amounts of their plant assets. Why? Because such sales may signal the businesses are in financial trouble and need cash. For example, downturns in the retail industry have caused some companies to close stores and sell fixtures, equipment, and real estate in order to generate cash.

Cash Flows from Financing Activities

Cash flows from financing activities include the following:

Proceeds from the Issuance of Stock and Debt (Notes and Bonds Payable). Issuing stock and borrowing money are two ways to finance a company. In Exhibit 11-13, The Red Roadster Superstore received $4,000 when it issued common stock. TRRS also received $94,000 cash when it issued long-term debt (such as a note payable) to borrow money.

Payment of Debt and Purchasing the Company's Own Stock. Paying debt (notes payable) is the opposite of borrowing. TRRS reported long-term debt payments of $11,000. TRRS did not purchase any treasury stock in 2018, but if it had, this expenditure would have appeared on the statement of cash flows.

Payment of Cash Dividends. Paying cash dividends is a financing activity, as shown by The Red Roadster Superstore's $17,000 payment in Exhibit 11-13. A stock dividend has no effect on cash, so it is *not* reported on the cash flow statement.

Noncash Investing and Financing Activities

Companies can buy plant assets and equipment by paying for them with something other than cash, such as issuance of stock or issuance of long-term debt. Exhibit 11-14 illustrates some noncash investing and financing activities a business could have engaged in (all amounts are assumed).

Exhibit 11-14 Noncash Investing and Financing Activities

	A	B
1		**Thousands**
2		
3	**Noncash investing and financing activities:**	
4	Acquisition of building by issuing common stock	$ 300
5	Acquisition of land by issuing note payable	70
6	Payment of long-term debt by issuing common stock	100
7	Total noncash investing and financing activities	$ 470
8		

These transactions would not be reported on a company's statement of cash flows because they don't involve cash. Instead, noncash investing and financing activities such as these appear in a separate schedule that follows the statement of cash flows.

TRY IT

(Answers are given on p. 667.)

Using the direct method, classify each of the following as an operating activity, an investing activity, or a financing activity. Also identify those items that are not reported on the statement of cash flows prepared using the direct method.

a. Net income
b. Payment of dividends
c. Borrowing long-term
d. Payment of cash to suppliers
e. Making a loan
f. Sale of treasury stock
g. Depreciation expense
h. Purchase of equipment with cash
i. Issuance of stock
j. Purchase of another company with cash
k. Payment of a long-term note payable
l. Payment of income taxes
m. Collections from customers
n. Accrual of interest revenue
o. Expiration of prepaid expense
p. Receipt of cash dividends

Computing Operating Cash Flows Using the Direct Method

Recall that the direct method format of the operating activities section on the statement of cash flows lists all of the individual cash receipts (collections from customers and receipts of interest and dividends) and cash disbursements (payments to suppliers and employees, and for interest and income taxes) to directly determine the net cash provided by a company's operating activities.

To compute operating cash flows using the direct method, we utilize a business's income statement and the *changes* in its balance-sheet accounts. Exhibit 11-15 diagrams the process. Exhibit 11-16 is The Red Roadster Superstore's income statement, and Exhibit 11-17 shows its comparative balance sheets.

Exhibit 11-15 Direct Method of Computing Cash Flows from Operating Activities

RECEIPTS / PAYMENTS	Income Statement Account	Change in Related Balance Sheet Account	
RECEIPTS:			
From customers	Sales Revenue	+ Decrease in Accounts Receivable − Increase in Accounts Receivable	
Of interest	Interest Revenue	+ Decrease in Interest Receivable − Increase in Interest Receivable	
PAYMENTS:			
To suppliers	Cost of Goods Sold	+ Increase in Inventory − Decrease in Inventory	+ Decrease in Accounts Payable − Increase in Accounts Payable
	Other Operating Expense	+ Increase in Prepaids − Decrease in Prepaids	+ Decrease in Accrued Liabilities − Increase in Accrued Liabilities
To employees	Salary (Wage) Expense	+ Decrease in Salary (Wage) Payable − Increase in Salary (Wage) Payable	
For interest	Interest Expense	+ Decrease in Interest Payable − Increase in Interest Payable	
For income tax	Income Tax Expense	+ Decrease in Income Tax Payable − Increase in Income Tax Payable	

Exhibit 11-16 Income Statement

	A	B	C
1	**The Red Roadster Superstore (TRRS)** **Income Statement** **Year Ended December 31, 2018**		
2		**(In thousands)**	
3	Revenues and gains:		
4	Sales revenue	$ 303	
5	Interest revenue	2	
6	Gain on sale of plant assets	8	
7	Total revenues and gains		$ 313
8	Expenses:		
9	Cost of goods sold	$ 150	
10	Salary and wage expense	56	
11	Depreciation expense	18	
12	Other operating expense	17	
13	Income tax expense	15	
14	Interest expense	7	
15	Total expenses		263
16	Net income		$ 50
17			

Computing Cash Collections from Customers. The Red Roadster Superstore's income statement in Exhibit 11-16 reports sales of $303,000. Accounts receivable increased from $81,000 at the beginning of the year to $96,000 at year-end, a $15,000 increase, as Exhibit 11-17 shows.

Exhibit 11-17 | Comparative Balance Sheets

	A	B	C	D	
1	**The Red Roadster Superstore (TRRS) Comparative Balance Sheets December 31, 2018 and 2017**				
2	**(In thousands)**	**2018**	**2017**	**Increase (Decrease)**	
3	**Assets**				
4	Current:				
5	Cash	$ 34	$ 42	$ (8)	
6	Accounts receivable	96	81	15	Changes in noncash current assets—Operating
7	Inventory	35	38	(3)	
8	Prepaid expenses	8	7	1	
9	Plant assets, net of depreciation	343	219	124	Changes in noncurrent assets—Investing
10	Notes receivable	21	—	21	
11	Total	$ 537	$ 387	$ 150	
12	**Liabilities**				
13	Current:				
14	Accounts payable	$ 91	$ 57	$ 34	Changes in current liabilities—Operating
15	Salary and wage payable	4	6	(2)	
16	Accrued liabilities	1	3	(2)	
17	Long-term debt	160	77	83	Changes in long-term liabilities and paid-in capital accounts—Financing
18	**Stockholders' Equity**				
19	Common stock	162	158	4	
20	Retained earnings	119	86	33	Change due to net income—Operating Change due to dividends—Financing
21	Total	$ 537	$ 387	$ 150	
22					

Based on those amounts, we can solve for TRRS's cash collections (X). The following calculations show that TRRS's cash collections equaled $288,000:

Accounts Receivable

Beginning balance	+	Sales	−	Collections	=	Ending balance
$81,000	+	$303,000		$-X$	=	$96,000
				$-X$	=	$96,000 − $81,000 − $303,000
				X	=	$288,000

The T-account for Accounts Receivable provides another view of the same computation.

Accounts Receivable

Beginning balance	81,000		
Sales	303,000	Collections	288,000
Ending balance	96,000		

Accounts Receivable increased, so collections must be less than sales.

All collections of receivables are computed this way. Let's turn now to TRRS's cash receipts of interest revenue. In our example, the company The Red Roadster Superstore earned interest revenue and collected cash of $2,000. The amounts of interest revenue and cash receipts of interest often differ. Exhibit 11-15 shows how to make this computation.

Computing Payments to Suppliers. This computation includes two parts:

- Payments for inventory
- Payments for operating expenses (other than salaries and wages)

Payments for inventory are computed by converting a company's cost of goods sold to the cash basis. To do so, we use Cost of Goods Sold, Inventory, and Accounts Payable. All the amounts come from Exhibits 11-16 and 11-17.

Cost of Goods Sold

Beginning inventory	+	Purchases	−	Ending inventory	=	Cost of goods sold
\$38,000	+	*X*	−	\$35,000	=	\$150,000
		X			=	\$150,000 − \$38,000 + \$35,000
		X			=	\$147,000

Now we can compute cash payments for inventory (*Y*), as follows:

Accounts Payable

Beginning balance	+	Purchases	−	Payments for inventory	=	Ending balance
\$57,000	+	\$147,000		−*Y*	=	\$91,000
				−*Y*	=	\$91,000 − \$57,000 − \$147,000
				Y	=	\$113,000

The T-accounts show where the data come from. Start with Cost of Goods Sold.

Cost of Goods Sold

Beg inventory	38,000	End inventory	35,000
Purchases	147,000		
Cost of goods sold	150,000		

Accounts Payable

Payments for inventory	113,000	Beg bal	57,000
		Purchases	147,000
		End bal	91,000

Accounts Payable increased, so payments for inventory are less than purchases.

Computing Payments for Other Operating Expenses. Payments for operating expenses other than salaries and wages are computed from three accounts: Prepaid Expenses, Accrued Liabilities, and Other Operating Expenses. All The Red Roadster Superstore data come from Exhibits 11-16 and 11-17.

Prepaid Expenses

Beginning balance	+	Payments	−	Expiration of prepaid expense (assumed)	=	Ending balance
\$7,000	+	*X*	−	\$7,000	=	\$8,000
		X			=	\$8,000 − \$7,000 + \$7,000
		X			=	\$8,000

Accrued Liabilities

Beginning balance	+	Accrual of expense at year-end (assumed)	−	Payments	=	Ending balance
\$3,000	+	\$1,000		−*X*	=	\$1,000
				−*X*	=	\$1,000 − \$3,000 − \$1,000
				X	=	\$3,000

Other Operating Expenses

Accrual of expense at year-end	+	Expiration of prepaid expense	+	Payments	=	Ending balance
$1,000	+	$7,000	+	X	=	$17,000
				X	=	$17,000 − $1,000 − $7,000
				X	=	$9,000
				Total payments for other operating expenses	=	$8,000 + $3,000 + $9,000
					=	$20,000

The T-accounts give another picture of the same data.

Prepaid Expenses

Beg bal	7,000	Expiration of prepaid expense	7,000
Payments	8,000		
End bal	8,000		

Accrued Liabilities

		Beg bal	3,000
Payment	3,000	Accrual of expense at year-end	1,000
		End bal	1,000

Other Operating Expenses

Accrual of expense at year-end	1,000		
Expiration of prepaid expense	7,000		
Payments	9,000		
End bal	17,000		

Total payments for other operating expenses = $20,000 ($8,000 + $3,000 + $9,000)

Now we can compute the payments to suppliers:

Payments to suppliers	=	Payments for inventory	+	Payments for other operating expenses
$133,000	=	$113,000	+	$20,000

Computing Payments to Employees. It is convenient to combine all payments to employees into one account, Salary and Wage Expense. To calculate the payments, we then adjust the expense for the change in Salary and Wage Payable, as shown here:

Salary and Wage Payable

Beginning balance	+	Salary and wage expense	−	Payments	=	Ending balance
$6,000	+	$56,000		$-X$	=	$4,000
				$-X$	=	$4,000 − $6,000 − $56,000
				X	=	$58,000

Salary and Wage Payable

		Beginning balance	6,000
Payments to employees	58,000	Salary and wage expense	56,000
		Ending balance	4,000

Computing Payments of Interest and Income Taxes. The Red Roadster Superstore's expense and payment amounts are the same for interest and income tax, so no analysis is required. If the expense and the payment differ, the payment can be computed as shown in Exhibit 11-15.

TRY IT

(Answers are given on p. 667.)

Fidelity Company reported the following for 2018 and 2017 (in millions):

At December 31,	2018	2017
Receivables, net	$3,500	$3,900
Inventory	5,200	5,000
Accounts payable	900	1,200
Income taxes payable	600	700

Year Ended December 31,	2018
Revenues	$23,000
Cost of goods sold	14,100
Income tax expense	900

Based on these figures, how much cash did

- **Fidelity collect from customers during 2018?**
- **Fidelity pay for inventory during 2018?**
- **Fidelity pay for income taxes during 2018?**

Computing Investing and Financing Cash Flows

Investing and financing activities are explained on pages 604–609. These computations are the same for both the direct and the indirect methods.

Measuring Cash Adequacy: Free Cash Flow

Some investors want to know how much cash a company can "free up" to pursue new opportunities. **Free cash flow** is the amount of cash available from operations after paying for planned investments in plant assets. A large amount of free cash flow is good because it means that a lot of cash is available for new investments that could ultimately generate more income. Free cash flow can be computed as follows:

$$\text{Free cash flow} = \begin{array}{c}\text{Net cash provided}\\ \text{by operating activities}\end{array} - \begin{array}{c}\text{Cash payments earmarked for}\\ \text{investments in plant assets}\end{array}$$

PepsiCo, Inc., uses free cash flow to manage its operations. Suppose PepsiCo expects net cash inflow of $2.3 billion from operations. Assume the company plans to spend $1.9 billion to modernize its bottling plants. In this case, PepsiCo's free cash flow would be $0.4 billion ($2.3 billion – $1.9 billion). If a good investment opportunity comes along, PepsiCo should have $0.4 billion to invest in the other company. **Shell Oil Company** also uses free cash flow analysis. The Decision Guidelines that follow show some ways to use cash flow and income data for investment and credit analysis.

Decision Guidelines

WHAT CASH FLOW FACTORS DIFFERENTIATE A HEALTHY COMPANY FROM AN UNHEALTHY COMPANY?

What are the signs of good financial health from the standpoint of cash flows? How can you differentiate a healthy company from an unhealthy one? Here are a few guidelines:

1. The primary source of cash inflows should be operations. In general, the cash flow a company generates should exceed its net income. When the indirect method is used, one of the largest positive adjustments to net income is usually the add-back for depreciation and amortization expense. Declining inventory and receivables balances can also be signs of healthy cash flows from operations. In contrast, a negative cash flow from operations is a danger sign. Companies that, over the long run, use rather than provide cash from operations, do not remain in business.
2. The net cash flow from investing activities is usually negative. To see cash flowing out of an entity for purchases of long-term assets is a sign that the company is focused on growth, and is investing for the future. Healthy companies can also be expected to sell long-term assets from time to time that they no longer need for their core business operations or to make room for new assets. This will result in some positive cash flow from investing activities for a company, but the amount will be relatively small and relatively rare. In contrast, weak companies often have positive net cash flows from investing activities because they are trying to generate cash by selling their fixed assets. Companies that do this as a primary source of cash are eroding their assets and, in effect, contracting their businesses, which hampers their ability to remain in business over the long run.
3. Cash flow from financing activities such as issuance of debt or capital stock provides cash on an as-needed basis for selective investing activities. However, net cash generated from financing activities should not exceed net cash provided by operating activities over extended periods of time. Companies that continually have to "return to the well" of external financing sometimes run into trouble later by expanding faster than they can sustain themselves by operating profitably. Negative cash flows in the financing activities section can also be signs of a healthy company if it's either paying off debts or returning cash to shareholders through stock repurchases or dividends.

Let's compare the financial health of two well-known U.S.-based retail businesses: **Sears Holdings Corporation** and **Wal-Mart Stores, Inc**, based on their fiscal year 2014–2016 Statements of Cash Flows shown below and on the next page. Both companies' fiscal years end on January 31 of the following year: So, fiscal 2014 year ends on January 31, 2015, and so forth.

A1

	A	B	C	D
1	**Sears Holdings Corporation Consolidated Statements of Cash Flows - USD ($) in Millions**	**Fiscal 2016**	**Fiscal 2015**	**Fiscal 2014**
2		**12 Months Ended**		
3		**Jan. 28, 2017**	**Jan. 30, 2016**	**Jan. 31, 2015**
4	**Cash Flows from Operating Activities**			
5	Net loss	$ (2,221)	$ (1,128)	$ (1,810)
6	Adjustments to convert to cash basis	840	(1,039)	423
7	Net cash used by operating activities	(1,381)	(2,167)	(1,387)
8	**Cash Flows from Investing Activities**			
9	Proceeds from sales of property and investments	386	2,730	424
10	Purchases of property and equipment	(142)	(211)	(270)
11	Other investing activities	–	–	173
12	Net cash provided by investing activities	244	2,519	327
13	**Cash Flows from Financing Activities**			
14	Proceeds from debt issuances	2,028	–	1,025
15	Repayments of debt	(66)	(1,405)	(80)
16	Other increases (decreases) in debt	(777)	1,041	(660)
17	Net cash provided by (used in) financing activities	1,185	(364)	285
18	Effect of exchange rate changes on cash and cash equivalents	–	–	(3)
19	Net Increase (Decrease) in Cash and Cash Equivalents	48	(12)	(778)
20	Cash and Cash Equivalents, Beginning of Year	238	250	1,028
21	Cash and Cash Equivalents, End of Period	$ 286	$ 238	$ 250
22				

Data from the U.S. Securities and Exchange Commission EDGAR Company filings, www.sec.gov

	A	B	C	D
1	**Wal-Mart Stores, Inc. Consolidated Statements of Cash Flows - USD ($) $ in Millions**	**Fiscal 2016**	**Fiscal 2015**	**Fiscal 2014**
2		**12 Months Ended**		
3		**Jan. 31, 2017**	**Jan. 31, 2016**	**Jan. 31, 2015**
4	**Cash Flows from Operating Activities:**			
5	Net income	$ 14,293	$ 15,080	$ 17,099
6	Adjustments to convert to cash basis	17,237	12,309	11,465
7	Net cash provided by operating activities	31,530	27,389	28,564
8	**Cash Flows from Investing Activities:**			
9	Purchases of property and equipment	(10,619)	(11,477)	(12,174)
10	Proceeds from the disposal of property and equipment	456	635	570
11	Proceeds from the disposal of certain operations	662	246	671
12	Purchase of available for sale securities	(1,901)	–	–
13	Other investing activities	(2,585)	(79)	(192)
14	Net cash used in investing activities	(13,987)	(10,675)	(11,125)
15	**Cash Flows from Financing Activities:**			
16	Net change in short-term borrowings	(1,673)	1,235	(6,288)
17	Proceeds from issuance of long-term debt	137	39	5,174
18	Payments of long-term debt	(2,055)	(4,432)	(3,904)
19	Dividends paid	(6,216)	(6,294)	(6,185)
20	Purchase of Company stock	(8,298)	(4,112)	(1,015)
21	Other financing activities	(824)	(2,558)	(2,853)
22	Net cash used in financing activities	(18,929)	(16,122)	(15,071)
23	Effect of exchange rates on cash and cash equivalents	(452)	(1,022)	(514)
24	Net increase (decrease) in cash and cash equivalents	(1,838)	(430)	1,854
25	Cash and cash equivalents at beginning of year	8,705	9,135	7,281
26	Cash and cash equivalents at end of year	$ 6,867	$ 8,705	$ 9,135
27				

Data from the U.S. Securities and Exchange Commission EDGAR Company filings, www.sec.gov

Guideline 1: Sears Holdings Corporation shows negative cash flows from operating activities for all three fiscal years, from 2014 through 2016. Thus, the company is spending more cash from its core business operations than it is taking in—not a good sign for a company that wants to stay in business. In contrast, Wal-Mart's largest single source of cash over the same period was operations. The company generated net cash from operating activities of over $31.5 billion in 2016 (over two times the amount of its net income) and had similar strong results for the two prior years.

Guideline 2: In all 3 years, Sears Holdings generated positive cash flow from investing activities, meaning that, on a net basis, it was selling more long-term assets than it was buying. This is a sign of a company in decline. In contrast, Wal-Mart's single most negative cash flow was from purchases of property and equipment. Although it disposed of some assets (which were likely obsolete or nonproductive), it purchased far more than it sold. In addition, Wal-Mart generated enough excess cash from its operating activities to enable the company to purchase some investment assets (see Appendix E for a further explanation of investments).

Guideline 3: In two of the three years, Sears Holdings issued large amounts of debt, far more than it repaid. Also, the proceeds from these debt issuances were not being used to purchase fixed assets, as is usually the case, but were probably used to finance operations. In contrast, in fiscal 2016 Wal-Mart used almost $19 billion from various financing activities. The company paid about $2 billion to long-term creditors, and about $1.7 billion to short-term creditors. In addition, Wal-Mart returned about $14.5 billion in cash to its shareholders: $6.2 billion in dividends and $8.3 billion in share repurchases.

Which of these retailers is stronger? There is hardly a comparison: Wal-Mart! In fact, it appears doubtful whether Sears Holdings Corporation will remain in business.

End-of-Chapter Summary Problems

Adeva Health Foods, Inc., reported the following comparative balance sheets for 2018 and 2017 and the income statement for 2018:

	A	B	C
1	**Adeva Health Foods, Inc.** **Comparative Balance Sheets** **December 31, 2018 and 2017**		
2		**2018**	**2017**
3	Cash	$ 19,000	$ 3,000
4	Accounts receivable	22,000	23,000
5	Inventories	34,000	31,000
6	Prepaid expenses	1,000	3,000
7	Equipment, net	90,000	79,000
8	Intangible assets	9,000	9,000
9	Total assets	$ 175,000	$ 148,000
10			
11	Accounts payable	$ 14,000	$ 9,000
12	Accrued liabilities	16,000	19,000
13	Income tax payable	14,000	12,000
14	Notes payable	45,000	50,000
15	Common stock	31,000	20,000
16	Retained earnings	64,000	40,000
17	Treasury stock	(9,000)	(2,000)
18	Total liabilities and stockholders' equity	$ 175,000	$ 148,000
19			

	A	B
1	**Adeva Health Foods, Inc.** **Income Statement** **Year Ended December 31, 2018**	
2	Sales revenue	$ 190,000
3	Gain on sale of equipment	6,000
4	Total revenue and gains	196,000
5	Cost of goods sold	85,000
6	Depreciation expense	19,000
7	Other operating expenses	36,000
8	Total expenses	140,000
9	Income before income tax	56,000
10	Income tax expense	18,000
11	Net income	$ 38,000
12		

Assume that **Berkshire Hathaway** is considering buying Adeva. Berkshire Hathaway requests the following cash flow data for 2018. There were no noncash investing and financing activities.

a. Collections from customers.
b. Cash payments for inventory.
c. Cash payments for other operating expenses.
d. Cash payment for income tax.
e. Cash received from the sale of equipment. Adeva paid $40,000 for new equipment during the year.
f. Issuance of common stock.
g. Issuance of notes payable. Adeva paid off $20,000 during the year.
h. Cash dividends. There were no stock dividends.

Provide the requested data. Show your work.

Answers

a. Analyze Accounts Receivable: Let *X* = Collections from customers:

Beginning Accounts Receivable	+	Sales	−	Collections	=	Ending Accounts Receivable
$23,000	+	$190,000	−	*X*	=	$22,000
				X	=	$191,000

b. Analyze Inventory and Accounts Payable: Let *X* = Purchases, and let *Y* = Payments for inventory:

Beginning Inventory	+	Purchases	−	Cost of Goods Sold	=	Ending Inventory
$31,000	+	*X*	−	$85,000	=	$34,000
				X	=	$88,000

Beginning Accounts Payable	+	Purchases	−	Payments	=	Ending Accounts Payable
$9,000	+	$88,000	−	*Y*	=	$14,000
				Y	=	$83,000

c. Start with Other Operating Expenses, and adjust for the changes in Prepaid Expenses and Accrued Liabilities:

Other Operating Expenses	− Decrease in Prepaid Expenses	+ Decrease in Accrued Liabilities	=	Payments for Other Operating Expenses
$36,000	− $2,000	+ $3,000	=	$37,000

d. Analyze Income Tax Payable: Let *X* = Payment of income tax:

Beginning Income Tax Payable	+	Income Tax Expense	−	Payments	=	Ending Income Tax Payable
$12,000	+	$18,000	−	*X*	=	$14,000
				X	=	$16,000

e. Analyze Equipment, Net: Let X = Book value of equipment sold. Then combine with the gain or loss to compute cash received from the sale:

Beginning Equipment, net	+	Acquisitions	−	Depreciation Expense	−	Book Value Sold	=	Ending Equipment, net
$79,000	+	$40,000	−	$19,000	−	X	=	$90,000
						X	=	$10,000

Cash Received from Sale	=	Book Value Sold	+	Gain on Sale
$16,000	=	$10,000	+	$6,000

f. Analyze Common Stock: Let X = Issuance:

Beginning Common Stock	+	Issuance	=	Ending Common Stock
$20,000	+	X	=	$31,000
		X	=	$11,000

g. Analyze Notes Payable: Let X = Issuance:

Beginning Notes Payable	+	Issuance	−	Payment	=	Ending Notes Payable
$50,000	+	X	−	$20,000	=	$45,000
				X	=	$15,000

h. Analyze Retained Earnings: Let X = Dividends:

Beginning Retained Earnings	+	Net Income	−	Dividends	=	Ending Retained Earnings
$40,000	+	$38,000	−	X	=	$64,000
				X	=	$14,000

REVIEW | Statement of Cash Flows

Accounting Vocabulary

direct method (p. 599) A format of the operating activities section of the statement of cash flows that lists the major categories of operating cash receipts (collections from customers and receipts of interest and dividends) and cash disbursements (payments to suppliers and employees, and for interest and income taxes).

financing activities (p. 598) Activities that obtain from investors and creditors the cash needed to launch and sustain a business; a section of the statement of cash flows.

free cash flow (p. 621) The amount of cash available from operations after paying for planned investments in plant assets.

indirect method (p. 599) A format of the operating activities section of the statement of cash flows; the indirect method starts with net income, which is then converted to the net cash provided by a company's operating activities.

investing activities (p. 598) Activities that increase or decrease the long-term assets available to the business; a section of the statement of cash flows.

operating activities (p. 598) Activities that create revenues, expenses, gains and losses; a section of the statement of cash flows. Operating activities affect the income statement.

statement of cash flows (p. 596) A statement that reports cash receipts and cash payments classified according to a company's major activities: operating, investing, and financing.

Quick Check (Answers are given on page 667.)

1. The statement of cash flows is designed for all of the following purposes *except*

a. to list all revenues and expenses.
b. to determine a company's ability to pay dividends and interest.
c. to predict future cash flows.
d. to provide information about cash receipts and cash payments during a period.

2. The statement of cash flows does *not* report

a. cash payments in the current year.
b. revenues and expenses for the current year.
c. cash receipts in the current year.
d. noncash investing and financing activities in the current year.

3. On the statement of cash flows, increases and decreases in long-term assets resulting from cash transactions are reported as:

a. operating activities.
b. investing activities.
c. financing activities.
d. noncash investing and financing activities.

4. Which of the three types of activities reported on the statement of cash flows is the most important to evaluate when analyzing a company's long-term survival?

a. Operating activities
b. Investing activities
c. Financing activities
d. Noncash investing and financing activities

5. Cash received from the issuance of common stock is reported on a statement of cash flows under

a. operating activities.
b. investing activities.
c. financing activities.
d. noncash investing and financing activities.

6. On the statement of cash flows, which of the following items is classified as a financing activity?

a. Borrowing cash by signing a long-term note
b. Purchasing investments with cash
c. Acquiring long-term assets with cash
d. Loaning money with a short-term note receivable

7. On the statement of cash flows, which of the following items is classified as an investing activity?

a. Borrowing cash from a bank
b. Issuing common stock
c. Repaying a loan with cash
d. Collecting cash on a long-term loan

8. When using the indirect method of preparing the statement of cash flows, the starting point to determine net cash provided by operating activities is

a. sales.
b. net income.
c. the beginning cash balance.
d. the ending cash balance.

9. In the current year, BOGO Company sold land for $80,000 cash, purchased a delivery van for $25,000 cash, and issued common stock for $100,000 cash. The net cash provided by investing activities is

a. $155,000.
b. $180,000.
c. $205,000.
d. $55,000.

10. Which of the following transactions does *not* affect cash during a period?

a. A write-off of an uncollectible account
b. A purchase of a building with cash
c. Issuing common stock
d. Paying an accounts payable

11. If the indirect method is used to calculate net cash provided by operating activities, a decrease in accounts receivable is

a. added to net income.
b. subtracted from net income.
c. ignored since it does not affect net income.
d. ignored since it does not affect expenses.

12. In 2018, Jubilee Company repurchased its own stock at a cost of $55,000. During the year, the company purchased land with cash for $120,000 and issued bonds payable for $500,000. Net cash provided by financing activities for the year would have been

a. $675,000.
b. $325,000.
c. $445,000.
d. $555,000.

13. When using the direct method of preparing the statement of cash flows, cash receipts from operating activities do *not* include

a. collections from customers.
b. collection of a long-term note receivable.
c. receipt of interest on investments.
d. receipt of dividends on investments.

14. The major difference between the way a statement of cash flows is prepared using the indirect method and the way the same statement is prepared using the direct method is how ____________ are reported.

a. operating activities
b. investing activities
c. financing activities
d. noncash activities

Excel Project
Autograded Excel Project available in **MyLab Accounting**

ASSESS YOUR PROGRESS

Ethics Check

EC11-1 Identify ethical principle violated

For each of the situations listed, identify which of three principles (integrity, objectivity and independence, or due care) from the AICPA Code of Professional Conduct is violated. Assume all persons listed in the situations are members of the AICPA. (Note: Refer to the AICPA Code of Professional Conduct contained on pages 25–27 in Chapter 1 for descriptions of the principles.)

a. Eleanor has been the CFO of Solaris Technologies for 15 years, and has never uncovered any material mistakes or fraud on its financial statements. Eleanor is sure this year that nothing has changed, so she signs off on the financial statements without reviewing them first because she has more urgent matters demanding her attention.

b. Patty is a newly hired accountant at Trucking Systems. Her responsibilities include preparing all of the company's financial statements including its statement of cash flows. Trucking Systems uses the direct method to prepare its statement of cash flows. Patty has not prepared a statement of cash flows in many years and cannot remember how to prepare it using the direct method. Patty prepares the statement of cash flows using the indirect method and hopes that no one will notice.

c. Reagan is the accounting manager of Velocity, Inc., and has approved the acquisition of expensive, new equipment without approval from her boss. She knows her boss will find out when looking at the financial statements so Reagan asks one of the staff accountants to hide the cash flow in another category where it will not be noticed.

d. Albert is an accountant who is close to retirement at Image Industries. Since he does not have much time left with the company, he has been a little careless with the preparation of the company's statement of cash flows. The ending cash balance does not match the cash balance on the balance sheet, but Albert forces it to balance with a plug figure.

Short Exercises

S11-1. *(Learning Objective 1: Explain the purposes of the statement of cash flows)* Describe how the statement of cash flows helps investors and creditors do each of the following: LO 1

a. Predict future cash flows
b. Evaluate management decisions

S11-2. *(Learning Objective 2: Evaluate operating cash flows—indirect method)* Examine CooperHall Company's statement of cash flows that follows. LO 2

	A	B	C
1	**CooperHall Company Consolidated Statement of Cash Flows (Adapted, In Millions) Year Ended December 31, 2018**		
2	**Cash flows from operating activities:**		
3	Net income	$ 875	
4	Adjustment to reconcile net income to net cash		
5	used in operating activities:		
6	Depreciation and amortization	222	
7	Change in assets and liabilities, net of acquired businesses:		
8	Increase in Accounts receivable	(470)	
9	Increase in Other current assets	(160)	
10	Decrease in Accounts payable	(167)	
11	Decrease in Accrued expenses and other liabilities	(238)	
12	Increase in Unearned revenue	25	
13	Decrease in Income taxes payable	(266)	
14	Increase in Other, net	26	
15	Net cash used in operating activities		$ (153)
16	**Cash flows from investing activities:**		
17	Purchase of property and equipment	$ (1,593)	
18	Purchase of investments	(21,282)	
19	Sale of investments	19,286	
20	Acquisitions of other companies	(363)	
21	Net cash used in investing activities		$ (3,952)
22	**Cash flows from financing activities:**		
23	Proceeds from the issuance of common stock, net	$ 835	
24	Other financing activities, net	378	
25	Net cash provided by financing activities		$ 1,213
26	Impact of foreign currency translation		18
27	Net increase (decrease) in cash and cash equivalents		$ (2,874)
28	Cash and cash equivalents at beginning of year		4,155
29	Cash and cash equivalents at end of year		$ 1,281
30			

Suppose CooperHall's operating activities *provided*, rather than *used*, cash. Identify three things if using the indirect method that could cause operating cash flows to be positive.

LO 2

S11-3. ***(Learning Objective 2: Use cash flow data to evaluate performance)*** The CEO and CFO from Lawrence Hotels, Inc., are reviewing company performance for 2018. The income statement reports a 25% increase in net income over 2017. However, most of the increase resulted from a gain on insurance proceeds from fire damage to a building. The balance sheet shows a large increase in receivables. The cash flows statement, in summarized form, reports the following:

Net cash used for operating activities	$(53,700)
Net cash provided by investing activities	39,300
Net cash provided by financing activities	17,500
Increase in cash during 2018	$ 3,100

Write a memo giving Lawrence's top executives your assessment of 2018 operations and your outlook for the future. Focus on the information content of the cash flow data.

LO 3

S11-4. ***(Learning Objective 3: Report cash flows from operating activities—indirect method)*** Westfall Industries began 2018 with its accounts receivable, inventory, and prepaid expenses totaling $50,000 and its total current liabilities totaling $36,000. At the end of the year, these same current assets totaled $48,000, while its total current liabilities totaled $40,000.

Net income for the year was $81,000. Included in net income were a $4,000 loss on the sale of land and depreciation expense of $8,000.

Show how Westfall should report cash flows from operating activities for 2018. The company uses the *indirect* method.

LO 2

S11-5. ***(Learning Objective 2: Distinguish among operating, financing, and investing activities—indirect method)*** Crater HVAC Systems is preparing its statement of cash flows (*indirect* method) for the year ended March 31, 2018. To follow, in no particular order, is a list of items that will be used in preparing the company's statement of cash flows. Identify each item as an operating activity addition to net income; an operating activity subtraction from net income; an investing activity; a financing activity; or an activity that is not used to prepare the cash flows statement.

a. Increase in inventory
b. Issuance of common stock
c. Decrease in accrued liabilities
d. Net income
e. Decrease in prepaid expense
f. Collection of cash from customers
g. Purchase of equipment with cash
h. Retained earnings
i. Payment of dividends
j. Increase in accounts payable
k. Decrease in accounts receivable
l. Gain on sale of a building
m. Loss on sale of land
n. Depreciation expense

LO 3

S11-6. ***(Learning Objective 3: Prepare operating cash flows—indirect method)*** Elan Corporation accountants have assembled the following data for the year ended June 30, 2018:

Net income	$?	Cost of goods sold	$115,000
Payment of dividends	6,300	Other operating expenses	41,000
Proceeds from the issuance of common stock	20,000	Purchase of equipment with cash	36,000
Sales revenue	223,000	Increase in current liabilities	6,000
Increase in current assets other than cash	37,000	Payment of note payable	31,000
Purchase of treasury stock	8,000	Proceeds from sale of land	34,000
		Depreciation expense	12,000

Prepare the *operating activities section* of Elan's statement of cash flows for the year ended June 30, 2018. The company uses the *indirect* method for operating cash flows.

S11-7. ***(Learning Objective 3: Prepare a statement of cash flows—indirect method)*** Use the data in Short Exercise 11-6 to prepare Elan Corporation's statement of cash flows for the year ended June 30, 2018. The company uses the *indirect* method for operating cash flows. LO 3

S11-8. ***(Learning Objective 3: Calculate investing cash flows)*** Thompson Turf Trimmers, Inc., reported the following financial statements for 2018: LO 3

	A	B
1	**Thompson Turf Trimmers, Inc. Income Statement Year Ended December 31, 2018**	
2	**(In thousands)**	
3	Service revenue	$ 790
4	Cost of goods sold	400
5	Salary expense	30
6	Depreciation expense	10
7	Other expenses	200
8	Total expenses	640
9	Net income	$ 150
10		

	A	B	C	D	E	F
1	**Thompson Turf Trimmers, Inc. Comparative Balance Sheets December 31, 2018 and 2017**					
2	**(In thousands)**					
3	**Assets**	**2018**	**2017**	**Liabilities**	**2018**	**2017**
4	Current:			Current:		
5	Cash	$ 24	$ 20	Accounts payable	$ 56	$ 46
6	Accounts receivable	53	48	Salary payable	29	25
7	Inventory	75	86	Accrued liabilities	16	19
8	Prepaid expenses	12	11	Long-term note payable	67	54
9	Plant assets, net	223	182			
10	Long-term investments	61	80	**Stockholders' Equity**		
11				Common stock	48	38
12				Retained earnings	232	245
13	Total	$ 448	$ 427	Total	$ 448	$ 427
14						

Calculate the following investing cash flows; enter all amounts in thousands.

a. Acquisitions of plant assets (all were for cash). Thompson Turf Trimmers sold no plant assets during the year.

b. Proceeds from the sale of investments. Thompson Turf Trimmers purchased no investments during the year.

LO 3 **S11-9.** ***(Learning Objective 3: Calculate financing cash flows)*** Use the Thompson Turf Trimmers data in Short Exercise 11-8 to calculate the following; enter all amounts in thousands.

a. New borrowing or payment of long-term notes payable. Thompson Turf Trimmers had only one long-term note payable transaction during the year.

b. Issuance of common stock or retirement of common stock. Thompson Turf Trimmers had only one common stock transaction during the year.

c. Payment of cash dividends (same as dividends declared).

LO 4 **S11-10.** ***(Learning Objective 4: Calculate operating cash flows—direct method)*** Use the Thompson Turf Trimmers data in Short Exercise 11-8 to calculate the following; enter all amounts in thousands.

a. Collections from customers

b. Payments for inventory

LO 4 **S11-11.** ***(Learning Objective 4: Calculate operating cash flows—direct method)*** Use the Thompson Turf Trimmers data in Short Exercise 11-8 to calculate the following; enter all amounts in thousands.

a. Payments to employees

b. Payments of other expenses

LO 4 **S11-12.** ***(Learning Objective 4: Prepare a statement of cash flows—direct method)*** Tally-Ho Horse Farms, Inc., began 2018 with cash of $170,000. During the year, Tally-Ho earned service revenue of $595,000 and collected $590,000 from customers. Expenses for the year totaled $395,000, with $380,000 paid in cash to suppliers and employees. Tally-Ho also paid $134,000 to purchase equipment and paid a cash dividend of $55,000 to stockholders. During 2018, Tally-Ho borrowed $20,000 by issuing a note payable. Prepare the company's statement of cash flows for the year ending December 31, 2018. Format operating activities using the *direct* method.

LO 4 **S11-13.** ***(Learning Objective 4: Computing operating cash flows—direct method)*** Middleburg Golf Club, Inc., has assembled the following data for the year ended September 30, 2018:

Cost of goods sold	$106,000	Payment of dividends	$ 6,500
Payments to suppliers	113,000	Proceeds from issuance	
Purchase of equipment with cash	42,000	of common stock	22,000
Payments to employees	79,000	Sales revenue	226,000
Payment of note payable	23,000	Collections from customers	208,000
Proceeds from sale of land	47,000	Payment of income tax	17,000
Depreciation expense	9,000	Purchase of treasury stock	5,700

Prepare the *operating activities* section of Middleburg Golf Club's statement of cash flows for the year ended September 30, 2018. The company uses the *direct* method for operating cash flows.

LO 4 **S11-14.** ***(Learning Objective 4: Preparing a statement of cash flows—direct method)*** Use the data in Short Exercise 11-13 to prepare Middleburg Golf Club's statement of cash flows for the year ended September 30, 2018. The company uses the *direct* method for operating cash flows.

Exercises MyLab Accounting

Group A

E11-15A. ***(Learning Objectives 2, 3: Distinguish among operating, investing, and financing activities for the statement of cash flows—indirect method)*** Aurum Investments specializes in low-risk government bonds. Identify each of Aurum's transactions as operating (O), investing (I), financing (F), noncash investing and financing (NIF), or a transaction that is not reported on the statement of cash flows (N). Indicate whether each item increases (+) or decreases (−) cash. The *indirect* method is used for operating cash flows.

LO **2, 3**

	a. Acquisition of equipment by issuance of note payable
	b. Purchase of long-term investment with cash
	c. Issuance of long-term note payable to borrow cash
	d. Increase in prepaid expenses
	e. Decrease in accrued liabilities
	f. Loss of sale of equipment
	g. Decrease in accounts receivable
	h. Depreciation of equipment
	i. Increase in accounts payable
	j. Amortization of intangible assets
	k. Purchase of treasury stock
	l. Payment of long-term debt
	m. Increase in salary payable
	n. Cash sale of land
	o. Sale of long-term investment
	p. Acquisition of building by cash payment
	q. Net income
	r. Issuance of common stock for cash
	s. Payment of cash dividend

E11-16A. ***(Learning Objectives 2, 3: Distinguish among operating, investing, and financing activities for the statement of cash flows—indirect method)*** A company uses the indirect method to prepare the statement of cash flows. Indicate whether each of the following transactions affects an operating activity, an investing activity, a financing activity, or a noncash investing and financing activity:

LO **2, 3**

A1

	A	B	C	D	E	F	G	H
1	a.	Cash	61,000		h.	Equipment	11,000	
2		Common Stock		10,000		Cash		11,000
3		Paid-in Capital in Excess of Par		51,000	i.	Furniture and Fixtures	18,000	
4	b.	Dividends Payable	13,000			Cash		18,000
5		Cash		13,000	j.	Cash	52,000	
6	c.	Cash	7,000			Accounts Receivable	11,000	
7		Long-Term Investment		7,000		Service Revenue		63,000
8	d.	Building	105,000		k.	Salary Expense	14,000	
9		Note Payable—Long-Term		105,000		Cash		14,000
10	e.	Treasury Stock	12,000		l.	Loss on Disposal of Equipment	1,000	
11		Cash		12,000		Equipment, Net		1,000
12	f.	Depreciation Expense	5,000		m.	Bonds Payable	35,000	
13		Accumulated Depreciation		5,000		Cash		35,000
14	g.	Land	15,000					
15		Cash		15,000				
16								

LO 3 **E11-17A.** ***(Learning Objective 3: Calculate cash flows from operating activities—indirect method)*** The accounting records of Kelly Corporation reveal the following:

Net income	$ 11,000	Depreciation expense	$ 9,000
Collection of dividend revenue	7,200	Decrease in current liabilities	19,000
Payment of interest	12,000	Decrease in current assets	
Sales revenue	180,000	other than cash	32,000
Loss on sale of land	28,000	Payment of dividends	7,600
Acquisition of land with cash	38,000	Payment of income tax	5,000

Requirements

1. Prepare the cash flows from operating activities section of the statement of cash flows using the *indirect* method.
2. Evaluate the operating cash flow of Kelly Corporation. Explain.

LO 3 **E11-18A.** ***(Learning Objective 3: Calculate cash flows from operating activities—indirect method)*** The accounting records of the Porter Trading Post Company include these accounts:

Cash

Dec 1	40,000		
Receipts	567,000	Payments	446,000
Dec 31	161,000		

Accounts Receivable

Dec 1	8,000		
Credit sales	538,000	Collections	537,000
Dec 31	9,000		

Inventory

Dec 1	4,000		
Purchases	437,000	Cost of Sales	434,000
Dec 31	7,000		

Equipment

Dec 1	183,000		
Acquisition	14,000		
Dec 31	197,000		

Accumulated Deprec.—Equipment

		Dec 1	51,000
		Depreciation	7,000
		Dec 31	58,000

Accounts Payable

		Dec 1	14,500
Payments	327,000	Purchases	437,000
		Dec 31	124,500

Accrued Liabilities

		Dec 1	18,000
Payments	25,000	Accruals	23,000
		Dec 31	16,000

Retained Earnings

Quarterly		Dec 1	62,000
Dividend	14,000	Net Income	20,000
		Dec 31	68,000

Requirement

1. Prepare the company's net cash provided by (used for) operating activities section of the statement of cash flows for the month of December. Use the *indirect* method. Do you see any potential problems in the company's cash flows from operations? How can you tell?

LO 3 **E11-19A.** ***(Learning Objective 3: Prepare the statement of cash flows—indirect method)*** The income statement and additional data of Barnaby Travel Products, Inc., follow:

A1

	A	B	C
1	**Barnaby Travel Products, Inc. Income Statement Year Ended December 31, 2018**		
2	Revenues:		
3	Service revenue	$ 236,000	
4	Dividend revenue	8,500	$ 244,500
5	Expenses:		
6	Cost of goods sold	96,000	
7	Salary expense	60,000	
8	Depreciation expense	28,000	
9	Advertising expense	4,700	
10	Interest expense	2,800	
11	Income tax expense	14,000	205,500
12	Net income		$ 39,000
13			

Additional data:

a. Acquisition of plant assets was $156,000. Of this amount, $104,000 was paid in cash and $52,000 was financed by signing a note payable.
b. Proceeds from the sale of land totaled $39,000.
c. Proceeds from the issuance of common stock totaled $31,000.
d. Payment of a long-term note payable was $16,000.
e. Payment of dividends was $8,000.
f. From the balance sheets:

	A	B	C
1		**December 31,**	
2		**2018**	**2017**
3	**Current assets:**		
4	Cash	$ 170,000	$ 33,200
5	Accounts receivable	47,000	63,000
6	Inventory	30,000	72,000
7	Prepaid expenses	9,000	8,800
8			
9	**Current liabilities:**		
10	Accounts payable	$ 34,000	$ 19,000
11	Accrued liabilities	90,000	35,000
12			

Requirements

1. Prepare Barnaby's statement of cash flows for the year ended December 31, 2018, using the *indirect* method.
2. Evaluate the company's cash flows for the year. In your evaluation, mention all three categories of cash flows and give the rationale for your evaluation.

E11-20A. ***(Learning Objective 3: Evaluate a statement of cash flows—indirect method)*** Consider three independent cases for the cash flows of Winter Merchandising Corporation. For each case, identify from the statement of cash flows how the company generated the cash to acquire new plant assets. Rank the three cases from the most healthy financially to the least healthy. LO 3

	A	B	C	D
1		**Case A**	**Case B**	**Case C**
2	Cash flows from operating activities:			
3	Net income	$ 25,000	$ 25,000	$ 25,000
4	Depreciation and amortization	11,000	11,000	11,000
5	Increase in current assets other than cash	(27,000)	(2,000)	(14,000)
6	Decrease in current liabilities	(12,000)	(5,000)	(1,000)
7		(3,000)	29,000	21,000
8	Cash flows from investing activities:			
9	Acquisition of plant assets	(102,000)	(102,000)	(102,000)
10	Sales of plant assets	11,000	46,000	111,000
11		(91,000)	(56,000)	9,000
12	Cash flows from financing activities:			
13	Issuance of stock	119,000	76,000	18,000
14	Payment of debt	(27,000)	(47,000)	(28,000)
15		92,000	29,000	(10,000)
16	Net increase (decrease) in cash	$ (2,000)	$ 2,000	$ 20,000
17				

LO 3, 4 **E11-21A.** ***(Learning Objectives 3, 4: Calculate investing and financing amounts for the statement of cash flows)*** Calculate the following items for the statement of cash flows:

a. Beginning and ending Plant Assets, Net, were $115,000 and $109,000, respectively. Depreciation for the period was $11,000, and purchases of new plant assets were $25,000. Plant assets were sold at a gain of $6,000. What were the cash proceeds of the sale?

b. Beginning and ending Retained Earnings were $37,000 and $72,000, respectively. Net income for the period was $63,000, and stock dividends were $9,000. How much were the cash dividends?

LO 4 **E11-22A.** ***(Learning Objective 4: Calculate cash flows from operating activities—direct method)*** The accounting records of Grand Pharmaceuticals, Inc., reveal the following:

Payment of salaries and wages	$33,000	Net income	$56,000
Depreciation expense	25,000	Payment of income tax	13,000
Decrease in current liabilities	13,000	Collection of dividend revenue	11,000
Decrease in current assets other than cash	23,000	Payment of interest	17,000
Payment of dividends	9,000	Cash sales	35,000
Collection of accounts receivable	115,000	Gain on sale of land	15,000
		Acquisition of land with cash	46,000
		Payment of accounts payable	59,000

Requirement

1. Prepare cash flows from operating activities using the *direct* method. Also evaluate Grand's operating cash flow. Give the rationale for your evaluation.

LO 4 **E11-23A.** ***(Learning Objective 4: Identify items for the statement of cash flows—direct method)*** Selected accounts of McKay Bricker Framing show the following:

Salaries Payable

		Beginning bal	8,000
Payments	23,000	Salary expense	21,000
		Ending bal	6,000

Buildings

Beginning bal	60,000	Depreciation	15,000
Acquisitions with cash	90,000	Book value of building sold	89,000*
Ending bal	46,000		

*Sale price was $112,000.

Notes Payable

		Beginning bal	176,000
Payments	50,000	Issuance of note payable for cash	56,000
		Ending bal	182,000

Requirement

1. For each account, identify the item or items that should appear on a statement of cash flows prepared using the *direct* method. State where to report the item.

E11-24A. ***(Learning Objective 4: Prepare the statement of cash flows—direct method)*** The income statement and additional data of Hapland Light, Inc., follow: LO 4

	A	B	C
1	**Hapland Light, Inc.** **Income Statement** **Year Ended June 30, 2018**		
2	**Revenues:**		
3	Sales revenue	$ 225,000	
4	Dividend revenue	11,000	$ 236,000
5	**Expenses:**		
6	Cost of goods sold	101,000	
7	Salary expense	42,000	
8	Depreciation expense	24,000	
9	Advertising expense	11,500	
10	Interest expense	4,000	
11	Income tax expense	10,000	192,500
12	Net income		$ 43,500
13			

Additional data:

a. Collections from customers are $15,500 less than sales.

b. Payments to suppliers are $1,500 more than the sum of cost of goods sold plus advertising expense.

c. Payments to employees are $2,400 more than salary expense.

d. Dividend revenue, interest expense, and income tax expense equal their cash amounts.

e. Acquisition of plant assets is $156,000. Of this amount, $108,000 is paid in cash and $48,000 is financed by signing a long-term note payable.

f. Proceeds from the sale of land totaled $26,000.

g. Proceeds from the issuance of common stock totaled $86,000.

h. Payment of a long-term note payable is $29,000.

i. Payment of dividends is $9,000.

j. Cash balance, June 30, 2017, was $38,000.

Requirements

1. Prepare Hapland Light's statement of cash flows and accompanying schedule of noncash investing and financing activities. Report operating activities using the *direct* method.
2. Evaluate the company's cash flows for the year. In your evaluation, mention all three categories of cash flows and give the rationale for your evaluation.

E11-25A. ***(Learning Objective 4: Calculate amounts for the statement of cash flows—direct method)*** Calculate the following items for the statement of cash flows: LO 4

a. Beginning and ending Accounts Receivable were $28,000 and $27,000, respectively. Credit sales for the period totaled $66,000. How much were the cash collections from customers?

b. Cost of Goods Sold was $75,000. Beginning Inventory was $25,000, and Ending Inventory was $24,000. Beginning and ending Accounts Payable were $16,000 and $13,000, respectively. How much were the cash payments for inventory?

Group B

LO **2, 3**

E11-26B. ***(Learning Objectives 2, 3: Distinguish among operating, investing, and financing activities for the statement of cash flows—indirect method)*** Vanderpool Investments specializes in low-risk government bonds. Identify each of Vanderpool's transactions as operating (O), investing (I), financing (F), noncash investing and financing (NIF), or a transaction that is not reported on the statement of cash flows (N). Indicate whether each item increases (+) or decreases (−) cash. The *indirect* method is used for operating cash flows.

	a. Issuance of long-term note payable to borrow cash
	b. Purchase of treasury stock
	c. Net income
	d. Loss on sale of equipment
	e. Decrease in accounts receivable
	f. Acquisition of equipment by issuance of note payable
	g. Increase in accounts payable
	h. Payment of cash dividend
	i. Purchase of long-term investment with cash
	j. Cash sale of land
	k. Increase in prepaid expenses
	l. Increase in salary payable
	m. Depreciation of equipment
	n. Sale of long-term investment
	o. Issuance of common stock for cash
	p. Decrease in accrued liabilities
	q. Amortization of intangible assets
	r. Acquisition of building by cash payment
	s. Payment of long-term debt

LO **2, 3**

E11-27B. ***(Learning Objectives 2, 3: Distinguish among operating, investing, and financing activities for the statement of cash flows—indirect method)*** A company uses the indirect method to prepare the statement of cash flows. Indicate whether each of the following transactions affects an operating activity, an investing activity, a financing activity, or a noncash investing and financing activity.

	A	B	C	D	E	F	G	H
1	a.	Equipment	28,000		h.	Dividends Payable	25,000	
2		Cash		28,000		Cash		25,000
3	b.	Bonds Payable	70,000		i.	Treasury Stock	12,000	
4		Cash		70,000		Cash		12,000
5	c.	Cash	110,000		j.	Land	123,000	
6		Common Stock		17,000		Cash		123,000
7		Paid-in Capital in Excess of Par		93,000	k.	Cash	74,000	
8	d.	Depreciation Expense	16,000			Accounts Receivable	13,000	
9		Accumulated Depreciation		16,000		Service Revenue		87,000
10	e.	Loss on Disposal of Equipment	2,000		l.	Salary Expense	36,000	
11		Equipment, Net		2,000		Cash		36,000
12	f.	Building	235,000		m.	Furniture and Fixtures	36,000	
13		Note Payable, Long-Term		235,000		Cash		36,000
14	g.	Cash	10,000					
15		Long-Term Investment		10,000				
16								

E11-28B. ***(Learning Objective 3: Calculate cash flows from operating activities—indirect method)*** The accounting records of Steven Corporation reveal the following: LO **3**

Net income	$ 38,000	Depreciation expense	$ 13,000
Collection of dividend revenue	6,900	Increase in current liabilities	15,000
Payment of interest	19,000	Increase in current assets other than cash	24,000
Sales revenue	215,000		
Loss on sale of land	20,000	Payment of dividends	7,400
Acquisition of land with cash	43,000	Payment of income tax	15,000

Requirements

1. Prepare the cash flows from operating activities section of the statement of cash flows using the *indirect* method.
2. Evaluate the operating cash flow of Steven Corporation. Explain.

E11-29B. ***(Learning Objective 3: Calculate cash flows from operating activities—indirect method)*** The accounting records of the Ashby Trading Post Company include these accounts: LO **3**

Cash

Jul 1	40,000		
Receipts	491,000	Payments	436,000
Jul 31	95,000		

Accounts Receivable

Jul 1	4,000		
Credit sales	531,000	Collections	401,000
Jul 31	134,000		

Inventory

Jul 1	1,000		
Purchases	402,000	Cost of Sales	312,000
Jul 31	91,000		

Equipment

Jul 1	185,000		
Acquisition	12,000		
Jul 31	197,000		

Accumulated Deprec.—Equipment

		Jul 1	53,000
		Depreciation	11,000
		Jul 31	64,000

Accounts Payable

		Jul 1	10,000
Payments	334,000	Purchases	402,000
		Jul 31	78,000

Accrued Liabilities

		Jul 1	19,000
Payments	32,000	Accruals	27,000
		Jul 31	14,000

Retained Earnings

		Jul 1	68,000
Quarterly Dividend	22,000	Net Income	17,000
		Jul 31	63,000

Requirement

1. Prepare the company's net cash provided by (used for) operating activities section of the statement of cash flows for the month of July. Use the *indirect* method. Do you see any potential problems in the company's cash flows from operations? How can you tell?

E11-30B. ***(Learning Objective 3: Prepare the statement of cash flows—indirect method)*** The income statement and additional data of Casey Travel Products, Inc., follow: LO **3**

A1

	A	B	C
1	**Casey Travel Products, Inc.** **Income Statement** **Year Ended December 31, 2018**		
2	Revenues:		
3	Service revenue	$ 239,000	
4	Dividend revenue	8,500	$ 247,500
5	Expenses:		
6	Cost of goods sold	100,000	
7	Salary expense	54,000	
8	Depreciation expense	26,000	
9	Advertising expense	4,600	
10	Interest expense	2,500	
11	Income tax expense	12,000	199,100
12	Net income		$ 48,400
13			

Additional data:

a. Acquisition of plant assets was $153,000. Of this amount, $102,000 was paid in cash and $51,000 was financed by signing a note payable.
b. Proceeds from the sale of land totaled $45,000.
c. Proceeds from the issuance of common stock totaled $80,000.
d. Payment of a long-term note payable was $18,000.
e. Payment of dividends was $14,000.
f. From the balance sheets:

	A	B	C
1		December 31,	
2		2018	2017
3	**Current assets:**		
4	Cash	$ 75,000	$ 8,700
5	Accounts receivable	40,000	58,000
6	Inventory	50,000	72,000
7	Prepaid expenses	9,200	8,100
8			
9	**Current liabilities:**		
10	Accounts payable	$ 32,000	$ 12,000
11	Accrued liabilities	21,000	79,000
12			

Requirements

1. Prepare Casey's statement of cash flows for the year ended December 31, 2018, using the *indirect* method.
2. Evaluate the company's cash flows for the year. In your evaluation, mention all three categories of cash flows and give the rationale for your evaluation.

LO **3**

E11-31B. ***(Learning Objective 3: Evaluate a statement of cash flows—indirect method)*** Consider three independent cases for the cash flows of Lucky Merchandise Company. For each case, identify from the statement of cash flows how the company generated the cash to acquire new plant assets. Rank the three cases from the most healthy financially to the least healthy.

	A	B	C	D
1		Case A	Case B	Case C
2	Cash flows from operating activities:			
3	Net income	$ 14,000	$ 14,000	$ 14,000
4	Depreciation and amortization	17,000	17,000	17,000
5	Increase in current assets other than cash	(7,000)	(3,000)	(1,000)
6	Decrease in current liabilities	(27,000)	(4,000)	(3,000)
7		(3,000)	24,000	27,000
8	Cash flows from investing activities:			
9	Acquisition of plant assets	(141,000)	(141,000)	(141,000)
10	Sales of plant assets	28,000	47,000	148,000
11		(113,000)	(94,000)	7,000
12	Cash flows from financing activities:			
13	Issuance of stock	149,000	104,000	26,000
14	Payment of debt	(28,000)	(45,000)	(38,000)
15		121,000	59,000	(12,000)
16	Net increase (decrease) in cash	$ 5,000	$ (11,000)	$ 22,000
17				

E11-32B. ***(Learning Objectives 3, 4: Calculate investing and financing amounts for the statement of cash flows)*** Calculate the following items for the statement of cash flows: LO 3, 4

a. Beginning and ending Plant Assets, Net, were $101,000 and $98,000, respectively. Depreciation for the period was $20,000, and purchases of new plant assets were $38,000. Plant assets were sold at a loss of $3,000. What were the cash proceeds of the sale?

b. Beginning and ending Retained Earnings were $46,000 and $70,000, respectively. Net income for the period was $63,000, and stock dividends were $15,000. How much were the cash dividends?

E11-33B. ***(Learning Objective 4: Calculate cash flows from operating activities—direct method)*** The accounting records of Pepperell Pharmaceuticals, Inc., reveal the following: LO 4

Payment of salaries and wages	$ 31,000	Net income	$40,000
Depreciation expense	21,000	Payment of income tax	11,000
Increase in current liabilities	23,000	Collection of dividend revenue	4,000
Increase in current assets other than cash	26,000	Payment of interest	19,000
Payment of dividends	3,000	Cash sales	20,000
Collection of accounts receivable	117,000	Loss on sale of land	4,000
		Acquisition of land with cash	25,000
		Payment of accounts payable	55,000

Requirement

1. Prepare cash flows from operating activities using the *direct* method. Also evaluate Pepperell's operating cash flow. Give the rationale for your evaluation.

E11-34B. ***(Learning Objective 4: Identify items for the statement of cash flows—direct method)*** Selected accounts of Roosevelt Framing Company show the following: LO 4

Salaries Payable

		Beginning bal	11,000
Payments	15,000	Salary expense	32,000
		Ending bal	28,000

Buildings

Beginning bal	75,000	Depreciation	17,000
Acquisitions with cash	116,000	Book value of building sold	88,000*
Ending bal	86,000		

*Sale price was $120,000.

Notes Payable

		Beginning bal	183,000
Payments	54,000	Issuance of note payable for cash	68,000
		Ending bal	197,000

Requirement

1. For each account, identify the item or items that should appear on a statement of cash flows prepared using the *direct* method. State where to report the item.

LO 4

E11-35B. ***(Learning Objective 4: Prepare the statement of cash flows—direct method)*** The income statement and additional data of Jubilee World, Inc., follow:

	A	B	C
1	**Jubilee World, Inc.** **Income Statement** **Year Ended June 30, 2018**		
2	**Revenues:**		
3	Sales revenue	$ 222,000	
4	Dividend revenue	11,500	$ 233,500
5	**Expenses:**		
6	Cost of goods sold	102,000	
7	Salary expense	42,000	
8	Depreciation expense	28,000	
9	Advertising expense	8,000	
10	Interest expense	2,500	
11	Income tax expense	10,500	193,000
12	Net income		$ 40,500
13			

Additional data:

a. Collections from customers are $15,500 more than sales.
b. Payments to suppliers are $1,700 less than the sum of cost of goods sold plus advertising expense.
c. Payments to employees are $2,200 less than salary expense.
d. Dividend revenue, interest expense, and income tax expense equal their cash amounts.
e. Acquisition of plant assets is $176,000. Of this amount, $122,000 is paid in cash and $54,000 is financed by signing a long-term note payable.
f. Proceeds from the sale of land totaled $24,000.
g. Proceeds from the issuance of common stock totaled $39,000.
h. Payment of a long-term note payable is $20,000.
i. Payment of dividends is $7,000.
j. Cash balance, June 30, 2017, was $32,000.

Requirements

1. Prepare Jubilee World's statement of cash flows and accompanying schedule of noncash investing and financing activities. Report operating activities using the *direct* method.
2. Evaluate the company's cash flows for the year. In your evaluation, mention all three categories of cash flows and give the rationale for your evaluation.

LO 4

E11-36B. ***(Learning Objective 4: Calculate amounts for the statement of cash flows—direct method)*** Calculate the following items for the statement of cash flows:

a. Beginning and ending Accounts Receivable were $25,000 and $24,000, respectively. Credit sales for the period totaled $69,000. How much were the cash collections from customers?
b. Cost of Goods Sold was $71,000. Beginning Inventory was $29,000, and Ending Inventory was $33,000. Beginning and ending Accounts Payable were $16,000 and $19,000, respectively. How much were the cash payments for inventory?

Quiz

Test your understanding of the statement of cash flows by answering the following questions. Select the best choice from among the possible answers given.

Q11-37. Paying off bonds payable is reported on the statement of cash flows under

a. noncash investing and financing activities.
b. financing activities.
c. operating activities.
d. investing activities.

Q11-38. The issuance of stock for cash is reported on the statement of cash flows under

a. financing activities.
b. operating activities.
c. noncash investing and financing activities.
d. investing activities.

Q11-39. Selling equipment for cash is reported on the statement of cash flows under

a. operating activities.
b. investing activities.
c. financing activities.
d. noncash investing and financing activities.

Q11-40. If the indirect method is used, which of the following items appears on a statement of cash flows?

a. Collections from customers
b. Payments to suppliers
c. Cash receipt of interest revenue
d. Depreciation expense

Q11-41. On an indirect method statement of cash flows, an increase in prepaid insurance is

a. added to net income.
b. added to increases in current assets.
c. deducted from net income.
d. included in payments to suppliers.

Q11-42. On an indirect method statement of cash flows, an increase in accounts payable is

a. deducted from net income in the operating activities section.
b. reported in the financing activities section.
c. added to net income in the operating activities section.
d. reported in the investing activities section.

Q11-43. On an indirect method statement of cash flows, a gain on the sale of plant assets is

a. added to net income in the operating activities section.
b. deducted from net income in the operating activities section.
c. reported in the investing activities section.
d. ignored, because the gain did not generate any cash.

Q11-44. A company uses the direct method to prepare the statement of cash flows. Select an activity for each of the following transactions:

1. Receiving cash dividends is a/an ____________ activity.
2. Paying cash dividends is a/an ____________ activity.

Q11-45. PhotoEase Camera Co. sold equipment with a cost of $19,000 and accumulated depreciation of $7,000 for an amount that resulted in a gain of $1,000. What amount should PhotoEase report on the statement of cash flows as "proceeds from sale of plant assets"?

a. $13,000
b. $11,000
c. $12,000
d. Some other amount

Questions 46–56 use the following data. Cramer Corporation formats operating cash flows using the ***indirect*** method in questions 46–54. Cramer uses the direct method in questions 55–56.

	A	B	C
1	**Cramer's Income Statement for 2018**		
2	Sales revenue	$ 170,000	
3	Gain on sale of equipment	10,000*	$ 180,000
4	Cost of goods sold	$ 110,000	
5	Depreciation	7,500	
6	Other operating expenses	27,000	144,500
7	Net income		$ 35,500
8			

*The book value of equipment sold during 2018 was $22,000.

	A	B	C	D	E	F
1	**Cramer's Comparative Balance Sheets December 31, 2018 and 2017**					
2		**2018**	**2017**		**2018**	**2017**
3	Cash	$ 3,500	$ 2,000	Accounts payable	$ 7,000	$ 8,000
4	Accounts receivable	6,000	11,000	Accrued liabilities	9,000	1,000
5	Inventory	8,000	7,000	Common stock	20,000	10,000
6	Plant and equipment, net	89,000	71,000	Retained earnings	70,500	72,000
7		$ 106,500	$ 91,000		$ 106,500	$ 91,000
8						

Q11-46. How many items enter the computation of Cramer's net cash provided by operating activities?

a. 2
b. 3
c. 7
d. 5

Q11-47. How do Cramer's accrued liabilities affect the company's statement of cash flows for 2018?

a. They increase cash used by financing activities.
b. They increase cash provided by operating activities.
c. They increase cash used by investing activities.
d. They don't because the accrued liabilities are not yet paid.

Q11-48. How do accounts receivable affect Cramer's cash flows from operating activities for 2018?

a. They increase cash provided by operating activities.
b. They don't because accounts receivable result from investing activities.
c. They decrease cash used by investing activities.
d. They decrease cash provided by operating activities.

Q11-49. Cramer's net cash provided by operating activities during 2018 was

a. $32,000.
b. $33,000.
c. $37,000.
d. $44,000.

Q11-50. How many items enter the computation of Cramer's net cash flow from investing activities for 2018?

a. 7
b. 2
c. 3
d. 5

Q11-51. The book value of equipment sold during 2018 was $22,000. Cramer's net cash flow from investing activities for 2018 was

a. net cash used of $10,000.
b. net cash used of $47,500.
c. net cash used of $15,500.
d. net cash used of $32,000.

Q11-52. How many items enter the computation of Cramer's net cash flow from financing activities for 2018?

a. 2
b. 5
c. 7
d. 3

Q11-53. Cramer's largest financing cash flow for 2018 resulted from (assume no stock dividends were distributed)

a. issuing common stock.
b. paying dividends.
c. purchasing equipment.
d. selling equipment.

Q11-54. Cramer's net cash flow from financing activities for 2018 was (assume no stock dividends were distributed)

a. net cash provided of $10,000.
b. net cash used of $26,500.
c. net cash used of $27,000.
d. net cash used of $45,000.

Q11-55. Assume Cramer uses the direct method to prepare the statement of cash flows. Credit sales totaled $750,000, accounts receivable increased by $40,000, and accounts payable decreased by $25,000. How much cash did the company collect from customers?

a. $710,000
b. $735,000
c. $790,000
d. $750,000

Q11-56. Assume Cramer uses the direct method to prepare the statement of cash flows. Income tax payable was $6,500 at the end of the year, and $3,100 at the beginning of the year. Income tax expense for the year totaled $58,900. What amount of cash did the company pay for income taxes during the year?

a. $55,500
b. $62,000
c. $58,900
d. $62,300

Problems MyLab Accounting

Group A

P11-57A. ***(Learning Objectives 2, 3: Prepare an income statement, balance sheet, and statement of cash flows—indirect method)*** Coleman Motors, Inc., was formed on January 1, 2018. The following transactions occurred during 2018: LO 2, 3

On January 1, 2018, Coleman issued its common stock for $350,000. Early in January, Coleman made the following cash payments:

a. $140,000 for equipment
b. $175,000 for inventory (five cars at $35,000 each)
c. $19,000 for 2018 rent on a store building

In February, Coleman purchased six cars for inventory on account. The cost of this inventory was $282,000 ($47,000 per car). Before year-end, the company paid off $197,400 of this debt. The company uses the first-in, first-out (FIFO) method to account for its inventory.

During 2018, Coleman sold six autos for a total of $426,000. Before year-end, it had collected 90% of this amount.

The business employs three people. The combined annual payroll is $90,000, of which Coleman owes $5,000 at year-end. At the end of the year, the company paid income taxes of $14,000.

Late in 2018, Coleman declared and paid cash dividends of $29,000.

For equipment, Coleman uses the straight-line depreciation method, over five years, with zero residual value.

Requirements

1. Prepare Coleman's income statement for the year ended December 31, 2018. Use the single-step format, with all revenues listed together and all expenses together.
2. Prepare Coleman's balance sheet at December 31, 2018.
3. Prepare Coleman's statement of cash flows for the year ended December 31, 2018. Format cash flows from operating activities using the *indirect* method.

LO 2, 4

P11-58A. ***(Learning Objectives 2, 4: Prepare an income statement, balance sheet, and statement of cash flows—direct method)*** Use the Coleman Motors data from P11-57A.

Requirements

1. Prepare Coleman's income statement for the year ended December 31, 2018. Use the single-step format, with all revenues listed together and all expenses together.
2. Prepare Coleman's balance sheet at December 31, 2018.
3. Prepare Coleman's statement of cash flows for the year ended December 31, 2018. Format cash flows from operating activities using the *direct* method.

LO 2, 3

P11-59A. ***(Learning Objectives 2, 3: Prepare the statement of cash flows—indirect method)*** Smither Software Corp. has assembled the following data for the years ending December 31, 2018 and 2017.

	A	B	C
1		December 31,	
2		2018	2017
3	**Current Accounts:**		
4	Current assets:		
5	Cash and cash equivalents	$ 66,500	$ 26,000
6	Accounts receivable	21,000	64,300
7	Inventories	89,500	79,000
8	Prepaid expenses	3,600	2,300
9	Current liabilities:		
10	Accounts payable	$ 58,100	$ 55,300
11	Income tax payable	18,500	16,200
12	Accrued liabilities	15,100	17,200
13			

Transaction Data for 2018:

Acquisition of land by issuing long-term note payable	$204,000	Purchase of treasury stock	$14,500
Stock dividends	31,400	Loss on sale of equipment	4,000
Collection of loan	11,000	Payment of cash dividends	19,000
Depreciation expense	21,000	Issuance of long-term note payable to borrow cash	24,400
Purchase of building with cash	97,000	Net income	66,000
Retirement of bonds payable by issuing common stock	60,000	Issuance of common stock for cash	37,000
Purchase of long-term investment with cash	44,700	Proceeds from sale of equipment	12,700
		Amortization expense	5,100

Requirement

1. Prepare Smither's statement of cash flows using the *indirect* method to report operating activities. Include a schedule of noncash investing and financing activities.

P11-60A. *(Learning Objectives 2, 3: Prepare the statement of cash flows—indirect method)* The comparative balance sheets of Bedford Movie Theater Company at November 30, 2018, and 2017, reported the following:

LO 2, 3

	A	B	C
1		November 30,	
2		2018	2017
3	**Current assets:**		
4	Cash and cash equivalents	$ 13,600	$ 15,500
5	Accounts receivable	14,400	21,600
6	Inventories	63,700	60,700
7	Prepaid expenses	3,500	8,000
8	**Current liabilities:**		
9	Accounts payable	$ 57,600	$ 56,100
10	Accrued liabilities	46,800	26,800
11	Income tax payable	6,600	10,600
12			

Bedford's transactions during the year ended November 30, 2018, included:

Acquisition of land by issuing note payable	$96,000	Proceeds from sale of long-term investment	$16,300
Amortization expense............	7,000	Depreciation expense	15,300
Payment of cash dividend......	25,000	Cash purchase of building.....	50,000
Cash purchase of equipment	56,700	Net income...........................	11,000
Issuance of long-term note payable to borrow cash.....	41,000	Issuance of common stock for cash....................	13,000
		Stock dividend......................	17,000

Requirements

1. Prepare Bedford Movie Theater Company's statement of cash flows for the year ended November 30, 2018, using the *indirect* method to report cash flows from operating activities. Report noncash investing and financing activities in an accompanying schedule.
2. Evaluate Bedford's cash flows for the year. Mention all three categories of cash flows, and give the rationale for your evaluation.

LO 2, 3

P11-61A. ***(Learning Objectives 2, 3: Prepare the statement of cash flows—indirect method)*** The 2018 and 2017 comparative balance sheets and 2018 income statement of Queen Supply Corp. follow:

	A	B	C	D
1	**Queen Supply Corp. Comparative Balance Sheets**			
2		**December 31,**		**Increase**
3		**2018**	**2017**	**(Decrease)**
4	Current assets:			
5	Cash and cash equivalents	$ 17,800	$ 9,000	$ 8,800
6	Accounts receivable	50,200	42,000	8,200
7	Inventories	56,700	43,300	13,400
8	Prepaid expenses	2,300	5,000	(2,700)
9	Plant assets:			
10	Land	68,500	30,800	37,700
11	Equipment, net	53,700	49,000	4,700
12	Total assets	$ 249,200	$ 179,100	$ 70,100
13	Current liabilities:			
14	Accounts payable	$ 35,700	$ 26,500	$ 9,200
15	Salary payable	27,000	18,100	8,900
16	Other accrued liabilities	21,200	23,900	(2,700)
17	Long-term liabilities:			
18	Notes payable	65,000	27,000	38,000
19	Stockholders' equity:			
20	Common stock, no-par	88,000	64,400	23,600
21	Retained earnings	12,300	19,200	(6,900)
22	Total liabilities and stockholders' equity	$ 249,200	$ 179,100	$ 70,100
23				

	A	B	C
1	**Queen Supply Corp. Income Statement Year Ended December 31, 2018**		
2	Revenues:		
3	Sales revenue		$ 439,000
4	Expenses:		
5	Cost of goods sold	$ 186,600	
6	Salary expense	77,000	
7	Depreciation expense	16,800	
8	Other operating expense	49,600	
9	Interest expense	24,800	
10	Income tax expense	28,700	
11	Total expenses		383,500
12	Net income		$ 55,500
13			

Queen Supply had no noncash investing and financing transactions during 2018. During the year, there were no sales of land or equipment, no payment of notes payable, no retirements of stock, and no treasury stock transactions.

Requirements

1. Prepare Queen Supply's 2018 statement of cash flows. Use the indirect method to format operating activities.
2. How can the concepts used in this problem help you evaluate an investment?

LO 2, 4

P11-62A. ***(Learning Objectives 2, 4: Prepare the statement of cash flows—direct method)*** Use the Queen Supply Corp. data from P11-61A.

Requirements

1. Prepare the company's 2018 statement of cash flows using the *direct* method.
2. How can the concepts used in this problem help you evaluate an investment?

LO 2, 4

P11-63A. ***(Learning Objectives 2, 4: Prepare the statement of cash flows—direct method)*** Rourke Furniture Gallery, Inc., provided the following data from the company's records for the year ended March 31, 2019:

a. Credit sales, $583,800
b. Loan to another company, $10,000
c. Cash payments to purchase plant assets, $89,300
d. Cost of goods sold, $282,900
e. Proceeds from the issuance of common stock, $5,000
f. Payment of cash dividends, $48,500
g. Collection of interest, $5,100
h. Acquisition of equipment by issuing a short-term note payable, $16,700
i. Payments of salaries, $78,500
j. Proceeds from the sale of plant assets, $22,200, including a $6,800 loss
k. Collections on accounts receivable, $421,000
l. Interest revenue, $3,300
m. Cash receipt of dividend revenue, $8,900
n. Payments to suppliers, $379,100
o. Cash sales, $199,400
p. Depreciation expense, $59,500
q. Proceeds from the issuance of note payable, $24,500
r. Payments of long-term notes payable, $52,000
s. Interest expense and payments, $12,900
t. Salary expense, $77,100
u. Loan collections, $11,300
v. Proceeds from the sale of investments, $9,100, including a $1,700 gain
w. Payment of a short-term note payable by issuing a long-term note payable, $60,000
x. Amortization expenses, $2,800
y. Income tax expense and payments, $38,100
z. Cash balance: March 31, 2018, $89,900; March 31, 2019, $88,000

Requirements

1. Prepare Rourke Furniture Gallery's statement of cash flows for the year ended March 31, 2019. Use the *direct* method for cash flows from operating activities. Include an accompanying schedule of noncash investing and financing activities.
2. Evaluate the company's fiscal year ended March 31, 2019, from a cash flow standpoint.

LO 2, 3, 4

P11-64A. *(Learning Objectives 2, 3, 4: Prepare the statement of cash flows—direct and indirect methods)* To prepare the statement of cash flows, accountants for Ronklin Electric Company have summarized 2018 activity in two accounts:

Cash

Beginning bal	34,900	Payments on accounts payable	387,000
Sale of long-term investment	18,700	Payments of dividends	27,000
Collections from customers	661,900	Payments of salaries and wages	143,100
Issuance of common stock	37,900	Payments of interest	23,100
Receipts of dividends	17,000	Purchase of equipment	31,500
		Payments of other operating expenses	34,700
		Payment of long-term note payable	41,500
		Purchase of treasury stock	21,200
		Payment of income tax	18,400
Ending Bal	42,900		

Common Stock

		Beginning bal	89,100
		Issuance for cash	37,900
		Issuance to acquire land	53,000
		Issuance to retire note payable	15,000
		Ending bal	195,000

Ronklin Electric's 2018 income statement and balance sheet data follow:

A1

	A	B	C
1	**Ronklin Electric Company** **Income Statement** **Year Ended December 31, 2018**		
2	Revenues:		
3	Sales revenue		$ 643,900
4	Dividend revenue		17,000
5	Total revenue		660,900
6	Expenses and losses:		
7	Cost of goods sold	$ 390,500	
8	Salary and wage expense	135,300	
9	Depreciation expense	19,400	
10	Other operating expense	45,200	
11	Interest expense	20,900	
12	Income tax expense	15,800	
13	Loss on sale of investments	20,300	
14	Total expenses and losses		647,400
15	Net income		$ 13,500
16			

	A	B
1	**Ronklin Electric Company** **Selected Balance Sheet Data** **December 31, 2018**	
2		**Increase (Decrease)**
3	Current assets:	
4	Cash and cash equivalents	$ 8,000
5	Accounts receivable	(18,000)
6	Inventories	(11,800)
7	Prepaid expenses	200
8	Land	53,000
9	Equipment, net	12,100
10	Long-term investments	(39,000)
11	Current liabilities:	
12	Accounts payable	(8,300)
13	Interest payable	(2,200)
14	Salary payable	(7,800)
15	Other accrued liabilities	10,700
16	Income tax payable	(2,600)
17	Long-term note payable	(56,500)
18	Common stock	105,900
19	Retained earnings	(13,500)
20	Treasury stock	21,200
21		

Requirements

1. Prepare the statement of cash flows of Ronklin Electric for the year ended December 31, 2018, using the *direct* method to report operating activities. Also prepare the accompanying schedule of noncash investing and financing activities.
2. Use Ronklin Electric's 2018 income statement and information from its selected balance sheet data to prepare a supplementary schedule of cash flows from operating activities using the *indirect* method.

LO **2, 3, 4**

P11-65A. ***(Learning Objectives 2, 3, 4: Prepare the statement of cash flows—indirect and direct methods)*** The comparative balance sheets of American-Davis Design Studio, Inc., at June 30, 2018, and 2017, and transaction data for fiscal 2018, are as follows:

	A	B	C	D
1	**American-Davis Design Studio, Inc.** **Comparative Balance Sheets**			
2		**June 30,**		**Increase**
3		**2018**	**2017**	**(Decrease)**
4	Current assets:			
5	Cash	$ 23,700	$ 19,000	$ 4,700
6	Accounts receivable	48,400	22,800	25,600
7	Inventories	98,300	50,200	48,100
8	Prepaid expenses	1,900	3,000	(1,100)
9	Land	42,900	89,900	(47,000)
10	Equipment, net	74,800	72,900	1,900
11	Long-term investment	22,000	6,200	15,800
12		$ 312,000	$ 264,000	$ 48,000
13	Current liabilities:			
14	Notes payable, short-term	$ 13,600	$ 18,500	$ (4,900)
15	Accounts payable	29,600	40,800	(11,200)
16	Income tax payable	13,000	15,300	(2,300)
17	Accrued liabilities	55,700	9,300	46,400
18	Interest payable	3,500	2,900	600
19	Salary payable	4,500	5,200	(700)
20	Long-term note payable	52,100	98,000	(45,900)
21	Common stock	65,800	52,600	13,200
22	Retained earnings	74,200	21,400	52,800
23		$ 312,000	$ 264,000	$ 48,000
24				

Transaction data for the year ended June 30, 2018, follows:

a. Net income, $60,500
b. Depreciation expense on equipment, $13,000
c. Purchased a long-term investment with cash, $15,800
d. Sold land for $39,900, including a $7,100 loss
e. Acquired equipment by issuing a long-term note payable, $14,900
f. Paid off a long-term note payable, $60,800
g. Received cash for the issuance of common stock, $8,300
h. Paid cash dividends, $7,700
i. Paid off a short-term note payable by issuing common stock, $4,900

Requirements

1. Prepare the statement of cash flows of American-Davis Design Studio for the year ended June 30, 2018, using the *indirect* method to report operating activities. Also prepare the accompanying schedule of noncash investing and financing activities. All current account changes except for the short-term Notes Payable changes result from operating transactions.
2. Prepare a supplementary schedule showing cash flows from operations using the *direct* method. The accounting records provide the following: collections from customers, $254,300; interest received, $2,000; payments to suppliers, $147,200; payments to employees, $49,200; payments for income tax, $13,500; and payment of interest, $5,600.

Group B

LO 2, 3

P11-66B. ***(Learning Objectives 2, 3: Prepare an income statement, balance sheet, and statement of cash flows—indirect method)*** Vintage Motors, Inc., was formed on January 1, 2018. The following transactions occurred during 2018:

On January 1, 2018, Vintage issued its common stock for $430,000. Early in January, Vintage made the following cash payments:

a. $160,000 for equipment
b. $234,000 for inventory (six cars at $39,000 each)
c. $18,000 for 2018 rent on a store building

In February, Vintage purchased four cars for inventory on account. The cost of this inventory was $192,000 ($48,000 per car). Before year-end, the company paid off $153,600 of this debt. The company uses the first-in, first-out (FIFO) method to account for its inventory.

During 2018, Vintage sold seven autos for a total of $504,000. Before year-end, it had collected 90% of this amount.

The business employs two people. The combined annual payroll is $60,000, of which Vintage owes $11,000 at year-end. At the end of the year, the company paid income taxes of $22,000.

Late in 2018, Vintage declared and paid cash dividends of $13,000.

For equipment, Vintage uses the straight-line depreciation method, over five years, with zero residual value.

Requirements

1. Prepare Vintage's income statement for the year ended December 31, 2018. Use the single-step format, with all revenues listed together and all expenses together.
2. Prepare Vintage's balance sheet at December 31, 2018.
3. Prepare Vintage's statement of cash flows for the year ended December 31, 2018. Format cash flows from operating activities using the *indirect* method.

LO 2, 4

P11-67B. ***(Learning Objectives 2, 4: Prepare an income statement, balance sheet, and statement of cash flows—direct method)*** Use the Vintage Motors data from P11-66B.

Requirements

1. Prepare Vintage's income statement for the year ended December 31, 2018. Use the single-step format, with all revenues listed together and all expenses together.
2. Prepare Vintage's balance sheet at December 31, 2018.
3. Prepare Vintage's statement of cash flows for the year ended December 31, 2018. Format cash flows from operating activities using the *direct* method.

LO 2, 3

P11-68B. ***(Learning Objectives 2, 3: Prepare the statement of cash flows—indirect method)*** Fortune Software Corp. has assembled the following data for the years ending December 31, 2018 and 2017:

A1

	A	B	C
1		December 31,	
2		2018	2017
3	**Current Accounts:**		
4	Current assets:		
5	Cash and cash equivalents	$ 95,900	$ 20,000
6	Accounts receivable	70,100	64,600
7	Inventories	8,800	80,000
8	Prepaid expenses	3,400	2,400
9	Current liabilities:		
10	Accounts payable	$ 57,300	$ 55,900
11	Income tax payable	29,000	16,400
12	Accrued liabilities	15,000	27,900
13			

Transaction Data for 2018:			
Acquisition of land by issuing long-term note payable	$195,000	Purchase of treasury stock	$11,800
Stock dividends	21,700	Gain on sale of equipment	2,000
Collection of loan	10,500	Payment of cash dividends	15,100
Depreciation expense	19,000	Issuance of long-term note payable to borrow cash	50,600
Purchase of building with cash	123,000	Net income	62,000
Retirement of bonds payable by issuing common stock	60,000	Issuance of common stock for cash	36,700
Purchase of long-term investment with cash	45,300	Proceeds from sale of equipment	24,300
		Amortization expense	4,200

Requirement

1. Prepare Fortune's statement of cash flows using the *indirect* method to report operating activities. Include a schedule of noncash investing and financing activities.

LO **2, 3**

P11-69B. ***(Learning Objectives 2, 3: Prepare the statement of cash flows—indirect method)*** The comparative balance sheets of Shaw Movie Theater Company at June 30, 2018 and 2017, reported the following:

	A	B	C
1		June 30,	
2		2018	2017
3	**Current assets:**		
4	Cash and cash equivalents	$ 3,600	$ 15,000
5	Accounts receivable	14,700	22,000
6	Inventories	63,400	60,300
7	Prepaid expenses	3,700	4,000
8	**Current liabilities:**		
9	Accounts payable	$ 58,100	$ 56,200
10	Accrued liabilities	23,900	16,900
11	Income tax payable	9,600	10,700
12			

Shaw's transactions during the year ended June 30, 2018, included the following:

Acquisition of land by issuing note payable	$96,000	Proceeds from sale of long-term investment	$ 12,300
Amortization expense	9,000	Depreciation expense	15,000
Payment of cash dividend	25,000	Cash purchase of building	52,000
Cash purchase of equipment	79,000	Net income	44,000
Issuance of long-term note payable to borrow cash	43,000	Issuance of common stock for cash	9,000
		Stock dividend	15,000

Requirements

1. Prepare Shaw Movie Theater Company's statement of cash flows for the year ended June 30, 2018, using the *indirect* method to report cash flows from operating activities. Report noncash investing and financing activities in an accompanying schedule.
2. Evaluate Shaw's cash flows for the year. Mention all three categories of cash flows, and give the rationale for your evaluation.

LO **2, 3**

P11-70B. ***(Learning Objectives 2, 3: Prepare the statement of cash flows—indirect method)*** The 2018 and 2017 comparative balance sheets and 2018 income statement of Mercedes Supply Corp. follow:

	A	B	C	D
1	**Mercedes Supply Corp.** **Comparative Balance Sheets**			
2		**December 31,**		**Increase**
3		**2018**	**2017**	**(Decrease)**
4	Current assets:			
5	Cash and cash equivalents	$ 17,600	$ 1,000	$ 16,600
6	Accounts receivable	38,500	43,500	(5,000)
7	Inventories	48,200	47,000	1,200
8	Prepaid expenses	1,600	4,800	(3,200)
9	Plant assets:			
10	Land	61,700	23,700	38,000
11	Equipment, net	63,200	49,400	13,800
12	Total assets	$ 230,800	$ 169,400	$ 61,400
13	Current liabilities:			
14	Accounts payable	$ 36,000	$ 31,300	$ 4,700
15	Salary payable	21,000	13,000	8,000
16	Other accrued liabilities	21,300	24,500	(3,200)
17	Long-term liabilities:			
18	Notes payable	56,000	34,000	22,000
19	Stockholders' equity:			
20	Common stock, no-par	88,500	63,700	24,800
21	Retained earnings	8,000	2,900	5,100
22	Total liabilities and stockholders' equity	$ 230,800	$ 169,400	$ 61,400
23				

	A	B	C
1	**Mercedes Supply Corp.** **Income Statement** **Year Ended December 31, 2018**		
2	Revenues:		
3	Sales revenue		$ 440,000
4	Expenses:		
5	Cost of goods sold	$ 185,500	
6	Salary expense	76,700	
7	Depreciation expense	14,600	
8	Other operating expense	50,600	
9	Interest expense	25,000	
10	Income tax expense	28,800	
11	Total expenses		381,200
12	Net income		$ 58,800
13			

Mercedes Supply had no noncash investing and financing transactions during 2018. During the year, there were no sales of land or equipment, no payment of notes payable, no retirements of stock, and no treasury stock transactions.

Requirements

1. Prepare Mercedes Supply's 2018 statement of cash flows. Use the indirect method to format operating activities.
2. How can the concepts used in this problem help you evaluate an investment?

LO 2, 4

P11-71B. ***(Learning Objectives 2, 4: Prepare the statement of cash flows—direct method)*** Use the Mercedes Supply Corp. data from P11-70B.

Requirements

1. Prepare the company's 2018 statement of cash flows using the *direct* method.
2. How can the concepts used in this problem help you evaluate an investment?

LO 2, 4

P11-72B. ***(Learning Objectives 2, 4: Prepare the statement of cash flows—direct method)*** Ballinger Furniture Gallery, Inc., provided the following data from the company's records for the year ended August 31, 2019:

a. Credit sales, $574,400
b. Loan to another company, $13,000
c. Cash payments to purchase plant assets, $37,600
d. Cost of goods sold, $382,700
e. Proceeds from the issuance of common stock, $8,000
f. Payment of cash dividends, $47,700
g. Collection of interest, $4,600
h. Acquisition of equipment by issuing a short-term note payable, $16,500
i. Payments of salaries, $96,900
j. Proceeds from the sale of plant assets, $22,200, including a $6,400 loss
k. Collections on accounts receivable, $378,500
l. Interest revenue, $1,800
m. Cash receipt of dividend revenue, $7,800
n. Payments to suppliers, $368,400
o. Cash sales, $201,000
p. Depreciation expense, $49,900
q. Proceeds from the issuance of note payable, $23,400
r. Payments of long-term notes payable, $83,000
s. Interest expense and payments, $12,900
t. Salary expense, $98,100
u. Loan collections, $12,600
v. Proceeds from the sale of investments, $10,000, including a $4,400 gain
w. Payment of a short-term note payable by issuing a long-term note payable, $78,000
x. Amortization expenses, $1,400
y. Income tax expense and payments, $36,800
z. Cash balance: August 31, 2018, $89,900; August 31, 2019, $61,700

Requirements

1. Prepare Ballinger Furniture Gallery's statement of cash flows for the year ended August 31, 2019. Use the *direct* method for cash flows from operating activities. Include an accompanying schedule of noncash investing and financing activities.
2. Evaluate the company's fiscal year ended August 31, 2019, from a cash flow standpoint.

LO 2, 3, 4

P11-73B. ***(Learning Objectives 2, 3, 4: Prepare the statement of cash flows—direct and indirect methods)*** To prepare the statement of cash flows, accountants for Dartmouth Electric Company have summarized 2018 activity in two accounts:

Cash

Beginning bal	90,100	Payments on accounts payable	387,000
Sale of long-term investment	32,400	Payments of dividends	62,000
Collections from customers	661,400	Payments of salaries and wages	143,500
Issuance of common stock	47,300	Payments of interest	26,800
Receipts of dividends	17,000	Purchase of equipment	31,900
		Payments of other operating expenses	34,300
		Payment of long-term note payable	41,700
		Purchase of treasury stock	28,900
		Payment of income tax	18,900
Ending Bal	73,200		

Common Stock

		Beginning bal	78,800
		Issuance for cash	47,300
		Issuance to acquire land	80,000
		Issuance to retire note payable	18,000
		Ending bal	224,100

Dartmouth Electric's 2018 income statement and balance sheet data follow:

A1

	A	B	C
1	**Dartmouth Electric Company Income Statement Year Ended December 31, 2018**		
2	Revenues:		
3	Sales revenue		$ 688,800
4	Dividend revenue		17,000
5	Total revenue		705,800
6	Expenses and losses:		
7	Cost of goods sold	$ 391,400	
8	Salary and wage expense	151,100	
9	Depreciation expense	17,500	
10	Other operating expense	45,300	
11	Interest expense	27,900	
12	Income tax expense	16,800	
13	Loss on sale of investments	8,600	
14	Total expenses and losses		658,600
15	Net income		$ 47,200
16			

	A	B
1	**Dartmouth Electric Company** **Selected Balance Sheet Data** **December 31, 2018**	
2		**Increase (Decrease)**
3	Current assets:	
4	Cash and cash equivalents	$ (16,900)
5	Accounts receivable	27,400
6	Inventories	(12,900)
7	Prepaid expenses	(500)
8	Land	80,000
9	Equipment, net	14,400
10	Long-term investments	(41,000)
11	Current liabilities:	
12	Accounts payable	(8,500)
13	Interest payable	1,100
14	Salary payable	7,600
15	Other accrued liabilities	10,500
16	Income tax payable	(2,100)
17	Long-term note payable	(59,700)
18	Common stock	145,300
19	Retained earnings	(14,800)
20	Treasury stock	28,900
21		

Requirements

1. Prepare the statement of cash flows of Dartmouth Electric for the year ended December 31, 2018, using the *direct* method to report operating activities. Also prepare the accompanying schedule of noncash investing and financing activities.
2. Use Dartmouth Electric's 2018 income statement and information from its selected balance sheet data to prepare a supplementary schedule of cash flows from operating activities using the *indirect* method.

LO **2, 3, 4**

P11-74B. ***(Learning Objectives 2, 3, 4: Prepare the statement of cash flows—indirect and direct methods)*** The comparative balance sheets of Mary McGuire Design Studio, Inc., at June 30, 2018, and 2017, and transaction data for fiscal 2018, are as follows:

	A	B	C	D
1	**Mary McGuire Design Studio, Inc.** **Comparative Balance Sheets**			
2		**June 30,**		**Increase**
3		**2018**	**2017**	**(Decrease)**
4	Current assets:			
5	Cash	$ 28,900	$ 1,600	$ 27,300
6	Accounts receivable	59,000	52,000	7,000
7	Inventories	97,700	60,500	37,200
8	Prepaid expenses	3,700	2,100	1,600
9	Land	22,200	92,800	(70,600)
10	Equipment, net	74,800	73,300	1,500
11	Long-term investment	22,000	5,200	16,800
12		$ 308,300	$ 287,500	$ 20,800
13	Current liabilities:			
14	Notes payable, short-term	$ 12,900	$ 19,000	$ (6,100)
15	Accounts payable	34,300	41,500	(7,200)
16	Income tax payable	13,400	14,800	(1,400)
17	Accrued liabilities	14,900	9,300	5,600
18	Interest payable	4,000	3,000	1,000
19	Salary payable	4,800	3,200	1,600
20	Long-term note payable	50,700	93,800	(43,100)
21	Common stock	68,100	61,500	6,600
22	Retained earnings	105,200	41,400	63,800
23		$ 308,300	$ 287,500	$ 20,800
24				

Transaction data for the year ended June 30, 2018, follows:

- **a.** Net income, $71,000
- **b.** Depreciation expense on equipment, $14,000
- **c.** Purchased a long-term investment with cash, $16,800
- **d.** Sold land for $63,600, including a $7,000 loss
- **e.** Acquired equipment by issuing a long-term note payable, $15,500
- **f.** Paid off a long-term note payable, $58,600
- **g.** Received cash for the issuance of common stock, $500
- **h.** Paid cash dividends, $7,200
- **i.** Paid off a short-term note payable by issuing common stock, $6,100

Requirements

1. Prepare the statement of cash flows of Mary McGuire Design Studio for the year ended June 30, 2018, using the *indirect* method to report operating activities. Also prepare the accompanying schedule of noncash investing and financing activities. All current account changes except for the short-term Notes Payable changes result from operating transactions.
2. Prepare a supplementary schedule showing cash flows from operations using the *direct* method. The accounting records provide the following: collections from customers, $260,000; interest received, $1,900; payments to suppliers, $158,600; payments to employees, $40,200; payments for income tax, $12,600; and payment of interest, $4,700.

Challenge Exercises and Problem

LO 3, 4

E11-75. ***(Learning Objectives 3, 4: Calculate cash flow amounts)*** Luxe, Inc., reported the following in its financial statements for the year ended May 31, 2018 (in thousands):

	A	B	C
1		**2018**	**2017**
2	Income Statement		
3	Net sales	$ 24,623	$ 21,555
4	Cost of sales	18,176	15,497
5	Depreciation	266	229
6	Other operating expenses	3,888	4,206
7	Income tax expense	534	488
8	Net income	$ 1,759	$ 1,135
9	Balance Sheet		
10	Cash and cash equivalents	$ 21	$ 18
11	Accounts receivable	599	606
12	Inventory	3,110	2,841
13	Property and equipment, net	4,342	3,423
14	Accounts payable	1,544	1,363
15	Accrued liabilities	939	631
16	Income tax payable	196	191
17	Long-term liabilities	480	472
18	Common stock	518	445
19	Retained earnings	4,395	3,786
20			

Requirement

1. Determine the following cash receipts and payments for Luxe during the fiscal year ended May 31, 2018 (enter all amounts in thousands):
   a. Collections from customers
   b. Payments for inventory
   c. Payments for other operating expenses
   d. Payment of income tax
   e. Proceeds from issuance of common stock
   f. Payment of cash dividends

LO 3

E11-76. ***(Learning Objective 3: Use the balance sheet and the statement of cash flows together)*** Delorme Specialties reported the following at December 31, 2018 (in thousands):

	A	B	C
1		2018	2017
2	From the comparative balance sheet:		
3	Property and equipment, net	$ 11,200	$ 9,580
4	Long-term notes payable	4,400	3,100
5	From the statement of cash flows:		
6	Depreciation	$ 1,950	
7	Capital expenditures	(4,100)	
8	Proceeds from sale of property and equipment	830	
9	Proceeds from issuance of long-term note payable	1,200	
10	Payment of long-term note payable	(110)	
11	Issuance of common stock	389	
12			

Requirement

1. Determine the following items for Delorme Specialties during 2018:
   a. Gain or loss on the sale of property and equipment
   b. Amount of long-term debt issued for something other than cash

LO 2, 3

P11-77. ***(Learning Objectives 2, 3: Prepare a balance sheet from a statement of cash flows)*** The December 31, 2017, balance sheet and the 2018 statement of cash flows for McFarland Corporation follow:

	A	B
1	**McFarland Corporation Balance Sheet December 31, 2017**	
2	**Assets:**	
3	Cash	$ 17,000
4	Accounts receivable (net)	78,400
5	Inventory	50,700
6	Prepaid expenses	2,200
7	Land	95,600
8	Machinery and equipment (net)	73,500
9	Total assets	$ 317,400
10	**Liabilities:**	
11	Accounts payable	$ 40,600
12	Unearned revenue	8,600
13	Income taxes payable	5,500
14	Long-term debt	86,000
15	**Total liabilities**	140,700
16	**Stockholders' equity:**	
17	Common stock, no par	51,200
18	Retained earnings	125,500
19	Total stockholders' equity	176,700
20	Total liabilities and stockholders' equity	$ 317,400
21		

	A	B	C
1	**McFarland Corporation** **Statement of Cash Flows** **Year Ended December 31, 2018**		
2	**Cash flows from operating activities:**		
3	Net income		$ 18,400
4	Adjustments to reconcile net income to net cash		
5	provided by operating activities:		
6	Depreciation	$ 13,900	
7	Loss on sale of equipment	18,000	
8	Gain on sale of land	(7,100)	
9	Change in assets and liabilities:		
10	Decrease in Accounts receivable	50,100	
11	Increase in Inventory	(17,600)	
12	Decrease in Prepaid expenses	1,300	
13	Increase in Accounts payable	1,200	
14	Decrease in Taxes payable	(4,100)	
15	Increase in Unearned revenue	11,400	67,100
16	Net cash provided by operating activities		$ 85,500
17	**Cash flows from investing activities:**		
18	Purchase of equipment	(15,000)	
19	Sale of equipment	14,000	
20	Sale of land	61,000	
21	Net cash provided by investing activities		60,000
22	**Cash flows from financing activities:**		
23	Repayment of long-term debt	(21,000)	
24	Issuance of common stock	17,700	
25	Dividends paid (dividends declared, $6,000)	(5,000)	
26	Net cash used for financing activities		(8,300)
27	Increase (decrease) in cash		137,200
28	Cash balance, December 31, 2017		17,000
29	Cash balance, December 31, 2018		$ 154,200
30			

Requirement

1. Prepare the December 31, 2018, balance sheet for McFarland.

APPLY YOUR KNOWLEDGE

Serial Case

C11-78 *(Learning Objectives 1, 2, 3: Analyze the statement of cash flows for a company in the restaurant industry)*

Note: This case is part of The Cheesecake Factory serial case contained in every chapter in this textbook.

The Cheesecake Factory has thousands of guests each day who pay immediately after finishing their meals. The Cheesecake Factory also spends cash to pay for the food it serves, employees' wages, and other expenses. The company might also use cash to set up new restaurant locations and renovate older facilities.

In addition, The Cheesecake Factory has the option to declare cash dividends and buy treasury stock. It might borrow cash via long-term loans or it might issue common stock for cash.

Below are the consolidated statements of cash flows for The Cheesecake Factory Incorporated for the fiscal years 2014–2016.[1]

	A	B	C	D
1	**The Cheesecake Factory Incorporated**	**Fiscal year**		
2	**Statement of Cash Flows (adapted for educational use)**			
3	**(In thousands)**	**2016**	**2015**	**2014**
4	Cash flows from operating activities:			
5	Net Income	$ 139,494	$ 116,523	$ 101,276
6	Adjustments to reconcile net income to cash	163,026	118,900	138,373
7	Cash provided by operating activities	$ 302,520	$ 235,423	$ 239,649
8	Cash flows from investing activities:			
9	Additions to property and equipment	(115,821)	(153,941)	(113,982)
10	Additions to intangible assets	(1,640)	(1,760)	(1,879)
11	Investments in unconsolidated affiliates	(42,000)	–	–
12	Cash used in investing activities	$ (159,461)	$ (155,701)	$ (115,861)
13	Cash flows from financing activities:			
14	Miscellaneous borrowings/repayments	55,764	51,454	43,294
15	Cash dividends paid	(42,371)	(35,969)	(30,332)
16	Treasury stock purchases	(146,467)	(109,371)	(140,483)
17	Cash used in financing activities	$ (133,074)	$ (93,886)	$ (127,521)
18	Net change in cash and cash equivalents	$ 9,985	$ (14,164)	$ (3,733)
19	Cash and cash equivalents at beginning of period	43,854	58,018	61,751
20	Cash and cash equivalents at end of period	$ 53,839	$ 43,854	$ 58,018
21				

Data from the U.S. Securities and Exchange Commission EDGAR Company Filings, www.sec.gov

Requirements

1. Which activity (operating, investing, or financing) generated the most cash for The Cheesecake Factory in 2016, 2015, and 2014?
2. What specific investing or financing activity used the most cash in 2016? In 2015? In 2014?
3. Did The Cheesecake Factory's overall cash and cash equivalents balance increase, decrease, or stay the same from 2014 to 2015? From 2015 to 2016?
4. Using only the statement of cash flows as evidence, does The Cheesecake Factory appear to be a healthy company? Why or why not?

[1]All statements have been condensed and adapted for educational purposes and should not be used for investment decisions.

Decision Cases

LO 3

C11-79. *(Learning Objective 3: Prepare and use the statement of cash flows to evaluate operations)* The 2018 income statement and the 2018 comparative balance sheet of Ghent River Camp, Inc., have just been distributed at a meeting of the camp's board of directors. The directors raise a fundamental question: Why is the cash balance so low? This question is especially troublesome since 2018 showed record profits. As the controller of the company, you must answer the question.

	A	B
1	**Ghent River Camp, Inc. Income Statement Year Ended December 31, 2018**	
2	**(In thousands)**	
3	Revenues:	
4	Sales revenue	$ 436
5	Expenses:	
6	Cost of goods sold	221
7	Salary expense	48
8	Depreciation expense	46
9	Interest expense	13
10	Amortization expense	11
11	Total expenses	339
12	Net income	$ 97
13		

	A	B	C
1	**Ghent River Camp, Inc. Comparative Balance Sheets December 31, 2018 and 2017**		
2	**(In thousands)**	**2018**	**2017**
3	**Assets:**		
4	Cash	$ 17	$ 63
5	Accounts receivable, net	72	61
6	Inventories	194	181
7	Property, plant, and equipment	369	259
8	Accumulated depreciation	(244)	(198)
9	Long-term investments	31	0
10	Patents	177	188
11	Totals	$ 616	$ 554
12	**Liabilities and stockholders' equity:**		
13	Accounts payable	$ 63	$ 56
14	Accrued liabilities	12	17
15	Notes payable, long-term	179	264
16	Common stock, no par	149	61
17	Retained earnings	213	156
18	Totals	$ 616	$ 554
19			

Requirements

1. Prepare a statement of cash flows for 2018 in the format that best shows the relationship between net income and operating cash flow. The company sold no plant assets or long-term investments and issued no notes payable during 2018. There were *no* noncash investing and financing transactions during the year. Show all amounts in thousands.
2. Answer the board members' question: Why is the cash balance so low? Point out the two largest cash payments during 2018. (Challenge)
3. Considering net income and the company's cash flows during 2018, was it a good year or a bad year? Give your reasons.

LO 1, 2

C11-80. *(Learning Objectives 1, 2: Use cash flow data to evaluate an investment)* Thompson Technology, Inc., and Beaudoin Catering Corporation are asking you to recommend their stock to your clients. Because Thompson and Beaudoin earn about the same net income and have similar financial positions, your decision depends on their statements of cash flows, which are summarized as follows:

	Thompson		Beaudoin	
Net cash provided by operating activities:		$ 30,000		$ 70,000
Cash provided by (used for) investing activities:				
Purchase of plant assets	$(20,000)		$(100,000)	
Sale of plant assets	40,000	20,000	10,000	(90,000)
Cash provided by (used for) financing activities:				
Issuance of common stock		—		30,000
Paying off long-term debt		(40,000)		—
Net increase in cash		$ 10,000		$10,000

Requirement

1. Based on their cash flows, which company looks better? Give your reasons.

Ethical Issues

Georgetown Motors is having a bad year. Net income is only $37,000 to date. Also, two important overseas customers are falling behind on their payments to Georgetown, and Georgetown's accounts receivable are ballooning. The company desperately needs a loan. The Georgetown board of directors is considering ways to put the best face on the company's financial statements. Georgetown's bank closely examines the company's cash flow from operations. Donna McDowell, Georgetown's controller, suggests reclassifying as long-term the receivables from the slow-paying clients. She explains to the board that removing the $80,000 rise in accounts receivable from current assets will increase net cash provided by operations. This approach may help Georgetown get the loan.

Requirements

1. Using only the amounts given, calculate Georgetown's net cash provided by operations, both without and with the reclassification of the receivables. Which reporting makes the company look better?
2. Identify the ethical issue(s).
3. Who are the stakeholders?
4. Analyze the issue from the (a) economic, (b) legal, and (c) ethical standpoints. What is the potential impact on all stakeholders?
5. What should the board do?
6. Under what conditions would reclassifying the receivables be considered ethical?

Focus on Financials | Apple Inc.

LO **1, 2, 3, 4**

(Learning Objectives 1, 2, 3, 4: Use the statement of cash flows) Use **Apple Inc.'s** consolidated statement of cash flows along with the company's other consolidated financial statements, all in Appendix A and online in the filings section of **www.sec.gov**, to answer the following questions.

Requirements

1. Which method does Apple use to report cash flows from operating activities? How can you tell?
2. What type of activity (operating, financing, or investing) generated the most cash flows for Apple in 2016? Which activity type(s) used cash in 2016? Judging by the statement of cash flows only, is Apple a healthy company? Explain your answer.
3. Suppose Apple reported net cash flows from operating activities using the direct method. Calculate the following amounts for the year ended September 24, 2016. (Ignore the statement of cash flows, and use only Apple's income statement and balance sheet.)
   a. Calculate collections from customers and others. Prepare a T-account for Gross Accounts Receivable. Prepare another T-account for Allowance for Doubtful Accounts. Calculate the beginning and ending gross amounts of Gross Accounts Receivable by adding the beginning and ending balances of Allowance for Doubtful Accounts ($63 million and $53 million, respectively) to the net accounts receivable at both the beginning and end of the year. Assume that all sales are on account. Also assume that the company uses the percentage of net sales method for estimating doubtful accounts expense and that the company estimates this amount at 0.5%. Determine write-offs by analyzing the Allowance for Uncollectible Accounts.
   b. Calculate payments to suppliers. Apple calls its cost of goods sold "Cost of Sales." Assume all inventory is purchased on account and that all cash payments to suppliers are made from accounts payable.
4. Calculate the change from 2015 to 2016 for Apple in terms of net income, total assets, stockholders' equity, cash flows from operating activities, and overall results. Be specific. (Challenge)

Focus on Analysis | Under Armour, Inc.

LO **1, 2, 3, 4**

(Learning Objectives 1, 2, 3, 4: Analyze cash flows) Retrieve the 2016 **Under Armour** financial statements at **www.sec.gov** by clicking on Filings and then searching for "Under Armour" under Company Filings. When you see the list of filings for the company, select the Form 10-K for 2016. Be sure to retrieve the 2016 financial statements, not another year.

Requirements

1. What is(are) Under Armour's main source(s) of cash in 2016? Is this good news or bad news for its managers, stockholders, and creditors? What is Under Armour's main use of cash in 2016? Is this good news or bad news? Discuss your reasoning.
2. Explain briefly the three most significant differences between net cash provided by operating activities and net income in 2016.
3. Did Under Armour buy or sell more plant assets during 2016 than in the previous two years? How can you tell?
4. Identify the largest item in the financing activities section of the Consolidated Statement of Cash Flows in 2016. Explain the company's probable reasoning behind this activity.
5. Evaluate Under Armour's overall performance for 2016 in terms of cash flows. Be as specific as you can. What other information would be helpful to you in making your evaluation?

Group Projects

Project 1. Each member of the group should obtain the annual report of a different company. Select companies in different industries. Evaluate each company's trend of cash flows for the most recent two years. You can use any other publicly available information—the companies' other financial statements (income statement, balance sheet, statement of stockholders' equity, and the related notes), and news stories from magazines and newspapers. Rank the companies' cash flows from best to worst, and write a two-page report on your findings.

Project 2. Select a company and obtain its annual report, including all the financial statements. Focus on the statement of cash flows and, in particular, the cash flows from operating activities. Specify whether the company uses the direct method or the indirect method to report operating cash flows. Next, use the other method to prepare the company's cash flows from operating activities. Use the other financial statements (income statement, balance sheet, and statement of stockholders' equity) as needed and the notes to the financial statements.

Quick Check Answers

1. *a*
2. *b*
3. *b*
4. *a*
5. *c*
6. *a*
7. *d*
8. *b*
9. *d [Sale of land $80,000 − Purchase equipment (delivery van) $25,000 = $55,000]*
10. *a*
11. *a*
12. *c [Issue bonds payable $500,000 − Purchase treasury stock $55,000 = $445,000]*
13. *b*
14. *a*

Try It Solutions

Page 608

a. Financing
b. Financing
c. Operating (included in net income)
d. Financing
e. Investing
f. Financing
g. Financing
h. Operating (included in net income)
i. Investing
j. Operating (included in net income)
k. Investing
l. Investing

Page 616

a. Not reported
b. Financing
c. Financing
d. Operating
e. Investing
f. Financing
g. Not reported
h. Investing
i. Financing
j. Investing
k. Financing
l. Operating
m. Operating
n. Not reported
o. Not reported
p. Operating

Page 621

	Beginning receivables	+	Revenues	−	Collections	=	Ending receivables
Collections from customers = $23,400:	$3,900	+	$23,000	−	$23,400	=	$3,500

	Cost of goods sold	+	Increase in inventory	+	Decrease in accounts payable	=	Payments
Payments for inventory = $14,600:	$14,100	+	($5,200 − $5,000)	+	($1,200 − $900)	=	$14,600

	Beginning income taxes payable	+	Income tax expense	−	Payment	=	Ending income taxes payable
Payment of income taxes = $1,000:	$700	+	$900	−	$1,000	=	$600

12 Financial Statement Analysis

LEARNING OBJECTIVES

1. **Perform** an industry and company analysis
2. **Perform** a horizontal analysis
3. **Perform** a vertical analysis
4. **Use** ratios to make business decisions
5. **Evaluate** the quality of earnings

SPOTLIGHT

Evaluating Under Armour, Inc., and Apple Inc., Using Different Financial Analysis Tools

Only one aspect of the course remains: financial statement analysis. How does a firm stack up to its competitors overall? By analyzing various aspects of their financial statements, you will be able to tell.

In the first half of this chapter, we will use horizontal and vertical analysis to analyze the financial statements of **Under Armour, Inc.** In the second half of the chapter, we will use ratios to analyze **Apple Inc.** You have seen most of these ratios in previous chapters. However, we have yet to use all of them in a comprehensive analysis of a company.

When you finish this chapter, you will understand the relationships among the data that reflect the results of operations, cash flows, and financial positions of these two companies. The skills you develop in this chapter are also transferrable: After studying this chapter, you will be able to analyze and understand the financial statements of any company you choose. ●

Tooykrub/Shutterstock

PERFORM AN INDUSTRY AND COMPANY ANALYSIS

1 Perform an industry and company analysis

Under Armour, Inc., is a competitor in the athletic apparel game. The company has developed an innovative alternative to the cotton T-shirt that provides compression and wicks perspiration off the skin rather than absorbs it. The result is a line of apparel engineered to keep athletes cool, dry, and light throughout the course of a game, practice, or workout. The technology behind Under Armour's diverse product assortment for men, women, and youth is complex, but the program for reaping the benefits is simple: Wear athletic gear that is suited to the seasons—hot, cold, and in-between. Under Armour has also made inroads into the "connected fitness" industry by acquiring online companies such as **Endomonto**, **MyFitnessPal**, and **MapMyFitness**. The company's Connected Fitness community now has over 130 million unique users across its combined electronic platforms, comprising the largest digital health and fitness community in the world. Let's look at Under Armour, Inc.'s Consolidated Statements of Operations for the three years ended December 31, 2016:

A1

	A	B	C	D
1	**Under Armour, Inc.** **Consolidated Statements of Income**	**12 Months Ended**		
2	**In thousands of $**	**Dec. 31, 2016**	**Dec. 31, 2015**	**Dec. 31, 2014**
3	Net revenues	$ 4,825,335	$ 3,963,313	$ 3,084,370
4	Cost of goods sold	2,584,724	2,057,766	1,572,164
5	Gross profit	2,240,611	1,905,547	1,512,206
6	Selling, general and administrative expenses	1,823,140	1,497,000	1,158,251
7	Income from operations	417,471	408,547	353,955
8	Interest expense, net	(26,434)	(14,628)	(5,335)
9	Other expense, net	(2,755)	(7,234)	(6,410)
10	Income before income taxes	388,282	386,685	342,210
11	Provision for income taxes	131,303	154,112	134,168
12	Net income	$ 256,979	$ 232,573	$ 208,042
13				

Data from the U.S. Securities and Exchange Commission EDGAR Company filings, www.sec.gov

Try It in Excel®

You can access the most current annual report of Under Armour, Inc., in Excel format at **www.sec.gov**. Using the "FILINGS" link on the toolbar at the top of the home page, select "Company Filings Search." This will take you to the "Edgar Company Filings" page. Type "Under Armour" in the company name box, and select "Search." This will produce the "EDGAR Search Results" page showing the company name. Click on the "CIK" link beside the company name. Doing so will pull up all of the reports the company has filed with the SEC. Under the "Filing Type" box, type "10-K" and click the search box. Form 10-K is the SEC form for the company's annual report. Find the year that you wish to view. Click on the "Interactive Data" box, which takes you to the "View Filing Data" page. Find and click on the "View Excel Document" link at the top of this page. You may choose to either open or download the Excel files containing the company's most recent financial statements.

Financial analysis involves more than just looking at financial reports and doing some math. A thorough analysis begins with understanding a company's business and industry. In other words, you need to see the "big picture." This usually entails quite a bit of reading and research, using all kinds of business publications and media. You can usually gain free access to this information via popular finance websites.

In addition, every public company's annual report filed with the SEC begins with a description of the company's business. This section of the annual report provides vital information about the company's products, its marketing and promotion, sales and distribution strategies, product design and development, manufacturing and quality assurance, and inventory management. Item 1 of an annual report (Business) describes how a company views its own operations and lends insight into why its management makes certain strategic decisions. Also, in the Management's Discussion and Analysis (MD&A) section of the annual report, you will find management's explanations for trends in sales and shipments, cost of sales and gross profit, selling, general and administrative expenses, and income taxes.

Learning about what's happening in the industry, markets, general economic conditions, trends in product development, and specific company strategies puts the numbers in context and helps you understand why they turned out as they did. After all, accounting data should paint a picture of the results of implementing a particular business strategy.

Let's look at the business of Under Armour and the trends in its industry. The athletic apparel industry is enjoying a period of booming expansion. The market for "activewear" or "athleisure" apparel (clothing people can wear both around town and to the gym) is estimated to reach $83 billion by 2020. Under Armour is enjoying its share of this boom but is facing major challenges in terms of growing its revenues and controlling its costs. During its early years, Under Armour's product innovations allowed it to make significant gains in revenue and gross margin percentage growth over its competitors. As a result, over the 10-year period ending in 2015, the company's stock price climbed by over 1,400%.

However, Under Armour is in an extremely competitive industry. Starting in 2016, its larger competitors, **Nike** and **Adidas** began to regain ground they had lost to Under Armour in earlier years. Upscale athletic retailers that sell their products at higher prices have traditionally been a large part of Under Armour's customer base, which has allowed the company to earn higher gross margins than its competitors. However, in recent years, several of these high-end retailers have been forced out of business. Consequently, Under Armour has had to find new markets for its products among more moderately priced retailers, thus discounting its selling prices and eroding its gross margins. Although Under Armour has landed some lucrative sponsorship deals from famous athletes and sports teams, Nike continues to dominate the market, particularly in footwear. All of these competitive pressures have begun to eat into Under Armour's income from operations.

The numbers in the graphs in Exhibit 12-1 are taken from Under Armour, Inc.'s comparative Consolidated Income Statements on page 669, and show the three-year trend of net revenues and income from operations. Reading from left to right, Under Armour's net revenues (panel A) increased from about $3.1 billion in fiscal 2014 to about $4.8 billion in fiscal 2016. At first glance, this looks like a really positive trend. However, a closer look shows that the year-to-year increase in net revenue declined from $878.9 million in fiscal 2015 to $862 million in 2016. So, although the general trend in revenues over the three years was positive, the *growth rate* in net revenues declined in 2016.

Now look at the trend in income from operations (Panel B). Income from operations (line 7 on page 669) is computed by subtracting Cost of Goods Sold (line 4 on page 669) and Selling, general and administrative expenses (line 6 on page 669) from Net Revenues (line 3 on page 669). Steadily increasing income from operations means that a company is growing its revenues while controlling its costs, which usually signals expansion and growth in the business's value in future years. Declining income from operations indicates a slowdown in business activity, which signals declining growth and a decline in a business's value. Income from Under Armour's operations grew from about $354 million in fiscal 2014 to about $409 million in 2015 (about $54.6 million, or about 15%). However, in fiscal 2016, income from operations grew by only about $8.9 million (about 2%). This tells us that the growth in Under Armour, Inc.'s revenues did not keep pace with the growth in its costs.

Exhibit 12-1 Comparative Net Revenues and Income from Operations for Under Armour (2014–2016)

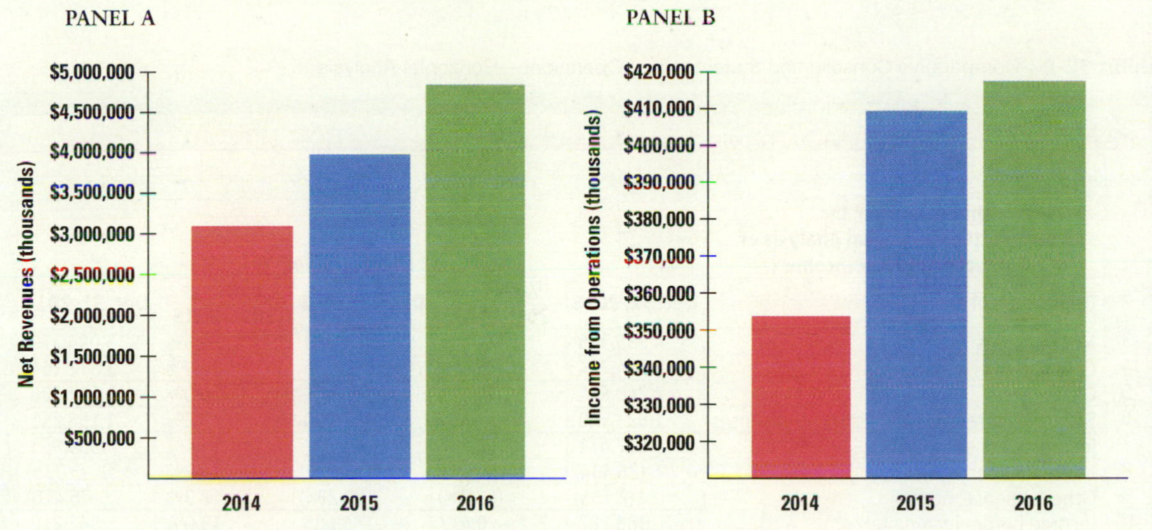

Data from the U.S. Securities and Exchange Commission EDGAR Company filings, www.sec.gov

PERFORM A HORIZONTAL ANALYSIS

2 Perform a horizontal analysis

We can learn more about what caused Under Armour's lower performance by doing a **horizontal analysis**, which is the study of percentage changes from year to year. Computing a percentage change takes two steps:

1. Compute the dollar amount of the change from one period (the base period) to the next.
2. Divide the dollar amount of change by the base-period amount.

A horizontal analysis of Under Armour's net revenues (using the 2015 and 2016 figures, dollars in thousands) reveals the following information:

			Increase (Decrease)	
	2016	2015	Amount	Percentage
Net revenues	$4,825,335	$3,963,313	$862,022	21.8%

Under Armour's net revenues (in thousands) increased by 21.8% during 2016. The percentage change is computed as follows:

Step 1 Compute the dollar amount of change from 2015 to 2016:

2016		2015		Increase
$4,825,335	−	$3,963,313	=	$862,022

Step 2 Divide the dollar amount of change by the base-period amount. This computes the percentage change for the period:

$$\text{Percentage change} = \frac{\text{Dollar amount of change}}{\text{Base-year amount}} \times 100$$

$$= \frac{\$862,022}{\$3,963,313} = 21.8\%$$

Exhibit 12-2 presents a line-by-line detailed horizontal analysis of Under Armour, Inc.'s comparative Consolidated Statements of Operations over the two-year period from December 31, 2014, through December 31, 2016.

Exhibit 12-2 Comparative Consolidated Statements of Operations—Horizontal Analysis

	A	B	C	D	E	F
1	**Under Armour, Inc. Comparative Horizontal Analysis of Consolidated Net Income**			**12 Months Ended**		
2	(thousands of $)	**Dec. 31, 2016**	**% change 2015–2016**	**Dec. 31, 2015**	**% change 2014–2015**	**Dec. 31, 2014**
3	Net revenues	$ 4,825,335	21.8%	$ 3,963,313	28.5%	$ 3,084,370
4	Cost of goods sold	2,584,724	25.6%	2,057,766	30.9%	1,572,164
5	Gross profit	2,240,611	17.6%	1,905,547	26.0%	1,512,206
6	Selling, general and administrative expenses	1,823,140	21.8%	1,497,000	29.2%	1,158,251
7	Income from operations	417,471	2.2%	408,547	15.4%	353,955
8	Interest expense, net	(26,434)	80.7%	(14,628)	174.2%	(5,335)
9	Other expense, net	(2,755)	(61.9%)	(7,234)	12.9%	(6,410)
10	Income before income taxes	388,282	0.4%	386,685	13.0%	342,210
11	Provision for income taxes	131,303	(14.8%)	154,112	14.9%	134,168
12	Net income	$ 256,979	10.5%	$ 232,573	11.8%	$ 208,042
13						

Data from the U.S. Securities and Exchange Commission EDGAR Company filings, www.sec.gov

Try It in Excel®

Formatting comparative financial statements for a horizontal analysis when the financial statements are in Excel format is quite easy. Try reconstructing Exhibit 12-2 in Excel.

1. Start with the Consolidated Statements of Operations in the opening figure of the chapter.
2. Change the labels to correspond with Exhibit 12-2. Your spreadsheet might be slightly different from Exhibit 12-2, so the cells in which you start to enter formulas might have to be modified accordingly.
3. Insert one column between the 2016 and 2015 columns and another column between the 2015 and 2014 columns. Label these "% change."
4. Compute the percentage change as follows. We start in cell C3 (blank). Change the format of the data in the cell to % by clicking on the % box in the number field in the top toolbar. In cell C3, type the following: =(B3–D3)/D3. The result of 21.8% should appear in the cell. Copy this cell formula through line 12 of the sheet to do this computation for all other income and expenses.
5. Repeat the process in (4) using blank cell E3 and using the formula: =(D3–F3)/F3. Copy this formula through line 12.
6. Pat yourself on the back. You've just performed a horizontal analysis using Excel!

	A	B	C	D	E
1	(In thousands)	2016	2015	$ Change	% Change
2	Apparel	$ 3,229,142	$ 2,801,062	$ 428,080	15.3%
3	Footwear	1,010,693	677,744	332,949	49.1
4	Accessories	406,614	346,885	59,729	17.2
5	Total net sales	4,646,449	3,825,691	820,758	21.5
6	License	99,849	84,207	15,642	18.6
7	Connected Fitness	80,447	53,415	27,032	50.6
8	Intersegment Eliminations	(1,410)	-	(1,410)	(100.0)
9	Total net revenues	$ 4,825,335	$ 3,963,313	$ 862,022	21.8%
10					

Data from the U.S. Securities and Exchange Commission EDGAR Company filings, www.sec.gov

Now focus on the "% change" column from 2014 to 2016 in Exhibit 12-2. A chart from the MD&A section of the company's annual report includes a more detailed discussion of these changes by category. Let's analyze the change in net revenues by category first.

The figure above shows that Under Armour, Inc.'s, net revenue consists of net sales of products (apparel, footwear, and accessories) as well as license and other revenues. Product sales are generated primarily from the wholesale of products to national, regional, independent, and specialty retailers, as well as direct sales through factory outlet stores. The overall 21.8% increase in net revenues was comprised of a 15.3% increase in apparel sales, a 49.1% increase in footwear, and a 17.2% increase in accessories. The Connected Fitness category, consisting of licenses and digital fitness platform licenses and subscriptions, grew by the largest percentage (50.6%). Although these percentage changes look impressive in isolation, they are down significantly from fiscal 2015, when overall sales increased by 28.5%.

Cost of goods sold (Exhibit 12-2, line 4) measures the direct cost of various products sold. Gross profit (line 5) measures the difference between net revenues and cost of goods sold. Exhibit 12-2 shows that cost of goods sold increased by 25.6% in 2016. When combined with only a 21.8% increase in net revenues, this brings the increase in gross profit down to only 17.6% over 2015. In MD&A, management explains that the decrease in gross profit was caused mostly by the increased liquidation and discounting of excess inventory, which includes products that typically don't sell quickly. The company cut the selling prices of these products in order to sell them, which reduced Under Armour's gross profit percentage.

Selling, general, and administrative expenses in 2016 (Exhibit 12-2, line 6) increased by 21.8% over 2015. MD&A reveals that these expenses consist of the following: marketing costs such as the sponsorships of professional teams and athletes; selling costs such as distribution, product innovation, and supply chain costs; and the cost of corporate services such as personnel and other administrative costs. These costs rose over the year at a higher rate than Under Armour's gross profit, bringing the increase in the company's income from operations (line 7) down to only 2.2%.

Under Armour's interest expense for 2016 (Exhibit 12-2, line 8) grew by 80.7% over 2015, primarily due to new long-term debt the company incurred during the year, which we will see when we analyze the balance sheet later. Other expense, net (line 9) consisted mostly of foreign currency exchange losses due to a relatively strong U.S. dollar. Line 11 contains the company's provision for income taxes. Under Armour, Inc's, income tax provision declined by 14.8% in 2016, ultimately causing the company's net income for fiscal 2016 to reflect a 10.5% increase over fiscal 2015. Overall, Under Armour, Inc.'s, profits continued to rise, but the *growth* in profits slowed because costs increased faster than revenues.

It's impossible to evaluate a company effectively by examining only one year's financial data. Studying year-to-year changes in balance-sheet accounts can enhance our total understanding of a company's current and long-term financial position. Let's look at a few balance-sheet changes in Exhibit 12-3.

Exhibit 12-3 | Horizontal Analysis: Consolidated Balance Sheets

	A	B	C	D	E
1	**Under Armour, Inc. Consolidated Balance Sheets**			**Increase (decrease)**	
2		**Dec. 31, 2016**	**Dec. 31, 2015**	**Amount**	**Percentage**
3	**Assets**				
4	Cash and cash equivalents	$ 250,470	$ 129,852	$ 120,618	92.9%
5	Accounts receivable, net	622,685	433,638	189,047	43.6%
6	Inventories	917,491	783,031	134,460	17.2%
7	Prepaid expenses and other current assets	174,507	152,242	22,265	14.6%
8	Total current assets	1,965,153	1,498,763	466,390	31.1%
9	Property and equipment, net	804,211	538,531	265,680	49.3%
10	Goodwill	563,591	585,181	(21,590)	(3.7%)
11	Intangible assets, net	64,310	75,686	(11,376)	(15.0%)
12	Deferred income taxes	136,862	92,157	44,705	48.5%
13	Other long-term assets	110,204	75,652	34,552	45.7%
14	Total assets	$ 3,644,331	$ 2,865,970	$ 778,361	27.2%
15	**Liabilities and Stockholders' Equity**				
16	Accounts payable	$ 409,679	$ 200,460	$ 209,219	104.4%
17	Accrued expenses	208,750	192,935	15,815	8.2%
18	Current maturities of long-term debt	27,000	42,000	(15,000)	(35.7%)
19	Other current liabilities	40,387	43,415	(3,028)	(7.0%)
20	Total current liabilities	685,816	478,810	207,006	43.2%
21	Long term debt, net of current maturities	790,388	624,070	166,318	26.7%
22	Other long term liabilities	137,227	94,868	42,359	44.7%
23	Total liabilities	1,613,431	1,197,748	415,683	34.7%
24	Commitments and contingencies (see Note 6)				
25	Stockholders' equity				
26	Common Stock	145	144	1	0.7%
27	Additional paid-in capital	823,484	636,558	186,926	29.4%
28	Retained earnings	1,259,414	1,076,533	182,881	17.0%
29	Accumulated other comprehensive income (loss)	(52,143)	(45,013)	7,130	15.8%
30	Total stockholders' equity	2,030,900	1,668,222	362,678	21.7%
31	Total liabilities and stockholders' equity	$ 3,644,331	$ 2,865,970	$ 778,361	27.2%
32					

Data from the U.S. Securities and Exchange Commission EDGAR Company filings, www.sec.gov

First, cash and cash equivalents (line 4) increased by an impressive 92.9% in 2016. Accounts receivable, net (line 5) increased by 43.6%, which is double the increase in net revenues (21.8%) we saw in Exhibit 12-2. Given that an account receivable is only as good as its collectability, and that some of the company's major customers went out of business during the year, we wonder if all of these receivables are collectible. Hopefully, Under Armour increased its allowance for doubtful accounts accordingly. Inventories (line 6) increased by 17.2%, indicating that the company was building up inventories. As we pointed out in Chapter 6, increasing inventories along with declining gross margins usually signal lower inventory turnover, raising questions about inventory obsolescence. If some inventories are in fact obsolete, the company will have to reduce their carrying value from cost to market values, producing more future losses.

Accounts payable (line 16) increased by 104.4%. This indicates that the company's rate of payments to its creditors is slowing. Overall, total current assets (line 8) increased at the rate of 31.1%, and total current liabilities (line 20) increased by 43.2%. Net working capital (current assets – current liabilities) increased from $1,020 million in 2015 to $1,279 million in 2016. The current ratio (current assets/current liabilities) was very strong in both years (3.13 in 2015, declining to 2.87 in 2016), indicating that, in spite of its operating challenges, the company maintained a strong ability to pay its short-term liabilities.

Property and equipment, net (line 9) increased by 49.3% ($265.7 million), indicating that the company invested significant amounts in long-term assets such as warehouses and technology. Long-term debt, net of current maturities (line 21), which consists largely of amounts borrowed to finance these assets, as well as debt related to capital lease obligations, increased by 26.7% ($166.3 million).

Overall, it appears that as of December 31, 2016, in spite of declining profitability, Under Armour, Inc.'s, financial position was still healthy, both from the current as well as the long-term standpoint. Management invested significant resources in the growth of the company through the end of 2016. The company also accumulated a substantial amount of cash and inventories. Under Armour was ready to grow in 2017, even if at a slower pace than in previous years.

Trend Percentages

Trend percentages are a form of horizontal analysis. Trends indicate the direction a business is taking. How have revenues changed over a five-year period? What trend does net income show? These questions can be answered by looking at trend percentages over a representative period, such as the most recent five years.

Trend percentages are computed by selecting a base year whose amounts are set equal to 100%. The amount for each following year is stated as a percentage of the base amount. To compute a trend percentage, divide an item for a later year by the base-year amount, and multiply by 100.

$$\text{Trend \%} = \frac{\text{Any year \$}}{\text{Base year \$}} \times 100$$

Under Armour's income from operations for 2014–2016 was as follows:

(In millions)	2016	2015	2014 (Base)
Income from operations	$417,471	$408,547	$353,955

We want to calculate a trend for the period 2014 through 2016. The first year in the series (2014) is set as the base year. Trend percentages are computed by dividing each successive year's amount by the 2014 amount. The resulting trend percentages follow (2014 = 100%):

	2016	2015	2014 (Base)
Income from operations	117.9%	115.4%	100%

This analysis highlights the declining trend in Under Armour's business over two years, and how quickly trends change in a highly competitive business environment. In 2015, income from operations jumped up 15.4% relative to the base year, but increased only 2.5% in 2016. In other words, relative to the base year, Under Armour's income from operations increased by a total of 17.9% during the two years. If we had the space to show a longer term trend, it would show a 70% increase in operating profits in the two years preceding 2014, which is a stark contrast to these results. You can perform a trend analysis on any item you consider important. Investors and stock analysts look at trends to try to predict future stock values. A horizontal analysis highlights changes over time in the line items in financial statements. However, no single technique gives a complete picture of a business.

PERFORM A VERTICAL ANALYSIS

3 Perform a vertical analysis

A **vertical analysis** shows the relationship of a financial statement item to its base, which is the 100% figure. All items on the financial statement are reported as a percentage of the base. For the income statement, net revenue (net sales) is usually the base.

The following equation shows how to calculate each income statement item relative to the base (net sales):

$$\text{Vertical analysis \%} = \frac{\text{Each income statement item}}{\text{Net sales (revenue)}} \times 100$$

Why is a vertical analysis important? Suppose investors have come to expect a company's net income to be greater than 8% of its net sales revenue. If the economy is good or improving, a drop to 4% over a period of two years could cause investors to become disappointed in the performance of the company. As a result, they might sell the company's stock, and its price could fall. Exhibit 12-4 shows a vertical analysis of Under Armour, Inc.'s, Consolidated Statements of Operations.

Exhibit 12-4 | Comparative Consolidated Statements of Operations—Vertical Analysis

	A	B	C	D	E	F	G
1	**Under Armour, Inc.** **Consolidated Statements of Income (Adapted)**	**Year ended**	**% of**	**Year ended**	**% of**	**Year ended**	**% of**
2	**($ in thousands)**	**Dec. 31, 2016**	**total**	**Dec. 31, 2015**	**total**	**Dec. 31, 2014**	**total**
3	Net revenues	$ 4,825,335	100.0%	$ 3,963,313	100.0%	$ 3,084,370	100.0%
4	Cost of goods sold	2,584,724	53.6%	2,057,766	51.9%	1,572,164	51.0%
5	Gross profit	2,240,611	46.4%	1,905,547	48.1%	1,512,206	49.0%
6	Selling, general and administrative expenses	1,823,140	37.8%	1,497,000	37.8%	1,158,251	37.6%
7	Income from operations	417,471	8.7%	408,547	10.3%	353,955	11.5%
8	Interest expense, net	(26,434)	(0.5%)	(14,628)	(0.4%)	(5,335)	(0.2%)
9	Other expense, net	(2,755)	(0.1%)	(7,234)	(0.2%)	(6,410)	(0.2%)
10	Income before income taxes	388,282	8.0%	386,685	9.8%	342,210	11.1%
11	Provision for income taxes	131,303	2.7%	154,112	3.9%	134,168	4.3%
12	Net income	$ 256,979	5.3%	$ 232,573	5.9%	$ 208,042	6.7%
13							

Data from the U.S. Securities and Exchange Commission EDGAR Company filings, www.sec.gov

» Try It in Excel®

Formatting comparative financial statements for a vertical analysis when the financial statements are in Excel format is just as easy as it was for horizontal analysis. Try reconstructing Exhibit 12-4 in Excel.

1. Start with the Consolidated Statements of Operations in the opening figure of the chapter. You will be ahead of the game if you have already prepared this in Excel.
2. Change the labels to correspond with Exhibit 12-4. Your spreadsheet might be slightly different than Exhibit 12-4, so the cells in which you start to enter formulas might have to be modified accordingly.
3. We are preparing three years of comparative data, so insert columns after each of the 2016, 2015, and 2014 financial columns. In our example, these become columns C, E, and G with blank cells; label these "% of total."
4. *Common-size* income statements set net revenues at 100% and express all other income and expenses as percentages of net revenues. To set net revenues at 100%, we start in cell C3 (blank). In the cell, type the following: =B3/B3. It is very important to insert the $ signs in the denominator both before and after the letter B. This "freezes" cell B3 to make it a constant denominator for the values in all other cells in the column. You can also use the F4 function key to freeze the cell value. The result of 100% should appear in the cell. To increase precision, use the "increase decimal" tab in the "number" field in the toolbar. We have adjusted to a precision of one decimal place. Copy this cell formula through line 12 of the sheet to do this computation for all other income and expenses.
5. Repeat the process in (4) for the 2015 and 2014 figures columns by entering corresponding formulas in columns E and G. Copy these formulas through line 12. Use the "borders" tab (under "font" in the toolbar) to format the cells to extend the proper underscoring as shown in Exhibit 12-4.
6. Pat yourself on the back. You're learning to use Excel for the very valuable function of vertical analysis! Now let's dig into the numbers to interpret what they mean.

The vertical analysis format in Exhibit 12-4 makes it easier for us to study trends in key financial statistics such as gross profit, operating income, and net income over time. The absolute numbers are converted to percentages, permitting us to see fluctuations we might not see otherwise. Let's begin with gross profit and proceed through operating expenses.

Under Armour, Inc.'s, gross profit percentages over the three-year period declined steadily (49.0% in 2014, 48.1% in 2015, and 46.4% in 2016). This means that its product costs were rising faster than its revenues. Under Armour's operating expenses increased slightly from 37.6% of net revenues in 2014 to 37.8% of net revenues in 2015 and 2016. This slight increase in operating expenses magnified the negative trend in the company's gross profit. The result was a steady decline in operating income as a percentage of net revenues, from 11.5% in 2014 to 8.7% in 2016. Notice that the overall picture of how the company is performing over time is consistent with the picture we saw with our horizontal analysis: Under Armour, Inc.,'s profits are shrinking because its costs are rising faster than its revenues. With a vertical analysis, we are just looking at the picture from a slightly different angle.

Exhibit 12-5 shows the vertical analysis of Under Armour, Inc.'s, Consolidated Balance Sheets. The base amount (100%) represents total assets for each year. The balance sheet reveals several things about Under Armour's financial position at December 31, 2016, relative to December 31, 2015:

Exhibit 12-5 | Comparative Consolidated Balance Sheets—Vertical Analysis

A1

	A	B	C	D	E
1	**Under Armour, Inc. Consolidated Balance Sheets (in thousands of USD)**		**% of total**		**% of total**
2		**Dec. 31, 2016**		**Dec. 31, 2015**	
3	**Assets**				
4	Cash and cash equivalents	$ 250,470	6.9%	$ 129,852	4.5%
5	Accounts receivable, net	622,685	17.1%	433,638	15.1%
6	Inventories	917,491	25.2%	783,031	27.3%
7	Prepaid expenses and other current assets	174,507	4.8%	152,242	5.3%
8	Total current assets	1,965,153	53.9%	1,498,763	52.3%
9	Property and equipment, net	804,211	22.1%	538,531	18.8%
10	Goodwill	563,591	15.5%	585,181	20.4%
11	Intangible assets, net	64,310	1.8%	75,686	2.6%
12	Deferred income taxes	136,862	3.8%	92,157	3.2%
13	Other long term assets	110,204	3.0%	75,652	2.6%
14	Total assets	$ 3,644,331	100.0%	$ 2,865,970	100.0%
15	**Liabilities and Stockholders' Equity**				
16	Accounts payable	$ 409,679	11.2%	$ 200,460	7.0%
17	Accrued expenses	208,750	5.7%	192,935	6.7%
18	Current maturities of long term debt	27,000	0.7%	42,000	1.5%
19	Other current liabilities	40,387	1.1%	43,415	1.5%
20	Total current liabilities	685,816	18.8%	478,810	16.7%
21	Long term debt, net of current maturities	790,388	21.7%	624,070	21.8%
22	Other long term liabilities	137,227	3.8%	94,868	3.3%
23	Total liabilities	1,613,431	44.3%	1,197,748	41.8%
24	Commitments and contingencies (see Note 7)				
25	Stockholders' equity				
26	Common Stock	145	0.0%	144	0.0%
27	Additional paid-in capital	823,484	22.6%	636,558	22.2%
28	Retained earnings	1,259,414	34.6%	1,076,533	37.6%
29	Accumulated other comprehensive income (loss)	(52,143)	(1.4%)	(45,013)	(1.6%)
30	Total stockholders' equity	2,030,900	55.7%	1,668,222	58.2%
31	Total liabilities and stockholders' equity	$ 3,644,331	100.0%	$ 2,865,970	100.0%
32					

Data from the U.S. Securities and Exchange Commission EDGAR Company filings, www.sec.gov

- Cash and cash equivalents increased in 2016 by 92.9% from 2015 (Exhibit 12-3, p. 674), and also increased as a percentage of total assets from 4.5% to 6.9% (line 4 in Exhibit 12-5).

- Accounts receivable, net increased by 43.6% from 2015 to 2016 (Exhibit 12-3, line 5), and also increased as a percentage of total assets from 15.1% in 2015 to 17.1% in 2016 (line 5 in Exhibit 12-5). The percentage increase in accounts receivable year over year was about double the 21.8% increase in net sales from line 4 in Exhibit 12-2. This is a signal that the company's accounts receivable were growing faster than its net sales, and that Under Armour should have started reviewing collections from customers more closely.
- Although inventories increased by 17.2% from 2014 to 2016 (Exhibit 12-3 line 6), they declined as a percentage of total assets, from 27.3% in 2015 to 25.2% in 2016 (Exhibit 12-5, line 6). Inventory turnover (cost of goods sold ÷ average inventory) decreased from about 3.12 times per year (once about every 117 days) in 2015 to about 3.04 times per year (once about every 120 days) in 2016.[1] Combining information from Exhibits 12-4 and 12-5, we see that gross profit declined in 2016 (46.4% vs. 48.1%), and inventory turned over about 3 days slower in 2016 than 2015. This means that the company's products were both less profitable and sold slower in 2016 than 2015—not a good trend.
- Property, plant and equipment (net) (line 9 of Exhibit 12-5) grew as a percentage of total assets from 18.8% in 2015 to 22.1% in 2016. So, we can infer that the company was investing in fixed assets in anticipation of future growth.
- The company's debt ratio (total liabilities ÷ total assets), reflected clearly in line 23, rose from 41.8% of total assets in 2015 to 44.3% of total assets in 2016. This increase was caused chiefly by an increase in current liabilities, principally accounts payable, which increased from 7.0% to 11.2% as a percentage of total assets. This means that the company took longer to pay off its accounts payable in 2016 than in 2015. However, as we discussed in Chapter 3, a debt ratio of 44.3% is considered quite low. The company will likely be able to expand operations and service its debt as long as its cash flow from operations remains healthy.

Overall, Under Armour, Inc.'s, financial position was strong as of December 31, 2016. The company was highly liquid, well invested in inventory and fixed assets, and had a relatively low level of leverage (debt).

Prepare Common-Size Financial Statements

Exhibits 12-4 and 12-5 can be modified to report only percentages (no dollar amounts). Such financial statements are called **common-size statements**. A common-size financial statement assists in the comparison of different companies because all amounts are stated in percentages, thus expressing the financial results of each company comparatively in terms of a common denominator.

TRY IT

(Answers are given on p. 743.)

Calculate the common-size percentages for the following income statement:

Net sales	$150,000
Cost of goods sold	60,000
Gross profit	90,000
Operating expense	40,000
Operating income	50,000
Income tax expense	15,000
Net income	$ 35,000

[1] For computation of inventory turnover, see Chapter 6. Inventory as of December 31, 2014 was $536.7 million.

Benchmarking

Benchmarking compares a company to standards set by another company or companies. The goal of benchmarking is improvement. Suppose you are a financial analyst for **Goldman Sachs**, a large investment bank. You are considering investing in one of two different retailers: Under Armour or Nike. A direct comparison of these companies' financial statements may not be meaningful, in part because Nike is so much larger than Under Armour. However, you can convert both companies' income statements to a common size and compare the percentages, making comparisons more meaningful.

Benchmarking Against a Key Competitor

Exhibit 12-6 presents the common-size income statement of Under Armour, Inc., benchmarked against the common-size income statement of Nike, Inc.

Exhibit 12-6 | Common-Size Income Statements Benchmarked Against Competitor

A1

	A	B	C
1	**Under Armour, Inc. Common-Size Income Statement for Comparison with Key Competitor (Adapted) Year Ended During 2016**		
2		**Under Armour, Inc.**	**Nike, Inc.**
3	Net sales	100.0%	100.0%
4	Cost of sales	53.6%	53.8%
5	Gross profit	46.4%	46.2%
6	Operating (selling, general and administrative) expenses	37.8%	32.3%
7	Operating income	8.6%	13.9%
8			

Data from the U.S. Securities and Exchange Commission EDGAR Company filings, www.sec.gov

In this comparison, the results of operations of the two companies are strikingly similar. However, if you studied the companies' long-term trends (not shown here because of space) you would see that from 2014 through 2016, Nike's gross margin statistics improved while Under Armour's deteriorated. Nike's sales are much larger because it has been selling to a wider range of customers, including big-box discount stores such as **Wal-Mart** and **Target**, for a longer period of time than Under Armour. Also, due to its size advantage, which produces economies of scale, Nike has lower operating (selling, general, and administrative) expense percentages than Under Armour. So, Nike is the overall winner in terms of operating income percentages.

Mid-Chapter | Summary Problem

Perform a horizontal analysis and a vertical analysis of the comparative income statement of Firm Stone Products, Inc., which makes metal detectors. State whether 2018 was a good year or a bad year compared with 2017, and give your reasons. We encourage you to use Excel to do your analysis.

	A	B	C
1	**Firm Stone Products, Inc.** **Comparative Income Statements** **Years Ended December 31, 2018 and 2017**		
2		**2018**	**2017**
3	Total revenues	$ 275,000	$ 225,000
4	Expenses:		
5	Cost of goods sold	194,000	165,000
6	Engineering, selling, and administrative expenses	54,000	48,000
7	Interest expense	5,000	5,000
8	Income tax expense	9,000	3,000
9	Other expense (income)	1,000	(1,000)
10	Total expenses	263,000	220,000
11	Net income	$ 12,000	$ 5,000
12			

Answer

The horizontal analysis shows that total revenues increased 22.2%. This was greater than the 19.5% increase in total expenses, resulting in a 140% increase in net income.

	A	B	C	D	E
1	**Firm Stone Products, Inc.** **Horizontal Analysis of Comparative Income Statements** **Years Ended December 31, 2018 and 2017**				
2		**2018**	**2017**	**Increase (Decrease)** **Amount**	 **Percent**
3	Total revenues	$ 275,000	$ 225,000	$ 50,000	22.2%
4	Expenses:				
5	Cost of goods sold	194,000	165,000	29,000	17.6
6	Engineering, selling, and				
7	administrative expenses	54,000	48,000	6,000	12.5
8	Interest expense	5,000	5,000	—	—
9	Income tax expense	9,000	3,000	6,000	200.0
10	Other expense (income)	1,000	(1,000)	2,000	—*
11	Total expenses	263,000	220,000	43,000	19.5
12	Net income	$ 12,000	$ 5,000	$ 7,000	140.0%
13					

*Percentage changes are typically not computed for shifts from a negative to a positive amount and vice versa.

The vertical analysis shows decreases in the percentages of net revenues consumed by the cost of goods sold (from 73.3% to 70.5%) and by the engineering, selling, and administrative expenses (from 21.3% to 19.6%). Because these two items are Firm Stone's largest dollar expenses, their percentage decreases are quite important. The relative reduction in expenses raised 2018 net income to 4.4% of revenues, compared with 2.2% the preceding year. The overall analysis indicates that 2018 was significantly better than 2017.

A1

	A	B	C	D	E
1	**Firm Stone Products, Inc.** **Vertical Analysis of Comparative Income Statements** **Years Ended December 31, 2018 and 2017**				
2		**2018** **Amount**	**Percent**	**2017** **Amount**	**Percent**
3	Total revenues	$ 275,000	100.0 %	$ 225,000	100.0 %
4	Expenses:				
5	Cost of goods sold	194,000	70.5	165,000	73.3
6	Engineering, selling, and				
7	administrative expenses	54,000	19.6	48,000	21.3
8	Interest expense	5,000	1.8	5,000	2.2
9	Income tax expense	9,000	3.3	3,000	1.4 **
10	Other expense (income)	1,000	0.4	(1,000)	(0.4)
11	Total expenses	263,000	95.6	220,000	97.8
12	Net income	$ 12,000	4.4 %	$ 5,000	2.2 %
13					

**Number rounded up.

USE RATIOS TO MAKE BUSINESS DECISIONS

4 **Use** ratios to make business decisions

Ratios are a major tool of financial analysis. In this section, we will look at Apple Inc., to review how ratios are computed and used to make business decisions. Apple Inc., was our spotlight company in Chapter 5, and is also featured in Appendix A of this text. Many companies include ratios in a special section of their annual reports. Exhibit 12-7 shows a summary of selected data from Apple's annual reports, along with most of the ratios we have studied in this text. Popular financial websites report many of these ratios as well.

The template in Exhibit 12-7, which was prepared in Excel, can be used to analyze any company's financial statements. Excel makes computing financial ratios easy. Interpreting what the ratios mean and using them to make decisions takes more time and effort.

Exhibit 12-7 Financial Summary: Apple Inc.

A1

	A	B	C	D	E	F
1	**Apple Inc. Financial Summary and Key Ratios**					
2	**In millions of $**	**FY 2016**	**FY 2015**	**FY 2014**	**FY 2013**	**FY 2012**
3	**Results of operations**					
4	Net sales	$ 215,639	$ 233,715	$ 182,795	$ 170,910	$ 156,508
5	Cost of sales	131,376	140,089	112,258	106,606	87,846
6	Gross margin	84,263	93,626	70,537	64,304	68,662
7	Gross margin as percent of net sales	39.1%	40.1%	38.6%	37.6%	43.9%
8	Operating income	60,024	71,230	52,503	48,999	55,241
9	Operating income as percent of net sales	27.8%	30.5%	28.7%	28.7%	35.3%
10	Net income after taxes	45,687	53,394	39,510	37,037	41,733
11	Net income/sales (Return on Sales or ROS)	21.2%	22.8%	21.6%	21.7%	26.7%
12	ROA (line 11 x line 29)	14.9%	20.5%	18.0%	19.3%	28.6%
13	ROE (line 12 x line 40)	36.90%	46.25%	33.61%	30.73%	42.93%
14	Times interest earned	41	97	137	360	N/A
15	Common shares outstanding (000)	5,470,820	5,753,421	6,085,572	6,477,320	6,543,726
16	Earnings per common share, basic	$ 8.35	$ 9.28	$ 6.49	$ 5.72	$ 6.38
17	Price/earnings multiple	13.70	12.3	15.50	12.00	14.93
18	Cash dividends	12,150	11,561	11,126	10,564	2,523
19	Dividends per common share	$ 2.18	$ 1.98	1.82	1.64	2.65
20	**Financial position**					
21	Accounts receivable	$ 15,754	$ 16,849	17,460	13,102	10,930
22	Average accounts receivable	16,302	17,155	15,281	12,016	8,150
23	Inventories	2,132	2,349	2,111	1,764	791
24	Average inventories	2,241	2,230	1,938	1,278	784
25	Current assets	106,869	89,378	68,531	73,286	57,653
26	Quick assets	82,909	58,450	42,537	53,648	40,059
27	Total assets	321,686	290,345	231,839	207,000	176,064
28	Average total assets	306,016	261,092	219,420	191,532	146,218
29	Asset turnover (line 4/line 28)	0.705	0.895	0.833	0.892	1.07
30	Accounts payable	37,294	35,490	30,196	22,367	21,175
31	Average accounts payable	36,392	32,843	26,282	21,771	17,904
32	Current liabilities	79,006	80,610	63,448	43,658	38,542
33	Total liabilities	193,437	170,990	120,292	83,451	57,854
34	Working capital (line 25-line 32)	27,863	8,768	5,083	29,628	19,111
35	Current ratio (line 25/line 32)	1.35	1.11	1.08	1.68	1.50
36	Quick ratio (line 26/line 32)	1.05	0.73	0.67	1.23	1.04
37	Debt ratio (line 33/line 27)	0.60	0.59	0.52	0.40	0.33
38	Total stockholders' equity	128,249	119,355	111,547	123,549	118,210
39	Average stockholders' equity	123,802	115,451	117,548	120,880	97,413
40	Leverage ratio (line 28/line 39)	2.472	2.261	1.867	1.584	1.501
41	Inventory turnover (line 5/ line 24)	58.64	62.82	57.94	83.45	112.12
42	Days inventory outstanding (DIO)(365/line 41)	6.22	5.81	6.30	4.37	3.26
43	Accounts receivable turnover (line 4/line 22)	13.23	13.62	11.96	14.22	19.2
44	Days sales outstanding (DSO)(365/line 43)	27.59	26.80	30.51	25.66	19.01
45	Accounts payable turnover (line 5/line 31)	3.61	4.27	4.27	4.90	4.91
46	Days payable outstanding (DPO)(365/line 45)	101.11	85.48	85.45	74.49	74.34
47	Cash conversion cycle (line 42+line44-line 46)	(67.3)	(52.9)	(48.6)	(44.5)	(52.1)
48						

Data from the U.S. Securities and Exchange Commission EDGAR Company filings, www.sec.gov

The ratios we discuss in this chapter are classified as follows:

1. Measuring the ability to pay current liabilities
2. Measuring turnover and the cash conversion cycle
3. Measuring leverage: the overall ability to pay debts
4. Measuring profitability
5. Analyzing stock as an investment

Remember to Start at the Beginning: Company and Industry Information

Apple Inc., has established itself as the world's leader in the consumer electronics and media sales industries. The company was founded in Cupertino, California, by Steve Jobs and Michael Wozniak and went public in 1977. For more than two decades, Apple mostly manufactured personal computers. It faced intense competition from companies such as **Dell, Inc**.

Apple experienced rocky sales and low market share during the 1990s. Jobs, who had been ousted from the company in 1985, returned to Apple in 1996 and became the company's CEO. Under his leadership, Apple began developing innovative products, including the iPhone, iPod Touch, iPad, and Apple TV, and sales skyrocketed.

Jobs died in 2011, but Apple continues to grow and prosper under the leadership of Tim Cook, its new CEO. In 2015, the company launched the Apple Watch, which was literally the world's first Internet-connected "wearable computer." Some people predict that virtually every device that we use will be connected to the Internet by 2020. The company's engineers are rumored to be working on an all-electric car that could be introduced by 2020 as well.

Due to its innovation strategy and expertise, Apple seems to be well positioned to prosper in the future. But how has all of this innovation affected the company's shareholders? Are they prospering? The discussion in the following paragraphs describes the company's business strategy from 2014 through 2016 and its effect on the financial information shown in Exhibit 12-7.

As of April 2017, Apple Inc. was the world's largest and most valuable company. With a total market capitalization of over $730 billion, it was larger than **Facebook** and **Exxon-Mobil** combined. As Exhibit 12-7 shows, during the fiscal years 2012 through 2016, worldwide net sales revenues (line 4) for Apple grew by 38%, from $156.5 billion to $215.6 billion. Net income after taxes (line 10) grew from $41.7 billion in 2012, to an all-time high of $53.4 billion in 2015, before settling back to $45.6 billion in 2016. At the end of its 2016 fiscal year, the company had generated an enormous stockpile of cash and marketable securities (refer to Appendix E). During this period of rapid growth, Apple increased its dividend per share by 10% and kept its debt levels respectably low.

The story behind Apple's decision to distribute its first corporate dividend in 2012 is interesting. The company's share price was approaching $700 per share. Profits were high, as was the company's stockpile of cash. Shareholders began to complain that, while the company was flush with profits and cash, they had not been allowed to participate adequately in the company's profitability through dividends or stock repurchases. Under pressure, the company's board of directors voted to pay Apple Inc.'s first dividend at the end of fiscal 2012, as well as to engage in an aggressive stock repurchase program over a period of several years, in order to allow shareholders to realize the pent-up appreciation in the prices they paid for their shares.

However, there was a problem getting the cash out of the company and to the shareholders. Most of the company's cash was sitting in the banks of the company's profitable subsidiaries located in foreign countries with much lower tax rates than the United States. To be distributed by Apple Inc. (the parent company), the cash and earnings would have to be "repatriated." That is, it would have to be distributed as dividends from the foreign subsidiaries and translated from foreign currencies to dollars. Repatriating the earnings would have subjected Apple Inc. to U.S. corporate income taxes at rates exceeding 30%.

How could Apple make the required distributions and still avoid taxes? The company's finance team went to work and came up with an innovative solution: borrow the money to pay shareholder dividends and to repurchase their shares rather than transfer it from the foreign subsidiaries. Consequently, in spite of its tremendous stockpile of cash, Apple took on a combination of short-term and long-term debt. The company used the proceeds from the debt instruments along with its vast holdings in short-term, marketable securities to provide almost $90 billion in new cash to pay the dividend and repurchase its shares over the next several years.

Because Apple has an excellent credit rating, the debt instruments have been snapped up by institutional investors such as pension funds. The interest Apple pays on these instruments is low and tax deductible. Dividend payments are not tax deductible. By using the proceeds from the debt instruments to pay the dividends, the company avoided the heavy tax burden associated with repatriation of its earnings. In addition, the company declared a 7-for-1 stock split in 2014, distributing 7 shares for each share owned by its existing shareholders. This stock split increased the number of Apple's outstanding shares sevenfold, and reduced the market price of the stock from over $700 per share to less than $100 per share. The company's share price as of April 2017 has increased yet another 40% in value. The impact of these decisions on the company's liquidity and profitability ratios over the past two years has been significant, as you will see.

Now Let's Do the Numbers

Once you gain knowledge about a company and its industry, how do you determine whether the company's performance has been strong or weak, based on its current-period ratios? You can make that decision only if you have the following ratios to compare against the current period: (1) prior-year ratios, and (2) industry comparables, either in the form of an industry average or the ratios of a strong competitor. So, in the following sections, we will compare Apple's current year ratios with (1) its prior years' ratios (see Exhibit 12-7), and (2) ratios for the industry (if available) or one or more of Apple's competitors.

It is difficult to find a single competitor for Apple, because its products span several different industries. Consequently, we have selected **Alphabet, Inc.**, the parent of **Google**, because it is Apple's main competitor in its primary market—smartphones.

Measuring the Ability to Pay Current Liabilities

Recall that working capital (which is also referred to as *net working capital*) is the amount of money a company has to pay its current liabilities with its current assets. The formula for working capital is as follows:

Working capital = Current assets − Current liabilities

In general, the larger the working capital, the better the ability to pay debts.

Consider two companies with equal amounts of working capital:

	Company	
	Jones	**Smith**
Current assets	$100,000	$200,000
Current liabilities	50,000	150,000
Working capital	$ 50,000	$ 50,000

Both companies have working capital of $50,000, but Jones's working capital is as large as its current liabilities. Smith's working capital is only one-third as large as its current liabilities. Jones is in a better position because its working capital is a higher percentage of its current liabilities.

As Exhibit 12-7 (line 34) shows, Apple Inc.'s working capital as of September 24, 2016 (the end of its 2016 fiscal year), was $27,863 million. This was over three times its working capital at the end of fiscal 2015 ($8,768), and it was mainly due to the fact that the company's cash position was growing enormously. Looking at the trend in line 34 across 5 years, you can see that working capital took a big dip in fiscal 2014 after the company made its strategic decision to use short-term borrowing in order to return cash to its shareholders. The company doubled its payments to shareholders in the form of stock repurchases from $22.9 billion in fiscal 2013 to $45 billion in fiscal 2014. The company also returned $11.1 billion more cash to shareholders in the form of cash dividends in 2014. This left Apple Inc.'s working capital substantially lower at the end of 2014, but still not depleted to a critical level, because the company has continued to generate billions of dollars in sales monthly, mostly for cash. By the end of 2016, working capital levels had returned to almost all-time high levels. Let's look at two key ratios now that help tell the rest of the story.

Current Ratio. The current ratio makes it easier to compare working capital amounts from firm to firm when you are trying to determine a company's ability to pay its current liabilities with its current assets. Recall that the formula for the current ratio is:

$$\text{Current ratio} = \text{Current assets} \div \text{Current liabilities}$$

In general, a higher current ratio indicates a stronger debt-paying ability. Exhibit 12-8 shows Apple's Comparative Consolidated Statements of Operations. Exhibit 12-9 shows Apple's Comparative Consolidated Balance Sheets.

Exhibit 12-8 Comparative Consolidated Statements of Operations—Apple Inc.

	A	B	C	D
1	**Apple Inc. Consolidated Statements of Operations**	**12 Months Ended**		
2	In millions, except share data	**Sep. 24, 2016**	**Sep. 26, 2015**	**Sep. 27, 2014**
3	Net sales	$ 215,639	$ 233,715	$ 182,795
4	Cost of sales	131,376	140,089	112,258
5	Gross margin	84,263	93,626	70,537
6	Operating expenses:			
7	Research and development	10,045	8,067	6,041
8	Selling, general and administrative	14,194	14,329	11,993
9	Total operating expenses	24,239	22,396	18,034
10	Operating income	60,024	71,230	52,503
11	Other income/(expense), net	1,348	1,285	980
12	Income before provision for income taxes	61,372	72,515	53,483
13	Provision for income taxes	15,685	19,121	13,973
14	Net income	$ 45,687	$ 53,394	$ 39,510
15	Earnings per share:			
16	Basic	$ 8.35	$ 9.28	$ 6.49
17	Diluted	$ 8.31	$ 9.22	$ 6.45
18	Shares used in computing earnings per share:			
19	Basic	5,470,820	5,753,421	6,085,572
20	Diluted	5,500,281	5,793,069	6,122,663
21	Cash dividends declared per common share	$ 2.18	$ 1.98	$ 1.82
22				

Data from the U.S. Securities and Exchange Commission EDGAR Company filings, www.sec.gov

Exhibit 12-9 Comparative Consolidated Balance Sheets—Apple Inc.

	A	B	C
1	**Apple Inc. Consolidated Balance Sheets**	**Sep. 24, 2016**	**Sep. 26, 2015**
2	in millions of $, unless otherwise specified		
3	**Current assets:**		
4	Cash and cash equivalents	$ 20,484	$ 21,120
5	Short-term marketable securities	46,671	20,481
6	Accounts receivable, less allowances of $86 and $99, respectively	15,754	16,849
7	Inventories	2,132	2,349
8	Vendor non-trade receivables	13,545	13,494
9	Other current assets	8,283	15,085
10	**Total current assets**	106,869	89,378
11	Long-term marketable securities	170,430	164,065
12	Property, plant and equipment, net	27,010	22,471
13	Goodwill	5,414	5,116
14	Acquired intangible assets, net	3,206	3,893
15	Other assets	8,757	5,422
16	**Total assets**	$ 321,686	$ 290,345
17	**Current liabilities:**		
18	Accounts payable	$ 37,294	$ 35,490
19	Accrued expenses	22,027	25,181
20	Deferred revenue	8,080	8,940
21	Commercial paper	8,105	8,499
22	Current portion of long-term debt	3,500	2,500
23	**Total current liabilities**	79,006	80,610
24	Deferred revenue - non-current	2,930	3,624
25	Long-term debt	75,427	53,329
26	Other non-current liabilities	36,074	33,427
27	**Total liabilities**	193,437	170,990
28	Commitments and contingencies		
29	**Shareholders' equity:**		
30	Common stock and additional paid-in capital, $0.00001 par value;		
31	12,600,000 shares authorized; 5,336,166 and 5,578,753 shares		
32	issued and outstanding, respectively	31,251	27,416
33	Retained earnings	96,364	92,284
34	Accumulated other comprehensive income/(loss)	634	(345)
35	**Total shareholders' equity**	128,249	119,355
36	**Total liabilities and shareholders' equity**	$ 321,686	$ 290,345
37			

Data from the U.S. Securities and Exchange Commission EDGAR Company filings, www.sec.gov

We can use the figures in Exhibit 12-9 to calculate Apple's current ratios at September 24, 2016, and September 26, 2015, which are as follows:

	Apple Inc.'s Current Ratio		
Formula (figures in millions)	**2016**	**2015**	**Competitor Alphabet, Inc.**
$\text{Current ratio} = \frac{\text{Current assets}}{\text{Current liabilities}}$	$\frac{\$106{,}869}{\$79{,}006} = 1.35$	$\frac{\$89{,}378}{\$80{,}610} = 1.11$	6.29

Apple Inc.'s current ratio increased during 2016, to 1.35 from 1.11 in 2015, for the same reason that its working capital increased: The company generated excess cash and marketable securities while holding its current liabilities relatively constant. Line 35 of Exhibit 12-7 shows that the current ratio increased significantly from 1.08 in 2014 to 1.35 in 2016. This occurred because current liabilities slightly declined in 2016 to $79,006 from $80,610 in 2015; current assets increased from $89,378 million to $106,869 million (about 20%). Virtually all of this increase was in cash, cash equivalents, and short-term marketable securities, which increased by $25 billion over the year.

However, Apple's current ratio of 1.35 was much lower than Alphabet's, partly because Alphabet is a newer company and hasn't yet paid a dividend or repurchased stock from its shareholders. Paying a dividend or repurchasing stock would have lowered Alphabet's current ratio.

Quick (Acid-Test) Ratio. As discussed in Chapter 5, the quick (acid-test) ratio tells us whether a business could pass the "acid test" of paying all its current liabilities if they came due immediately (quickly). The quick ratio uses a narrower base to measure liquidity than the current ratio does.

To compute the quick ratio, we add up a business's cash, short-term investments, and accounts receivable (net of allowances), and divide the sum by the business's current liabilities. Inventory and prepaid expenses are excluded because they are less liquid (take longer to convert to cash). A low quick ratio indicates that a company's cash conversion cycle is short. A quick ratio of 0.90 to 1.00 is acceptable in most industries.

Using the information in Exhibits 12-7 (line 36) and 12-9, Apple Inc.'s quick ratios for 2016 and 2015 are (in millions of $):

	Formula	*Apple Inc.'s Quick Ratio* 2016	2015
Quick ratio =	$\dfrac{\text{Cash and cash equivalents} + \text{Short-term investments} + \text{Net current receivables}}{\text{Current liabilities}}$	$\dfrac{\$20{,}484 + \$46{,}671 + \$15{,}754}{\$79{,}006} = 1.05$	$\dfrac{\$21{,}120 + \$20{,}481 + \$16{,}849}{\$80{,}610} = 0.73$
Quick ratio of competitor	Alphabet, Inc.	6.0	

Like the current ratio, the company's quick ratio declined somewhat from 2013 through 2015 but recovered in 2016. Alphabet, Inc.'s quick ratio is much larger than Apple's for the same reasons that its current ratio is higher: It is a younger company that has yet to pay dividends or repurchase any of its stock.

Measuring Turnover and the Cash Conversion Cycle

The ability to sell inventory and collect receivables, as well as effectively manage payments on accounts payable, is the lifeblood of any retail, wholesale, or manufacturing concern. In this section, we discuss three ratios that measure this ability—inventory turnover, accounts receivable turnover, and accounts payable turnover—as well as the relationship among them, which is called the *cash conversion cycle*.

Inventory Turnover. Companies generally strive to sell their inventory as quickly as possible. The faster inventory sells, the sooner cash comes in. Inventory turnover, discussed in Chapter 6, measures the number of times a company sells its average level of inventory during a year. A fast turnover indicates ease in selling inventory; a low turnover indicates difficulty. A value of 6 means that the company's average level of inventory has been sold six times during the year, and that's usually better than a turnover of three times. But too high a value can mean that the business is not keeping enough inventory on hand, which can lead to lost sales if the company can't fill orders. Therefore, a business strives for the most *profitable* turnover rate, not necessarily the *highest* turnover rate.

To compute inventory turnover, divide a company's cost of goods sold by its average inventory for the period. We use the cost of goods sold—not sales—in the computation because both cost of goods sold and inventory are stated *at cost*. Apple Inc.'s inventory turnover for 2016 is

Formula	*Apple Inc.'s Inventory Turnover*	Competitor (Alphabet, Inc.)
Inventory turnover $= \dfrac{\text{Cost of goods sold}}{\text{Average inventory}}$	$\dfrac{\$131{,}376 \text{ million}}{\$2{,}241 \text{ million}} = 58.64$	131
Days' inventory outstanding (DIO) $= \dfrac{365}{\text{Turnover}}$	$\dfrac{365}{58.64} = 6.2$ days	2.8 days

Apple's cost of goods sold is found on the Consolidated Statements of Operations (see Exhibit 12-8). Average inventory (from the balance sheets, Exhibit 12-9) is the average of beginning inventory ($2,349 million) and ending inventory ($2,132 million). If inventory levels vary greatly from month to month, you can compute the monthly average by adding up the 12 monthly balances and dividing the sum by 12.

Inventory turnover varies widely with the nature of the business. For example, Apple's inventory turned over 58.6 times in 2016, which is once every 6.2 days (365/58.6). In 2015, Apple Inc.'s inventory turned over 62.8 times. Line 41 in Exhibit 12-7 shows that between 2012 and 2016, inventory turnover fluctuated between 58 and 112 times per year. In contrast, Alphabet, Inc.'s inventory turned over 131 times in 2016 (about once every 3 days). Computer and electronics manufacturers purposely keep very low inventory levels and produce products quickly because the components they use to make them can quickly become obsolete as newer technology is developed.

To evaluate a company's inventory turnover, compare the ratio over time as well as with industry averages or competitors' ratios. Steadily increasing inventory turnover is a positive sign, particularly if gross margins (gross profits) are also increasing. A sharp decline in inventory turnover suggests the need to take action to increase sales, usually by lowering prices. Unfortunately, this will reduce a business's gross margins.

Accounts Receivable Turnover. Accounts receivable turnover, which was discussed in Chapter 5, measures a company's ability to collect cash from its credit customers. The ratio tells how many times during the year average receivables were turned into cash. In general, the higher this ratio is, the better. However, a receivable turnover that is too high could indicate that a company's credit terms are too tight, which may cause it to lose sales to potentially good customers.

To compute accounts receivable turnover, divide net sales (assumed all on credit) by average net accounts receivable. Apple Inc.'s accounts receivable turnover ratio for 2016 was

Formula		*Apple Inc.'s Accounts Receivable Turnover*	Competitor (Alphabet, Inc.)
Accounts receivable turnover	$= \dfrac{\text{Net credit sales}}{\text{Average net accounts receivable}}$	$\dfrac{\$215{,}639\text{ million}}{\$16{,}302\text{ million}} = 13.23$	7.03
Days' sales outstanding (DSO) (or days'-sales-in-receivables)	$= \dfrac{365}{\text{Turnover}}$	$\dfrac{365}{13.23} = 27.59$ days	52 days

Net sales comes from Exhibit 12-8 and from line 4 of Exhibit 12-7. Average net accounts receivable (line 22 of Exhibit 12-7) is figured by adding beginning ($16,849 million) and ending receivables ($15,754 million) from Exhibit 12-9, and then dividing by 2. If accounts receivable vary widely during the year, compute the average by using the 12 monthly balances. Apple collected its average accounts receivable 13.23 times during 2016. According to Exhibit 12-7 (line 43), accounts receivable turnover fluctuated between 12 and 19 times over the course of 5 years. In comparison, Alphabet, Inc.'s accounts receivable turnover for 2016 was 7.03 times.

Apple Inc.'s accounts receivable turnover of 13.23 times per year is much faster than the industry average. Apple owns and operates a large number of retail stores, and much of its sales are for cash, which makes the company's receivables balance very low relative to its sales.

Days' Sales Outstanding. Businesses must convert accounts receivable to cash. All else being equal, the lower the receivable balance, the better the cash flow. Days' sales outstanding (DSO), or *days sales in receivables*, also discussed in Chapter 5, shows how many days it takes to collect an average account receivable. If you have already calculated a company's receivables turnover (see the previous section), simply divide it by 365. For Apple, DSO works out to about 27.6 days (365/13.23). Exhibit 12-7 (line 44) shows that DSO fluctuated between 19 and 31 days over the 5 years, which is similar to an average company's credit cycle of 30 days. By comparison, Alphabet, Inc.'s, DSO in 2016 was 52 days (365/7.03 turnover).

Accounts Payable Turnover. Discussed in Chapter 8, accounts payable turnover measures the number of times per year a business pays off an average account payable. To compute accounts payable turnover, divide the company's cost of goods sold by its average accounts payable.[2] For Apple Inc., this ratio is

Formula			*Apple Inc.'s Accounts Payable Turnover*	Competitor (Alphabet, Inc.)
Accounts payable turnover	=	$\frac{\text{Cost of goods sold}}{\text{Average accounts payable}}$	$\frac{\$131{,}376 \text{ million}}{\$36{,}392 \text{ million}} = 3.61$	17.7
Days' payable outstanding (DPO)	=	$\frac{365}{\text{Turnover}}$	$\frac{365}{3.61} = 101.1$ days	20.6 days

Apple's cost of goods sold (cost of sales) comes from Exhibit 12-8 and line 5 of Exhibit 12-7, whereas the company's average accounts payable comes from line 31 of Exhibit 12-7. On average, Apple pays off its accounts payable 3.61 times per year, which is about every 101 days. To convert accounts payable turnover to days' payable outstanding (DPO), divide the turnover into 365 (365 ÷ 3.61 = 101.1 days). In comparison, Alphabet, Inc.'s accounts payable turnover is 17.7 times per year, or about every 21 days. Apple's financial summary (Exhibit 12-7, line 46) shows that DPO fluctuated between 74 and 101 days over the 5-year period, and at the end of fiscal 2016 was at its highest point.

Cash Conversion Cycle. By expressing the three turnover ratios in days, we can compute Apple's **cash conversion cycle** as follows:

Formula			*Apple Inc.'s Cash Conversion Cycle*	Competitor (Alphabet, Inc.)
Cash conversion cycle	=	DIO + DSO − DPO	6.2 + 27.6 − 101.1 = −67.3 days	34 days
where DIO	=	Days' inventory outstanding		
DSO	=	Days' sales outstanding		
DPO	=	Days' payable outstanding		

A negative amount for the cash conversion cycle looks odd. What does it mean? Apple is in the enviable position of being able to sell inventory and collect from its customers 67.3 days before it pays the suppliers that provided the parts and materials to produce those inventories. As a result, Apple can stock less inventory and hold on to cash longer than other companies. It also helps explain why the company could afford to keep almost $47 billion in short-term marketable securities (Exhibit 12-9) to "sop up" its excess cash, using it to make still more money while waiting to pay off suppliers. According to Exhibit 12-7, line 47, Apple's negative cash conversion cycle increased (became more favorable) by 15 days from 2012 through 2016. Apple's competitor, Alphabet, Inc., had a positive cash conversion cycle of 34 days in 2016.

Under Armour, Inc., featured earlier in this chapter, had a positive cash conversion cycle in 2016 of about 117 days, meaning that it took the company 117 days (almost a third of a year) to sell its inventory, collect the cash for it, and pay off its accounts payable. Retail companies that have a more "seasonal" inventory turnover (about four times per year, or about every 90 days) have cash conversion cycles in the range of 30 to 120 days. Because service businesses typically do not carry inventory, their cash conversion cycles consist only of DSO – DPO and are generally shorter.

[2] For manufacturing or product-oriented companies, it is appropriate to use purchases rather than cost of goods sold as the numerator of the fraction. This requires adjusting cost of goods sold for the difference between beginning and ending inventories. See Chapter 8 for details. When inventories are small in relation to cost of goods sold, and/or when there is virtually no change between beginning and ending inventories (as is the case for Apple Inc.), this adjustment is insignificant. Therefore, to simplify, cost of goods sold may be used without adjustment.

Measuring Leverage: The Overall Ability to Pay Debts

The ratios discussed so far relate to current assets and current liabilities. They measure the ability to sell inventory, collect receivables, and pay current liabilities. Two indicators of the ability to pay total liabilities are the debt ratio and the times-interest-earned ratio.

Debt Ratio. Suppose you are a bank loan officer and you have received loan applications for \$500,000 from two similar companies. The first company already owes \$600,000, and the second owes only \$250,000. Which company gets the loan? Company 2 may look like the stronger candidate, because it owes less.

This relationship between total liabilities and total assets is called the debt ratio. Discussed in Chapters 3 and 9, the debt ratio tells us the proportion of a company's assets financed with debt. A debt ratio of 1 reveals that debt has financed all the assets. A debt ratio of 0.50 means that debt finances half the assets. The higher the debt ratio, the greater the pressure to pay interest and principal. The lower the debt ratio, the lower the company's credit risk.

The debt ratios for Apple Inc. in 2016 and 2015 follow (\$ in millions):

	Apple Inc.'s Debt Ratio		
Formula	**2016**	**2015**	**Competitor (Alphabet, Inc.)**
Debt ratio $= \dfrac{\text{Total liabilities}}{\text{Total assets}}$	$\dfrac{\$193{,}437}{\$321{,}686} = 0.60$	$\dfrac{\$170{,}990}{\$290{,}345} = 0.59$	0.17

Line 37 of Exhibit 12-7 shows that Apple's debt ratio increased substantially between fiscal 2012 and fiscal 2016. However, it was still about average compared with many other public companies. Debt ratios vary substantially between industries. Companies in industries such as advertising and aerospace usually have higher debt ratios than those in the manufacturing or retail industries.

Times-Interest-Earned Ratio. Analysts use a second ratio—the times-interest-earned ratio (introduced in Chapter 9)—to relate operating income to interest expense. To compute the times-interest-earned ratio, divide income from operations (operating income) by interest expense. Interest expense is a component of other income (expense) and is disclosed separately in Note 3 of the financial statements. This ratio measures the number of times operating income can cover a company's interest expense and is also called the *interest-coverage ratio*. A high ratio indicates ease in paying interest; a low value suggests difficulty.

	Apple Inc.'s Times-Interest-Earned Ratio		
Formula	**2016**	**2015**	**Competitor (Alphabet, Inc.)**
Times-interest-earned ratio $= \dfrac{\text{Income from operations}}{\text{Interest expense}}$	$\dfrac{\$60{,}024}{\$1{,}456} = 41$	$\dfrac{\$71{,}230}{\$733} = 97$	196

Apple Inc.'s interest expense for fiscal 2016 was \$1,456 million, up from \$733 million in 2015. Income from operations in 2016 was down from 2015 by over \$11 billion, but covered interest charges by 41 times, as compared to 97 times in 2015. The company's operating income was clearly sufficient to cover its interest charges. In comparison, Alphabet, Inc. had a very low debt ratio (17%). Therefore, its times-interest-earned ratio was quite a bit higher (196). In summary, like so many other factors of financial statement analysis, whether a company's times-earned-interest ratio is adequate depends on the company being studied and the industry in which it competes.

Measuring Profitability

The fundamental goal of business is to earn a profit, and so the ratios that measure profitability are reported widely.

Gross Margin (Profit) Percentage. In Chapter 6, we defined *gross (profit) margin* as net sales – cost of goods sold. That is, gross margin is the amount of profit a business makes from merely selling a product before other operating costs are subtracted. Let's look at Apple Inc.'s gross margin percentages (see line 7 in Exhibit12-7, and Exhibit 12-8 for details):

Formula			*Apple Inc.'s Gross Margin %* 2016	2015	Competitor (Alphabet, Inc.)
Gross Margin %	=	$\frac{\text{Gross margin}}{\text{Net sales}}$	39.1%	40.1%	61%

Do you remember the last time you visited an Apple store (perhaps when a new version of the iPhone was introduced)? How much were you willing to pay for your new iPhone, iPad, or iMac? Do you remember how crowded the store was? As we discussed in Chapter 7, because of the creative talents of their people, some companies have been able to adopt a "product differentiation" business strategy, which allows them to sell their products at a higher price than their competitors. When everyone wants the product, people are usually willing to pay more for it. Apple's gross margin percentage of 39.1% in 2016 was 1% less than it was in 2015. Alphabet, Inc., which is largely a service business with very little inventory, has a much higher gross margin of 61%. Most of Alphabet's expenses are operating expenses, which are below the gross margin line in its income statement.

Operating Income (Profit) Percentage. **Operating income (profit) percentage** is income from operations as a percentage of net sales. It is an important statistic because it measures the percentage of profit earned from each sales dollar a company brings in. The first component of having high operating earnings is having a high gross margin percentage. The second component is keeping operating expenses as low as possible, given the product quality and customer service levels a business wants to maintain. Apple and Alphabet's operating income percentages were as follows:

Formula			*Apple Inc.'s Operating Income %* 2016	2015	Competitor (Alphabet, Inc.)
Operating Income %	=	$\frac{\text{Operating Income}}{\text{Net sales}}$	27.8%	30.5%	26.3%

Apple's operating income percentage of 27.8% is similar to Alphabet's, which is 26.3%. Exhibit 12-7 (lines 7 and 9) shows that Apple's gross margin and operating income percentages both declined since 2012. The decline was mostly due to increased competition from Alphabet in the smartphone market.

DuPont Analysis. Recall from Chapter 10 that the ultimate goal of DuPont Analysis is to explain the rate of return on common stockholders' equity (see the far right-hand column in Exhibit 12-10) by breaking it down into its component elements: rate of return on sales, asset turnover, and leverage ratio.

Exhibit 12-10 | DuPont Analysis Calculations

ROA			×	Leverage ratio (Equity multiplier)	=	ROE
Rate of return on sales (Net profit margin ratio)	×	Asset turnover ratio	×	Leverage ratio (Equity multiplier)	=	Return on equity (ROE)
$\frac{\text{Net income*}}{\text{Net sales}}$	×	$\frac{\text{Net sales}}{\text{Average total assets}}$	×	$\frac{\text{Average total assets}}{\text{Average common stockholders' equity}}$	=	$\frac{\text{Net income*}}{\text{Average common stockholders' equity}}$

*minus preferred dividends, if any

The first two components in Exhibit 12-10 combine to give rate of return on total assets (ROA). When the last component (the leverage ratio) is incorporated into the calculations, it produces (by cross-cancellation) the rate of return on common stockholders' equity (ROE). We now explain each component using figures for Apple Inc., to illustrate.

Rate of Return on Sales (Net Profit Margin Ratio). The first element of a DuPont Analysis is the **rate of return on net sales**, or simply *return on sales (ROS)*. (The word *net* is usually omitted for convenience.) This ratio shows the percentage of each sales dollar earned as net income. (In Chapter 7, we referred to this ratio as the *net profit margin ratio*.) The fiscal 2016 return-on-sales ratios for Apple, compared with those of its competitor Alphabet, were as follows (using figures in millions from Exhibits12-7 and 12-8):

Formula	*Apple Inc.'s Rate of Return on Sales* 2016	2015	Competitor (Alphabet, Inc.)
Rate of return on sales (Net profit margin ratio) $= \dfrac{\text{Net income} - \text{Preferred dividends}}{\text{Net sales}}$	$\dfrac{\$45{,}687}{\$215{,}639} = 21.2\%$	$\dfrac{\$53{,}394}{\$233{,}715} = 22.8\%$	21.6%

Companies strive for a high rate of return on sales. The higher the percentage, the more profit is being generated by sales dollars. According to Exhibit 12-7 (line 11), Apple Inc.'s return on sales was high in 2016 (21.2%). But again, looking at the five-year trend, we see that Apple's ROS sank back to this level in 2013 after reaching an all-time high in 2012 of 26.7%. Again, this was primarily due to the decline in Apple's gross margins as a result of competition from Alphabet (Google). Interestingly, Apple's return on sales in 2016 almost matched Alphabet's (21.6%).

Asset Turnover. As discussed in Chapter 7, asset turnover measures the amount of net sales generated for each dollar invested in assets. Consequently, asset turnover is a measure of how efficiently management is operating the company. A company with a high asset turnover tends to be more productive than a company with a low asset turnover. Let's examine Apple's asset turnover for 2016 compared with 2015 and then compare it to competitor Alphabet's asset turnover (see Exhibit 12-7, line 28, for average total assets, and line 29 for asset turnover).

Formula	*Apple Inc.'s Asset Turnover* 2016	2015	Competitor (Alphabet, Inc.)
Asset turnover ratio $= \dfrac{\text{Net sales}}{\text{Average total assets}}$	$\dfrac{\$215{,}639 \text{ million}}{306{,}016 \text{ million}} = 0.705$	$\dfrac{\$233{,}715 \text{ million}}{\$261{,}092 \text{ million}} = 0.895$	0.57

Both Apple and Alphabet have invested a significant amount in assets per dollar of sales. This is often the case with innovative companies, as opposed to companies that focus on selling products at a low cost. To make major product innovations requires a significant investment in both tangible and intangible assets.

Rate of Return on Total Assets (ROA). Having computed the rate of return on net sales and asset turnover, we are now prepared to combine them into the first two elements of our DuPont Analysis to compute the rate of return on total assets (ROA):[3]

Rate of return on assets (ROA)	*Apple Inc.'s ROA* 2016	2015	Competitor (Alphabet, Inc.)
Rate of return on sales	21.2%	22.8%	21.6%
×	×	×	×
Asset turnover ratio	0.705	0.895	0.57
=	=	=	=
ROA	14.9%	20.5%	12.3%

[3] Some analysts use net income before interest expense to compute ROA because interest expense measures the return earned by creditors who provide the portion of total assets for which the company has used borrowed capital.

Again, the raw figures for our computations are based on income and asset figures in Exhibits 12-7 (line 12), 12-8, and 12-9. However, the component ratios are based on the previous two illustrations. We see from these computations that for both Apple and Alphabet, ROA was driven primarily by the high profitability of the companies due to their product innovation strategies rather than their operating efficiency. That said, Apple's 0.705 turnover indicates that the company was slightly more efficiently run than Alphabet, which has an asset turnover of 0.57. Therefore, Apple's ROA is slightly higher than Alphabet's (14.9% vs. 12.3%).

Leverage (Equity Multiplier) Ratio. The final element of a DuPont Analysis is the leverage ratio. Recall that it measures the impact of debt financing on profitability. You learned in Chapters 9 and 10 that it can be advantageous to use borrowed capital to finance a business. Companies like Apple that finance operations with debt are said to *leverage* their positions.

Earlier, we expressed the debt ratio as the ratio of total liabilities to total assets. The leverage ratio, or equity multiplier, measures the number of dollars of assets provided by each dollar of invested capital in stockholders' equity. Because Total assets − Stockholders' equity = Total liabilities, the leverage ratio is a way of inversely expressing the debt ratio—it merely looks at financing from the other side of the basic accounting equation. Let's compare Apple's leverage ratios for 2016 and 2015 to Alphabet's (see Exhibit 12-7, line 28, for average total assets and line 39 for average stockholders' equity).

Formula	*Apple Inc.'s Leverage Ratios* 2016	2015	Competitor (Alphabet, Inc.)
Leverage ratio = $\frac{\text{Average total assets}}{\text{Average common stockholders' equity}}$	$\frac{\$306{,}016 \text{ million}}{\$123{,}802 \text{ million}} = 2.472$	$\frac{\$261{,}092 \text{ million}}{115{,}451 \text{ million}} = 2.261$	1.22

Over the last few years, Apple has built up a debt ratio of about 0.60. This translates to leverage ratios of 2.472 for 2016 and 2.261 for 2015, respectively. The ratios are listed on line 40 of Exhibit 12-7. By comparison, Alphabet had a very low debt ratio of only about 17% in 2016. Therefore, Apple used more borrowed capital than equity capital to finance its operations, so its leverage ratio was much higher than Alphabet's (2.472 compared to only 1.22).

Rate of Return on Common Stockholders' Equity (ROE). A popular measure of profitability is rate of return on common stockholders' equity, often shortened to *return on equity* (ROE). Discussed in Chapter 10, this ratio shows the relationship between net income and common stockholders' investment in the company—how much income is earned for every \$1 invested by common stockholders. Apple's ROE is shown on line 13 of Exhibit 12-7.

To compute this ratio by itself, first subtract preferred dividends, if any, from net income to measure the income available to the common stockholders. Then divide the income available to common stockholders by average common equity during the year. Common equity is total equity minus preferred equity. The vast majority of companies have no preferred equity, so common equity makes up the total. The 2016 return on common stockholders' equity, computed the traditional way, for Apple was

Formula	*Apple Inc.'s 2016 Rate of Return on Common Stockholders' Equity*	Competitor (Alphabet, Inc.)
Rate of return on common stockholders' equity = $\frac{\text{Net income} - \text{Preferred dividends}}{\text{Average common stockholders' equity}}$	$\frac{\$45{,}687 \text{ million} - \$0}{\$123{,}802 \text{ million}} = 36.9\%$	15%

A DuPont Analysis ultimately reaches the same result (except for rounding error), but using it allows us to see much more information about the interaction among profitability (return on sales), asset utilization (turnover), and leverage:

Rate of Return on Stockholders' Equity (ROE)	*Apple Inc.'s ROE* 2016	2015	Competitor (Alphabet, Inc.)
ROA	14.9%	20.5%	12.3%
×	×	×	×
Leverage ratio	2.472	2.261	1.22
=	=	=	=
ROE	36.83%*	46.35%*	15.0%

* figures differ slightly from Exhibit 12–7 because of rounding.

Apple's ROA was slightly higher than Alphabet's ROA. In addition, Apple Inc. used quite a bit more debt, or leverage, to finance its operations than Alphabet. To be sure, use of leverage is often a good thing in business, as long as it is kept within reasonable limits. The practice of using leverage is called *trading on the equity* because it acts as a compounding factor for ROA. However, as we pointed out in Chapter 10, leverage is a double-edged sword. It increases profits during good times but also magnifies losses during bad times.

Earnings per Share of Common Stock. As discussed in Chapter 10, earnings per share of common stock, or simply *earnings per share (EPS)*, is the amount of net income earned for each share of outstanding common stock. EPS is the most widely quoted of all financial statistics. It's the only ratio that appears on the income statement.

Earnings per share is computed by dividing net income available to common stockholders by the weighted-average number of common shares outstanding during the year. Preferred dividends are subtracted from net income because the preferred stockholders have a prior claim to their dividends. Like most other companies, Apple Inc., has no preferred stock and thus has no preferred dividends. The firm's EPS for 2016 and 2015 follow (based on Exhibits12-7 (line 16) and 12-8):

		Apple Inc.'s Earnings per Share (Basic)	
Formula		**2016**	**2015**
Earnings per share of common stock	= (Net income − Preferred dividends (in thousands)) / (Average number of shares of common stock outstanding (in thousands))	$\frac{\$45{,}687{,}000 - \$0}{5{,}470{,}820} = \$8.35$	$\frac{\$53{,}394{,}000 - \$0}{5{,}753{,}421} = \$9.28$

Apple's EPS fell 10% (from $9.28 to $8.35) during 2016. Sales revenue fell by a little over $18 billion, as a result of weaker-than-anticipated sales. Gross margin declined, as did operating income. The company repurchased 300 million shares, but not enough to keep EPS from declining by $0.93 per share. Nevertheless, Apple's shares continue to appreciate. In mid-2017, a common share sold for about $140. That's more than 50% appreciation from the price of the stock in 2014.

Where is the stock headed currently? Would purchasing Apple's shares at $140 per share be a wise business decision? The next section gives you some information on how analysts make this decision.

Analyzing Stock as an Investment

Investors buy stock to earn a return on their investment. This return consists of two parts: (1) gains (or losses) from selling the stock and (2) dividends.

Price-Earnings Ratio (Multiple). Recall from Chapter 10 that the price-earnings ratio (multiple) is the ratio of common stock price per share to earnings per share. Abbreviated P/E, the ratio appears in stock listings and online. It shows the market price of $1 of earnings. Exhibit 12-7 (line 17) shows historical P/E multiples of Apple's stock at various times from 2012 through 2016.

Calculations for Apple's P/E ratios follow. The market price of Apple's common stock was $114.42 at September 24, 2016 (the end of its 2016 fiscal year) and $113.85 at September 26, 2015 (the end of its 2015 fiscal year). Stock prices can be obtained from a company's website or various other financial websites.

	Apple Inc.'s Price/Earnings Ratio	
Formula	**2016**	**2015**
P/E ratio = Market price per share of common stock / Earnings per share	$\frac{\$114.42}{\$8.35} = 13.7$	$\frac{\$113.85}{\$9.28} = 12.3$

Given Apple Inc.'s 2016 P/E ratio of 13.7, we would say that the company's stock is selling at 13.7 times earnings. In other words, each $1 of Apple's earnings is worth $13.70 to the stock market.

Stocks trade in ranges, and public companies report updated EPS values quarterly. The earnings are annualized and projected for the upcoming year (quarterly earnings multiplied by 4). During 2016, Apple's stock traded in the range of $89 to $145 per share. Things change fast in the technology industry. Competitors like Alphabet are threatening Apple with smart devices that perform comparably for a lower price. The market prices of stocks are based on consensus estimations of what may happen in the future. The health of the global economy, business cycles, competition, government policies (both domestic and abroad), new-product announcements, foreign trade deals, foreign currency fluctuations, and even the health of key company executives may significantly impact the estimates. Markets run on sentiment and are very difficult to predict.

Some analysts study past trends in P/E multiples and try to estimate future trading ranges. If the P/E multiple of a particular stock drifts toward the low end of a range, and if its projected earnings are increasing, it means that the price of the stock is becoming more attractive, which is a signal to buy. As P/E multiples drift higher, given projected earnings, the stock becomes too expensive, and an analyst would recommend investors either "hold" or "sell" the stock, but not buy it. In April 2017, Apple's stock was selling for about $142 per share. The stock's projected (forward) P/E multiple from one popular website in April 2017 was 15.7. Projected earnings per share for fiscal 2017 from the same website, based on the estimates of many stock analysts, was about $9. Therefore, the projected price of Apple Inc.'s stock as of April 2017 would have been only $141.30 (15.7 × $9). Were Apple's shares overvalued at the price of $142 per share? In April 2017, four out of six analysts recommended "hold" decisions at best. However, these recommendations are very subjective and can change overnight. Only time will tell whether purchasing Apple Inc.'s stock for $142 per share will prove profitable. Investing in stocks is a game of chance.

Dividend Yield. Recall also from Chapter 10 that dividend yield is the ratio of dividends per share of stock to the stock's market price per share. This ratio measures the percentage of a stock's market value returned annually to the stockholders as dividends. Although dividends are never guaranteed, some well-established companies continue to pay dividends even through turbulent economic times. Preferred stockholders pay special attention to this ratio because they invest primarily to receive dividends. However, certain companies, such as **The Home Depot, Inc., Merck Pharmaceuticals**, and Apple Inc. also pay attractive dividends on their common stock. In periods of low interest rates on certificates of deposit or money-market funds, dividend-paying stocks become more attractive alternatives for conservative investors.

Since paying its first quarterly dividend in 2012, Apple has paid regular dividends. For the year ended September 24, 2016, Apple Inc.'s stock paid $2.18 per share in dividends. Based on the stock's price of $114.42 on September 24, 2016, the dividend yield for Apple's common shareholders on that date was

Formula	*Dividend Yield on Apple Inc. Common Stock* September 24, 2016
Dividend yield on common stock* $= \dfrac{\text{Dividend per share of common stock}}{\text{Market price per share of common stock}}$	$\dfrac{\$2.18}{\$114.42} = 0.019$

*Dividend yields may also be calculated for preferred stock in a similar manner.

The company's dividend yield at the end of its 2016 fiscal year was about 1.9%. If you think a dividend yield of 1.9% is low, you'd be correct, but compared to current yields on certificates of deposit or bonds, it's attractive. Dividend yields vary widely. They are generally higher for older, established firms (such as **Procter & Gamble** and **General Electric**) and lower to nonexistent for young, growth-oriented companies like Alphabet. Historically, Apple investors purchased the stock hoping it would appreciate, which it has. However, in recent years, they have been rewarded with healthy dividends as well.

What is the future outlook for Apple? Some people claim the company has had its day and that the appeal of its stock may have peaked. But people have said that before about Apple, and they have been proven wrong. Apple's track record over the past decade has been astounding. Its earnings per share are solid, and its ROS, ROA, and ROE lead the industry. From the standpoint of liquidity and leverage, the company is in great shape. It has a negative cash conversion cycle, meaning that it sells inventory and collects cash from customers weeks before accounts payable are due. At the end of fiscal 2016, Apple had a debt ratio that was about average for a public company and no problems servicing existing debt. The company's recent P/E ratio of about 15.7 was relatively low. That said, Apple's financial ratios and its share price do fluctuate. Many investors have profited handsomely over the years by buying (and selling) the company's stock at the right time.

The Limitations of Ratio Analysis

Business decisions are made in a world of uncertainty. As useful as ratios are, they aren't a cure-all. Consider a physician's use of a thermometer. A reading of 102.0° Fahrenheit tells a doctor that something is wrong with the patient but doesn't indicate what the problem is or how to cure it.

Similarly, a sudden drop in a firm's profitability, for example, signals that *something* is wrong, but it doesn't identify the problem. A manager must analyze the figures to learn what caused the ratio to fall. A drop in profitability may mean that sales are slowing or that costs are rising. The manager must evaluate all the ratios in the light of factors such as increased competition or a slowdown in the economy. Legislation, international affairs, scandals, and other factors can turn profits into losses.

To be useful, ratios should be analyzed over a period of years to consider all relevant factors. Any one year, or even any two years, may not represent the company's performance over the long term. An investment decision, whether it's related to stocks, bonds, real estate, cash, or more exotic instruments, depends on one's tolerance for risk, and risk is the one factor that is always certain!

EVALUATE THE QUALITY OF EARNINGS

5 Evaluate the quality of earnings

A corporation's net earnings (including earnings per share), receive more attention than any other single item in a financial statement. To stockholders, the larger the net income, the greater the likelihood of dividends. In addition, a steady and upward trend in persistent *operating* earnings generally translates to a higher stock price down the road.

A knowledgeable investor tries to assess **earnings quality**—that is, whether a company's earnings have been conservatively computed and are attributable to higher sales or lower costs rather than accounting manipulations. The higher the quality of operating earnings in the current period compared to its recent past, the more likely it is that the company is executing a successful business strategy to generate healthy earnings in the future, which is a key component in predicting the stock price. There are many components of earnings quality. Among the most prominent are (1) conservative revenue and expense recognition, (2) a high and persistently improving gross profit percentage and declining or stable operating expenses compared to sales, and (3) the separation of ongoing operating earnings from discontinued operations.

The first component of earnings quality is the conservative recognition of net revenues. In Chapter 1, you learned that the two fundamental qualitative characteristics of accounting information are: (1) relevance and (2) faithful representation. All revenue should be recorded conservatively and clearly, and must faithfully represent the facts so the company's financial position and operational results are not distorted. The *revenue principle*, discussed in Chapter 3 (pp. 123–124), states that revenue should be recognized when it is earned, and not before. In Chapter 4 (pp. 211–212), you learned about the importance of internal controls over the processes by which revenue is recognized and by which cash collections are entered into the accounting system. In Chapter 5 (pp. 258–263), you learned that credit sales, or sales on account, have to go through the process of collection, that some will ultimately not be collectible, and that a company must make an appropriately conservative allowance for doubtful accounts in order to state receivables at net realizable value. All of these principles must be followed to properly recognize revenues. Recall in Chapter 5 how OCZ Technology Group "cooked its books" by improperly accounting for its shipping terms, sales discounts, and sales returns, thus overstating net revenues.

After revenue, the next two important earnings-quality components are the cost of goods sold and the resulting gross profit. All expenses need to be accurately, completely, and transparently included in the computation of gross profit (and net income). We saw in Chapter 7 what happened when WorldCom manipulated its reported earnings by deliberately understating its expenses. Without full and complete disclosures of all existing expenses, and without recognizing those expenses in the proper periods, trends in earnings are at best meaningless and, at worst, downright misleading.

A trend of high and persistently improving operating earnings in relation to a company's net sales reflects increasing earnings quality. Operating earnings are earnings from the company's core business; they are a key factor that analysts use to predict the future earnings of the company, which in turn is the key ingredient in determining a company's stock price. Operating earnings are a function of all of its individual elements: sales revenue, cost of goods sold, gross margin (gross profit), and operating expenses.

Operating earnings should be separated from items that represent isolated or nonrecurring events, such as *discontinued operations*. For example, if a company discontinues a segment or line of business within a particular period, the earnings from that segment should be separated from earnings from continuing operations on the income statement. Financial analysts typically do not include discontinued operations in predictions of future corporate income because the discontinued segments will not continue to generate income for the company. The details of this topic are covered in more advanced accounting classes.

An Audit Adds Credibility to Financial Statements

All public companies are required to have their financial statements audited annually by a firm of independent certified public accountants (CPAs). An audit is the systematic process of gathering evidence to verify the assertions a company's management includes in its financial statements. Those assertions include:

- That asset, liability, equity, revenue, and expense accounts exist, and that the transactions that produced the account balances are accurately recorded.
- That no items, transactions, or events that impact the business in a significant way are omitted.
- That the business has the title to all of its assets (legally owns them), and recognizes all of the obligations for its liabilities.
- That all accounts and transactions are valued at the proper stated amounts—either at cost or, where required, fair values.
- That all transactions have been allocated to the proper time periods and are classified in the proper categories in the financial statements.
- That all disclosures necessary for fairness of presentation are included either in the body or the footnotes to the financial statements.

Verifying these assertions allows the company's independent auditor to issue an "opinion on the fairness of presentation of the financial statements." The opinion is included with the financial statements in the annual report the company submits to the SEC. The components of the auditor's opinion include:

- That the auditor is independent (not connected with the company as either owner or management).
- That an audit of the financial statements was conducted.
- That the financial statements are the responsibility of management and that the responsibility of the auditor is to express an opinion on the financial statements based on the audit.
- That the audit was conducted in accordance with a rigorous set of professional standards.
- That the audit included examining evidence supporting the amounts and disclosures in the financial statements, as well as evaluating management's significant estimates and disclosures.
- That, in the auditor's opinion, the financial statements are fairly presented in accordance with generally accepted accounting principles.

The auditor is also required to audit the public company's system of internal controls and to express an opinion as to how adequate the controls are when it comes to their use in preventing, detecting, and correcting material misstatements in the financial statements. Independent auditors' reports are required for all companies that are registered with the SEC. Other companies that are not required to be audited nevertheless may have their financial statements audited by independent CPAs. Audited financial statements help give investors and creditors assurance as to the integrity and reliability of reported financial information, and thus play an important role in the financial reporting process.

Red Flags in Financial Statement Analysis

An important aspect of conducting a financial analysis is being able to spot *red flags*—potential financial troubles or irregularities—when evaluating a company. The following conditions may mean a company is very risky:

- *Earnings problems.* Has income from continuing operations and net income decreased for several years in a row? Did the company experience a net loss? These conditions may be okay for a company in a cyclical industry, such as an airline company or a home builder, but a struggling small or under-capitalized company in an industry with larger competitors may be unable to survive consecutive loss years.
- *Decreased cash flow.* Is borrowed money or the sale of plant assets the major source of cash? Is the net cash provided by operations consistently lower than net income? Cash flow validates earnings. Conversely, declining cash flow from operations over long periods of time signals trouble. If the answers to the above questions are affirmative, the company may be facing a cash shortage.
- *Too much debt.* How does the company's debt ratio compare to that of major competitors and to the industry average? If the company's debt ratio is much higher than average, the company may be unable to pay its debts during tough times.
- *Inability to collect receivables.* Are days' sales in receivables growing faster than they are for other companies in the industry? If so, a cash shortage may occur.
- *Buildup of inventories.* Is inventory turnover slowing down? If so, the company may be having trouble selling its products, or it may be overstating its inventory on its balance sheet. Recall from the cost-of-goods-sold model that one of the easiest ways to overstate net income is to overstate ending inventory.
- *Trends of sales, inventory, and receivables.* Do the relationships between the trends in sales, receivables, and inventory make sense? Sales, receivables, and inventory generally move together. Increased sales lead to higher receivables and require more inventory to meet demand. Strange movements among these items may spell trouble.

Efficient Markets

An **efficient capital market** is one in which market prices fully reflect all information available to the public. Because stock prices reflect all publicly accessible data, it can be argued that the stock market is efficient. If the information is available, the market as a whole can set a "fair" price for the company's stock.

Market efficiency has implications for the actions a firm's managers take and for investors' decisions. It means that unless managers are willing to engage in financial fraud, they cannot fool the market with accounting gimmicks. For example, suppose you are the president of Vitacomp Corporation. Reported earnings per share are $2, and the stock price is $40—so the P/E ratio is 20. You believe Vitacomp's stock is underpriced. To correct the situation, you are considering changing your depreciation method from accelerated to straight-line. The accounting change will increase earnings per share to $3. Will the stock price then rise to $60? Probably not; the company's stock price will probably remain at $40 because the market can understand the accounting change. After all, the company merely changed its method of computing depreciation. The change has no effect on Vitacomp's cash flows or the company's economic position.

In an efficient market, the search for "underpriced" stock is fruitless unless the investor has relevant private information. However, it is unlawful as well as unethical to sell or buy the shares of a company on the basis of information not available to the general public. In general, the most appropriate investment strategy seeks to manage risk, diversify investments, and minimize transaction costs. Financial analysis helps mainly to identify the risks of various stocks and then to manage the risk.

The Decision Guidelines feature summarizes the most widely used ratios.

Decision Guidelines

USING RATIOS IN FINANCIAL STATEMENT ANALYSIS

Bobby and Kaye Simpson operate a financial services firm. They manage other people's money and do most of their own financial statement analysis. How do they measure the ability of companies to pay bills, sell inventory, collect receivables, and so on? The Simpsons do so by using the standard ratios we have covered throughout this book.

Ratio	Computation	Information Provided
Measuring ability to pay current liabilities:		
1. Current ratio	$\dfrac{\text{Current assets}}{\text{Current liabilities}}$	Measures the ability to pay current liabilities with current assets
2. Quick (acid-test) ratio	$\dfrac{\text{Cash and cash equivalents} + \text{Short-term investments} + \text{Net current receivables}}{\text{Current liabilities}}$	Shows the ability to pay all current liabilities if they come due immediately
Measuring turnover and cash conversion cycle:		
3. Inventory turnover and days' inventory outstanding (DIO)	$\text{Inventory turnover} = \dfrac{\text{Cost of goods sold}}{\text{Average inventory}}$ $\text{Days' inventory outstanding (DIO)} = \dfrac{365}{\text{Inventory turnover}}$	Indicates the salability of inventory—the number of times a company sells its average level of inventory during a year. DIO converts inventory turnover to the number of days it takes to sell average inventory.
4. Accounts receivable turnover	$\dfrac{\text{Net credit sales}}{\text{Average net accounts receivable}}$	Measures the ability to collect cash from credit customers
5. Days' sales in receivables or days' sales outstanding (DSO)	$\dfrac{365}{\text{Accounts receivable turnover}}$	Shows how many days' sales remain in accounts receivable—how many days it takes to collect the average level of receivables
6. Accounts payable turnover and days' payable outstanding (DPO)	$\text{Accounts payable turnover} = \dfrac{\text{Cost of goods sold}}{\text{Average accounts payable}}$ Days' payable outstanding (DPO) = 365/Accounts payable turnover	Shows how many times a year accounts payable turns over and how many days it takes the company to pay off accounts payable
7. Cash conversion cycle	Cash conversion cycle = DIO + DSO − DPO where DIO = Days' inventory outstanding DSO = Days' sales outstanding DPO = Days' payable outstanding	Shows overall liquidity by computing the total days it takes to convert inventory to receivables and back to cash, minus the days to pay off suppliers

Ratio	Computation	Information Provided
Measuring ability to pay long-term debt:		
8. Debt ratio	$\frac{\text{Total liabilities}}{\text{Total assets}}$	Indicates the percentage of assets financed with debt
9. Times-interest-earned ratio	$\frac{\text{Income from operations}}{\text{Interest expense}}$	Measures the number of times operating income can cover interest expense
Measuring profitability:		
10. Gross margin %	$\frac{\text{Gross margin}}{\text{Net sales}}$	Shows the percentage of profit that a company makes from merely selling products, before any other operating costs are subtracted
11. Operating income %	$\frac{\text{Income from operations}}{\text{Net sales}}$	Shows the percentage of profit earned from each dollar of sales in the company's core business, after operating costs have been subtracted
12. DuPont model	Exhibit 12-10	A detailed analysis of return on assets (ROA) and return on common stockholders' equity (ROE)
13. Rate of return on net sales	$\frac{\text{Net income} - \text{Preferred dividends}}{\text{Net sales}}$	Shows the percentage of each sales dollar earned as net income
14. Asset turnover ratio	$\frac{\text{Net sales}}{\text{Average total assets}}$	Measures the amount of net sales generated for each dollar invested in assets
15. Rate of return on total assets	DuPont method: Rate of return on net sales × Asset turnover or $\frac{\text{Net income} - \text{Preferred dividends}}{\text{Average total assets}}$	Measures how profitably a company uses its assets
16. Leverage ratio	$\frac{\text{Average total assets}}{\text{Average common stockholders' equity}}$	Otherwise known as the *equity multiplier*, it measures the ratio of average total assets to average common stockholders' equity
17. Rate of return on common stockholders' equity	DuPont method: ROA × Leverage ratio or $\frac{\text{Net income} - \text{Preferred dividends}}{\text{Average common stockholders' equity}}$	Measures how much income is earned for every dollar invested by the company's common shareholders
18. Earnings per share of common stock	$\frac{\text{Net income} - \text{Preferred dividends}}{\text{Average number of shares of common stock outstanding}}$	Measures the amount of net income earned for each share of the company's common stock outstanding
Analyzing stock as an investment:		
19. Price-earnings ratio	$\frac{\text{Market price per share of common stock}}{\text{Earnings per share}}$	Indicates the market price of $1 of earnings
20. Dividend yield	$\frac{\text{Dividend per share of common (or preferred) stock}}{\text{Market price per share of common (or preferred) stock}}$	Shows the percentage of a stock's market value returned as dividends to stockholders each period

End-of-Chapter | Summary Problems

The following financial data are adapted from the annual reports of Leargear Corporation:

	A	B	C	D	E
1	**Leargear Corporation Four-Year Selected Financial Data Years Ended December 31, 2018, 2017, 2016, and 2015**				
2	**Operating Results***	**2018**	**2017**	**2016**	**2015**
3	Net Sales	$ 13,848	$ 13,673	$ 11,635	$ 9,054
4	Cost of goods sold	8,715	8,599	6,775	5,318
5	Interest expense	109	75	45	46
6	Income from operations	1,675	1,445	1,817	1,333
7	Net earnings (net loss)	1,450	877	1,127	824
8	Cash dividends	76	75	76	77
9					
10	**Financial Position**				
11	Merchandise inventory	1,550	1,904	1,462	1,056
12	Total assets	7,591	7,012	5,189	3,963
13	Current ratio	1.48	0.95	1.25	1.20
14	Stockholders' equity	3,010	2,928	2,630	1,574
15	Average number of shares of				
16	common stock outstanding				
17	(in thousands)	850	879	895	576
18					

*Dollar amounts are in thousands.

Requirement

1. Compute the following ratios for 2016 through 2018, and evaluate Leargear's operating results. Use the DuPont formula for ROA and ROE. Are operating results strong or weak? Did they improve or deteriorate during the three-year period?

   a. Inventory turnover
   b. Gross margin (profit) percentage
   c. Operating income (profit) percentage
   d. Rate of return on sales
   e. Asset turnover
   f. Rate of return on assets
   g. Leverage ratio
   h. Rate of return on stockholders' equity
   i. Times interest earned
   j. Earnings per share

Answer

	2018	2017	2016
a. Inventory turnover	$\frac{\$8{,}715}{(\$1{,}550 + \$1{,}904)/2} = 5.05$ times	$\frac{\$8{,}599}{(\$1{,}904 + \$1{,}462)/2} = 5.1$ times	$\frac{\$6{,}775}{(\$1{,}462 + \$1{,}056)/2} = 5.4$ times
b. Gross profit percentage	$\frac{\$13{,}848 - \$8{,}715}{\$13{,}848} = 37.1\%$	$\frac{\$13{,}673 - \$8{,}599}{\$13{,}673} = 37.1\%$	$\frac{\$11{,}635 - \$6{,}775}{\$11{,}635} = 41.8\%$
c. Operating income percentage	$\frac{\$1{,}675}{\$13{,}848} = 12.1\%$	$\frac{\$1{,}445}{\$13{,}673} = 10.6\%$	$\frac{\$1{,}817}{\$11{,}635} = 15.6\%$
d. Rate of return on sales	$\frac{\$1{,}450}{\$13{,}848} = 10.5\%$	$\frac{\$877}{\$13{,}673} = 6.4\%$	$\frac{\$1{,}127}{\$11{,}635} = 9.7\%$
e. Asset turnover	$\frac{\$13{,}848}{(\$7{,}591 + \$7{,}012)/2} = 1.897$	$\frac{\$13{,}673}{(\$7{,}012 + \$5{,}189)/2} = 2.241$	$\frac{\$11{,}635}{(\$5{,}189 + \$3{,}963)/2} = 2.543$
f. Rate of return on assets*	$10.5\% \times 1.897 = 19.9\%$	$6.4\% \times 2.241 = 14.3\%$	$9.7\% \times 2.543 = 24.7\%$
g. Leverage ratio	$\frac{\$7{,}301.50}{(\$3{,}010 + \$2{,}928)/2} = 2.459$	$\frac{\$6{,}100.50}{(\$2{,}928 + \$2{,}630)/2} = 2.195$	$\frac{\$4{,}576}{(\$2{,}630 + \$1{,}574)/2} = 2.177$
h. Rate of return on stockholders' equity*	$19.9\% \times 2.459 = 48.9\%$	$14.3\% \times 2.195 = 31.4\%$	$24.7\% \times 2.177 = 53.8\%$
i. Times-interest-earned ratio	$\frac{\$1{,}675}{\$109} = 15.4$ times	$\frac{\$1{,}445}{\$75} = 19.3$ times	$\frac{\$1{,}817}{\$45} = 40.4$ times
j. Earnings per share	$\frac{\$1{,}450}{850} = \$1.71$	$\frac{\$877}{879} = \$1.00$	$\frac{\$1{,}127}{895} = \$1.26$

* Used DuPont model in Exhibit 12–10.

Evaluation: After dipping a little in 2017, some of Leargear's operating results started to recover in 2018. The company's gross profit percentage is consistent with 2017, and its operating income percentage and all the return measures improved in 2018. Asset turnover fell a little, but the rate of return on assets was headed in the right direction because of the increases in profitability that the company experienced in 2018. The final result in 2018 was a healthy net income and earnings per share for the year. This yielded a positive ROA and, because of leverage, an even more positive ROE.

REVIEW | Financial Statement Analysis

Accounting Vocabulary

benchmarking (p. 679) The comparison of a company to a standard set by other companies, with a view toward improvement.

cash conversion cycle (p. 689) The number of days it takes to convert inventory to receivables, and receivables into cash, after paying off payables. The formula is Days' inventory outstanding + Days' sales outstanding – Days' payables outstanding.

common-size statement (p. 678) A financial statement that reports only percentages (no dollar amounts).

earnings quality (p. 696) Conservatively computed earnings, attributable to higher sales or lower costs rather than accounting manipulations.

efficient capital market (p. 698) A capital market in which market prices fully reflect all information available to the public.

horizontal analysis (p. 671) The study of percentage changes in line items on comparative financial statements.

operating income (profit) percentage (p. 691) Income from operations as a percentage of net sales.

rate of return on net sales (p. 692) A ratio that shows the percentage of each sales dollar earned as net income. Also called *return on sales (ROS)*.

trend percentages (p. 675) A form of horizontal analysis that indicates the direction a business is taking.

vertical analysis (p. 675) Analysis of a financial statement that reveals the relationship of each statement item to a specified base, which is the 100% figure.

Quick Check (Answers are given on page 743.)

1. Which of the following can be used to do an industry and company analysis?
   a. Business publications
   b. Description of the company's business in the annual report
   c. Management's Discussion and Analysis section of the annual report
   d. All of the listed options

2. The primary focus of horizontal analysis is
   a. the income statement only.
   b. the balance sheet only.
   c. the percentage changes in line items on the comparative financial statements.
   d. the individual line items on the financial statements as a percentage of a related base, such as total sales or total assets.

3. When performing a horizontal analysis on an income statement, the percentage change in any individual item is calculated by dividing the dollar amount of the change from the base period to the current period by
   a. the base period amount.
   b. the current period amount.
   c. the amount estimated for the future period.
   d. the average of the base and the current period amounts.

4. Randall Corporation reported the following revenue data:

Year	Net revenues (in millions)
2016	$6,800
2017	$7,004
2018	$6,732
2019	$7,276

   Use 2016 as the base year. The trend percentage in 2019 is closest to
   a. 93%.
   b. 104%.
   c. 107%.
   d. 112%.

5. Expressing accounts receivable as a percentage of total assets is an example of
   a. ratio analysis.
   b. vertical analysis.
   c. horizontal analysis.
   d. trend analysis.

6. Kincaid Company reported the following data (in millions) for the past two years:

	2019	2018
Net revenues	$280	$250
Cost of goods sold	$150	$140
Gross profit	$130	$110
Operating expenses	$ 90	$ 75
Operating income	$ 40	$ 35

   In a vertical analysis of 2019, the operating expenses percentage is closest to
   a. 225%.
   b. 69%.
   c. 14%.
   d. 32%.

7. The base for inventory in a vertical analysis is:
   a. total current assets.
   b. inventory.
   c. total liabilities.
   d. total assets.

8. Ratios that measure liquidity include all of the following *except*:
   a. the leverage ratio.
   b. inventory turnover.
   c. the current ratio.
   d. the quick ratio.

9. Verba Corporation has an inventory turnover of 15 times per year, while the industry average is 4.0 times per year. What does this indicate about Verba's inventory turnover?
   a. Verba may have obsolete inventory on hand.
   b. Verba may not be keeping enough inventory on hand, which could lead to lost sales.
   c. Verba has too much inventory on hand.
   d. Verba is experiencing difficulties in selling the inventory.

10. The measure of a company's ability to collect cash from its customers who purchase on account is the
   a. accounts payable turnover.
   b. cash conversion cycle.
   c. accounts receivable turnover.
   d. days' payable outstanding.

11. A ratio that measures a company's profitability is the
   a. leverage ratio.
   b. gross margin percentage.
   c. current ratio.
   d. times-interest-earned ratio.

12. Steadily increasing cost of goods sold as a percentage of net revenues is an indication of
   a. decreasing earnings quality.
   b. increasing earnings quality.
   c. financial statement fraud.
   d. increasing production efficiencies.

13. Increasing earnings quality could be indicated by
   a. an improving operating earnings/sales ratio.
   b. a declining operating expenses/sales ratio.
   c. an improving gross margin/sales ratio.
   d. all of the above.

14. An auditors' report by independent accountants
   a. gives investors assurance that the company's financial statements conform to GAAP.
   b. is ultimately the responsibility of the management of the client company.
   c. ensures that the financial statements are error-free.
   d. gives investors assurance that the company's stock is a safe investment.

Excel Project
Autograded Excel Project available in **MyLab Accounting**

ASSESS YOUR PROGRESS

Ethics Check

EC12-1. Identify ethical principle violated

For each of the situations listed, identify which of three principles (integrity, objectivity and independence, or due care) from the AICPA Code of Professional Conduct is violated. Assume all persons listed in the situations are members of the AICPA. (Note: Refer to the AICPA Code of Professional Conduct contained on pages 25–27 in Chapter 1 for descriptions of the principles.)

a. Cindy is an accountant for Caperton, Inc., and is stressed by the amount of work her boss has been giving her. Yesterday, Cindy's boss asked that she perform a financial statement analysis on the company's previous five years of financial statements and write a report explaining any inconsistencies. Cindy is busy, so she quickly throws together the report, without double checking the data used and the related calculations.

b. Deneen is the senior accounting manager for Kent Co. and is in charge of preparing quarterly reports for the CEO and CFO. These reports compare a variety of Kent's financial ratios to industry averages. This quarter, Kent has done poorly compared to its competitors, so some of its ratios were not favorable. Because of their legendary tempers, Deneen does not want to upset the CEO and CFO. She decides to include only favorable ratios in her report.

c. Malik is the accounting manager for Belmont Global and knows the company must maintain working capital in excess of $50,000 to stay in accordance with its debt covenants. This past year, Belmont's working capital fell below $50,000 for a short period of time. Malik created fictitious entries to hide the violation of its debt covenants.

d. Matt was recently hired as a senior audit manager at the firm of Marjenin & Vena, but did not disclose that his wife is the CFO for one of its clients.

Short Exercises

S12-1. ***(Learning Objective 2: Perform horizontal analysis of revenues, expenses, and net income)*** Regan Corporation reported the following amounts on its 2018 comparative income statements: LO 2

(In thousands)	2018	2017	2016
Revenues	$20,477	$20,997	$18,600
Expenses	10,915	10,238	10,100
Net income	$ 9,562	$10,759	$ 8,500

Perform a horizontal analysis of revenues, expenses, and net income—both in dollar amounts and in percentages—for 2018 and 2017.

S12-2. ***(Learning Objective 2: Perform trend analysis of sales and net income)*** LeBlanc, Inc., reported the following sales and net income amounts: LO 2

(In thousands)	2018	2017	2016	2015
Sales	$10,492	$9,804	$9,288	$8,600
Net income	1,232	960	896	800

Show LeBlanc's trend percentages for sales and net income. Use 2015 as the base year.

S12-3. ***(Learning Objective 3: Perform vertical analysis to analyze cash)*** Sokolsky Designs reported the following amounts on its balance sheets at December 31, 2018, 2017, and 2016: LO 3

	2018	2017	2016
Cash	$ 10,000	$ 4,440	$ 3,990
Receivables, net	35,000	23,200	23,940
Inventory	240,000	177,600	131,670
Prepaid expenses	15,000	21,200	15,960
Property, plant, and equipment, net	200,000	217,560	223,440
Total assets	$500,000	$444,000	$399,000

Sales and profits are high. Nevertheless, Sokolsky is experiencing a cash shortage. Perform a vertical analysis of the company's assets at the end of years 2018, 2017, and 2016. Use the analysis to explain the reason for the cash shortage.

LO 3 **S12-4.** ***(Learning Objective 3: Compare common-size income statements for two companies)*** Madison Company and Orwell Corporation are competitors. Compare the two companies by converting their condensed income statements to common-size statements.

(In millions)	Madison	Orwell
Net sales	$17,000	$10,000
Cost of goods sold	10,166	6,540
Selling and administrative expenses	4,828	2,220
Interest expense	68	80
Other expenses	102	40
Income tax expense	748	320
Net income	$ 1,088	$ 800

Which company earned more net income? Which company's net income was a higher percentage of its net sales? Explain your answer.

LO 4 **S12-5.** ***(Learning Objective 4: Evaluate the trend in a company's current ratio)*** Examine the financial data of Musketeer Corporation.

Year Ended December 31	2018	2017	2016
Operating Results			
Net income	$ 250	$ 340	$ 342
Earnings per common share	$1.37	$1.68	$1.99
Net income as a percent of sales	19.9%	17.9%	19.3%
Return on average stockholders' equity	21.0%	18.0%	19.0%
Financial Position			
Current assets	$ 712	$ 489	$ 434
Current liabilities	$ 400	$ 326	$ 350
Working capital	$ 312	$ 163	$ 84

Calculate Musketeer's current ratio for each year from 2016 through 2018. Is the company's ability to pay its current liabilities improving or deteriorating?

S12-6. ***(Learning Objective 4: Evaluate a company's quick ratio)*** To follow are the balance sheets for Metro Corporation and selected comparative competitor data. LO 4

	A	B	C	D	E
1	**Metro Corporation Balance Sheets (Adapted) December 31, 2018 and 2017**				
2				**Increase (Decrease)**	
3	**(Dollar amounts in millions)**	**2018**	**2017**	**Amount**	**Percentage**
4	**Assets**				
5	**Current assets:**				
6	Cash and cash equivalents	$ 1,210	$ 980	$ 230	23.5%
7	Short-term investments	14	48	(34)	(70.8)
8	Receivables, net	230	268	(38)	(14.2)
9	Inventories	102	70	32	45.7
10	Prepaid expenses and other assets	292	302	(10)	(3.3)
11	Total current assets	1,848	1,668	180	10.8
12	Property, plant, and equipment, net	3,660	3,386	274	8.1
13	Intangible assets	1,020	848	172	20.3
14	Other assets	826	730	96	13.2
15	Total assets	$ 7,354	$ 6,632	$ 722	10.9%
16	**Liabilities and Stockholders' Equity**				
17	**Current liabilities:**				
18	Accounts payable	$ 966	$ 860	$ 106	12.3%
19	Income tax payable	42	66	(24)	(36.4)
20	Short-term debt	128	116	12	10.3
21	Other	66	68	(2)	(2.9)
22	Total current liabilities	1,202	1,110	92	8.3
23	Long-term debt	3,648	2,970	678	22.8
24	Other liabilities	1,128	1,096	32	2.9
25	Total liabilities	5,978	5,176	802	15.5
26	**Stockholders' equity:**				
27	Common stock	2	2	—	—
28	Retained earnings	1,534	1,640	(106)	(6.5)
29	Accumulated other comprehensive (loss)	(160)	(186)	26	14.0
30	Total stockholders' equity	1,376	1,456	(80)	(5.5)
31	Total liabilities and stockholders' equity	$ 7,354	$ 6,632	$ 722	10.9%
32					

Company	Quick (acid-test) Ratio
Orleans Electric, Inc. (Utility)	0.74
O'Neil Company (Department store)	0.63
Lavallee Foods Corporation (Grocery store)	0.66

Use the data to answer the following questions.

1. Calculate Metro's quick (acid-test) ratio at December 31, 2018, and 2017.
2. Use the comparative information from the table given for Orleans Electric, Inc., O'Neil Company, and Lavallee Foods Corporation. Is Metro's quick (acid-test) ratio for 2018 and 2017 strong, average, or weak in comparison?

LO 4

S12-7. *(Learning Objective 4: Calculate and evaluate turnover and the cash conversion cycle)* The Metro 2018 income statement follows.

	A	B	C
1	**Metro Corporation Statements of Income (Adapted) Year Ended December 31, 2018 and 2017**		
2	**(Dollar amounts in millions)**	**2018**	**2017**
3	Net revenues	$ 9,500	$ 9,319
4	Cost of goods sold	4,589	4,851
5	Gross profit	4,911	4,468
6	Selling, general and administrative expenses	3,607	3,456
7	Income from operations	1,304	1,012
8	Interest expense, net	204	178
9	Income before income taxes	1,100	834
10	Provision for income taxes	389	251
11	Net income	$ 711	$ 583
12			

Use the preceding income statement and the balance sheet from S12-6 to calculate the following:

a. Metro's rate of inventory turnover and days' inventory outstanding for 2018.
b. Days' sales in average receivables (days' sales outstanding) during 2018 (round dollar amounts to one decimal place). Assume all sales are made on account.
c. Accounts payable turnover and days' payables outstanding for 2018. For this purpose, assume that the impact of inventories on cost of goods sold is immaterial, allowing you to use cost of goods sold rather than purchases in your computations.
d. Length of cash conversion cycle in days for 2018.

Do these measures look strong or weak? Give the reason for your answer.

LO 4

S12-8. *(Learning Objective 4: Measure ability to pay long-term debt)* Use the financial statements of Metro Corporation in S12-6 and S12-7.

1. Calculate the company's debt ratio at December 31, 2018.
2. Calculate the company's times-interest-earned ratio for 2018. For operating income, use income from operations.
3. Is Metro's ability to pay liabilities and interest expense strong or weak? Comment on the value of each ratio calculated for questions 1 and 2.

LO 4

S12-9. *(Learning Objective 4: Measure profitability using DuPont Analysis)* Use the financial statements of Metro Corporation in S12-6 and S12-7 to calculate these profitability measures for 2018. Show each calculation.

a. Rate of return on sales
b. Asset turnover ratio
c. Rate of return on total assets
d. Leverage (equity multiplier) ratio
e. Rate of return on common stockholders' equity
f. Is Metro's profitability strong, medium, or weak?

S12-10. ***(Learning Objective 4: Calculate EPS and the price-earnings ratio)*** The annual report of Salem Cars, Inc., for the year ended December 31, 2018, included the following items (in millions): LO 4

Preferred stock outstanding, 3%	$ 1,000
Net income	$ 700
Average number of shares of common stock outstanding	500

1. Calculate earnings per share (EPS) and the price-earnings ratio for Salem Cars' stock. Round to the nearest cent. The price of a share of the company's stock is $18.
2. How much does the stock market say $1 of Salem Cars' net income is worth?

S12-11. ***(Learning Objective 4: Use ratio data to reconstruct an income statement)*** A skeleton of Canton Auto Corporation's income statement appears as follows (amounts in thousands): LO 4

	A	B
1	**Income Statement**	
2	Net sales	$ 7,100
3	Cost of goods sold	(a)
4	Selling expenses	1,513
5	Administrative expenses	1,334
6	Interest expense	(b)
7	Other expenses	151
8	Income before taxes	1,046
9	Income tax expense	(c)
10	Net income	$ (d)
11		

Use the following ratio data to complete Canton Auto's income statement:

a. The inventory turnover was 3 (beginning inventory was $790; ending inventory was $770).

b. The rate of return on sales (after income taxes) was 0.09.

S12-12. ***(Learning Objective 4: Use ratio data to reconstruct a balance sheet)*** A skeleton of Gunner Corporation's balance sheet appears as follows (amounts in thousands): LO 4

	A	B	C	D
1	**Balance Sheet**			
2	Cash	$ 250	Total current liabilities	$ 2,190
3	Receivables	(a)	Long-term debt	(e)
4	Inventories	1,364	Other long-term liabilities	820
5	Prepaid expenses	(b)		
6	Total current assets	(c)		
7	Plant assets, net	(d)	Common stock	180
8	Other assets	2,275	Retained earnings	2,944
9	Total assets	$ 7,100	Total liabilities and equity	$ (f)
10				

Use the following ratio data to complete Gunner's balance sheet:

a. The debt ratio was 0.56.

b. The current ratio was 1.60.

c. The quick (acid-test) ratio was 0.700.

LO 4

S12-13. ***(Learning Objective 4: Analyze a company based on its ratios)*** Take the role of an investment analyst. It is your job to recommend investments for your client. The only information you have is the following ratio values for two companies in the data analytics industry:

Ratio	Abbott Co.	Stellar Corporation
Days' sales in receivables	48	41
Inventory turnover	11	7
Gross profit percentage	58%	67%
Net income as a percent of sales	13%	12%
Times interest earned	13	19
Return on equity	30%	35%
Return on assets	19%	14%

Recommend one company's stock over the other. State the reasons for your recommendation.

LO 1, 5

S12-14. ***(Learning Objectives 1, 5: Evaluate quality of earnings)*** To follow is the 2018 income statement of Kurzic Imports, Inc.

A1

	A	B	C
1	**Kurzic Imports, Inc. Consolidated Statement of Operations (Adapted)**		
2		**Year Ended**	
3	**(In thousands except per share amounts)**	**2018**	**2017**
4			
5	Net sales	$ 1,806,092	$ 1,825,975
6	Operating costs and expenses:		
7	Cost of sales (including buying and store occupancy costs)	1,045,880	1,121,690
8	Selling, general, and administrative expenses	526,060	549,850
9	Depreciation and amortization	48,750	55,675
10	Total operating costs and expenses	1,620,690	1,727,215
11	Operating income (loss)	185,402	98,760
12	Nonoperating (income) and expenses:		
13	Interest and investment income	(2,740)	(2,675)
14	Interest expense	1,640	1,725
15	Interest income, net	(1,100)	(950)
16	Income (loss) from continuing operations before income taxes	186,502	99,710
17	Provision (benefit) for income taxes	69,315	34,700
18	Income (loss) from continuing operations	$ 117,187	$ 65,010
19	Discontinued operations:		
20	Income (loss) from discontinued operations	210	(2,300)
21	Net income (loss)	$ 117,397	$ 62,710
22			
23	Earnings (loss) per share from continuing operations: Basic	$ 1.52	$ 0.85
24			
25	Earnings (loss) per share from discontinued operations: Basic	$ 0.00	$ (0.03)
26			
27	Earnings (loss) per share: Basic	$ 1.52	$ 0.83
28			

1. How much gross profit did Kurzic earn on the sale of its products in 2018? How much was income from continuing operations? How much net income did the company earn?
2. At the end of 2018, what dollar amount of income would most sophisticated investors use to predict Kurzic's net income for 2019 and beyond? Name this item, give its amount, and state your reason.

LO 5

S12-15. ***(Learning Objective 5: Evaluate quality of earnings)*** Research has shown that over 50% of financial statement frauds are committed by companies that recognize revenue improperly. What does this mean? Describe the most common ways companies improperly recognize revenue.

Exercises MyLab Accounting

Group A

E12-16A. ***(Learning Objective 2: Perform a horizontal analysis of an income statement)*** Prepare a horizontal analysis of the comparative income statements of Norman Music Co. Round percentage changes to the nearest one-tenth percent (three decimal places). LO 2

	A	B	C
1	**Norman Music Co. Comparative Income Statements Years Ended December 31, 2018 and 2017**		
2		**2018**	**2017**
3	Total revenue	$ 1,080,000	$ 919,000
4	Expenses:		
5	Cost of goods sold	$ 479,000	$ 400,450
6	Selling and general expenses	289,000	260,000
7	Interest expense	24,500	14,500
8	Income tax expense	106,500	86,850
9	Total expenses	899,000	761,800
10	Net income	$ 181,000	$ 157,200
11			

E12-17A. ***(Learning Objective 2: Calculate trend percentages)*** Calculate trend percentages for Blueberry Valley Sales & Service's total revenue and net income for the following five-year period, using year 0 as the base year. Round to the nearest full percent. LO 2

(In thousands)	Year 4	Year 3	Year 2	Year 1	Year 0
Total revenue	$1,412	$1,251	$1,090	$1,017	$1,020
Net income	129	120	102	98	85

Which grew faster during the period, total revenue or net income?

E12-18A. ***(Learning Objective 3: Perform a vertical analysis of a balance sheet)*** Perform a vertical analysis of Beta Golf Company's balance sheet to determine the component percentages of its assets, liabilities, and stockholders' equity. LO 3

	A	B
1	**Beta Golf Company Balance Sheet December 31, 2018**	
2	**Assets**	
3	Total current assets	$ 44,100
4	Property, plant, and equipment, net	213,600
5	Other assets	42,300
6	Total assets	$ 300,000
7		
8	**Liabilities**	
9	Total current liabilities	$ 48,300
10	Long-term debt	113,100
11	Total liabilities	161,400
12		
13	**Stockholders' Equity**	
14	Total stockholders' equity	138,600
15	Total liabilities and stockholders' equity	$ 300,000
16		

LO 3

E12-19A. ***(Learning Objective 3: Prepare a common-size income statement)*** Prepare a comparative common-size income statement for Norman Music Co., using the 2018 and 2017 data of E12-16A and rounding to four decimal places.

LO 4

E12-20A. ***(Learning Objective 4: Calculate year-to-year changes in working capital)*** The following information is for Nature Lodge. What were the dollar amounts of change and the percentage of each change in Nature Lodge's net working capital during 2018 and 2017? Is this trend favorable or unfavorable?

	2018	2017	2016
Total current assets	$424,950	$259,800	$260,000
Total current liabilities	410,000	200,000	130,000

LO 4

E12-21A. ***(Learning Objective 4: Calculate ratios; evaluate turnover, liquidity, and current debt-paying ability)*** The financial statements of Explorer News, Inc., include the following items:

	2018	2017	2016
Balance sheet:			
Cash	$ 77,000	$103,000	
Short-term investments	18,000	20,000	
Net receivables	81,000	84,000	35,000
Inventory	96,000	70,000	58,000
Prepaid expenses	7,000	6,000	
Total current assets	279,000	283,000	
Accounts payable	45,000	35,000	40,000
Total current liabilities	130,000	97,000	
Income statement:			
Net credit sales	$493,000	$507,000	
Cost of goods sold	280,000	278,000	

Requirements

1. Calculate the following ratios for 2018 and 2017. When calculating days, round your answer to the nearest whole number.
   - **a.** Current ratio
   - **b.** Quick (acid-test) ratio
   - **c.** Inventory turnover and days' inventory outstanding (DIO)
   - **d.** Accounts receivable turnover
   - **e.** Days' sales in average receivables or days' sales outstanding (DSO)
   - **f.** Accounts payable turnover and days' payable outstanding (DPO). Use cost of goods sold in the formula for accounts payable turnover.
   - **g.** Cash conversion cycle (in days)
2. Evaluate the company's liquidity and current debt-paying ability for 2018. Has it improved or deteriorated from 2017?
3. As a manager of this company, what would you try to improve next year?

LO 4

E12-22A. ***(Learning Objective 4: Analyze a company's ability to pay its liabilities)*** Jalbert Furniture Company has asked you to determine whether the company's ability to pay its current liabilities and long-term debts improved or deteriorated during 2018. To answer this question, calculate the following ratios for 2018 and 2017. Round your answers to two decimal places. Summarize the results of your analysis in a short paragraph.

a. Net working capital
b. Current ratio
c. Quick (acid-test) ratio
d. Debt ratio
e. Times-interest-earned ratio

	2018	2017
Cash	$ 50,000	$ 49,000
Short-term investments	29,000	11,000
Net receivables	123,000	129,000
Inventory	239,000	266,000
Prepaid expenses	20,000	4,000
Total assets	560,000	470,000
Total current liabilities	217,000	262,000
Long-term debt	77,000	104,000
Income from operations	250,000	148,000
Interest expense	40,000	38,000

LO 4

E12-23A. ***(Learning Objective 4: Analyze the profitability of a company)*** For 2018 and 2017, calculate return on sales, asset turnover, return on assets (ROA), leverage, return on common stockholders' equity (ROE), gross profit percentage, operating income percentage, and earnings per share to measure the ability to earn profits for Durham Decor, Inc., whose comparative income statements follow. Perform a DuPont Analysis for ROA and ROE, and round each component ratio to three decimal places; for other ratio computations, round to two decimal places.

A1

	A	B	C
1	**Durham Decor, Inc.** **Comparative Income Statements** **Years Ended December 31, 2018 and 2017**		
2		**2018**	**2017**
3	Net sales	$ 250,000	$ 199,000
4	Cost of goods sold	123,000	102,000
5	Gross profit	127,000	97,000
6	Selling and general expenses	55,000	51,000
7	Income from operations	72,000	46,000
8	Interest expense	14,000	18,000
9	Income before income tax	58,000	28,000
10	Income tax expense	20,000	10,000
11	Net income	$ 38,000	$ 18,000
12			

Additional data:

	2018	2017	2016
Total assets	$ 310,000	$ 305,000	$300,000
Common stockholders' equity	$ 196,000	$ 194,000	$192,000
Preferred dividends	$ 2,000	$ 1,000	$ 0
Average common shares outstanding during the year	15,000	14,000	13,000

Did the company's operating performance improve or deteriorate during 2018?

LO 4

E12-24A. ***(Learning Objective 4: Calculate earnings per share)*** Palace Loan Company's balance sheet at December 31, 2018, reports the following:

Preferred stock, $50 par value, 10%, 10,000 shares issued	$ 500,000
Common stock, $0.75 par, 1,000,000 shares issued	750,000
Treasury stock, common, 80,000 shares at cost	720,000

During 2018, Palace Loan earned net income of $6,300,000. Calculate Palace Loan's earnings per common share (EPS) for 2018. (Round EPS to two decimal places.) Assume the number of shares issued and outstanding did not change during the year.

LO 4

E12-25A. ***(Learning Objective 4: Evaluate a stock as an investment)*** Evaluate the common stock of Carver Distributing Company as an investment. Specifically, use the two common stock ratios to determine whether the common stock became more or less attractive during the past year. (The number of common stock shares was the same in 2017 and 2018.) Round calculations and your final answer to three decimal places.

	2018	2017
Net income	$ 114,000	$ 70,500
Dividends to common	13,000	16,000
Total stockholders' equity at year-end	400,000	500,000
(includes 43,500 shares of common stock)		
Preferred stock, 5%	105,000	105,000
Market price per share of common stock at year-end	$ 23.50	$ 17.25

LO 4, 5

E12-26A. ***(Learning Objectives 4, 5: Prepare an income statement; calculate earnings per share; evaluate quality of earnings; evaluate a company as an investment)*** The Calloway Book Company's accounting records include the following for 2018 (in thousands):

Other revenues	$ 2,300
Income tax expense	7,950
Sales revenue	129,000
Total operating expenses	104,800

Requirements

1. Prepare Calloway Book Company's single-step income statement for the year ended December 31, 2018, including earnings per share (EPS). Calloway had 1,000,000 shares of common stock and no preferred stock outstanding during the year.
2. Assume Calloway Book Company's income from operations indicates that its core business has steadily increased by about 10% per year over the past three years and that none of its operations have been discontinued. What does this say about the quality of the company's earnings?

Group B

E12-27B. ***(Learning Objective 2: Perform a horizontal analysis of an income statement)*** Prepare a horizontal analysis of the comparative income statements of Monroe Music Co. Round percentage changes to the nearest one-tenth percent (three decimal places). LO 2

	A	B	C
1	**Monroe Music Co.** **Comparative Income Statements** **Years Ended December 31, 2018 and 2017**		
2		**2018**	**2017**
3	Total revenue	$ 844,000	$ 934,000
4	Expenses:		
5	Cost of goods sold	$ 404,000	$ 400,000
6	Selling and general expenses	234,000	270,000
7	Interest expense	9,300	12,000
8	Income tax expense	84,000	86,000
9	Total expenses	731,300	768,000
10	Net income	$ 112,700	$ 166,000
11			

E12-28B. ***(Learning Objective 2: Calculate trend percentages)*** Calculate trend percentages for Oak View Sales & Service's total revenue and net income for the following five-year period, using year 0 as the base year. Round to the nearest full percent. LO 2

(In thousands)	Year 4	Year 3	Year 2	Year 1	Year 0
Total revenue	$1,400	$1,246	$1,093	$999	$1,025
Net income	129	120	107	95	87

Which grew faster during the period, total revenue or net income?

E12-29B. ***(Learning Objective 3: Perform a vertical analysis of a balance sheet)*** Perform a vertical analysis of Chapel Hill Golf Company's balance sheet to determine the component percentages of its assets, liabilities, and stockholders' equity. LO 3

	A	B
1	**Chapel Hill Golf Company** **Balance Sheet** **December 31, 2018**	
2	**Assets**	
3	Total current assets	$ 45,440
4	Property, plant, and equipment, net	229,760
5	Other assets	44,800
6	Total assets	$ 320,000
7		
8	**Liabilities**	
9	Total current liabilities	$ 53,440
10	Long-term debt	119,360
11	Total liabilities	172,800
12		
13	**Stockholders' Equity**	
14	Total stockholders' equity	147,200
15	Total liabilities and stockholders' equity	$ 320,000
16		

LO 3 **E12-30B.** ***(Learning Objective 3: Prepare a common-size income statement)*** Prepare a comparative common-size income statement for Monroe Music Co. using the 2018 and 2017 data of E12-27B and rounding to four decimal places.

LO 4 **E12-31B.** ***(Learning Objective 4: Calculate year-to-year changes in working capital)*** The following information is for Leary Lodge. What were the dollar amount of change and the percentage of each change in Leary Lodge's net working capital during 2018 and 2017? Is this trend favorable or unfavorable?

	2018	2017	2016
Total current assets	$880,800	$395,000	$320,000
Total current liabilities	360,000	115,000	160,000

LO 4 **E12-32B.** ***(Learning Objective 4: Calculate ratios; evaluate turnover, liquidity, and current debt-paying ability)*** The financial statements of Big City News, Inc., include the following items:

	2018	2017	2015
Balance sheet:			
Cash	$ 53,000	$ 89,000	
Short-term investments	10,000	33,000	
Net receivables	77,000	80,000	35,000
Inventory	91,000	75,000	58,000
Prepaid expenses	6,000	6,000	
Total current assets	237,000	283,000	
Accounts payable	55,000	45,000	50,000
Total current liabilities	134,000	91,000	
Income statement:			
Net credit sales	$497,000	$ 503,000	
Cost of goods sold	275,000	286,000	

Requirements

1. Calculate the following ratios for 2018 and 2017. When calculating days, round your answer to the nearest whole number.
   - **a.** Current ratio
   - **b.** Quick (acid-test) ratio
   - **c.** Inventory turnover and days' inventory outstanding (DIO)
   - **d.** Accounts receivable turnover
   - **e.** Days' sales in average receivables or days' sales outstanding (DSO)
   - **f.** Accounts payable turnover and days' payable outstanding (DPO). Use cost of goods sold in the formula for accounts payable turnover.
   - **g.** Cash conversion cycle (in days)
2. Evaluate the company's liquidity and current debt-paying ability for 2018. Has it improved or deteriorated from 2017?
3. As a manager of this company, what would you try to improve next year?

LO 4

E12-33B. ***(Learning Objective 4: Analyze a company's ability to pay its liabilities)*** Evansville Furniture Company has asked you to determine whether the company's ability to pay its current liabilities and long-term debts improved or deteriorated during 2018. To answer this question, calculate the following ratios for 2018 and 2017. Round your answers to two decimal places. Summarize the results of your analysis in a short paragraph.

a. Net working capital
b. Current ratio
c. Quick (acid-test) ratio
d. Debt ratio
e. Times-interest-earned ratio

	2018	2017
Cash	$ 35,000	$ 47,000
Short-term investments	32,000	4,000
Net receivables	115,000	128,000
Inventory	240,000	270,000
Prepaid expenses	21,000	12,000
Total assets	510,000	500,000
Total current liabilities	187,000	252,000
Long-term debt	157,000	48,000
Income from operations	196,000	155,000
Interest expense	59,000	46,000

LO 4

E12-34B. ***(Learning Objective 4: Analyze the profitability of a company)*** For 2018 and 2017, calculate return on sales, asset turnover, return on assets (ROA), leverage, return on common stockholders' equity (ROE), gross profit percentage, operating income percentage, and earnings per share to measure the ability to earn profits for Rolling Hills Decor, Inc., whose comparative income statements follow. Perform a DuPont Analysis for ROA and ROE, and round each component ratio to three decimal places; for other ratio computations, round to two decimal places.

A1

	A	B	C
1	**Rolling Hills Decor, Inc.** **Comparative Income Statements** **Years Ended December 31, 2018 and 2017**		
2		**2018**	**2017**
3	Net sales	$ 190,000	$ 240,000
4	Cost of goods sold	102,000	134,000
5	Gross profit	88,000	106,000
6	Selling and general expenses	44,000	49,000
7	Income from operations	44,000	57,000
8	Interest expense	9,000	7,000
9	Income before income tax	35,000	50,000
10	Income tax expense	12,000	16,000
11	Net income	$ 23,000	$ 34,000
12			

Additional data:

	2018	2017	2016
Total assets	$300,000	$270,000	$250,000
Common stockholders' equity	$104,000	$103,000	$102,000
Preferred dividends	$ 15,000	$ 14,000	$ 3,000
Average common shares outstanding during the year	24,000	23,000	22,000

Did the company's operating performance improve or deteriorate during 2018?

LO 4

E12-35B. ***(Learning Objective 4: Calculate earnings per share)*** Altar Loan Company's balance sheet at December 31, 2018, reports the following:

Preferred stock, $100 par value, 6%, 9,000 shares issued	$ 900,000
Common stock, $0.75 par, 900,000 shares issued	675,000
Treasury stock, common, 70,000 shares at cost	630,000

During 2018, Altar Loan earned net income of $6,200,000. Calculate Altar Loan's earnings per common share (EPS) for 2018; round EPS to two decimal places. Assume the number of shares issued and outstanding did not change during the year.

LO 4

E12-36B. ***(Learning Objective 4: Evaluate a stock as an investment)*** Evaluate the common stock of Tristan Distributing Company as an investment. Specifically, use the two common stock ratios to determine whether the common stock became more or less attractive during the past year. (The number of common stock shares was the same in 2017 and 2018.) Round calculations and your final answer to three decimal places.

	2018	2017
Net income	$114,000	$ 70,500
Dividends to common	28,000	24,000
Total stockholders' equity at year-end	300,000	495,000
(includes 43,500 shares of common stock)		
Preferred stock, 5%	105,000	105,000
Market price per share of common stock at year-end	$ 23.50	$ 17.25

LO 4, 5

E12-37B. ***(Learning Objectives 4, 5: Prepare an income statement; calculate earnings per share; evaluate quality of earnings; evaluate a company as an investment)*** The Hooper Book Company's accounting records include the following for 2018 (in thousands):

Other revenues	$ 1,600
Income tax expense	5,640
Sales revenue	122,000
Total operating expenses	104,800

Requirements

1. Prepare Hooper Book Company's single-step income statement for the year ended December 31, 2018, including earnings per share (EPS). Hooper had 1,000,000 shares of common stock and no preferred stock outstanding during the year.
2. Assume Hooper Book Company's income from operations indicates that its core business has steadily increased by about 10% per year over the past three years and that none of its operations have been discontinued. What does this say about the quality of the company's earnings?

Quiz

Test your understanding of financial statement analysis concepts by answering the following questions. Select the best choice from among the possibilities.

Q12-38. A public company's annual report filed with the SEC includes
- **a.** a description of the business.
- **b.** financial statements.
- **c.** management's explanations for trends in sales.
- **d.** All of the above are included in an annual report.

Q12-39. If you want an indication of the direction a business is taking, you would use
- **a.** benchmarking.
- **b.** trend percentages.
- **c.** industry analysis.
- **d.** vertical analysis.

Q12-40. Bond Company reported the following inventory data:

Year	Inventory (in millions)
2016	$2,500
2017	$2,350
2018	$2,600
2019	$2,170

Use 2016 as the base year. The trend percentage in 2019 is closest to
- **a.** 83%.
- **b.** 87%.
- **c.** 92%.
- **d.** 115%.

Q12-41. Movens Company gathered the following data (in millions) for the past two years:

	2019	2018
Net revenues	$280	$250
Cost of goods sold	$150	$140
Gross profit	$130	$110
Operating expenses	$ 90	$ 75
Operating income	$ 40	$ 35

In a vertical analysis of 2019, the gross profit percentage would be closest to
- **a.** 18%.
- **b.** 46%.
- **c.** 100%.
- **d.** 325%.

Use the Orlando Medical Corporation financial statements that follow to answer questions 12-42 through 12-53.

	A	B	C
1	**Orlando Medical Corporation** **Consolidated Statements of Financial Position**		
2		**December 31,**	
3	**(In Millions)**	**2018**	**2017**
4	**Assets:**		
5	Current Assets		
6	Cash and cash equivalents	$ 4,333	$ 4,226
7	Short-term investments	845	520
8	Accounts and notes receivable	3,400	2,403
9	Inventories, at cost	433	411
10	Prepaid expense and other current assets	1,638	1,226
11	Total current assets	10,649	8,786
12	Property and equipment, net	1,555	907
13	Investments	6,804	5,199
14	Other non-current assets	303	155
15	Total assets	$ 19,311	$ 15,047
16	**Liabilities and stockholders' equity:**		
17	Current liabilities		
18	Accounts payable	$ 7,708	$ 6,009
19	Accrued and other liabilities	3,676	3,033
20	Total current liabilities	11,384	9,042
21	Long-term debt	304	305
22	Other non-current liabilities	1,701	1,179
23	Total liabilities	13,389	10,526
24	Stockholders' equity		
25	Preferred stock and capital in excess of $0.02 par value;		
26	shares issued and outstanding: none	—	—
27	Common stock and capital in excess of $0.05 par value;		
28	shares authorized: 6,000; shares issued: 2,163 and		
29	1,903, respectively	7,803	7,001
30	Treasury stock, at cost: 183 and 123 shares, respectively	(6,444)	(4,401)
31	Retained earnings	4,676	1,990
32	Other comprehensive loss	(79)	(25)
33	Other	(34)	(44)
34	Total stockholders' equity	5,922	4,521
35	Total liabilities and stockholders' equity	$ 19,311	$ 15,047
36			

	A	B	C	D
1	**Orlando Medical Corporation** **Consolidated Statements of Income**			
2		**Year ended December 31,**		
3	**(In Millions, Except per Share Amounts)**	**2018**	**2017**	**2016**
4	Net Revenue	$ 42,666	$ 35,220	$ 31,111
5	Cost of goods sold	35,147	29,255	25,492
6	Gross profit	7,519	5,965	5,619
7	Operating expenses:			
8	Selling, general, and administrative	3,341	3,250	2,985
9	Research, development, and engineering	544	553	536
10	Special charges	—	—	512
11	Total operating expenses	3,885	3,803	4,033
12	Operating income	3,634	2,162	1,586
13	Investment and other income (loss), net	153	196	(30)
14	Income before income taxes	3,787	2,358	1,556
15	Income tax expense	1,136	940	472
16	Net income	$ 2,651	$ 1,418	$ 1,084
17	Earnings per common share:			
18	Basic	$ 1.41	$ 0.95	$ 0.37
19				

Q12-42. During 2018, Orlando Medical's total assets

a. increased by \$1,863 million.
b. increased by 28.3%.
c. Both a and b.
d. increased by 22.1%.

Q12-43. Orlando Medical's current ratio at year-end 2018 is closest to

a. \$735.
b. \$8,578.
c. 0.94.
d. 1.2.

Q12-44. Orlando Medical's quick (acid-test) ratio at year-end 2018 is closest to

a. 0.68.
b. \$8,578 million.
c. 0.45.
d. 0.75.

Q12-45. What is the largest single item included in Orlando Medical's debt ratio at December 31, 2018?

a. Accounts payable
b. Cash and cash equivalents
c. Common stock
d. Investments

Q12-46. Using the earliest year available as the base year, the trend percentage for Orlando Medical's net revenue during 2018 was

a. 121%.
b. up by 21.1%.
c. up by \$11,555 million.
d. 137%.

Q12-47. Orlando Medical's common-size income statement for 2018 would report cost of goods sold as

a. 82.4%.
b. \$35,147 million.
c. up by 20.1%.
d. 137.9%.

Q12-48. Orlando Medical's days' sales in receivables during 2018 was (assuming all revenue is on credit)

a. 137.9 days.
b. 25 days.
c. 35 days.
d. 20.1 days.

Q12-49. Orlando Medical's inventory turnover during fiscal year 2018 was

a. \$35,147.
b. very slow.
c. 83 times.
d. 137.9 times.

Q12-50. Orlando Medical's long-term debt carries an annual interest rate of 11%. During the year ended December 31, 2018, Orlando's times-interest-earned ratio was

a. 137.9 times.
b. \$35,147.
c. 20.1 times.
d. 108.7 times.

Q12-51. Orlando Medical's trend of return on sales is

a. improving.
b. declining.
c. stuck at 22.1%.
d. worrisome.

Q12-52. How many shares of common stock did Orlando Medical have outstanding, on average, during 2018? (*Hint*: Calculate earnings per share.)

a. 137.9 million
b. 1,880 million
c. 20.1 million
d. 35,147 million

Q12-53. Book value per share[1] of Orlando Medical's common stock outstanding at December 31, 2018, was

a. 137.9.
b. \$35,147.
c. \$2.99.
d. 20.1.

Q12-54. The quality of earnings concept indicates that

a. stockholders want the corporation to earn enough income to be able to pay its debts.
b. net income is the best measure of the results of operations.
c. continuing operations and one-time transactions are of equal importance.
d. income from continuing operations is a more relevant predictor of future performance than income from one-time transactions.

[1] $\text{Book value per share of common stock} = \dfrac{\text{Total stockholders' equity} - \text{Preferred equity}}{\text{Number of shares of common stock outstanding}}$

Q12-55. A company with high earnings quality is more likely to experience ____________ than a company with low earnings quality.

a. low revenue levels in the future
b. increasing operating expenses, compared to sales, in the future
c. high earnings in the future
d. low earnings in the future

Problems MyLab Accounting

Group A

LO 1, 2, 4

P12-56A. ***(Learning Objectives 1, 2, 4: Calculate trend percentages, return on sales, asset turnover, and ROA and compare with industry averages)*** Net sales, net income, and total assets for Azul Shipping, Inc., for a five-year period follow:

(In thousands)	2018	2017	2016	2015	2014
Net sales	$498	$327	$352	$315	$296
Net income	30	10	28	41	25
Total assets	314	266	248	224	204

Requirements

1. Calculate trend percentages for each item for 2015 through 2018. Use 2014 as the base year and round to the nearest percent.
2. Calculate the rate of return on net sales for 2016 through 2018, rounding to three decimal places. Explain what this means.
3. Calculate asset turnover for 2016 through 2018. Explain what this means.
4. Use a DuPont Analysis to calculate the rate of return on average total assets (ROA) for 2016 through 2018.
5. How does Azul Shipping's return on net sales for 2018 compare with previous years? How does it compare with that of the industry? In the shipping industry, rates above 9% are considered good, and rates above 11% are outstanding.
6. Evaluate the company's ROA for 2018, compared with previous years and against an 18% benchmark for the industry.

P12-57A. ***(Learning Objectives 1, 3, 4: Prepare common-size statements; analyze profitability; make comparisons to the industry)*** Top managers of Caffrey Products, Inc., have asked you to compare the company's profit performance and financial position with the average for the industry. The company's accountant has given you the business's income statement, balance sheet, and industry data:

LO 1, 3, 4

	A	B	C
1	**Caffrey Products, Inc.** **Income Statement Compared with Industry Average** **Year Ended December 31, 2018**		
2		**Caffrey**	**Industry Average**
3	Net sales	$ 960,000	100.0%
4	Cost of goods sold	662,400	57.3
5	Gross profit	297,600	42.7
6	Operating expenses	211,200	29.4
7	Operating income	86,400	13.3
8	Other expenses	14,400	2.5
9	Net income	$ 72,000	10.8%
10			

	A	B	C
1	**Caffrey Products, Inc.** **Balance Sheet Compared with Industry Average** **December 31, 2018**		
2		**Caffrey**	**Industry Average**
3	Current assets	$ 501,600	72.1%
4	Plant assets, net	120,120	19.0
5	Intangible assets, net	22,440	4.8
6	Other assets	15,840	4.1
7	Total	$ 660,000	100.0%
8			
9	Current liabilities	$ 257,400	47.2%
10	Long-term liabilities	141,240	21.0
11	Stockholders' equity	261,360	31.8
12	Total	$ 660,000	100.0%
13			

Requirements

1. Prepare a common-size income statement and balance sheet for Caffrey Products. The first column of each statement should present the company's common-size statement, and the second column should show the industry averages.
2. For the profitability analysis, compare the company's (a) ratio of gross profit to net sales, (b) ratio of operating income to net sales, and (c) ratio of net income to net sales with the industry averages. Is the company's profit performance better or worse than the average for the industry?
3. For the analysis of financial position, calculate Caffrey Products' (a) ratios of current assets and current liabilities to total assets and (b) ratio of stockholders' equity to total assets. Compare these ratios with the industry averages. Is the company's financial position better or worse than the average for the industry?

LO 4

P12-58A. ***(Learning Objective 4: Calculate the effects of business transactions on selected ratios)*** Financial statement data of Greatland Engineering include the following items:

Cash	$ 26,000	Accounts payable	$107,000
Short-term investments	36,000	Accrued liabilities	32,000
Accounts receivable, net	85,000	Long-term notes payable	163,000
Inventories	147,000	Other long-term liabilities	34,000
Prepaid expenses	6,000	Net income	99,000
Total assets	677,000	Number of common shares outstanding	46,000
Short-term notes payable	49,000		

Requirements

1. Calculate Greatland's current ratio, debt ratio, and earnings per share. Round all ratios to two decimal places.
2. Calculate the three ratios after evaluating the effect of each transaction that follows. Consider each transaction *separately*.
   a. Borrowed $105,000 on a long-term note payable
   b. On January 1, issued 40,000 shares of common stock, receiving cash of $360,000
   c. Paid off short-term notes payable, $28,000
   d. Purchased $43,000 of merchandise on account, debiting Inventory
   e. Received cash on account, $17,000

LO 4

P12-59A. ***(Learning Objective 4: Use ratios to evaluate a stock investment)*** Comparative financial statement data of Hamden Optical Mart follow:

	A	B	C
1	**Hamden Optical Mart Comparative Income Statements Years Ended December 31, 2018 and 2017**		
2		**2018**	**2017**
3	Net sales	$ 673,000	$ 595,000
4	Cost of goods sold	382,000	278,000
5	Gross profit	291,000	317,000
6	Operating expenses	125,000	145,000
7	Income from operations	166,000	172,000
8	Interest expense	35,000	49,000
9	Income before income tax	131,000	123,000
10	Income tax expense	40,000	52,000
11	Net income	$ 91,000	$ 71,000
12			

A1			
Hamden Optical Mart **Comparative Balance Sheets** **December 31, 2018 and 2017**			
	2018	**2017**	**2016***
Current assets:			
Cash	$ 39,000	$ 43,000	
Current receivables, net	214,000	152,000	$ 139,000
Inventories	293,000	280,000	188,000
Prepaid expenses	9,000	30,000	
Total current assets	555,000	505,000	
Property, plant, and equipment, net	287,000	279,000	
Total assets	$ 842,000	$ 784,000	700,000
Accounts payable	$ 120,000	$ 98,000	108,000
Other current liabilities	141,000	195,000	
Total current liabilities	261,000	293,000	
Long-term liabilities	243,000	232,000	
Total liabilities	504,000	525,000	
Common stockholders' equity, no par	338,000	259,000	197,000
Total liabilities and stockholders' equity	$ 842,000	$ 784,000	

*Selected 2016 amounts.

Other information:

1. Market price of Hamden Optical Mart common stock: $48.15 at December 31, 2018, and $39.96 at December 31, 2017
2. Common shares outstanding: 17,000 during 2018 and 16,000 during 2017
3. All sales on credit
4. Cash dividends paid per share: $1.10 in 2018 and $0.80 in 2017

Requirements

1. Calculate the following ratios for 2018 and 2017:
   a. Current ratio
   b. Quick (acid-test) ratio
   c. Receivables turnover and days' sales outstanding (DSO)—round to the nearest whole day
   d. Inventory turnover and days' inventory outstanding (DIO)—round to the nearest whole day
   e. Accounts payable turnover and days' payable outstanding (DPO)—use cost of goods sold in the numerator of the turnover ratio and round DPO to the nearest whole day
   f. Cash conversion cycle (in days)
   g. Times-interest-earned ratio
   h. Return on assets—use DuPont Analysis
   i. Return on common stockholders' equity—use DuPont Analysis
   j. Earnings per share of common stock
   k. Price-earnings ratio
2. Decide whether (a) Hamden Optical Mart's financial position improved or deteriorated during 2018 and (b) whether the investment attractiveness of the company's common stock appears to have increased or decreased from 2017 to 2018.
3. How will what you learned in this problem help you evaluate an investment?

LO 4

P12-60A. ***(Learning Objective 4: Use ratios to decide between two stock investments)*** Assume that you are considering purchasing stock as an investment. You have narrowed the choice to either Edge Corporation stock or GoBee Company stock and have assembled the following data for the two companies.

Selected income statement data for the current year:

	Edge	GoBee
Net sales (all on credit)	$595,000	$524,000
Cost of goods sold	452,000	388,000
Income from operations	89,000	73,000
Interest expense	—	13,000
Net income	69,000	36,000

Selected balance sheet and market price data at the *end* of the current year:

	Edge	GoBee
Current assets:		
Cash	$ 21,000	$ 35,000
Short-term investments	4,000	18,000
Current receivables, net	186,000	167,000
Inventories	212,000	181,000
Prepaid expenses	17,000	9,000
Total current assets	440,000	410,000
Total assets	985,000	930,000
Total current liabilities	368,000	333,000
Total liabilities	663,000	689,000
Preferred stock, 5%, $125 par		25,000
Common stock, $1 par (150,000 shares)	150,000	
$5 par (20,000 shares)		100,000
Total stockholders' equity	322,000	241,000
Market price per share of common stock	$ 5.52	$ 38.28

Selected balance sheet data at the *beginning* of the current year:

	Edge	GoBee
Balance sheet:		
Current receivables, net	$142,000	$198,000
Inventories	202,000	199,000
Total assets	843,000	911,000
Long-term debt	—	309,000
Preferred stock, 5%, $125 par		25,000
Common stock, $1 par (150,000 shares)	150,000	
$5 par (20,000 shares)		100,000
Total stockholders' equity	261,000	222,000

Your strategy is to invest in companies that have low price-earnings ratios but appear to be in good shape financially. Assume that you have analyzed all other factors and that your decision depends on the results of your ratio analysis.

Requirements

1. Calculate the following ratios for both companies for the current year, and decide which company's stock better fits your investment strategy.
   - **a.** Quick (acid-test) ratio
   - **b.** Inventory turnover
   - **c.** Days' sales in average receivables
   - **d.** Debt ratio
   - **e.** Times-interest-earned ratio
   - **f.** Return on common stockholders' equity
   - **g.** Earnings per share of common stock
   - **h.** Price-earnings ratio

P12-61A. ***(Learning Objectives 2, 4, 5: Analyze trends; calculate and interpret ratios; evaluate earnings quality)***

LO **2, 4, 5**

Selected data from Tompkin Furniture, Inc., follows.

Selected balance sheet data	2018	2017	2016	2015
Cash	$ 2,800	$ 3,000	$ 4,200	
Marketable securities	400	600	500	
Accounts receivable, net	6,700	6,300	5,100	$ 4,800
Inventory	6,000	4,200	3,200	3,000
Total current assets	15,900	14,100	13,000	
Long-term assets	6,900	7,800	9,200	
Total assets	22,800	21,900	22,200	
Accounts payable	3,500	2,300	1,500	1,900
Short-term notes payable	6,000	4,600	3,750	
Total current liabilities	9,500	6,900	5,250	
Total long-term liabilities	265	2,725	6,982	

Selected income statement data	2018	2017	2016	2015
Net sales revenue *(assume all sales are credit sales)*	$ 34,500	$ 33,000	$ 32,100	$ 31,500
Cost of goods sold	20,700	15,840	14,445	
Operating expenses	12,500	13,500	13,700	
Interest expense	150	255	300	
Income taxes	390	1,098	1,187	

Industry averages have been gathered for several ratios.

Furniture industry averages	
Current ratio	2.3
Quick ratio	1.0
Days' inventory outstanding	80.0
Days' sales outstanding	60.0
Days' payable outstanding	32.0
Debt ratio	62%
Times-interest-earned ratio	12.0
Gross margin percentage	51%
Operating income percentage	10%

Requirements

1. Perform a trend analysis on Tompkin's sales revenue, inventory, and receivables over the past three years, using 2015 as the base. Is the trend in each of these areas favorable or unfavorable for the company?
2. Using the industry averages as benchmarks, analyze Tompkin's performance over the past three years in the following areas:
   - **a.** Liquidity
   - **b.** Turnover
   - **c.** Overall debt payment ability
   - **d.** Profitability
3. Evaluate Tompkin's quality of earnings. Are there any red flags in your analysis? Explain.

Group B

LO **1, 2, 4**

P12-62B. ***(Learning Objectives 1, 2, 4: Calculate trend percentages, return on sales, asset turnover, and ROA, and compare with industry averages)*** Net sales, net income, and total assets for Suburban Shipping, Inc., for a five-year period follow:

(In thousands)	2018	2017	2016	2015	2014
Net sales	$616	$502	$354	$311	$301
Net income	54	34	11	35	34
Total assets	308	272	258	232	203

Requirements

1. Calculate trend percentages for each item for 2015 through 2018. Use 2014 as the base year and round to the nearest percent.
2. Calculate the rate of return on net sales for 2016 through 2018, rounding to three decimal places. Explain what this means.
3. Calculate asset turnover for 2016 through 2018. Explain what this means.
4. Use a DuPont Analysis to calculate the rate of return on average total assets (ROA) for 2016 through 2018.
5. How does Suburban Shipping's return on net sales for 2018 compare with previous years? How does it compare with that of the industry? In the shipping industry, rates above 9% are considered good, and rates above 11% are outstanding.
6. Evaluate the company's ROA for 2018, compared with previous years and against an 18% benchmark for the industry.

P12-63B. ***(Learning Objectives 1, 3, 4: Prepare common-size statements; analyze profitability; make comparisons to the industry)*** Top managers of Ryan Products, Inc., have asked you to compare the company's profit performance and financial position with the average for the industry. The company's accountant has given you the business's income statement, balance sheet, and industry data:

LO 1, 3, 4

	A	B	C
1	**Ryan Products, Inc.** **Income Statement Compared with Industry Average** **Year Ended December 31, 2018**		
2		**Ryan**	**Industry Average**
3	Net sales	$ 500,000	100.0%
4	Cost of goods sold	355,000	57.3
5	Gross profit	145,000	42.7
6	Operating expenses	120,000	29.4
7	Operating income	25,000	13.3
8	Other expenses	7,500	2.5
9	Net income	$ 17,500	10.8%
10			

	A	B	C
1	**Ryan Products, Inc.** **Balance Sheet Compared with Industry Average** **December 31, 2018**		
2		**Ryan**	**Industry Average**
3	Current assets	$ 496,400	72.1%
4	Plant assets, net	121,040	19.0
5	Intangible assets, net	27,200	4.8
6	Other assets	35,360	4.1
7	Total	$ 680,000	100.0%
8			
9	Current liabilities	$ 266,560	47.2%
10	Long-term liabilities	144,160	21.0
11	Stockholders' equity	269,280	31.8
12	Total	$ 680,000	100.0%
13			

Requirements

1. Prepare a common-size income statement and balance sheet for Ryan Products. The first column of each statement should present the company's common-size statement, and the second column should show the industry averages.
2. For the profitability analysis, compare the company's (a) ratio of gross profit to net sales, (b) ratio of operating income to net sales, and (c) ratio of net income to net sales with the industry averages. Is the company's profit performance better or worse than the average for the industry?
3. For the analysis of financial position, calculate Ryan Products' (a) ratios of current assets and current liabilities to total assets and (b) ratio of stockholders' equity to total assets. Compare these ratios with the industry averages. Is the company's financial position better or worse than the average for the industry?

LO 4

P12-64B. ***(Learning Objective 4: Calculate the effects of business transactions on selected ratios)*** Financial statement data of Highland Engineering include the following items:

Cash	$ 22,000	Accounts payable	$102,000
Short-term investments	33,000	Accrued liabilities	37,000
Accounts receivable, net	87,000	Long-term notes payable	162,000
Inventories	145,000	Other long-term liabilities	32,000
Prepaid expenses	9,000	Net income	95,000
Total assets	675,000	Number of common shares outstanding	50,000
Short-term notes payable	44,000		

Requirements

1. Calculate Highland's current ratio, debt ratio, and earnings per share. Round all ratios to two decimal places.
2. Calculate the three ratios after evaluating the effect of each transaction that follows. Consider each transaction *separately*.
   - **a.** Borrowed $140,000 on a long-term note payable
   - **b.** On January 1, issued 30,000 shares of common stock, receiving cash of $367,000
   - **c.** Paid off short-term notes payable, $27,000
   - **d.** Purchased $41,000 of merchandise on account, debiting Inventory
   - **e.** Received cash on account, $15,000

LO 4

P12-65B. ***(Learning Objective 4: Use ratios to evaluate a stock investment)*** Comparative financial statement data of Stow Optical Mart follow:

	A	B	C
1	**Stow Optical Mart Comparative Income Statements Years Ended December 31, 2018 and 2017**		
2		**2018**	**2017**
3	Net sales	$ 686,000	$ 595,000
4	Cost of goods sold	382,000	276,000
5	Gross profit	304,000	319,000
6	Operating expenses	132,000	150,000
7	Income from operations	172,000	169,000
8	Interest expense	38,000	45,000
9	Income before income tax	134,000	124,000
10	Income tax expense	40,000	46,000
11	Net income	$ 94,000	$ 78,000
12			

A1	A	B	C	D
1	**Stow Optical Mart** **Comparative Balance Sheets** **December 31, 2018 and 2017**			
2		**2018**	**2017**	**2016***
3	Current assets:			
4	Cash	$ 42,000	$ 82,000	
5	Current receivables, net	212,000	155,000	$132,000
6	Inventories	299,000	288,000	180,000
7	Prepaid expenses	12,000	27,000	
8	Total current assets	565,000	552,000	
9	Property, plant, and equipment, net	287,000	275,000	
10	Total assets	$852,000	$827,000	704,000
11				
12	Accounts payable	$140,000	$114,000	108,000
13	Other current liabilities	137,000	176,000	
14	Total current liabilities	277,000	290,000	
15	Long-term liabilities	244,000	234,000	
16	Total liabilities	521,000	524,000	
17	Common stockholders' equity, no par	331,000	303,000	195,000
18	Total liabilities and stockholders' equity	$852,000	$827,000	
19				

*Selected 2016 amounts.

Other information:

1. Market price of Stow Optical Mart common stock: $122.91 at December 31, 2018, and $165.75 at December 31, 2017
2. Common shares outstanding: 13,000 during 2018 and 8,000 during 2017
3. All sales on credit
4. Cash dividends paid per share: $2.75 per share in 2018 and $4.00 in 2017

Requirements

1. Calculate the following ratios for 2018 and 2017:
   a. Current ratio
   b. Quick (acid-test) ratio
   c. Receivables turnover and days' sales outstanding (DSO)—round to the nearest whole day
   d. Inventory turnover and days' inventory outstanding (DIO)—round to the nearest whole day
   e. Accounts payable turnover and days' payable outstanding (DPO)–use cost of goods sold in the turnover ratio and round DPO to the nearest whole day
   f. Cash conversion cycle (in days)
   g. Times-interest-earned ratio
   h. Return on assets—use DuPont Analysis
   i. Return on common stockholders' equity—use DuPont Analysis
   j. Earnings per share of common stock
   k. Price-earnings ratio
2. Decide whether (a) Stow Optical Mart's financial position improved or deteriorated during 2018 and (b) whether the investment attractiveness of the company's common stock appears to have increased or decreased from 2017 to 2018.
3. How will what you learned in this problem help you evaluate an investment?

LO 4

P12-66B. ***(Learning Objective 4: Use ratios to decide between two stock investments)*** Assume that you are considering purchasing stock as an investment. You have narrowed the choice to either Border Corporation stock or Celebration Company stock and have assembled the following data for the two companies.

Selected income statement data for the current year:

	Border	Celebration
Net sales (all on credit)	$601,000	$517,000
Cost of goods sold	458,000	388,000
Income from operations	94,000	70,000
Interest expense	—	10,000
Net income	63,000	32,000

Selected balance sheet and market price data at the *end* of the current year:

	Border	Celebration
Current assets:		
Cash	$ 26,000	$ 35,000
Short-term investments	9,000	18,000
Current receivables, net	185,000	167,000
Inventories	211,000	187,000
Prepaid expenses	18,000	12,000
Total current assets	449,000	419,000
Total assets	985,000	933,000
Total current liabilities	367,000	342,000
Total liabilities	671,000	700,000
Preferred stock: 9%, $175 par		35,000
Common stock, $1 par (115,000 shares)	115,000	
$5 par (20,000 shares)		100,000
Total stockholders' equity	314,000	233,000
Market price per share of common stock	$ 5.50	$ 30.24

Selected balance sheet data at the *beginning* of the current year:

	Border	Celebration
Balance sheet:		
Current receivables, net	$141,000	$198,000
Inventories	205,000	199,000
Total assets	844,000	910,000
Long-term debt	—	310,000
Preferred stock, 9%, $175 par		35,000
Common stock, $1 par (115,000 shares)	115,000	
$5 par (20,000 shares)		100,000
Total stockholders' equity	263,000	219,000

Your strategy is to invest in companies that have low price-earnings ratios but appear to be in good shape financially. Assume that you have analyzed all other factors and that your decision depends on the results of your ratio analysis.

Requirements

1. Calculate the following ratios for both companies for the current year, and decide which company's stock better fits your investment strategy.
   - **a.** Quick (acid-test) ratio
   - **b.** Inventory turnover
   - **c.** Days' sales in average receivables
   - **d.** Debt ratio
   - **e.** Times-interest-earned ratio
   - **f.** Return on common stockholders' equity
   - **g.** Earnings per share of common stock
   - **h.** Price-earnings ratio

P12-67B. ***(Learning Objectives 2, 4, 5: Analyze trends; calculate and interpret ratios; evaluate earnings quality)*** LO **2, 4, 5**

Selected data from Switzer Furniture, Inc., follows.

Selected balance sheet data	2018	2017	2016	2015
Cash	$ 2,750	$ 3,200	$ 4,100	
Marketable securities	425	550	550	
Accounts receivable, net	6,800	6,400	5,200	$ 4,900
Inventory	6,100	4,300	3,300	2,900
Total current assets	16,075	14,450	13,150	
Long-term assets	7,050	7,800	9,150	
Total assets	23,125	22,250	22,300	
Accounts payable	3,750	2,450	1,700	1,800
Short-term notes payable	5,950	4,750	3,625	
Total current liabilities	9,700	7,200	5,325	
Total long-term liabilities	551	2,933	6,958	

Selected income statement data	2018	2017	2016	2015
Net sales revenue (*assume all sales are credit sales*)	$ 34,025	$ 33,050	$ 32,200	$ 31,300
Cost of goods sold	20,755	16,195	14,812	
Operating expenses	11,975	13,490	13,650	
Interest expense	150	255	300	
Income taxes	388	1,010	1,121	

Industry averages have been gathered for several ratios.

Furniture industry averages	
Current ratio	2.4
Quick ratio	1.0
Days' inventory outstanding	80.0
Days' sales outstanding	60.0
Days' payable outstanding	32.0
Debt ratio	61%
Times-interest-earned ratio	13.0
Gross margin percentage	52%
Operating income percentage	12%

Requirements

1. Perform a trend analysis on Switzer's sales revenue, inventory, and receivables over the past three years, using 2015 as the base. Is the trend in each of these areas favorable or unfavorable for the company?
2. Using the industry averages as benchmarks, analyze Switzer's performance over the past three years in the following areas:
   a. Liquidity
   b. Turnover
   c. Overall debt payment ability
   d. Profitability
3. Evaluate Switzer's quality of earnings. Are there any red flags in your analysis? Explain.

Challenge Exercises and Problem

LO 4

E12-68. ***(Learning Objective 4: Use ratio data to reconstruct a company's balance sheet)*** The following data (dollar amounts in millions) are taken from the financial statements of Quantrill Industries, Inc.:

Total liabilities	$11,800
Total current assets	$11,900
Accumulated depreciation	$ 2,100
Debt ratio	40%
Current ratio	1.70

Requirement

1. Complete the following condensed balance sheet. Report amounts to the nearest million dollars.

		(In millions)
Current assets		
Property, plant, and equipment		
Less: Accumulated depreciation		
Total assets		
Current liabilities		
Long-term liabilities		
Stockholders' equity		
Total liabilities and stockholders' equity		

LO 4

E12-69. ***(Learning Objective 4: Use ratio data to reconstruct a company's income statement)*** The following data (dollar amounts in millions) are from the financial statements of Hill Corporation:

Average stockholders' equity	$3,500
Interest expense	$ 200
Operating income as a percent of sales	25%
Rate of return on stockholders' equity	21%
Income tax rate	30%

Requirement

1. Complete the following condensed income statement. Report amounts to the nearest million dollars.

Sales	
Operating expense	
Operating income	
Interest expense	
Income before taxes	
Income tax expense	
Net income	

LO **2, 3, 4**

P12-70. ***(Learning Objectives 2, 3, 4: Use trend percentages, common-size percentages, and ratios to reconstruct financial statements)*** An incomplete comparative income statement and balance sheet for Ivy Corporation follow:

Ivy Corporation
Comparative income Statements
Years Ended December 31, 2018 and 2017

		2018	2017
3	Sales revenue	$2,300,000	$1,800,000
4	Cost of goods sold	?	990,000
5	Gross profit	?	810,000
6	Operating expense	?	660,000
7	Operating income	?	150,000
8	Interest expense	15,300	15,300
9	Income before income tax	?	134,700
10	Income tax expense (30%)	?	33,675
11	Net income	?	$ 101,025

Ivy Corporation
Balance Sheet
December 31, 2018 and 2017

		2018	2017
3	ASSETS		
4	Current:		
5	Cash	$?	$ 37,000
6	Accounts receivable, net	?	120,000
7	Inventory	?	190,000
8	Total current assets	?	347,000
9	Plant and equipment, net	?	303,000
10	Total assets	$?	$650,000
11	LIABILITIES		
12	Current liabilities	$150,000	$160,000
13	10% Bonds payable	?	90,000
14	Total liabilities	?	250,000
15	STOCKHOLDERS' EQUITY		
16	Common stock, $5 par	?	154,700
17	Retained earnings	?	245,300
18	Total stockholders' equity	?	400,000
19	Total liabilities and stockholders' equity	$?	$650,000

Requirement

1. Using the ratios, common-size percentages, and trend percentages given, complete the income statement and balance sheet for Ivy for 2018. Additional information:

	A	B	C
1	**Additional information:**	**2018**	**2017**
2	Common size cost of goods sold %	70%	55%
3	Comon size common stock %	20%	23.80%
4	Trend percentage for operating income	125%	100%
5	Asset turnover	1.25	
6	Accounts receivable turnover	20.00	
7	Quick (acid-test) ratio	2.50	
8	Current ratio	2.75	
9	Return on equity (DuPont model)	20.50%	
10			

APPLY YOUR KNOWLEDGE

Serial Case

LO 4, 5

C12-71 *(Learning Objectives 4, 5: Calculate and analyze ratios and earnings quality for a company in the restaurant industry)*

Note: This case is part of The Cheesecake Factory serial case contained in every chapter in this textbook.

To follow are **The Cheesecake Factory Incorporated**'s financial statements from its 2016 Form 10-K.

	A	B	C	D	E
1	**The Cheesecake Factory Incorporated** **Consolidated Statements of Income: Condensed and adapted for educational use** ***(In thousands)***				
2		**Fiscal Year**			
3		**2016**	**2015**	**2014**	**2013**
4	Revenues	$ 2,275,719	$ 2,100,609	$ 1,976,624	$ 1,877,910
5	Costs and expenses:				
6	Cost of sales	526,628	504,031	490,306	455,685
7	Labor expenses	759,998	684,818	646,102	603,069
8	Depreciation and amortization expense	88,010	660,951	82,835	78,558
9	Other expenses	700,090	85,563	612,650	579,644
10	Total costs and expenses	2,074,726	1,935,363	1,831,893	1,716,956
11	Income from operations	200,993	165,246	144,731	160,954
12	Interest and other expense, net	(9,225)	(5,894)	(6,187)	(4,504)
13	Income before income taxes	191,768	159,352	138,544	156,450
14	Income tax expense	52,274	42,829	37,268	42,094
15	Net income	$ 139,494	$ 116,523	$ 101,276	$ 114,356
16					
17	*Note: Financial information presented here should not be used for investment decisions.*				
18					

Data from the U.S. Securities and Exchange Commission EDGAR Company filings, www.sec.gov

	A	B	C	D
1	**The Cheesecake Factory Incorporated** **Consolidated Balance Sheets: Condensed and adapted for educational use** ***(In thousands, except share data)***			
2		**January 3, 2017**	**December 29, 2015**	**December 30, 2014**
3	**Assets**			
4	Current assets:			
5	Cash and cash equivalents	$ 53,839	$ 43,854	$ 58,018
6	Accounts receivable	15,632	14,159	15,170
7	Income tax receivable	–	18,739	17,383
8	Other receivables	64,592	72,658	62,327
9	Inventories	34,926	34,010	33,255
10	Prepaid expenses	52,438	41,976	38,233
11	Total current assets	221,427	225,396	224,386
12	Property and equipment, net	910,134	892,191	828,305
13	Other assets:			
14	Intangible assets, net	23,054	21,972	20,781
15	Prepaid rent	42,162	46,881	46,212
16	Other assets	96,542	46,906	41,692
17	Total other assets	161,758	115,759	108,685
18	Total assets	$ 1,293,319	$ 1,233,346	$ 1,161,376
19				
20	**Liabilities and Stockholders' Equity**			
21	Current liabilities:			
22	Accounts payable	$ 41,564	$ 47,770	$ 57,325
23	Other accrued expenses	334,962	302,456	264,686
24	Total current liabilities	376,526	350,226	322,011
25	Noncurrent liabilities	313,586	294,581	282,855
26	Stockholders' equity:			
27	Preferred stock	–	–	–
28	Common stock	947	931	918
29	Additional paid-in capital	774,137	710,242	654,033
30	Retained earnings	1,238,012	1,140,788	1,060,211
31	Treasury stock	(1,409,889)	(1,263,422)	(1,158,652)
32	Total stockholders' equity	603,207	588,539	556,510
33	Total liabilities and stockholders' equity	$ 1,293,319	$ 1,233,346	$ 1,161,376
34				
35	*Note: Financial information presented here should not be used for investment decisions.*			

Data from the U.S. Securities and Exchange Commission EDGAR Company filings, www.sec.gov

The preceding financial statements have been condensed and adapted for educational use and should not be used for investment decisions.

Requirements

1. Calculate The Cheesecake Factory's net working capital for 2015 and 2016. What does the net working capital figure mean? Did The Cheesecake Factory's net working capital increase or decrease from 2015 to 2016? Explain.
2. Calculate The Cheesecake Factory's current ratio for 2015 and 2016. Did the current ratio improve or deteriorate?
3. Calculate The Cheesecake Factory's quick ratio for 2015 and 2016. Did the quick ratio improve or deteriorate?
4. How would you assess The Cheesecake Factory's overall ability to pay its current liabilities? Explain.
5. Calculate inventory turnover for 2016. Next, calculate days' inventory outstanding. What does this number mean?
6. Calculate accounts receivable turnover for 2016. Assume all net revenue is from credit sales. Next, calculate days' sales outstanding. What does this number mean?
7. Calculate accounts payable turnover for 2016. Next, calculate days' payable outstanding. What does this number mean?

8. Calculate the cash conversion cycle (in days). Explain what this cash conversion cycle number means.
9. Calculate the debt ratio for 2016 and for 2015. Has the debt ratio increased or decreased?
10. Calculate the times-interest-earned ratio for 2016. Use "interest and other expense, net" as interest expense. What does this ratio mean?
11. Calculate the following profitability ratios for 2016:
    a. Gross margin percentage
    b. Operating income percentage
    c. Rate of return on sales
    d. Rate of return on assets
12. Comment on The Cheesecake Factory's profitability in 2016 based on the profitability ratios you just calculated.
13. How would you evaluate the company's earnings quality?

Decision Cases

LO 4, 5

C12-72. *(Learning Objective 4, 5: Assess the effects of transactions on a company)* Suppose United Cable and Entertainment, Inc., is having a bad year in 2018, because the company has incurred a $4.9 billion net loss. The loss has pushed most of the company's return measures into the negative column, and its current ratio dropped below 1.0. The company's debt ratio is still only 0.27. Top management of United Cable and Entertainment is considering ways to improve the company's ratios, including the following possible transactions:

1. Selling off the cable television segment of the business for $30 million (receiving half in cash and half in the form of a long-term note receivable). The book value of the cable television business is $27 million.
2. Borrowing $100 million on long-term debt.
3. Purchasing treasury stock for $500 million cash.
4. Writing off one-fourth of the goodwill carried on the books at $128 million.
5. Selling advertising at the normal gross profit of 60%. The advertisements run immediately.
6. Purchasing trademarks from **NBC**, paying $20 million cash and signing a one-year note payable for $80 million.

Requirements

1. Top management wants to know the effects of these transactions (increase, decrease, or no effect) on the following ratios of United Cable and Entertainment:
    a. Current ratio
    b. Debt ratio
    c. Times-interest-earned ratio (measured as [Net income + Interest expense]/Interest expense)
    d. Return on equity
2. Some of these transactions have an immediate positive effect on the company's financial condition. Some are negative. Others are neither clearly positive nor clearly negative. Evaluate each transaction's effect as positive, negative, or unclear. (Challenge)

C12-73. ***(Learning Objectives 3, 4: Identify action to cut losses and establish profitability)*** Suppose you manage High Peaks Performance, Inc., a Vermont sporting goods store that lost money during the past year. To turn the business around, you must analyze the company and industry data for the current year to learn what is wrong. The company's data follow:

LO 3, 4

	A	B	C
1	**High Peaks Performance, Inc.** **Common-Size Balance Sheet Data**		
2		**High Peaks**	**Industry Average**
3	Cash and short-term investments	3.0%	6.8%
4	Trade receivables, net	15.2	11.0
5	Inventory	64.2	60.5
6	Prepaid expenses	1.0	0.0
7	Total current assets	83.4%	78.3%
8	Fixed assets, net	12.6	15.2
9	Other assets	4.0	6.5
10	Total assets	100.0%	100.0%
11			
12	Notes payable, short-term, 12%	17.1%	14.0%
13	Accounts payable	21.1	25.1
14	Accrued liabilities	7.8	7.9
15	Total current liabilities	46.0	47.0
16	Long-term debt, 11%	19.7	16.4
17	Total liabilities	65.7	63.4
18	Common stockholders' equity	34.3	36.6
19	Total liabilities and stockholders' equity	100.0%	100.0%
20			

	A	B	C
1	**High Peaks Performance, Inc.** **Common-Size Income Statement Data**		
2		**High Peaks**	**Industry Average**
3	Net sales	100.0%	100.0%
4	Cost of sales	(68.2)	(64.8)
5	Gross profit	31.8	35.2
6	Operating expense	(37.1)	(32.3)
7	Operating income (loss)	(5.3)	2.9
8	Interest expense	(5.8)	(1.3)
9	Other revenue	1.1	0.3
10	Income (loss) before income tax	(10.0)	1.9
11	Income tax (expense) benefit	4.4	(0.8)
12	Net income (loss)	(5.6)%	1.1%
13			

Requirement

1. Based on your analysis of these figures, suggest four courses of action High Peaks might take to reduce its losses and establish profitable operations. Give your reason for each suggestion. (Challenge)

Ethical Issues

C12-74. Greensboro Golf Corporation's long-term debt agreements make certain demands on the business. For example, Greensboro may not purchase treasury stock in excess of the balance of retained earnings. Also, long-term debt may not exceed stockholders' equity, and the current ratio may not fall below 1.50. If Greensboro fails to meet any of these requirements, the company's lenders have the authority to take over management of the company.

Changes in consumer demand have made it hard for Greensboro to attract customers. The company's current liabilities have grown faster than its current assets, causing the current ratio to fall to 1.47. Before releasing financial statements, managers are scrambling to improve the current ratio. The controller points out that the company owns an investment that is currently classified as long-term. The investment can be classified as either long-term or short-term, depending on management's intention. By deciding to convert an investment to cash within one year, Greensboro can classify the investment as short-term—a current asset. On the controller's recommendation, Greensboro's board of directors votes to reclassify long-term investments as short-term.

Requirements

1. What is the accounting issue in this case? What ethical decision needs to be made?
2. Who are the stakeholders?
3. Analyze the potential impact on the stakeholders from the following standpoints: (a) economic, (b) legal, and (c) ethical.
4. Shortly after the financial statements are released, sales improve; so, too, does the current ratio. As a result, Greensboro management decides not to sell the investments it had reclassified as short-term. Accordingly, the company reclassifies the investments as long-term. Has management acted unethically? Give the reason for your answer.

Focus on Financials | Apple Inc.

LO **1, 2, 3, 4, 5**

(Learning Objectives 1, 2, 3, 4, 5: Calculate standard financial ratios; measure liquidity and profitability; analyze earnings quality; vertical and horizontal analysis) Use the consolidated financial statements and the data in **Apple Inc.'s** annual report in Appendix A and online in the filings section of **www.sec.gov** to evaluate the company's comparative performance for 2016 versus 2015.

Requirements

1. Perform a horizontal and a vertical analysis of the following information on the company's comparative income statements for 2016 and 2015:
   a. Net sales
   b. Gross margin
   c. Operating income
   d. Net income

   Did the company appear to be performing better or worse on these dimensions in 2016, relative to 2015? Explain.
2. Perform horizontal and vertical analysis of the company's balance sheets for 2016 and 2015. In what areas did the company's balance sheet appear to be improving? Deteriorating? Explain.
3. Calculate the trends in the major elements of the company's cash flow statement (operations, investing, and financing) for 2016 relative to 2015. From where does the company generate most of its cash? What did the company spend most of its cash on?
4. Describe the information in Apple's annual report that can be used to analyze the company's earnings quality. What is your overall evaluation of Apple's earnings quality?

Focus on Analysis | Under Armour, Inc.

LO **1, 2, 4**

(Learning Objectives 1, 2, 4: Analyze trend data; calculate the standard financial ratios and use them to make decisions) Retrieve the 2016 **Under Armour** financial statements at **www.sec.gov** by clicking on Filings and then searching for "Under Armour" under Company Filings. When you see the list of filings for the company, select the Form 10-K for 2016. Be sure to retrieve the 2016 financial statements, not another year.

Requirements

1. Calculate ratios for 2015 and 2016 to determine the following for Under Armour:
   a. The company's ability to pay its current liabilities. Was 2016 stronger or weaker than 2015?
   b. The company's inventory turnover and days inventory outstanding (DIO); accounts receivable turnover and days sales outstanding (DSO), accounts payable turnover and days payable outstanding (DPO), and the number of days in its cash conversion cycle. 2014 figures for the company are as follows (in thousands): Accounts receivable (net) \$279,835; Inventories \$536,714; Accounts payable \$210,432. Was 2016 stronger or weaker than 2015 based on these measures? (Assume all sales were on account.)
   c. The company's rates of return on sales (ROS), average total assets (ROA), and average stockholders' equity (ROE), using DuPont analysis. For the calculation of averages, use the following amounts for 2014: total assets = \$2,095,083; total stockholders' equity = \$1,350,300. Did these ratios get stronger or weaker in 2016 compared to 2015?
2. Find Under Armour, Inc.'s, annual report for 2017 at **www.sec.gov**. Also research the company using an Internet site such as MSN Money or Yahoo! Finance to update the information in question 1. (Challenge)
3. What in your opinion is the company's outlook for the future? Would you buy the company's stock as an investment? Why or why not? (Challenge)

Group Project

Project 1. Select an industry in which you are interested, and use the leading company in that industry as the benchmark. Then select two other companies in the same industry. For each category of ratios in the Decision Guidelines feature on pages 699–700, calculate at least two ratios for all three companies. Write a two-page report that compares the two companies with the benchmark company.

COMPREHENSIVE FINANCIAL STATEMENT ANALYSIS PROJECT

The objective of this exercise is to develop your ability to perform a comprehensive analysis on a set of financial statements. Obtain a copy of the 2016 annual report (Form 10-K) of **Kohl's Corporation** (year ended January 28, 2017) from **www.sec.gov**. (Use "Kohl's" in the company search box.)

Requirement 1: Compile basic information (provide sources for your answers)

a. Using a site such as Yahoo! Finance or Hoover's Inc., research the discount variety store industry. List two competitors of Kohl's Corporation.
b. Describe Kohl's business and risk factors.
c. List three Kohl's brands.
d. At January 28, 2017, what is Kohl's largest asset? Largest liability?
e. At January 28, 2017, how many shares of common stock are authorized? Issued? Outstanding?
f. Did Kohl's repurchase any shares of common stock during its fiscal year ended January 28, 2017?
g. When does Kohl's record revenue?
h. What inventory method does Kohl's use?
i. Does Kohl's have any business interests in foreign countries? Explain your answer.

Requirement 2: Evaluate profitability

Using information you have learned in the text and elsewhere, evaluate Kohl's profitability for 2016 compared with 2015. (Remember that the 2016 year-end is January 28, 2017.) In your analysis, you should calculate the following ratios and then comment on what those ratios indicate. Note: You will have to look up the 10-K for 2015 to obtain total assets and stockholders' equity for 2014. See **www.sec.gov**.

a. Rate of return on sales
b. Asset turnover
c. Return on assets (DuPont model)
d. Leverage ratio
e. Return on equity (DuPont model)
f. Gross margin percentage
g. Earnings per share (show computation)

Requirement 3: Evaluate turnover

Evaluate Kohl's ability to sell inventory and pay debts during 2016 and 2015. Please note that the company does not hold traditional accounts receivable because it sells all of its receivables to **Capital One**, which is a credit card company. Therefore, it is impossible to calculate accounts receivable turnover and days sales to collection. However, in your analysis, you should calculate the following ratios and then comment on what those ratios indicate. Because the 2016 annual report contains only the balance sheets for 2016 and 2015, you will need to look up Kohl's 10-K for 2015 for information about 2014 inventory and accounts payable.

a. Inventory turnover and days' inventory outstanding (DIO)
b. Accounts payable turnover and days' payable outstanding (DPO)
c. Cash conversion cycle (DIO-DPO)
d. Current ratio
e. Quick (acid-test) ratio
f. Debt ratio
g. Times interest earned

Requirement 4: Perform other financial analysis

a. Calculate common-size percentages for sales, gross profit, operating income, and net income for 2013–2016. Comment on your results.

b. Find the selected financial data in the 10-K where Kohl's reports selected information since 2013. Calculate trend percentages, using 2013 as the base year, for total revenues and net earnings. Comment on your results.

Requirement 5: Evaluate Kohl's Corporation stock as an investment

a. What was the closing market price of Kohl's Corporation stock on January 30, 2017, the next trading day after the balance-sheet date of January 28, 2017?

b. Calculate the price-earnings ratio using your EPS calculation and the market price you just determined.

Quick Check Answers

1. *d*
2. *c*
3. *a*
4. *c [($7,276 ÷ $6,800) × 100 = 107%]*
5. *b*
6. *d ($90 ÷ $280 × 100 = 32%)*
7. *d*
8. *a*
9. *b*
10. *c*
11. *b*
12. *a*
13. *d*
14. *a*

Try It Solutions

Page 678

Net sales	100%	(= $150,000 ÷ $150,000)
Cost of goods sold	40	(= $ 60,000 ÷ $150,000)
Gross profit	60	(= $ 90,000 ÷ $150,000)
Operating expense	27	(= $ 40,000 ÷ $150,000)
Operating income	33	(= $ 50,000 ÷ $150,000)
Income tax expense	10	(= $ 15,000 ÷ $150,000)
Net income	23%	(= $ 35,000 ÷ $150,000)

Remember that you can use Excel to quickly and easily convert dollar-denominated data to percentages. You might want to practice doing this with the data above to assure yourself that you have mastered it.

Appendix A

2 0 1 6

Apple Inc.

ANNUAL REPORT

Author's Note: Information in the narrative component of these financial statements has been greatly abbreviated, though should be sufficient to complete the requirements of the Focus on Financials activities.

To view the report in its entirety, visit:
U.S. Securities and Exchange Commission EDGAR Company Filings, www.sec.gov

UNITED STATES
SECURITIES AND EXCHANGE COMMISSION
Washington, D.C. 20549

Form 10-K

☒ **ANNUAL REPORT PURSUANT TO SECTION 13 OR 15(d) OF THE SECURITIES EXCHANGE ACT OF 1934**

For the fiscal year ended September 24, 2016

or

☐ **TRANSITION REPORT PURSUANT TO SECTION 13 OR 15(d) OF THE SECURITIES EXCHANGE ACT OF 1934**

For the transition period from ________ to ________

Commission File Number: 001-36743

APPLE INC.

(Exact name of Registrant as specified in its charter)

California	**94-2404110**
(State or other jurisdiction of incorporation or organization)	(I.R.S. Employer Identification No.)
1 Infinite Loop **Cupertino, California**	**95014**
(Address of principal executive offices)	(Zip Code)

(408) 996-1010

(Registrant's telephone number, including area code)

Securities registered pursuant to Section 12(b) of the Act:

Common Stock, $0.00001 par value per share	**The NASDAQ Stock Market LLC**
1.000% Notes due 2022	**New York Stock Exchange LLC**
1.375% Notes due 2024	**New York Stock Exchange LLC**
1.625% Notes due 2026	**New York Stock Exchange LLC**
2.000% Notes due 2027	**New York Stock Exchange LLC**
3.050% Notes due 2029	**New York Stock Exchange LLC**
3.600% Notes due 2042	**New York Stock Exchange LLC**
(Title of class)	(Name of exchange on which registered)

Securities registered pursuant to Section 12(g) of the Act: None

Indicate by check mark if the Registrant is a well-known seasoned issuer, as defined in Rule 405 of the Securities Act.

Yes ☒ No ☐

Indicate by check mark if the Registrant is not required to file reports pursuant to Section 13 or Section 15(d) of the Act.

Yes ☐ No ☒

Indicate by check mark whether the Registrant (1) has filed all reports required to be filed by Section 13 or 15(d) of the Securities Exchange Act of 1934 during the preceding 12 months (or for such shorter period that the Registrant was required to file such reports), and (2) has been subject to such filing requirements for the past 90 days.

DOCUMENTS INCORPORATED BY REFERENCE

PART I

Item 1. Business

Company Background

The Company designs, manufactures and markets mobile communication and media devices, personal computers and portable digital music players, and sells a variety of related software, services, accessories, networking solutions and third-party digital content and applications. The Company's products and services include iPhone®, iPad®, Mac®, iPod®, Apple Watch®, Apple TV®, a portfolio of consumer and professional software applications, iOS, macOS™, watchOS® and tvOS™ operating systems, iCloud®, Apple Pay® and a variety of accessory, service and support offerings. The Company sells and delivers digital content and applications through the iTunes Store®, App Store®, Mac App Store, TV App Store, iBooks Store™ and Apple Music® (collectively "Internet Services"). The Company sells its products worldwide through its retail stores, online stores and direct sales force, as well as through third-party cellular network carriers, wholesalers, retailers and value-added resellers. In addition, the Company sells a variety of third-party Apple compatible products, including application software and various accessories through its retail and online stores. The Company sells to consumers, small and mid-sized businesses and education, enterprise and government customers. The Company's fiscal year is the 52 or 53-week period that ends on the last Saturday of September. The Company is a California corporation established in 1977.

Business Strategy

The Company is committed to bringing the best user experience to its customers through its innovative hardware, software and services. The Company's business strategy leverages its unique ability to design and develop its own operating systems, hardware, application software and services to provide its customers products and solutions with innovative design, superior ease-of-use and seamless integration. As part of its strategy, the Company continues to expand its platform for the discovery and delivery of digital content and applications through its Internet Services, which allows customers to discover and download digital content, iOS, Mac, Apple Watch and Apple TV applications, and books through either a Mac or Windows personal computer or through iPhone, iPad and iPod touch® devices ("iOS devices"), Apple TV and Apple Watch. The Company also supports a community for the development of third-party software and hardware products and digital content that complement the Company's offerings. The Company believes a high-quality buying experience with knowledgeable salespersons who can convey the value of the Company's products and services greatly enhances its ability to attract and retain customers. Therefore, the Company's strategy also includes building and expanding its own retail and online stores and its third-party distribution network to effectively reach more customers and provide them with a high-quality sales and post-sales support experience. The Company believes ongoing investment in research and development ("R&D"), marketing and advertising is critical to the development and sale of innovative products and technologies.

Business Organization

The Company manages its business primarily on a geographic basis. The Company's reportable operating segments consist of the Americas, Europe, Greater China, Japan and Rest of Asia Pacific. The Americas segment includes both North and South America. The Europe segment includes European countries, as well as India, the Middle East and Africa. The Greater China segment includes China, Hong Kong and Taiwan. The Rest of Asia Pacific segment includes Australia and those Asian countries not included in the Company's other reportable operating segments. Although the reportable operating segments provide similar hardware and software products and similar services, each one is managed separately to better align with the location of the Company's customers and distribution partners and the unique market dynamics of each geographic region. Further information regarding the Company's reportable operating segments may be found in Part II, Item 7 of this Form 10-K under the subheading "Segment Operating Performance," and in Part II, Item 8 of this Form 10-K in the Notes to Consolidated Financial Statements in Note 11, "Segment Information and Geographic Data."

[...]

Markets and Distribution

The Company's customers are primarily in the consumer, small and mid-sized business, education, enterprise and government markets. The Company sells its products and resells third-party products in most of its major markets directly to consumers and small and mid-sized businesses through its retail and online stores and its direct sales force. The Company also employs a variety of indirect distribution channels, such as third-party cellular network carriers, wholesalers, retailers and value-added resellers. During 2016, the Company's net sales through its direct and indirect distribution channels accounted for 25% and 75%, respectively, of total net sales.

The Company believes that sales of its innovative and differentiated products are enhanced by knowledgeable salespersons who can convey the value of the hardware and software integration and demonstrate the unique solutions that are available on its products. The Company further believes providing direct contact with its targeted customers is an effective way to demonstrate the advantages of its products over those of its competitors and providing a high-quality sales and after-sales support experience is critical to attracting new and retaining existing customers.

To ensure a high-quality buying experience for its products in which service and education are emphasized, the Company continues to build and improve its distribution capabilities by expanding the number of its own retail stores worldwide. The Company's retail stores are typically located at high-traffic locations in quality shopping malls and urban shopping districts. By operating its own stores and locating them in desirable high-traffic locations the Company is better positioned to ensure a high quality customer buying experience and attract new customers. The stores are designed to simplify and enhance the presentation and marketing of the Company's products and related solutions. The retail stores employ experienced and knowledgeable personnel who provide product advice, service and training and offer a wide selection of third-party hardware, software and other accessories that complement the Company's products.

The Company has also invested in programs to enhance reseller sales by placing high-quality Apple fixtures, merchandising materials and other resources within selected third-party reseller locations. Through the Apple Premium Reseller Program, certain third-party resellers focus on the Apple platform by providing a high level of product expertise, integration and support services.

The Company is committed to delivering solutions to help educators teach and students learn. The Company believes effective integration of technology into classroom instruction can result in higher levels of student achievement and has designed a range of products, services and programs to address the needs of education customers. The Company also supports mobile learning and real-time distribution of, and access to, education related materials through iTunes U, a platform that allows students and teachers to share and distribute educational media online. The Company sells its products to the education market through its direct sales force, select third-party resellers and its retail and online stores.

The Company also sells its hardware and software products to enterprise and government customers in each of its reportable operating segments. The Company's products are deployed in these markets because of their performance, productivity, ease of use and seamless integration into information technology environments. The Company's products are compatible with thousands of third-party business applications and services, and its tools enable the development and secure deployment of custom applications as well as remote device administration.

No single customer accounted for more than 10% of net sales in 2016, 2015 and 2014.

Competition

The markets for the Company's products and services are highly competitive and the Company is confronted by aggressive competition in all areas of its business. These markets are characterized by frequent product introductions and rapid technological advances that have substantially increased the capabilities and use of mobile communication and media devices, personal computers and other digital electronic devices. The Company's competitors that sell mobile devices and personal computers based on other operating systems have aggressively cut prices and lowered their product margins to gain or maintain market share. The Company's financial condition and operating results can be adversely affected by these and other industry-wide downward pressures on gross margins. Principal competitive factors important to the Company include price, product features (including security features), relative price and performance, product quality and reliability, design innovation, a strong third-party software and accessories ecosystem, marketing and distribution capability, service and support and corporate reputation.

The Company is focused on expanding its market opportunities related to personal computers and mobile communication and media devices. These markets are highly competitive and include many large, well-funded and experienced participants. The Company expects competition in these markets to intensify significantly as competitors attempt to imitate some of the features of the Company's products and applications within their own products or, alternatively, collaborate with each other to offer solutions that are more competitive than those they currently offer. These markets are characterized by aggressive pricing practices, frequent product introductions, evolving design approaches and technologies, rapid adoption of technological and product advancements by competitors and price sensitivity on the part of consumers and businesses.

The Company's digital content services have faced significant competition from other companies promoting their own digital music and content products and services, including those offering free peer-to-peer music and video services.

The Company's future financial condition and operating results depend on the Company's ability to continue to develop and offer new innovative products and services in each of the markets in which it competes. The Company believes it offers superior innovation and integration of the entire solution including the hardware (iOS devices, Mac, Apple Watch and Apple TV), software (iOS, macOS, watchOS and tvOS), online services and distribution of digital content and applications (Internet Services). Some of the Company's current and potential competitors have substantial resources and may be able to provide such products and services at little or no profit or even at a loss to compete with the Company's offerings.

[…]

Research and Development

Because the industries in which the Company competes are characterized by rapid technological advances, the Company's ability to compete successfully depends heavily upon its ability to ensure a continual and timely flow of competitive products, services and technologies to the marketplace. The Company continues to develop new technologies to enhance existing products and to expand the range of its product offerings through R&D, licensing of intellectual property and acquisition of third-party businesses and technology. Total R&D expense was $10.0 billion, $8.1 billion and $6.0 billion in 2016, 2015 and 2014, respectively.

Patents, Trademarks, Copyrights and Licenses

The Company currently holds rights to patents and copyrights relating to certain aspects of its hardware devices, accessories, software and services. The Company has registered or has applied for trademarks and service marks in the U.S. and a number of foreign countries. Although the Company believes the ownership of such patents, copyrights, trademarks and service marks is an important factor in its business and that its success does depend in part on such ownership, the Company relies primarily on the innovative skills, technical competence and marketing abilities of its personnel.

[…]

Foreign and Domestic Operations and Geographic Data

During 2016, the Company's domestic and international net sales accounted for 35% and 65%, respectively, of total net sales. Information regarding financial data by geographic segment is set forth in Part II, Item 7 of this Form 10-K under the subheading "Segment Operating Performance," and in Part II, Item 8 of this Form 10-K in the Notes to Consolidated Financial Statements in Note 11, "Segment Information and Geographic Data."

While some Mac computers are manufactured in the U.S. and Ireland, substantially all of the Company's hardware products are currently manufactured by outsourcing partners that are located primarily in Asia. The supply and manufacture of a number of components is performed by sole-sourced outsourcing partners in the U.S., Asia and Europe. Margins on sales of the Company's products in foreign countries and on sales of products that include components obtained from foreign suppliers, can be adversely affected by foreign currency exchange rate fluctuations and by international trade regulations, including tariffs and antidumping penalties. Information regarding concentration in the available sources of supply of materials and products is set forth in Part II, Item 8 of this Form 10-K in the Notes to Consolidated Financial Statements in Note 10, "Commitments and Contingencies."

Business Seasonality and Product Introductions

The Company has historically experienced higher net sales in its first quarter compared to other quarters in its fiscal year due in part to seasonal holiday demand. Additionally, new product introductions can significantly impact net sales, product costs and operating expenses. Product introductions can also impact the Company's net sales to its indirect distribution channels as these channels are filled with new product inventory following a product introduction, and often, channel inventory of a particular product declines as the next related major product launch approaches. Net sales can also be affected when consumers and distributors anticipate a product introduction. However, neither historical seasonal patterns nor historical patterns of product introductions should be considered reliable indicators of the Company's future pattern of product introductions, future net sales or financial performance.

Warranty

The Company offers a limited parts and labor warranty on most of its hardware products. The basic warranty period is typically one year from the date of purchase by the original end-user. The Company also offers a 90-day basic warranty for its service parts used to repair the Company's hardware products. In certain jurisdictions, local law requires that manufacturers guarantee their products for a period prescribed by statute, typically at least two years. In addition, where available, consumers may purchase APP or AC+, which extends service coverage on many of the Company's hardware products.

[…]

Employees

As of September 24, 2016, the Company had approximately 116,000 full-time equivalent employees.

CONSOLIDATED STATEMENTS OF OPERATIONS

(In millions, except number of shares which are reflected in thousands and per share amounts)

	Years ended		
	September 24, 2016	**September 26, 2015**	**September 27, 2014**
Net sales	$ 215,639	$ 233,715	$ 182,795
Cost of sales	131,376	140,089	112,258
Gross margin	84,263	93,626	70,537
Operating expenses:			
Research and development	10,045	8,067	6,041
Selling, general and administrative	14,194	14,329	11,993
Total operating expenses	24,239	22,396	18,034
Operating income			
Other income/(expense), net	60,024	71,230	52,503
Income before provision for income taxes	1,348	1,285	980
Provision for income taxes	61,372	72,515	53,483
Net income	15,685	19,121	13,973
	$ 45,687	$ 53,394	$ 39,510
Earnings per share:			
Basic	$ 8.35	$ 9.28	$ 6.49
Diluted	$ 8.31	$ 9.22	$ 6.45
Shares used in computing earnings per share:			
Basic	5,470,820	5,753,421	6,085,572
Diluted	5,500,281	5,793,069	6,122,663
Cash dividends declared per share	$ 2.18	$ 1.98	$ 1.82

See accompanying Notes to Consolidated Financial Statements.

CONSOLIDATED STATEMENTS OF COMPREHENSIVE INCOME
(In millions)

	Years ended		
	September 24, 2016	September 26, 2015	September 27, 2014
Net income	$ 45,687	$ 53,394	$ 39,510
Other comprehensive income/(loss):			
Change in foreign currency translation, net of tax effects of $8, $201 and $50, respectively	75	(411)	(137)
Change in unrealized gains/losses on derivative instruments:			
Change in fair value of derivatives, net of tax benefit/(expense) of $(7), $(441) and $(297), respectively	7	2,905	1,390
Adjustment for net (gains)/losses realized and included in net income, net of tax expense/(benefit) of $131, $630 and $(36), respectively	(741)	(3,497)	149
Total change in unrecognized gains/losses on derivative instruments, net of tax	(734)	(592)	1,539
Change in unrealized gains/losses on marketable securities:			
Change in fair value of marketable securities, net of tax benefit/(expense) of $(863), $264 and $(153), respectively	1,582	(483)	285
Adjustment for net (gains)/losses realized and included in net income, net of tax expense/(benefit) of $(31), $(32) and $71, respectively	56	59	(134)
Total change in unrealized gains/losses on marketable securities, net of tax	1,638	(424)	151
Total other comprehensive income/(loss)	979	(1,427)	1,553
Total comprehensive income	$ 46,666	$ 51,967	$ 41,063

See accompanying Notes to Consolidated Financial Statements.

CONSOLIDATED BALANCE SHEETS

(In millions, except number of shares which are reflected in thousands and par value)

	September 24, 2016	September 26, 2015
ASSETS:		
Current assets:		
Cash and cash equivalents	$ 20,484	$ 21,120
Short-term marketable securities	46,671	20,481
Accounts receivable, less allowances of $53 and $63, respectively	15,754	16,849
Inventories	2,132	2,349
Vendor non-trade receivables	13,545	13,494
Other current assets	8,283	15,085
Total current assets	106,869	89,378
Long-term marketable securities	170,430	164,065
Property, plant and equipment, net	27,010	22,471
Goodwill	5,414	5,116
Acquired intangible assets, net	3,206	3,893
Other non-current assets	8,757	5,422
Total assets	$ 321,686	$ 290,345
LIABILITIES AND SHAREHOLDERS' EQUITY:		
Current liabilities:		
Accounts payable	$ 37,294	$ 35,490
Accrued expenses	22,027	25,181
Deferred revenue	8,080	8,940
Commercial paper	8,105	8,499
Current portion of long-term debt	3,500	2,500
Total current liabilities	79,006	80,610
Deferred revenue, non-current	2,930	3,624
Long-term debt	75,427	53,329
Other non-current liabilities	36,074	33,427
Total liabilities	193,437	170,990
Commitments and contingencies		
Shareholders' equity:		
Common stock and additional paid-in capital, $0.00001 par value: 12,600,000 shares authorized; 5,336,166 and 5,578,753 shares issued and outstanding, respectively	31,251	27,416
Retained earnings	96,364	92,284
Accumulated other comprehensive income/(loss)	634	(345)
Total shareholders' equity	128,249	119,355
Total liabilities and shareholders' equity	$ 321,686	$ 290,345

See accompanying Notes to Consolidated Financial Statements.

CONSOLIDATED STATEMENTS OF SHAREHOLDERS' EQUITY
(In millions, except number of shares which are reflected in thousands)

	Common Stock and Additional Paid-In Capital		Retained	Accumulated Other Comprehensive	Total Shareholders'
	Shares	Amount	Earnings	Income/(Loss)	Equity
Balances as of September 28, 2013	6,294,494	$ 19,764	$ 104,256	$ (471)	$ 123,549
Net income	—	—	39,510	—	39,510
Other comprehensive income/(loss)	—	—	—	1,553	1,553
Dividends and dividend equivalents declared	—	—	(11,215)	—	(11,215)
Repurchase of common stock	(488,677)	—	(45,000)	—	(45,000)
Share-based compensation	—	2,863	—	—	2,863
Common stock issued, net of shares withheld for employee taxes	60,344	(49)	(399)	—	(448)
Tax benefit from equity awards, including transfer pricing adjustments	—	735	—	—	735
Balances as of September 27, 2014	5,866,161	23,313	87,152	1,082	111,547
Net income	—	—	53,394	—	53,394
Other comprehensive income/(loss)	—	—	—	(1,427)	(1,427)
Dividends and dividend equivalents declared	—	—	(11,627)	—	(11,627)
Repurchase of common stock	(325,032)	—	(36,026)	—	(36,026)
Share-based compensation	—	3,586	—	—	3,586
Common stock issued, net of shares withheld for employee taxes	37,624	(231)	(609)	—	(840)
Tax benefit from equity awards, including transfer pricing adjustments	—	748	—	—	748
Balances as of September 26, 2015	5,578,753	27,416	92,284	(345)	119,355
Net income	—	—	45,687	—	45,687
Other comprehensive income/(loss)	—	—	—	979	979
Dividends and dividend equivalents declared	—	—	(12,188)	—	(12,188)
Repurchase of common stock	(279,609)	—	(29,000)	—	(29,000)
Share-based compensation	—	4,262	—	—	4,262
Common stock issued, net of shares withheld for employee taxes	37,022	(806)	(419)	—	(1,225)
Tax benefit from equity awards, including transfer pricing adjustments	—	379	—	—	379
Balances as of September 24, 2016	5,336,166	$ 31,251	$ 96,364	$ 634	$ 128,249

See accompanying Notes to Consolidated Financial Statements.

CONSOLIDATED STATEMENTS OF CASH FLOWS
(in millions)

	Years ended		
	September 24, 2016	**September 26, 2015**	**September 27, 2014**
Cash and cash equivalents, beginning of the year	$ 21,120	$ 13,844	$ 14,259
Operating activities:			
Net income	45,687	53,394	39,510
Adjustments to reconcile net income to cash generated by operating activities:			
Depreciation and amortization	10,505	11,257	7,946
Share-based compensation expense	4,210	3,586	2,863
Deferred income tax expense	4,938	1,382	2,347
Changes in operating assets and liabilities:			
Accounts receivable, net	1,095	611	(4,232)
Inventories	217	(238)	(76)
Vendor non-trade receivables	(51)	(3,735)	(2,220)
Other current and non-current assets	1,090	(179)	167
Accounts payable	1,791	5,400	5,938
Deferred revenue	(1,554)	1,042	1,460
Other current and non-current liabilities	(2,104)	8,746	6,010
Cash generated by operating activities	65,824	81,266	59,713
Investing activities:			
Purchases of marketable securities	(142,428)	(166,402)	(217,128)
Proceeds from maturities of marketable securities	21,258	14,538	18,810
Proceeds from sales of marketable securities	90,536	107,447	189,301
Payments made in connection with business acquisitions, net	(297)	(343)	(3,765)
Payments for acquisition of property, plant and equipment	(12,734)	(11,247)	(9,571)
Payments for acquisition of intangible assets	(814)	(241)	(242)
Payments for strategic investments	(1,388)	—	(10)
Other	(110)	(26)	26
Cash used in investing activities	(45,977)	(56,274)	(22,579)
Financing activities:			
Proceeds from issuance of common stock	495	543	730
Excess tax benefits from equity awards	407	749	739
Payments for taxes related to net share settlement of equity awards	(1,570)	(1,499)	(1,158)
Payments for dividends and dividend equivalents	(12,150)	(11,561)	(11,126)
Repurchases of common stock	(29,722)	(35,253)	(45,000)
Proceeds from issuance of term debt, net	24,954	27,114	11,960
Repayments of term debt	(2,500)	—	—
Change in commercial paper, net	(397)	2,191	6,306
Cash used in financing activities	(20,483)	(17,716)	(37,549)
Increase/(Decrease) in cash and cash equivalents	(636)	7,276	(415)
Cash and cash equivalents, end of the year	$ 20,484	$ 21,120	$ 13,844

See accompanying Notes to Consolidated Financial Statements.

Notes to Consolidated Financial Statements

Note 1 – Summary of Significant Accounting Policies

Apple Inc. and its wholly-owned subsidiaries (collectively "Apple" or the "Company") designs, manufactures and markets mobile communication and media devices, personal computers and portable digital music players, and sells a variety of related software, services, accessories, networking solutions and third-party digital content and applications. The Company sells its products worldwide through its retail stores, online stores and direct sales force, as well as through third-party cellular network carriers, wholesalers, retailers and value-added resellers. In addition, the Company sells a variety of third-party Apple-compatible products, including application software and various accessories through its retail and online stores. The Company sells to consumers, small and mid-sized businesses and education, enterprise and government customers.

Basis of Presentation and Preparation

The accompanying consolidated financial statements include the accounts of the Company. Intercompany accounts and transactions have been eliminated. In the opinion of the Company's management, the consolidated financial statements reflect all adjustments, which are normal and recurring in nature, necessary for fair financial statement presentation. The preparation of these consolidated financial statements in conformity with U.S. generally accepted accounting principles ("GAAP") requires management to make estimates and assumptions that affect the amounts reported in these consolidated financial statements and accompanying notes. Actual results could differ materially from those estimates. Certain prior period amounts in the consolidated financial statements have been reclassified to conform to the current period's presentation.

The Company's fiscal year is the 52 or 53-week period that ends on the last Saturday of September. The Company's fiscal years 2016, 2015 and 2014 ended on September 24, 2016, September 26, 2015 and September 27, 2014, respectively, and each spanned 52 weeks. An additional week is included in the first fiscal quarter approximately every five or six years to realign fiscal quarters with calendar quarters, which will next occur in the first quarter of the Company's fiscal year ending September 30, 2017. Unless otherwise stated, references to particular years, quarters, months and periods refer to the Company's fiscal years ended in September and the associated quarters, months and periods of those fiscal years.

During 2016, the Company adopted an accounting standard that simplified the presentation of deferred income taxes by requiring deferred tax assets and liabilities be classified as noncurrent in a classified statement of financial position. The Company has adopted this accounting standard prospectively; accordingly, the prior period amounts in the Company's Consolidated Balance Sheets within this Annual Report on Form 10-K were not adjusted to conform to the new accounting standard. The adoption of this accounting standard was not material to the Company's consolidated financial statements

[…]

Revenue Recognition

Net sales consist primarily of revenue from the sale of hardware, software, digital content and applications, accessories, and service and support contracts. The Company recognizes revenue when persuasive evidence of an arrangement exists, delivery has occurred, the sales price is fixed or determinable and collection is probable. Product is considered delivered to the customer once it has been shipped and title, risk of loss and rewards of ownership have been transferred. For most of the Company's product sales, these criteria are met at the time the product is shipped. For online sales to individuals, for some sales to education customers in the U.S., and for certain other sales, the Company defers revenue until the customer receives the product because the Company retains a portion of the risk of loss on these sales during transit. For payment terms in excess of the Company's standard payment terms, revenue is recognized as payments become due unless the Company has positive evidence that the sales price is fixed or determinable, such as a successful history of collection, without concession, on comparable arrangements. The Company recognizes revenue from the sale of hardware products, software bundled with hardware that is essential to the functionality of the hardware and third-party digital content sold on the iTunes Store in accordance with general revenue recognition accounting guidance. The Company recognizes revenue in accordance with industry specific software accounting guidance for the following types of sales transactions: (i) standalone sales of software products, (ii) sales of software upgrades and (iii) sales of software bundled with hardware not essential to the functionality of the hardware.

For the sale of most third-party products, the Company recognizes revenue based on the gross amount billed to customers because the Company establishes its own pricing for such products, retains related inventory risk for physical products, is the primary obligor to the customer and assumes the credit risk for amounts billed to its customers. For third-party applications sold through the App Store and Mac App Store and certain digital content sold through the iTunes Store, the Company does not determine the selling price of the products and is not the primary obligor to the customer. Therefore, the Company accounts for such sales on a net basis by recognizing in net sales only the commission it retains from each sale. The portion of the gross amount billed to customers that is remitted by the Company to third-party app developers and certain digital content owners is not reflected in the Company's Consolidated Statements of Operations.

The Company records deferred revenue when it receives payments in advance of the delivery of products or the performance of services. This includes amounts that have been deferred for unspecified and specified software upgrade rights and non-software services that are attached to hardware and software products. The Company sells gift cards redeemable at its retail and online stores, and also sells gift cards redeemable on iTunes Store, App Store, Mac App Store, TV App Store and iBooks Store for the purchase of digital content and software. The Company records deferred revenue upon the sale of the card, which is relieved upon redemption of the card by the customer. Revenue from AppleCare service and support contracts is deferred and recognized over the service coverage periods. AppleCare service and support contracts typically include extended phone support, repair services, web-based support resources and diagnostic tools offered under the Company's standard limited warranty.

The Company records reductions to revenue for estimated commitments related to price protection and other customer incentive programs. For transactions involving price protection, the Company recognizes revenue net of the estimated amount to be refunded. For the Company's other customer incentive programs, the estimated cost of these programs is recognized at the later of the date at which the Company has sold the product or the date at which the program is offered. The Company also records reductions to revenue for expected future product returns based on the Company's historical experience. Revenue is recorded net of taxes collected from customers that are remitted to governmental authorities, with the collected taxes recorded as current liabilities until remitted to the relevant government authority.

[…]

Shipping Costs

Amounts billed to customers related to shipping and handling are classified as revenue, and the Company's shipping and handling costs are classified as cost of sales.

Warranty Costs

The Company generally provides for the estimated cost of hardware and software warranties in the period the related revenue is recognized. The Company assesses the adequacy of its accrued warranty liabilities and adjusts the amounts as necessary based on actual experience and changes in future estimates.

Software Development Costs

Research and development ("R&D") costs are expensed as incurred. Development costs of computer software to be sold, leased, or otherwise marketed are subject to capitalization beginning when a product's technological feasibility has been established and ending when a product is available for general release to customers. In most instances, the Company's products are released soon after technological feasibility has been established and as a result software development costs were expensed as incurred.

Advertising Costs

Advertising costs are expensed as incurred and included in selling, general and administrative expenses.

[…]

Earnings Per Share

Basic earnings per share is computed by dividing income available to common shareholders by the weighted-average number of shares of common stock outstanding during the period. Diluted earnings per share is computed by dividing income available to common shareholders by the weighted-average number of shares of common stock outstanding during the period increased to include the number of additional shares of common stock that would have been outstanding if the potentially dilutive securities had been issued. Potentially dilutive securities include outstanding stock options, shares to be purchased by employees under the Company's employee stock purchase plan, unvested restricted stock and unvested RSUs. The dilutive effect of potentially dilutive securities is reflected in diluted earnings per share by application of the treasury stock method. Under the treasury stock method, an increase in the fair market value of the Company's common stock can result in a greater dilutive effect from potentially dilutive securities.

The following table shows the computation of basic and diluted earnings per share for 2016, 2015 and 2014 (net income in millions and shares in thousands):

	2016	2015	2014
Numerator:			
Net income	$ 45,687	$ 53,394	$ 39,510
Denominator:			
Weighted-average shares outstanding	5,470,820	5,753,421	6,085,572
Effect of dilutive securities	29,461	39,648	37,091
Weighted-average diluted shares	5,500,281	5,793,069	6,122,663
Basic earnings per share	$ 8.35	$ 9.28	$ 6.49
Diluted earnings per share	$ 8.31	$ 9.22	$ 6.45

Potentially dilutive securities whose effect would have been antidilutive are excluded from the computation of diluted earnings per share.

Financial Instruments

Cash Equivalents and Marketable Securities

All highly liquid investments with maturities of three months or less at the date of purchase are classified as cash equivalents. The Company's marketable debt and equity securities have been classified and accounted for as available-for-sale. Management determines the appropriate classification of its investments at the time of purchase and reevaluates the classifications at each balance sheet date. The Company classifies its marketable debt securities as either short-term or long-term based on each instrument's underlying contractual maturity date. Marketable debt securities with maturities of 12 months or less are classified as short-term and marketable debt securities with maturities greater than 12 months are classified as long-term. Marketable equity securities, including mutual funds, are classified as either short-term or long-term based on the nature of each security and its availability for use in current operations. The Company's marketable debt and equity securities are carried at fair value, with unrealized gains and losses, net of taxes, reported as a component of accumulated other comprehensive income ("AOCI") in shareholders' equity, with the exception of unrealized losses believed to be other-than-temporary which are reported in earnings in the current period. The cost of securities sold is based upon the specific identification method.

[...]

Allowance for Doubtful Accounts

The Company records its allowance for doubtful accounts based upon its assessment of various factors, including historical experience, age of the accounts receivable balances, credit quality of the Company's customers, current economic conditions and other factors that may affect the customers' abilities to pay.

Inventories

Inventories are stated at the lower of cost, computed using the first-in, first-out method and net realizable value. Any adjustments to reduce the cost of inventories to their net realizable value are recognized in earnings in the current period. As of September 24, 2016 and September 26, 2015, the Company's inventories consist primarily of finished goods.

Property, Plant and Equipment

Property, plant and equipment are stated at cost. Depreciation is computed by use of the straight-line method over the estimated useful lives of the assets, which for buildings is the lesser of 30 years or the remaining life of the underlying building; between one to five years for machinery and equipment, including product tooling and manufacturing process equipment; and the shorter of lease terms or useful life for leasehold improvements. The Company capitalizes eligible costs to acquire or develop internal-use software that are incurred subsequent to the preliminary project stage. Capitalized costs related to internal-use software are amortized using the straight-line method over the estimated useful lives of the assets, which range from three to five years. Depreciation and amortization expense on property and equipment was $8.3 billion, $9.2 billion and $6.9 billion during 2016, 2015 and 2014, respectively.

Long-Lived Assets Including Goodwill and Other Acquired Intangible Assets

The Company reviews property, plant and equipment, inventory component prepayments and identifiable intangibles, excluding goodwill and intangible assets with indefinite useful lives, for impairment. Long-lived assets are reviewed for impairment whenever events or changes in circumstances indicate the carrying amount of an asset may not be recoverable. Recoverability of these assets is measured by comparison of their carrying amounts to future undiscounted cash flows the assets are expected to generate. If property, plant and equipment, inventory component prepayments and certain identifiable intangibles are considered to be impaired, the impairment to be recognized equals the amount by which the carrying value of the assets exceeds its fair value.

The Company does not amortize goodwill and intangible assets with indefinite useful lives, rather such assets are required to be tested for impairment at least annually or sooner whenever events or changes in circumstances indicate that the assets may be impaired. The Company performs its goodwill and intangible asset impairment tests in the fourth quarter of each year. The Company did not recognize any impairment charges related to goodwill or indefinite lived intangible assets during 2016, 2015 and 2014.

[…]

The Company amortizes its intangible assets with definite useful lives over their estimated useful lives and reviews these assets for impairment. The Company typically amortizes its acquired intangible assets with definite useful lives over periods from three to seven years.

Fair Value Measurements

The Company applies fair value accounting for all financial assets and liabilities and non-financial assets and liabilities that are recognized or disclosed at fair value in the financial statements on a recurring basis. The Company defines fair value as the price that would be received from selling an asset or paid to transfer a liability in an orderly transaction between market participants at the measurement date. When determining the fair value measurements for assets and liabilities, which are required to be recorded at fair value, the Company considers the principal or most advantageous market in which the Company would transact and the market-based risk measurements or assumptions that market participants would use to price the asset or liability, such as risks inherent in valuation techniques, transfer restrictions and credit risk. Fair value is estimated by applying the following hierarchy, which prioritizes the inputs used to measure fair value into three levels and bases the categorization within the hierarchy upon the lowest level of input that is available and significant to the fair value measurement:

Level 1 – Quoted prices in active markets for identical assets or liabilities.

Level 2 – Observable inputs other than quoted prices in active markets for identical assets and liabilities, quoted prices for identical or similar assets or liabilities in inactive markets, or other inputs that are observable or can be corroborated by observable market data for substantially the full term of the assets or liabilities.

Level 3 – Inputs that are generally unobservable and typically reflect management's estimate of assumptions that market participants would use in pricing the asset or liability.

The Company's valuation techniques used to measure the fair value of money market funds and certain marketable equity securities were derived from quoted prices in active markets for identical assets or liabilities. The valuation techniques used to measure the fair value of the Company's debt instruments and all other financial instruments, all of which have counterparties with high credit ratings, were valued based on quoted market prices or model-driven valuations using significant inputs derived from or corroborated by observable market data.

[…]

Note 2 – Financial Instruments

Cash, Cash Equivalents and Marketable Securities

The following tables show the Company's cash and available-for-sale securities' adjusted cost, gross unrealized gains, gross unrealized losses and fair value by significant investment category recorded as cash and cash equivalents or short- or long-term marketable securities as of September 24, 2016 (in millions):

	2016						
	Adjusted Cost	Unrealized Gains	Unrealized Losses	Fair Value	Cash and Cash Equivalents	Short-Term Marketable Securities	Long-Term Marketable Securities
Cash	$ 8,601	$ —	$ —	$ 8,601	$ 8,601	$ —	$ —
Level 1:							
Money market funds	3,666	—	—	3,666	3,666	—	—
Mutual funds	1,407	—	(146)	1,261	—	1,261	—
Subtotal	5,073	—	(146)	4,927	3,666	1,261	—
Level 2:							
U.S. Treasury securities	41,697	319	(4)	42,012	1,527	13,492	26,993
U.S. agency securities	7,543	16	—	7,559	2,762	2,441	2,356
Non-U.S. government securities	7,609	259	(27)	7,841	110	818	6,913
Certificates of deposit and time deposits	6,598	—	—	6,598	1,108	3,897	1,593
Commercial paper	7,433	—	—	7,433	2,468	4,965	—
Corporate securities	131,166	1,409	(206)	132,369	242	19,599	112,528
Municipal securities	956	5	—	961	—	167	794
Mortgage- and asset-backed securities	19,134	178	(28)	19,284	—	31	19,253
Subtotal	222,136	2,186	(265)	224,057	8,217	45,410	170,430
Total	$ 235,810	$ 2,186	$ (411)	$ 237,585	$ 20,484	$ 46,671	$ 170,430

The Company considers the declines in market value of its marketable securities investment portfolio to be temporary in nature. The Company typically invests in highly-rated securities, and its investment policy generally limits the amount of credit exposure to any one issuer. The policy generally requires investments to be investment grade, with the primary objective of minimizing the potential risk of principal loss. Fair values were determined for each individual security in the investment portfolio. When evaluating an investment for other-than-temporary impairment the Company reviews factors such as the length of time and extent to which fair value has been below its cost basis, the financial condition of the issuer and any changes thereto, changes in market interest rates and the Company's intent to sell, or whether it is more likely than not it will be required to sell the investment before recovery of the investment's cost basis. As of September 24, 2016, the Company does not consider any of its investments to be other-than-temporarily impaired.

[...]

Accounts Receivable

Trade Receivables

The Company has considerable trade receivables outstanding with its third-party cellular network carriers, wholesalers, retailers, value-added resellers, small and mid-sized businesses and education, enterprise and government customers. The Company generally does not require collateral from its customers; however, the Company will require collateral in certain instances to limit credit risk. In addition, when possible, the Company attempts to limit credit risk on trade receivables with credit insurance for certain customers or by requiring third-party financing, loans or leases to support credit exposure. These credit-financing arrangements are directly between the third-party financing company and the end customer. As such, the Company generally does not assume any recourse or credit risk sharing related to any of these arrangements.

As of September 24, 2016 and September 26, 2015, the Company had one customer that represented 10% or more of total trade receivables, which accounted for 10% and 12%, respectively. The Company's cellular network carriers accounted for 63% and 71% of trade receivables as of September 24, 2016 and September 26, 2015, respectively.

[...]

Note 3 – Consolidated Financial Statement Details

The following tables show the Company's consolidated financial statement details as of September 24, 2016 and September 26, 2015 (in millions):

Property, Plant and Equipment, Net

	2016	2015
Land and buildings	$ 10,185	$ 6,956
Machinery, equipment and internal-use software	44,543	37,038
Leasehold improvements	6,517	5,263
Gross property, plant and equipment	61,245	49,257
Accumulated depreciation and amortization	(34,235)	(26,786)
Total property, plant and equipment, net	$ 27,010	$ 22,471

Other Non-Current Liabilities

	2016	2015
Deferred tax liabilities	$ 26,019	$ 24,062
Other non-current liabilities	10,055	9,365
Total other non-current liabilities	$ 36,074	$ 33,427

Other Income/(Expense), Net

The following table shows the detail of other income/(expense), net for 2016, 2015 and 2014 (in millions):

	2016	2015	2014
Interest and dividend income	$ 3,999	$ 2,921	$ 1,795
Interest expense	(1,456)	(733)	(384)
Other expense, net	(1,195)	(903)	$ (431)
Total other income/(expense), net	$ 1,348	$ 1,285	980

[...]

Note 5 – Income Taxes

The provision for income taxes for 2016, 2015 and 2014, consisted of the following (in millions):

	2016	2015	2014
Federal:			
Current	$ 7,652	$ 11,730	$ 8,624
Deferred	5,043	3,408	3,183
	12,695	15,138	11,807
State:			
Current	990	1,265	855
Deferred	(138)	(220)	(178)
	852	1,045	677
Foreign:			
Current	2,105	4,744	2,147
Deferred	33	(1,806)	(658)
	2,138	2,938	1,489
Provision for income taxes	$ 15,685	$ 19,121	$ 13,973

The foreign provision for income taxes is based on foreign pre-tax earnings of $41.1 billion, $47.6 billion and $33.6 billion in 2016, 2015 and 2014, respectively. The Company's consolidated financial statements provide for any related tax liability on undistributed earnings that the Company does not intend to be indefinitely reinvested outside the U.S. Substantially all of the Company's undistributed international earnings intended to be indefinitely reinvested in operations outside the U.S. were generated by subsidiaries organized in Ireland, which has a statutory tax rate of 12.5%. As of September 24, 2016, U.S. income taxes have not been provided on a cumulative total of $109.8 billion of such earnings. The amount of unrecognized deferred tax liability related to these temporary differences is estimated to be $35.9 billion.

As of September 24, 2016 and September 26, 2015, $216.0 billion and $186.9 billion, respectively, of the Company's cash, cash equivalents and marketable securities were held by foreign subsidiaries and are generally based in U.S. dollar-denominated holdings. Amounts held by foreign subsidiaries are generally subject to U.S. income taxation on repatriation to the U.S.

A reconciliation of the provision for income taxes, with the amount computed by applying the statutory federal income tax rate (35% in 2016, 2015 and 2014) to income before provision for income taxes for 2016, 2015 and 2014, is as follows (dollars in millions):

	2016	2015	2014
Computed expected tax	$ 21,480	$ 25,380	$ 18,719
State taxes, net of federal effect	553	680	469
Indefinitely invested earnings of foreign subsidiaries	(5,582)	(6,470)	(4,744)
Domestic production activities deduction	(382)	(426)	(495)
Research and development credit, net	(371)	(171)	(88)
Other	(13)	128	112
Provision for income taxes	$ 15,685	$ 19,121	$ 13,973
Effective tax rate	25.6%	26.4%	26.1%

[...]

Note 6 – Debt

Commercial Paper

The Company issues unsecured short-term promissory notes ("Commercial Paper") pursuant to a commercial paper program. The Company uses net proceeds from the commercial paper program for general corporate purposes, including dividends and share repurchases. As of September 24, 2016 and September 26, 2015, the Company had $8.1 billion and $8.5 billion of Commercial Paper outstanding, respectively, with maturities generally less than nine months. The weighted-average interest rate of the Company's Commercial Paper was 0.45% as of September 24, 2016 and 0.14% as of September 26, 2015.

The following table provides a summary of cash flows associated with the issuance and maturities of Commercial Paper for 2016 and 2015 (in millions):

	2016	2015
Maturities less than 90 days:		
Proceeds from (repayments of) commercial paper, net	$ (869)	$ 5,293
Maturities greater than 90 days:		
Proceeds from commercial paper	3,632	3,851
Repayments of commercial paper	(3,160)	(6,953)
Maturities greater than 90 days, net	472	(3,102)
Total change in commercial paper, net	$ (397)	$ 2,191

Long-Term Debt

As of September 24, 2016, the Company had outstanding floating- and fixed-rate notes with varying maturities for an aggregate principal amount of $78.4 billion (collectively the "Notes"). The Notes are senior unsecured obligations, and interest is payable in arrears, quarterly for the U.S. dollar-denominated and Australian dollar-denominated floating-rate notes, semi-annually for the U.S. dollar-denominated, Australian dollar-denominated, British pound-denominated and Japanese yen-denominated fixed-rate notes and annually for the euro-denominated and Swiss franc-denominated fixed-rate notes.

The following table provides a summary of the Company's term debt as of September 24, 2016 and September 26, 2015:

		2016		2015	
	Maturities	Amount (in millions)	Effective Interest Rate	Amount (in millions)	Effective Interest Rate
2013 debt issuance of $17.0 billion:					
Floating-rate notes	2018	$ 2,000	1.10%	$ 3,000	0.51%–1.10%
Fixed-rate 1.000%–3.850% notes	2018–2043	12,500	1.08%–3.91%	14,000	0.51%–3.91%
2014 debt issuance of $12.0 billion:					
Floating-rate notes	2017–2019	2,000	0.86%–1.09%	2,000	0.37%–0.60%
Fixed-rate 1.050%–4.450% notes	2017–2044	10,000	0.85%–4.48%	10,000	0.37%–4.48%
2015 debt issuances of $27.3 billion:					
Floating-rate notes	2017–2020	1,781	0.87%–1.87%	1,743	0.36%–1.87%
Fixed-rate 0.350%–4.375% notes	2017–2045	25,144	0.28%–4.51%	24,958	0.28%–4.51%
Second quarter 2016 debt issuance of $15.5 billion:					
Floating-rate notes	2019	500	1.64%	—	—
Floating-rate notes	2021	500	1.95%	—	—
Fixed-rate 1.300% notes	2018	500	1.32%	—	—
Fixed-rate 1.700% notes	2019	1,000	1.71%	—	—
Fixed-rate 2.250% notes	2021	3,000	1.91%	—	—
Fixed-rate 2.850% notes	2023	1,500	2.58%	—	—
Fixed-rate 3.250% notes	2026	3,250	2.51%	—	—
Fixed-rate 4.500% notes	2036	1,250	4.54%	—	—
Fixed-rate 4.650% notes	2046	4,000	4.58%	—	—
Third quarter 2016 Australian dollar-denominated debt issuance of A$1.4 billion:					
Fixed-rate 2.650% notes	2020	493	1.92%	—	—
Fixed-rate 3.350% notes	2024	342	2.61%	—	—
Fixed-rate 3.600% notes	2026	247	2.84%	—	—
Third quarter 2016 debt issuance of $1.4 billion:					
Fixed-rate 4.150% notes	2046	1,377	4.15%	—	—
Fourth quarter 2016 debt issuance of $7.0 billion:					
Floating-rate notes	2019	350	0.91%	—	—
Fixed-rate 1.100% notes	2019	1,150	1.13%	—	—
Fixed-rate 1.550% notes	2021	1,250	1.40%	—	—
Fixed-rate 2.450% notes	2026	2,250	2.15%	—	—
Fixed-rate 3.850% notes	2046	2,000	3.86%	—	—
Total term debt		78,384		55,701	
Unamortized premium/(discount) and issuance costs, net		(174)		(248)	
Hedge accounting fair value adjustments		717		376	
Less: Current portion of long-term debt, net		(3,500)		(2,500)	
Total long-term debt		$ 75,427		$ 53,329	

Note 7 – Shareholders' Equity

Dividends

The Company declared and paid cash dividends per share during the periods presented as follows:

	Dividends Per Share	Amount (in millions)
2016:		
Fourth quarter	$ 0.57	$ 3,071
Third quarter	0.57	3,117
Second quarter	0.52	2,879
First quarter	0.52	2,898
Total cash dividends declared and paid	$ 2.18	$ 11,965
2015:		
Fourth quarter	$ 0.52	$ 2,950
Third quarter	0.52	2,997
Second quarter	0.47	2,734
First quarter	0.47	2,750
Total cash dividends declared and paid	$ 1.98	$ 11,431

Future dividends are subject to declaration by the Board of Directors.

Share Repurchase Program

In April 2016, the Company's Board of Directors increased the share repurchase authorization from $140 billion to $175 billion of the Company's common stock, of which $133 billion had been utilized as of September 24, 2016. The Company's share repurchase program does not obligate it to acquire any specific number of shares. Under the program, shares may be repurchased in privately negotiated and/or open market transactions, including under plans complying with Rule 10b5-1 under the Securities Exchange Act of 1934, as amended (the "Exchange Act").

[...]

Note 10 – Commitments and Contingencies

Accrued Warranty and Indemnification

The following table shows changes in the Company's accrued warranties and related costs for 2016, 2015 and 2014 (in millions):

	2016	2015	2014
Beginning accrued warranty and related costs	$ 4,780	$ 4,159	$ 2,967
Cost of warranty claims	(4,663)	(4,401)	(3,760)
Accruals for product warranty	3,585	5,022	4,952
Ending accrued warranty and related costs	$ 3,702	$ 4,780	$ 4,159

[...]

The Company has entered into indemnification agreements with its directors and executive officers. Under these agreements, the Company has agreed to indemnify such individuals to the fullest extent permitted by law against liabilities that arise by reason of their status as directors or officers and to advance expenses incurred by such individuals in connection with related legal proceedings. It is not possible to determine the maximum potential amount of payments the Company could be required to make under these agreements due to the limited history of prior indemnification claims and the unique facts and circumstances involved in each claim. However, the Company maintains directors and officers liability insurance coverage to reduce its exposure to such obligations.

[...]

Other Off-Balance Sheet Commitments

Operating Leases

The Company leases various equipment and facilities, including retail space, under noncancelable operating lease arrangements. The Company does not currently utilize any other off-balance sheet financing arrangements. As of September 24, 2016, the Company's total future minimum lease payments under noncancelable operating leases were $7.6 billion. The Company's retail store and other facility leases are typically for terms not exceeding 10 years and generally contain multi-year renewal options.

Rent expense under all operating leases, including both cancelable and noncancelable leases, was $939 million, $794 million and $717 million in 2016, 2015 and 2014, respectively. Future minimum lease payments under noncancelable operating leases having remaining terms in excess of one year as of September 24, 2016, are as follows (in millions):

2017	$ 929
2018	919
2019	915
2020	889
2021	836
Thereafter	3,139
Total	$ 7,627

Contingencies

The Company is subject to various legal proceedings and claims that have arisen in the ordinary course of business and that have not been fully adjudicated, as further discussed in Part I, Item 1A of this Form 10-K under the heading "Risk Factors" and in Part I, Item 3 of this Form 10-K under the heading "Legal Proceedings." In the opinion of management, there was not at least a reasonable possibility the Company may have incurred a material loss, or a material loss in excess of a recorded accrual, with respect to loss contingencies for asserted legal and other claims. However, the outcome of litigation is inherently uncertain. Therefore, although management considers the likelihood of such an outcome to be remote, if one or more of these legal matters were resolved against the Company in a reporting period for amounts in excess of management's expectations, the Company's consolidated financial statements for that reporting period could be materially adversely affected.

Apple Inc. v. Samsung Electronics Co., Ltd., et al.

On August 24, 2012, a jury returned a verdict awarding the Company $1.05 billion in its lawsuit against Samsung Electronics Co., Ltd. and affiliated parties in the United States District Court, Northern District of California, San Jose Division. On March 6, 2014, the District Court entered final judgment in favor of the Company in the amount of approximately $930 million. On May 18, 2015, the U.S. Court of Appeals for the Federal Circuit affirmed in part, and reversed in part, the decision of the District Court. As a result, the Court of Appeals ordered entry of final judgment on damages in the amount of approximately $548 million, with the District Court to determine supplemental damages and interest, as well as damages owed for products subject to the reversal in part. Samsung paid $548 million to the Company in December 2015, which was included in net sales in the Condensed Consolidated Statement of Operations. Because the case remains subject to further proceedings, the Company has not recognized any further amounts in its results of operations. On October 11, 2016, the United States Supreme Court heard arguments in Samsung's request for appeal related to the $548 million in damages.

[…]

Appendix B

TYPICAL CHARTS OF ACCOUNTS FOR DIFFERENT TYPES OF BUSINESSES

A Simple Service Corporation

Assets	Liabilities	Stockholders' Equity
Cash	Accounts Payable	Common Stock
Accounts Receivable	Notes Payable, Short-Term	Retained Earnings
Allowance for Uncollectible Accounts	Salary Payable	Dividends
Notes Receivable, Short-Term	Wages Payable	
Interest Receivable	Payroll Taxes Payable	**Revenues and Gains**
Supplies	Employee Benefits Payable	Service Revenue
Prepaid Rent	Interest Payable	Interest Revenue
Prepaid Insurance	Unearned Service Revenue	Gain on Sale of Land (Furniture, Equipment, or Building)
Notes Receivable, Long-Term	Notes Payable, Long-Term	
Land		**Expenses and Losses**
Building		Salary Expense
Accumulated Depreciation—Building		Payroll Tax Expense
Equipment		Employee Benefits Expense
Accumulated Depreciation—Equipment		Rent Expense
Furniture		Insurance Expense
Accumulated Depreciation—Furniture		Supplies Expense
		Uncollectible Accounts Expense
		Depreciation Expense—Furniture
		Depreciation Expense—Equipment
		Depreciation Expense—Building
		Income Tax Expense
		Interest Expense
		Miscellaneous Expense
		Loss on Sale (or Exchange) of Land (Furniture, Equipment, or Building)

A Service Partnership

Same as service corporation, except for owners' equity

Owners' Equity

Partner 1, Capital
Partner 2, Capital
.
.
.
Partner *N*, Capital

Partner 1, Drawing
Partner 2, Drawing
.
.
.
Partner *N*, Drawing

TYPICAL CHARTS OF ACCOUNTS FOR DIFFERENT TYPES OF BUSINESSES (continued)

A Complex Merchandising Corporation

Assets

- Cash
- Investments in Trading Debt Securities or Investments in Available-for-Sale Debt Securities
- Accounts Receivable
- Allowance for Uncollectible Accounts
- Notes Receivable, Short-Term
- Interest Receivable
- Inventory
- Supplies
- Prepaid Rent
- Prepaid Insurance
- Notes Receivable, Long-Term
- Equity-Method Investment
- Investments in Available-for-Sale Debt Securities
- Investment in Held-to-Maturity Bonds
- Other Receivables, Long-Term
- Land
- Land Improvements
- Buildings
- Accumulated Depreciation—Buildings
- Equipment
- Accumulated Depreciation—Equipment
- Furniture and Fixtures
- Accumulated Depreciation—Furniture and Fixtures
- Franchises
- Patents
- Leasehold Improvements
- Goodwill

Liabilities

- Accounts Payable
- Notes Payable, Short-Term
- Current Portion of Bonds Payable
- Salary Payable
- Wages Payable
- Payroll Taxes Payable
- Employee Benefits Payable
- Interest Payable
- Income Tax Payable
- Unearned Sales Revenue
- Notes Payable, Long-Term
- Bonds Payable
- Lease Liability

Stockholders' Equity

- Preferred Stock
- Paid-in Capital in Excess of Par—Preferred
- Common Stock
- Paid-in Capital in Excess of Par—Common
- Paid-in Capital from Treasury Stock Transactions
- Paid-in Capital from Retirement of Stock
- Retained Earnings
- Accumulated Other Comprehensive Income (or Loss)
- Treasury Stock
- Noncontrolling Interest

Revenues and Gains

- Sales Revenue
- Interest Revenue
- Dividend Revenue
- Equity-Method Investment Revenue
- Unrealized Gain on Equity Securities
- Gain on Sale of Investments
- Gain on Sale of Land (Furniture and Fixtures, Equipment, or Buildings)
- Discontinued Operations—Gain

Expenses and Losses

- Cost of Goods Sold
- Salary Expense
- Wage Expense
- Commission Expense
- Payroll Tax Expense
- Employee Benefits Expense
- Rent Expense
- Insurance Expense
- Supplies Expense
- Uncollectible Accounts Expense
- Depreciation Expense—Land Improvements
- Depreciation Expense—Furniture and Fixtures
- Depreciation Expense—Equipment
- Depreciation Expense—Buildings
- Organization Expense
- Amortization Expense—Franchises
- Amortization Expense—Leasehold Improvements
- Amortization Expense—Patent
- Income Tax Expense
- Unrealized Loss on Equity Securities
- Loss on Sale of Investments
- Loss on Sale (or Exchange) of Land (Furniture and Fixtures, Equipment, or Buildings)
- Discontinued Operations—Loss

A Manufacturing Corporation

Same as merchandising corporation, except for assets

Assets

- Inventories:
  - Raw Materials Inventories
  - Work-in-Process Inventories
  - Finished Goods Inventories
- Manufacturing Wages
- Manufacturing Overhead

Appendix C

SUMMARY OF U.S. GENERALLY ACCEPTED ACCOUNTING PRINCIPLES (GAAP)

Every technical area has professional associations and regulatory bodies that govern the practice of the profession. Accounting is no exception. In the United States, generally accepted accounting principles (GAAP) are written by the Financial Accounting Standards Board (FASB). The FASB has seven full-time members and a large staff. An independent organization with no government or professional affiliation, the FASB is subject to oversight by the Financial Accounting Foundation (FAF), which selects its members and funds its work. In order to ensure impartiality, FASB members are required to sever all ties to previous firms and institutions that they may have served prior to joining the FASB. Each member is appointed for a five-year term and is eligible for one additional five-year term.

FASB pronouncements are called *Statements of Financial Accounting Standards.* Once issued, these pronouncements are added to the *Accounting Standards Codification*™, which is the single source of authoritative nongovernmental U.S. GAAP. The codification organizes the many pronouncements that constitute U.S. GAAP—each of which specifies how to measure and report a particular type of business event or transaction—into a consistent, searchable format. U.S. GAAP is the "accounting law of the land." In the same way that our laws draw authority from their acceptance by the people, U.S. GAAP depends on general acceptance by the business community. Throughout this book, we refer to U.S. GAAP as the proper way to measure and report business activity.

In 2002, the FASB and the International Accounting Standards Board (IASB) announced a convergence project, whereby both bodies agreed to combine international financial reporting standards (IFRS) and U.S. GAAP into one set of global, compatible, high-quality standards. All new FASB and IASB standards written since that time have been written to measure and report various types of business activities in compatible (if not identical) ways. However, some differences between the two sets of standards still exist. Those differences are discussed in Appendix D.

The U.S. Congress has given the Securities and Exchange Commission (SEC), a government organization that regulates the trading of investments, ultimate responsibility for establishing accounting rules for companies that are owned by the general investing public. However, the SEC has delegated much of its rule-making power to the FASB. Exhibit C-1 outlines the flow of authority for developing U.S. GAAP.

Exhibit C-1 | Flow of Authority for Developing U.S. GAAP

The Objective of Financial Reporting

The basic objective of financial reporting is to provide information that is useful in making investment and lending decisions. The FASB believes that accounting information can be useful in decision making only if it is *relevant* and if it *faithfully represents* economic reality.

Relevant information is useful in making predictions and for evaluating past performance—that is, the information has feedback value. For example, PepsiCo's disclosure of the profitability of each of its lines of business is relevant for investor evaluations of the company. To be relevant, information must be timely. To faithfully represent, the information must be complete, neutral (free from bias), and without material error (accurate). Accounting information must focus on the *economic substance* of a transaction, event, or circumstance, which may or may not always be the same as its legal form. Faithful representation makes the information *reliable* to users. Exhibit 1-3 on page 6 of Chapter 1 presents the objective of accounting, its fundamental and enhancing qualitative characteristics, and its constraint. These characteristics and constraint combine to shape the concepts and principles that make up U.S. GAAP. Exhibit C-2 summarizes the assumptions, concepts, and principles that accounting has developed to provide useful information for decision making.

Exhibit C-2 | Summary of Important Accounting Concepts, Principles, and Financial Statements

Assumptions, Concepts, Principles, and Financial Statements	Quick Summary	Text Reference
Assumptions and Concepts		
Entity assumption	Accounting draws a boundary around each organization to be accounted for.	Chapter 1, page 7
Continuity (going-concern) assumption	Accountants assume the business will continue operating for the foreseeable future.	Chapter 1, page 7
Stable-monetary-unit assumption	Accounting information is expressed primarily in monetary terms that ignore the effects of inflation.	Chapter 1, page 8
Time-period concept	Ensures that accounting information is reported at regular intervals.	Chapter 3, page 122
Principles		
Historical cost principle	Assets are recorded at their actual historical cost.	Chapter 1, pages 7–8
Revenue principle	Tells accountants when to record revenue (only after it has been earned) and the amount of revenue to record (the cash value of what has been received).	Chapter 3, page 123 Chapter 5, pages 250–251 and Chapter 12, page 696
Expense recognition (matching) principle	Directs accountants to (1) identify and measure all expenses incurred during the period and (2) match the expenses against the revenues earned during the period. The goal is to measure net income.	Chapter 3, page 124
Consistency principle	Businesses should use the same accounting methods from period to period.	Chapter 6, page 320
Disclosure principle	A company's financial statements should report enough information for outsiders to make informed decisions about the company.	Chapter 6, page 320
Financial Statements		
Balance sheet	Assets = Liabilities + Owners' Equity at a point in time.	Chapter 1
Income statement	Revenues and gains − Expenses and losses = Net income or net loss for the period	Chapters 1 and 3
Statement of cash flows	Cash receipts − Cash payments = Increase or decrease in cash during the period, grouped under operating, investing, and financing activities	Chapters 1 and 11
Statement of retained earnings	Beginning retained earnings + Net income (or − Net loss) − Dividends Declared = Ending retained earnings	Chapters 1 and 10
Statement of stockholders' equity	Shows the reason for the change in each stockholders' equity account, including retained earnings.	Chapter 10, page 551
Financial statement notes	Provide information that cannot be reported conveniently on the face of the financial statements. The notes are an integral part of the statements.	Chapter 12

Appendix D

SUMMARY OF DIFFERENCES BETWEEN U.S. GAAP AND IFRS CROSS REFERENCED TO CHAPTER

The following table describes some of the current differences between U.S. generally accepted accounting principles (GAAP) and International Financial Reporting Standards (IFRS) that relate to topics (by chapter) covered in this textbook. Because of the globalization of business, there are theoretical advantages to adopting a single uniform set of global accounting standards. However, for practical reasons, most people feel that is unlikely. The last column of the table explains what could happen if the U.S. GAAP of today were to switch to IFRS as they currently exist. This will help you assess the impact of these changes on U.S. financial statements.

Accounts	Topic	U.S. GAAP Position	IFRS Position	Implications of Switch to IFRS
Inventory and Cost of Goods Sold Chapter 6	Inventory costing	Companies can choose to use LIFO inventory costing, if desired. A large portion of U.S. companies currently use LIFO for its tax benefits.	LIFO is not allowed under any circumstances.	LIFO could be eliminated. Companies could still choose to use FIFO, average, or specific identification methods.
	Lower-of-cost-or market (LCM)	For companies that use LIFO, market is usually determined to be replacement cost. For companies that use FIFO or average costing, market is defined as net realizable value (estimated selling price less cost of completion, disposal, and transportation). LCM write-downs cannot be reversed.	Since LIFO is not allowed, market is always net realizable value (fair market value). LCM write-downs can be reversed under certain conditions.	Some write-downs might be reversed over time.
Property, Plant, and Equipment Chapter 7	Asset impairment and revaluation	If long-term assets are impaired, they are written down by a two-step process, using different computations in each step: (1) recognizing that an asset has been impaired; and (2) making the adjustment to lower of cost or fair value. Once impairment has been recorded, it can never be reversed.	Long-term assets may be written up or down, based on fair market value (appraisals). Adjustments may be potentially reversed, up to a limited amount. There is only a one-step process to impair an asset. Once impairment is recognized, the adjustment is the amount of the impairment.	The cost principle might not apply to long-term assets as strongly. Assets could be evaluated by independent appraisers and adjusted either up or down.
	Depreciation	Assets are depreciated by classes (i.e., buildings, equipment, etc.).	Assets are depreciated by component (much more detailed than by classes).	Much more detailed records would have to be kept over depreciation.
Research and Development Chapter 7	Development costs	All research and development costs are expensed. Only exception is for computer software development costs, which can be capitalized and amortized over future sales revenues.	All research is expensed, but development costs are capitalized if six criteria are met, and amortized over future sales revenues.	Standards already developed by U.S. GAAP might be extended to apply to all development costs, not just computer software development.

Accounts	Topic	U.S. GAAP Position	IFRS Position	Implications of Switch to IFRS
Intangible Assets Chapter 7	Capitalization and recognition of intangible assets on balance sheet	Only recognized when purchased. Internally developed not recognized.	Recognized if future benefit is probable and reliably measurable (same criteria as recognition of contingencies). May be purchased or internally developed.	More intangible assets could be recognized on balance sheet. Adjusted for amortization or impairment over time.
Contingent Liabilities Chapter 8	Recording of contingent liabilities	Accrued (recorded in journal entry) if "probable" and if a "reasonable estimate" of the amount of loss can be made. Contingent liabilities that are "reasonably possible" are disclosed in notes to financial statements.	Contingencies are not considered "probable" to occur in the future. Therefore, they can, by definition, only be disclosed in the financial statement footnotes. However, if it is "more likely than not" (i.e., greater than a 50% probability) that an obligation is going to arise, and if an estimate can be made of the amount, IFRS requires that a "provision" be recorded by making an accrual journal entry.	More contingent liabilities could be accrued.
Leases Chapter 9	Accounting for lease assets and lease liabilities	Definition of lease is limited to specific property, plant, or equipment. Virtually all leases have to be capitalized as assets, and corresponding liabilities have to be recognized, on the balance sheet. The present value of all future payments on leased assets must be capitalized under the category of "right to use" assets. The related obligations will be reported as obligations for "future lease payment" long-term liabilities. There are two categories of leases for lessees: (1) finance; and (2) operating. These types of leases are accounted for differently in the income statement, impacting income in different time periods.	Definition of lease is different than GAAP, not restricted to specific property, plant and equipment. There is only one category of lease, of which the recording is similar to the FASB's finance lease.	More leases will be capitalized, resulting in more frequent recognition of long-term assets as well as long-term liabilities.
Interest Revenue and Interest Expense Chapter 11	Indirect method cash flows statement presentation Direct method cash flows statement presentation	Interest revenue and interest expense are part of net income, and as such are included in operating activities (as part of net income) on an indirect method cash flows statement. Interest income is not reported under investing activities.	Interest revenue and interest expense are removed from net income (as an adjustment, similar to the adjustment for depreciation expense) in the operating activities section of the indirect method cash flows statement. Interest income is reported under investing activities, and interest expense is reported under financing activities for both direct and indirect methods.	Interest revenue and interest expense reclassified to different sections of the cash flows statement.

Appendix E—Investments

1 **Explain** why companies invest in other companies

1 **Explain** why companies invest in other companies

2 **Account for** investments in equity securities when the investor has *insignificant influence*

3 **Account for** investments in equity securities when the investor has *significant influence*

4 **Account for** investments in equity securities when the investor has *controlling influence*

5 **Account for** investments in debt securities

EXPLAIN WHY COMPANIES INVEST IN OTHER COMPANIES

Apple Inc. presents one of the best examples of companies that invest significant amounts of money in the securities of other companies, such as their stocks, bonds, and notes. Examine the following excerpt from Apple Inc.'s Consolidated Balance Sheets as of September 24, 2016 and September 26, 2015:

	A	B	C
1	**Apple Inc. CONSOLIDATED BALANCE SHEETS - USD ($) $ in Millions**	**Sep. 24, 2016**	**Sep. 26, 2015**
2	Current assets:		
3	Cash and cash equivalents	$ 20,484	$ 21,120
4	Short-term marketable securities	46,671	20,481
5	Accounts receivable, less allowances of $53 and $63, respectively	15,754	16,849
6	Inventories	2,132	2,349
7	Vendor non-trade receivables	13,545	13,494
8	Other current assets	8,283	15,085
9	Total current assets	106,869	89,378
10	Long-term marketable securities	170,430	164,065
11	Property, plant and equipment, net	27,010	22,471
12	Goodwill	5,414	5,116
13	Acquired intangible assets, net	3,206	3,893
14	Other non-current assets	8,757	5,422
15	Total assets	$ 321,686	$ 290,345
16	CONSOLIDATED STATEMENTS OF OPERATIONS - $ in Millions	Fiscal 2016	Fiscal 2016
17	Other income, net	$ 1,348	$ 1,285
18			

Data from the Securities and Exchange Commission EDGAR Company filings, www.sec.gov

Notice that, of the $107 billion of total current assets Apple Inc. owned as of September 24, 2016, about $67.2 billion (62.8%) is in cash and cash equivalents ($20.5 billion), as well as short-term marketable securities ($46.7 billion). In addition, the company owns investments of $170.4 billion in long-term marketable securities. In all, cash and investments of various types in stocks and bonds of other companies makes up about 74% [($20,484 + $46,671 + $170,430)/$321,686] of Apple's total assets! Together, these investments earned Apple about $1.35 billion in extra income as well as cash in fiscal 2016.

Companies invest in the securities of other companies for at least two reasons:

1. They may have excess cash that they do not need immediately and so they invest on a short-term basis, hoping to earn additional income and raise additional cash to use later in their operations. The additional income can consist of interest and dividends plus gains (or losses) on the sales of these securities.
2. They may have long-term strategic reasons for investing, such as gaining influence or control of other companies. For example, Apple Inc. might acquire stock in a supplier in order to influence its operating decisions and be assured a steady stream of good-quality, reasonably priced raw material to use in production of its products.

As Apple's Consolidated Balance Sheets on page 772 show, investments in securities may be classified as either short term or long term. Short-term investments are reported as current assets on a company's balance sheet, and long-term investments are classified as long-term assets. To be classified as a current asset, an investment must meet *both* of the following criteria:

- The investment must be liquid (easily convertible to cash).
- The investor must intend to either convert the investment to cash within one year or the current operating cycle, whichever is longer, or use the proceeds from the sale of the investment to pay a current liability.

Otherwise, the investment is classified as a long-term asset.

GAAP rules for investments differ based on whether an investment is composed of equity securities or debt securities. **Equity securities** are investments in capital stock. **Debt securities** are investments in either bonds or notes payable. In this appendix, we will look at each of these categories of investments.

Investments in Equity Securities

According to GAAP, the proper way to account for equity investments depends on the percentage of the voting stock the investor owns, and hence, the degree of influence the investor has over the company in which it invested (the investee). As Exhibit E-1 shows, if an investor owns less than 20% of the voting stock of the investee, the investor is presumed to have **insignificant influence**, and the fair value method of reporting the investment must be used. If an investor owns more than 20% but less than 50% of the voting stock of the investee, the investor is presumed to have **significant influence** over the investee, and the equity method of accounting is used to account for the investment. Finally, if the investor owns more than 50% of the voting stock of the investee, the investor is presumed to have *controlling influence* over the investee, and the consolidation method of accounting is used for the investment.

Exhibit E-1 | Methods of accounting for equity investments by Percentage of ownership

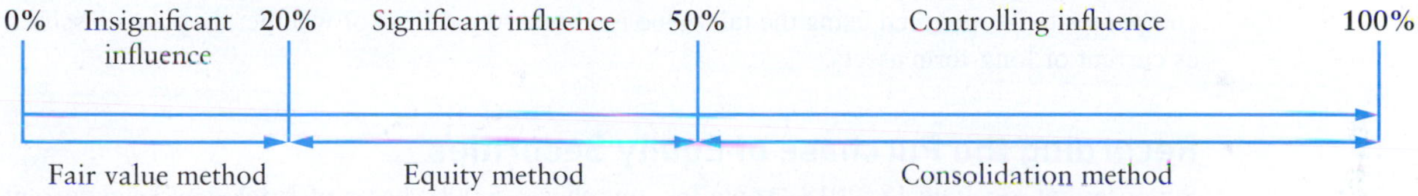

ACCOUNT FOR INVESTMENTS IN EQUITY SECURITIES WHEN THE INVESTOR HAS *INSIGNIFICANT INFLUENCE*

2 Account for investments in equity securities when the investor has *insignificant influence*

Investments in equity securities (stock) can be classified as either current or long-term assets, depending on the company's ability and intent to hold or sell them. Short-term investments in equity securities are generally purchased with excess cash, and are generally bought and sold frequently in order to take advantage of market fluctuations, for the purpose of generating more cash for use in the company's operations. Other investments in equity securities may be held for reasons other than to profit on a short-term basis, and may be classified as either current or long-term assets.

Let's examine how Apple Inc. describes its investments (from Note 1, *Summary of Significant Accounting Policies*):

Cash Equivalents and Marketable Securities

All highly liquid investments with maturities of three months or less at the date of purchase are classified as cash equivalents. Management determines the appropriate classification of its investments at the time of purchase and reevaluates the designations at each balance sheet date. The Company classifies its marketable debt securities as either short-term or long-term based on each instrument's underlying contractual maturity date. Marketable debt securities with maturities of 12 months or less are classified as short-term and marketable debt securities with maturities greater than 12 months are classified as long-term. The Company classifies its marketable equity securities, including mutual funds, as either short-term or long-term based on the nature of each security and its availability for use in current operations. The cost of securities sold is based upon the specific identification method.

Source: Data from the Securities and Exchange Commission EDGAR Company filings, www.sec.gov

This description encompasses the following securities on Apple's balance sheet:

- Line 3, "cash and cash equivalents," \$20,484 million, includes debt securities with maturities of three months or less. These were discussed in Chapter 4.
- Line 4, "short-term marketable securities," \$46,671 million, includes both debt and equity securities as described in Note 1 above. These are current assets because they are highly liquid and the company intends to convert them to cash within the next fiscal year.
- Line 10, "long-term marketable securities," \$170,430 million, includes investment assets that don't meet at least one of the criteria for being classified as current. The company has made these investments for long-term strategic purposes. It does not plan to sell these investments within the next fiscal year and/or the investments are not liquid.

GAAP requires equity securities (stocks) that comprise an insignificant influence in other companies to be recorded using the fair value method—regardless of whether they are classified as current or long-term assets.

Recording the Purchase of Equity Securities

Suppose that, on June 18, 2018, Apple Inc., purchases 5,000 shares of **Intel** stock as a current asset. Apple now owns less than 1% of Intel's outstanding shares, and thus has insignificant influence over Intel. Apple buys the stock for \$20 per share, paying \$100,000 cash, and records the purchase of the investment at cost:

	A	B	C	D
1	2018			
2	June 18	Investment in Equity Securities	100,000	
3		Cash		100,000
4		*Purchased investment.*		
5				

Investment in Equity Securities	
100,000	

Recording Cash Dividends

Suppose that, on June 30, Apple Inc., receives a cash dividend of $4,000 from Intel. Apple Inc., records the dividend revenue as:

	A	B	C	D
1	June 30	Cash	4,000	
2		Dividend Revenue		4,000
3		*Received cash dividend.*		
4				

Adjusting Equity Investments to Their Fair Value

Fair (market) value is the amount for which the owner of a security can sell it. Apple's 2018 fiscal year ends on September 29. Suppose that on this date, the fair market value of Intel's stock is $22. Intel's stock has risen in value. Consequently, on September 29, Apple's investment in the stock has a current fair value of $110,000.

Unrealized Gains and Losses. Apple's investment in Intel results in a gain because the fair value of the Intel stock ($110,000) is greater than what Apple paid for it ($100,000). However, the gain is *unrealized* because Apple hasn't actually sold the stock for a profit:

- **Unrealized gains** are gains that arise before securities are sold, because their fair market value exceeds their cost.
- **Unrealized losses** are losses that arise before securities are sold, because their fair market value drops below their cost.

Regardless of whether they result in unrealized gains or losses for a company, investments in equity securities must be reported on the balance sheet at their current fair values. So, prior to preparing financial statements on September 29, 2018, Apple uses this year-end journal entry to adjust the Intel securities to their current fair value:[1]

	A	B	C	D
1	Sept 29	Investment in Equity Securities	10,000	
2		Unrealized Gain on Equity Securities		10,000
3		*Adjusted investment to fair value.*		
4				

Investment in Equity Securities		Unrealized Gain on Equity Securities (other income)	
100,000			
10,000			10,000
110,000			

After the adjustment, Apple's Investment in Equity Securities account, reflecting its investment in Intel stock, is ready to be reported on the balance sheet at the current fair value.

Suppose Apple decides to keep the Intel stock for another year, and during that time, it declines in value. On September 28, 2019, the end of Apple's fiscal year, the fair value of Intel

[1]Although our simple example contains only one investment in one stock, fair value adjustments should be made to the entire portfolio on an aggregate basis.

stock is $21 per share. In preparation for its 2019 balance sheet, Apple makes the following adjusting entry:

	A	B	C	D
1	2019			
2	Sept 28	Unrealized Loss on Equity Securities	5,000	
3		Investment in Equity Securities		5,000
4		*Adjusted investment to fair value.*		
5				

Investment in Equity Securities	
100,000	5,000
10,000	
105,000	

Unrealized Loss on Equity Securities (other income)	
5,000	

At the end of each period, because they are reported on the income statement, unrealized gains and losses on equity securities are closed along with other revenue and expense accounts and eventually become a part of retained earnings on the balance sheet. Apple's unrealized gain of $10,000 is reported on the company's 2018 income statement and is closed to retained earnings at the end of that year. In 2019, an unrealized loss is reported on 2019's income statement and is closed to retained earnings at the end of that year. Consequently, the company's retained earnings balance at the end of 2019 includes a net $5,000 unrealized gain from the Intel stock (a $10,000 unrealized gain in 2018, and a $5,000 unrealized loss in 2019).

Recording the Sale of an Equity Investment

Suppose Apple sells its Intel stock on June 19, 2020. The sale price is $107,000, so Apple makes this journal entry:

	A	B	C	D
1	2020			
2	June 19	Cash	107,000	
3		Investment in Equity Securities		105,000
4		Gain on Sale of Equity Securities (other income)		2,000
5		*Sold investments at a gain.*		
6				

Realized Gains and Losses. By selling its Intel stock for $107,000, Apple *realizes* a gain:

- **Realized gains** are gains earned because the sales price from the sold securities is greater than their carrying value on the balance sheet.
- **Realized losses** are losses incurred because the sales price from the sold securities is less than their carrying value on the balance sheet.

A realized gain or loss occurs only when the investor sells an investment. However, accountants rarely use the word *realized* in an account title. Instead, a gain (or a loss) is understood to have occurred as a result of the sales transaction. In contrast, unrealized gains and losses are clearly labeled as *unrealized*. The fair value method for investments in equity securities with insignificant influence over investees requires that both realized and unrealized gains and losses on investments in equity securities be reported in "other income" on the income statement.

TRY IT

(Answers are given on page 797.)

The largest current asset on Waverly Corporation's balance sheet at December 31, 2018, is Investment in Equity Securities. The investments consist of stock in other corporations and cost Waverly $8,660 (amounts in millions). At the balance sheet date, the fair value of these securities is $9,000.

(1) Suppose Waverly holds the equity investments in the hope of trading them actively for a profit and converting them to cash within four to six months. How will Waverly classify the investments? What will Waverly report on the balance sheet at December 31, 2018? What will Waverly report on its 2018 income statement? Show a T-account for Investment in Equity Securities.

(2) Suppose Waverly sells the investment in securities for $8,700 in 2019. Journalize the sale and then show the Investment in Equity Securities T-account as it appears after the sale.

ACCOUNT FOR INVESTMENTS IN EQUITY SECURITIES WHEN THE INVESTOR HAS *SIGNIFICANT INFLUENCE*

3 Account for investments in equity securities when the investor has *significant influence*

An investor owning between 20% and 50% of the investee's voting stock or other ownership interests has significant influence over the business activities of the investee (such as its dividend policies, product lines, and other important decisions) because it will more than likely hold one or more seats on the board of directors of the investee company. As Exhibit E-1 shows, GAAP requires the use of the equity method to account for these types of investments. With the **equity method**, profits and losses of the investee are recorded as part of the investor's income on its income statement. The equity method investment is classified as a long-term asset on the investor's balance sheet.

As an example, let's consider the investing activities of another large corporation. Intel Corporation holds equity-method investments in **IM Flash Technologies, LLC**, and **Intel-GE Care Innovations, LLC**. These investee companies are referred to as *affiliates* because the investor's ownership percentage in them is significant enough to influence their operations. Because Intel has a voice in shaping the policy and operations of these companies, Intel's share of their profits and losses should be included in Intel's income.

Purchase of Equity-Method Investments

Investments accounted for using the equity method are recorded initially at cost. Suppose that, on January 1, 2018, Intel pays $490 million for a 49% ownership of IM Flash Technologies, LLC. Intel's entry to record the purchase of this investment follows (figures assumed, in millions):

A1

	A	B	C	D
1	2018			
2	Jan 1	Equity-method Investment	490	
3		Cash		490
4		*To purchase equity-method investment.*		
5				

The Investor's Percentage of Investee Income. Under the equity method, Intel, as the investor, applies its percentage of ownership—49% in our example—to record its share of the investee's net income and dividends. If IM Flash Technologies reports net income of $300 million for 2018, Intel records 49% of this amount as follows (in millions):

A1			
A	B	C	D
2018			
Dec 31	Equity-method Investment (300 × 0.49)	147	
	Equity-method Investment Revenue		147
	To record investment revenue.		

Intel increases the Equity-method Investment account and records Equity-method Investment Revenue when IM Flash Technologies reports income. As IM Flash's stockholders' equity increases, so does the Equity-method Investment account on Intel's books.

Recording Dividends on Equity-Method Investments. Intel records its proportionate part of cash dividends received from IM Flash. When IM Flash declares and pays a cash dividend of $200 million, Intel receives 49% of this dividend and records this entry (in millions):

A1			
A	B	C	D
2018			
Dec 31	Cash ($200 × 0.49)	98	
	Equity-method Investment		98
	To receive cash dividend on equity-method investment.		

The Equity-method Investment account is decreased by the dividend because it decreases the investee's owners' equity and thus the investor's investment.

After the preceding entries are posted, Intel's Equity-method Investment account at December 31, 2018, shows Intel's equity in the net assets of IM Flash Technologies (in millions):

Equity-method Investment

Jan 1	Purchase	490	Dec 31	Dividends	98
Dec 31	Net income	147			
Dec 31	Balance	539			

On December 31, 2018, Intel would report the Equity-method investment as a long-term asset on its balance sheet and the Equity-method investment revenue on its income statement as follows:

	Millions
Balance sheet (partial):	
Assets	
Total current assets	$XXX
Property, plant, and equipment, net	XXX
Equity-method investment	539
Income statement (partial):	
Income from operations	$XXX
Other revenue:	
Equity-method investment revenue	147
Net income	$XXX

The following T-account summarizes how equity-method investments are recorded:

Equity-method Investment

Original cost	Share of losses
Share of income	Share of dividends
Balance	

TRY IT

(Answers are given on p. 797.)

An investor paid $67,900 to acquire a 40% investment in the common stock of an investee. At the end of the first year, the investee's net income was $80,000, and the company declared and paid cash dividends of $55,000. What is the investor's ending balance in its Equity-Method Investment account? Use a T-account to answer this question.

ACCOUNT FOR INVESTMENTS IN EQUITY SECURITIES WHEN THE INVESTOR HAS *CONTROLLING INFLUENCE*

4 **Account for** investments in equity securities when the investor has *controlling influence*

Most large corporations own controlling equity interests in other companies. A **controlling (or majority) interest** is the ownership of more than 50% of the investee's voting stock. Such an investment enables the investor to elect a majority of the members of the investee's board of directors and thus control the investee's policies, such as its production, distribution (supply chain), financing, and investing decisions. The investor is called the **parent company**, and the investee company is called the **subsidiary**. For example, **McAfee, Inc.**, a computer data security company, is a subsidiary of Intel Corporation, the parent. Therefore, the stockholders of Intel control McAfee, Inc., as diagrammed in Exhibit E-2.

Exhibit E-2 | Ownership Structure of Intel Corporation and McAfee, Inc.

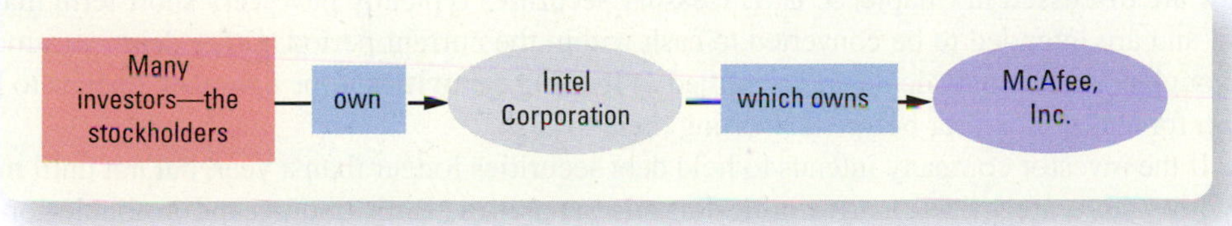

Intel owned controlling equity interests in almost 30 other subsidiary corporations as of the end of fiscal 2016. Exhibit E-3 shows some of these other subsidiaries.

Exhibit E-3 | Selected Subsidiaries of Intel Corporation

Intel Capital	Intel Americas, Inc.
Componentes Intel de Costa Rica, S.A.	Intel Europe, Inc.
Intel Asia Holding Limited	Wind River Systems, Inc.

Consolidation Accounting

Consolidation accounting is a method of combining the financial statements of all the companies controlled by the same stockholders. This method reports a single set of financial statements for the consolidated entity, which carries the name of the parent company.

Consolidated financial statements combine the balance sheets, income statements, statements of stockholders' equity, and cash flow statements of the parent company with those of its subsidiaries. The result is a single set of statements as if the parent and its subsidiaries were one company. Investors can gain a better perspective on total operations from these statements than they could by examining the reports of the parent and each individual subsidiary.

In consolidated financial statements, the assets, liabilities, revenues, and expenses of each subsidiary are added to the parent's accounts. For example, the balance in Intel Capital's Cash account is added to the balance in the Intel Corporation's Cash account and to the cash of all other subsidiaries. The sum of all of the cash amounts is presented as a single amount in Intel's consolidated balance sheet. Each account balance of a subsidiary, such as **Intel Capital** or **Intel Europe, Inc.**, loses its identity in the consolidated statements, which bear the name of the parent, Intel Corporation. After a subsidiary's financial statements become consolidated into the parent company's statements, the subsidiary's statements are no longer available to the public.

ACCOUNT FOR INVESTMENTS IN DEBT SECURITIES

5 Account for investments in debt securities

Accounting for debt securities such as bonds, from the issuer's (borrower's) point of view was covered in Chapter 9. This section looks at debt securities from the investor's point of view. The major investors in debt securities such as bonds are financial institutions—pension funds, mutual funds, and insurance companies. The relationship between the issuing corporation and the investor (bondholder) is diagrammed as follows:

Appendix E Investor (Bondholder)		Chapter 9 Issuing Corporation
Investment in bonds	←——→	Bonds payable
Interest revenue	←——→	Interest expense

Investments in debt securities, such as bonds or notes, can be placed in any one of three categories: trading, available-for-sale, or held to maturity, depending on the intent and ability of the investor. Some debt securities such as U.S. Treasury securities are considered cash equivalents. They are discussed in Chapter 4. U.S. Treasury securities typically have very short-term maturities, and are intended to be converted to cash within the current period. Other debt instruments, although not cash equivalents, are classified as **trading securities** if the company intends to hold them for less than a year before converting them to cash.

If the investor company intends to hold debt securities longer than a year, but not until maturity, they are categorized as **available-for-sale securities**. Both trading and available-for-sale investments in debt securities are accounted for using the fair value method in a way that's similar to how investments in equity securities are accounted for.[2]

If the investor intends and has the ability to hold a debt security until maturity, the investor accounts for the security at amortized cost, as a **held-to-maturity security**. Held-to-maturity debt securities are reported by the **amortized cost method**, which determines the carrying amount. Bond investments are initially recorded at cost (market price as a percentage × par value of bonds issued). At each semiannual interest payment date, the investor records interest revenue (one-half

[2] If debt securities are considered trading securities, accounting for them is identical to that of equity securities with insignificant influence, described earlier. The fair value method requires that unrealized gains or losses on these investments be included in other income. Available-for-sale debt securities are accounted for under the fair value method and must be adjusted to their market values at the end of each accounting period. However, the periodic adjustment for unrealized gains and losses on available-for-sale debt securities is not treated as current income, but rather as part of "other comprehensive income." Thus, such unrealized gains and losses are allowed to bypass the income statement, and eventually become part of "accumulated other comprehensive income," a separate element of Stockholders' Equity. Other comprehensive income and accumulated other comprehensive income are mentioned briefly in Chapter 10, but are considered largely beyond the scope of this text. They are covered in detail in later accounting courses.

the annual face interest rate × the face amount of the bond). In addition, whenever there is an issue premium or discount, it is amortized by adjusting the carrying amount of the bond upward or downward toward its par or face value, with an offsetting entry being made to interest revenue. Years later, at maturity, the carrying amount will have been adjusted from the original issue amount to its par or face value, and the investor will receive the face amount when redeeming the bond.

Bonds of publicly traded companies are traded on the open market, just as stocks are. Like other forms of debt, bonds pay investors interest, usually semiannually (twice a year). The (face) interest rate of a particular bond is quoted on the face of the instrument and determines the cash amount of semiannual interest the debtor company pays. Bonds are usually issued in $1,000 face (par) denominations, but they typically do not sell at par value. The price of a bond at a particular time is quoted as a percentage of its par value. Market prices of bonds fluctuate inversely with market interest rates. If market rates on competing instruments are higher than the face rate of interest on a particular bond, the bond sells at a discount (below 100% of par, or face value). For example, a quoted bond price of 96.5 means that the $1,000 bond is selling for 96.5% of par, or $965 (discounted from par value). If market rates are lower than the face rate of interest on the bond being considered, the bond sells at a premium (above 100% of par). For example, a quoted bond price of 102.5 means that the bond is selling for 102.5% of par, or $1,025 (a premium over par value).

Held-to-maturity investments are reported by the amortized cost method, which determines the carrying amount. Bond investments are initially recorded at cost (market price as a percentage × par value of bonds issued). At each semiannual interest payment date, the investor records interest revenue (one-half the annual face interest rate × the face amount of the bond). In addition, whenever there is a premium or discount at issue, it is amortized by adjusting the carrying amount of the bond upward or downward toward its par or face value, with an offsetting entry being made to interest revenue. Years later, at maturity, the carrying amount will have been adjusted from the original issue amount to its par or face value, and the investor will receive the face amount upon redemption of the bond.

As an example, suppose Intel Capital purchases $10,000 of 6% **CBS** bonds at a price of 95.2 on April 1, 2018. Intel Capital intends to hold the bonds until their maturity date, which is April 1, 2022. Interest is paid semiannually, on April 1 and October 1. Because these bonds mature on April 1, 2022, they will be outstanding for four years (48 months). In this case, Intel Capital pays a discount price for the bonds (95.2% of face value), because the market rates of interest for other similar instruments are higher than 6%.[3] The initial purchase price and carrying value of the investment is $9,520 (95.2% × $10,000). Intel Capital must amortize the discount of $480 and thus adjust the bonds' carrying amount from cost of $9,520 up to $10,000 over their 48-month term to maturity. Assume Intel Capital amortizes the discount on the bonds using the straight-line method. The entries for this bond investment on April 1 and October 1, 2018, the issue date and the first interest payment date are as follows:

A1

	A	B	C	D
1	2018			
2	Apr 1	Held-to-Maturity Investment in Bonds ($10,000 × 0.952)	9,520	
3		Cash		9,520
4		*To purchase bond investment.*		
5				
6	Oct 1	Cash ($10,000 × 0.06 × 6/12)	300	
7		Interest Revenue		300
8		*To receive semiannual interest.*		
9				
10	Oct 1	Held-to-Maturity Investment in Bonds [($10,000 – $9,520)/48] × 6	60	
11		Interest Revenue		60
12		*To amortize discount on bond investment.*		
13				

[3] The time value of money impacts the price of an investment. The time value of money is covered in Appendix F.

At December 31, 2018, Intel Capital's year-end adjustments are

	A	B	C	D
1	2018			
2	Dec 31	Interest Receivable ($10,000 × 0.06 × 3/12)	150	
3		Interest Revenue		150
4		*To accrue interest revenue.*		
5				
6	Dec 31	Held-to-Maturity Investment in Bonds [($10,000 − $9,520)/48] × 3	30	
7		Interest Revenue		30
8		*To amortize discount on bond investment.*		
9				

This amortization entry has two effects:

- It increases the Held-to-Maturity Investment in Bonds account on its march toward its maturity value, which will be $10,000 on April 1, 2022.
- It records the interest revenue earned from the increase in the carrying amount of the investment.

The financial statements of Intel Capital at December 31, 2018, would report the following for this investment in bonds:

Balance sheet at December 31, 2018:		
Current assets:		
Interest receivable	$	150
Long-term assets:		
Property, plant, and equipment		X,XXX
Held-to-maturity investment in bonds ($9,520 + $60 + $30)		9,610
Income statement for the year ended December 31, 2018:		
Other revenues:		
Interest revenue ($300 + $60 + $150 + $30)	$	540

By April 1, 2022, the maturity date of the bonds, the carrying value will have been adjusted to equal the face value of $10,000, and Intel Capital will redeem the bonds for this amount.

If market interest rates are below the face rate on these bonds on the date of purchase, they will sell at a premium, with an initial carrying value of something above $10,000. On each interest payment date, as interest revenue is recorded, the premium on the bonds will be amortized as well, reducing the amount of interest revenue and gradually reducing the carrying value of the bonds over the period of the investment to its maturity value of $10,000.

REVIEW | Investments

Accounting Vocabulary

amortized-cost method (p. 780) The method of accounting used to account for held-to-maturity investments in debt securities.

available-for-sale securities (p. 780) Debt securities that are not classified as held-to-maturity or trading securities. These securities are held for reasons other than to profit on a short-term basis, and may be classified as either current or long-term assets.

consolidated financial statements (p. 780) Financial statements that combine those of the parent company plus those of more than 50%-owned subsidiaries as if the combined entities were a single entity.

controlling interest (p. 779) Ownership of more than 50% of an investee company's voting stock. Also called *majority interest*.

debt securities (p. 773) Investments in either bonds or notes payable.

equity method (p. 777) The accounting method used to account for investments when the investor has the ability to significantly influence the operating decisions of the investee.

equity securities (p. 773) Investments in capital stock.

fair value (p. 775) The amount for which an investment can be sold to a willing purchaser on a given date. Equity securities with insignificant influence are valued at fair value on the balance sheet date.

held-to-maturity securities (p. 780) Debt securities the investor intends to and is able to hold until their maturity dates.

insignificant influence (p. 773) An ownership interest of less than 20% of the voting stock of another company.

parent company (p. 779) An investor company that owns more than 50% of the voting stock of another company.

realized gains (p. 776) Gains earned because the cash proceeds from the sale of securities exceeds their carrying value on the balance sheet.

realized losses (p. 776) Losses incurred because the cash proceeds from the sale of securities is less than their carrying value on the balance sheet.

significant influence (p. 773) An ownership interest of between 20% and 50% of the voting stock of another company.

subsidiary (p. 779) A company whose voting stock is more than 50% owned by another company.

trading securities (p. 780) Debt investments that the entity expects to sell in the near future, usually purchased with excess cash that has been generated from operations, with the intent of generating profits on the sale. Trading securities are classified as current assets.

unrealized gains (p. 775) Gains that arise before securities are sold, because the fair market value of the securities exceeds their cost.

unrealized losses (p. 775) Losses that arise before securities are sold, because the fair market value of securities drops below their cost.

Quick Check (Answers are given on page 796.)

1. Why might a company invest in another company?

a. To earn dividend income
b. To earn interest revenue
c. To ensure a steady supply of raw materials if the company being purchased is a supplier of those raw materials
d. All of the above

2. Rolling Hills Productions held investments in equity securities (in Elban Company) with a fair value of $75,000 at December 31, 2018. These investments cost Rolling Hills Productions $68,000 on January 1, 2018. What is the appropriate amount for Rolling Hills Productions to report for these investments on its December 31, 2018, balance sheet? (Assume that Rolling Hills has insignificant influence over Elban Company.)

a. $68,000
b. A $7,000 gain
c. $75,000
d. Cannot be determined from the data given

3. Return to Rolling Hills Productions in question 2. What should appear on the company's income statement for the year ended December 31, 2018, for the equity securities?

a. $75,000
b. $68,000
c. $7,000 unrealized gain
d. Cannot be determined from the data given

4. Crandall's investment is in less than 2% of **Mobil**'s stock, which Crandall expects to hold for three years and then sell. What type of investment is this?

a. Debt
b. Equity with significant influence
c. Equity with insignificant influence
d. Consolidation

5. Dumois Corporation purchased 1,500 shares of Southwest Supplies stock for $26 per share. Southwest Supplies had 100,000 shares of stock outstanding. On the next balance sheet date, Southwest Supplies stock is quoted at $25 per share. Dumois' *balance sheet* should report

a. an unrealized gain of $37,500.
b. an unrealized loss of $1,500.
c. investments of $37,500.
d. investments of $39,000.

6. Use the Dumois Corporation data in question 5. Dumois' *income statement* should report

a. an unrealized gain of $1,500.
b. an unrealized loss of $1,500.
c. investments of $37,500.
d. nothing, because Dumois hasn't sold the investment.

7. Use the Dumois Corporation data in question 5. Dumois sold the Southwest Supplies stock for $55,000 two months later. Dumois' *income statement* for the period of the sale should report a(n)

a. investment of $55,000.
b. gain on sale of $17,500.
c. unrealized gain of $1,500.
d. loss on sale of $17,500.

8. Jackson Moving & Storage Co. paid $120,000 for 25% of the common stock of McDonough Co. at the beginning of the year. During the year, McDonough earned net income of $50,000 and paid dividends of $20,000. The carrying value of Jackson's investment in McDonough at the end of the year is

a. $150,000.
b. $170,000.
c. $120,000.
d. $127,500.

9. Tide Corp. owns 40% of Granite Corporation and 30% of Rourke Company. During 2018, these companies' net incomes are as follows:

- Tide, $100,000
- Granite, $64,000
- Rourke, $35,000

How much net income should Tide report for 2018?

a. $136,100
b. $100,000
c. $199,000
d. $36,100

10. Majestic Corporation holds an investment in Cromwell bonds that pays interest each October 31. Majestic's *balance sheet* at December 31 should report

a. interest expense.
b. interest revenue.
c. interest payable.
d. interest receivable.

Excel Project
Autograded Excel Project available in **MyLab Accounting**.

ASSESS YOUR PROGRESS

Short Exercises

E-S-1. ***(Learning Objective 2: Account for investments in equity securities when the investor has insignificant influence)*** Newcomb Corporation holds a portfolio of equity securities. On September 15, Newcomb paid $83,000 for an investment in Sarelli Company stock, representing 5% of Sarelli Company stock. Newcomb plans on holding the securities a few months. On October 31, the market value of Newcomb's Sarelli investment is $90,000. For this situation, show everything Newcomb would report on its October 31 balance sheet and on its income statement for the year ended October 31. LO 2

E-S-2. ***(Learning Objective 2: Account for investments in equity securities when the investor has insignificant influence)*** Ardmore Investments purchased Columbia Corporation shares on December 16 for $110,000. Ardmore plans on holding the securities a few months. Ardmore owns less than 2% of the outstanding shares of Columbia. LO 2

1. Suppose the Columbia shares decreased in value to $88,000 at December 31. Make the Ardmore journal entry to adjust the Investment in Equity Securities account to fair value.
2. Show how Ardmore would report the Investment in Equity Securities account on its balance sheet and the unrealized gain or loss on its income statement.

E-S-3. ***(Learning Objective 2: Record an equity investment and related dividend revenue)*** Flores Company purchases 900 shares of Sherman Express common stock at the market price of $79.24 on March 23, 2018. (Flores' investment in Sherman represents less than 5% of the outstanding stock of Sherman; Flores does not have significant influence over Sherman.) Flores intends to hold this investment for more than one year. On June 22, 2018, Flores receives a cash dividend of $0.31 per share of the Sherman stock. Record the entries to (1) record the initial investment; and (2) record the receipt of the cash dividend. LO 2

E-S-4. ***(Learning Objective 2: Adjust an equity investment to fair value)*** Use the data from E-S-3 for this exercise. At year-end on December 31, 2018, the Sherman common stock that Flores holds has a market price of $88.13 per share. Assuming that Flores has no other investments, record the entry to adjust the Sherman common stock to fair value. LO 2

E-S-5. ***(Learning Objective 2: Record the sale of an equity investment)*** Use the data from E-S-3 and E-S-4 for this exercise. Flores sells its entire investment of the Sherman common stock on November 22, 2019, for a total of $67,050. Record the entries for the sale. LO 2

E-S-6. ***(Learning Objective 2: Analyze and report an equity investment)*** Athens Company completed these long-term equity investment transactions during 2018: LO 2

2018	
Apr 10	Purchased 400 shares of Technomite stock (less than 10% of Technomite's outstanding stock), paying $18 per share. Athens Company intends to hold the investment indefinitely.
Jul 22	Received a cash dividend of $1.21 per share on the Technomite stock.
Dec 31	Adjusted the Technomite investment to its current market value of $4,900.

1. Journalize Athens Company's investment transactions. Explanations are not required.
2. Assume the Technomite stock is Athens Company's only investment. Explain how these transactions will be reflected on Athens Company's income statement for the year ended December 31, 2018.
3. Show how to report the investment on Athens Company's balance sheet at December 31, 2018. Ignore income taxes.

LO 2 **E-S-7.** ***(Learning Objective 2: Account for the sale of an equity investment)*** Use the data given in E-S-6. On May 21, 2019, Athens Company sold its investment in Technomite stock for $28 per share.

1. Journalize the sale. No explanation is required.
2. How does the gain or loss you recorded differ from the gain or loss recorded on December 31, 2018?

LO 3 **E-S-8.** ***(Learning Objective 3: Analyze and report an investment in an affiliate)*** On January 1, 2018, Western Motors paid $450 million for a 40% investment in Yaza Motors. Yaza earned net income of $65 million and declared and paid cash dividends of $45 million during 2018.

1. What method should Western Motors use to account for the investment in Yaza? Give your reason.
2. Journalize these three transactions on the books of Western Motors. Show all amounts in millions of dollars (rounded to the closest million), and include an explanation for each entry.
3. Post to the Equity-Method Investment T-account. What is its balance after all the transactions are posted?

LO 3 **E-S-9.** ***(Learning Objective 3: Account for the sale of an equity-method investment)*** Use the data given in E-S-8. On January 1, 2019, Western Motors sold half of its investment in Yaza Motors. The sale price was $135 million. Calculate Western Motors' gain or loss on the sale.

LO 4 **E-S-10.** ***(Learning Objective 4: Define and explain controlling interests and consolidated financial statements)*** Answer these questions about consolidation accounting:

1. Define *parent company*. Define *subsidiary company*.
2. How do consolidated financial statements differ from the financial statements of a single company?
3. Which company's name appears on the consolidated financial statements? How much of the subsidiary's shares must the parent own before using consolidated statements?

LO 5 **E-S-11.** ***(Learning Objective 5: Record a held-to-maturity bond investment and interest when issued at par)*** On January 1, 2018, Downtown Industries purchased $8,000 of 4% JMK bonds at a price of 100 (par). Downtown intends to hold the bonds until their maturity date of January 1, 2021. The bonds pay interest semiannually on each January 1 and July 1. Record the initial purchase of the bonds on January 1, 2018, and the receipt of the interest on the first interest payment date of July 1, 2018.

LO 5 **E-S-12.** ***(Learning Objective 5: Record a held-to-maturity bond investment and interest when issued at a discount)*** Brackett Insurance purchased $60,000 of 10% AMS bonds on January 1, 2018, at a price of 85 when the market rate of interest was 12%. Brackett intends to hold the bonds until their maturity date of January 1, 2038. The bonds pay interest semiannually on each January 1 and July 1. Record the initial purchase of the bonds by Brackett on January 1, 2018, and the receipt of the interest on the first interest payment date of July 1, 2018.

LO 5 **E-S-13.** ***(Learning Objective 5: Calculate and record interest on a bond investment issued at a discount)*** Using the data from E-S-12, calculate the amount of discount amortization (using the straight-line amortization method) on July 1, 2018, and record the related journal entry. What is the total interest revenue for the first six months of 2018? (Hint: include both the interest received in E-S-12 and the discount amortization from this exercise.)

LO 5 **E-S-14.** ***(Learning Objective 5: Report a bond investment issued at a discount)*** Using the data from E-S-12, make the adjusting entries that Brackett Insurance would need to make on December 31, 2018, related to the investment in AMS bonds. How would the bonds be reported on Brackett Insurance's balance sheet as of December 31, 2018? What amount of interest revenue would be reported on Brackett Insurance's income statement for the year ended December 31, 2018, related to the AMS bonds?

E-S-15. ***(Learning Objective 5: Calculate and record interest on a bond investment issued at a premium)*** Glimmer Pools purchased $50,000 of 7% AKL bonds on January 1, 2018, at a price of 104.2 when the market rate of interest was 6%. Glimmer intends to hold the bonds until their maturity date of January 1, 2023. The bonds pay interest semiannually on each January 1 and July 1. Calculate the amount of premium amortization (using the straight-line amortization method) on July 1, 2018, and record the related journal entries. What is the total interest revenue for the first six months of 2018? LO 5

E-S-16. ***(Learning Objective 5: Report a bond investment issued at a premium)*** Using the data from E-S-15, make the adjusting entries that Glimmer Pools would need to make on December 31, 2018, related to the investment in AKL bonds. How would the bonds be reported on Glimmer Pools' balance sheet as of December 31, 2018? What amount of interest revenue related to the AKL bonds would be reported on Glimmer Pools' income statement for the year ended December 31, 2018? LO 5

Exercises MyLab Accounting

Group A

E-E-17A. ***(Learning Objective 2: Apply GAAP for equity investments)*** Lancaster Corporation, an investment banking company, often has extra cash to invest. Suppose Lancaster buys 500 shares of Knight Corporation stock at $40 per share, representing less than 5% of Knight's outstanding stock. Lancaster expects to hold the Knight stock for one month and then sell it. The purchase occurs on December 15, 2018. On December 31, the market price of one share of Knight stock is $47 per share. LO 2

Requirements

1. What type of investment is this for Lancaster? Give the reason for your answer.
2. Record Lancaster's purchase of the Knight stock on December 15 and the adjustment to market value on December 31.
3. Show how Lancaster would report this investment on its balance sheet at December 31 and any gain or loss on its income statement for the year ended December 31, 2018.

E-E-18A. ***(Learning Objective 2: Record transactions for equity securities)*** LO 2
Journalize the following long-term, equity security transactions of Jeakin Department Stores:

- **a.** Purchased 450 shares of Fordham Fine Foods common stock at $33 per share (less than 10% of Fordham's outstanding stock), with the intent of holding the stock for the indefinite future.
- **b.** Received a cash dividend of $1.30 per share on the Fordham investment.
- **c.** At year-end, adjusted the investment account to fair value of $39 per share.
- **d.** Sold the Fordham stock for $28 per share.

E-E-19A. ***(Learning Objective 2: Analyze and report investments in equity securities)*** LO 2
During the most recent year, Quinn Co. bought 2,800 shares of Germana-Hall Corporation common stock at $35, 590 shares of Barlengo Corporation stock at $45.50, and 1,000 shares of Frumley Corporation stock at $70. At December 31, Hoover's Online reports Germana-Hall stock at $28.13, Barlengo at $48.00, and Frumley at $63.25. Quinn does not own more than 10% of the outstanding stock in any of its investments.

Requirements

1. Determine the cost and the fair value of the long-term investment portfolio at December 31.
2. Record Quinn's adjusting entry at December 31.
3. What would Quinn report on its income statement and balance sheet at year-end for the information given? Ignore income taxes.

LO 3

E-E-20A. ***(Learning Objective 3: Account for transactions using the equity method)*** Shay Corporation owns equity-method investments in several companies. Shay paid $1,600,000 to acquire a 25% investment in Faulk Software Company. Faulk reported net income of $620,000 for the first year and declared and paid cash dividends of $480,000.

Requirements

1. Record the following in Shay's journal: (a) the purchase of the investment, (b) Shay's proportion of Faulk's net income, and (c) the receipt of the cash dividends.
2. What is the ending balance in Shay's investment account?

LO 3

E-E-21A. ***(Learning Objective 3: Analyze gains or losses on equity-method investments)*** Without making journal entries, record the transactions of E-E-20A directly in the Shay T-account, Equity-method Investment. Assume that after all the noted transactions took place, Shay sold its entire investment in Faulk for cash of $1,600,000. How much is Shay's gain or loss on the sale of the investment?

LO 3

E-E-22A. ***(Learning Objective 3: Apply the appropriate accounting method for a 30% investment)*** Kingman Financial paid $590,000 for a 30% investment in the common stock of Cavalier, Inc. For the first year, Cavalier reported net income of $240,000, and at year-end declared and paid cash dividends of $110,000. On the balance-sheet date, the fair value of Kingman's investment in Cavalier stock was $390,000.

Requirements

1. Which method is appropriate for Kingman to use in accounting for its investment in Cavalier? Why?
2. Show everything that Kingman would report for the investment and any investment revenue in its year-end financial statements.

LO 5

E-E-23A. ***(Learning Objective 5: Analyze and report held-to-maturity security transactions)*** On September 30, 2018, Baytex, Inc., purchased 6.8% bonds of Whitmore Corporation at 98 as a long-term, held-to-maturity investment. The maturity value of the bonds will be $35,000 on September 30, 2023. The bonds pay interest on March 31 and September 30. Baytex's fiscal year end is December 31.

Requirements

1. What method should Baytex use to account for its investment in the Whitmore Corp. bonds?
2. Using the straight-line method of amortizing the discount on bonds, journalize all of Baytex's transactions on the bonds for 2018.
3. Show how Baytex would report everything related to the bond investment on its balance sheet at its year-end, December 31, 2018.

Group B

LO 2

E-E-24B. ***(Learning Objective 2: Apply GAAP for equity investments)*** Amherst Corporation, an investment banking company, often has extra cash to invest. Suppose Amherst buys 900 shares of Hurricane Corporation stock at $57 per share, representing less than 5% of Hurricane's outstanding stock. Amherst expects to hold the Hurricane stock for one month and then sell it. The purchase occurs on December 15, 2018. On December 31, the market price of a share of Hurricane stock is $58 per share.

Requirements

1. What type of investment is this for Amherst? Give the reason for your answer.
2. Record Amherst's purchase of the Hurricane stock on December 15 and the adjustment to market value on December 31.
3. Show how Amherst would report this investment on its balance sheet at December 31 and any gain or loss on its income statement for the year ended December 31, 2018.

LO 2

E-E-25B. ***(Learning Objective 2: Record transactions for equity securities)*** Journalize the following long-term, equity investment transactions of Johnson Department Stores:

a. Purchased 420 shares of Gates Fine Foods common stock at $35 per share (less than 10% of Gates' outstanding stock), with the intent of holding the stock for the indefinite future.
b. Received a cash dividend of $1.90 per share on the Gates investment.
c. At year-end, adjusted the investment account to fair value of $37 per share.
d. Sold the Gates stock for $24 per share.

LO 2

E-E-26B. ***(Learning Objective 2: Analyze and report investments in equity securities)*** During the most recent year, Smither Travelers Co. bought 3,400 shares of German Corporation common stock at $37, 630 shares of British Corporation stock at $47.00, and 1,400 shares of Milan Corporation stock at $76. At December 31, Hoover's Online reports German stock at $28.88, British at $49.00, and Milan at $69.25. Smither Travelers does not own more than 10% of the outstanding stock in any of its investments.

Requirements

1. Determine the cost and the fair value of the long-term investment portfolio at December 31.
2. Record Smither Travelers' adjusting entry at December 31.
3. What would Smither Travelers report on its income statement and balance sheet at year-end for the information given? Ignore income taxes.

LO 3

E-E-27B. ***(Learning Objective 3: Account for transactions using the equity method)*** McCloud Corporation owns equity-method investments in several companies. McCloud paid $1,800,000 to acquire a 30% investment in Brown Software Company. Brown reported net income of $660,000 for the first year and declared and paid cash dividends of $460,000.

Requirements

1. Record the following in McCloud's journal: (a) the purchase of the investment, (b) McCloud's proportion of Brown's net income, and (c) the receipt of the cash dividends.
2. What is the ending balance in McCloud's investment account?

LO 3 **E-E-28B.** ***(Learning Objective 3: Analyze gains or losses on equity-method investments)*** Without making journal entries, record the transactions of E-E-27B directly in the McCloud T-account, Equity-method Investment. Assume that after all the noted transactions took place, McCloud sold its entire investment in Brown for cash of $1,400,000. How much is McCloud's gain or loss on the sale of the investment?

LO 3 **E-E-29B.** ***(Learning Objective 3: Apply the appropriate accounting method for a 20% investment)*** Conroy Financial paid $530,000 for a 20% investment in the common stock of Maverick, Inc. For the first year, Maverick reported net income of $270,000, and at year-end declared and paid cash dividends of $115,000. On the balance-sheet date, the fair value of Conroy's investment in Maverick stock was $410,000.

Requirements

1. Which method is appropriate for Conroy to use in its accounting for its investment in Maverick? Why?
2. Show everything that Conroy would report for the investment and any investment revenue in its year-end financial statements.

LO 5 **E-E-30B.** ***(Learning Objective 5: Analyze and report held-to-maturity security transactions)*** On September 30, 2018, Rittex, Inc., purchased 5% bonds of McPhee Corporation at 97 as a long-term, held-to-maturity investment. The maturity value of the bonds will be $46,000 on September 30, 2023. The bonds pay interest on March 31 and September 30. Rittex's fiscal year end is December 31.

Requirements

1. What method should Rittex use to account for its investment in the McPhee Corp. bonds?
2. Using the straight-line method of amortizing the discount on bonds, journalize all of Rittex's transactions on the bonds for 2018.
3. Show how Rittex would report everything related to the bond investment on its balance sheet at its year-end, December 31, 2018.

Quiz

Test your understanding of investments by answering the following questions. Select the best choice from among the possible answers given.

E-Q-31. For an investment to be classified as a current asset,

a. the investment must be easily convertible to cash.
b. the investor must intend to convert the investment to cash within one year or current operating cycle, whichever is longer, or use it to pay a current liability.
c. both a and b must be met for the investment to be classified as a current asset.
d. neither a nor b are relevant to the classification of an investment as a current asset.

E-Q-32. Continental Bank, a nationwide banking company, owns many types of investments. Continental paid $550,000 for equity securities on December 5. Continental owns less than 10% of the stock of the companies in which it invests. Two weeks later, Continental received a $37,000 cash dividend. On December 31, these equity securities were quoted at a market price of $554,000. Continental's December income statement would include an

a. unrealized loss of $4,000.
b. unrealized gain of $41,000.
c. unrealized gain of $4,000.
d. unrealized loss of $41,000.

E-Q-33. Refer to the Continental data in E-Q-32. On December 31, Continental's balance sheet should report

a. dividend revenue of $37,000.
b. investment in equity securities of $554,000.
c. investment in equity securities of $550,000.
d. an unrealized gain of $4,000.

Questions 34–35 use the following data:

Reliable Networks owns the following long-term equity investments (it does not have significant influence over any of its investments):

Company	Number of Shares	Cost per Share	Year-end Fair Value per Share	Dividend per Share
Brine Corp.	1,000	$56	$77	$2.20
Signality, Inc.	200	8	10	1.70
Solo Ltd.	700	16	30	1.20

E-Q-34. Reliable's balance sheet at year-end should report

a. investments of $100,000.
b. an unrealized loss of $11,600.
c. investments of $68,800.
d. dividend revenue of $3,380.

E-Q-35. Reliable's income statement for the year should report

a. investments of $68,800.
b. an unrealized loss of $31,200.
c. dividend revenue of $3,380.
d. a gain on sale of investment of $31,200.

E-Q-36. Dividends received on an equity-method investment

a. decrease the investment account.
b. increase stockholders' equity.
c. increase dividend revenue.
d. increase the investment account.

E-Q-37. Consolidation accounting

a. eliminates all liabilities.
b. reports the receivables and payables of the parent company only.
c. combines the accounts of the parent company and its subsidiary companies.
d. all of the above

E-Q-38. On November 1, 2018, Sigma Inc. invests in $1,000,000 of 5%, 10-year bonds issued by **Microsoft Corporation**, intending to hold the bonds until their maturity. The bonds pay interest each January 1 and July 1. What account related to the bonds will be on Sigma's income statement for the year ended December 31, 2018?

a. Interest revenue
b. Interest expense
c. Interest receivable
d. Interest payable

Problems MyLab Accounting

Group A

LO 2

E-P-39A. *(Learning Objective 2: Apply GAAP to short-term investments)* During the fourth quarter of 2018, Rainbarrel, Inc. generated excess cash, which the company invested in equity securities as follows:

2018	
Nov 16	Purchased 1,200 common shares as an investment in equity securities, paying $6 per share. Rainbarrel owns less than 10% of the outstanding stock in the companies in which it invests.
Dec 16	Received cash dividend of $0.35 per share on the equity securities.
Dec 31	Adjusted the equity securities to fair value of $4 per share.

Requirements

1. Open T-accounts for Cash (including its beginning balance of $23,000), Investment in Equity Securities, Dividend Revenue, and Unrealized Gain (Loss) on Equity Securities.
2. Journalize the foregoing transactions and post to the T-accounts.
3. Show how to report the short-term investment on Rainbarrel's balance sheet at December 31, 2018.
4. Show how to report whatever should appear on Rainbarrel's income statement for the year ended December 31, 2018.
5. Rainbarrel sold the equity securities for $6,000 on January 14, 2019. Journalize the sale.

LO **2, 3**

E-P-40A. ***(Learning Objectives 2, 3: Analyze and report various long-term investment transactions on the balance sheet and income statement)*** Oregon Exchange Company completed the following long-term investment transactions during 2018:

2018	
May 12	Purchased 18,200 shares, which make up 25% of the common stock of Nashua Corporation at total cost of $340,000.
Jul 9	Received annual cash dividend of $1.23 per share on the Nashua investment.
Sep 16	Purchased 1,000 shares of Columbus, Inc., common stock (less than 5% of its outstanding stock) paying $41.50 per share.
Oct 30	Received cash dividend of $0.33 per share on the Columbus investment.
Dec 31	Received annual report from Nashua Corporation. Net income for the year was $540,000.

At year-end, the fair value of the Columbus stock is $30,100. The fair value of the Nashua stock is $658,000.

Requirements

1. For which investment is fair value used in the accounting? Why is fair value used for one investment and not the other?
2. Show what Oregon Exchange would report on its year-end balance sheet and income statement for these investment transactions. It is helpful to use a T-account for the Equity-method Investment account. Ignore income tax.

LO **2, 3**

E-P-41A. ***(Learning Objectives 2, 3: Analyze and report equity and equity-method investments)*** The beginning balance sheet of Homesby Corporation included the following long-term asset:

Equity-method Investment in Jasmine Software	$618,000

Homesby completed the following investment transactions during the year:

Mar 16	Purchased 2,700 shares Lowell, Inc. common stock (10% of Lowell's stock) as a long-term equity investment, paying $12.50 per share.
May 21	Received a cash dividend of $2.25 per share on the Lowell investment.
Aug 17	Received a cash dividend of $83,000 from Jasmine Software.
Dec 31	Received annual reports from Jasmine Software; net income for the year was $550,000. Of this amount, Homesby's share was 27%.

At year-end, the fair values of Homesby's investments were as follows: Lowell, $39,000; Jasmine, $747,000.

Requirements

1. Record the transactions in the journal of Homesby.
2. Post entries to the T-account for Equity-method Investment in Jasmine Software, and determine its balance at December 31.
3. Show how to report the Investment in Equity Securities and the Equity-method Investment in Jasmine Software accounts on Homesby's balance sheet at December 31.

LO 5

E-P-42A. ***(Learning Objective 5: Analyze and report held-to-maturity investments purchased at a discount)*** Insurance companies and pension plans hold large quantities of bond investments. Sea Insurance Corp. purchased $2,000,000 of 9% bonds of Sheehan, Inc., for 96 on January 1, 2018. These bonds pay interest on January 1 and July 1 each year. They mature on January 1, 2022. Sea Insurance's fiscal year end is October 31.

Requirements

1. Journalize Sea's purchase of the bonds as a long-term investment on January 1, 2018 (to be held to maturity), receipt of cash interest, and amortization of the bond discount at July 1, 2018. The straight-line method is appropriate for amortizing the bond investment.
2. Journalize the accrual of interest receivable and amortization of the discount on October 31, 2018 (round the answer to the nearest whole number).

Group B

LO 2

E-P-43B. ***(Learning Objective 2: Apply GAAP to short-term investments)*** During the fourth quarter of 2018, Harvestology, Inc. generated excess cash, which the company invested in equity securities as follows:

2018	
Nov 17	Purchased 1,300 common shares as an investment in equity securities, paying $6 per share. Harvestology owns less than 10% of the outstanding stock in the companies in which it invests.
Dec 19	Received cash dividend of $0.28 per share on the equity securities.
Dec 31	Adjusted the equity securities to fair value of $4 per share.

Requirements

1. Open T-accounts for Cash (including its beginning balance of $21,000), Investment in Equity Securities, Dividend Revenue, and Unrealized Gain (Loss) on Equity Securities.
2. Journalize the foregoing transactions and post to the T-accounts.
3. Show how to report the short-term investment on Harvestology's balance sheet at December 31, 2018.
4. Show how to report whatever should appear on Harvestology's income statement for the year ended December 31, 2018.
5. Harvestology sold the equity securities for $6,500 on January 14, 2019. Journalize the sale.

LO 2, 3

E-P-44B. ***(Learning Objectives 2, 3: Analyze and report various long-term investment transactions on the balance sheet and income statement)*** Illinois Exchange Company completed the following long-term investment transactions during 2018:

2018	
May 12	Purchased 21,000 shares, which make up 45% of the common stock of Exeter Corporation at total cost of $340,000.
Jul 9	Received annual cash dividend of $1.21 per share on Exeter investment.
Sep 16	Purchased 1,100 shares of Amsterdam, Inc., common stock (less than 5% of its outstanding stock) paying $42.25 per share.
Oct 30	Received cash dividend of $0.34 per share on the Amsterdam investment.
Dec 31	Received annual report from Exeter Corporation. Net income for the year was $580,000.

At year-end, the fair value of the Amsterdam stock is $30,900. The fair value of the Exeter stock is $652,000.

Requirements

1. For which investment is fair value used in the accounting? Why is fair value used for one investment and not the other?
2. Show what Illinois Exchange would report on its year-end balance sheet and income statement for these investment transactions. It is helpful to use a T-account for the Equity-method Investment account. Ignore income tax.

E-P-45B. ***(Learning Objectives 2, 3: Analyze and report equity and equity-method investments)*** The beginning balance sheet of Lansing Corporation included the following long-term asset: LO 2, 3

Equity-method Investment in Rockaway Software	$615,000

Lansing completed the following investment transactions during the year:

Mar 16	Purchased 1,500 shares of Lowell, Inc. common stock (10% of Lowell's stock) as a long-term equity investment, paying $12.75 per share.
May 21	Received a cash dividend of $2.50 per share on the Lowell investment.
Aug 17	Received a cash dividend of $88,000 from Rockaway Software.
Dec 31	Received annual reports from Rockaway Software; net income for the year was $500,000. Of this amount, Lansing's share was 21%.

At year-end, the fair values of Lansing's investments were as follows: Lowell, $26,100; Rockaway Software, $749,000.

Requirements

1. Record the transactions in the journal of Lansing.
2. Post entries to the T-account for Equity-method Investment in Rockaway Software, and determine its balance at December 31.
3. Show how to report the Investment in Equity Securities and the Equity-method Investment in Rockaway Software accounts on Lansing's balance sheet at December 31.

E-P-46B. ***(Learning Objective 5: Analyze and report held-to-maturity investments purchased at a discount)*** Insurance companies and pension plans hold large quantities of bond investments. Rainy Day Corp. purchased $1,500,000 of 8% bonds of Quantrill, Inc., for 95 on January 1, 2018. These bonds pay interest on January 1 and July 1 each year. They mature on January 1, 2022. Rainy Day's fiscal year end is October 31. LO 5

Requirements

1. Journalize Rainy Day's purchase of the bonds as a long-term investment on January 1, 2018 (to be held to maturity), receipt of cash interest, and amortization of the bond discount at July 1, 2018. The straight-line method is appropriate for amortizing the bond investment.
2. Journalize the accrual of interest receivable and amortization of the discount on October 31, 2018 (round answer to the nearest whole number).

APPLY YOUR KNOWLEDGE

Decision Case

LO 2, 3, 5

E-C-47. ***(Learning Objectives 2, 3, 5: Make an investment sale decision)*** Callie Tarres is the general manager of Brennon Company, which provides data-management services for physicians in the Columbus, Ohio, area. Brennon Company is having a rough year. Net income trails projections for the year by almost $75,000. This shortfall is especially important because Brennon plans to issue stock early next year and needs to show investors that the company can meet its earnings targets.

Brennon holds several investments purchased a few years ago. Even though investing in stocks is outside of Brennon's core business of data-management services, Tarres thinks these investments may help the company meet its net income goal for the year. She is considering what to do with the following investments:

1. Brennon owns 50% of the common stock of Ohio Office Systems, which provides the business forms Brennon uses. Ohio Office Systems has lost money for the past two years but still has a retained earnings balance of $550,000. Tarres thinks she can get the Ohio Office Systems' treasurer to declare a $160,000 cash dividend, half of which would go to Brennon.
2. Brennon owns a bond investment purchased eight years ago for $250,000. The purchase price represents a discount from the bonds' maturity value of $400,000. These bonds mature two years from now, and Brennon purchased them as a long-term investment intending to hold them until they matured. Their current market value is $380,000. Tarres has checked with an investment representative, and she is considering selling the bonds. The investment firm would charge a 1% commission on the sale transaction.
3. Brennon owns 5,000 shares of Microsoft stock valued at $73 per share as a long-term investment. One year ago, Microsoft stock was worth only $54 per share. Brennon purchased the Microsoft stock for $37 per share. Tarres wonders whether Brennon should sell the Microsoft stock.

Requirement

1. Evaluate all three actions as a way for Brennon Company to generate the needed amount of income. Recommend the best way for Brennon to achieve its net income goal.

Quick Check Answers

1. *d*	5. *c*	8. *d*
2. *c*	6. *b*	9. *a*
3. *c*	7. *b*	10. *d*
4. *c*		

Try It Solutions

Page 777

1.

Investment in Equity Securities

	8,660	
	340	
Balance	9,000	

These investments in equity securities are current assets as reported on the 2018 balance sheet, and Waverly's 2018 income statement will report as follows (amounts in millions):

Balance sheet		Income statement	
Current assets:		Other revenue and expense:	
Cash	$ XX	Unrealized Gain on Equity Securities	
Investment in Equity Securities	9,000	($9,000 − $8,660)	$ 340

2.

		(In millions)
Cash	8,700	
Loss on Sale of Equity Securities	300	
Investment in Equity Securities		9,000
Sold investments at a loss.		

Investment in Equity Securities

	8,660	
	340	9,000
Balance	-0-	

Page 779

Equity-method Investment

Cost	67,900	Dividends	22,000**
Income	32,000*		
Balance	77,900		

*$80,000 × .40 = $32,000
**$55,000 × .40 = $22,000

Appendix F —Time Value of Money

EXPLAIN THE IMPACT THE TIME VALUE OF MONEY HAS ON CERTAIN TYPES OF INVESTMENTS

1 **Explain** the impact the time value of money has on certain types of investments

Which would you rather have: $1,000 received today, or $1,000 received a year from now? A logical person would answer: "I'd rather have the cash now, because I can invest it at some interest rate and have more money a year from now." The term **future value** means the sum of money that an investment will be "worth" at a specified time in the future, assuming a certain interest rate. The term *time value of money* refers to the fact that money earns interest over time. *Interest* is the cost of using money. To borrowers, interest is the fee paid to the lender for the period of the loan. To lenders, interest is the revenue earned from allowing someone else to use their money for a period of time.

Whether making investments or borrowing money, we must always recognize the interest we receive or pay. Otherwise, we overlook an important part of the transaction. Suppose you invest $4,545 in corporate bonds that pay 10% interest (based on the original amount invested) each year. After one year, the value of your investment will have grown to $5,000, as shown in Exhibit F-1:

Exhibit F-1 | Future Value of an Investment

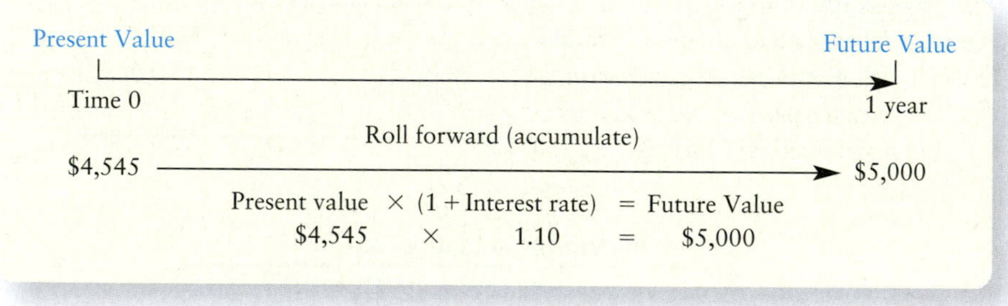

The difference between your original (present) investment ($4,545) and its future value ($5,000) is the amount of interest revenue you will earn during the year ($455). The amount of interest depends on the amount of time the money is invested. The time value of money plays a key role in measuring the value of certain long-term investments as well as long-term debt.

If the money were invested for five years, you would have to perform five calculations like the one described in Exhibit F-1 to determine the investment's value. You would also have to consider the compound interest your investment would earn. *Compound interest* is not only the interest you earn on your principal amount but also the interest you receive on the interest you have already earned.

To calculate the future value of an investment, we need three inputs:

1. The *amount of the initial payment* (or *receipt)*
2. The *length of time* between investment and future receipt (or payment)
3. The *interest rate*

The following table shows the interest revenue earned on the original $4,545 investment each year for five years when the interest rate is 10%:

End of Year	Interest	Future Value
0	—	$4,545
1	$4,545 × 0.10 = $455	5,000
2	5,000 × 0.10 = 500	5,500
3	5,500 × 0.10 = 550	6,050
4	6,050 × 0.10 = 605	6,655
5	6,655 × 0.10 = 666	7,321

As the table shows, earning 10% compounded annually, a $4,545 investment grows to $5,000 at the end of one year, to $5,500 at the end of two years, and to $7,321 at the end of five years.

Present Value

Often a person knows or is able to estimate a future amount and needs to determine the related present value (PV). The term **present value** means today's value of a future payment or series of future payments, assuming that those payments include interest at the current market rate. In Exhibit F-1, the present value and future value are on opposite ends of the same timeline. Suppose an investment promises to pay you $5,000 at the end of one year. How much would you pay now to acquire this investment? You would be willing to pay the present value of the $5,000 future amount, which, at 10% interest, is $4,545.

Like future value, present value depends on three factors:

1. The *amount of payment* (or *receipt*)
2. The *length of time* between investment and future receipt (or payment)
3. The *interest rate*

The process of computing a present value is called **discounting** because the present value is *less* than the future value.

In our investment example, the future receipt is $5,000. The investment period is one year. Assume that you demand an annual interest rate of 10% on your investment. With all three factors specified, you can compute the present value of $5,000 at 10% for one year as follows:

$$\text{Present value} = \frac{\text{Future value}}{1 + \text{Interest rate}} = \frac{\$5{,}000}{1.10} = \$4{,}545$$

By turning the data around into a future-value problem, we can verify the present-value computation:

Amount invested (present value)	$4,545
Expected earnings ($4,545 × 0.10)	455
Amount to be received one year from now (future value)	$5,000

This example illustrates that present value and future value are based on variations of the same equation:

$$\text{Future value} = \text{Present value} \times (1 + \text{Interest rate})^n$$

$$\text{Present value} = \frac{\text{Future value}}{(1 + \text{Interest rate})^n}$$

Where n = number of periods

If the $5,000 is to be received two years from now, you will pay only $4,132 for the investment, as Exhibit F-2 shows.

Exhibit F-2 | Present Value: An Example

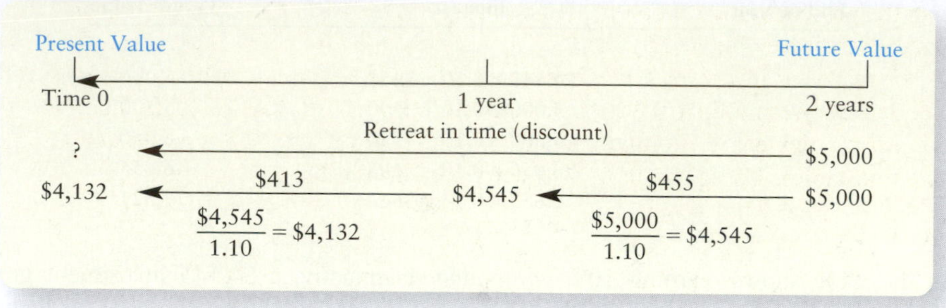

By turning the data around, we verify that $4,132 accumulates to $5,000 at 10% for two years:

Amount invested (present value)	$4,132
Expected earnings for first year ($4,132 × 0.10)	413
Value of investment after one year	4,545
Expected earnings for second year ($4,545 × 0.10)	455
Amount to be received two years from now (future value)	$5,000

$$\text{Formula: Present value} = \frac{\text{Future value}}{(1 + \text{Interest rate})^n}$$

$$4{,}132 = \frac{5{,}000}{(1 + 0.10)^2}$$

$$\text{Future value} = \text{Present value} \times (1 + \text{Interest rate})^n$$

$$5{,}000 = \$4{,}132 \times (1 + 0.10)^2$$

You would pay $4,132—the present value of $5,000—to receive the $5,000 at the end of two years if the interest rate is 10% per year. The $868 difference between the amount invested ($4,132) and the amount to be received ($5,000) is the return on the investment, and the sum of the two interest receipts: $413 + $455 = $868.

Present-Value Tables

Calculating the present value of an investment spanning many years "by hand" is time consuming and presents too many opportunities for arithmetic errors. Present-value tables simplify our work. Let's review our examples of present value by using Exhibit F-3, Present Value of $1.

Exhibit F-3 | Present Value of $1

Present Value of $1

Periods	4%	5%	6%	7%	8%	10%	12%	14%	16%
1	0.962	0.952	0.943	0.935	0.926	0.909	0.893	0.877	0.862
2	0.925	0.907	0.890	0.873	0.857	0.826	0.797	0.769	0.743
3	0.889	0.864	0.840	0.816	0.794	0.751	0.712	0.675	0.641
4	0.855	0.823	0.792	0.763	0.735	0.683	0.636	0.592	0.552
5	0.822	0.784	0.747	0.713	0.681	0.621	0.567	0.519	0.476
6	0.790	0.746	0.705	0.666	0.630	0.564	0.507	0.456	0.410
7	0.760	0.711	0.665	0.623	0.583	0.513	0.452	0.400	0.354
8	0.731	0.677	0.627	0.582	0.540	0.467	0.404	0.351	0.305
9	0.703	0.645	0.592	0.544	0.500	0.424	0.361	0.308	0.263
10	0.676	0.614	0.558	0.508	0.463	0.386	0.322	0.270	0.227
11	0.650	0.585	0.527	0.475	0.429	0.350	0.287	0.237	0.195
12	0.625	0.557	0.497	0.444	0.397	0.319	0.257	0.208	0.168
13	0.601	0.530	0.469	0.415	0.368	0.290	0.229	0.182	0.145
14	0.577	0.505	0.442	0.388	0.340	0.263	0.205	0.160	0.125
15	0.555	0.481	0.417	0.362	0.315	0.239	0.183	0.140	0.108
16	0.534	0.458	0.394	0.339	0.292	0.218	0.163	0.123	0.093
17	0.513	0.436	0.371	0.317	0.270	0.198	0.146	0.108	0.080
18	0.494	0.416	0.350	0.296	0.250	0.180	0.130	0.095	0.069
19	0.475	0.396	0.331	0.277	0.232	0.164	0.116	0.083	0.060
20	0.456	0.377	0.312	0.258	0.215	0.149	0.104	0.073	0.051

For the 10% investment for one year, we find the junction of the 10% column and row 4 (corresponding to period 1) in Exhibit F-3. The figure 0.909 is computed as follows: 1/1.10 = 0.909. This work has been done for us, and only the present value factors are given in the table. To figure the present value for $5,000, we multiply 0.909 by $5,000. The result is $4,545, which matches the result we obtained by hand.

For the two-year investment, we read down the 10% column and across row 5 (corresponding to period 2). We multiply 0.826 (computed as $1/1.10^2 = 0.826$) by $5,000 and get $4,130, which confirms our earlier computation of $4,132 (the difference is due to rounding in the present-value table). Using the table, we can compute the present value of any single future amount.

Present Value of an Ordinary Annuity

The investment illustrated in Exhibit F-2 provided the investor with only a single future receipt ($5,000 at the end of two years). In contrast, an ordinary annuity is an investment that provides multiple receipts of an equal amount at fixed year-end intervals over the investment's duration. How is an ordinary annuity calculated? Consider an investment that promises annual cash receipts of $10,000 to be received at the end of each year for three years. Assume that you demand a 12% return on your investment. What is the investment's present value? That is, what would you pay today to acquire the investment? The investment spans three periods, and you would pay the sum of three present values. The computation follows:

Year	Annual Cash Receipt	Present Value of $1 at 12% (Exhibit F-3)	Present Value of Annual Cash Receipt
1	$10,000	0.893	$ 8,930
2	10,000	0.797	7,970
3	10,000	0.712	7,120
Total present value of investment..............			$24,020

The present value of this annuity is $24,020. By paying this amount today, you will receive $10,000 at the end of each of the three years while earning 12% on your investment.

This example illustrates the repetitive computations that must be made to determine the three present amounts. One way to ease the computational burden is to add the three successive present value factors (0.893 + 0.797 + 0.712) and multiply their sum (2.402) by the annual cash receipt ($10,000) to obtain the present value of the annuity ($10,000 × 2.402 = $24,020).

An easier approach is to use a present value of an ordinary annuity table. Exhibit F-4 shows the present value of $1 to be received periodically for a given number of periods, at the end of each period. The present value factor for a three-period annuity at 12% is 2.402 (the junction of row 6 [corresponding to period 3] and the 12% column). Thus, $10,000 received annually at the end of each of three years, discounted at 12%, is $24,020 ($10,000 × 2.402), which is the present value.

Exhibit F-4 | Present Value of Ordinary Annuity of $1

Present Value of Ordinary Annuity of $1

Periods	4%	5%	6%	7%	8%	10%	12%	14%	16%
1	0.962	0.952	0.943	0.935	0.926	0.909	0.893	0.877	0.862
2	1.886	1.859	1.833	1.808	1.783	1.736	1.690	1.647	1.605
3	2.775	2.723	2.673	2.624	2.577	2.487	2.402	2.322	2.246
4	3.630	3.546	3.465	3.387	3.312	3.170	3.037	2.914	2.798
5	4.452	4.329	4.212	4.100	3.993	3.791	3.605	3.433	3.274
6	5.242	5.076	4.917	4.767	4.623	4.355	4.111	3.889	3.685
7	6.002	5.786	5.582	5.389	5.206	4.868	4.564	4.288	4.039
8	6.733	6.463	6.210	5.971	5.747	5.335	4.968	4.639	4.344
9	7.435	7.108	6.802	6.515	6.247	5.759	5.328	4.946	4.608
10	8.111	7.722	7.360	7.024	6.710	6.145	5.650	5.216	4.833
11	8.760	8.306	7.887	7.499	7.139	6.495	5.938	5.453	5.029
12	9.385	8.863	8.384	7.943	7.536	6.814	6.194	5.660	5.197
13	9.986	9.394	8.853	8.358	7.904	7.103	6.424	5.842	5.342
14	10.563	9.899	9.295	8.745	8.244	7.367	6.628	6.002	5.468
15	11.118	10.380	9.712	9.108	8.559	7.606	6.811	6.142	5.575
16	11.652	10.838	10.106	9.447	8.851	7.824	6.974	6.265	5.668
17	12.166	11.274	10.477	9.763	9.122	8.022	7.120	6.373	5.749
18	12.659	11.690	10.828	10.059	9.372	8.201	7.250	6.467	5.818
19	13.134	12.085	11.158	10.336	9.604	8.365	7.366	6.550	5.877
20	13.590	12.462	11.470	10.594	9.818	8.514	7.469	6.623	5.929

Using Microsoft Excel to Calculate Present Value

While tables such as Exhibits F-3 and F-4 are helpful, they are limited to the interest rates in the columns or the periods of time in the rows. A computer program like Microsoft Excel allows us to use an infinite range of interest rates and periods. For that reason, most businesspeople solve present-value problems quickly and easily using Excel rather than tables.

- *To compute the present value of a single payment*, the following formula applies:

$$= \text{Payment}/(1 + i)^n$$

where i = interest rate
n = number of periods

- In Excel, we use the ^ symbol to indicate the exponent. To illustrate, suppose you expect to receive a $500,000 payment four years from now, and the interest rates is 8%. You would enter the following formula in Excel:

= 500000/(1.08)^4

You should calculate a present value of $367,514.93 (rounded to $367,515).

■ *To compute the present value of an annuity (stream of payments)*, open an Excel spreadsheet to a blank cell. Click the insert function button (f_x). Then select the "Financial" category from the drop-down box. The following box will appear:

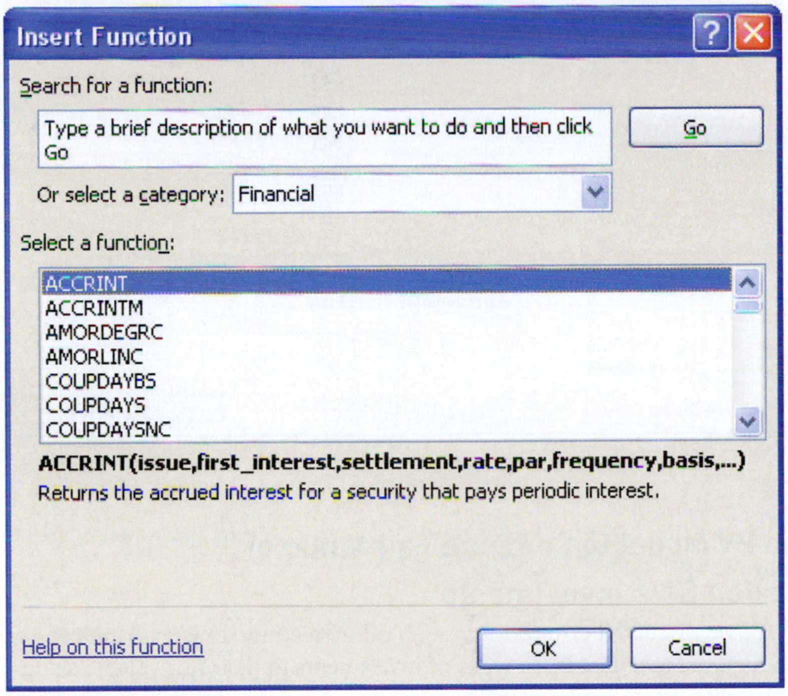

Windows 10, Microsoft Corporation

Scroll down the function list and select "PV." A description of the PV function will display beneath the function list, along with the following line: **PV (rate, nper, pmt, fv, type)**. Double-click PV, and the following box will appear:

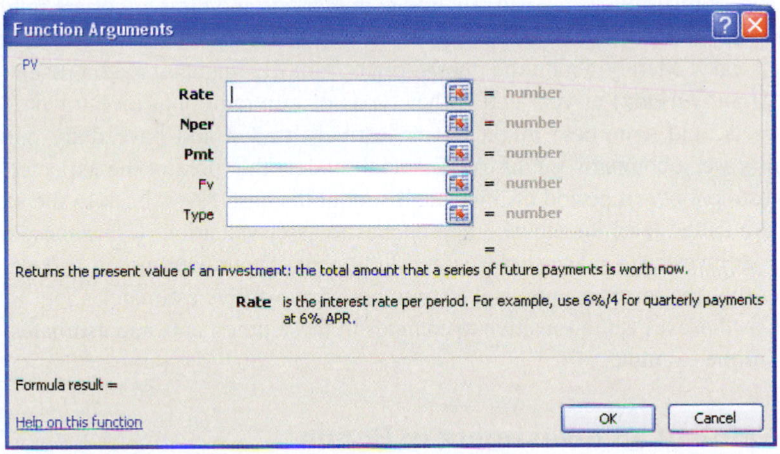

Windows 10, Microsoft Corporation

Enter the interest rate, the number of periods, and the payment (as a negative number). The present value of the annuity will appear at the bottom of the box after the "=" sign.

To illustrate, notice that we have assumed an investment that is expected to return $20,000 per year for 20 years, and that the interest rate is 8%. The present value of this annuity (rounded to the nearest cent) is $196,362.95. It is computed with Excel as follows:

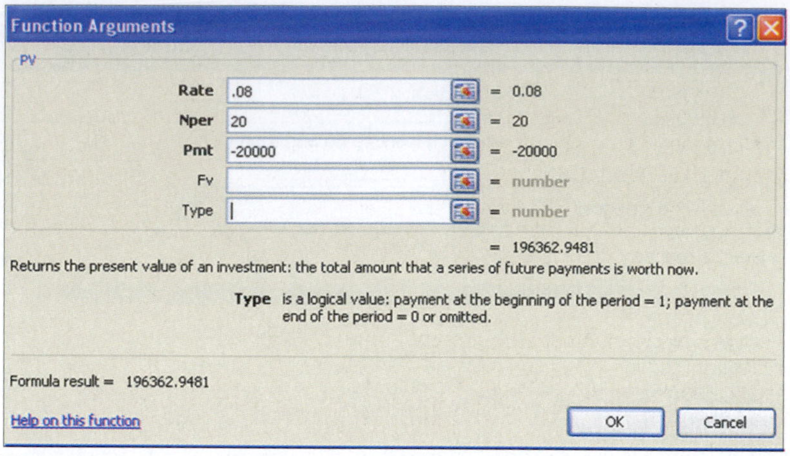

Windows 10, Microsoft Corporation

Using the PV Model to Compute Fair Value of Available-for-Sale Investments

In Appendix E, we discussed GAAP for available-for-sale investments. At the end of each year, investors are required to adjust these types of investments to their fair values, using one of three different approaches (in this order of preference):

- Level 1: Quoted prices in active markets for identical assets
- Level 2: Estimates based on other observable inputs (e.g., the prices for similar assets)
- Level 3: Estimates based on unobservable estimates (the company's own estimates based on certain assumptions)

Some types of investments are actively traded in markets and their prices are publicly quoted daily. Publicly traded stocks and bonds are an example. Determining the fair value for these investments is easy: Merely obtain the quoted price from the financial media (usually the Internet or *Wall Street Journal*) at year-end. Other types of nontraditional investments (e.g., notes, bonds, contracts, and annuities) might not be actively traded and have daily quoted market prices. In this case, a company might use financial models that predict the expected cash flows from the investment over a period of time and discount the cash flows back to the balance-sheet date. These are called level 2 or level 3 approaches to asset valuation. Using these models usually requires an investor to make sophisticated judgments about the amount and timing of cash flows. Sometimes the investor must make a number of subjective estimates about interest rates. Models such as these are quite sensitive to changes in these judgments and estimates. Let's illustrate with a simple example.

Present Value of an Investment in Bonds

The present value of a bond—its market price—is the present value of the future principal amount at maturity plus the present value of the future stated interest payments. The principal is a single amount to be received by the investor and paid by the debtor at maturity. The interest is an *annuity* because it occurs periodically.

Let's compute the present value of 9% five-year bonds of **Southwest Airlines** from the standpoint of an investor. The face value of the bonds is $100,000, and the face interest rate is 9% annually. Bonds typically pay interest twice per year. So, let's assume the Southwest Airlines bonds pay 4.5% interest semiannually. Suppose that at issuance, the market interest rate is 10% annually. Therefore, the effective (market) interest rate for each of the 10 semiannual periods is

5% (because the bonds pay interest twice a year). Consequently, we use 5% to compute the present value of the sum of the principal and stream of interest payments. The market price of the bonds is $96,149. It is calculated as follows:

	Annual Market Interest Rate ÷ 2	Number of Semiannual Interest Payments	
PV of principal:			
$100,000 × PV of single amount at 5%		for 10 periods	
$100,000 × 0.614 (Exhibit F-3)			$61,400
PV of stated (cash) interest:			
$100,000 × 0.045 × PV of annuity at 5%		for 10 periods	
$4,500 × 7.722 (Exhibit F-4)			34,749
PV (market price) of bonds			$96,149

The inputs needed to calculate the present value in Excel are[1]

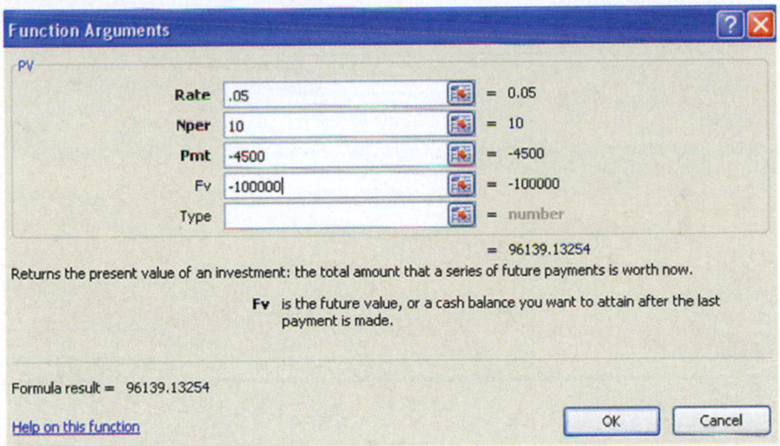

Windows 10, Microsoft Corporation

The fair value of the Southwest bonds on the investor's balance sheet would be $96,139 using Excel.[2] Amounts calculated from the PV tables ($96,149) and Excel ($96,139) differ merely by rounding. We discuss accounting for these bonds from the debtor's point of view in Chapter 9 on pages 476–480. It may be helpful for you to reread this section before you study those pages.

As an example, **Intel Corporation** reported the fair value of its long-term investments and other assets in a (partial) footnote to its 2016 financial statements as follows (in millions):

	Level 1	Level 2	Level 3
Marketable equity securities	$7,097	$ 0	$ 0
Other long-term assets	717	1,540	39

Some of the level 2 and level 3 fair value estimates use discounted cash flow projections such as the ones we have described in this section.

[1] Assume that all payments of interest and principal occur at the end of the period, rather than the beginning. Therefore, it is appropriate to leave the Excel table field labeled "Type" blank.

[2] In the real world, bond investments in public companies are typically classified as level 1 investments because they are usually traded in active markets with quoted prices. We use an investment in bonds here to illustrate the valuation computation for level 3 investments because bonds are easier to understand than the more complex types of level 3 investments. The process of estimating fair value using discounted cash flow models is similar for all types of investments.

Summary Problem

You have invested in a commercial building that you are leasing to a national retail chain. The tenant has signed a 10-year lease agreement that cannot be canceled. You expect to collect $8,000 per month for the full term of the lease. Payments occur at the end of each month. What is the present value of this investment if the interest rate is 12% and compounded monthly?

Answer

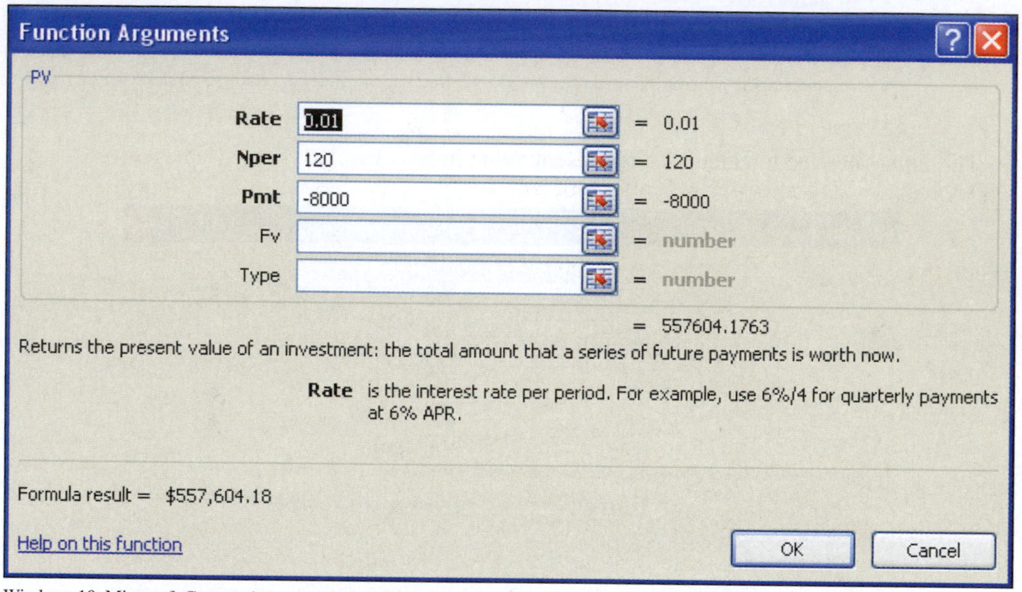

The interest compounds monthly, so it is appropriate to use 120 periods, the number of months in the lease, rather than 10 years. In addition, the yearly interest rate must be adjusted to a monthly rate of 1% (12% ÷ 12). The net present value of this lease is $557,604. Note that you cannot use Exhibit F-4 since it does not include 1% and does not have 120 periods. The Excel PV function easily gives the result.

REVIEW | Appendix F: Time Value of Money

Accounting Vocabulary

discounting (p. 799) The process of computing a present value.

future value (p. 798) A measure of the future sum of money that a given current investment is "worth" at a specified time in the future assuming a certain interest rate.

present value (p. 799) Today's value of a future payment or series of future payments, assuming that those payments include interest at the current market rate.

Quick Check (Answers are given on page 809.)

1. You are calculating the present value of $1,000 that you will receive five years from now. Which table will you use to obtain the present value factor to multiply to calculate the present value of that $1,000?
   a. Present Value of $1 table
   b. Future Value of $1 table
   c. Present Value of Ordinary Annuity of $1
   d. Future Value of Ordinary Annuity of $1

2. You are calculating the present value of $5,000 that you will receive at the end of every year for the next ten years. Which table will you use to obtain the present value factor to calculate the total present value of those $5,000 payments you will be receiving?
   a. Present Value of $1 table
   b. Future Value of $1 table
   c. Present Value of Ordinary Annuity of $1
   d. Future Value of Ordinary Annuity of $1

3. You have received a settlement offer from an automobile manufacturer due to mechanical problems with your automobile. The manufacturer will pay you $20,000 in one lump sum five years from now. You can earn 4% on your investments. The present value of the manufacturer's settlement offer is closest to
   a. $20,000.
   b. $19,200.
   c. $24,330.
   d. $16,440.

4. You have won $1,000,000 in a lottery. Your winnings will be paid to you in equal annual year-end installments of $50,000 over 20 years. You estimate that you can earn 5% on your investments. The present value of your $1,000,000 winnings would be closest to
   a. $377,000.
   b. $623,100.
   c. $1,000,000.
   d. $1,050,000.

5. Albert Financing leases airplanes to airline companies. Albert has just signed a 5-year lease agreement that requires annual year-end lease payments of $1,400,000. What is the present value of the lease using a 12% interest rate?
   a. $793,800
   b. $5,047,000
   c. $50,470,000
   d. $7,938,000

Excel Project
Autograded Excel Project available at **MyLab Accounting**.

ASSESS YOUR PROGRESS

F-S-1. ***(Learning Objective 1: Calculate present value of various amounts)*** Calculate the present value of the following amounts: LO 1

1. $6,000 at the end of twenty years at 10%
2. $6,000 a year at the end of the next twenty years at 10%

F-S-2. ***(Learning Objective 1: Calculate the present value of an investment using present-value tables)*** McGee Leasing leased a car to a customer. McGee will receive $300 a month, at the end of each month, for 36 months. Use the PV function in Excel® to calculate the asnw-ers to the following questions LO 1

1. What is the present value of the lease if the annual interest rate in the lease is 18%?
2. What is the present value of the lease if the car can likely be sold for $6,000 at the end of three years?

Exercises MyLab Accounting

LO 1 **F-E-3A.** ***(Learning Objective 1: Calculate the present value of a bond investment)*** Haddock Corp. purchased fifteen $1,000 7% bonds of Galvan Corporation when the market rate of interest was 8%. Interest is paid semiannually, and the bonds will mature in nine years. Using the PV function in Excel®, compute the price Haddock paid (the present value) for the bond investment.

LO 1 **F-E-4B.** ***(Learning Objective 1: Calculate the present value of a bond investment)*** Hodson Corp. purchased ten $1,000 8% bonds of Eagle Corporation when the market rate of interest was 6%. Interest is paid semiannually, and the bonds will mature in four years. Using the PV function in Excel®, compute the price Hodson paid (the present value) for the bond investment.

Quiz

Test your understanding of time value of money concepts by answering the following questions. Select the best choice from among the possible answers given.

F-Q-5. The present value of $3,000 at the end of seven years at 8% interest is

a. $2,228.
b. $1,749.
c. $3,000.
d. $15,618.

F-Q-6. Which of the following is not needed to compute the present value of an investment?

a. The length of time between the investment and future receipt
b. The interest rate
c. The rate of inflation
d. The amount of the receipt

F-Q-7. What is the present value of bonds with a face value of $6,000, a stated interest rate of 7%, a market rate of 5%, and a maturity date three years in the future? Interest is paid semiannually. Use Excel®.

a. $5,614
b. $7,060
c. $6,000
d. $6,330

Problems MyLab Accounting

LO 1 **F-P-8A.** ***(Learning Objective 1: Explain the impact of the time value of money on valuation of investments)*** Annual cash inflows from two competing investment opportunities are given. Each investment opportunity will require the same initial investment.

	Investment	
Year	A	B
1	$11,000	$14,000
2	6,000	$14,000
3	25,000	14,000
	$42,000	$42,000

Requirement

1. Assuming a 12% interest rate, which investment opportunity would you choose?

LO 1

F-P-9B. ***(Learning Objective 1: Explain the impact of the time value of money on the valuation of investments)*** Annual cash inflows from two competing investment opportunities are given. Each investment opportunity will require the same initial investment.

	Investment	
Year	A	B
1	$10,000	$13,000
2	13,000	$13,000
3	16,000	13,000
	$39,000	$39,000

Requirement

1. Assuming a 12% interest rate, which investment opportunity would you choose?

Challenge Exercise

LO 1

F-E-10. ***(Learning Objective 1: Calculate present values of competing investments)*** Which option is better: receive $160,000 now or $50,000, $25,000, $55,000, $30,000, and $40,000, respectively, over the next five years? The cash flows are at the end of each year except for $160,000.

Requirements

1. Assuming a 6% interest rate, which investment opportunity would you choose?
2. If you could earn 10%, would your choice change?
3. Assuming a 10% interest rate, what would the cash flow in year 5 have to be in order for you to be indifferent to the two plans?

Quick Check Answers

1. *a*
2. *c*
3. *d [$20,000 × 0.822 = $16,440]*
4. *b [$50,000 × 12.462 = $623,100]*
5. *b [$1,400,000 × 3.605 = $5,047,000]*

Company Index

*Note: Company names in **bold** are real companies.*

J

K

L

M

N

O

P

R

S

T

U

Glindex A Combined Glossary and Subject Index

B

C

D

E

F

J

K

L

Q

R

T

U

V

W